The Beach Boys

The Beach Boys

The Men Who Flew With 514 Squadron RAF

Simon Hepworth
Roger Guernon
Andrew Porrelli

Edited by Stephen Kingham

MENTION
THE WAR
PUBLICATIONS

Cover design: Topics – The Creative Partnership
www.topicdesign.co.uk

Cover illustration: Chas McHugh

A CIP catalogue reference for this book is available from the British Library.

ISBN 9781911255475

Other books in the History of 514 Squadron RAF series

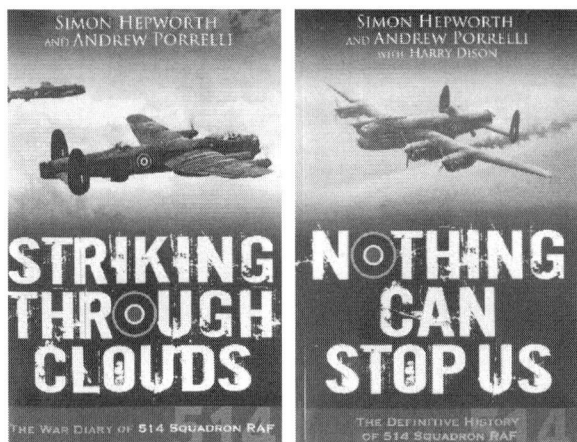

Striking Through Clouds is the War Diary of 514 Squadron RAF, containing the daily entries from the squadron's Operational Record Book, together with additional information about losses and the context of each day's activities.

Nothing Can Stop Us is the narrative history of 514 Squadron, including details from the RAF Waterbeach Station Record Book along with many personal anecdotes from squadron members, as collated by 514 Squadron flight engineer Sgt. Harry Dison.

Available on Amazon worldwide, or the publisher's website, www.bombercommandbooks.com

Contents

Return to Ops, RAF Waterbeach

F/Sgt. Geoffrey Payne - 2014

F/Sgt. Geoffrey Albert Payne in 1944 (left and 2014 (right)

514 Squadron was formed at RAF Foulsham in September 1943 as part of 3 Group and began operations in November 1943 flying Bristol Hercules radial engined Mk2 Lancasters before re-locating to RAF Waterbeach for the rest of the war until disbanded in August 1945.

I arrived at Waterbeach and was deposited on the ground floor of one of the H Blocks. RAF Waterbeach was a pre-war aerodrome which had all the facilities one could wish for. Hot and cold water, baths and showers within the billet and only fifty yards to the Sergeant's Mess, luxury indeed as opposed to the spartan conditions which prevailed at Witchford. The rest of the inhabitants of my billet were all aircrew awaiting medical assessment prior to being re-admitted to operational duties and were known as the "Odd Bods". Some were recovering from wounds, frostbite, or illness and would be joining other crews when declared fit. In the meantime, we were all allocated some useful tasks to keep us fully occupied until we were returned to operational duties. Together with another air gunner and as senior NCOs we were allocated airfield defence which meant on occasions being in charge of the perimeter guard or manning the guns at either end of the main runway when the squadron was operating. This duty was necessary due to the frequency of German intruders who followed the bomber stream back their bases. One night as I was manning the guns on the downwind end of the main runway awaiting the return of the squadron I saw a twin engined aircraft approaching the runway and got a bead on it. As it carne closer I noticed that it had its port undercarriage down but to my relief this aircraft turned out to be a Mosquito, obviously in trouble, coming in downwind. It must have landed half way down the runway in a shower of sparks then, a terrific bang and flames lit up the sky. After about five minutes the field phone rang to inform me that I could stand down as the squadron had been diverted. Three days later the station adjutant informed me that as I had recently been promoted to Flight Sergeant I was to take the funeral parade for the two airmen that had perished in the Mosquito crash.

During my time "convalescing", there was ample time to get involved with the many recreational activities on the station. One such time was the visit by a dramatic soap with Margaret Lockwood taking the lead in a play by and directed by Terrance Rattigan. On another occasion, the RAF film unit arrived on camp to film some aspects of an operational squadron. Among the group was the famous American actor Edward G Robinson with a retinue of lowly airmen who were to participate in this documentary/film. In later years some would become famous such as Dickie Attenborough, George Cole, David Tomlinson and a few others. This film became a box office success entitled "Journey Together", a copy of which I now treasure.

Very soon the "honeymoon" would be over, as a message came over the tannoy for me to report to the Medical Officer who told me to pick up transport the following day and report to the RAF hospital at Ely for my final medical assessment. A friendly type of third degree took place and, eventually I was passed fit for flying and would return to Waterbeach operational. Back at Waterbeach I reported to the Gunnery Leader and had a pleasant chat with him concerning my interview with the Medical Board. He told me that they were trying to ascertain if I was "swinging the lead" as frostbite was considered, in the first instance, a self- inflicted wound and that the recipient had to prove otherwise. With that, I was given first option of joining a crew when a vacancy arose and ordered to report at the gunnery office the following day and every day.

D-Day came and went and as I was now operational I was excused normal station duties, so I spent much of my time flying the Link Trainer or knocking about in the cricket nets or even swimming in the River Cam. Bomber Command had switched from attacking the industrial cities of Germany to supporting the advancing allied armies by attacking German troop concentrations, communications, flying bomb sites/storage areas, as well the many oil plants.

The 514 Squadron Operational Records:

The source of the information contained in this book is the Operational Records Book (ORB) of 514 Squadron, RAF. The unit was formed at RAF Foulsham on 1st September 1943, and disbanded on 22nd August 1945, the week after VJ Day.

The 514 Squadron ORB is available in digital image format through the National Archives website, www.nationalarchives.gov.uk or in microfiche format for public viewing at the Public Records Office, Kew, London. However the full content is reproduced as the daily record by crew in this book and the summary of events is contained in the companion volume *Striking Through Clouds*. The material is Crown Copy right and is reproduced under Government Open Licence v 2.0. The ORB was the official record of the squadron's operations. Every crew and aircraft was listed for each attack, together with details of bomb load, target and time airborne. After the sortie, the returning crew was debriefed and a short account of their efforts entered in the ORB, including time over target and landing time at base, combats and any other noteworthy incidents. If the aircraft was lost, a concise entry simply stated, 'Aircraft Missing'.

It should be noted that the ORB was completed as meticulously as possible, usually by the squadron's administrative officer. However, it is apparent from further research that there were inaccuracies when the official record is compared with individual crew log books, much work in this vein being undertaken by Roger Guernon, who has carefully compiled and maintained an archive of documents, records and photographs on behalf of the veterans, friends and family of those who served with the unit.

The original ORB material was transcribed by Andrew Porrelli and collated by Simon Hepworth, originally for *Striking Through Clouds*. A narrative history was added by Simon Hepworth to add context and anecdotal material, mostly contributed by Harry ison, who flew a tour of operations with the squadron in 1944. The relevant information in each record is summarised for each sortie, exactly as it appears in the official records. It is in a consistent format as far as possible:

Date	Aircraft	Duty	Target	Up	Drop	Down
13/02/1945	NG298 JI-E	Bombing	Dresden	21.42	01.30	06.07

Date: Operational Date according to the ORB. This typicaly ran from 0600 hrs to 0559 hrs the following morning. For that reason, sorties flown prior to 0600hrs would be included under the previous day's records. This is most noticeable in the raids in support of the D-Day landings, which are show in the ORB n as occurring on 5th June 1944.

Aircraft: The identity of the aircraft flown by the crew is given as the aircraft serial number, which stayed with the aircraft throughout its operational life, followed by the three-letter squadron code. 'JI-' was used by 514 Squadron's 'A' and 'B' Flights whilst 'C' Flight aircraft were designated 'A2-'. Individual aircraft were then allocated a final letter, usually that of an aircraft they were replacing after it was lost.

Duty: The majority of the squadron's operations were bombing raids. Some early sorties were 'Gardening' (sea-mining), whilst at the end of the war the squadron participated in a number of non-hostile tasks. These included Manna (dropping food packs to Dutch civilians), Exodus (returning liberated POWs from France aand the Low Countries), Dodge (returning POWs from Italy) and Post Mortem (testing the effectiveness of captured German radar equipment).

Target: Usually a city or town in which the specific target was located. Occasionally it would be small site, especially the storage or launch sites for V1 or V2 weapons.

Up: Time of take-off from originating airfield, usually Waterbeach or, for early raids, Foulsham.

Drop: Time at which bombs were released.

Down: Time of landing on return. This was usually Waterbeach or Foulsham, but in an emergency would be a convenient RAF or other British airfield.

The authors hope that the individual records of the crews go some way towards preserving the story of the heroic men who flew into battle with 514 Squadron, and of the 437 who lost their lives.

Simon Hepworth

Merthyr Tydfil, South Wales
June 2019.

P/O. Stephen Abel, DFC

191247 (1581759) P/O. Stephen "Steve" Abel, DFC.   Pilot.
NZ422419 F/S. B.D. Cramp, RNZAF.   A/Bomber.
165339 F/O. John Verley Francis. Navigator.
A434801   F/S. Terence Francis O'Neill, RAAF. WOP/AG.
1606238 Sgt. Frederick George Gillett. MU/Gunner.
Sgt. C.A. Cook.   R/Gunner.
Sgt. R.O. Thomas.   F/Engineer.

Passenger: 05/05/1945

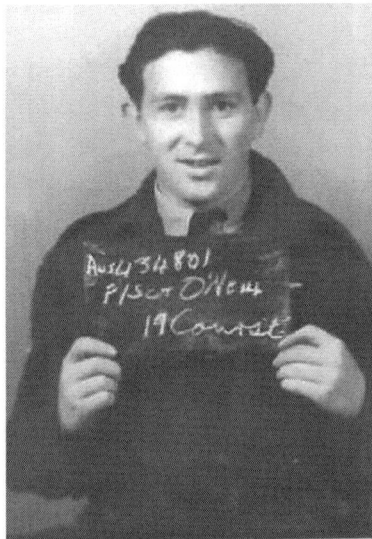

L to R: C.A. Cook, Steve Abel, Freddy   *F/S Terence Francis O'Neill, RAAF*
Gillett (courtesy Ken Staveley).

13/02/1945 NG298 JI-E Bombing Dresden   21.42   01.30   06.07
   Bomb load 1 x 4000 HC, 7 x No. 14 Clusters. Primary target: Dresden.
Weather 5/10ths cloud over target. Bombed at 01.30 hours from 20,000 feet.
Overshot Green T.I.s.
   P/O. Stephen "Steve" Abel flew the mission as 2nd pilot with F/L. Royston
Worthing's crew.
16/02/1945 PB902 JI-A Bombing Wesel   12.26   16.00   17.48
   Bomb load 1 x 4000 HC, 4 x 500 GP, 2 x 500 MC L/Delay, 4 x 250 GP, 6 x
500 ANM64. Primary target: Wesel. Weather clear. Bombed at 16.00 hours

from 20,000 feet on leading aircraft.

P/O. Stephen "Steve" Abel flew the mission as 2nd pilot with F/L. Royston Worthing's crew.

27/02/1945 LM275 JI-C Bombing Gelsenkirchen 11.0714.28   16.42

Bomb load 1 x 4000 HC, 2 x 500 MC (L/D 37B), 9 x 500 ANM64, 4 x 250 GP. Primary target: Gelsenkirchen (Alma Pluts) Benzin plant. Weather 10/10ths cloud, 6/10,000 feet tops. Bombed at 14.28 hours from 20,000 feet on leading aircraft.

01/03/1945 LM275 JI-C Bombing Kamen   11.49   15.05½ 17.44

Bomb Load 1 x 4000 HC, 9 x 500 ANM64, 2 x 500 MC L/Delay and 4 x 500 GP. Primary target: Kamen, Coking plant. Weather 10/10ths cloud. Bombed at 15.05½ hours from 19,500 feet on leading aircraft.

02/03/1945 LM275 JI-C Bombing Koln   12.43 16.03 18.27½

Bomb load 1 x 4000 HC, 12 x 500 ANM64. Primary target: Koln. Weather 10/10ths cloud over Koln, South and South-East of Koln clear. Bombed at 15.05½ hours from 21,000 feet. Visual, built up area.

06/03/1945 LM285 JI-A Bombing Salzbergen 08.21½ 12.14   14.16

Bomb load 1 x 4000 HC, 12 x 500 ANM64, 2 x 500 MC. Primary target: Salzbergen, Wintershall oil plant. Weather 10/10ths cloud over target, tops 10,000 feet. Bombed at 12.14 hours from 21,000 feet on G.H. Leader. Whole Squadron compact over target.

07/03/1945 LM285 JI-A Bombing Dessau   17.10   22.16   02.23

Bomb load 1 x 4000 HC, 6 x Mk.17 Clusters. Primary target: Dessau. Weather 5 to 10/10ths thin cloud. Bombed at 22.16 hours from 21,000 feet on red flares with green stars.

12/03/1945 NN782 JI-F Bombing Dortmund 13.05 16.57½ 19.06

Bomb load 1 x 4000 HC, 13 x 500 ANM64. Primary target: Dortmund. Weather 10/10ths cloud over target, tops 6/10,000 feet. Bombed at 16.57½ hours from 18,500 feet on G.H. Leader.

17/03/1945 LM285 JI-A Bombing Auguste Viktoria 11.42   15.07   17.18

Bomb load 1 x 4000 HC, 13 x 500 ANM64, 2 x 500 MC. Primary target: Auguste Viktoria, Marl-Hüls coal mine. Weather 10/10ths cloud, tops and contrails up to 23,000 feet. Bombed 15.07 hours from 21,500 feet on leading aircraft.

20/03/1945 ME535 JI-G Bombing Hamm   10.01   13.15   15.55

Bomb load 7 x 1000 MC, 9 x 500 ANM64. Primary target: Hamm, Marshalling yards. Weather 5/10ths cloud. Bombed at 13.15 hours from 18,000 feet on G.H. Leader.

09/04/1945 LM627 JI-D Bombing Kiel 19.53 22.44   02.05

Primary target: Kiel, Submarine Buildings Yards. Weather clear with slight haze. Bomb load 1 x 4000 HC and 12 x 500 ANM64. Bombed at 22.44 hours from 20,000 feet on centre of Green T.I.s per Master Bomber's instructions. Two clear patches of marking. Many fires and much smoke over area. Good raid, huge fires among the T.I.s seen past Sylt.

18/04/1945 LM285 JI-A Bombing Heligoland 09.40 13.08 15.04

6 x 1000 MC and 10 x 500 ANM64. Primary target: Heligoland, Naval base. Weather no cloud, slight haze. Bombed visually on Red T.I.s at 13.08 hours from 18,500 feet. Pickwick per Master Bomber's orders. Oil fire and bags of smoke. 4 small boats getting to hell out of it. Excellent raid. Formation rather poor.

22/04/1945 LM285 JI-A Bombing Bremen 15.04 18.42 21.00

Bomb load 1 x 4000 HC, 2 x 500 MC and 14 x 500 ANM64. Primary target: Bremen, in support of Troop concentration. Weather on approaching target 4-5/10ths cloud. Bombed on leading aircraft "M" 514 at 18.42 hours from 19,000 feet.

Sustained structural damage at Wilhelmshaven on outward journey and further damage on the run up to the target. Rear Turret damaged. Port Wing Petrol Tank holed. Hole in fuselage. Starboard wing damaged. A/C escorted by JI-D and JI-N. A/C Port inner engine feathered. A/C finally crash landed near Venlo, due to loss of control about 1930 hours on 22.4.45. Crew returned Waterbeach evening 25th April 1945.

01/05/1945 RF231 JI-A Manna The Hague 13.22 x 15.40

Weather clear over target. 5 Panniers dropped.

05/05/1945 RF231 JI-A Manna The Hague 06.03 07.14 08.15

LAC Terry passenger on this op. Dropping area The Hague. Dropped 5 panniers on Red T.I. and White Cross. Low cloud. Slightly overshot by 150 yards - Red T.I. badly placed.

10/05/1945 RF231 JI-A Exodus Juvincourt - Ford 11.06 x 17.45

Duration 3.18. Outward 1.27 hours. Collected 24 ex POWs. Homeward 1.51 hours. Better facilities for starting up at Juvincourt.

F/L. Anthony Ralph Adams

133712 F/L. Anthony Ralph Adams. Pilot.
W/O. S.G. Barnes.   A/Bomber.
W/O. T.M. Casey.   Navigator.
155960 F/O.   John Lawrence Boulter, DFC. WOP/AG.
F/S. A.C. Smith.   MU/Gunner.
178238 F/O. William Oseman   R/Gunner.
F/S. R. Willey.   F/Engineer.

Passengers: 28/06/1945

28/06/1945 ME422 JI-Q Baedeker Tour over Continent 15.20   x 19.46
Passengers – P/O. Farrar, S/O. Dyson, LAC. Moore, LAC. Billing, Cpl. Cope.
29/06/1945 ME359 JI-T Post MortemSpecial mission 09.52 x 15.56

F/O. Leslie A. Adams

NZ414255   F/O. Leslie A. "Les" Adams, RNZAF. Pilot.
Sgt. Peter D. "Pete" Banyard.   A/Bomber.
Sgt. Robert J. "Bob" Talbot.   Navigator.
2220687 Sgt.   Leslie Alfred Joseph "Les" Holt. WOP/AG.
Sgt. J.H. "Jack" Blandford.   MU/Gunner.
Sgt. F.J. "Fred" Blandford.   R/Gunner.
Sgt. John Ronald Currie "Jock" Brouwer. F/Engineer.

Passengers: 19/06/1945, 20/06/1945, 28/06/1945, 30/07/1945

17/03/1945 NN782 JI-F Bombing Auguste Viktoria 11.37   15.06½ 17.22
    Bomb load 1 x 4000 HC, 13 x 500 ANM64, 2 x 500 MC. Primary target:
Auguste Viktoria, Marl-Hüls coal mine. Weather 10/10ths cloud, tops and
contrails up to 23,000 feet. Bombed at 15.06½ hours from 20,400 feet on G.H.
Leader.
    F/O. Leslie A. "Les" Adams flew the mission as 2nd Pilot with P/O. W.A.F.
Winkworth's crew.
18/03/1945 LM724 JI-H Bombing Bruchstrasse   12.02   15.00   17.21
    Bomb load 1 x 4000 HC, 13 x 500 ANM64, 2 x 500 MC. Primary target:
Bruchstrasse, Coal mine and coking plant. Weather 10/10ths cloud, tops 6-
12,000 feet. Bombed at 15.00 hours from 18,500 feet on leading G.H. aircraft.
Blue puffs in evidence.

29/03/1945 NN782 JI-F Bombing Salzgitter 12.15 16.44   19.14

23

Bomb load 1 x 4000 HC and 8 x 500 ANM64. Primary target: Salzgitter, Hallendorf works. Weather 10/10ths cloud. Bombed at 16.44 hours from 20,500 feet on G.H. Leader.

04/04/1945 NG298 JI-F Bombing Merseburg (Leuna) 18.37 22.43½ 02.33

Weather 5-10/10ths cloud, and 10/10ths over Merseburg. Bombed Magdeburg. Bomb load 1 x 4000 HC, 6 x 500 ANM64 on Red and Green T.I.s. at 22.43½ hours from 20,000 feet. 1 x 500 ANM64 hung up, brought back. H2S U/S. Very good attack, after turning at Halberstadt, towards Merseburg saw P.F.F. start attack and bombed in T.I.s. No other target marked after bombing saw Merseburg attack commence.

F/O. Leslie A. "Les" Adams flew the mission as 2nd Pilot with F/O. C.G. Fiset's crew.

18/04/1945 NN782 JI-K Bombing Heligoland 09.46 13.08 15.14

Bomb load 6 x 1000 MC and 10 x ANM64. Primary target: Heligoland, Naval base. Weather no cloud, slight haze. Bombed visually on upwind edge of smoke at 13.08 hours from 18,500 feet. Island covered with smoke. Very concentrated raid. No troubles.

20/04/1945 ME530 JI-C Bombing Regensburg 09.31 14.07 17.30

Bomb load 16 x 500 ANM64. Primary target: Regensburg. Weather clear over target and whole route. Followed G.H. aircraft 'J2' but he did not bomb. Bombed Oil Storage Tanks, visually at 14.07 hours from 19,000 feet. Our G.H. Leader did not bomb on first run, nor after orbiting, so we bombed visually. Bombing concentrated but tending to undershoot.

24/04/1945 ME363 JI-R Bombing Bad-Oldesloe 07.05 10.44½ 12.59

Bomb load 6 x 1000 ANM64 and 10 x 500 ANM64. Primary target: Bad-Oldesloe, Rail and road junction and Marshalling Yards. Weather 3/10ths to nil cloud. Bombed visually at 10.44½ hours from 16,900 feet on Rail Tracks, concentration of bomb bursts. Much smoke seen and many bomb bursts seen, small explosions on the railway. Good trip. Satisfactory attack. Could not keep up with leading A/C so bombed visually.

01/05/1945 ME535 JI-G Manna The Hague 13.14 14.40 15.50

Weather clear over target. Dropped 5 Panniers on Visual and T.I.s of race course. No trouble whatever. Pin points easily picked up. Bags concentrated. Usual greetings from the crowd.

17/05/1945 RF231 JI-A Exodus Brussels – Westcott 10.23 x 14.50

Duration 2 hrs. 39 mins. Out, 1 hr. 26 mins. In, 1 hr. 13 mins. 10 Belgian refugees taken over to Brussels, H/P faulty (Hydraulic Pressure) reducing efficiency of Flying Control.

18/05/1945 RF231 JI-A Exodus Brussels - Oakley 11.58 x 17.11

Duration 3 hrs. Out, 1 hr. 13 mins. In, 1 hr. 47 mins. 11 Belgians taken to Brussels. 24 ex POWs returned. No troubles.

23/05/1945 RF231 JI-A Exodus Brussels - Oakley 11.55 x 17.05

Duration 2.56 hours. Out, 1.09 hours. In, 1.47 hours. 9 Belgian refugees returned to Brussels. 24 ex POWs evacuated. Organisation excellent.

24/05/1945 RE137 JI-D Exodus Brussels 12.01 x 15.21

Duration 2.24 hours. Out 1.06 hours. In 1.18 hours. 10 Belgian refugees returned to Brussels. No POWs available. All OK.

25/05/1945 ME530 JI-C Exodus Brussels 11.55 x 15.07

Duration 2.17 hours. Out 1.04 hours. In 1.13 hours. 9 Belgian refugees to Brussels. No POWs. home.

26/05/1945 ME530 JI-C Exodus Brussels - Ford 11.47 x 17.02

Duration 3.14 hours. Out 1.13 hours. In 2.01 hours. 10 Belgian refugees to Brussels. 24 ex POWs all military brought back.

19/06/1945 RF231 JI-A Baedeker Tour over Continent 09.45 x 14.06

Passengers – F/O. Boosamra, LAC. Coates, LAC. Parish.

20/06/1945 RF231 JI-A Baedeker Tour over Continent 08.15 x 13.09

Passengers – Sgt. Philip, LAC. Scott, LAC. Smith and LAC. Davis.

25/06/1945 RF231 JI-A Post Mortem Special mission.09.49 x 15.56

28/06/1945 ME380 JI-E Baedeker Tour over Continent 15.26 x 19.30

No Bomber and no Rear Gunner listed for this mission. Passengers – Grandy, Bendon, Parnell and Hatton.

05/07/1945 RF231 JI-A Post Mortem Special mission.13.25 x 17.59

30/07/1945 RF230 JI-B Baedeker Tour over Continent 15.10 x 19.27

Passengers Edmunds, Butcher, Brickle, Blandford.

F/O. William Allan

153171 F/O. William "Bill" Allan. Pilot.

F/O. K. or A.G. Walker. A/Bomber.

164287 F/O. Anthony Kellman Legge.   Navigator.

Sgt. H. Tyson.   WOP/AG.

1595278 Sgt. Albert Craddock. MU/Gunner.

179813 F/O. John Campbell Mitchell. R/Gunner.

Sgt. G. Richards.   F/Engineer.

Passengers: 07/05/1945, 05/06/1945, 22/06/1945, 21/07/1945

14/03/1945 NF968 JI-B Bombing Heinrichshutte 13.02   16.40   18.33

Bomb load 1 x 4000 HC, 11 x 500 ANM64, 1 Skymarker Red Puff. Primary target: Heinrichshutte, Hattingen Steel works and Benzol plant. Weather 10/10ths cloud, tops 7/12,000 feet. Bombed at 16.40 hours from 17,500 feet on G.H. Aircraft hit by heavy flak.

Left: Sgt. Albert Craddock (Alcan MacOne). Right: F/O. Bill Allan (Jacqui McIntosh).

F/O. William Allan flew the mission as 2nd Pilot with F/L. R. Worthing's crew.

17/03/1945 NG118 A2-H Bombing Auguste Viktoria 11.33 x 17.34

Bomb load 1 x 4000 HC, 13 x 500 ANM64, 2 x 500 MC. Primary target: Auguste Viktoria, Marl-Hüls coal mine. Weather 10/10ths cloud, tops and contrails up to 23,000 feet. Abortive sortie. Farthest point reached 5123N 0532E at 14.43 hours. Port outer engine went unserviceable at 14.40 hours, could not keep up on three engines. Jettisoned 1 x 4000 HC, 2 x 500 MC, 2 x 500 ANM64 at 5223N 0316E at 16.22 hours from 10,000 feet. 11 x 500 ANM64 brought back to Base.

18/03/1945 NN776 A2-D Bombing Bruchstrasse 11.40 15.05 17.25

Bomb load1 x 4000 HC, 13 x 500 ANM64 and 2 x 500 MC. Primary target: Bruchstrasse, Coal mine and coking plant. Weather 10/10ths cloud, tops 6-12,000 feet. Bombed at 15.05 hours from 19,000 feet on leading G.H aircraft.

04/04/1945 PD389 A2-J Bombing Merseburg (Leuna) 18.49 x 02.52

Weather 5-10/10ths cloud, and 10/10ths over Merseburg. Bombed Magdeburg area. Bomb load 1 x 4000 HC, 6 x 500 ANM64 on Red and Green markers. Two attacks by enemy aircraft. Near collision with Lancaster over target with Nav. lights on. Attack rather scattered, many markers seen. (Patchy cloud). F/O. William Allan flew the mission as 2nd Pilot with F/L. E.S. Henderson's crew.

18/04/1945 PB426 A2-E Bombing Heligoland 09.56 13.08 15.31

Bomb load 6 x 1000MC and 10 x 500 ANM64. Primary target: Heligoland, Naval base. Weather no cloud, slight haze. Bombed visually at 13.08 hours from 18,500 feet. Whole Island obscured by smoke, 1 x 1000 MC hang up. Very good effort. Flames seen from the submarine harbour.

22/04/1945 ME529 A2-F   Bombing Bremen   15.06   18.41½ 20.52

Bomb Load 1 x 4000 HC, 2 x 500 MC and 14 x 500 ANM64. Primary target: Bremen, in support of Troop concentration. Weather on approaching target 4-5/10ths cloud. Bombed on leading A/C at 18.41½ hours from 18,500 feet. Smoke seen on east bank of river. Appeared to be a good raid. Congested over target.

07/05/1945 ME529 A2-F   Manna The Hague   12.10½ 13.37½ 14.48

Dropped 5 Packs on White Cross and Red T.I.s. Clear - Bags concentrated on airfield. *NB Due to inconsistency in the ORB there is some uncertainty as to the precise composition of the crew on this op.*

No Air Bomber for this operation. Passenger AC. L. Couchman.

11/05/1945 PD389 A2-J Exodus Juvincourt - Wing   17.30   x   22.01

Duration 3.08. Outward 1.33 hours. No POW returned. Homeward 1.35 hours. Aircraft could not take off with POWs before 20.00 hours so ordered to return empty.

13/05/1945 PD389 A2-J Exodus Juvincourt - Tangmere 13.16   x   16.18

Duration 3.02 hours. "Return to Base" heard at 14.50 hours.

05/06/1945 RE123 A2-K   Baedeker Tour over Germany 08.00   x   12.27

Passengers Sgt. G. Reed, Sgt. T. Sawyer, Sgt. B Batts.

22/06/1945 NF966 A2-G   Baedeker Tour over Continent 09.52   x   14.29

Passengers F/L. Chapman, Cpl. Bruce, LAC. Smith, LAC. Davis, LAC. Hogh.

25/06/1945 ME355 A2-G   Post Mortem   Special mission 09.51 x 16.16

05/07/1945 RE120 A2-C   Post Mortem   Special mission 13.28 x 18.22

21/07/1945 ME355 A2-G   Baedeker Tour over Continent 15.08   x   19.30

Passengers G/Capt. Harston, F/O. Whisman, Sgt. Butler, LAC. Tolley, LAC. Ward.

02 to 04/08/1945 ME363 JI-R Dodge Italy (Bari)   06.45   14.15   17.15

Waterbeach 06.45, Bari 14.15 – Returned Waterbeach 04 Aug. 17.15.

20 ex POWs. brought back to U.K.

11-13/08/1945 ME364 JI-P Dodge Italy (Bari)   07.45   x 16.45

Waterbeach 07.45, Bari ? – Returned Waterbeach 13 Aug. 16.45.

20 ex POWs. brought back to U.K.

F/L. John Beaumont Allen

145076 (1399691) F/L. John Beaumont Allen. Pilot.
164085 (1282279) F/O. Barney Power. A/Bomber.
181482 (1807320) F/O. Leonard Ernest Wey. Navigator.
Sgt. W.R. Ayres. WOP/AG.
Sgt. D.C. Bradbury. WOP/AG.
Sgt. L.A. Davis. MU/Gunner.
Sgt. J. Kirkham. R/Gunner.
Sgt. W.I. Wilson. F/Engineer.
Sgt. W.I. Inglis. F/Engineer.

Passengers: 16/07/1945.

01/07/1945 RE137 JI-D Post Mortem Special mission 11.56 x18.10
06/07/1945 ME535 JI-G Baedeker Tour over Continent 10.34 x 14.49
16/07/1945 RE137 JI-D Baedeker Tour over Continent 09.57 x14.16

Passengers Cpl. Ing, LAC. Sharrill, LAC. Hembrow, F/L. Grandy.

F/L. Montague Grosvenor Tynsdale Allen

122112 F/L. Montague Grosvenor Tynsdale Allen. Pilot.
 F/S. W.P. Hooper. A/Bomber.
173555 (1012770) F/O. Stanley Ellis, DFC. A/Bomber. 1 op
197094 (1207677) P/O. Lionel Ernest Slade. Navigator.
164442 (1583325) F/O. Robert Arthur Edward Tidmarsh. Navigator. 1 op
125989 (1248870) F/L. Alexander Sharp Smith, DFC. Navigator. 1 op
148374 (1442933) F/L. George Robert Baker. Navigator. 2 ops
 F/S. R.W. Kirk. WOP/AG.
 F/S. K. Jeffery. MU/Gunner.
 F/O. E. Smith. MU/Gunner. 1 op
Sgt. L.S. King. R/Gunner.
Sgt. G. Sacker. F/Engineer.
196041 (1581940) F/S. Harry Glyn Huyton. 2nd Pilot. 14/03/1945
J9442 F/L. H.J. Clark, RCAF 2nd Pilot. 04/04/1945
NZ40429 P/O. D.T. Pettit, RNZAF 2nd Pilot. 16/08/1945

Passengers: 01/06/1945, 25/06/1945, 06/07/1945.

The Allen crew with their Lancaster 'Ot-az-Ell' (Hugh Allen).

19/02/1945 ME354 JI-M Bombing Wesel 12.53 16.36 18.20

Bomb load 1 x 4000 HC, 6 x 500 MC, 6 x 500 ANM64, 3 x 250 GP, 1 Skymarker Red puff. Primary target: Wesel. Weather over target 5-7/10ths cloud. Bombed at 16.36 hours from 18,700 feet on G.H. Wesel communications.

F/L. M.G.T. Allen flew the mission as 2nd pilot with F/L. M.D. Muggeridge's crew.

20/02/1945 ME355 JI-L Bombing Dortmund 21.44 01.06 03.38

Bomb load 1 x 4000HC, 6 x 500 Type 14 Clusters, 6 x 750 Type 15 Clusters. Primary target: Dortmund. Weather 8-10/10ths thin cloud at about 5,000 feet. Bombed at 01.06 hours from 20,300 feet on glow of Red T.I. through thin cloud. 010/10 Cloud 5000' - 3/4 Moon - Strong fighter reaction.

F/L. M.G.T. Allen flew the mission as 2nd pilot with F/L. M.D. Muggeridge's crew.

22/02/1945 ME358 JI-O Bombing Osterfeld 12.23 16.01 18.00

Bomb load 1 x 4000 HC, 9 x 500 ANM64, 2 x 500 MC, 4 x 250 GP. Primary target: Osterfeld, Coking ovens. Weather at target clear, but hazy. Bombed Starboard of leading G.H. aircraft. Coking ovens. Clear. Heavy Flak.

26/02/1945 ME358 JI-O Bombing Dortmund 11.09 14.02½ 16.15

Bomb load 1 x 4000 HC, 2 x 500 MC L/Delay 37B, 9 x 500 ANM64, 4 x 250 GP. Primary target: Dortmund, Hoesch Benzin plant. Weather 10/10ths cloud, tops 8/10,000 feet. On G.H. Benzine plant. 10/10 cloud, 8000'-

29

Moderate Flak.

27/02/1945 ME358JI-O Bombing Gelsenkirchen 11.02   14.28   16.38

Bomb load 1 x 4000 HC, 2 x 500 MC (L/D 37B), 9 x 500 ANM64, 4 x 250 GP. Primary target: Gelsenkirchen (Alma Pluts) Benzin plant. Weather 10/10ths cloud, 6/10,000 feet tops. Bombed at 14.28 hours from 20,000 feet on leading aircraft. Moderate Flak.

01/03/1945 ME354JI-M Bombing Kamen 11.54 15.06   17.53

Bomb load 1 x 4000 HC, 9 x 500 ANM64, 2 x 500 MC L/D, 4 x 250 GP. On centre of 4 Blue markers. Primary target: Kamen, Coking plant. Weather 10/10ths cloud, 13,000'. No Flak.

F/O. R.A.E. Tidmarsh Navigator for this operation.

07/03/1945 ME422JI-Q Bombing Wesel 02.45   05.31   07.38

Bomb load 1 x 4000 HC, 13 x 500 ANM64, 2 x 500 GP. Primary target: Wesel, Troop and Transport concentration. Weather 10/10ths cloud, thin in places. Bombed at 05.31 hours from 18,000 feet on G.H. "Bomb flashes indicate bombing concentrated. No Flak or fighters."

09/03/1945 ME422JI-Q Bombing Datteln 11.10 14.03   16.01

Bomb load 1 x 4000 HC, 13 x 500 ANM64, 2 x 500 MC L/Delay37. Primary target: Datteln, Synthetic oil plant. Weather 10/10ths cloud, tops 8-10,000 feet. Bombed at 14.03 hours from 20,100 feet on G.H. Moderate Flak.

11/03/1945 ME358JI-O Bombing Essen 11.34   15.27   17.25

Bomb load 1 x 4000 HC, 13 x 500 ANM64, 2 x 500 MC, 1 Skymarker Blue Puff. Primary target: Essen, Marshalling yards. Weather 10/10ths cloud, tops 7/8000 feet. Bombed at 15.27 hours from 18,700 feet on G.H. Blue smoke puff hang up and brought back to Base.

"1000 Bomber raid. Negligeable Flak".

14/03/1945 ME364JI-P Bombing Heinrichshutte 13.05   16.40   18.35

Bomb load 1 x 4000 HC, 12 x 500 ANM64. Primary target: Heinrichshutte, Hattingen Steel works and Benzol plant. Weather 10/10ths cloud, tops 7/12,000 feet. Bombed at 16.40 hours from 18,000 feet on G.H. Considerable flak after crossing battle front. Patchy clouds.

F/S. H.G. Huyton was 2nd Pilot that day.

18/03/1945 ME358JI-O Bombing Bruchstrasse 11.58 15.04   17.23

Bomb load 1 x 4000 HC, 13 x 500 ANM64, 2 x 500 MC. Primary target: Bruchstrasse, Coal mine and coking plant. Weather 10/10ths cloud, tops 6-12,000 feet. Bombed at 15.04 hours from 17,900 feet on G.H. Bombing appeared concentrated. Accurate Flak over target.

21/03/1945 ME358JI-O Bombing Munster 09.38   13.18   15.28

Bomb load 1 x 4000 HC, 13 x 500 ANM64, 2 x 500 MC, 1 Skymarker Blue Puff. Primary target Munster Viaduct and Marshalling Yards. Weather cloud nil to 2/10ths. Attacked area 5144N 0703E (near Dorsten) at 13.08 hours from 18,000 feet visually. Stream off track before G.H. run. When aircraft started this it was too late and target was overshot, aircraft orbitted, and bombed built up area near Dorsten. Heavy Flak. Bombed secondary target.

04/04/1945 ME358 JI-O Bombing Merseburg (Leuna) 18.53 22.5303.15

Bomb load 1 x 4000 HC, 6 x 500 ANM64. 10/10th cloud. Bombed primary Target: Merseburg, Synthetic oil plant. on Red T.I.s at 22.53 hours from 20,300 feet. Very scattered marking but reasonable concentration of markers that have bombed. H2S 1196, Front turret U/S. No Skymarkers seen on arrival, orbited and bombed on red T.I.s as skymarkers had disappeared. Moderate Flak.

F/L. H.J. Clark, RCAF was 2nd Pilot that day.

13/04/1945 ME358 JI-O Bombing Kiel 20.32 23.31 02.25

Bomb load 1 x 4000 HC and 12 x 500 ANM64. Primary target: Kiel, Docks and ship yards. Weather 10/10ths cloud low and thin. Bombed on centre of bunch of Green T.I.s on M.B.'s instructions. Well lit up under cloud. 3 lots of green glows of markers. Large explosion at 23.30. Attack looked concentrated, fires seemed to have started.

Docks and ship yards. 10/10ths Cloud. Light Flak. P.F.F. attack, good concentration.

22/04/1945 ME358 JI-O Bombing Bremen 15.20 18.42 20.59

Bomb load 1 x 4000 HC, 2 x 500 MC, 14 x 500 ANM 64. Primary target: Bremen, in support of Troop concentration. Weather on approaching target 4-5/10ths cloud. Bombed on G.H. at 18.42 hours from 18,400 ft. Smoke obscured vision. Formation good and average concentration of bombing.

Troop concentrations. 8/10ths Cloud. Very accurate Flak on approach.

01/05/1945 ME358 JI-O Manna The Hague 13.26 14.43 15.50

6,200 lbs. food. Weather clear over target. Dropped 4 Panniers on Red T.I.'s and White cross. One Pannier hung up. Successful delivery. Usual enthusiastic reception.

14/05/1945 ME358 JI-O Exodus Juvincourt - Oakley 10.29 x 18.31

Base - Juvincourt near Reims - Oakley - Base. Duration 3.18 hours. Outward 1.39 hours. Collected 24 POWs. Homeward 1.39 hours. We had to wait 3 hours before POWs were available. Well organised both at Juvincourt and Oakley.

17/05/1945 ME363 JI-R Exodus Brussels - Westcott 10.09 x 16.13

Base - Brussels (Melsbroeck) - Wescott - Base. Duration 3 hrs 6 mins. Out 1 hr 15 mins. In 1 hr 51 mins. 10 Belgian refugees returned to Brussels. 24 Ex POWs taken to Westcott. Everything satisfactory at Westcott.

18/05/1945 PB142 JI-N Exodus Brussels - Oakley 12.04 x 17.10

Base - Brussels (Melsbroeck) - Dunsfold - Base. Duration 3 hrs 04 mins. Out 1 hr 13 mins. In 2 hrs 6 mins. 10 Belgian refugees taken to Brussels. 24 ex POWs Returned to U.K. Good organisation.

23/05/1945 RE139 JI-M Exodus Brussels - Oakley 12.15 x 18.37

Base - Brussels (Melsbroeck) - Oakley - Base. Duration 3.14 hours. Out 1.24 hours. In 1.50 hours. 10 Belgian refugees returned to Brussels. 15 ex POWs evacuated. All O.K.

24/05/1945 RE139 JI-M Exodus Brussels 11.57 x 14.57

Base - Brussels (Melsbroeck) - Base. Duration 2.18 hours. Out 1.07 hours.

In 1.11 hours. 10 Belgian refugees returned to Brussels. No POWs available. All O.K.

25/05/1945 RE139 JI-M Exodus Brussels 11.50 x 14.51

Base - Brussels (Melsbroeck) - Base. Duration 2.20 hours. Out 1.02 hours. In 1.18 hours. 10 Belgian refugees returned to Brussels. No POWs home. No troubles.

F/O. A.S. Smith Navigator for this operation.

26/05/1945 RE139 JI-M Exodus Brussels - Ford 12.03 x 17.52

Base - Brussels (Melsbroeck) - Ford - Base. Duration 3.18 hours. Out 1.15 hours. In 2.03 hours. 10 Belgian refugees to Brussels. 24 ex POWs all military brought back to Ford.

01/06/1945 RE139 JI-M Baedeker Tour over Germany 10.29 x 15.22

Tour of Ruhr.

Passengers F/O. D.J. Bose, AC. G. Thomas, LAC. Hopkins, Cpl. K. Woodleigh.

25/06/1945 ME358 JI-O Post Mortem Special mission. 09.52 x 15.51

To Flensburg, test of German Radar, 16,000ft due to St. inner trouble could not reach 20,000ft.

Passenger AC. Doran. F/O. S. Ellis Bomb Aimer, F/O. E. Smith Air Gunner for this operation.

03/07/1945 ME358 JI-O Post Mortem Special mission.14.36 x 19.52

To Flensburg, Testing German radar.

06/07/1945 ME530 JI-C Baedeker Tour over Continent

Baedeker Tour of Ruhr. Passengers Cpl. Round, LACW. Crewe, LACW. Copping, AC. Cornish, LAC. Haley. No Bomb Aimer, no Rear Gunner.

24 to 26/07/1945

ME358 JI-O Dodge Italy 06.34 17.56 17.45

24/07/1945 Waterbeach 06.34 - Italy 17.56 - Returned 26/07/1945. Italy 10.08 - Waterbeach 17.45

No Rear Gunner that day.

16/08/1945 ME355 A2-G Dodge Italy (Bari) ca.07.06 to 10.53 x x

Recalled VHF U/S. Mission described in ORB summary only. The following details and crew composition for 16 and 16 to 20 August come from M.G.T. Allen's logbook.

No Bomb Aimer, no Mid Upper Gunner.

F/L. G.R. Baker was navigator that day and P/O. D.T. Pettit 2nd Pilot.

16 to 20/08/1945

LM544 JI-A Dodge Italy A.M. ca. 20.20 PM

16/08/1945 Waterbeach ca. 07.06 to 10.53, Bari ca. 20.20, - Returned 20/08/1945 Bari xx.xx, Waterbeach ca. 15.19 to 17.14.

No Bomb Aimer, no Mid Upper Gunner.

F/L. G.R. Baker was navigator that day and P/O. D.T. Pettit 2nd Pilot.

Repatriation of 20 Army personnel. 14 a/c airborne for Italy. One a/c went u/s. All aircrew landed safely at Bari, Italy.

F/O. Stanley Milton Anderson

170283 (1373407)   F/O. Stanley, Milton Anderson. Pilot.
J.93786 P/O.   Kenneth Earl Rhodes, RCAF. A/Bomber.
J.89982 P/O.   William Oswald Derry Larmouth, RCAF.   Navigator.
1233064 Sgt.   Raymond Percival Whitehall.   WOP/AG.
J.93712 P/O.   Kenneth Arthur Jeffery, RCAF.   MU/Gunner.
J.94395 P/O.   Charles Nott Samson, RCAF. R/Gunner.
615819   Sgt. A. Wilson.   F/Engineer.

20/07/1944 HK571 JI-L Bombing Homberg   23.07 01.24 x
   Bomb load 1 x 4000 HC, 2 x 500 MC, 14 x 500 GP. Primary target:
Homberg, Oil plant.
Crashed at Daubenspeckhof. Probably shot down by Hptm. Hermann Greiner,
11./NJG1, crashing at 01.24 21/07/1944 at Daubenspeckhof 1 km W. of Moers
(in target area).
   All crew KIA and are now buried in the Reichswald Forest War Cemetery.

F/O. Leonard Nixon Arkless

152343 (1802198) F/O. Leonard Nixon Arkless. Pilot.
152967 (1396186) F/O. Alec Jabez Desmond Teece. A/Bomber.
156772 (1681220) F/O. Ian Partington.   Navigator.
1271373 Sgt. Thomas Edward Jones. WOP/AG.
1853662 Sgt. James Harman. MU/Gunner.
1825696 Sgt. Robert Duncan Dumbreck Shields. R/Gunner.
1868535 Sgt. Alan Howard White. F/Engineer.

31/08/1944 LM285 JI-K Bombing Pont-Remy 16.02   18.11   19.32
Bomb load 11 x 1000 MC, 4 x 500 GP Mk IV Long Delay. Primary target: Pont Remy, Dump. Weather cloudy. Bombed from 15,000 feet on G.H.
05/09/1944 LM285 JI-K Bombing Le Havre   17.27   19.24   20.27
Bomb load 11 x 1000 MC and 4 x 500 GP. Bombed from 13,500 feet on red T.I.
06/09/1944 LM285 JI-K Bombing Le Havre   16.35   18.49   20.09
Bomb load 11 x 1000 MC and 4 x 500 GP Mk IV Long Delay. Weather cloudy. Bombed from 15,000 feet on G.H.
08/09/1944 PB426 JI-J Bombing Le Havre   05.53   07.58   09.20
Bomb load 11 x 1000 MC and 4 x 500 GP. Bombed from 5,000 feet on red and green T.I.s.
12/09/1944 LM724 JI-B Bombing Frankfurt   18.31   23.03   01.09
Bomb load 1 x 4000 HC, 14 x 500 Clusters 4lb. Primary target: Frankfurt - Main. Weather clear over the target. Bombed at 23.03 hours from 17,000 feet centre of clusters of red and green T.I.s.
20/09/1944 LM277 JI-F Bombing Calais 14.48
Bomb load 11 x 1000 MC and 4 x 500 GP. Weather clear over target. Aircraft Missing.

Crashed in the sea near the target. JI-F was the only aircraft lost on the Calais raid, which involved 646 aircraft in total. It is clear that this was the aircraft reported to have crashed into the sea off Calais. It is not clear from the description in the ORB (above) whether JI-F was in fact hit by flak or bombs from another aircraft. Sadly there were no survivors from the crew. Four have no known graves, but F/O. Partington and Sgt. Jones are buried in Calais Canadian War Cemetery and Sgt. Harman is buried at Wissant Communal Cemetery.

F/S. Paul Michael Ashpitel, DFM

1378365 F/S. Paul Michael Ashpitel, DFM. Pilot.

1450549 F/S. Bryan George Green. A/Bomber.

135670 (1464986) F/O. William Llewellyn Wynn Jones. Navigator.

1175873 Sgt. Richard Alan Hounsome, DFM. WOP/AG. 1 op

169554 (1076809) Sgt. James Morton Hydes. WOP/AG. 1 op

1387235 Sgt. Robert Samuel Cole. WOP/AG. 15ops

143598 (1397354) F/O. Harold Cherberd Bryant, DFC. MU/Gunner. 13ops

1586017 Sgt. G.R. Hutton. MU/Gunner. 4 ops

1618730 Sgt. George Henry Thornton. R/Gunner. 1 op

976475 W/O. Raymond Frank Joseph Cyril "Ray" Hall. R/Gunner. 16ops

1032632 Sgt. Stanley Frank Martin. F/Engineer. 15ops

173829 (1393193) Sgt. Donald Albert Winterford. F/Engineer. 1 op

1330027 Sgt. M.C.L. Bristow. F/Engineer. 1 op

11/11/1943 DS822 JI-T Gardening La Tranche 17.35 01.19
Gardening. Bomb Load 2 x G714 and 2 x H802. No cloud.

02/12/1943 DS822 JI-T Bombing Berlin 17.04 20.23 23.27
Bomb load 1 x 2000 HC, 40 x 30 incendiaries, 810 x 4 incendiaries and 90 x 4 incendiaries. Clear, cloud nil. Bombed with total load on green T.I. from 20,000 feet. Good number of incendiaries catching hold as we left target area. Well concentrated. Very little trouble with flak, and no fighters seen over the route.

03/12/1943 DS822 JI-T Bombing Leipzig 00.49 07.09
Bomb load 1 x 2000 HC, 48 x 30 incendiaries, 800 x 4 incendiaries and 100 x 4 incendiaries. Satisfactory route, markers seen, no troubles. 10/10ths cloud over target, starting to break on aircraft's left. Bombed with total load on release flares.

16/12/1943 DS822 JI-T Bombing Berlin 16.52 20.04 23.44
Bomb load 1 x 4000, 11 cans incendiaries. 10/10ths cloud over target. Red and green flares seen. Bombed from 19,000 feet. Glows of fires seen through cloud. Photographs attempted. Landed at Little Snoring.

24/12/1943 DS822 JI-T Bombing Berlin 00.52 04.04 07.48
Bomb load 1 x 4000, 32 x 30 incendiaries, 450 x 4 incendiaries and 90 x 4 incendiaries. 5/10ths cloud, visibility otherwise OK. Skymarkers and fires with green T.I.s near it. Bombed from 19,500 feet. Concentration good and a promising attack. No photo attempted.

14/01/1944 LL683 JI-P Bombing Brunswick 16.57 19.39
Bomb load 1 x 4000 and 48 x 30 incendiaries. Returned early. Intercom U/S. Farthest point reached 5220N 0210E. Load jettisoned.

20/01/1944 DS822 JI-T Bombing Berlin 16.11 19.42 23.45
Bomb load 1 x 4000, 32 x 30, 540 x 4 and 60 x 4 incendiaries. There was

10/10ths cloud. Bombed from 20,000 feet on red flares with green stars. T.I.s well concentrated. Orange glow seen.

21/01/1944 DS822 JI-T Bombing Magdeburg 19.57 23.04 02.47

Bomb load 1 x 4000, 720 x 4, 90 x 4 and 32 x 30 incendiaries. Clear patch over Magdeburg, remainder 10/10ths cloud. Bombed from 19,000 feet. Red and green T.I.s seen also incendiaries and numerous fires. Route across coast too lively.

27/01/1944 DS822 JI-T Bombing Berlin 17.47 20.31 02.12

Bomb load 1 x 4000, 32 x 30, 450 x 4 and 90 x 4 incendiaries. There was 10/10ths cloud. Bombed from 19,000 feet. Quiet trip, good route. Photo taken. One fighter seen over target.

30/01/1944 DS822 JI-T Bombing Berlin 17.18 20.27 23.24

Bomb load 1 x 4000, 600 x 4, 90 x 4 and 32 x 30 incendiaries. There was 10/10ths cloud. Bombed from 18,000 feet. Big glow of fires seen through clouds. Route good. Bright moon above clouds. Numerous fighters seen. Had encounter with an enemy aircraft

15/02/1944 DS822 JI-T Bombing Berlin 17.28 21.23 00.19

Bomb load 1 x 2000, 1 x 1000, 24 x 30 and 900 x 4 incendiaries. There was 10/10ths cloud. Bombed from 20,000 feet. Area well lit up with whitish glow. Route very good. Too early over target to give good description, but fires appeared to be increasing on leaving target area.

19/02/1944 DS822 JI-T Bombing Leipzig 23.55 04.08 06.48

Bomb load 1 x 4000, 32 x 30, 510 x 4 and 90 x 4 incendiaries. There was 10/10ths cloud. Bombed from 20,000 feet. Sky markers well concentrated. P.Q.R. very scattered and valueless. Route very good. Photo attempted.

21/02/1944 DS822 JI-T Bombing Stuttgart 00.16 04.06 07.26

Bomb load 1 x 4000, 40 x 30, 690 x 4 and 90 x 4 incendiaries. There was 4/10ths cloud, broken over target. Bombed from 20,000 feet. Fires appeared to be converging into one large conflagration. Route good, practically flak and fighter free.

24/02/1944 DS822 JI-T Bombing Schweinfurt 20.46 01.08 04.38

Bomb load 1 x 4000, 24 x 30, 320 x 4 and 90 x 4 incendiaries. Weather was clear. Bombed from 20,000 feet. Whole of town in N.W. bank of river was a mass of fires. No one could be left alive there, terrific fires. Little opposition. Route very satisfactory.

07/03/1944 DS822 JI-T Bombing Le Mans 19.36 21.47 00.02

Bomb load 10 x 1000 and 4 x 500 lb. bombs. There was 10/10ths cloud, tops at 5,500/6,000 feet. Bombed from 5,000 feet. Bombed in centre of 4 red T.I.s. Marshalling Yards seen below. Believed to have been a good effort.

15/03/1944 DS822 JI-T Bombing Stuttgart 19.21 23.16 03.34

Bomb load 1 x 1000, 72 x 30, 1050 x 4 and 90 x 4 incendiaries. There was 7/10ths cloud. White flares and green T.I.s on approach, red T.I.s on arrival. Bombed from 19,000 feet. Built up area seen. Number of incendiaries appeared to undershoot. Good route. P.F.F. Markers in open country south of target.

22/03/1944 DS822 JI-T Bombing Frankfurt   18.34   21.54   00.33

Bomb load 1 x 1000, 64 x 30, 1161 x 4 and 129 x 4 incendiaries. There was 5/10ths thin cloud. Bombed from 19,000 feet. 2 x Incendiaries from another aircraft fell into the mid upper turret, severing oxygen mask of Mid Upper Gunner. There were many searchlights, Wireless Operator counted 127.

F/L.   Bertram Arthur Audis

125416 (1389496)   F/L. Bertram Arthur Audis. Pilot.
F/S. T. Burns.   A/Bomber.
164206 (1804805)   F/O. Alan Dron Lacey.   Navigator.
F/S. K.G. Summerfield. WOP/AG.
Sgt. A.J. Mackness.   MU/Gunner.
Sgt. A. Kallick.   R/Gunner.
Sgt. E.G. "Ted" Key.   F/Engineer.
J41845 F/O. E. "Eddie" Monahan RCAF. 2nd Pilot.09/04/1945

Passengers 08/05/1945, 22/06/1945, 12/07/1945, 18/07/1945.

28/01/1945 LM724JI-H Bombing Cologne-Gremberg 10.19   14.12 16.06

Bomb load 1 x 4000 HC, 10 x 500 ANM64, 2 x 500 GP, 3 x 250 GP. Primary target: Koln- Gremberg, Marshalling yards. Weather 10/10ths cloud en route clearing on apprach to target where visibility was good and nil cloud. Bombed at 14.12 hours from 19,500 feet on G.H. Leader.

F/L. B. A. Audis flew the mission as 2nd pilot with S/L. K.G. Condict crew.

29/01/1945 LM285A2-K   Bombing Krefeld   10.28   14.00   15.54

Bomb load 1 x 4000 HC, 10 x 500 ANM64, 2 x 500 GP, 4 x 250 GP. Primary target: Krefeld Marshalling Yards. Weather 10/10ths low thin cloud over target although clear patches en-route. Bombed at 14.00 hours from 20,000 feet.

01/02/1945 LM285A2-K   Bombing Munchen Gladbach 13.16 16.35 18.28

Bomb load 1 x 4000 HC, 14 x No 14 Clusters. Primary target: Munchen-Gladbach, Marshalling yards. Bombed at 16.35 hours from 18,900 feet.

02/02/1945 PD334 A2-D Bombing Wiesbaden 20.40   00.01   03.15

Bomb load 1 x 4000 HC, 10 x 500 ANM64, 2 x 500 GP, 4 x 250 GP. Primary target: Wiesbaden. Weather 10/10ths cloud, winds very erratic. Bombed from 16,000 feet on glow of flares. Explosion beneath at 00.02 hours, causing aircraft to spin down - pulled out at 3000 feet

03/02/1945 LM285A2-K   Bombing Dortmund-Huckarde.16.19 19.50 21.25

Bomb load 1 x 4000 HC, 2 x 500 MC, 2 x 500 MC I/Delay, 6 x 500 ANM64,

2 x 500 GP, 3 x 250 GP. Primary target Dortmund-Huckarde, Coking plant. Weather clear with slight haze. Bombed at 19.50 hours from 19,300 feet.on Red T.Is. Holes in perspex and bomb doors over target due to heavy flak.

08/02/1945 PB482 A2-K Bombing Hohenbudberg 03.35   06.25   08.09

Bomb load 1 x 4000 HC, 2 x 500 MC, 4 x 250 GP, 4 x 500 GP, 6 x 500 ANM64. Primary target: Hohenbudberg, Marshalling yards. Weather 8/10ths cloud over target. Bombed at 06.25 hours from 18,200 feet.on Red T.Is. Bombing concentrated on T.Is.

13/02/1945 PB482 A2-K Bombing Dresden 21.44   01.36   07.00

Bomb load 1 x 500 MC, 15 x No. 14 Clusters. Primary target: Dresden. Weather 5/10ths cloud over target. Bombed at 01.36 hours from 20,000 feet. on Red T.Is. Aircraft attacked by fighter on outward journey.

14/02/1945 PB482 A2-K Bombing Chemnitz 20.26 00.33   04.29

Bomb load 1 x 500 MC, 15 x No. 14 Clusters. Primary target: Chemnitz. Weather 8-10/10ths cloud, tops 15-16,000 feet with occasinal breaks. Bombed from 19,200 feet. on Green flare with Red star.

16/02/1945 PB482 A2-K Bombing Wesel 12.30   16.01½ 17.38

Bomb load 1 x 4000 HC, 4 x 500 GP, 2 x 500 MC L/Delay, 4 x 250 GP, 6 x 500 ANM64. Primary target: Wesel. Weather clear. Bombed from 19,000 feet. on leading aircraft.

18/02/1945 PB482 A2-K Bombing Wesel x x x

Bomb load 1 x 4000 HC, 4 x 500 GP, 2 x 500 MC L/Delay, 4 x 250 GP, 6 x 500 ANM64. Primary target: Wesel. Weather 10/10ths cloud. Failed to take off. Unserviceable port inner engine.

19/02/1945 PB482 A2-K Bombing Wesel 13.01   16.36   19.19

Bomb load 1 x 4000 HC, 6 x 500 MC, 6 x 500 ANM64, 4 x 250 GP. Primary target: Wesel. Weather over target 5-7/10ths cloud. Bombed at 16.36 hours from 19,000 feet. on G.H. Leader. Landed at Moreton in Marsh.

25/02/1945 PB419 A2-B Bombing Kamen   09.34   12.46   14.59

Bomb load 1 x 4000 HC, 9 x 500 ANM64, 2 x 500 MC, 4 x 250 GP. Primary target: Kamen. Weather 6-8/10ths cloud. Bombed at 12.46 hours from 20,000 feet. on G.H. Leader

27/02/1945 PB482 A2-K Bombing Gelsenkirchen 10.49   14.27½ 16.38

Bomb load 1 x 4000 HC, 2 x 500 MC (L/D 37B), 9 x 500 ANM64, 4 x 250 GP. Primary target: Gelsenkirchen (Alma Pluts) Benzin plant. Weather 10/10ths cloud, 6/10,000 feet tops. Bombed at 14.27½ hours from 20,000 feet. on G.H. Leader.

10/03/1945 PB482 A2-K Bombing Gelsenkirchen 12.13   15.37   17.32

Bomb load 1 x 4000 HC, 13 x 500 ANM64, 2 x 500 MC. Primary target: Gelsenkirchen. Weather 10/10ths cloud at target, tops 8,000 feet. Bombed at 15.37 hours from 19,000 feet. on G.H. Leader.

12/03/1945 NN781 A2-B Bombing Dortmund 13.04 16.57 19.07

Bomb load 1 x 4000 HC, 13 x 500 ANM64. Primary target: Dortmund. Weather 10/10ths cloud over target, tops 6/10,000 feet. Bombed at 16.57 hours from 19,100 feet followed G.H. aircraft. one hole through trailing edge of port wing by heavy flak at 16.55 hours.

14/03/1945 NN781 A2-B Bombing Heinrichshutte 13.17 16.40 18.46

Bomb load 1 x 4000 HC, 12 x 500 ANM64. Primary target: Heinrichshutte, Hattingen Steel works and Benzol plant. Weather 10/10ths cloud, tops 7/12,000 feet. Bombed at 16.40 hours from 18,700 feet on leading G.H. aircraft.

20/03/1945 NN781 A2-B Bombing Hamm 09.49 13.14¾ 15.38

Bomb load 7 x 1000 ANM59, 9 x 500 ANM64. Primary target: Hamm, Marshalling yards. Weather 5/10ths cloud. Bombed at 13.14¾ hours from 18,000 feet. on leading G.H. aircraft.

27/03/1945 ME336 JI-S Bombing Hamm Sachsen 10.45 14.03 16.22

Bomb load 1 x 4000 HC, 13 x 500 ANM64, 2 x 500 MC. Primary target: Hamm Sachsen, Benzol plant. Weather 10/10ths cloud. Bombed at 14.03 hours from 17,000 feet. on leading aircraft, H2S U/S.

04/04/1945 NN776 A2-D Bombing Merseburg (Leuna) 18.49 22.52 02.47

Bomb load 1 x 4000 HC, 6 x 500 ANM64. Bombed primary target Merseburg at 22.52 hours from 20,000 feet on centre of 3 Red and 1 Green T.I.'s. 10/10th cloud. Bombs seen to explode in target area. No T.I.'s on arrival. Target area orbited, second run bombed on T.I.'s. Attack was concentrated on T.I.'s. H.2.S. of area fixed position of target as accurate.

09/04/1945 PB482 A2-K Bombing Kiel 19.36 22.42 01.31

Bombed primary target: Kiel, Submarine Buildings Yards. Weather clear with slight haze. Bomb load 1 x 4000 HC and 12 x 500 ANM64. Bombed centre of Green T.I.'s. at 22.42 hours from 20,000 feet. M/B heard. Visual of Canal and harbour. Many fires started. Huge explosion orange coloured 22.35½. Concentration of bombing seemed to be on the North of marking. Good attack. Fires seen from Sylt outward.

22/04/1945 PD389 A2-J Bombing Bremen 15.10 18.42½ 20.51

Bomb load 1 x 4000 HC, 2 x 500 MC, 14 x 500 ANM 64. Primary target: Bremen, in support of Troop concentration. Weather on approaching target 4-5/10ths cloud. Bombed at 18.42½ hours from 18,000 feet. on G.H. G.H. working well. Appeared a concentrated raid. HF damage between starboard and inner and fuselage. Quiet a concentrated raid - much smoke and fires seen.

29/04/1945 ME529 A2-F Manna The Hague 12.36 13.58 15.15

Weather broken cloud above and clear below. Dropped 5 packs. Difficult to release food packs. Vociferous welcome by crowds of people.

01/05/1945 ME529 A2-F Manna The Hague 13.09 14.30 15.29

Weather clear over target. Dropped 5 Panniers on T.I.'s and White Cross. Had to skirt one rainstorm. It would have been difficult to locate the dropping area without the P.F.F. Bags were confined to the area. Seemed better than last time. Usual greeting from the populace. Guns on coast were manned, there was no opposition.

08/05/1945 NN781 A2-B Manna Rotterdam 12.43 14.13 15.15

Dropped 5 Packs on T.I.'s and White. Clear. Packs well concentrated. Some fell in water on the field.

Passenger LAC. Sumering

11/05/1945 NN781 A2-B   Exodus Juvincourt - Tangmere.11.10 x 17.43

Duration 3.29. Outward 1.39 hours. Collected 24 ex POWs. Homeward 1.50 hours. No R.T. at Tangmere ¾ landing procedure worked very smoothly.

12/05/1945 NN781 A2-B   ExodusBrussels - Tangmere 12.15 x 18.30

Duration 3.15. Outward 1.23 hours. Homeward 1.23 hours. 10 Refugees to Brussels, 24 POW to Tangmere. All OK.

14/05/1945 PD389 A2-J Exodus Juvincourt - Oakley 10.04 x 15.30

Duration 3 hours 42 minutes. Outward 1 hr 33 mins. Collected 24 POWs. Homeward 2.09 hrs. Organisation fine.

17/05/1945 RE123 A2-K   Exodus Brussels - Westcott 10.17 x 16.26

Duration 3 hrs 7 mins. Out 1 hr 23 mins. In 1 hr 47 mins. 10 Belgian refugees out. 24 Ex POWs. Brought back to Westcott. Everything O.K. with exception of poor R.T. at Brussels. Organisation perfect at Westcott.

19/05/1945 RE159 A2-E   Exodus Brussels - Oakley   12.07 x 20.28

Duration 2 hrs 47 mins. Out 1 hr 16 mins. In 1 hr 41 mins. 10 refugees taken to Brussels. 24 POWs. evacuated.

22/06/1945 RA599 JI-L Baedeker Tour over Continent 15.17 x 19.27

Passengers Vaughan, Baron, Haws, Lithgow, Hutchison.

25/06/1945 ME529 A2-F   Post Mortem Special mission 10.04   x 16.06

12/07/1945 ME529 A2-B   Baedeker Tour over Continent 10.08   x 14.30

Passengers F/S. G. Phillips, Sgt. I. Ponder, AC. K. Webster, ACW. Shernon.

18/07/1945 RF272 A2-F   Baedeker Tour over Continent 09.53   x 15.10

Passengers Sgt. Niblett, LAC. Wynne, LAC. Orkley, ACW. Gallagher, ACW. Tride.

F/L. William Gilson Bainbridge

131794 (1109283)   F/L. William Gilson Bainbridge. Pilot.
154912 (1622182)   F/O. Donald Hugh Snazle. A/Bomber.
164716 (1685742)   F/O. Terence Charles Warham.   Navigator.
176988 (1892590)   F/O. Norman Sydney Warren. WOP/AG.   17 ops
   F/S. R.V. Rudling.   WOP/AG.   6 ops
Sgt. H. Spence.   MU/Gunner.   22 ops
Sgt. H. Nicholson.   R/Gunner.
   F/S. D. Robertson.   F/Engineer.

Passengers 03/05/1945, 12/06/1945, 17/06/1945, 26/06/1945, 03/07/1945, 20/07/1945.

01/03/1945 ME387 JI-N Bombing Kamen 11.48 15.05   17.54
   Bomb load 1 x 4000 HC, 11 x 500 ANM64, 2 x 500 MC L/Delay37. Primary target: Kamen, Coking plant. Weather 10/10ths cloud. Bombed at 15.05 hours from 18,500 feet on leading G.H. aircraft and Blue puffs. 1x 500 ANM64 hung up and brought back.
   F/L. W.G. Bainbridge flew the mission as 2nd pilot with S/L. H.C.G. Wilcox crew.
02/03/1945 NG118 A2-H Bombing Koln   12.58 x 17.04
   Bomb load 1 x 4000 HC, 12 x 500 ANM64. Primary   target: Koln. Weather 10/10ths cloud over Koln, South and South-East of Koln clear. Abortive sortie. Farthest point reached 5050N 0400E. Jettisoned 1 x 4000 HC, 8 x 500 ANM64 at 16.07 hours from 10,000 at 5209N 0308E. Remainder of bomb load brought back. Port inner engine unserviceable and had to be feathered. Could not get height or speed so returned to Base.
05/03/1945 ME365 JI-T Bombing Gelsenkirchen 10.22 14.09½   16.07
   Bomb load 1 x 4000 HC, 12 x 500 ANM64. Primary target: Gelsenkirchen, Benzol plant. Weather 10/10ths cloud over target with cirrus cloud at bombing height. Bombed at 14.09½ hours from 21,000 feet on G.H. Leader.
07/03/1945 ME387 JI-N Bombing Dessau 17.11 21.58   01.52
   Bomb load 1 x 4000 HC, 6 x Mk.17 Clusters. Primary target: Dessau. Weather 5 to 10/10ths thin cloud. Bombed at 21.58 hours from 20,000 feet on Red flares with Green stars.
   F/L. W.G. Bainbridge flew the mission as 2nd pilot with S/L. H.C.G. Wilcox crew.
18/03/1945 ME359 JI-T Bombing Bruchstrasse 11.35 15.05   16.50
   Bomb load 1 x 4000 HC, 13 x 500 ANM64, 2 x 500 MC. Primary target: Bruchstrasse, Coal mine and coking plant. Weather 10/10ths cloud, tops 6-12,000 feet. Bombed at 15.05 hours from 18,000 feet on leading G.H. aircraft.
20/03/1945 ME358 JI-O Bombing Hamm 09.50 13.15   15.37

Bomb load 7 x 1000 ANM65, 9 x 500 ANM64. Primary target: Hamm, Marshalling yards. Weather 5/10ths cloud. Bombed at 13.15 hours from 18,250 feet on leading aircraft.

27/03/1945 ME358 JI-O Bombing Hamm Sachsen 10.25 14.02   15.50

Bomb load 1 x 4000 HC, 13 x 500 ANM64, 2 x 500 MC. Primary target: Hamm Sachsen, Benzol plant. Weather 10/10ths cloud. Bombed at 14.02 hours from 17,900 feet on G.H. Leader.

09/04/1945 PB419 JI-L Bombing Kiel   19.42   22.41   02.02

Bomb load 1 x 4000 HC and 12 x 500 ANM64. Primary target: Kiel, Submarine Buildings Yards. Weather clear with slight haze. Bombed at 22.41 hours from 20,000 feet on centre of Green T.I.'s. per M/B. Two marked areas clearly seen. Southern area well on fire burning red. Good attack. Bombing accurate on markers.

18/04/1945 ME422 JI-Q Bombing Heligoland 10.0013.07   15.09

Bomb load 6 x 1000 MC, 10 x 500 ANM64. Primary target: Heligoland, Naval base. Weather no cloud, slight haze. Bombed on smoke, yellow markers and Master Bomber at 13.07 hours from 18,700 feet. Overshot yellow T.I.s by two secs. On M/B's instructions. Mass of smoke and flames. Only harbour to south visible. Seemed like and oil fire in centre of target. Good attack.

30/04/1945 ME358 JI-O Manna Rotterdam 16.49 18.15   19.28

Weather intermittent showers and low cloud. Load 5 packs. Dropped 5 packs on white cross and green very light fired by A/C. Visual. Warm reception from inhabitants. Packs fell short pf A/P on dry land.

03/05/1945 ME358 JI-O Manna The Hague 11.06 x 13.29

Dropped 4 Panniers visually on White Cross and T.I. smoke. Clear over dropping area. Bad over sea. Bags well together. Some flour bags appeared to burst. Usual enthusiastic crowds.

No Mid/Up Gunner that day. Passenger LAC. Constantine

10/05/1945 ME359 JI-T Exodus Juvincourt - Ford 11.10 x 22.10

Duration 3.53. Outward 1.53 hours. Collected 24 ex POWs. Homeward 2.00 hours. Organisation OK.

12/05/1945 ME358 JI-O Exodus   Juvincourt - Wing 09.00   x 13.47

Duration 3.26. Outward 1.32 hours. Collected 24 POWs. Homeward 1.54 hours. Everything O.K.

15/05/1945 ME358 JI-O Exodus Juvincourt - Wing 15.54 x 21.40

Duration 3 hrs 51 mins. Outward 1 hr 45 mins. Collected 24 POWs. Homeward 2 hrs 6 mins. Organisation O.K.

18/05/1945 ME363 JI-R Exodus Brussels - Oakley 12.03 x 18.06

Duration 3 hrs 05 mins. Out 1 hr 12 mins. In 1 hr 53 mins. 10 Belgians refugees taken to Brussels. 24 ex POWs. returned to U.K. No difficulties.

19/05/1945 ME363 JI-R Exodus Brussels - Oakley   12.04   x 18.51

Duration 2 hrs 59 mins. Out 1 hr 56 mins. In 1 hr 43 mins. 10 Belgian refugees to Brussels. 24 ex POWs. evacuated, all military.

24/05/1945 ME380JI-E Exodus Brussels 12.40 x 16.04

Duration 2.15 hours. Out 1.09 hours. In 1.06 hours. 10 Belgian refugees to Brussels. No ex POWs. to be returned.

25/05/1945 ME380JI-E Exodus Brussels 11.58 x 15.58

Duration 2.21 hours. Out 1.13 hours. In 1.08 hours. 10 Belgian refugees returned to Brussels. No POWs. home. Dakotas taking off as a/c about to land, causing own a/c to overshoot and make another circuit.

26/05/1945 ME380JI-E Exodus Brussels - Ford 11.51 x 17.39

Duration 3.05 hours. Out 1.07 hours. In 2.58 hours. 10 Belgian refugees to Brussels. 24 ex POWs. all military brought back.

12/06/1945 ME358JI-O Baedeker Tour over Continent 12.33 x 17.26

Passengers Sgt. R. Simpson, AC. C. Wigley, LAC. M. McCurrie.

17/06/1945 ME358JI-O Baedeker Tour over Continent 14.44 x 18.48

Passengers W/O. Redford, Sgt. Gregory, Sgt. Davidson, Sgt. Murray, LAC. Wolfe.

26/06/1945 ME364JI-P Baedeker Tour over Continent 09.56 x 14.08

Passengers W/O. Bird, Sgt. Box, LAC. Watt, Cpl. Bush, AC. Hunter.

29/06/1945 RE159 A2-E Post Mortem Special mission 09.55 x 15.49

03/07/1945 RE123 A2-K Baedeker Tour over Continent 09.24 x 12.57

Passengers LACW. Schartz, LACW. MacKintosh, LAC. Thomson, LAC. Huggins, Cpl. Smith.

20/07/1945 RE159 A2-E Baedeker Tour over Continent 09.38 x 13.47

Passengers Cpl. Muggeridge, LAC. Green, LAC. Prebble, ACW. Longland, ACW. Graham.

S/L. Acting W/C. Sidney Baker, DSO & Bar, DFC & Bar

115867 (919349) W/C. Sidney Baker. DSO Bar. DFC Bar. Pilot.

    Nil   A/Bomber.

144209 (1109872) S/L. Ronald Duncan MacKay, DFM Navigator.

    F/L. G.K. Baxter.   2nd Navigator.

176988 (1892590) F/O. Norman Sydney Warren. WOP/AG.

    F/S. J.C. Tilley.   WOP/AG.

177174 (1870300) F/O. John Frederick "Johnny" Channell. WOP/AG.

186190 (1895997) F/O. James Handley.   MU/Gunner.

    Nil   R/Gunner.

191847 (962612) P/O. Ralph Swift.   F/Engineer.

    F/S. R.H. Sherwood.   F/Engineer.

Passengers 13/06/1945, 09/07/1945, 30/07/1945.

13/06/1945 RE139 JI-M Baedeker Tour over Continent 10.20 x 14.49

Passengers 76056 W/C. William Harold Nelson Shakespeare MC AFC, LAC. Rice, LAC. Prosser, LAC. Drain.

09 to 14/07/1945

RE158 A2-J Dodge Italy   07.38   12.25   15.40

09/07/1945 Waterbeach 07.38 - Italy 12.25 - Returned 14/07/1945 Italy 09.05 - Waterbeach 15.40

2nd Navigator F/L. G.K. Baxter.

Passengers G/Capt. Innes, W/C. Foden, W/C. Bennett, Cpl. Round, LAC. Haynes.

30/07/1945 ME530 JI-C Baedeker Tour over Continent 13.47 x 18.02

Passengers W/C. Harris, S/O. May, F/S. Keep, LAC. Crossley, LACW. Pilcher.

F/O Acting F/L. Leonard Claude Baines, DFC

NZ39076 F/L. Leonard Claude Baines, DFC RNZAF.   Pilot.

NZ422419 F/O.   W.J. McLay, RNZAF   A/Bomber.

F/S. D.D. or B.D. Cramp.   A/Bomber. 1 op

197275 (1608171)   P/O. George Albert Thomas Mills.   A/Bomber. 1 op

F/S. M.S. Anderson.   Navigator.

P/O. E. Williams.   Navigator. 1 op

164196 (1624262) F/O. George Edward Kiley. Navigator. 1 op

Sgt. H.W. Picton.   WOP/AG.

A425363 W/O.   John Rutherford, RAAF   WOP/AG. 2 ops

Sgt. M. Molyneux.   MU/Gunner.

W/O. George Edgar Sales.   MU/Gun. 2 ops

Sgt. G.E. Lacey-Hatton.   R/Gunner.

Sgt. D. Sawyer.   R/Gunner. 2 ops

Sgt. W.R "Bill". Fletcher.   F/Engineer.

F/L. T. Wake.   F/Engineer. 1 op

191847 (962612) P/O. Ralph Swift.   F/Engineer. 1 op

196313 (1601963)   F/S Ronald Frederick Etherington. 2nd Pilot. 23/03/1945

27/11/1944 NN717 JI-E Bombing Cologne   12.31   15.04   16.15

Bomb load 1 x 4000 HC, 16 x 500 GP. Primary target: Cologne, Marshalling Yards. Weather patchy cloud. Bombed at 15.04 hours from 19,000 feet on G.H. aircraft.

F/O. L.C. Baines flew the mission as 2nd pilot with F/O. T.B. Carpenter crew.

29/11/1944 PB767 JI-G Bombing Neuss 02.58 05.40 07.10

Bomb load 1 x 4000 HC, 6 x 1000 HC, 6 x 500 GP. Primary target: Neuss. Weather 10/10ths cloud over target but the glow of fires was seen through cloud. Bombed at 05.40 hours from 21,000 feet. Sky markers. Sky markers well concentrated, glow of fires through cloud.

F/O. L.C. Baines flew the mission as 2nd pilot with F/O. T.B. Carpenter crew.

30/11/1944 LM733 JI-F Bombing Osterfeld 10.53 13.06 14.57

Bomb load 1 x 4000 HC and 16 x 500 GP. Primary target: Osterfeld, Coking plant. Weather 10/10ths cloud. Bombed at 13.06 hours from 19,000 feet on G.H. Leader.

04/12/1944 PB767 JI-G Bombing Oberhausen 11.55 14.07 16.24

Bomb load 1 x 4000 HC, 6 x 1000 MC and 6 x 500 GP. Primary target: Oberhausen, Built up area. Weather 10/10ths cloud. Bombed at 14.07 hours from 20,000 feet on G.H. Leader.

05/12/1944 PB767 JI-G Bombing Hamm 08.55 11.29 13.46

Bomb load 1 x 4000 HC and 1950 x 4 lb incendiaries. Primary target: Hamm. Weather 10/10ths cloud over target, but otherwise varying from 6-10/10ths. Bombed at 11.29 hours from 20,000 feet on G.H. Leader.

06/12/1944 PB482 JI-P Bombing Merseburg 16.56 20.53 00.19

Bomb load 1 x 4000 HC, 8 x 500 GP and 1 x 500 GP Long Delay. Primary target: Merseburg. Weather 10/10ths cloud with odd breaks. Bombed at 20.53 hours from 20,000 feet on Red/Green flares.

08/12/1944 LM734 JI-U Bombing Duisburg 08.34 11.04 12.59

Bomb load 14 x 1000 ANM59. Primary target: Duisberg. Weather 10/10ths cloud. Bombed at 11.04 hours from 20,000 feet on G.H. Leader.

11/12/1944 PB767 JI-G Bombing Osterfeldt 08.37 11.07 12.56

Bomb load 12 x 1000 ANM65 and 2 x 1000 ANM59. Primary target: Osterfeld. Weather 10/10ths cloud, tops 16,000 feet. Bombed at 11.07 hours from 20,000 feet on G.H. Leader.

28/12/1944 LM685 JI-K Bombing Cologne Gremberg 12.21 15.05 17.00

Bomb load 1 x 4000 HC, 10 x 500 GP and 6 x 250 GP. Primary target: Koln Gremberg, Marshalling yards. Weather 10/10ths cloud or fog. Bombed 15.05 hours from 20,000 feet on G.H. Leader.

01/01/1945 LM717 JI-C Bombing Vohwinkle 16.23 19.47 21.47

Bomb load 1 x 4000 HC, 10 x 500 ANM58 and 2 x 500 GP. Primary target: Vohwinkel. Weather clear. Bombed at 19.47 hours from 19,000 feet on centre of Red T.I.s.

02/01/1945 NF968 JI-B Bombing Nuremburg 15.27 19.37 22.42

Bomb load: 1 x 4000 HC and 7 x 500 Clusters. Primary target: Nuremburg. Weather clear. Bombed at 19.37 hours from 18,000 feet. Undershot T.I.s on Master Bomber's instructions

05/01/1945 LM275 JI-F Bombing Ludwigshafen 11.19 15.08 17.20

Bomb load 1 x 4000 HC, 10 x 500 ANM58, 64, 2 x 500 GP. Primary target:

Ludwigshafen, Marshalling yards. Weather clear over target. Bombed at 15.08 hours from 20,000 feet on leading aircraft. Aircraft hit by flak, port fin damaged.

07/01/1945 PB902 JI-A Bombing Munich   18.53   22.28   02.37

Bomb load 1 x 4000 HC and 7 x 500 clusters. Primary target: Munich. Weather 10/10ths cloud over target 6-8,000 feet with a thin layer altitude 16,000 feet. Bombed at 22.28 hours from 20,000 feet on Red and Green flares.

11/01/1945 PB902 JI-A Bombing Krefeld   11.50 15.16   16.31

Bomb load 1 x 4000 HC, 10 x 500 ANM64 and 4 x 250 GP. Primary target: Krefeld. Weather 10/10ths cloud above and below. Visibility poor. Bombed at 15.16 hours from 20,000 feet on G.H. Leader.

13/01/1945 PB902 JI-A Bombing Saarbrucken   11.48   15.22   17.46

Bomb load 1 x 4000 HC, 10 x 500 ANM58 or 64 and 4 x 250 GP. Primary target: Saarbrucken. Weather 3-5/10ths cloud, tops 4/5,000 feet. Bombed at 15.22 hours from 20,000 feet on G.H. Leader. All aircrafts of this ops were diverted on return to Exeter as weather at base was unfit to land.

15/01/1945 PB902 JI-A Bombing Lagendreer   11.48   15.02   16.44

Bomb load 1 x 4000 HC, 10 x 500 ANM64 and 4 x 250 GP. Primary target: Lagendreer. Weather 10/10ths cloud. Bombed at 15.02 hours from 18,500 feet on G.H. Leader.

16/01/1945 PB902 JI-A Bombing Wanne-Eickel   23.20   02.29   04.30

Bomb load 1 x 4000 HC, 10 x 500 ANM58 and 4 x 250 GP. Primary target: Wanne-Eickel, Benzol plant. Weather 10/10ths thin low cloud. Bombed at 02.29 hours from 18,000 feet on Red and Green sky markers.

22/01/1945 PB902 JI-A Bombing Hamborn   16.56   20.06   21.49

Bomb load 1 x 4000 HC, 7 x 500 ANM58 or 64, 2 x 500 GP (L/Delay), 3 x 250 GP. Primary target: Hamborn, Thyssen works. Weather over target clear and almost as bright as day. Bombed at 20.06½ hours from 20,000 feet on U concentrated Green T.I.

03/02/1945 NN773 JI-K Bombing Dortmund-Huckarde 16.16   19.37 21.26

Bomb load 1 x 4000 HC, 2 x 500 MC, 2 x 500 MC L/Delay, 6 x 500 ANM64, 2 x 500 GP and 3 x 250 GP. Primary target Dortmund-Huckarde, Coking plant. Weather clear with slight haze. Bombed at 19.37 hours from 19,500 feet on centre of Red T.Is. Bombing concentrated, much smoke.

08/02/1945 PB142 JI-G Bombing Hohenbudberg 03.31   06.42   08.40

Bomb load 1 x 4000 HC, 2 x 500 MC, 4 x 250 GP, 4 x 500 GP, 6 x 500 ANM64. Primary target: Hohenbudberg, Marshalling yards. Weather 8/10ths cloud over target. Bombed 06.42 hours from 19,000 feet on Red T.I.

13/02/1945 PB142 JI-G Bombing Dresden   21.40   01.31   06.47

Bomb load 1 x 4000 HC, and 7 x No. 14 Clusters. Primary target: Dresden. Weather 5/10ths cloud over target. Bombed 01.31 hours from 19,000 feet on Green T.I.

14/02/1945 PB902 JI-A Bombing Chemnitz   20.25   01.05   04.59

Bomb load 1 x 4000 HC and 8 x No. 14 Clusters. Primary target: Chemnitz.

Weather 8-10/10ths cloud, tops 15-16,000 feet with occasional breaks. Attacked last resort 49.35N, 11.55E (Built up area). Bombed at 01.05 hours from 11,000 feet on H2S. Master Bomber not heard and no markers seen.

16/02/1945 PB142 JI-G Bombing Wesel 12.25 16.00 17.46

Bomb load 1 x 4000 HC, 4 x 500 GP, 2 x 500 MC L/Delay, 4 x 250 GP, 6 x 500 ANM64. Primary target: Wesel. Weather clear. Bombed at 16.00 hours from 20,000 feet on G.H.

18/02/1945 PB142 JI-G Bombing Wesel 11.25 15.24 16.55

Bomb load 1 x 4000 HC, 4 x 500 GP, 2 x 500 MC L/Delay, 3 x 250 GP, 6 x 500 ANM64. Primary target: Wesel. Weather 10/10ths cloud. Bombed at 15.24 hours from 20,000 feet on G.H.

23/02/1945 LM724 JI-H Bombing Gelsenkirchen 11.19 15.01½ 18.12

Bomb load 1 x 4000 HC, 9 x 500 ANM64, 2 x 500 MC and 4 x 250 GP. Primary target Gelsenkirchen. Weather 10/10ths cloud. Bombed at 15.01½ hours from 19,500 feet on G.H.

26/02/1945 ME351 JI-U Bombing Dortmund 10.29 14.03 16.10

Bomb load 1 x 4000 HC, 2 x 500 MC L/Delay 37B, 9 x 500 ANM64, 3 x 250 GP. Primary target: Dortmund, Hoesch Benzin plant. Weather 10/10ths cloud, tops 8/10,000 feet. Bombed at 14.03 hours from 20,000 feet on G.H. equipment.

28/02/1945 PB142 JI-G Bombing Nordstern 08.41 12.04½ 14.01

Bomb load 1 x 4000 HC, 9 x 500 ANM64, 2 x 500 MC L/Delay, 3 x 250 GP and 1 Green Puff. Primary target: Nordstern (Gelsenkirchen). Weather 10/10ths cloud. Bombed at 12.04½ hours from 21,000 feet on G.H.

11/03/1945 PB142 JI-G Bombing Essen 11.28 15.25¼ 17.12

Bomb load 1 x 4000 HC, 13 x 500 ANM64, 2 x 500 MC and 1 Skymarker Blue Puff. Primary target: Essen, Marshalling yards. Weather 10/10ths cloud, tops 7/8000 feet. Bombed at 15.25¼ hours from 19,000 feet on G.H. 3 Blue smoke puffs seen after bombing in target area.

14/03/1945 LM285 JI-A Bombing Heinrichshutte 13.11 16.41 18.45

Bomb load 1 x 4000 HC, 11 x 500 ANM64 and 1 Skymarker Red Puff. Primary target: Heinrichshutte, Hattingen Steel works and Benzol plant. Weather 10/10ths cloud, tops 7/12,000 feet. Bombed at 16.41 hours from 18,500 feet on G.H.

18/03/1945 LM285 JI-A Bombing Bruchstrasse 11.37 15.05 17.00

Bomb load 1 x 4000 HC, 13 x 500 ANM64, 2x 500 MC and 1 Skymarker Blue Puff. Primary target: Bruchstrasse, Coal mine and coking plant. Weather 10/10ths cloud, tops 6-12,000 feet. Bombed at 15.05 hours from 19,000 feet on G.H.

21/03/1945 LM285 JI-A Bombing Munster 10.16 13.08 15.30

Bomb load 1 x 4000 HC, 13 x 500 ANM64, 2 x 500 MC, 1 Skymarker Blue Puff. Primary target Munster Viaduct and Marshalling Yards. Weather cloud nil to 2/10ths. Bombed at 13.08 hours from 18,500 feet on G.H. and visual. Bomb bursts concentrated on Railway Junctions.

23/03/1945 LM285 JI-A Bombing Wesel 14.21 17.38½ 19.01

Bomb load 13 x 1000 MC. Primary target: Wesel, in support of ground troops. Weather perfect. Bombed at 17.38½ hours from 19,500 feet on G.H. All bombs appeared to fall in town.

2nd pilot that day was F/S. Ronald Frederick Etherington.

29/03/1945 LM285 JI-A Bombing Salzgitter 12.18 16.43½ 19.03

Bomb load 1 x 4000 HC and 8 x 500 ANM64. Primary target: Salzgitter, Hallendorf works. Weather 10/10ths cloud. Bombed 16.43½ hours from 22,500 feet on G.H. Leader.

09/04/1945 LM285 JI-A Bombing Kiel 19.27½ 22.40 01.59

Bomb load 1 x 4000 HC and 12 x 500 ANM64. Primary target: Kiel, Submarine Buildings Yards. Weather clear with slight haze. Bombed on red and green T.I.'s at 22.40 hours from 19,500 feet. Undershot green T.I.s by 1 sec on Master Bomber's instructions. Two attacks seen when bombing, but merged into one attack later. Gee u/s on return. Good attack.

18/05/1945 RE137 JI-D Exodus Brussels - Oakley 11.57 x 16.59

Duration 3 hrs 18 mins. Out 1 hr 14 mins. In 2 hrs 02 mins. 8 Belgian refugees taken to Brussels. 24 ex POWs. returned. Everything satisfactory
. Crew that day D.D. or B.D. Cramp. A/Bomber, P/O. E. Williams. Navigator, W/O. John Rutherford, RAAF WOP/AG., W/O. George Edgar Sales. MU/Gunner., Sgt. D. Sawyer. R/Gunner., F/L. T. Wake. F/Engineer.

19/05/1945 RE116 JI-F Exodus Brussels - Oakley 11.48 x 19.32

Duration 2 hrs 54 mins. Out 1 hr 13 mins. In 1 hr 41 mins. 10 Belgians taken to Brussels. 24 ex POWs. returned to U.K.

Crew that day P/O. George Albert Thomas Mills. A/Bomber, F/O. George Edward Kiley Navigator, W/O. John Rutherford, RAAF WOP/AG., W/O. George Edgar Sales. MU/Gunner., Sgt. D. Sawyer. R/Gunner., P/O. Ralph Swift. F/Engineer.

F/O.   Donald Beaton, DSO

1st crew.

179980 (1344715)   P/O Donald "Don" Beaton. DSO.   Pilot.
752638 W/O. Frederick Donovan "Don" Say, DFC   A/Bomber.
A428080 F/O. Geoffrey Alan Trollope, RAAF   A/Bomber.1 op
55949 (627877)   P/O. Bernard Cecil Ogilwy Baynes.   Navigator.
161741 (657060) F/O. Alfred Ernest Nye. DFC   Navigator.1 op
179828 (1124503)   P/O. Bernard Alban James Hargreaves, DFC   WOP/AG.
103538 (902785) F/L. Vivian George Ivor Outen. DFC WOP/AG.1 op
1316691 Sgt. T.W. or E.M. Temple.   MU and R/Gun.
1485238 Sgt. R. or T. Rutherford.   MU and R/Gun.
1825315 Sgt. James Sherry. DFM   F/Engineer.

W/O. Frederick Donovan
"Don" Say, DFC

P/O. Robert MacPherson
"Bob" Toms
(courtesy Toms family)

24/06/1944 DS786 A2-F   Bombing Rimeux 23.20 00.33   01.59
   Bomb load 18 x 500 GP. Primary target: Rimeux, Flying bomb installations.
Weather clear. Bombed at 0033 hours from 12,200 feet, centre of cluster of
Red T.I.s. Bomb burst well on Red T.I.s. Yellow fires seen 2 or 3 miles away.
Many searchlights.
30/06/1944 LL716 A2-G   Bombing Villers Bocage 18.15   20.00   21.32
   Bomb load 11 x 1000 MC and 3 x 500 GP. Primary target: Villers Bocage.
Weather 10/10ths cloud, but a good break over the target. Bombed at2000
hours from 12,000 feet on Red T.I. Target obscured by smoke. Bombing was

49

OK but flying discipline bad. Many stragglers.

02/07/1944 LL677 A2-E   Bombing Beauvoir 12.59   14.37   15.54

Bomb load 11 x 1000 MC, 4 x 500 GP. Primary target: Beauvoir, Flying bomb supply site. Bombed from 8,500 feet on Yellow T.I.s.

05/07/1944 LL677 A2-E   Bombing Watten   22.52   00.10   01.09

Bomb load 11 x 1000 ANM 65, 4 x 500 GP. Primary target: Watten, Constructional works. Bombed at 0010 hours from 8,500 feet Red and Green T.I.s.

07/07/1944 DS787 A2-D   Bombing Vaires 22.49   00.23

Bomb load 7 x 1000 MC, 4 x 500 GP. To attack Vaires, Marshalling yards. Abortive Sortie. Returned early, Rear turret U/S. Jettisoned at 23.37 hours from 4,500 feet. Position 52.18N, 02.13E, 4 x 500 GP.

10/07/1944 LL677 A2-E   Bombing Nucourt 04.30 06.06   07.30

Bomb load 11 x 1000 ANM 65, 4 x 500 GP. Primary target: Nucourt, Constructional works. Bombed at 0606 hours from 15,500 feet on Gee.

12/07/1944 LL677 A2-E   Bombing Vaires 18.02 21.40

Bomb load 18 x 500 GP. To attack Vaires, Marshalling yards. Abandoned mission as ordered by Master Bomber. Jettisoned at 20.44 hours 4 x 500 GP from 19,000 feet, position 49.45N, 00.43E.

15/07/1944 LL677 A2-E   Bombing Chalons sur Marne 21.47   02.47

Bomb load 18 x 500 GP. Primary target: Chalons sur Marne, Railway centre. Returned early Starboard inner engine feathered due to fire. The fire suspected to have led to an attack by two twin-engined enemy aircraft, 1 from starboard quarter down. Lancaster corkscrewed, Rear Gunner fired long burst. Then the Second aircraft was seen on Port quarter down, Rear Gunner again firing. Lancaster evaded in cloud and kept losing height and airspeed, so jettisoned at 48.10N, 10.40E at 00.42 hours from 10,000 feet. Furthest point reached 48.12N, 01.54E.

No claim. According combat report T.W. (or E.M.) Temple was Rear Gunner that day."

18/07/1944 LL677 A2-E   Bombing Emieville 04.21   06.05   07.13

Bomb load 11 x 1000 MC, 4 x 500 GP. Primary target: Emieville, Troop concentration. Weather clear. Bombed at 0605 hours from 7,000 feet South East corner of wood. A good attack.

20/07/1944 LL677 A2-E   Bombing Homburg 23.37   01.24   03.08

Bomb load 1 x 4000 HC, 2 x 500 MC, 14 x 500 GP. Primary target: Homberg, Oil plant. Slight haze. Bombed at 0124 hours from 17,500 feet red T.I. Terrific explosion at 01.23 hours. Head-on attack by single engine fighter just after leaving target. According Baynes logbook "2 combats".

23/07/1944 LL677 A2-E   Bombing Kiel 22.30   01.27   04.00

Bomb load 6 x 1000 MC and 10 x 500GP. Primary target: Kiel, Warehouses and docks. Weather 10/10ths low cloud. Bombed at 0127 hours from 19,000 feet centre of Red and Green T.I.s. Very bright orange explosion seen in target area.

24/07/1944 LL677 A2-E   Bombing Stuttgart 21.44 23.00

Bomb load 5 x 1000 ANM65 and 3 x 500 GP. Returned early with Rear Turret U/S. Jettisoned 52.19N, 02.30E.

25/07/1944 LL677 A2-E   Bombing Stuttgart 21.44   01.59   05.29

Bomb Load 5 x 1000 MC and 3 x 500 GP. Weather clear, slight haze. Bombed at 0159 hours from 20,000 feet centre of Red T.I.s. Marking scattered.

04/08/1944 LL677 A2-E   Bombing Bec d'Ambes 13.43 18.01   21.12

Bomb load 5 x 1000 MC and 2 x 500 GP. Primary target: Bec d'Ambes depot. Weather clear. Bombed at 1801 hours from 8,200 feet on Yellow T.I.s. Many tanks seen to explode with much flame and black smoke.

07/08/1944 DS787 A2-G   Bombing Mare de Magne   22.00   23.48 01.04

Bomb load 9 x 1000 MC and 4 x 500 GP. Primary target: Mare de Magne (just past Caen). Weather clear, slight haze. Bombed at 2348 hours from 7,000 feet port of Red T.I.s as ordered. Fair concentration of T.I.s. Bombing concentrated.

11/08/1944 LL677 A2-E   Bombing Lens 14.18 16.34   17.52

Bomb load 11 x 1000 MC and 4 x 500 GP. Primary target: Lens, Marshalling yards. Small patches of cloud. Bombed at 1634 hours from 14,300 feet, Yellow and Red T.I.s. Concentrated attack, many bomb bursts on northern part of yards.

15/08/1944 LL677 A2-E   Bombing St Trond 10.08   12.09   13.25

Bomb load 11 x 1000 MC and 4 x 500 GP. Primary target St. Trond Airfield. Weather clear. Bombed at 1209 hours from 17,000 feet on intersection of runways. Satisfactory attack.

16/08/1944 LL677 A2-E   Bombing Stettin   21.18   00.10

Bomb Load 1 x 2000 HC and 9 x 500lb 'J' type clusters. Returned early, failure of both generators. Jettisoned 9 x 500lb 'J' type clusters at 23.05 hours from 3,000 feet, position 54.28N, 04.45E.

18/08/1944 LL677 A2-E   Bombing Bremen 21.44 00.42   02.39

Bomb load 1 x 2000 HC, 96 x 30, 810 x 4 and 9 x 40 incendiaries. Weather 10/10ths cloud. Bombed at 0042 hours from 18,000 feet. Centre of general flak area. Markers not seen. Navigation trouble caused us to be late over Bremen. Nothing in view and all quiet so set course and bombed first flak area – Emden.

25/08/1944 LL677 A2-E   Bombing Vincly   18.36   20.36   21.58

Bomb load 11 x 1000 MC, 2 x 500 GP MK-IV and 2 x 500 GP MK-IV Long Delay. Weather, cloud clearing. Bombed at 2036 hours from 14,600 feet, visual of G.H. Leader.

26/08/1944 LL677 A2-E   Bombing Kiel 20.22 23.12   01.26

Bomb load 1 x 4000 HC, 72 x 30 IB, 600 x 4, 90 x 4lb. Primary target: Kiel. Weather clear. Bombed at 2312 hours from 20,000 feet, centre of Red T.I.s. Yellow explosion in target area 23.11 hours. Splendid attack, fires getting a good hold.

31/08/1944 LL677 A2-E   Bombing Pont-Remy 16.10   18.10   19.37

Bomb load 11 x 1000 MC, 2 x 500 GP MK-IV Long Delay. Primary target: Pont Remy, Dump. Weather cloudy, bombed at 1810 hours from 14,800 feet on G.H.

03/09/1944 LL677 A2-E Bombing Eindhoven 15.19 17.29 18.47

Bomb load 11 x 1000 MC, 4 x 500 GP. Primary target: Eindhoven airfield. Bombed at 1729 hours from 17,000 feet, visually.

08/09/1944 LL677 A2-E Bombing Le Havre 05.56 08.05 08.52

Bomb load 11 x 1000 MC, 4 x 500 GP. Primary target: Le Havre. Weather 10/10ths cloud down to 3000 feet. Bombed at 0805 hours from 4,500 feet, 400 yards short of T.I.s.

Detailed to bomb strong points near the beleaguered German Garrison. Hit by Flak and very severely damaged. Crash-landed 0852 at Tangmere airfield, Sussex. The pilot and Flight Engineer were very seriously injured, but P/O Nye is thought to have escaped with only minor wounds.

F/O. G.A. Trollope, A/Bomber, P/O. A.E. Nye, Navigator and F/L. V.G.L. Outen, WOP/AG on this op.

2nd crew.

179980 (1344715) F/O. Donald "Don" Beaton. DSO. Pilot.
J40946 F/O. Joe A Speare, RCAF A/Bomber.5 ops
J40778 F/O. Ray Bertram Hilchey, RCAF Navigator.
1892880 F/S. John Goodworth Brittain. WOP/AG.
J95536 (R279032) P/O. Orval Clare "Shorty" Evers, RCAF MU
and R/G.5 ops
J95531 (R271567) P/O. Robert MacPherson. "Bob" Toms, RCAF
MU and R/G.5 ops
939832 F/S. Alfred "Alf" McMurrugh. F/Engineer

Passengers 02/05/1945, 05/05/1945, 09/05/1945.

20/04/1945 RE116 JI-F Bombing Regensburg 09.35 13.56 17.18

Bomb load 16 x 500 ANM64. Primary target: Regensburg. Weather clear over target and whole route. Bombed on leading aircraft at 13.56 hours from 19,300 feet. A good deal of smoke. Bombs seen straddling Danube. Some bombs falling short. Would have been better to bomb on the Oil dock and not so leaders. Weather perfect.

24/04/1945 NN782 JI-K Bombing Bad Oldesloe 06.59 10.43 12.47

Bomb load 6 x 1000 ANM65 and 10 x 500 ANM 64. Primary target: Bad-Oldesloe, Rail and road junction and Marshalling Yards. Weather 3/10ths to nil cloud. Bombed at 10.43 hours from 18,000 feet on 514/S. Several bombs seen to burst in yard and along railway line. Heavy flak. Large explosion seen in target area. Well concentrated formation. Closed in target area.

30/04/1945 RE116 JI-F Manna Rotterdam 16.47 18.13 19.22

Weather intermittent showers and low cloud. Load 5 packs. Dropped 4 packs in fields surrounded by people where all other packets were dropped. One pack hung up brought back. Visibility very bad. No identification seen. DRC u/s. Populace gave great welcome. Dropping very scattered some in water. Submarine in pens appeared to be undergoing repairs.

02/05/1945 RF230 JI-B Manna The Hague 11.28 12.31 13.38

Weather over dropping zone clear below cloud for the first arrivals changing later to heavy showers which marred visibility. Dropped 5 panniers on smoke from T.I. and White Cross. Heavy shower made visibility poor. Rain at time marred visibility. Panniers dropped slightly to the west.

No MU/Gunner (O.C. Evers) that day.

Passenger LAC. Fleckney.

05/05/1945 RF230 JI-B Manna The Hague 05.58   07.16½ 08.13

No R/Gunner (R.M. Toms) that day. Dropped 5 panniers on Red T.I. and White Cross. Low cloud. Some rain. Perfectly O.K. - Fires caused by Red T.I.

Passenger Cpl. Hall.

09/05/1945 RF230 JI-B Exodus Juvincourt - Dunsfold 07.26 x 12.30

No A/Bomber (J.A. Speare) that day. Passenger Wing Commander Sidney Baker (Only flew on outbound flight. Returned with another aircraft).

The aircraft took off at 07.26 hours from Waterbeach. Returning to base, took off from Juvincourt in France at 12.15 hours with 24 POWs and six crew. A message giving their estimated time of arrival was received at RAF Waterbeach at 1219 and shortly afterwards the pilot reported he was experiencing trouble with the controls and was putting back to Juvincourt. A further message sent by the aircraft at 1225 stated that it was making a forced landing. Flares were fired off from an airfield on route indicating permission to land but no acknowledgment was received.

"At 12.30 hours this aircraft was seen by a number of witnesses on the ground to approach Roye-Amy airfield from the west at a height of 10,000 feet. After circling the airfield twice the aircraft was seen to go into a steep bank to port, before going into a flat spin and crashing to the ground into a wooded area, 2 miles east-south-east of Roye-Amy where it was destroyed by fire On investigation into the crash, it was not possible to account for the necessity for a forced land, as the aircraft seemed to be fully serviceable or to establish definitely the cause of the crash. It was noted, that after the aircraft crew sent a brief message saying that they were going to make a forced landing, the pilot applied full flap, to which the aircraft then went out of control, entering the spin from which it did not recover. It appears that several of the passengers had moved from their allotted places in the aircraft, causing centre of gravity problems, their positions to the rear of the fuselage would have indicated that the aircraft have been tail heavy, resulting in the pilot finding the aircraft to be dangerously heavy, believing that there was something seriously wrong with the aircraft. The pilot had already used 8 divisions of elevator trim to keep the aircraft in balance. However, the application of full flap caused loss of control to which the aircraft lost control. RF230 crashed at 1230 hours one mile ESE of Roye Amy, killing all crew and passengers on board. All buried in Clichy New Communal Cemetery, on the northern boundary of Paris. This was possibly the highest loss of life in any Lancaster crash." (John Ball)

Crew:
F/O.   Donald "Don" Beaton. DSO.   Pilot.
F/O.   Ray Bertram Hilchey, RCAF   Navigator.
F/S. John Goodworth Brittain.   WOP/AG.
P/O.   Robert MacPherson. "Bob" Toms, RCAF MU/Gunner.
P/O.   Orval Clare "Shorty" Evers, RCAF R/Gunner.
F/S. Alfred "Alf" McMurrugh.   F/Engineer

Passengers:
5111739 Sgt. Ronald Arthur Adams.   Royal Warwickshire Regt.
2940187 Pte. Thomas Anderson. Queen's Own Cameron Highlanders.
804169 Pte. William Leonard Ball.   Queens Royal Regt.
4751822 Pte. Samuel James Bayston.   Green Howards.
2650397 Cpl. Emanuel L. Belshaw.   East Surrey Regt.
4032985 Pte. Roland Albert Betton. Kings Shropshire Light Infantry
124175 Lt.   Patrick Archibald Tomlin Campbell Royal West Kent Regt.
5954856 Pte   Ronald Ernest Clark.   Royal Scots.
2185985 Pte   Walter Croston.   Pioneer Corps.
840450 Gnr. Alfred James Spencer Crowe. Royal Artillery.
3461448 Fus. Harold Cummings.   Lancashire Fusiliers.
3392078 Pte. Richard Danson.   East Surrey Regt.
6912680 Rfn. Thomas James Edwards.   Rifle Brigade.
6844798 L/Cpl. George William Franks.   Kings Royal Rifle.
45537 Gnr. A. N. Labotske.   South African Artillery
PAL/12055 Pnr. W.L. Lindheimer   Pioneer Corps.
PAL/12056 Pnr. Mordhai Maschit.   Pioneer Corps.
3448706 Fus. Owen Parkin.   Lancashire Fusiliers.
2719806 Gdsm. James Arthur Roe.   Irish Guards.
94190 Lt. Eric Thomas Theodore Snowdon. Royal Artillery.
5253245 Cpl. Albert George Thompson.   Worcestershire Regt.
4451208 Pte. Ralph Turnbull.   Durham Light Infantry.
85759 Capt. Robert Worsley Wheeler.   Royal Engineers.
14208422 Pte. Patrick Yates.   Leicestershire Regt.

P/O. Richard Albert John Bennett

J87679 (R150540) P/O. Richard Albert John Bennett, RCAF   Pilot.
J92601 (R168202) P/O. William Leroy Baker, RCAF A/Bomber.
J87616 (R128222) P/O. Thomas Wilfred Dodd, RCAF Navigator.
1336538 F/S. Peter William Upton. WOP/AG.
1493262 Sgt. Arthur Brettell.   MU/Gunner.
1312982 W/O. Dennis James Hughes. R/Gunner.
1622243 Sgt. Kenneth Arthur Lowery. F/Engineer.

29/12/1943 DS816 JI-O Bombing Berlin 17.07 20.16   00.14
Bomb load 1 x 4000, 24 x 30 incendiaries, 540 x 4 incendiaries, 90 x 4 incendiaries. Primary target: Berlin. There was 10/10 cloud with tops 8/10000. Bombed at 2016 hours at 18000 ft. 8 x 30 incendiaries hung up and brought back. Cloud prevented observation other than bomb flashes. Flak rather heavier than usual.

P/O. R.A.J. Bennett flew the mission as 2nd pilot with S/L. A.L. Roberts crew.

21/01/1944 LL627 JI-U Bombing Magdeburg 20.00 x   x
Bomb load 1 x 4000, 720 x 4, 90 x 4, 24 x 30 incendiaries. Aircraft missing. Lost in the same area (Ijsselmeer) as DS824, with the loss of the entire crew. It is possible that this aircraft was also shot down by Ofw. Heinz Vinke at the same time as DS824 was shot down by Oblt. Drewes. The crew was lost on its first operation.

F/S Upton and Sgt Brettell are buried in Harlingen General Cemetery; the others are commemorated on the Runnymede Memorial. Their average age was 21.

Comments: The first major raid on Magdeburg was plagued by enemy night fighters. Opposition was fierce causing havoc and many losses. Some crews arrived ahead of Pathfinders and bombed using H2S. Marking was sparse which resulted in a scattered attack. Most of the bombs are believed to have fallen outside the city. 514 Sqn suffered its biggest single losses on operations so far, 4 aircraft failing to return.

F/O. Keith John Dene Bickmore

187524 (1332734) F/O. Keith John Dene Bickmore.   Pilot.
Sgt. J. Rice.   A/Bomber.
144921 (1473518) F/L. Sidney Eric Stanley Whitby. Navigator.
F/S. S. Collar.   WOP/AG.
188653 (1117093) F/O. Matthew Craig Sutherland Paterson.   MU/Gunner.
W/O. D.J. Ellis.   R/Gunner.
Sgt. W.G. Harris.   F/Engineer.

Passengers 16/07/1945, 17/07/1945, 19/07/1945, 21/07/1945

Date Aircraft Duty   Target   Up Drop Down
29/06/1945 ME529 A2-F   Post Mortem Special mission. 10.02 x 16.02
03/07/1945 ME355 A2-G   Post Mortem Special mission 14.09 x 20.04
05/07/1945 ME529 A2-B   Post Mortem Special mission 13.24 x 18.27
16/07/1945 ME358 JI-O Baedeker Tour over Continent 09.51 x 14.21
    Passengers ACW. Otten, LACW. Abermand, LAC. Biscombe, Cpl.
Buckingham, Sgt. Mercer.
17/07/1945 ME355 A2-G Baedeker Tour over Continent 14.53   x 19.08
    Passengers Sgt. Bevan(WAAF), LACW. Ford(WAAF), Cpl. Probert, Cpl.
Santi, LAC. Thompson.
19/07/1945 RE120 A2-C Baedeker Tour over Continent 15.14   x 19.23
    Passengers LAC. Bishop, LAC. Cook, LAC. Curthays, LACW. Chipping,
LACW. McKintosh.
21/07/1945 RE158 A2-J Baedeker Tour over Continent 15.05   x 19.13
    Passengers Sgt. Aspen, Cpl. Collier, LAC. Jack, LAC. Robinson, LACW.
Zenner.

P/O. Arthur Bilbrough, DFC

172766 (1104586)   P/O. Arthur Bilbrough, DFC   Pilot.
R89830 W/O. George Wesley Metcalfe. RCAF, DFC A/Bomber.
J23343   F/O. Henry Charles Heaney, RCAF DFC   Navigator.13ops
1559148 Sgt.   David Kellock   Navigator. 5 ops
201703 (1487389)   F/S. Louis Lionel Stanforth.   WOP/AG.
1812034 F/S.   G.R.W. Braithwaite.   MU/Gunner.
A418572 F/S.   Roy Maurice Rogers, RAAF   R/Gunner.
1692069 Sgt.   Walter Terry Barber.   F/Engineer.

24/12/1943 LL653 A2-F   Bombing Berlin 00.42   04.09   07.43
Bomb load 1 x 4000, 32 x 30 incendiaries, 450 x 4 incendiaries and 90 x 4 incendiaries. Dense cloud with one or two breaks. Bombed from 20,000 feet. Six green T.I.s clearly seen. Scattered fires seen. Special equipment OK. Results rather scattered. Photo Attempted.

20/01/1944 LL678 A2-L   Bombing Berlin 16.16   19.39   23.30
Bomb load 1 x 4000, 32 x 30, 540 x 4 and 60 x 4 incendiaries. 10/10ths cloud. Bombed from 20,500 feet on Red and Green sky marker. T.I.s concentrated and faint glow seen below cloud.

21/01/1944 LL674 A2-D   Bombing Magdeburg 19.54   23.02   03.12
Bomb load 1 x 4000, 720 x 4, 90 x 4 and 32 x 30 incendiaries. There was 6/10ths cloud. Bombed from 20,000 feet. Scattered fires and tending to overshoot. Monica u/s. Fires beginning to obtain hold. Route not too good.

28/01/1944 LL727 A2-C   Bombing Berlin 00.17   03.19   08.04
Bomb load 1 x 4000 lb bomb, 24 x 30, 180 x 4 and 90 x 4 incendiaries. There was 10/10ths cloud. Bombed from 20,000 feet. When coming into target, sky lit up by huge explosion. Long line of fires running NW/SE, terminating in a large concentration line of fires spreading West. Should have been a very good attack. No trouble from fighters.

30/01/1944 DS786 A2-F   Bombing Berlin 17.21 23.25
Dropped time not stated approximately 20.20 hours. Bomb load 1 x 4000 lb bomb, 600 x 4, 90 x 4 and 32 x 30 incendiaries. There was 10/10ths cloud with 5000 ft. (tops). Cloud prevented visual. Monica u/s. Markers more concentrated than I have ever seen before – if they were OK, we were "Bang On".

21/02/1944 LL684 A2-B   Bombing Stuttgart 00.26   04.09   07.13
Bomb load 1 x 4000 lb. bomb, 40 x 30, 690 x 4 and 90 x 4 incendiaries. There was thin wispy cloud. Bombed from 20,000 feet. Bombed on visual bend of river as Green T.I.s seemed to be South of target. Nine or ten cherry Red flares burning along the river, the first had been undershooting. Marking fairly concentrated but slightly S.E. working into the town as we bombed. River could be seen clearly, also the city through fall of snow.

24/02/1944 LL620 A2-G Bombing Schweinfurt 20.51   01.24   04.38

Sgt. D. Kellock, navigator for 4 missions. Bomb load 1 x 4000 lb. bomb, 24 x 30, 420 x 4, and 90 x 4 incendiaries. Weather was clear. Bombed from 20,000 feet. There was a good concentration of fires. Monica u/s. Aircraft mostly North of track on outward, as D.R. Compass u/s and P.4 Compass u/s. Good show, no trouble on route although aircraft was alone on route.

01/03/1944 LL620 A2-G Bombing Stuttgart 23.40   03.10   07.25

Bomb load 1 x 8000 lb. bomb, 8 x 30 and 90 x 4 incendiaries. There was 10/10ths cloud. Bombed from 20,000 feet. Fires seen through clouds, if anything, rather to South of aiming point. Monica unreliable. Sky markers appeared at first to be slightly South of aiming point but moved nearer centre as we made run up. Route very good. Photo attempted.

07/03/1944 LL620 A2-G Bombing Le Mans 19.52   00.11

Bomb load 10 x 1000, and 4 x 500 lb bombs. No Attack. Target not identified. Aircraft sent down to 5,700 feet and still slightly above cloud. Red T.I. seen. Some red glow seen reflected on clouds. 2 x 1000, 2 x 500 lb. bombs jettisoned. 8 x 1000 lbs. brought back.

15/03/1944 LL620 A2-G Bombing Stuttgart 19.36   23.20   02.41

Bomb load 1 x 8000 lb bomb and 90 x 4 incendiaries. There was 7/10ths cloud with 6000 feet tops. Bombed from 20,000 feet. Attack very scattered. Fires seemed to be burning red on leaving. Markers too scattered and few.

18/03/1944 LL620 A2-G Bombing Frankfurt 19.41 22.03   00.32

F/O. N.C. Heaney navigator. Bomb load 1 x 8000 lb. bomb and 32 x 30 incendiaries. There was wispy cloud with much haze. Bombed from 20,000 feet. Too hazy and too early for results. Gee u/s. Route OK. Explosions seen at 22.03 hours.

24/03/1944 LL620 A2-G Bombing Berlin 18.42   22.30   01.30

Sgt. D. Kellock, navigator. Bomb load 1 x 8000 lb. bomb. There was 4-5/10ths cloud. Bombed from 20,000 feet. Flares seen lighting up ground detail, a few scattered incendiaries burning. Monica u/s Hanover to Base. Searchlights rather troublesome, visual of target showed T.I.s were definitely on the city.

10/04/1944 LL620 A2-G Bombing Laon   01.31 03.48   05.53

F/O. N.C. Heaney returns as navigator. Bomb load 9 x 1000 and 4 x 500 lb bombs. Weather was clear. Bombed from 10,000 feet. T.I.s very well concentrated. Some bomb bursts seen South of T.I.s. Raid well concentrated.

18/04/1944 LL620 A2-G Bombing Rouen   22.31   00.46   02.04

Bomb load 8 x 1000 MC, 2 x 1000 GP and 5 x 500 lb bombs. There was slight haze. Bombed from 10,500 feet. Visual of river and yards seen. T.I.s were bang on the yards. Target very well marked and illuminated. The M of C giving excellent guidance especially during period when a bunch of mixed T.I.s went down in town area. A good show. Own bombs seen bursting in the yards.

20/04/1944 LL620 A2-G Bombing Cologne 00.07 02.15   04.12

Bomb load 1 x 1000, 1026 x 4, 114 x 4 and 103 x 30 incendiaries. There was 10/10ths cloud. Bombed from 20,000 feet. Markers were few and scattered. Large explosion below cloud at 02.33 hours, the flash coming above the cloud in target area.

22/04/1944 LL620 A2-G Bombing Dusseldorf 23.01 01.21 02.55

Bomb load 9 x 1000 and 5 x 500 lb bomb. There was slight haze. Bombed from 19,000 feet. Bombing bend in river seen clearly. P.P.F. slightly late, causing us to orbit for correct bombing run. Attack well concentrated Cookies seen to explode around T.I.s.

24/04/1944 LL620 A2-G Bombing Karlsruhe 22.22 00.46 04.01

Bomb load 1 x 1000 lb bomb, 1026 x 4, 114 x 4 and 108 x 30 incendiaries. There was 10/10ths cloud at 18,000 feet, visibility below cloud good. Bombed from 15,500 feet. Town visible in light of flares. T.I.s scattered to North at first, but later concentrated over town. Several bombs seen well away to the North not near to T.I.s

26/04/1944 LL620 A2-G Bombing Essen 23.00 01.31 03.01

Bomb load 1 x 8000 lb bomb, 60 x 30, 405 x 4 and 45 x 4 lb incendiaries. Weather was clear with slight haze. Bombed from 20,000 feet. Good concentration of bombing round the T.I.s spreading slightly westward. A good attack if T.I.s were on. Searchlights were rather ineffective due to presence of many vapour trails.

19/05/1944 LL716 A2-G Bombing Le Mans 22.25 00.26 02.50

Bomb load 4 x 1000 USA, 5 x 1000 MC, 1 x 1000 GP and 4 x 500 GP. Cloudy over target extending from 8,500 feet to 10,000 feet. Bombed Green T.I. markers from 7,000 feet, as instructed by Master Bomber. Marshalling Yards seen and large explosion with orange flames observed south of aiming point. Considered a good attack.

21/05/1944 LL716 A2-G Bombing Duisburg 22.55 01.20 03.10

Bomb load 1 x 8000 lb bomb and 96 x 30 incendiaries. There was wispy cloud up to 20,000 feet. Bombed Red T.I.s from 20,000 feet. Believe attack very scattered and questionable.

22/05/1944 LL716 A2-G Bombing Dortmund 22.55 00.40

Bomb load 1 x 8000 lb bomb, 96 x 30, 540 x 4 and 60 x 4 incendiaries. Very severe icing, both aerials broken, unable to climb above 9,000 feet and therefore returned early. Furthest point reached 52.27N, 03.20E and all bombs jettisoned safe at that position at 23.46 hours.

24/05/1944 LL716 A2-G Bombing Boulogne 00.10 01.16 02.10

Bomb load 9 x 1000 MC, 1 x 1000 GP, 1 x 1000 ANM and 4 x 500 GP. Clear over target. Bombed Green T.I.s from 9,000 feet. Sortie considered successful and no troubles experienced.

28/05/1944 LL716 A2-G Bombing Angers 18.50 23.55 01.40

Bomb load 5 x 1000 MC, 1 x 1000 USA and 4 x 500 MC. Clear at target. Bombed from 9,000 feet. Number of fires seen and large explosion at 23.54 ½ hours followed by smaller explosions. Good attack.

F/O. Irvine Joseph Bittner, DFC

J86219   F/O.   Irvine Joseph Bittner. RCAF DFC.   Pilot.
R154052   W/O.   J.W. Minshall. RCAF   A/Bomber.
R181695   W/O.   F.G. Ursel. RCAF   Navigator.
Sgt. M.C. Murphy   WOP/AG.
Sgt. G.A. Brown   WOP/AG.1 op
201216 (1470138)   Sgt. James Albert Smith   WOP/AG.1 op
R223513   F/S. G.M. Durant RCAF   MU/Gunner.
Sgt. E.A. Mason   R/Gunner.
   F/S. R.E.G. Collins   F/Engineer.
Sgt. W.H. "Paddy" Mills   F/Eng 2 ops

18/08/1944 HK572 JI-T Bombing Bremen   21.26   00.17   02.49
   Bomb load 1 x 8000 HC, 48 x 30 incendiaries, 540 x 4 incendiaries, 60 x 4?
Primary target: Bremen. Weather clear. Bombed at 0017 hours, from 18,000
feet on Red T.I.s. Decoys in action. Good attack. Marking good.
   F/O. I.J. Bittner flew the mission as 2nd pilot with F/L. T.A. Lever crew.
31/08/1944 LM684 JI-O Bombing Pont-Remy 16.18   18.11   19.34
   Bomb load 11 x 1000 MC, 4 x 500 GP Mk IV LD. Primary target: Pont
Remy, Dump. Weather cloudy. Bombed at 1811 hours from 15000 feet on
release of leading aircraft's bombs.
20/09/1944 PB482 JI-P Bombing Calais 14.49   16.01   17.51
   Bomb load 11 x 1000 MC, 4 x 500 GP, Primary target: Calais. Weather clear
over target. Bombed at 1601 hours from 2500 feet, red T.I.s.
23/09/1944 NF968 JI-L Bombing Neuss 19.21   21.25   23.21
   Bomb load 11 x 1000 ANM 59, 4 x 500 GP. Primary target: Neuss. Weather
10/10ths cloud over target, tops 8/10,000 feet. Bombed at 2125 hours from
19000 feet on red glow beneath cloud.
25/09/1944 NF968 JI-L Bombing Pas de Calais   08.17   11.21
   Bomb load 11 x 1000 MC, 4 x 500 GP. Primary target: Calais. Abandoned
on Master Bomber's orders. Jettisoned 2x1000 MC.
27/09/1944 LM288 JI-C(?) Bombing Calais 17.28   08.43   10.15
   Bomb load 11 x 1000 MC, 4 x 500 GP. Primary target: Calais 15. Weather,
cloud 5,500 feet 10/10ths. Bombed at 0843 hours from 5500 feet, overshot red
T.I. by 1 second.
   (?) In ORBs F/O N. Jennings crew is noted using the same A/C at the same
time, with comment as follows:
"Primary target: Calais. Bombed at 08.49 hours from 5,500 feet, overshot red
T.I."

07/10/1944 PD334 A2-D   Bombing Emmerich   12.16   14.28   16.18

Bomb load 1 x 4000 HC. 10 x No.14 clusters. 4 x (150x4). Primary target Emmerich. Weather clear with cloud at 13,000 feet. Bombed at 1428 hours from 13,000 feet on south of town as ordered.

14/10/1944 LM728 JI-U Bombing Duisburg   22.45   01.35   03.43

Bomb load 1 x 4000 HC. 14 x no. 14 clusters. Primary target: Duisburg. Weather was clear with small amount of cloud over the target. Bombed at 01.35 hours from 21,000 feet. Red and green T.I.s.

15/10/1944 LM275 JI-M Bombing Wilhelmshaven 17.13 19.51   21.54

Bomb load 11 x 1000 MC, 4 x 500 GP. Primary target: Wilhelmshaven. Weather haze and thin cloud at first with thick cloud later. Bombed at 19.51 hours from 20,000 feet. Centre of cluster of Red and Green T.I.s.

19/10/1944 LM728 JI-U Bombing Stuttgart 17.25 22.19

Bomb load 1x4000 HC. 3x500 Clusters. 7 x 150 x4, 1 x 90 x 4 I.B. Aircraft returned early - Oxygen supply to rear turret unserviceable - Rear Gunner sick. Jettisoned safe at 5218N 0135E.

21/10/1944 LM728 JI-U Bombing Flushing 10.52   12.29   13.37

Bomb load 12x1000 MC. 2x500 GP. Primary target: Flushing 'B'. Weather clear. Bombed at 12.29½ hours from 9,000 feet. Area of A/P.

23/10/1944 LM727 JI-S Bombing Essen 16.31   19.48   22.01

Bomb load 1 x 4000 HC. 6 x 1000 MC. 6 x 500 GP. Primary target: Essen. Weather 10/10ths cloud over target - tops 12/14,000 feet with most appalling weather on route. Bombed at 19.48 hours from 20,000 feet. Red Wanganui sky marker.

25/10/1944 LM728 JI-U Bombing Essen 13.18   15.46   17.27

Bomb load 1 x 4000 HC. 6 x 1000 MC. 6 x 500 GP. Primary target: Essen. Weather over target 10/10ths low cloud, with one clear patch which appeared to fill up later in the attack. Bombed at 15.46 hours from 20,000 feet. Red sky marker.

28/10/1944 LM728 JI-U Bombing Flushing 08.51   10.17   11.22

Bomb load 11 x 1000 MC. 4 x 500 GP. Primary target: Flushing. Weather over the target quite clear and conditions perfect, although believed to be only local, and some low cloud approaching. Bombed at 10.17 hours from 9,000 feet. Visual of A/P.

29/10/1944 LM728 JI-U Bombing Westkapelle 09.52 11.37   12.28

Bomb load 11 x 1000 ANM 59, 4 x 500 GP. MC. Primary target: Flushing, Gun installations. Weather clear over target. Bombed at 11.37 hours from 6,500 feet. One second overshot on smoke as directed by Master Bomber.

31/10/1944 LM728 JI-U Bombing Bottrop 11.56 15.01   16.45

Bomb load 1 x 4000 HC. 16 x 500 GP. Primary target: Bottrop, Synth. Oil plants. Weather 10/10ths cloud over target. Bombed at 15.01 hours from 18,000 feet on leading G.H. aircraft. Aircraft fuselage damaged by heavy flak.

02/11/1944 LM728 JI-U Bombing Homberg   11.40   14.10   15.35

Bomb load 1 x 4000 HC, 6 x 1000 ANM59, 6 x 500 MC. Primary target: Homberg. Weather variable cloud but clear for bombing. Target obscured by pall of smoke rising to 10,000 feet. Bombed at 14.10 hours from 19,000 feet. Centre of flares and smoke.

05/11/1944 LM728 JI-U Bombing Solingen 10.32 13.02 14.58
Bomb load 1 x 4000 HC, 14 x 500 Clusters. Primary target: Solingen. Weather 10/10ths cloud over target. Bombed at 13.02 hours from 18,500 feet on leading aircraft.

08/11/1944 LM728 JI-U Bombing Homberg   07.59 10.33 12.18
Bomb load 1 x 4000 HC, 14 x No. 14 Clusters. Primary target: Homberg. Weather clear. Bombed at 10.33 hours from 17,500 feet on leading aircraft. Aircraft damaged by flak.

16/11/1944 LM734 JI-U Bombing Heinsburg 13.15 15.30 17.05
Bomb load 1 x 4000 HC, 6 x 1000 MC, 6 x 500 GP. Primary target: Heinsburg. Weather - nil cloud with slight haze over target. Bombed at 15.30 hours from 9,000 feet. Centre of town.

29/11/1944 LM627 JI-R Bombing Neuss 03.10 05.35 07.25
Bomb load 1 x 4000 HC, 6 x 1000 MC, 4 x 500 GP, 4 x 250 T.I.s. Primary target: Neuss. Primary target: Neuss. Weather 10/10ths cloud over target but the glow of fires was seen through cloud. Bombed at 15.35 hours from 19,000 feet on G.H. Markers fairly concentrated.

30/11/1944 LM627 JI-R Bombing Osterfeld   10.55 13.11 14.55
Bomb load 1 x 4000 HC, 15 x 500 GP, 1 Red/Green flare. Primary target: Osterfeld, Coking plant. Weather 10/10ths cloud. Bombed at 13.11 hours from 19,000 feet, Red flares. G.H. ineffective.

02/12/1944 NG118 A2-E Bombing Dortmund 13.07 14.58 17.05
Bomb load 14 x 1000 HC. Primary target: Dortmund, Benzol plant. Weather 10/10ths cloud. Bombed at 14.58 hours from 20,000 feet on leading aircraft.

05/12/1944 NF966 JI-R Bombing Hamm 09.00 11.29 13.40
Bomb load 1 x 4000 HC, 9 x 500 ANM58, 4 x 500 MC, 2 x 500 GP Long Delay, 1 Flare. Primary target: Hamm. Weather 10/10ths cloud over target, but otherwise varying from 6-10/10ths. Bombed at 11.29 hours from 20,000 feet on G.H.

08/12/1944 NF968 JI-L Bombing Duisburg   08.35 11.05 12.45
Bomb load 13 x 1000 ANM59, 1 Red/Green flare. Primary target: Duisberg. Weather 10/10ths cloud. Bombed at 11.05 hours from 21,000 feet on G.H.

11/12/1944 NF968 JI-L Bombing Osterfeld   08.39 11.08 12.55
Bomb load 1 x 4000 HC, 12 x 500 GP, 2 x 500 GP Long Delay, 1 Flare, Primary target: Osterfeld. Weather 10/10ths cloud, tops 16,000 feet. Bombed at 11.08½ hours from 20,000 feet on leading aircraft.

12/12/1944 NF968 JI-L Bombing Witten 11.44 14.55
Bomb load 1 x 4000 HC, 5 x 500 GP, 6 x 500 ANM58, 4 x 500 ANM64, 1 Flare. Primary target: Witten. Weather 10/10ths cloud, tops 14/16,000 feet.

Abortive sortie, returned early with port outer and starboard inner engines unserviceable.

15/12/1944 LM275 JI-M Bombing Siegen ca.11.30 x ca.14.00

Between 11.19 to 11.36 hours 19 aircraft took off to attack Siegen. At 12.30 hours, all aircraft recalled as Fighters were unable to take off. Operation only reported in ORBs "Summary of events", no trace in ORBs "Detail of Work carried out - Details of sorties of flight". Operation noted in I.J. Bittner logbook.

16/12/1944 LM275 JI-M Bombing Siegen 11.38 15.00 16.54

Bomb load 1 x 4000 HC. 5 x 1000 MC. 7 x 500 GP. 1 Flare. Primary target: Siegen. Bombed at 15.00 hours from 18,000 feet on G.H. Leader.

21/12/1944 ME841 JI-J Bombing Trier 12.16 14.57 17.08

Bomb load 1 x 4000 HC. 10 x 500 GP. 2 x 250 GP. 4 x 250 T.I.s. Primary target: Trier, Marshalling yards. Weather 10/10 cloud, tops 6/9000 feet. Bombed at 14.57 hours from 18,000 feet on M.B.s release.

23/12/1944 LM717 JI-C Bombing Trier 11.44 14.28 16.10

Bomb load 1 x 4000 HC. 10 x 500 GP. 6 x 250 GP. Primary target: Trier. Weather clear over target. Bombed at 14.28 hours from 18,000 feet visually aided by G.H.

27/12/1944 LM717 JI-C Bombing Rheydt 12.50 14.59 16.30

Bomb load 7 x 1000 MC, 6 x 500 GP, 3 x 250 GP. Primary target: Rheydt, Marshalling yards. Weather clear. Bombed at 14.59 hours from 20,000 feet. Red T.I.s.

F/O. Robert Owen Blackall

150868 (1805085)   F/O. Robert Owen "Robin" Blackall. Pilot.
164708 (1608267)   F/O. Jean Paul Pettavel.   A/Bomber.
164280 (1615723)   F/O. John Foll.   Navigator.
Sgt. S. Beevers or Beavers.   WOP/AG.
Sgt. K.W. Atkins.   MU/Gunner.
F/S. A.T. Waller.   R/Gunner.
F/S. D.E. Ell.   F/Engineer.

Passengers 07/05/1945, 08/06/1945, 08/07/1945, 18/07/1945.

23/03/1945 ME425 A2-L   Bombing Wesel 14.30   17.40   19.15
Bomb load 1 x 1000 ANM65, 12 x 1000 MC. Primary target: Wesel, in support of ground troops. Weather perfect. Bombed at 17.40 hours from 19,600 feet on G.H. 1 x 1000 ANM65 hung up and brought back to Base.
F/O. R.O. Blackall flew the mission as 2nd pilot with F/L. H.C. Mottershead's crew.
27/03/1945 PB423 A2-C   Bombing Hamm Sachsen   10.35   14.04
16.09
Bomb load 1 x 4000 HC, 13 x 500 ANM64, 2x 500 MC. Primary target, Hamm Sachsen, Bombed on G.H. Leader. at 14.04 hours at 18,500 feet.
09/04/1945 PD389 A2-J Bombing Kiel   19.40   22.42   01.30
Bombed secondary target Hamburg. Bomb load 1 x 4000 HC and 12 x 500 ANM64. Bombed centre of Red/Green T.I.'s. at 22.42 hrs. from 18,000 feet. Large fire seen on approach. 4 large fires seen on leaving target. One very large explosion seen. No fire after 21.48 hrs. D/R until 22.15 hrs when yellow illuminations were seen ahead. There were considerable Decoys. M/B heard to instruct bomb nearest green flares. These were seen to fall well to starboard. 22.30 turned starboard 190 degs ran in on 170 and bombed centre of Green T.Is. G East chain U/S. Several 4000 lbs seen to fall in the sea from 0300 degs.
F/O. R.O. Blackall flew the mission as 2nd pilot with F/L. T.W. Hurley crew.
18/04/1945 ME529 A2-F   Bombing Heligoland 09.52   13.09   15.22
Bombed primary target, Heligoland. Bomb load 6 x 1000 MC, 10 x 500 ANM64. Primary target: Heligoland, Naval base. Weather no cloud, slight haze. Bombed visually at 13.09hours from 18,200 ft. Smoke on north end of Island. Whole target covered with smoke and fires. Only north tip of island visible. Very few bombs fell in sea. Bang-on. Mass of grey-black smoke with white plume in centre.
20/04/1945 NG118 A2-H   Bombing Regensburg 09.32   13.56½ 17.17
Bomb load 16 x 500 ANM64. Primary target: Regensburg. Weather clear over target and whole route. Bombed on following G.H. A/C 514 'E' and visual. at 1356½ from 18,500 feet. Bombed Road Bridge, own bombs

straddled river, other bombs seen to undershoot. Some Grey smoke from target area. Very good trip but could not catch G.H. Leader. Unable to bomb A.P. on account of congestion of A/C to port. Nuremburg still on fire. 1 x 500 brought back.

24/04/1945 ME425 A2-L Bombing Bad Oldesloe 07.06 10.44 13.03

Bomb load 6 x 1000 ANM65, 10 x 500 ANM 64. Primary target: Bad-Oldesloe, Rail and road junction and Marshalling Yards. Weather 3/10ths to nil cloud. Bombed visually on leading aircraft at 10.44 hours from 18,700 ft. Explosion as if ammunition train had been hit, much smoke and flames. Accurate flak from Ijmuiden. - Bombed visually on account of a/c above with bomb doors open.

07/05/1945 NN781 A2-B Manna The Hague 12.20 13.33 14.50

Dropping area The Hague. Dropped 4 Packs on Red T.I.s to port of White Cross. Clear. Slight haze. Deliver O.K. Usual cheerful reception accompanied by the message "Thank you boys".

No MidUp Gunner in this mission.

Passenger Sgt. Cox.

12/05/1945 RE159 A2-E Exodus Juvincourt - Wing 09.04 x 14.42

Duration 4.10. Outward 2.06 hours. Collected 24 POWs. Homeward 2.04 hours. Delay of 40 mins after landing at Juvincourt due to other a/c taking off.

08/06/1945 RE158 A2-J Baedeker Tour over Continent 09.59 x 14.39

Passengers F/Lt. R. West, AC. K. Jaye, LAC. S. McLaughlan.

03/07/1945 RE117 A2-D Post Mortem Special mission.14.11 x 20.01

05/07/1945 RE117 A2-D Post Mortem Special mission 13.26 x 18.19

08/07/1945 ME529 A2-B Baedeker Tour over Continent 10.01 x 14.33

Passengers F/S. Stephens (WAAF), Cpl. Killick, LAC. Jubb, S/L. Flewitt, F/L. Tavlin (3Grp.).

18/07/1945 RE158 A2-J Baedeker Tour over Continent 09.45 x 14.07

Passengers S/L. Parkin, Cpl. Skinner, LAC. Trace, LAC. Cook, LAC. Bryling.

F/L. Joseph Michael John Bourke

J20220 F/L. Joseph Michael John "Joe" Bourke, RCAF Pilot.
J22620 F/O. James Earl Scott Clare. RCAF   A/Bomber.
1320287 Sgt. S.G. or S.E. "Sid" Cuttler.   Navigator.
1322308 Sgt. Ronald Leslie "Ron" Smith.   WOP/AG.
1867200 Sgt. Jack Brewer.   MU/Gunner.
R176589 F/S. Albert Alexander "Al" Williston. RCAF R/Gunner.
1802314 Sgt. Peter "Pete" McQueeney.   F/Engineer.
29/12/1943 LL672 A2-C Bombing Berlin 17.15   20.18   00.04
   Bomb load 1 x 4000, 24 x 30 incendiaries, 540 x 4 incendiaries, 90 x 4
incendiaries. Primary target Berlin. 10/10ths cloud. Bombed at 2018 hours at
22000 feet. 3 or 4 red flares with green stars seen. Circle of fires seen with
glow on clouds. The route was O.K. Photo attempted.
02/01/1944 LL672 A2-C Bombing Berlin 00.15   02.56   07.15
   Bomb load 1 x 2000, 40 x 30, 900 x 4 incendiaries. Primary target Berlin.
There was 10/10ths cloud with tops 10/1200 feet. Bombed at 0256 hours at
20000 ft. in centre of good concentration of red and green markers. Occasional
bursts on the cloud, tending to undershoot. Photo attempted. Two encounters
with enemy aircraft reported.
14/01/1944 LL672 A2-C Bombing Brunswick 17.01   19.19   22.28
   Bomb load 1 x 4000, 48 x 30 incendiaries. Primary target Brunswick. There
was 10/10ths cloud over the target. Bombed at 1919 hours at 20000 ft. Terrific
explosion from below. Red glow changing to white approximately 1 ½ miles
to starboard of concentration, over target. Very quiet route. Very big glow in
sky on leaving target area.
20/01/1944 LL674 A2-D Bombing Berlin 16.12   19.40   23.49
   Bomb load 1 x 4000, 32 x 30, 540 x 4, 60 x 4 incendiaries. Primary target
Berlin. There was 10/10ths cloud. Bombed at 1940 hours at 20,000 feet on red
T.I.s glowing through cloud. Bomb sight U/S.
21/01/1944 LL672 A2-C Bombing Magdeburg 20.01
   Bomb load 1 x 4000, 720 x 4, 90 x 4, 32 x 30 incendiaries. Aircraft Missing.
Hit by flak near Perlesberg and crashed. Shot down outbound from 21,000 feet
over Perleberg by Maj Prinz Heinrich zu Sayn Wittgenstein, the Luftwaffe's
top night-fighter ace.
The information regarding the loss and the fighter ace are provided by Mr
Williston, brother to the rear gunner who was killed, Sgts McQueeney and
Williston were KIA,
   The two airmen killed are buried in the Berlin 1939-45 War Cemetery. The
other crew members survived as POW - JMJ Bourke POW N°3344 camp L3
- JES Clare POW N°3353 camp L3 - SE Cuttler POW N°878 camp L6/357 -
RL Smith POW N°39982 camp 9C/L3 - J Brewer POW N°920 camp L6/357

F/L.   George Kilpatrick Boyd, DFC

125427 (1060543)   F/L. George Kilpatrick Boyd, DFC Pilot.
1454683 F/S. Peter Drake Martindale. A/Bomber.
1600694 Sgt. Lawrence Sidney John Adkin. Navigator.
1382810 Sgt. John Dowding.   WOP/AG.
1338959 Sgt. Reginald Arthur Duncan Mirams.   MU/Gunner.
981579Sgt. Alexander Nicholson. R/Gunner.
1815316 Sgt. Peter William Webb. F/Engineer.

27/01/1944 DS706 JI-G Bombing Berlin
17.45 21.23
   Bomb Load 1 x 4000, 32 x 30, 450 x 4, 90
x 4 incendiaries. Returned early. Farthest
point reached 5315N 0610E. Both port
engines overheating and starboard wing
flying low. Load jettisoned.
28/01/1944 DS706 JI-G Bombing Berlin
00.08 03.25 08.24
   Bomb load 1 x 2000 lb. bomb. Primary
target: Berlin. There was 10/10ths cloud.
Bombed at 0325 hours at 20000 ft. Several
large fires seen from German coast. Route
and attack very good.
30/01/1944 DS706 JI-G Bombing Berlin
17.23

Sgt. John Dowding

   Bomb load 1 x 4000 lb. bomb, 600 x 4, 90 x 4, 32 x 30 incendiaries. Aircraft
Missing. Lost without trace. Possibly one of two Lancasters shot down over
the North Sea by Lt. Guido Krupinski and Ofw. Heinz Vinke, both of
11./NJG1.

   No survivors amongst crew. All are commemorated on the Runnymede
Memorial. NB: Aircraft wrongly shown as DS708 JI-G in ORB.

F/O. George Bradford, DFC

156933 (1074130)   F/O. George Bradford, DFC Pilot.
J29692   F/O.   J.V. Price, RCAF   A/Bomber.
1567211   Sgt.   John McCune Gilmour. Navigator.
Sgt. E. Peake.   WOP/AG.
Sgt. R.C. or A.C. Potipher.   MU/Gunner.
F/S. W.S. Nicol.   R/Gunner.   13 Ops
Sgt. H. Francis.   R/Gunner.   7 Ops
W/O.   J.W. Hughes.   R/Gunner.   15 Ops
Sgt. J. Forrester   F/Engineer.
128551   F/L. Kenneth Godfrey Condict, DFC 2nd pilot 14/10/1944

30/06/1944 LM180JI-G Bombing Villers Bocage 18.06   20.03   21.49
Bomb load 10 x 1000 MC, 3 x 500 GP. Primary target: Villers Bocage. Weather was clear. Bombed at 2003 hours from 12000 feet. Nothing but palls of smoke seen.
02/07/1944 LM180JI-G Bombing Beauvoir   12.42   14.38   16.23
Bomb load 11 x 1000 MC, 4 x 500 GP. Primary target: Beauvoir, Flying bomb supply site. Bombed at 1438 hours from 12000 feet visual
05/07/1944 LM180JI-G Bombing Watten 22.43 00.09   00.54
Bomb load 11 x 1000 ANM 65, 4 x 500 GP. Primary target: Watten, Constructional works. Bombed at 0009 hours from 10,000 feet red T.I.s.
10/07/1944 ME842JI-K Bombing Nucourt   04.10   06.04   07.39
Bomb load 11 x 1000 ANM 65, 4 x 500 GP. Primary target: Nucourt, Constructional works. Bombed at 0604½ hours from 16000 feet, Gee Fix.
15/07/1944 LM206JI-C Bombing Chalons sur Marne 21.36 22.17
Bomb load 18 x 500 GP. Primary target: Chalons sur Marne, Railway centre. Port outer engine revs and boost dropped after take off. Unable to jettison petrol. Jettisoned bombs at 2220 hours from 5000 feet in Wash.
18/07/1944 PB142 JI-A Bombing Emieville   04.13   06.06   07.27
Bomb load 11 x 1000 MC, 4 x 500 GP. Primary target: Emieville, Troop concentration. Weather clear. Bombed at 0606 hours from 6,800 feet, centre of two yellow T.I.s. Bombing well concentrated.
20/07/1944 PB143 JI-B Bombing Homburg   23.05   01.21   02.55
Bomb load 1 x 4000 HC, 2 x 500 MC, 14 x 500 GP. Primary target: Homberg, Oil plant. Weather clear. Bombed at 0122 hours from 20,000 feet North East side of green T.I.s. Much smoke and fire with explosions.
27/07/1944 HK577JI-E Bombing Les Catelliers 16.54   18.50   20.08
Bomb load 18 x 500 GP. Primary target: Les Catelliers, Flying bomb site. Bombed at 1850 hours from 16000 feet on Mosquito.
28/07/1944 HK577JI-E Bombing Stuttgart 21.37   01.53   05.33
Bomb load 17 x 500 GP. Primary target: Stuttgart. Weather 9/10ths cloud. Bombed at 0153 hours from 2000 feet green T.I.s. No Trouble on route.

30/07/1944 ME841 JI-H Bombing Caen 06.00 07.50 10.03

Bomb load 18 x 500 GP. Primary target: Caen 'B'. Weather 10/10ths cloud. Bombed at 0750 hours from 2300 feet red T.I.s. Good trip believed successful. Landed at Woodbridge.

01/08/1944 LM180 JI-G Bombing Foret de Nieppe 19.13 20.47 21.39

Bomb load 11 x 1000 MC, 4 x 500 GP. Primary target: De Nieppe, constructional works. Bombed at 2047 hours from 11000 feet, on Gee Fix.

12/08/1944 PB142 JI-A Bombing Brunswick 21.43 01.18 03.10

Bomb load 1 x 2000 HC. 12 x 500 'J' type clusters. Primary target: Brunswick. Last resort - Eastern tip of Terschelling. Weather 10/10ths. Bombed at 0001 hours from 18,500 feet. Bomb door would not open over target Photo flash taken of Brunswick. Fuselage and hydraulic shot away.

03/09/1944 PD265 JI-G Bombing Eindhoven 15.09 17.30 18.53

Bomb load 11 x 1000 MC, 4 x 500 GP. Primary target: Eindhoven airfield. Bombed at 1730 hours from 18500 feet, red T.I.

05/09/1944 ME841 JI-H Bombing Le Havre 17.16 19.23 20.17

Bomb load 11 x 1000 MC, 4 x 500 GP. Primary target: Le Havre. Bombed at 1923 hours from 13000 feet red T.I.

06/09/1944 LM275 JI-E Bombing Le Havre 16.33 18.40 19.53

Bomb load 11 x 1000 MC, 4 x 500 GP. Primary target: Le Havre. Bombed at 1840 hours from 7000 feet red T.I.s.

10/09/1944 LM684 JI-O Bombing Le Havre 15.50 17.38 19.09

Bomb load 11 x 1000 MC, 4 x 500 GP. Primary target: Le Havre. Weather clear. Bombed at 1738 hours from 10000 feet. Undershot red T.I.s by 200 yards.

12/09/1944 LM275 JI-E Bombing Frankfurt 18.27 22.54 01.33

Bomb load 1 x 4000 HC, 14 x 500 Clusters 4lb. Target: Frankfurt - Main. Weather clear over the target. Jettisoned 10 miles S.W. of Frankfurt at 2254 hours from 17000 feet owing to attack by fighter in which Rear Gunner was wounded. During the attack, the Rear Gunner received head injuries and Rear Turrett was put u/s. There were also numerous holes in the fuselage and tailplane,

17/09/1944 LM627 JI-D Bombing Boulogne 10.50 12.16 13.38

Bomb load 11 x 1000 MC, 4 x 500 GP. Primary target: Boulogne, Aiming point 2. Weather clear below cloud. Bombed at 1216 hours from 4000 feet, starboard of red T.I., which were port of target.

20/09/1944 LM627 JI-D Bombing Calais 14.37 16.01 17.08

Bomb load 11 x 1000 MC, 4 x 500 GP. Primary target: Calais. Weather clear over target. Bombed at 1601 hours from 2700 feet, red T.I.

03/10/1944 NN717 JI-E Bombing Westkapelle 12.28   16.51   14.45

Bomb load 1 x 4000 HC. 6 x 1000 MC. 1 x 500 GP. L/Delay. Primary target: Westkapelle (Walcheren). Weather patchy-scattered cloud with base 5000 feet. Bombed at 13.51 hours from 4,200 feet, visually.

05/10/1944 NN717 JI-E Bombing Saarbrucken 17.15   20.35   22.30

Bomb load 11 x 1000 MC. 1 x 500 GP. Primary target: Saarbrucken. Bombed at 20.35½ hours from 18,000 feet on Green T.I.

07/10/1944 NN717 JI-E Bombing Emmerich 11.57 14.25   16.06

Bomb load 1 x 4000 HC. 10 x no. 14 clusters, 4 x (150x4). Primary target: Emmerich. Weather clear with cloud at 13,000 feet. Bombed at 14.26 hours from 12,600 feet starboard of smoke and visual means.

14/10/1944 NN717 JI-E Bombing Duisburg   06.56   09.05   10.55

Bomb load 11 x 1000 MC. 4 x 500 GP Long Delay. Primary target: Duisburg. Weather patchy cloud with gaps for bombing. Bombed at 09.05 hours from 20,000 feet. Docks

K.D. Condict was 2nd pilot that day.

14/10/1944 NN717 JI-E Bombing Duisburg   22.50   01.29   03.17

Bomb load 11 x 1000 MC. 4 x 500 GP Long Delay. Primary target: Duisburg. Weather was clear with small amount of cloud over the target. Bombed at 01.29 hours from 23,000 feet. Between red and green T.I.s.

18/10/1944 LM285 JI-K Bombing Bonn 08.15   11.00   13.03

Bomb load 1 x 4000 HC. 5 x 12 x 30 - 2 x 12 x 30 modified. 9 x No.14 Clusters. Primary target: Bonn. Weather varying cloud 2-7/10ths with break for bombing. Weather varying cloud 2-7/10ths with break for bombing. Bombed at 11.00 hours from 17,500 feet. On G.H. G.H. corroborated by visual as falling in Northern centre of town.

19/10/1944 NN717 JI-E Bombing Stuttgart 22.01   01.05   03.55

Bomb load 1 x 4000 HC. 3 x 500 Clusters. 7 x 150 x 4, 1 x 90 x 4. Primary target: Stuttgart, A/P 'E' 2nd attack. Weather 10/10ths low cloud over target and all crew arrived late owing to winds not as forecast. Bombed at 01.05 hours from 20,000 feet. Read and Yellow markers.

21/10/1944 NN717 JI-E Bombing Flushing 10.43   12.27   13.31

Bomb load 12 x 1000 MC. 2 x 500 GP. Primary target: Flushing 'B'. Weather clear. Bombed at 12.27 hours from 8,000 feet. Visual of coast.

23/10/1944 NN717 JI-E Bombing Essen 16.13   19.29   21.16

Bomb load 1 x 4000 HC. 6 x 1000 MC. 6 x 500 GP. Primary target: Essen. Weather 10/10ths cloud over target - tops 12/14,000 feet with most appalling weather on route. Bombed at 19.29 hours from 22,500 feet. Red flares.

26/10/1944 PD265 JI-G Bombing Leverkusen 13.05   15.29   17.17

Bomb load 1 x 4000 HC, 6 x 1000 MC, 4 x 500 GP, 2 x 500 GP Long Delay. Primary target: Leverkusen. Weather over target and on route was 10/10ths cloud. Bombed at 15.29 hours from 16,000 feet on G.H.

29/10/1944 NN717 JI-E Bombing Flushing 09.55 11.38 12.24

Bomb load 11 x 1000 ANM59. 4 x 500 GP.MC. Primary target: Flushing, Gun installations. Weather clear over target. Bombed at 11.38 hours from 6,000 feet. Slightly to starboard of Green T.I.s. as instructed.

31/10/1944 LM717 JI-B Bombing Bottrop 11.45 15.01 16.31

Bomb load 1 x 4000 HC. 15 x 500 GP. 1 Flare. Primary target: Bottrop, Synth. Oil plants. Weather 10/10ths cloud over target. Bombed at 15.01 hours from 17,500 feet on G.H.

11/11/1944 PD265 JI-G Bombing Castrop Rauxel 08.26 11.07 12.47

Bomb load 1 x 4000 HC. 15 x 500 GP. 1 Flare. Primary target: Castro Rauxel. Primary target: Castrop Rauxel, Oil refineries. Weather 10/10ths cloud. Bombed at 11.07 hours from 21,000 feet on G.H.

15/11/1944 PD265 JI-G Bombing Dortmund 12.38 15.41 17.11

Bomb load 1 x 4000 HC. 15 x 500 GP. 1 Red with Green star Flare. Primary target: Hoesch-Benzin Dortmund, Oil refineries. Weather 10/10ths cloud over the target. Bombed at 15.41 hours from 17,000 feet on G.H.

16/11/1944 PD265 JI-G Bombing Heinsburg 13.20 15.37 16.55

Bomb load 1 x 4000 HC, 6 x 1000 MC, 4 x 500 GP, 4 x 250 lb T.Is. Primary target: Heinsburg. Weather - nil cloud with slight haze over target. Bombed at 15.37 hours from 12,500 feet. Visual and starboard of Red T.Is. per Master Bomber.

20/11/1944 PD265 JI-G Bombing Homberg 12.33 15.15 16.50

Bomb load 1 x 4000 HC, 15 x 500 GP, 1 Red-Green Flare. Primary target: Homberg. Weather 10/10ths cloud over target. Bombed at 15.15 hours from 21,500 feet on G.H.

F/O. William Douglas Brickwood

179791 (1384035) F/O. William Douglas Brickwood. Pilot.
NZ416861 F/O. Harold Thomas Crampton. RNZAF A/Bomber.
1230758 F/S. Robert James Rigden. A/Bomber.5 ops
NZ421784 F/S. Keith Varndell Stafford. RNZAF Navigator.
NZ416419 P/O. Ronald Gordon Collender. RNZAF WOP/AG.
972379Sgt. William Percy Blake   MU/Gunner.
A428331   P/O. James Samuel Lupton. RAAF R/Gunner.
182295 (1831748) P/O. Colin Oliver Turner   F/Engineer.

30/06/1944 LL670 A2-K   Bombing Villers Bocage 18.11   19.55   21.21
   Bomb load 10 x 1000 MC, 2 x 500 GP. Primary target: Villers Bocage.
Weather 5/10ths about 9,000. Bombed at 19.55 hours at 13,000 feet. Overshot red T.I.s by one second directed by the Master Bomber. Should be a good attack.

02/07/1944 LL728 A2-L Bombing Beauvoir 12.57 14.36 16.16
Bomb load 11 x 1000 MC, 4 x 500 GP. Primary target: Beauvoir, Flying bomb supply site. Bombed at 14.36 hours from 8,000 feet on red T.I.s and visual.

07/07/1944 LL726 A2-H Bombing Vaires 22.48 01.34 03.26
Bomb load 7 x 1000 MC, 4 x 500 GP. Primary target: Vaires, Marshalling yards. Weather clear. Bombed at 01.34 hours from 12,000 feet centre of red and green T.I.s. Bombing concentrated, opposition slight.

10/07/1944 LL726 A2-H Bombing Nucourt 04.29 06.04   07.49
Bomb load 11 x 1000 ANM 65, 4 x 500 GP.   Primary   target: Nucourt, Constructional works. Bombed at 0604 hours from 16000 feet on Gee.

F/S. K.V. Stafford – Detroit USA – 27 June 1943
(courtesy Eamon Stafford)

   23/07/1944 DS786 A2-H Bombing Kiel 22.28½ 01.23 04.08
   Bomb load 6 x 1000 MC, 10 x 500 GP, Special Nickels. Primary target: Kiel, Warehouses and docks. Weather 10/10ths thin cloud. Bombed at 01.23 hours from 19,000 feet centre of green T.I.s. Defences moderate, good trip.
24/07/1944 DS786 A2-H Bombing Stuttgart 21.50 02.34

Bomb load 5 x 1000 ANM 65, 3 x 500 GP. Returned early starboard inner engine u/s. Jettisoned 5218N 0220E.

27/07/1944 DS620 A2-D Bombing Les Catelliers 16.43 18.53 20.02
Bomb load 18 x 500 GP. Primary target: Les Catelliers, Flying bomb site. Bombed at 18.53 hours from 16,500 feet on Mosquito.

30/07/1944 DS786 A2-H Bombing Caen 06.12 07.49 09.01
Bomb load 18 x 500 GP. Primary target: Caen 'B'. Weather 10/10yths cloud. Bombed at 07.49 hours from 2,000 feet red T.I. Fairly large stone building on fire. Too early in attack to assess results. Master Bomber clear and helpful.

01/08/1944 DS786 A2-H Bombing Foret de Nieppe 19.25 20.46
21.34
Bomb load 11 x 1000 MC, 4 x 500 GP. Primary target: De Nieppe, constructional works. Bombed at 20.46 hours from 11,500 feet on leading aircraft.

04/08/1944 DS786 A2-H Bombing Bec D'Ambes 13.15 18.02 21.06
Bomb load 5 x 1000 MC, 4 x 500 GP. Primary target: Bec d'Ambes depot. Weather clear. Bombed at 18.02 hours from 8,000 feet. Storage tanks South of fires. Master Bomber instructed crews to bomb yellow T.I.s which were not visible. Column of black smoke up to 8000 feet.

08/08/1944 DS786 A2-H Bombing Foret de Lucheux 21.49 23.50
01.07
Bomb load 18 x 500 GP. Primary target: Foret de Lucheux, Petrol dump. Slight haze. Bombed at 23.50 hours, 12,000 feet, ½ second undershoot on fires as instructed by Master Bomber. T.I.s obliterated by fires and pall of black smoke.

11/08/1944 LL697 A2-B Bombing Lens 14.13 16.33 17.30
Bomb load 11 x 1000 MC. 4 X 500 GP. Primary target: Lens, Marshalling yards. Weather 3/10ths cloud. Bombed at 16.33 hours, 14,000 feet.

Bomb aimer had given 'Steady' when Lancaster was hit in nose by bombs from Lancaster above. The bomb aimer and equipment were hurled from aircraft. Pilot tried to jettison bombs, but believed already gone. All instruments on panel u/s except altimeter. Aircraft was assisted back to Woodbridge by 'E2'. The bomb aimer's parachute failed to deploy, probably because he was killed or knocked out when the bomb hit. He is buried in the Loos British Cemetery at Loos-en-Gohelle, 3km NW of Lens. His six comrades, including RNZAF navigator Flt Sgt K V Stafford and wireless operator Wt Off R G Collender, returned safely to England, the badly damaged LL697 touching down at Woodbridge, Suffolk, at 17.30. The Lancaster did not fly again, however, being struck off charge as beyond economical repair.
Air Bomber KIA: NZ416861 F/O. Harold Thomas Crampton, RNZAF - Age 27. 315hrs. 22nd op.

18/08/1944 PB426 JI-J Bombing Bremen 21.39 00.16 03.01
Bomb load 1 x 4000 HC, 96 x 30 lb incend, 1080 x 4lb incend, 120 x 4lb x incend. Primary target: Bremen. Weather clear over target. Bombed at 00.16

hours, 2,000 feet, red T.Is. Many fires, two large explosions in target area. Very successful prang.

05/09/1944 DS826 A2-C Bombing Le Havre 17.31 19.23 20.34

Bomb load 11 x 1000 MC, 4 x 500 GP. Primary target: Le Havre. Bombed at 19.23 hours from 13,500 feet red T.I.

08/09/1944 LL726 A2-H Bombing Le Havre 06.07 09.38

Bomb load 11 x 1000 MC, 4 x 500 GP. Primary target: Le Havre. Weather 10/10ths cloud down to 3,000 feet. Abandoned mission on Master Bomber's instructions.

11/09/1944 LL726 A2-H Bombing Kamen 16.12 18.44 20.30

Bomb load 1 x 4000 HC, 16 x 500 GP. Weather clear. Primary target: Kamen. Bombed at 18.44 hours from 17,000 feet between red and yellow T.I.s.

12/09/1944 LL731 JI-U Bombing Frankfurt 18.44 23.30

Bomb load 1 x 8000 HC, 1 x 500 Cluster 4lb. Primary target: Frankfurt - Main. Weather clear over the target. Aircraft missing

. Crashed at 23.30 hours at Kordel, a small town in the Ehranger Wald, 8 km NW of Trier. Shot down by Lt. Fred Hromadnik of 9./NJG4. Those killed are buried in Rheinberg War Cemetery.

F/O W.D. Brickwood KIA, P/O C.O. Turner PoW, F/S K.V. Stafford RNZAF KIA, F/S R.J. Rigden PoW, P/O R.G. Collender RNZAF KIA, Sgt W.P. Blake KIA, P/O J.S. Lupton RAAF KIA.

F/S R.J. Rigden was interned in Camp L7, PoW No.944. P/O C.O. Turner in Camp L1, PoW No.5872.

F/L. Ronald Burnett

119534 (1213146) F/L. Ronald Burnett. Pilot.

F/S. F.A. Dufoe. A/Bomber.

Sgt. W.B. Long. Navigator.

Sgt. A.A. Berry. WOP/AG.

F/S. P.G. Fitzpatrick. MU/Gunner.

F/S T.B.C. Strong. R/Gunner.

Sgt. T.L. Kenrick. F/Engineer.

14/03/1945 PB142 JI-G Bombing Heinrichshutte 13.14 16.40 19.05

Bomb load 1 x 4000 HC, 12 x 500 ANM64. Primary target: Heinrichshutte, Hattingen Steel works and Benzol plant. Weather 10/10ths cloud, tops 7/12,000 feet. Bombed at 16.40 hours from 18,000 feet on G.H. Leader. 1 Red marker as aircraft bombed. Port outer engine holed by flak at 16.33 hours and had to be feathered. Mid upper turret holed and Hydraulics unserviceable.

F/L. R. Burnett flew the mission as 2nd pilot with F/O. C.G. Fiset crew.

17/03/1945 LM627JI-D Bombing August Viktoria 11.42 15.10 17.43

Bomb load 1 x 4000 HC, 13 x 500 ANM64, 2 x 500 MC. Primary target:

Auguste Viktoria, Marl-Hüls coal mine. Weather 10/10ths cloud, tops and contrails up to 23,000 feet. Reached August Victoria at 15.10 hours following G.H. aircraft. He signalled G.H. unserviceable. We tried to bomb on formation in front but contrails obscured it any by the time we reached height to bomb the formation had turned West for home. All bombs brought back to Base.

F/L. W.F. Burrows

J20986 F/L. W.F. Burrows. RCAF Pilot.
159990 (1650697) F/O. David Philip Bartlett. A/Bomber.
J40541 F/O. E.G. "Ed" Commeford. RCAF Navigator.
Sgt. G.D. Tough. WOP/AG.
Sgt. F.C. Vincent. MU/Gunner.
Sgt. J.A. Walker. R/Gunner.
1677111 Sgt. C.R. Ingham. F/Engineer.
134136 F/L. Frank Raymond Wilton England. 2nd pilot. 06/03/1945
J9442 F/L H.J. Clark, RCAF   2nd pilot. 14/03/1945

Passengers 03/05/1945, 08/05/1945.

29/11/1944 LM285 JI-K Bombing Neuss 03.08   05.40   07.29
Bomb load 1 x 4000 HC, 6 x 1000 MC, 4 x 500 GP, 4 x 250 Green T.I.s. Primary target: Neuss. Weather 10/10ths cloud over target but the glow of fires was seen through cloud. Bombed at 05.40 hours from 19,000 feet. Red flares with green stars. Glow observed through cloud, successful raid. F/L. W.F. Burrows flew the mission as 2nd pilot with P/O. W.R. Foreman crew.
30/11/1944 PB756 JI-B Bombing Osterfeld   11.00   13.11   15.13
Bomb load 1 x 4000 HC, 16 x 500 GP. Primary target: Osterfeld, Coking plant. Weather 10/10ths cloud. Bombed at 13.110 hours from 20,000 feet on G.H. Leader. Smoke billowing up through cloud.
04/12/1944 PB756 JI-B Bombing Oberhausen 11.58 14.09   16.02
Bomb load 1 x 4000 HC, 2100 x 4 lb incendiaries. Primary target: Oberhausen, Built up area. Weather 10/10ths cloud. Bombed at 14.09 hours from 20,000 feet on leaders release.
05/12/1944 PB756 JI-B Bombing Hamm 09.06 11.30   13.53
Bomb load 1 x 4000 H.C, 1950 x 4 lb incendiaries. Primary target: Hamm. Weather 10/10ths cloud over target, but otherwise varying from 6-10/10ths. Bombed at 11.30 hours from 20,000 feet on G.H. Leader,
06/12/1944 PB426 JI-D Bombing Merseburg 17.02 22.45
Bomb load 1 x 4000 HC, 8 x 500 GP, 1 x 500 GP Long Delay. Primary target: Merseburg. Weather 10/10ths cloud with odd breaks. Returned early with A.S.I. and Gee unserviceable. Jettisoned at 19.55 hours from 16,000 feet

at 5045N 0759E. Landed at Oakington.

08/12/1944 LM627A2-H Bombing Duisburg 08.45 11.05 13.07

Bomb load 12 x 1000 MC, 2 x 1000 ANM59. Primary target: Duisberg. Weather 10/10ths cloud. Bombed at 11.05 hours from 20,000 feet on G.H. Leader.

12/12/1944 NN717JI-E Bombing Witten 11.20 14.04 15.59

Bomb load 1 x 4000 HC, 14 x 500 4lb Clusters. Primary target: Witten. Weather 10/10ths cloud, tops 14/16,000 feet. Bombed at 14.04 hours from 20,000 feet on G.H. Leader.

15/12/1944 PB426 JI-D Bombing Siegen ca.11.30 x ca.14.00

Between 11.19 to 11.36 hours 19 aircraft took off to attack Siegen. At 12.30 hours, all aircraft recalled as Fighters were unable to take off. Operation only reported in ORBs "Summary of events", no trace in ORBs "Detail of Work carried out - Details of sorties of flight". Operation noted in C.R. Ingham logbook.

16/12/1944 NN717JI-E Bombing Siegen 11.28 15.00 17.25

Bomb load 1 x 4000 HC. 14 x No.14 clusters. Primary target: Siegen. Weather very bad on route with icing and cloud. Bombed at 15.00 hours from 18,500 feet on leading aircraft.

13/01/1945 NF968 JI-B Bombing Saarbrucken 12.00 15.24 18.12

Bomb load 1 x 4000 HC, 10 x 500 ANM58 or 64, 4x250 GP. Primary target: Saarbrucken. Weather 3-5/10ths cloud, tops 4/5,000 feet. Bombed at 15.24 hours from 19,500 feet on G.H. Leader. All aircrafts of this ops were diverted on return to Exeter as weather at base was unfit to land.

19/02/1945 ME355JI-L Bombing Wesel 13.23 16.35 19.38

Bomb load 1 x 4000 HC, 6 x 500 MC, 6 x 500 ANM64, 4 x 250 GP. Primary target: Wesel. Weather over target 5-7/10ths cloud. Bombed at 16.35 hours from 20,000 feet on G.H. Landed at Moreton in Marsh.

22/02/1945 ME363JI-Q Bombing Osterfeld 12.14 15.59 17.53

Bomb load 1 x 4000 HC, 9 x 500 ANM64, 2 x 500 MC, 4 x 250 GP. Primary target: Osterfeld, Coking ovens. Weather at target clear, but hazy. Bombed at 15.59 hours from 20,000 feet on G.H. equipment.

25/02/1945 ME358JI-O Bombing Kamen 09.38 12.46 15.00

Bomb load 1 x 4000 HC, 9 x 500 ANM64, 2 x 500 MC, 4 x 250 GP. Primary target: Kamen. Weather 6-8/10ths cloud. Bombed at 12.46 hours from 20,000 feet on G.H. equipment.

27/02/1945 ME336JI-S Bombing Gelsenkirchen 10.53 14.28½16.27

Bomb load 1 x 4000 HC, 2 x 500 MC (L/D 37B), 9 x 500 ANM64, 3 x 250 GP, 1x 250 Blue Puff. Primary target: Gelsenkirchen (Alma Pluts) Benzin plant. Weather 10/10ths cloud, 6/10,000 feet tops. Bombed at 14.28½ hours from 20,000 feet on G.H.

06/03/1945 ME358JI-O Bombing Wesel 18.26 21.10 23.29

Bomb load 1 x 4000 HC, 13 x 500 ANM64, 2 x 500MC. Primary target: Wesel. Weather 10/10ths cloud, tops 16,000 feet preventing visual. Bombed at

21.10 hours from 18,000 feet on G.H.

2nd pilot F/L. F.R.W. England.

09/03/1945 ME355JI-L Bombing Datteln 10.35 14.00 15.55

Bomb load 1 x 4000 HC, 13 x 500 ANM64, 13 x 500 MC L/Delay37B. Primary target: Datteln, Synthetic oil plant. Weather 10/10ths cloud, tops 8-10,000 feet. Bombed at 14.00 hours from 21,000 feet on G.H. Leader.

14/03/1945 ME336JI-S Bombing Heinrichshutte 13.07 16.40 18.39

Bomb load 1 x 4000 HC, 11 x 500 ANM64, 1 Skymarker Red Puff. Primary target: Heinrichshutte, Hattingen Steel works and Benzol plant. Weather 10/10ths cloud, tops 7/12,000 feet. Bombed at 16.40 hours from 18,500 feet on G.H. Aircraft holed by flak in tail and port inner engine.

2nd pilot H.J. Clark RCAF.

21/03/1945 ME336JI-S Bombing Munster 09.26 13.08 15.43

Bomb load 1 x 4000 HC, 13 x 500 ANM64, 2 x 500 MC, 1 Skymarker Blue Puff. Primary target Munster Viaduct and Marshalling Yards. Weather cloud nil to 2/10ths. Bombed at 13.08 hours from 18,000 feet on G.H.

23/03/1945 ME336JI-S Bombing Wesel 14.29 17.38 19.24

Bomb load 13 x 1000 MC. Primary target: Wesel, in support of ground troops. Weather perfect. Bombed at 17.38 hours from 19,500 feet on G.H.

29/03/1945 ME358JI-O Bombing Salzgitter 12.25 16.44 19.22

Bomb load 1 x 4000 HC, 8 x 500 ANM64. Primary target: Salzgitter, Hallendorf works. Weather 10/10ths cloud. Bombed at 16.44 hours from 22,000 feet on G.H. Leader. Too much cloud to assess result. Special Equipment very good.

09/04/1945 ME358JI-O Bombing Kiel 19.44 22.38 01.49

Bombed primary target Kiel, Submarine Buildings Yards. Weather clear with slight haze. Bomb load 1 x 4000 HC and 12 x 500 ANM64. Bombed centre of Green T.I.'s. per M.B.'s instructions at 22.38 hours from 20,000 feet. T.I.'s appeared well placed. Good visual of harbour. Bombing very accurate. Good raid. Marking clear and concentrated. Large fire area seen from Sylt outwards.

18/04/1945 ME336JI-S Bombing Heligoland 09.3813.08 15.13

Bomb load 4 x 1000 MC, 2 x 1000 GP, 10 x 500 ANM64. Primary target: Heligoland, Naval base. Weather no cloud, slight haze. Bombed visually in centre of smoke at 13.08 hours from 18,000 feet. Whole island covered in smoke. Raid very successful. Island of Dune obliterated.

24/04/1945 ME422JI-Q Bombing Bad Oldesloe 07.34 10.43 13.09

Bomb load 6 x 1000 ANM65, 10 x 500 ANM 64. Primary target: Bad-Oldesloe, Rail and road junction and Marshalling Yards. Weather 3/10ths to nil cloud. Bombed on leading aircraft 514/S at 10.43 hours from 18,000 ft. Smoke and fires. Good effort. Formation rather straggly. Attack good. G.H. u/s.

01/05/1945 ME336JI-S Manna The Hague 13.31 14.50 15.57

Weather clear over target. Dropped 5 Panniers at 14.50 hours on Red T.I.'s and White Cross (Partly covered). Delivery effected in the right spot. The word 'Thanks' written on top of tenement building in what appeared to be sawdust. One flak burst 20 miles to south of track, not fired at aircraft, from a point 51.43 N. 03.41 E.

03/05/1945 ME336 JI-S Manna The Hague 11.08 12.36 13.42

Dropping area The Hague. Dropped 4 panniers clear on Red T.I.'s and White Cross at 12.36 hours. One Pannier returned to Base due to hang -up. Delivery O.K. Numerous cattle visible in the field on route.

Passenger AC. Watling.

08/05/1945 ME336 JI-S Manna Rotterdam 12.47 14.10 15.13

Dropping area Rotterdam. Dropped 5 Packs on Red T.I. and visually at 1410 hours. Clear. Bad dropping area due to small rivulets intersecting at numerous points - many packs seen to cause a splash when reaching deck.

Passenger LAC. Kampion.

10/05/1945 ME336 JI-S Exodus Juvincourt - Ford 11.17 x 18.02

Duration 3.42. Outward 1.45 hours. Collected 24 ex POWs. Homeward 1.57 hours. Organisation very good.

P/O.   Harry Stanley Butcher

191610 (1394302)   P/O. Harry Stanley Butcher.   Pilot.
164827 (1584399)   F/O. Geoffrey M. O. Briegel. A/Bomber.
197467 (1629088)   P/O. Anthony L.E. Thoday.   Navigator.
Sgt. E.R. Thompson.   WOP/AG.
Sgt. W.M. Mortensen   MU/Gunner.11 ops
Sgt. F.C. Wright   MU and R/G.3 ops
F/S. A. Balderstone.   MU and R/Gunner.
202304 (3006111)   Sgt. Harry Joseph John Wrenn.   F/Engineer.

Passengers 01/06/1945, 05/07/1945, 20/07/1945.

16/02/1945 NN717 A2-E   Bombing Wesel 12.32½ 16.01   17.48

Bomb load 1 x 4000 HC, 4 x 500 GP, 2 x 500 MC L/Delay, 4 x 250 GP, 6 x 500 ANM64. Primary target: Wesel. Weather clear. Bombed at 16.01 hours from 20,500 feet on leading aircraft.

P/O. H.S. Butcher flew the mission with F/O. C.I.H. Nicholl crew.

18/02/1945 NN717 A2-E   Bombing Wesel 11.29   15.23   17.08

Bomb load 1 x 4000 HC, 4 x 500 GP, 2 x 500 MC L/Delay, 4 x 250 GP, 6 x 500 ANM64. Primary target: Wesel. Weather 10/10ths cloud. Bombed at 15.23 hours from 20,000 feet on leading aircraft.

19/02/1945 NN717 A2-E   Bombing Wesel 13.03   16.36   19.17

Bomb load 1 x 4000 HC, 6 x 500 MC, 6 x 500 ANM64, 4 x 250 GP. Primary target: Wesel. Weather over target 5-7/10ths cloud. Bombed at 16.36 hours from 19,800 feet on leading aircraft. Landed at Moreton in Marsh.

22/02/1945 NN717 A2-E   Bombing Osterfeld 12.17 16.02 18.04

Bomb load 1 x 4000 HC, 9 x 500 ANM64, 2 x 500 MC, 4 x 250 GP. Primary target: Osterfeld, Coking ovens. Weather at target clear, but hazy. Bombed at 16.02 hours from 18,000 feet on G.H. Leader. (1x 500 ANM64 hang-up brought back).

05/03/1945 NN717 A2-E   Bombing Gelsenkirchen 10.34 14.08 16.23

Bomb load 1 x 4000 HC, 12 x 500 ANM64. Primary target: Gelsenkirchen, Benzol plant. Weather 10/10ths cloud over target with cirrus cloud at bombing height. Bombed at 14.08 hours from 21,000 feet on Red Puffs.

06/03/1945 NN717 A2-E   Bombing Salzbergen 08.25 12.15 14.18

Bomb load 1 x 4000 HC, 12 x 500 ANM64, 2 x 500MC. Primary target: Salzbergen, Wintershall oil plant. Weather 10/10ths cloud over target, tops 10,000 feet. Bombed at 12.15 hours from 21,000 feet on G.H. Leader. MidUp turret and various other minor damage done by fragments from aircraft exploding.

09/03/1945 NN717 A2-E   Bombing Datteln   10.38 14.00 15.57

Bomb load 1 x 4000 HC, 13 x 500 ANM64, 13 x 500 MC L/Delay37B. Primary target: Datteln, Synthetic oil plant. Weather 10/10ths cloud, tops 8-10,000 feet. Bombed at 14.00 hours from 21,000 feet on G.H. Leader.

11/03/1945 NN717 A2-E   Bombing Essen   11.32 15.25 17.21

Bomb load 1 x 4000 HC, 13 x 500 ANM64, 2 x 500 MC. Primary target: Essen, Marshalling yards. Weather 10/10ths cloud, tops 7/8000 feet. Bombed at 15.25 hours from 19,000 feet on leading G.H. aircraft.

17/03/1945 NN717 A2-E   Bombing August Viktoria 11.30 15.06 17.08

Bomb load 1 x 4000 HC, 13 x 500 ANM64, 2x 500 MC. Primary target: Auguste Viktoria, Marl-Hüls coal mine. Weather 10/10ths cloud, tops and contrails up to 23,000 feet. Bombed at 15.06 hours from 21,800 feet on leading G.H. aircraft.

20/03/1945 PD389 A2-J Bombing Hamm 10.31 13.14½ 15.58

Bomb load 7 x 1000 ANM65, 9 x 500 ANM64. Primary target: Hamm, Marshalling yards. Weather 5/10ths cloud. Bombed at 13.14½ hours from 18,800 feet on leading aircraft. 1 x 1000 ANM65 Jettisoned in the Herbern area at 13.17 hours from 18,800 feet.

13/04/1945 PB426 A2-E   Bombing Kiel 20.22 23.37 02.26

Bombed primary target. Bomb load 18 x 500 ANM64. Primary target: Kiel, Docks and ship yards. Weather 10/10ths cloud low and thin. Bombed Green T.I.'s on M/B's instructions at 23.37 hours from 19,700 feet.   Left hand edge of green glow. Several heavy explosions near green glow seen through the cloud. Large fire burning as we left. Good attack if marking was O.K. Very concentrated.

20/04/1945 PB426 A2-E   Bombing Regensburg 09.47 13.59 17.23

Bomb load 16 x 500 ANM64. Primary target: Regensburg. Weather clear over target and whole route. Bombed on G.H. aircraft 514 'H' and visually at

13.59 hours from 18,500 feet. G.H. release pulse not received. M. 'Y' just S of tanks. Concentration of bombing on each side of river at east end of target. Trip was a pleasure one.

01/06/1945 RA602 A2-H   Baedeker Tour over Germany 11.05   x 15.36
Passengers Sgt. A. Kinselle, Cpl. B. Brown, AC. W. Pitt, AC. K. Dyer.

05/07/1945 RF272 A2-F   Baedeker Tour over Continent 14.17   x 18.52
By error n ORBs this aircraft is noted as RE272.
Passengers F/S. Williams, F/S. King, LAC. Denton, ACW. Gallagher 828, Cpl. Baker (WAAF).

20/07/1945 RA602 A2-H   Baedeker Tour over Continent 09.28   x 14.06
Passengers Cpl. Smith, Cpl. Orr, Cpl. Wilson, LACW. Hayes, LACW. Scott.

P/O. Joseph McLaws McLellan Cameron

196042 (1564681)   P/O. Joseph McLaws McLellan Cameron.   Pilot.
Sgt. William C. "Bill" "Flip" Legon.   A/Bomber.
Sgt. J.H. Milan.   Navigator.
Sgt. R. Barnes.   WOP/AG.
Sgt. L.R. Whitehouse.   MU/Gunner.
Sgt. A.J. Aldridge.   R/Gunner.
Sgt. D.G. Thomas.   F/Engineer.

Passenger 02/05/1945, 02/06/1945, 14/06/1945, 13/07/1945, 23/07/1945, 24/07/1945, 26/07/1945.

17/03/1945 ME336 JI-S Bombing August Viktoria 11.36½ 15.06   17.14
Bomb load 1 x 4000 HC, 13 x 500 ANM64, 2x 500 MC. 1 Skymarker Blue Puff. Primary target: Auguste Viktoria, Marl-Hüls coal mine. Weather 10/10ths cloud, tops and contrails up to 23,000 feet. Bombed at 15.06 hours from 20,000 feet on G.H.
P/O. J.McL.McL. Cameron flew the mission as 2nd pilot with F/O. J.A. Chadwell crew.

18/03/1945 PB482 A2-K   Bombing Bruchstrasse   11.43   15.05   17.12
Bomb load 1 x 4000 HC, 13 x 500 ANM64, 2 x 500 MC. Primary target: Bruchstrasse, Coal mine and coking plant. Weather 10/10ths cloud, tops 6-12,000 feet. Bombed at 15.05 hours from 20,000 feet on G.H. Leader.   2 Blue Puffs to starboard.

04/04/1945 ME363 JI-R Bombing Merseburg (Leuna) 18.46   22.48   03.08
Weather 5-10/10ths cloud, and 10/10ths over Merseburg. Bombed primary Target: Merseburg. Bomb load 1 x 4000 HC, 6 x 500 ANM64. Bombed on Red T.I. on ground at 22.48 hrs from 19,900 feet. 1 x 500 ANM64 jettisoned live at 01.53 hrs from 7,000 feet. 5018N 0000E. Timing rather poor - Red and Green T.I. seen dropped to port in Magdeberg area. Master bomber not heard.

P/O. J.McL.McL. Cameron flew the mission as 2nd pilot with F/O. F.E. Sider's crew.

18/04/1945 ME364 JI-P Bombing Heligoland 09.42 13.07 15.07

Bomb load 4 x 1000 MC, 2 x 1000 GP, 10 x 500 ANM64. Primary target: Heligoland, Naval base. Weather no cloud, slight haze. Bombed visually at 13.07 hours from 18500 ft. Markers only faintly discernible. Bombs burst upwind edge of smoke. Island covered with smoke, very successful raid. M/B ordered to bomb on T.I. then on Pickwick.

20/04/1945 ME364 JI-P Bombing Regensburg 09.36 13.56½ 17.15

Bomb load 16 x 500 ANM64. Primary target: Regensburg. Weather clear over target and whole route. Bombed visually at 13.56½ from 19,000 feet.

Visually as leader had turned off too sharply. Bombs seen to burst across the oil tanks on north side of harbour. Some smoke or dust cloud rising. Should be a good raid.

22/04/1945 ME363 JI-R Bombing Bremen 15.16 18.42 20.57

Bomb load 1 x 4000 HC, 2 x 500 MC, 14 x 500 ANM 64. Primary target: Bremen, in support of Troop concentration. Weather on approaching target 4-5/10ths cloud. Bomb following 514/S. at 18.42 hrs. from 19.000 ft. Bombs seen to fall in target area north of river. One bomb in river. Flak. Good attack.

02/05/1945 ME363 JI-R Manna The Hague 11.02 12.15½ 13.21

Weather over dropping zone clear below cloud for the first arrivals changing later to heavy showers which marred visibility. Dropped 5 panniers visually on T.I.s and white cross at 12.15½ hours. Fortress seen on beach E. point of Overplothe.

No Mid Upper Gunner that day.

Passenger LAC. Jenkins.

02/06/1945 ME336 JI-S Baedeker Tour over Germany 09.53 x 15.27

Passengers Sgt. C. Fletcher, AC. A. Gunn, Cadet J. Orwisher.

14/06/1945 ME363 JI-R Baedeker Tour over Continent 12.14 x 16.43

Passengers S/L. Pidgeon, LAC. Ayres, LAC. Forbes, LAC. Bradley.

01/07/1945 ME363 JI-R Post Mortem Special mission 12.07 x 18.02

05/07/1945 ME363 JI-R Post Mortem Special mission 13.23 x 18.17

13/07/1945 ME363 JI-R Baedeker Tour over Continent 09.40 x 14.00

Passengers Sgt. Levy, LAC. Bailey, Cpl. Naylor, LACW. Burnett, LACW. Jamieson.

23/07/1945 ME363 JI-R Baedeker Tour over Continent 15.05 x 19.11

Passengers S/O. London, S/L. Pawsey, LAC. Elliott, LAC. Meese, LAC. Marner.

24/07/1945 ME363 JI-R Baedeker Tour over Continent 09.54 x 14.04

Passengers Cpl. Hutchinson (WAAF), LACW. Belling, Cpl. Stansfield, Cpl. Williams, LAC. Washington.

26/07/1945 RF231 JI-A Baedeker Tour over Continent 09.52 x 14.04

Passengers S/O. Denver, Cpl. Tester, ACW. Flaving, AC. Washington, AC. Burrows.

F/L. Edward Alexander Campbell, DFC

Insets: FS. E.R. Jones (left), F/O. R.R. Giffin.
L to R (front): F/S. S.A. Harvey, F/S. E.F. Garland.
L to R (back): Sgt. W.A. Donaldson, F/L. E.A. Campbell, F/O. J.E. Chapman, Sgt. A.R. Lyons.

J25414   F/L. Edward Alexander "Red" Campbell, RCAF DFCPilot.
J29670   F/O. John Ernest "Chappie" Chapman, RCAF A/Bomber.
R153444 F/S. Earl Frederick "Judy" Garland, RCAF   Navigator.
1397284 Sgt. Arthur Robert "Ben" Lyons.   WOP/AG.
R211833 F/S. Earl Russel "Jonesy" Jones, RCAF MU/Gunner.
R215180 F/S. Sam A. Harvey, RCAF   R/Gunner.
761328 (1821127) Sgt.William A. "Jock" Donaldson, DFM   F/Engineer.
178865(1476474)F/S. John Backhouse Topham, DFC   Captain. 19/05/1944
J23078   F/O Robert Roy "Bob" Giffin, RCAF 2nd Pilot. 28/07/1944

19/05/1944 DS842 JI-F Bombing Le Mans 22.21   00.28   03.10
    Bomb load 4 x 1000 USA, 5 x 1000 MC, 1 x 1000 GP, 4 x 500 GP. Primary
target: Le Mans. Cloud extended from 8500 feet upwards. Bombed as
instructed by Master Bomber at 00.28 hours from 7,500 feet. Arrived rather

early and made orbit. Attack thought to be good. At 00.59 hours F.W.190 seen about 250 yards away but become lost in clouds. When 30 miles from Le Mans on outward journey J.U.88 approached and Rear Gunner fired short burst at it. Enemy aircraft approached again and both Gunners fired bursts claiming several hits.

F/S. J.B. Topham accompanied the crew, taking the Flight Engineer's seat.

21/05/1944 LL677 A2-E   Bombing Duisburg 22.50 01.20 03.30

Bomb load 1 x 2000 lb. Bomb, 120 x 30, 600 x 4 incendiaries. Primary target: Duisburg. There was 10/10 cloud at target Red T.I.s scattered. Bombed at 01.20 hours from 20,000 feet. Explosions seen through cloud and some H.F. bursts. Orbited at target.

22/05/1944 LL727 A2-C   Bombing Dortmund 22.55 00.59 03.20

Bomb load 1 x 2000 lb. Bomb, 96 x 30, 810 x 4, 90 x 4 incendiaries. Primary target: Dortmund. Clear with few cloud patches over target. Bombed fires and markers at 00.59 hours from 19,000 feet. Huge explosion seen in target area and raid thought to be successful. Flak negligible but many fighters seen in target area. Unidentified aircraft approached from astern and followed for ten minutes before disappearing. Heavy icing, Slight opposition over target.

According E.F. Garland's logbook: "Heavy icing, Slight opposition over target".

27/05/1944 LL716 A2-G   Bombing Boulogne 00.15 01.16½02.20

Bomb load 7 x 1000 MC, 4 x 1000 ANM, 4 x 500 GP. Primary target Boulogne, gun batteries. Clear at target. Bombed at 01.16½ hours from 9,000 feet. Own bombs fell rather to North of the centre of the T.I.s. Trouble free route.

28/05/1944 LL726 A2-H   Bombing Angers   19.02 23.57 02.00

Bomb load 5 x 1000 MC, 1 x 1000 USA, 4 x 500 MC. Primary target: Angers. Clear at target. Bombed at 23.57 hours from 10,000 feet. Visual obtained of river. Satisfactory route.

According E.F. Garland's logbook: "light flak, Slight opposition".

30/05/1944 DS795 A2-J Bombing Boulogne   23.00   00.06½01.20

Bomb load 6 x 1000 MC, 4 x 500 MC. Primary target: Boulogne gun batteries. Clear at target. Bombed at 00.06½ hours from 8,000 feet. Burst seen rather north of T.I.s. Spasmodic bursts of heavy flak which came uncomfortably close.

31/05/1944 DS795 A2-J Bombing Trappes   00.05   02.02   03.38

Bomb load 8 x 1000 MC, 8 x 500 MC. Primary target: Trappes. Clear at target. Bombed at 02.02 hours from 10,000 feet. Large fire seen with clouds of smoke. Master Bomber heard very clearly. Monica u/s. A single engine aircraft was seen at 0204 hours 10 miles S.E. of Trappes.

05/06/1944 LL670 A2-K   Bombing Ouistreham 03.56   05.10   06.52

Bomb load 9 x 1000 MC and 2 x 500 MC. Primary target: Ouistreham. There was 5/10 thin cloud at target. Bombed at 05.10 hours from 10,000 feet. Only one bomb was released when the bomb-tit was depressed. Remainder of bombs were released immediately afterwards by means of jettison bar. Cloud prevented an effective visual. Quiet trip.

According E.F. Garland's logbook: "Flak hole Port, Fuel low".

06/06/1944 LL670 A2-K   Bombing Lisieux   00.27   01.43   03.15

Bomb load 16 x 500 MC Nose Inst. and 2 x 500 MC LD. Primary target: Lisieux. Weather clear for bombing. Bombed as instructed by Master Bomber at 01.43 hours from 5,500 feet. Heard Master Bomber clearly and came down below cloud to bomb. Yellow T.I.s accurately placed according to Master Bomber.

08/06/1944 LL670 A2-K   Bombing Fougeres 21.51   00.45   02.27

Bomb load 16 x 500 GP and 2 x 500 MC LD. Primary target: Fougeres. Bombed as instructed by Master Bomber at 00.45 hours from 8,000 feet. Fires and clouds of smoke were seen. One stick of bombs undershot and 1 x 500 GP hung up. Weather bad on route.

According E.F. Garland's logbook: "2 attacks by F.W.190".

11/06/1944 DS786 A2-F   Bombing Nantes   23.53   02.46   05.06

Bomb load 16 x 500 GP. 2 x 500 LD. Primary target: Nantes. Bombed as instructed by Master Bomber at 02.46 hours from 2,300 feet. Saw bomb bursts overshooting T.I.s. Coned in searchlights while over the target area, lost height. According E.F. Garland's logbook: "Heavy flak over searchlights coned- 2000' ".

12/06/1944 DS786 A2-F   Bombing Gelsenkirchen 23.13   01.07   02.58

Bomb load 1 x 4000 HC, 12 x 500 GP, 4 x 500 MC. Primary target: Gelsenkirchen. Clear over target. Bombed at 01.07 hours from 20,000 feet. Large orange explosion seen at 0105 hours and good fires and smoke seen. S/L very active. Moderate H/F.

According E.F. Garland's logbook: "2 attacks J.U.88 - Heavy flak over searchlights".

15/06/1944 LL692 A2-C   Bombing Valenciennes 23.11   00.44   02.11

Bomb load 16 x 500 GP, 2 x 500 MC. Primary target: Valenciennes. Layer of cloud 9/10ths 9,500 feet to 11,000 feet, clear above cloud and good visibility below. Bombed at 00.44 hours from 9,000 feet undershooting green markers.

23/06/1944 LL670 A2-K   Bombing L'Hey   23.11   00.20   01.36

Bomb load 11 x 1000 MC, 4 x 500 GP. Primary target: L'Hey, Flying bomb installations. There was 10/10ths cloud. Bombed at 00.20 hours from 9,000 feet on instructions from Master Bomber, on N.W. part of red glow. Good route, trouble free, flak negligible.

27/06/1944 LL692 A2-C   Bombing Biennais 23.32   01.13   02.37

Bomb load 16 x 500 GP. 2 x 500 ANM 64 GP. Primary target: Biennais, Flying bomb installations. There was 10/10 cloud. Bombed at 01.13 hours from 13,000 feet red glow.

30/06/1944 LL692 A2-C   Bombing Villers Bocage 18.10   20.00   21.12

Bomb load 11 x 1000 MC, 3 x 500 GP. Primary target: Villers Bocage. Weather 5/10ths cloud, clear for bombing. Bombed at 20.00 hours from 12,000 feet, red T.I.s. Many bomb bursts all around aiming point, and thick clouds of smoke. Target well plastered.

02/07/1944 LL692 A2-C   Bombing Beauvoir 12.54   14.36   15.55

Bomb load 11 x 1000 MC, 4 x 500 GP. Primary target: Beauvoir, Flying bomb supply site. Bombed at 14.36 hours from 13,000 feet visual.

07/07/1944 LL716 A2-G   Bombing Vaires 22.54   01.33   03.28

Bomb load 7 x 1000 MC, 4 x 500 GP. Primary target: Vaires, Marshalling yards. Weather clear. Bombed at 01.33 hours from 13,000 feet, red T.I.s. T.I.s well placed, visual of river, bomb doors damaged but bombs finally dropped in target area.

10/07/1944 LL692 A2-C   Bombing Nucourt 04.30 06.02   07.25

Bomb load 11 x 1000 ANM 65, 4 x 500 GP. Primary target: Nucourt, Constructional works. Bombed at 06.02 hours from 16,000 feet on red T.I.s.

12/07/1944 LL692 A2-C   Bombing Vaires 17.55   19.59   22.29

Bomb load 18 x 500 GP. Primary target: Vaires, Marshalling yards. Reached target 19.59 hours at 16,000 feet, told to abandon mission. Jettisoned 30 miles E of Southwold 21.59 hours from 10,000 feet 4 x 500 GP.

According E.F. Garland's logbook: "Target obscured, bombs jettisoned".

15/07/1944 LL692 A2-C   Bombing Chalons sur Marne 21.46   01.31   04.03

Bomb load 18 x 500 GP. Primary target: Chalons sur Marne, Railway centre. Weather 10/10ths cloud. Bombed at 01.31 hours from 9,000 feet, red T.I.s. Quiet trip. Rear Gunner fired short burst at M.E. 410.

According E.A. Campbell logbook: "Two attacks by ME410 and 110".

18/07/1944 LL692 A2-C   Bombing Aulnoye 22.35   00.58   02.25

Bomb load 18 x 500 GP. Primary target: Aulnoye, Railway junction. Weather clear. Bombed at 00.58 hours from 9,000 feet green T.I.s.

20/07/1944 LL692 A2-C   Bombing Homberg 23.22   01.20   02.47

Bomb load 1 x 4000 HC, 2 x 500 MC, 14 x 500 GP. Primary target: Homberg, Oil plant. Weather clear, slight haze. Bombed at 01.20 hours from 19,000 feet red T.I. Bombs well concentrated, large pillar of thick black smoke.

According E.F. Garland's logbook: "2 attacks F.W.190".

25/07/1944 LL692 A2-C   Bombing Stuttgart 21.40   01.56   05.18

Bomb load 5 x 1000 MC, 3 x 500 GP. Primary target: Stuttgart. Weather clear, slight haze. Bombed at 01.56 hours from 19,000 feet red T.I.s. One good fire in target area. Landed at Ford, short of petrol.

According E.F. Garland's logbook: "Hit by flak - Fuel supply low".

28/07/1944 LL692 A2-C   Bombing Stuttgart 21.47½ 23.55

Aircraft called "Charlie Squared" also "Charlie Two".

Report on file. Bomb load 13 x 500 GP. Aircraft missing.

E.F. Garland noted in his logbook "Fire 2 Stbd engs, Abandoned A/C 23.55".

The first aircraft to be shot down that night, LL692 was brought down at 0001 hours by the JU88 G1 4R+AK flown by Lt. Johannes Strassner of 2./NJG2.

The location was 4 km. East of Chateaudun. F/L Campbell and most of his crew fortunately survived and their tale is told in a short film produced by his son.

Crashed near the village of St-Cloud-en-Dunois (Eure-et-Loir), 8 km SSE of Chateaudun. F/O Giffin is buried in St-Cloud- en-Dunois Communal Cemetery.

F/L. E.A. Campbell RCAF Evd, F/O. R.R. Giffin RCAF (2nd pilot) KIA, Sgt. W.A. Donaldson Evd, F/S. E.F. Garland RCAF PoW, F/O. J.E. Chapman RCAF Evd, Sgt. A.R. Lyons Evd, F/S. E.R. Jones RCAF Evd, F/S. S.A. Harvey RCAF Evd.

F/S. E.F. Garland was interned in Camp L7, PoW No.580.

F/O. Ian Roderick Campbell, DFC

A418521   F/O. Ian Roderick Campbell. RAAF, DFC Pilot.
   F/S. R.P. Newman.   A/Bomber.
187501(1555050)   P/O. Alexander Archibald Stuart.   Navigator.
A427301   F/S. Ronald Clemitson Currey, RAAF   WOP/AG.
   Sgt. E.S.W. Langlands.   MU/Gunner.
196933 (1333763) W/O.   Harold George Everest Friend.   MU/Gun.1 op
R157096   W/O.   N.F. Cook, RCAF   R/Gunner.
   Sgt. R.H. Partridge.   F/Engineer.

27/07/1944 LL731 JI-U Bombing Les Catelliers 17.03   18.53   20.13
   Bomb load 18 x 500 GP. Primary target: Les Catelliers, Flying bomb site. Bombed at 1853 hours from 16,300 feet on Mosquito.
30/07/1944 HK577 JI-P Bombing Caen   06.03   07.50   09.32
   Bomb load 18 x 500 GP. Primary target: Caen 'B'. Weather 10/10ths cloud, with breaks. Bombed at 07.50 hours from 3,000 feet, red T.I. as instructed. Much jamming on P/T. Landed at Woodbridge.
03/08/1944 HK577 JI-P Bombing Bois de Cassan   11.46   14.06   15.45
   Bomb load 11 x 1000 MC, 4 x 500 GP. Primary target: Bois de Cassan, Flying bomb supply depot. Bombed at 14.06 hours from 15,000 feet centre of smoke.
05/08/1944 LL624 JI-R Bombing Bassen 14.19 19.05   22.17
   Bomb load 5 x 1000 MC, 4 x 500 GP. Primary target: Bassen Oil Depot. Weather clear. Bombed at 19.05 hours from 5,000 feet port of fires as instructed by Master Bomber. 2 areas of fire in target area, 2 columns of black smoke up to 2000 feet. Appeared a good attack.
14/08/1944 LL666 JI-Q Bombing Hamel (Falaise) 13.57 15.51   17.16
   Bomb load 11 x 1000 MC. 4 x 500 GP. Primary target: Hamel. Weather

hazy. Bombed at 15.51 hours from 8,500 feet, red T.I.s instructed.
Satisfactory raid, much smoke. Bombing of troop concentrations.

25/08/1944 PB419 JI-N Bombing Russelsheim 20.39 01.03 04.53
Bomb load 1 x 4000 HC, 11 x 500 LB Clusters. Primary target: Russelsheim. Weather clear. Bombed at 01.03 hours from 18,000 feet, undershot red and green T.I.s. Scattered fires seen. Starboard inner engine feathered while outbound due to lack of oil pressure. Coned by searchlights on run-up.

17/09/1944 PB419 JI-N Bombing Boulogne 10.42 12.15 13.32
Bomb load 11 x 1000 MC, 4 x 500 GP. Primary target: Boulogne Aiming Point 2. Weather clear below cloud. Bombed at 12.15 hours from 4,000 feet, 100 yards port of red T.I.s.

23/09/1944 PB419 JI-N Bombing Neuss 19.18 21.24 23.20
Bomb load 11 x 1000 ANM 59, 4 x 500 GP. Primary target: Neuss. Weather 10/10ths cloud over target, tops 8/10,000 feet. Bombed at 21.24 hours from 19,500 feet on centre of glow.

25/09/1944 PB419 JI-N Bombing Pas de Calais 08.11 11.02
Bomb load 11 x 1000 MC, 4 x 500 GP. Primary target: Calais. Abandoned on Master Bomber's orders. Jettisoned 4 x 1000 at 5023N 0108E.

27/09/1944 PB419 JI-N Bombing Calais 17.26 08.42½ 08.54
Bomb load 11 x 1000 MC, 4 x 500 GP. Primary target: Calais 15. Weather, cloud 5,500 feet 10/10ths. Bombed at 08.42½ hours from 5,500 feet on green T.I. + 1 second.

07/10/1944 LM684 JI-O Bombing Emmerich 12.15 14.28 15.53
Bomb load 1 x 4000 HC. 10 x No. 14 Clusters. 4 x (150x4). Primary target: Emmerich. Weather clear with cloud at 13,000 feet. Bombed at 14.28 hours from 13,900 feet on south side of pall of smoke as instructed by Master Bomber.

14/10/1944 PB419 JI-N Bombing Duisburg 06.57 09.04 10.50
Bomb load 11 x 1000 MC. 4 x 500 GP Long Delay. Primary target Duisburg. Weather patchy cloud with gaps for bombing. Bombed at 09.04 hours from 18,000 feet. River Docks.

14/10/1944 PB419 JI-N Bombing Duisburg 22.41 01.28 03.08
Bomb load 11 x 1000 MC. 4 x 500 GP Long Delay. Primary target Duisburg. Weather was clear with small amount of cloud over the target. Bombed at 01.28 hours from 21,500 feet. Centre of red T.I.s.

15/10/1944 PB419 JI-N Bombing Wilhelmshaven 17.15 19.47 21.33
Bomb load 11 x 1000 MC, 4 x 500 GP. Primary target: Wilhelmshaven. Weather haze and thin cloud at first with thick cloud later. Bombed at 19.47 hours from 20,000 feet. Between T.I.s - red and green.

18/10/1944 PB419 JI-N Bombing Bonn 08.30 11.00 12.55
Bomb load 1 x 4000 HC. 5 x 12 x 30 - 2 x 12 x 30 modified. 9 x No.14 Clusters. Primary target: Bonn. Primary target: Bonn. Weather varying cloud

2-7/10ths with break for bombing. Bombed at 11.00 hours from 17,000 feet. On G.H. South part of the town.

34 Avro Lancasters of No.3 Group reported flak damaged to varying degrees. LM724 is reported to have received 33 flak hits, this included splinters and fragments of all sizes. In all No.514 Squadron had 5 aircraft hit by flak.

21/10/1944 PB419 JI-N Bombing Flushing 10.59 12.27 13.17

Bomb load 12 x 1000 MC. 2 x 500 GP. Primary target: Flushing 'B'. Weather clear. Bombed at 12.27 hours from 8,300 feet. Visually.

22/10/1944 PB419 JI-N Bombing Neuss 13.10 15.55 17.07

Bomb load 1 x 4000 HC. 14 x No.14 Clusters. Primary target: Neuss. Weather 10/10ths cloud over target. Bombed at 15.55 hours from 18,000 feet on GH Leader.

25/10/1944 PB419 JI-N Bombing Essen 13.10 15.37 16.52

Bomb load 1 x 4000 HC. 6 x 1000 MC. 6 x 500 GP. Primary target: Essen. Weather over target 10/10ths low cloud, with one clear patch which appeared to fill up later in the attack. Bombed at 15.37 hours from 21,700 feet. Red sky markers.

05/11/1944 PB419 JI-N Bombing Solingen 10.18 13.01 14.37

Bomb load 1 x 4000 HC, 6 x 1000 ANM59, 4 x 500 GP, 2 x 500 GP (L/Delay), 3 Flares. Primary target: Solingen. Weather 10/10ths cloud over target. Bombed at 13.01 hours from 17,500 feet on instruments.

06/11/1944 PB419 JI-N Bombing Koblenz 16.50 21.00

Bomb load 1 x 4000 HC, 12 x 500 Clusters, 2 x 250 T.I.s. Primary target: Koblenz. Abortive. Returned early with port inner engine unserviceable.

08/11/1944 NF966 JI-R Bombing Homberg 08.07 10.30 12.04

Bomb load 1 x 4000 HC, 6 x 1000 GP, 6 x 500 GP. Primary target: Homberg. Weather clear. Bombed at 10.30 hours from 17,000 feet on instruments. Aircraft hit by flak. Windscreen damaged.

15/11/1944 PB419 JI-N Bombing Dortmund 12.37 15.40 17.05

Bomb load 1 x 4000 HC, 2 x 500 MC, 13 x 500 GP, 1 Red with Green star Flare. Primary target: Hoesch-Benzin Dortmund, Oil refineries. Weather 10/10ths cloud over the target. Bombed at 15.40 hours from 17,000 feet on G.H. Markers appeared well concentrated.

16/11/1944 PB419 JI-N Bombing Heinsburg 13.26 17.30

Bomb load 1 x 4000 HC, 6 x 1000 MC, 4 x 250 lb T.I.s. Primary target: Heinsburg. Weather - nil cloud with slight haze over target. Abortive sortie, jettisoned safe 4 miles East of Southwold, due to hang up. Aircraft hit by flak. Mid upper turret damaged.

20/11/1944 PB419 JI-N Bombing Homberg 12.47 15.15 16.15

Bomb load 1 x 4000 HC, 15 x 500 GP, 1 Red-Green Flare. Primary target: Homberg. Weather 10/10ths cloud over target. Weather - nil cloud with slight haze over target. Bombed at 15.15 hours from 19,500 feet on G.H.

21/11/1944 PB419 JI-N Bombing Homberg 12.43 15.08 16.27

Bomb load 1 x 4000 HC, 15 x 500 GP, 1 Red-Green Flare. Primary target: Homberg. Weather about 5/10ths cloud but clear for bombing. Bombed at 15.08 hours from 20,000 feet to port of target.

27/11/1944 LM285 JI-K Bombing Cologne 12.33   15.05   16.47

Bomb load 1 x 4000 HC, 14 x 500 GP, 1 x 500 MC. Primary target: Cologne, Marshalling Yards. Weather patchy cloud. Bombed at 15.05 hours from 20,000 feet on G.H.

30/11/1944 PB419 JI-N Bombing Osterfeld   10.54   13.10   14.36

Bomb load 1 x 4000 HC, 15 x 500 GP, 1 Red/Green Flare. Primary target: Osterfeld, Coking plant. Weather 10/10ths cloud. Bombed at 13.10 hours from 20,000 feet on G.H.

05/12/1944 PB419 JI-N Bombing Hamm 08.56 11.30   13.35

Bomb load 1 x 4000 HC, 2 x 500 MC, 11 x 500 GP, 2 x 500 GP Long Delay, 1 Flare. Primary target: Hamm. Weather 10/10ths cloud over target, but otherwise varying from 6-10/10ths. Bombed at 11.30 hours from 20,000 feet on G.H.

12/12/1944 PB419 JI-N Bombing Witten 11.27 14.04   15.37

Bomb load 1 x 4000 HC, 5 x 500 GP, 6 x 500 ANM58, 4 x 500 ANM64, 1 Flare. Primary target: Witten. Weather 10/10ths cloud, tops 14/16,000 feet. Bombed at 14.04 hours from 20,000 feet on G.H.

F/O. Maurice Raoul Cantin

J20214. F/O.   Maurice Raoul Cantin, RCAF Pilot.
R161620. F/S. Stuart Elmer Smith, RCAF A/Bomber.
1346909. F/S. William George Fyfe Saddler. Navigator.
1576668. Sgt. Francis Beardsley Vallance.   WOP/AG.   1 op.
1388185 Sgt.   William Eric Thomas Michell. WOP/AG.   1 op.
1287750. Sgt. Robert Neville Walne.   MU/Gunner.
928328. Sgt. Leslie Frank Eyre.   R/Gunner. 1 op.
1821076. Sgt. William Lannigan. R/Gunner.   1 op.
577808. Sgt. Kerry George King.   F/Engineer.

L to R: Unknown; W.G.F. Saddler; W.E.T. Michell; M.R. Cantin; R.N. Walne; S.E. Smith.

11/11/1943 DS814 JI-M Gardening   La Tranche 17.38 00.56
  Aircraft carried 2 x D404, 2 x G710. Primary area La Tranche No cloud. Visibility good. Route very good. An uneventful trip in good weather.
26/11/1943 DS814 JI-M Bombing Berlin   17.48
  Bomb load 1 x 4000 HC. 24 x 30 incendiaries, 405 x 4 incendiaries, 45 x 4 X. Aircraft missing. No news.
Crashed at Germendorf, 4 km w of Oranienburg. All crew KIA and buried at Germendorf 29 November 43. They have been subsequently re-interred in the Berlin 1939-45 War Cemetery.
  F/O. M.R. Cantin RCAF KIA, Sgt. K.G. King KIA, Sgt. W.G.F. Saddler KIA, F/S. S.E. Smith RCAF KIA, Sgt. W.E.T. Michell KIA, Sgt. R.N. Walne KIA, Sgt. L.F. Eyre KIA

F/O. Thomas Bruce Carpenter, DFC

146719 (1260362) F/O. Thomas Bruce Carpenter, DFC   Pilot.
Sgt. E.D. Horne.   A/Bomber.21 ops
Sgt. J. Murray.   A/Bomber. 8 ops.
A422606 F/S. William Alexander Mayger, RAAF Navigator.
125480 (798669) F/O. Sebastian Farrell.   WOP/AG.25 ops
J19707   F/O. Frank Harold Rowan, DFC RCAF. WOP/AG. 4 ops.
Sgt. D.H. Penfold.   MU/Gunner.
Sgt. C. Clark.   R/Gunner.
Sgt. E. Smith   F/Engineer.
NZ39076 F/O. Leonard C. Baines, DFC RNZAF. 2nd Pilot. 2 ops.

Back row 2nd from left: F/O S. Farrell; Front row middle: F/O T.B. Carpenter.

(Debbie Murphy (Farrell))

10/09/1944 PB142 JI-A Bombing Le Havre   15.51   17.39   19.11
Bomb load 11 x 1000 MC, 4 x 500 GP. Primary target: Le Havre. Weather clear. Bombed at 1739 hours from 10000 feet. Undershot T.I.s red by 200 yards.
14/09/1944 PB142 JI-A Bombing Wassenaar 12.53 14.30   15.42
Bomb load 11 x 1000 MC, 4 x 500 GP. Primary target: Wassenaar. Weather was good, nil cloud. Bombed at 1430 hours from 11500 feet, red T.I.s.
17/09/1944 LM724 JI-B Bombing Boulogne   10.52 13.40
Bomb load 11 x 1000 MC, 4 x 500 GP. Primary target: Boulogne Aiming Point 2. Weather clear below cloud. Abortive sortie. At 1215 hours order given by Master Bomber to abandon mission. Jettisoned 24 x 1000 MC brought remainder back.

20/09/1944 PD265 JI-G Bombing Calais 17.50 16.03 17.44

Bomb load 11 x 1000 MC, 4 x 500 GP. Primary target: Calais. Weather clear over target. Bombed at 1603 hours from 4000 feet, red T.I.

23/09/1944 LM724 JI-B Bombing Neuss 19.22 21.33 23.38

Bomb load 11 x 1000 ANM 44, 4 x 500 GP. Primary target: Neuss. Weather 10/10ths cloud over target, tops 8/10,000 feet. Bombed at 2133 hours from 20000 feet on glow of red T.I.s.

25/09/1944 NG142 A2-H Bombing Pas de Calais 08.24 x 11.03

Bomb load 11 x 1000 MC, 4 x 500 GP. Primary target: Calais. Abandoned on Master Bomber's orders. Jettisoned 3 x 1000, 2 x 500 GP.

27/09/1944 PD265 JI-G Bombing Calais 07.40 08.43 10.21

Primary target: Calais. Bomb load 11 x 1000 MC, 4 x 500 GP. Primary target: Calais 15. Weather, cloud 5,500 feet 10/10ths. Bombed at 0843 hours from 5500 feet on port of green T.I.

03/10/1944 PD265 JI-G Bombing Westkapelle (Walcheren) 12.30 13.55 15.05

Bomb load 1 x 4000 MC, 6 x 1000 MC, 1 x 500 GP. L/Delay. Primary target: Westkapelle. Weather patchy-scattered cloud with base 5000 feet. Bombed at 13.55 hours, 6,500 feet between T.I.s and coast.

05/10/1944 PD265 JI-G Bombing Saarbrucken 17.27 x 22.50

Bomb load 11 x 1000 MC, 1 x 500 GP, 3 x 500 GP. Long Delay. Abandoned mission on instructions from Master Bomber heard to say they were unable to locate target and called "Abandon Mission - our troop in vicinity". Jettisoned 1 x 1000 MC and 3 x 500 GP. At position 5220N 0227E at 22.11 hours from 8,000 feet. Remainder brought back.

06/10/1944 NG121 JI-H Bombing Dortmund 16.32 20.30 22.34

Bomb load 1 x 4000 HC. 12 x No. 14 Clusters. Primary target: Dortmund, Town and Railways. Weather over the target was clear with slight ground haze. Bombed at 20.30 hours from 18,000 feet on red T.I.s.

14/10/1944 LM724 JI-B Bombing Duisburg 07.05 09.07 11.27

Bomb load 11 x 1000 MC. 4 x 500 GP. Long Delay. Primary target: Duisburg. Weather patchy cloud with gaps for bombing. Bombed at 09.07 hours from 18,000 feet. Built up area 2 miles North of Docks.

14/10/1944 PD265 JI-G Bombing Duisburg 23.06 01.50 03.44

Bomb load 11 x 1000 MC. 4 x 500 GP. Long Delay. Primary target: Duisburg. Weather was clear with small amount of cloud over the target. Bombed at 01.50 hours from 18,000 feet. Centre of red T.I.s.

19/10/1944 PD265 JI-G Bombing Stuttgart 22.04 01.05 03.58

Bomb load 1 x 4000 HC. 6 x 1000 MC. 1 x 500 GP. Primary target: Stuttgart, A/P 'E' 2nd attack. Weather 10/10ths low cloud over target and all crew arrived late owing to winds not as forecast. Bombed at 01.05 hours from 19,600 feet. Red and Yellow markers.

28/10/1944 PD265 JI-G Bombing Cologne 13.16 15.48 17.47

Bomb load 1 x 4000 HC. 8 x 150 x 4. Primary target: Cologne. Weather clear over target. Bombed at 12.48 hours from 22,000 feet. Centre of 4 fires on Master Bomber's instructions.

Sgt. J. Murray was A/Bomber from that day, until 21/11/1944

30/10/1944 NN717 JI-E Bombing Wesseling 09.23 11.57 13.20

Bomb load 1 x 4000 HC. 16 x 500 GP. Primary target: Wesseling. Weather was 10/10ths cloud - tops about 7,000 feet. Bombed at 11.57 hours from 18,000 feet on G.H. Leader's release bombs.

02/11/1944 LM733 JI-F Bombing Homberg 11.32 14.06 15.44

Bomb load 1 x 4000 HC, 6 x 1000 ANM59, 6 x 500 MC. Primary target: Homberg. Weather variable cloud but clear for bombing. Target obscured by pall of smoke rising to 10,000 feet. Bombed at 14.06 hours from 21,000 feet. Centre of pall of smoke.

04/11/1944 NN717 JI-E Bombing Solingen 11.40 14.09 15.53

Bomb load 1 x 4000 HC, 14 x 500 Clusters. Primary target: Solingen. Weather 8-10/10ths cloud. Bombed at 14.09 hours from 19,500 feet between 2 red flares.

15/11/1944 NN717 JI-E Bombing Dortmund 12.46 15.40 17.41

Bomb load 1 x 4000 HC, 16 x 500 GP. Primary target: Hoesch-Benzin Dortmund, Oil refineries. Weather 10/10ths cloud over the target. Bombed at 15.40 hours from 16,800 feet on leading aircraft.

16/11/1944 NN717 JI-E Bombing Heinsburg 13.12 15.31 17.08

Bomb load 1 x 4000 HC, 6 x 1000 MC, 6 x 500 GP. Primary target: Heinsburg. Weather - nil cloud with slight haze over target. Bombed at 15.31½ hours from 9,000 feet. Centre of town.

F/O. F.H. Rowan was WOP/AG from that day until 23/11/1944.

20/11/1944 NN717 JI-E Bombing Homberg 12.51 15.15 17.14

Bomb load 1 x 4000 HC, 16 x 500 MC. Primary target: Homberg. Weather 10/10ths cloud over target. Bombed at 15.15 hours from 20,000 feet on G.H. Leader.

21/11/1944 NN717 JI-E Bombing Homberg 12.38 15.08 17.44

Bomb load 1 x 4000 HC, 16 x 500 GP. Primary target: Homberg. Weather about 5/10ths cloud but clear for bombing. Bombed at 15.08½ hours from 20,000 feet on Red T.I.s.

23/11/1944 LM733 JI-F Bombing Nordstern 13.00 15.21 17.07

Bomb load 1 x 4000 HC, 16 x 500 GP. Primary target: Nordstern, Gelsenkirchen Oil refineries. Weather 10/10ths cloud. Bombed at 15.21½ hours from 20,000 feet with leading G.H. aircraft.

According F.H. Rowan logbook target "Gelsenkirchen". Nordstern is industrial place at Gelsenkirchen.

Sgt. E.D. Horne returns A/Bomber until 31/12/1944.

27/11/1944 NN717 JI-E Bombing Cologne 12.31 15.04 16.15

Bomb load 1 x 4000 HC, 16 x 500 GP. Primary target: Cologne, Marshalling Yards. Weather patchy cloud. Bombed at 15.04 hours from 19,000 feet on G.H. aircraft.

F/O. Leonard Claude Baines, DFC RNZAF. 2nd Pilot.

F/O. Sebastian Farrell returns WOP/AG until 31/12/1944.

29/11/1944 PB767 JI-G Bombing Neuss 02.58 05.40 07.10

Bomb load 1 x 4000 HC, 6 x 1000 HC, 6 x 500 GP. Primary target: Neuss. Weather 10/10ths cloud over target but the glow of fires was seen through cloud. Bombed at 05.40 hours from 21,000 feet. Sky markers. Sky markers well concentrated, glow of fires through cloud.

F/O. Leonard Claude Baines, DFC RNZAF was 2nd Pilot that day.

16/12/1944 PB767 JI-G Bombing Siegen 11.39 14.59 16.57

Bomb load 1 x 4000 HC. 14 x No. 14 clusters. Primary target: Siegen. Weather very bad on route with icing and cloud. Bombed at 14.59 hours from 18,000 feet on G.H. Leader.

21/12/1944 PB767 JI-G Bombing Trier 12.23 15.03 16.51

Bomb load 1 x 4000 HC. 10 x 500 GP. 6 x 250 GP. Primary target: Trier, Marshalling yards. Weather 10/10 cloud, tops 6/9000 feet. Bombed at 15.03½ hours from 18,000 feet on G.H. Leader.

23/12/1944 PB767 JI-G Bombing Trier 11.50 14.32 16.03

Bomb load 1 x 4000 HC. 10 x 500 GP. 6 x 250 GP. Primary target: Trier. Weather clear over target. Bombed at 14.32 hours from 18,000 feet on T.I. Red.

27/12/1944 LM685 JI-K Bombing Rheydt 12.46 15.04 17.05

Bomb load 7 x 1000 MC, 6 x 500 GP, 3 x 250 GP. Primary target: Rheydt, Marshalling yards. Weather clear. Bombed at 15.04 hours from 19,000 feet. Upwind edge of smoke.

31/12/1944 PB142 JI-G Bombing Vohwinkle 11.40 14.42 17.17

Bomb load 1 x 4000 HC, 12 x 500 M64, 2 x 500 GP. Primary target: Vohwinkel. Weather 10/10ths cloud on approaching target although the target itself was clear. Bombed at 14.42 hours from 20,000 feet on leading G.H. aircraft.

P/O (Acting F/O.) P.F. Carter

NZ422367 F/O. Percy Francis Carter, RNZAF   Pilot.
  Sgt. F. Newton.   A/Bomber.
NZ429034 F/S. Donald Alexander "Don" Barron, RNZAF Navigator.
NZ417210 F/S. Richard George Hall "Dick" Jefferis, RNZAF WOP/AG.
A437188 F/S. Raymond Morris "Ray" Wilson, RAAF   MU/Gunner.
  Sgt. Edward John "Ted" Neale.   R/Gunner.
  Sgt. J. Carruthers.   F/Engineer.

08/05/1944 DS786 A2-F Bombing Cap Gris Nez 23.02 23.52 00.41

Bomb load 14 x 1000 lb. Bombs. Primary target: Cap Gris Nez. Weather was clear. Bombed at 2352 hours from 8000 feet. Numerous bomb bursts seen in vicinity of lighthouse an W/T station. Bulk of attack concentrated on tip of Cape Gris Nez. Green T.I.s not seen until 2358 hours as aircraft left. Route

O.K.

09/05/1944 DS786 A2-F   Bombing Cap Gris Nez 03.10 04.06   05.05

Bomb load 1 x 1000 GP. 13 x 1000 MC. Primary target Cape Gris Nez. Skies clear and visual of coastline was obtained and also of green T.I.s. Bombed at 0406½ hours from 7000 feet. The green T.I.s were overshot lightly to the left on instructions of Master Bomber. Reddish fire observed in target area and bomb bursts appeared concentrated. Master Bomber instructions proved helpful and attack appeared successful.

10/05/1944 DS786 A2-F   Bombing Courtrai 22.15 23.28   00.55

Bomb load 7 x 1000 GP, 7 x 1000 MC. Primary target: Courtrai. Hazy conditions but yellow T.I.s seen. Bombed on instructions of Master Bomber at 2328 hours from 10000 feet. Bombs appeared to fall in concentration around yellow T.I.s. Successful attack.

27/05/1944 LL670 A2-K   Bombing Boulogne 00.10 01.15   02.15

Bomb load 7 x 1000 MC, 4 x 1000 ANM, 4 x 500 GP. Primary target: Boulogne Gun Batteries. Clear over target. Bombed at 0115 hours from 9000 feet. Many green fighter flares seen in target area. 1 x 1000 MC bomb hung up and was jettisoned live at 5037N 0128E at 0122 hours from 9000 feet.

28/05/1944 LL733 JI-S Bombing Angers   19.05 23.58   02.15

Bomb load 5 x 1000 MC, 1 x 1000 USA, 4 x 500 MC. Primary target: Angers. Clear at target. Bombed at 2358 hours from 9000 feet. Two or three bursts of heavy flak over target. Arrived at targets 5 minutes early orbited twice. A.S.I. was sticking during climb from 1000 feet to 9000 feet.

30/05/1944 LL670 A2-K   Bombing Boulogne 23.00 00.06   01.00

Bomb load 6 x 1000 MC, 4 x 500 MC. Primary target: Boulogne Gun Batteries. Bombed at 0006 hours from 8000 feet T.I.s were concentrated and bombs fell close to them. Good attack if markers accurately placed.

31/05/1944 LL726 A2-H   Bombing Trappes 00.02 02.02   04.33

Bomb load 8 x 1000 MC, 8 x 500 MC. Primary target: Trappes. Clear at target, with some smoke. Bombed as instructed by Master Bomber at 0202 hours from 10000 feet. No visual of marshalling yards obtained, only yellow fire and smoke. Should be a good attack. Route satisfactory. Weather better than it was anticipated.

02/06/1944 LL716 A2-G   Bombing Wissant 01.25 02.12   03.10

Bomb load 1 x 1000 GP, 10 x 1000 MC, 4 x 500 MC. Primary target: Wissant Gun Positions. There was 10/10 cloud at target. Bombed markers at 0212½ hours from 7000 feet. Red T.I. seen distinctly in the cloud, bomb flashes were also seen. Appeared to be a satisfactory attack.

05/06/1944 LL727 A2-C   Bombing Ouistreham 03.54 05.11   07.00

Bomb load 9 x 1000 MC and 2 x 500 MC. Primary target: Ouistreham. There was broken cloud at target. Bombed at 0511 hours from 10,000 feet. Unable to see the ground and could not therefore judge the effectiveness of the attack.

06/06/1944 LL727 A2-C   Bombing Lisieux   00.14   01.39   03.03

L to R, Back row: E.J. Neale, P.F. Carter, D.A. Barron, F. Newton
front row: R.M. Wilson, R.G.H. Jefferis, J. Carruthers

(Caren Wilson via Pat Neale)

Bomb load 16 x 500 MC Nose Inst. and 2 x 500 MC LD. Primary target: Lisieux. Broken cloud but clear for bombing. Bombed markers at 0139 hours from 6000 feet. Bomb bursts seen on T.I. Master Bomber could not be heard owing to chatter of another aircraft.

08/06/1944 DS786 A2-F   Bombing Fougeres 21.50 00.20 02.18

Bomb load 16 x 500 GP and 2 x 500 MC LD. Primary target: Fougeres. Bombed as instructed by Master Bomber at 0020 hours from 7600 feet. There seemed to be scattered ground markers with a fire at some road junctions near open country at the position of the white T.I. which everyone bombed. Considerable smoke. No fighters seen. Weather bad on route.

10/06/1944 DS787 A2-D Bombing Dreux 23.11 01.02 03.26

Bomb load 16 x 500 GP, 2 x 500 LD. Primary target: Dreux. Bombed yellow T.I. as instructed by Master Bomber at 0102 hours from 7000 feet. Much interference, otherwise satisfactory trip. Clear below cloud.

12/06/1944 LL692 JI-A Bombing Gelsenkirchen 23.06 01.07 02.50

Bomb load 1 x 4000 HC, 12 x 500 GP, 4 x 500 MC. Primary target: Gelsenkirchen. Weather clear. Bombed red and green T.I.s at 0107 hours from 20000 feet. Concentrated fires and much smoke were observed. The attack appeared a good one. No troubles were experienced except when fired on by another Lancaster in Eindhoven area.

15/06/1944 LL728 A2-L Bombing Valenciennes 23.03 00.39 02.34

Bomb load 16 x 500 GP, 2 x 500 MC. Primary target: Valenciennes. Weather clear below 10/10ths cloud. Bombed at 0039 hours from 8000 feet mixture of red and green markers with two seconds overshoot. Markers scattered at first but concentration improved later. Successful attack, no trouble.

30/06/1944 LL728 A2-L Bombing Villers Bocage 18.15 20.00 21.53

Bomb load 11 x 1000 MC, 3 x 500 GP. Primary target: Villers Bocage. Weather clear. Bombed at 2000 hours from 4000 feet red T.I.s. Target covered with smoke. Good show, no trouble.

02/07/1944 ME841 JI-H Bombing Beauvoir 12.40 14.36 15.52

Bomb load 11 x 1000 MC, 4 x 500 GP. Primary target: Beauvoir, Flying bomb supply site. Bombed at 1436 hours from 8,000 feet on yellow T.I.s.

05/07/1944 LM627 JI-D Bombing Watten 22.46 00.11 01.28

Bomb load 11 x 1000 ANM 65, 4 x 500 GP. Primary target: Watten, Constructional works. Bombed at 0011 hours from 9000 feet red T.I.s.

07/07/1944 ME858 JI-J Bombing Vaires 22.38 00.10

Bomb load 11 x 1000 ANM65. To attack Vaires, Marshalling yards. Abortive sortie. Jettisoned safe 8 x 1000 MC at 2330 hours from 4000 feet 5220N 0224E. Port inner engine u/s on take-off.

12/07/1944 LM627 JI-D Bombing Vaires 17.54 20.09 22.00

Bomb load 18 x 500 GP. Primary target: Vaires, Marshalling yards. Target area reached 2002 hours at 16000 feet, Master Bomber ordered abandon mission.

18/07/1944 LM627 JI-D Bombing Emieville 04.18 06.08 07.33

Bomb load 11 x 1000 MC, 4 x 500 GP. Primary target: Emieville, Troop concentration. Weather clear. Bombed at 0608 hours from 6,500 feet yellow T.I.s. Much smoke, seemed a good attack.

18/07/1944 LM181 JI-E Bombing Aulnoye 22.27 00.59 02.35

Bomb load 18 x 500 GP. Primary target: Aulnoye, Railway junction. Weather clear. Bombed at 0059 hours from 9000 feet green T.I.s. Attack satisfactory. Master Bomber concise.

20/07/1944 LM627 JI-D Bombing Homberg 23.10 01.21 02.39

Bomb load 1 x 4000 HC, 2 x 500 MC, 16 x 500 GP. Primary target: Homberg, Oil plant. Oil plant. Weather clear. Bombed at 0121 hours from 20,000 feet red T.I.s. Fires and clouds of black smoke.

25/07/1944 ME841 JI-H Bombing Stuttgart 21.32 02.16 05.54

Bomb load 7 x 1000 MC, 4 x 500 GP. Primary target: Stuttgart. Weather clear. Bombed at 0216 hours from 14000 feet centre of fires. Very large fire in centre of target, smaller fires covering an area approx radius 5 miles.

28/07/1944 LM627 JI-D Bombing Stuttgart 21.42 01.54 05.27

Bomb load 7 x 1000 MC, 2 x 500 GP. Primary target: Stuttgart. Weather 10/10ths cloud. Bombed at 0154 hours from 19000 feet, glow of red T.I.s.

Master Bomber not heard. Not very satisfactory, T.I.s. too scattered.

30/07/1944 LM627 JI-D Bombing Caen   06.05   07.50   10.12
Bomb load 18 x 500 GP. Primary target: Caen 'B'. Weather breaks in cloud. Bombed at 07.50 hrs. 3000 feet. Red T.I. as instructed. Much jamming on R/T. Landed at Woodbridge.

01/08/1944 LM627 JI-D Bombing Foret de Nieppe 19.15 20.45   21.48
Bomb load 11 x 1000 MC, 4 x 500 GP. Primary target: De Nieppe, constructional works. Bombed at 2045 hours from 11000 feet, leading aircraft.

03/08/1944 LM627 JI-D Bombing Bois de Cassan   11.38   14.07   15.53
Bomb load 11 x 1000 MC, 4 x 500 GP. Primary target: Bois de Cassan, Flying bomb supply depot. Bombed at 1407 hours from 15,500 feet centre of smoke.

04/08/1944 LM627 JI-D Bombing Bec D'Ambes 13.13   17.59   21.02
Bomb load 8 x 1000 MC, 2 x 500 GP. Primary target: Bec d'Ambes Depot. Weather clear. Bombed at 1759 hours from 8000 feet. Bombs seen straddling target. Yellow Flames bursting from oil tanks. Satisfactory effort. Uneventful trip.

05/08/1944 LM627 JI-D Bombing Bassen   14.28 18.59   22.09
Bomb load 8 x 1000 MC, 2 x 500 GP. Primary target: Bassen Oil Depot. Weather cloud down to 5000 feet, clear below. Bombed at 1859 hours from 5000 feet visually, at base of smoke. Large fires with yellow flame, bursts seen across target. Aircraft hit by heavy flak over target, main plane holed.

07/08/1944 PB143 JI-B Bombing Mare de Magne 21.45 23.39   00.50
Bomb load 11 x 1000 MC, 4 x 500 GP. Primary target: Mare de Magne (just past Caen). Weather clear. Bombed at 2339 hours from 9000 feet red T.I.s. Bomb bursts seen across T.I.s.

F/L. John Allan Chadwell

155512 (1208559)   F/L. John Allan Chadwell. Pilot.
173555 (1012770)   F/O. Stanley Ellis, DFC   A/Bomber.
NZ42832   F/O. N. Simmons, RNZAF A/Bomber.   1 op.
125989 (1248870)   F/L. Alexander Sharp Smith, DFC   Navigator.
   W/O.   S. or H. Bean.   WOP/AG.
171721 (926944) F/O. Edwin Charles Smith, DFC MU/Gunner. 13 ops.
   F/S. E.D.A. Dixon.   MU/Gunner. 15 ops.
53671 (581285) F/O.   Douglas David Higham, DFC R/Gunner.
   F/S. S. Sowerby.   F/Engineer.
   W/O.   W. Coe.   2nd WOP. 1 op.
196042 (1564681)   F/S. Joseph McL. Cameron.   2nd Pilot. 1 op.

Passengers 02/05/1945, 07/05/1945, 09/06/1945, 17/06/1945.

02/02/1945 LM627 A2-H   Bombing Wiesbaden 21.11   23.48   02.41

Bomb load 1 x 4000 HC, 12 x 500 GP, 4 x 250 GP. Primary target: Wiesbaden. Primary target: Wiesbaden. Weather 10/10ths cloud, winds very erratic. Bombed at 23.48 hours from 20,000 feet. Reflexion of fires on cloud.

03/02/1945 LM627A2-H Bombing Dortmund-Huckarde 16.39 x 21.15

Bomb load 1 x 4000 HC, 2 x 500 MC, 2 x 500 MC L/Delay, 6 x 500 ANM64, 2 x 500 GP, 3 x 250 GP. Primary target Dortmund-Huckarde, Coking plant. Weather clear with slight haze. Farthest point reached 5030N 0440E. Jettisoned load at 5213N 0310E at 20.07 hours from 13,000 feet. Reason of early return, starboard outer engine over-heating.

20/02/1945 ME364JI-P Bombing Dortmund   21.48   01.07   03.42

Bomb load 1 x 2000 HC, 12 x 750 Type 15 Clusters. Primary target: Dortmund. Weather 8-10/10ths thin cloud at about 5,000 feet. Bombed at 01.07 hours from 21,000 feet on centre of Red/Green flares.

22/02/1945 ME364JI-P Bombing Osterfeld   11.58   16.03   18.08

Bomb load 1 x 4000 HC, 9 x 500 ANM64, 2 x 500 MC, 4 x 250 GP. Primary target: Osterfeld, Coking ovens. Weather at target clear, but hazy. Bombed at 16.03 hours from 20,000 feet. Bombed visually.

25/02/1945 ME364JI-P Bombing Kamen   09.46 12.46½14.56

Bomb load 1 x 4000 HC, 9 x 500 ANM64, 2 x 500 MC, 4 x 250 GP. Primary target: Kamen. Weather 6-8/10ths cloud. Bombed at 12.46½ from 19,500 feet on G.H. Leader,

27/02/1945 ME364JI-P Bombing Gelsenkirchen 10.47   14.27½16.36

Bomb load 1 x 4000 HC, 2 x 500 MC (L/D 37B), 9 x 500 ANM64, 4 x 250 GP.   Primary target: Gelsenkirchen (Alma Pluts) Benzin plant. Weather 10/10ths cloud, 6/10,000 feet tops. Bombed at 14.27½ hours from 19,300 feet on G.H.

W/O. W. Coe was 2nd WOP that day.

01/03/1945 ME364JI-P Bombing Kamen   11.40 15.05   17.34

Bomb load 1 x 4000 HC, 10 x 500 ANM64, 2 x 500 MC L/Delay37, 1 SM Blue puff. Primary target: Kamen, Coking plant. Weather 10/10ths cloud. Bombed at 15.05 hours from 18,700 feet on G.H.

10/03/1945 ME422JI-Q Bombing Gelsenkirchen 12.21   15.36   17.34

Bomb load 1 x 4000 HC, 13 x 500 ANM64, 1 x 500 MC, 1 x 500 GP. Primary target: Gelsenkirchen. Weather 10/10ths cloud at target, tops 8,000 feet. Bombed at 15.36 hours from 18,800 feet on G.H. Squadron formation good.

12/03/1945 ME351JI-U Bombing Dortmund   12.56   16.58   18.51

Bomb load 1 x 4000 HC, 13 x 500 ANM64. Primary target: Dortmund. Weather 10/10ths cloud over target, tops 6/10,000 feet. Bombed at 16.58 hours from 18,500 feet on G.H. Leader.

17/03/1945 ME336JI-S Bombing August Viktoria 11.36½   15.06   17.14

Bomb load 1 x 4000 HC, 13 x 500 ANM64, 2x 500 MC. 1 Skymarker Blue Puff. Primary target: Auguste Viktoria, Marl-Hüls coal mine. Weather 10/10ths cloud, tops and contrails up to 23,000 feet. Bombed at 15.06 hours from 20,000 feet on G.H.

F/S. Joseph McLaws McLellan Cameron was 2nd Pilot that day.

20/03/1945 ME354 JI-M Bombing Hamm 09.49 13.15 15.35

Bomb load 7 x 1000 ANM65, 8 x 500 ANM64, 1 Skymarker Green Puff. Primary target: Hamm, Marshalling yards. Weather 5/10ths cloud. Bombed at 13.15 hours from 17,800 feet on G.H.

29/03/1945 ME364 JI-P Bombing Salzgitter 12.17 16.43 19.10

Bomb load 1 x 4000 HC, 8 x 500 ANM64. Primary target: Salzgitter, Hallendorf works. Weather 10/10ths cloud. Bombed at 16.43 hours on leading aircraft from 20,500 feet.

09/04/1945 ME364 JI-P Bombing Kiel 19.45 22.42 01.36

Bombed primary target: Kiel, Submarine Buildings Yards. Weather clear with slight haze. Bomb load 1 x 4000 HC and 12 x 500 ANM64. Bombed on large concentration of Green by instructions of M/B at 22.42 hours from 20,000 feet. Fairly good concentration one very large fire seen. Few scattered bombs.

22/04/1945 ME364 JI-P Bombing Bremen 15.27 18.41½ 21.08

Bomb load 1 x 4000 HC, 2 x 500 MC, 14 x 500 ANM 64. Primary target: Bremen, in support of Troop concentration. Weather on approaching target 4-5/10ths cloud. Bombed on G.H. Leader 514/M. at 1841½ from 19,000 feet. Excellent concentration of bombing in built up area. North of river EFN-several fires and a huge brown/black smoke pall. G.H. u/s. Picked up G.H. Leader as our own was u/s. Excellent raid.

F/S. E.D.A. Dixon was MU/Gunner from that day.

29/04/1945 ME364 JI-P Manna The Hague 12.29 13.52½ 15.05

Weather broken cloud above and clear below. Dropped 5 packs on red T.I. to port of airfield and white cross at 1352½ hrs. Thousands of cheering civilians gave hearty welcome.

02/05/1945 ME364 JI-P Manna The Hague 10.57 12.15 13.16

Weather over dropping zone clear below cloud for the first arrivals changing later to heavy showers which marred visibility. Dropped 5 panniers on Red T.I. and White Cross at 12.15 hours. Usual reception from inhabitants.

No Mid Upper Gunner that day.

Passenger LAC. Hardman.

07/05/1945 ME364 JI-P Manna The Hague 12.16 13.42 14.44

Dropped 5 Packs on White Cross and Red T.I.'s at 1342 hours. Clear - slight ground haze. Good concentration.

No Mid Upper Gunner that day.

Passenger Sgt. Blamiers.

09/05/1945 ME364 JI-P Exodus Juvincourt - Dunsfold 07.30 x 12.41

Outward 1.29 hours. Collected 24 POW Homeward 1.47 hrs. Everything went smoothly - organisation efficient.

11/05/1945 ME336 JI-S Exodus Juvincourt - Tangmere 11.14 x 18.38

Duration 3.40. Outward 1.32 hours. Collected 24 ex POWs. Homeward 2.08

hours. No snags.

12/05/1945 ME380 JI-E Exodus Brussels - Tangmere 11.35 x 18.05

Duration 3.19. Outward 1.21 hours. Homeward 1.58 hours. 10 Refugees to Brussels, 24 POW to Ford.

16/05/1945 ME364 JI-P Exodus Brussels - Westcott 13.27 x 19.20

Duration 2 hrs 50 mins. Out 1 hr 8 mins. In 1 hr 42 mins. Arrived overseas A/F 14.36½. Arrived reception A/F 18.13. 10 Belgian refugees taken to Brussels / Melsbroeck. 24 ex POW all military to Westcott.

18/05/1945 ME364 JI-P Exodus Brussels - Oakley 12.02 x 16.43

Duration 2 hrs 55 mins. Out 1 hr 07 mins. In 1 hr 48 mins. 10 Belgian refugees taken to Brussels. 24 POW returned. Organisation good. Dunsfold much improved.

19/05/1945 ME364 JI-P Exodus Brussels - Oakley 12.02 x 17.14

Duration 2 hrs 52 mins. Out 1 hr 33 mins. In 1 hr 19 mins. 10 refugees out. 24 ex POWs. All military evacuated.

24/05/1945 ME364 JI-P Exodus Brussels 12.00 x 15.10

Duration 2.15½ hours. Out 1.06½ hours. In 1.09 hours. 10 Belgian refugees returned to Brussels. No POW available.

25/05/1945 ME364 JI-P Exodus Brussels 12.03 x 15.13

Duration 2.13 hours. Out 1.06 hours. In 1.07 hours. 10 Belgian refugees returned to Brussels. No POWs home. Organisation O.K.

26/05/1945 ME364 JI-P Exodus Brussels - Ford 11.59 x 17.31

Duration 3.03 hours. Out 1.05 hours. In 1.58 hours. 10 Belgian refugees to Brussels. 24 ex POWs. all military brought back

09/06/1945 ME364 JI-P Baedeker Tour over Continent 09.45 x 15.01

Passengers F/O. P. Cunningham, AC. N. Neiter, Cpl. O. Irwin.

17/06/1945 ME422 JI-Q Baedeker Tour over Continent 09.55 x 13.39

Passengers LAC. Butcher, LAC. Briggs, Cpl. Chapman, Cpl. Woodleigh, Sgt. Rowley, Cpl. Grilby.

03/07/1945 ME364 JI-P Post Mortem Special mission 14.27 x 19.43

24 to 26/07/1945

ME364 JI-P Dodge Italy 06.29 17.58 17.46

24/07/1945 Waterbeach 06.29 - Italy 17.58 - 26/07/1945 Italy 10.12 - Waterbeach 17.46.

F/O. N. Simmons, RNZAF was A/Bomber that day.

P/O. Thomas Trevor Charlton

183027 (1562353)   P/O. Thomas Trevor Charlton Pilot.
1398590 Sgt. Kenneth Martin Goodman. A/Bomber.
1523782 Sgt. Norman Stevens. Navigator.
J38561 F/O. Ronald Frank Dell, RCAF WOP/AG.
1673439 Sgt. Peter T. Devlin. MU/Gunner.
169764 (1593371) F/O. Walter Ernest Gibbs. R/Gunner.
1893522 Sgt. Reginald William Pomroy. F/Engineer.

11/08/1944 PB142 JI-A Bombing Lens   14.08   16.33   17.32
Bomb load 11 x 1000 MC, 4 x 500 GP. Primary target: Lens, Marshalling yards. Weather 5/10ths patchy cloud. Bombed at 1633 hours 14,500 feet, cluster of red T.I.s. Sticks of bombs seen to burst on target.
29/08/1944 PB143 JI-B Bombing Stettin 21.05 00.12
   Bomb load 1 x 500 GP, 1 x 1000 HC, 84 x 30, 756 x 4, 84 x 4 lb. incendiaries. Aircraft Missing.
Shot down at 0012 hours en route to the target, by Oblt. Fritz Brandt of Stab II./NJG3. Crashed into the sea off the small Danish village of Estrupland, Denmark where six are buried in the local churchyard. There were no survivors amongst the crew.
On 6 September, the body of F/O Dell was taken from the water and he is buried in Frederikshaven Cemetery. At 36, F/O Gibbs was above the average age for Bomber Command aircrew.
   F/S T.T. Charlton KIA, Sgt. R.W. Pomroy KIA, Sgt. N. Stevens KIA, Sgt. K.M. Goodman KIA, F/O. R.F. Dell RCAF KIA, Sgt. P.T. Devlin KIA, F/O. W.E. Gibbs KIA.

F/L. George Joseph Chequer

J21428. F/L.George Joseph Chequer. RCAF   Pilot.
1391252 F/S. E.J. Wallington.   A/Bomber.
1431168 F/S. Kenneth "Ken" Mortimer. Navigator.
1366420 Sgt. Robert Montgomery. WOP/A.G.
A425740. F/S. John Leo O'Brien, RAAF   MU/Gunner.
A418509 F/S. Alexander John Robertson, RAAF R/Gunner.
575818   Sgt. J.S. Carey.   F/Engineer.
   F/O. J. Doig.   2nd Pilot   1 op. 01/01/1944
1317103 F/S. R.L. Gulliford.   2nd Pilot 1 op. 30/01/1944

07/11/1943 DS735 JI-A Gardening   La Rochelle 23.52 x 07.02
   Aircraft carried 3 x G710 (8.9.12). Primary area La Rochelle. 10/10 cloud. Base 4,000 feet. Monica was U/S. Successful trip with no opposition from ground or air.

18/11/1943 DS735 JI-A
   Bombing Mannheim
17.29 20.46
   Took off to attack Mannheim but was forced to return to base with inter-com in Rear Turret U/S. 1 x 4000 was jettisoned and 720 x 4 and 16 x 30 were brought back to base.
16/12/1943 DS735 JI-A
   Bombing Berlin 16.45
   20.06   00.01
   Bomb load 1 x 2000, 630 x 4 incendiaries, 40 x 30 incendiaries. Primary target: Berlin. 10/10 cloud. Red and green T.I.s and Markers seen. Bombed at 20.08 at 21,000 ft. Landed at Downham Market.
24/12/1943 DS735 JI-A
   Bombing Berlin 00.31
   04.08   07.39
   Bomb load 1 x 4000, 4 x 30 x 8, 6x 4 x90 incendiaries. Primary target: Berlin. 5/10

F/L George Joseph Chequer

cloud, visibility 2 to 3 miles. Bombed at 04.08 hrs at 21,000 feet. Greens rather scattered. Bombing fairly well concentrated. Good concentrated fires in South of Berlin. Photos taken. Landed at Foulsham owing to petrol leakage.

01/01/1944 LL624 JI-B Bombing Berlin 00.32 03.20 07.53

Bomb load 1 x 4000, 24 x 30, 430 x 4, 90 x 4 lbs. Incendiaries. Primary target: Berlin. There was 10/10 cloud with tops at 20000 feet. Bombed at 0010 hours at 21000 feet. Bombed in centre of red and green markers. Some reflections of fires seen with columns of smoke above cloud tops. Monica u/s on homeward journey.

F/O. J. Doig was 2nd Pilot that day.

02/01/1944 LL624 JI-B Bombing Berlin 00.10 02.45 06.13

Bomb load 1 x 4000, 24 x 30, 450 x 4, 90 x 4 Incendiaries. Primary target: Berlin. There was 10/10 cloud. Bombed at 0245 hours at 21000 feet. Total load dropped on target.

14/01/1944 DS735 JI-A Bombing Brunswick 16.53 19.15 22.17

Bomb load 1 x 4000, 32 x 30 incendiaries. Primary target: Brunswick. There was 8-10/10 cloud. Bombed at 1915 hours at 20000 ft. Clouds lit up with yellow T.I.s. Very well concentrated. Monica u/s, working only at extreme ranges. Perfect show - Photo attempted.

20/01/1944 DS735 JI-A Bombing Berlin 16.17 19.29 23.09

Bomb load 1 x 4000, 32 x 30, 540 x 4, 60 x 4 incendiaries. Primary target: Berlin. There was haze and 8/10 cloud. Bombed at 1929 hours at 21000 ft. Bombed on E.T.A. arriving before Pathfinders. Saw T.I.s on leaving target and believed to have dropped bombs approx 3 miles S. of T.I.s.

21/01/1944 DS735 JI-A Bombing Magdeburg 20.08 22.20

Bomb load 1 x 4000, 720 x 4, 90 x 4, 32 x 30 incendiaries. Returned early inter-com u/s. Farthest point reached 53° 40'N 02° 00E. Total load jettisoned.

27/01/1944 DS735 JI-A Bombing Berlin 17.40 20.33 02.00

Bomb load 1 x 8000 lb bomb. Primary target: Berlin. There was 10/10 cloud. Bombed at 2033 hours at 20000 ft. Glow of fires and S/Ls below cloud. Concentration of sky markers. Route quiet but long. P.F.F. well grouped. Little flak.

30/01/1944 DS735 JI-A Bombing Berlin 17.22

Bomb load 1 x 4000 lb bomb, 600 x 4, 90 x 4, 32 x 30. Aircraft missing. Aircraft was shot down approximately 10 miles North of Brandenburg. There were numerous unidentified aircraft shot down by night fighters in the Berlin area on this op and it is probable that DS735 was one such.

F/S. R.L. Gulliford was 2nd Pilot that day.

F/L. George Joseph Chequer. RCAF, Sgt. Robert Montgomery, F/S. John Leo O'Brien. RAAF, killed and buried in Berlin War Cemetery alongside Sgt. Robert Montgomery who was subsequently killed on The March when Typhoons shot up a PoW column near Gresse, 6 km NNE of Boizenburg 19 Apr. 45.

Sgt J. Carey was interned in Camp L6/357 PoW No.1011, with F/S. R.L.

Gulliford PoW No.1096, F/S. A.J. Robertson PoW No.1095, F/S E.J. Wallington PoW No.1051 and F/S K. Mortimer, PoW No.1094.

F/S. Robertson survived the war and was discharged from the RAAF as a Warrant Officer.

F/L. Walter Evan Chitty

1st crew.

A410039   F/L. Walter Evan Chitty, RAAF Pilot.
J94414 (R125845)   P/O. Allen Bruce Pattison, RCAF A/Bomber. 2 ops
1539935 F/S. Ronald Fox.   Navigator.   2 ops.
189643 (1504777) Sgt. Colin Pratt.   WOP/AG.   2 ops.
2209614 Sgt. Joseph Shepherd.   MU/Gunner. 2 ops.
1565396 Sgt. Robert Calder "Bert" Guy. R/Gunner.   2 ops.
1714996 Sgt. Leonard Arthur "Len" Ive. F/Engineer. 2 ops.

22/03/1944 LL731 JI-U Bombing Frankfurt   18.42 22.04 00.51
Bomb load 1 x 8000 lb. Bomb, there was 6/10 thin cloud. Primary target: Frankfurt. Bombed at 22.04 hours from 20,000 feet. Good fires coinciding with position of markers with a slight undershoot. A good attack, fires seen from over 100 miles. Route O.K.
F/L. W.E. Chitty flew the mission as 2nd pilot with P/O. N.W.F. Thackray crew.
26/03/1944 DS816 JI-O Bombing Essen 20.04 22.04 00.31
Bomb load 1 x 2000 lb. Bomb, 56 x 30, 1080 x 4, 120 x 4 incendiaries. Primary target: Essen. There was 10/10 cloud over the target. Bombed at 22.04 hours from 20,000 feet. Red glow seen through cloud, Red and green T.I.s seen above cloud. Monica and Gee u/s. Glow of fires seen about 50 miles away. Little opposition, no fighters.
30/03/1944 LL645 JI-R Bombing Nuremburg 22.19 05.50
Bomb load 1 x 8000 lb. bomb, 90 x 4. Primary target Nuremburg.
Crashed 31/03/1944 05:50 hours, 2 miles South West of Waterbeach Aerodrome. While trying to land, another aircraft jumped its turn, pilot tried to go round again and crash landed, ripping the undercarriage off.
Sgt. A. Pattison RCAF (Bomb aimer) and Sgt. J. Shepherd (MidUp gunner) were KIA.
Crew injured and suffered from shock and admitted Station Sick Quarters. P/O Chitty was injured but recovered to fly again, sadly failing to return from Caen on 30-Jul-44.
Rear Gunner Robert Calder Guy noted in his logbook:
"OPS-NUREMBURG - 1/2 Moon- Crashed on return- MID-UPPER and BOMB AIMER killed. Rest of crew confined to hospital - F/E Broken ankle,

Left: F/L Walter Evan Chitty, London August 1943. Right: P/O. Allen Bruce Pattison

concussion, etc.- W/Op broken clavicule, concussion, etc. - Pilot split scalp, cuts + bruises on hands and body+ concussion, R/AG + Nav bruises + abrasions+ slight concussion. Everybody badly shaken up"

2nd crew.

A410039 F/L. Walter Evan Chitty, RAAF Pilot.
J20915 F/O John Peake, DFC RCAF. A/Bomber. 13 ops.
1380408 W/O. Leslie Arthur Ding. A/Bomber. 3 ops.
J24522 F/O. William Stewart Bonnell, RCAF Nav.&A/B. 3 ops.
1420245 F/S. Cecil David Williams, DFM Navigator. 15 ops.
1485703 F/S. John Edward "Johnny" Richardson. WOP/AG. 17 ops.
1811733 F/S. Edward William Jenner. MU/Gunner. 17 ops
R161431 W/O. S.J. Everitt, RCAF R/Gunner. 8 ops.
1334325 F/S. George Charles Wells. R/Gunner. 9 ops.
  Sgt. G.H. or G.S. Homer. F/Engineer. 11 ops.
1820355 Sgt. Charles Mathieson "Charlie" Guy. F/Engineer. 7 ops.

10/06/1944 LL635 JI-M Bombing
Dreux 23.02 01.01 03.47
Bomb load 16 x 500 GP, 2 x 500 LD. Primary target Dreux. Bombed on yellow T.I.s on instructions of Master Bomber at 01.01 hours from 5,500 feet. Fire seen burning to N. end of target. Much air/air activity seen before reaching target. Bombs seen to burst on yards. Weather slightly cloudy.

11/06/1944 LL620 JI-T Bombing
Nantes 23.44 02.54 05.26
Bomb load 16 x 500 GP, 2 x 500 LD. Primary target: Nantes. Bombed at 02.54 hours from 4,000 feet. Heard Master Bomber instruct to bomb yellow T.I.s after orbiting to port. At 4,000 feet slight break in cloud showed up yellow T.I.s and enabled to bomb.

14/06/1944 LL620 JI-T Bombing
Le Havre 23.39 01.17
02.48

Sgt C.M. "Charlie" Guy (F/Engineer)
(Sinclair and Jean Ronald (Guy))

Bomb load 11 x 1000 MC, 4 x 500 GP. Primary target: Le Havre. Weather clear. Bombed at 01.17 hours from 14,000 feet on red T.I.s. Fires seen burning in dock area - a good attack. Quiet trip, flak negligible - two or three searchlights in action, ineffectively.

15/06/1944 LL620 JI-T Bombing Valenciennes 22.56 00.39 02.27
Bomb load 16 x 500 GP, 2 x 500 MC. Primary target: Valenciennes. Weather clear; Bombed at 00.39½ hours from 6,500 feet on centre of red T.I.s. Bomb bursts near Marshalling Yards.

21/06/1944 LL620 JI-T Bombing Domleger 18.04 20.50
Bomb load 18 x 500 MC. Primary target: Domleger near Abbeville, V-1 flying bomb launch site. Sortie abandoned in accordance with Master Bomber's instructions Jettisoned safe 8 x 500 MC at 19.41 hours from 11,000 feet 5124N 0119E.

23/06/1944 LL624 JI-R Bombing L'Hey 23.03 00.16 01.45
Bomb load 11 x 1000 MC, 4 x 500 GP. Primary target: L'Hey, Flying bomb installations. There was 10/10ths cloud. Bombed at 00.16 from 8,000 feet. Bombed centre of red T.I.s. Quiet trip. Little opposition.

27/06/1944 DS813 JI-N Bombing Biennais 23.28 01.12 02.32
Bomb load 16 x 500 GP, 2 x 500 ANM 64 GP. Primary target: Biennais, Flying bomb installations. There was 10/10ths cloud. Bombed at 01.12 hours

107

from 12,000 feet red glow.

30/06/1944 DS813 JI-N Bombing Villers Bocage 18.20   20.04   21.46

Bomb load 11 x 1000 MC, 3 x 500 GP. Primary target: Villers Bocage. Weather clear for bombing. Bombed at 20.04 hours from 12,500 feet green T.I. as ordered by Master Bomber. Target obscured by smoke, bomb bursts concentrated in smoke. Moderate heavy flak. Spitfires whizzing all aroud us.

02/07/1944 DS813 JI-N Bombing Beauvoir   12.50   14.38   16.24

Bomb load 11 x 1000 MC, 4 x 500 GP. Primary target: Beauvoir. Bombed at 14.38 hours from 10,000 feet visual.

05/07/1944 DS813 JI-N Bombing Watten 22.59 00.12   01.29

Bomb load 11 x 1000 ANM 65, 4 x 500 GP. Primary target: Watten, Constructional works. Bombed at 00.12 hours from 8,600 feet green T.I.s.

07/07/1944 DS813 JI-N Bombing Vaires 22.45   01.32   03.36

Bomb load 7 x 1000 MC, 4 x 500 GP. Primary target: Vaires, Marshalling yards. Weather clear. Bombed at 01.32 hours from 12,000 feet, green T.I.s. Bomb bursts around T.I.s. Terrific explosion at 01.35 hours. Satisfactory attack, clear and precise.

10/07/1944 DS813 JI-N Bombing Nucourt   04.23   06.06   08.00

Bomb load 11 x 1000 ANM 65, 4 x 500 GP. Primary target: Nucourt, Constructional works. Bombed at 06.06 hours from 15,500 feet, on Gee.

12/07/1944 DS813 JI-N Bombing Vaires 17.56 20.02 22.08

Bomb load 18 x 500 GP. Primary target: Vaires, Marshalling yards. Target reached 20.02 hours from 15,000 feet, Master Bomber ordered abandon mission. Very good concentration on route out until flak started when formation dispersed. Jettisoned at 20.45 hours from 12,000 feet, position 4951N 0036E, 3 x 500 GP. Abandoned on Master Bomber's orders.

23/07/1944 DS813 JI-N Bombing Kiel   22.29   01.26   04.02

Bomb load 10 x 1000 MC, 5 x 500 GP. Primary target: Kiel, Warehouses and docks. Weather 10/10ths thin cloud. Bombed at 01.26 hours from 18,000 feet centre of red T.I.s. Markers rather scattered.

24/07/1944 DS813 JI-N Bombing Stuttgart 21.35 01.50 15.16

Bomb load 5 x 1000 ANM 65, 3 x 500 GP. Primary target Stuttgart. Weather 10/10ths cloud. Bombed at 01.50 hours from 20,000 feet on S. E. group of green and yellow markers. Glows seen under the clouds.

27/07/1944 DS813 JI-N Bombing Les Catelliers 16.56 18.50 20.19

Bomb load 18 x 500 GP. Primary target: Les Catelliers, Flying bomb site. Bombed at 18.50 hours from 16,000 feet on Mosquito.

30/07/1944 LL733 JI-S Bombing Caen   06.13 07.50

Bomb load 18 x 500 GP. Aircraft missing.

Daylight raid to bomb enemy strong points at Caen. It was carrying 18 x 500lb GP bombs and 1710 gallons of petrol which allowed for approx 7:30 hours of flying time, with an anticipated flying time of approx 3 hours. Lost without trace.

All crew killed: F/L. Walter Evan Chitty. RAAF, W/O. Leslie Arthur Ding,

F/O. William Stewart Bonnell. RCAF, F/S. John Edward Richardson, F/S. Edward William Jenner, F/S. George Charles Wells, Sgt. Charles Mathieson Guy. All are commemorated on the Runnymede Memorial.

In a letter from Air Ministry to C.M. Guy parents: "British Naval authorities have reported that his body was recovered from the sea off the coast of Normandy by one of His Majesty's ships and was buried at sea". F/L Chitty and Sgt Guy's twin brother Robert Guy had been involved in a very serious crash on return from Nürenberg on 31 Mar 1944.

F/L. Acting S/L. Ralph Campbell Chopping, DFC

1st crew

70126   S/L. Ralph   C. Chopping, DFC Pilot.
178003 (1388280)   F/S. Herbert John Friend, DFM A/Bomber.
132035 (1391511)   F/O. Ivan George Barham, DFC Navigator.
1368303 Sgt. John Cameron Wilson, DFM   WOP/AG.
1823102 F/S. Thomas Smith Combe. MU&R/Gun.14 ops.
130154 (1312409) F/O. Henry William May.   MU&R/Gun. 3 ops.
1382982 F/S. P.J. Fox.   MU&R/Gun.14 ops.
1437285 F/S. Leslie James Henry Whitbread. R/Gunner.   1 op.
177638 (1807915) P/O. Desmond C. Hughes, DFC F/Engineer
1337754 F/S. Charles James "Charlie" Medland, DFM 2nd Pilot.24/03/1944
32221 S/L.   William George Devas. AFC.   2nd Pilot. 20/04/1944
105193 (1378130) F/L. Philip Barber Clay, DFC 2nd Pilot. 19/05/1944

15/02/1944 LL728 JI-B Bombing Berlin 17.24 21.25 00.11
Bomb load 1 x 4000 lbs bomb 32 x 30, 540 x 4, 90 x 4 x incendiaries. Primary target: Berlin. There was 10/10 cloud with tops at 1000 ft. Bombed at 21.25 hrs. At 21,000 ft. P.F.F. scattered. Few results noticed. Believed decoy dark green markers S. W. of Berlin.
F/L. Chopping flew the mission as 2nd Pilot with S/L. E.G.B. Reid crew.
21/02/1944 DS842 JI-F Bombing Stuttgart 00.24 04.02 06.56
Bomb load 1 x 8000 lbs. Bomb. 16 x 30, 90 x 4 incendiaries. Primary target: Stuttgart. There was 4 -5/10 broken cloud. Bombed at 04.02 hours at 20,000 ft. Several scattered fires East and West. Largest concentration believed North of the city. Average attack. Main weight believed to fall North of the city.
24/02/1944 LL733 JI-G Bombing Schweinfurt 20.56 01.12   04.51
Bomb load 1 x 2000 lb. Bomb, 32 x 30, 900 x 4 incendiaries. Weather, haze and much smoke. Primary target: Schweinfurt. Bombed at 01.12 hours from 20,000 feet. Conflagration of numerous fires seen. Route O.K. Aircraft passed too near on reciprocal. Very good attack. Had encountered with enemy aircraft

and it is claimed as damaged.

25/02/1944 LL733 JI-G Bombing Augsburg   21.34   01.14   05.07

Bomb load 1 x 2000 lb. Bomb, 48 x 30, 900 x 4 incendiaries. Primary target: Augsburg. Weather good with 2/10 cloud. Bombed at 01.14 hours at 20,000 ft. Fires very concentrated at river junction. Arrived 10 mins early. Very good attack. Route good. Had 3 encounters with enemy aircraft one of which is claimed as damaged.

15/03/1944 LL625 JI-C Bombing Stuttgart   19.20   23.17   02.47

Bomb load 1 x 8000 lb. Bomb, 90 x 4 incendiaries. Primary target: Stuttgart. There was 6/10 cloud. Bombed at 23.17 hours from 21,000 feet. Bomb sight u/s, used emergency sitting. P.F.F. markers were late. Red T.I.s dropped before P.F.F., incendiaries widely scattered. Buildings seen lit up by fire after leaving.

22/03/1944 LL733 JI-G Bombing Frankfurt   18.38   21.54   00.10

Bomb load 1 x 8000 lb. Bomb, 56 x 30 incendiaries. Primary target: Frankfurt. There was thin cloud over the target. Bombed at 21.54 hours from 20,000 feet. Concentration of T.I., red. Concentrated along banks of river clearly seen. Good fires seen on leaving. Good effort. Red markers very concentrated along banks of river. Green markers on the outside of red. Route good.

24/03/1944 LL733 JI-G Bombing Berlin   18.26   22.46   01.54

Bomb load 1 x 8000 lb. Bomb. Primary target: Berlin. There was 7/10 cloud, tops 6,000 feet. Bombed at 22.46 hours from 20,000 feet. Not a great deal seen in area and fires seemed wide spread. Monica u/s. Change not heard.

F/S. Charles James "Charlie" Medland, DFM was 2nd Pilot that day

10/04/1944 LL733 JI-G Bombing Laon   01.16   03.38   05.16

Bomb load 9 x 1000, 4 x 500 lb. Bombs. Primary target: Laon. There was 3/10 cloud with slight haze. Bombed at 03.38hours from 10,700 feet. Good concentration of T.I.s and many explosions seen. Attack appeared successful. Some fires seen and many bombs bursting over target.

18/04/1944 LL733 JI-G Bombing Rouen   22.37   00.48   02.41

Bomb load 8 x 1000, 2 x 1000, 5 x 500 lb. Bombs. Primary target: Rouen. There was some cloud and haze. Bombed at 00.48 hours from 12,000 feet. Aircraft bombed slightly east as directed by M of G. Scattered fires seen. Attack believed scattered. Route O.K.

20/04/1944 LL733 JI-G Bombing Cologne   00.01   02.13   04.04

Bomb load 1 x 8000 lb. Bomb, 216 x 4, 24 x 4 incendiaries. Primary target: Koln. There was 10/10 cloud. Bombed at 02.13 hours from 19,000 feet. 3 flares (green with yellow stars) seen to fall before arrival. - none during attack so bombed red glow under cloud. Markers very few and very scattered. 1st. sky markers seen to illuminate. Bomb doors damages by falling 1 x 8000 lb. bomb.

S/L. William George Devas AFC was 2nd Pilot that day.

22/04/1944 LL733 JI-G Bombing Dusseldorf 23.1801.16   02.50

Bomb load 9 x 1000, 5 x 500 lb. Bombs. Primary target: Dusseldorf. There was slight haze. Bombed at 01.16 hours from 19,500 feet. Bend of river seen and T.I. appeared to be on marshalling yard, but major part of attack seemed to undershoot. More cloud on route than expected. Hazy over target. Many searchlights over target, moderate flak.

24/04/1944 LL733 JI-G Bombing Karlsruhe   22.28   00.50   04.04

Bomb load 1 x 1000 lb. Bomb, 1026 x 4, 114 x 4, 108 x 30 lb. Incendiaries. Primary target 15 Miles S.E. of Mannheim. There was 8/10 cloud. Aircraft had been lost. ETA already passed. Bombs dropped at 00.50 hours from 17,500 feet. After bombs dropped we ran over Karlsruhe and saw ground markers, attack believed moderate with several jettisons to North of target.

27/04/1944 LL733 JI-G Bombing Friedrichshafen 22.57 02.06   03.19

Bomb load 1 x 4000, 2 x 1000, 1 x 500 lb. Bombs. Primary target: Friedrichshafen. Weather was hazy, no cloud. Bombed at 02.06 hours from 19,000 feet. P.F.F. marker well placed. Attack very successful in the town. Route satisfactory.

09/05/1944 LL733 JI-G Bombing Cap Gris Nez   03.00   04.07   04.40

Bomb load 1 x 1000 GP, 13 x 1000 MC. Primary target: Cape Gris Nez. Clear conditions and visuals of coast and green T.I.S to east of target were obtained. Bombs released when slightly inland from curve pf coastline at 04.07 hours from 5,000 feet. Target very well illuminated by flares. T.I.s seemed to be off target and after orbiting on instructions of Master Bomber target was bombed visually.

19/05/1944 LL733 JI-S Bombing Le Mans 22.25   00.27   03.00

Bomb load 4 x 1000 USA, 3 x 1000 MC, 1 x 1000 GP, 4 x 500GP. Primary target: Le Mans. Cloud at 8000 feet over target but clear below. Bombed at 00.27 hours from 7,800 feet. Attack thought moderate, and fires seen appeared to be oil fires; Port wing holed by heavy flak at Le Havre.

F/L. Philip Barber Clay, DFC was 2nd Pilot that day.

21/05/1944 LL733 JI-S Bombing Duisburg   22.55   01.14   03.10

Bomb load 1 x 8000 lb. Bomb, 96 x 30 incendiaries. Primary target: Duisburg. There was 10/10 cloud at target. Bombed red and yellow flares at 01.14 hours from 21,000 feet. Attack covered a wide area and aircraft approached from all angles. 8 x 30 incendiaries hung up.

22/05/1944 LL733 JI-S Bombing Dortmund   22.54 23.45

Bomb load 1 x 8000 lb. Bomb, 96 x 30, 540 x 4, 60 x 4 incendiaries. Primary target: Dortmund. Returned early. Badly iced up, holes in perspex from ice and made emergency landing at Woodbridge. Crew ordered to bale out beforehand and pilot subsequently made successful landing. Body of mid-upper gunner found, his parachute having failed to open but reason unknown. Bombs jettisoned safe.

31/05/1944 DS822 JI-T Bombing Trappes   23.55   02.06   04.50

Bomb load 8 x 1000 MC, 8 x 500 MC. Primary target: Trappes. Clear at target. Bombed as instructed by Master Bomber at 02.06 hours from 10,000 feet. Concentrated attacks obscured by smoke. Master Bomber good and sortie successful. Route O.K. but long.

S/L. R.C. Chopping flew this mission with the crew of F/S. J.E.K. Hannesson, who was 2nd Pilot.

70126 S/L. Ralph Campbell Chopping, DFC Pilot.
J87269 (R162636) F/S. Jack E K Hannesson.RCAF. 2nd Pilot.
R118249 Sgt. Thomas Stanley Colbeck, RCAF A/Bomber.
1670036 Sgt. James Bryson. Navigator.
1126909 Sgt. Bert A. Brown WOP/AG.
646041Sgt. Harry James Morgan. MU/Gunner.
J89894 (R178139) Sgt. Andrew Lorne George, RCAF R/Gunner.
2201592 Sgt. Kenneth Edward Arthur Fox. F/Engineer.

2nd crew

70126 S/L. Ralph Campbell Chopping, DFC Pilot.
R151814 W/O.R.W. Deans, RCAF A/Bomber.
185519 (1387106) F/S. Dennis Arthur Newman. Navigator.
1235332 Sgt. Norman Walter Cringle, DFM WOP/AG.
1382982 F/S. P.J. Fox. MU/Gunner.
1301325 Sgt. J.S. Johnson. R/Gunner.
177638 (1807915) P/O. Desmond Connell Hughes, DFC F/Engineer.

06/06/1944 LL733 JI-S Bombing Lisieux 00.32 01.42 03.17
Bomb load 16 x 500 MC tail fused and 2 x 500 MC LD. Primary target: Lisieux. There was patchy cloud at target. Bombed red T.I. at 01.42 hours from 4,200 feet. Instructed by Master Bomber to bomb red T.I. Markers and bombs well concentrated. Everything dependent upon accuracy of the markers. A fire was seen on the sea at 02.12 hours believed to be an aircraft possibly shot down by trace from ships.
08/06/1944 LL733 JI-S Bombing Fougeres 21.58 00.17 02.18
Bomb load 16 x 500 GP and 2 x 500 MC LD. Primary target: Fougeres. Bombed as instructed by Master Bomber at 00.17 hours from 6,200 feet. Visual built-up area obtained. T.I.s were scattered but attack seemed good. No trouble experienced.
11/06/1944 LL733 JI-S Bombing Nantes 23.45 02.50 05.16
Bomb load 16 x 500 GP, 2 x 500 LD. Primary target: Nantes. Bombed at 02.50 hours from 4,000 feet in 10/10ths cloud. Heard Master Bomber's instructions to bomb red and green T.I.s but could not see them at 2,500 feet, so went up to 4000 feet and bombed glow in cloud over target as briefed.
12/06/1944 LL733 JI-S Bombing Gelsenkirchen 23.07 01.09 03.15
Bomb load 1 x 4000 HC, 12 x 500 GP, 4 x 500 MC. Primary target: Gelsenkirchen. Clear over target. Bombed at 01.09 hours from 18,000 feet. Fires and huge column of smoke seen. Several aircraft seen shot down on

route.

14/06/1944 LL733 JI-S Bombing Le Havre   23.46   01.16   02.50

Bomb load 11 x 1000 MC, 4 x 500 GP. Primary target: Le Havre. Weather clear. Bombed at 01.16 hours from 15,000 feet on red and green T.I.S identified as aiming point. Bombs seen bursting on the Quay. Target burning well from first attack - second should be good. Had combat enemy aircraft.

17/06/1944 LL733 JI-S Bombing Montdidier 01.12 04.38

Bomb load 16 x 500 GP, 2 x 500 ANM 64 GP. Primary target: Montdidier. 10/10ths thick cloud tops 6,000 feet. Master Bomber heard give order to return to base. Jettisoned 4 x 500 GP at 03.23 hours from 9,000 feet 5002N 0058E.

21/06/1944 LL733 JI-S Bombing Domleger   18.03 20.59

Bomb load 18 x 500 MC. Primary target: Domleger near Abbeville, V-1 flying bomb launch site. There was 9/10ths cloud 2,000 feet thick, tops 3/4000 feet. Reached target area at 19.30 hours at 13000 feet. No T.I.s seen, abandoned sortie as ordered by Master bomber. Jettisoned safe 8 x 500 MC. at 19.43 hours from 12,000 feet, 5020N 0122E. Had combat with E/A.

30/06/1944 LL733 JI-S Bombing Villers Bocage 18.00   19.59   21.41

Bomb load 10 x 1000 MC, 3 x 500 GP. Primary target: Villers Bocage. Weather 5/10ths cloud at 5-7,000 feet. Bombed at 19.59 hours from 4,000 feet, red T.I.s. This aircraft led 3 Group formation. Mess of aircraft owing to changes of course before target, and differences of speed. Many aircraft did not come down to 4,000 feet as ordered by Master Bomber.

07/07/1944 LL733 JI-S Bombing Vaires 22.46 01.32 03.22

Bomb load 7 x 1000 MC, 4 x 500 GP. Primary target: Vaires, Marshalling yards. Weather, clear. Bombed at 01.32 hours from 12,000 feet, green T.I.s. Attack believed satisfactory, fair amount of fighter activity. Two combats, no claims.

Note: R.C. Chopping was subsequently KIA 26/08/1944 whilst with No.7 Sqn.

F/L. H.J. Clark

J9442   F/L. H.J. Clark, RCAF.   Pilot.
J41528   F/O. Manley Foster Adams, RCAF. A/Bomber.
164038 (1621350) F/O. Bertram "Bert" Evans.   Navigator.
177179   F/O. Terence "Locky" Lockwood. WOP/AG.
J45710   F/O. Samuel "Sam" English, RCAF   MU/Gunner.
J46089 (R308432) F/O. Thomas J. "Tom" Casey, RCAF. R/Gun. 13 ops.
Sgt. W.S. Craig.   F/Engineer.

Passengers: 07/05/1945.

14/03/1945 ME336 JI-S Bombing Heinrichshutte 13.07   16.40   18.39
   Bomb load 1 x 4000 HC, 11 x 500 ANM64, 1 Skymarker Red Puff. Primary target: Heinrichshutte, Hattingen Steel works and Benzol plant. Weather 10/10ths cloud, tops 7/12,000 feet. Bombed at 16.40 hours from 18,500 feet on G.H.   Aircraft holed by flak in tail and port inner engine.
   F/L. H.J. Clark flew the mission as 2nd Pilot with F/L. W.F. Burrows' crew.
17/03/1945 ME364 JI-P Bombing Auguste Viktoria 11.27   15.07   17.12
   Bomb load 1 x 4000 HC, 13 x 500 ANM64, 2 x 500 MC. Primary target: Auguste Viktoria, Marl-Hüls coal mine. Weather 10/10ths cloud, tops and contrails up to 23,000 feet. Bombed at 15.07 hours from 23,000 feet on G.H. leading aircraft.
   From M.F. Adams' logbook: "Huls, Coke-ovens, 9/10 cloud, light flak".
20/03/1945 ME363 JI-R Bombing Hamm 09.52   13.15   15.41
   Bomb load 7 x 1000 ANM65, 9 x 500 ANM64. Primary target: Hamm, Marshalling yards. Weather 5/10ths cloud. Bombed at 13.15 hours from 17,000 feet on G.H. aircraft. Crew saw bombs burst on Marshalling Yards.
   From M.F. Adams' logbook: "Hamm, Marshalling Yards, 3/10 cloud, hit by flak".
21/03/1945 ME354 JI-M Bombing Munster 09.28   13.07   15.20
   Bomb load 1 x 4000 HC, 13 x 500 ANM64, 2 x 500 MC. Primary target: Munster Viaduct. Bombed at 13.07 hours from 18,000 feet on G.H. Leader and visual.
   From M.F. Adams' logbook: "Munster, Marshalling Yards, 2/10 cloud, heavy flak".
27/03/1945 ME364 JI-P Bombing Hamm Sachsen 10.31 14.03   15.53
   Bomb load 1 x 4000 HC, 13 x 500 ANM64, 2 x 500 MC. Primary target: Hamm Sachsen, Benzol plant. Weather 10/10ths cloud. Bombed at 14.03 hours at 18,200 feet on G.H. Leader.
   From M.F. Adams' logbook: "Hamm, Benzol plant, 10/10 cloud, light flak".
04/04/1945 ME358 JI-O Bombing Merseburg (Leuna) 18.53   22.53
03.15
Weather 5-10/10ths cloud, and 10/10ths over Merseburg. Bombed primary

114

L to R: Unknown, F/O. T. Lockwood, F/O. S. English, F/L. H.J. Clark, Unknown, F/O. T.J. Casey, F/O. M.F. Adams. (Carol Smith (Adams))

target: Merseburg. Bomb load 1 x 4000 HC, 6 x 500 ANM64. 10/10th cloud. Bombed on Red T.I.s at 22.53 hours from 20,300 feet. Very scattered marking but reasonable concentration of markers that have been bombed. H2S 1196, Front turret U/S. No Skymarkers seen on arrival, orbited and bombed on red T.I.s as skymarkers had disappeared.

Synthetic oil plant. 7/10 Cloud. Moderate Flak. P.F.F. Sky markers scattered attack.

F/L. H.J. Clark flew the mission as 2nd Pilot with F/L. M.G.T. Allen's crew.

09/04/1945 PB426 A2-E Bombing Kiel 19.54 22.40 01.54

Primary target: Kiel, Submarine Buildings Yards. Weather clear with slight haze. Bomb load 1 x 4000 HC and 12 x 500 ANM64. Bombed at 22.40 hours at 20,000 feet on centre of Green T.I.s. Visual of target confirmed M/B's instructions to bomb slightly short of Green T.I.s. H2S on fire. Very good attack. From M.F. Adams' logbook: "Admiral Scheer sunk, 2/10 cloud, heavy flak, raid OK".

18/04/1945 ME359JI-T Bombing Heligoland 09.39 13.07½ 15.01

Bomb load 6 x 1000 MC, 10 x 500 ANM64. Primary target: Heligoland, Naval base. Weather no cloud, slight haze. Bombed visually at 13.07½ from 18,500 feet. Smoke on north edge of town. Target entirely obscured by smoke. Oil leak in starboard engine. Returned on three engines. Noticed two minutes before bombing. Well concentrated attack. Our M/B not heard.

From M.F. Adams' logbook: "Heligoland, Naval base".

22/04/1945 PB419 JI-L Bombing Bremen   15.18   18.41   21.00

Bomb load 1 x 4000 HC, 2 x 500 MC, 14 x 500 ANM 64. Primary target: Bremen, in support of Troop concentration. Weather on approaching target 4-5/10ths cloud. Bombed on G.H. Leader at 18.41 hours from 19,000 ft. Bomb bursts seen amid smoke north of river, pall rising to 8,000 ft. Large fire seen near A/P. Good raid. Formation good.

From M.F. Adams' logbook: "Bremen, 1 x 4000, 1 x 500, troop concentrations, very accurate flak".

07/05/1945 ME363 JI-R Manna The Hague Rotterdam 12.17
13.45½ 14.48

Dropped 5 packs on White Cross. Clear. Bags dropped well together away from water. Many flags flying.

No Rear Gunner that day.

Passenger F/O. Jones.

From M.F. Adams' logbook: "Rotterdam, food supply".

09/05/1945 ME529 A2-F Exodus Juvincourt - Dunsfold 07.36 x 13.40

Outward 1.22 hours. Collected 24 ex POWs. Homeward 2.28 hours. Organisation good at Juvincourt but poor at Dunsfold.

From M.F. Adams' logbook: "POW transport, Juvincourt - Dunsfold".

11/05/1945 RA599 JI-L Exodus Juvincourt - Tangmere 11.12 x 18.20

Returned to base at 18.20 hours on 12 May.

Duration 3.01. Outward 1.42 hours. Collected 24 ex POWs. Homeward 1.19 hours. Tractor ran into Lanc. at Tangmere - Crew returned with 514/D.

From M.F. Adams' logbook: "POWs Juvincourt - Tangmere".

13/05/1945 ME359 JI-T Exodus Juvincourt - Tangmere 13.26 x 16.12

Duration 2.47 hours. "Return to Base" heard at 14.46 hrs.

From M.F. Adams' logbook: "POWs Juvincourt, ordered 'Return to Base' ".

16/05/1945 RE139 JI-M Exodus   Brussels - Westcott   13.36 x 19.14

Duration 2 hrs 58 mins. Out 1 hr 13 mins. In 1 hr 45 mins. Arrived overseas A/F 14.49. Arrived reception A/F 18.42. 11 Belgian refugees taken to Brussels / Melsbroeck. 24 ex POWs all military to Westcott.

From M.F. Adams' logbook: "Belgiums to Brussels, POWs to Westcott".

18/05/1945 RE139 JI-M Exodus   Brussels - Oakley   12.06   x 16.50

Duration 3 hrs 05 mins. Out 1 hr 15 mins. In 1 hr 50 mins. 10 Belgian refugees taken to Brussels. 24 ex POWs. Returned to U.K. Organisation good.

From M.F. Adams' logbook: "Belgiums to Brussels, POWs to Oakley".

19/05/1945 RE139 JI-M Exodus   Brussels - Oakley   11.57   x 18.50

Duration 3 hrs. Out 1 hr 18 mins. In 1 hr 42 mins. 10 Belgian refugees taken to Brussels. 24 ex POWs evacuated.

M.F. Adams did not note this sortie in his logbook, but in ORBs he is clearly mentioned in the crew that day.

F/L. (Acting S/L.) Philip Barber Clay, DFC

105193 (1378130) S/L. Philip Barber Clay, DFC Pilot.
J29880 F/O. R.E. Bayliss, RCAF   A/Bomber.
1566160 F/S. Ronald James Wilson, DFM Navigator.
153266 (1487602) F/O. John Rogers, DFC WOP/AG. 26 ops.
189643 (1504777) F/S. Colin Pratt. WOP/AG. 4 ops.
187639 (1896360) F/S. Thomas Henry Cousins. MU/Gunner.
3040512 F/S. D. Cox.   R/Gunner.
55894 (643636) P/O. Roy Douglas Simpson. F/Engineer.
37994 W/C. Michael "Mike" Wyatt, DFC Captain. 05/06/1944
186325 (1318539) F/S. Donald Crome, DFC 2nd Pilot. 05/10/1944
Passenger 08/08/1944, 14/10/1944.

19/05/1944 LL733 JI-S Bombing Le Mans 22.25 00.27 03.00
   Bomb load 4 x 1000 USA, 3 x 1000 MC, 1 x 1000 GP, 4 x 500 GP. Primary target: Le Mans. Cloud at 8000 feet over target but clear below. Bombed at 00.27 hours from 7,800 feet. Attack thought moderate, and fires seen appeared to be oil fires; Port wing holed by heavy flak at Le Havre.
S/L. P.B. Clay flew the mission as 2nd Pilot with F/L. R.C. Chopping's crew.

21/05/1944 DS826 JI-U Bombing Duisburg   22.48 01.12 03.48
   Bomb load 1 x 2000 lb. Bomb, 120 x 30, 600 x 4 incendiaries. Primary target: Duisburg. There was 10/10 cloud at target. Bombed red and yellow flares at 01.12 hours from 20,000 feet. Red glow observed through the cloud. Only a few markers seen and they disappeared rapidly into the cloud. Little flak and no fighters seen.

22/05/1944 DS822 JI-T Bombing Dortmund 22.45 01.20
   Bomb load 1 x 2000 lb. Bomb, 96 x 30, 810 x 4 incendiaries. Primary target: Dortmund. Returned early. Severe icing encountered and unable to climb above 9,500 feet. Aerials broken, starboard cutter prop. And perspex broken. All bombs jettisoned safe. Farthest point reached 5226N 0257E.

24/05/1944 LL620 JI-N Bombing Boulogne   00.05 01.14 02.45
   Bomb load 9 x 1000 MC, 1 x 1000 GP, 1 x 1000 ANM, 4 x 500 GP. Primary Target: Boulogne, Gun Battery. Very slight haze over target. Bombed at 01.14 hours from 8,100 feet. No visual obtained and bombs aimed at markers. Bombs seen to burst between two clusters of green T.I.s.

28/05/1944 LL731 JI-L Bombing Angers 19.00 23.59 02.25
   Bomb load 5 x 1000 MC, 1 x 1000 USA, 4 x 500 MC. Primary target: Angers. Clear over target. Clear over target. Bombed at 23.59 hours from 9,000 feet, target well lit up. Much smoke from T.I.s which obscured railway.

30/05/1944 LL731 JI-L Bombing Boulogne   23.09 00.04½ 01.39
   Bomb load 6 x 1000 MC, 4 x 500 MC. Primary target: Boulogne gun batteries. Haze over target. Bombed red T.I.s at 00.04½ hours from 7,400 feet.

Bombs seemed to be falling well on the markers. Defences strengthened since earlier attacks.

05/06/1944 LL731 JI-L Bombing Ouistreham 03.45 05.09 06.45

Bomb load 9 x 1000 MC and 2 x 500 MC. Primary target: Ouistreham. There was 4/10ths cloud at target. Bombed marker at 05.09 hours from 9,000 feet. Cloud prevented a visual. Marking seemed concentrated as did the bombing. Opposition negligible and route quiet.

W/C. M. Wyatt was Captain of this crew that day and S/L. P.B. Clay 2nd Pilot.

07/06/1944 LL731 JI-L Bombing Massy Palaiseau 00.31 02.13 04.27

Bomb load 18 x 500 MC. Primary target: Massy Palaiseau. Clear below cloud. Bombed as instructed by Master Bomber at 02.13 hours from 6,400 feet. Many bomb bursts amongst T.I.s. Good concentrated raid and much activity in target area both from ground and fighters. Some icing on outward journey between 9/10,000 feet. At 02.05 hours was attacked by a single-engined fighter, own gunners did not reply,

17/06/1944 LL666 JI-D Bombing Montdidier 01.01 02.58 04.30

Bomb load 16 x 500 GP, 2 x 500 ANM64 GP. Primary target: Montdidier. Weather 10/10ths thin cloud. Bombed at 02.58 hours from 10,000 feet red T.I.s. Arrived early and did an orbit of target, voice heard instructing return to base but no call sign given at this period.

21/06/1944 PB143 JI-B Bombing Domleger   17.53 20.39

S/L Philip Barber Clay (centre) with his crew and Lancaster Mk II LL692 A2-C (David Clay).

Bomb load 18 x 500 MC. Primary target: Domleger near Abbeville, V-1 flying bomb launch site. T.I.s not visible obeyed Master Bomber instructions to return to base. Jettisoned 9 x 500 MC at 19.43 hours from 12,000 feet 5028N 0117E.

23/06/1944 PB143 JI-B Bombing L'Hey 23.01 00.15 01.08

Bomb load 11 x 1000 MC, 4 x 500 GP. Primary target: L'Hey, Flying bomb installations. There was 10/10ths cloud, tops 4-5,000 feet. Bombed at 00.15 hours from 8,900 feet glow of red T.I.s. Raid appeared concentrated, bomb bursts seen amid glow of red T.I.s. Heavy flak intense and fairly accurate.

24/06/1944 PB143 JI-B Bombing Rimeux 23.31 00.35 01.45

Bomb load 18 x 500 GP. Primary target: Rimeux, Flying bomb installations. Weather clear. Bombed at 00.35 hours from 10,000 feet on red T.I.s. Target well marked, green markers rather wide. Searchlights very active, some heavy flak.

27/06/1944 PB143 JI-B Bombing Biennais 23.30 01.11 02.50

Bomb load 16 x 500 GP. 2 x 500 ANM64 GP. Primary target: Biennais, Flying bomb installations. There was 10/10ths cloud. Bombed at 01.11 hours from 13000 feet, red glow.

30/06/1944 PB143 JI-B Bombing Villers-Bocage 18.01 20.00 21.19

Bomb load 10x1000 MC, 3x500 GP. Primary target: Villers-Bocage. Weather clear. Bombed at 20.00 hours from 6,000 feet. Bombed on red T.I.s. as instructed by Master Bomber. Bombing excellent.

02/07/1944 PB143 JI-B Bombing Beauvoir 12.36 14.35 15.49

Bomb load 11 x 1000 MC, 4 x 500 GP. Primary target: Beauvoir, Flying bomb supply site. Broken drifting cloud. Bombed at 14.35 hours from 9,000 feet on yellow T.I.s.

05/07/1944 PB143 JI-B Bombing Watten 22.49 00.07 01.18

Bomb load 11 x 1000 ANM65, 4 x 500 GP. Primary target: Watten, Constructional works. Bombed at 00.07 hours from 8,000 feet red T.I.s.

07/07/1944 PB143 JI-B Bombing Vaires 22.36 01.34 03.18

Bomb load 7 x 1000 MC, 4 x 500 GP. Primary target: Vaires, Marshalling yards. Weather clear. Bombed at 01.34 hours from 11,000 feet centre of all T.I.s. Red and green T.I.s concentrated, whites widely scattered. Flak surprisingly light. Violent explosions at 01.38 hours.

15/07/1944 PB143 JI-B Bombing Chalons sur Marne 21.38 01.34 04.09

Bomb load 18 x 500 GP. Primary target: Chalons sur Marne, Railway centre. Weather 5/10ths cloud below 10/10ths above, clear for bombing. Bombed at 01.34 hours from 12,000 feet green T.I.s. Markers well placed on Marshalling Yards, bombing good. A.S.I. u/s shortly after take-off also starboard outer engine out on route to target.

18/07/1944 LL692 A2-C Bombing Emieville 04.22 06.06 07.56

Bomb load 11 x 1000 MC, 4 x 500 GP. Primary target: Emieville, Troop concentration. Weather clear. Bombed at 06.06 hours from 7,900 feet yellow T.I.s. Considerable heavy and light flak in target area. Bombing concentrated.

30/07/1944 PB143 JI-B Bombing Caen   06.01   07.50   10.00

Bomb load 18 x 500 GP. Primary target Caen 'B'. Weather 10/10ths cloud. Bombed at 07.50 hours from 2,000 feet, red T.I.s. Bursts well concentrated on smoke and T.I.s. Landed at Woodbridge.

05/08/1944 PB143 JI-B Bombing Bassen   14.16 19.02   22.05

Bomb load 8 x 1000 MC, 2 x 500 GP. Primary target: Bassen Oil Depot. Weather: cum nimbus, 7,000 feet over target. Bombed visually at 19.02 hours from 6,000 feet oil storage tanks. Two large explosions seen with flames up to 800/1000 feet followed by dense black smoke. Bombing concentrated,

08/08/1944 PB143 JI-B Bombing Foret de Lucheux 21.40   23.48   01.01

Bomb load 18 x 500 GP. Primary target: Foret de Lucheux, Petrol dump. Weather clear, slight haze. Bombed at 23.48 hours, 12,000 feet, port of fires as ordered by Master Bomber. Large fires in target area with huge cloud of black smoke up to 6,000 feet.

G/C. Cyril Montague Heard was a passenger.

15/08/1944 PB143 JI-B Bombing St Trond   09.51   12.09   13.20

Bomb load 11 x 1000 MC. 4 x 500 GP. Primary target St. Trond Airfield. Weather perfect. Bombed at 12.09 hours, 17,000 feet, red T.I.s and intersection of runways. Very successful attack, accurate bombing.

05/09/1944 PB482 JI-P Bombing Le Havre   17.14   19.23   20.32

Bomb load 11 x 1000 MC, 4 x 500 GP. Primary target: Le Havre. Bombed at 19.23 hours from 13,000 feet red T.I. Jettisoned 1 x 1000 MC which hung up at 5010N on track.

20/09/1944 LM724 JI-B Bombing Calais   14.39   16.05   17.12

Bomb load 11 x 1000 MC, 4 x 500 GP. Primary target: Calais. Weather clear over target. Bombed at 16.05 hours from 3,000 feet, red T.I.s.

05/10/1944 LM724 JI-B Bombing Saarbrucken   17.06 22.44

Bomb load 11 x 1000 MC. 1 x 500 GP. 3 x 500 GP. Long delay. Abandoned mission on instructions from Master Bomber heard to say they were unable to locate target and called "Abandon Mission - our troops in vicinity". 3 x 500 GP Long delay jettisoned at 22.12 hours at 5220N 0236E from 8,000 feet.

F/S. Donald Crome was 2nd pilot that day.

07/10/1944 NG121 JI-H Bombing Emmerich 12.09 14.26   16.07

Bomb load 1 x 4000 HC. 10 x No. 14 clusters. 4 x (150 x 4). Primary target Emmerich. Weather clear with cloud at 13,000 feet. Bombed at 14.26 hours from 13,200 feet on south edge of smoke.

14/10/1944 LM724 JI-B Bombing Duisburg   23.02   01.30   03.39

Bomb load 11 x 1000 MC. 4 x 500 GP long delay. Primary target Duisburg. Weather was clear with small amount of cloud over the target. Bombed at 01.30 hours from 19,000 feet. Red T.I.

Daily Express War correspondent William M. Troughton aboard.

From that day F/S. Colin Pratt was WOP/AG.

15/10/1944 LM724 JI-B Bombing Wilhelmshaven 17.16   19.55   21.44

Bomb load 11 x 1000 MC, 4 x 500 GP. Primary target: Wilhelmshaven.

Weather haze and thin cloud at first with thick cloud later. Bombed at 19.55 hours from 17,000 feet. Red T.I.s.

05/11/1944 NG121 JI-H Bombing Solingen 10.16 13.05 14.47

Bomb load 1 x 4000 HC, 6 x 1000 ANM59, 4 x 500 GP, 2 x 500 GP (L/Delay). Primary target: Solingen. Weather 10/10ths cloud over target. Bombed at 13.05 hours from 17,000 feet on leading aircraft.

06/11/1944 LM728 JI-U Bombing Koblenz 16.45 19.32 21.33

Bomb load 1 x 4000 HC, 2100 x 4 lb I.B. Primary target: Koblenz. Weather clear over target. Bombed at 19.32 hours from 18,200 feet on Red and Green T.I.s.

F/O. Ronald Cyril Saville Clements.

Detailed for mission with F/L. J.T. Anderson and crew of No.115 Squadron in Lancaster MkII DS725 KO-F.

127890 F/L. John Thomas Anderson. Pilot.
134106 (1066632) F/O. Ronald Cyril Saville Clements. 2nd Pilot.
134073 F/O. Frank George Andrews. A/Bomber.
1387726 F/S. Derrick Leslie Walter Horn. Navigator.
132413 F/O. Douglas James Boston. WOP/AG.
1577754 Sgt. Ernest Alfred Gibbs. A/Gunner.
1252153 F/S. Frank Norman Simpson Cowie. A/Gunner.
621459 Sgt. Gilbert Herbert McDonald Batten. F/Engineer.

20/10/1943 DS725 KO-F Bombing Leipzig 18.17 x 20.00

Weather: Very bad, raining heavily, cold with high winds.

F/O. R.S. Clements who was second pilot to F/L. Anderson in 'F' for Freddie of 115 Squadron has been reported as missing. Nothing has been heard of this aircraft after take-off.

F/O. R.S. Clements is listed on the 514 Squadron Roll of Honour as having lost his life on 20th October 1943. He was flying in DS725, KO-F, which had taken off at 18.17 hours from Little Snoring. Shot down at 20.00 hours by Lt. Paul Fehre of 5./NJG3 at Engersen, 12 km ESE of Klötze, near Gardelegen. There were no survivors from the crew. All are buried in the Berlin 1939-45 War Cemetery.

F/L, Acting S/L. Kenneth Godfrey Condict, DFC

128551 (1288450) S/L. Kenneth Godfrey Condict, DFC. Pilot.
  F/S. E.L. Thistlewood. A/Bomber.
  F/S. E.G. Winterborne. Navigator.
1218696 F/S. William Joseph Sparkes. WOP/AG. 32 ops
103538 (902785) F/L. Vivian George Ivor Outen, DFC. WOP/AG. 1 op.
J19707   F/O. Frank Harold Rowan, DFC RCAF. WOP/AG. 1 op.
  F/S. P.L. Capon.   MU and R/Gunner.
 Sgt. E. Cornwell. (32 ops.)   MU and R/Gunner.
  F.S. George Edgar Sales. R/Gunner. 2 ops
  F/S. R. Leischman.   F/Engineer.
J28322 F/O. Campbell G. Fiset, DFC RCAF. 2nd Pilot. 29/11/44
116005 (1379910) F/L. Royston Worthing. 2nd Pilot. 21/12/44
47225 (549527) F/L. Roy Henry Marks. 2nd Pilot. 02/01/45
125416 (1389496) F/L. Bertram Arthur Audis.   2nd Pilot. 28/01/45
J41105   F/O. C.A. Dunn, RCAF. 2nd Pilot. 03/02/45
130171 (1335758) F/L. Harold Thomas Lunson. 2nd Pilot. 07/03/45

14/10/1944 NN717 JI-E Bombing Duisburg   06.56   09.05   10.55
Bomb load 11 x 1000 MC. 4 x 500 GP Long Delay. Primary target: Duisburg. Weather patchy cloud with gaps for bombing. Bombed at 09.05 hours from 20,000 feet. Docks.
S/L. K.G. Condict flew the mission as 2nd Pilot with F/O. G. Bradford's crew.

23/10/1944 LM733 JI-F Bombing Essen 16.22   19.39   21.59
Bomb load 1 x 4000 HC, 6 x 1000 MC, 2 x 500 GP. Primary target: Essen. Weather 10/10ths cloud over target - tops 12/14,000 feet with most appalling weather on route. Bombed at 19.39 hours from 20,000 feet. Green sky markers.

25/10/1944 ME841 JI-C Bombing Essen 12.59   15.30   17.01
Bomb load 1 x 4000 HC, 6 x 1000 MC, 6 x 500 GP. Primary target: Essen. Weather over target 10/10ths low cloud, with one clear patch which appeared to fill up later in the attack. Bombed at 15.30 hours from 22,000 feet. Visual means of built up area.

28/10/1944 NG121 JI-H Bombing Flushing 09.03   10.15   11.16
Bomb load 11 x 1000 MC, 4 x 500 GP. Primary target: Flushing. Weather over the target quite clear and conditions perfect, although believed to be only local, and some low cloud approaching. Bombed at 10.15 hours from 8,000 feet. Saucer shaped indentation on neck of land.

29/10/1944 NG121 JI-H Bombing Flushing 09.45   11.37   12.30
Bomb load 11 x 1000 ANM59, 4 x 500 GP. Primary target: Flushing, Gun installations. Weather clear over target. Bombed at 11.37 hours from 6,000

feet. Starboard of Green T.I.s as instructed.

31/10/1944 NG203 JI-A Bombing Bottrop 11.49 15.00 16.39
Bomb load 1 x 4000 HC, 16 x 500 GP. Primary target: Bottrop, Synth. Oil plants. Weather 10/10ths cloud over target. Bombed at 15.00 hours from 16,500 feet on G.H. Leader.

02/11/1944 NG121 JI-H Bombing Homberg 11.27 14.08 15.37
Bomb load 1 x 4000 HC, 6 x 1000 ANM59, 6 x 500 MC. Primary target: Homberg. Weather variable cloud but clear for bombing. Target obscured by pall of smoke rising to 10,000 feet. Bombed at 14.08 hours from 20,000 feet. Green flares.

04/11/1944 NG121 JI-H Bombing Solingen 11.36 14.20 16.04
Bomb load 1 x 4000 HC, 14 x 500 Clusters. Primary target: Solingen. Weather 8-10/10ths cloud. Bombed at 14.20 hours from 20,500 feet on upwind edge of wide area of flares.

11/11/1944 NG121 JI-H Bombing Castrop Rauxel 08.17 11.06 12.56
Bomb load 1 x 4000 HC, 16 x 500 GP. Primary target: Castrop Rauxel, Oil refineries. Weather 10/10ths cloud. Bombed at 11.06 hours from 19,500 feet. Upwind edge of Red flares.

15/11/1944 ME841 JI-J Bombing Dortmund 12.45 15.40 17.35
Bomb load 1 x 4000 HC, 2 x 500 MC, 13 x 500 GP, 1 Red with Green star flare. Primary target: Hoesch-Benzin Dortmund, Oil refineries. Weather 10/10ths cloud over the target. Bombed at 15.40 hours from 16,800 feet on G.H. Good concentration of bombs.

16/11/1944 ME841 JI-J Bombing Heinsburg 13.06 15.31 17.18
Bomb load 1 x 4000 HC, 6 x 1000 MC, 6 x 500 GP. Primary target: Heinsburg. Weather - nil cloud with slight haze over target. Bombed at 15.31 hours from 9,500 feet. Upwind edge of smoke.

27/11/1944 LM724 JI-H Bombing Cologne 12.18 15.05 17.08
Bomb load 1 x 4000 HC, 15 x 500 GP, 1 Flare. Primary target: Cologne, Marshalling Yards. Weather patchy cloud. Bombed at 15.05 hours from 19,500 feet. Visually.

29/11/1944 LM724 JI-H Bombing Neuss 03.07 05.32 07.23
Bomb load 1 x 4000 HC, 6 x 1000 MC, 4 x 500 GP, 4 x 250 Green T.I.s. Primary target: Neuss. Weather 10/10ths cloud over target but the glow of fires was seen through cloud. Bombed at 05.32 hours from 19,000 feet on G.H. Glow observed through cloud. T.I.s well concentrated.

F/O. Campbell George "Cam" Fiset, DFC RCAF was 2nd Pilot that day

30/11/1944 LM724 JI-H Bombing Osterfeld 10.55 13.06 14.56
Bomb load 1 x 4000 HC, 15 x 500 GP, 1 Red/Green flare. Primary target: Osterfeld, Coking plant. Weather 10/10ths cloud. Bombed at 13.06 hours from 20,000 feet on G.H.

F/O. Campbell George "Cam" Fiset, DFC RCAF was 2nd Pilot that day. In his logbook, C.G. Fiset noted that he was 2nd Pilot with K.G. Condict as Captain, not J.S. Parnell as recorded in the ORBs.

02/12/1944 ME841 JI-J Bombing Dortmund 13.06 14.58 17.06

Bomb load 13 x 1000 HC, 1 Red/Green flare. Primary target: Dortmund, Benzol plant. Weather 10/10ths cloud. Bombed at 14.58 hours from 19,000 feet on G.H. Leader.

04/12/1944 LM724 JI-H Bombing Oberhausen 11.50 14.08 16.14

Bomb load 1 x 4000 HC, 15 x 500 GP, 1 Flare. Primary target: Oberhausen, Built up area. Weather 10/10ths cloud. Bombed at 14.08 hours from 20,000 feet on G.H.

06/12/1944 LM724 JI-H Bombing Merseburg 16.58 20.48 00.11

Bomb load 1 x 4000 HC, 8 x 500 GP, 1 x 500 GP Long Delay. Primary target: Merseburg. Weather 10/10ths cloud with odd breaks. Bombed at 20.48 hours from 22,000 feet on Red/Green flare.

11/12/1944 LM724 JI-H Bombing Osterfeld 08.42 11.04 12.59

Bomb load 1 x 4000 HC, 14 x 500 GP, 1 x 500 GP Long Delay, 1 Flare. Primary target: Osterfeld. Weather 10/10ths cloud, tops 16,000 feet. Bombed at 11.04 hours from 19,500 feet on G.H.

21/12/1944 LM724 JI-H Bombing Trier 12.15 x 17.12

Bomb load 1 x 4000 HC, 10 x 500 GP, 2 x 250 GP, 4 x 250 GP. Primary target: Trier, Marshalling yards. Weather 10/10 cloud, tops 6/9000 feet. Abortive - bombs could not be released on target.

F/L. Royston Worthing was 2nd Pilot that day.

28/12/1944 LM724 JI-H Bombing Cologne-Gremberg 12.18 15.06 16.53

Bomb load 7 x 1000 MC, 6 x 500 GP, 2 x 250 GP, 1 Flare. Primary target: Koln-Gremberg, Marshalling yards. Weather 10/10ths cloud or fog. Bombed at 15.06 hours from 19,600 feet on G.H.

02/01/1945 LM724 JI-H Bombing Nuremburg 15.26 19.33 22.44

Bomb load: 1 x 1000 ANM65, 1 x 500 ANM58, 10 x 80 x 4 IB., 120 x 4 lb. Primary target: Nuremburg. Weather clear. Bombed at 19.33 hours from 17,000 feet, - overshot Red T.I.s as instructed by Master Bomber.

22/01/1945 LM724 JI-H Bombing Hamborn 17.02 20.07 21.47

Bomb load 1 x 4000 HC, 7 x 500 ANM58 or 64, 2 x 500 GP (L/Delay), 3 x 250 GP. Primary target: Hamborn, Thyssen works. Weather over target clear and almost as bright as day. Bombed at 20.07 hours from 21,200 feet on centre of Green T.I.s.

28/01/1945 LM724 JI-H Bombing Cologne-Gremberg 10.19 14.12 16.06

Bomb load 1 x 4000 HC, 10 x 500 ANM64, 2 x 500 GP, 3 x 250 GP. Primary target: Koln-Gremberg, Marshalling yards. Weather 10/10ths cloud en route clearing on approach to target where visibility was good and nil cloud. Bombed at 14.12 hours from 19,500 feet on G.H. Leader.

F/L. Bertram Arthur Audis was 2nd Pilot that day.

29/01/1945 LM724 JI-H Bombing Krefeld 10.20 13.59 15.40

Bomb load 1 x 4000 HC, 10 x 500 ANM64, 2 x 500 GP, 3 x 250 GP, 1 Flare. Primary target: Krefeld Marshalling Yards. Weather 10/10ths low thin cloud over target although clear patches en-route. Bombed at 13.59 hours from

20,000 feet on G.H.

01/02/1945 LM724 JI-H Bombing Munchen-Gladbach 13.12   16.33 18.18

Bomb load 1 x 4000 HC, 10 x 500 ANM64, 2 x 500 GP, 3 x 250 GP, 1 Blue smoke T.I. Primary target: Munchen-Gladbach, Marshalling yards. Bombed at 16.33 hours from 18,500 feet on G.H.

02/02/1945 LM724 JI-H Bombing Wiesbaden 20.47 23.45   02.30

Bomb load 1 x 4000 HC, 12 x 500 GP, 4 x 250 GP. Primary target: Wiesbaden. Weather 10/10ths cloud, winds very erratic. Bombed at 23.45 hours from 20,000 feet on G.H.

F/L. Roy Henry Marks was 2nd Pilot that day.

03/02/1945 NF968 JI-B Bombing Dortmund-Huckarde 16.21 19.46 21.41

Bomb load 1 x 4000 HC, 2 x 500 MC, 2 x 500 MC L/Delay, 6 x 500 ANM64, 6 x 500 GP, 3 x 250 GP, 1 Red/Green Flare. Primary target Dortmund-Huckarde, Coking plant. Weather clear with slight haze. Bombed at 19.46 hours from 19,600 feet on G.H. Good concentration of T.I.s.

F/O. C.A. Dunn, RCAF was 2nd Pilot and F.S. George Edgar Sales R/Gunner that day.

08/02/1945 LM724 JI-H Bombing Hohenbudberg 03.40   06.22   08.40

Bomb load 1 x 4000 HC, 2 x 500 MC, 3 x 250 GP, 4 x 500 GP, 6 x 500 ANM64, 1 Red/Green Flare. Primary target: Hohenbudberg, Marshalling yards. Weather 8/10ths cloud over target. Bombed at 06.22 hours from 20,000 feet on G.H. Fires and reflection of fires seen on leaving target.

14/02/1945 NG298 JI-E Bombing Chemnitz   20.34   00.32   04.28

Bomb load 1 x 4000 HC, 8 x No. 14 Clusters. Primary target: Chemnitz. Weather 8-10/10ths cloud, tops 15-16,000 feet with occasional breaks. Bombed at 00.32 hours from 20,000 feet.

F.S. George Edgar Sales was R/Gunner that day.

16/02/1945 NF968 JI-B Bombing Wesel   12.25   16.00   17.37

Bomb load 1 x 4000 HC, 4 x 500 GP, 2 x 500 MC L/Delay, 3 x 250 GP, 6 x 500 ANM64, 1 Red Puff. Primary target: Wesel. Weather clear. Bombed at 16.00 hours from 20,000 feet on G.H.

22/02/1945 LM724 JI-H Bombing Osterfeld   12.26   16.01   18.10

Bomb load 1 x 4000 HC, 9 x 500 ANM64, 2 x 500 MC, 3 x 250 GP, 1 x 250 Blue Puff. Primary target: Osterfeld, Coking ovens. Weather at target clear, but hazy. Bombed at 16.01 hours from 19,500 feet on G.H.

07/03/1945 LM724 JI-H Bombing Wesel   02.47   05.30   07.43

Bomb load 1 x 4000 HC, 13 x 500 ANM64, 2 x 500 GP. Primary target: Wesel, Troop and Transport concentration. Weather 10/10ths cloud, thin in places. Bombed at 05.30 hours from 18,000 feet on G.H.

F/L. Harold Thomas Lunson was 2nd Pilot that day.

14/03/1945 LM724 JI-H Bombing Heinrichshutte 13.16   16.40   18.29

Bomb load 1 x 4000 HC, 11 x 500 ANM64, 1 Skymarker Red Puff. Primary target: Heinrichshutte, Hattingen Steel works and Benzol plant. Weather

10/10ths cloud, tops 7/12,000 feet. Bombed at 16.40 hours from 18,500 feet on G.H. 1 Red smoke Puff as we bombed. At 16.42 hours North of Hattingen, a burst of heavy flak caught the aircraft killing the Wireless Operator instantly. Squadron formation good.

21/03/1945 NF968 JI-B Bombing Munster   09.29   13.08   15.08

Bomb load 1 x 4000 HC, 13 x 500 ANM64, 2 x 500 MC, 1 Skymarker Blue Puff. Primary target Munster Viaduct and Marshalling Yards. Weather cloud nil to 2/10ths. Bombed at 13.08 hours from 18,500 feet on G.H. Slight damage to port inner engine at Dorstern.

F/L. Vivian George Ivor Outen, DFC was WOP/AG that day.

09/04/1945 LM724 JI-H Bombing Kiel   19.35   22.39   01.30

Primary target: Kiel, Submarine Buildings Yards. Weather clear with slight haze. Bomb load 1 x 4000 HC and 12 x 500 ANM64. Bombed centre of Green T.I.s at 22.39 hours from 20,000 feet. Harbour seen by flares. Marking appeared correctly placed. Markers broken up by bomb bursts. Bombing concentrated and huge fires seen 100 miles distant. M/B heard and obeyed.

F/O. Frank Harold Rowan, DFC RCAF was WOP/AG that day.

P/O, Acting F/O. Edward Thomas Cossens, DFC

NZ421683 F/O. Edward Thomas Cossens, DFC RNZAF. Pilot.
152735 (1063122) F/O. William Grier "Bill" Lees. A/Bomber.
152314 (1348235) F/O. James Robertson "Jimmie" Gould. Navigator.
158611 (1132014) F/O. Eric John Hayden. WOP/A.G.
Sgt. Dennis "the Menace" Young. MU/Gunner. 23 ops.
141271 (1386976) F/O. Herbert Henry Wright, DFM. MU/Gunner. 1 op.
F/S. E.C. Francis. MU/Gunner. 7 ops.
Sgt. Peter Guthrie Brown. Rear Gunner. 8 ops.
1584931 F/S. Geoffrey A."Geoff" Payne. Rear Gunner. 23 ops.
Sgt. R.G. Flint. F/Engineer.
NZ425302 F/O. Alfred D J Uffindell. 2nd Pilot. 04/08/1944
J88101 F/S. G.A. Wark, DFC RCAF.   2nd Pilot. 12/08/1944
128922 (1432982) F/O. Ronald Arthur Pickler DFC. 2nd Pilot. 18/08/1944

"F/O Cossens' crew were: Navigator F/O. Jimmie Gould, a Scot from Kilmarnock, Flight Engineer Sgt. R.J. Flint from Motherwell, Bomb Aimer F/O. Billie Lees of Canada, WOP/A.G.   F/O. Hayden, MU/Gunner Sgt. Dennis Young, with myself as Rear Gunner. As there were four officers in the crew, socialising as a crew never arose, however, Mid Upper Gunner Dennis Young became firm friends until he passed away in 2008."
Geoffrey Payne - 2014.

08/05/1944 DS818 JI-Q Bombing Cap Gris Nez 22.55 23.54 00.59

Bomb Load 14 x 1000 lb Bombs. Primary target: Cape Gris Nez. Weather was clear. Bombed at 23.54 hours from 8000 feet. Smoke and bomb bursts seen. A good attack. Markers not seen until after bombing.

19/05/1944 DS818 JI-Q Bombing Le Mans 22.25 01.25

Bomb Load 4 x 1000 USA, 5 x 10000 MC, 1 x 1000 GP, 4 x 500 GP. Primary target: Le Mans. Due to certain of the aircraft equipment not functioning properly, farthest point reached was 5023N 0003E. All bombs were brought back to Base. Fuel jettisoned from No. 1 tank to reduce weight.

21/05/1944 DS818 JI-Q Bombing Duisburg 22.48 01.12 03.45

Bomb load 1 x 2000 lb. Bomb, 120 x 30, 600 x 4 incendiaries. Primary target: Duisburg. There was 10/10ths cloud with small breaks. Bombed markers at 01.12 hours from 20,000 feet. Saw fires through cloud break but unable to assess results. One aircraft with lights on seen.

22/05/1944 DS816 JI-O Bombing Dortmund 22.50 00.45 02.25

Bomb load 1 x 2000 lb bomb, 96 x 30, 810 x 4, 90 x 4 incendiaries. Primary target: Dortmund. Clear over target. Bombed markers at 00.45 hours from 20,000 feet. Attack seemed very good, many fires visible. On return landed at Woodbridge owing to icing.

24/05/1944 LL733 JI-S Bombing Boulogne 00.05 01.16 02.40

Bomb load 9 x 1000 GP, 1 x 1000 ANM, 4 x 500 GP. Primary target: Boulogne Gun Battery. Clear over target. Bombed green T.I.s at 01.16 hours from 7,500 feet. Trouble free trip and flak negligible.

31/05/1944 DS816 JI-O Bombing Trappes 00.01 01.58 03.35

Bomb load 8 x 1000 MC, 8 x 500 MC. Primary target: Trappes. Clear at target. Bombed as instructed by Master Bomber at 01.58 hours from 8,600 feet. Whole yards illuminated by flares, and bombs seen to strike in the yards. Sortie was successful. Quiet trip. Fires seen at Rouen. At 01.56 hours a single engine aircraft was seen and at 01.54 hours a twin-engined aircraft was seen.

06/06/1944 LL624 JI-R Bombing Lisieux 00.09 01.43 03.33

Bomb load 16 x 500 MC tail fused and 2 x 500 MC LD. Primary target: Lisieux. There was 3/10 - 5/10ths cloud at target. Bombed as instructed by Master Bomber at 01.43 hours from 2000 feet. Partial visual of the target area was obtained and some bombs were seen bursting around the markers. Appeared to be a successful attack. Master Bomber was heard clearly. Another aircraft had its transmitter on during their bombing and conversations were heard clearly, interfering with the Master Bomber's instructions.

07/06/1944 LL624 JI-R Bombing Massy Palaiseau 00.28 02.16 03.35

Bomb load 18 x 500 MC. Primary target: Massy Palaiseau. Clear below cloud. Bombed as instructed by Master Bomber at 02.16 hours from 5,000 feet. Starboard wing damaged by light flak. Rear turret damaged in a fighter attack. Rear Gunner seriously injured. Captain too busy elsewhere to pay attention to raid. Landed at Manston.

NOTE - The Rear Gunner injured was Sgt. Peter Brown. Although he had been listed as MU Gunner in the unit ORBs – it is apparent he was Rear Gunner. His replacement, Sgt. Geoffrey Albert Payne informed me on 29 September 2014 that, Sgt. Brown did not take part in further operations. He sadly lost his leg below the knee and was subsequently invalided from service.

15/07/1944 DS813 JI-N Bombing Chalons-sur-Marne 21.47 01.34
03.50

Bomb load 18 x 500 GP. Primary target: Chalons-sur-Marne. Railway centre. Weather clear below 9,000 feet. Bombed at 01.34 hours from 8,800 feet, green T.I.s bursts seen across Marshalling Yards.

Sgt. Geoffrey A. Payne takes over as Rear Gunner.

F/Sgt Geoffrey Payne - 2014. "15/16th July 1944: My first trip with my new crew was a night operation to Chalons-sur-Marne a railway marshalling yard, a trip of six and a half hours."

17/07/1944 DS813 JI-N Bombing Paris

514 Squadron Operational Record Books (ORBs) do not make any mention of this raid, reported as a DNC (Did Not Complete) mission in some 514 Sqn crew's logbooks and by F/Sgt. Geoffrey Payne as follows:

F/Sgt. Geoffrey Payne - 2014. "This is recorded in my Log Book (as a DNC), Flying Bomb Sites and, I remember it well. The raid was aborted and, as when we were returning back over the coast, I saw German soldiers running to an AA gun and, as we crossed the coast light flak came up then, a heavy flak shell burst well to our starboard. Soon out of range then jettisoned our bombs in the sea according to instructions."

W.G. Lees did not register this mission in his logbook and F/Sgt. Geoffrey Payne told me on 6 Dec. 2015: "There is a good possibility that W.G. Lees was not flying on that day."

Bomber Command War Diaries Stated for that day -

"Flying Bomb Sights - 132 Aircraft. 72 Halifaxes, 28 Sterlings, 20 Lancasters, 11 Mosquitos, and 1 Mustang attacked 3 V-weapons sites without loss. Few details of results were recorded."

18/07/1944 DS813 JI-N Bombing Emieville   04.32   06.05   07.40

Bomb load 11 x 1000 MC, 4 x 500 GP. Primary target: Emieville, Troop concentration. Weather clear. Bombed at 06.05 hours from 6,500 feet, yellow T.I.s. A good show. Bombing Troop concentrations.

F/Sgt. Geoffrey Payne - 2014. "18 July 1944. Daylight raid to Emieville to attack troop concentrations. Arriving at base at 07.40 hours and informed to be ready for operations again that night."

18/07/1944 DS813 JI-N Bombing Aulnoye 22.43   00.59   02.27

Bomb load 18 x 500 GP. Primary target: Aulnoye, Railway junction. Weather Hazy. Bombed at 00.59 hours from 9,000 feet, green T.I.s. Much smoke. Bombing Railway junction.

The 'original' Cossens crew.   L to R Back row: D.G. Young, E.J. Hayden or A.J. Flint, J.R. Gould, W.G. Lees. Front row: P.G. Brown, E.T. Cossens, E.J. Hayden or A.J. Flint (Allan and Beata Lees)

" Pictured above in the Sergeants Mess at Waterbeach. Seated front left - Sgt. Willie McDonald (Rear Gunner with the F/O. Holland crew). Next is my long time friend, Sgt. Dennis Young, and his dear wife" - F/Sgt Geoffrey Payne- 2014.

F/Sgt. Geoffrey Payne - 2014. "18/19th July 1944. Night attack on the rail junctions at Aulnoye. Flak was moderate but in the distance, another attack was taking place at the rail junction of Revigny, with fighter rockets seen. Back at base 02.27 hrs. Very tired but ready for a seven-day leave."

28/07/1944 LL733 JI-S Bombing Stuttgart 21.44 01.51 05.46

Bomb load 13 x 500 GP. Primary target: Stuttgart. Weather 10/10ths thin cloud. Bombed at 01.51 hours from 18,000 feet, green marker and yellow stars. Little evidence of bombing.

F/Sgt. Geoffrey Payne - 2014. "28/29th July 1944. Back from leave, we practised formation flying for a few days in preparation of deep penetration behind the German lines but once again Bomber Harris still wanted to continue his attacks against German industrial towns, hence another night trip into the heart of Germany. Detailed to attack Stuttgart which was to be the third heavy raid by Bomber Command against Stuttgart in seven days. Fairly clear moonlight night, fighter flares began to illuminate the sky as we approached the French/German border with a number of combats taking place north of our tack. It seems as though the German Radar had correctly forecast our target owing to the number of searchlights waving about the target area. Very heavy flak as we went into bomb with usual buffeting about, turning for home I spotted a number of Bf-109s scurrying about, silhouetted against the fires. The return journey was uneventful, although these were the times that a fighter could catch you unawares. After an eight-hour flight we landed back at base at 05.46 hrs. Later we were to learn that 39 aircraft had been lost on this raid against the five hundred that had participated."

30/07/1944 LL666 JI-Q Bombing Caen 06.14 07.50 09.09

Bomb load 18 x 500 GP. Primary target: Caen 'B'. Weather 10/10ths cloud. Bombed at 07.50 hours from 2,500 feet, group of red markers beside long L shaped grey building. Good concentration.

F/Sgt. Geoffrey Payne - 2014. "30th July 1944. Daylight raid to Normandy in support of our ground troops who were ready to advance against the stubborn resistance of a German mechanised division. Caen target area B was our aiming point. Orange smoke was deployed as the British front line, and we were to bomb east of that line at 4000 ft. Going in to attack we were met by a lot of light flak which subsided appreciably as the Germans took cover. I don't know how anyone could have survived such a concentrated battering that I had witnessed."

03/08/1944 LL635 JI-M Bombing Bois de Cassan 11.51 14.07 15.48

Bomb load 11 x 1000 MC, 4 x 500 GP. Primary target: Bois de Cassan, Flying bomb supply depot. Bombed at 14.07 hours from 16,000 feet, centre of red T.I.s.

F/Sgt. Geoffrey Payne - 2014. "3rd August 1944. Daylight operation to Bois de Cassan flying bomb storage sites. Four hours flying time."

04/08/1944 LL624 JI-R Bombing Bec d'Ambes 13.28 18.04 21.17

Bomb load 5 x 1000 MC, 4 x 500 GP. Primary target: Bec d'Ambes Depot.

Weather - visibility very good. Bombed at 18.04 hours from 8000 feet. Yellow T.I.s in the midst of much black smoke and yellow flames. 3 tanks exploded as our bombs were going down. Very good attack, smoke from attack up to 12,000 feet.

F/Sgt. Geoffrey Payne - 2014. "4th August 1944. Daylight raid Bec d Ambes oil storage port on the Gironde Estuary (of The Cockleshell Heroes fame) leading into Bordeaux. Take-off time 13.30hrs to avoid being detected by the German radar we were detailed to fly out below 4000 ft. Setting course in close formation, we joined up with other squadrons at Falmouth, Cornwall, then out to sea heading for the Bay of Biscay, an area notorious for patrols of Ju 88's. Nearing the French coast we climbed to our bombing height then went into bomb. The attack was extremely successful as I could see the storage tanks on fire and a tanker alongside the jetty listing badly. Very strange that there was only light flak in the vicinity, it being obvious that we had caught the defences unawares. Relatively pleasant journey on the way back but it must have been quite a strain for our pilot flying at that low level. A couple of our Mosquito escorts buzzed us on the way home which was gratifying. Back at base after an eight-hour flight and ready for a 48hr pass."

08/08/1944 LL734 JI-O Bombing Foret de Lucheux 21.54 23.50 01.20

Bomb load 18 x 500 GP. Primary target: Foret de Lucheux, Petrol dump. Weather clear. Bombed at 23.50 hours from 12,000 feet, red T.I.s. Fires beginning to take hold. Attack on petrol dump.

Foret de Lucheux is a forest between Lille and Amiens. During WWII, important fuel tanks were there.

F/Sgt. Geoffrey Payne - 2014. "8/9th August 1944. Night operation Foret de Lacheux. Munitions storage dumps and depots."

12/08/1944 LL635 JI-M Bombing Russelsheim 21.57 00.15 02.41

Bomb load 1 x 8000 HC, 6 x 500 No. 14 clusters. Primary target: Russelsheim. Weather clear. Bombed at 00.15 hours from 17,500 feet. Red T.I.s. Large number of flares seen over target. Markers appeared to be well concentrated. Master Bomber not clearly heard.

F/S. G.A. Wark was 2nd Pilot for this mission.

F/Sgt. Geoffrey Payne - 2014. "12/13th August 1944. Back to the German industrial towns with a night operation to Russelsheim by Frankfurt on Main. Target was the Opal factories, who were manufacturing aircraft and military vehicles. Very apprehensive as, this was my third visit to Frankfurt and held many unpleasant memories. Clear night with heavy flak and many searchlights and fighter flares. Incident free trip but losses were high, losing thirty aircraft. A loss rate of 6.7%."

16/08/1944 LL635 JI-M Bombing Stettin 21.05 01.07 05.19

Bomb load 1 x 2000 HC, 9 x 500 lb "J" type clusters. Primary target: Stettin. Weather 7/10ths cloud. Bombed at 01.07 hours from 17,000 feet centre of red and green T.I.s. Bomb bursts seen across T.I.s.

F/Sgt. Geoffrey Payne - 2014. "16-17th August 1944. Loud groans from the assembled crews as the target Stettin was revealed, a Polish port away in the Baltic. We were to adopt the same tactics as employed in the successful daylight raid on Bec de Ambes and to fly out below 4000 ft under the radar screen. A diversionary raid would also take place against Kiel in an attempt to confuse the German defences. Take off time 21.05hrs we set out over the North Sea. Crossing over the northern tip of Denmark, to the north we could see the lights of Stockholm with one or two searchlights wafting about, accompanied by a few bursts of flak. I think they were warning us to keep clear although, I knew that some of our aircraft had wandered into Swedish neutral airspace. Continuing on over the Baltic we began to gain height in preparation to attack. Not many searchlights about with a moderate amount of flak, we bombed and turned away dropping very quickly down to almost sea level for our flight back home. Uneventful trip back to base after an eight-and-a-half-hour flight. It seemed as though the tactics employed on that raid were successful, with Stettin being very badly damaged. Unfortunately, our squadron lost one aircraft, crashing in Denmark on the return flight. Five aircraft were lost on that raid."

18/08/1944 LL635 JI-M Bombing Bremen   21.41   00.15   02.40

Bomb load 1 x 2000 HC, 96 x 30 lb incendiaries, 810 x 4 lb incendiaries, 90 x 4 lb incendiaries. Primary target: Bremen. Weather clear over target. Bombed at 00.15 hours from 17,500 feet red T.I.s. T.I.s well concentrated. Long rows of fires burning. Excellent concentrated attack.

F/Sgt. Geoffrey Payne - 2014. "19th August 1944. Night operation to Bremen. Very heavily defended and reports indicate that this raid on Bremen was the most devastating of the war. Uneventful trip.

21st August 1944: Converted to Lancaster Mk IIIs. Merlin engines."

25/08/1944 LL635 JI-M Bombing Vincly 18.32 20.35 22.03

Bomb load 11 x 1000 MC, 2 x 500 GP MK IV, 2 x 500 GP MK IV, LD. Primary target: Vincly. Weather - cloud patches. Bombed at 20.35 hours from 15,000 feet, visual of G.H. Leader. Damaged by flak over target, no injuries. Severely damaged and declared a write-off at base.

26/08/1944 PB423 JI-S Bombing Kiel   20.08   23.20   02.01

Bomb load 1 x 4000 HC, 96 x 30 lb, 900 x 4 lb. Primary target: Kiel. Weather clear. Bombed at 23.20 hours from 19,000 feet, centre of red T.I.s and fires. Plenty of fires.

F/Sgt. Geoffrey Payne - 2014. "26/27 August 1944. Night attack on Kiel."

05/09/1944 LL731 JI-U Bombing Le Havre   17.30   19.24   20.49

Bomb load 11 x 1000 MC, 4 x 500 GP. Primary target: Le Havre. Weather clear. Bombed at 19.24 hours from 13,500 feet and 19.28 hours from 13,500 red T.I.s on second run up owing to hang up of 2 x 1000.

F/Sgt. Geoffrey Payne - 2014. "6th September 1944. Operations Le-Havre. German fortifications and transport."

20/09/1944 LM728 JI-U Bombing Calais 14.54 16.02   17.40

Bomb load 11 x 1000 MC, 4 x 500 GP. Primary target: Calais. Weather clear

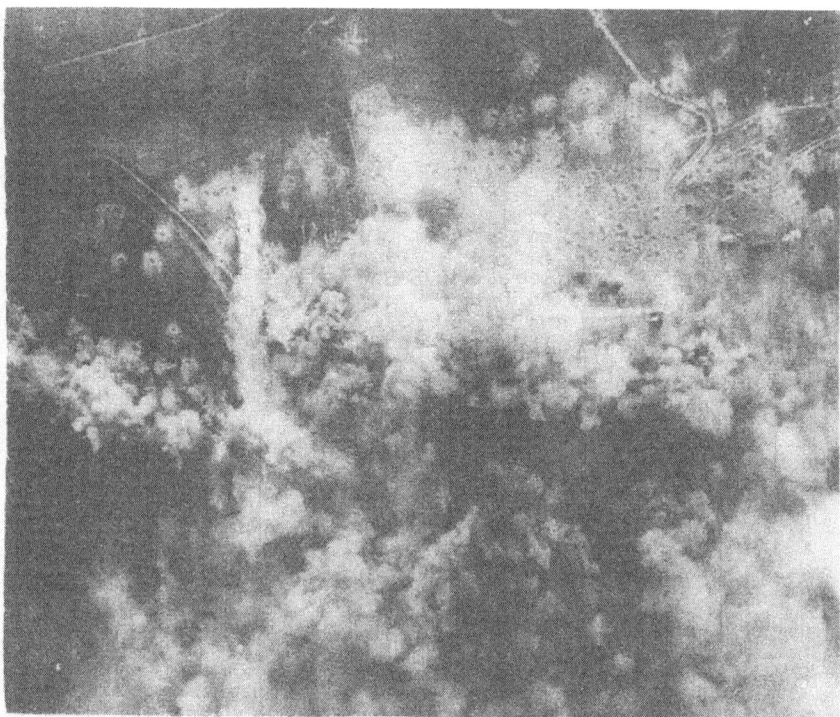

Under the pall of smoke lie heavily defended positions four miles West of Calais. The picture was taken during R.A.F. Bomber Command's attack on 20.9.1944 when large forces of Lancasters and Halifaxes bombarded Calais for nearly two and a half hours. Two aircraft can be seen flying over the target. The craters at the top of the photograph were caused by bombs dropped from aircraft in the opening stages of the attack. (Picture issued September 1944).

(British Official Photograph No. CL. 1200. Crown Copyright, courtesy of F/Sgt Geoffery Payne.

over target. Bombed at 1602½ hours from 3,500 feet red T.I.

F/Sgt. Geoffrey Payne - 2014. "20th September 1944. Operations Calais enemy troop concentrations."

Picture shows: -

23/09/1944 LM728JI-U Bombing Neuss 19.31 21.26 23.13

Bomb load 4 x 1000 ANM59, 7 x 1000 ANM44, 3 x 500 GP. Weather 10/10ths cloud over target, tops 8/10,000 feet. Bombed at 21.26 hours from 20,000 feet. Overshot slightly on green T.I.

F/Sgt. Geoffrey Payne - 2014 "23/24 September 1944. Night attack on Neuss (Ruhr). Heavily defended."

25/09/1944 LM728JI-U Bombing Pas de Calais 08.16 10.50

Bomb load 11 x 1000 MC, 4 x 500 GP. Primary target: Calais. Primary target: Calais. Abandoned on Master Bomber's orders. Jettisoned 4 x 1000

MC.

F/Sgt. Geoffrey Payne - 2014 "25th September 1944. Operations Calais enemy troop positions. "Sgt Francis and myself lived in the same billet while we were both recovering from frostbite and we developed a great friendship, Dennis Young broke his wrist and did not operate after his 23rd operation. Sgt. Frances took over from Dennis Young as M/U gunner and did 7

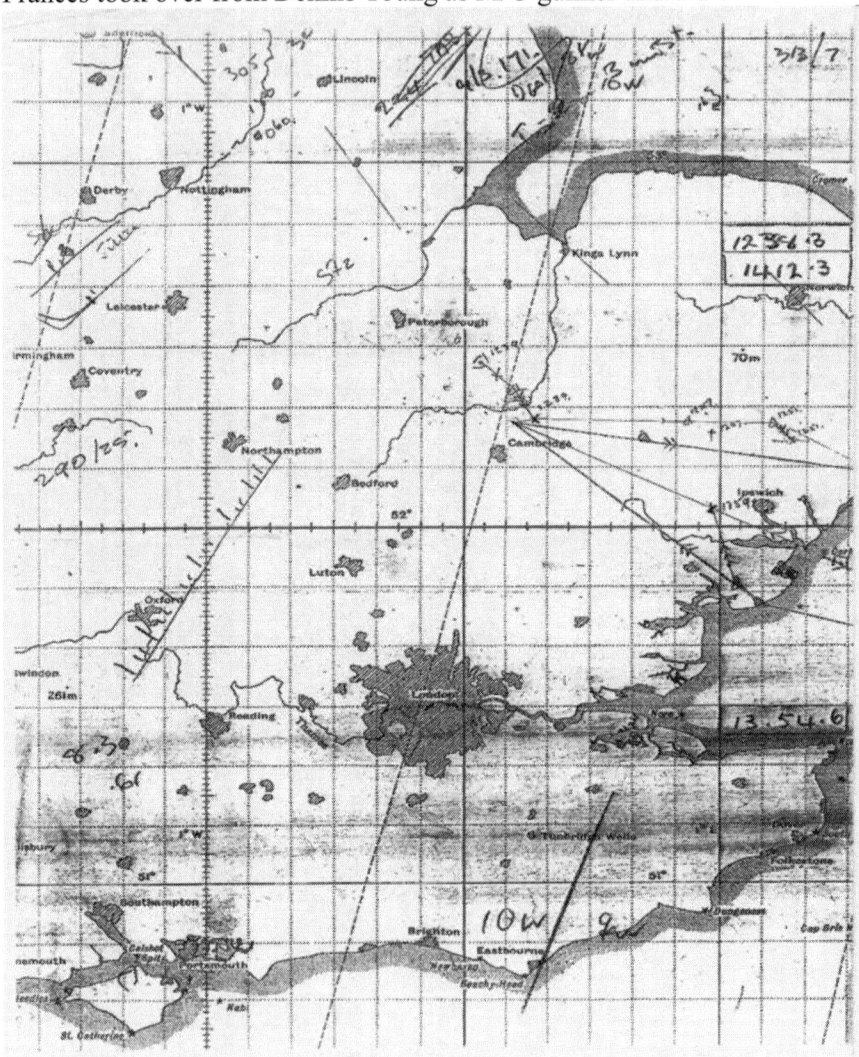

Image courtesy of F/S. G. Payne – 2014
F/L. Nye Navigation Plot – Westkapelle 3/10/1944

Image courtesy of F/S. G. Payne – 2014
F/L. Nye Navigation Plot – Westkapelle 3/10/1944

135

operations to complete Cossens crew's tour of operations."

26/09/1944 LM728 JI-U Bombing Calais 11.28 12.46 14.01

Bomb load 11 x 1000 MC, 4 x 500 GP. Primary target: Calais. Bomb load 11 x 1000 MC, 4 x 500 GP. Primary target: Calais 7D. Weather clear below cloud which was 3,500 feet. Bombed at 12.46 hours from 3700 ft on red T.I.

F/Sgt. Geoffrey Payne - 2014. "26th September 1944. Operations Cap Gris Nez enemy troop concentrations."

28/09/1944 LM728 JI-U Bombing Calais 07.58 09.21 10.34

Bomb load 11 x 1000 MC, 4 x 500 GP. Primary target: Calais 19. Bombed at 09.21 hours from 9,500 feet red T.I.

F/Sgt. Geoffrey Payne - 2014. "28th September 1944. Operations Calais enemy troop concentrations."

03/10/1944 LM728 JI-U Bombing Westkapelle 12.07 13.22 14.17

Bomb load 1 x 4000 MC, 6 x 1000 MC, 1 x 500 GP long delay. Primary target: Westkapelle. Weather patchy-scattered cloud with base 5000 feet. Bombed at 13.22 hours from 6,000 feet visually.

F/Sgt. Geoffrey Payne - 2014. "3rd October 1944. Daylight operation to Westkapelle. The target shown was the Dutch island of Walcheren at the approaches to the port of Antwerp on the River Scheldt. We were informed that the target was strategically important as the Germans were denying the Allies the use of the port of Antwerp and was required for the supply of material for our advancing armies. The object of the raid was to breach the dykes and to flood the island purposely to neutralise the German forces established there.

I was feeling rather disturbed that we were going to flood vast tracts of land that had taken years to establish and concern for the population who had suffered four years of hardship and deprivation during the German occupation. Take-off time was 12.07hrs. Reaching our rendezvous point there seemed to be hundreds of four engined aircraft converging before heading out over the North Sea. Dropping down to our bombing height we approached our target and dropped our 8000 lb bomb which according to our bomb aimer, got a direct hit on the dyke. Passing over the target I saw that the dyke had been breached with the sea gushing through the gaps."

"Due to the concentration of German forces on the island there was an enormous amount of light and heavy flak as we turned for home, however it was thankful that no enemy fighters were seen over the target area but we still had to keep a watchful eye open as there were many enemy fighter airfields in Holland. Back at base after a two-and-a-half-hour flight, after "interrogation" we repaired to our mess for a meal and a pint to celebrate our Mid-uppers 20th birthday. Sometime later I was to learn that my best friend, a Marine, was killed during the assault on the island of Walcheren at Westkapelle. They attacked through the breaches that we had made in the dyke."

Breaching the Dyke at Westkapelle
Westkapelle 3/10/1944 (courtesy F/S. G. Payne - 2014)

05/10/1944 LM728 JI-U Bombing Saarbrucken 17.25 22.50

Bomb load 11 x 1000 MC, 1 x 500 GP, 3 x 500 GP Long Delay. Abandoned mission on instructions from Master Bomber heard to say they were unable to locate target and called "Abandon Mission - our troops in vicinity". Jettisoned 4 x 500 GP at position 5230N 0226E at 22.22 hours from 4,000 feet. Remainder brought back.

F/Sgt. Geoffrey Payne - 2014. "5/6th October 1944. Night operation to Saabrucken to attack marshalling yards and steelwork installations. This raid was at the request of General Patton in preparation for the American forces offensive along the Southern front, in an attempt to stem the flow of German reinforcements to that front. Heavy flak in the target area, no fighters seen."

07/10/1944 LM728 JI-U Bombing Emmerich 12.14 14.27 16.01

Bomb load 1 x 4000 H.C. 10 x No. 14 clusters, 4 x (150 x 4). Primary target: Emmerich. Weather clear with cloud at 13,000 feet. Bombed at 14.27 hours from 13,000 feet south of smoke as instructed by Master Bomber.

F/Sgt. Geoffrey Payne - 2014. "7th October 1944. Daylight operation to Emmerich, a German town on the border with Holland. Synthetic oil installations and German supply were to be attacked. It was the first time that we had been ordered to fly in formation, our two sister squadrons, 115 ahead and 75 New Zealand Squadron behind us. Other groups and squadrons had made similar arrangements. As we neared the German/Dutch border very accurate flak opened up which immediately dispersed the bomber stream. The lead Lancaster of 75 Squadron, who was following us, took a direct hit and completely disintegrated, the wreckage slowly drifting to earth. A very disconcerting sight."

"Clear skies over the target which we bombed on the PFF flares, but as we closed our bomb door, an enormous crump shook our aircraft and shrapnel

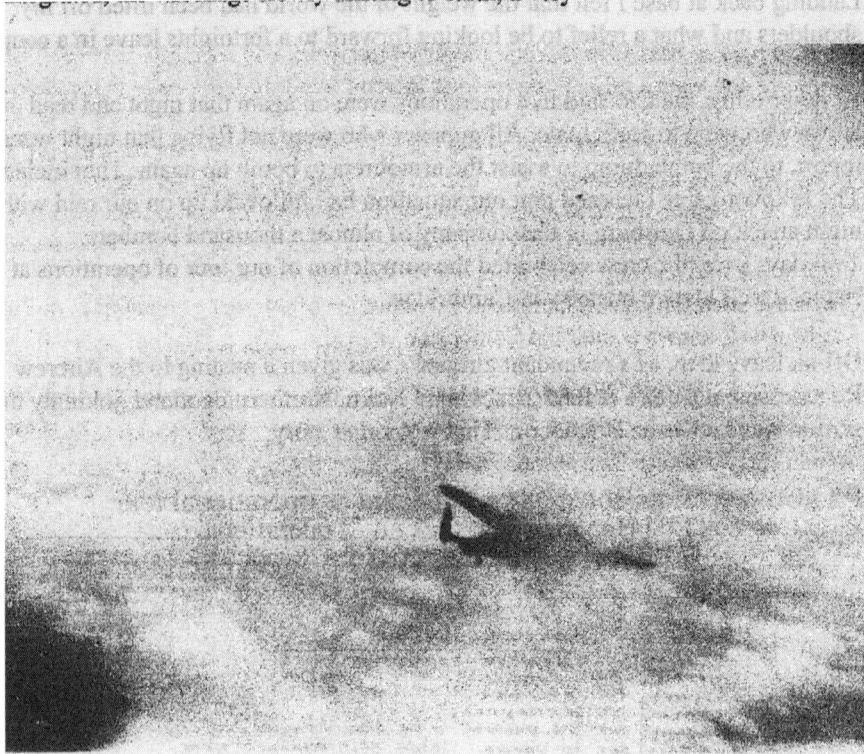

75 (NZ) Squadron Lancaster taking a direct hit.
(courtesy F/S. G. Payne - 2014)

rattled along the fuselage, putting my turret and Mid-uppers out of action. The hydraulics had been severed somewhere leaving us to operate our turrets by hand, not a good position to be in, although we were supposed to have an escort of Mosquitos. Arriving back at base there was some concern that we would be unable to activate the undercarriage, owing to the problem with the hydraulic. However, the undercarriage dropped down perfectly. We delivered U for Uncle to the hanger for repair and said a fond farewell to the lady. That was my 29th operation and keeping my fingers crossed that number 30 would be an easy one."

14/10/1944 LM728 JI-U Bombing Duisburg   07.14   09.06   10.43

Bomb load 11 x 1000 MC, 4 x 500 GP Long Delay. Primary target: Duisburg. Weather patchy cloud with gaps for bombing. Bombed at 09.06 hours from 19,000 feet Red T.I. in centre of built up area.

F/Sgt. Geoffrey Payne - 2014. "14th October 1944. Briefing 05.00 hrs. Taken aback when the target was revealed, a daylight attack on the Ruhr town of Duisburg, one of the most heavily defended areas in Germany, dangerous enough at night. This is me going out with a bang one way or another. As we were to have a fighter escort, the flight out was uneventful until we were approaching the target area. There were nearly a thousand heavy bombers converging towards, then passing through what seemed to be a black-haze intermingled with deep red flashes of exploding flak shells. As we dropped our bombs, I looked down to see the fires and the ground erupting, a truly awesome site. Soon we were out of the Ruhr defences heading back to Waterbeach feeling slightly more relaxed but still scanning the skies for the unexpected fighter to jump us. Landing back at base I felt that the weight of the world had been lifted off my shoulders and what a relief to be looking forward to a fortnight's leave in a couple of days' time. At de-briefing, the C/O said that operations were on again that night and read out the crews who were to participate. All gunners who were not flying that night were to report, to the bomb dump to assist the armourers to bomb up again. That included me. The following day I learned that our squadron had followed up on our raid with a night attack on Duisburg in the company of almost a thousand bombers. Two days later, the crew celebrated the completion of our tour of operations at The Eagle, a well-known hostelry in Cambridge.
Off on leave then, as a redundant airman, I was given a posting to the Aircrew Reassessment Centre at RAF Brackla by Nairn, Northern Scotland. Jokingly this station was known as Brigadoon."

"But that is another story!"

F/Sgt. Geoffrey Payne other operations.
Source – F/Sgt. Geoffrey Payne - 2014

115 Squadron Witchford operations

P/O. Speirenburg Flying Time
Augsburg   7.30 hrs   Night

F/O. Martin Flying Time
Stuttgart 6.30 hrs   Night
Air Sea Rescue   5.20 hrs   Daylight
Frankfurt   5.30 hrs   Night
Frankfurt   6.10 hrs   Night

514 Squadron RAF Waterbeach other operations

F/Sgt Whitwood Flying Time (see at § F/O. J.A. Whitwood)
Vaires   4.45 hrs   Night
Nucourt 3.40 hrs   Daylight

P/O. William McDill Coyle, DFC.

183028 (1374928)   P/O. William McDill "Bill" Coyle, DFC Pilot.
   F/S. L. John Boffin.   A/Bomber.
A422170 W/O.Douglas Frederick George Gray, RAAF   Navigator.
   Sgt. J.E. Parker.   WOP/AG. 3 ops.
18964 (1504777) Sgt. Colin Pratt.   WOP/AG. 1 op.
636773   W/O. George Beadle Stratford, DFC   WOP/AG. 25 ops.
   F/S. W. Harry Fuller.   MU/Gunner.
R184009 W/O.G.C. "Moe" MacPhee, RCAF R/Gunner.
   Sgt. William James "Curly" Watts. F/Engineer.
186502 (1128949)   P/O. Alfred William Tasker. 2nd Pilot. 11/12/1944

09/08/1944 DS826 A2-C Bombing Fort d'Englos 21.52 23.20   00.36
   Bomb load 13 x 1000 MC. Primary target: Fort d'Englos (Lille), Petrol
dump. Weather clear, bombed at 23.20 hours, 13,100 feet, yellow and green
T.I.s. Master Bomber changed bombing instructions four times between pilot
getting visual of large black building and actual release of bombs.
   Sgt. J.E. Parker was WOP/AG that day.
   The fort of Ennetières-en-Weppes, or "fort d'Englos" is one of a set of six
forts surrounding Lille.

From left: "Bill" Coyle, John Boffin, Douglas Gray, George Stratford, "Moe" MacPhee, Harry Fuller, "Curly" Watts.

18/08/1944 LL726 A2-H Bombing Bremen 21.34 00.15 02.43

Bomb load 1 x 8000 HC, 40 x 30 inc., 350 x 4, 40 x 4 inc. Primary target: Bremen. Weather clear. Bombed at 00.15 hours 18,000 feet. Centre of red T.I.s. Searchlights very accurate, but did not seem to hold. Bombing concentrated.

Sgt. J.E. Parker was WOP/AG that day.

26/08/1944 LL666 A2-K Bombing Kiel 20.25 23.15 02.00

Bomb load 1 x 8000 HC, 180 x 4lb. Primary target: Kiel. Weather clear. Bombed at 23.15 hours from 17,800 feet red T.I.s. Bombing well concentrated round T.I.s.

Sgt. Colin Pratt was WOP/AG that day

31/08/1944 LL666 A2-K Bombing Pont-Remy 16.14 18.11 19.50

Bomb load 11 x 1000 MC, 2 x 500 GP Mk IV LD. Primary target: Pont Remy, Dump. Weather cloudy. Bombed at 18.11 hours from 15,000 feet on visual of target.

Sgt. J.E. Parker was WOP/AG that day.

06/09/1944 LL666 A2-K Bombing Le Havre 16.44 18.40 20.04

Bomb load 11 x 1000 MC, 4 x 500 GP. Primary target: Le Havre. Bombed at 18.40 hours from 7,300 feet red T.I.s.

10/09/1944 LL666 A2-K Bombing Le Havre 15.55 17.39 19.15

Bomb load 11 x 1000 MC, 4 x 500 GP. Primary target: Le Havre. Bomb load 11 x 1000 MC, 4 x 500 GP. Primary target: Le Havre. Weather clear. Bombed at 17.39 hours from 11,000 feet. Undershot red T.I.s by 150 yards.

12/09/1944 LL666 A2-K Bombing Frankfurt 18.47 23.06 01.31

Bomb load 1 x 1000 MC, 16 x 500 Clusters 4lb. Primary target: Frankfurt - Main. Weather clear over the target. Bombed at 23.06 hours from 15,500 feet on red and green T.I.s. Had combat with an enemy aircraft.

17/09/1944 LL666 A2-K Bombing Boulogne 10.58 13.50

Bomb load 11 x 1000 MC, 4 x 500 GP. Bomb load 11 x 1000 MC, 4 x 500 GP. Primary target: Boulogne Aiming Point 2. Weather clear below cloud. Abortive sortie. At 12.15 hours order given by Master Bomber to abandon mission. Jettisoned 6 x 1000 MC, brought remainder back.

23/09/1944 LL666 A2-K Bombing Neuss 19.32 21.34 23.41

Bomb load 8 x 1000 ANM59, 3 x 1000 ANM44, 3 x 500 GP. Primary target: Neuss. Weather 10/10ths cloud over target, tops 8/10,000 feet. Bombed at 21.34 hours from 17,400 feet on centre of dull red glow.

26/09/1944 LM286 A2-F Bombing Calais 11.30 12.44 14.00

Bomb load 11 x 1000 MC, 4 x 500 GP. Primary target: Calais 7D. Weather clear below cloud which was 3,500 feet. Bombed at 12.44 hours from 3000 feet on red T.I.

28/09/1944 PD333 A2-K Bombing Calais 08.04 10.49

Bomb load 11 x 1000 MC, 4 x 500 GP. Primary target: Calais 19. Abortive sortie. At 09.28 hours Master Bomber gave abandon mission. Jettisoned 5 x 1000 MC.

07/10/1944 PB423 JI-Z Bombing Emmerich 12.31 14.28 15.57

Bomb load 1 x 4000 HC, 1 x No. 14 Clusters, 4 x (150 x 4). Primary target: Emmerich. Weather clear with cloud at 13,000 feet. Bombed at 14.28 hours from 12,900 feet to the West of a large pall of smoke.

14/10/1944 PD333 A2-K Bombing Duisburg 06.48 09.06 11.31

Bomb load 11 x 1000 MC, 4 x 500 GP Long Delay. Primary target: Duisburg. Weather patchy cloud with gaps for bombing. Bombed at 09.06 hours from 19,000 feet. Built up area about 2 miles North-east of Docks.

14/10/1944 PD333 A2-K Bombing Duisburg 22.58 01.28 03.32

Bomb load 11 x 1000 MC, 4 x 500 GP Long Delay. Primary target: Duisburg. Weather was clear with small amount of cloud over the target. Bombed at 01.28 hours from 20,500 feet. Centre of mixed red and green T.I.s.

15/10/1944 PD333 A2-K Bombing Wilhelmshaven   17.08 19.48
21.35

Bomb load 11 x 1000 MC, 4 x 500 GP. Primary target: Wilhelmshaven. Weather haze and thin cloud at first with thick cloud later. Bombed at 19.48 hours from 17,000 feet. Red and Green T.I.s.

23/10/1944 PD333 A2-K Bombing Essen 17.02 19.40 21.34

Bomb load 1 x 4000 HC, 6 x 1000 MC, 6 x 500 GP. Primary target: Essen. Weather 10/10ths cloud over target - tops 12/14,000 feet with most appalling weather on route. Bombed at 19.40 hours from 18,200 feet. Green flares.

25/10/1944 PD333 A2-K Bombing Essen 13.15 15.48 17.20

Bomb load 1 x 4000 HC, 10 x No. 14 Clusters, 4 x 150 x 4. Primary target: Essen. Weather over target 10/10ths low cloud, with one clear patch which appeared to fill up later in the attack. Bombed at 15.48 hours from 20,000 feet. Red flares - 2 seconds overshot.

28/10/1944 PD333 A2-K Bombing Flushing 08.57 10.16 11.12

Bomb load 1 x 4000 HC, 6 x 1000 MC, 4 x 500 GP. Primary target:

Flushing. Weather over the target quite clear and conditions perfect, although believed to be only local, and some low cloud approaching. Bombed at 10.16 hours from 8,000 feet. Visual.

29/10/1944 PD333 A2-K Bombing Flushing 09.58   11.36   12.28
Bomb load 11 x 1000 ANM59, 4 x 500 GP. Primary target: Flushing, Gun installations. Weather clear over target. Bombed at 11.36 hours from 6.000 feet, slightly to starboard of Red T.I.s as instructed.

30/10/1944 PD333 A2-K Bombing Wesseling 09.21 12.01   13.55
Bomb load 1 x 4000 HC, 12 x 500 GP. Primary target: Wesseling. Weather was 10/10ths cloud - tops about 7,000 feet. Bombed at 12.01 hours from 17,500 feet on release of G.H. leader.

27/11/1944 PD333 A2-K Bombing Cologne 12.2915.05 16.54
Bomb load 1 x 4000 HC, 13 x 500 GP, 2 x 500 MC. Primary target: Cologne, Marshalling Yards. Weather patchy cloud. Bombed at 15.05 hours from 21,400 feet on Marshalling Yards.

29/11/1944 PD333 A2-K Bombing Neuss 03.00   05.37   07.19
Bomb load 1 x 4000 HC, 6 x 1000 MC, 6 x 500 GP, 3 Red/Green flares. Primary target: Neuss. Weather 10/10ths cloud over target but the glow of fires was seen through cloud. Bombed at 05.37 hours from 20,000 feet. Upwind edge of Red and Green sky markers. Believed good attack.

02/12/1944 PD333 A2-K Bombing Dortmund 13.00 14.56   16.58
Bomb load 14 x 1000 HC. Primary target: Dortmund, Benzol plant. Weather 10/10ths cloud. Bombed at 14.56 hours from 20,000 feet on leading aircraft. Aircraft hit by flak - tail plane and fuselage damaged.

05/12/1944 PD324 A2-B Bombing Hamm   08.52   11.30   13.54
Bomb load 1 x 4000 HC, 2 x 500 MC, 12 x 500 GP, 2 x 500 GP Long Delay. Primary target: Hamm. Weather 10/10ths cloud over target, but otherwise varying from 6-10/10ths. Bombed at 11.30 hours from 20,000 feet on G.H. Leader.

06/12/1944 PD324 A2-B Bombing Merseburg 16.58 20.48 00.03
Bomb load 1 x 4000 HC, 8 x 500 GP, 1 x 500 GP Long Delay. Primary target: Merseburg. Weather 10/10ths cloud with odd breaks. Bombed at 20.48 hours from 20,000 feet on upwind edge of sky markers.

08/12/1944 PD324 A2-B Bombing Duisburg 08.39   11.04   12.43
Bomb load 14 x 1000 MC. Primary target: Duisberg. Weather 10/10ths cloud. Bombed at 11.04 hours from 20,000 feet on G.H. Leader.

11/12/1944 PA186 A2-G Bombing Osterfeld 08.46   11.05   12.52
Bomb load 1 x 4000 HC, 13 x 500 GP, 2 x 500 MC. Primary target: Osterfeld. Weather 10/10ths cloud, tops 16,000 feet. Bombed at 11.05 hours from 20,000 feet on G.H. Leader.

P/O. A.W. Tasker was 2nd Pilot that day.

16/12/1944 NG298 A2-K Bombing Siegen   11.33   14.59   17.01
Bomb load 1 x 4000 HC, 5 x 1000 MC, 7 x 500 GP. Primary target: Siegen. Weather very bad on route with icing and cloud. Bombed at 14.59 hours from

17,500 feet on G.H. Leader. Aircraft hit by flak. Elevator smashed. M/U Turret damaged.

21/12/1944 NG142 A2-C Bombing Trier 12.17 15.00 16.48

Bomb load 1 x 4000 HC, 10 x 500 GP, 8 x 250 GP. Primary target: Trier, Marshalling yards. Weather 10/10 cloud, tops 6/9000 feet. Bombed at 15.00 hours from 18,000 feet on leading aircraft.

S/L. Ernest Brazier Cozens, DFC.

J16010   S/L. Ernest Brazier Cozens, DFC RCAF. Pilot.

J17715   F/O. Paul Shaughnessy, DFC RCAF. A/Bomber.

J17977   F/O. James Murray Phillip O'Brien, DFC RCAF. Navigator.

J19331   F/O. John McCrindle, DFC RCAF. WOP/AG.

J85630   F/O. J.H. Rothwell, RCAF.   MU/Gunner.

R133293 W/O. J.S. Hatton, RCAF.   R/Gunner.

147694 (1295209)   F/O. William Jack Humphries, DFC. F/Engineer.

J10781   F/L. E.S. "Ted" Henderson, RCAF. 2nd Pilot 03/02/1945

185226 (1482503)

P/O. Holman Gordon Stanley Kerr, RCAF 2nd Pilot 13&16/02/1945

J37983   F/O. William Mark Wiseman, RCAF 2nd Pilot 04/04/1945

Passengers 04/05/1945, 09/05/1945

30/11/1944 PD389 JI-Q Bombing Osterfeld 10.55 13.09 14.36

Bomb load 1 x 4000 HC, 15 x 500 GP, 1 Red/Green flare. Primary target: Osterfeld, Coking plant. Weather 10/10ths cloud. Bombed at 13.09 hours from 20,000 feet on G.H.

S/L. E.B. Cozens flew the mission as 2nd Pilot with F/O. H.L. Merrett crew.

04/12/1944 LM734 JI-U Bombing Oberhausen 11.54 14.09 15.56

Bomb load 1 x 4000 HC, 6 x 1000 MC, 6 x 500 GP. Primary target: Oberhausen, Built up area. Weather 10/10ths cloud. Bombed at 14.09 hours from 20,000 feet on leading G.H. aircraft.

05/12/1944 LM734 JI-U Bombing Hamm   09.03 11.29 13.50

Bomb load 1 x 4000 HC, 1950 x 4 lb incendiaries. Primary target: Hamm. Weather 10/10ths cloud over target, but otherwise varying from 6-10/10ths. Bombed at 11.29 hours from 20,000 feet on G.H. Leader.

06/12/1944 LM734 JI-U Bombing Merseburg 17.05 20.56 00.55

Bomb load 1 x 4000 HC, 8 x 500 GP, 1 x 500 GP Long Delay. Primary target: Merseburg. Weather 10/10ths cloud with odd breaks. Bombed at 20.56 hours from 20,000 feet on Red/Green flares.

16/12/1944 ME336 A2-F Bombing Siegen   11.34 15.00 16.58

Bomb load 1 x 4000 HC, 14 x No. 14 Clusters. Primary target: Siegen. Weather very bad on route with icing and cloud. Bombed at 15.00 hours from

18,000 feet on leading aircraft.

01/01/1945 NG142 A2-C   Bombing Vohwinkle   16.17   19.44   21.46

Bomb load 1 x 4000 HC, 12 x 500 ANM58, 2 x 500 GP. Primary target: Vohwinkel. Weather clear. Bombed at 19.44 hours from 20,000 feet. Red and Green T.I.s.

07/01/1945 PA186 A2-G   Bombing Munich   19.23   22.47   02.55

Bomb load 1 x 4000 HC, 7 x 500 clusters. Primary target: Munich. Weather 10/10ths cloud over target 6-8,000 feet with a thin layer altitude 16,000 feet. Bombed at 22.47 hours from 20,000 feet on centre of Red glow.

03/02/1945 PA186 A2-G   Bombing Dortmund-Huckarde   16.28   19.46   21.48

Bomb load 1 x 4000 HC, 2 x 500 MC, 2 x 500 MC L/Delay, 6 x 500 ANM64, 2 x 500 GP, 3 x 250 GP. Primary target: Dortmund-Huckarde, Coking plant. Weather clear with slight haze. Bombed at 19.46 hours from 20,000 feet on red T.I.s. Bombing concentrated markers. Starboard flap damaged by heavy flak.

F/L. E.S. Henderson, RCAF was 2nd Pilot that day.

08/02/1945 PB419 A2-B   Bombing Hohenbudberg 03.36   06.28   08.12

Bomb load 1 x 4000 HC, 2 x 500 MC, 4 x 250 GP, 4 x 500 GP, 6 x 500 ANM64. Primary target: Hohenbudberg, Marshalling yards. Weather 8/10ths cloud over target. Bombed at 06.28 hours from 19,000 feet on Red T.I.s.
Severe icing encountered.

13/02/1945 PB419 A2-B   Bombing Dresden 22.00 01.31   07.53

Bomb load 1 x 400 MC, 15 x No. 14 Clusters. Primary target: Dresden. Weather 5/10ths cloud over target. Bombed at 01.31 hours from 20,000 feet on Red T.I.s.

P/O. Holman Gordon Stanley Kerr, RCAF was 2nd Pilot that day.

14/02/1945 PB419 A2-B   Bombing Chemnitz 20.30   00.32   04.25

Bomb load 1 x 500 MC, 15 x No. 14 Clusters. Primary target: Chemnitz. Weather 8-10/10ths cloud, tops 15-16,000 feet with occasional breaks. Bombed at 00.32 hours from 19,500 feet on H2S per Master Bomber's instructions.

16/02/1945 PB419 A2-B   Bombing Wesel   12.35   16.01   17.52

Bomb load 1 x 4000 HC, 4 x 500 GP, 2 x 500 MC L/Delay, 4 x 250 GP, 6 x 500 ANM64. Primary target: Wesel. Weather clear. Bombed at 16.01 hours from 20,000 feet on G.H. Leader.

P/O. Holman Gordon Stanley Kerr, RCAF was 2nd Pilot that day.

23/02/1945 NN717 A2-E   Bombing Gelsenkirchen 11.13 15.01   18.14

Bomb load 1 x 4000 HC, 9 x 500 ANM64, 2 x 500 MC, 4 x 250 GP. Primary target: Gelsenkirchen. Weather 10/10ths cloud. Bombed at 15.01 hours from 20,000 feet on G.H. Leader. On return landed at Chipping Ongar.

12/03/1945 PD389 A2-J Bombing Dortmund 13.02 16.56   18.53

Bomb load 1 x 4000 HC, 13 x 500 ANM64. Primary target: Dortmund. Weather 10/10ths cloud over target, tops 6/10,000 feet. Bombed at 16.56 hours from 19,000 feet on G.H. Leader.

27/03/1945 NN781 A2-B   Bombing Hamm Sachsen   10.32   14.03
16.04

Bomb load 1 x 4000 HC, 13 x 500 ANM64, 2 x 500 MC. Primary target: Hamm Sachsen, Benzol plant. Weather 10/10ths cloud. Bombed on G.H. Leader at 14.03 hours at 18,500 feet.

04/04/1945 NN781 A2-B   Bombing Merseburg (Leuna) 18.43 22.38
03.12

Weather 5-10/10ths cloud, and 10/10ths over Merseburg. Target not attacked. Bomb load 1 x 4000 HC, 6 x 500 ANM64 brought back. Arrived at 22.38, orbited as no markers were down - saw skymarkers go down at 22.45 by the time we got on correct heading they had disappeared. Accurately engaged by intense flak we had to take evasive action after which there were no markers visible. Decided to bring bombs back owing to proximity of bomb line. Second bombing run at approx 23.05.

F/O. William Mark Wiseman, RCAF was 2nd Pilot that day.

13/04/1945 NG118 A2-H   Bombing Kiel   20.10 23.31   02.15

Bomb load 18 x 500 ANM64. Primary target: Kiel, Docks and ship yards. Weather 10/10ths cloud low and thin. Bombed centre of Green T.I.s (emergency bomb sights) at 23.31 from 20,000ft. Marking concentrated. Bombing appeared good. Mark (XIV) Bomb sight U/S. Believed good attack, orbited in target area having arrived too early.

24/04/1945 NN781 A2-B   Bombing Bad Oldesloe 07.03 10.43   12.51

Bomb load 6 x 1000 ANM65, 10 x 500 ANM 64. Primary target: Bad-Oldesloe, Rail and road junction and Marshalling Yards. Weather 3/10ths to nil cloud. Bombed on G.H. leader 514/S. at 1043 hours from 18,000ft. Southern part of target covered with smoke - bomb bursts in the built up area. Good formation both squadrons and group. Should be an OK attack. Two red explosions burning red afterwards, 10.45 hrs.

01/05/1945 NN781 A2-B   Manna The Hague 13.07 14.20   15.26

Weather clear over target. Dropped 5 Panniers on Red T.I. and White Cross. Crowds in Grandstand gave good welcome. Target easy to identify.

04/05/1945 NN781 A2-B   Manna The Hague 12.06 13.24   14.36

Dropping area The Hague. 5 Panniers dropped on White Cross. Clear. 5148 N 0418 E notice in large letters "TABAC S.V.P.".

No Rear Gunner that day.

Passenger Cpl. Gottinson.

09/05/1945 NN781 A2-B   Exodus Juvincourt - Dunsfold 07.34   x 12.57

Outward 1.35 hours. Collected 24 ex POWs. Homeward 1.50 hours. Organisation good.

No Bomb aimer that day.

Passenger S/L. H.F. Cronin.

11/05/1945 ME425 A2-L   Exodus Juvincourt - Wing   7.19 x 22.32

Duration 3.30. Outward 1.50 hours. Collected 24 ex POWs. Homeward 1.40

hours. Landing by Flying control at Wing very slow.

14/05/1945 NN781 A2-B   Exodus Juvincourt - Oakley 10.00 x 11.40
Starboard inner u/s. Returned to Base.

17/05/1945 ME425 A2-L   Exodus Brussels - Westcott 10.03 x 15.47
Duration 3 hrs 27 mins. Out 1 hr 16 mins. 10 Belgian refugees taken to Brussels. 20 Ex POWs returned to Westcott. No troubles.

18/05/1945 RE117 A2-D   Exodus Brussels - Oakley   12.01 x 17.17
Duration 3 hrs 19 mins. Out 1 hr 16 mins. In 2 hrs 03 mins. 10 Belgian refugees taken to Brussels. 24 ex POWs. Returned to U.K. Everything O.K.

P/O. Donald Charles Cameron Crombie

A414654 P/O. Donald Charles Cameron "Don" Crombie, RAAF. Pilot.
137547 (1579731) F/O. Harry George Darby. A/Bomber.
1392000 F/S. Andy "Jock" McPhee.   Navigator.
642170 Sgt. Edward Leo Humes.   Navigator.   1 op.
1323748 Sgt. Morris Joseph Tyler.   WOP/AG.
1811733 Sgt. Edward William Jenner.   MU/Gunner. 2 ops.
1238470 Sgt. Geoffrey Clewlow, DFM.   MU/Gunner. 2 ops.
1134608 Sgt. Claude Charles Payne.   MU/Gunner. 10 ops.
1586017 Sgt. G.R. Hutton.   MU/Gunner. 2 ops.
1579675 Sgt. Harold Roy Hill.   R/Gunner.
1509891 Sgt. Bernard Peter "Ben" Le Neve Foster. F/Engineer.
51707 (570208) F/O. Howard Hall.   F/Engineer.   1 op.
1421544 Sgt. James "Jim" McGahey.   F/Engineer.   1 op.

16/12/1943 DS820 JI-R Bombing Berlin 16.49 20.06 00.13
Bomb load 1 x 2000, 40 x 30 incendiaries, 630 x 4 incendiaries. Primary target: Berlin. 10/10 cloud over target. Bombed at 20.06 at 18,500 feet. Flats appeared to be burning well below from fires seen through cloud. Returned on 3 engines. Good trip for the weather conditions. Had combat over Berlin with F.W.190 which was claimed as damaged. No damage to our aircraft. Landed at Downham Market.
Sgt. Edward William Jenner was MU/Gunner that day.

20/12/1943 DS818 JI-Q Bombing Frankfurt   17.30   19.49   22.36
Bomb load 1 x 4000, 48 x 30 incendiaries, 950 x 4 incendiaries, 100 x 4 incendiaries. Primary target: Frankfurt. 8/10 cloud. Route markers scattered, no real help. Good trip. No trouble. Good effort but rather scattered. Bombed target at 19.49 at 20,000 ft.
Sgt. Edward William Jenner was MU/Gunner that day.

24/12/1943 DS818 JI-Q Bombing Berlin 00.26 03.21
Bomb load 1 x 4000, 32 x 30, 450 x 4, 90 x 4 incendiaries. Primary target: Berlin. Sortie abandoned. Port inner engine overheating. Oil pressure drop.

Inter-com rear turret U/S. All bombs jettisoned.

Sgt. Geoffrey Clewlow, DFM was MU/Gunner that day.

01/01/1944 DS822 JI-T Bombing Berlin 00.33 03.19 07.48

Bomb load 1 x 2000, 40 x 30, 900 x 4 lbs. Incendiaries. Primary target: Berlin. There was 10/10 cloud with tops 15,000 feet. Bombed at 03.19 hours at 21,000 feet. No T.I.s. Two sky markers 7 miles apart. Vague red glow seen through cloud. Attack scattered.

Sgt. Edward Leo Humes was Navigator that day.

Sgt. Geoffrey Clewlow, DFM was MU/Gunner that day.

02/01/1944 DS822 JI-T Bombing Berlin 00.12 02.25

Bomb load 1 x 2000, 40 x 30, 900 x 4 lb incendiaries. Returned early. Bomb Aimer sick. Impossible to carry on. Load jettisoned.

14/01/1944 LL734 JI-S Bombing Brunswick 16.59 19.18 22.00

Bomb load 1 x 4000, 48 x 30 incendiaries. Primary target: Brunswick. There was 8-9/10 cloud. Bombed at 19.18 hours at 21,500 ft. Skymarkers appeared to be beyond T.I.s. Few fires developing. Route good. Photo attempted.

20/01/1944 DS823 JI-M Bombing Berlin 16.13 19.36 23.27

Bomb load 1 x 4000, 32 x 30, 540 x 4, 60 x 4 incendiaries. Primary target: Berlin. 10/10 cloud. Bombed at 19.36 from 23,000 feet. Bombed between clusters of sky markers. Skymarkers well concentrated.

21/01/1944 DS823 JI-M Bombing Magdeburg 19.55 23.32

Bomb load 1 x 4000, 720 x 4, 90 x 4, 960 x 30 incendiaries. Returned early. Rear turret oxygen failure. Rear Gunner semi-conscious, revived on losing height to 17,000 feet. Farthest point reached 5430N 0640E. 1 x 4000 bomb jettisoned. Incendiaries brought back to base.

27/01/1944 LL734 JI-S Bombing Berlin 17.56 20.36 02.08

Bomb load 1 x 8000 lb, bomb. Primary target: Berlin. There was 8/10 cloud. Bombed at 20.36 hours at 21,000 ft. Glow reflected through cloud. Quite uneventful trip. Route satisfactory. Attack should develop.

30/01/1944 LL734 JI-S Bombing Berlin 17.16 20.22 23.20

Bomb load 1 x 4000 lb bomb, 600 x 4, 90 x 4, 32 x 30 incendiaries. Primary target: Berlin. There was 10/10 cloud. Bombed at 20.22 hours at 22,000 ft. Target area ringed with fighter flares. Route markers well placed helpful. Moon quite bright, aircraft could be seen about two miles away.

15/02/1944 DS736 A2-D Bombing Berlin 17.48 21.33 00.30

Bomb load 1 x 4000 lbs bomb, 32 x 30, 540 x 4, 90 x 4 incendiaries. Primary target: Berlin. There was 10/10 cloud. Bombed at 21.33 hrs at 22,000 ft. About three lots of green ground markers seen just after bombing. Glow of several fires nicely concentrated seen through cloud. Markers well concentrated,

19/02/1944 LL734 JI-S Bombing Leipzig 23.53 03.55 06.29

Bomb load 1 x 4000 lbs bomb, 32 x 30, 510 x 4, 90 x 4 incendiaries. Primary target: Leipzig. There was 10/10 cloud. Bombed at 03.55 hours at 21,000 ft. Winds not as forecast, had to orbit over sea to fill in time. Good concentration of sky markers seen after leaving target.

01/03/1944 LL734 JI-S Bombing Stuttgart 23.46 03.17 07.31

Bomb load 1 x 4000 lb. bomb, 24 x 30, 600 x 4, 90 x 4 incendiaries. Primary target: Stuttgart. There was 9/10 cloud. Bombed at 03.17 hours at 21,000 feet. Good carpet of orange fires on target. Skymarkers well concentrated. Weak pulses. C giving false readings, no B pulse. Quiet trip. Route good.

Sgt. G.R. Hutton MU/Gunner was that day.

22/03/1944 LL645 JI-R Bombing Frankfurt   18.37 21.55 00.14

Bomb load 1 x 8000 lb bomb, 56 x 30 incendiaries. Primary target: Frankfurt. There was 6/10 cloud. Bombed at 21.55 hours from 22,000 feet. Good concentration of red T.I.s. Incendiary fires burning among concentration. Flak came through front perspex panel killing the Engineer Sgt. Bernard Peter Le Neve Foster.

26/03/1944 LL645 JI-R Bombing Essen 20.01 22.03 00.27

Bomb load 1 x 8000 lb bomb, 96 x 30 incendiaries. Primary target: Essen. There was 10/10 cloud over the target. Bombed at 22.03 hours from 21,000 feet. Decoy sky markers seen, red/green stars. Attack judging by glow seemed concentrated. Many cookies landing among the glow. Good route.

F/O. Howard Hall was F/Engineer and Sgt. G.R. Hutton MU/Gunner that day.

30/03/1944 DS836 JI-L Bombing Nuremburg 22.22

Bomb load 1 x 1000 lb bomb, 96 x 30, 810 x 4, 90 x 4 incendiaries. Aircraft missing.

Whilst approaching turning point on to final leg at 22,000 feet, intercepted by a night-fighter, probably that of Lt. Wilhelm Seuss of 11./NJG5 at 00.56 hours and coming down at Wulfershausen 9 km east of Bad Neustadt.

P/O. D.C.C. Crombie RAAF KIA, Sgt. J. McGahey KIA, F/S. A. McPhee PoW, P/O. H.G. Darby PoW, Sgt. M.J. Tyler KIA, Sgt. C.C. Payne KIA, Sgt. H.R. Hill KIA.

P/O. H.G. Darby was interned in Camp L1. PoW No. and F/S. A. McPhee in Camp L6/357, PoW No.3464.

Crew KIA are commemorated on the Runnymede Memorial

P/O. Donald Crome, DFC

186325 (1318539) P/O. Donald Crome, DFC.   Pilot.
J29677 (*) F/O. John Robert "Buck" Bennett, RCAF. A/Bomber.
R180349   W/O. M. Brickman, RCAF. Navigator.
Sgt. C.E. Robinson.   WOP/AG.
Sgt. Arthur Wilfred "Pip" Joyce.   MU/Gunner.
R197461   F/S. E.E. "Doc" Strathdee, RCAF. R/Gunner.
Sgt. P. Mann.   F/Engineer.

(*): incoherencies in ORBs about A/Bomber J.R. Bennett who is noted in
both Harland's and Crome's crew on 04 and 08/11/1944 at the same time.

Date Aircraft Duty Target   Up Drop Down
05/10/1944 LM724 JI-B Bombing Saarbrucken 17.06 22.44
   Bomb load 11 x 1000 MC, 1 x 500 GP, 3 x 500 GP long delay. Abandoned
mission on instructions from Master Bomber heard to say they were unable to
locate target and called "Abandon Mission - our troop in vicinity". 3 x 500 GP
Long delay jettisoned at 22.12 hours at 5220N 0236E from 8,000 feet.
   P/O. Donald Crome flew the mission as 2nd Pilot with S/L. P.B. Clay's
crew.
07/10/1944 LM724 JI-B Bombing Emmerich 12.07 14.30 16.19
   Bomb load 1 x 4000 HC, 10 x No. 14 Clusters, 4 x (150x4). Primary target:
Emmerich. Weather clear with cloud at 13,000 feet. Bombed at 14.30 hours
from 14,000 feet on centre of smoke. Master Bomber not heard.
14/10/1944 NG121 JI-H Bombing Duisburg   23.05 01.36 03.44
   Bomb load 11 x 1000 MC, 4 x 500 GP Long Delay. Primary target:
Duisburg. Weather was clear with small amount of cloud over the target.
Bombed at 01.36 hours from 20,000 feet. Centre of Green T.I.s.
15/10/1944 LM734 A2-C Bombing Wilhelmshaven 17.07 19.47
   22.01
   Bomb load 11 x 1000 MC, 4 x 500 GP. Primary target: Wilhelmshaven.
Weather haze and thin cloud at first with thick cloud later. Bombed at 19.47
hours from 17,000 feet. Bombed on H2S - no results seen.
19/10/1944 PD333 A2-K Bombing Stuttgart 17.33 20.38 23.14
   Bomb load 1 x 4000 HC, 3 x 500 Clusters, 7 x 150 x 4, 1 x 90 x 4lb. Primary
target: Stuttgart, A/P 'D' 1st attack. Weather 10/10ths cloud which broke to
6/10ths at the end of the period. Bombed at 20.38 hours from 16,000 feet.
Centre of mixed red and green T.I.s.
21/10/1944 ME841 JI-Y Bombing Flushing 10.42 12.29 13.47
   Bomb load 12 x 1000 MC, 2 x 500 GP. Primary target: Flushing 'B'. Weather
clear. Bombed at 12.29 hours from 9,000 feet. Visual.
23/10/1944 NG203 JI-A Bombing Essen 16.17 19.31 21.31
   Bomb load 1 x 4000 HC, 6 x 1000 MC, 6 x 500 GP. Primary target: Essen.

Weather 10/10ths cloud over target - tops 12/14,000 feet with most appalling weather on route. Bombed at 19.31 hours from 20,000 feet. Red T.I.s.

28/10/1944 NG118 A2-E Bombing Cologne 13.12 15.47 18.02

Bomb load 1 x 4000 HC, 12 x 500 lb. Clusters. 2 x 150 x 4. Primary target: Cologne. Weather clear over target. Bombed at 15.47 hours from 20,000 feet. Upward edge of smoke as instructed.

31/10/1944 LM733 JI-F Bombing Bottrop 11.50 15.00 16.35

Bomb load 1 x 4000 HC, 16 x 500 GP. Primary target: Bottrop, Synth. Oil plants. Weather 10/10ths cloud over target. Bombed at 15.00 hours from 16,500 feet on G.H. Leader.

04/11/1944 NG203 JI-A Bombing Solingen 11.33 13.18

Bomb load 1 x 4000 HC, 14 x 500 Clusters. Primary target: Solingen. Weather 8-10/10ths cloud. Abortive sortie. Returned early with CSU control cable broken.

08/11/1944 NG203 JI-A Bombing Homberg 07.55 10.32 12.27

Bomb load 1 x 4000 HC, 14 x No. 14 Clusters. Primary target: Homberg. Weather clear. Bombed at 10.32 hours from 16,500 feet. Visually.

27/11/1944 NG203 JI-A Bombing Cologne 12.19 15.04 16.52

Bomb load 1 x 4000 HC, 16 x 500 GP. Primary target: Cologne, Marshalling Yards. Weather patchy cloud. Bombed at 15.04 hours from 20,000 feet. Centre of Marshalling Yard. Aircraft hit by flak - Windscreen and fuselage damaged.

04/12/1944 LM733 JI-F Bombing Oberhausen 11.53 14.08 16.06

Bomb load 1 x 4000 HC, 6 x 1000 MC, 6 x 500 GP. Primary target: Oberhausen, Built up area. Weather 10/10ths cloud. Bombed at 14.08 hours from 20,000 feet on upwind edge of red flares.

06/12/1944 PB142 JI-O Bombing Merseburg 16.55 20.50 00.50

Bomb load 1 x 4000 HC, 8 x 500 GP, 1 x 500 GP. Long Delay. Primary target: Merseburg. Weather 10/10ths cloud with odd breaks. Bombed at 10.50 hours from 20,000 feet on centre of Wanganui flares.

08/12/1944 LM285 JI-K Bombing Duisburg 09.02 11.05 12.58

Bomb load 13 x 1000 ANM59, 1 Red/Green Flare. Primary target: Duisberg. Weather 10/10ths cloud. Bombed at 11.05 hours from 20,000 feet on upwind edge of flares.

11/12/1944 NG203 JI-A Bombing Osterfeld 08.44 11.08 13.01

Bomb load 1 x 4000 HC, 14 x 500 GP Long Delay, 1 Flare. Primary target: Osterfeld. Weather 10/10ths cloud, tops 16,000 feet. Bombed at 11.08 hours from 20,000 feet on green flare.

12/12/1944 NG203 JI-A Bombing Witten 11.22 14.08 16.07

Bomb load 1 x 4000 HC, 1 x 500 GP, 6 x 500 ANM58, 4 x 500 ANM64, 1 Flare. Primary target: Witten. Weather 10/10ths cloud, tops 14/16,000 feet. Bombed at 14.08 hours from 21,000 feet on G.H.

23/12/1944 PB426 JI-D Bombing Trier 11.41 14.32 16.15

Bomb load 1 x 4000 HC, 10 x 500 GP, 6 x 250 GP. Primary target: Trier. Weather clear over target. Bombed at 14.32 hours from 18,000 feet visually and on Red T.I.

28/12/1944 NG203 JI-A Bombing Cologne Gremberg 12.21   15.06
17.07

Bomb load 7 x 1000 MC, 6 x 500 GP, 2 x 250 GP, 1 Flare. Primary target: Koln Gremberg, Marshalling yards. Weather 10/10ths cloud or fog. Bombed at 15.06 hours from 20,000 feet on G.H.

31/12/1944 NG203 JI-A Bombing Vohwinkle 11.27 14.40   16.27

Bomb load 1 x 4000 HC, 3 x 1000 M65, 2 x 500 GP, 2 x 500 ANM58, 2 x 500 GP L/Delay, 4 x 250 GP. Primary target: Vohwinkel. Weather 10/10ths cloud on approaching target although the target itself was clear. Bombed at 14.40 hours from 20,000 feet on G.H.

01/01/1945 PB426 JI-D Bombing Vohwinkle 16.22 19.38   21.37

Bomb load 1 x 4000 HC, 12 x 500 ANM58, 2 x 500 GP. Primary target: Vohwinkel. Weather clear. Bombed at 19.38 hours from 21,000 feet on G.H.

03/01/1945 PB426 JI-D Bombing Dortmund Buckarde 12.50   15.33
17.36

Bomb load 1 x 4000 HC, 12 x 500 ANM58 or 64, 3 x 500 GP, 1 Flare. Primary target: Dortmund Buckarde. Weather 10/10ths cloud over target. Bombed at 15.33 hours from 20,000 feet on G.H.

05/01/1945 PB426 JI-D Bombing Ludwigshafen 11.26   15.08   17.15

Bomb load 1 x 4000 HC, 10 x 500 ANM58 or 64, 2 x 500 GP, 1 Flare. Primary target: Ludwigshafen, Marshalling yards. Weather clear over target. Bombed at 15.08 hours from 20,000 feet on G.H. Aircraft hit by flak - Air Bomber's perspex and Pilot's wind screen shattered.

F/L. John Duncan Kay Crooks, DFC

140921 (1348106)   F/L. John Duncan Kay Crooks, DFC. Pilot.
NZ413026   F/O. Willis Livingstone Combs, DFC RNZAF. A/Bomber.
148374 (1442933)   F/L. George Robert Baker. Navigator. 14 ops.
134705 (1324447)   F/L. John Bruce Jarvis. Navigator. 15 ops.
W/O.   A.R.W. Smith.   WOP/AG.
Sgt. A. "Andy" Deighton.   MU/Gunner. 21 ops.
F/S. J.E. Dawson.   MU/Gunner. 8 ops.
1353916 W/O. George William "Curly" Copland, DFC. R/Gunner.
56710 (620482)   P/O. Walter Edward "Wiz" Wiseman, DFC. F/Engineer.
47481 (523741) F/L.   Arthur Charles Southward. 2nd Pilot. 04/04/1945

Passengers 05/05/1945, 08/05/1945, 03/07/1945.

16/12/1944 PB419 JI-N Bombing Siegen   11.38   16.54

Lancaster III ME535 JI-G – May 1945. F/L J.D.K. Crooks (back 3rd from left)

Bomb load 1 x 4000 HC, 5 x 1000 MC, 7 x 500 GP, 1 Flare. Primary target: Siegen. Weather very bad on route with icing and cloud. Abortive sortie. Aircraft made no contact with bomber stream due to 10/10 cloud up to 21,000 feet. Jettisoned 1 x 4000 HC at 5218N 0312E. Brought remainder back.

18/02/1945 NG142 JI-J Bombing Wesel 11.21 15.24 16.59

Bomb load 1 x 4000 HC, 4 x 500 GP, 2 x 500 MC L/Delay, 4 x 250 GP, 6 x 500 ANM64. Primary target: Wesel. Primary target: Wesel. Weather 10/10ths cloud. Bombed at 15.24 hours from 19,000 feet on G.H. Leader.

19/02/1945 PB902 JI-A Bombing Wesel 13.08 16.36 19.25

Bomb load 1 x 4000 HC, 6 x 500 MC, 6 x 500 ANM64, 4 x 250 GP. Primary target: Wesel. Weather over target 5-7/10ths cloud. Bombed at 16.36 hours from 18,500 feet on leading aircraft. Landed at Moreton in Marsh.

20/02/1945 PB142 JI-G Bombing Dortmund 21.50 01.07 03.36

Bomb load 1 x 2000 HC, 12 x 750 Type 15 Clusters. Primary target: Dortmund. Weather 8-10/10ths thin cloud at about 5,000 feet. Bombed at 01.17 hours from 21,000 feet on centre of Red T.I.s.

22/02/1945 PB902 JI-A Bombing Osterfeld 12.22 16.01 18.02

Bomb load 1 x 4000 HC, 9 x 500 ANM64, 2 x 500 MC, 4 x 250 GP. Primary target: Osterfeld, Coking ovens. Weather at target clear, but hazy. Bombed at 16.01 hours from 20,000 feet on G.H. Leader.

28/02/1945 NN773 JI-K Bombing Nordstern 08.54 12.05 14.21

Bomb load 1 x 4000 HC, 9 x 500 ANM64, 2 x 500 MC L/D, 4 x 250 GP.

Primary target: Nordstern (Gelsenkirchen). Weather 10/10ths cloud. Bombed at 12.05 hours from 20,500 feet on leading aircraft.

02/03/1945 NG203 A2-C Bombing Koln 12.51 x 18.35

Bomb load 1 x 4000 HC, 11 x 500 ANM64. Primary target: Koln. Weather 10/10ths cloud over Koln, South and South-East of Koln clear. Abortive sortie. Jettisoned 1 x 4000 HC at 17.45 hours from 15,000 feet at 5213N 0307E. Brought back 12 x 500 ANM64.

05/03/1945 LM275 JI-C Bombing Gelsenkirchen 10.28 14.05 16.12

Bomb load 1 x 4000 HC, 12 x 500 ANM64. Primary target: Gelsenkirchen, Benzol plant. Weather 10/10ths cloud over target with cirrus cloud at bombing height. Last resort target: Wesel. Bombed at 14.05 hours from 16,000 feet. G. fix, Map reading, 2 previous visits. Bombs seen to burst across railway at the South-East corner of the town.

07/03/1945 PB142 JI-G Bombing Dessau 17.10 22.05 02.21

Bomb load 1 x 500 ANM64, 15 x No.15 Clusters. Primary target: Dessau. Weather 5 to 10/10ths thin cloud. Bombed at 22.05 hours from 20,000 feet on Red flares with Green stars.

10/03/1945 NN773 JI-K Bombing Gelsenkirchen 12.05 15.37 17.25

Bomb load 1 x 4000 HC, 13 x 500 ANM64, 2 x 500 MC. Primary target: Gelsenkirchen. Weather 10/10ths cloud at target, tops 8,000 feet. Bombed at 15.37 hours from 19,000 feet on G.H. Leader.

12/03/1945 LM275 JI-C Bombing Dortmund 13.03 16.57 18.59

Bomb load 1 x 4000 HC, 13 x 500 ANM64. Primary target: Dortmund. Weather 10/10ths cloud over target, tops 6/10,000 feet. Bombed at 16.57 hours from 19,000 feet on G.H. Leader.

14/03/1945 LM275 JI-C Bombing Heinrichshutte 13.19 16.41 19.04

Bomb load 1 x 4000 HC, 12 x 500 ANM64. Primary target: Heinrichshutte, Hattingen Steel works and Benzol plant. Weather 10/10ths cloud, tops 7/12,000 feet. Bombed at 16.41 hours from 17,500 feet on G.H. Leader.

27/03/1945 LM285 JI-A Bombing Hamm Sachsen 10.39 14.02 16.12

Bomb load 1 x 4000 HC, 13 x 500 ANM64, 2 x 500 MC. Primary target: Hamm Sachsen, Benzol plant. Weather 10/10ths cloud. Bombed at 14.02, at 18,300 on G.H. Leader. Markers only. Smoke from another target. Attack very concentrated. Smoke rising above cloud after leaving.

04/04/1945 LM724 JI-H Bombing Merseburg (Leuna) 18.43 22.53 02.50

Bombed Magdeburg area. Bomb load 1 x 4000 HC, 6 x 500 ANM64. Bombed on Red and Green T.I.s and River Elbe. Cloud 5/10th. Bombed at 22.53 hours from 20,000 feet. Attack on Merseburg opened late. Red/Green T.I. dropped N.E. of Target. A/C circled three times for further means of identifying sky markers later seen at Merseburg.

F/L. Arthur Charles Southward was 2nd Pilot that day.

13/04/1945 NF968 JI-B Bombing Kiel 20.31 23.31 02.21

Bomb load 1 x 4000 MC and 12 x 500 ANM64. Primary target: Kiel, Docks

154

and ship yards. Weather 10/10ths cloud low and thin. Bombed centre of Green glow on M/B's instructions at 23.31 hours from 19,000 feet. Glow of fires seen through cloud. Two targets separately marked. Merged into one large glow after bombing. H2S u/s. Very good attack. Marking concentrated. M/B clear and helpful.

29/04/1945 RF230 JI-B Manna The Hague 12.26 13.49 14.55

Weather broken cloud above and clear below. Dropping zone: The Hague. Dropped 5 packs on red T.I. and white circle. Bomb bays damaged by the pack. Had hearty reception from inhabitants. Food packs covered the dropping zone.

05/05/1945 ME535 JI-G Manna The Hague 06.04 07.23 08.27

Dropping area: The Hague. Dropped 5 Panniers on Red T.I. Visibility poor - low cloud 7-800 ft. Slightly to port of racecourse on dry ground. Union Jack and Dutch flag flown out of windows.

Passengers Cpl. Naylor.

08/05/1945 ME535 JI-G Manna Rotterdam 12.40 14.09 15.10

Dropping area: Rotterdam. Dropped 5 Packs on T.I.s and White Cross. Clear. Bags dropped well together.

Passengers LAC. Boney.

10/05/1945 ME535 JI-G Exodus Juvincourt - Ford 11.09 x 18.15

Duration 3.36. Outward 1.42 hours. Collected 24 ex POWs. Homeward 1.52 hours. Organisation OK.

12/05/1945 ME535 JI-G Exodus Juvincourt - Wing 08.58 x 14.40

Duration 4.13. Outward 2.13 hours. Collected 24 POWs. Homeward 2.00 hours. Organisation good.

14/05/1945 ME535 JI-G Exodus Juvincourt - Oakley 10.12 x 15.59

Duration 3.56 hours. Outward 1.33 hours. Collected 24 POWs. Homeward 2.23 hours. No trouble.

17/05/1945 ME535 JI-G Exodus Brussels - Westcott 10.53 x 14.55

Duration 2 hrs 28 mins. Out 1 hr 15 mins. In 1 hr 13 mins. 10 Belgian refugees taken over to Brussels. No POWs available. No troubles.

18/05/1945 ME535 JI-G Exodus Brussels - Oakley 11.46 x 20.07

Duration 3 hrs 19 mins. Out 1 hr 11 mins. In 2 hrs 8 mins. 10 Belgian refugees taken to Brussels. 24 ex POWs. Returned to U.K. All OK.

24/05/1945 ME535 JI-G Exodus Brussels 11.59 x 16.13

Duration 2.28 hours. Out 1.14 hours. In 1.14 hours. 10 Belgian refugees to Brussels. No ex POWs. brought back.

25/05/1945 ME535 JI-G Exodus Brussels 11.56 x 15.17

Duration 2.24 hours. Out 1.12 hours. In 1.12 hours. 9 Belgian refugees returned to Brussels. No POWs home. No troubles except Dakotas taxiing on to runway when our a/c on approach.

26/05/1945 ME535 JI-G Exodus Brussels - Ford 11.49 x 17.50

Duration 3.44 hours. Out 1.34 hours. In 2.10 hours. 10 Belgian refugees to Brussels. 24 ex POWs all military brought back.

25/06/1945 ME535 JI-G Post Mortem Special mission 10.01 x 16.07

03/07/1945 ME535 JI-G Baedeker Tour over Continent 09.16 x 13.45
Passengers F/O. McCutcheon, Sgt. Danby, Sgt. Burton, Cpl. Mitchell, LAC. Scutt.
05/07/1945 ME535 JI-G Post Mortem Special mission 13.27 x 18.23

P/O. Argyle Bruce Cunningham

NZ424433 P/O. Argyle Bruce "Sly" Cunningham, RNZAF. Pilot.
144333 (1350747) F/O. Reginald Ford "Reg" Brailsford. A/Bomber.
148745 (1324809) F/O. Robert John "Bob" Ramsey. Navigator.
656855 F/S. John Wallace Stone. WOP/AG.
1819401 Sgt. Bleddyn Lloyd "Bob" "Taffy" Roberts. MU and R/Gunner.
1350401 Sgt. Fred W. Brown. MU and R/Gunner.
1377661 Sgt. J.F. Gordon "Jock" Hay. F/Engineer. 7 ops
173829 (1393193) P/O. Donald Albert "Don" Winterford. F/Engineer. 3 ops

07/03/1944 DS816 JI-O Bombing Le Mans 19.31 23.38
Bomb load 10 x 1000, 4 x 500 lb bomb. No attack made, bombs brought back. Target not identified visually. 2 x 1000, 2 x 500 lb bombs jettisoned safe to reduce weight for landing.
P/O. A.B. Cunningham flew the mission as 2nd Pilot with S/L. A.L. Roberts' crew.
22/03/1944 DS816 JI-O Bombing Frankfurt 18.41 21.05
Bomb load 1 x 1000 lb bomb, 63 x 30, 1161 x 4, 129 x 4 incendiaries. Returned early. Furthest point reached 5340N 0303E. Total load jettisoned safe. Starboard inner engine feathered and aircraft returned on 3 engines.
24/03/1944 LL645 JI-R Bombing Berlin 18.32 22.36 02.11
Bomb load 1 x 8000 lb bomb. Primary target: Berlin. Weather was clear. Bombed at 22.36 hours from 20,000 feet. Many fighter flares seen over whole route. Flak was slight. No fighters seen. Few fires were seen.
11/04/1944 LL624 JI-P Bombing Aachen 20.58 22.44 00.26
Bomb load 10 x 1000 lb bomb, 160 x 4, 20 x 4 incendiaries. Primary target: Aachen. There was scattered cloud. Bombed at 22.44 hours from 19,000 feet. Slight undershoot of incendiaries falling on target. Very successful attack. Route OK.
18/04/1944 LL739 JI-M Bombing Rouen 22.42 00.47 02.58
Bomb load 8 x 1000 MC, 2 x 1000 GP, 5 x 500 lb bombs. Primary target: Rouen. There was ground haze but no cloud. Visual of river loop and bridge. Bombed at 00.47 hours from 13,500 feet. Some bombs appeared to burst on town. M of C gave useful aid over target. A concentrated raid. Photo attempted.

L to R, Back: "Reg" Brailsford, Fred Brown; "Jock" Hay, John Stone.
Front: "Taffy" Roberts, "Sly" Cunningham, "Bob" Ramsey.

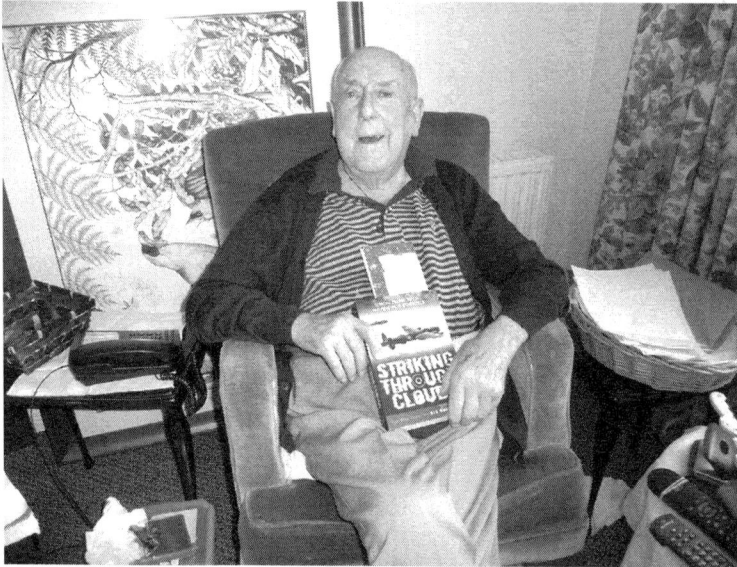

Argyle Bruce "Sly" Cunningham at home January 2015

157

20/04/1944 LL739 JI-M Bombing Cologne   23.52   02.02   03.46
Bomb load 1 x 1000 lb bomb. 1026 x 4, 114 x 4, 108 x 30 lb incendiaries. Primary target: Koln. There was 10/10 cloud. Bombed at 02.02 hours from 21,000 feet. Bombed 2 minutes after zero hour and no P.F.F. markers visible. Impossible to estimate results.

22/04/1944 DS816 JI-O Bombing Dusseldorf 23.05 01.15
Bomb load 9 x 1000, 5 x 500 lb bombs. Returned early. Starboard inner engine overheating. Mid upper turret U/S. Furthest point reached 5127N 0232E at 00.07 hours, 12,500 feet. 3 x 1000, 5 x 500 brought back to base, remainder jettisoned safe at 5140N 0221E at 0013 hours, 12500 feet.

24/04/1944 DS816 JI-O Bombing Karlsruhe   22.16   00.44   03.45
Bomb load 1 x 8000 lb bomb, 24 x 30, 216 x 4, 24 x 4 lb incendiaries. Primary target: Karlsruhe. There was patchy cloud. Bombed at 00.44 hours from 20,000 feet. Bombed in centre of concentration of green T.I.s. T.I.s appeared concentrated but bombs seen burst well outside the area marked. Completely 10/10 cloud Aachen to Karlsruhe. Moderate icing conditions and static electricity over this part of route. Attack very scattered. Route good except Aachen to Karlsruhe when cloud and icing conditions made flying wholly dependent on instruments. Flight Engineer wounded in face by ice smashing through the windscreen.

P/O. A.B. Cunningham stated in July 2015: "Our engineer was a fellow called Hay whose first name I have forgotten. He was injured on a trip to Karlsruhe. Severe icing and some came off the prop through the perspex and laid him out. When he came around another lot hit him. We thought he was going to lose his sight but that did not occur."

01/05/1944 LL734 JI-S Bombing Chambly   22.43   00.25   02.06
Bomb load 10 x 1000, 5 x 500 lb. bombs. Primary target: Chambly. Weather was clear with slight haze. Bombed at 00.25 hours from 8500 feet. Bombed on visual by light of flares. Greens seen to be off the target, on M of C's instructions greens were avoided. A good attack, flak negligible.

10/05/1944 LL739 JI-M Bombing Courtrai 22.05 23.28 00.35
Bomb load 7 x 1000 GP, 7 x 1000 MC. Primary target: Courtrai. Moderate haze over target. T.I.s seen. No visual identification possible. Bombed as ordered by Master Bomber at 23.28 hours from 11,000 feet. Bombing appeared well concentrated. Route satisfactory.

11/05/1944 LL739 JI-M Bombing Louvain 23.00
Bomb load 5 x 1000 MC, 5 x 1000 GP, 5 x 500 MC. Aircraft missing.
To bomb the railway yards at Louvain. Damaged by a night fighter. Starboard inner engine set on fire. Report on file. Aircraft attacked by a FW 190, possibly flown by Ofw. Vinzenz Glessuebel while leaving the target area. LL739 crashed in Brussels area. Starboard inner engine caught fire which spread to entire wing. All baled out. All crew members survived.

P/O. Cunningham landed on the roof of a cafe at Rixensart (Brabant),

Belgium. P/O. Winterford landed on a railway line, drew fire from a German patrol who initially thought he was a saboteur, was shot through the shoulder at point blank range after giving himself, was robbed of his cigarettes and escape kit, and left for dead. Later was found by another German patrol and taken to hospital. F/O. Ramsey and Sgt. Brown evaded capture until betrayed by Rene van Muylem to the Antwerp Gestapo and arrested in Brussels 16 Jun 1944.

Sgt. F.W. Brown was eventually interned in Camp L7. PoW No.207, P/O. A.B. Cunningham in Camp L3, PoW No.5150 with F/O. R.J. Ramsey, PoW No.6305, and F/O. D.A. Winterford, PoW No.6510. F/O. Brailsford, Sgt. Stone and Sgt. Roberts successfully evaded, took shelter with the Réseau Comète and were liberated in Sept 1944 in Brussels, Porcheresse and Bellevaux, respectively.

F/L. Leo Lloyd Currie, DFC

J9582 F/L. Leo Lloyd Currie, DFC RCAF. Pilot.
A428080 P/O. Geoffrey Alan Trollope, RAAF. A/Bomber.
J40945 F/O. H.D. Fulcher, RCAF. A/Bomber. 16/12/1944
NZ421405 P/O. E.D. Vallance, RNZAF. Navigator.
J40779 F/O. E.S. MacTier, RCAF. Navigator. 16/12/1944
A428421 F/S. Arthur Leslie Newnham. RAAF. WOP/AG.
Sgt. B.A. Robus. WOP/AG. 16/12/1944
Sgt. J. Doran. MU/Gunner.
R264534 F/S. W.G. Wheeler, RCAF. MU/Gunner.16/12/1944
Sgt. H.R. or R. Cammell. R/Gunner.
F/S. E.D. Dixon. R/Gunner. 08/12/1944
R217362 Sgt. J.A. Moran, RCAF. R/Gunner. 16/12/1944
Sgt. K.G. Haynes. F/Engineer.
Sgt. J. Taylor-Lowen. F/Engineer. 16/12/1944
J41105 F/O. C.A. Dunn, RCAF. 2nd Pilot. 11/12/1944
J29301 F/O. F.E. Sider, RCAF. 2nd Pilot. 16/12/1944

26/08/1944 ?? Bombing Kiel
According to his logbook F/L. Leo Lloyd Currie, DFC RCAF did this mission 5.20 hours flying time. Crew unknown, probably as 2nd pilot.
31/08/1944 HK572 JI-T Bombing Pont-Remy 16.08 18.17 19.58
Bomb load 11 x 1000 MC, 4 x 500 GP Mk IV LD. Primary target: Pont Remy, Dump. Weather cloudy. Bombed at 1817 hours from 15,000 feet on Leading aircraft.
According L.L. Currie's logbook target "Abbeville", Abbeville is the great town very close to Pont-Remy.
17/09/1944 PB482 JI-P Bombing Boulogne 10.46 12.15 13.35
Bomb load 11 x 1000 MC, 4 x 500 GP. Primary target: Boulogne Aiming

Point 2. Weather clear below cloud. Bombed at 12.15 hours from 3500 feet, red T.I.s in centre of smoke.

20/09/1944 PB419 JI-N Bombing Calais 14.40 16.03 17.32

Bomb load 11 x 1000 MC, 4 x 500 GP. Primary target: Calais. Weather clear over target. Bombed at 16.03 hours from 3500 feet, red T.I.s.

23/09/1944 LM717JI-T Bombing Neuss 19.13 23.50

Bomb load 11 x 1000 ANM59, 4 x 500 GP. Weather 10/10ths cloud over target, tops 8/10,000 feet. No attack. Indicators not seen, circled but unable to locate target. Bombs brought back.

05/10/1944 LM727JI-S Bombing Saarbrucken 17.21 22.57

Bomb load 11 x 1000 MC, 1 x 500 GP, 3 x 500 GP. Long Delay. Abandoned mission on instructions from Master Bomber heard to say they were unable to locate target and called "Abandon Mission - our troop in vicinity". Jettisoned 3 x 500 GP at 5254N 0240E at 22.10 hours from 4,000 feet. Brought remainder back.

06/10/1944 LM684 JI-O Bombing Dortmund 16.51 20.32 22.33

Bomb load 1 x 4000 HC, 12 x No. 14 Clusters. Primary target: Dortmund, Town and Railways. Weather over the target was clear with slight ground haze. Bombed at 20.32 hours from 19,500 feet on Green T.I.

07/10/1944 LM717JI-T Bombing Emmerich 12.21 14.27 16.09

Bomb load 1 x 4000 HC, 10 x No. 14 Clusters. 4 x (150 x 4). Primary target: Emmerich. Weather clear with cloud at 13,000 feet. Bombed at 14.27 hours from 13,000 feet on South of smoke as ordered.

22/10/1944 NF966 JI-R Bombing Neuss 13.14 15.56 17.25

Bomb load 1 x 4000 HC, 6 x 1000 MC, 6 x 500 GP. Primary target: Neuss. Weather 10/10ths cloud over target. Bombed at 15.56 hours from 17,000 feet on GH. Overshoot of 3 seconds due to having to use jettison bars. Small hole through Mid-upper turret perspex. The GH was not satisfactory.

23/10/1944 NF966 JI-R Bombing Essen 16.35 19.45 21.55

Bomb load 1 x 4000 HC, 2 x 1000 MC, 10 x 500 GP, 3 x 500 MC. Primary target: Essen. Weather 10/10ths cloud over target - tops 12/14,000 feet with most appalling weather on route. Bombed at 19.45 hours from 20,000 feet on GH which coincided with Red flares.

25/10/1944 NF966 JI-R Bombing Essen 13.09 15.43 17.09

Bomb load 1 x 4000 HC, 6 x 1000 MC, 6 x 500 GP. Primary target: Essen. Weather over target 10/10ths low cloud, with one clear patch which appeared to fill up later in the attack. Bombed at 15.43 hours from 22,000 feet. Centre of 5 red flares.

26/10/1944 NF966 JI-R Bombing Leverkusen 13.03 15.30 17.16

Bomb load 1 x 4000 HC, 6 x 1000 MC, 4 x 500 GP, 2 x 500 GP Long Delay. Primary target: Leverkusen. Weather over target and on route was 10/10ths cloud. Bombed at 15.30 hours from 18,000 feet on GH.

28/10/1944 NF966 JI-R Bombing Cologne 13.08 15.46 17.45

Bomb load 1 x 4000 HC, 8 x 150 x 4. Primary target: Cologne. Weather clear over target. Bombed at 15.46 hours from 20,000 feet. Middle of cloud of smoke on Master Bomber's instructions.

30/10/1944 NF966 JI-R Bombing Wesseling   09.09   12.00   13.34

Bomb load 1 x 4000 HC, 15 x 500 GP. Primary target: Wesseling. Weather was 10/10ths cloud - tops about 7,000 feet. Bombed at 12.00 hours from 17,500 feet on small group of red flares.

31/10/1944 NF966 JI-R Bombing Bottrop   11.55 15.00   16.25

Bomb load 1 x 4000 HC, 15 x 500 GP, 1 Flare. Primary target: Bottrop, Synth. Oil plants. Weather 10/10ths cloud over target. Bombed at 15.00 hours from 18,000 feet on G.H.

02/11/1944 NF966 JI-R Bombing Homberg   11.11   14.05   15.27

Bomb load 1 x 4000 HC, 6 x 1000 ANM59, 6 x 500 MC. Primary target: Homberg. Weather variable cloud but clear for bombing. Target obscured by pall of smoke rising to 10,000 feet. Bombed at 14.05 hours from 20,000 feet on instruments checked by visual.

05/11/1944 NF966 JI-R Bombing Solingen 10.13   13.05   14.53

Bomb load 1 x 4000 HC, 6 x 1000 ANM59, 4 x 500 GP, 2 x 500 GP (L/Delay), 3 Flares. Primary target: Solingen. Weather 10/10ths cloud over target. Bombed at 13.05 hours from 17,500 feet on red flares with green stars.

06/11/1944 PD334 A2-D Bombing Koblenz 17.11 19.32   21.52

Bomb load 1 x 4000 HC, 2100 x 4 lb. Primary target: Koblenz. Weather clear over target. Bombed at 19.32 hours from 18,000 feet on centre of Red T.I.

11/11/1944 NF966 JI-R Bombing Castrop Rauxel 08.05   11.10   12.47

Bomb load 1 x 4000 HC, 15 x 500 GP, 1 Flare. Primary target: Castrop Rauxel, Oil refineries. Weather 10/10ths cloud. Alternative target: Wuppertal. Bombed at 11.10 hours from 19,250 feet. GH. was unserviceable so aircraft followed another aircraft which did not bomb, so they bombed Wuppertal on H2S.

According to L.L. Currie's logbook target "Wuppertal".

15/11/1944 NF966 JI-R Bombing Dortmund   12.35   15.41   17.40

Bomb load 1 x 4000 HC, 16 x 500 GP. Primary target: Hoesch-Benzin Dortmund, Oil refineries. Weather 10/10ths cloud over the target. Bombed at 15.41 hours from 17,000 feet on leading aircraft.

16/11/1944 PB423 A2-G Bombing Heinsburg   13.24   15.43   17.15

Bomb load 1 x 4000 HC, 6 x 1000 MC, 4 x 500 GP, 4 x 250 lb T.I.s. Primary target: Heinsburg. Weather - nil cloud with slight haze over target. Bombed at 15.43 hours from 9,000 feet. Visual.

20/11/1944 NF966 JI-R Bombing Homberg   12.35   15.15   16.55

Bomb load 1 x 4000 HC, 15 x 500 GP, 1 Red-Green Flare. Primary target: Homberg. Weather 10/10ths cloud over target. Bombed at 15.15 hours from 20,000 feet on leading aircraft. Jettisoned 2 x 500 GP safe 5129N 0234E at 16.15 hours from 5,000 feet. Damage to fuselage due to aircraft exploding.

21/11/1944 LM275 JI-M Bombing Homberg   12.30   15.07   16.35

Bomb load 1 x 4000 HC, 15 x 500 GP, 1 Red and Green Flare. Primary target: Homberg. Weather about 5/10ths cloud but clear for bombing. Bombed at 15.07 hours from 20,000 feet on GH.

27/11/1944 LM275 JI-M Bombing Cologne 12.14 15.04 16.55

Bomb load 1 x 4000 HC, 15 x 500 GP, 1 Flare. Primary target: Cologne, Marshalling Yards. Weather patchy cloud. Bombed at 15.04 hours from 20,000 feet on GH.

29/11/1944 LM275 JI-M Bombing Neuss 02.51 05.31 07.13

Bomb load 1 x 4000 HC, 6 x 1000 MC, 4 x 500 GP, 4 x 250 Green T.I.s. Primary target: Neuss. Weather 10/10ths cloud over target but the glow of fires was seen through cloud. Bombed at 05.31 hours from 19,000 feet on GH. Aircraft first to attack, no results seen.

08/12/1944 PA186 A2-G Bombing Duisburg 08.48 11.05 12.37

Bomb load 14 x 1000 MC. Primary target: Duisberg. Weather 10/10ths cloud. Bombed at 11.05 hours from 20,000 feet on GH Leader.

F/S. E.D. Dixon R/Gunner was that day.

11/12/1944 LM275 JI-M Bombing Osterfeld 08.36 11.06 12.45

Bomb load 1 x 4000 HC, 12 x 500 GP, 2 x 500 GP Long Delay, 2 x 500 MC. Primary target: Osterfeld. Weather 10/10ths cloud, tops 16,000 feet. Bombed at 11.06 hours from 19,500 feet on GH.

12/12/1944 NF966 JI-R Bombing Witten 11.23 14.06 15.48

Bomb load 1 x 4000 HC, 4 x 500 GP, 6 x 500 ANM58, 4 x 500 ANM64, 1 Flare. Primary target: Witten. Weather 10/10ths cloud, tops 14/16,000 feet. Bombed at 14.06 hours from 20,500 feet on GH.

16/12/1944 NF966 JI-R Bombing Siegen 11.22 14.59 16.55

Bomb load 1 x 4000 HC, 5 x 1000 MC, 7 x 500 GP. 1 Flare. Primary target: Siegen. Weather very bad on route with icing and cloud. Bombed at 14.59 hours from 17,750 feet on GH Leader.

F/L. L.L. Currie flew the mission as Captain of aircraft with 2nd Pilot F.E. Sider. Remaining crew was that of F.E. Sider (see F/O. F.E. Sider).
Crew that day:
J9582 F/L. Leo Lloyd Currie, DFC RCAF. Pilot.
J29301 F/O. F.E. Sider, RCAF. 2nd Pilot.
J40945 F/O. H.D. Fulcher, RCAF. A/Bomber.
J40779 F/O. E.S. MacTier, RCAF. Navigator.
Sgt. B.A. Robus. WOP/AG.
R264534 F/S. W.G. Wheeler, RCAF. MU/Gunner.
R217362 Sgt. J.A. Moran, RCAF. R/Gunner.
Sgt. J. Taylor-Lowen. F/Engineer.

21/12/1944 NF966 JI-R Bombing Trier 12.13 14.58 17.00

Bomb load 1 x 4000 HC, 10 x 500 GP, 2 x 250 GP, 4 x 250 T.I.s. Primary target: Trier, Marshalling yards. Weather 10/10 cloud, tops 6/9000 feet. Bombed at 14.58 hours from 18,500 feet on leading aircraft.

F/L. Robert Julian Curtis, DFM

First crew

120090 (742232) F/L. Robert Julian Curtis, DFM. Pilot.
158650 (1387983) F/O. Donald McLeod. A/Bomber.
155105 (1392225) F/O. Reginald "Reg" Davey. Navigator.
157984 (1123282) P/O. Charles Ernest Baud, DFC. WOP/AG.
1389975 F/S. Ronald Harle Marshall, DFC. MU/Gunner.
1560436 F/S. William James Clubb, DFC. R/Gunner.
1086096 F/S. Peter G. Cooper. F/Engineer. 7 ops.
1330027 Sgt. M.C.L. Bristow or Bristowe. F/Engineer. 5 ops.

14/01/1944 DS823 JI-M Bombing Brunswick 16.56 19.17 22.05
Bomb load 1 x 4000, 48 x 30 incendiaries. Primary target: Brunswick. There was 8/10 cloud. Bombed at 19.17 hours at 21,000 feet. Some fires seen rather scattered. Monica u/s. P.F.F. opened attack too early and T.I. very scattered, appeared to be scattered raid. Photo attempted.
F/L. R.J. Curtis flew the mission as 2nd Pilot with S/L. A.L. Roberts' crew.
20/01/1944 LL683 JI-P Bombing Berlin 16.15 19.39 23.35
Bomb load 1 x 4000, 32 x 30, 540 x 4, 60 x 4 incendiaries. Primary target: Berlin. There was 10/10 cloud. Bombed at 19.39 hours at 21,000ft on green T.I.s. Fires seen concentrated on leaving target.
21/01/1944 LL683 JI-P Bombing Magdeburg 19.49 23.02 03.14
Bomb load 1 x 4000, 720 x 4, 90 x 4, 32 x 30 incendiaries. Primary target: Magdeburg. Scattered patchy cloud. Bombed at 23.02 hours at 20,000 ft. Fires seen on starboard of river. Route good except for entering and leaving coast. Attack should develop well.
28/01/1944 DS822 JI-T Bombing Berlin 23.57 03.15 07.44
Bomb load 1 x 2000 lb bomb. 16 x 30, 750 x 4 incendiaries. Primary target: Berlin. There was 8-9/10 cloud. Bombed at 03.15 hours at 21,000 ft. Concentrated fires in target area, burning red. Marking flares and T.I.s well concentrated. Huge explosion with an orange coloured flash at 03.14 hours and a further one to the N.E. at 03.26 hours.
30/01/1944 DS818 JI-Q Bombing Berlin 17.13 20.23 23.31
Bomb load 1 x 4000 lb bomb, 600 x 4, 90 x 4, 32 x 30 incendiaries. Primary target: Berlin. There was 10/10 cloud. Concentration of sky markers red with green stars. Bombed at 20.23 hours at 20,000 ft. Target area surrounded by fighter flares. Glow of fires seen through cloud. Attack appeared concentrated if P.F.F. OK. No troubles.

F/S. G.J. Davis (front, 3rd from left) and crew. Sgt. E.J. Roberts back row far right.
(Courtesy of Calvin Davis)

F/S. Graham John "Roger" Davis

24/02/1944 LL732 JI-R Bombing Schweinfurt 20.44 01.14 04.41

Bomb load 1 x 4000 lb bomb, 24 x 30, 420 x 4, 90 x 4 x incendiaries. Primary target: Schweinfurt. Bombed at 01.14 hours at 21,000 ft. Weather very smoky. There was a large mass of fire seen obscured by smoke. Arrived early and had to stand off about 5 minutes. Very concentrated attack. Fires of 1st attack seen 100 miles away. Good route.

01/03/1944 LL732 JI-R Bombing Stuttgart 23.47 03.16 07.36

Bomb load 1 x 8000 lb bomb, 8 x 30, 90 x 4 incendiaries. Primary target: Stuttgart. There was 10/10 cloud in the area with odd breaks. Bombed at 03.16 hours at 20,000 ft. Definite undershooting to the west of target. Red glow seen after leaving target. Large explosion SE of Stuttgart at 03.21 hours with 5 seconds orange flash coming up through clouds.

07/03/1944 LL645 A2-H Bombing Le Mans 19.47 23.39

Bomb load 10 x 1000, 4 x 500 lb bombs. There was 10/10 cloud. No attack. Aiming point could not be seen, nor were any T.I.s visible. 4 x 500 jettisoned at 22.34 hours. 1 x 1000 jettisoned at 22.45 hours. 9 x 1000 brought back to Base. Target circled for 10 minutes, no markers seen although we descended to 6500 feet.

18/03/1944 LL732 A2-H Bombing Frankfurt 19.39 22.07 00.51

Bomb load 1350 x 4, 90 x 4, 32 x 30 incendiaries. Primary target: Frankfurt. There was thin cloud. Bombed at 22.07 hours from 20,000 feet. Rather early to judge effect of attack. Markers were well concentrated. Route good.

22/03/1944 LL732 A2-H Bombing Frankfurt 18.26 21.59 00.44

Bomb load 1 x 8000 lb bomb, 56 x 30 incendiaries. Primary target: Frankfurt. There was 7/10 cloud; Bombed at 21.59 hours from 20,000 feet. Concentrated fires and red T.I.s intermingled. Fires burning orange had good hold, majority being on the North back of river seen reflected in glare. Marking good.

24/03/1944 LL732 A2-H Bombing Berlin 18.38 22.49 02.16

Bomb load 1 x 1000 lb bomb, 88 x 30, 810 x 4, 90 x 4 incendiaries. Primary target: Berlin. There was 8/10 cloud with gaps. Bombed at 22.49 hours from 20,000 feet. Considered P.F.F. late, but attack developed successfully later - concentrated around T.I.s. Overshot first run then orbited and made second run.

26/03/1944 LL732 A2-H Bombing Essen 20.11 22.11 00.36

Bomb load 1 x 8000 lb bomb, 96 x 30 incendiaries. Primary target: Essen. There was 10/10 cloud with tops 15,000 feet. Bombed at 22.11 hours from 20,000 feet. Glow of red and green T.I.s seen disappearing into cloud. No evidence of fire. Route good. Effort marred by cloud.

30/03/1944 LL732 A2-H Bombing Nuremburg 22.04 00.15

Bomb load 1 x 8000 lb bomb, 90 x 4 incendiaries. Returned early. Farthest point reached 5148N 6250E. Bomb jettisoned safe. Starboard outer engine u/s. Engine feathered and aircraft returned on 3 engines.

Second crew

120090 (742232) F/L. Robert Julian Curtis, DFM.   Pilot.
1450549 F/S. Bryan George Green.   A/Bomber.
135670 (1464986)   F/O. William Llewellyn Wynn Jones. Navigator.
1387235 F/S. Robert Samuel Cole.   WOP/AG.
143598 (1397354)   F/O. Harold Cherberd Bryant, DFC.   MU/Gunner.
976475   W/O.   Raymond Frank Joseph Cyril "Ray" Hall.   R/Gunner.
1032632 Sgt. Stanley Frank Martin.   F/Engineer.

11/04/1944 LL691 A2-D Bombing Aachen   20.59   22.43   00.27
Bomb load 10 x 1000, 2 x 500 lb bomb, 160 x 4, 20 x 4 incendiaries. Primary target: Aachen. There was 6/10 cloud. Bombed 22.43 hours from 20,000 feet; T.I.s very concentrated. Many bomb bursts seen appeared to be breaking up T.I.s. Attack very successful. Incendiaries seemed to be slightly undershooting.

18/04/1944 LL732 A2-H Bombing Rouen   22.32   00.49   03.08
Bomb load 8 x 1000 MC, 2 x 1000 GP, 5 x 500 MC lb bombs. Primary target: Rouen. There was thin cloud. Bombed at 00.49 hours from 13,500 feet. T.I.s appeared concentrated. Bombs appeared to burst within area marked. Photo attempted.

20/04/1944 LL732 A2-H Bombing Cologne 00.1002.13   04.42
Bomb load 1 x 8000 lb bomb, 24 x 30, 216 x 4, 24 x 4 lb incendiaries. Primary target: Cologne. There was 10/10 cloud over target. Bombed at 02.13 hours from 20,000 feet. Nothing seen except one red flare. Scarcity of markers, what were seen were scattered.

22/04/1944 LL732 A2-H Bombing Dusseldorf 23.02   01.16   03.10
Bomb load 9 x 1000, 5 x 500 lb bombs. Primary target: Dusseldorf. Weather was clear with slight haze. Bombed at 01.16 hours from 19,000 feet. T.I.s concentrated, bombs appeared to burst in area marked, but incendiaries later appeared scattered over wider area. Successful raid. Good route, easy trip.

27/04/1944 LL732 A2-H Bombing Friedrichshafen 21.52   02.05   05.33
Bomb load 1 x 4000, 2 x 1000, 1 x 500 lb bombs. Primary target Friedrichshafen. Weather was clear with slight haze. Bombed at 02.05 hours from 19,000 feet. Fires were seen burning well among T.I.s. Green T.I.s seemed to go down before the reds, however a good attack developed. Two large orange explosions seen at 02.05 hours. A route good. Had encounter with enemy aircraft.

01/05/1944 LL732 A2-H Bombing Chambly 22.47
Bomb load 10 x 1000, 5 x 500 lb bombs. Primary target: Chambly. Aircraft missing.
Tasked to destroy the railway and stores depot. On the home leg shot down N.W. of Paris, in a near vertical dive some 3 km S.W. of Chaumont-en-Vexin (Oise), 25 km S.W. of Beauvais by a night-fighter flown by Oblt. Jakob

Schauss of 4./NJG4. No survivors from the crew. All are buried in the Department of Seine-Maritime at Rouen in extension to the St-Sever Cemetery.

F/L. Curtis, whose award was Gazetted on 23rd September 1944, had previously flown Hampdens with 144 Squadron, logging 31 sorties. By his death he had flown another seventeen operations. F/O. Jones had been a Scholar of Trinity College, Caermarthen. F/O. Bryant's parents lived in the little island of Dominica (Commonwealth of Dominica).

F/S. Graham John Davis

1553150 F/S. Graham John "Roger" Davis.   Pilot.
1445550 Sgt. Reginald Derek Seddon.   A/Bomber.
1452782 Sgt. Eric James Roberts.   Navigator.
1334931 Sgt. Hugh Morris.   WOP/AG.
1407182 Sgt. Arthur Reginald Bird.   MU/Gunner.
A418558 Sgt. Walter David Barry "Wally" O'Dea, RAAF. R/Gunner.
1062645 Sgt. James Smethurst.   F/Engineer.

20/12/1943 DS817 JI-P Bombing Frankfurt   17.32
Bomb load 1 x 4000, 48 x 30 incendiaries, 950 x 4 incendiaries, 100 x 4 incendiaries. Aircraft missing.
The aircraft exploded in mid-air after a night fighter attack and crashed at Rettert, WNW of the target, at approx 20.00hrs on 20/12/43. Shot down by the late Hauptmann Wilhelm Herget over Frankfurt am Main.
All the crew were killed except F/S. Davis who was a POW in Camp IVB POW No. 269762.

G.J. Davis' son, Calvin Davis tells: "My father Pilot Flight Sgt. G.J. (Roger) Davis, flew DS817 out of Waterbeach, the last time was 20/12/43. He was shot down over Frankfurt by Hauptmann Wilhelm Herget, after evading 5 earlier attacks. His crew all perished except him. He fell from 21,000 feet to around 600 feet before he got his parachute open, and was only wearing a Pilot's 'chute due a series of lucky circumstances. He was taken PoW in Dulag Luft and Stalag IVB, after several days hiding in the trees and snow with serious injuries, and held for 17 months, during which he escaped 3 or 4 times, and was recaptured each time. On one occasion he and his fellow escapees hid inside, and destroyed, a top secret Warzburg Radio Location set mounted on a rail wagon. After reprocessing at Dulag Luft each time he was recaptured, because he lied and said he'd been shot down the previous night, he'd be returned to Stalag IVB and put in solitary for a week.
Eventually, as a habitual escapee, he was marched along with many others, (I believe about 250,000), through Poland to a secure facility up on the Silesian

167

Plateau to Stalag 7. During the march many of the 250,000 prisoners and guards perished in the freezing conditions."

F/O. Peter Geoffrey Dean

A417741 (O35137) F/O. Peter Geoffrey Dean, RAAF. Pilot.
F/S. William "Bill" Elliott.   A/Bomber.
1608171 (197275)   P/O. George Albert Thomas Mills. Navigator.
A39024   W/O.   John Charles Kemp, RAAF. WOP/AG.
Sgt. Martin Golightly.   MU/Gunner. 20 Ops.
Sgt. E. Roy Griffiths.   R/Gunner.
Sgt. Basil D. Holiday.   F/Engineer.

Passenger: 02/05/1945.

Note: after WWII, P.G. Dean served in the RAAF notably in the Korean War until 15/09/1953, then in the RAF as a F/L. ID No. 505194 until 12/02/1962.

16/02/1945 NG203 A2-C Bombing Wesel 12.27   16.01   17.42
Bomb load 1 x 4000 HC, 4 x 500 GP, 2 x 500 MC L/Delay, 4 x 250 GP, 6 x 500 ANM64. Primary target: Wesel. Weather clear. Bombed at 16.01 hours from 19,000 feet on G.H. Bomb bay hit by flak over Wesel.
F/O. P.G. Dean flew the mission as 2nd Pilot with F/O. G.A. Hanson's crew.
18/02/1945 NN782 JI-F Bombing Wesel 11.24   15.23   16.56
Bomb load 1 x 4000 HC, 4 x 500 GP, 2 x 500 MC L/Delay, 4 x 250 GP, 6 x 500 ANM64. Primary target: Wesel. Primary target: Wesel. Weather 10/10ths cloud. Bombed at 15.23 hours from 20,000 feet on G.H. Leader.
19/02/1945 NN782 JI-F Bombing Wesel 13.07   16.36   19.26
Bomb load 1 x 4000 HC, 6 x 500 MC, 6 x 500 ANM64, 3 x 250 GP. Primary target: Wesel. Weather over target 5-7/10ths cloud. Bombed at 16.36 hours from 19,400 feet on G.H. Leader. Landed at Moreton in Marsh.
22/02/1945 NN782 JI-F Bombing Osterfeld   12.25   16.01   17.59
Bomb load 1 x 4000 HC, 9 x 500 ANM64, 2 x 500 MC, 4 x 250 GP. Primary target: Osterfeld, Coking ovens. Weather at target clear, but hazy. Bombed at 16.01 hours from 20,000 feet on G.H. Leader.
26/02/1945 NN773 JI-K Bombing Dortmund   10.17   14.02   16.10
Bomb load 1 x 4000 HC, 2 x 500 MC L/Delay 37B, 9 x 500 ANM64, 4 x 250 GP. Primary target: Dortmund, Hoesch Benzin plant. Weather 10/10ths cloud, tops 8/10,000 feet. Bombed at 14.02 hours from 20,000 feet on G.H. Leader.
28/02/1945 ME387 JI-N Bombing Nordstern   08.43   12.04   14.03
Bomb load 1 x 4000 HC, 9 x 500 ANM64, 2 x 500 MC L/D, 4 x 250 GP. Primary target: Nordstern (Gelsenkirchen). Weather 10/10ths cloud. Bombed

at 12.04 hours from 20,300 feet on leading aircraft.

02/03/1945 PB142 JI-G Bombing Koln   12.42   16.03   18.43

Bomb load 1 x 4000 HC, 12 x 500 ANM64. Primary target: Koln. Weather 10/10ths cloud over Koln, South and South-East of Koln clear. Attacked Bonn. Bombed at 16.03 hours from 21,400 feet. Centre of town and Railways Marshalling Yards

05/03/1945 PB142 JI-G Bombing Gelsenkirchen 10.25   14.07   16.22

Bomb load 1 x 4000 HC, 12 x 500 ANM64. Primary target: Gelsenkirchen, Benzol plant. Weather 10/10ths cloud over target with cirrus cloud at bombing height. Bombed at 14.07 hours from 20,600 feet on G.H. Leader.

07/03/1945 NN773 JI-K Bombing Dessau 16.55 22.06 02.17

Bomb load 1 x 500 ANM64, 15 x No.15 Clusters. Primary target: Dessau. Weather 5 to 10/10ths thin cloud. Bombed at 22.06 hours from 20,000 feet on Red/Green flares.

F/O. P.G. Dean flew the mission as 2nd Pilot with P/O. L.J.W. Sutton's crew.

09/03/1945 NN782 JI-F Bombing Datteln 10.31 14.00   15.49

Bomb load 1 x 4000 HC, 13 x 500 ANM64, 2 x 500 MC L/Delay. Primary target: Datteln, Synthetic oil plant. Weather 10/10ths cloud, tops 8-10,000 feet. Bombed at 14.00 hours from 20,700 feet on G.H. Leader.

11/03/1945 LM275 JI-C Bombing Essen   11.24   15.25   17.07

Bomb load 1 x 4000 HC, 13 x 500 ANM64, 2 x 500 MC. Primary target: Essen, Marshalling yards. Weather 10/10ths cloud, tops 7/8000 feet. Bombed at 15.25 hours from 19,300 feet on G.H. Leader.

14/03/1945 NN782 JI-F Bombing Heinrichshutte 13.03 16.40   18.31

Bomb load 1 x 4000 HC, 12 x 500 ANM64. Primary target: Heinrichshutte, Hattingen Steel works and Benzol plant. Weather 10/10ths cloud, tops 7/12,000 feet. Bombed at 16.40 hours from 18,200 feet on leading G.H. aircraft.

18/03/1945 NN782 JI-F Bombing Bruchstrasse 11.37 15.04   17.06

Bomb load 1 x 4000 HC, 13 x 500 ANM64, 2 x 500 MC. Primary target: Bruchstrasse, Coal mine and coking plant. Weather 10/10ths cloud, tops 6-12,000 feet. Bombed at 15.04 hours from 19,000 feet on G.H. aircraft.

21/03/1945 NN782 JI-F Bombing Munster 09.34   13.07   15.28

Bomb load 1 x 4000 HC, 13 x 500 ANM64, 2 x 500 MC. Primary target Munster Viaduct and Marshalling Yards. Weather cloud nil to 2/10ths. Bombed at 13.07 hours from 18,300 feet on leading G.H. aircraft and visual. Small hole, heavy flak, between port inner and port outer engines.

09/04/1945 NG298 JI-F Bombing Kiel   19.30   22.40   01.40

Bombed primary target Kiel, Submarine Buildings Yards. Weather clear with slight haze. Bomb load 1 x 4000 HC and 12 x 500 ANM64. Bombed at 22.40 hours from 19,900 feet on Green T.I. Marking   very   concentrated. Attack appeared to fall well within area marked. H2S u/s. Good concentrated attack. Large white-red explosion at 22.37 in Northern A/P.

13/04/1945 LM724 JI-H Bombing Kiel   20.25 x 00.13

Bomb load 1 x 4000 HC and 12 x 500 ANM64. Primary target: Kiel, Docks and ship yards. Weather 10/10ths cloud low and thin. This aircraft returned early. Farthest point reached 5451N 0535E. Bombs jettisoned at 5451N 0535E. Starboard inner went u/s and was feathered. Port outer giving trouble. Fluctuation of revs.

24/04/1945 ME380 JI-E Bombing Bad Oldesloe 07.02 10.45 12.55

Bomb load 6 x 1000 ANM65, 10 x 500 ANM 64. Primary target: Bad-Oldesloe, Rail and road junction and Marshalling Yards. Weather 3/10ths to nil cloud. Bombed on G.H. at 10.45 hours from 17,900 ft. Good G.H. run. Large explosion seen in target area. Well concentrated. Bomb bursts seen in target area. Formation straggled over target.

30/04/1945 ME380 JI-E Manna Rotterdam   16.43   18.12   19.22

Weather intermittent showers and low cloud. Dropping area: Rotterdam. Load 5 packs. Dropped 4 packs on white cross. Visibility bad and most of the packs fell short of the white cross on south side of road dry land. One house seen on fire. Good reception from natives.

02/05/1945 RE116 JI-F Manna The Hague 11.11   12.32   13.39

Weather over dropping zone clear below cloud for the first arrivals changing later to heavy showers which marred visibility. Dropped 5 panniers on Red T.I. Rain storm made visibility very poor. Transmitters u/s. Released in field to west between railway and wood.

No Mid Upper Gunner that day.

Passenger LAC. Starkes.

14/05/1945 RF231 JI-A Exodus Juvincourt - Oakley 10.27 x 19.53

Duration 3.23 hours. Outward 1.47 hours. Collected 24 POWs. Homeward 1.36 hours. Organisation good. Had to wait for a "supply" of POW

17/05/1945 RE116 JI-F Exodus Brussels - Westcott 10.13 x 15.59

Duration 3 hrs 05 mins. Out 1 hr 23 mins. In 1 hr 22 mins. 10 Belgian refugees taken to Brussels. 24 Ex POWs returned to Westcott. Organisation O K.

18/05/1945 RE116 JI-F Exodus Brussels - Oakley 11.56 x 16.48

Duration 2 hrs 46 mins. Out 1 hr 06 mins. In 1 hr 40 mins. 10 Belgians taken to Brussels. 24 ex POWs returned to U.K. Everything OK.

23/05/1945 RE137 JI-D Exodus Brussels - Oakley 12.07 x 17.27

Duration 3.09 hours. Out 1.11 hours. In 1.58 hours. 10 Belgian refugees returned to Brussels. 24 ex POWs evacuated. Organisation OK.

P/O. Herbert Samuel Delacour

A425136 P/O. Herbert Samuel "Bertie" Delacour, RAAF Pilot.
1433141 F/S. George Palamountain.   A/Bomber.
151087 (1511958) F/O. Roy Geoffrey Picton. Navigator.

1580616 Sgt. Albert Clifford Benham.   WOP/AG.

J87116 (R197190)

  Sgt. Spurgeon Francis "Pop" Williams, RCAF   MU/Gunner.

1523833 F/S. George Donald "Don" Savage. R/Gunner.

1625906 Sgt. Gerald Edward "Gerry" Martin. F/Engineer.

J16550 F/O. Samuel Alexander "Alex" Phillips, RCAF   2nd Pilot. 12/06/44

14/01/1944 LL680 A2-H Bombing Brunswick 16.58   19.21   22.25

Bomb load 1 x 4000, 48 x 30 incendiaries. Primary target: Brunswick. There was 8/10 cloud. Bombed at 19.21 hours at 20,000 ft. Large glow of fires seen while over target and still visible 60 miles away on homeward journey. Very good and effective effort. Photo attempted.

P/O. H.S. Delacour did the mission as 2nd Pilot with P/O. V.H.J. Vizer's crew.

21/01/1944 LL678 A2-L Bombing Magdeburg 20.04 23.11   03.18

Bomb load 1 x 4000, 90 x 4, 32 x 30 incendiaries. Primary target: Magdeburg. There was 7/10 cloud. Bombed at 23.11 hours at 20,000 ft. Good attack. Route satisfactory. Fires over Berlin area.

27/01/1944 LL678 A2-L   Bombing Berlin 18.00 x   x

Did Not Complete Operation due to Oxygen failure.

28/01/1944 LL678 A2-L Bombing Berlin 00.12   03.26   08.12

Bomb load 1 x 2000 lb bomb, 16 x 30, 750 x 4 incendiaries. Primary target: Berlin. There was 10/10 cloud. Bombed at 03.26 hours at 20,000 ft. Fires and explosions seen through cloud, S/Ls below. Route quiet. Photo attempted. Had two encounters with enemy aircraft.

30/01/1944 LL678 A2-L   Bombing Berlin 17.17   20.19   23.29

Bomb load 1 x 2000 lb bomb, 10 x 500 lb bombs, 900 x 4, 48 x 30 incendiaries. Primary target: Berlin. There was 10/10 solid cloud. Bombed at 20.19 hours at 21,000 ft. Too early to see anything except sky markers. 48 x 30 incendiaries hung up. Very quiet and uneventful. 50 miles from target saw glow of fires.

15/02/1944 LL727 A2-C Bombing Berlin 17.25   21.19   00.53

Bomb load 1 x 4000 lb bomb, 32 x 30, 540 x 4, 90 x 4 incendiaries. Primary target: Berlin. There was 10/10 cloud. Bombed at 21.19 hrs at 21,000 ft. 2 distinct concentration of sky markers, which were rather scattered. 32 x 30 incendiaries hung up. R.M.s rather scattered but helpful. Visual monica u/s. Route very good. LL727 A2-C "C for Charlie".

21/02/1944 LL670 A2-K   Bombing Stuttgart 00.30   04.04   07.03

Bomb load 1 x 8000 lb bomb, 16 x 30, 90 x 4 incendiaries. Primary target: Stuttgart. There was 5/10 cloud, clear patches. Bombed at 04.04 hours at 20,000 ft. Whitish fires seen and appeared to be gaining hold when we left target. T.I.s well concentrated. Route very quiet but arrived too early on target. Photo attempted.

24/02/1944 LL678 A2-L   Bombing Schweinfurt 21.00   01.12   04.45

Bomb load 1 x 4000 lb bomb, 24 x 30, 420 x 4, 90 x 4 incendiaries. Primary target: Schweinfurt. Weather clear, much smoke. Bombed at 01.12 hours at 21,000 ft. Mass of fires and billows of smoke to SW. 90 x 4 incendiaries hung up. Monica u/s. Good route.

25/02/1944 LL678 A2-L   Bombing Augsburg 22.02   01.16   04.55

Bomb load 1 x 4000 lb bomb, 32 x 30, 510 x 4, 90 x 4 incendiaries. Primary target: Augsburg. Weather clear, but pall of smoke hanging over town. Monica u/s. Fires burning on arrival, appeared to be increasing on departure. 90 x 4lb inc, hung up. D.R. (Dead reckoning) compass went u/s when crossing English coast on return. Landed at R.A.F. Oakington. Bombed at 01.16 hours at 21,000 ft.

01/03/1944 LL678 A2-L   Bombing Stuttgart 23.37 x 03.31

Bomb load 1 x 4000 lb bomb, 24 x 30, 600 x 4, 90 x 4 incendiaries. Returned early. Furthest point reached on course 4825N 0120E. W/T receiver u/s. Pilot's oxygen unreliable. Jettisoned bomb to reduce load for landing.

15/03/1944 LL678 A2-L   Bombing Stuttgart 19.24 x 03.22

Bomb load 1 x 1000 lb bomb, 72 x 30, 1050 x 4, 90 x 4 incendiaries. Primary target: Stuttgart. There was 7-9/10 cloud with tops 10,000 feet. Fires and marking seemed to be in two centres. One on port and one on starboard. Monica went u/s at Chartres. A very scattered attack. Route trouble free.

18/03/1944 LL678 A2-L   Bombing Frankfurt 19.40   22.05   00.45

Bomb load 1 x 4000 lb bomb, 40 x 30, 1350 x 4 incendiaries. Primary target: Frankfurt. Weather was hazy. Bombed at 22.05 hours from 20,000 feet. Large area of fires seen. Considered P.F.F. a little late. Attack slightly scattered but successful.

22/03/1944 LL678 A2-L   Bombing Frankfurt 18.27   21.59   00.46

Bomb load 1 x 1000 lb. bomb, 1161 x 4, 129 x 4, 64 x 30 incendiaries. Primary target: Frankfurt. There was 3/10 cloud. Bombed at 21.59 hours from 21,000 feet. Red and green T.I.s and many small scattered fires seen. P.F.F. good - on time. Glow of fires seen for 200 miles. Attack considered successful.

24/03/1944 LL678 A2-L   Bombing Berlin 18.37 x 23.31

Bomb load 1 x 1000 lb bomb, 88 x 30, 810 x 4, 90 x 4 incendiaries. Returned early. 1 x 1000 lb bomb jettisoned safe. Navigator ill, lack of oxygen suspected. Furthest point reached 5453N 0855E.

26/03/1944 LL678 A2-L   Bombing Essen 20.12   22.11   00.45

Bomb load 1 x 2000 lb bomb, 56 x 30, 1080 x 4, 120 x 4 incendiaries. Primary target: Essen. There was 10/10 cloud. Bombed at 22.11 hours from 21,000 feet. Some glow seen. Sky markers to port. Route OK. Success or otherwise difficult to ascertain owing to cloud.

10/04/1944 LL678 A2-L   Bombing Laon 01.39 03.51   05.48

Bomb load 9 x 1000, 4 x 500 lb bomb. Primary target: Laon. Weather was clear. Bombed at 03.51 hours from 11,000 feet. Some fires seen. Good attack and perfect bombing. Route good.

26/04/1944 LL678 A2-L Bombing Essen 22.55 01.30 03.06

Bomb load 1 x 2000 lb bomb, 84 x 30, 945 x 4, 105 x 4 lb incendiaries. Primary target: Essen. Weather was clear. Bombed at 01.30 hours from 20,000 feet. There was plenty of searchlight, little flak. Main fires round markers. Few scattered incendiaries. Good route. Ruhr searchlights an impressive sight. Fires developed quickly as we left.

27/04/1944 LL678 A2-L Bombing Friedrichshafen 21.57 02.04 05.34

Bomb load 1 x 4000, 2 x 1000, 1 x 500 lb bombs. Primary target: Friedrichshafen. Weather was clear. Bombed at 02.04 hours from 20,000 feet. No fires seen on arrival. Cones of searchlights with flak which diminished when attack started. There was a concentration of fires on leaving.

01/05/1944 LL677 A2-E Bombing Chambly 22.59 00.23 01.57

Bomb load 10 x 1000, 5 x 500 lb bombs. Primary target: Chambly. Weather was clear. Bombed at 00.23 hours from 8,500 feet. Yellow T.I. seen and bombs seen to burst. Should be a good effort. Route satisfactory.

08/05/1944 LL678 A2-L Bombing Cap Gris Nez 22.57 23.55 00.50

Bomb load 14 x 1000 lb. bombs. Primary target: Cape Gris Nez. Weather was clear. Bombed at 23.55 hours from 7,000 feet. Smoke covered bomb bursts seen through smoke. Attack would have been better if markers had been on time.

09/05/1944 LL678 A2-L Bombing Cap Gris Nez 03.10 04.18 05.00

Bomb load 1 x 1000 GP, 13 x 1000 MC. Primary target: Cape Gris Nez. Slight haze over target. Bombed as instructed by Master Bomber at 04.18 hours from 6,000 feet. Appeared to be more successful raid than on previous night and believed target was well pranged.

11/05/1944 LL678 A2-L Bombing Louvain 22.55 00.18 01.35

Bomb load 5 x 1000 GP, 5 x 1000 MC, 5 x 500 MC. Primary target: Louvain. Hazy conditions over target. Bombed markers at 00.18 hours from 8,500 feet. Pall of smoke over target. Believed only moderate attack, markers rather scattered and smoke obscured vision.

15/05/1944 LL727 A2-C Bombing Rushford Range 23.00 x x

Only noted in ORB summary. Sortie not detailed. G.D. Savage noted in his logbook "I.R. Bombing and X-Country".

CATAMOUNT - Special Night Navigation Exercise in which was incorporated Infra-red photography and Night Bombing.

19/05/1944 LL678 A2-L Bombing Le Mans 22.40 00.26 03.00

Bomb load 4 x 1000 USA, 5 x 1000 MC, 1 x 1000 GP, 4 x 500 GP. Primary target: Le Mans. 10/10 cloud over target. Bombed on T.I. markers at 00.26 hours from 7,500 feet. Narrowly missed collision with another Lancaster over target. Hazy conditions below cloud and little to be seen of the attack.

21/05/1944 LL728 JI-B Bombing Duisburg 23.00 01.14 02.45

Bomb load 1 x 8000 lb bomb, 96 x 30 incendiaries. Primary target: Duisberg. There was 10/10 cloud with tops at 19,000 feet. Bombed general glow and red T.I. at 01.14 hours from 20,000 feet. Seemed a poor attack with much indiscriminate bombing.

22/05/1944 LL678 A2-L Bombing Dortmund 23.00 x 00.20

Bomb load 1 x 2000 lb bomb, 96 x 30, 810 x 4, 90 x 4 incendiaries. Primary target: Dortmund. Returned early because of severe icing. Could not climb above 9,000 feet. Farthest point reached 5217N 0040E. All bombs jettisoned safe at Rushford Range at 00.04 hours.

02/06/1944 LL678 A2-L Bombing Wissant 01.25 x 03.25

Bomb load 1 x 1000 GP, 10 x 1000 MC, 4 x 500 MC. Primary target: Wissant Gun Positions. Target not identified because of 10/10 cloud and did not bomb therefore. On the way into target one red T.I. was seen but this had disappeared on arrival. 1 x 1000 GP, 2 x 1000 MC, and 4 x 500 MC jettisoned safe at 5219N 0223E. Remainder of bombs brought back.

05/06/1944 LL678 A2-L Bombing Ouistreham 03.58 05.11 06.57

Bomb load 9 x 1000 MC and 2 x 500 MC. Primary target: Ouistreham. There was 5/10 cloud at target. Bombed red and green T.I.s at 05.11 hours from 9,000 feet. Markers were well grouped but bombing did not seem too good. Results of raid doubtful. Route quiet and opposition practically nil. Landed at Woodbridge on return, due to lack of brake pressure.

07/06/1944 LL678 A2-L Bombing Massy Palaiseau 00.25 02.09 03.47

Bomb load 18 x 500 MC. Primary target: Massy Palaiseau. 8/10 cloud above. Bombed on Master Bomber's instructions at 02.09 hours from 6,500 feet. Was first aircraft to bomb and saw no activity. Had combat with enemy aircraft.

10/06/1944 DS786 A2-F Bombing Dreux 23.13 00.56 03.06

Bomb load 16 x 500 GP, 2 x 500 LD. Primary target: Dreux. Bombed on instructions of Master Bomber at 00.56 hours from 7,000 feet. Rear Gunner reported large red explosion at 00.59 hours.

12/06/1944 LL678 A2-L Bombing Gelsenkirchen 23.12 x 01.24

Bomb load 1 x 4000 HC, 12 x 500 GP, 4x 500 MC. Primary target: Gelsenkirchen. Aircraft missing.

Shot down by a night fighter, crashing near Bathmen. According to www.lostaircraft.com, shot down by a night-fighter of Oblt. Dietrich Schmidt, II/NJG1, crashing at 01.24 hours at Zuid Loo (Overjssel), a small hamlet 3 km SE of Bathmen, where those who died are buried in the general cemetery. However, Nachtjagd War Diaries credits Hptm. Gerhard Friedrich, 1/NJG6, with shooting down LL678.

F/O. S.A. Phillips was 2nd Pilot that day.

P/O. H.S. Delacour RAAF KIA, F/O. S.A. Phillips RCAF (P2) KIA, Sgt. G.E. Martin Evaded, F/O. R.G. Picton KIA, F/S. A.C. Palamountain Evaded, Sgt. A.C. Benham KIA, Sgt. F.S. Williams RCAF Evaded, F/S. G.D. Savage KIA.

S/L. William George Devas, AFC DFC

William George Devas

32221 S/L. William George Devas. AFC, DFC.   Pilot.
NZ416861   F/O. Harold Thomas Crampton, RNZAF.   A/Bomber.
NZ421874   F/S. Keith Varndell Stafford, RNZAF. Navigator.
NZ416419   W/O. Ronald Gordon Collender, RNZAF. WOP/AG.
972379   Sgt. William Percy Blake.   MU/Gunner.
A428331   F/S. James Samuel Lupton, RAAF.   R/Gunner.
182295 (1831748) Sgt. Colin Oliver Turner.   F/Engineer.
20/04/1944 LL733 JI-G Bombing Cologne 00.01 02.13 04.04
    Bomb load 1 x 8000 lb bomb, 216 x 4, 24 x 4 incendiaries. Primary target: Koln. There was 10/10 cloud. Bombed at 02.13 hours from 19,000 feet. 3 flares (green with yellow stars) seen to fall before arrival. - none during attack so bombed red glow under cloud. Markers very few and very scattered. 1st sky markers seen to illuminate. Bomb doors damaged by falling 1 x 8000 lb bomb.
    Of his usual crew; only S/L. W.G. Devas flew the mission as 2nd Pilot with

F/L. R.C. Chopping's crew.

22/04/1944 LL728 JI-B Bombing Dusseldorf 23.0801.32 03.31

Bomb load 1 x 2000 lb bomb, 84 x 30, 1050 x 4 incendiaries. Weather was clear, much smoke. Bombed at 01.32 hours from 20,000 feet. Terrific number of fires coinciding with position of markers. Very good attack. Route satisfactory.

24/04/1944 LL728 JI-B Bombing Karlsruhe 22.21 00.45 03.37

Bomb load 1 x 8000 lb bomb, 24 x 30, 216 x 4, 24 x 4 lb incendiaries. Primary target: Karlsruhe. There was patchy cloud. Bombed at 00.45 hours from 20,000 feet. T.I.s appeared very scattered - bombs bursting over a very wide area. Air Speed Indicator frozen - could not be used - moderate icing. Disappointing trip - bombed after E.T.A. to obtain better identification of target. Route good.

26/04/1944 LL728 JI-B Bombing Essen 22.52 01.35 03.29

Bomb load 1 x 1000 lb bomb, 60 x 30, 405 x 4, 45 x 4 lb incendiaries. Primary target: Essen. There was thin cloud with patches in layers. Bombed at 01.35 hours from 21,000 feet. Good concentration of T.I.s and incendiaries, smoke column up to 15,000 feet. Considered very good raid. Slightly early. Target well alight as we left area.

27/04/1944 LL728 JI-B Bombing Friedrichshafen 21.54 02.21 06.01

Bomb load 810 x 4, 80 x 30 lb incendiaries. Primary target: Friedrichshafen. Weather was clear. Bombed at 02.21 hours from 20,000 feet. Well concentrated fires seen. Bombed 10 minutes late - no markers. Very successful raid. Very large flames seen from hangar roofs. Explosion seen at 02.19 hours. Good route.

08/05/1944 LL728 JI-B Bombing Cap Gris Nez 22.59 23.54 00.54

Bomb load 14 x 1000 lb bombs. Primary target: Cape Gris Nez. Weather was clear. Bombed at 23.54 hours from 8,000 feet. Smoke and small explosions seen also muzzle bursts from A.A. Guns. Successful attack. Aircraft arrived in time and orbited to starboard before bombing. P.F.F. Markers first dropped at 23.57 hours.

09/05/1944 LL728 JI-B Bombing Cap Gris Nez 03.00 04.14 05.05

Bomb load 1 x 1000 GP, 13 x 1000 MC. Primary target: Cape Gris Nez. Conditions were clear and visual obtained of coast line and red T.I.s. Red T.I.s bombed at 04.14 hours from 6,000 feet. Bomb burst, smoke and dust seen. No opposition and attack seemed successful. Enemy aircraft sighted at 04.09 hours, but no combat.

19/05/1944 LL728 JI-B Bombing Le Mans 22.15 x 03.25

Bomb load 4 x 1000 USA, 5 x 1000 MC, 1 x 1000 GP, 4 x 500 GP. Primary target: Le Mans. Orbited the target five times but difficulty experienced in obtaining definite instructions from Master Bomber. No T.I.s were visible and as target was not identified with certainty, decided not to bomb. 4 x 500 GP jettisoned safe at 4916N 0256W. Remainder of bombs brought back to Base.

02/06/1944 LL728 JI-B Bombing Wissant 01.25 02.14 03.15

Bomb load 1 x 1000 GP, 10 x 1000 MC, 4 x 500 MC. Primary target: Wissant Gun Positions. 8/10ths cloud with a gap. Bombed between red and green T.I.s at 02.14½ hours from 6,000 feet. Success of attack difficult to ascertain but red T.I. believed to be too far inland.

06/06/1944 LL728 JI-B Bombing Lisieux 00.13 01.37 03.21

Bomb load 16 x 500 MC tail fused and 2 x 500 MC LD. Primary target: Lisieux. Clear below 6000 feet. Bombed red T.I. at 01.37 hours from 6,000 feet as directed by Master Bomber. Aircraft orbited in target area waiting for Master Bomber. Glows of fires were seen through smoke. Everything dependent upon accuracy of the markers.

07/06/1944 LL728 JI-B Bombing Massy Palaiseau 00.22 02.14 04.06

Bomb load 18 x 500 MC. Primary target: Massy Palaiseau. Hazy below and 10/10 cloud above. Bombed as directed by Master Bomber at 02.14 hours 6,000 feet. Bombing seemed accurate and several explosions seen in target area; Starboard outer was feathered before reaching target and came home on 3 engines. Fighters active around target.

10/06/1944 LL728 JI-B Bombing Dreux 23.06 00.56 03.23

Bomb load 16 x 500 GP, 2 x 500 LD. Primary target: Dreux. Bombed as instructed by Master bomber to starboard of green T.I. at 00.56 hours from 8,000 feet. Master Bomber rather faint. Believed very accurate but vision obscured by smoke. Weather clear.

F/L. Acting S/L. Marcus Dods, DFC

66013 (1057899) S/L. Marcus Dods, DFC.   Pilot.
182294 (1610232) P/O. Roy Perkins.   A/Bomber.
A424502   P/O. Douglas Leslie Wright, RAAF. Navigator.
A424380   F/S. Brian McLennan Crapp, RAAF. WOP/AG.
1180797 Sgt. R.K. Redfern.   MU/Gunner.
909712 Sgt. J. Edwards.   R/Gunner.
12893311   Sgt. F. Widowson.   F/Engineer.
37994 W/C. Michael "Mike" Wyatt, DFC. Captain. 10/06/1944

10/06/1944 LL731 JI-L Bombing Dreux 23.03 00.57 03.53

Bomb load 16 x 500 GP; 2 x 500 LD. Primary target: Dreux. Bombed as instructed by Master Bomber at 00.57 hours from 7500 feet. Results appeared to be good and attack concentrated. Trouble free trip. Weather clear.

W/C. M. Wyatt was Captain of this crew that day and S/L. Marcus Dods 2nd Pilot.

12/06/1944 LL731 JI-L Bombing Gelsenkirchen 23.06 x 02.15

Bomb load 1 x 4000 HC, 12 x 500 GP, 4 x 500 MC. Starboard outer engine feathered as Lancaster unable to maintain height and would have been 20 minutes late over target so returned early. Furthest point reached 35 E

Westkapelle. Bombs jettisoned at 5150N 0430E from 15,000 feet.

Above: A/S/L Marcus Dods (centre) with crew, Dalmatian dog and Lancaster LM685 JI-Q. Below left: A portrait of Marcus Dods. After the war he found fame as a composer and conductor. Below right: A GH 'vic' photographed from Dods' Lancaster, date unknown. (Waterbeach Military Heritage Museum).

14/06/1944 LL731 JI-L Bombing Le Havre   23.40   01.15   02.53

Bomb load 11 x 1000 MC, 4 x 500 GP. Primary target: Le Havre. Weather clear. Bombed at 01.15 hours from 15,000 feet. Fires seen on arrival. T.I.s well placed. Master Bomber said bomb red and green - believed enemy said bomb yellow - no yellow visible. Little opposition. Attack good. Had combat with M.E.110.

15/06/1944 LL731 JI-L Bombing Valenciennes 23.05   00.37   02.15

Bomb load 16 x 500 GP, 2 x 500 MC. Primary target: Valenciennes. Weather clear below cloud. Bombed at 00.37 hours from 7,800 feet on centre of red and green T.I.s. Crossed coast at Orfordness owing to compass fault, joining stream on the enemy coast. D.R. Compass u/s. Bomb bursts amongst T.I.

17/06/1944 LL731 JI-L Bombing Montdidier 01.06 x 04.37

Bomb load 16 x 500 GP, 2 x 500 ANM64 GP. Primary target: Montdidier. Arrived over target and heard Master Bomber order return to Base. Jettisoned safe 10 x 500 GP at 03.21 hours from 10,000 feet 5003N 0052E.

21/06/1944 LL731 JI-L Bombing Domleger   18.05 x 20.51

Bomb load 18 x 500 MC. Primary target: Domleger near Abbeville, V-1 flying bomb launch site. 8/10 - 10/10ths cloud. No T.I.s seen, ordered to return to Base by Master Bomber. Very meagre bursts of heavy flak. Jettisoned 8 x 500 MC at 19.40 hours from 11,000 feet, 5025N 0122E.

24/06/1944 LL624 JI-R Bombing Rimeux   23.22   00.34   02.08

Bomb load 18 x 500 GP. Primary target: Rimeux, Flying bomb installations. Weather clear. Bombed at 00.34 hours from 10,600 feet centre of red T.I.s. Bomb bursts seen on red T.I.s. Many searchlights, 3 aircraft seen coned. No flak.

27/06/1944 LL731 JI-L Bombing Biennais 23.29 01.12 02.30

Bomb load 16 x 500 GP. 2 x 500 ANM64 GP. Primary target: Biennais, Flying bomb installations. There was 10/10ths cloud. Bombed at 01.12 hours from 13,000 feet red glow.

30/06/1944 LL731 JI-L Bombing Villers Bocage 18.22 19.59 21.38

Bomb load 11 x 1000 MC, 3 x 500 GP. Primary target: Villers Bocage. Weather clear below, 5/10ths cloud above. Bombed at 19.59 hours from 4,000 feet on red T.I.s. Bombing very concentrated, moderate, heavy and light flak. Fighter cover well in evidence.

02/07/1944 LL733 JI-S Bombing Beauvoir   12.46   14.35   16.09

Bomb load 11 x 1000 MC, 4 x 500 GP. Primary target: Beauvoir, Flying bomb supply site. Bombed at 14.35 hours from 8,000 feet on yellow T.I.s.

05/07/1944 LL733 JI-S Bombing Watten 23.00 00.09 01.24

Bomb load 11 x 1000 ANM65, 4 x 500 GP. Primary target: Watten, Constructional works. Bombed at 00.09 hours from 8,700 feet red T.I.s.

10/07/1944 LL733 JI-S Bombing Nucourt 04.17 06.06 08.03

Bomb load 11 x 1000 ANM65, 4 x 500 GP. Primary target: Nucourt, Constructional works. Bombed at 06.06 hours from 15,500 feet, Gee.

12/07/1944 LL733 JI-S Bombing Vaires 17.58 20.03 21.57

Bomb load 18 x 500 GP. Primary target: Vaires, Marshalling yards. Target reached 20.03 hours from 14,500 feet. Some yellow T.I.s seen but Master Bomber had ordered to abandon mission. Much flak North of Paris. Jettisoned at 20.41 hours from 12000 feet, position 4955N 0035E, 4 x 500 GP.

23/07/1944 LL733 JI-S Bombing Kiel 22.27 01.26 04.07

Bomb load 10 x 1000 MC, 5 x 500 GP. Primary target: Kiel, Warehouses and docks. Weather 10/10ths cloud. Bombed at 01.26 hours from 20,000 feet green T.I. Large orange fire seen to port of target markers.

25/07/1944 LL733 JI-S Bombing Stuttgart 21.42 01.40 05.35

Bomb load 5 x 1000 MC, 3 x 500 GP. Primary target: Stuttgart. Weather clear, ground haze. Bombed at 01.40 hours from 19,000 feet on red T.I. T.I.s rather scattered, but considered within limits of built up area. Large red glow seen in sky 80 miles away.

01/08/1944 LL635 JI-M Bombing Foret de Nieppe 19.10 x 21.53

Bomb load 11 x 1000 MC, 4 x 500 GP. Target: De Nieppe, constructional works. Jettisoned at 20.55 hours from 11,000 feet 4 x 1000 MC, position 5112N 0223E. Abandoned on Master Bomber's orders.

08/08/1944 LL635 JI-M Bombing Foret de Lucheux 21.59 23.49 01.21

Bomb load 18 x 500 GP. Primary target: Foret de Lucheux, Petrol dump. Weather clear, slight ground haze. Bombed at 23.49 hours from 12,600 feet, undershot by ½ second large central fire as instructed by Master Bomber. Very large concentrated mass of fires observed.

"Foret de Lucheux" is a forest between Lille and Amiens. During WWII, important fuel tanks were there.

15/08/1944 LL635 JI-M Bombing St Trond 10.00 12.09 13.27

Bomb load 11 x 1000 MC, 4 x 500 GP. Primary target St. Trond Airfield. Slight haze over target. Bombed at 12.09 hours from 16,400 feet intersection of runways. A very successful attack, many craters seen on airfield.

29/08/1944 LM685 JI-Q Bombing Stettin 21.10 02.06 06.53

Bomb load 1 x 4000 HC, 52 x 30, 486 x 4, 54 x 4 lb. incendiaries. Primary target: Stettin. Weather clear. Bombed at 02.06 hours from 17,000 feet, red and green T.I.s. 02.05 hours large column black smoke following an explosion. Very good attack. Master Bomber enthusiastic.

17/09/1944 LM685 JI-Q Bombing Boulogne 10.40 12.15 13.30

Bomb load 11 x 1000 MC, 4 x 500 GP. Primary target: Boulogne Aiming Point 2. Weather clear below cloud. Bombed at 12.15 hours from 3,500 feet, 300 yards port of red T.I.s.

25/09/1944 LM685 JI-Q Bombing Pas de Calais 08.12 x 10.58

Bomb load 11 x 1000 MC, 4 x 500 GP. Primary target: Calais. Abandoned mission on Master Bomber's instructions. Jettisoned 3 x 1000 MC, 2 x 500 GP.

05/10/1944 LM685 JI-Q Bombing Saarbrucken 17.08 20.31 22.20

Bomb load 11 x 1000 MC, 1 x 500 GP, 3 x 500 GP. Long Delay. Primary target: Saarbrucken, Marshalling yards. This aircraft was a P.F.F. supporter. Weather clear over target. Bombs dropped at 20.31 hours from 15,000 feet on green T.I.

07/10/1944 LM685 JI-Q Bombing Emmerich 12.11 14.27 15.54

Bomb load 1 x 4000 HC, 10 x No.14 clusters, 4 x (150 x 4). Primary target Emmerich. Weather clear with cloud at 13,000 feet. Bombed at 14.27 hours from 12,500 feet on built up area North West of harbour.

14/10/1944 LM685 JI-Q Bombing Duisburg 22.24 01.31 03.12

Bomb load 11 x 1000 MC, 4 x 500 GP Long Delay. Primary target: Duisburg. Weather was clear with small amount of cloud over the target. Bombed at 01.31 hours from 19,800 feet. Centre of red T.I.s.

18/10/1944 LM719 A2-E Bombing Bonn 08.28 11.03 13.19

Bomb load 1 x 4000 HC, 5 x 12 x 30 - 2 x 12 x 30 modified, 9 x No.14 Clusters. Primary target: Bonn. Weather varying cloud 2-7/10ths with break for bombing. Bombed at 11.03 hours from 19,000 feet. Area of town South-west of the bridge.

30/10/1944 LM685 JI-Q Bombing Wesseling 09.10 12.04 13.31

Bomb load 1 x 4000 HC, 15 x 500 GP. Primary target: Wesseling. Weather was 10/10ths cloud - tops about 7,000 feet. Bombed at 11.58 hours from 17,300 feet on G.H.

04/11/1944 LM685 JI-Q Bombing Solingen 11.16 14.07 16.10

Bomb load 1 x 4000 HC, 6 x 1000 ANM59, 4 x 500 GP, 2 x 500 MC (L/Delay), 3 Flares. Primary target: Solingen. Weather 8-10/10ths cloud. Bombed at 14.07 hours from 20,000 feet on upwind edge of red flares.

06/11/1944 LM685 JI-Q Bombing Koblenz 16.49 19.34 21.53

Bomb load 1 x 4000 HC, 12 x 500 Clusters, 2 x 250 T.I.s. Primary target: Koblenz. Weather clear over target. Bombed at 19.34 hours from 17,500 feet on G.H.

15/11/1944 PD389 JI-Q Bombing Dortmund 12.34 15.41 17.29

Bomb load 1 x 4000 HC, 2 x 500 MC, 10 x 500 GP, 4 x 250 T.I. Red. Primary target: Hoesch-Benzin Dortmund, Oil refineries. Weather 10/10ths cloud over the target. Bombed at 15.41 hours from 17,000 feet. Had to feather 1 engine on way out over English coast. Completed trip on 3 engines.

P/O. Leslie Samuel Drew, DFC

182355 (1387020) P/O. Leslie Samuel Drew, DFC. Pilot.
  F/S. R.S. Williams. A/Bomber.
  F/S. W.F.T. Reid. Navigator.
Sgt. S.E. Jarvis. WOP/AG. 26 ops.
201216 (1470138) Sgt. James Albert Smith. WOP/AG. 2 ops.
J19707 F/O. Frank Harold Rowan, DFC RAAF. WOP/AG. 1 op.
Sgt. K.V. Henry. MU/Gunner. 26 ops.
196933 (1333763)
  W/O. Harold George Everest Friend. MU/Gunner. 2 ops.
  F/S. George Edgard Sales. MU/Gunner.1 op.
Sgt. W.A. Abbott. R/Gunner. 28 ops.
  F/S. I.M. Davies. R/Gunner. 1 op.
Sgt. R.C. Tween. F/Engineer.

03/08/1944 LM265 JI-E Bombing Bois de Cassan   11.15   14.07   15.51
  Bomb load 11 x 1000 MC, 4 x 500 GP. Primary target: Bois de Cassan, Flying bomb supply depot. Bombed at 14.07 hours from 15,000 feet centre of smoke.
04/08/1944 LM288 JI-C Bombing Bec d'Ambes 13.23   18.03   21.22
  Bomb load 8 x 1000 MC, 2 x 500 GP. Primary target: Bec d'Ambes depot. Weather clear. Bombed at 18.03 hours from 8,000 feet, NW edge of smoke pall as instructed by Master Bomber. Port inner feathered at 19.07 hours. Quite good effort.
05/08/1944 LM277 JI-F Bombing Bassen 14.24 19.02 22.14
  Bomb load 8 x 1000 MC, 2 x 500 GP. Primary target: Bassen Oil Depot. Cloud base 4,000 feet over target. Bombed at 19.02 hours from 4,000 feet visually long buildings on North side of target. Bombing concentrated large fires. Aircraft damaged by flak, rear turret u/s, hydraulics and oxygen system.
07/08/1944 LM288 JI-C Bombing Mare de Magne 21.44 23.41   01.07
  Bomb load 11 x 1000 MC, 4 x 500 GP. Primary target: Mare de Magne (just past Caen). No cloud. Bombed at 23.41 hours from 9000 feet red T.I.s. Only results seen were clouds of smoke. Mare-de-Magne: place between Caen and Fontenay le Marmion.
29/08/1944 LM627 JI-D Bombing Stettin 21.19 02.06   06.26
  Bomb load 1 x 4000 HC, 52 x 30, 486 x 4, 54 x 4 lb incendiaries. Primary target: Stettin. Weather clear. Bombed at 02.06 hours from 11,300 feet between two red T.I.s slight N of main T.I. concentration. T.I.s appeared to cover whole target area. Fires taking good hold, several small explosions seen. Master Bomber's instructions helpful.
05/09/1944 LM627 JI-D Bombing Le Havre   17.20   19.23   20.37
  Bomb load 11 x 1000 MC, 4 x 500 GP. Primary target: Le Havre. Bombed

at 19.23 hours from 13,000 feet red T.I.

06/09/1944 LM627 JI-D Bombing Le Havre   16.36   18.40   19.57

Bomb load 11 x 1000 MC, 4 x 500 GP. Primary target: Le Havre. Bombed at 18.40 hours from 7,000 feet red T.I.s.

08/09/1944 LM627 JI-D Bombing Le Havre   06.05   08.05   09.28

Bomb load 11 x 1000 MC, 4 x 500 GP. Primary target: Le Havre. Weather 10/10ths cloud down to 3,000 feet. Bombed at 08.05 hours from 3,000 feet, red T.I.s.

12/09/1944 LM627 JI-D Bombing Frankfurt   18.28   23.03   01.12

Bomb load 1 x 4000 HC, 14 x 500 Clusters 4lb. Target: Frankfurt am Main. Weather clear over the target. Bombed at 23.03 hours from 16,500 feet on centre of red T.I.s partially obscured by smoke.

23/09/1944 LM627 JI-D Bombing Neuss 19.20   21.31   23.30

Bomb load 8 x 1000 ANM59, 3 x 1000 ANM44, 4 x 500 GP. Primary target: Neuss. Weather 10/10ths cloud over target, tops 8/10,000 feet. Bombed at 21.31 hours from 19,500 feet at centre of dull red glow.

05/10/1944 LM627 JI-D Bombing Saarbrucken 17.16 20.35   22.18

Bomb load 11 x 1000 MC, 1 x 500 GP. Primary target: Saarbrucken, Marshalling yards. Weather clear over target. Bombed at 20.35 hours from 14,500 feet on the centre of close triangle on 1 red and 2 green T.I.s.

07/10/1944 LM627 JI-D Bombing Emmerich 12.05 14.27   15.50

Bomb load 1 x 4000 HC. 10 x No.14 clusters. 4 x (150 x 4). Primary target Emmerich. Weather clear with cloud at 13,000 feet. Bombed at 14.27 hours from 12,500 feet on red T.I.s.

14/10/1944 LM627 JI-D* Bombing Duisburg 06.51 09.04   11.10

Bomb load 11 x 1000 MC. 4 x 500 GP Long Delay. Primary target: Duisburg. Weather patchy cloud with gaps for bombing. Bombed at 09.04 hours from 17,700 feet. North of Docks.

(*) Note: by error in ORBs LM627 JI-D is also noted at the same hours for P/O. E. Hill crew. At this period LM627 was L.S. Drew's usual aircraft.

14/10/1944 LM627 JI-D Bombing Duisburg   23.00   01.29   03.07

Bomb load 11 x 1000 MC. 4 x 500 GP Long Delay. Primary target: Duisburg. Weather was clear with small amount of cloud over the target. Bombed at 01.29 hours from 20,000 feet. Centre of red T.I.s.

18/10/1944 LM627 JI-D Bombing Bonn   08.19   11.00   12.54

Bomb load 1 x 4000 HC. 5 x 12 x 30 - 2 x 12 x 30 modified. 9 x No.14 Clusters. Primary target: Bonn. Weather varying cloud 2-7/10ths with break for bombing. Bombed at 11.00 hours from 17,000 feet. Visually. Bombing accurate about A/P.

19/10/1944 LM627 JI-D Bombing Stuttgart 22.14   01.05   03.51

Bomb load 1 x 4000 HC. 6 x 1000 MC. 1 x 500 GP. Primary target: Stuttgart, A/P 'E' 2nd attack. Weather 10/10ths low cloud over target and all crew arrived late owing to winds not as forecast. Bombed at 01.05 hours from 19,700 feet. Centre of flames. Red with Yellow stars.

21/10/1944 LM627 JI-D Bombing Flushing 10.45 12.27 13.21

Bomb load 12 x 1000 MC, 2 x 500 GP. Primary target: Flushing 'B'. Weather clear. Bombed at 12.27 hours from 8,000 feet. Visual.

23/10/1944 LM627 JI-D Bombing Essen 16.49 19.50 21.30

Bomb load 1 x 4000 HC. 14 x 500 Clusters. Primary target: Essen. Weather 10/10ths cloud over target - tops 12/14,000 feet with most appalling weather on route. Bombed at 19.50 hours from 20,600 feet on GH.

Sgt. J. A. Smith was WOP/AG and F/S. I.M. Davies R/Gunner that day.

25/10/1944 LM627 JI-D Bombing Essen 13.01 15.30 16.50

Bomb load 1 x 4000 HC. 6 x 1000 MC. 6 x 500 GP. Primary target: Essen. Weather over target 10/10ths low cloud, with one clear patch which appeared to fill up later in the attack. Bombed at 15.30 hours from 21,000 feet. Red T.I.s.

Sgt. J. A. Smith was WOP/AG and W/O. H. G. E. Friend MU/Gunner that day.

05/11/1944 LM627 JI-D Bombing Solingen 10.25 13.05 14.46

Bomb load 1 x 4000 HC, 6 x 1000 ANM59, 4 x 500 GP, 2 x 500 GP (L/Delay), 3 Flares. Primary target: Solingen. Weather 10/10ths cloud over target. Bombed at 13.05 hours from 18,000 feet on instruments.

06/11/1944 LM627 JI-D Bombing Koblenz 16.52 19.33 21.42

Bomb load 1 x 4000 HC, 12 x 500 Clusters, 2 x 250 T.I.s. Primary target: Koblenz. Weather clear over target. Bombed at 19.33 hours from 17,500 feet on G.H.

F/S. G. E. Sales was MU/Gunner that day.

08/11/1944 LM627 JI-D Bombing Homberg 08.12 10.30 12.11

Bomb load 1 x 4000 HC, 6 x 1000 GP, 6 x 500 GP. Primary target: Homberg. Weather clear. Bombed at 10.30 hours from 17,500 feet. Visual target area.

W/O. H. G. E. Friend was MU/Gunner that day.

11/11/1944 LM627 JI-D Bombing Castrop Rauxel 08.28 11.06 12.39

Bomb load 1 x 4000 HC, 15 x 500 GP, 1 Flare. Primary target: Castrop Rauxel, Oil refineries. Weather 10/10ths cloud. Bombed at 11.06 hours from 19,000 feet on G.H.

F/O. F. H. Rowan was WOP/AG that day.

15/11/1944 LM627 JI-D Bombing Dortmund 12.53 15.39 17.10

Bomb load 1 x 4000 HC, 15 x 500 GP, 1 Red with Green star Flare. Primary target: Hoesch-Benzin Dortmund, Oil refineries. Weather 10/10ths cloud over the target. Bombed at 15.39 hours from 17,000 feet on G.H. Aircraft damaged by flak. Bomb Aimer wounded in head.

20/11/1944 ME841 JI-J Bombing Homberg 12.52 15.16 17.07

Bomb load 1 x 4000 HC, 15 x 500 GP, 1 Red-Green Flare. Primary target: Homberg. Weather 10/10ths cloud over target. Bombed at 15.16 hours from 19,000 feet on G.H.

21/11/1944 ME841 JI-J Bombing Homberg 12.42 15.07 16.28

Bomb load 1 x 4000 HC, 15 x 500 GP, 1 Red and Green Flare. Primary target: Homberg. Last resort target: Rheinberg. Weather about 5/10ths cloud but clear for bombing. Bombed at 15.07 hours from 20,000 feet visually.

27/11/1944 PB426 JI-D Bombing Cologne 12.30 15.05 17.36

Bomb load 1 x 4000 HC, 15 x 500 GP, 1 Flare. Primary target: Cologne, Marshalling Yards. Weather patchy cloud. Bombed at 15.05 hours from 19,500 feet. Visually on Marshalling Yards.

30/11/1944 LM728 JI-T Bombing Osterfeld 11.01 13.11 14.41

Bomb load 1 x 4000 HC, 15 x 500 GP, 1 Red/Green flare. Primary target: Osterfeld, Coking plant. Weather 10/10ths cloud. Bombed at 13.11 hours from 19,500 feet on G.H. Aircraft seemed well concentrated.

16/12/1944 PB426 JI-D Bombing Siegen 11.38 14.59 16.50

Bomb load 1 x 4000 HC, 5 x 1000 MC, 7 x 500 GP, 1 Flare. Primary target: Siegen. Weather very bad on route with icing and cloud. Bombed at 14.59 hours from 17,500 feet on G.H. Leader. Appalling weather conditions on outward journey.

P/O. Derek Anthony Duncliffe

174413 (1238964) P/O. Derek Anthony Duncliffe. Pilot.
1586150 F/S. Harry J. Bourne. A/Bomber.
658833 F/S. Gordon Florence Lewis. Navigator.
1536327 Sgt. J. Hollis. WOP/AG. 20 ops.
103538 (902785) F/L. Vivian George Ivor Outen, DFC WOP/AG. 1 op.
1520541 Sgt. George Kennedy Brown. WOP/AG. 2 ops.
2209357 Sgt. W. Saxon. MU/Gunner. 7 ops.
1586017 F/S. G.R. Hutton. MU/Gunner. 14 ops.
1852412 Sgt. Keith Russel Baker. MU and R/Gunner.
2208713 Sgt. William Edward Steger. R/Gunner. 2 ops.
1820355 Sgt. Charles Mathieson "Charlie" Guy. F/Engineer. 6 ops.
1642480 Sgt. W. Webb. F/Engineer. 14 ops.
51707 (570208) F/O. Howard Hall. F/Engineer. 1 op.
1086096 Sgt. Peter G. Cooper. F/Engineer. 2 ops.

Passenger
05/06/1944 Herald War Correspondent. Mr. G. Bray.

19/02/1944 DS816 JI-O Bombing Leipzig 23.54 03.59 06.38

Bomb load 1 x 4000 lb bomb. 32 x 30, 510 x 4, 90 x 4 incendiaries. Primary target Leipzig. There was 10/10 cloud. Bombed at 03.59 hours at 21,000 ft. Aircraft arrived 12½ minutes early on target - orbited. Route O.K. Photo attempted.

P/O. D.A. Duncliffe flew the mission as 2nd Pilot with S/L. A.L. Roberts' crew.

24/02/1944 LL734 JI-S Bombing Schweinfurt 18.47 x 22.32

Bomb load 1 x 2000 lb bomb, 32 x 30, 900 x 4, 90 x 4 incendiaries. Primary target: Schweinfurt. Returned early. Furthest point reached 5012N 0128E. Inter-comm u/s, Gee u/s. Load jettisoned.

Sgt. C. M. "Charlie" Guy F/Engineer until 15/03/1944.

Sgt. J. Hollis WOP/AG until 07/06/1944.

Sgt. W. Saxon MU/Gunner until 26/03/1944.

25/02/1944 LL734 JI-S Bombing Augsburg 21.49 01.24 05.03

Derek Anthony Duncliffe (courtesy Phillip Duncliffe)

Bomb load 1 x 2000 lb bomb, 48 x 30, 900 x 4 incendiaries. Primary target: Augsburg. Weather clear. Bombed at 01.24 hours at 20,000 ft. There were many fires seen. River identified. Mass of fires seemed well placed. T.I.s concentrated. Defences appeared to be saturated.

01/03/1944 LL703 JI-L Bombing Stuttgart 23.48½ 03.11 07.35

Bomb load 1 x 2000, 1 x 500 lb bomb, 40 x 30, 900 x 4 incendiaries. Primary target: Stuttgart. There was 10/10 cloud, broken in patches. Bombed at 03.11 hours at 21,000 ft. Fires appeared to be reflected on clouds - white, caused by incendiaries.

07/03/1944 LL734 JI-S Bombing Le Mans 19.39 21.50 23.45

Bomb load 10 x 1000, 4 x 500 lb bombs. Primary target: Le Mans. There was 10/10 cloud. Bombed at 21.50 hours from 13,000 feet. Some fires seen reflected on clouds further south. Monica u/s. 10/10 cloud made observation difficult. Red T.I.s coincided with position of earlier attack.

15/03/1944 LL703 JI-L Bombing Stuttgart 19.18 23.24 02.43

Bomb load 1 x 1000 lb bomb, 72 x 30, 1050 x 4, 4 x 90 incendiaries. Primary target: Stuttgart. There was 9/10 thin cloud, Bombed at 23.24 hours from 21,000 feet. T.I.s appeared scattered. Many fires seen. Monica u/s. Attack appeared scattered.

18/03/1944 LL670 A2-K Bombing Frankfurt 19.42 x 22.01

Bomb load 1 x 4000 lb bomb, 1350 x 4, 90 x 4, 32 x 30 incendiaries. Returned early. Total bomb load jettisoned. Mid Upper Gunner sick. Wireless u/s.

Sgt. W. Webb was F/Engineer that day.

26/03/1944 LL683 JI-P Bombing Essen 20.03 22.02 00.38

Bomb load 1 x 2000 lb bomb, 56 x 30, 1080 x 4, 120 x 4 incendiaries. Primary target: Essen. There was 10/10 cloud. Bombed at 22.02 hours from 20.000 feet. Little evidence - some glows. Route satisfactory. Result of raid difficult to ascertain.

Sgt. C. M. "Charlie" Guy was F/Engineer that day.

10/04/1944 DS826 JI-L Bombing Laon 01.21 03.40 05.31

Bomb load 9 x 1000, 4 x 500 lb bomb. Primary target: Laon. Weather was clear. Bombed at 03.40 hours from 10,500 feet; Bomb bursts and one fire seen. Successful attack. Perfect marking. Route satisfactory.

Sgt. W. Webb F/Engineer until 31/05/1944.

F/S. G.R. Hutton MU/Gunner until 08/06/1944.

11/04/1944 DS826 JI-L Bombing Aachen 21.07 22.45 00.15

Bomb load 10 x 1000, 2 x 500 lb bombs, 160 x 4, 20 x 4 incendiaries. Primary target: Aachen. There was 9/10 cloud. Bombed at 22.45 hours from 20,000 feet. T.I.s red and green fairly concentrated. Attack considered successful. T.I.s visible on ground.

18/04/1944 DS826 JI-L Bombing Rouen 23.05 00.48 02.35

Bomb load 8 x 1000 MC, 2 x 1000 GP, 5 x 500 lb bombs. Primary target: Rouen. There was ground haze, but no cloud. Bombed at 00.48 hours from 14,000 feet. T.I.s were scattered. Bombs seen to fall in town. A scattered raid. M of C gave valuable assistance. Photo attempted.

20/04/1944 DS826 JI-L Bombing Cologne 23.57 02.09 04.20

Bomb load 1 x 1000 lb bomb, 1026 x 4, 114 x 4, 108 x 30 lb incendiaries. Primary target: Koln. There was 10/10 cloud. Bombed at 02.09 hours from 20,000 feet. Bombed in centre of red flares with yellow stars. No comments, too much cloud.

27/04/1944 LL734 JI-S Bombing Friedrichshafen 22.07 02.10 05.30

Bomb load 1 x 4000 lb bomb, 32 x 30,324 x 4, 86 x 4 lb incendiaries. Weather was clear with slight haze. Bombed at 02.10 hours from 18,000 feet. There was a good concentration of T.I.s. Fires seen gaining hold. Searchlights were ineffective. Should be a good attack.

07/05/1944 DS826 JI-L Bombing Nantes 00.32 03.01 05.59

Bomb load 1 x 4000, 14 x 500 lb bombs. Primary target: Nantes. Weather was clear. Bombed at 03.01 hours from 10,000 feet. Some fires and palls of smoke seen. Successful effort, raid concentrated. Route good.

09/05/1944 DS826 JI-L Bombing Cap Gris Nez 03.00 04.05 05.00

Bomb load 1 x 1000 GP, 13 x 1000 MC. Primary target: Cape Gris Nez. Hazy conditions over target. T.I. Markers and coastline seen. Bombed estimated position of gun site at 04.05 hours from 6,000 feet. Target well illuminated and bombs well placed if P.F.F. marking was accurate.

10/05/1944 DS633 A2-B Bombing Courtrai 22.12 23.28 00.42

Bomb load 14 x 1000lb MC bombs. Primary target: Courtrai. Conditions rather hazy. Red T.I. and white flares seen. Bombed on Master Bomber's instructions. Bombed at 23.28 hours from 10,000 feet. Bombing seemed well concentrated on aiming point. Route satisfactory. No opposition over target.

27/05/1944 DS818 JI-Q Bombing Aachen   00.35 02.29   04.10

Bomb load 7 x 1000 MC, 4 x 1000 ANM, 4 x 500 MC. Primary target: Aachen. Clear over target. Bombed at 02.29 hours from 14,000 feet. Concentrated bomb bursts seen. Good attack if markers well placed. Unidentified aircraft passed overhead from port to starboard at 03.25 hours.

28/05/1944 DS818 JI-Q Bombing Angers   19.05 23.58   01.35

Bomb load 5 x 1000 MC, 1 x 1000 USA, 4 x 500 MC. Primary target: Angers. Clear over target. Bombed at 23.58 hours from 9,000 feet. Visual obtained of river and bursts seen around the T.I.s. Good attack and good route.

31/05/1944 DS818 JI-Q Bombing Trappes   23.59   02.00   04.20

Bomb load 8 x 1000 MC, 8 x 500 MC. Primary target: Trappes. Clear at target. Bombed at 02.00 hours from 9,000 feet. Sticks seen to burst south of the T.I.s. Slight light flak. Route quiet.

05/06/1944 DS818 JI-Q Bombing Ouistreham 03.44   05.10   06.49

Bomb load 9 x 1000 MC and 2 x 500 MC. Primary target: Ouistreham. There was 5/10 cloud. Obtained visual of markers and inlet. Bombed at 05.10 hours from 9,500 feet. Green T.I.s were over the target. One red T.I. seen in the sea.

Sgt. C. M. "Charlie" Guy was F/Engineer that day and Herald War Correspondent Mr. G. Bray was aboard.

According to Herald newspaper article, the flight engineer was C. M. Guy contrary to that is noted in ORBs.

07/06/1944 DS818 JI-Q Bombing Massy Palaiseau 00.30 x 02.45

Bomb load 18 x 500 MC. Returned early, because D.R. compass repeater was u/s. All bombs were jettisoned safe. Ran into cloud soon after leaving base, climbed to 10,000 feet and met with some icing.

Sgt. W. Webb was F/Engineer that day.

08/06/1944 DS818 JI-Q Bombing Fougeres   21.56   00.22   02.30

Bomb load 16 x 500 GP and 2 x 500 MC LD. Primary target: Fougeres. Bombed as instructed by Master Bomber at 00.22 hours from 8,000 feet. White T.I.s appeared to be in westerly part of a built-up area, with concentration of bombs rear markers. No fires seen at target after leaving, merely a glow. Quiet trip. Very cloudy.

F/O. Howard Hall was F/Engineer that day and F/L. V.G.I. Outen WOP/AG.

11/06/1944 LL731 JI-L Bombing Nantes   23.50   02.46   05.07

Bomb load 16 x 500 GP, 2 x 500 LD. Primary target: Nantes. Bombed on T.I.s as Master Bomber not heard at 02.46 hours from 6,500 feet in 10/10ths cloud. Much light flak.

From that day, Sgt. P.G. Cooper was F/Engineer, Sgt. G.K. Brown WOP/AG, and Sgt. W.E. Steger R/Gunner.

12/06/1944 DS818 JI-Q Bombing Gelsenkirchen 23.11 x x

Bomb load 1 x 4000 HC, 12 x 500 GP, 4 x 500 MC. Aircraft missing.

DS818 JI-Q "Maggie" cause of loss not established. Possibly shot down by

Hptm. Joachim Boehner, 2/NJG6 who claimed an unidentified 4-engine aircraft 20 km S of Deelen. Nunspeet is approx. 50 km North of that location, crashed at Nunspeet (Gelderland), where those killed are buried in Ermelo (Nunspeet) New General Cemetery."

P/O. D.A. Duncliffe Evaded, Sgt. P.G. Cooper POW, F/S. G.F. Lewis KIA, F/S. H.J. Bourne POW, Sgt. G.K. Brown KIA, Sgt. W.E. Steger KIA, Sgt. K.R. Baker KIA.

F/S. H.J. Bourne (also recorded as M.J. Bourne) was interned in Camp L7. POW No.205, with Sgt. P.G. Cooper, POW No.211.

F/O. C.A. Dunn

J41105 F/O. C.A. Dunn, RCAF. Pilot.
R191984   F/S. A.F. Garrity, RCAF. A/Bomber. 24 ops.
J37188 (R191984)
    F/O. Joseph Edward "Ted" Morrey, RCAF. A/Bomber. 1 op.
J40817 F/O. S.M. Roberts, RCAF. Navigator.
Sgt. J.J. Jones. WOP/AG.
R258160   F/S. W.H. Wylie, RCAF.   MU/Gunner. 23 ops.
R283152   F/S. I.P. Cahill, RCAF. R/Gunner.
1810744 Sgt. Reginald Ernest "Reg" Sieloff. F/Engineer.
188927 (1612704)   P/O. Victor Reginald Thompson. 2nd Pilot. 17/03/1945

Passengers: 03/05/1945, 08/05/1945.

11/12/1944 LM275 JI-M Bombing Osterfeld   08.36   11.06   12.45
    Bomb load 1 x 4000 HC, 12 x 500 GP, 2 x 500 GP Long Delay, 2 x 500 MC.
Primary target: Osterfeld. Bombed at 11.06 hours from 19,500 feet on G.H.
    F/O. C.A. Dunn flew the mission as 2nd Pilot with F/L. L.L. Currie's crew.
12/12/1944 LM728 JI-T Bombing Witten 11.25 14.06   16.02
    Bomb load 1 x 4000 HC, 1890 x 4 lb Incendiaries, 210 x 4 lb Incendiaries.
Primary target: Witten. Weather 10/10ths cloud, tops 14/16,000 feet. Bombed at 14.06 hours from 20,000 feet on G.H. Leader.
03/02/1945 NF968 JI-B Bombing Dortmund-Huckarde 16.21 19.46
    21.41
    Bomb load 1 x 4000 HC, 2 x 500 MC, 2 x 500 MC L/Delay, 6 x 500 ANM64, 6 x 500 GP, 3 x 250 GP, 1 Red/Green Flare. Primary target

Reginald Ernest "Reg" Sieloff (courtesy Paul Sieloff)

Dortmund-Huckarde, Coking plant. Weather clear with slight haze. Bombed at 19.46 hours from 19,600 feet on G.H. Good concentration of T.I.s.

F/O. C.A. Dunn flew the mission as 2nd Pilot with S/L. K.G. Condict's crew.

19/02/1945 ME358JI-O Bombing Wesel 12.58 16.36 19.35

Bomb load 1 x 4000 HC, 6 x 500 MC, 6 x 500 ANM64, 4 x 250 GP. Primary target: Wesel. Weather over target 5-7/10ths cloud. Bombed at 16.36 hours from 18,900 feet on leading aircraft. Landed at Moreton in Marsh.

20/02/1945 ME351JI-U Bombing Dortmund 21.53 01.07 03.30

Bomb load 1 x 2000 HC, 12 x 750 Type 15 Clusters. Primary target: Dortmund. Weather 8-10/10ths thin cloud at about 5,000 feet. Bombed at 01.07 hours from 21,000 feet on Skymarkers Red/Green.

23/02/1945 ME358JI-O Bombing Gelsenkirchen 11.21 15.01 18.05

Bomb load 1 x 4000 HC, 9 x 500 ANM64, 2 x 500 MC, 4 x 250 GP. Primary target Gelsenkirchen. Weather 10/10ths cloud. Bombed at 15.01 hours from 20,000 feet on leading aircraft. According ORBs on return landed at Acklington, but Sgt. Sieloff noted in his logbook "ASI u/s during trip, landed at Woodbridge" and the next day "Woodbridge to Base".

26/02/1945 LM285JI-A Bombing Dortmund 10.18 14.03 16.02

Bomb load 1 x 4000 HC, 2 x 500 MC L/Delay 37B, 9 x 500 ANM64, 4 x 250 GP. Primary target: Dortmund, Hoesch Benzin plant. Weather 10/10ths cloud, tops 8/10,000 feet. Bombed at 14.03 hours from 20,100 feet on leading aircraft.

27/02/1945 ME355JI-L Bombing Gelsenkirchen 11.01 14.28 16.39

Bomb load 1 x 4000 HC, 2 x 500 MC (L/D 37B), 9 x 500 ANM64, 4 x 250 GP. Primary target: Gelsenkirchen (Alma Pluts) Benzin plant. Weather 10/10ths cloud, 6/10,000 feet tops. Bombed at 14.28 hours from 20,200 feet on leading aircraft.

190

01/03/1945 PD389 A2-J Bombing Kamen 11.37 15.06 17.38

Bomb load 1 x 4000 HC, 11 x 500 ANM64, 2 x 500 MC L/Delay 37. Primary target: Kamen, Coking plant. Weather 10/10ths cloud. Bombed at 15.06 hours from 17,500 feet on G.H. Leader.

05/03/1945 ME358 JI-O Bombing Gelsenkirchen 10.33 14.08 16.14

Bomb load 1 x 4000 HC, 12 x 500 ANM64. Primary target: Gelsenkirchen, Benzol plant. Weather 10/10ths cloud over target with cirrus cloud at bombing height. Bombed at 14.08 hours from 20,900 feet on G.H.

06/03/1945 PD334 A2-B Bombing Salzbergen 08.22 12.15 14.20

Bomb load 1 x 4000 HC, 12 x 500 ANM64, 2 x 500 MC. Primary target: Salzbergen, Wintershall oil plant. Weather 10/10ths cloud over target, tops 10,000 feet. Bombed at 12.15 hours from 20,500 feet on G.H. Leader. "Aircraft badly damaged by explosion of 'T'.

According Sieloff's logbook: "bomb aimer hit" - "A/C severely damaged" Paul Sieloff, nephew of E. Sieloff told author: "F/O. Flack's aircraft was just ahead of Dunn's causing the damage mentioned in log book. Reg (Sieloff) grabbed legs of bomb aimer to stop him falling out. Bomb aimer's bubble blown off canopy above pilot and Reg lost the bomb doors, which were unable to be closed and undercarriage had to be lowered by hand on return. "

07/03/1945 ME422 JI-Q Bombing Dessau 17.26 21.57 02.02

Bomb load 1 x 4000 HC, 6 x Mk.17 Clusters. Primary target: Dessau. Weather 5 to 10/10ths thin cloud. Bombed at 21.57½ hours from 20,000 feet on Red flares with Green stars. Master Bomber heard and helpful.

According R.E. Sieloff and J.E. Morrey logbooks: "ME.109 attack".

17/03/1945 ME422 JI-Q Bombing August Viktoria 12.04 15.03 17.20

Bomb load 1 x 4000 HC, 13 x 500 ANM64, 2 x 500 MC. Primary target: Auguste Viktoria, Marl-Hüls coal mine. Weather 10/10ths cloud, tops and contrails up to 23,000 feet. Bombed at 15.03 hours from 21,500 feet on G.H.

According Sieloff's logbook: target "Huls".

P/O. V. R. Thompson was 2nd Pilot that day.

20/03/1945 ME422 JI-Q Bombing Hamm 09.51 13.15 15.40

Bomb load 7 x 1000 MC, 9 x 500 ANM64. Primary target: Hamm, Marshalling yards. Weather 5/10ths cloud. Bombed at 13.15 hours from 17,500 feet on G.H.

23/03/1945 ME354 JI-M Bombing Wesel 14.22 17.40 19.10

Bomb load 5 x 1000 ANM65, 8 x 1000 MC. Primary target: Wesel, in support of ground troops. Weather perfect. Bombed at 17.40 hours from 19,200 feet on G.H. Brown smoke covered town but all bombs fall in the area.

According R.E. Sieloff's logbook: "in support of Monty" - Bernard Law Montgomery's ground troops.

29/03/1945 ME422 JI-Q Bombing Salzgitter 12.24 16.43 19.20

Bomb load 1 x 4000 HC, 8 x 500 ANM64. Primary target: Salzgitter, Hallendorf works. Weather 10/10ths cloud. Bombed at 16.43 hours from 22,200 feet on G.H. and H2S. No Green Puffs seen.

191

According to Sieloff's logbook: target "Hallendorf - Longest RAF daylight raid".

09/04/1945 ME422 JI-Q Bombing Kiel   19.38   22.41   01.38

Bomb load 1 x 4000 HC and 12 x 500 ANM64. Primary target: Kiel, Submarine Buildings Yards. Weather clear with slight haze. Bombed at 22.41 hours from 20,300 feet on Green T.I. on M/B's instructions. All bombing appeared to fall in area of both A/Ps which had become one target. Very good effort. M/B gave varying instructions - but helpful generally.

"According Sieloff's logbook: "Scheer sunk".

Admiral Scheer is Germany's 10,000 ton battleship attacked at Kiel by RAF planes.

22/04/1945 ME422 JI-Q Bombing Bremen   15.22   18.42   21.03

Bomb load 1 x 4000 HC, 2 x 500 MC, 14 x 500 ANM 64. Primary target: Bremen, in support of Troop concentration. Weather on approaching target 4-5/10ths cloud. Bombed on leading A/C at 18.42 hours from 18,500 ft. G.H. no release pulse. Bomb bursts on east bank of river. Slight damage to front turret. Appeared good concentration of bombs.

According Sieloff's logbook: "again Monty". See 23 March.

30/04/1945 ME422 JI-Q Manna Rotterdam   16.55   18.18   19.30

Dropping area: Rotterdam. Weather intermittent showers and low cloud. Load 5 packs. Dropped 4 visually at 18.18 hours. Seemed a good effort in spite of weather visibility being poor. Bags were dropped well together. Cheering populace. House seen on fire.

03/05/1945 ME422 JI-Q Manna The Hague   11.11   12.24   13.27

Dropping area The Hague. Dropped 4 Panniers visually on White Cross and T.I.s at 12.24 hours. 8/10 base, 1,500 Hazy. One Pannier brought back. Broken lead to release clips cause of one Pannier brought back. Dropping concentrated.

That day A.C. Vowler was a passenger and there was no M/U Gunner.

08/05/1945 ME422 JI-Q Manna Rotterdam   12.45   14.06   15.04

Dropping area Rotterdam. Dropped 5 Packs on Red T.I. and visually at 14.06 hours. Clear. Much water in area - dropping area appeared dry but intersected by small rivulets.

That day Cpl. Scrace was a passenger and there was no M/U Gunner.

10/05/1945 ME422 JI-Q Exodus Juvincourt - Ford   11.16 x 17.30

Duration 3.49. Outward 1.50 hours. Collected 24 ex POWs. Homeward 1.59 hours. Tyre burst on landing at Ford, but nobody hurt.

11/05/1945 ME422 JI-Q Exodus Juvincourt - Wing   17.22 x 22.35

Duration 4.00. Outward 2.23 hours. Collected 24 ex POWs. Homeward 1.37 hours. Organisation OK.

14/05/1945 ME364 JI-P Exodus Juvincourt - Oakley   10.22 x 16.23

Duration 4.05 hours. Outward 1.40 hours. Collected 24 POWs. Homeward 2.25 hours. All OK.

17/05/1945 ME422 JI-Q Exodus Brussels - Westcott   10.20 x 16.29

Duration 3 hrs 10 mins. Out 1 hr 25 mins. In 1 hr 45 mins. 10 Belgian refugees taken to Brussels. 22 POWs returned to Westcott. Westcott well organised. R.T. troublesome at Brussels.

19/05/1945 ME359 JI-T Exodus Brussels - Oakley 12.50 x 19.38

Duration 3 hrs 10 mins. Out 1 hr 20 mins. In 1 hr 50 mins. 10 Belgians taken to Brussels. 24 ex POWs evacuated.

23/05/1945 ME422 JI-Q Exodus Brussels - Oakley 12.05 x 17.42

Duration 3.10 hours. Out 1.15 hours. In 1.55 hours. 10 Belgian refugees returned to Brussels. 24 ex POWs evacuated. Organisation OK.

F/O. Ronald Hinde Edmundson, DFC

172604 (1336585) F/O. Ronald Hinde "Eddie" Edmundson, DFC. Pilot.
Sgt. George H. Colledge. A/Bomber.
184805 (1577553) P/O. Reginald Dan "Reg" Waldram. Navigator.
 F/S. Frank Addison. WOP/AG.
Sgt. John G. "Ivan" Carpenter. MU/Gunner.
Sgt. Eric R. Bishop. R/Gunner.
Sgt. John P. or R. Lambourn. F/Engineer.

L to R kneeling: George Colledge, Reginald Waldram. Standing: Eric Bishop, Frank Addison, Ronald Edmundson, John Lambourn, John Carpenter.

14/08/1944 ME841JI-H Bombing Hamel (Falaise) 13.59 15.55 17.27

Bomb load 11 x 1000 MC, 4 x 500 GP. Primary target: Hamel. Weather clear. Bombed at 15.55 hours from 8,600 feet red T.I.s. Bomb bursts well concentrated around T.I.s which were well placed. Bombing of troop concentrations.

15/08/1944 LL731 JI-U Bombing St Trond 10.04 12.10 13.30

Bomb load 11 x 1000 MC, 4 x 500 GP. Primary target St. Trond Airfield. Weather clear over target. Bombed at 12.10 hours from 16,600 feet, red T.I.s. Bombing accurate, no interference.

25/08/1944 PB423 JI-S Bombing Russelsheim 20.28 01.02 04.42

Bomb load 1 x 4000 HC, 11 x 500 LB Clusters. Primary target: Russelheim. Weather clear. Bombed at 01.02 hours from 18,000 feet, centre of 3 red T.I.s. Bomb bursts well within area of concentration.

26/08/1944 LM285JI-K Bombing Kiel 20.07 23.15 01.52

Bomb load 1 x 4000 HC, 96 x 30 IB, 900 x 4 IB. Primary target: Kiel. Weather clear. Bombed at 23.15 hours from 18,000 feet red T.I.s. Well concentrated and fires developing.

29/08/1944 PD265 JI-G Bombing Stettin 21.14 02.09 06.48

Bomb load 1 x 4000 HC, 52 x 30, 486 x 4, 54 x 4 lb incendiaries. Primary target: Stettin. Weather thin cloud 4/10ths. Bombed at 02.09 hours from 17,000 feet, centre of red T.I.s. T.I.s clearly seen. Good area of fires seen. Good attack.

03/09/1944 HK572JI-T Bombing Eindhoven 15.18 17.35 19.04

Bomb load 11 x 1000 MC, 4 x 500 GP. Primary target: Eindhoven airfield. Bombed at 17.35 hours from 16,000 feet, red T.I.s.

17/09/1944 LM719JI-M Bombing Boulogne 10.46 x 13.34

Bomb load 11 x 1000 MC, 4 x 500 GP. Primary target: Boulogne, Aiming point 2. Weather clear below cloud. At 12.15 hours order given by Master Bomber to abandon mission. Jettisoned 2 x 1000 MC, brought remainder back.

20/09/1944 NF966 JI-R Bombing Calais 14.53 16.03 17.42

Bomb load 11 x 1000 MC, 4 x 500 GP. Primary target: Calais. Weather clear over target. Bombed at 16.03 hours from 2,500 feet, red T.I.s.

25/09/1944 NF966 JI-R Bombing Pas de Calais 08.14 x 11.11

Bomb load 11 x 1000 MC, 4 x 500 GP. Primary target: Calais. Abandoned mission on Master Bomber's instructions. Jettisoned 3 x 1000 MC, 1 x 500 GP.

26/09/1944 LM719JI-M Bombing Calais 11.35 12.47 14.12

Bomb load 11 x 1000 MC, 4 x 500 GP. Primary target: Calais 7D. Weather clear below cloud which was 3,500 feet. Bombed at 12.47 hours from 3,000 feet on red T.I. + 1 second.

05/10/1944 LM719JI-M Bombing Saarbrucken 17.21 x 22.41

Bomb load 11 x 1000 MC, 1 x 500 GP, 3 x 500 GP Long Delay. Primary target: Saarbrucken, Marshalling yards. Weather clear over target. Abandoned mission on instructions from Master Bomber heard to say they were unable to locate target and called "Abandon Mission - our troop in vicinity". Jettisoned 1 x 1000 MC, 3 x 500 GP Long Delay 40 miles East of Southwold at 22.06

hours from 5,000 feet. Remainder brought back.

14/10/1944 ME841 JI-Y Bombing Duisburg 07.17 09.06 11.20

Bomb load 11 x 1000 MC, 4 x 500 GP Long Delay. Primary target: Duisburg. Weather patchy cloud with gaps for bombing. Bombed at 09.04 hours from 18,000 feet. East position of Airport.

14/10/1944 ME841 JI-Y Bombing Duisburg 22.48 01.30 03.59

Bomb load 11 x 1000 MC, 4 x 500 GP Long Delay. Primary target: Duisburg. Weather was clear with small amount of cloud over the target. Bombed at 01.30 hours from 20,000 feet. Red T.I.

19/10/1944 LM275 JI-M Bombing Stuttgart 21.59 01.08 04.02

Bomb load 1 x 4000 HC, 3 x 500 Clusters, 7 x (150 x 4), 1 x (90 x 4). Primary target: Stuttgart, A/P 'E' 2nd attack. Weather 10/10ths low cloud over target and all crew arrived late owing to winds not as forecast. Bombed at 01.08 hours from 18,500 feet. Glow of fires.

21/10/1944 LM727 JI-S Bombing Flushing 10.56 12.29 13.10

Bomb load 12 x 1000 MC, 2 x 500 GP. Primary target: Flushing 'B'. Weather clear. Bombed at 12.29 hours from 8,000 feet. A/P.

23/10/1944 LM275 JI-M Bombing Essen 16.52 19.46 22.08

Bomb load 1 x 4000 HC, 14 x 500 Clusters. Primary target: Essen. Weather 10/10ths cloud over target - tops 12/14,000 feet with most appalling weather on route. Bombed at 19.46 hours from 20,000 feet. Yellow glow through cloud.

25/10/1944 LM275 JI-M Bombing Essen 13.06 15.37 17.10

Bomb load 1 x 4000 HC, 6 x 1000 MC, 6 x 500 GP. Primary target: Essen. Weather over target 10/10ths low cloud, with one clear patch which appeared to fill up later in the attack. Bombed at 15.37 hours from 20,500 feet. White smoke as instructed.

28/10/1944 LM275 JI-M Bombing Flushing 09.00 10.17 11.13

Bomb load 11 x 1000 MC, 6 x 1000 MC, 4 x 500 GP. Primary target: Flushing. Weather over the target quite clear and conditions perfect, although believed to be only local, and some low cloud approaching. Bombed at 10.17 hours from 8,500 feet. Smoke.

29/10/1944 LM275 JI-M Bombing Flushing 10.01 11.36 12.31

Bomb load 11 x 1000 ANM59, 4 x 500 GP. Primary target: Flushing, Gun installations. Weather clear over target. Bombed at 11.36 hours from 6,000 feet. Overshot 1 second and starboard of Green T.I.s.

31/10/1944 LM275 JI-M Bombing Bottrop 11.57 14.45 16.45

Bomb load 1 x 4000 HC 15 x 500 GP, 1 Flare. Primary target: Bottrop, Synth. Oil plants. Weather 10/10ths cloud over target. Bombed at 14.45 hours from 15,500 feet on G.H. Aircraft hit by flak over the target. M.U. turret and starboard outer engine damaged.

04/11/1944 NF966 JI-R Bombing Solingen 11.18 14.08 16.08

Bomb load 1 x 4000 HC, 6 x 1000 ANM59, 4 x 500 GP, 2 x 500 MC (L/Delay), 3 Flares. Primary target: Solingen. Weather 8-10/10ths cloud. Bombed at 14.08 hours from 20,000 feet on G.H.

05/11/1944 LM684 JI-O Bombing Solingen 10.23   13.05   14.54

Bomb load 1 x 4000 HC, 6 x 1000 ANM59, 4 x 500 GP, 2 x 500 GP (L/Delay), 3 Flares. Primary target: Solingen. Weather 10/10ths cloud over target. Bombed at 13.05 hours from 17,500 feet on instruments.

08/11/1944 NF968 JI-L Bombing Homberg   08.04   10.31   12.19

Bomb load 1 x 4000 HC, 6 x 1000 GP, 6 x 500 GP. Primary target: Homberg. Weather clear. Bombed at 10.31 hours from 17,000 feet. Factory.

11/11/1944   PB419 JI-N Bombing Castrop Rauxel 08.10 x 11.20

Bomb load 1 x 4000 HC, 15 x 500 GP, 1 Flare. Primary target: Castrop Rauxel, Oil refineries. Weather 10/10ths cloud. Abortive sortie. Aircraft returned early with port outer engine unserviceable. Jettisoned safe 40 miles East of Southwold.

15/11/1944   LM275 JI-M Bombing Dortmund   12.47   15.40   17.25

Bomb load 1 x 4000 HC, 2 x 500 MC, 13 x 500 GP, 1 Red with Green star Flare. Primary target: Hoesch-Benzin Dortmund, Oil refineries. Weather 10/10ths cloud over the target. Bombed at 15.40 hours from 17,000 feet on G.H.

16/11/1944   LM275 JI-M Bombing Heinsburg 13.27 15.42   17.33

Bomb load 1 x 4000 HC, 6 x 1000 MC, 6 x 500 GP.   Primary target: Heinsburg. Weather - nil cloud with slight haze over target. Bombed at 15.42 hours from 9,000 feet. Centre of town.

20/11/1944   LM285 JI-K Bombing Homberg   12.57   15.15   17.00

Bomb load 1 x 4000 HC, 15 x 500 GP, 1 Red-Green Flare. Primary target: Homberg. Weather 10/10ths cloud over target. Bombed at 15.15 hours from 20,000 feet on G.H.

23/11/1944   LM275 JI-M Bombing Nordstern   12.40   15.19   17.08

Bomb load 1 x 4000 HC, 12 x 500 GP, 4 x 250 Red T.I.s. Primary target: Nordstern, Gelsenkirchen Oil refineries. Weather 10/10ths cloud. Bombed at 15.19 hours from 20,000 feet on G.H.

05/12/1944 PB426 JI-D Bombing Hamm 09.04 11.30   13.41

Bomb load 1 x 4000 HC, 2 x 500 MC, 11 x 500 GP, 2 x 500 GP Long Delay, 1 Flare. Primary target: Hamm. Weather 10/10ths cloud over target, but otherwise varying from 6-10/10ths. Bombed at 11.30 hours from 20,000 feet on G.H.

08/12/1944 PD389 JI-Q Bombing Duisburg   09.00   11.04   12.42

Bomb load 11 x 1000 MC, 2 x 1000 ANM65, 1 Flare. Primary target: Duisberg. Weather 10/10ths cloud. Bombed at 11.04 hours from 20,000 feet on flares.

F/O. Norman James Eley

163588 (1802442)   F/O. Norman James "Jim" Eley.   Pilot.
154076 (1494455)   F/O. John William "Jack" Eykyn.   A/Bomber.
Sgt. Thomas A. "Tom" Barker.   Navigator.
Sgt. Denis F. L. "Den" Fox.   WOP/AG.
Sgt. Leslie E. "Les" Austin.   MU/Gunner. 6 ops.
Sgt. William J. "Johnny" Cook.   R/Gunner.
Sgt. Ronald W. "Ron" Pugh.   F/Engineer.

Passengers: 02/05/1945.

L to R: "Ron" Pugh, "Johnny" Cook, "Tom" Barker, "Jim" Eley, "Den" Fox, "Les" Austin, "Jack" Eykyn. (courtesy Jim Eley, June 2014)

17/03/1945 ME535 JI-G Bombing August Viktoria 11.29 15.06   16.56
Bomb load 1 x 4000 HC, 13 x 500 ANM64, 2 x 500 MC. Primary target: Auguste Viktoria, Marl-Hüls coal mine. Weather 10/10ths cloud, tops and contrails up to 23,000 feet. Bombed at 15.06 hours from 20,000 feet on G.H. Leader. Aircraft congested over target. Risk of collision.
F/O. N.J. Eley flew the mission as 2nd Pilot with F/O. W.G.H.T. Gibson's crew.
According to Blakemore's logbook: "Light flak. Heavy vapour trails over target."
18/03/1945 NG298 JI-E Bombing Bruchstrasse 11.39 15.06   17.18
Bomb load 1 x 4000 HC, 13 x 500 ANM64, 2 x 500 MC. Primary target: Bruchstrasse, Coal mine and coking plant. Weather 10/10ths cloud, tops 6-12,000 feet. Bombed at 15.06 hours from 18,000 feet on G.H. Leader.

29/03/1945 LM627 JI-D Bombing Salzgitter   12.29   16.45   19.25

Bomb load 1 x 4000 HC, 8 x 500 ANM64. Primary target: Salzgitter, Hallendorf works. Weather 10/10ths cloud. Bombed at 16.45 hours from 19,500 feet on leading aircraft G.H. Cloud prevented accurate bombing.

04/04/1945 ME535 JI-G Bombing Merseburg (Leuna) 18.37   22.45 02.40

Weather 5-10/10ths cloud, and 10/10ths over Merseburg. Bombed primary target. Bomb load 1 x 4000 HC and 6 x 500 ANM64. 9/10 cloud. Bombed on single red T.I. at 22.45 hours from 20,000 feet. Glow seen through cloud appeared to be fires. Excessive vibration caused star inner on return. Numerous dummies over a large area including Magdeberg. Bombing rather scattered.

F/O. N.J. Eley flew the mission as 2nd Pilot with P/O. L.J.W. Sutton's crew.

18/04/1945 LM724 JI-H Bombing Heligoland 09.49 13.10   15.21

Bomb load 6 x 1000 MC, 10 x 500 ANM64. Primary target: Heligoland, Naval base. Weather no cloud, slight haze. Bombed visually on Leader of Vic at 13.10 hours from 18,200 ft. Whole Island covered in smoke. 1 x 500 ANM64 hang up. Markers not shown. No troubles.

20/04/1945 NG142 JI-J Bombing Regensburg 09.33   13.56   17.20

Bomb load 16 x 500 ANM64. Primary target: Regensburg. Weather clear over target and whole route. Bombed on blue markers visually at 13.56 hours from 19,000 ft visually due to G.H. leaders marking too sharp a turn before the target. Bomb bursts seen across the target, much undershooting seen. Formation good, should be a successful raid. Fair amount of smoke.

30/04/1945 RF231 JI-A Manna Rotterdam   16.44   18.13   19.26

Dropping area: Rotterdam. Weather intermittent showers and low cloud. Load 5 packs. Dropped 4 packs visually on white cross at 18.13 hours. Bags well together. Saw people gathering them and stacking them up. Saw house on fire. Populace waving to us from streets and roof tops.

02/05/1945 ME535 JI-G Manna The Hague 11.12   12.35   13.43

Dropping area The Hague. Weather over dropping zone clear below cloud for the first arrivals changing later to heavy showers which marred visibility. Dropped 4 panniers on Red T.I.s at 12.35 hours. Rain storm and poor visibility over target. 1 pannier returned to Base due to hang-up. Delivery OK although much undershooting into the wood. Many flags flying in Hague.

AC. Winns was a passenger and there was no Mid Upper Gunner that day.

05/07/1945 RF230 JI-B Post Mortem   Special mission   13.21   x 18.28

198

F/L. K.L. Ellwood

J20086   F/L. K.L. Ellwood, RCAF. Pilot.
J42263   F/O. P.A. Clarke, RCAF. A/Bomber.
J40813   F/O. J.F. Evans, RCAF. Navigator.
  Sgt. J.K. Webster. WOP/AG.
R285659 F/S. F.L. Ward, RCAF. MU/Gunner.
R198015 F/S. L.A. Richardson, RCAF. R/Gunner.
  F/S. E.G. Watson. F/Engineer.

14/03/1945 ME422 JI-Q Bombing Heinrichshutte 13.00   16.39   18.30
  Bomb load 1 x 4000 HC, 12 x 500 ANM64. Primary target: Heinrichshutte, Hattingen Steel works and Benzol plant. Weather 10/10ths cloud, tops 7/12,000 feet. Bombed at 16.39 hours from 18,500 feet on Red markers.
  F/L. K.L. Ellwood flew the mission as 2nd Pilot with F/L. R.H. Marks' crew.
17/03/1945 PB426 A2-L   Bombing August Viktoria   12.20   15.10
  17.30
  Bomb load 1 x 4000 HC, 13 x 500 ANM64, 2 x 500 MC. Primary target: Auguste Viktoria, Marl-Hüls coal mine. Weather 10/10ths cloud, tops and contrails up to 23,000 feet. Bombed at 15.10 hours from 21,500 feet on leading G.H. aircraft.

F/L. Frank Raymond Wilton England

134136 (1436422)   F/L. Frank Raymond Wilton "Lofty" England. Pilot.
162203 (1801527)   F/O. Harry Alfred George Saville. A/Bomber. 9 ops.
158679 (964177)
  F/O. Wilfred Alfred Edward Peake, DFM. A/Bomber. 14 ops.
165214 (1339645)   F/O. Alfred David George Wallen. Navigator.
  F/S. W.D. Cuckow. WOP/AG.
Sgt. C.W. Potton. MU/Gunner. 22 ops.
Sgt. R. Blackburn. R/Gunner.
Sgt. H.E. Emms. F/Engineer. 22 ops.
  F/S. M.S. Jenner. F/Engineer. 2 ops.

Passengers: 03/05/1945, 03/06/1945, 28/06/1945, 17/07/1945.

25/02/1945 PB423 A2-L Bombing Kamen   09.35   12.46   15.02
  Bomb load 1 x 4000 HC, 9 x 500 ANM64, 2 x 500 MC, 4 x 250 GP. Primary target: Kamen. Weather 6-8/10ths cloud. Bombed at 12.46 hours from 19,700 feet on G.H. Leader
  F/L. F.R.W. England flew the mission as 2nd Pilot with F/L. H.C.

Frank Raymond Wilton "Lofty" England

Mottershead's crew.

26/02/1945 PB423 A2-L Bombing Dortmund 10.14 14.04 16.20

Bomb load 1 x 4000 HC, 2 x 500 MC L/Delay 37B, 9 x 500 ANM64, 4 x 250 GP. Primary target: Dortmund, Hoesch Benzin plant. Weather 10/10ths cloud, tops 8/10,000 feet. Bombed at 14.04 hours from 20,100 feet on leading aircraft.

28/02/1945 PB423 A2-L Bombing Nordstern 08.50 12.05 14.12

Bomb load 1 x 4000 HC, 9 x 500 ANM64, 2 x 500 MC L/D, 4 x 250 GP. Primary target: Nordstern (Gelsenkirchen). Weather 10/10ths cloud. Bombed at 12.05 hours from 20,100 feet on Green markers.

02/03/1945 PB423 A2-L Bombing Koln 12.46 16.04 18.25

Bomb load 1 x 4000 HC, 12 x 500 ANM64. Primary target: Koln. Weather 10/10ths cloud over Koln, South and South-East of Koln clear. Bombed at 16.04 hours from 21,100 feet. Followed G.H. aircraft and identified visually.

05/03/1945 NF968 JI-B Bombing Gelsenkirchen 10.26 14.07 15.57

Bomb load 1 x 4000 HC, 12 x 500 ANM64. Primary target: Gelsenkirchen, Benzol plant. Weather 10/10ths cloud over target with cirrus cloud at bombing height. Bombed at 14.07 hours from 21,800 feet on leading aircraft.

06/03/1945 ME358 JI-O Bombing Wesel 18.26 21.10 23.29

Bomb load 1 x 4000 HC, 13 x 500 ANM64, 2 x 500 MC. Primary target: Wesel. Weather 10/10ths cloud, tops 16,000 feet preventing visual. Bombed at 21.10 hours from 18,000 feet on G.H.

F/L. F.R.W. England flew the mission as 2nd Pilot with F/L. W.F. Burrows' crew.

09/03/1945 NG203 A2-C Bombing Datteln 10.27 14.01 15.47

Bomb load 1 x 4000 HC, 13 x 500 ANM64, 2 x 500 MC L/Delay 37. Primary target: Datteln, Synthetic oil plant. Weather 10/10ths cloud, tops 8-10,000 feet. Bombed at 14.01 hours from 20,300 feet on G.H.

21/03/1945 ME425 A2-L Bombing Munster 09.25 13.08 15.03

Bomb load 1 x 4000 HC, 13 x 500 ANM64, 2 x 500 MC. Primary target Munster Viaduct and Marshalling Yards. Weather cloud nil to 2/10ths. Bombed at 13.08 hours from 18,000 feet on G.H.

04/04/1945 ME425 A2-L Bombing Merseburg (Leuna) 18.35 22.47 03.19

Weather Bomb load 1 x 4000 HC, 6 x 500 ANM64. Weather 5/10 Broken cloud. Bombed primary target Merseburg on centre of four green ground markers at 22.47 hrs from 19,900 feet. Red explosions seen. Several sticks seen to fall in T.I. area. P.F.F. markings too scattered.

18/04/1945 ME425 A2-L Bombing Heligoland 09.45 13.09 15.17

Bomb load 6 x 1000 MC, 10 x 500 ANM64. Primary target: Heligoland, Naval base. Weather no cloud, slight haze. Bombed visually at 13.09 hours from 16,500 ft. Overshoot - pickwick one sec. Area covered in smoke. Oil fire burning amid smoke on leaving. Formation poor. Raid very good.

22/04/1945 RE123 A2-K Bombing Bremen 15.02 x 20.40

Bomb load 1 x 4000 HC, 2 x 500 MC, 14 x 500 ANM64. Primary target: Bremen, in support of Troop concentration. Weather on approaching target 4-5/10ths cloud. All brought back. G.H. Master switch knocked off. Instruments therefore u/s. Stream too compact to go round again.

29/04/1945 ME425 A2-L Manna The Hague 12.31 13.55 15.16

Dropping area: The Hague. Weather broken cloud above and clear below. Dropped 5 packs rations at 13.55 hours. Many sacks appeared to burst on obstructional stakes on airfield. Our bags dropped on starboard side of white cross. We saw no T.I.s. We made a second orbit for the benefit of file unit.

Thousands of civilians waving and cheering. We observed a Freya on coast E of Hague. Red Cross train in Selft. Flooding extensive to S of Hague. Unmanned gun was on the a/field.

01/05/1945 ME425 A2-L Manna The Hague 13.08 14.28 15.33

Dropping area The Hague. Weather clear over target. Dropped 5 Panniers at 14.28 hrs. on Red T.I.s and White Cross. Successful delivery - Usual cheering crowds forming reception committee. German tanks 2 miles west of Brielles.

03/05/1945 NN781 A2-B Manna The Hague 11.10 12.27 13.28

Dropping area The Hague. Dropped 5 panniers at 12.27 hrs on smoke from T.I. and White Cross. Cloud at 1,000 ft, visibility below O.K. Good collection of Food packs in dropping zone. A.G.R.

That day LAC. Dodd was a passenger and there was no Mid Upper Gunner.

15/05/1945 RE120 A2-C Exodus Juvincourt - Wing 15.56 x 21.27

Duration 3 hrs 34 mins. Outward 1 hr 43 mins. Collected 24 POWs. Homeward 1 hr 51 mins. All OK.

17/05/1945 RE140 JI-H Exodus Brussels - Westcott 11.19 x 15.12

Duration 2 hrs 16 mins. Out 1 hr 03 mins. In 1 hr 13 mins. 10 Belgian refugees taken over to Brussels. No troubles.

19/05/1945 ME425 A2-L Exodus Brussels - Oakley 12.58 x 19.27

Duration 2 hrs 55 mins. Out 1 hr 53 mins. In 1 hr 42 mins. 10 Belgian refugees taken to Brussels. 24 ex POWs all military evacuated.

24/05/1945 ME425 A2-L Exodus Brussels 12.08 x 14.58

Duration 2.14 hours. Out 1.30 hours. In 1.11 hours. No ex POWs to be brought back. 10 Belgian refugees to Brussels.

25/05/1945 ME425 A2-L Exodus Brussels 11.53 x 14.48

Duration 2.10 hours. Out 1.04 hours. In 1.06 hours. 10 Belgian refugees to

Brussels. No POWs home. No difficulties.

26/05/1945 ME425 A2-L Exodus Brussels - Ford 12.19 x 18.33
Duration 3.04 hours. Out 1.09 hours. In 1.55 hours. 10 Belgian refugees to Brussels. 23 ex POWs all military brought back. 1 Nursing orderly taken to escort stretcher case.

03/06/1945 RE159 A2-E Baedeker Tour over Germany 09.38 x 13.37
Passengers: Sgt. H. Balls, Sgt. T. Huggard, LAC. V. Moody.

25/06/1945 RA602 A2-H Post Mortem Special mission 10.00 x 16.02

28/06/1945 RE158 A2-J Baedeker Tour over Continent 14.59 x 19.12
No Bomb Aimer and no Mid Upper Gunner that day.
Passengers: LAC. Burton, Cpl. Wilcox, LAC. A.T. Carter, LAC. W.H. Kiantia, LAC. J.T. Khann.

03/07/1945 RF272 A2-F Post Mortem Special mission 14.31 x 19.59

17/07/1945 RE120 A2-C Baedeker Tour over Continent 09.29 x 13.37
Passengers: Cpl. Harris, Cpl. Litchfield, Sgt. Dobson, ACW. McCreight, ACW. Pemble 875.

24 to 26/07/1945
RE120 A2-C Dodge Italy 06.27 18.10 x
24/07/1945 Waterbeach 06.27 - Italy 18.10 - 26/07/1945 Italy aircraft u/s at Bari, Italy.

P/O. Ronald Frederick Etherington

196313 (1601963) P/O. Ronald Frederick Etherington. Pilot.
F/S. J.W. Lowe. A/Bomber.
F/S. D.D. Hatton. Navigator. 5 ops.
154876 (1583815) F/O. Robert William Simons. Navigator. 2 ops.
165037 or 172468 F/O. William John Graham. Navigator. 2 ops.
Sgt. W. Williams. WOP/AG.
Sgt. W.A. Hogg. MU/Gunner. 7 ops.
Sgt. P.R. Hall. R/Gunner.
F/S. F.G. Rusbridge. F/Engineer.

Passengers: 03/05/1945, 07/05/1945, 08/06/1945, 14/07/1945, 30/07/1945.

23/03/1945 LM285 JI-A Bombing Wesel 14.21 17.38 19.01
Bomb load 13 x 1000 MC. Primary target: Wesel, in support of ground troops. Weather perfect. Bombed at 17.38 hours from 19,500 feet on G.H. All bombs appeared to fall in town.
P/O. Ronald Frederick Etherington flew the mission as 2nd Pilot with F/O. L.C. Baines' crew.

27/03/1945 ME535 JI-G Bombing Hamm Sachsen 10.31 14.03 16.05

Bomb load 1 x 4000 HC, 13 x 500 ANM64, 2 x 500 MC. Primary target: Hamm Sachsen, Benzol plant. Weather 10/10ths cloud. Bombed at 14.03 hours from 18,000 feet on G.H. Leader.

04/04/1945 ME354 JI-M Bombing Merseburg (Leuna) 18.55 22.54 02.55

Weather 5-10/10ths cloud, and 10/10ths over Merseburg. Bombed primary target. Bomb load 1 x 4000 HC, 6 x 500 ANM64. 9/10th cloud. Bombed on Sky-markers at 22.54 hours from 19,500 feet. 1 x 4000 jettisoned 45 secs after all other bombs released. Markings late and very widely dispersed. Master Bomber said "Bomb Skymarkers" then "Bomb visually" - not helpful.

P/O. Ronald Frederick Etherington flew the mission as 2nd Pilot with F/L. R.H. Marks' crew.

18/04/1945 NG142 JI-J Bombing Heligoland 09.47 13.10 15.16

Bomb load 6 x 1000 MC, 10 x 500 ANM64. Primary target: Heligoland, Naval base. Weather no cloud, slight haze. Bombed visually on smoke at 13.10 hours from 18,400 ft. Pickwick overshoot 2 secs. Cloud of smoke. Red dust obscured the whole island. 2 large explosins 13.15 hours also several fires. Good effort.

20/04/1945 ME535 JI-G Bombing Regensburg 09.41 14.00 17.22

Bomb load 16 x 500 ANM64. Primary target: Regensburg. Weather clear over target and whole route. Bombed on leading aircraft at 14.00 hours from 18,700 ft. Smoke and bomb bursts covering a wide area. A/C was following J/514 who could not bomb, A/C after orbiting tacked on to another formation.

03/05/1945 ME535 JI-G Manna The Hague 11.05 12.20 13.25

Dropping area The Hague. Dropped 5 Panniers visually on White Cross and Red T.I.s at 12.20 hrs. 8/10 Base 1,500 ft. Hazy.

That day AC. Constantine was a passenger and there was no Mid Upper Gunner. F/O. R. W. Simons was Navigator.

07/05/1945 ME535 JI-G Manna The Hague 12.28 13.57 14.58

Dropping area The Hague. Dropped 5 Packs on White Cross and Red T.I.s at 13.57 hours.

That day AC. Faulkner was a passenger and there was no Mid Upper Gunner. F/O. R. W. Simon Navigator.

08/06/1945 RE139 JI-M Baedeker Tour over Continent 14.41 x 18.38

F/O. W.J. Graham Navigator.

Passengers: S/L. J. Hilliard, S/L. O. Riley, F/Lt. V. Vernon, AC. E. Adams.

01/07/1945 RE116 JI-F Post Mortem Special mission 12.09 x 15.35

F/O. W.J. Graham was Navigator that day.

14/07/1945 RE140 JI-H Baedeker Tour over Continent 09.50 x 14.02

Passengers: LAC. Crawley, AC. Adams, Cpl. Edwards (WAAF), ACW. Watford, ACW. Melling.

30/07/1945 RE117 ? A2-D ? Baedeker Tour over Continent 15.21 x 16.53

Aircraft returned early from tour. By error, in ORBs, two crews are recorded with the same plane at the same time.

Passengers: Butler, Weaver, Stacey, Preston, Bailey. (Bomber Command personnel ranks and initials not given).

F/L. R.E. Farvolden

J7741 F/L. R.E. Farvolden, RCAF. Pilot.
J40365 F/O. B.H. Goodwin, RCAF. A/Bomber.
J40468 F/O. P.D. Bedson, RCAF. Navigator.
R250599 F/S. G.M. Wilson, RCAF. WOP/AG.
R208212 F/S. G.T. Carroll, RCAF. MU/Gunner. 19 ops.
 Sgt. F.C. Wright. R/Gunner.
 Sgt. T. Wilson. F/Engineer.
J41845 F/O. E. "Eddie" Monahan, RCAF. 2nd Pilo.t 14/03/1945

Passenger: 04/05/1945

18/02/1945 PA186 A2-G Bombing Wesel 11.28 15.22 17.30
 Bomb load 1 x 4000 HC, 4 x 500 GP, 2 x 500 MC L/Delay, 4 x 250 GP, 6 x 500 ANM64. Primary target: Wesel. Weather 10/10ths cloud. Bombed at 15.22 hours from 18,500 feet on leading aircraft.
 F/L. R.E. Farvolden flew the mission as 2nd Pilot with F/O. J.N. Gallicano crew.
19/02/1945 NN775 A2-F Bombing Wesel 12.55 16.36 19.25
 Bomb load 1 x 4000 HC, 6 x 500 MC, 6 x 500 ANM64, 4 x 250 GP. Primary target: Wesel. Weather over target 5-7/10ths cloud. Bombed at 16.36 hours from 19,000 feet on G.H. Leader. Landed at Moreton in Marsh.
22/02/1945 PB482 A2-K Bombing Osterfeld 12.13 16.01 17.50
 Bomb load 1 x 4000 HC, 9 x 500 ANM64, 2 x 500 MC, 4 x 250 GP. Primary target: Osterfeld, Coking ovens. Weather at target clear, but hazy. Bombed at 16.01 hours from 19,000 feet on G.H. Leader.
23/02/1945 PB482 A2-K Bombing Gelsenkirchen 11.2015.00 17.18
 Bomb load 1 x 4000 HC, 9 x 500 ANM64, 2 x 500 MC, 4 x 250 GP. Primary target Gelsenkirchen. Weather 10/10ths cloud. Bombed at 15.00 hours from 20,200 feet on G.H. Leader. On return landed at Witchford.
26/02/1945 NF966 A2-G Bombing Dortmund 10.14 14.02 16.10
 Bomb load 1 x 4000 HC, 2 x 500 MC L/Delay 37B, 9 x 500 ANM64, 4 x 250 GP. Primary target: Dortmund, Hoesch Benzin plant. Weather 10/10ths cloud, tops 8/10,000 feet. Bombed at 14.02 hours from 20,300 feet on leading aircraft.
27/02/1945 NF966 A2-G Bombing Gelsenkirchen 10.49 14.27 16.20
 Bomb load 1 x 4000 HC, 2 x 500 MC (L/D 37B), 9 x 500 ANM64, 4 x 250

GP. Primary target: Gelsenkirchen (Alma Pluts) Benzin plant. Weather 10/10ths cloud, 6/10,000 feet tops. Bombed at 14.27 hours from 20,000 feet on G.H. Leader.

01/03/1945 NF966 A2-G Bombing Kamen   11.45   15.06   17.40
Bomb load 1 x 4000 HC, 11 x 500 ANM64, 2 x 500 MC L/Delay37. Primary target: Kamen, Coking plant. Weather 10/10ths cloud. Bombed at 15.06 hours from 19,000 feet on G.H. aircraft.

05/03/1945 NF966 A2-G Bombing Gelsenkirchen 10.20   14.07   15.57
Bomb load 1 x 4000 HC, 12 x 500 ANM64. Primary target: Gelsenkirchen, Benzol plant. Weather 10/10ths cloud over target with cirrus cloud at bombing height. Bombed at 14.07 hours from 21,000 feet on G.H. Leader.

07/03/1945 PD389 A2-J Bombing Dessau   17.01   22.18   02.09
Bomb load 1 x 500 ANM64, 15 x No.15 Clusters. Primary target: Dessau. Weather 5 to 10/10ths thin cloud. Bombed at 22.18 hours from 20,300 feet on Skymarkers and Master Bomber.

F/L. R.E. Farvolden flew the mission as 2nd Pilot with F/O. C.I.H. Nicholl's crew.

09/03/1945 NF966 A2-G Bombing Datteln   10.38   14.00   15.40
Bomb load 1 x 4000 HC, 13 x 500 ANM64, 13 x 500 MC L/Delay 37B. Primary target: Datteln, Synthetic oil plant. Weather 10/10ths cloud, tops 8-10,000 feet. Bombed at 14.00 hours from 21,000 feet on G.H. Leader.

11/03/1945 NN776 A2-D Bombing Essen 11.27   15.26   17.09
Bomb load 1 x 4000 HC, 13 x 500 ANM64, 2 x 500 MC. Primary target: Essen, Marshalling yards. Weather 10/10ths cloud, tops 7/8000 feet. Bombed at 15.26 hours from 20,000 feet on leading G.H. aircraft.

14/03/1945 NF966 A2-G Bombing Heinrichshutte 13.58 x 16.08
Bomb load 1 x 4000 HC, 12 x 500 ANM64. Primary target: Heinrichshutte, Hattingen Steel works and Benzol plant. Weather 10/10ths cloud, tops 7/12,000 feet. Farthest point reached 5023N 0008W. Port inner engine unserviceable. Jettisoned 1 x 4000 HC, 12 x 500 ANM64 at 5023N 0008W at 15.07 hours from 5,200 feet.

F/O. E. Monahan was 2nd Pilot that day.

17/03/1945 NN781 A2-B Bombing August Viktoria   11.33   15.08   17.17
Bomb load 1 x 4000 HC, 13 x 500 ANM64, 2 x 500 MC. Primary target: Auguste Viktoria, Marl-Hüls coal mine. Weather 10/10ths cloud, tops and contrails up to 23,000 feet. Bombed at 15.08 hours from 21,500 feet on G.H. Leader.

29/03/1945 ME523 A2-G Bombing Salzgitter 12.15   16.43   19.09
Bomb load 1 x 4000 HC, 8 x 500 ANM64. Primary target: Salzgitter, Hallendorf works. Weather 10/10ths cloud. Bombed at 16.43 hours from 21,000 feet on leading aircraft. Lost touch with Leader due to cloud.

09/04/1945 NN781 A2-B Bombing Kiel 19.40   22.42   02.05
Bombed primary target: Kiel. Bomb load 1 x 4000 HC and 12 x 500

ANM64. Bombed at 22.42 hours at 20,000 feet on centre of Green T.I.s. Concentrated marking and bombing. Very good concentration. Four very large explosions seen as Lanc left target. Lanc underneath as 514/B2 was about to bomb so veered over to port to bomb.

F/L. R.E. Farvolden flew the mission as 2nd Pilot with F/L. E.S. Henderson's crew.

13/04/1945 ME523 A2-G   Bombing Kiel   20.12   23.30   01.56

Bomb load 1 x 4000 HC and 12 x 500 ANM64. Primary target: Kiel, Docks and ship yards. Weather 10/10ths cloud low and thin. Bombed on centre of Green T.I.s at 23.30 hours from 21,000 feet. Red and Green T.I.s fell in same place quite concentratedly. 1 x 500 ANM64 hang up, brought back. Good attack.

20/04/1945 ME523 A2-G   Bombing Regensburg   09.39   13.57   17.16

Bomb load 15 x 500 ANM64. Primary target: Regensburg. Weather clear over target and whole route. Bombed on G.H. at 13.57 hours from 19,000 feet. Had a good run. We were first over target looking back smoke cloud could be seen rising, but not black. Very nice trip.

24/04/1945 RE117 A2-D   Bombing Bad Oldesloe   07.11   10.44   13.02

Bomb load 6 x 1000 ANM65, 10 x 500 ANM64. Primary target: Bad-Oldesloe, Rail and road junction and Marshalling Yards. Weather 3/10ths to nil cloud. Bombed on G.H. at 10.44 hours from 18,000 ft. Good G.H. run. Concentrated attack. Photo should be good.

29/04/1945 RE117 A2-D   Manna The Hague   12.33 13.56   15.12

Dropping area: The Hague. Weather broken cloud above and clear below. Carried 5 packs. Dropped 4 packs at 13.56 hrs. 1 pack hang up not known till visual check over sea on return.

01/05/1945 RE117 A2-D   Manna The Hague   13.11 14.22   15.25

Dropping area The Hague. Weather clear over target. Dropped 5 Panniers on Red T.I.s at 14.22 hours (rather too scattered). Dropping concentrated. Some aircraft must have been ahead of time. Hague crowds very enthusiastic, even the grandstand being utilised for the show. Green and Red lights still invisible.

04/05/1945 RE117 A2-D   Manna The Hague   12.07 13.28   14.38

Dropping area The Hague. Dropped 5 Panniers on White Cross and T.I. Visually at 13.28 hours. 10/10 cloud, 1000 Base good visibility.

That day Cpl. Brunham was a passenger and there was no Mid Upper Gunner.

09/05/1945 RE117 A2-D   Exodus Juvincourt - Dunsfold   07.35   x 13.24

Outward 1.40 hours. Collected 24 ex POWs. Homeward 2.04 hours. Aircraft kept too long in air at Dunsfold, otherwise organisation good at Juvincourt.

11/05/1945 RE120 A2-C   Exodus Juvincourt - Tangmere 11.02   x 16.35

Duration 3.40. Outward 1.41 hours. Collected 24 ex POWs. Homeward 1.59 hours. No comment.

F/O. Campbell George Fiset, DFC

J28322   F/O. Campbell George "Cam" Fiset, DFC RCAF.   Pilot.
R170632 W/O.Robert J. "Bob" Hamilton, RCAF. A/Bomber.
J93778 (R189208) P/O. G.D. Kay, RCAF.   Navigator.
A425363 W/O.John Rutherford, RAAF. WOP/AG. 25 ops.
159964 (1605076) F/O. Kenneth Dundonald Bailey.   WOP/AG. 4 ops.
J19707   F/O. Frank Harold Rowan, DFC RCAF. WOP/AG. 6 ops.
NZ412324   F/O. Oliver Lawrence Goldsmith, DFC RNZAF.WOP/AG. 0 ops.
   F/S. E.D. Dixon.   MU/Gunner. 0 ops.
R258925 W/O.W.J. May, RCAF.   MU&R/Gunner. 34 ops.
R201136 W/O.Larry R. Mulhall, RCAF. MU&R/Gunner. 35 ops.
   F/S. J. Tranter.   R/Gunner.   1 op.
   Sgt. E.B. Swaffield.   F/Engineer.
J29301   F/O. F.E. Sider, RCAF.   2nd Pilot. 08/02/1945
119534 (1213146) F/L. Ronald Burnett. 2nd Pilot. 14/03/1945
NZ414255 NZ1102112   F/O. L.A. Adams, RNZAF. 2nd Pilot. 04/04/1945

29/11/1944 LM724 JI-H Bombing Neuss   03.07   05.32   07.23
   Bomb load 1 x 4000 HC, 6 x 1000 MC, 4 x 500 GP, 4 x 250 Green T.I.s.
Primary target: Neuss. Weather 10/10ths cloud over target but the glow of fires
was seen through cloud. Bombed at 05.32 hours from 19,000 feet on G.H.
Glow observed through cloud. T.I.s well concentrated.
   F/O. C.G. Fiset flew the mission as 2nd Pilot with F/L. K.G. Condict's crew.
30/11/1944 PB767 JI-G Bombing Osterfeld   11.00   13.11   14.41
   Bomb load 1 x 4000 HC, 16 x 500 GP. Primary target: Osterfeld, Coking
plant. Weather 10/10ths cloud. Bombed at 13.11 hours from 19,500 feet on
G.H. Leader.
   F/O. C.G. Fiset flew the mission as 2nd Pilot with F/O. J.S. Parnell's crew.
Though contrary to ORBs, in his logbook F/O. Fiset reported that he was with
F/L. K.G. Condict's crew.
02/12/1944 LM733 JI-F Bombing Dortmund   12.56   14.57   17.30
   Bomb load 14 x 1000 HC. Primary target: Dortmund, Benzol plant. Weather
10/10ths cloud. Bombed at 14.57 hours from 20,000 feet on leading aircraft.
Aircraft hit by flak - perspex damaged.
05/12/1944 NN717 JI-E Bombing Hamm   09.10   11.19   12.59
   Bomb load 1 x 4000 HC, 1950 x 4 lb incendiaries. Primary target: Hamm.
Weather 10/10ths cloud over target, but otherwise varying from 6-10/10ths.
Bombed Bochalt at 11.19 hours from 20,000 feet on built up area. Did not
bomb primary target owing to oxygen failure, returned early.
06/12/1944 PB767 JI-G Bombing Merseburg 17.05 20.51   00.43

ME380 JI-E in background was used by the crew once for a training sortie. L to R standing: J. Rutherford, R.J. Hamilton, E.B. Swaffield, C.G. Fiset, W.J. May. Kneeling: G.D. Kay, L.R. Mulhall. (courtesy Karen Russel nee Hamilton)

Bomb load 1 x 4000 HC, 8 x 500 GP, 1 x 500 GP Long Delay. Primary target: Merseburg. Weather 10/10ths cloud with odd breaks. Bombed at 20.51 hours from 20,000 feet on Red/Green flares.

W/O. L.R. Mulhall was MU/Gunner that day and F/S. J. Tranter R/Gunner.

08/12/1944 PB756 JI-B Bombing Duisburg   08.46   11.05   13.07

Bomb load 14 x 1000 ANM59. Primary target: Duisberg. Weather 10/10ths cloud. Bombed at 11.05 hours from 20,000 feet on G.H. Leader.

W/O. L.R. Mulhall was MU/Gunner that day and F/S. J. Tranter R/Gunner. Contrary to ORBs, in his logbook F/O. Fiset noted his usual crew. In this case the Rear Gunner would be W/O. W.J. May and not F/S. J. Tranter.

11/12/1944 LM727JI-S Bombing Osterfeld   08.47   11.05   12.50

Bomb load 6 x 1000 ANM65, 7 x 1000 ANM59, 1 x 1000 MC. Primary target: Osterfeld. Weather 10/10ths cloud, tops 16,000 feet. Bombed at 11.05 hours from 20,000 feet on release by G.H. Leader.

12/12/1944 NG118 A2-E Bombing Witten   11.15   14.07   16.08

Bomb load 1 x 4000 HC, 1890 x 4 lb incendiaries, 210 x 4 lb incendiaries. Primary target: Witten. Weather 10/10ths cloud, tops 14/16,000 feet. Bombed at 14.07 hours from 21,000 feet on G.H. Leader.

21/12/1944 NN717 JI-E Bombing Trier   12.26   15.03   16.55

Bomb load 1 x 4000 HC, 10 x 500 GP, 6 x 250 GP. Primary target: Trier, Marshalling yards. Weather 10/10 cloud, tops 6/9000 feet. Bombed at 15.03

hours from 18,000 feet on G.H. Leader.

27/12/1944 NG142 A2-C Bombing Rheydt 12.49 15.00 16.43

Bomb load 7 x 1000 MC, 6 x 500 GP, 3 x 250 GP. Primary target: Rheydt, Marshalling yards. Weather clear. Bombed at 15.00 hours from 20,000 feet. North port of M/Y.

28/12/1944 NG118 A2-E Bombing Cologne Gremberg 12.28 15.06 16.55

Bomb load 1 x 4000 HC, 10 x 500 GP, 6 x 250 GP. Primary target: Koln Gremberg, Marshalling yards. Weather 10/10ths cloud or fog. Bombed at 15.06 hours from 20,000 feet on G.H. Leader.

07/01/1945 NG298 JI-E Bombing Munich 19.05 x 00.14

Bomb load 1 x 1000 ANM65, 1 x 500 ANM58, 1080 x 4 lb I.B, 120 x 4 I.B. Primary target: Munich. Weather 10/10ths cloud over target 6-8,000 feet with a thin layer altitude 16,000 feet. Abortive sortie. Returned early with D/R Compass unserviceable. All bombs brought back.

F/O. K.D. Bailey was WOP/AG from that day until 13/01/1944.

11/01/1945 NG298 JI-E Bombing Krefeld 11.48 15.16 16.50

Bomb load 1 x 4000 HC, 10 x 500 ANM64, 4 x 250 GP. Primary target: Krefeld. Weather 10/10ths cloud above and below. Visibility poor. Bombed at 15.06 hours from 20,000 feet on G.H. Leader.

13/01/1945 NG298 JI-E Bombing Saarbrucken 11.50 15.22 17.42

Bomb load 1 x 4000 HC, 10 x 500 ANM58 or 64, 4 x 250 GP. Primary target: Saarbrucken. Weather 3-5/10ths cloud, tops 4/5,000 feet. Bombed at 15.22 hours from 20,000 feet on leading aircraft. All aircraft on this op were diverted on return to Exeter as weather at base was unfit to land.

F/S. E.D. Dixon was MU/Gunner that day and W/O. W.J. May was R/Gunner. However, contrary to ORBs, F/S. Dixon does not appear in C.G. Fiset's logbook suggesting that the MU/Gunner would have been W/O. L.R. Mulhall as usual.

15/01/1945 NG298 JI-E Bombing Lagendreer 11.45 15.01 16.35

Bomb load 1 x 4000 HC, 10 x 500 ANM64, 4 x 250 GP. Primary target: Lagendreer. Weather 10/10ths cloud. Bombed at 15.01 hours from 18,900 feet on G.H. Leader.

16/01/1945 NG298 JI-E Bombing Wanne-Eickel 23.30 02.24 04.26

Bomb load 1 x 4000 HC, 10 x 500 ANM58, 4 x 250 GP. Primary target: Wanne-Eickel, Benzol plant. Weather 10/10ths thin low cloud. Bombed at 02.24 hours from 20,000 feet on Red and Green flares.

22/01/1945 NG298 JI-E Bombing Hamborn (Duisburg) 17.08 20.02 21.49

Bomb load 1 x 4000 HC, 7 x 500 ANM58 or 64, 2 x 500 GP (L/Delay), 3 x 250 GP. Primary target: Hamborn, Thyssen works. Weather over target clear and almost as bright as day. Bombed at 20.02 hours from 20,000 feet on centre of Red T.I.

28/01/1945 NG298 JI-E Bombing Cologne-Gremberg 10.22 14.27

16.07

Bomb load 1 x 4000 HC, 10 x 500 ANM64, 2 x 500 GP, 3 x 250 GP. Primary target: Koln- Gremberg, Marshalling yards. Weather 10/10ths cloud en route clearing on approach to target where visibility was good and nil cloud. Bombs hung over target area but jettisoned over MUNSTEREIFEL area at 14.27 hours from 19,000 feet.

29/01/1945 NG298 JI-E Bombing Krefeld 10.27 x 15.56

Bomb load 1 x 4000 HC, 10 x 500 ANM64, 2 x 500 GP, 4 x 250 GP. Primary target: Krefeld Marshalling Yards. Weather 10/10ths low thin cloud over target although clear patches en-route. Unable to bomb primary target - Bombs hung up and jettisoned 1 x 4000 HC at 15.10 from 10,000 feet at 5215N 0315E. Remainder of bombs brought back.

02/02/1945 NG142 JI-J Bombing Wiesbaden 20.49 23.43 02.30

Bomb load 1 x 4000 HC, 10 x 500 ANM64, 2 x 500 GP, 4 x 250 GP. Primary target: Wiesbaden. Weather 10/10ths cloud, winds very erratic. Bombed at 23.43 hours from 20,000 feet on Gee.

03/02/1945 NG142 JI-J Bombing Dortmund-Huckarde 16.18 19.34
21.25

Bomb load 1 x 4000 HC, 2 x 500 MC, 2 x 500 MC L/Delay, 6 x 500 GP, 3 x 250 GP. Primary target Dortmund-Huckarde, Coking plant. Weather clear with slight haze. Bombed at 19.34 hours from 19,500 feet on centre of Red T.Is. Good fires and explosions.

08/02/1945 NG142 JI-J Bombing Hohenbudberg 03.29 06.23 08.08

Bomb load 1 x 4000 HC, 2 x 500 MC, 4 x 250 GP, 4 x 500 GP, 6 x 500 ANM64. Primary target: Hohenbudberg, Marshalling yards. Weather 8/10ths cloud over target. Bombed at 06.23 hours from 19,500 feet on Red T.I.s. Bombing fairly concentrated.

F/O. F.E. Sider was 2nd Pilot that day.

18/02/1945 NG298 JI-E Bombing Wesel 11.28 15.24 16.57

Bomb load 1 x 4000 HC, 4 x 500 GP, 2 x 500 MC L/Delay, 4 x 250 GP, 6 x 500 ANM64. Primary target: Wesel. Weather 10/10ths cloud. Bombed at 15.24 hours from 19,500 feet on leading aircraft.

19/02/1945 NF968 JI-B Bombing Wesel 13.30 16.36 18.25

Bomb load 1 x 4000 HC, 6 x 500 MC, 6 x 500 ANM64, 4 x 250 GP. Primary target: Wesel. Weather over target 5-7/10ths cloud. Bombed at 16.16 hours from 19,000 feet on G.H. Leader.

20/02/1945 NG298 JI-E Bombing Dortmund   21.50 x 03.03

Bomb load 1 x 4000HC, 5 x 500 Type 14 Clusters, 6 x 750 Type 15 Clusters. Primary target: Dortmund. Weather 8-10/10ths thin cloud at about 5,000 feet. Returned early. Jettisoned complete bomb load. Feathered starboard outer engine at 00.24 hours, could not keep height and reach target on time after engine failure, so returned.

22/02/1945 NN773 JI-K Bombing Osterfeld   12.42 16.00 17.46

Bomb load 1 x 4000 HC, 9 x 500 ANM64, 2 x 500 MC, 4 x 250 GP. Primary target: Osterfeld, Coking ovens. Weather at target clear, but hazy. Bombed at 16.00 hours from 19,500 feet on G.H. Leader.

Contrary to ORBs, in his logbook F/O. Fiset noted F/O. Bailey as WOP/AG that day.

26/02/1945 NG298 JI-E Bombing Dortmund   10.28   14.03   16.04

Bomb load 1 x 4000 HC, 2 x 500 MC L/Delay 37B, 9 x 500 ANM64, 4 x 250 GP. Primary target: Dortmund, Hoesch Benzin plant. Weather 10/10ths cloud, tops 8/10,000 feet. Bombed at 14.03 hours from 20,000 feet on G.H. Leader.

F/O. F.H. Rowan was WOP/AG from that day until 11/03/1945, except for 02/03.

28/02/1945 NG298 JI-E Bombing Nordstern   08.52   12.04   14.15

Bomb load 1 x 4000 HC, 9 x 500 ANM64, 2 x 500 MC L/D, 4 x 250 GP. Primary target: Nordstern (Gelsenkirchen). Weather 10/10ths cloud. Bombed at 12.04 hours from 20,300 feet on leading aircraft.

According F.H. Rowan's logbook target "Gelsenkirchen". Nordstern is an industrial place at Gelsenkirchen.

02/03/1945 NG298 JI-E Bombing Koln   12.40   16.03   18.22

Bomb load 1 x 4000 HC, 12 x 500 ANM64. Primary target: Koln. Weather 10/10ths cloud over Koln, South and South-East of Koln clear. Bombed at 16.03 hours from 20,500 feet on leading aircraft.

There is probably a typing error in R.J. Hamilton's logbook where this mission is noted as the next day: 03/03/1945.

Contrary to ORBs, in his logbook F/O. Fiset noted F/O. F.H. Rowan as WOP/AG that day, confirmed by F/O. Rowan's logbook.

06/03/1945 NG298 JI-E Bombing Saltzbergen 08.10   12.15   14.03

Bomb load 1 x 4000 HC, 12 x 500 ANM64, 2x 500MC. Primary target: Salzbergen, Wintershall oil plant. Weather 10/10ths cloud over target, tops 10,000 feet. Bombed at 12.15 hours from 20,500 feet on G.H. Leader. Slight damage to aircraft due to explosion of 'T'.

07/03/1945 NG298 JI-E Bombing Dessau   17.00 22.02   02.10

Bomb load 1 x 4000 HC, 6 x Mk.17 Clusters. Primary target: Dessau. Weather 5 to 10/10ths thin cloud. Bombed at 22.02 hours from 20,000 feet on Red/Green flares.

11/03/1945 NN773 JI-K Bombing Essen   11.36   15.25   17.23

Bomb load 1 x 4000 HC, 13 x 500 ANM64, 2 x 500 MC. Primary target: Essen, Marshalling yards. Weather 10/10ths cloud, tops 7/8000 feet. Bombed at 15.25 hours from 19,000 feet. Followed G.H. Leader.

14/03/1945 PB142 JI-G Bombing Heinrichshutte 13.14   16.40   19.05

Bomb load 1 x 4000 HC, 12 x 500 ANM64. Primary target: Heinrichshutte, Hattingen Steel works and Benzol plant. Weather 10/10ths cloud, tops 7/12,000 feet. Bombed at 16.40 hours from 18,000 feet on G.H. Leader. 1 Red marker as aircraft bombed. Port outer engine holed by flak at 16.33 hours and had to be feathered. Mid upper turret holed and Hydraulics unserviceable.

F/L. R. Burnett was 2nd Pilot that day.

27/03/1945 NN782 JI-F Bombing Hamm Sachsen 10.35 14.02 16.05

Bomb load 1 x 4000 HC, 13 x 500 ANM64, 2 x 500 MC. Primary target: Hamm Sachsen, Benzol plant. Weather 10/10ths cloud. Bombed on G.H. Leader at 14.02 hrs at 18,000 feet.

04/04/1945 NG298 JI-F Bombing Merseburg (Leuna) 18.37 22.43 02.33

Weather 5-10/10ths cloud, and 10/10ths over Merseburg. Bombed Magdeburg. Bomb load 1 x 4000 HC, 6 x 500 ANM64 on Red and Green T.I.s. at 22.43 hours from 20,000 feet. 1 x 500 ANM64 hung up, brought back. H2S U/S. Very good attack, after turning at Halberstadt, towards Merseberg saw P.F.F. start attack and bombed in T.I.s. No other target marked after bombing saw Merseberg attack commence.

F/O. L.A. Adams was 2nd Pilot that day.

13/04/1945 NG298 JI-F Bombing Kiel 20.26 23.54 02.05

Bomb load 1 x 4000 HC and 12 x 500 ANM64. Primary target: Kiel, Docks and ship yards. Weather 10/10ths cloud low and thin. Bombed centre of area of Green T.I.s on M/B's instructions at 23.54 from 20,000 ft. Bomb bursts seen through cloud. We were early to bomb but attack seemed good after leaving. M/B was clear and did not have to make corrections.

F/O. O.L. Goldsmith was WOP/AG from that day. Contrary to ORBs though, in his logbook F/O. Fiset noted usual crew. In this case the WOP/AG would have been W/O. J. Rutherford and not F/O. O.L. Goldsmith.

18/04/1945 NF968 JI-B Bombing Heligoland 09.50 13.08 14.55

Bomb load 6 x 1000 MC, 10 x 500 ANM64. Primary target: Heligoland, Naval base. Weather no cloud, slight haze. Bombed visually on upwind edge of smoke as instructed at 13.08 from 18,000 ft. Whole Island covered with smoke. Bomb bursts across island. Complete success and no troubles. Small boats leaving harbour trying to evade bombs.

F/O. O.L. Goldsmith was WOP/AG that day. Contrary to ORBs though, in his logbook F/O. Fiset noted usual crew. In this case the WOP/AG would be W/O. J. Rutherford and not F/O. O.L. Goldsmith.

F/O. Warren James Keating Fisher

J41106 F/O. Warren James Keating Fisher, RCAF. Pilot.

J40767 F/O. Donald Edward Stephens, RCAF. A/Bomber.

J41672 F/O. Alan Quilliam Downward, RCAF. Navigator.

A429799 F/S. Ronald Hardy, RAAF. WOP/AG.

R7729 Sgt. Albert Richard McWhinney, RCAF. MU/Gunner.

J95454 (R278031) P/O. Alfred Hector Morrison, RCAF. R/Gunner.

1399495 F/S. William Barclay Warr. F/Engineer.

Alan Quilliam Downward (courtesy Janet Murphy)

Ronald Hardy (NAA)

13/01/1945 LM724 JI-H Bombing Saarbrucken 11.53 15.25 18.06

Bomb load 1 x 4000 HC, 10 x 500 ANM58 or 64, 4 x 250 GP. Primary target: Saarbrucken. Weather 3-5/10ths cloud, tops 4/5,000 feet. Bombed at 15.25 hours from 19,500 feet on G.H. All aircrafts on this op were diverted on return to Exeter as weather at base was unfit to land.

F/O. W.J.K. Fisher flew the mission as 2nd Pilot with P/O. W.R. Foreman's crew.

15/01/1945 NG203 JI-C Bombing Lagendreer 11.40 15.00 17.00

Bomb load 1 x 4000 HC, 10 x 500 ANM64, 4 x 250 GP. Primary target: Lagendreer. Weather 10/10ths cloud. Bombed at 15.00 hours from 19,000 feet on G.H. Leader.

16/01/1945 LM724 JI-H Bombing Wanne-Eickel 23.25 02.22 04.31

Bomb load 1 x 4000 HC, 10 x 500 ANM58, 4 x 250 GP. Primary target: Wanne-Eickel, Benzol plant. Weather 10/10ths thin low cloud. Bombed at 02.22 hours from 19,400 feet on G.H.

F/O. W.J.K. Fisher flew the mission as 2nd Pilot with P/O. W.R. Foreman's crew.

22/01/1945 NN776 JI-F Bombing Hamborn (Duisburg) 17.00 20.10 21.55

Bomb load 1 x 4000 HC, 7 x 500 ANM58 or 64, 2 x 500 GP (L/Delay), 3 x 250 GP. Primary target: Hamborn, Thyssen works. Weather over target clear and almost as bright as day. Bombed at 20.10 hours from 21,000 feet on Green T.I.s.

213

28/01/1945 NN773 JI-K Bombing Cologne-Gremberg 10.20 14.11 16.20

Bomb load 1 x 4000 HC, 10 x 500 ANM64, 2 x 500 GP, 3 x 250 GP. Primary target: Koln-Gremberg, Marshalling yards. Weather 10/10ths cloud en route clearing on apprach to target where visibility was good and nil cloud. Bombed at 14.11 hours from 20,000 feet on G.H. Leader.

29/01/1945 NN773 JI-K Bombing Krefeld 10.16 x 15.44

Bomb load 1 x 4000 HC, 10 x 500 ANM64, 2 x 500 GP, 4 x 250 GP. Primary target: Krefeld Marshalling Yards. Weather 10/10ths low thin cloud over target although clear patches en-route. Unable to bomb primary target due to hang up - Jettisoned 1 x 4000 HC at 14.55 from 12,000 feet at 5215N 0320E. Remainder of bombs brought back.

01/02/1945 PB426 JI-D Bombing Munchen-Gladbach 13.18 16.33 18.25

Bomb load 1 x 4000 HC, 14 x No 14 Clusters. Primary target: Munchen-Gladbach, Marshalling yards. Bombed at 16.33 hours from 18,000 feet on leading aircraft.

03/02/1945 LM685 A2-B Bombing Dortmund-Huckarde 16.19 x x

Bomb load 1 x 4000 HC, 2 x 500 MC, 2 x 500 MC L/Delay, 6 x 500 ANM64, 2 x 500 GP, 3 x 250 GP. Primary target Dortmund-Huckarde, Coking plant, Hansa benzol plant. Weather clear with slight haze. Aircraft missing.

Nachtjagd War Diaries states 'Two Lancasters, HK688 (AP-W of 186 Sqn.) and LM685, were lost during the run up to the target, probably to the Flak, in combination with the searchlights, though the same source notes that the aircraft was possibly shot down by Maj. Heinz-Wolfgang Schnaufer of Stab NJG4. There were no survivors from the crew, who are buried in Reichswald Forest War Cemetery.

F/O. Leslie Flack

J29160 F/O. Leslie "Les" Flack, RCAF. Pilot.
1800217 F/S. Frederick Albert "Max" Wall. A/Bomber.
J37531 (R149932) F/O. Roy Aubry Young, RCAF. Navigator.
A426796 F/S. Patrick Francis "Paddy" O'Donohue, RAAF. WOP/AG.
2222184 Sgt. Andrew "Andy" Reilly. MU/Gunner.
1594663 Sgt. Dennis "Joe" Heeley. R/Gunner.
1595208 Sgt. William John "Billy" Watson. F/Engineer.

27/11/1944 LM734 JI-U Bombing Cologne 12.23 15.03 17.01

Bomb load 1 x 4000 HC, 16 x 500 GP. Primary target: Cologne, Marshalling Yards. Weather patchy cloud. Bombed at 15.03 hours from 19,500 feet with G.H. Leader.

29/11/1944 LM727 JI-S Bombing Neuss 02.55 05.33 07.05

Bomb load 1 x 4000 HC, 14 x 150 x 4 incendiaries. Primary target: Neuss.

Weather 10/10ths cloud over target but the glow of fires was seen through cloud. Bombed at 05.33 hours from 20,000 feet on H2S.

F/O. Leslie Flack flew the mission as 2nd Pilot with F/O. E.E. Williams' crew.

30/11/1944 LM727 JI-S Bombing Osterfeld   10.44   13.11   14.47

Bomb load 1 x 4000 HC, 15 x 500 GP, 1 Red/Green flare. Primary target: Osterfeld, Coking plant. Weather 10/10ths cloud. Bombed at 13.11 hours from 19,500 feet on G.H. Leader.

04/12/1944 LM727 JI-S Bombing Oberhausen 11.45   14.09   16.02

Bomb load 1 x 4000 HC, 2100 x 4 lb incendiaries. Primary target: Oberhausen, Built up area. Weather 10/10ths cloud. Bombed at 14.09 hours from 19,500 feet on G.H. Leader.

05/12/1944 PA186 A2-G Bombing Hamm   08.50   11.30   14.00

Bomb load 1 x 4000 HC, 1950 x 4 lb incendiaries. Primary target: Hamm. Weather 10/10ths cloud over target, but otherwise varying from 6-10/10ths. Bombed at 11.30 hours from 20,000 feet on G.H. Leader.

06/12/1944 LM727 JI-S Bombing Merseburg 16.55 20.47   00.35

Bomb load 1 x 4000 HC, 8 x 500 GP and 1 x 500 GP Long Delay. Primary target: Merseburg. Weather 10/10ths cloud with odd breaks. Bombed at 20.47 hours from 20,000 feet on centre of flares.

15/12/1944 NN717 JI-E Bombing Siegen ca 11.30 x ca 14.00

Between 11.19 to 11.36 hours 19 aircraft took off to attack Siegen. At 12.30 hours, all aircraft were recalled as Fighters were unable to take off. Operation only reported in ORB's "Summary of events", no trace in ORB's "Detail of Work carried out - Details of sorties of flight". Operation also recorded in R.A. Young's logbook.

01/02/1945 LM275 JI-C Bombing Munchen-Gladbach 13.20   16.35
18.11

Bomb load 1 x 4000 HC, 10 x 500 ANM64, 2 x 500 GP, 4 x 250 GP. Primary target: Munchen-Gladbach, Marshalling yards. Bombed at 16.35 hours from 18,500 feet on G.H. Bombed at 16.33 hours from 17,500 feet on G.H.

02/02/1945 LM685 A2-B Bombing Wiesbaden 20.54   23.44   02.29

Bomb load 1 x 4000 HC, 12 x 500 GP, 4 x 250 GP. Primary target: Wiesbaden. Weather 10/10ths cloud, winds very erratic. Bombed at 23.44 hours from 19,500 feet on Gee fix.

19/02/1945 ME363 JI-Q Bombing Wesel 13.00   16.36   18.24

Bomb load 1 x 4000 HC, 6 x 500 MC, 6 x 500 ANM64, 4 x 250 GP. Primary target: Wesel. Weather over target 5-7/10ths cloud. Bombed at 16.36 hours from 19,000 feet on G.H.

20/02/1945 ME363 JI-Q Bombing Dortmund   21.40   01.07   03.27

Bomb load 1 x 4000 HC, 6 x 500 Type 14 Clusters, 6 x 750 Type 15 Clusters. Primary target: Dortmund. Weather 8-10/10ths thin cloud at about 5,000 feet. Bombed at 01.07 hours from 20,800 feet on centre of Red/Green T.I.s.

Patrick Francis "Paddy" O'Donohue

(AWM P05549.001)

Leslie "Les" Flack

(courtesy Leona)

Roy Aubry Young (courtesy Cory Young)

05/03/1945 ME422 JI-Q Bombing Gelsenkirchen 10.21 14.07 16.07

Bomb load 1 x 4000 HC, 12 x 500 ANM64. Primary target: Gelsenkirchen, Benzol plant. Weather 10/10ths cloud over target with cirrus cloud at bombing height. Bombed at 14.07 hours from 20,600 feet on G.H.

06/03/1945 ME365 JI-T Bombing Salzbergen 08.19 x x

Bomb load 1 x 4000 HC, 11 x 500 ANM64, 2 x 500MC, 1 Skymarker Blue Puff. Primary target: Salzbergen, Wintershall oil plant. Weather 10/10ths cloud over target, tops 10,000 feet. Aircraft missing.

Seen to explode over target at 12.04 hours. No survivors from the crew who are buried at Reichswald Forest War Cemetery.

F/O. R.C. Foord

J26041 F/O.   R.C. Foord, RCAF. Pilot.
J44600 F/O.   H.S. Morris, RCAF. A/Bomber.
R190150 F/S. H.W.S. Harding, RCAF. Navigator.
NZ4210989 F/S. W.F. Dowdle, RNZAF.   WOP/AG.
R290373 F/S. J.G. Hearn.   MU/Gunner. 4 ops.
R283454 F/S. J.H. McCready.   R/Gunner.
  F/S. W. Hopps. F/Engineer.

Passenger: 02/05/1945.

04/04/1945 ME530 JI-C Bombing Merseburg (Leuna) 18.40 22.46 02.39

Weather 5-10/10ths cloud, and 10/10ths over Merseburg. Bombed primary target. Bomb load 1 x 4000 HC, 6 x 500 ANM64. 5/10th to 10/10th thin cloud. Glow of fires and bursting bombed. Bombed at 22.46 hours from 20,000 feet. Bombed glow of fires, Red and Green Decoy Markers seen to port of track near target. W/T U/S and H2S U/S. Fires seen at Magdeberg on leg into target. No markers seen in our A/P so orbited on glow of fires.

F/O. R.C. Foord flew the mission as 2nd Pilot with F/O. H. MacLean's crew.

09/04/1945 ME535 JI-G Bombing Kiel   19.35 22.40 02.10

Bomb load 1 x 4000 HC and 12 x 500 ANM64. Primary target: Kiel, Submarine Buildings Yards. Weather clear with slight haze. Bombed at 22.40 hours from 20,000 feet on Green T.I. on M/B's instructions. Bombed Hamburg (uncertain) but H2S photograph taken. Several explosions well concentrated. Bomb bursts well concentrated. Other target seen after bombing.

20/04/1945 ME380 JI-E Bombing Regensburg 09.30 13.57 17.07

Bomb load 15 x 500 ANM64. Primary target: Regensburg. Weather clear over target and whole route. Bombed on G.H. at 13.57 hours from 18,500 feet. Good runs, bombs appeared to be falling N and S of oil plant. No black smoke. Success of attack doubtful, otherwise good trip. Perfect conditions for G.H.

run.

F/O. R.C. Foord flew the mission as 2nd Pilot with F/O. H. MacLean's crew.

22/04/1945 RE116 JI-F Bombing Bremen   15.13   18.40   21.06

Bomb load 1 x 4000 HC, 2 x 500 MC, 14 x 500 ANM64. Primary target: Bremen, in support of Troop concentration. Weather on approaching target 4-5/10ths cloud. Bombed following 514/H2 at 18.40 hours from 19,000 ft. Bombs seen to burst in close area north of river, two good fires seen. Flak. Effective attack. Falling shrapnel pierced radiator of starboard inner, feathered lost 10 m.p.h. Released on 4th bomb of leader.

30/04/1945 ME535 JI-G Manna Rotterdam   16.46   18.20   19.38

Dropping area: Rotterdam. Weather intermittent showers and low cloud. Load 5 packs. Dropped 4 packs on white cross at 18.20 hours. 3 packs brought back due to hang up. Turning point before target. Much too congested. Successful delivery. Very enthusiastic reception.

02/05/1945 ME530 JI-C Manna The Hague   11.09   12.38   13.45

Dropping area The Hague. Weather over dropping zone clear below cloud for the first arrivals changing later to heavy showers which marred visibility. Dropped 4 packs at 12.38 hours on White Cross and Red T.I.s. Showers.

That day LAC. Puttnam was a passenger and no Mid Upper Gunner.

18/05/1945 RA601 JI-J Exodus Brussels - Oakley 11.49 x 16.45

Duration 3 hrs 05 mins. Out 1 hr 17 mins. In 1 hr 48 mins. 9 Belgian refugees taken to Brussels. 24 ex POWs returned to U.K. Perfect organisation. Dunsfold very good.

P/O. William Raymond Foreman

184505 (1322359)   P/O. William Raymond "Ray" Foreman. Pilot.

Sgt. R.P. "Ron" McGowan.   A/Bomber.

F/S. R.A. "Tony" Baxter.   Navigator.

Sgt. R.E. "Ron" Taylor.   WOP/AG.

Sgt. Edward Kenneth "Ken" Grieves. MU/Gunner.

F/S. J. Tranter.   R/Gunner. 10 ops.

Sgt. A. "Andy" Deighton.   R/Gunner. 19 ops.

NZ425546

F/O. Albert George "Chatty" Chatfield, DFC RNZAF. R/Gunner. 1 op.

Sgt. John Goldthorp.   F/Engineer.

J20986 F/O. W.F. Burrows, RCAF. 2nd Pilot. 29/11/1944

J41106

F/O.Warren James Keating Fisher, RCAF. 2nd Pilot. 13&16/01/1945

06/10/1944 PB142 JI-A Bombing Dortmund   16.39   20.29   22.30

Bomb load 1 x 4000 HC, 12 x No. 14 Clusters. Primary target: Dortmund, Town and Railways. Weather over the target was clear with slight ground haze. Bombed at 20.29 hours from 20,000 feet on green T.I.s. Smoke and fires. Good raid.

07/10/1944 PB142 JI-A Bombing Emmerich 12.08 14.28   16.15

Bomb load 1 x 4000 HC. 10 x No.14 clusters, 4 x (150 x 4). Primary target Emmerich. Weather clear with cloud at 13,000 feet. Bombed at 14.28 hours from 14,000 feet on red T.I. side of town.

14/10/1944 LM733 JI-F Bombing Duisburg   23.03   01.32   03.42

Bomb load 11 x 1000 MC, 4 x 500 GP Long Delay. Primary target: Duisburg. Weather was clear with small amount of cloud over the target. Bombed at 01.32 hours from 20,000 feet, Green T.I.

15/10/1944 LM627 JI-D Bombing Wilhelmshaven 17.18 19.47   21.47

Bomb load 11 x 1000 MC, 4 x 500 GP. Primary target: Wilhelmshaven. Weather haze and thin cloud at first with thick cloud later. Bombed at 19.47 hours from 20,500 feet. Centre of T.I.s.

19/10/1944 ME841 JI-C Bombing Stuttgart 22.07   01.03   04.16

Bomb load 1 x 4000 HC. 6 x 1000 MC. 1 x 500 GP. Primary target: Stuttgart, A/P 'E' 2nd attack. Weather 10/10ths low cloud over target and all crew arrived late owing to winds not as forecast. Bombed at 01.03 hours from 17,500 feet. Red and Yellow markers.

21/10/1944 PD265 JI-G Bombing Flushing 10.47   12.28   13.37

Bomb load 12 x 1000 MC, 2 x 500 GP. Primary target: Flushing 'B'. Weather clear. Bombed at 12.28 hours from 8,000 feet. Building running parallel to the jetty.

25/10/1944 NG203 JI-A Bombing Essen 12.58   15.35   17.06

Bomb load 1 x 4000 HC, 6 x 1000 MC, 6 x 500 GP. Primary target: Essen. Weather over target 10/10ths low cloud, with one clear patch which appeared to fill up later in the attack. Bombed at 15.35 hours from 19,500 feet. Red sky markers.

28/10/1944 PD324 A2-B   Bombing Flushing 08.55   10.14   11.18

Bomb load 11 x 1000 MC, 4 x 500 GP. Primary target: Flushing. Weather over the target quite clear and conditions perfect, although believed to be only local, and some low cloud approaching. Bombed at 10.14 hours from 8,000 feet. Between two Piers.

30/10/1944 LM733 JI-F Bombing Wesseling   09.06   11.58   13.38

Bomb load 1 x 4000 HC, 16 x 500 GP. Primary target: Wesseling. Weather was 10/10ths cloud - tops about 7,000 feet. Bombed at 11.58 hours from 18,500 feet on release of bombs by G.H. Leader.

11/11/1944 LM733 JI-F Bombing Castrop Rauxel 08.26 11.08   12.57

Bomb load 1 x 4000 HC, 16 x 500 GP. Primary target: Castrop Rauxel, Oil refineries. Weather 10/10ths cloud. Bombed at 11.08 hours from 22,000 feet on G.H. Leader.

15/11/1944 LM733 JI-F Bombing Dortmund   12.38   15.40   17.35

Bomb load 1 x 4000 HC, 16 x 500 GP. Primary target: Hoesch-Benzin Dortmund, Oil refineries. Weather 10/10ths cloud over the target. Bombed at 15.40 hours from 16,700 feet. Upwind of Red flares.

16/11/1944 LM733 JI-F Bombing Heinsburg 13.17 15.32   17.29

Bomb load 1 x 4000 HC, 6 x 1000 MC, 6 x 500 GP.   Primary target: Heinsburg. Weather - nil cloud with slight haze over target. Bombed at 15.32 hours from 6,700 feet. Building on West side of town. Aircraft hit by flak. Mid upper turret damaged.

29/11/1944 LM285 JI-K Bombing Neuss   03.08   05.40   07.29

Bomb load 1 x 4000 HC, 6 x 1000 MC, 4 x 500 GP, 4 x 250 Green T.I.s. Primary target: Neuss. Weather 10/10ths cloud over target but the glow of fires was seen through cloud. Bombed at 05.40 hours from 19,000 feet. Red flares with green stars. Glow observed through cloud, successful raid.

F/O. W.F. Burrows was 2nd Pilot that day.

30/11/1944 NN717 JI-E Bombing Osterfeld   11.08   13.10   14.54

Bomb load 1 x 4000 HC, 16 x 500 GP. Primary target: Osterfeld, Coking plant. Weather 10/10ths cloud. Bombed at 13.10 hours from 19,000 feet. Upwind edge of sky markers.

04/12/1944 NG203 JI-A Bombing Oberhausen 11.57   14.10   16.11

Bomb load 1 x 4000 HC, 15 x 500 GP, 1 Flare. Primary target: Oberhausen, Built up area. Weather 10/10ths cloud. Bombed at 14.10 hours from 19,000 feet on G.H.

05/12/1944 NG203 JI-A Bombing Hamm   09.07   11.31   13.59

Bomb load 1 x 4000 HC, 9 x 500 ANM58, 4 x 500 MC, 2 x 500 GP Long Delay 37, 1 Flare. Primary target: Hamm. Weather 10/10ths cloud over target, but otherwise varying from 6-10/10ths. Bombed at 11.31 hours from 19,000 feet on G.H.

06/12/1944 LM733 JI-F Bombing Merseburg 17.02 x 20.28

Bomb load 1 x 4000 HC, 8 x 500 GP and 1 x 500 GP Long Delay. Primary target: Merseburg. Weather 10/10ths cloud with odd breaks. Returned early with Rear gunner sick. Jettisoned safe at 19.40 hours from 7,000 feet at 5222N 0223E.

08/12/1944 LM724 JI-H Bombing Duisburg   08.39   11.04   12.57

Bomb load 13 x 1000 ANM59, 1 Red/Green flare. Primary target: Duisberg. Weather 10/10ths cloud. Bombed at 11.04 hours from 19,500 feet on G.H.

F/O. A.G. Chatfield was R/Gunner that day.

11/12/1944 LM285 JI-K Bombing Osterfeld   08.44   11.06   12.57

Bomb load 1 x 4000 HC, 12 x 500 GP, 2 x 500 GP Long Delay, 1 Flare. Primary target: Osterfeld. Weather 10/10ths cloud, tops 16,000 feet. Bombed at 11.06 hours from 19,000 feet on G.H.

12/12/1944 LM275 JI-M Bombing Witten 11.25 14.05   15.55

Bomb load 1 x 4000 HC, 5 x 500 GP, 6 x 500 ANM58, 4 x 500 ANM64, 1

Flare. Primary target: Witten. Weather 10/10ths cloud, tops 14/16,000 feet. Bombed at 14.05 hours from 20,000 feet on G.H.

16/12/1944 LM724 JI-H Bombing Siegen 11.36 15.00 17.03

Bomb load 1 x 4000 HC, 5 x 1000 MC, 7 x 500 GP, 1 Flare. Primary target: Siegen. Weather very bad on route with icing and cloud. Bombed at 15.00 hours from 17,500 feet on G.H. Leader.

From that day F/S. J. Tranter was R/Gunner.

28/12/1944 LM275 JI-F Bombing Cologne Gremberg 12.30 15.04 17.09

Bomb load 7 x 1000 MC, 6 x 500 GP, 2 x 250 GP, 1 Flare. Primary target: Koln Gremberg, Marshalling yards. Weather 10/10ths cloud or fog. Bombed at 15.04 hours from 18,600 feet on G.H.

06/01/1945 PB419 JI-J Bombing Neuss 15.52 18.47 20.31

Bomb load 1 x 4000 HC, 2 x 500 ANM58, 12 x 500 ANM64, 1 flare. Primary target: Neuss. Weather 8-10/10ths cloud over target. Bombed at 18.47 hours from 19,500 feet on G.H.

07/01/1945 PB419 JI-J Bombing Munich 18.54 22.33 02.35

Bomb load 1 x 1000 ANM65, 1 x 500 ANM58, 1080 x 4 lb I.B, 120 x 4 I.B. Primary target: Munich. Weather 10/10ths cloud over target 6-8,000 feet with a thin layer altitude 16,000 feet. Bombed at 22.33 hours from 19,000 feet on Red and Green flares.

11/01/1945 LM724 JI-H Bombing Krefeld 11.44 15.12 16.41

Bomb load 1 x 4000 HC, 2 x 500 ANM58, 8 x 500 ANM64, 4 x 250 GP, 1 Flare. Primary target: Krefeld. Weather 10/10ths cloud above and below. Visibility poor. Bombed at 15.12 hours from 19,500 feet on G.H.

13/01/1945 LM724 JI-H Bombing Saarbrucken 11.53 15.25 18.06

Bomb load 1 x 4000 HC, 10 x 500 ANM58 or 64, 4 x 250 GP. Primary target: Saarbrucken. Weather 3-5/10ths cloud, tops 4/5,000 feet. Bombed at 15.25 hours from 19,500 feet on G.H. All aircraft on this op were diverted on return to Exeter as weather at base was unfit to land.

F/O. W.J.K. Fisher was 2nd Pilot that day.

15/01/1945 LM724 JI-H Bombing Lagendreer 11.40 15.02 16.44

Bomb load 1 x 4000 HC, 10 x 500 ANM64, 4 x 250 GP. Primary target: Lagendreer. Weather 10/10ths cloud. Bombed at 15.02 hours from 18,500 feet on G.H.

16/01/1945 LM724 JI-H Bombing Wanne-Eickel 23.25 02.22 04.31

Bomb load 1 x 4000 HC, 10 x 500 ANM58, 4 x 250 GP. Primary target: Wanne-Eickel, Benzol plant. Weather 10/10ths thin low cloud. Bombed at 02.22 hours from 19,400 feet on G.H.

F/O. W.J.K. Fisher was 2nd Pilot that day.

22/01/1945 PB142 JI-G Bombing Hamborn (Duisburg) 17.05 20.07 21.50

Bomb load 1 x 4000 HC, 7 x 500 ANM58 or 64, 2 x 500 GP (L/Delay), 3 x 250 GP. Primary target: Hamborn, Thyssen works. Weather over target clear and almost as bright as day. Bombed at 20.07 hours from 19,500 feet on centre of cluster of Green T.I.s.

28/01/1945 PB142 JI-G Bombing Cologne-Gremberg 10.24 14.11 15.52

Bomb load 1 x 4000 HC, 10 x 500 ANM64, 2 x 500 GP, 3 x 250 GP, 1 Flare. Primary target: Koln- Gremberg, Marshalling yards. Weather 10/10ths cloud en route clearing on approach to target where visibility was good and nil cloud. Bombed at 14.11 hours from 19,500 feet on G.H.

F/L. Alba Fletcher Fowke

J24970   F/L. Alba Fletcher Fowke, RCAF.   Pilot.
J28685   F/O. Richard Jack Bennett, RCAF.   A/Bomber.
J27493   F/O. James Terence Daly, RCAF.   Navigator.
1586848 Sgt. Sydney Arthur Picton.   WOP/AG.
86817   F/L. Henry Charles Alfred Chapman. MU/Gunner.   10 ops.
1179859 Sgt. J.F. Lewis.   MU/Gunner.   9 ops.
R87920 W/O. William Ernest Egri, DFM RCAF.   MU& R/Gun. 2 ops.
J36596   F/O. Gordon Reginald Murphy, RCAF.   R/Gunner.
546667 Sgt. Harold Gordon Carter. F/Engineer.

30/04/1944 LL734 JI-S Bullseye x   22.25 x 3.20

Only described in ORB summary. Op not detailed.

W.E. Egri noted in his logbook "Rear Gunner - Bullseye". Rest of crew unknown, but probably: F/O. R.J. Bennett, F/O. J.T. Daly, Sgt. S.A. Picton, Sgt. J.F. Lewis, Sgt. H.G. Carter.

22/05/1944 DS826 JI-U Bombing Dortmund   23.00   00.49   02.50

Bomb load 1 x 2000 lb bomb, 96 x 30, 810 x 4, 90 x 4 incendiaries. Primary target: Dortmund. Clear to 2/10 cloud at target. Bombed red T.I.s at 00.49 hours from 19.800 feet. Visual of streets outlined by fire. Many small fires near aiming point and attack thought fairly concentrated. Severe icing beginning at Base and continuing up to 13,000 feet before clearing. Sighted a JU88 on homeward journey from target.

24/05/1944 DS826 JI-U Bombing Boulogne   00.10   01.19   02.35

Bomb load 9 x 1000 MC, 1 x 1000 GP, 1 x 1000 ANM, 4 x 500 GP. Primary target: Boulogne, Gun Battery. Slight haze over the target. Bombed green T.I.s at 01.19 hours from 7000 feet. T.I.s well concentrated and could be seen from English coast. Smoke seen rising from target area. Unidentified aircraft sighted homeward from target.

Above left: James Terence Daly; right Sydney Arthur Picton (courtesy Debbie Howe Edwards). Below left: Gordon Reginald Murphy; right: Henry Charles Alfred Chapman.

Harold Gordon Carter (courtesy Mark Carter)

First graves at Deinvillers (courtesy Deinvillers Mayor)

27/05/1944 DS826 JI-U Bombing Boulogne 00.05 01.16 02.30

Bomb load 7 x 1000 MC, 4 x 1000 ANM, 4 x 500 GP. Primary target: Boulogne Gun Batteries. Clear at target. Bombed at 01.16 hours from 8,800 feet. One T.I. marker was burst with own bombs. Concentrated attack. When nearing Dungeness on return, twin-engined aircraft approached from 350 yards. Mid-upper gunner fired two short bursts.

28/05/1944 DS826 JI-U Bombing Angers 18.50 23.58 02.15

Bomb load 5 x 1000 MC, 1 x 1000 USA, 4 x 500 MC. Primary target: Angers. Clear over target. Bombed at 23.58 hours from 10,000 feet, as instructed by Master Bomber. Large vivid flash seen in target area at 00.03 hours. A good attack. Heavy flak at Nantes hit port tail plane.

30/05/1944 DS818 JI-Q Bombing Boulogne 23.16 x 00.31

Bomb load 6 x 1000 MC, 4 x 500 MC. Primary target: Boulogne Gun Batteries. Port inner engine out on take-off. Bombs jettisoned safe at 5320N 0057E at 23.52 hours, and aircraft then returned to base.

05/06/1944 LL733 JI-S Bombing Ouistreham 03.45 05.11 06.35

Bomb load 9 x 1000 MC and 2 x 500 MC. Primary target: Ouistreham. There was 7/10 broken cloud over target. Bombed at 05.11 hours from 9800 feet. Red and green T.I.s seen whilst over target. Bombs seen bursting all around T.I.s and attack thought successful. Visual of target obtained after bombing.

06/06/1944 DS818 JI-Q Bombing Lisieux 00.10 01.39 03.00

Bomb load 16 x 500 MC tail fused and 2 x 500 MC LD. Primary target: Lisieux. Weather was clear below but cloud above. Bombed at 01.39 hours from 6000 feet. Sticks seen to burst across red T.I.s. Attack thought to be good. Cloud on route gave trouble. 2 aircraft with Navigation lights on were seen over target.

17/06/1944 DS826 JI-U Bombing Montdidier 01.02 x 04.39

Bomb load 16 x 500 GP, 2 x 500 ANM, 64 GP. Primary target: Montdidier. Over target 02.51 hours and orbited until 02.59 hours when Master Bomber was heard to order return to Base. Jettisoned safe entire load. Four aircraft seen to bomb glow of T.I.s.

24/06/1944 DS826 JI-U Bombing Rimeux 23.26 00.35 01.54

Bomb load 18 x 500 GP. Primary target: Rimeux, Flying bomb installations. Weather hazy. Bombed at 00.35 hours from 11,000 feet centre of red T.I.s. Bomb bursts seen right across red T.I.s, which were concentrated. Intense searchlights activity.

27/06/1944 LL635 JI-M Bombing Biennais 23.50 01.09 02.18

Bomb load 16 x 500 GP, 2 x 500 ANM 64 GP. Primary target: Biennais, Flying bomb installations. There was 10/10ths cloud. Bombed at 01.09 hours from 13,500 feet red glow.

F/L. H.C.A. Chapman was MU/Gunner from that day except 30/06/1944.

30/06/1944 DS826 JI-U Bombing Villers Bocage 18.17 19.59 21.30

Bomb load 11 x 1000 MC, 2 x 500 GP. Primary target: Villers Bocage. Weather clear. Bombed at 19.59 hours from 4,000 feet, red T.I.s as instructed by the Master Bomber. At one period the Master Bomber said Monkey Nuts on account of smoke. Marvellous attack.

In his logbook E.W. Egri noted he was Mid Upper Gunner that day.

02/07/1944 DS826 JI-U Bombing Beauvoir   12.48   14.38   16.18

Bomb load 11 x 1000 MC, 4 x 500 GP. Primary target: Beauvoir, Flying bomb supply site. Bombed at 14.38 hours from 11,500 feet visual.

05/07/1944 DS826 JI-U Bombing Watten 22.58 00.09   00.59

Bomb load 11 x 1000 ANM 65, 4 x 500 GP. Primary target: Watten, Constructional works. Bombed at 00.09 hours from 10,000 feet red T.I.s.

07/07/1944 DS826 JI-U Bombing Vaires 22.52   01.37   03.34

Bomb load 7 x 1000 MC, 4 x 500 GP. Primary target: Vaires, Marshalling yards. Weather clear. Bombed at 01.37 hours from 12,500 feet, centre of T.I.s. Bombing concentrated. JU88 claimed destroyed.

10/07/1944 LL635 JI-M Bombing Nucourt   04.22   06.05   07.43

Bomb load 11 x 1000 ANM 65, 4 x 500 GP. Primary target: Nucourt, Constructional works. Bombed at 06.05 hours from 15,500 feet, Gee.

12/07/1944 HK571 JI-L Bombing Vaires   17.57 x 21.48

Master Bomber ordered "Abandon mission". Jettisoned 4 x 500 GP, at 20.42 hours from 12,000 feet position 4953N 0034E.

15/07/1944 HK571 JI-L Bombing Chalons Sur Marne 21.39 x 00.35

Bomb load 18 x 500 GP. Primary target: Chalons sur Marne, Railway centre. Returned early with both Mid upper and rear turrets u/s. Jettisoned at 23.58 hours from 9,000 feet 3 miles East of Lowestoft.

18/07/1944 HK571 JI-L Bombing Emieville   04.15   06.07   07.17

Bomb load 11 x 1000 MC, 4 x 500 GP. Primary target: Emieville, Troop concentration. Weather clear. Bombed at 06.07 hours from 8,000 feet yellow T.I.s.

18/07/1944 HK571 JI-L Bombing Aulnoye 22.28   00.56   02.02

Bomb load 18 x 500 GP. Primary target: Aulnoye, Railway junction. Weather clear. Bombed at 00.56 hours from 7,800 feet between green and red T.I.s.

28/07/1944 DS813 JI-N Bombing Stuttgart   21.54 x 01.30

Bomb load 13 x 500 GP. Target: Stuttgart. Crashed at Deinvillers, near St. Die, circumstances not known. Possibly shot down by Ofhr. Walter Swoboda, 2./NJG6, who claimed a Lancaster in the St. Die area 29 July 1944 at 01.30 hours. All the crew were killed and this is where all were first buried. They have been subsequently re-interred in the Choloy War Cemetery. F/L. Chapman was the Squadron Gunnery Leader.

F/O. Geoffrey Charles France

179705 (1511708)   P/O. Geoffrey Charles "Geoff" France.   Pilot.
J29701   F/O.   Kenneth Hubert "Ken" Barker, RCAF.   A/Bomber.
161585 (1605263)   F/O. Frederick James "Fred" Eisberg.   Navigator.
1705084   Sgt.   Ronald William "Ron" Harding.   WOP/AG.
 Sgt. William John "Bill" Meredith. MU/Gunner. 24 ops
172026 (655843) F/O. Peter Slater.   MU/Gunner. 10 ops.
NZ425592
   F/O. Albert George "Chatty" Chatfield. RNZAF, DFC.   MU/Gunner. 1
op.
1894366 Sgt. Leslie Peter "Pete" Coles.   R/Gunner.
1891510 Sgt. Peter Andrew "Pete" Gosnold.   F/Engineer.
37994 W/C.   Michael "Mike" Wyatt, DFC. Captain. 05/07/1944

05/07/1944 ME841 JI-H Bombing Watten 22.47 00.09   01.13
   Bomb load 11 x 1000 ANM65, 4 x 500 GP. Primary target: Watten,
Constructional works. Bombed at 00.09 hours from 11,000 feet red T.I.s.
   W/C. M. Wyatt was Captain of this crew that day and F/S. later F/O. G.C.
France 2nd Pilot.
07/07/1944 ME842 JI-K Bombing Vaires 22.49 01.34 03.15
   Bomb load 11 x 1000 ANM65. Primary target: Vaires, Marshalling yards.
Weather 8/10ths cloud at 13,000 feet. Bombed at 01.34 hours from 12,600 feet
centre of group of green T.I.s on edge of red markers as instructed by Master
Bomber. Large fires started. Good trip, combat with FW190, no claims.
10/07/1944 ME841 JI-H Bombing Nucourt 04.07 06.07   07.57
   Bomb load 11 x 1000 ANM65, 4 x 500 GP. Primary target: Nucourt,
Constructional works. Bombed at 06.07 hours from 16,000 feet Gee Fix.
12/07/1944 ME842 JI-K Bombing Vaires 17.49 x 21.50
   Bomb load 18 x 500 GP. Primary target: Vaires, Marshalling yards. Master
Bomber's instructions to abandon mission obeyed, bombs brought back to
Base.
15/07/1944 LM627 JI-D Bombing Chalons Sur Marne 21.37 x 22.30
   Bomb load 18 x 500 GP. Primary target: Chalons sur Marne, Railway centre.
Petrol leak noticed after take-off, jettisoned sufficient fuel to land.
18/07/1944 LM180 JI-G Bombing Emieville   04.06 06.07 07.24
   Bomb load 11 x 1000 MC, 4 x 500 GP. Primary target: Emieville, Troop
concentration. Weather clear. Bombed at 06.07 hours from 10,500 feet, South
East corner of smoke as directed by Master Bomber. A good attack.
18/07/1944 ME858 JI-J Bombing Aulnoye 22.26 00.54 02.13
   Bomb load 18 x 500 GP. Primary target: Aulnoye, Railway junction.
Weather clear. Bombed at 00.54 hours from 10,000 feet red and green T.I.s. A
quiet trip, bombing good.
23/07/1944 PB143 JI-B Bombing Kiel   22.19 01.21 03.57

L to R: Sgt. Ron Harding (WOP/AG), Sgt Pete Coles (Rear Gunner), Sgt Pete Gosnold (Flight Engineer), F/S Geoff France (Pilot), F/O Ken Barker RCAF (Bomb Aimer), Sgt Bill Meredith (MU Gunner), F/O Freddie Eisberg (Navigator). Probably taken at 3LFS, Feltwell, June 1943. (Simon Hepworth/ Molly Gosnold)

Bomb load 10 x 1000 MC, 5 x 500 GP. Primary target: Kiel, Warehouses and docks. Weather 10/10ths cloud. Bombed at 01.20 hours from 20,000 feet centre of red and green T.I.s. Large explosion giving an orange glow at 01.21 hours.

24/07/1944 PB143 JI-B Bombing Stuttgart 21.42 01.48 05.20

Bomb load 7 x 1000 MC, 4 x 500 GP. Primary target: Stuttgart. Weather 10/10ths cloud. Bombed at 01.48 hours from 20,000 feet south east corner of green and yellow star sky markers. Glow seen beneath cloud.

28/07/1944 PB143 JI-B Bombing Stuttgart 21.35 02.00 05.19

Bomb load 7 x 1000 MC, 2 x 500 GP. Primary target: Stuttgart. Weather 9/10 thin layer of cloud. Bombed at 02.00 hours from 20,000 feet glow of green T.I.s. Uneventful trip.

30/07/1944 LM180JI-G Bombing Caen 05.58 07.49 09.08

Bomb load 18 x 500 GP. Primary target: Caen 'B'. Weather 10/10ths cloud. Bombed at 07.49 hours from 2,000 feet, red T.I.s as instructed. Clouds of yellowish smoke. Bomb bursts seen across the reds. A good trip. Damage to fuselage from bomb bursts. Landed at Woodbridge.

01/08/1944 LM277JI-F Bombing Foret de Nieppe 19.18 x 21.38

Bomb load 11 x 1000 MC, 4 x 500 GP. Target: De Nieppe, constructional works. Jettisoned 3 x 1000 MC, 2 x 500 GP at 20.54 hours from 11,000 feet, position 5110N 0230E. Abandoned on Master Bomber's orders.

03/08/1944 PB142 JI-A Bombing Bois de Cassan 11.42 14.06 15.27

Bomb load 11 x 1000 MC, 4 x 500 GP. Primary target: Bois de Cassan, Flying bomb supply depot. Bombed at 14.06 hours from 16,000 feet on smoke of yellow T.I.

12/08/1944 LM286 A2-F   Bombing Brunswick   21.38   00.05   02.30

Bomb load 1 x 2000 HC. 12 x 500 'J' type clusters. Primary target: Brunswick. Weather 10/10ths cloud. Bombed at 00.05 hours from 20,000 feet. Glow of fires seen through cloud. Bombing appeared rather scattered. Black smoke up to 6/8,000 feet. Good trip.

06/09/1944 LM277 JI-F Bombing Le Havre   16.34   18.40   19.51

Bomb load 11 x 1000 MC, 4 x 500 GP. Primary target: Le Havre. Bombed at 18.40 hours from 9,000 feet red T.I.s.

08/09/1944 NF966 JI-R Bombing Le Havre   06.00 x 10.04

Bomb load 11 x 1000 MC, 4 x 500 GP. Primary target: Le Havre. Weather 10/10ths cloud down to 3,000 feet. Abandoned mission on Master Bomber's instructions.

11/09/1944 LM277 JI-F Bombing Kamen   16.08 18.42   20.24

Bomb load 1 x 4000 HC, 16 x 500 GP. Weather clear. Primary target: Kamen. Bombed at 18.42 hours from 16,500 feet on red fires per Master Bomber's instructions.

12/09/1944 LM277 JI-F Bombing Frankfurt   18.26   22.58   01.06

Bomb load 1 x 4000 HC, 14 x 500 Clusters 4lb. Target: Frankfurt - Main. Weather clear over the target. Bombed at 22.58 hours from 16,000 feet on red and green T.I.s.

17/09/1944 LM277 JI-F Bombing Boulogne   10.49 x 13.38

Bomb load 11 x 1000 MC, 4 x 500 GP. Primary target: Boulogne, Aiming point 2. Weather clear below cloud. At 12.15 hours order given by Master Bomber to abandon mission. Jettisoned 3 x 1000 MC, 2 x 500 GP, brought remainder back.

03/10/1944 LM733 JI-F Bombing Westkapelle 12.31 13.57   14.49

Bomb load 1 x 4000 MC, 6 x 1000 MC, 1 x 500 GP. L/Delay. Primary target: Westkapelle (Walcheren). Weather patchy-scattered cloud with base 5,000 feet. Bombed at 13.57½ hours from 5,700 feet, undershot red T.I. on instructions.

05/10/1944 LM733 JI-F Bombing Saarbrucken 17.19 20.34   22.27

Bomb load 11 x 1000 MC, 1 x 500 GP, 3 x 500 GP. Long Delay. Primary target: Saarbrucken, Marshalling yards. Weather clear over target. Dummies very active in Saarbrucken area. "514 Sqdn. 'F' (LM733 JI-F) attacked Rail tracks 5-6 miles East of Saarbrucken at 20.34 hours from 15,000 feet dropping 11 x 1000 MC, 1 x 500 GP, 1 x 500 GP L/Delay".

06/10/1944 LM733 JI-F Bombing Dortmund   16.47   20.32   22.19

Bomb load 1 x 4000 HC, 12 x No. 14 Clusters. Primary target: Dortmund, Town and Railways. Weather over the target was clear with slight ground haze. Bombed at 20.32 hours from 22,500 feet on red T.I.s.

18/10/1944 PD265 JI-G Bombing Bonn   08.22   11.01   13.01

Bomb load 1 x 4000 HC, 5 x 12 x 30 - 2 x 12 x 30 modified. 9 x No.14

Clusters. Primary target: Bonn. Weather varying cloud 2-7/10ths with break for bombing. Bombed at 11.01 hours from 19,000 feet. West side of bridge.

F/O. P. Slater was MU/Gunner from that day until 25/10/1944.

19/10/1944 LM733 JI-F Bombing Stuttgart 21.51 01.10 03.53

Bomb load 1 x 4000 HC, 6 x 1000 MC, 1 x 500 GP. Primary target: Stuttgart, A/P 'E' 2nd attack. Weather 10/10ths low cloud over target and all crew arrived late owing to winds not as forecast. Bombed at 01.10 hours from 20,000 feet. Estimated position of Wanganui flares, which died out ½ minute before aircraft bombing.

21/10/1944 LM733 JI-F Bombing Flushing 10.34 12.30 13.30

Bomb load 12 x 1000 MC, 2 x 500 GP. Primary target: Flushing 'B'. Weather clear. Bombed at 12.30 hours from 5,000 feet. Coastal tip of target area.

22/10/1944 PD265 JI-G Bombing Neuss 13.01 15.57 17.23

Bomb load 1 x 4000 HC, 6 x 1000 MC, 6 x 500 GP. Primary target: Neuss. Weather 10/10ths cloud over target. Bombed at 15.57 hours from 16,400 feet. Following aircraft 'E2'.

25/10/1944 LM733 JI-F Bombing Essen 12.54 15.32 17.07

Bomb load 1 x 4000 HC, 6 x 1000 MC, 6 x 500 GP. Primary target: Essen. Weather over target 10/10ths low cloud, with one clear patch which appeared to fill up later in the attack. Bombed at 15.32 hours from 21,500 feet. White smoke as ordered by Master Bomber.

29/10/1944 NG203 JI-A Bombing Flushing 09.42 11.37 12.26

Bomb load 11 x 1000 ANM59, 4 x 500 GP. Primary target: Flushing, Gun installations. Weather clear over target. Bombed at 11.37 hours from 7,000 feet. Starboard of Green T.I. as instructed.

31/10/1944 LM285 JI-K Bombing Bottrop 11.47 15.00 16.26

Bomb load 1 x 4000 HC, 15 x 500 GP. 1 Flare. Primary target: Bottrop, Synth. Oil plants. Weather 10/10ths cloud over target. Bombed at 15.00 hours from 18,000 feet on G.H.

02/11/1944 PD265 JI-G Bombing Homberg 11.14 14.06 15.26

Bomb load 1 x 4000 HC, 6 x 1000 ANM59, 6 x 500 MC. Primary target: Homberg. Weather variable cloud but clear for bombing. Target obscured by pall of smoke rising to 10,000 feet. Bombed at 14.06 hours from 20,000 feet on instruments.

F/O. A.G. Chatfield was MU/Gunner that day.

04/11/1944 LM719 JI-B Bombing Solingen 11.22 14.06 15.50

Bomb load 1 x 4000 HC, 6 x 1000 ANM59, 4 x 500 GP, 2 x 500 MC (L/Delay), 3 Flares. Primary target: Solingen. Weather 8-10/10ths cloud. Bombed at 14.06 hours from 20,000 feet on red flares.

F/O. P. Slater was MU/Gunner from that day.

05/11/1944 PB423 A2-G Bombing Solingen 10.07 x 12.55

Bomb load 1 x 4000 HC, 6 x 1000 ANM59, 4 x 500 GP, 2 x 500 GP (L/Delay), 3 Flares. Primary target: Solingen. Aircraft returned early with port outer engine unserviceable. Jettisoned at 5220N 0243E at 12.00 hours from

7,500 feet.

08/11/1944 ME841 JI-J Bombing Homberg   08.00   10.31   12.10

Bomb load 1 x 4000 HC, 12 x No. 14 Clusters, 2 x 150 x 4. Primary target: Homberg. Weather clear. Bombed at 10.31 hours from 17,500 feet on instruments.

20/11/1944 LM733 JI-F Bombing Homburg   12.37   15.14   16.57

Bomb load 1 x 4000 HC, 4 x 500 GP, 12 x 500 MC. Primary target: Homberg. Weather 10/10ths cloud over target. Bombed at 15.14½ hours from 19,000 feet on G.H. Leader.

21/11/1944 PD265 JI-G Bombing Homberg   12.28 x   x

Bomb load 1 x 4000 HC, 15 x 500 GP, 1 Red and Green Flare. Primary target: Homberg. Weather about 5/10ths cloud but clear for bombing. Aircraft missing.

Approaching the target the aircraft (although another source says after bombing the target) was hit by flak between the starboard inner engine and the cockpit. A fire started in at least one engine causing injury to most of the crew. F/O. France believed the aircraft was also hit in the tail as it had become uncontrollable. He remembered bracing his feet on the instrument panel whilst attempting to pull the aircraft out of its dive. F/O. France was subsequently unclear about how he escaped, and could only conclude that he was thrown clear when the aircraft broke up. Baling out at more than 20,000 feet, he saw another parachute, the navigator F/O. Frederick Eisberg having also been thrown clear, fortunately wearing his parachute. F/O. France noted the tail becoming detached, and the aircraft eventually exploding though whether this was on or above the ground he does not know. He landed in a cabbage field, breaking his left leg, so was unable to affect an escape.

F/O. Eisberg also landed in farmland whilst the aircraft came down in the moat surrounding the Grafschafter Castle in the centre of Moers. Both were captured, although separately.

After his release F/O. Eisberg wrote to the family of Sgt. Peter Gosnold, the Flight Engineer, explaining what had happened and apologising for not having been able to save the other crew members, but everything had happened very quickly. F/O. France subsequently lost his right leg due to the untreated wounds turning gangrenous. He spent the rest of the war as a POW, left the RAF and was eventually ordained as a clergyman.

Those of the crew who lost their lives are buried in Reichswald Forest War Cemetery, in a communal grave with members of the crew of JI-C, shot down at the same time. The loss was also witnessed by F/L Harry Yates, who wrote an account in 'Luck and a Lancaster'.

F/O. Kenneth Hubert "Ken" Barker KIA
Sgt. Ronald William "Ron" Harding KIA
F/O. Peter Slater KIA
Sgt. Leslie Peter "Les" Coles KIA
Sgt. Peter Andrew "Pete" Gosnold KIA

F/O. Joseph Norman Gallicano, DFC

J88748 F/O.   Joseph Norman "Joe" Gallicano RCAF, DFC. Pilot.
R169804 F/S. D.L. "Del" Cressman, RCAF. A/Bomber. 21 ops.
Sgt. J.A. Murray.   A/Bomber. 10 ops.
Sgt. R.A. Barrett.   Navigator. 4 ops.
Sgt. W.E. Harradine.   Navigator. 9 ops.
J40778 F/O.   Ray Bertram Hilchey, RCAF. Navigator.1 op.
528335 W/O. Peter Vincent James Lowen, DFM. Navigator. 19 ops.
R184404 F/S. R.C.C. Robertson, RCAF.   WOP/AG.
R195975 Sgt. M.C. Willard, RCAF.   MU/Gunner. 2 ops.
 W/O. I.M. Davies.   MU/Gunner. 1 op.
1126875 F/S. Jack Swindlehurst, DFM. MU/Gunner. 27ops
 W/O. George Edgar Sales.   MU/Gunner. 1 op.
Sgt. D.W.F. Sawyer.   MU/Gunner. 1 op.
R264534 F/S. W.G. Wheeler.   MU/Gunner. 1 op.
R268502 F/S. Louis Gadsby Watson, RCAF. R/Gunner.
195232 (1595309) P/O. Frank Walker Leslie Ellis.   F/Engineer.
174335 (1430412) F/O. George Robertson. 2nd Pilot. 16/02/1945
J7741 F/L. R.E. Farvolden, RCAF. 2nd Pilot. 18/02/1945

L to R: G.E. Sales, L.G. Watson, D.L. Cressman, J.N. Gallicano, F.W.L. Ellis, R.C.C. Robertson, P.V.J. Lowen. (courtesy Gord Watson)

29/11/1944 PD324 A2-B Bombing Neuss 02.48 05.36 07.02

Bomb load 1 x 4000 HC, 14 x 150 x 4 incendiaries. Primary target: Neuss. Weather 10/10ths cloud over target but the glow of fires was seen through cloud. Bombed at 05.36 hours from 20,000 feet, Centre of flares.

P/O. J.N. Gallicano flew the mission as 2nd Pilot with F/O. G.D. Orr's crew.

30/11/1944 NG142 A2-H Bombing Osterfeld 10.45 13.10 14.56

Bomb load 1 x 4000 HC, 16 x 500 GP. Primary target: Osterfeld, Coking plant. Weather 10/10ths cloud. Bombed at 13.10 hours from 20,000 feet on leading G.H. aircraft. Markers well concentrated. Flak holes in starboard wing. Landed at Mildenhall 14.56 hours by mistake owing to lack of local geographical knowledge. 1st daylight trip from this Station. Landed later at 15.50 hours at Waterbeach.

Sgt. R.A. Barrett Navigator from this day until 12/12/1944.

F/S. D.L. Cressman A/Bomber from this day until 19/02/1945.

Sgt. M.C. Willard MU/Gunner from this day until 06/12/1944.

06/12/1944 NG236 A2-C Bombing Merseburg 17.03 x 19.05

Bomb load 1 x 4000 HC, 8 x 500 GP, 1 x 500 GP Long Delay. Primary target: Merseburg. Weather 10/10ths cloud with odd breaks. Returned early with Rear Gunner sick. Jettisoned safe at 18.11 hours from 12,000 feet at 5337N 0221E.

08/12/1944 NG118 A2-E Bombing Duisburg 08.37 11.06 13.03

Bomb load 14 x 1000 ANM59. Primary target: Duisberg. Weather 10/10ths cloud. Bombed at 11.06 hours from 20,000 feet on timed run from G fix. Navigational aids unserviceable through icing.

W/O. I.M. Davies was MU/Gunner that day.

12/12/1944 NG141 A2-J Bombing Witten 11.44 14.04 15.57

Bomb load 1 x 4000 HC, 14 x 500 Clusters. Primary target: Witten. Weather 10/10ths cloud, tops 14/16,000 feet. Bombed at 14.04 hours from 20,000 feet on G.H. Leader.

F/S. Jack Swindlehurst was MU/Gunner from that day until 21/03/1945.

01/01/1945 PD334 A2-D Bombing Vohwinkle 16.28 19.46 21.39

Bomb load 1 x 4000 HC, 12 x 500 ANM64, 2 x 500 GP. Primary target: Vohwinkel. Weather clear. Bombed at 19.46 hours from 20,000 feet. Centre of Red T.I.s.

Sgt. W.E. Harradine was Navigator from that day until 22/01/1945.

02/01/1945 PD334 A2-D Bombing Nuremburg 15.32 19.30 22.34

Bomb load: 1 x 4000 HC, 7 x 500 Clusters. Primary target: Nuremburg. Weather clear. Bombed at 19.30 hours from 19,000 feet on Red T.I.s.

05/01/1945 PD334 A2-D Bombing Ludwigshafen 11.21 15.08 17.30

Bomb load 1 x 4000 HC, 10 x 500 ANM58 or 64, 2 x 500 GP. Primary target: Ludwigshafen, Marshalling yards. Weather clear over target. Bombed at 15.08 hours from 21,000 feet on leading G.H. aircraft. Aircraft hit by flak - Mid-upper turret damaged.

06/01/1945 PD334 A2-D Bombing Neuss 15.54 18.49 20.16

Bomb load 1 x 4000 HC, 2 x 500 ANM58, 12 x 500 ANM64. Primary target: Neuss. Weather 8-10/10ths cloud over target. Bombed at 18.49 hours from 20,000 feet on Red T.I.

11/01/1945 NN717 A2-E Bombing Krefeld 11.45 15.14 16.45

Bomb load 1 x 4000 HC, 10 x 500 ANM64, 4 x 250 GP. Primary target: Krefeld. Weather 10/10ths cloud above and below. Visibility poor. Bombed at 15.14 hours from 20,000 feet on G.H. Leader.

13/01/1945 PD334 A2-D Bombing Saarbrucken 11.55 15.23 17.41

Bomb load 1 x 4000 HC, 10 x 500 ANM58 or 64, 4 x 250 GP. Primary target: Saarbrucken. Weather 3-5/10ths cloud, tops 4/5,000 feet. Bombed at 15.23 hours from 19,000 feet on leading aircraft. All aircrafts on this op were diverted on return to Exeter as weather at base was unfit to land.

15/01/1945 PD334 A2-D Bombing Lagendreer 11.41 15.01 16.39

Bomb load 1 x 4000 HC, 10 x 500 ANM64, 4 x 250 GP. Primary target: Lagendreer. Weather 10/10ths cloud. Bombed at 15.01 hours from 19,000 feet on G.H. Leader.

16/01/1945 PD334 A2-D Bombing Wanne-Eickel 23.15 02.20 04.02

Bomb load 1 x 4000 HC, 10 x 500 ANM58, 4 x 250 GP. Primary target: Wanne-Eickel, Benzol plant. Weather 10/10ths thin low cloud. Bombed at 02.20 hours from 19,500 feet on Red flare with Green stars.

22/01/1945 NN772 A2-C Bombing Hamborn 17.09 20.04 21.37

Bomb load 1 x 4000 HC, 7 x 500 ANM58 or 64, 2 x 500 GP (L/Delay), 3 x 250 GP. Primary target: Hamborn (Duisburg), Thyssen works. Weather over target clear and almost as bright as day. Bombed at 20.04 hours from 20,500 feet on centre of Red and Green T.Is.

28/01/1945 PD334 A2-D Bombing Cologne 10.32 14.10 16.00

Bomb load 1 x 4000 HC, 10 x 500 ANM64, 2 x 500 GP, 3 x 250 GP. Primary target: Koln- Gremberg, Marshalling yards. Weather 10/10ths cloud en route clearing on approach to target where visibility was good and nil cloud. Bombed at 14.10 hours from 19,000 feet on G.H. Leader.

F/O. Ray Bertram Hilchey was Navigator that day.

16/02/1945 NN776 A2-D Bombing Wesel 12.30 16.00 18.10

Bomb load 1 x 4000 HC, 4 x 500 GP, 2 x 500 MC L/Delay, 4 x 250 GP, 6 x 500 ANM64. Primary target: Wesel. Weather clear. Bombed at 16.00 hours from 21,000 feet on leading aircraft. Aircraft hit by flak - port inner engine damaged and had to be feathered.

F/O. George Robertson was 2nd Pilot that day.

W/O. Peter Vincent James Lowen was Navigator from that day.

18/02/1945 PA186 A2-G Bombing Wesel 11.28 15.22 17.30

Bomb load 1 x 4000 HC, 4 x 500 GP, 2 x 500 MC L/Delay, 4 x 250 GP, 6 x 500 ANM64. Primary target: Wesel. Weather 10/10ths cloud. Bombed at 15.22 hours from 18,500 feet on leading aircraft.

F/L. R.E. Farvolden was 2nd Pilot that day.

19/02/1945 PA186 A2-G Bombing Wesel 13.07 16.37 19.15

Bomb load 1 x 4000 HC, 6 x 500 MC, 6 x 500 ANM64, 4 x 250 GP. Primary target: Wesel. Weather over target 5-7/10ths cloud. Bombed at 16.37 hours from 19,000 feet G.H. Leader. Landed at Moreton in Marsh.

22/02/1945 ME365 JI-T Bombing Osterfeld   12.16   16.00   17.48

Bomb load 1 x 4000 HC, 9 x 500 ANM64, 2 x 500 MC, 4 x 250 GP. Primary target: Osterfeld, Coking ovens. Weather at target clear, but hazy. Bombed at 16.00 hours from 19,500 feet on G.H. Leader.

Sgt. J.A. Murray A/Bomber from this day until 14/03/1945.

25/02/1945 NN781 A2-D Bombing Kamen   09.40   12.46   14.52

Bomb load 1 x 4000 HC, 9 x 500 ANM64, 2 x 500 MC, 3 x 250 GP and Smoke Puff. Primary target: Kamen. Weather 6-8/10ths cloud. Bombed at 12.46 hours from 19,000 feet on G.H. Leader.

27/02/1945 NN781 A2-D Bombing Gelsenkirchen 10.55   14.28   16.25

Bomb load 1 x 4000 HC, 2 x 500 MC (L/D 37B), 9 x 500 ANM64, 4 x 250 GP. Primary target: Gelsenkirchen (Alma Pluts) Benzin plant. Weather 10/10ths cloud, 6/10,000 feet tops. Bombed at 14.28 hours from 19,500 feet on G.H. Leader.

01/03/1945 NN781 A2-D Bombing Kamen   11.44   15.09   17.55

Bomb load 1 x 4000 HC, 11 x 500 ANM64, 2 x 500 MC L/Delay 37. Primary target: Kamen, Coking plant. Weather 10/10ths cloud. Bombed at 15.09 hours from 19,500 feet on Blue puffs.

02/03/1945 NN781 A2-D Bombing Koln 12.54 16.03   18.30

Bomb load 1 x 4000 HC, 12 x 500 ANM64. Primary target: Koln. Weather 10/10ths cloud over Koln, South and South-East of Koln clear. Bombed at 16.03 hours from 20,000 feet on leading G.H. aircraft.

06/03/1945 NN781 A2-D Bombing Salzbergen 08.12   12.15   14.01

Bomb load 1 x 4000 HC, 12 x 500 ANM64, 2 x 500MC. Primary target: Salzbergen, Wintershall oil plant. Weather 10/10ths cloud over target, tops 10,000 feet. Bombed at 12.15 hours from 21,000 feet on G.H. Leader.

07/03/1945 NN781 A2-D Bombing Dessau   17.01   22.06   01.46

Bomb load 1 x 4000 HC, 6 x Mk.17 Clusters. Primary target: Dessau. Weather 5 to 10/10ths thin cloud. Bombed at 22.06 hours from 21,000 feet on Red flares with Green stars.

10/03/1945 NN776 A2-D Bombing Gelsenkirchen 12.12   15.37   17.37

Bomb load 1 x 4000 HC, 13 x 500 ANM64, 2 x 500 GP. Primary target: Gelsenkirchen. Weather 10/10ths cloud at target, tops 8,000 feet. Bombed at 15.37 hours from 19,000 feet on leading G.H. aircraft.

12/03/1945 NN776 A2-D Bombing Dortmund 12.58 16.58   18.57

Bomb load 1 x 4000 HC, 13 x 500 ANM64. Primary target: Dortmund. Weather 10/10ths cloud over target, tops 6/10,000 feet. Bombed at 16.58 hours from 19,000 feet. Followed G.H. aircraft.

14/03/1945 NN776 A2-D Bombing Heinrichshutte 13.11   16.41   18.47

Bomb load 1 x 4000 HC, 12 x 500 ANM64. Primary target: Heinrichshutte, Hattingen Steel works and Benzol plant. Weather 10/10ths cloud, tops

7/12,000 feet. Bombed at 16.41 hours from 18,500 feet on G.H. Leader. 1 x 500 ANM64 brought back to Base.

17/03/1945 NN776 A2-D   Bombing August Viktoria   11.27   15.08   17.57

Bomb load 1 x 4000 HC, 13 x 500 ANM64, 2 x 500 MC. Primary target: Auguste Viktoria, Marl-Hüls coal mine. Weather 10/10ths cloud, tops and contrails up to 23,000 feet. Bombed at 15.08 hours from 20,500 feet on leading G.H. aircraft.

F/S. D.L. Cressman was A/Bomber from this day until 09/04/1945.

20/03/1945 NN776 A2-D   Bombing Hamm   09.46   13.14   15.29

Bomb load 7 x 1000 ANM65, 9 x 500 ANM64. Primary target: Hamm, Marshalling yards. Weather 5/10ths cloud. Bombed at 13.14 hours from 18,000 feet on leading G.H. aircraft. Perspex holed by heavy flak.

21/03/1945 NN776 A2-D   Bombing Munster 09.33 13.08   15.14

Bomb load 1 x 4000 HC, 13 x 500 ANM64, 2 x 500 MC. Primary target Munster Viaduct and Marshalling Yards. Weather cloud nil to 2/10ths. Bombed at 13.08 hours from 18,000 feet on G.H. aircraft and visual. 1 x 4000 HC seen to hit a bridge.

09/04/1945 NN776 A2-D   Bombing Kiel 19.51 22.43   01.51

Bomb load 1 x 4000 HC and 12 x 500 ANM64. Primary target: Kiel, Submarine Buildings Yards. Weather clear with slight haze. Bombed at 22.43 hours from 19,500 feet on Red and Green T.I.s. Well concentrated explosions and large columns of black smoke seen.

F/S. George Edgar Sales was MU/Gunner that day.

13/04/1945 NN776 A2-D   Bombing Kiel 20.20 23.37   02.30

Bomb load 1 x 4000 HC and 12 x 500 ANM64. Primary target: Kiel, Docks and ship yards. Weather 10/10ths cloud low and thin. Bombed on centre of Green T.I.s at 23.37 hours from 19,500 feet. Good concentration of Green T.I.s. H2S U/S. Arrived early and orbited. Both A/Ps marked distinctly but merged into one green glow when Lanc bombed.

Sgt. J.A. Murray was A/Bomber from that day.

Sgt. D.W.F. Sawyer was MU/Gunner that day.

20/04/1945 ME529 A2-F   Bombing Regensburg 09.25   13.55   17.09

Bomb load 15 x 500 ANM64. Primary target: Regensburg. Weather clear over target and whole route. Bombed visually at 13.55 hours from 19,500 feet. on end of docks. Leading aircraft tending to overshoot, so bombed visually. Bombs seen to straddle oil dock. Raid tending to overshoot. Railway Bridge seen hit.

F/S. W.G. Wheeler was MU/Gunner that day.

F/S.   Thomas Lipsey Gibson

984464   F/S. Thomas Lipsey Gibson. Pilot.
1585541 Sgt.   James Laird Dunbar.   A/Bomber.
1670597 Sgt.   Alexander Henry Freeburn. Navigator.
1614503 Sgt.   Lawrence Buxton. WOP/AG.
1592001 Sgt.   George Henry Kemp. MU/Gunner.
1823530 Sgt.   J. Gallagher. R/Gunner.
935291   Sgt. James Fraser. F/Engineer.

20/04/1944 DS813 JI-H Bombing Cologne 23.59 02.08 04.04
    Bomb load 1 x 1000 lb bomb, 1026 x 4, 108 x 30, 114 x 4 incendiaries.
Primary target: Koln. There was 10/10 cloud. Bombed at 02.08 hours from
20,000 feet. Red flares and yellow stars scarcely distinguishable. Cloud too
thick. Not much evidence. Route OK.
    F/S. T.L. Gibson flew the mission as 2nd Pilot with P/O. E.A. Greenwood's
crew.

24/04/1944 DS786 A2-F   Bombing Karlsruhe 22.31 00.51 04.13
    Bomb load 1 x 1000 lb bomb, 1026 x 4, 114 x 4, 108 x 30 incendiaries.
Primary target: Karlsruhe. There was 5/10 cloud - broken in patches. Bombed
at 00.51 hours from 19,000 feet. Large fires in centre of area marked by T.I.s.
T.I.s appeared scattered but fires have good hold in whole area - large pillars
of smoke to 5,000 feet. Monica u/s over enemy territory. Dense cloud before
and after target area with moderate icing causing speed indicator to freeze up.
Had combat with an enemy aircraft.

26/04/1944 LL732 A2-H   Bombing Essen 23.03 01.33 03.34
    Bomb load 1 x 2000 lb bomb, 84 x 30, 945 x 4, 108 x 4 lb incendiaries.
Primary target: Essen. Weather was clear. Bombed at 01.33 hours from 19,000
feet. T.I.s were concentrated. Fires covered whole area. Very successful attack.
Route good.

07/05/1944 LL727 A2-C   Bombing Nantes   00.31 03.02 05.47
    Bomb load 1 x 4000, 14 x 500 lb bombs. Primary target: Nantes. Weather
was very clear. Bombed at 03.02 hours from 10,000 feet. Bombs seen bursting
in area, appeared concentrated, pall of smoke to 6000 feet.

09/05/1944 LL727 A2-C   Bombing Cap Gris Nez 02.55 04.13   04.55
    Bomb load 1 x 1000 GP, 13 x 1000 MC. Primary target: Cape Gris Nez.
Conditions haze, but visual of coast, lighthouse and road obtained. Bombs fell
along coast line at 04.15 hours from 5,000 feet. Bomb bursts were seen and
there appeared to be bursts and smoke from explosions. T.I.s were erratic.

10/05/1944 LL716 A2-G   Bombing Courtrai 22.20 23.27   01.05
    Bomb load 14 x 1000 MC. Primary target: Courtrai. Slight haze over target,

but marker flares visible. Bombed on Master Bomber's instructions at 23.27 hours from 10,000 feet. T.I.s were going down well and several sticks of bombs were seen bursting between them. Very concentrated attack which should prove successful. Route very good. Little opposition.

19/05/1944 DS633 A2-B Bombing Le Mans 22.20   00.34   03.15

Bomb load 4 x 1000 USA, 5 x 1000 MC, 1 x 1000 GP, 4 x 500 GP. Primary target: Le Mans. 10/10 cloud at about 8/10000 feet. Bombed green T.I.s at 00.34 hours from 7,000 feet. Target well illuminated and three sticks of bombs seen to burst followed by a succession of explosions.

21/05/1944 DS633 A2-B Bombing Duisburg 22.50 x   x

Bomb load 1 x 2000 lb bomb, 120 x 30, 600 x 4 incendiaries. Aircraft missing believed crashed in the sea.

After abandoning the mission and on the return to base, instructions were given to jettison the bomb load. Nothing else was ever heard. The circumstances are unclear but Squadron ORB states aircraft is believed to have crashed in The Wash. A fix on this aircraft was obtained by Waterbeach at 03.03 hours on 22 May 44 and about six minutes later base ordered the crew to jettison their bombs.

It is possible that the aircraft was one of three unidentified heavy bombers claimed by Fw. Johann Trenke who was flying a Me410 on an intruder mission over Northern Norfolk at this precise time between 03.05 and 03.22 hours. Source of claim is Nachtjagd War Diaries.

All crew KIA and recovered. They are buried in various UK cemeteries.

F/O. William George Henry Thomas Gibson

150651 (1795353)

F/O. William George Henry Thomas "Gerry" Gibson. Pilot.

154311 (1398362)   F/O. Ronald "Ron" Goulding.   A/Bomber. 5 ops.

154616 (1494072)   F/O. David Craig "Dinty" Taylor.   A/Bomber. 24 ops.

55403 (590960) F/O. Leslie "Les" Moore.   Navigator.

175938 (1819442)   F/O. Leslie "Red" Blakemore.   WOP/AG.

F/S. Jim J. "Blondie" Ellson.   MU/Gunner. 28 ops.

1836615 Sgt. William Thomas "Taffy" Williams. R/Gunner.

F/S. R.J. "Johnnie" Layzell.   F/Engineer.

163588 (1802442)   F/O. Norman James "Jim" Eley.   2nd Pilot.

17/03/1945

Passengers: 07/05/1945, 20/06/1945, 09/07/1945, 29/07/1945.

1945 - 514 Squadron RAF Lancaster III ME350 JI-C

L to R (front): F/S. R.J. Layzell, F/O. L. Blakemore, F/S. J.J. Ellson. L to R (back): F/O. L. Moore, Sgt. W.T. Williams, F/O. W.G.H.T. Gibson, F/O. D.C. Taylor. (courtesy Nicola J. Pole)

18/02/1945 NN773 JI-K Bombing Wesel 11.21 15.24 16.51

Bomb load 1 x 4000 HC, 4 x 500 GP, 2 x 500 MC L/Delay, 4 x 250 GP, 6 x 500 ANM64. Primary target: Wesel. Weather 10/10ths cloud. Bombed at 15.24 hours from 19,400 feet on G.H. Leader.

F/O. W.G.H.T. "Gerry" Gibson flew the mission as 2nd Pilot with F/L. R. Worthing's crew.

19/02/1945 NG142 JI-J Bombing Wesel 13.02 16.35 19.08

Bomb load 1 x 4000 HC, 6 x 500 MC, 6 x 500 ANM64, 4 x 250 GP. Primary target: Wesel. Weather over target 5-7/10ths cloud. Bombed at 16.35 hours from 18,500 feet on leading aircraft. Landed at Moreton in Marsh.

Blakemore's logbook note: "Diverted. Light flak."

22/02/1945 PB426 JI-D Bombing Osterfeld 12.19 x 17.20

Bomb load 1 x 4000 HC, 9 x 500 ANM64, 2 x 500 MC, 4 x 250 GP. Primary target: Osterfeld, Coking ovens. Weather at target clear, but hazy. Abortive sortie. Furthest point reached 5027N 0440E. All bombs jettisoned at 16.23 hours from 5,000 feet at 5024N 0000.

Blakemore's logbook note: "STBD Outer engine U/S. Ret to base (emergency)"

23/02/1945 NN773 JI-K Bombing Gelsenkirchen 11.17 15.00 17.20

Bomb load 1 x 4000 HC, 9 x 500 ANM64, 2 x 500 MC, 4 x 250 GP. Primary target Gelsenkirchen. Weather 10/10ths cloud. Bombed at 15.00 hours from 20,200 feet on G.H. Leader. On return landed at Witchford.

Blakemore's logbook note: "No flak. Diverted."

26/02/1945 NG142 JI-J Bombing Dortmund 10.20 14.06 16.24

Bomb load 1 x 4000 HC, 2 x 500 MC L/Delay 37B, 9 x 500 ANM64, 4 x 250 GP. Primary target: Dortmund, Hoesch Benzin plant. Weather 10/10ths cloud, tops 8/10,000 feet. Bombed at 14.06 hours from 17,000 feet on G.H. Leader. From Blakemore's logbook "Heavy flak. Bomb Det. fell into tail unit (OK)"

28/02/1945 ME354 JI-M Bombing Nordstern 08.45 12.05 14.04

Bomb load 1 x 4000 HC, 9 x 500 ANM64, 2 x 500 MC L/D, 4 x 250 GP. Primary target: Nordstern (Gelsenkirchen). Weather 10/10ths cloud. Bombed at 12.05 hours from 20,000 feet on leading aircraft.

Blakemore's logbook note: "Target Gelsenkirchen. Mod flak."

02/03/1945 NN773 JI-K Bombing Koln 12.40 x 18.38

Bomb load 1 x 4000 HC, 12 x 500 ANM64. Primary target: Koln. Weather 10/10ths cloud over Koln, South and South-East of Koln clear. Abortive sortie. Jettisoned 1 x 4000 HC at 17.53 hours from 6,500 feet 5212N 0309E. Brought back 12 x 500 ANM64.

Blakemore's logbook note: "7/10 cloud. Dummy run. Mod flak. "

05/03/1945 LM285 JI-A Bombing Gelsenkirchen 10.25 14.08 16.00

Bomb load 1 x 4000 HC, 12 x 500 ANM64. Primary target: Gelsenkirchen, Benzol plant. Weather 10/10ths cloud over target with cirrus cloud at bombing height. Bombed at 14.18 hours from 21,000 feet on leading aircraft.

Blakemore's logbook note: "Mod flak."

06/03/1945 ME354 JI-M Bombing Wesel 18.11 21.10 23.20

Bomb load 1 x 4000 HC, 13 x 500 ANM64, 2 x 500 MC. Primary target: Wesel. Weather 10/10ths cloud, tops 16,000 feet preventing visual. Bombed at 21.10 hours from 18,000 feet on G.H. Bombing concentrated.

F/O. W.G.H.T. "Gerry" Gibson flew the mission as 2nd Pilot with F/L. M.D. Muggeridge's crew.

09/03/1945 PD389 A2-J Bombing Datteln 10.26 14.00 15.39

Bomb load 1 x 4000 HC, 13 x 500 ANM64, 2 x 500 MC L/Delay37. Primary target: Datteln, Synthetic oil plant. Weather 10/10ths cloud, tops 8-10,000 feet. Bombed at 14.00 hours from 21,000 feet on G.H. Leader.

Blakemore's logbook note: "A/C NG141. 10/10 cloud. Light flak". NG141 A2-J was badly damaged by the explosion of another aircraft at base on 29/12/1944 and was not used later by the Squadron. Probably Leslie Blakemore confused both aircraft due to the same code A2-J. Also error in ORBs that day with Munro's crew being noted twice at the same time in 2 different planes whereas Gibson's crew was missed in records.

11/03/1945 NG142 JI-J Bombing Essen 11.34 15.26 17.20

Bomb load 1 x 4000 HC, 13 x 500 ANM64, 2 x 500 MC. Primary target:

Essen, Marshalling yards. Weather 10/10ths cloud, tops 7/8000 feet. Bombed at 15.26 hours from 19,000 feet on leading G.H. aircraft. 12 Blue smoke puffs seen together and showing attack concentrated.

Blakemore's logbook note: "1000 Bomber Raid. No flak. Good effort."

17/03/1945 ME535 JI-G Bombing August Viktoria 11.29 15.06 16.56

Bomb load 1 x 4000 HC, 13 x 500 ANM64, 2 x 500 MC. Primary target: Auguste Viktoria, Marl-Hüls coal mine. Weather 10/10ths cloud, tops and contrails up to 23,000 feet. Bombed at 15.06 hours from 20,000 feet on G.H. Leader. Aircraft congested over target. Risk of collision.

Blakemore's logbook note: "Light flak. Heavy vapour trails over target".

F/O. N. Eley was 2nd Pilot that day.

20/03/1945 LM627 JI-D Bombing Hamm 09.55 13.14 15.55

Bomb load 7 x 1000 ANM65, 9 x 500 ANM64. Primary target: Hamm, Marshalling yards. Weather 5/10ths cloud. Bombed at 13.14 hours from 18,500 feet on leading G.H. aircraft. Bomb craters straddled whole area. 3 heavy flak holes in fuselage. 1 hole in bomb door.

Blakemore's logbook note: "Mod flak (5 holes). Good Prang".

21/03/1945 ME535 JI-G Bombing Munster 09.23 13.08 15.03

Bomb load 1 x 4000 HC, 13 x 500 ANM64, 2 x 500 MC. Primary target Munster Viaduct and Marshalling Yards. Weather cloud nil to 2/10ths. Bombed at 13.08 hours from 18,500 feet on G.H. aircraft and visually. Aircraft hit by flak.

Blakemore's logbook note: "No Cloud. Heavy flak. M/U hit – OK - Home first".

18/04/1945 ME530 JI-C Bombing Heligoland 09.37 13.08 15.03

Bomb load 6 x 1000 MC, 10 x 500 ANM64. Primary target: Heligoland, Naval base. Weather no cloud, slight haze. Bombed visually on markers on upwind edge of smoke at 13.08 hours from 18,500 ft. Whole Island covered in smoke. Return visit not necessary.

Blakemore's logbook note: "900 A/C. No flak".

22/04/1945 ME530 JI-C Bombing Bremen 13.05 18.42 20.43

Bomb load 1 x 4000 HC, 2 x 500 MC, 14 x 500 ANM 64. Primary target: Bremen, in support of Troop concentration. Weather on approaching target 4-5/10ths cloud. Bombed on G.H. at 18.42 hours from 18,300 ft. Bombs seen bursting north of river bend among built up area - much smoke. H.F. holed bomb bay. Should be an excellent raid. G.H. perfect.

Blakemore's logbook note: "Mod flak. Good prang".

07/05/1945 ME530 JI-C Manna The Hague 12.25 13.51 14.55

Dropping area The Hague. Dropped 5 packs at 13.51 hours. Clear. Cloud above. Bags concentrated. Some bags appeared to break up. "Drop shag" and "Many thanks" written on roof tops

. Blakemore's logbook note: "Supply dropping on airfield".

No Mid Upper Gunner that day.

Passenger: Sgt. P. Burton.

11/05/1945 RF231 JI-A Exodus Juvincourt - Tangmere 11.19 x 19.05
Duration 4.00. Outward 1.47 hours. Collected 24 ex POWs. Homeward 2.13 hours. Magneto drop on port inner dropped. Take off at Juvincourt.

13/05/1945 ME530 JI-C Exodus Juvincourt - Tangmere 13.11 x 16.10
Duration 3 hours. Message "return to Base" received 14.50 hrs.
Blakemore's logbook note: "Airfield U/S. Returned to base".

17/05/1945 ME530 JI-C Exodus Brussels - Westcott 11.20   x 14.54
Duration 2 hrs 24 mins. Out 1 hr 10 mins. In 1 hr 14 mins. 10 Belgian refugees taken to Brussels. No troubles.

18/05/1945 ME530 JI-C Exodus Brussels - Oakley 11.50 x 16.47
Duration 2 hrs 55 mins. Out 1 hr 04 mins. In 1 hr 51 mins. 10 Belgian refugees taken to Brussels. 24 ex POWs. returned. Satisfactory trip.

23/05/1945 ME530 JI-C Exodus Brussels - Oakley 12.03 x 17.11
Duration 3 hours. Out 1.10 hours. In 1.50 hours. 10 Belgian refugees returned to Brussels. 24 ex POWs evacuated. All OK.

24/05/1945 ME530 JI-C Exodus Brussels 12.07 x 15.56
Duration 2.20 hours. Out 1.05 hours. In 1.15 hours. 10 Belgian refugees returned to Brussels. No ex POWs evacuated.

29/05/1945 ME530 JI-C Baedeker Tour over Germany 10.01 x 14.17
Only described in ORB summary. Operation not detailed.
Blakemore's logbook note: "Tour of Ruhr damage".

20/06/1945 ME530 JI-C Baedeker Tour over Continent 08.10 x 12.42
Blakemore's logbook note: "Baedeker Ruhr."
Passengers: Sgt. Sheldon, Sgt. Henry, LAC. McGowan, Sgt. Cox.

29/06/1945 ME530 JI-C Post Mortem   Special mission 10.15 x 15.46
Blakemore's logbook note: "Post Mortem 'Δ' Flensburg".

03/07/1945 ME530 JI-C Post Mortem   Special mission 14.37 x 19.38
Blakemore's logbook note: "Post Mortem 'Δ' Flensburg".

09/07/1945 ME530 JI-C Baedeker Tour over Continent 09.56 x 14.15
Blakemore's logbook note: "Baedeker Ruhr".
Passengers: Sgt. Lewis, Cpl. Baraclough, LAC. Potter, LACW. Starking, ACW. Williamson.

29/07/1945 ME535 JI-G Baedeker Tour over Continent 10.07 x 14.37
Blakemore's logbook note "Baedeker Ruhr".
Passengers: LAC. Parker, LAC. Yates, AC. Hobbs, ACW. Cutting, ACW. Sharpe.

02 to 04/08/1945
RA601 JI-J Dodge Italy (Bari)   06.15 x 20.05
Only described in ORB summary.
Blakemore's logbook note:
Waterbeach-Bari take-off 02/08/1945 06.15 for 6.40 hours flying time.
Bari-Tibbenham take-off 04/08/1945 08.00 for 7.00 hours flying time carried 20 Army Personel. Tibbenham-Base take-off 19.45 for 0.20 hours flying time.

11 to 15/08/1945

ME363 JI-R and PB914 Dodge Italy (Bari) 08.55 x 22.05

Only described in ORB summary. On 13 August 1945 aircraft "R" not returned from Italy with the other aicraft. Returned on 15/08/1945 with aircraft PB914.

Details from Blakemore's logbook:

Waterbeach-Bari take-off 11/08/1945 08.55 for 6.20 hours flying time.
Bari-Tibbenham take-off 15/08/1945 13.15 for 7.50 hours flying time carried 20 Army Personel. Tibbenham-Base take-off 21.45 for 0.20 hours flight time.

F/S. John Clare Gilbertson-Pritchard

1084862 F/S. John Clare Gilbertson-Pritchard. Pilot.
R155985 F/S. William Earle Brown, RCAF. A/Bomber.
1549227 Sgt. Gordon Kenneth Woodward. Navigator.
1516394 Sgt. Ernest "Sunny" Gledhill.   WOP/AG.
1585622 Sgt. George "Hawkeye" Henry. MU/Gunner. 2 ops.
811039   Sgt. Ernest Walter "Ernie" Haigh. MU/Gunner. 1 op.
1600760 Sgt. Jack Birch.   R/Gunner.
1421544 Sgt. James "Jim" McGahey.   F/Engineer.

24/02/1944 DS816 JI-O Bombing Schweinfurt 20.42 01.07 04.48

Bomb load 1 x 8000 lb. Primary target: Schweinfurt. Weather clear, much smoke. Bombed at 01.07 hours at 11,000 ft. Bomb jettisoned on Schweinfurt at 01.07 hours - as 4 lb incendiary dropped from above fell in aircraft by Navigator's table and thrown to safety by WOP. Slight damage to Navigator's table. Inter-com I.F.F. Fuselage holed by incendiaries from above. Pilot's nerves affected by falling incendiary. Wonderful attack. Route good. Aircraft flew at 11,000 ft whole sortie on account of oxygen failure.

F/S. J.C. Gilbertson-Pritchard flew the mission as 2nd Pilot with S/L. A.L. Roberts' crew.

01/03/1944 LL683 JI-P Bombing Stuttgart 23.41 x 02.05

Bomb load 1 x 2000, 1 x 500 lb bomb, 40 x 30, 900 x 4 incendiaries. Returned early. Furthest point reached on course - Cambridge. W/T receiver u/s. Jettisoned bombs to reduce load for landing.

15/03/1944 LL734 JI-S Bombing Stuttgart 19.14 23.20 02.39

Bomb load 1 x 1000 lb bomb, 72 x 30, 1050 x 4, 90 x 4 incendiaries. Primary target: Stuttgart. There was very thin cloud. Bombed at 23.20 hours from 21,000 feet. Attack not concentrated. Holes in fuselage due to flak homeward near French coast.

18/03/1944 DS822 JI-T Bombing Frankfurt   19.30 22.04 01.04

Bomb load 1 x 4000 lb bomb, 1350 x 4, 90 x 4, 32 x 30 incendiaries. Primary target: Frankfurt. Weather hazy. Bombed at 22.04 hours from 21,000 feet.

Incendiaries scattered round T.I.s. Fires to South and East. Monica and Gee u/s homeward. Holes in port wing by heavy flak.

Sgt. E.W. Haigh was MU/Gunner that day.

J.C. Gilbertson-Pritchard later became a fighter pilot with 154 Sqn, and was KIA at sea 2 miles East of Lowestoft on 31 March 1945.

P/O. Thomas Gilchrist

186330 (1682052) P/O. Thomas Gilchrist.   Pilot.
1520986 Sgt.   Thomas Fenwick.   A/Bomber.
934280   W/O. Gerald James Manlow.   Navigator.
A419844 F/S. Stanley McLean, RAAF.   WOP/AG.
Sgt. W.A. Dabbs.   MU/Gunner. 1 op.
1819401 Sgt.   Bleddyn Lloyd "Bob" "Taffy" Roberts.   MU/Gunner. 1 op.
1798718 Sgt.   Patrick Joseph Sheehy.   R/Gunner.
1867701 Sgt.   Henry Robert Knight.   F/Engineer.

05/10/1944 LM286 A2-F   Bombing Saarbrucken   17.09 22.39

Bomb load 11 x 1000 MC, 1 x 500 GP, 3 x 500 GP. Long Delay. Abandoned mission at position 5918N 0705E on instructions from Master Bomber heard to say they were unable to locate target and called "Abandon Mission - our troop in vicinity". Jettisoned 4 x 500 GP. At 20.38 from 9,000 feet - live, Remainder brought back.

P/O. T. Gilchrist flew the mission as 2nd Pilot with F/L. B.K. McDonald's crew.

"Flak damage" according H.E. Bentley logbook (F/L. B.K. McDonald crew).

06/10/1944 NG141 A2-J Bombing Dortmund   16.30   20.30   22.40

Bomb load 1 x 4000 HC, 12 x No. 14 Clusters. Primary target: Dortmund, Town and Railways. Weather over the target was clear with slight ground haze. Bombed at 20.30 hours from 22,000 feet on red T.I.s.

Sgt. W.A. Dabbs was MU/Gunner that day.

07/10/1944 LM735 A2-G   Bombing Emmerich   12.25 x   x

Bomb load 1 x 4000 HC, 10 x No.14 clusters. 4 x (150 x 4). Primary target Emmerich. Weather clear with cloud at 13,000 feet. Aircraft missing.

The circumstances are not known. It is considered most likely that LM735 was hit either by flak or by 'friendly' bombs. There is no record of hostile fighter activity on this daylight operation.

Sgt. B.L. Roberts was MU/Gunner that day.

All the crew were KIA. The first six crewmen are now buried in the Reichswald Forest War Cemetery. Sgt. Sheehy, who came from Corbally, Limerick in the Republic of Ireland, has no known grave, and is commemorated on Panel 237 of the Runnymede Memorial.

F/O. Ronald Tembey Gill

150919 (1586715) F/O. Ronald Tembey "Ron" Gill.   Pilot.
165158 (1795462) F/O. Norman Samuel Browne. A/Bomber.
1543962 F/S. Frederick Herbert "Fred" Stogdale. Navigator.
  F/S. R. "Roy" Pitt.   WOP/AG.
1593349 Sgt. Bernard Longson Hellewell. MU/Gunner.
1899134 Sgt. Eric Frank Cousins. R/Gunner.
  Sgt. P.C.H. "Pete" Childs. F/Engineer.

Passengers: 22/06/1945, 05/07/1945, 17/07/1945, 19/07/1945.

11/03/1945 NG203 A2-C Bombing Essen 11.31   15.25   17.17
  Bomb load 1 x 4000 HC, 13 x 500 ANM64, 2 x 500 MC. Primary target:
Essen, Marshalling yards. Weather 10/10ths cloud, tops 7/8,000 feet. Bombed
at 15.25 hours from 18,500 feet. Followed G.H. Leader. 3 Blue Puffs seen on
aiming point and flares seen to port from the other attack.
  F/O. R.T. Gill flew the mission as 2nd Pilot with F/O. G. Robertson's crew.
12/03/1945 NN717 A2-E   Bombing Dortmund 12.55 17.07   19.13
  Bomb load 1 x 4000 HC, 13 x 500 ANM64. Primary target: Dortmund.
Weather 10/10ths cloud over target, tops 6/10,000 feet. Bombed at 17.07 hours
from 19,000 feet on G.H. Leader.
29/03/1945 PB482 A2-K Bombing Salzgitter 12.39 16.42   19.29
  Bomb load 1 x 4000 HC, 8 x 500 ANM64. Primary target: Salzgitter,
Hallendorf works. Weather 10/10ths cloud. Bombed at 16.42 hours from
22,000 feet on leading G.H. aircraft.
18/04/1945 PB423 A2-C Bombing Heligoland 09.48   13.09   15.19
  Bomb load 6 x 1000 MC, 10 x 500 ANM64. Primary target: Heligoland,
Naval base. Weather no cloud, slight haze. Bombed visually upwind edge of
smoke pall at 13.09 hours from 18,800 ft. Whole Island covered in smoke.
Raid very successful and no troubles.
20/04/1945 PB423 A2-C Bombing Regensburg 09.34 13.56   17.12
  Bomb load 16 x 500 ANM64. Primary target: Regensburg. Weather clear
over target and whole route. Bombed on leading aircraft at 13.56 hours from
19,500 feet. Bomb bursts. Bombs seen to fall in target area.
24/04/1945 ME529 A2-F Bombing Bad Oldesloe 07.32 10.43   13.08
  Bomb load 6 x 1000 ANM65, 10 x 500 ANM 64. Primary target: Bad-
Oldesloe, Rail and road junction and Marshalling Yards. Weather 3/10ths to
nil cloud. Bombed on G.H. leader 514/Q at 10.43 hours from 17,900 ft. Several
bomb bursts seen across railway track. Much smoke over southern part of
target. Large burst of flame at 10.45 in target.
07/05/1945 PD389 A2-J Manna The Hague 12.30   13.39   14.45
  Dropping area The Hague. Dropped 5 Packs on Red T.I.s and White Cross
at 13.39 hours. Clear. Usual crowds on ground. T.I.s O.K.

L to R (back): P.C.H. Childs, N.S. Browne, R.T. Gill, F.H. Stogdale. L to R (front): R. Pitt, E.F. Cousins. B.L. Hellewell missed the photo due to frost bite on his hip. (courtesty Yvonne Cousins)

12/05/1945 ME529 A2-F   Exodus Juvincourt - Wing   09.05 x 16.11

Duration 4.08. Outward 2.09 hours. Collected 24 POWs. Homeward 1.59 hours. Difficulty experienced in starting up at Juvincourt - practically 2 hours delay.

26/05/1945 ME529 A2-F   Baedeker Tour over Germany 09.33   x 14.02

Only described in ORB summary. Op not detailed.

Tour of Ruhr according E.F. Cousins' logbook.

22/06/1945 RE158 A2-J Baedeker Tour over Continent 15.16   x 19.40

Ruhr Tour.

The passengers were members of Bomber Command, ranks and initials not recorded: Scattergood, Saman, Swinden, Peotake, Truscott.

25/06/1945 PD389 A2-J Post Mortem   Special mission 09.48 x 16.12

Special exercise target Flensburg.

01/07/1945 PD389 A2-J Post Mortem   Special mission 12.06 x 17.45

Special exercise target Flensburg.

05/07/1945 RE123 A2-K   Baedeker Tour over Continent 15.29   x 20.06

Contrary to ORBs, according E.F. Cousins' logbook it would have been an air test starting at 15.29 for 2.05 flying time.

The passengers were members of Bomber Command, ranks and initials not recorded: Smith, Gough, Row, Jackson, Mead.

12/07/1945 ME529 A2-B   Bullseye ??   21.46 x 03.46

Quoted in ORB summary and E.F. Cousins' logbook. Op not detailed.

17/07/1945 ME363 JI-R Baedeker Tour over Continent 15.05 x 19.09
Ruhr Tour.

Passengers: LACW. Robinson, Cpl. Ashton (WAAF), AC. Turner, Mr. Maughin.

19/07/1945 RF272 A2-F   Baedeker Tour over Continent 15.15   x 19.29
Ruhr Tour.

Passengers: Cpl. Russell, LAC. Bennett, ACW. Lidbetter, Cpl. Turner (WAAF), ACW. Rivett.

02 to 04/08/1945

ME364 JI-P Dodge Italy (Bari) 06.44 x 19.30

Operation Dodge to Bari, only described in ORB summary.

Details from E.F. Cousins' logbook:

Waterbeach-Bari take-off 02/08/1945 06.44 for 7 hours flying time.

Bari-Tibbenham take-off 04/08/1945 09.23 for 7.25 hours flying time.

Tibbenham-Base take-off 19.10 for 0.20 hours flying time.

11/08/1945 RE158 A2-J Dodge Italy (Bari) 08.00 x 16.50

Operation Dodge to Bari.

Details from E.F. Cousins' logbook:

Waterbeach-Bari take-off 08.00 for 6 hours flying time.

Bari-Tibbenham take-off 07.10 for 7.35 hours flying time.

Tibbenham-Base take-off 16.30 for 0.20 hours flying time.

F/O. Donald Carlos Gordon, DFC

A418944   F/O. Donald Carlos "Don" Gordon, DFC RAAF. Pilot.
J29370 F/O. S. Smitten, RCAF   A/Bomber.
J14261 (R14201) F/O. J.W. Mundy, RCAF   Navigator. 27 ops.
149340 (1562280) F/O. Talbot William "Bill" Ledingham, DFC. Nav. 3 ops.
NZ427888 F/O. F.E. Cooper, RNZAF   WOP/AG.
NZ42836   F/S. G. Burke, RNZAF   MU/Gunner.
 Sgt. Harry Dobinson.   R/Gunner.
 Sgt. F.J. Saunders.   F/Engineer.

F/O. 'Don' Gordon subsequently died in Australia in a Spitfire crash on 4 October 1945.

Just after landing from the Duisburg raid on 14th October 1944 – Lancaster Mk.III PB142 JI-A. L to R: F.J. Saunders, G. Burke, H. Dobinson, S. Smitten, F.E. Cooper, J.W. Mundy, D.C. Gordon. (courtesy Dan Ellin)

28/07/1944 PB142 JI-A Bombing Stuttgart 21.39 01.57 05.51

Bomb load 7 x 1000 MC, 2 x 500 GP. Primary target: Stuttgart. Weather 8/10ths cloud. Bombed at 01.57 hours from 19,000 feet green T.I.s as instructed. Much fighter activity. Should be a good attack.

30/07/1944 PB142 JI-A Bombing Caen 06.59 07.49 10.16

Bomb load 18 x 500 GP. Primary target: Caen 'B'. Weather low cloud. Bombed at 07.49 hours from 2,800 feet red T.I. as instructed. Clouds of smoke, visual of main road. Our bombs south of this. Satisfactory attack.

01/08/1944 PB142 JI-A Bombing Foret de Nieppe 19.16 20.45 21.42

Bomb load 11 x 1000 MC, 4 x 500 GP. Primary target: De Nieppe, constructional works. Bombed at 20.45 hours from 12,000 feet smoke from red T.I.s.

05/08/1944 LM265 JI-E Bombing Bassen 14.20 19.00 22.07

Bomb load 8 x 1000 MC, 2 x 500 GP. Primary target: Bassen Oil Depot. Weather clear below cloud base at 5,000 feet. Bombed at 19.00 hours from 4,200 feet visually, large hangar in SW corner of target. Bombing very concentrated.

07/08/1944 LM265 JI-E Bombing Mare de Magne 21.46 23.40 00.59

Bomb load 11 x 1000 MC, 4 x 500 GP. Primary target: Mare de Magne (just past Caen). Weather clear over target. Bombed at 23.40 hours from 8,500 feet red T.I.s. Bomb bursts seen in the centre of red T.I.s and appeared concentrated, fires seen.

Mare-de-Magne: place between Caen and Fontenay le Marmion.

09/08/1944 LM265 JI-E Bombing Fort d'Englos 21.42 23.17 00.13

Bomb load 14 x 1000 MC. Primary target: Fort d'Englos (Lille), Petrol dump. Weather clear. Bombed at 23.17 hours from 13,000 feet, undershot red T.I.s as instructed by Master Bomber. Pall of smoke seen on leaving.

The fort of Ennetières-en-Weppes, or "fort d'Englos" is one of a set of six forts surrounding Lille.

11/08/1944 LM265 JI-E Bombing Lens 14.08 16.32 17.36

Bomb load 11 x 1000 MC. 4 X 500 GP. Primary target: Lens, Marshalling yards. Weather 4/10ths cloud. Bombed at 16.32 hours from 16,000 feet, red T.I.s. Two fires seen in marshalling yards, many sticks across yards.

06/09/1944 PB426 JI-J Bombing Le Havre 16.37 18.40 19.55

Bomb load 11 x 1000 MC, 4 x 500 GP. Primary target: Le Havre. Bombed at 18.40 hours from 9,000 feet red and green T.I.s.

08/09/1944 PB142 JI-A Bombing Le Havre 05.54 07.55 09.11

Bomb load 11 x 1000 MC, 4 x 500 GP. Primary target: Le Havre. Weather 10/10ths cloud down to 3,000 feet. Abandoned mission on Master Bomber's instructions.

11/09/1944 PB142 JI-A Bombing Kamen 16.04 18.43 19.55

Bomb load 1 x 4000 HC, 16 x 500 GP. Weather clear. Primary target: Kamen. Bombed at 18.43 hours from 16,500 feet. Fire and yellow T.I.s.

12/09/1944 PB142 JI-A Bombing Frankfurt   18.25   23.03   01.14

Bomb load 1 x 4000 HC, 14 x 500 Clusters 4lb. Target: Frankfurt - Main. Weather clear over the target. Bombed at 23.03 hours from 17,000 feet on centre of red and green T.I.s. Had combat with enemy aircraft.

17/09/1944 PB142 JI-A Bombing Boulogne   10.48 x 13.36

Bomb load 11 x 1000 MC, 4 x 500 GP. Primary target: Boulogne, Aiming point 2. Weather clear below cloud. At 12.15 hours order given by Master Bomber to abandon mission. Jettisoned 4 x 1000 MC brought remainder back.

20/09/1944 PB142 JI-A Bombing Calais   14.51   16.02   17.22

Bomb load 11 x 1000 MC, 4 x 500 GP. Primary target: Calais. Weather clear over target. Bombed at 16.02 hours from 2,500 feet, red T.I.s.

23/09/1944 PB142 JI-A Bombing Neuss   19.25 x 20.58

Bomb load 11 x 1000 ANM44, 4 x 500 GP. Primary target: Neuss. Abortive sortie. Returned early with W/T receiver u/s. Jettisoned load.

25/09/1944 PB142 JI-A Bombing Pas de Calais   08.23 x 10.57

Bomb load 11 x 1000 MC, 4 x 500 GP. Primary target: Calais. Abandoned mission on Master Bomber's instructions. Jettisoned 3 x 1000, 1 x 500 safe at 5025N 0105E. Brought remainder back.

26/09/1944 PB142 JI-A Bombing Calais   11.39   12.44   13.54

Bomb load 11 x 1000 MC, 4 x 500 GP. Primary target: Calais 7D. Weather clear below cloud which was 3,500 feet. Bombed at 12.44 hours from 3,400 feet on red T.I. + ½ second.

28/09/1944 LM627 JI-D Bombing Calais   07.58 x 10.43

Bomb load 11 x 1000 MC, 4 x 500 GP. Primary target: Calais 19. Abortive sortie. At 09.28 hours Master Bomber gave abandon mission. Jettisoned 5 x 1000. Brought remainder back.

03/10/1944 PB142 JI-A Bombing Westkapelle 12.32   14.01   15.04

Bomb load 1 x 4000 MC, 6 x 1000 MC, 1 x 500 GP L/Delay. Primary target: Westkapelle (Walcheren). Weather patchy-scattered cloud with base 5,000 feet. Bombed at 14.01 hours from 5,000 feet on red T.I.s and visual of wall.

05/10/1944 PB142 JI-A Bombing Saarbrucken 17.28   20.30   22.25

Bomb load 11 x 1000 MC, 1 x 500 GP, 3 x 500 GP Long Delay. Primary target: Saarbrucken, Marshalling yards. Weather clear over target. Bombed at 20.30 hours from 15,000 feet on flares. 1 x 500 GP Long Delay brought back due to hang up.

14/10/1944 PB142 JI-A Bombing Duisburg   07.08   09.04   10.54

Bomb load 11 x 1000 MC, 4 x 500 GP Long Delay. Primary target: Duisburg. Weather patchy cloud with gaps for bombing. Bombed at 09.04 hours from 18,000 feet. Built up area North of Docks.

26/10/1944 LM719 JI-B Bombing Leverkusen 13.00   15.28   17.07

Bomb load 1 x 4000 HC, 6 x 1000 MC, 4 x 500 GP, 2 x 500 GP Long Delay. Primary target: Leverkusen. Weather over target and on route was 10/10ths cloud. Bombed at 15.28 hours from 16,500 feet on G.H.

28/10/1944 LM733 JI-F Bombing Cologne   13.07   15.46   17.36

Bomb load 1 x 4000 HC, 8 x 150 x 4. Primary target: Cologne. Weather clear over target. Bombed at 15.46 hours from 19,000 feet. Visually.

30/10/1944 LM719 JI-B Bombing Wesseling   09.21   11.58   13.18

Bomb load 1 x 4000 HC, 15 x 500 GP. Primary target: Wesseling. Weather was 10/10ths cloud - tops about 7,000 feet. Bombed at 11.58 hours from 17,500 feet on G.H.

02/11/1944 LM719 JI-B Bombing Homberg   11.13   14.07   15.22

Bomb load 1 x 4000 HC, 6 x 1000 ANM59, 6 x 500 MC. Primary target: Homberg. Weather variable cloud but clear for bombing. Target obscured by pall of smoke rising to 10,000 feet. Bombed at 14.07 hours from 20,000 feet visually. Aircraft damaged by flak.

04/11/1944 LM627 JI-D Bombing Solingen 11.27   14.07   15.49

Bomb load 1 x 4000 HC, 6 x 1000 ANM59, 4 x 500 GP, 2 x 500 MC (L/Delay), 3 Flares. Primary target: Solingen. Weather 8-10/10ths cloud. Bombed at 14.07 hours from 20,000 feet on upwind edge of red flares.

05/11/1944 PD265 JI-G Bombing Solingen 10.30   13.03   14.44

Bomb load 1 x 4000 HC, 6 x 1000 ANM59, 4 x 500 GP, 2 x 500 GP (L/Delay), 3 Flares. Primary target: Solingen. Weather 10/10ths cloud over target. Bombed at 13.03 hours from 18,000 feet on instruments.

06/11/1944 PD265 JI-G Bombing Koblenz 17.00   19.33   21.32

Bomb load 1 x 4000 HC, 12 x 500 Clusters, 2 x 250 T.I.s. Primary target: Koblenz. Weather clear over target. Bombed at 19.33 hours from 18,000 feet on Red and Green T.I.s.

02/12/1944 NG350 JI-C Bombing Dortmund   13.00   14.58   16.52

Bomb load 14 x 1000 HC. Primary target: Dortmund, Benzol plant. Weather 10/10ths cloud. Bombed at 14.58 hours from 20,000 feet. Red flare with Green star. Aircraft hit by flak. Fuselage damaged.

F/O. T.W. Ledingham was Navigator from that day.

05/12/1944 NG350 JI-C Bombing Hamm 08.55 11.30   13.40

Bomb load 1 x 4000 HC, 1950 x 4 lb incendiaries. Primary target: Hamm. Weather 10/10ths cloud over target, but otherwise varying from 6-10/10ths. Bombed at 11.30 hours from 20,500 feet on G.H. Leader.

06/12/1944 NG350 JI-C Bombing Merseburg 17.05 20.46   23.59

Bomb load 1 x 4000 HC, 8 x 500 GP and 1 x 500 GP Long Delay. Primary target: Merseburg. Weather 10/10ths cloud with odd breaks. Bombed at 20.46 from 22,000 feet on centre of red/green flares.

F/O. David Anthony Athelston Gray, DFC

131090 (1322890). F/O. David Anthony Athelston "Dave" Gray, DFC. Pilot.
177561 (1315709) P/O. Edward William Russell "Tiny" Brazier.
   A/Bomber.
177966 (1610618) P/O. Ronald Robert "Brownie" Brown. Navigator.
1175873. F/S. Richard Alan "Shorty" Hounsome, DFM. WOP/AG.
1283278.   F/S. R.A. "Dicky" Hoddle-Wrigley. MU/Gunner.   27 ops
1586017 Sgt. G.R. Hutton. MU/Gunner. 2 ops.
1105921 Sgt. Eric Gordon Moorhouse, DFM. MU/Gunner. 1 op.
J85651 (R142559) P/O. Howard Gray "Pip" Sharp, RCAF. R/Gunner.
1002381.   Sgt. Ronald "Ronnie" Helliwell.   F/Engineer.

This was the first crew to finish a tour with 514 Squadron.

L to R (standing): R.R. Brown, R. Helliwell, E.W.R. Brazier, D.A.A. Gray, H.G. Sharp. L to R (kneeling) R.A. Hounsome, R.A. Hoddle-Wrigley.

11/11/1943 DS736 JI-L Gardening La Tranche 17.49 x 01.07
   Aircraft carried bomb load and fusing 4 Mines. Primary target: La Tranche, 4607 N O 1313/4N. According H.G. Sharp's logbook target "Gardening - La Rochelle". Landed at Hixon 01.07 hours. No cloud. Visibility good. No photograph attempted. Starboard inner engine U/S from start point to 48 Degs N 060W and with that Theatbd Generator became U/S. VR 101 on receiver and Gee ceased to function at 20.04 hours. Monica switched on at 21.40 hours

and on testing proved U/S. Telephone wire to Rear Gunner's intercom went faulty during part of turret rotation. Otherwise a satisfactory trip. Good clear weather all the way.

26/11/1943 DS818 JI-Q Bombing Berlin 17.49 21.27 01.04
Bomb load 1 x 4000 HC, 24 x 30 incendiaries, 405 x 4 incendiaries, 45 x 4. Primary target: Berlin. Weather clear. Target attacked at 21.27 hrs at 21,000 feet. Target area appeared to be a mass of flames. Controls stiff with ice. All route markers were seen.

02/12/1943 DS817 JI-P Bombing Berlin 17.04 20.23 00.24
Bomb load 1 x 8000, 160 x 4 incendiaries, 20 x 4 incendiaries. Primary target: Berlin. 3/10 cloud, target attacked 20.23 hours, 20,000 feet. Concentrated fires. Was hit by flak and dinghy blown out of wings South of Berlin. D.R. compass u/s. Returned via Hanover, N of Ruhr, S of Point Hant Blanc, Beachy Head, Base, trouble with winds. Short of fuel landed at Tangmere.

20/12/1943 DS820 JI-R Bombing Frankfurt 17.34 19.45 22.33
Bomb load 1 x 4000, 48 x 30 incendiaries, 950 x 4 incendiaries, 100 x 4 incendiaries. Primary target: Frankfurt. 7/10 cloud. Bombed target at 19.45 at 18,000 ft. Very scattered fires with large fires believed target area. Port outer engine u/s just short of target which caused aircraft to jettison bomb a few miles short of aiming point. Returned on 3 engines. Photo attempted.

29/12/1943 DS822 JI-T Bombing Berlin 17.06 20.10 23.29
Bomb load 1 x 4000, 24 x 30 incendiaries, 540 x 4 incendiaries. Primary target: Berlin. There was 10/10 cloud with tops 8/9000 ft. Bombed at 20.10 hours at 20,000 ft. Reflection of fires seen through clouds. Sky markers appeared in circle. Route outward was good. 90 x 4 incendiaries hung up and brought back. Monica U/S on return. Very easy trip. Little opposition. Magazine not fitted.

20/01/1944 LL703 JI-L Bombing Berlin 16.21 x 19.00
Bomb load 1 x 4000, 32 x 30, 540 x 4, 60 x 4 incendiaries. Primary target: Berlin. Returned early due to oxygen supply being u/s. Farthest point reached 53°45N 03°10E. Jettisoned 1 x 4000, 450 x 4, 16 x 30 incendiaries.

21/01/1944 LL703 JI-L Bombing Magdeburg x 23.04 x
Bomb load 1 x 4000, 90 x 4, 32 x 30 incendiaries. Primary target: Magdeburg. There was 5/10 cloud. Bombed at 23.04 hours at 20,000 ft. T.I.s very scattered in length over target area. Well lit up. No red markers seen - one green with yellow stars. More cloud than anticipated.

30/01/1944 DS816 JI-O Bombing Berlin 17.20 20.26 23.38
Bomb load 1 x 4000 lb bomb, 600 x 4, 90 x 4, 32 x 30 incendiaries. Primary target: Berlin. There was 9-10/10 cloud. Bombed at 20.26 hours at 20,000 ft. Orange glow of fires and sky well lit up with fighter flares. Easy trip though unmolested much fighter activity.

15/02/1944 LL653 JI-E Bombing Berlin 17.35 21.27 00.34
Bomb load 1 x 8000 lbs bomb. Primary target: Berlin. There was 10/10

cloud. Bombed at 21.27 hrs at 20,000 ft. Reddish glows seen beneath clouds stretching East to West tending to undershoot. Monica u/s. Route easy. Some fighter flares seen in target area. Occasional flares on route. P.F.F. flares rather scattered.

19/02/1944 LL703 JI-L Bombing Leipzig 00.02 x 02.54

Bomb load 1 x 4000 lbs bomb, 32 x 30, 510 x 4, 90 x 4 incendiaries. Returned early. Farthest point reached 5253N 0439E. Port outer engine u/s. Severe vibration throughout aircraft. Starboard outer engine running rough. Bomb load jettisoned.

24/02/1944 LL703 JI-L Bombing Schweinfurt 18.46 23.18 02.05

Bomb load 1 x 2000 lb bomb, 32 x 30, 900 x 4, 90 x 4 incendiaries. Primary target: Schweinfurt. Weather clear no cloud. Bombed at 23.18 hours at 20,000 ft. One large conflagration. White incendiaries on ground. T.I.s were concentrated. Whole well lit up and T.I.s were placed accurately the job was well done.

Sgt. G.R. Hutton was MU/Gunner that day.

25/02/1944 LL703 JI-L Bombing Augsburg   21.35 01.17 04.25

Bomb load 1 x 2000 lb bomb, 48 x 30, 900 x 4 incendiaries. Primary target: Augsburg. There was no cloud. Bombed at 01.17 hours at 20,000 ft. Western side of town solid mass of flame. Eastern side beginning to take hold. The whole area included in the S/Ls was well ablaze as we left. Target seen burning before reaching Lake Constance. Several small explosions seen at 01.15 hours.

Sgt. G.R. Hutton was MU/Gunner that day.

07/03/1944 LL703 JI-L Bombing Le Mans 19.34 x 23.34

Bomb load 10 x 1000, 4 x 500 lb bombs. Primary target: Le Mans. There was 10/10 cloud. Cloud prevented visual. During run up first attack could be seen. Several Yellowish explosions seen at 21.20 hours. Bombed on reflection through cloud of red T.I.s which coincided with E.T.A. (Estimated Time of Arrival) at target. No results of the attack were visible.

Sgt. E.G. Moorhouse was MU/Gunner that day.

24/03/1944 LL683 JI-P Bombing Berlin 18.34 22.38 02.03

Bomb load 1 x 1000 lb bomb, 88 x 30, 810 x 4, 90 x 4 incendiaries. Primary target: Berlin. There was 6/10 cloud with gaps. Bombed at 22.38 hours from 20,500 feet. Good concentrations of fires around ground markers. Attack considered successful.

10/04/1944 LL670 A2-K Bombing Laon 01.32 03.51 06.00

Bomb load 9 x 1000, 4 x 500 lb bomb. Primary target: Laon. There was a slight haze. Bombed at 03.51 hours from 11,100 feet. Many T.I.s seen and bombing seemed to be concentrated. Railway line leading to yard seen. Attack quite successful.

18/04/1944 DS818 JI-Q Bombing Rouen 22.45 00.48 02.09

Bomb load 10 x 1000 MC, 5 x 500 MC lb bombs. Primary target: Rouen. There was 5/10 thin cloud. Bombed at 00.48 hours from 13,500 feet. There was a huge concentration of T.I.s which seemed nearer town than Marshalling

Yards. Church seen in built up area. Monica not used. Many flares, T.I.s and flak of first attack seen from coast. M of C directed us to bomb south of main concentration of flares. A.A. seen over London.

22/04/1944 DS818 JI-Q Bombing Dusseldorf 22.5401.16 02.57

Bomb load 9 x 1000, 5 x 500 lb bombs. Primary target: Dusseldorf. There was slight haze. Bombed at 01.16 hours from 19,000 feet. Red T.I.s visual of river. Held in searchlights for 3 minutes. Flak heavy and accurate. Route good.

09/05/1944 LL734 JI-S Bombing Cap Gris Nez 03.00 04.10 05.00

Bomb load 1 x 1000 GP, 13 x 1000 MC. Primary target: Cape Gris Nez. Clear conditions with slight ground haze. Bombed visually on T.I.s and instructions of Master Bomber at 04.10 hours from 6,000 feet. Bombs appeared very concentrated in area marked. Attack believed very good.

19/05/1944 LL703 JI-L Bombing Le Mans 22.30 00.28 03.00

Bomb load 4 x 1000 USA, 5 x 1000 MC, 1 x 1000 GP, 4 x 500 GP. Primary target: Le Mans. Clear conditions below aircraft. Bombed at 00.28 hours from 8,000 feet. In the act of bombing, aircraft was hit by light flak riddling the underfloor through open bomb door causing brilliant orange flash and small fire. Further bursts hit aircraft through mainplane from port to starboard along fuselage. Remainder of bombs jettisoned and whilst jettisoning further burst of flak holed one of the petrol tanks, putting out of order electrical system to port prop system. Landed at Gravely on two engines with starboard tyre burst and flap joined in raised position.

22/05/1944 DS818 JI-Q Bombing Dortmund 22.58 00.51 02.58

Bomb load 1 x 2000 lb, bomb, 96 x 30, 810 x 4, 90 x 4 incendiaries. Primary target: Dortmund. Slight haze over target. Bombed markers at 00.51 hours from 20,500 feet. Weather proved reverse of that anticipated and attack considered poor.

24/05/1944 DS818 JI-Q Bombing Boulogne 00.20 01.16 02.20

Bomb load 9 x 1000 MC, 1 x 1000 GP, 1 x 1000 ANM, 4 x 500 GP. Primary target: Boulogne, Gun Battery. Hazy over target. Bombed green T.I.s at 00.16 hours from 8,400 feet. Coastline seen and bombs burst amongst and around the markers. Uneventful trip.

27/05/1944 LL620 JI-N Bombing Aachen 00.40 02.32 04.20

Bomb load 7 x 1000 MC, 4 x 1000 ANM, 4 x 500 MC. Primary target: Aachen. Haze over target but route clear. Bombed at 02.32 hours from 13,200 feet. Visual of built up area by light of photo flash. Two large explosions seen at 02.28½ hours. Flak was fairly accurate for light, bursting in barrage form.

28/05/1944 LL620 JI-N Bombing Angers 19.03 23.57 02.10

Bomb load 5 x 1000 MC, 1 x 1000 USA, 4 x 500 MC. Primary target: Angers. Clear over target, but for smoke. Bombed as instructed by Master Bomber at 23.57 hours from 10,000 feet. Many bombs seen bursting around T.I.s.

30/05/1944 DS822 JI-T Bombing Boulogne 23.15 00.06 00.55

Bomb load 6 x 1000 MC, 4 x 500 MC. Primary target: Boulogne Gun

Batteries. Hazy over target. Bombed red T.I.s at 00.06 hours from 8,000 feet. Bomb bursts seemed generally scattered to N and W of markers.

10/06/1944 LL733 JI-S Bombing Dreux 23.06 01.01 03.38

Bomb load 16 x 500 GP, 2 x 500 LD. Primary target: Dreux. Bombed to E. of yellow T.I.s as instructed by Master Bomber at 01.01 hours from 8,000 feet. Uneventful trip.

12/06/1944 LL690 JI-J Bombing Gelsenkirchen 23.09 01.04 02.53

Bomb load 1 x 4000 HC, 12 x 500 GP, 4 x 500 MC. Primary target: Gelsenkirchen. Slight haze over target. Bombed red and green T.I.s at 01.04 hours from 19,000 feet. Saw large columns of black smoke. Numerous S/Ls in area but not over target.

15/06/1944 LL733 JI-S Bombing Valenciennes 23.13 00.38 02.05

Bomb load 16 x 500 GP, 2 x 500 MC. Primary target: Valenciennes. Weather clear below cloud - base 8000 feet. Bombed at 00.38 hours from 7,500 feet on red and green T.I.s per Master Bomber's instructions. Cloud over whole route.

21/06/1944 DS813 JI-N Bombing Domleger 18.06 x 20.48

Bomb load 18 x 500 MC. Primary target: Domleger near Abbeville, V-1 flying bomb launch site. According H.G. Sharp's logbook target "Abbeville". There was 10/10ths cloud. Reached target 19.28 hours at 13,000 feet. Abandoned sortie in accordance with Master Bomber's instructions.

23/06/1944 LL620 JI-N Bombing L'Hey 23.12 00.16 01.28

Bomb load 11 x 1000 MC, 4 x 500 GP. Primary target: L'Hey, Flying bomb installations. Bombed at 00.16 hours from 9,000 feet. There was 10/10ths cloud. Bomb flashes seen in glow. Several red T.I.s seen 5-6 miles south of target. No troubles.

24/06/1944 DS813 JI-N Bombing Rimeux 23.32 00.35 02.12

Bomb load 18 x 500 GP. Primary target: Rimeux, Flying bomb installations. Weather clear. Bombed at 00.35 hours from 11,000 feet centre of red T.I.s. Bomb bursts seen on markers, good concentration. Searchlights troublesome.

F/O. Louis Greenburgh DFC & Bar

1st Crew:

49803 (542422) F/O. Louis "Lou" Greenburgh. DFC & Bar.   Pilot.
A417149 Sgt. Donald Lloyd "Don" Bament, RAAF.   A/Bomber.
1313839 Sgt. David Patrick Gervase "Pat""Geordie" Butler. Navigator.
1386539 F/S. Gordon Henry "Strommy" Stromberg.   WOP/AG.
900040   Sgt. Fred J. Carey.   MU/Gunner. 7 ops
1804303 Sgt. Richard Jack "Andy" Woosnam. MU/Gunner. 2 ops.
A420925 F/S. Colin Albert "Connie" Drake, RAAF R/Gunner.
1673443 Sgt. Leslie "Les" Weddle.   F/Engineer.
177517 (1334210)
  F/S. Charles James Johnson, DFM.   2nd Pilot. 07/03/1944
178865 (1476474)
  F/S. John Backhouse "Toppy" Topham, DFC. 2nd Pilot. 18/03/1944

L to R (back): Gordon Stromberg, Leslie Weddle, Fred Carey, Pat Butler. L to R (front): Colin Drake, Lou Greenburgh, Don Bament. (courtesy Ed Greenburgh)

29/12/1943 DS821 JI-S Bombing Berlin 17.01 x   x
  Bomb load 1 x 2000, 40 x 30, 900 x 4, 90 x 4 incendiaries. Primary target: Berlin. Aircraft ditched at about 10pm short of petrol owing to fuel tanks holed during a combat with enemy aircraft flown by Ofw. Karl-Heinz Scherling of 12./NJG 30 km South of Texel.

Fifteen hours later, 30/12/1943 at about 2.30pm all crew rescued by an ASR HSL and taken to Royal Navy hospital at Great Yarmouth.

According another source, P.G. Butler received a heavy bang on the head whilst Colin Drake remained in hospital for a week due to a foot injury.

27/01/1944 LL727 A2-C   Bombing Berlin 17.54 20.41 01.46

Bomb load 1 x 4000. There was 10/10 cloud. Bombed at 20.41 hours at 20,000 ft. Red haze seen through clouds. P.Q.R. seen rather scattered. Attack progressing well. Photo attempted. Hole in Mid Upper turret perspex.

30/01/1944 LL727 A2-C   Bombing Berlin 17.19 20.24 23.40

Bomb load 1 x 4000 lb. bomb, 600 x 4, 90 x 4, 32 x 30 incendiaries. Primary target: Berlin. There was 10/10 cloud with tops 8-10,000 ft. Bombed at 20.24 hours at 20,000 ft. Bombed in centre of rather scattered red and green markers. Weather clear above cloud. Target area illuminated by all types of coloured flares and rockets - Route too tricky. Had encounter with enemy aircraft.

01/03/1944 LL727 A2-C   Bombing Stuttgart 23.30 03.15 07.33

Bomb load 1 x 8000 lb bomb, 8 x 30, 90 x 4 incendiaries. Primary target: Stuttgart. There was 9/10 cloud. Bombed at 03.15 hours at 20,000 ft. Terrific seen covering a wide area. An excellent attack. Route O.K. Inter-comm u/s for most of the way.

07/03/1944 LL727 A2-C   Bombing Le Mans 19.43 x 23.33

Bomb load 10 x 1000, 4 x 500 lb. Bomb. No attack. Could not identify the target. There was 10/10 cloud with tops 4/5000 feet. 4 x 500 lb bombs jettisoned. 6 x 1000 lb bombs brought back to Base. Aircraft came down to 9,000 feet over the target. Other aircraft seen at 6,000 feet still above cloud. Saw no red T.I. hence brought bombs back.

F/S. C.J. Johnson was 2nd Pilot that day.

15/03/1944 LL691 A2-D   Bombing Stuttgart 19.25   23.15   02.32

Bomb load 1 x 1000 lb bomb, 1050 x 4, 90 x 4 incendiaries. There was 8/10 cloud. Primary target: Stuttgart. Bombed at 23.15 hours from 20,000 feet. On arrival few fires seen which appeared to spread immediately after bombing. Weather not as forecast, patches of cloud building up to target.

Sgt. R.J. Woosnam was MU/Gunner that day.

18/03/1944 LL727 A2-C   Bombing Frankfurt 19.44 x 00.49

Bomb load 1 x 8000 lb bomb, 450 x 4, 90 x 4, 32 x 30 incendiaries. No attack. Markers not seen while in target area. Monica u/s from take off. A poor show. After we had been over target for 5 minutes we were coned by S/Ls. Fighter flares round us so we let the load go, but no T.I.s visible at the time.

Sgt. R.J. Woosnam was MU/Gunner that day, and F/S. J.B. Topham 2nd Pilot.

22/03/1944 LL727 A2-C   Bombing Frankfurt 18.28 22.03 00.41

Bomb load 1 x 8000 lb bomb, 56 x 30 incendiaries. Primary target: Frankfurt. Weather was clear. Bombed at 22.03 hours from 20,000 feet. Red T.I.s and many fires seen. After leaving target had to corkscrew continually to avoid fighter.

24/03/1944 LL727 A2-C Bombing Berlin 18.40 22.30 02.00

Bomb load 1 x 8000 lb. bomb. Primary target: Berlin. There was 7-8/10 cloud over the target. Bombed at 22.30 hours from 20,000 feet. Medium concentration of fires seen. Caught in searchlights over Denmark. Attacked by a JU88, Engineer and Bomb Aimer baled out after orders.

2nd Crew:

49803 (542422) F/O. Louis "Lou" Greenburgh. DFC & Bar. Pilot.
1392790 F/S. Eric George Rippingale. A/Bomber.
1539935 F/S. Ronald Fox. Navigator.
1386539 F/S. Gordon Henry "Strommy" Stromberg. WOP/AG.
900040 Sgt. Fred J. Carey. MU/Gunner.
1804303 Sgt. Richard Jack "Andy" Woosnam. R/Gunner. 10 ops.
A420925 F/S. Colin Albert "Connie" Drake, RAAF. R/Gunner. 1 op.
J85651 (R142559) P/O. Howard Gray "Pip" Sharp, RCAF. R/Gunner. 2 ops
1623947 Sgt. Frank Collingwood. F/Engineer.
186268 (1289916)
   W/O. Leslie John William "Les" Sutton. 2nd Pilot. 07/06/1944

20/04/1944 LL727 A2-C Bombing Cologne 00.0902.17 05.23

Bomb load 1 x 8000 lb bomb, 24 x 30, 216 x 4, 24 x 4 lb incendiaries. Primary target: Koln. There was 10/10 cloud. Bombed at 02.17 hours from 18,500 feet. Cloud prevented visual. Monica u/s. Starboard outer supercharger u/s after crossing English Coast out. Trip completed with 3 engines. Could only get height with difficulty. Glow beneath cloud seen from English Coast out.

According E.G. Rippingale's logbook: "Ops Koln Railway Yard and Chemical Works. Bombed glow 1 x 8000 lb".

P/O. H.G. Sharp was R/Gunner that day.

22/04/1944 LL727 A2-C Bombing Dusseldorf 23.06 00.59 02.40

Bomb load 1 x 8000 lb. bomb, 48 x 30, 486 x 4, 54 x 4 incendiaries. Did not bomb Dusseldorf, Pilot mistook new course and Navigator failed to check Pilot and so bombed opportunity target, aerodrome 4911N 0253E dgs. Bombed at 00.59 hours from 15,000 feet.

Sgt. R.J. Woosnam was R/Gunner that day.

Eric George Rippingale
(courtesy Mark Rippingale)

Howard Gray "Pip" Sharp

24/04/1944 LL727 A2-C   Bombing Karlsruhe 22.15 00.53 03.52

Bomb load 1 x 8000 lb bomb, 24 x 30,216 x 4, 24 x 4 lb incendiaries. Primary target: Karlsruhe. Weather was hazy. Bombed at 00.53 hours from 19,800 feet. Red T.I.s well concentrated. Successful attack, many large fires coinciding with position of markers. Many explosions seen.

P/O. H.G. Sharp was R/Gunner that day.

27/04/1944 LL727 A2-C   Bombing Friedrichshafen   21.59   02.18 05.53

Bomb load 810 x 4, 80 x 30 lb incendiaries. Primary target: Friedrichshafen. Weather was clear but hazy. Bombed at 02.18 hours from 19,000 feet. Most satisfactory sortie. Route O.K.

Sgt. R.J. Woosnam was R/Gunner that day.

01/05/1944 LL727 A2-C   Bombing Chambly 22.50 00.23 01.59

Bomb load 10 x 1000, 4 x 500 lb bombs. Primary target: Chambly. Weather was clear. Bombed at 00.23 hours from 8,000 feet. Visual of target illuminated by yellow flare. Green T.I.s seen but Master Bomber gave orders to ignore them. Yellow flare seen in target centre. Bombs appeared to burst in this area. Very successful attack. Route good.

260

F/S. C.A. Drake was R/Gunner that day.

10/05/1944 LL727 A2-C   Bombing Courtrai 22.20 23.28   01.00

Bomb load 7 x 1000 GP, 7 x 1000 MC. Primary target: Courtrai. Slight haze over target. Bombed on instructions of Master Bomber at 23.28 hours from 10,000 feet. Bomb bursts concentrated around yellow T.I. Seemed to be a good attack. Sighted enemy aircraft at 10,000 feet and 2,000 yards astern, no combat.

Sgt. R.J. Woosnam R/Gunner from that day.

11/05/1944 LL727 A2-C   Bombing Louvain 22.52 x 01.45

Bomb load 5 x 1000 GP, 5 x 1000 MC, 5 x 500 MC. Primary target: Louvain. Reached position 5131N 0235E but AP unidentified. White and yellow T.I.s seen. At 00.58 hours identified target by yellow flares but was told by the Master Bomber to bomb green T.I.s. As no green T.I.s were visible bombs were brought back and jettisoned. Bomb bursts seen around target area were very scattered. Unidentified aircraft with Navigation lights on seen at 00.21 hours travelling in opposite direction 1,500 feet below.

19/05/1944 LL677 A2-E   Bombing Le Mans 22.30   00.26   03.00

Bomb load 4 x 1000 USA, 5 x 1000 MC, 1 x 1000 GP, 4 x 500 GP. Primary target: Le Mans. Clear conditions below 8,000 feet. Bombed green T.I.s as instructed at 00.26 hours from 7,600 feet. Clouds of smoke appeared to be over railway marshalling yards and explosion seen at 00.40 hours. Appeared to be a good attack. Route satisfactory.

21/05/1944 LL727 A2-C   Bombing Duisburg 22.50   01.13   02.45

Bomb load 1 x 2000 lb bomb, 120 x 30, 600 x 4 incendiaries. Primary target: Duisberg. There was 10/10 cloud. Bombed a red glow through the cloud on ETA at 01.13 hours from 20,000 feet. Saw no markers but red glow seen through cloud.

24/05/1944 LL727 A2-C   Bombing Boulogne 00.15   01.16   02.10

Bomb load 9 x 1000 MC, 1 x 1000 GP, 1 x 1000 ANM, 4 x 500 GP. Primary target: Boulogne, Gun Battery. Clear over target except for slight haze. Bombed at 01.16 hours from 4,700 feet and bomb bursts coincided with T.I.s. Starboard inner engine u/s on take-off and sortie completed on three engines. 4,700 feet was maximum height obtained.

28/05/1944 LL727 A2-C   Bombing Angers   19.05   23.58   02.05

Bomb load 5 x 1000 MC, 1 x 1000 USA, 4 x 500 MC. Primary target: Angers. Slight haze over target. Bombed at 23.58 hours from 10,000 feet. Target seen clearly. Did not hear Master Bomber because of interference. At 00.32 hours FW190 passed 500 yards on port side.

31/05/1944 LL727 A2-C   Bombing Trappes 00.07 01.58   04.40

Bomb load 8 x 1000 MC, 8 x 500 MC. Primary target: Trappes. Clear at target, but slight haze. Bombed at 01.58 hours from 8,000 feet. Bursts seen in target area, opposition slight and trip trouble free. Attack thought good.

07/06/1944 LL727 A2-C   Bombing Massy Palaiseau 00.27 x 02.55

Bomb load 18 x 500 MC. Primary target: Massy Palaiseau, Marshalling

Yards. Set on fire by a night fighter over the target area, the crew escaped from their attacker, received further flak damage before finally being shot down by the JU88 of Hptm. Herbert Lorenz of 1/NJG2. Crashed 08/06/1944 02.55 hours at St-Eusoye (Oise), 20 km NE of Beauvais.

W/O. L.J.W. Sutton was 2nd Pilot that day.

F/O. L. Greenburgh Evaded, W/O. L.J.W. Sutton (P2) Evaded, F/S. R. Fox Evaded, F/S. E.G. Rippingale Evaded.

There is an unconfirmed report that Sgt F.J. Carey evaded until captured on the 6th July 1944 and interned in Camp L7. PoW No.384, with Sgt F. Collingwood, PoW No.80059.

F/S R.J. Woosnam initially evaded until captured on the 3rd July 1944 and interned in Camp L7, PoW No.424.

The sole casualty, F/S. G.H. Stromberg who died of his injuries in Amiens Hospital on the 9th June 1944, is buried at Amiens St-Pierre Cemetery.

P/O. Edward Alfred Greenwood, DFC

J19060 R85412 P/O.   Edward Alfred Greenwood, DFC.   Pilot.
121738 (1387265)   F/O. David Kennedy Lang. B/Aimer. 4 ops.
170457 (1585089)   Sgt. Victor Francis Dobell Meade. B/Aimer. 1 op.
1044234 Sgt. Jack Knights.   B/Aimer. 1 op.
1585341 Sgt. William Alexander Bates. B/Aimer. 4 ops.
R151814   F/S. R.W. Deans, RCAF   B/Aimer. 17 ops.
147709 (1288759) F/O. Douglas Arthur Nicol. Navigator. 10 ops.
185519 (1387106) F/S. Dennis Arthur Newman. Navigator.   17 ops.
143911 (928281) F/O. John Kenworthy Dawes. WOP/AG. 14 ops.
1578078 Sgt. D. Thom   WOP/AG.   1 op.
1235332 Sgt. Norman Walter Cringle. WOP/AG.   12 ops.
1585622 F/S. George "Hawkeye" Henry. MU/Gunner. 10 ops.
R161431   W/O. S.J. Everitt, RCAF MU/Gunner. 1 op.
J19355 (R128609)
        P/O. Edward Wolfe "Ed" Bourne, RCAF. MU&R/Gunner.
J89407 (R190270)
        Sgt. John Joseph McNeill, RCAF.   MU&R/Gunner. 16 ops
173348 (1629747) P/O. Frederick John Thornton F/Engineer.
552769 (54223) F/S.   Elmer Protheroe. 2nd Pilot. 29/12/1943
Sgt. M. Miller.   2nd Pilot. 01/01/1944
984464 F/S. Thomas Lipsey Gibson. 2nd Pilot. 20/04/1944

07/11/1943 DS813 JI-H Gardening   La Rochelle 23.56 x 06.57

Aircraft carried 3 x G714 (11, 10 and 8). Primary area La Rochelle. 10/10 cloud. Base about 4,000 feet. Very quiet route. No troubles, successful pin point. No opposition.

F/O. D.A. Nicol was Navigator from that day until 02/01/1944.

F/O. D.K Lang was B/Aimer from that day until 22/11/1943.

F/O. J.K. Dawes was WOP/AG from that day until 30/01/1944.

P/O. E.W. Bourne was MU/Gunner from that day until 20/12/1943.

Sgt. J.J. McNeill was R/Gunner from that day until 20/12/1943.

18/11/1943 DS813 JI-H Bombing Mannheim 17.20 20.41 23.24

Bomb load 1 x 4000, 16 x 30, 720 x 4. Primary target Mannheim. Weather was good with no cloud. Bombed Green T.I.s at 20.41 hours, 19,000 feet. Monica U/S. and 4 x 30 lb incendiaries hung up and were brought back.

22/11/1943 DS823 JI-K Bombing Berlin 17.39 20.21   23.44

Bomb load 1 x 4000, 360 x 4 incendiaries, 90 x 4 incendiaries, 24 x 30 incendiaries. Primary target: Berlin. 10/10 cloud with tops about 12,000, Red flares cascading Green Sparks. Red flare seen disappearing in cloud. Several flares seen over target on near up two patches of fire seen below cloud and a very bad explosion lasting 10 seconds at 20.21.

03/12/1943 DS820 JI-R Bombing Leipzig 00.41 x 07.13

Bomb load 1 x 2000 HC, 48 x 30 incendiaries, 800 x 4 incendiaries, 100 x 4 incendiaries. Primary target: Leipzig. Quiet trip. 10/10 cloud obscuring target area. Fire reflection through clouds. Bombed total load on release flares. If flares were in right position they had it down below.

Sgt. V.F.D. Meade was B/Aimer that day.

16/12/1943 DS813 JI-H Bombing Berlin 16.55 20.02 00.16

Bomb load 1 x 2000, 40 x 30 incendiaries, 630 x 4 incendiaries. Primary target: Berlin. 10/10 cloud, Tops approx 6,000. Bombed at 20.02 at 19,000 ft. Markers OK. No results seen owing to cloud. Landed at Downham Market.

Sgt. J. Knights was B/Aimer that day.

20/12/1943 DS813 JI-H Bombing Frankfurt   17.39 19.46 22.34

Bomb load 1 x 8000, 16 x 30 incendiaries, 330 x 4 incendiaries, 30 x 4 incendiaries. Primary target: Frankfurt. 7/10 cloud, Tops 5,000 ft. Bombed target at 19.46 at 20,000 ft. Many good fires, tending to undershoot. Cloudy over target.

F/O. D.K. Lang was B/Aimer that day.

24/12/1943 DS813 JI-H Bombing Berlin 00.29 04.02 08.45

Bomb load 1 x 4000, 32 x 30 incendiaries, 450 x 4 incendiaries, 90 x 4 incendiaries. Primary target: Berlin. 4-5/10 cloud below. Bombed at 04.02 hrs at 19,000 ft (incendiaries only). 1 x 4000 bomb hung up, due to icing up of release. No fires seen burning in vicinity of markers. Route satisfactory. Photo attempted.

Sgt. W.A. Bates was B/Aimer from that day until 02/01/1944.

George "Hawkeye" Henry

(courtesy Joan Henry)

Sgt. J.J. McNeill was MU/Gunner from that day until 15/03/1944.

P/O. E.W. Bourne was R/Gunner from that day.

29/12/1943 DS813 JI-H Bombing Berlin 17.13 20.07 23.58

Bomb load 1 x 2000, 40 x 30 incendiaries, 900 x 4 incendiaries, 90 x 4 incendiaries. Primary target: Berlin. There was 10/10 cloud. Bombed at 20.07 hours at 19,000 feet. Route was OK. Photo attempted.

F/S. E. Protheroe was 2nd Pilot that day.

01/01/1944 DS813 JI-H Bombing Berlin 00.45 03.20 07.20

Bomb load 1 x 4000, 24 x 30, 450 x 4, 90 x 4 lbs incendiaries. Primary target: Berlin. There was 10/10 cloud, visibility OK above. Sky markers and green T.I.s seen. Bombed at 03.10 hours at 19,500 feet. Bombed in centre of rather scattered group of sky markers. Some 4000 lbs exploding, but no fires seen. Attack not quite so well concentrated as usual.

Sgt. M. Miller was 2nd Pilot that day.

02/01/1944 DS813 JI-H Bombing Berlin 00.20 02.34 06.47

Bomb load 1 x 2000, 40 x 30, 900 x 4 incendiaries. Primary target: Berlin. There was 10/10 cloud with tops 17/18,000 ft. Bombed at 02.54 hours at 20,000 ft. In centre of red and green sky markers. Some glows reflected on clouds. Markers better placed than last night. Should be better show. Photo attempted.

27/01/1944 DS842 JI-F Bombing Berlin 17.46 20.37 02.19

Bomb load 1 x 4000, 32 x 30, 450 x 4, 90 x 4 incendiaries. Primary target: Berlin. There was 10/10 cloud. Bombed at 20.37 hours at 20,000 ft. Bombed in centre of two green and red markers. Attack should develop well. Photo flash failed.

F/S. D.A. Newman was Navigator from that day.

F/S. R.W. Deans was B/Aimer from that day.

28/01/1944 DS813 JI-H Bombing Berlin 00.10 03.24 08.28

Bomb load 1 x 2000 lb bomb, 16 x 30, 750 x 4 incendiaries. Primary target: Berlin. There was 10/10 cloud. Bombed at 03.24 hours at 20,000 ft. Very good fires and seen from Rostock. Monica u/s. Route and attack good.

30/01/1944 DS813 JI-H Bombing Berlin 17.14 20.22 23.49

Bomb load 1 x 8000 lb bomb. Primary target: Berlin. There was 10/10 cloud. Bombed at 20.22 hours at 20,000 ft. There was good concentration of sky markers. Monica u/s. Route too hot - Attack not as good as previous night.

15/02/1944 DS813 JI-H Bombing Berlin 17.30 21.22 00.24

Bomb load 1 x 8000 lbs bomb. Primary target: Berlin. There was 10/10 cloud. Bombed at 21.22 hrs. At 20,000 ft. Small hole in Mid Upper turret, flak bursting all round. Attack seemed rather poor due to scattered sky marking. Flak was heavier than usual.

Sgt. D. Thom was WOP/AG that day.

19/02/1944 DS813 JI-H Bombing Leipzig 00.11 04.12 07.03

Bomb load 1 x 2000, 1 x 500 lb bomb. 40 x 30, 900 x 4 incendiaries. Primary target: Leipzig. There was 10/10 cloud. Bombed at 04.12 hours at 20,000 ft. One large fire noticed spreading out around. Should be OK if P.F.F. were correct. Northern route satisfactory. Had encounter with enemy aircraft, but no damage is claimed. Lancaster suffered no damage.

F/O. J.K. Dawes was WOP/AG that day.

15/03/1944 DS813 JI-H Bombing Stuttgart 19.32 23.29 02.34

Bomb load 1 x 1000 lb bomb, 1050 x 4, 90 x 4, 64 x 30 incendiaries. Primary target: Stuttgart. There was 7/10 cloud. Bombed at 23.29 hours from 20,000 feet. Many fires burning when we left. Mid Upper turret blown off. Attacked over Stuttgart by enemy aircraft resulted in death of Mid Upper Gunner.

Sgt. N.W. Cringle was WOP/AG from that day.

30/03/1944 DS813 JI-H Bombing Nuremburg 22.33 01.30 05.14

Bomb load 1 x 8000, 90 x 4 incendiaries. Primary target: Nuremberg. There was 8-10/10 cloud in layers. Bombed at 01.30 hours from 20,000 feet. Bombed centre of fires with 2 red markers. Success of raid doubtful. Bombed the Easterly of 2 large fire areas about 20 miles apart. Little opposition but many combats over Ruhr.

F/S. G. Henry was MU/Gunner from that day until 01/05/1944.

11/04/1944 DS813 JI-H Bombing Aachen 20.55 22.44 00.38

Bomb load 10 x 1000, 2 x 500 lb bombs, 160 x 4, 20 x 4 incendiaries. Primary target: Aachen. There was a thin layer of cloud. Bombed at 22.44 hours from 20,000 feet. Bombs appeared to be bursting all around T.I.s. One explosion seen on leaving target area.

18/04/1944 DS813 JI-H Bombing Rouen 22.28 00.45 02.30

Bomb load 8 x 1000 MC, 2 x 1000 GP, 5 x 500 lb bomb. Primary target: Rouen. Weather was hazy. Bombed at 00.45 hours from 12,500 feet. Bomb bursts and much black smoke seen. If T.I.s were correct - attack should be successful.

20/04/1944 DS813 JI-H Bombing Cologne 23.59 02.08 04.04

Bomb load 1 x 1000 lb bomb, 1026 x 4, 108 x 30, 114 x 4 incendiaries. Primary target: Koln. There was 10/10 cloud. Bombed at 02.08 hours from 20,000 feet. Red flares and yellow stars scarcely distinguishable. Cloud too thick. Not much evidence. Route O.K.

F/S. T.L. Gibson was 2nd Pilot that day.

24/04/1944 DS813 JI-H Bombing Karlsruhe   22.15   00.44   03.52

Bomb load 1 x 1000 lb bomb, 1026 x 4, 114 x 4, 108 x 30 lb incendiaries. Primary target: Karlsruhe. Weather was hazy, cloud base about 18/19,000 feet. Bombed at 00.44 hours from 17,000 feet. Ground markers very concentrated and bombing and fires coinciding. Successful effort. Route OK. Sky markers seen above coinciding also with position of ground markers.

27/04/1944 DS813 JI-H Bombing Friedrichshafen 21.58 02.11   05.52

Bomb load 1 x 4000 lb bomb, 32 x 30, 36 x 4, 36 x 4 lb incendiaries. Primary target Friedrichshafen. Weather was clear. Bombed at 02.11 hours from 20,000 feet. Large fires seen concentrated round markers. One of the best attacks experienced. Markers well placed. Route good.

01/05/1944 DS813 JI-H Bombing Chambly   22.58   00.21   02.24

Bomb load 10 x 1000, 5 x 500 lb bombs. Primary target: Chambly. Weather was clear but slight haze. Visibility moderate. Bombed at 00.21 hours from 8,500 feet. There was much smoke, river only visible. T.I.s rather scarce, only 3 seen. Bombing was early and most of bombs jettisoned SE of the 3 T.I.s seen.

11/05/1944 DS818 JI-Q Bombing Louvain   22.30   00.22   01.50

Bomb load 5 x 1000 GP, 5 x 1000 MC. Primary target: Louvain. Clear conditions at target but ground haze. Bombed at 00.22 hours from 8,500 feet. Very few markers seen and bomb bursts scattered. Fuselage damaged by flak.

W/O. S.J. Everitt was MU/Gunner that day.

19/05/1944 DS813 JI-H Bombing Le Mans 22.15 x 03.15

Bomb load 4 x 1000 USA, 5 x 1000 MC, 1 x 1000 GP, 4 x 500 GP. Primary target: Le Mans. Target not identified with certainty. Green T.I.s were seen but seemed scattered and as Master Bomber's instructions were not heard clearly, decided not to bomb. Jettisoned 4 x 500 GP and 1 x 1000 GP safe at 4922N 0323W and brought back remainder of bombs.

F/S. G. Henry was MU/Gunner from that day.

02/06/1944 DS813 JI-H Bombing Wissant   01.30 x 03.40

Bomb load 1 x 1000 GP, 10 x 1000 MC, 4 x 500 MC. Primary target: Wissant Gun Positions. Target not identified. 3 x 1000 MC and 4 x 500 MC jettisoned safe at position 5220N 0230E. Remainder of bomb load brought back.

05/06/1944 DS813 JI-H Bombing Ouistreham 03.40   05.10   06.55

Bomb load 9 x 1000 MC and 2 x 500 MC. Primary target: Ouistreham. There was slight dispersed cloud. Bombed markers at 05.10 hours from 9,200 feet. Bombing seemed concentrated around aiming point and attack thought to be successful. Observed some red T.I.s to the East, possibly out at sea.

F/S. Frederick Gregory

1283636 F/S. Frederick "Fred" Gregory. Pilot.
J89471 (R164086)
     P/O. James Duncan "Jimmy" McCreary, RCAF. A/Bomber.
R143361 P/O. C. Gordon E. MacDonald, RCAF. Navigator.
1320161 Sgt. Eric Raymond William Pond. WOP/AG.
1105202 Sgt. Robert Byth. MU/Gunner.
2209173 Sgt. Alfred Cooke. R/Gunner.
1589935 Sgt. Sanford Peter Frith. F/Engineer.

19/02/1944 LL670 A2-K Bombing Leipzig 00.15 04.06 06.54
Bomb load 1 x 4000 lbs bomb. 32 x 30, 510 x 4, 90 x 4 x incendiaries.
Primary target: Leipzig. There was 10/10 cloud. Bombed at 04.06 hours at
20,000 ft. Four large fires and smaller ones seen over a wide area. Northern
route OK. Aircraft arrived too early and had to waste time in Willenberg area.
Attack very widespread.
F/S. Frederick Gregory flew the mission as 2nd Pilot with F/S. E.R.
Protheroe's crew.
21/02/1944 LL727 A2-C Bombing Stuttgart 00.28 04.20 07.10
Bomb load 1 x 4000 lbs bomb, 40 x 30, 690 x 4, 90 x 4 incendiaries. Primary
target: Stuttgart. There was 9/10 cloud. Bombed at 04.20 hours at 20,000 ft.
Large fires seen, smoke billowing up through the cloud. Ran past and had to
do a reciprocal so turned again. Fires had a good hold when leaving target.
24/02/1944 LL727 A2-C Bombing Schweinfurt 18.49 23.18 02.44
Bomb load 1 x 8000 lb bomb. Primary target: Schweinfurt. Weather was
clear with some ground haze or smoke. Bombed at 23.18 hours at 21,000 ft.
There were good fires concentrated round the markers. Several good Monica
reactions on way to target. Photo. Run spilt by FW190 just below and
corkscrew action.
25/02/1944 LL620 A2-G Bombing Augsburg 22.01 01.19 04.33
Bomb load 1 x 4000 lb bomb, 32 x 30, 510 x 4, 90 x 4 incendiaries. Primary
target: Augsburg. There was 7/10 cloud - clear patches. Bombed at 01.19 hours
at 19,000 ft. Fires already raging in city when we arrived. T.I.s appeared rather
scattered. Arrived too early and orbited to lose time. D.R. compass u/s. Attack
appeared to be successful. Dummy target to South of Augsburg helpful to
Pilot.
01/03/1944 DS786 A2-F Bombing Stuttgart 23.45 03.16 07.07
Bomb load 1 x 2000, 1 x 500 lb bomb. Primary target: Stuttgart. There was
10/10 cloud. Bombed at 03.16 hours at 20,000 ft. Glow of fires seen through
cloud. Windscreen obscured by icing from half way along second leg until
until return. Much H.F. over target.
07/03/1944 LL678 A2-L Bombing Le Mans 19.50 22.09 23.58

Bomb load 9 x 1000, 4 x 500 lb bombs. Primary target: Le Mans. There was 10/10 cloud over the target. Bombed at 22.09 hours from 11,000 feet. Fires and river visual through break in cloud. No markers seen, target located by visual means after circling for 17 minutes. Previous seemed concentrated as seen from 40 miles away.

15/03/1944 LL698 A2-J Bombing Stuttgart 19.35 23.24 03.08

Bomb load 1 x 1000 lb bomb, 1050 x 4, 90 x 4 incendiaries. Primary target: Stuttgart. There was 8/10 cloud. Bombed at 23.24 hours from 20,000 feet. Some good fires seen rather scattered, tending to overshoot. No visual means, attack satisfactory if on correct place.

18/03/1944 LL698 A2-J Bombing Frankfurt 19.45 22.09 01.07

Bomb load 1 x 8000 lb bomb, 32 x 30 incendiaries. Primary target: Frankfurt. Weather hazy. Bombed at 22.09 hours from 20,000 feet. Target seemed well alight when we left.

30/03/1944 LL698 A2-J Bombing Nuremburg 22.13 x x

Bomb load 1 x 1000 lb bomb, 96 x 30, 810 x 4, 90 x 4 incendiaries. Aircraft missing.

Outbound, brought down by night-fighter, possibly flown by Uffz. Lorenz Gerstmayr of 4/NJG3 on 31/03/1944 at 00.38 hours, near Oberpleis, 12 km ESE of Bonn. All crew KIA except F/S. C.G.E. MacDonald. Those killed were buried within 24 hours of the crash at Oberpleis. They have been subsequently re-interred in the Rheinberg War Cemetery.

C.G.E. MacDonald was interned in Camp L6/357, PoW No.3474.

F/L. Acting S/L. Charles Walter Gwilliam

102568 (1057922) S/L. Charles Walter Gwilliam. Pilot.
138828 (927579) F/L. Reginald Lawrence Ross. A/Bomber. 9 ops.
171186 (1212306) F/O. Horace Hassall. Navigator. 9 ops.
131603 (1508455) F/L. Alan Hope Deadman, DFC. Navigator. 1 op.
158668 (1376850) F/O. Reginald George Gaisford, DFC. WOP/AG.
NZ426075 F/O. I.D.H. Terry, RNZAF. MU/Gunner.
162525 (1140570) F/O. Anthony John Abbott. R/Gunner.
W/O. T.A. Carr. F/Engineer. 9 ops.

Passengers: 19/06/1945, 22/06/1945, 30/06/1945, 09/07/1945.

L to R (back): H. Hassall, C.W. Gwillam, I.D.H. Terry, A.J. Abbott, R.L. Ross, R.G. Gaisford, T.A. Carr. (courtesy Brian Hassall)

19/05/1945 RA601 JI-J Exodus Brussels - Oakley 11.58 x 19.15
Duration 3 hrs 08 mins. Out 1 hr 19 mins. In 1 hr 49 mins. 11 Belgian refugees taken to Brussels. 24 ex POWs all military evacuated.
Mission not noted in H. Hassall's logbook.
23/05/1945 ME425 A2-L Exodus Brussels - Oakley 12.09 x 18.11
Duration 3 hrs 17 mins. Out 1 hr 10 mins. In 2 hrs 07 min. 11 Belgian refugees returned to Brussels. 24 ex POWs evacuated. Organisation good.
24/05/1945 RA600 JI-B Exodus Brussels 12.03 x 16.35
Duration 2.25 hours. Out 1.11 hours. In 1.14 hours. 10 Belgian refugees to Brussels. No ex POWs to be returned.
Mission not noted in H. Hassall's logbook.
25/05/1945 RE120 A2-C Exodus Brussels 11.52 x 16.13
Duration 2.25 hours. Out 1.10 hours. In 1.15 hours. 10 Belgian refugees to Brussels. No POWs home. No troubles.
26/05/1945 RE120 A2-C Exodus Brussels - Ford 11.53 x 17.15
Duration 3.15 hours. Out 1.10 hours. In 2.05 hours. 10 Belgian refugees to Brussels. 24 ex POWs all military returned.
19/06/1945 RE120 A2-C Baedeker Tour over Continent 09.46 x 14.30

"Rhineland Tour".

Passengers: S/L. Denning, LAC. Hall, LAC. Harris, AC. Lamb, AC. Brooks.

22/06/1945 RA602 A2-H Baedeker Tour over Continent 09.41 x 13.52
"Ruhr Tour".

Passengers: W/C. Young, Cpl. Howells, Cpl. Bagley, LAC. Robinson, LAC. Fuller.

25/06/1945 ME364 JI-P Post Mortem Special mission x x x
Burst tyre on take off.

30/06/1945 RE120 A2-C Baedeker Tour over Continent 12.45 x 17.04
"Ruhr Tour"

Passengers: LAC. Watson, AC. Slater, S/O. Lunson.

09 to 13/07/1945

RE159 A2-E Dodge Italy 07.40 12.30 17.55
09/07/1945 Waterbeach 07.40 - Italy 12.30 - 13/07/1945 Italy 10.00 - Waterbeach 17.55.

No F/Engineer and no Bomb Aimer for that mission.

Passengers: G/Capt. Marwood-Elton, W/C. Carr, W/C. Peake, W/C. Lawson, S/L. Warren, Cpl. Fish, LAC. Salt.

F/S. Norman Hall

978968 F/S. Norman Hall. Pilot.
1338713 Sgt. Kenneth Leonard Cragg. A/Bomber.
1585416 Sgt. John Roland Williams. Navigator.
1419042 Sgt. Frank Reginald Lewis. WOP/AG.
1651897 Sgt. William Kenneth Watkins. MU/Gunner.
1806800 Sgt. Thomas Samuel Woodford. R/Gunner.
1582498 Sgt. Arthur Reginald Hodson. F/Engineer.

27/01/1944 LL674 A2-D Bombing Berlin 17.10 x 20.20

Aborted the operation, overran the runway and crashed into a ditch on return. Touched down at 20.20 hours. No injuries reported. Apart from the names of the two pilots, taken from the accident record card the Squadron ORB omits all reference to the incident. Such omissions, although not unique, are relatively uncommon. F/S. H.A. Symmons was Captain and F/S. N. Hall 2nd pilot.

Both the Rear Gunner R.C. Guy and the Bomb Aimer E.G. Rippingale of H.A. Symmons' crew noted simply in their logbooks "OPS E/R PRANGED BERLIN".

The RAF Waterbeach ORB notes that F/S. Symmons was sick, and the aircraft was flown home by F/S. Norman Hall who, fortuitously, was flying as 'second dickie'. On landing LL674 overran the runway, coming to rest in a ditch with the wing obstructing the Ely road, fortunately without injury to the crew or passing motorists. The aircraft was SOC on 26/02/1944.

From his normal crew, only F/S. Norman Hall did the mission as 2nd Pilot with F/S. H.A. Symmons' crew.

19/02/1944 DS736 A2-D Bombing Leipzig 00.20 x x

Bomb load 1 x 2000, 1 x 500 lb bomb, 40 x 30, 900 x 4 incendiaries. Primary target: Leipzig. Aircraft missing. No news. Lost 20/02/1944 without trace. Probably the victim of an unidentified night fighter. All crew KIA and commemorated on the Runnymede Memorial.

P/O. Jack Edward Kristjan Hannesson

J87269 (R162636) P/O. Jack Edward Kristjan Hannesson, RCAF. Pilot.
R118427 Sgt. Thomas Stanley "Tommy" Colbeck, RCAF. A/Bomber.
1670036 Sgt. James Bryson.   Navigator. 6 ops.
A426753 F/S. Beverley Gordon Lee, RAAF.   Navigator. 3 ops.
1126909 F/S. Bert A. Brown.   WOP/AG.
J89894 (R178139) P/O. Andrew Lorne George, RCAF. MU/Gunner.
646041   Sgt. Harry James Morgan.   R/Gunner.
2201592 Sgt. Kenneth Edward Arthur Fox.   F/Engineer.
70126 S/L. Ralph Campbell Chopping, DFC. Captain. 31/05/1944

31/05/1944 DS822 JI-T Bombing Trappes 23.55 02.06 04.50

Bomb load 8 x 1000 MC, 8 x 500 MC. Primary target: Trappes. Clear at target. Bombed as instructed by Master Bomber at 02.06 hours from 10,000 feet. Concentrated attacks obscured by smoke. Master Bomber good and sortie successful. Route O.K. but long.

S/L. R.C. Chopping was Captain of this crew that day and F/S. J.E.K. Hannesson 2nd Pilot.

02/06/1944 DS818 JI-Q Bombing Wissant 01.26 x 03.38

Bomb load 1 x 1000 GP, 10 x 1000 MC, 4 x 500 MC. Primary target: Wissant Gun Positions. Could not identify target at 8,000 feet. 2 x 1000 MC and 4 x 500 MC jettisoned safe at 5225N.

Thomas Stanley "Tommy" Colbeck   Beverley Gordon Lee

06/06/1944 LL731 JI-L Bombing Lisieux 00.07 01.36 03.28

Bomb load 16 x 500 MC tail fused and 2 x 500 MC LD. Primary target: Lisieux. Weather was clear below 6,000 feet. Bombed red T.I. at 01.36 hours from 6,000 feet. Visual obtained of river. On leaving, fires were seen through clouds of smoke. Very good concentration of bombs around markers. Master Bomber unintelligible. Visibility poor over England on return.

07/06/1944 LL733 JI-S Bombing Massy Palaiseau 00.26 02.15 04.44

Bomb load 18 x 500 MC. Primary target: Massy Palaiseau, Marshalling Yards. Slight haze below, 10/10 cloud above. Bombed on Master Bomber's instructions at 02.15 hours from 6,500 feet. Bombing seen was accurately aimed on markers. Attack thought good. Fighters active over target area.

10/06/1944 DS813 JI-H Bombing Dreux 23.16 00.56 03.40

Bomb load 16 x 500 GP, 2 x 500 LD. Primary target: Dreux. Bombed on green T.I.s on instructions of Master Bomber at 00.56 hours from 8,000 feet. Illuminating flares lit up Lancaster as well as target. Weather clear.

12/06/1944 LL728 JI-B Bombing Gelsenkirchen 23.05 01.07 03.17

Bomb load 1 x 4000 HC, 12 x 500 GP, 4 x 500 MC. Primary target: Gelsenkirchen. Visibility was good. Bombed on green T.I. at 01.07 hours from 18,000 feet. Bombing appeared very concentrated. Experienced icing at 9,000 feet over North Sea on returning but climbed again to 9,500 feet where conditions were satisfactory.

15/06/1944 DS826 JI-U Bombing Valenciennes 23.09 00.36 02.19

Bomb load 16 x 500 GP, 2 x 500 MC. Primary target: Valenciennes. Weather clear below cloud. Bombed at 00.36 hours from 9,500 feet on centre of Red and Green T.I.s, bomb bursts seen. Weather clear below cloud. TR.1196 aerial lost due to icing over the Channel. Uneventful trip.

17/06/1944 LL635 JI-M Bombing Montdidier 01.10 x 04.30

Bomb load 16 x 500 GP, 2 x 500 ANM64 GP. Primary target: Montdidier. Arrived over target and heard Master Bomber order return to Base. Jettisoned safe 10 x 500 GP at 03.21 hours from 10,000 feet 5003N 0052E.

F/S. B.G. Lee Navigator from that day.

21/06/1944 LL635 JI-M   Bombing Domleger 18.07 x 19.41

Bomb load 18 x 500 MC. Primary target: Domleger near Abbeville, V-1 flying bomb launch site. Starboard inner had to be feathered owing to violent backfiring whilst over base. Jettisoned safe 18 x 500 MC at 18.09 hours from 3,000 feet, 5219N 0225E.

30/06/1944 PB178 JI-P Bombing Villers Bocage 18.18 x 19.27

Bomb load 9 x 1000 MC, 2 x 500 GP. Target Villers Bocage to destroy a flying-bomb site but at 19.25 hours collided over Tangmere with a 15 Squadron Lancaster (ME695), blew up in the air and crashed at Pittsham Farm near Midhurst in Sussex. ME695 landed safely, was repaired and continued in service until SOC on 29 August 1946.

From the crew of PB178 JI-P, Sgt. T.S. Colbeck, Bomb Aimer and Sgt. C.A. Brown, Wireless Operator were the only survivors. Those killed are buried in their home towns.

F/O. Glen A. Hanson

J36160 F/O. Glen A. Hanson, RCAF.   Pilot.
R188320 F/S. Doug J. Marsh, RCAF.   A/Bomber.
J39982 F/O.   Frederick E. "Fred" Coleman, RCAF. Navigator.
 F/S. Bruce E. Derriman   WOP/AG.
R273556 F/S. L.G. "Gord" Rollason, RCAF. MU/Gunner. 30 ops.
R269384 F/S. Frank R. Stanley, RCAF. R/Gunner. 29 ops.
 F/S. E.D. Dixon.   R/Gunner.   2 ops.
 Sgt. J. Bruce Pattullo.   F/Engineer. 29 ops.
 Sgt. W.H. Mills.   F/Engineer.   2 ops.
A417741 (O35137) P/O. Peter Geoffrey Dean, RAAF.   2nd Pilot.
16/02/1945

Passengers: 04/05/1945.

11/12/1944 NG141 A2-J Bombing Osterfeld 08.45 11.05 12.50
Bomb load 9 x 1000 ANM65, 5 x 1000 ANM59. Primary target: Osterfeld. Weather 10/10ths cloud, tops 16,000 feet. Bombed at 11.05 hours from 20,000 feet on G.H. Leader.
From his normal crew, only F/O. G.A. Hanson did the mission as 2nd Pilot with P/O. H.C. Richford's crew.
12/12/1944 PD334 A2-D Bombing Witten 11.17 14.04 16.04
Bomb load 1 x 4000 HC, 14 x 500 Clusters. Primary target: Witten. Weather 10/10ths cloud, tops 14/16,000 feet. Bombed at 14.04 hours from 20,700 feet on G.H. Leader.
16/12/1944 NG142 A2-C Bombing Siegen 11.25 x 14.36
Bomb load 1 x 4000 HC, 5 x 1000 MC, 7 x 500 GP. Primary target: Siegen. Weather very bad on route with icing and cloud. Aircraft returned early due to icing. Port wing dropped and aircraft dived rapidly losing height, so jettisoned 4000 HC at 11,000 feet. Jettisoned

L to R (back): B.E. Derriman, F.R. Stanley, J.B. Pattullo, L.G. Rollason. L to R (front): F.E. Coleman, D.J. Marsh, G.A. Hanson. (courtesy Fred Coleman)

274

safe 1 x 4000 HC, 2 x 500 GP, 5030N 0050E, 13.15 hours.

21/12/1944 PD324 A2-B Bombing Trier 12.27 15.03 17.01

Bomb load 1 x 4000 HC, 10 x 500 GP, 6 x 250 GP. Primary target: Trier, Marshalling yards. Weather 10/10 cloud, tops 6/9,000 feet. Bombed at 15.03 hours from 17,800 feet on G.H. Leader.

23/12/1944 LM727 A2-F Bombing Trier 11.47 14.32 16.17

Bomb load 1 x 4000 HC, 10 x 500 GP, 6 x 250 GP. Primary target: Trier. Weather clear over target. Bombed at 14.32 hours from 18,200 feet on smoke over centre of town.

05/01/1945 LM285 A2-F Bombing Ludwigshafen 11.30 15.08 18.08

Bomb load 1 x 4000 HC, 10 x 500 ANM58 or 64, 2 x 500 GP. Primary target: Ludwigshafen, Marshalling yards. Weather clear over target. Bombed at 15.08 hours from 20,000 feet on Red flares. Aircraft hit by flak - port wing and Rear turret damaged.

07/01/1945 NF966 A2-F Bombing Munich 19.08 22.33 03.17

Bomb load 1 x 4000 HC, 7 x 500 clusters. Primary target: Munich. Weather 10/10ths cloud over target 6-8,000 feet with a thin layer altitude 16,000 feet. Bombed at 22.33 hours from 20,000 feet on Red and Green flares.

11/01/1945 NF966 A2-F Bombing Krefeld 11.43 15.11 16.50

Bomb load 1 x 4000 HC, 10 x 500 ANM64, 4 x 250 GP. Primary target: Krefeld. Weather 10/10ths cloud above and below. Visibility poor. Bombed at 15.11 hours from 19,000 feet on G.H. Leader. Landed at Woodbridge.

15/01/1945 NN717 A2-E Bombing Lagendreer 11.44 x 15.23

Bomb load 1 x 4000 HC, 10 x 500 ANM64, 4 x 250 GP. Primary target: Lagendreer. Weather 10/10ths cloud. Landed at Manston with oil leak in both starboard engines and all Navigational aids unserviceable. Jettisoned 10 x 500 ANM64, 4 x 250 GP at 5120N 0248E at 14.33 hours. Brought 1 x 4000 HC back.

28/01/1945 NN717 A2-E Bombing Cologne 10.29 14.13 15.57

Bomb load 1 x 4000 HC, 10 x 500 ANM64, 2 x 500 GP, 3 x 250 GP. Primary target: Koln - Gremberg, Marshalling yards. Weather 10/10ths cloud en route clearing on approach to target where visibility was good and nil cloud. Bombed at 14.13 hours from 20,000 feet on G.H. Leader.

29/01/1945 PD334 A2-D Bombing Krefeld x x x

Failed to take off due to brake pressure unserviceable.

01/02/1945 NN717 A2-E Bombing Munchen-Gladbach 13.22 16.35

18.21

Bomb load 1 x 4000 HC, 14 x No 14 Clusters. Primary target: Munchen-Gladbach, Marshalling yards. Bombed at 16.35 hours from 18,700 feet on leading aircraft.

02/02/1945 NN717   A2-E   Bombing Wiesbaden 20.45 23.50 02.32

Bomb load 1 x 4000 HC, 12 x 500 GP, 4 x 250 GP. Primary target: Wiesbaden. Weather 10/10ths cloud, winds very erratic. Bombed at 23.50 hours from 20,000 feet on Gee fix.

Sgt. W.H. Mills F/Engineer and F/S. E.D. Dixon R/Gunner on that day.

16/02/1945 NG203   A2-C   Bombing Wesel   12.27 16.01 17.42

Bomb load 1 x 4000 HC, 4 x 500 GP, 2 x 500 MC L/Delay, 4 x 250 GP, 6 x 500 ANM64. Primary target: Wesel. Weather clear. Bombed at 16.01 hours from 19,000 feet on G.H. Bomb bay hit by flak over Wesel.

P/O. P.G. Dean 2nd Pilot, Sgt. W.H. Mills F/Engineer and F/S. E.D. Dixon R/Gunner that day.

18/02/1945 NG203   A2-C   Bombing Wesel   11.29 15.23 16.53

Bomb load 1 x 4000 HC, 4 x 500 GP, 2 x 500 MC L/Delay, 4 x 250 GP, 6 x 500 ANM64. Primary target: Wesel. Weather 10/10ths cloud. Bombed at 15.23 hours from 20,000 feet on G.H. Leader.

19/02/1945 NG203   A2-C   Bombing Wesel   12.53 16.36 18.33

Bomb load 1 x 4000 HC, 6 x 500 MC, 6 x 500 ANM64, 3 x 250 GP, 1 Skymarker Red puff. Primary target: Wesel. Weather over target 5-7/10ths cloud. Bombed at 16.36 hours from 19,000 feet on leading G.H. aircraft.

22/02/1945 PA186 A2-G   Bombing Osterfeld 12.09 16.00 17.44

Bomb load 1 x 4000 HC, 9 x 500 ANM64, 2 x 500 MC, 3 x 250 GP, 1 x 250 Blue Puff. Primary target: Osterfeld, Coking ovens. Weather at target clear, but hazy. Bombed at 16.00 hours from 19,500 feet on G.H. equipment.

05/03/1945 PD389 A2-J   Bombing Gelsenkirchen   10.31 14.07 15.59

Bomb load 1 x 4000 HC, 11 x 500 ANM64, 1 Skymarker Red Puff. Primary target: Gelsenkirchen, Benzol plant. Weather 10/10ths cloud over target with cirrus cloud at bombing height. Bombed at 14.07 hours from 21,000 feet on G.H.

07/03/1945 PB482 A2-K   Bombing Dessau   17.04 22.09 02.06

Bomb load 1 x 500 ANM64, 15 x No.14 Clusters. Primary target: Dessau. Weather 5 to 10/10ths thin cloud. Bombed at 22.09 hours from 20,000 feet on Red/Green flares.

17/03/1945 NG203   A2-C   Bombing August Viktoria 11.44   15.07
17.01

Bomb load 1 x 4000 HC, 13 x 500 ANM64, 2 x 500 MC, 1
Skymarker Blue Puff. Primary target: Auguste Viktoria, Marl-Hüls
coal mine. Weather 10/10ths cloud, tops and contrails up to 23,000
feet. Bombed at 15.07 hours from 21,500 feet on G.H. Leader.   1
Skymarker Blue Puff brought back to Base.

20/03/1945 PB482 A2-K   Bombing Hamm   09.47   13.14   15.31

Bomb load 7 x 1000 MC, 8 x 500 ANM64, 1 Skymarker Green
Puff. Primary target: Hamm, Marshalling yards. Weather 5/10ths
cloud. Bombed at 13.14 hours from 17,500 feet on G.H. Aircraft hit by
heavy flak.

23/03/1945 ME355   JI-L Bombing Wesel 14.28 17.38   19.39

Bomb load 13 x 1000 ANM59. Primary target: Wesel, in support of
ground troops. Weather perfect. Abortive sortie. Bombs failed to fall
on Navigator's release over target at 17.38 hours. 2 x 1000 ANM59
jettisoned at 5234N 0309E at 18.35 hours from 11,000 feet. 11 x 1000
ANM59 brought back to Base.

18/04/1945 RE123 A2-K   Bombing Heligoland 09.43   13.09   15.08

Bomb load 6 x 1000 MC, 10 x 500 ANM64. Primary target:
Heligoland, Naval base. Weather no cloud, slight haze. Bombed visual
on yellow T.I.s. in water at 13.09 hours from 18,200 ft. Smoke on
north edge of town. Whole Island covered with smoke. North shore
line covered with bomb craters.

29/04/1945 NN781   A2-B   Manna The Hague 11.32   13.53   15.10

Dropping area: The Hague. Weather broken cloud above and clear
below. Carried 5 packs. Dropped 4 packs at 13.53 & 13.55 hours. 1
pack hang up despite 2 runs over target. People gave great welcome.

02/05/1945 NN781   A2-B   Manna The Hague 11.04 12.21   13.23

Dropping area: The Hague. Weather over dropping zone clear below
cloud for the first arrivals changing later to heavy showers which
marred visibility. Dropped 5 panniers on Red T.I. and White Cross at
12.21 hours. Everything satisfactory.

04/05/1945 RE120 A2-C   Manna The Hague 12.09 13.28 14.37

Dropping area: The Hague. Dropped 5 panniers on Red T.I.s and
White Cross at 13.28 hours. Clear. Delivery perfect. Reception rather
more colourful - many flags and much enthusiasm.

LAC. Pollick was a passenger that day and no Mid Upper Gunner.

10/05/1945 ME230   A2-G   Exodus Juvincourt - Ford 11.12 x 17.31
      Duration 3.43. Outward 1.55 hours. Collected 24 ex POWs.
Homeward 1.48 hours. Delay occurred at Ford as aircraft parked
behind 2 other aircraft which became u/s.

12/05/1945 RE120 A2-C   Exodus   Juvincourt - Wing 09.06 x 13.43
      Duration 3.21. Outward 1.51 hours. Collected 24 POWs. Homeward
1.30 hours. Organisation good.

14/05/1945 RE120 A2-C   Exodus   Juvincourt - Oakley 10.05 x 15.43
      Duration 3 hours 23 minutes. Outward 1 hr 31 mins. Collected 24
POWs. Good organisation at both airfields.

17/05/1945 RE120 A2-C   Exodus   Brussels - Westcott 09.58 x 14.28
      Duration 2 hrs 56 mins. Out 1 hr 9½ mins. In 1 hr 46½ mins. 10
Belgian refugees taken out. 24 Ex POWs. Brought back. Reception at
Westcott perfect.

19/05/1945 RE120 A2-C   Exodus   Brussels - Oakley 11.56 x 19.01
      Duration 3 hrs 2½ mins. Out 1 hr 18 mins. In 1 hr 44½ mins. 10
Belgian refugees taken to Brussels. 24 ex POWs all military
evacuated.

23/05/1945 RE120 A2-C   Exodus   Brussels - Oakley 11.59 x 17.02
      Duration 2 hrs 45 mins. Out 1 hr 06 mins. In 1 hr 39 min. 10
Belgian refugees returned to Brussels. 24 ex POWs. evacuated. All
OK.

P/O.   Robert Hardwick, DFC

182006 (1490078) P/O. Robert Hardwick, DFC.   Pilot.
J29663   F/O. T.B. Searles, RCAF.   A/Bomber.
 Sgt. J.W. Whyke.   Navigator.
A414981   F/S. Jack Edward Archer, RAAF.   WOP/AG.
R207916   Sgt. E.H. Bradshaw, RCAF.   MU/Gunner.
R200528   Sgt. D.E. Holland, RCAF. R/Gunner.
 Sgt. C. Matthews.   F/Engineer.

24/06/1944 LL726 A2-H   Bombing Rimeux   23.33 00.37 02.24
      Bomb load 18 x 500 GP. Primary target: Rimeux, Flying bomb
installations. Weather clear. Bombed at 00.37 hours from 12,000 feet
centre of red T.I.s.

30/06/1944 DS787 A2-D   Bombing Villers Bocage 18.12 19.59 21.16

Bomb load 11 x 1000 MC, 3 x 500 GP. Primary target: Villers Bocage. Weather 10/10 high stratus. Bombed at 19.59 hours from 12,000 feet. As we left, others bombed and the target was a mass of smoke, and flame. More heavy flak than was expected especially as we left. A very good prang.

05/07/1944 LL692 A2-C Bombing Watten   22.53   00.08   01.02

Bomb load 11 x 1000 ANM65, 4 x 500 GP. Primary target: Watten, Constructional works. Bombed at 00.08 hours from 9,000 feet red T.I.s.

07/07/1944 LL670 A2-K Bombing Vaires   22.50   01.36   03.31

Bomb load 7 x 1000 MC, 4 x 500 GP. Primary target: Vaires, Marshalling yards. Weather clear. Bombed at 01.34 hours from 12,000 feet, green T.I.s. 2 large explosions with flames up to 4-5.000 feet at 01.36 hours. No Fighters.

10/07/1944 LL666 JI-Q Bombing Nucourt 04.20   06.04   07.51

Bomb load 11 x 1000 ANM65, 4 x 500 GP. Primary target: Nucourt, Constructional works. Bombed at 06.04 hours from 15,000 feet on Gee.

15/07/1944 DS842 A2-J   Bombing Chalons Sur Marne   21.48   01.33   04.17

Bomb load 18 x 500 GP. Primary target: Chalons sur Marne, Railway centre. Weather clear below. Bombed at 01.33 hours from 11,000 feet green T.I.s as instructed. A good concentrated attack.

18/07/1944 DS786 A2-F   Bombing Emieville 04.25   06.12   07.52

Bomb load 11 x 1000 MC, 4 x 500 GP. Primary target: Emieville, Troop concentration. Weather clear. Bombed at 06.12 hours from 9,000 feet yellow T.I.s. Numerous fires, splendid concentration of bombing.

28/07/1944 DS620 A2-D   Bombing Stuttgart 21.49 01.57 05.42

Bomb load 13 x 500 GP. Primary target: Stuttgart. Weather 9/10ths cloud. Bombed at 01.57 hours from 18,000 feet, centre of green T.I.s. per Master Bomber. Many large explosions seen. Glow of fires seen through cloud - appeared to be built up area. If Marking was accurate, the bombing was concentrated.

01/08/1944 DS620 A2-D   Bombing Foret de Nieppe 19.26 x 22.00

Bomb load 11 x 1000 MC, 4 x 500 GP. Target: De Nieppe, constructional works. Abandoned on Master Bomber's orders. Jettisoned at 21.22 hours from 11,500 feet 3 x 1000 MC, 1 x 500 GP, position 5216N 0237E.

03/08/1944 LL697 A2-B   Bombing Bois de Cassan 11.59   14.08

15.37

Bomb load 11 x 1000 MC, 4 x 500 GP. Primary target: Bois de Cassan, Flying bomb supply depot. Bombed at 14.08 hours from 16,000 feet, centre of smoke.

04/08/1944 DS620 A2-D Bombing Bec D'Ambes 13.21 18.00 21.20

Bomb load 5 x 1000 MC, 4 x 500 GP. Primary target: Bec d'Ambes depot. Weather 2/10ths cloud at 6,000 feet. Bombed at 18.00 hours from 8,100 feet. Smoke and oil seen on water. Best trip crew have had.

11/08/1944 DS620 A2-D Bombing Lens 14.15 16.34 17.43

Bomb load 11 x 1000 MC. 4 x 500 GP. Primary target: Lens, Marshalling yards. Weather 2/10ths cloud. Bombed at 16.34 hours from 15,000 feet yellow T.I.s. Bomb bursts seen well concentrated in target area.

15/08/1944 DS620 A2-D Bombing St. Trond 10.05 12.09 13.23

Bomb load 11 x 1000 MC, 4 x 500 GP. Primary target St. Trond Airfield. Weather clear. Bombed at 12.09 hours from 17,200 feet, red T.I.s. Very concentrated attack.

16/08/1944 DS620 A2-D Bombing Stettin 21.17 01.12 05.31

Bomb load 1 x 2000 HC, 9 x 500 lb 'J' type clusters. Primary target: Stettin. 4/10ths cloud up to 20,000 feet. Bombed at 01.12 hours from 15,800 feet, red T.I.s. T.I.s scattered. Bombing appeared concentrated on T.I.s.

18/08/1944 DS620 A2-D Bombing Bremen 21.45 00.18 03.05

Bomb load 1 x 2000 HC, 96 x 30 lb inc, 810 x 4lb inc, 90 x 4lb inc. Primary target: Bremen. Weather clear, slight haze. Bombed at 00.18 hours from 17,500 feet. Large square of fires and red T.I.s. 180 x 4 hung up, jettisoned 01.34 hours positioned 5412N 0430E. Good attack.

25/08/1944 DS620 A2-D Bombing Vincly 18.34½ 20.37 22.08

Bomb load 11 x 1000 MC, 2 x 500 GP MK IV, 2 x 500 GP MK IV LD. Primary target: Vincly. Weather: cloud clearing towards target. Bombed at 20.37 hours from 15,000 feet, visual of G.H. Leader.

26/08/1944 DS620 A2-D Bombing Kiel 20.17 x 01.43

Bomb load 1 x 4000 HC, 72 x 30 IB, 600 x 4 IB. Primary target: Kiel. Weather clear slight haze. Hung up of total load. Jettisoned 1 x 4000 HC at 5432N 0820E at 23.52 hours from 5,000 feet. Raid seemed good.

10/09/1944 LL731 JI-U Bombing Le Havre 16.16 17.38 19.05

Bomb load 11 x 1000 MC, 4 x 500 GP. Primary target: Le Havre. Weather clear. Bombed at 17.38 hours from 10,000 feet. Undershot

T.I.s red by 200 yards.

12/09/1944 DS786 A2-L Bombing Frankfurt 18.48 23.02 01.25

Bomb load 1 x 8000 HC, 1 x 500 Clusters 4lb. Target: Frankfurt - Main. Weather clear over the target. Bombed at 23.02 hours from 16,500 feet at centre of concentration of red and green T.I.s. Had combat with enemy aircraft.

17/09/1944 LL670 A2-D Bombing Boulogne 10.56 x 13.42

Bomb load 11 x 1000 MC, 4 x 500 GP. Primary target: Boulogne Aiming Point 2. Weather clear below cloud. At 12.15 hours order given by Master Bomber to abandon mission. Jettisoned 4 x 1000 MC, 2 x 500 GP, brought remainder back.

20/09/1944 LL670 A2-D Bombing Calais 14.58 16.08 17.24

Bomb load 11 x 1000 MC, 4 x 500 GP. Primary target: Calais. Weather clear over target. Bombed at 16.08 hours from 2,400 feet, red T.I.s.

25/09/1944 PD334 A2-D Bombing Pas de Calais 08.30 x 11.17

Bomb load 11 x 1000 MC, 4 x 500 GP. Primary target: Calais. Abandoned mission on Master Bomber's instructions. Jettisoned 3 x 1000 MC.

27/09/1944 LM734 A2-C Bombing Calais 07.38 08.51 10.20

Bomb load 11 x 1000 MC, 4 x 500 GP. Primary target: Calais 15. Weather, cloud 5,500 feet 10/10ths. Bombed at 08.51 hours from 5,500 feet on red T.I. + 1 second.

14/10/1944 PD334 A2-D Bombing Duisburg 07.02 09.04 11.06

Bomb load 11 x 1000 MC. 4 x 500 GP Long Delay. Primary target: Duisburg. Weather patchy cloud with gaps for bombing. Bombed at 09.04 hours from 19,000 feet. Green T.I. overshot 300 yards as instructed.

14/10/1944 PD334 A2-D Bombing Duisburg 22.55 01.28 03.45

Bomb load 11 x 1000 MC, 4 x 500 GP Long Delay. Primary target: Duisburg. Weather was clear with small amount of cloud over the target. Bombed at 01.28 hours from 20,000 feet. Green and red T.I.s.

F/O. John Herbert Gerard Harland

171813 (1553846) F/O. John Herbert Gerard "Johnnie" Harland.
Pilot.
Sgt. J. Talbot.   A/Bomber. 7 ops.
1586607 F/S. R.B.G. Scrase.   A/Bomber. 14 ops.
J2967 F/O. John Robert "Buck" Bennett, RCAF. A/Bomber. 6 ops.
NZ424402 P/O. Thomas Gordon Huie Adams, RNZAF. A/Bomber. 1
op.
1090796 F/S. Robert Irwin Gray.   Navigator.
1029427 W/O. Matthew Glyn George.   WOP/AG.
952787 Sgt. Stanley Douglas "Stan" Lucas. MU/Gunner. 21 ops.
Sgt. W.A. Dabbs.   MU/Gunner.   7 ops.
860307 Sgt. Leonard Slocombe.   R/Gunner.
1823505 Sgt. Robert McKinstray Paterson. F/Engineer.
146132 (1380396) F/O. Frederick Phineas Hendy, DFC. 2nd
Pilot. 04/11/44

L to R (back): S.D. Lucas, L. Slocombe, J.H.G. Harland, Unknown, M.G. George. L to R (front): Unknown, R.I. Gray. Inset: T.G.H. Adams. (crew photo courtesy Martin Runnacles)

Date Aircraft Duty Target Up Drop Down

01/08/1944 LL677 A2-E Bombing Foret de Nieppe 19.22 21.46 2.25

Bomb load 11 x 1000 MC, 4 x 500 GP. Primary target: De Nieppe, constructional works. Jettisoned at 20.55 hours from 10,000 feet 4 x 1000 MC, 4 x 500 GP at Position 5110N 0225E. Abandoned on Master Bomber's orders.

From his normal crew only F/O. J.H.G. Harland did the mission as 2nd pilot with F/L. B.K. McDonald's crew.

03/08/1944 DS786 A2-H Bombing Bois de Cassan 11.56 14.07 15.50

Bomb load 11 x 1000 MC, 4 x 500 GP. Primary target: Bois de Cassan, Flying bomb supply depot. Bombed at 14.07 hours from 15,300 feet, centre of smoke.

Sgt. J. Talbot A/Bomber from that day until 16/08/1944.

04/08/1944 LM277 JI-F Bombing Bec D'Ambes 13.21 18.01 21.20

Bomb load 8 x 1000 MC, 2 x 500 L/D. Primary target: Bec d'Ambes Depot. Weather clear. Bombed at 18.01 hours from 7,500 feet. Storage tanks at extreme tip of target. Large explosion seen during bombing. Starboard inner petrol gauge u/s. Very good attack.

05/08/1944 LL728 A2-L Bombing Bassen 14.29 19.01 22.24

Bomb load 5 x 1000 MC, 4 x 500 GP. Primary target: Bassen Oil Depot. Weather clear below 5,000 feet. Bombed at 19.01 hours from 4,000 feet visual of flat roofed building. Many bomb bursts mainly north of aiming point.

07/08/1944 LL728 A2-L Bombing Mare de Magne 21.50 23.41 01.13

Bomb load 9 x 1000 MC, 4 x 500 GP. Primary target: Mare de Magne (just past Caen). Weather clear. Bombed at 23.47 hours from 7,000 feet, port side of red T.I.s as instructed by Master Bomber. FW190 claimed and confirmed destroyed.

Mare-de-Magne: place between Caen and Fontenay le Marmion.

09/08/1944 LM286 A2-F Bombing Fort d'Englos 21.51 23.17 00.30

Bomb load 14 x 1000 MC. Primary target: Fort d'Englos (Lille), Petrol dump. Weather clear, bombed at 23.17 hours from 15,000 feet, undershot red T.I.s by two seconds, centre of fires. Two separate runs up had to be made owing to hang up. Bomb bursts concentrated over T.I.s.

The fort of Ennetières-en-Weppes, or "fort d'Englos" is one of a set of six forts surrounding Lille.

12/08/1944 DS787 A2-G Bombing Russelsheim 21.54 00.17 02.46
Bomb load 1 x 2000 HC, 12 x 500 No. 14 Clusters. Primary target: Russelsheim. Weather clear, bombed at 00.17 hours from 15,500 feet, centre of red T.I.s. Bombing appeared scattered. Result of attack - rather doubtful.

16/08/1944 DS787 A2-G Bombing Stettin 21.00 01.08 05.13
Bomb load 1 x 2000 HC, 9 x 500 lb 'J' type clusters. Primary target: Stettin. Broken cloud over target. Bombed at 01.08 hours from 19,000 feet, red T.I.s. Raid appeared scattered.

18/08/1944 DS787 A2-G Bombing Bremen 21.42 00.19 02.57
Bomb load 1 x 8000 HC, 40 x 30 inc, 350 x 4 inc, 40 x 4 inc. Primary target: Bremen. Weather clear, slight haze. Bombed at 00.19 hours from 19,000 feet, overshot of river, red T.I. One concentrated mass of flame. Good attack.

F/S. R.B.G. Scrase A/Bomber from that day until 23/10/1944.

26/08/1944 DS787 A2-G Bombing Kiel 20.13 23.13 01.56
Bomb load 1 x 8000 HC, 180 x 4 IB, 16 x 30 IB. Primary target: Kiel. Weather clear. Bombed at 23.13 hours from 19,000 feet red and green T.I.s. A very good attack.

31/08/1944 DS787 A2-G Bombing Pont-Remy 16.10 18.10 19.38
Bomb load 11 x 1000 MC, 2 x 500 GP Mk IV LD. Primary target: Pont Remy, Dump. Weather cloudy. Bombed at 18.10 hours from 15,000 feet on Leading aircraft.

06/09/1944 DS826 A2-C Bombing Le Havre 16.45 18.43 20.07
Bomb load 11 x 1000 MC, 4 x 500 GP. Primary target: Le Havre. Bombed at 18.43 hours from 7,000 feet, red T.I.s.

17/09/1944 DS786 A2-L Bombing Boulogne 10.25 11.45 12.50
Bomb load 11 x 1000 MC, 4 x 500 GP. Primary target: Boulogne Aiming Point 3. Weather clear below cloud. Bombed at 11.45 hours from 2,700 feet, red T.I.

23/09/1944 LM735 A2-G Bombing Neuss 19.29 21.36 23.34
Bomb load 11 x 1000 ANM59, 4 x 500 GP. Primary target: Neuss. Weather 10/10ths cloud over target, tops 8/10,000 feet. Bombed at 21.36 hours from 19,500 feet on centre of red glow.

26/09/1944 LM735 A2-G Bombing Calais 11.33 12.56 14.07
Bomb load 11 x 1000 MC, 4 x 500 GP. Primary target: Calais 7D. Weather clear below cloud which was 3,500 feet. Bombed at 12.56 hours from 3,000 feet on red T.I.

03/10/1944 LM735 A2-G Bombing Westkapelle 11.56 13.29

14.27

Bomb load 1 x 4000 MC, 6 x 1000 MC, 1 x 500 GP L/Delay. Primary target: Westkapelle (Walcheren). Weather patchy-scattered cloud with base 5000 feet. Bombed at 13.29 hours from 4,000 feet at sea wall between 2 lots of T.I. reds.

05/10/1944 LM735 A2-G Bombing Saarbrucken 17.18 x 23.00

Bomb load 11 x 1000 MC, 1 x 500 GP, 3 x 500 GP L/D. Primary target: Saarbrucken, Marshalling yards. Weather clear over target. Abandoned mission on instructions from Master Bomber heard to say they were unable to locate target and called "Abandon Mission - our troop in vicinity". 3 x 500 GP jettisoned 35 miles East of Southwold. Remainder brought back.

14/10/1944 PB423 A2-G Bombing Duisburg 07.00 09.04 11.03

Bomb load 11 x 1000 MC, 4 x 500 GP Long Delay. Primary target: Duisburg. Weather patchy cloud with gaps for bombing. Bombed at 09.04 hours from 18,000 feet. Northern edge of Docks.

14/10/1944 PB423 A2-G Bombing Duisburg 22.56 01.29 03.26

Bomb load 11 x 1000 MC, 4 x 500 GP Long Delay. Primary target: Duisburg. Weather was clear with small amount of cloud over the target. Bombed at 01.29 hours from 20,000 feet. Port of centre of Red T.I.s.

Sgt. W.A. Dabbs MU/Gunner from that sortie until 05/11/1944.

19/10/1944 PB423 A2-G Bombing Stuttgart 17.21 20.36 23.42

Bomb load 1 x 4000 HC, 3 x 500 Clusters, 7 x 150 x 4, 1 x 90 x 4 IB. Primary target: Stuttgart, A/P 'D' 1st attack. Weather 10/10ths cloud which broke to 6/10ths at the end of the period. Bombed at 20.36 hours from 16,000 feet. Centre of Red and Green T.I.s.

21/10/1944 NG142 A2-H Bombing Flushing 10.54 12.28 13.21

Bomb load 12 x 1000 MC, 2 x 500 GP. Primary target: Flushing 'B'. Weather clear. Bombed at 12.28 hours from 8,000 feet. Visual of A/P.

23/10/1944 PD324 A2-B Bombing Essen 16.39 19.38 21.53

Bomb load 1 x 4000 HC, 6 x 1000 MC, 6 x 500 GP. Primary target: Essen. Weather 10/10ths cloud over target - tops 12/14,000 feet with most appalling weather on route. Bombed at 19.38 hours from 18,500 feet. Green flares.

25/10/1944 PB423 A2-G Bombing Essen 13.20 15.41 17.05

Bomb load 1 x 4000 HC, 6 x 1000 MC, 6 x 500 GP. Primary target: Essen. Weather over target 10/10ths low cloud, with one clear patch which appeared to fill up later in the attack. Bombed at 15.41 hours from 22,000 feet. Red flares as instructed by the Master Bomber.

F/O. J.R. Bennett, RCAF A/Bomber from that day until 16/11/1944 (with uncertainty for 04 & 08/11/1944 owing to incoherency in ORBs - F/O. J.R. Bennett being noted at the same time in both Harland's and Crome's crews).

04/11/1944 PD325 A2-L Bombing Solingen 11.38 14.12 15.57
 Bomb load 1 x 4000 HC, 6 x 1000 ANM59, 4 x 500 GP, 2 x 500 MC (L/Delay). Primary target: Solingen. Weather 8-10/10ths cloud. Bombed at 14.12 hours from 19,500 feet on A/P visually.
 F/O. F.P. Hendy 2nd Pilot that day.

05/11/1944 PD325 A2-L Bombing Solingen 10.14 13.02 14.40
 Bomb load 1 x 4000 HC, 6 x 1000 ANM59, 4 x 500 GP, 2 x 500 GP (L/Delay). Primary target: Solingen. Weather 10/10ths cloud over target. Bombed at 13.02 hours from 18,500 feet on leading aircraft.

08/11/1944 PD333 A2-K Bombing Homberg 07.57 10.32 12.15
 Bomb load 1 x 4000 HC, 6 x 1000 GP, 6 x 500 GP. Primary target: Homberg. Weather clear. Bombed at 10.32 hours from 18,000 feet on leading aircraft. Aircraft damaged by flak.
 Sgt. S.D. Lucas MU/Gunner from that day.

15/11/1944 PD333 A2-K Bombing Dortmund 12.22 15.41 17.14
 Bomb load 1 x 4000 HC, 16 x 500 GP. Primary target: Hoesch-Benzin Dortmund, Oil refineries. Weather 10/10ths cloud over the target. Bombed at 15.41 hours from 17,000 feet on flares.

16/11/1944 LM286 A2-F Bombing Heinsburg 13.05 15.34 17.12
 Bomb load 1 x 4000 HC, 6 x 1000 MC, 6 x 500 GP. Primary target: Heinsburg. Weather - nil cloud with slight haze over target. Bombed at 15.34 hours from 8,500 feet. Church.

20/11/1944 LM286 A2-F Bombing Homburg 12.35 x x
 Bomb load 1 x 4000 HC, 16 x 500 GP. Primary target: Homberg. Weather 10/10ths cloud over target. Aircraft missing.
 Aircraft crashed in the target area, possibly as a result of being struck by "friendly" bombs from above. There is an uncorroborated suggestion that the aircraft exploded over the target (probably as mentioned by F/L. Currie who reported "Damage to fuselage due to aircraft exploding").
 P/O. T.G.H. Adams A/Bomber that day.
The crew were all KIA.
 F/O. John Herbert Gerard Harland.   Pilot.
 P/O. Thomas Gordon Huie Adams, RNZAF.   A/Bomber.
 F/S. Robert Irwin Gray.   Navigator.
 W/O. Matthew Glyn George.   WOP/AG.

Sgt. Stanley Douglas "Stan" Lucas.   MU/Gunner.
Sgt. Leonard Slocombe.   R/Gunner.
Sgt. Robert McKinstray Paterson. F/Engineer.
They are buried in the Reichswald Forest War Cemetery. Sgt. Slocombe was a member of the pre-war auxiliary Air Force.

P/O. John Douglas Harrison

54541 (569023) P/O.John Douglas Harrison. Pilot.
J87621 (R165242)F/S. Roy Nixon Kirkpatrick, RCAF. A/Bomber.
1451051   F/S. Edward Wilde.   Navigator.
1610167   Sgt. Frederick Desmond Nash.   WOP/AG.
1804303   Sgt. Richard Jack "Andy" Woosnam. MU/Gunner. 5 ops
1893040   Sgt. Lewis Harold David Warren. MU/Gunner. 1 op
1544912   Sgt. William Wilson. MU/Gunner. 4 ops
1891917   Sgt. Anthony George Buttling.   R/Gunner.
1801492   Sgt. Ronald William Norris. F/Engineer.

24/02/1944 LL670 A2-K Bombing
Schweinfurt 20.53 01.15 04.54
Bomb load 1 x 4000 lb bomb, 24 x 30, 420 x 4, 90 x 4 incendiaries. Primary target: Schweinfurt. Weather clear, visibility good. Bombed at 01.15 hours at 20,000 ft. Mass of fires, heavy pall of smoke rising to 10,000 ft. Monica u/s. halfway to target. Target burning fiercely on arrival. If the marking was accurate Schweinfurt has 'had it'. Route trouble before.
Sgt. R.J. Woosnam MU/Gunner that day.

Roy Nixon Kirkpatrick

01/03/1944 LL691 A2-D Bombing
Stuttgart 23.43 03.15 06.59
Bomb load 1 x 8000 lb bomb. Primary target: Stuttgart. There was 10/10 cloud with one or two breaks. Bombed at 03.15 hours at 21,000 ft. Pilot's Repeater u/s after leaving Stuttgart. Fires could be seen over

100 miles away on leaving. If markers were 'On' the bombing was.

Sgt. R.J. Woosnam MU/Gunner that day.

07/03/1944 LL677 A2-E Bombing Le Mans 19.51 21.50 00.04

Bomb load 10 x 1000, 4 x 500 lb bombs. There was 10/10 cloud. No attack. All bombs brought back to Base. Over target at 21.50 hours at 9,000 feet. Aircraft in stream seen outward and homeward. Red glare seen some distance from target also red and green tracer. Nothing to be seen over target.

Sgt. L.H.D. Warren MU/Gunner that day.

15/03/1944 LL669 JI-K Bombing Stuttgart 19.34 23.30 03.19

Bomb load 1 x 1000 lb bomb, 72 x 30, 1050 x 4, 90 x 4 incendiaries. Primary target: Stuttgart. There was 9/10 cloud. Bombed at 23.30 hours from 20,000 feet. Scattered fires seen burning orange. Route satisfactory. Fires seemed to be in two main groups. Aircraft late due to fighter attack, so made second run up. Did not see a concentrated effort.

Sgt. W. Wilson MU/Gunner that day.

22/03/1944 LL696 JI-A Bombing Frankfurt 18.35 21.56 00.29

Bomb load 1 x 1000 lb bomb, 64 x 30, 1161 x 4, 129 x 4 incendiaries. Primary target: Frankfurt. There was thin cloud. Bombed at 21.56 hours from 20,000 feet. Good concentration of fires seen. Should be a good show. Route OK. except that other aircraft jettisoned incendiaries after leaving target.

Sgt. R.J. Woosnam MU/Gunner that day.

24/03/1944 LL696 JI-A Bombing Berlin 18.30 x 02.19

Bomb load 1 x 1000 lb bomb, 88 x 30, 810 x4, 90 x 4 incendiaries. Coned by searchlights and Monica reacting constantly. Did not reach target, red and green T.I.s seen in target area but from a distance of approx. 100 miles SW. Uncertain at all time of exact position. First fix gave position as over Jersey. Crossed Southern end of Cherbourg Peninsular then to English coast, landed at Ford, shortage of petrol.

Sgt. R.J. Woosnam MU/Gunner that day.

26/03/1944 LL696 JI-A Bombing Essen 20.02 22.12 00.53

Bomb load 1 x 2000 lb bomb, 56 x 30, 1080 x 4, 120 x 4 incendiaries. Primary target: Essen. There was 8/10 cloud. Bombed at 22.12 hours from 18,000 feet. Cloud prevented visual. Uneventful trip. Flak moderate, mostly L.F. which did not come above the cloud. Large red glow seen on leaving.

Sgt. W. Wilson MU/Gunner that day.

30/03/1944 DS669 JI-C Bombing Nuremburg 22.10 x 00.06

Bomb load 1 x 8000 lb bomb, 90 x 4 incendiaries. Returned early. Farthest point reached 5207N 0240E. Bomb jettisoned safe. Oxygen u/s M.U. Turret. Mid Upper Gunner passed out at 17,000 feet.

Sgt. R.J. Woosnam MU/Gunner that day.

20/04/1944 DS669 JI-C Bombing Cologne   00.03 02.13 04.02

Bomb load 1 x 1000 lb bomb, 1026 x 4, 114 x 4, 108 x 30 lb incendiaries. Primary target: Cologne. There was 10/10 cloud over target. Bombed at 02.12 hours from 20,000 feet. Red flares only visible, nothing else seen. Owing to density of cloud nothing seen. P.F.F. were late, what flares were visible were concentrated. We orbited for minutes awaiting flares.

Sgt. W. Wilson MU/Gunner that day.

22/04/1944 DS669 JI-C Bombing Dusseldorf 23.16 x x

Bomb load 1 x 8000 lb bomb, 48 x 30, 486 x 4, 54 x 4 incendiaries. Aircraft missing. Believed hit by Flak, or may have collided with another Squadron Lancaster DS828, crashing 23/04/1944 in the target area at Ecke Rethel and Schubert-Strasse.

Sgt. W. Wilson MU/Gunner that day.

All crew KIA. Funerals were held 25th April and 26th April in the Nordfriedhof. Six of the crew have subsequently been re-interred in the Reichswald Forest War Cemetery. Sgt. Nash is commemorated on Panel 235 of the Runnymede Memorial.

P/O. Ronald Richard Harvey

172307 (1181161) P/O. Ronald Richard Harvey. Pilot.
1575361   F/S. J. Eley.   A/Bomber.
134705 (1324447) F/O. John Bruce Jarvis. Navigator.
1284583   F/S. P.J. Edwards. WOP/AG.
1439002   Sgt. D.F. Acaster.   MU/Gunner.
R174733   F/S. E.D. Reid.   R/Gunner.
1802938   Sgt. E.J. McIntyre. F/Engineer.

22/03/1944 LL677 A2-E Bombing Frankfurt 18.47 21.53 00.39

Bomb load 1 x 1000 lb bomb, 64 x 30, 1161 x 4, 129 x 4 incendiaries. Primary target: Frankfurt. There was 3/10 cloud over the target. Bombed at 21.53 hours from 20,000 feet. A few incendiary fires burning. Route quiet, attack seemed to be going well.

26/03/1944 LL670 A2-K Bombing Essen [2] 20.17 22.07 00.50

Bomb load 1 x 2000 lb bomb, 56 x 30, 1080 x 4, 120 x 4 incendiaries. Primary target: Essen. There was 10/10 cloud. Bombed at 22.07 hours from 20,000 feet. Glow of T.I.s seen through cloud. Little to be seen. Moderate heavy flak.

26/04/1944 DS795 A2-J Bombing Essen 23.02 01.41 03.36

Bomb load 1 x 2000 lb bomb, 84 x 30, 945 x 4, 105 x 4 lb incendiaries. Primary target: Essen. There was no cloud but plenty of smoke. Bombed at 01.41 hours from 19,500 feet. One large fire seen. Successful attack. Route OK. 1 red T.I. believed 20 miles West.

27/04/1944 DS795 A2-J Bombing Friedrichshafen 23.02 02.15 03.36

Bomb load 810 x 4, 80 x 30 lb incendiaries. Primary target: Friedrichshafen. Weather was clear with slight haze. Bombed at 02.15 hours from 19,000 feet. Target area well alight, fires very concentrated. Quiet route. A good attack.

01/05/1944 DS795 A2-J Bombing Chambly 22.54 00.31 02.09

Bomb load 10 x 1000, 5 x 500 lb bombs. Primary target: Chambly. Weather was clear. Bombed at 00.31 hours from 7,500 feet. Small red fires seen burning in target area. Good effort. T.I.s were over the target area. Route good.

07/05/1944 DS795 A2-J Bombing Nantes 00.26 03.02 05.44

Bomb load 1 x 4000, 14 x 500 lb. bombs. Primary target: Nantes. Weather was clear. Bombed at 03.02 hours from 9,500 feet. Large explosion seen at 03.14 hours on leaving target. Raid successful and route good.

09/05/1944 DS795 A2-J Bombing Cap Gris Nez 03.10 04.07 04.55

Bomb load 1 x 1000 GP, 13 x 1000 MC. Primary target: Cape Gris Nez. Skies were clean and a visual of coastline and red T.I.s were obtained. Bombed at 04.07 hours from 7,000 feet in position slightly to left of red T.I. on the instructions of Master Bomber. Bombs appeared to burst in concentration around red T.I. Area well lit up and Master Bomber's instructions helpful. Photo attempted.

10/05/1944 DS795 A2-J Bombing Courtrai 22.15 23.28 00.40

Bomb load 7 x 1000 GP, 7 x 1000 MC. Primary target: Courtrai. Thick haze over target but marker flares visible. Bombed as instructed by Master Bomber at 23.28 hours from 10,000 feet. Flares quite concentrated but no visual of target possible. Bombing appeared to be around markers. One fairly large fire seen on leaving target.

19/05/1944 DS795 A2-J   Bombing Le Mans   22.25 00.27 02.50

Bomb load 4 x 1000 USA, 5 x 1000 MC, 1 x 1000 GP, 4 x 500 GP. Primary target: Le Mans. 6/10 cloud over target. Bombed at 00.27 hours from 8,000 feet. Master Bomber's instructions spoiled by too much interference from the aircraft calling up. Several large explosions seen whilst at target but unable to assess value of attack.

21/05/1944 DS795 A2-J   Bombing Duisburg   22.55 01.16 02.40

Bomb load 1 x 2000 lb bomb, 120 x 30, 600 x 4 incendiaries. Primary target: Duisberg. There was 10/10 cloud at target. Bombed red T.I. at 01.16 hours from 20,000 feet. Cloud prevented visual. Many fighters thought to be on route home over the sea.

27/05/1944 DS795 A2-J or LL727 A2-C

Bombing Aachen   00.40 02.28 04.00

Bomb load 7 x 1000 MC, 4 x 1000 ANM, 4 x 500 MC. Primary target: Aachen. Slight ground haze. Bombed centre of markers at 02.28 hours from 12,000 feet. Bomb bursts seen amongst T.I.s. Could not climb above 15,000 feet so jettisoned 4 x 1000 MC safe at 5147N 0407E at 01.54 hours. Gained height after this. At 02.26 hours evaded a fighter and carried on with bombing run. Both Mid-upper and Rear gunners fired a burst but made no claim. Another unidentified aircraft sighted at 03.05 hours and took evasive action.

Note: ORBs indicates DS795 A2-J, but according to combat report signed Captain P/O. Harvey the aircraft would be LL727 A2-C.

28/05/1944 DS795 A2-J   Bombing Angers   18.55 23.58 02.20

Bomb load 5 x 1000 MC, 1 x 1000 USA, 4 x 500 MC. Primary target: Angers. Clear at target. Bombed at 23.58 hours from 9,000 feet. Visual of river obtained. Successful attack and route O.K.

10/06/1944 DS795 A2-J   Bombing Dreux   23.14 00.58 03.30

Bomb load 16 x 500 GP, 2 x 500 LD. Primary target: Dreux. Bombed as instructed by Master Bomber at 00.58 hours from 7,000 feet. Bomb burst amongst T.I.s with much smoke. Lancaster damaged by fighter.

11/06/1944 LL677 A2-E   Bombing Nantes x x x

Bomb load 16 x 500 GP. 2 x 500 LD. Failed to take off.

17/06/1944 LL692 A2-C   Bombing Montdidier   01.14 02.58 04.43

Bomb load 16 x 500 GP, 2 x 500 ANM64 GP. Primary target: Montdidier. Bombed at 02.58 hours from 9,000 feet on red glow of T.I.s 10/10ths cloud marred vision. Master Bomber heard only faintly.

21/06/1944 LL692 A2-C   Bombing Domleger 18.02 x 20.38

Bomb load 18 x 500 MC. Primary target: Domleger near Abbeville,

V-1 flying bomb launch site. There was 10/10ths cloud. No markers seen obeyed Master Bomber's instructions to return to Base. Jettisoned safe at 19.45 hours from 12,000 feet at 5025N 0120E.

23/06/1944 LL728 A2-L Bombing L'Hey   23.09 00.18 01.38

Bomb load 11 x 1000 MC, 4 x 500 GP. Primary target: L'Hey, Flying bomb installations. There was 10/10ths cloud. Bombed at 00.18 hours from 9,000 feet on glow of red T.I.s. T.I.s well maintained and concentrated.

30/06/1944 DS842 A2-J   Bombing Villers Bocage 18.13 20.01 21.09

Bomb load 11 x 1000 MC, 3 x 500 GP. Primary target: Villers Bocage. Weather 3/10ths cloud at 9,000 feet. Bombed at 20.01 hours from 12,000 feet centre of smoke which completely covered village. Concentration very good.

02/07/1944 DS842 A2-J   Bombing Beauvoir   12.58 14.37 16.04

Bomb load 11 x 1000 MC, 4 x 500 GP. Primary target: Beauvoir, Flying bomb supply site. Bombed at 14.37 hours from 12,000 feet on yellow T.I.s.

05/07/1944 DS842 A2-J   Bombing Watten   22.56½ 00.08 01.14

Bomb load 11 x 1000 ANM65, 4 x 500 GP. Primary target: Watten, Constructional works. Bombed at 00.08 hours from 8,000 feet red T.I.s.

07/07/1944 DS842 A2-J   Bombing Vaires   22.51 01.31 03.16

Bomb load 7 x 1000 MC, 4 x 500 GP. Primary target: Vaires, Marshalling yards. Weather clear. Bombed at 01.31 hours from 12,000 feet red and green T.I.s coinciding with visual. Several explosions seen from considerable distance. Good raid. Fighters foxed.

10/07/1944 DS842 A2-J   Bombing Nucourt 04.34 06.03 07.34

Bomb load 11 x 1000 ANM65, 4 x 500 GP. Primary target: Nucourt, Constructional works. Bombed at 06.03 hours from 15,500 feet on Gee.

12/07/1944 DS842 A2-J   Bombing Vaires   18.03 x 21.42

Bomb load 18 x 500 GP. Primary target: Vaires, Marshalling yards. Abandoned mission as instructed by Master Bomber. Jettisoned 4 x 500 GP at 20.41 hours from 12,500 feet, position 4953N 0037E.

23/07/1944 LL692 A2-C   Bombing Kiel   22.37 01.20 03.54

Bomb load 6 x 1000 MC, 10 x 500 GP. Primary target: Kiel, Warehouses and docks. Weather 10/10ths low thin cloud. Bombed at 01.20 hours from 19,000 feet red T.I. Jettisoned 4 x 500 GP at 00.59 hours from 17,000 feet, position Arnrurn Island as aircraft could not climb. Sky markers scattered.

24/07/1944 LL692 A2-C Bombing Stuttgart 21.51 x 23.52

Bomb load 5 x 1000 ANM65, 3 x 500 GP. Returned early. Rear gunner sick. Jettisoned at 5217N 0231E.

25/07/1944 DS786 A2-H Bombing Stuttgart 21.52 x 01.40

Bomb load 5 x 1000 MC, 3 x 500 GP. Abortive sortie, jettisoned at 00.57 hours safe 40 miles east of Southwold from 4,000 feet. Port inner caught fire - rapid drop in oil pressure.

27/07/1944 LL716 A2-G Bombing Les Catelliers 16.52 18.52 20.05

Bomb load 18 x 500 GP. Primary target: Les Catelliers, Flying bomb site. Bombed at 18.52 hours from 16,000 feet on Mosquito.

30/07/1944 LL716 A2-G Bombing Caen 06.10 07.51 09.06

Bomb load 18 x 500 GP. Primary target: Caen 'B'. Weather cloud base 1500 feet. Bombed at 07.51 hours from 1,800 feet, smoke of red T.I.s as instructed.

01/08/1944 DS842 A2-J Bombing Foret de Nieppe 19.24 20.45 21.37

Bomb load 11 x 1000 MC, 4 x 500 GP. Primary target: De Nieppe, constructional works. Bombed at 20.45 hours from 11,500 feet on leading aircraft.

F/O. Brian Haslam DFC

175191 (1055448) F/O. Brian Haslam, DFC.   Pilot.

R197691   F/S. Kingsley F. Harris, RCAF.   A/Bomber.

153454 (1622730) F/O. Raymond Eric "Ray" Hemmings, DFC.
    Navigator.

    F/S. J.G. Wilcox.   WOP/AG. 28 ops.

Sgt. W.H.E. Gray.   WOP/AG.   1 op.

Sgt. H. Marshall.   MU/Gunner.

R182992   Sgt. A. "Red" Page, RCAF.   R/Gunner.

Sgt. Douglas F. Locke.   F/Engineer.

18/08/1944 PB419 JI-N Bombing Bremen 21.30 00.15 02.50

Bomb load 1 x 4000 HC, 96 x 30 lb inc, 1080 x 4 lb inc, 120 x 4 lb inc. Primary target: Bremen. Weather clear over target. Bombed at 00.15 hours from 19,000 feet, red T.I.s. Bombing appeared very concentrated, many fires seen.

31/08/1944 LM685 JI-Q Bombing Pont-Remy 16.03 18.07 19.41

F/O. Brian Haslam DFC

Bomb load 11 x 1000 MC, 4 x 500 GP Mk IV LD. Primary target: Pont Remy, Dump. Weather cloudy. Bombed at 18.07 hours from 15,200 feet on Gee H Leading aircraft.

12/09/1944 PB419 JI-N Bombing Frankfurt 18.28 23.02 01.18

Bomb load 1 x 4000 HC, 14 x 500 Clusters 4lb. Target: Frankfurt - Main. Weather clear over the target. Bombed at 23.02 hours from 18,000 feet on centre of red and green T.I.s.

17/09/1944 LM717 JI-T Bombing Boulogne 10.53 x 13.43

Bomb load 11 x 1000 MC, 4 x 500 GP. Primary target: Boulogne Aiming Point 2. Weather clear below cloud. At 12.15 hours order given by Master Bomber to abandon mission. Jettisoned 2 x 1000 MC, brought remainder back.

20/09/1944 LM717 JI-T Bombing Calais 14.38 16.02 17.27

Bomb load 11 x 1000 MC, 4 x 500 GP. Primary target: Calais. Weather clear over target. Bombed at 16.02 hours from 3,000 feet, red T.I.s.

05/10/1944 LM717 JI-T Bombing Saarbrucken 17.05 x 22.33

Bomb load 11 x 1000 MC, 1 x 500 GP, 3 x 500 GP. Long Delay. Primary target: Saarbrucken, Marshalling yards. Weather clear over target. On arrival at 20.32 hours saw white flares going down. Made one orbit during which Green T.I. went down and abandoned mission on instructions from Master Bomber heard to say they were unable to locate target and called "Abandon Mission - our troop in vicinity". Jettisoned 3 x 500 Long Delay at 22.02 hours from 8,000 feet position 5157N 0218E.

06/10/1944 LM717 JI-T Bombing Dortmund 16.36 20.30 22.31

Bomb load 1 x 4000 HC. 12 x No. 14 Clusters. Primary target: Dortmund, Town and Railways. Weather over the target was clear with slight ground haze. Bombed at 20.30 hours from 19,000 feet on green T.I.s.

14/10/1944 LM717   JI-T Bombing Duisburg   07.06 09.06 11.23

Bomb load 11 x 1000 MC. 4 x 500 GP Long Delay. Primary target: Duisburg. Weather patchy cloud with gaps for bombing. Bombed at 09.06 hours from 18,000 feet. North of Docks.

15/10/1944 ME841   JI-Y Bombing Wilhelmshaven 17.14   19.53 21.55

Bomb load 11 x 1000 MC, 4 x 500 GP. Primary target: Wilhelmshaven. Weather haze and thin cloud at first with thick cloud later. Bombed at 19.53 hours from 18,500 feet. Glow of green T.I.s.

18/10/1944 LM717   JI-T Bombing Bonn   08.16 11.02 13.07

Bomb load 1 x 4000 HC. 5 x 12 x 30 - 2 x 12 x 30 modified, 9 x No.14 Clusters. Primary target: Bonn. Weather varying cloud 2-7/10ths with break for bombing. Bombed at 11.02 hours from 17,000 feet on G.H. Bombs believed fallen North part of town.

19/10/1944 LM717   JI-T Bombing Stuttgart   21.54 01.05 03.50

Bomb load 1 x 4000 HC, 3 x 500 Clusters, 7 x 150 x 4, 1 x 90 x 4. Primary target: Stuttgart, A/P 'E' 2nd attack. Weather 10/10ths low cloud over target and all crew arrived late owing to winds not as forecast. Bombed at 01.05 hours from 19,000 feet. Red and Yellow markers.

21/10/1944 LM717   JI-T Bombing Flushing   11.00 12.28 13.43

Bomb load 12 x 1000 MC, 2 x 500 GP. Primary target: Flushing 'B'. Weather clear. Bombed at 12.28 hours from 8,500 feet. Target area along Jetty.

23/10/1944 LM717   JI-T Bombing Essen   16.26 19.39 22.07

Bomb load 1 x 4000 HC, 2 x 1000 MC, 10 x 500 GP, 3 x 500 MC. Primary target: Essen. Weather 10/10ths cloud over target - tops 12/14,000 feet with most appalling weather on route. Bombed at 19.39 hours from 19,700 feet between 2 Green Wanganui flares.

25/10/1944 LM717   JI-T Bombing Essen   13.10 15.42 17.25

Bomb load 1 x 4000 HC, 6 x 1000 MC, 6 x 500 GP. Primary target: Essen. Weather over target 10/10ths low cloud, with one clear patch which appeared to fill up later in the attack. Bombed at 15.42 hours from 21,500 feet. Group of red markers.

28/10/1944 LM717   JI-T Bombing Cologne   13.10 15.47 17.46

Bomb load 1 x 4000 HC, 8 x 150 x 4. Primary target: Cologne. Weather clear over target. Bombed at 15.47 hours from 19,500 feet. A/P coinciding with position of bridge. Red T.I. slightly to East of A/P.

30/10/1944 LM717   JI-T Bombing Wesseling 09.01   12.03   13.42
Bomb load 1 x 4000 HC, 15 x 500 GP. Primary target: Wesseling.
Weather was 10/10ths cloud - tops about 7,000 feet. Bombed at 12.03
hours from 16,000 feet on G.H.

31/10/1944 LM717   JI-T Bombing Bottrop   11.46   15.02   16.36
Bomb load 1 x 4000 HC, 15 x 500 GP, 1 Flare. Primary target:
Bottrop, Synth. Oil plants. Weather 10/10ths cloud over target.
Bombed at 15.02 hours from 18,000 feet on G.H.

04/11/1944 LM717   JI-T Bombing Solingen   11.17   14.09   15.58
Bomb load 1 x 4000 HC, 6 x 1000 ANM59, 4 x 500 GP, 2 x 500
MC (L/Delay), 3 Flares. Primary target: Solingen. Weather 8-10/10ths
cloud. Bombed at 14.09 hours from 19,500 feet on G.H.

05/11/1944 LM717   JI-T Bombing Solingen   10.17   13.07   15.06
Bomb load 1 x 4000 HC, 6 x 1000 ANM59, 4 x 500 GP, 2 x 500 GP
(L/Delay), 3 Flares. Primary target: Solingen. Weather 10/10ths cloud
over target. Bombed at 13.07 hours from 17,000 feet on instruments.

08/11/1944 LM717   JI-T Bombing Homberg   08.02   10.30   12.22
Bomb load 1 x 4000 HC, 6 x 1000 GP, 6 x 500 GP. Primary target:
Homberg. Weather clear. Bombed at 10.30 hours from 18,000 feet on
instruments.

20/11/1944 NF968 JI-L Bombing Homberg   12.46   15.15   17.02
Bomb load 1 x 4000 HC, 15 x 500 GP, 1 Red - Green Flare. Primary
target: Homberg. Weather 10/10ths cloud over target. Bombed at 15.15
hours from 21,000 feet on leading G.H. aircraft.

21/11/1944 PB423 A2-G Bombing Homberg 12.34 15.09 17.04
Bomb load 1 x 4000 HC, 15 x 500 GP, 1 Red - Green Flare. Primary
target: Homberg. Weather about 5/10ths cloud but clear for bombing.
Bombed at 15.09 hours from 20,000 feet on centre of target area.

23/11/1944 PB482 JI-P Bombing Nordstern   12.32   15.19   17.14
Bomb load 1 x 4000 HC, 15 x 500 GP, 1 Red flare with Green stars.
Primary target: Nordstern, Gelsenkirchen Oil refineries. Weather
10/10ths cloud. Bombed at 15.19 hours from 20,000 feet on G.H.

29/11/1944 LM728   JI-T Bombing Neuss   02.46 05.35   07.16
Bomb load 1 x 4000 HC, 6 x 1000 MC, 6 x 500 GP, 3 Flares Red
with Green stars. Primary target: Neuss. Weather 10/10ths cloud over
target but the glow of fires was seen through cloud. Bombed at 05.35
hours from 19,000 feet. Red flares. A successful trip. G.H.
unserviceable.

04/12/1944 LM728   JI-T Bombing Oberhausen 11.44 14.09   16.05
Bomb load 1 x 4000 HC, 15 x 500 GP, 1 Flare. Primary target:

Oberhausen, Built up area. Weather 10/10ths cloud. Bombed at 14.09 hours from 20,000 feet on Flares.

05/12/1944 LM728 JI-T Bombing Hamm 09.10 11.29 13.49
Bomb load 1 x 4000 HC, 13 x 500 GP, 2 x 500 GP Long Delay, 1 Flare. Primary target: Hamm. Weather 10/10ths cloud over target, but otherwise varying from 6-10/10ths. Bombed at 11.29 hours from 20,000 feet on G.H.

06/12/1944 LM728 JI-T Bombing Merseburg 17.14 x 19.59
Bomb load 1 x 4000 HC, 8 x 500 GP and 1 x 500 GP Long Delay. Primary target: Merseburg. Weather 10/10ths cloud with odd breaks. Returned early with Mid upper turret unserviceable. Jettisoned load safe at 18.51 hours from 4,000 feet at 5220N 0240E.

08/12/1944 LM728 JI-T Bombing Duisburg 08.33 11.04 13.03
Bomb load 13 x 1000 ANM59, 1 Red/Green flare. Primary target: Duisberg. Weather 10/10ths cloud. Bombed at 11.04 hours from 20,000 feet on G.H.

11/12/1944 LM728 JI-T Bombing Osterfeld 08.34 11.06 13.10
Bomb load 13 x 1000 ANM65, 1 x Flare. Primary target: Osterfeld. Weather 10/10ths cloud, tops 16,000 feet. Bombed at 11.06 hours from 20,000 feet on G.H.

Sgt. W.H.E. Gray WOP/AG that day.

F/O. acting F/L.Ian Charles Scott Hay, DFC

151536 (1553675) F/L. Ian Charles Scott Hay, DFC. Pilot.
1396973 F/S. S.H.W. Bryant. A/Bomber.
151336 (992963) F/O. Hamish Cran MacLennan, DFC. Navigator.
183620 (1578694) F/S. Rupert William Morris. WOP/AG.
1803047 Sgt. W.E. Baldwin. MU/Gunner.
1592002 Sgt. W.H. Tate. R/Gunner.
1286251 Sgt. D.W. Farley. F/Engineer.

15/02/1944 LL645 A2-H Bombing Berlin 17.37 21.31 00.48
Bomb load 1 x 2000, 1 x 1000 lb bomb, 24 x 30, 900 x 4 incendiaries. Primary target: Berlin. There was 10/10 cloud. Bombed at 21.31 hrs. At 20,000 ft. Only sky markers seen and those rather scattered. Dull glow of fires seen through cloud with occasional flashes of small explosions. Not many fighters about.

L to R (back): 2nd Ian Charles Scott Hay. L to R (front): 1st Rupert W. Morris.

(courtesy Bob Morris)

19/02/1944 LL645 A2-H Bombing Leipzig 00.05 04.03 06.55
   Bomb load 1 x 2000, 1 x 500 lb bomb, 40 x 30, 900 x 4
incendiaries. Primary target: Leipzig. There was 6/10 cloud. Bombed
at 04.03 hours at 20,000 ft. Saw dull red glow beneath cloud in
circular shape. Smoke rising to approx. 9,000 ft. Very good
concentration of A/C over target. Markers appeared effectively
clustered.

21/02/1944 LL645 A2-H Bombing Stuttgart 00.35 04.04 06.41
   Bomb load 1 x 4000 lb bomb, 690 x 4, 90 x 4 incendiaries. Primary
target: Stuttgart. There was 9/10 cloud as we bombed - after - clear.
Bombed at 04.04 hours at 19,000 ft, 90 x 4 inc, not connected. Good
concentration of T.I.s but cloud prevented visual of area bombed
afterwards. Glow was turning red as we left.

24/02/1944 LL645 A2-H Bombing Schweinfurt 18.45 23.10 02.07
   Bomb load 1 x 8000 lb bomb. Primary target: Schweinfurt. Weather
clear no cloud. Bombed at 23.10 hours at 20,000 ft. White light of
incendiaries falling in sticks on target - following by reddish glow and
occasional flashes. Whole area one great sheet of flame turning to red
with smoke rising to about 12,000 ft.

25/02/1944 LL645 A2-H Bombing Augsburg 22.04 01.21 05.23
   Bomb load 1 x 2000 lb bomb, 48 x 30, 900 x 4 incendiaries.
Primary target: Augsburg. Good visibility. Bombed at 01.21 hours at
21,000 ft. North of target well ablaze, fires rather were scattered

towards Southern part of town. 50 x 4 inc. brought back, electrical fault. Effort did not seem quite so good, some incendiaries seemed at least 3 minutes away from the concentration of markers. Dense black smoke spreading over target.

07/03/1944 LL683 JI-P Bombing Le Mans   19.35 21.44 23.49

Bomb load 10 x 1000, 4 x 500 lb bombs. Primary target: Le Mans. There was 10/10 cloud with tops 6,000 feet. Bombed at 21.44 hours from 12,700 feet. Red glow of T.I.s seen through cloud. Made first run up hoping to see T.I. fall but saw none, on second run bombed good concentration of what were definitely T.I.s. Photo attempted.

15/03/1944 LL645 JI-R Bombing Stuttgart   19.15 23.20 03.25

Bomb load 1 x 1000 lb bomb, 72 x 30, 1050 x 4, 90 x 4 incendiaries. Primary target: Stuttgart. There was 10/10 cloud. Bombed at 23.20 hours from 21,000 feet. Monica u/s. Heavy flak more concentrated than on previous attacks. Fires were scattered over a wide area.

10/04/1944 DS682 JI-N Bombing Laon   01.15 03.38 05.29

Bomb load 9 x 1000, 4 x 500 lb bombs. Primary target: Laon. There was no cloud, but slight haze. Bombed at 03.38 hours from 8,900 feet. Attack considered very successful, best concentration of T.I.s yet seen. Opposition slight, no searchlights or flak.

20/04/1944 DS682 JI-N Bombing Cologne   23.53 02.10 04.21

Bomb load 1 x 8000 lb bomb, 24 x 30, 216 x 4, 24 x 4 lb incendiaries. Primary target: Koln. There was 10/10 cloud. Bombed at 02.10 hours from 20,000 feet. Glow of searchlights on cloud base broken by small red spots, possibly flares or fires below. Poor effort. Markers very scattered and not as briefed.

24/04/1944 LL731 JI-U Bombing Karlsruhe   22.32 01.03 04.09

Bomb load 1 x 1000 lb bomb, 1026 x 4, 114 x 4, 108 x 30 lb incendiaries. Primary target: Karlsruhe. There was 10/10 cloud above - haze below. Bombed at 01.03 hours from 16,300 feet. Red T.I. seen when 15 miles away but had burnt out on arrival. Severity of cold great than forecast. Leading edge and A.S.I. icing. Target could be identified from below cloud. Attack concentrated and winds not as forecast.

27/04/1944 DS633 A2-B Bombing Friedrichshafen 22.06 02.09 05.40

Bomb load 1 x 4000 lb bomb, 32 x 30, 324 x 4, 36 x 4 incendiaries. Primary target: Friedrichshafen. Weather was clear with some haze. Bombed at 02.09 hours from 20,000 feet. Numerous large fires seen.

Good successful attack. Many combats over target. Route O.K.

01/05/1944 DS633 A2-B Bombing Chambly 22.46 00.26 02.15

Bomb load 10 x 1000, 5 x 500 lb bombs. Primary target: Chambly. There was no cloud but little haze. Bombed at 00.26 hours from 7,200 feet. Markers well placed according to Master Bomber and all bombs fell in area marked. Bombs appeared to straddle target effectively. Route good.

19/05/1944 DS786 A2-F Bombing Le Mans 22.25 00.36 03.35

Bomb load 4 x 1000 USA, 5 x 1000 MC, 1 x 1000 GP, 4 x 500 GP. Primary target: Le Mans. 10/10 cloud at 7/9,000 feet. Bombed at 00.36 hours from 6,400 feet. Visual obtained of fires and built up area. Heavy concentration of fires with pall of black smoke and several large explosions seen. 1 x 1000 bomb brought back.

21/05/1944 DS786 A2-F Bombing Duisburg 22.50 01.15 03.10

Bomb load 1 x 8000 lb bomb, 96 x 30, 600 x 4 incendiaries. Primary target: Duisberg. There was 10/10 cloud at target. Bombed at 01.15 hours from 21,000 feet. Cloud prevented a visual. Flak heavy and over a wide area. Many fighter flares on homeward route.

24/05/1944 DS795 A2-J Bombing Boulogne 00.10 01.15 02.15

Bomb load 9 x 1000 MC, 1 x 1000 GP, 1 x 1000 ANM, 4 x 500 GP. Primary target: Boulogne, Gun Battery. Misty over target. Bombed at 01.15 hours from 7,500 feet. Bombed markers and visual obtained by light of photo flash. Attack thought good, and bombs bursting close to markers.

27/05/1944 DS786 A2-F Bombing Aachen 00.25 02.30 04.05

Bomb load 7 x 1000 MC, 4 x 1000 ANM, 4 x 500 MC. Primary target: Aachen. Misty over target. Bombed markers at 02.30 hours from 14,000 feet. Visual of the town obtained by light of photo flash. Moderate amount of light flak. Fighter opposition heavy to and from target. Enemy aircraft seen dropping flares at 02.30 hours.

28/05/1944 DS786 A2-F Bombing Angers 18.55 23.55 01.45

Bomb load 5 x 1000 MC, 1 x 1000 USA, 4 x 500 MC. Primary target: Angers. Slight ground haze at target. Bombed on Master Bomber's instructions at 23.55 hours from 9,500 feet. Visual obtained of marshalling yards and bombs seen to burst in the area. Good attack.

31/05/1944 LL677 A2-E Bombing Trappes 00.02 02.00 04.05

Bomb load 8 x 1000 MC, 8 x 500 MC. Primary target: Trappes. Clear with slight haze. Bombed at 02.00 hours from 10,000 feet. Visual obtained of the yards and white markers seemed in position. Bombs seen falling N and NE of yards. Light flak very slight and no searchlights. Route quiet. Vibration and rise in oil pressure necessitated feathering of starboard inner engine.

05/06/1944 DS786 A2-F   Bombing Ouistreham   03.55 05.10 07.03
Bomb load 9 x 1000 MC and 2 x 500 MC. Primary target: Ouistreham. There was 2/10 to 5/10 broken cloud at target. Bombed markers at 05.10 hours from 10,000 feet. Results not observed but on leaving the target, T.I.s were estimated to be on Le Havre. Defences were active.

06/06/1944 DS786 A2-F   Bombing Lisieux   00.30 01.39 03.13
Bomb load 16 x 500 MC Nose Inst. and 2 x 500 MC LD. Primary target: Lisieux. Weather was clear over target. Bombed red T.I.s at 01.39 hours from 6,500 feet. A good visual of built-up area was obtained and also of flares and red T.I.s around which a number of bursts were seen. Master Bomber was not heard even after orbiting. Many large flashes seen in target and attack considered successful.

17/06/1944 DS786 A2-F   Bombing Montdidier   00.59 x 04.52
Bomb load 16 x 500 GP, 2 x 500 ANM64 GP. Primary target: Montdidier. There was 10/10ths cloud. On ETA heard Master Bomber say "come below cloud". Orbited to do so then heard him order return to Base. Jettisoned safe 03.39 hours from 9,000 feet 5002N 0057E 3 x 500 GP.

23/06/1944 DS786 A2-F   Bombing L'Hey   23.00 00.19 01.40
Bomb load 11 x 1000 MC, 4 x 500 GP. Primary target: L'Hey, Flying bomb installations. There was 10/10ths cloud at 5,000 feet. Bombed at 00.19 hours from 8,100 feet, centre of glow of T.I.s as instructed by Master Bomber.

27/06/1944 DS786 A2-F   Bombing Biennais 23.25 01.15 02.27
Bomb load 16 x 500 GP, 2 x 500 ANM64 GP. Primary target: Biennais, Flying bomb installations. There was 10/10ths cloud. Bombed at 01.15 hours from 12,000 feet red glow.

30/06/1944 DS786 A2-F   Bombing Villers Bocage 18.07 20.03 21.43
Bomb load 11 x 1000 MC, 2 x 500 GP. Primary target: Villers Bocage. Weather clear. Bombed at 20.03 hours from 12,000 feet. One large mass of smoke, very good attack.

02/07/1944 DS786 A2-F   Bombing Beauvoir 12.52 14.35 15.48
Bomb load 11 x 1000 MC, 4 x 500 GP. Primary target: Beauvoir, Flying bomb supply site. Bombed at 14.35 hours from 9,000 feet on yellow T.I.s.

05/07/1944 DS786 A2-F   Bombing Watten   22.51 00.11 01.16
Bomb load 11 x 1000 ANM65, 4 x 500 GP. Primary target: Watten,

Constructional works. Bombed at 00.11 hours from 8,700 feet red T.I.s.

10/07/1944 DS786 A2-F Bombing Nucourt 04.27 06.05 07.55

Bomb load 11 x 1000 ANM65, 4 x 500 GP. Primary target: Nucourt, Constructional works. Bombed at 06.05 hours from 16,200 feet on Gee.

12/07/1944 DS786 A2-F Bombing Vaires 17.54 x 21.54

Bomb load 18 x 500 GP. Primary target: Vaires, Marshalling yards. Target area reached 20.02 hours at 15,000 feet. Mission abandoned as instructed by Master Bomber. Jettisoned 3 x 500 GP at 20.44 hours from 15,000 feet, position 4953N 0033E.

15/07/1944 DS786 A2-F Bombing Chalons sur Marne 21.42 01.30 03.37

Bomb load 18 x 500 GP. Primary target: Chalons sur Marne, Railway centre. Weather clear for bombing, otherwise 3-4/10ths cloud. Bombed at 01.30 hours from 9,400 feet, red T.I.s. Marshalling Yards, river and town could be recognized. No searchlights, Master Bomber very clear.

F/L. Malcom Robert Head, DSO DFC

NZ413414 F/L. Malcom Robert "Mac" Head, DSO DFC RNZAF. Pilot.

1582472 Sgt. Alfred Bert "Fossie" Foster, DFM. A/Bomber.

153447 (1621807) F/O. Derek William "Derrick" Woodall. Navigator. 27 ops.

J16828 (*) F/O. Allan Harry Fallis, DFC, RCAF. Navigator. 13 ops.

112635 F/S. J.L. "Jack" Whincup. WOP/AG. 35 ops.

NZ412324 F/O. Oliver Lawrence Goldsmith, DFC RNZAF. WOP/AG. 5 ops.

F/S. E.C. Francis. MU/Gunner. 5 ops.

1808451 Sgt. Albert Francis "Bert" Beckford, DFM. MU&R/Gunner.

56018 (624463) P/O. Ronald "Ron" Craig, DFC. MU&R/Gun. 35 ops.

1642480 Sgt. W. Webb. F/Engineer. 22 ops.

54152 (630356) F/O. John Daniel "Kil" Kilgallon, DFM. F/Engineer. 18 ops.

179987 (970882)   P/O. Frank Heald, DFC.   2nd Pilot.   12/08/1944

(*) see at 05/10/1944.

21/06/1944 DS787 A2-D   Bombing Domleger   18.02 x 20.55

Bomb load 18 x 500 MC. Primary target: Domleger near Abbeville, V-1 flying bomb launch site. Master Bomber instructed return to Base if no T.I.s seen. No T.I.s visible, jettisoned safe 19.42 hours from 12,000 feet at 5023N 0125E.

Sgt. W. Webb F/Engineer until 29/08/1944.

F/O. D.W. Woodall Navigator until 26/09/1944 (can be until 05/10).

Sgt. A.F. Beckford MU/Gunner that day.

P/O. R. Craig R/Gunner that day.

24/06/1944 DS787 A2-D   Bombing Rimeux   23.24   00.36   02.17

Bomb load 18 x 500 GP. Primary target: Rimeux, Flying bomb installations. Slight haze. Bombed at 00.36 hours from 10,000 feet centre of four red T.I.s. Good raid, bombs seen falling amongst red T.I.s.

Sgt. A.F. Beckford MU/Gunner that day.

P/O. R. Craig R/Gunner that day.

L to R (back): A.F. Beckford, J.L. Whincup, M.R. Head, J.D. Kilgallon, D.W. Woodall. L to R (front): R. Craig, A.B. Foster.

27/06/1944 LL697 A2-B Bombing Biennais 23.26 01.17 02.39

Bomb load 16 x 500 GP, 2 x 500 ANM64 GP. Primary target: Biennais, Flying bomb installations. There was 10/10ths cloud. Bombed at 01.17 hours from 5,500 feet red T.I.s. Bombed below cloud.

P/O. R. Craig MU/Gunner until 18/07/1944.

Sgt. A.F. Beckford MU/Gunner until 18/07/1944.

30/06/1944 LL697 A2-B Bombing Villers Bocage 18.12 20.00 21.20

Bomb load 11 x 1000 MC, 3 x 500 GP. Primary target: Villers Bocage. Weather clear. Bombed at 20.00 hours from 13,000 feet on visual of the village. Bomb bursts across the town and railway line. Very good raid.

02/07/1944 LL697 A2-B Bombing Beauvoir 12.53 14.37 16.17

Bomb load 11 x 1000 MC, 4 x 500 GP. Primary target: Beauvoir, Flying bomb supply site. Bombed at 14.37 hours from 7,500 feet on yellow T.I.s.

05/07/1944 LL697 A2-B Bombing Watten 22.50 00.12 01.51

Bomb load 11 x 1000 ANM 65, 4 x 500 GP. Primary target: Watten, Constructional works. Bombed at 00.12 hours from 8000 feet red T.I.s.

07/07/1944 DS786 A2-F Bombing Vaires 22.44 01.35 03.29

Bomb load 7 x 1000 MC, 4 x 500 GP. Primary target: Vaires, Marshalling yards. Weather clear. Bombed at 01.35 hours from 12,000 feet centre of green T.I.s as per Master Bomber. Marking seemed concentrated on the right spot. Explosions seen at 01.33 hours.

10/07/1944 LL697 A2-B Bombing Nucourt 04.26 06.06 07.58

Bomb load 11 x 1000 ANM65, 4 x 500 GP. Primary target: Nucourt, Constructional works. Bombed at 06.06 hours from 16,000 feet on T.I. red.

12/07/1944 LL697 A2-B Bombing Vaires 17.59 x 21.51

Bomb load 18 x 500 GP. Primary target: Vaires, Marshalling yards. Master Bomber ordered abandon mission. Jettisoned 4 x 500 GP at 20.44 hours from 14,000 feet, position 4952N 0025E.

15/07/1944 LL697 A2-B Bombing Chalons Sur Marne 21.44 01.32 04.23

Bomb load 16 x 500 GP, 2 x 500 GP LD. Primary target: Chalons sur Marne, Railway centre. Weather clear below cloud. Bombed at 01.32 hours from 8,000 feet, green T.I.s. T.I.s well placed, a good attack, no trouble.

18/07/1944 LL697 A2-B Bombing Emieville 04.35 06.08 07.37

Bomb load 11 x 1000 MC, 4 x 500 GP. Primary target: Emieville,

Troop concentration. Weather clear. Bombed at 06.08 hours from 10,000 feet green T.I.s. Bomb bursts around green T.I.s. Had combat with enemy aircraft.

18/07/1944 LL697 A2-B Bombing Aulnoye 22.33 00.58 02.20

Bomb load 18 x 500 GP. Primary target: Aulnoye, Railway junction. Weather clear. Bombed at 00.58 hours from 10,000 feet, green T.I.s. Bomb bursts around green T.I.s.

23/07/1944 LL697 A2-B Bombing Kiel 22.33 01.30 04.03

Bomb load 6 x 1000 MC, 10 x 500 GP. Primary target: Kiel, Warehouses and docks. Weather 10/10 cloud, thin. Bombed at 01.30 hours from 19,500 feet green T.I. Small explosions.

Sgt. A.F. Beckford MU/Gunner that day.

P/O. R. Craig R/Gunner that day.

24/07/1944 LL697 A2-B Bombing Stuttgart 21.50 01.50 05.04

Bomb load 5 x 1000 ANM65, 3 x 500 GP. Primary target Stuttgart. Weather 6/10ths cloud tops 5,000 feet. Bombed at 01.50 hours from 20,700 feet on S.E. group of Wanganui flares as instructed. Attack believed to be scattered.

P/O. R. Craig MU/Gunner until 22/10/1944.

Sgt. A.F. Beckford MU/Gunner until last operation on 30/10/1944.

04/08/1944 LM286 A2-F Bombing Bec d'Ambes 13.14 18.02 21.01

Bomb load 5 x 1000 MC, 4 x 500 GP. Primary target: Bec d'Ambes depot. Weather clear. Bombed at 18.02 hours from 8,000 feet, oil tanks. Most of the bombs were falling well on the target. Considered a successful attack. Bombing well concentrated, but aircraft not too well placed.

05/08/1944 LM286 A2-F Bombing Bassen 14.15 18.59 21.55

Bomb load 8 x 1000 MC, 2 x 500 GP. Primary target: Bassen Oil Depot. Patch of cloud down to 4000 feet clear below. Bombed at 18.59 hours from 3,500 feet visual of target. Large oil explosion at 18.55 hours. Good trip.

08/08/1944 LM286 A2-F Bombing Foret de Lucheux 21.45 23.50 01.02

Bomb load 18 x 500 GP. Primary target: Foret de Luchcux, Petrol dump. Weather clear, ground haze. Bombed at 23.50 hours from 11,700 feet, north of fires as instructed by Master Bomber. Black pall of smoke over target, scattered fires.

"Foret de Lucheux" is a forest between Lille and Amiens. During WWII, important fuel tanks were there.

12/08/1944 LL677 A2-E Bombing Russelsheim 21.56 00.13 02.37

Bomb load 1 x 2000 HC, 12 x 500 No. 14 clusters. Primary target: Russelsheim. Weather clear. Bombed at 00.13 from 18,000 feet, red and green T.I.s. Very scattered fires. Master Bomber not heard until after bombing - who ordered to bomb on centre of T.I.s. Much interference over R/T. FW190 claimed destroyed by Rear Gunner.

P/O. Frank Heald 2nd Pilot that day.

16/08/1944 HK577 JI-P Bombing Stettin 20.55 01.06 05.11

Bomb load 1 x 2000 HC, 12 x 500 lb clusters. Primary target: Stettin. Weather clear. Bombed at 01.06 hours from 17,500 feet centre of cluster of red and green T.I.s on Master Bomber's instructions. Bomb bursts concentrated in area marked by T.I.s.

25/08/1944 LL734 A2-B Bombing Vincly 18.33 20.34 22.01

Bomb load 11 x 1000 MC, 2 x 500 GP MK IV, 2 x 500 GP MK IV, LD. Primary target: Vincly. Weather: cloud patches. Bombed at 20.34 hours from 15,000 feet, visual of G.H. leader. Slight flak.

26/08/1944 LL734 A2-B Bombing Kiel 20.09 23.13 01.36

Bomb load 1 x 8000 HC, 16 x 30 IB, 180 x 4 IB. Primary target: Kiel. Weather low status. Bombed at 23.13 hours from 18,300 feet, centre of red and green T.I.s. Attack rather scattered, no large fires. Rocket projectiles over target bursting in clusters of 3.

29/08/1944 LM275 JI-E Bombing Stettin 21.07 02.08 06.38

Bomb load 1 x 500 GP LD 37A, 1 x 1000 MC, 84 x 30, 756 x 4, 84 x 4 lb incendiaries. Primary target: Stettin. Weather clear below 11,000 feet. Bombed at 02.08 hours from 10,700 feet, centre of red T.I.s. Incendiary fires taking hold round both areas of markers. Good marking, good raid.

03/09/1944 LL734 A2-B Bombing Eindhoven 15.21 17.31 18.50

Bomb load 11 x 1000 MC, 4 x 500 GP. Primary target: Eindhoven airfield. Bombed at 17.31 hours from 15,500 feet, visually.

F/O. J.D. Kilgallon F/Engineer from that day.

10/09/1944 LM724 JI-B Bombing Le Havre 15.42 17.38 19.02

Bomb load 11 x 1000 MC, 4 x 500 GP. Primary target: Le Havre. Weather clear. Bombed at 17.38 hours from 10,000 feet. Undershot red T.I.s by 200 yards.

12/09/1944 LL734 A2-B Bombing Frankfurt 18.46 23.01 01.03

Bomb load 1 x 1000 MC, 16 x 500 Clusters 4lb. Primary target: Frankfurt - Main. Weather clear over the target. Bombed at 23.01 hours from 17,400 feet on centre of red and green T.I.s.

23/09/1944 LM286 A2-F Bombing Neuss 19.12 21.28 23.09

Bomb load 11 x 1000 ANM44, 4 x 500 GP. Primary target: Neuss. Weather 10/10ths cloud over target, tops 8/10,000 feet. Bombed at 21.28 hours from 21,000 feet on glow of fires.

26/09/1944 PD324 A2-B Bombing Calais   11.37 12.44 13.52
Bomb load 11 x 1000 MC, 4 x 500 GP. Primary target: Calais 7D. Weather clear below cloud which was 3,500 feet. Bombed at 12.44 hours from 3,000 feet on red T.I.

05/10/1944 PD324 A2-B Bombing Saarbrucken 17.01 20.32 22.16
Bomb load 11 x 1000 MC, 1 x 500 GP, 3 x 500 GP. Long Delay. Primary target: Saarbrucken, Marshalling yards. Visibility clear with slight ground haze. Dropped all bombs at 20.32 hours from 13,500 feet. Sticks seen to burst round single green T.I.

F/O. A.H. Fallis Navigator from that day or from the next day.

(*) In ORBs on 05/10/1944 A.H. Fallis is noted at the same time in both PD324 A2-B of F/L M.R. Head's crew and in NG142 A2-H of F. Heald's crew. In summer 2015 Corb Stewart told the author that A.H. Fallis was in F. Heald crew "Alan Violet was stood down medically and replaced by Fallis in my diary".

06/10/1944 PD324 A2-B Bombing Dortmund 17.06 20.31 22.10
Bomb load 1 x 4000 HC, 12 x No. 14 Clusters. Primary target: Dortmund, Town and Railways. Weather over the target was clear with slight ground haze. Bombed at 20.31 hours from 23,300 feet on centre of green T.I.s.

07/10/1944 PD324 A2-B Bombing Emmerich 12.19 14.28 15.55
Bomb load 1 x 4000 HC, 10 x No.14 clusters, 4 x (150 x 4). Primary target Emmerich. Weather clear with cloud at 13,000 feet. Bombed at 14.28 hours from 13,000 feet on visual of town south of smoke as instructed.

14/10/1944 PD324 A2-B Bombing Duisburg 06.44 09.03 10.56
Bomb load 11 x 1000 MC, 4 x 500 GP Long Delay. Primary target: Duisburg. Weather patchy cloud with gaps for bombing. Bombed at 09.03 hours from 18,000 feet. Area North of Docks.

14/10/1944 PD324 A2-B Bombing Duisburg 22.37 01.26 03.01
Bomb load 11 x 1000 MC, 4 x 500 GP Long Delay. Primary target: Duisburg. Weather was clear with small amount of cloud over the target. Bombed at 01.26 hours from 23,000 feet. Red T.I.s.

19/10/1944 PD324 A2-B Bombing Stuttgart 17.15 20.32 23.14
Bomb load 1 x 4000 HC, 3 x 500 Clusters, 7 x 150 x 4, 1 x 90 x 4 IB. Primary target: Stuttgart, A/P 'D' 1st attack. Weather 10/10ths cloud which broke to 6/10ths at the end of the period. Bombed at

20.32 hours from 17,500 feet. Red flares with yellow stars. Checked by H2S.

21/10/1944 PD324 A2-B Bombing Flushing 10.49 12.26 13.16
Bomb load 12 x 1000 MC, 2 x 500 GP. Primary target: Flushing 'B'. Weather clear. Bombed at 12.26 hours from 8,000 feet. Visual of A/P.

22/10/1944 NG118 A2-E Bombing Neuss 13.01 15.57 17.22
Bomb load 1 x 4000 HC, 6 x 1000 MC, 6 x 500 GP. Primary target: Neuss. Weather 10/10ths cloud over target. Bombed at 15.57 hours from 16,000 feet on Gee H.

23/10/1944 PB423 A2-G Bombing Essen 16.38 19.49 22.04
Bomb load 1 x 4000 HC. 15 x 500 Clusters. Primary target: Essen. Weather 10/10ths cloud over target - tops 12/14,000 feet with most appalling weather on route. Bombed at 19.49 hours from 22,000 feet on Gee H.

F/O. O.L. Goldsmith WOP/AG from that day.

F/S. E.C. Francis MU/Gunner from that day.

25/10/1944 PD324 A2-B Bombing Essen 12.57 15.35 16.56
Bomb load 1 x 4000 HC, 10 x No. 14 Clusters, 4 x 15 x 4. Primary target: Essen. Weather over target 10/10ths low cloud, with one clear patch which appeared to fill up later in the attack. Bombed at 15.35 hours from 22,000 feet. Pall of smoke.

26/10/1944 PB423 A2-G Bombing Leverkusen 12.51 15.30 17.06
Bomb load 1 x 4000 HC, 6 x 1000 MC,4 x 500 GP, 2 x 500 GP Long Delay. Primary target: Leverkusen. Weather over target and on route was 10/10ths cloud. Bombed at 15.30 hours from 17,000 feet on G.H. Leader of another formation.

29/10/1944 NG142 A2-H Bombing Flushing 09.49 11.37 12.20
Bomb load 11 x 1000 ANM59, 4 x 500 GP. Primary target: Flushing, Gun installations. Weather clear over target. Bombed at 11.37 hours from 5,800 feet. Starboard of Green T.I.s. as instructed.

30/10/1944 PD324 A2-B Bombing Wesseling 09.00 11.58 13.25
Bomb load 1 x 4000 HC, 16 x 500 GP. Primary target: Wesseling. Weather was 10/10ths cloud - tops about 7,000 feet. Bombed at 11.58 hours from 17,400 feet on Red flares.

P/O. Frank Heald, DFC

179987 (970882) P/O.   Frank Heald, DFC.   Pilot.
R191783 F/S.   Cecil Corbett "Corb" Stewart, RCAF. A/Bomber.
   Sgt. Alan "Al" Violet.   Navigator. 27 ops.
J16828   (*)   F/O. Allan Harry Fallis, DFC RCAF. Navigator.   1 op.
   F/S. Leslie "Les" Baldwin.   WOP/AG.
   Sgt. James A. "Jim" Turner.   MU/Gunner.
   Sgt. John Shaughnessy.   R/Gunner.
   Sgt. George Cuthbertson.   F/Engineer.

(*) see at 05/10/1944.

*L to R (back): C.C. Stewart, J.A. Turner, F. Heald, G Cuthbertson. L to R (front): A. Violet,
J. Shaughnessy, L. Baldwin. (courtesy Corb Stewart)*

12/08/1944 LL677 A2-E   Bombing Russelsheim   21.56   00.13   02.37
   Bomb load 1 x 2000 HC, 12 x 500 No. 14 clusters. Primary target:
Russelsheim. Weather clear. Bombed at 00.13 from 18,000 feet, red
and green T.I.s. Very scattered fires. Master Bomber not heard until
after bombing - who ordered to bomb on centre of T.I.s. Much
interference over R/T. FW190 claimed destroyed by Rear Gunner.
   From his normal crew, only P/O. Frank Heald did the mission as
2nd Pilot with F/L. Malcom Robert Head crew.

14/08/1944 HK572   JI-T Bombing Hamel (Falaise) 13.58 15.51 17.26
Bomb load 11 x 1000 MC, 4 x 500 GP. Primary target: Hamel, troop concentrations. Weather clear. Bombed at 15.51 hours from 8,500 feet, red T.I.s. Bombing concentrated.
According to logbooks: G.A. Wark (pilot) - target "Falaise", T.C. Clayton's (Wark crew) - target 'Hamel'. Corbett Stewart testimony (Heald crew) - target 'Falaise'. There are several places named "Le Hamel" near Falaise.

18/08/1944 DS842 A2-J   Bombing Bremen 21.35 00.19 02.52
Bomb load 1 x 2000 HC, 96 x 30 lb inc, 810 x 4lb inc, 90 x 4lb x inc. Primary target: Bremen. Weather nil cloud, haze. Bombed at 00.19 hours from 17,000 feet, red T.I.s very concentrated. Glow in the sky seen from a considerable distance.

05/09/1944 LL726 A2-H   Bombing Le Havre 17.18 19.23 20.46
Bomb load 11 x 1000 MC, 4 x 500 GP. Primary target: Le Havre. Bombed at 19.23 hours from 14,000 feet red T.I.

06/09/1944 LL726 A2-H   Bombing Le Havre 16.32 18.40 20.05
Bomb load 11 x 1000 MC, 4 x 500 GP. Primary target: Le Havre. Bombed at 18.40 hours from 7-3000 feet, red T.I.s.

08/09/1944 DS826 A2-C   Bombing Le Havre 06.08 x 09.37
Bomb load 11 x 1000 MC, 4 x 500 GP. Primary target: Le Havre. Weather 10/10ths cloud down to 3,000 feet. Abandoned mission on Master Bomber's instructions.

11/09/1944 LL670 A2-D   Bombing Kamen   16.10 18.42 20.28
Bomb load 1 x 4000 HC, 16 x 500 GP. Weather clear. Primary target: Kamen. Bombed at 18.42 hours from 16,500 feet on flames and smoke per Master Bomber's instructions.

14/09/1944 DS826 A2-C   Bombing Wassenaar 12.51 14.30 15.40
Bomb load 11 x 1000 MC, 4 x 500 GP. Primary target: Wassenaar. Weather was good, nil cloud. Bombed at 14.30 hours from 12,000 feet, red T.I.s.

20/09/1944 LL726 A2-H   Bombing Calais   14.47 16.01 17.31
Bomb load 11 x 1000 MC, 4 x 500 GP. Primary target: Calais. Weather clear over target. Bombed at 16.01 hours from 2,500 feet, red T.I.s.

25/09/1944 LM286   A2-F   Bombing Pas de Calais 08.27 x 11.14
Bomb load 11 x 1000 MC, 4 x 500 GP. Primary target: Calais. Abandoned mission on Master Bomber's instructions. Jettisoned 4 x 1000 MC.

26/09/1944 NG142   A2-H   Bombing Calais   11.23 12.50 14.18

Bomb load 11 x 1000 MC, 4 x 500 GP. Primary target: Calais 7D. Weather clear below cloud which was 3,500 feet. Bombed at 12.50 hours from 3,000 feet on red T.I.

According Corbett Stewart's testimony the target was "Cap Gris Nez".

28/09/1944 NG142   A2-H   Bombing Calais   08.06 x 10.53

Bomb load 11 x 1000 MC, 4 x 500 GP. Primary target: Calais 19. Abortive sortie. At 09.28 hours Master Bomber gave abandon mission. Jettisoned 4 x 1000 MC.

03/10/1944 NG142   A2-H   Bombing Westkapelle   11.59   13.19   14.22

Bomb load 1 x 4000 MC, 6 x 1000 MC, 1 x 500 GP L/Delay. Primary target: Westkapelle (Walcheren). Weather patchy-scattered cloud with base 5,000 feet. Bombed at 13.19 hours from 5,000 feet undershot red T.I.s.

05/10/1944 NG142   A2-H   Bombing Saarbrucken   17.20   20.31   22.25

Bomb load 11 x 1000 MC, 1 x 500 GP. Primary target: Saarbrucken, Marshalling yards. Weather clear over target. Bombed at 20.31 hours from 15,000 feet on green T.I.s. Bomb bursts round the single green T.I. Master Bomber seemed unable to identify target so gave "Abandon mission" at 20.32 hours.

F/O. A.H. Fallis Navigator that day.

(*) In ORBs on 05/10/1944 A.H. Fallis is noted at the same time in both PD324 A2-B of F/L M.R. Head's crew and in NG142 A2-H of F. Heald's crew. In summer 2015 Corb Stewart told the author that A.H. Fallis was really in F. Heald crew "Alan Violet was stood down medically and replaced by Fallis in my diary".

06/10/1944 NG142   A2-H   Bombing Dortmund   17.06   20.31   22.10

Bomb load 1 x 4000 HC, 12 x No. 14 Clusters. Primary target: Dortmund, Town and Railways. Weather over the target was clear with slight ground haze. Bombed at 20.31 hours from 21,000 feet on green and red T.I.s.

07/10/1944 NG142   A2-H   Bombing Emmerich   12.23   14.29   16.10

Bomb load 1 x 4000 HC, 10 x No. 14 clusters, 4 x (150 x 4). Primary target: Emmerich. Weather clear with cloud at 13,000 feet. Bombed at 14.29 hours from 13,000 feet on port of red T.I.s.

23/10/1944 NG142   A2-H   Bombing Essen   16.20   19.41   21.29

Bomb load 1 x 4000 HC, 6 x 1000 MC, 6 x 500 GP. Primary target: Essen. Weather 10/10ths cloud over target - tops 12/14,000 feet with most appalling weather on route. Bombed at 19.41 hours from 22,000 feet. Green flares.

25/10/1944 NG142   A2-H   Bombing Essen   13.14   15.44   17.17

Bomb load 1 x 4000 HC, 6 x 1000 MC, 6 x 500 GP. Primary target: Essen. Weather over target 10/10ths low cloud, with one clear patch which appeared to fill up later in the attack. Bombed at 15.44 hours from 22,000 feet. Red sky markers.

28/10/1944 NG142   A2-H   Bombing Flushing   08.53   10.15   11.18

Bomb load 1 x 4000 HC, 6 x 1000 MC, 4 x 500 GP. Primary target: Flushing. Weather over the target quite clear and conditions perfect, although believed to be only local, and some low cloud approaching. Bombed at 10.15 hours from 8,500 feet. Visual of jetty.

30/10/1944 NG142   A2-H   Bombing Wesseling   09.14   12.00   13.30

Bomb load 1 x 4000 HC, 16 x 500 GP. Primary target: Wesseling. Weather was 10/10ths cloud - tops about 7,000 feet. Bombed at 12.00 hours from 17,200 feet on G.H. aircraft ahead.

31/10/1944 NG142   A2-H   Bombing Bottrop   12.03   14.59   16.57

Bomb load 1 x 4000 HC, 16 x 500 GP. Primary target: Bottrop, Synth. Oil plants. Weather 10/10ths cloud over target. Bombed at 14.59 hours from 17,500 feet on G.H. Leader. Aircraft hit by flak. Bomb Aimer's panel damaged.

02/11/1944 NG142   A2-H   Bombing Homberg   11.22 14.10   15.48

Bomb load 1 x 4000 HC, 6 x 1000 ANM59, 6 x 500 MC. Primary target: Homberg. Weather variable cloud but clear for bombing. Target obscured by pall of smoke rising to 10,000 feet. Bombed at 14.10 hours from 20,500 feet. Centre of black smoke.

06/11/1944 NG142   A2-H   Bombing Koblenz   16.57   19.32   21.39

Bomb load 1 x 4000 HC, 2100 x 4 lb I.B. Primary target: Koblenz. Weather clear over target. Bombed at 19.32 hours from 17,500 feet on centre of Red and Green T.I.s.

08/11/1944 NG142   A2-H   Bombing Homberg   08.03 10.29   12.08

Bomb load 1 x 4000 HC, 6 x 1000 GP, 6 x 500 GP. Primary target: Homberg. Weather clear. Bombed at 10.29 hours from 18,000 feet on leading aircraft. Aircraft hit by flak. Windscreen smashed.

11/11/1944 NG142   A2-H   Bombing Castrop Rauxel   08.24   11.06   12.10

Bomb load 1 x 4000 HC, 16 x 500 GP. Primary target: Castrop Rauxel, Oil refineries. Weather 10/10ths cloud. Bombed at 11.06 hours from 20,000 feet on G.H. Leader.

16/11/1944 NG142   A2-H   Bombing Heinsburg   13.07   15.35   17.11

Bomb load 1 x 4000 HC, 6 x 1000 MC, 6 x 500 GP. Primary target: Heinsburg. Weather - nil cloud with slight haze over target. Bombed at 15.35 hours from 9,000 feet. Upwind edge of smoke.

20/11/1944 NG142   A2-H   Bombing Homberg   12.24 15.13   16.51
Bomb load 1 x 4000 HC, 15 x 500 MC, 1 x 500 GP. Primary target: Homberg. Weather 10/10ths cloud over target. Bombed at 15.13 hours from 20,000 feet on G.H. Leader.

21/11/1944 NG142   A2-H   Bombing Homberg   12.42 15.08   16.31
Bomb load 1 x 4000 HC, 16 x 500 GP. Primary target: Homberg. Weather about 5/10ths cloud but clear for bombing. Bombed at 15.08 hours from 20,500 feet on centre of target area.

23/11/1944 NG142   A2-H   Bombing Nordstern   12.45   15.08   17.03
Bomb load 1 x 4000 HC, 16 x 500 GP. Primary target: Nordstern, Gelsenkirchen Oil refineries. Weather 10/10ths cloud. Bombed at 15.21 hours from 20,000 feet. Centre of Red flares.

29/11/1944 NG142   A2-H   Bombing Neuss   02.57   05.35   07.05
Bomb load 1 x 4000 HC, 6 x 1000 MC, 6 x 500 GP, 3 Flares Red with Green stars. Primary target: Neuss. Weather 10/10ths cloud over target but the glow of fires was seen through cloud. Bombed at 05.35 hours from 20,000 feet. Upwind edge of sky markers. D.R. compass unserviceable. Believed good attack.

F/O. Frank Fearnley Hebditch

168829 (1333586)   F/O. Frank Fearnley Hebditch. Pilot.
153236 (1577479)   F/O. Kenneth Stanley Robinson. A/Bomber.
183728 (1323958)   P/O. Clifford George Washington. Navigator.
1113619   W/O. James Patterson Edwards. WOP/AG.
2220842   Sgt. Cecil Amos Clarke.   MU/Gunner.
148029/148022 (1071308) F/O. Stanley Edwards Jones.   R/Gunner.
1896100   Sgt. Joseph Raymond Plant. F/Engineer.

05/08/1944 DS786 A2-H   Bombing Bassen   14.19 19.03 22.26
Bomb load 5 x 1000 MC, 4 x 500 GP. Primary target: Bassen Oil Depot. Blaye-et-Sainte-Luce (now renamed Blaye since 1961) attacked in error. Cloud down to 8,000 feet clear below. Bombed at 19.03 hours from 8,000 feet, yellow T.I. as per Master Bomber's instructions. Flames and smoke seen in target area. Altering course as T.I.s were seen to go down plus hearing Master Bomber's instructions to bomb at 8,000 feet caused error in bombing target.

313

07/08/1944 LM286　A2-F　Bombing Mare de Magne 21.48　23.47 01.17

Bomb load 11 x 1000 MC, 4 x 500 GP. Primary target: Mare de Magne (just past Caen). Weather clear, some haze. Bombed at 23.47 hours from 7,000 feet centre of red T.I.s. Bombing accurate on T.I.s.

Mare-de-Magne: place between Caen and Fontenay le Marmion.

08/08/1944 DS842 A2-J　Bombing Foret de Lucheux 21.50　23.49 01.19

Bomb load 18 x 500 GP. Primary target: Foret de Lucheux, Petrol dump. Weather very hazy, no cloud. Bombed at 23.49 hours from 10,000 feet, green T.I.s. Looked like really good prang.

"Foret de Lucheux" is a forest between Lille and Amiens. During WWII, important fuel tanks were there.

12/08/1944 LL728 A2-L　Bombing Russelsheim 21.46　00.14　00.39

Bomb load 1 x 8000 HC, 6 x 500 No. 14 Clusters. Primary target: Russelsheim. Weather 2/10ths cloud. Bombed at 00.14 hours from 17,000 feet, centre of red T.I.s. If T.I.s were on, we were on. No trouble.

15/08/1944 LL728 A2-L　Bombing St Trond 10.09　12.09　13.18

Bomb load 11 x 1000 MC, 4 x 500 GP. Primary target St. Trond Airfield. Weather clear. Bombed at 12.09 hours from 17,000 feet red T.I.s. Good attack. Clouds of smoke.

18/08/1944 LL728 A2-L　Bombing Bremen 21.43　00.17　02.53

Bomb load 1 x 2000 HC, 96 x 30 lb inc, 810 x 4lb inc, 90 x 4lb x inc. Primary target: Bremen. Weather nil cloud, haze. Bombed at 00.17 hours from 19,000 feet triangle of red T.I.s. Glow in the sky seen from a considerable distance.

25/08/1944 LL728 A2-L　Bombing Vincly　18.37　20.37　22.13

Bomb load 11 x 1000 MC, 2 x 500 GP MK IV, 2 x 500 GP MK IV, LD. Primary target: Vincly. Weather: cloud clearing near target. Bombed at 20.37 hours from 15,000 feet, visual of G.H. Leader. 1 x 1000 MC hung up.

26/08/1944 LL728 A2-L　Bombing Kiel　20.21 x 23.45

Bomb load 1 x 8000 HC, 180 x 4 IB, 16 x 30 IB. Primary target: Kiel. Aircraft missing.

Shot down by the night-fighter of Fw. Gottfried Schneider, 1/NJG3, crashing near Kleve at 23.45hrs, 10 km SSE of Friedrichstadt. LL728, one of three successes for Fw. Schneider that night, was lost on its return from the target area.

All crew KIA except F/O. K.S. Robinson who as a POW was

interned in Camp L1, POW No. 5300. Those killed are buried in Kiel War Cemetery. At 35, Sgt. Plant was well above the average age for Bomber Command aircrew.

F/L. E.S. Henderson

J10781 F/L. E.S. "Ted" Henderson, RCAF. Pilot.
J40445 F/O. M.S. Modlinsky, RCAF. A/Bomber.
R74354 W/O. C.G.K. Eagley, RCAF. Navigator.
R204630   Sgt. C.W. Bingham, RCAF.   WOP/AG.
Sgt. L. Brennan.   MU/Gunner.
R270464   F/S. G.S. Killingbeck, RCAF. R/Gunner.
Sgt. D. Homer.   F/Engineer.
153171 (1562823) F/O. William "Bill" Allan.   2nd Pilot. 04/04/1945
J7741 F/O.R.E. Farvolden, RCAF. 2nd Pilot. 09/04/1945

Passenger: 07/05/1945.

03/02/1945   PA186 A2-G Bombing Dortmund-Huckarde 16.28 19.46 21.48
   Bomb load 1 x 4000 HC, 2 x 500 MC, 2 x 500 MC L/Delay, 6 x 500 ANM64, 2 x 500 GP, 3 x 250 GP. Primary target Dortmund-Huckarde, Coking plant. Weather clear with slight haze. Bombed at 19.46 hours from 20,000 feet on red T.I.s. Bombing concentrated markers. Starboard flap damaged by heavy flak.
   From his normal crew, only F/L. E.S. Henderson did the mission as 2nd Pilot with S/L. E.B. Cozens' crew.
13/02/1945 NN775   A2-F Bombing Dresden 21.43 x 05.58
   Bomb load 1 x 500 MC, 15 x No. 14 Clusters. Primary target: Dresden. Weather 5/10ths cloud over target. Abortive sortie. Aircraft landed at Manston, short on fuel, oil leak and Gee unserviceable.
19/02/1945 NF966 A2-H Bombing Wesel   12.59 16.37 19.30
   Bomb load 1 x 4000 HC, 6 x 500 MC, 6 x 500 ANM64, 4 x 250 GP. Primary target: Wesel. Weather over target 5-7/10ths cloud. Bombed at 16.39 hours from 20,600 feet on centre of Red puffs.
   From his normal crew, only F/L. E.S. Henderson did the mission as 2nd Pilot with F/L. T.W. Hurley's crew.
20/02/1945 NG203   A2-C Bombing Dortmund 21.47 01.07 04.56
   Bomb load 1 x 4000HC, 6 x 500 Type 14 Clusters, 6 x 750 Type 14

Clusters. Primary target: Dortmund. Weather 8-10/10ths thin cloud at about 5,000 feet. Bombed at 01.07 hours from 21,000 feet on centre of Red/Green T.I.s.

22/02/1945 PD389 A2-J Bombing Osterfeld 12.17 16.03 18.15
Bomb load 1 x 4000 HC, 9 x 500 ANM64, 2 x 500 MC, 4 x 250 GP. Primary target: Osterfeld, Coking ovens. Weather at target clear, but hazy. Bombed at 16.03 hours from 19,700 feet on leading aircraft.

25/02/1945 NN717 A2-E Bombing Kamen 09.30 12.47 14.58
Bomb load 1 x 4000 HC, 9 x 500 ANM64, 2 x 500 MC, 4 x 250 GP. Primary target: Kamen. Weather 6-8/10ths cloud. Bombed at 12.47 hours from 20,200 feet on G.H. Leader.

06/03/1945 LM724 JI-H Bombing Salzbergen 08.18 12.15 14.11
Bomb load 1 x 4000 HC, 12 x 500 ANM64, 2 x 500MC. Primary target: Salzbergen, Wintershall oil plant. Weather 10/10ths cloud over target, tops 10,000 feet. Bombed at 12.15 hours from 20,300 feet on G.H.

09/03/1945 NG118 A2-H Bombing Datteln 10.30 14.00 15.50
Bomb load 1 x 4000 HC, 13 x 500 ANM64, 2 x 500 MC L/Delay37. Primary target: Datteln, Synthetic oil plant. Weather 10/10ths cloud, tops 8-10,000 feet. Bombed at 14.00 hours from 20,600 feet on G.H.

11/03/1945 NG118 A2-H Bombing Essen 11.25 15.27 17.11
Bomb load 1 x 4000 HC, 13 x 500 ANM64, 2 x 500 MC. Primary target: Essen, Marshalling yards. Weather 10/10ths cloud, tops 7/8,000 feet. Bombed at 15.27 hours from 19,500 feet on G.H.

12/03/1945 NG118 A2-H Bombing Dortmund 12.54 17.06 19.03
Bomb load 1 x 4000 HC, 13 x 500 ANM64. Primary target: Dortmund. Weather 10/10ths cloud over target, tops 6/10,000 feet. Bombed at 17.06 hours from 19,000 feet on G.H.

14/03/1945 NG118 A2-H Bombing Heinrichshutte 13.09 16.40 18.45
Bomb load 1 x 4000 HC, 12 x 500 ANM64. Primary target: Heinrichshutte, Hattingen Steel works & Benzol plant. Weather 10/10ths cloud, tops 7/12,000 feet. Bombed at 16.40 hours from 18,500 feet on G.H.

04/04/1945 PD389 A2-J Bombing Merseburg (Leuna) 18.49 x 02.52
Weather 5-10/10ths cloud, and 10/10ths over Merseburg. Bombed Magdeburg area. Bomb load 1 x 4000 HC, 6 x 500 ANM64. on Red and Green markers. Two attacks by enemy aircraft. Near collision with Lancaster over target with Nav. lights on. Attack rather scattered, many markers seen. (Patchy cloud.)

F/O. William Allan 2nd Pilot that day.

09/04/1945 NN781 A2-B Bombing Kiel 19.40 22.42 02.05

Bombed primary target: Kiel, Submarine Buildings Yards. Weather clear with slight haze. Bomb load 1 x 4000 HC and 12 x 500 ANM64. Bombed at 22.42 hours at 20,000 feet on centre of Green T.I.s. Concentrated marking and bombing. Very good concentration. Four very large explosions seen as Lanc left target. Lanc underneath as 514/B2 was about to bomb so veered over to port to bomb.

F/O. R.E. Farvolden 2nd Pilot that day.

18/04/1945 ME358 JI-O Bombing Heligoland 10.00 13.09 15.34

Bomb load 4 x 1000 MC, 2 x 1000 GP, 10 x 500 ANM64. Primary target: Heligoland, Naval base. Weather no cloud, slight haze. Bombed visually up-wind edge of smoke at 13.09 hours from 18,700 feet. Island obscured with flames and smoke. Wizard effort, no troubles.

22/04/1945 NG118 A2-H Bombing Bremen 15.01 18.40 20.43

Bomb load 1 x 4000 HC, 2 x 500 MC, 14 x 500 ANM64. Primary target: Bremen, in support of Troop concentration. Weather on approaching target 4-5/10ths cloud. Bombed on G.H. at 18.40 hours from 18,500 ft. Smoke seen rising from target area, and bombs to fall together. Flak hole through front turret. Concentrated and accurate good G.H. run, A/C was very much bumped about by flak along the river approaching the target.

07/05/1945 RE120 A2-C Manna The Hague 12.23 13.39 14.57

Dropping area The Hague. Dropped 4 Packs visually on White Cross and T.I.s at 13.39 hours. 4/10, 3,000 hazy, 1 pack brought back. Dropping concentrated. Lanc seen to leave bomber stream and orbit at 5144N 0300E. Large oil patch on sea. Time 13.10.

Passenger: Cunningham.

10/05/1945 RE117 A2-D Exodus Juvincourt - Ford 11.20 x 20.55

Duration 3.51. Outward 1.45 hours. Collected 24 ex POWs. Homeward 2.06 hours. Organisation good. Very short staff.

12/05/1945 RE117 A2-D Exodus Juvincourt - Wing 09.04 x 13.40

Duration 3.28. Outward 1.58 hours. Collected 24 POWs. Homeward 1.30 hours. Good organisation.

14/05/1945 RE117 A2-D Exodus Juvincourt - Oakley 10.03 x 15.03

Duration 3 hours 29 minutes. Outward 1 hr 29 mins. Collected 24 POWs. Homeward 2.00 hrs. Everything O.K.

17/05/1945 RA602 A2-H Exodus Brussels - Westcott 10.06 x 16.24

Duration 3 hrs 12 mins. Out 1 hr 17 mins. In 1 hr 55 mins. 10

Belgian refugees taken to Brussels.24 Ex POW Brought back to Westcott. R.T. at Brussels not very good.

19/05/1945 RE117A2-D Exodus Brussels - Oakley 12.11 x 19.23
Duration 3 hrs 2 mins. Out 1 hr 15 mins. In 1 hr 47 mins. 11 Belgian refugees taken to Brussels. 24 ex POWs. all military evacuated.

23/05/1945 RE117A2-D Exodus Brussels - Oakley 13.03 x 18.39
Duration 2 hrs 32 mins. Out 1 hr 09 mins. In 1 hr 24 min. 10 Belgian refugees returned to Brussels. No POWs available. All O.K.

F/L.   Frederick Phineas Hendy, DFC

146132 (1380396) F/L. Frederick Phineas "Fred" Hendy, DFC. Pilot.
190364 (1600658) P/O. Patrick Edwin Jackson. A/Bomber.
154876 (1583815) F/O. Robert William "Rob" Simons. Navigator. 24 ops.
161741 (657060) F/O. Alfred Ernest Nye. DFC. Navigator. 2 ops.
134705 (1324447) F/L. John Bruce Jarvis. Navigator. 1 op.
Sgt. J.E. Banham. Navigator. 11 ops.
F/S. Frank Bell. WOP/AG.
Sgt. F.J.B. Sharvin. MU/Gunner. 4 ops.
Sgt. I.R.B. "Ron" Clarke. MU/Gunner. 19 ops.
Sgt. K.J. Harris. MU&R/Gunner. F/S. George Edgar Sales.
MU&R/Gunner. 15 ops.
F/S. J. Tranter. R/Gunner. 1 op.
Sgt. E.W. Wall. F/Engineer.
J37099 F/O. Merlin Leigh Matkin, RCAF. 2nd Pilot. 13/01/1945
40160 later RCAF C94073
S/L. Hugh Clayton George Wilcox. 2nd Pilot. 16/01/1945
F/O. E. Jones. 2nd Pilot. 13/02/1945
191303 (1386380)
P/O. William Allwright Frederick Winkworth. 2nd Pilot.
16/02/1945
130318 (656066) F/L. Robert Geoffrey Keen Rice. 2nd Pilot.
07/03/1945

04/11/1944 PD325A2-L Bombing Solingen 11.38 14.12 15.57
Bomb load 1 x 4000 HC, 6 x 1000 ANM59, 4 x 500 GP, 2 x 500 MC (L/Delay). Primary target: Solingen. Weather 8-10/10ths cloud. Bombed at 14.12 hours from 19,500 feet on A/P visually.

L to R: 4th F.P. Hendy, 5th G.E. Sales. All other crew members unidentified.

From his normal crew, only F/O. F.P. Hendy did the mission as 2nd Pilot with F/O. J.H.G. Harland's crew.

05/11/1944 NG142 A2-H Bombing Solingen 10.08 13.04 14.59

Bomb load 1 x 4000 HC, 6 x 1000 ANM59, 4 x 500 GP, 2 x 500 GP (L/Delay). Primary target: Solingen. Weather 10/10ths cloud over target. Bombed at 13.04 hours from 17,500 feet on leading aircraft.

F/O. R.W. Simons Navigator until 22/01/1945.

Sgt. K.J. Harris MU/Gunner that day.

F/S. J. Tranter R/Gunner that day.

11/11/1944 PD324 A2-B Bombing Castrop Rauxel 08.07 11.07 12.54

Bomb load 1 x 4000 HC, 16 x 500 GP. Primary target: Castrop Rauxel, Oil refineries. Weather 10/10ths cloud. Bombed at 11.07 hours from 19,000 feet on G.H. Leader.

Sgt. F.J.B. Sharvin MU/Gunner from that day until 23/11/1944.

Sgt. K.J. Harris R/Gunner from that day until 27/03/1945.

16/11/1944 PD324 A2-B Bombing Heinsburg 13.04 15.31 17.25

Bomb load 1 x 4000 HC, 6 x 1000 MC, 6 x 500 GP. Primary target: Heinsburg. Weather - nil cloud with slight haze over target. Bombed at 15.31 hours from 9,000 feet. Church - Master Bomber said don't bomb T.I.s.

20/11/1944 PD334 A2-D Bombing Homberg 12.42 15.14 17.13

Bomb load 1 x 4000 HC, 3 x 500 GP, 13 x 500 MC. Primary target: Homberg. Weather 10/10ths cloud over target. Bombed at 15.14 hours from 20,000 feet on G.H. Leader.

23/11/1944 PD325 A2-L Bombing Nordstern 12.33 15.23 17.25

Bomb load 1 x 4000 HC, 16 x 500 GP. Primary target: Nordstern, Gelsenkirchen Oil refineries. Weather 10/10ths cloud. Bombed at 15.23 hours from 20,000 feet with leading aircraft and Red flares.

27/11/1944 PD325 A2-L Bombing Cologne 12.22 15.05 17.00

Bomb load 1 x 4000 HC, 16 x 500 GP. Primary target: Cologne, Marshalling Yards. Weather patchy cloud. Bombed at 15.05 hours from 20,000 feet with G.H. Leader.

Sgt. I.R.B. Clarke MU/Gunner from that day until 22/01/1945.

29/11/1944 PD325 A2-L Bombing Neuss 02.47 05.38 07.22

Bomb load 1 x 4000 HC, 6 x 1000 MC, 6 x 500 GP, 3 Flares Red/Green flares. Primary target: Neuss. Weather 10/10ths cloud over target but the glow of fires was seen through cloud. Bombed at 05.38 hours from 20,000 feet. Red flares with Green stars. T.I.s very well concentrated.

04/12/1944 PD334 A2-D Bombing Oberhausen 11.39 14.08 16.00

Bomb load 1 x 4000 HC, 6 x 1000 MC, 6 x 500 GP. Primary target: Oberhausen, Built up area. Weather 10/10ths cloud. Bombed at 14.08 hours from 20,000 feet on release of G.H. Leader.

05/12/1944 PD334 A2-D Bombing Hamm 08.52 11.29 13.55

Bomb load 1 x 4000 HC, 14 x 500 GP, 2 x 500 GP Long Delay. Primary target: Hamm. Weather 10/10ths cloud over target, but otherwise varying from 6-10/10ths. Bombed at 11.29 hours from 20,000 feet on G.H. Leader.

06/12/1944 PD334 A2-D Bombing Merseburg 16.52 20.50 00.22

Bomb load 1 x 4000 HC, 8 x 500 GP, 1 x 500 GP Long Delay. Primary target: Merseburg. Weather 10/10ths cloud with odd breaks. Bombed at 20.50 hours from 21,000 feet on upwind edge of flares.

16/12/1944 LM627 A2-H Bombing Siegen 11.21 15.01 17.00

Bomb load 1 x 4000 HC, 5 x 1000 MC, 7 x 500 GP. Primary target: Siegen. Weather very bad on route with icing and cloud. Bombed at 15.01 hours from 18,000 feet on G.H. Leader.

21/12/1944 NG118 A2-E Bombing Trier 12.14 15.01 17.03

Bomb load 1 x 4000 HC, 10 x 500 GP, 6 x 250 GP. Primary target: Trier, Marshalling yards. Weather 10/10 cloud, tops 6/9000 feet. Bombed at 15.01 hours from 18,000 feet on G.H.

23/12/1944 NG118   A2-E   Bombing Trier   11.46   14.33   16.11

Bomb load 1 x 4000 HC, 10 x 500 GP, 6 x 250 GP. Primary target: Trier. Weather clear over target. Bombed at 14.33 hours from 17,000 feet on centre of town.

28/12/1944 PA186 A2-G   Bombing Cologne   12.14   15.04   16.51

Bomb load 1 x 4000 HC, 10 x 500 GP, 4 x 250 Red T.I.s. Primary target: Koln Gremberg, Marshalling yards. Weather 10/10ths cloud or fog. Bombed at 15.04 hours from 19,500 feet on G.H.

31/12/1944 PB482 A2-K   Bombing Vohwinkle   11.30   14.42   16.26

Bomb load 1 x 4000 HC, 2 x 500 M58, 10 x 500 M64, 2 x 500 GP, 1 Flare. Primary target: Vohwinkel. Weather 10/10ths cloud on approaching target although the target itself was clear. Bombed at 14.42 hours from 19,500 feet on G.H.

01/01/1945 PB482 A2-K   Bombing Vohwinkle   16.20   19.34   21.30

Bomb load 1 x 4000 HC, 12 x 500 ANM64, 2 x 500 GP. Primary target: Vohwinkel. Weather clear. Bombed at 19.34 hours from 20,500 feet on G.H.

03/01/1945 PA186 A2-G   Bombing Dortmund   12.42   15.32   17.27

Bomb load 1 x 4000 HC, 12 x 500 ANM58 or 64, 3 x 500 GP, 1 Flare. Primary target: Dortmund Buckarde. Weather 10/10ths cloud over target. Bombed at 15.32 hours from 21,000 feet on G.H.

05/01/1945 PA186 A2-G   Bombing Ludwigshafen 11.18 15.08   17.17

Bomb load 1 x 4000 HC, 10 x 500 ANM58 or 64, 2 x 500 GP, 1 Flare. Primary target: Ludwigshafen, Marshalling yards. Weather clear over target. Bombed at 15.08 hours from 20,000 feet on G.H. Aircraft hit by flak, fuselage damaged.

06/01/1945 PA186 A2-G   Bombing Neuss   15.47   18.47   20.14

Bomb load 1 x 4000 HC, 10 x 500 ANM64, 4 x 250 Red T.I.s. Primary target: Neuss. Weather 8-10/10ths cloud over target. Bombed at 18.47 hours from 19,800 feet on G.H.

11/01/1945 LM627   A2-H   Bombing Krefeld   11.42   15.12   16.40

Bomb load 1 x 4000 HC, 10 x 500 ANM64, 4 x 250 GP, 1 Flare. Primary target: Krefeld. Weather 10/10ths cloud above and below. Visibility poor. Bombed at 15.11 hours from 19,500 feet on G.H.

13/01/1945 PA186 A2-G   Bombing Saarbrucken   11.52   15.24   17.32

Bomb load 1 x 4000 HC, 10 x 500 ANM58 or 64, 4 x 250 GP. Primary target: Saarbrucken. Weather 3-5/10ths cloud, tops 4/5,000 feet. Bombed at 15.24 hours from 19,500 feet on G.H. All aircrafts on this operation were diverted on return to Exeter as weather at base was unfit to land.

F/O. M.L. Matkin 2nd Pilot that day.

15/01/1945 PA186 A2-G Bombing Lagendreer   11.42 15.01 16.35
   Bomb load 1 x 4000 HC, 10 x 500 ANM64, 4 x 250 GP, 1 Flare.
Primary target: Lagendreer. Weather 10/10ths cloud. Bombed at 15.01
hours from 19,000 feet on G.H.

16/01/1945 PA186 A2-G Bombing Wanne-Eickel 23.10 02.27 04.19
   Bomb load 1 x 4000 HC, 10 x 500 ANM58, 4 x 250 GP, 1 Flare.
Primary target: Wanne-Eickel, Benzol plant. Weather 10/10ths thin
low cloud. Bombed at 02.27 hours from 18,000 feet on G.H.

   S/L. H.C.G. Wilcox 2nd Pilot that day.

22/01/1945 PA186 A2-G Bombing Hamborn 16.56 20.08 21.43
   Bomb load 1 x 4000 HC, 7 x 500 ANM58 or 64, 2 x 500 GP
(L/Delay), 3 x 250 GP. Primary target: Hamborn, Thyssen works.
Weather over target clear and almost as bright as day. Bombed at 20.08
hours from 20,000 feet on centre of red T.I.s.

08/02/1945 NG203   A2-C Bombing Hohenbudberg 03.30 06.26
   08.15
   Bomb load 1 x 4000 HC, 2 x 500 MC, 4 x 250 GP, 4 x 500 GP, 6 x
500 ANM64. Primary target: Hohenbudberg, Marshalling yards.
Weather 8/10ths cloud over target. Bombed at 06.26 hours from
18,300 feet on Red T.I.s. Large fires seen on target area.

   F/O. A.E. Nye Navigator that day.

   F/S. G.E. Sales MU/Gunner from that day until 27/03/1945.

13/02/1945 PA186 A2-G Bombing Dresden 21.38 01.38 06.45
   Bomb load 1 x 500 MC, 15 x No. 14 Clusters. Primary target:
Dresden. Weather 5/10ths cloud over target. Bombed at 01.38 hours
from 19,500 feet on centre of fires.

   F/O. E. Jones was 2nd Pilot that day and F/O. A.E. Nye Navigator.

14/02/1945 NN776   A2-D Bombing Chemnitz 20.17   00.34 04.23
   Bomb load 1 x 500 MC, 15 x No. 14 Clusters. Primary target:
Chemnitz. Weather 8-10/10ths cloud, tops 15-16,000 feet with
occasional breaks. Bombed at 00.34 hours from 19,300 feet on
Red/Green flares.

   F/O. R.W. Simons Navigator until that day.

16/02/1945 NG298   JI-E Bombing Wesel 12.26 16.00 17.33
   Bomb load 1 x 4000 HC, 4 x 500 GP, 2 x 500 MC L/Delay, 4 x 250
GP, 6 x 500 ANM64. Primary target: Wesel. Weather clear. Bombed at
16.00 hours from 20,000 feet on centre of built up area.

   P/O. W.A.F. Winkworth was 2nd Pilot that day and F/L. J.B. Jarvis
Navigator.

23/02/1945 NN781   A2-D   Bombing Gelsenkirchen 11.15 15.00 18.05

Bomb load 1 x 4000 HC, 9 x 500 ANM64, 2 x 500 MC, 4 x 250 GP. Primary target Gelsenkirchen. Weather 10/10ths cloud. Bombed at 15.00 hours from 20,000 feet on leading aircraft. On return landed at Hutton Cranswick.

Sgt. J.E. Banham Navigator from that day.

27/02/1945 NG203   A2-C   Bombing Gelsenkirchen 10.48 14.27 16.24

Bomb load 1 x 4000 HC, 2 x 500 MC (L/D 37B), 9 x 500 ANM64, 4 x 250 GP. Primary target: Gelsenkirchen (Alma Pluts) Benzin plant. Weather 10/10ths cloud, 6/10,000 feet tops. Bombed at 14.27 hours from 20,000 feet on G.H. Leader.

28/02/1945 NG203   A2-C   Bombing Nordstern 08.52   12.05 14.15

Bomb load 1 x 4000 HC, 9 x 500 ANM64, 2 x 500 MC L/D, 4 x 250 GP. Primary target: Nordstern (Gelsenkirchen). Weather 10/10ths cloud. Bombed at 12.05 hours from 20,100 feet on leading aircraft.

02/03/1945 NN717   A2-E   Bombing Koln   12.45 x 18.20

Bomb load 1 x 4000 HC, 12 x 500 ANM64. Primary target: Koln. Weather 10/10ths cloud over Koln, South and South-East of Koln clear. Abortive sortie. Total bomb load brought back to Base.

06/03/1945 NF966 A2-G   Bombing Salzbergen 08.14   12.14   14.10

Bomb load 1 x 4000 HC, 12 x 500 ANM64, 2 x 500MC. Primary target: Salzbergen, Wintershall oil plant. Weather 10/10ths cloud over target, tops 10,000 feet. Bombed at 12.14 hours from 21,000 feet on leading G.H. aircraft.

07/03/1945 NF966 A2-G   Bombing Dessau   17.07 22.08 02.28

Bomb load 1 x 4000 HC, 6 x Mk.17 Clusters. Primary target: Dessau. Weather 5 to 10/10ths thin cloud. Bombed at 22.08 hours from 19,500 feet on Red T.I.s.

F/L. R.G.K. Rice 2nd Pilot that day.

10/03/1945 ME529   A2-F   Bombing Gelsenkirchen 12.02 15.37 17.20

Bomb load 1 x 4000 HC, 13 x 500 ANM64, 2 x 500 MC. Primary target: Gelsenkirchen. Weather 10/10ths cloud at target, tops 8,000 feet. Bombed at 15.37 hours from 19,000 feet on leading G.H. aircraft. Squadron formation good. Attack should be accurate.

12/03/1945 ME529   A2-F   Bombing Dortmund 12.53 16.57 18.42

Bomb load 1 x 4000 HC, 13 x 500 ANM64. Primary target: Dortmund. Weather 10/10ths cloud over target, tops 6/10,000 feet.

Bombed at 16.57 hours from 19,000 feet on G.H. Leader.

14/03/1945 PD389 A2-J Bombing Heinrichshutte 13.08 16.40 18.43

Bomb load 1 x 4000 HC, 12 x 500 ANM64. Primary target: Heinrichshutte, Hattingen Steel works & Benzol plant. Weather 10/10ths cloud, tops 7/12,000 feet. Bombed at 16.40 hours from 18,100 feet on leading G.H. aircraft.

27/03/1945 NN776 A2-D Bombing Hamm Sachsen 10.23 14.02 15.49

Bomb load 1 x 4000 HC, 13 x 500 ANM64, 2 x 500 MC. Primary target: Hamm Sachsen, Benzol plant. Weather 10/10ths cloud. Bombed at 14.02 hours at 18,400 feet on leading aircraft.

04/04/1945 ME529 A2-F Bombing Merseburg 18.33 22.52 03.43

Bomb load 1 x 4000 HC, 6 x 500 ANM64. Weather 10/10th cloud, tops 8,000 feet. Bombed primary target Merseburg (Leuna) on centre of 3 Red flares & Green stars at 22.52 hours from 20,000 feet. Orange glow seen through the clouds. Arrived on time, no gound markings visible so we did in orbit until the skymarkers were placed. M.B. reception indistinct, bombing rather scattered.

Sgt. K.J. Harris MU/Gunner that day.

F/S. G.E. Sales R/Gunner that day.

P/O. Walter Henry

171394 (1345806) P/O. Walter Henry.   Pilot.
J86161 (R120852) F/S. William Sidney Ball, RCAF.   A/Bomber.
1323954   Sgt. Stanley William Ricketts.   Navigator.
1576668   Sgt. Francis Beardsley Vallance. WOP/AG.
542541 Sgt. Douglas Kenny.   MU/Gunner.
1821076   Sgt. William Lannigan.   R/Gunner.
1603741   Sgt. Alfred Edwin Bennett.   F/Engineer.

20/12/1943 DS823 JI-M Bombing Frankfurt 17.29 19.50 22.52

Bomb load 1 x 4000, 48 x 30 incendiaries, 950 x 4 incendiaries, 100 x 4 incendiaries. Primary target: Frankfurt. 5-7/10 cloud, visibility above cloud good. Bombed target at 19.50 at 20,000. 16 x 30 hung up, brought back to Base. Effort appeared too wide spread and fires burning short of target. Shortage of T.I.s may have had a lot to do with this.

24/12/1943 DS823 JI-M   Bombing Berlin   00.20 04.09   08.02

Bomb load 1 x 4000, 32 x 30 incendiaries, 450 x 4 incendiaries, 90 x 4 incendiaries. Primary target: Berlin. 5/10 cloud. Bombed at 04.09 at 20,000 ft. Many good fires seen on leaving, reflected through clouds. Quite concentrated. Good attack. Route OK but rather long. Photo attempted.

01/01/1944 DS815 JI-N Bombing Berlin   00.28 03.12   07.20

Bomb load 1 x 4000, 24 x 30, 450 x 4, 90 x 4 lb incendiaries. Primary target: Berlin. There was 10/10 cloud. Bombed at 03.12 hours at 20,000 feet. Concentration of red and green markers. Route OK. Photo attempted. No troubles.

02/01/1944 DS815 JI-N Bombing Berlin   00.03 02.56   07.03

Bomb load 1 x 2000, 40 x 30, 900 x 4 incendiaries. Primary target: Berlin. There was 10/10 cloud. Bombed at 02.56 hours at 20,000 ft. In centre of red T.I.s with green stars - good concentration. Glow under cloud on leaving target. Icing on way over sea. Route pretty good. Better than previous nights' raids.

27/01/1944 DS823 JI-M   Bombing Berlin   17.42 20.36   02.05

Bomb load 1 x 4000, 32 x 30, 450 x 4, 90 x 4 incendiaries. Primary target: Berlin. There was 10/10 cloud. Bombed at 20.36 hours at 20,000 ft. One cluster of green/red markers with two others nearby. Should be alright if P.F.F. were correct.

28/01/1944 DS823 JI-M   Bombing Berlin   23.59 03.23   08.07

Bomb load 1 x 4000 lb bomb, 24 x 30, 180 x 4, 90 x 4 incendiaries. Primary target: Berlin. There was 10/10 cloud. Bombed at 03.23 hours at 20,000 ft. Very good raid. Many numerous fires seen from German coast. Route OK and good raid. Large explosion at 03.19 hours.

15/02/1944 DS823 JI-M   Bombing Berlin   17.33 21.36   00.53

Bomb load 1 x 4000 lb bomb, 32 x 30, 540 x 4, 90 x 4 incendiaries. Primary target: Berlin. There was 10/10 cloud with tops 10,000 ft. Bombed at 21.36 hrs. at 20,000 ft. One good concentration with another smaller about 3 miles eastward. There were times when no markers were visible. One big glow seen still visible 50 miles away.

19/02/1944 DS823 JI-M   Bombing Leipzig   23.51 x 02.30

Bomb load 1 x 3000, 1 x 500 lb bomb, 900 x 4, 40 x 30 incendiaries. Aircraft missing. No news.

Shot down by a night-fighter and crashed 02.30hrs on the 20th February 1944 at Essern-Osterloh on the SW edge of Grosses Moor, 11 km NE of Rahden. Possibly attributable to Lt. Hans Raum, 9./NJG3. All crew KIA. All are buried in Rheinberg War Cemetery.

F/O. Ellis Hill

185478 (1147002) F/O. Ellis Hill.   Pilot.
1684645   F/S. Frank Guest.   A/Bomber.
R179821   F/S. R. Kimpton, RCAF.   Navigator. 5 ops.
   F/S. R.G. Wilson.   Navigator. 1 op.
156559 (1392560)
   F/O. Reginald Clifford Andrew "Reg" Cowles, DFC.   Navigator. 5
ops.
NZ412324
   F/O. Oliver Lawrence Goldsmith. DFC. RNZAF. WOP/AG. 3 ops.
1817884   Sgt. Cyril Ernest Atter.   WOP/AG. 8 ops.
1852397   Sgt. John Henry Balman.   MU/Gunner.
1877102   Sgt. Alan George Bowen.   R/Gunner.
2221251   Sgt. Norman Arthur Readman.   F/Engineer.

23/09/1944 LM285   JI-K Bombing Neuss   19.26 21.30 00.28
   Bomb load 8 x 1000 ANM59, 3 x 1000 ANM44, 4 x 500 GP.
Primary target: Neuss. Weather 10/10ths cloud over target, tops
8/10,000 feet. Bombed at 21.30 hours from 20,000 feet on red glow
through cloud.
   F/S. R. Kimpton RCAF Navigator until 14/10/1944.
   F/O. O.L. Goldsmith DFC WOP/AG until 26/09/1944.
25/09/1944 PD265 JI-G Bombing Pas de Calais 08.20 x 10.45
   Bomb load 11 x 1000 MC, 4 x 500 GP. Primary target: Calais.
Abandoned mission on Master Bomber's instructions. Jettisoned 2 x
1000, 3 x 500 at 5025N 0105E.
26/09/1944 PD265 JI-G Bombing Calais 11.32 12.45 14.13
   Bomb load 11 x 1000 MC, 4 x 500 GP. Primary target: Calais 7D.
Weather clear below cloud which was 3,500 feet. Bombed at 12.45
hours from 3,000 feet on red T.I. + 1 second.
14/10/1944 LM627   JI-D* Bombing Duisburg 06.54 09.06 10.45
   Bomb load 11 x 1000 MC, 4 x 500 GP Long Delay. Primary target:
Duisburg. Weather patchy cloud with gaps for bombing. Bombed at
09.06 hours from 18,700 feet. Large building on neck of land in Dock
area.
   (*) Note: Due to an error in the ORBs LM627 JI-D is also noted at

the same hours for P/O. L.S. Drew's crew. At this period LM627 was L.S. Drew's usual aircraft.

Sgt. C.E. Atter WOP/AG from that day.

14/10/1944 PB142 JI-A
BombingDuisburg   23.04 01.33   03.36

Bomb load 1 x 4000 HC. 14 x No. 14 Clusters. Primary target: Duisburg. Weather was clear with small amount of cloud over the target. Bombed at 01.33 hours from 23,500 feet. Centre of green T.I.s.

25/10/1944 NN717   JI-E
BombingEssen   12.56 15.31   16.55

Bomb load 1 x 4000 HC, 6 x 1000 MC, 6 x 500 GP. Primary target: Essen. Weather over target 10/10ths

Reginald Clifford Andrew "Reg" Cowles

(courtesy Maureen Kristjanson)

low cloud, with one clear patch which appeared to fill up later in the attack. Bombed at 15.31 hours from 22,500 feet. Red flares.

F/S. R.G. Wilson Navigator that day.

29/11/1944 NG350   JI-C BombingNeuss 02.56 05.35 07.10

Bomb load 1 x 4000 HC, 2100 x 4 incendiaries. Primary target: Neuss. Weather 10/10ths cloud over target but the glow of fires was seen through cloud. Bombed at 05.35 hours from 20,000 feet. Red flares with green stars. Cloud obscured ground.

F/O. R.C.A. Cowles Navigator from that day.

02/12/1944 NN717   JI-E BombingDortmund 12.51 14.57 16.55

Bomb load 14 x 1000 HC. Primary target: Dortmund, Benzol plant. Weather 10/10ths cloud. Bombed at 14.57 hours from 20,000 feet on Red sky markers.

06/12/1944 LM285   JI-K BombingMerseburg 17.06 20.54 00.30

Bomb load 1 x 4000 HC, 8 x 500 GP and 1 x 500 GP Long Delay. Primary target: Merseburg. Weather 10/10ths cloud with odd breaks. Bombed at 20.54 hours from 21,800 feet on Red/Green flare.

08/12/1944 LM733   JI-F Bombing Duisburg   08.42 11.04 12.40
   Bomb load 14 x 1000 ANM59. Primary target: Duisberg. Weather 10/10ths cloud. Bombed at 11.04 hours from 20,200 feet on G.H. Leader.
11/12/1944 NG350   JI-C Bombing Osterfeld   08.33 x   x
   Bomb load 1 x 4000 HC, 15 x 500 GP, 1 x 500 GP Long Delay. Primary target: Osterfeld. Weather 10/10ths cloud, tops 16,000 feet. Aircraft missing.
   Hit by Flak and fell into a built up area of Sterkrade, destroying several houses. Sadly none of the crew survived. All are buried in the Reichswald Forest War Cemetery. The two Air Gunners Sgts Balman and Bowen were 19 years old. F/O. E. Hill KIA, Sgt. N.A. Readman KIA, F/O. R.C.A. Cowles DFC KIA, F/S. F. Guest KIA, Sgt. C.E. Atter KIA, Sgt J.H. Balman KIA, Sgt. A.G. Bowen KIA.

F/O. acting F/L.Guy Harold Dudley Hinde

80476 (778644) F/L. Guy Harold Dudley Hinde. Pilot.
A422366 (O22045) F/S. John David Alford, RAAF. A/Bomber.
143850 (859619) F/O. Maurice Stanley Colston Emery. Navigator.
1578078. Sgt. D. Thom.   WOP/AG. 4 ops.
115327 (1059813) F/L. Ronald Thompson. DFC. WOP/AG. 1 op.
1311211   Sgt. W. Muskett.   WOP/AG. 1 op.
1672756.   Sgt. Ronald "Ron" Galloway. MU/Gunner.
1568236.   Sgt. Robert Curle. R/Gunner.
1566577.   Sgt. W.J. Stephen. F/Engineer.

03/11/1943 DS738 JI-J Gardening Frisian Islands 18.05 x 20.09
   Aircraft carried 2 x B218, 4 x 200. Primary area Frisian Islands. No cloud. Visibility good. 6 Vegetables planted successfully in ordered position.
18/11/1943 DS738 JI-J Bombing Mannheim 17.19 20.39 23.40
   Bomb load 1 x 8000. Primary target Mannheim attacked. Some high cloud visibility good. Green T.I.s seen. A number of incendiaries burning. Yellow T.I.s seen at 20.22 when about 36 miles west of Turn Point. Attacked target at 20.39 at 18,000 feet.
22/11/1943 DS738 JI-J Bombing Berlin 17.38 20.18 23.09
   Bomb load 1 x 4000, 360 x 4 incendiaries, 90 x 4 incendiaries. Primary target: Berlin. Green T.I. Markers seen. Large Red glow seen

through the cloud 20.18 hours. 60 x 4 hung up probably due to electrical fault. Pretty good cloud making visual report difficult, although the terrific glow reported at 20.18 came up so suddenly that it seemed like an explosion.

23/11/1943 DS738 JI-J Bombing Berlin 17.36 x 00.01

Bomb load 1 x 4000 HC, 32 x 30 incendiaries, 540 x 4 incendiaries, 90 x 4. Primary target: Berlin. 10/10 cloud. Tops 8/10,000 feet. Visibility good. Bombed target at 20.13 hours at 20,000 feet. Glow of fires visible under cloud for considerable distance on return route.

26/11/1943 DS738 JI-J Bombing Berlin 17.50 21.20 00.25

Bomb load 1 x 4000 HC, 24 x 30 incendiaries, 405 x 4 incendiaries, 45 x 4. Primary target: Berlin. No cloud, visibility good. Target attacked at 21.20 hrs. At 20,000 feet. Route markers seen as briefed, all effective. Monica OK. Gee OK. Photo flash failed. No flak in centre of Berlin.

F/L. R. Thompson WOP/AG that day.

02/12/1943 DS738 JI-J Bombing Berlin 17.03 x x

Bomb load 1 x 8000, 160 x 4 incendiaries, 20 x 4 incendiaries. Primary target: Berlin. Aircraft missing.

Sgt. W. Muskett WOP/AG that day.

Shot down by a night fighter over Potsdam approaching the target area. Possibly the Lancaster claimed by Lt. Alfred Koerver of Stab.II or 7/JG302 at 20.11 hours.

According to the Bomb Aimer, F/S. JD Alford RAAF, port fin and rudder were shot away, port wing tank set on fire, undercarriage hydraulics damaged, probable damage to rear turret. Order to bale out given by skipper by intercom and lights acknowledged by all except Rear Gunner who was probably shot up. Port wing was on fire and beginning to dive. It is thought that the pilot, F/L. Hinde from Rhodesia, was thrown clear. All crew survived as POWs except for Sgt. Curle. His body was not recovered and he is commemorated on Panel 146 of the Runnymede Memorial.

F/L. G.H.D. Hinde was interned in Camp L1, POW No.1676, Sgt. J.D. Alford in Camp 4B, POW No.267145, P/O. M.S.C. Emery in Camp L1, POW No.1756, Sgt. R. Galloway was confined to Hospital due to injuries so had no POW No, Sgt. W.J. Stephen was held in the Dulag Luft Interrogation Centre and also had no POW No.

P/O. Oliver Joseph Tate Hodgson

NZ4213260 P/O.   Oliver Joseph Tate Hodgson, RNZAF. Pilot.
NZ4212790 F/S.   Vivian Francis Dufty, RNZAF.   A/Bomber.
NZ438691 F/S. John Gower Hughes, RNZAF.   Navigator.
NZ4215138 F/S.   Barry Gordon Ballingall, RNZAF. WOP/AG.
NZ423107 (*)   F/S. Roy Newling Spence, RNZAF. MU/Gunner.
NZ427034 F/S. P. Turner, RNZAF.   R/Gunner.
1397533 F/S. M.S. Jenner.   F/Engineer.

(*) recorded as NZ423107 in 514 Sqn ORBs and NZ427107 in another source.

29/06/1945 RE231 JI-A Post Mortem Special mission 10.12 x 15.59
05/07/1945 RE137 JI-D Post Mortem Special mission 13.35 x 18.32
12/07/1945 RA601   JI-J Bullseye Orleans-Nantes ca.21.30 x
   ca.04.00 Only noted in ORB summary. Op not detailed. This is according O.J.T. Hodgson's logbook "Bullseye Ex. Base-Orleans-Nantes-Swindon".

F/O. Arthur John Holland, DFC

A427474 F/O. Arthur John Holland. DFC. RAAF.   Pilot.
 (*) F/S. Szilard Henrik Knotz   A/Bomber.
 F/S.   A. "Mike" Mulholland.   Navigator.
 Sgt.   George W. Halliwell.   WOP/AG.
 Sgt.   Charles O'Brien.   MU/Gunner. 35 ops.
1819401 Sgt. Bleddyn Lloyd Roberts.   MU/Gunner. 1 op.
 Sgt. William Gruer Carnagie "Bill" "Willie" MacDonald.   R/Gunner.
 Sgt.   A. Donald Douglas.   F/Engineer.

 (*): F/Sgt. Szilard Henrik Knotz (Hungarian Jew from Budapest) known as "Silard" or "Silard Henry", A.K.A. "Roy Barrett".

Back, 3rd from left, and below: J.G. Hughes
(courtesy Oliver Hodgson)

20/07/1944 DS787 A2-D Bombing   Homberg 23.28 01.25 03.08
  Bomb load 1 x 4000 HC, 2 x 500 MC, 14 x 500 GP. Primary target: Homberg, Oil plant. Weather clear, slight haze. Bombed at 01.25 hours from 18,000 feet green T.I. Huge clouds of black smoke up to 10,000 feet. Had combat with enemy aircraft.
23/07/1944 PB185 A2-F Bombing Kiel 22.35 01.25 04.14
  Bomb load 10 x 1000 MC, 6 x 500 GP. Primary target: Kiel,

Warehouses and docks. Weather 10/10ths cloud. Bombed at 01.25 hours from 18,000 feet green T.I. T.I.s widely scattered. Had combat with enemy aircraft.

25/07/1944 LL670 A2-K Bombing Stuttgart 21.48 x 00.39
Bomb load 5 x 1000 MC, 3 x 500 GP. Abortive sortie. Port inner engine u/s. Aircraft overshot runway on landing on 3 engines. Fuselage damaged.

27/07/1944 LL677 A2-E Bombing Les Catelliers 16.52 18.52 20.15
Bomb load 18 x 500 GP. Primary target: Les Catelliers, Flying bomb site. Bombed at 18.52 hours from 16,600 feet on Mosquito.

28/07/1944 LL697 A2-B Bombing Stuttgart 21.48 01.50 05.31
Bomb load 13 x 500 GP. Primary target: Stuttgart. Weather 10/10ths cloud. Bombed at 01.50 hours from 19,500 feet green T.I.s. Master Bomber not heard. Some glows of fires, appeared to be a moderate raid.

30/07/1944 LL697 A2-B Bombing Caen 06.07 07.51 10.07
Bomb load 18 x 500 GP. Primary target: Caen 'B'. Weather 10/10ths cloud. Bombed at 07.51 hours from 1,700 feet South end of smoke and dust as instructed by Master Bomber. Bombing very concentrated, should be a good attack. Master Bomber very clear.

01/08/1944 LL697 A2-B Bombing Foret de Nieppe 19.27 20.46 21.52
Bomb load 11 x 1000 MC, 4 x 500 GP. Primary target: De Nieppe, constructional works. Bombed at 20.46 hours from 11,500 feet on leading aircraft.

03/08/1944 DS842 A2-J Bombing Bois de Cassan 12.00 14.08 15.56
Bomb load 11 x 1000 MC, 4 x 500 GP. Primary target: Bois de Cassan, Flying bomb supply depot. Bombed at 14.08 hours from 15,000 feet, Red T.I.s.

07/08/1944 DS842 A2-J Bombing Mare de Magne 21.56 23.48 01.11
Bomb load 9 x 1000 MC, 4 x 500 GP. Primary target: Mare de Magne (just past Caen). Weather clear over target. Bombed at 23.48 hours from 7,000 feet red T.I.s. Bombing concentrated.
Mare-de-Magne: place between Caen and Fontenay le Marmion.

09/08/1944 DS842 A2-J Bombing Fort d'Englos 21.54 23.17 00.35
Bomb load 13 x 1000 MC. Primary target: Fort d'Englos (Lille), Petrol dump. Weather clear. Bombed at 23.17 hours from 13,000 feet, 4 green T.I.s. Bombing did not appear too concentrated, Master

Bomber indistinct.

The fort of Ennetières-en-Weppes, or "fort d'Englos" is one of a set of six forts surrounding Lille.

11/08/1944 DS842 A2-J Bombing Lens 14.13 16.33 17.39

Bomb load 11 x 1000 MC, 4 X 500 GP. Primary target: Lens, Marshalling yards. Weather 3/10ths cloud. Bombed at 16.33 hours from 14,000 feet, red T.I. Bomb bursts well concentrated in yards.

12/08/1944 LM285 JI-K Bombing Russelsheim 21.50 00.19 02.53

Bomb load 1 x 4000 HC, 6 x 500 No. 14 clusters, 6 x (150 x 4) 10% X1 B. Primary target: Russelsheim. Weather clear. Bombed at 00.19 hours from 18,000 feet. Red T.I.s. Bombing seemed concentrated. Master Bomber heard talking to Deputy but no instructions heard.

16/08/1944 LL728 A2-L Bombing Stettin 21.16 01.09 05.39

Bomb load 1 x 2000 HC, 9 x 500 lb 'J' type clusters. Primary target: Stettin. Weather 9/10ths cloud. Bombed at 01.09 hours from 19,000 feet, centre of concentration of fires as no markers were visible. Large 'L' shaped fire seen in built up area.

05/09/1944 DS842 A2-J Bombing Le Havre 17.34 19.23 20.48

Bomb load 11 x 1000 MC, 4 x 500 GP. Primary target: Le Havre. Bombed at 19.23 hours from 14,000 feet red T.I.

08/09/1944 LL666 A2-K Bombing Le Havre 06.09 x 08.40

Bomb load 11 x 1000 MC, 4 x 500 GP. Primary target: Le Havre. Weather 10/10ths cloud down to 3,000 feet. Returned early with starboard outer engine u/s.

11/09/1944 DS842 A2-J Bombing Kamen 16.12 18.43 20.33

Bomb load 1 x 4000 HC, 16 x 500 GP. Weather clear. Primary target: Kamen. Bombed at 18.43 hours from 16,900 feet on yellow T.I.s.

14/09/1944 DS842 A2-J Bombing Wassenaar 12.48 14.30 15.34

Bomb load 11 x 1000 MC, 4 x 500 GP. Primary target: Wassenaar. Weather was good, nil cloud. Bombed at 14.30 hours from 12,000 feet, 200 yards to port of red T.I.s.

17/09/1944 DS842 A2-J Bombing Boulogne 10.25 11.46 13.02

Bomb load 11 x 1000 MC, 4 x 500 GP. Primary target: Boulogne Aiming Point 3. Weather clear below cloud. Bombed at 11.46 hours from 2,400 feet, starboard of red T.I.s.

20/09/1944 DS786 A2-L Bombing Calais 14.57 16.02 17.38

Bomb load 11 x 1000 MC, 4 x 500 GP. Primary target: Calais. Weather clear over target. Bombed at 16.02 hours from 2,400 feet, red T.I.s.

25/09/1944 NG141   A2-J   Bombing Pas de Calais 08.28 x 11.13
   Bomb load 11 x 1000 MC, 4 x 500 GP. Primary target: Calais. Abandoned mission on Master Bomber's instructions. Jettisoned 3 x 1000 MC, 1 x 500 GP.
26/09/1944 NG141   A2-J   Bombing Calais   11.28 12.49 14.09
   Bomb load 11 x 1000 MC, 4 x 500 GP. Primary target: Calais 7D. Weather clear below cloud which was 3,500 feet. Bombed at 12.49 hours from 3,000 feet on red T.I. + 1 second.
27/09/1944 LM735   A2-G   Bombing Calais   07.25 08.43 10.18
   Bomb load 11 x 1000 MC, 4 x 500 GP. Primary target: Calais 15. Weather, cloud 5,500 feet 10/10ths. Bombed at 08.43 hours from 5500 feet to port of red T.I.
03/10/1944 NG141   A2-J   Bombing Westkapelle 12.01   13.21 14.23
   Bomb load 1 x 4000 MC, 6 x 1000 MC, 1 x 500 GP L/Delay. Primary target: Westkapelle (Walcheren). Weather patchy-scattered cloud with base 5,000 feet. Bombed at 13.21 hours from 5,500 feet visually.
05/10/1944 NG141   A2-J   Bombing Saarbrucken 17.25   20.32 22.29
   Bomb load 11 x 1000 MC, 1 x 500 GP. Primary target: Saarbrucken, Marshalling yards. Weather clear over target. Bombed at 20.32 hours at 13,500 feet green T.I.s. Defences fairly heavy. Searchlights in action. Master Bomber gave instructions not to bomb as we bombed.
   Sgt. B.L. Roberts MU/Gunner that day.
07/10/1944 NG141   A2-J   Bombing Emmerich 12.22 14.29 16.14
   Bomb load 1 x 4000 HC, 10 x No. 14 clusters, 4 x (150 x 4). Primary target: Emmerich. Weather clear with cloud at 13,000 feet. Bombed at 14.29 hours from 13,000 feet on South-west corner of smoke on town.
21/10/1944 NG141   A2-J   Bombing Flushing   10.55 12.28 13.35
   Bomb load 12 x 1000 MC, 2 x 500 GP. Primary target: Flushing 'B'. Weather clear. Bombed at 12.28 hours from 8,000 feet. Centre of target area.
23/10/1944 NG141   A2-J   Bombing Essen   16.39 19.46 22.09
   Bomb load 1 x 4000 HC, 6 x 1000 MC, 6 x 500 GP. Primary target: Essen. Weather 10/10ths cloud over target - tops 12/14,000 feet with most appalling weather on route. Bombed at 19.46 hours from 22,500 feet. Green Wanganui flares.
25/10/1944 NG141   A2-J   Bombing Essen   13.14 15.45 17.16

Bomb load 1 x 4000 HC, 10 x No.14 Clusters, 4 x 150 x 4. Primary target: Essen. Weather over target 10/10ths low cloud, with one clear patch which appeared to fill up later in the attack. Bombed at 15.45 hours from 22,500 feet. Centre of smoke and fires.

28/10/1944 NG141   A2-J   Bombing Flushing   08.59   10.16   11.23
Bomb load 1 x 4000 HC, 6 x 1000 MC, 4 x 500 GP. Primary target: Flushing. Weather over the target quite clear and conditions perfect, although believed to be only local, and some low cloud approaching. Bombed at 10.16 hours from 10,000 feet. A/P.

29/10/1944 PD324 A2-B   Bombing Flushing 09.57 11.38   12.34
Bomb load 11 x 1000 ANM59, 4 x 500 GP. MC. Primary target: Flushing, Gun installations. Weather clear over target. Bombed at 11.38 hours from 6,000 feet. Starboard of Green T.I.s on Master Bomber's instructions.

30/10/1944 NG141   A2-J   Bombing Wesseling 09.20   12.00   13.25
Bomb load 1 x 4000 HC, 16 x 500 GP. Primary target: Wesseling. Weather was 10/10ths cloud - tops about 7,000 feet. Bombed at 12.00 hours from 17,000 feet on release of G.H. aircraft.

02/11/1944 NG141   A2-J   Bombing Homberg   11.20   14.09   15.45
Bomb load 1 x 4000 HC, 6 x 1000 ANM59, 6 x 500 MC. Primary target: Homberg. Weather variable cloud but clear for bombing. Target obscured by pall of smoke rising to 10,000 feet. Bombed at 14.09 hours from 21,000 feet visually. Aircraft hit by flak. Mid upper turret and flap on port wing damaged.

06/11/1944 NG141   A2-J   Bombing Koblenz   16.55   19.34   22.00
Bomb load 1 x 4000 HC, 2100 x 4 lb I.B. Primary target: Koblenz. Weather clear over target. Bombed at 19.34 hours from 17,000 feet on centre of Red and Green T.I.s.

08/11/1944 NG141   A2-J   Bombing Homberg   07.58   10.30   12.14
Bomb load 1 x 4000 HC, 6 x 1000 GP, 6 x 500 GP. Primary target: Homberg. Weather clear. Bombed at 10.30 hours from 19,000 feet. Visual of Factory.

23/11/1944 NG141   A2-J   Bombing Nordstern   12.38   15.22   17.22
Bomb load 1 x 4000 HC, 16 x 500 GP. Primary target: Nordstern, Gelsenkirchen Oil refineries. Weather 10/10ths cloud. Bombed at 15.22 hours from 20,000 feet. Centre of Red flares.

27/11/1944 NG141   A2-J   Bombing Cologne   12.27   15.06   16.50
Bomb load 1 x 4000 HC, 16 x 500 GP. Primary target: Cologne, Marshalling Yards. Weather patchy cloud. Bombed at 15.06 hours from 21,000 feet on G.H. Leader.

29/11/1944 NG141   A2-J   BombingNeuss   02.50 05.34   06.59

Bomb load 1 x 4000 HC, 6 x 1000 MC, 6 x 500 GP, 3 Flares Red with Green stars. Primary target: Neuss. Weather 10/10ths cloud over target but the glow of fires was seen through cloud. Bombed at 05.34 hours from 20,000 feet. Centre of Red and Green sky markers. Single engine aircraft seen over target - believed hostile.

F/O. Peter James Kendrick Hood

125519 (1321297) F/O.Peter James Kendrick Hood. Pilot.
131993 (1318355) F/O.Robert John Samson Wilton. A/Bomber. 6 ops.
A415482   F/S. John Russel Moulsdale, RAAF. A/Bomber. 1 op.
1397083   F/S. H.J. Cosgrove.   Navigator.
1379466   F/S. V.J. Rollings.   WOP/AG.
2201271   Sgt. Clarence Dunkin Fraser MacKenzie. MU/Gunner.
US10601612 T/S. Maurice George Lanthier, USAAF. R/Gunner.
1430638   Sgt. H.H. Wickson.   F/Engineer.
1388915   F/S. Edward Henry Shearing. 2nd Pilot. 15/03/1944

02/01/1944 LL653 A2-F   BombingBerlin   00.21   03.02   06.53

Bomb load 1 x 4000, 24 x 30, 450 x 4, 90 x 4 incendiaries. Primary target: Berlin. There was 10/10 cloud, very thick. Bombed at 03.02 hours at 9,000 ft. Sky markers (red) very scattered but green T.I. nicely concentrated. Orange glow through cloud but could identify it as fires etc. M/U Turret u/s. Hit by flak.

From his normal crew, only F/O. P.J.K. Hood did the mission as 2nd Pilot with P/O. V.H.J. Vizer crew.

15/02/1944 DS820JI-A BombingBerlin   17.26 21.30   00.55

Bomb load 1 x 4000 lb bomb, 32 x 30, 540 x 4, 90 x 4 incendiaries. Primary target: Berlin. There was 10/10 cloud with tops 10,000 ft. Bombed at 21.30 hrs at 20,000 ft. Quiet route. Flak over Berlin fairly heavy, otherwise no bother. Explosion seen over Berlin at 21.26 hrs.

25/02/1944 LL690 JI-J   BombingAugsburg   21.46 x 23.48

Bomb load 1 x 2000 lb bomb, 48 x 30, 900 x 4 incendiaries. Returned early. Furthest point reached 5225N 0331E. D.R. (Dead Reckoning) Compass u/s, R/G's (Rear Gunner) and B/A's (Bomb Aimer) inter-comm u/s. Aircraft sluggish and not climbing properly.

01/03/1944 DS820 JI-A Bombing Stuttgart   23.51 03.11 07.29

Bomb load 1 x 4000 lb. bomb, 24 x 30, 600 x4, 90 x 4 incendiaries. Primary target: Stuttgart. There was 10/10 cloud, with occasional breaks. Bombed at 03.11 hours at 21,000 ft. There were good fires over a wide area, tending to undershoot. Mass of flames and fires seen from 150 miles over wide area.

07/03/1944 DS820 JI-A Bombing Le Mans   19.41 x 00.13

Bomb load 10 x 1000, 4 x 500 lb bomb. There was 10/10 cloud. No attack made. 2 x 1000 lb bomb jettisoned safe, remainder brought back to base. Red glow seen through cloud, died on hearing some explosions. Could not identify the target.

15/03/1944 DS820 JI-A Bombing Stuttgart   19.30 23.36 03.28

Bomb load 1 x 1000 lb bomb, 1050 x 4, 90 x 4 x incendiaries. Primary target: Stuttgart. There was a thin cloud. Bombed at 23.36 hours from 20,000 feet. Monica u/s over 2000 feet. Fires were scattered. Several large ones, tending to undershoot. Route satisfactory.

F/S. J.R. Moulsdale was A/Bomber that day and F/S. E.H. Shearing 2nd Pilot.

18/03/1944 LL738 JI-D Bombing Frankfurt   19.35 x 22.20

Bomb load 1 x 4000 lb bomb, 1350 x 4, 90 x 4, 32 x 30 incendiaries. Returned early. Furthest point reached 12 miles WSW Ghent. Total bomb load jettisoned safe 15 miles SW Dunkirk. Defect in both starboard engines. Inner picked up later. 4 enemy aircraft seen but no attack.

30/03/1944 LL696 JI-A Bombing Nuremburg 22.26 x x

Bomb load 1 x 1000 lb bomb, 96 x 30, 810 x 4, 90 x 4 incendiaries. Aircraft missing 31/03/1944.

'Bomber Command Losses 1944' (WR Chorley) states: 'Believed shot down while on final leg to target by JU88 of Fw. Emil Nonnenmacher, III./NJG2, crashing near Memmelsdorf'. Memmelsdord is 6.5 km NE of Bamberg. According to the Nachtjagd War Diaries (Dr. Theo Boiten) Nonnenmacher, who was actually with 9./NJG2, made no verified claim in that area; however, Lt. Achim Woeste, Stab III./NJG3 was credited with an unidentified 4-engined bomber in the Schesslitz area, 10 km NE of Bamberg at a time consistent with 514 Sqn aircraft being in that area. It therefore more likely that the loss of LL696 was due to being shot down by Woeste.

Sgt. Mckenzie is buried in Durnbach War Cemetery. F/S. H.J. Cosgrove was interned in Camps L6/357 POW No.3493 with F/S.

R.J.S. Rollings POW No.3495 and Sgt. H.H. Wickson Camp L6 POW No.3494 or 3496. F/O. P.J.K. Hood was interned in Camp L1 POW No.4101 and F/O. R.J.S. Wilton Camp L1 No POW No. T/S. M.G. Lanthier was confined to Hospital due to his injuries (Stalag XVII B Barrack 30b) so had no POW No.

F/O. Frederick Louis Hookway

NZ429076 F/O.Frederick Louis "Freddie" Hookway, RNZAF. Pilot.
 Sgt. A.R. "Sandy" Somerville.   A/Bomber.
 Sgt. Harry Biggins (or Riggins or Higgins)   Navigator.
 Sgt. Dennis J. Hoskin.   WOP/AG.
R273636 Sgt. George E. Stafford, RCAF.   MU/Gunner. 4 ops.
 Sgt. L. Brennan.   MU/Gunner.5 ops.
 Sgt. R.D.T. "Bobbie" Baxter.   R/Gunner.
 Sgt. Cyril O.G. Burdett.   F/Engineer.

Passengers: 03/05/1945, 07/05/1945, 08/05/1945, 23/05/1945.

23/03/1945 ME351   JI-U Bombing Wesel   14.27 17.38 19.11
 Bomb load 13 x 1000 ANM65. Primary target: Wesel, in support of ground troops. Weather perfect. Bombed at 17.38 hours from 19,900 feet on G.H.
 From his normal crew, only F/O. F.L. Hookway did the mission as 2nd Pilot with F/L. J.F. Knight's crew.
27/03/1945 NN773   JI-K Bombing Hamm Sachsen 10.35   14.03
 16.15
 Bomb load 1 x 4000 HC, 13 x 500 ANM64, 2 x 500 MC. Primary target: Hamm Sachsen, Benzol plant. Weather 10/10ths cloud. Bombed at 14.03 hrs at 18,000 feet on G.H. Leader.
 Sgt. George E. Stafford MU/Gunner until 01/05/1945.
04/04/1945 ME380   JI-E Bombing Merseburg (Leuna)   18.40 22.55
 02.53
 Weather 5-10/10ths cloud, and 10/10ths over Merseburg. Bombed primary target. Bomb load 1 x 4000 HC, 6 x 500 ANM64. 10/10th cloud. Bombed on Sky Markers at 22.55 hours from 20,000 feet in centre of red flares with green stars. Very concentrated bombing, H2S. D.R. Compass U/S. Marking not good had to bomb on incorrect heading in order to get bombs away before flares died out.

From his normal crew, only F/O. F.L. Hookway did the mission as 2nd Pilot with F/O. H.C. Snow's crew.

18/04/1945 ME535   JI-G Bombing Heligoland 09.53 13.09 15.25

Bomb load 6 x 1000 MC, 10 x 500 ANM64. Primary target: Heligoland, Naval base. Weather no cloud, slight haze. Bombed visually on upwind edge of smoke at 13.09 hours from 18,000 ft.

Smoke palls obscured island. Good trip and no troubles.

22/04/1945 ME535   JI-G Bombing Bremen 15.14 18.45 20.55

Bomb load 1 x 4000 HC, 2 x 500 MC, 14 x 500 ANM64. Primary target: Bremen, in support of Troop concentration. Weather on approaching target 4-5/10ths cloud. Bombed following on 514/H at 18.45 hours from 18,800 ft. Pall of reddish smoke through cloud. A/C well packed and concentrated.

01/05/1945 RF230 JI-B Manna The Hague   13.16 14.33 15.43

Dropping area The Hague. Weather clear over target. 5 Panniers dropped at 14.33 hrs. Clear, good visibility. Smoke from Red T.I. - White cross. Terrific reception from populace.

03/05/1945 RF230 JI-B Manna The Hague   11.03   12.22   13.31

Dropping area The Hague. Dropped 5 panniers, clear, at 12.22 hrs. Smoke from T.I.'s and visual of Racecourse. Weather was bad over the sea, otherwise good trip. Bags dropped well together. Usual enthusiastic crowds to greet us.

No Mid Upper Gunner that day.

Passenger: AC. Baxter

07/05/1945 RF231 JI-A Manna The Hague   12.26   13.48   15.00

Dropping area The Hague. Dropped 3½ Panniers on smoke from T.I.'s and White Cross at 13.48 hours. Cheerful crowds waving flags and bunting, colour of T.I.s not seen. Clear.

No Mid Upper Gunner that day.

Passenger: Sgt. A. Greenwood.

08/06/1945 ME336   JI-S Baedeker Tour over Continent 14.45 x 19.01

Sgt. L. Brennan MU/Gunner from that day.

Passengers: Cpl. H. Clift, AC. N. Bisasor, Sgt. A. Butman, Cpl. E. Edwards.

23/06/1945 ME535   JI-G Baedeker Tour over Continent 09.50 x 14.08

Passengers: Sgt. Du Foe, LAC. Thompson, LAC. Cooke, AC. Beatson, A/C. Hardcastle.

25/06/1945 ME336   JI-S Post Mortem Special mission 10.15 x 11.08

Landed at Gromer Base. Starboard inner u/s.

29/06/1945 ME380   JI-E Post Mortem Special mission 10.13 x 16.01

03/07/1945 LM724   JI-H Post Mortem Special mission 14.30 x 19.58

F/S. John Gordon Hudson

NZ41150   F/S. John Gordon Hudson, RNZAF.   Pilot.
1049548   Sgt. Geoffrey Goddard.   A/Bomber.
1563542   F/S. Patrick Millar Constable.   Navigator.
1176863   W/O. Henry Thomas Rolph.   WOP/AG.
J89445 (R182020) P/O. Colin Alexander Campbell, RCAF.
MU/Gunner.
J89454 (R181176) P/O. Wallace Lawrence Granbois, RCAF.
    R/Gunner.
1811331   Sgt. Graham Randall Jones.   F/Engineer.

22/03/1944 LL728 JI-B
    Bombing Frankfurt   18.40
    21.49 00.35
    Bomb load 1 x 1000 lb
bomb, 64 x 30, 1161 x 4, 129
x 4 incendiaries. Primary
target: Frankfurt. There was
3/10 cloud about 8,000 feet.
Bombed at 21.49 hours from
20,000 feet. Smoke fires
starting and smoke rising
from W side of town. Monica
did not react until enemy
Aircraft were within 200/300
yards. 2 reactions in Lille
area. Seemed an effective
attack on the town with a big
explosion at 21.50 hours and
another at 21.59 hours seen
from 50 miles away.

John Gordon Hudson

Starboard inner engine caught
fire in Lille area and aircraft returned to Base on 3 engines.
26/03/1944 LL690 JI-J Bombing Essen 19.58 22.09 00.43
    Bomb load 1 x 2000 lb bomb, 56 x 30, 1080 x 4, 120 x 4
incendiaries. Primary target: Essen. There was 10/10 cloud with
broken patches. Bombed at 22.09 hours from 20,000 feet. Nothing
seen. Uneventful trip. Route OK.

30/03/1944 LL690 JI-J Bombing Nuremburg 22.35 x 00.16

Bomb load 1 x 1000 lb bomb, 96 x 30, 810 x 4, 90 x 4 incendiaries. Returned early. Farthest point reached 5150N 0230E. Intercom u/s in Rear Turret. Bomb jettisoned.

18/04/1944 DS828 JI-D Bombing Rouen 22.50 00.51 02.36

Bomb load 10 x 1000, 5 x 500 lb. bombs. Primary target: Rouen. Visibility was good. Bombed at 00.51 hours from 12,500 feet. Black smoke covered target area. 1 x 1000 lb bomb brought back - hang up. If the markers were in the right spot the yards have had it.

22/04/1944 DS828 JI-D Bombing Dusseldorf 23.15 x x

Bomb load 1 x 2000 lb bomb, 84 x 30, 1050 x 4 incendiaries. Aircraft missing.

Believed to have been hit by flak, or possibly collided with DS669, crashing 23/04/1944 in the target area. All crew KIA. Like their comrades from DS669, five were buried in the Dusseldorf North Cemetery (Nordfriedhof), the burial of Sgt. Granbois being reported as late as 2nd May 44. They have been subsequently re-interred in the Reichswald Forest War Cemetery.

F/S. Hudson and W/O. Rolph are commemorated on Panels 264 and 214 respectively on the Runnymede Memorial. In civilian life, 33-year-old F/S. Constable of Edinburgh had been a Chartered Accountant.

P/O. Garth Stewart Hughes, DFC

A413614 P/O.   Garth Stewart Hughes, DFC RAAF. Pilot.
NZ427199 F/S. A.D. Hall. RNZAF.   A/Bomber.
NZ416587 P/O. Llewellyn Selwyn Smith, RNZAF. Navigator.
A421267 W/O. Osmond John Goddard, RAAF. WOP/A.G.
1105921 Sgt. Eric Gordon Moorhouse, DFM. MU/Gunner. 17 ops.
1437285 F/S. Leslie James Henry Whitbread. MU&R/Gunner. 8 ops.
1618730 Sgt. George Henry Thornton. R/Gunner. 10 ops.
R165360 Sgt. Leo Wilton, RCAF.   R/Gunner. 1 op.
1523926 Sgt. Harry West.   F/Engineer. 16 ops.
1579492 Sgt. Philip Charles Knill Bennett. F/Engineer. 1 op.
1531244 Sgt. Joseph Black.   F/Engineer.   1 op.
174119 (1216258) F/S. Ernest Arthur Kingham. 2nd Pilot. 15/02/1944

G.S. Hughes (left) and O.J. Goddard

03/11/1943 DS785 JI-D Bombing Dusseldorf 17.58 19.45 21.11

Aircraft carried 1 x 4000, 720 x 4 lb incendiaries, 32 x 30 lb incendiaries (including 60 x 4 lb). Attacked target at 19.45 hours, height 20,000 feet. 032 Degs. Industrial haze. No cloud. Report combat with an enemy aircraft.

Sgt. E.G. Moorhouse MU/Gunner until 24/03/1944.

18/11/1943 DS787 JI-F Bombing Berlin 17.54 21.01 00.45

Bomb load 1 x 4000, 16 x 30, 270 x 4. Primary target Berlin. Visibility was poor with 10/10 low cloud. Red T.I.s were well separated and there were no Green T.I.s visible so the bombs were aimed at the centre of the Reds at 21.01 hours. 20,000 feet. A scattered raid with P.F.F. late over the target area.

22/11/1943 DS785 JI-D Bombing Berlin 17.38 20.19 23.30

Bomb load 1 x 4000, 360 x 4 incendiaries, 90 x 4 incendiaries, 24 x 30 incendiaries. Primary target: Berlin. 10/10 cloud. No flares or markers seen. Large glow seen through clouds: 30 x 4, 2 Miles Wells 4500 hung up presumed electrical fault. Large glow seen through clouds 20.19 showed that good fires had caught hold below.

23/11/1943 DS783 JI-B Bombing Berlin 17.38 x 23.30

Bomb load 1 x 4000 HC, 32 x 30 incendiaries, 540 x 4 incendiaries, 90 x 4. Primary target: Berlin. 8/10 cloud estimated 16,000 ft. Visibility fair. Sky markers red flares green stars. Over target saw many red flares and green stars going dim as we approached, and over target saw a good concentration of green T.I.s. Good size fires going well over a fairly wide area. 30 x 4 incendiaries hung up over target. Received diversion to proceed to Cranfield at 22.32 hours.

26/11/1943 DS783 JI-B Bombing Berlin   17.53 21.20   00.52

Bomb load 1 x 4000 HC, 24 x 30 incendiaries, 405 x 4 incendiaries, 45 x 4 X. Primary target: Berlin. No cloud, some haze. Target attacked at 21.20 hrs. At 20,000 feet. Approaching target ring of S/Ls all round. Glow of fires visible for some considerable distance on return route. Flak very active.

02/12/1943 DS783 JI-B Bombing Berlin   17.06 20.25   23.59

Bomb load 1 x 8000, 160 x 4 incendiaries, 20 x 4 incendiaries. Primary target: Berlin. 5-6/10 cloud. Bombed on Green T.I.s 20.25 at 20,000 ft. Attacked by fighter in target area and Rear Gunner killed. Aircraft sustaining severe damage. Hydraulics, rear turret, mid-upper turret, oxygen u/s. Port tyre, port inner engine damaged. Landed safely on 3 engines.

Sgt. L. Wilton RCAF R/Gunner that day.

16/12/1943 DS787 JI-F Bombing Berlin   16.47 20.06   23.26

Bomb load 1 x 4000, 40 x 430 incendiaries, 540 x 4 incendiaries. Primary target: Berlin. 10/10 cloud over target. Bombed at 20.06 at 20,000 ft. Pretty good trip. Fires could be seen in target area from considerable distance. Landed at Downham Market.

Sgt. P.C.K. Bennett was F/Engineer that day and F/S. L.J.H. Whitbread R/Gunner.

24/12/1943 DS785 JI-D Bombing Berlin   00.39 04.09   07.25

Bomb load 1 x 4000, 32 x 30 incendiaries, 450 x 4 incendiaries, 90 x 4 incendiaries. Primary target: Berlin. 6/10 cloud, Tops 15/16,000 ft. Bombed at 04.09 hrs at 20,000 ft. Good fires beginning to obtain hold, seen from 100 miles on leaving. F.M. on return badly placed.

F/S. L.J.H. Whitbread R/Gunner that day.

14/01/1944 DS785 JI-D Bombing Brunswick   17.23 19.30   22.03

Bomb load 1 x 4000 bomb. Primary target: Brunswick. There was 10/10 cloud. Bombed at 19.20 hours at 20,000 ft. Fires visible through cloud. Well concentrated fires below cloud. Broadcast wind good. Fighters appeared to drop red flares and flak opened up on these. Photo flash hung up.

20/01/1944 DS816 JI-O Bombing Berlin   16.14 19.37   23.30

Bomb load 1 x 4000, 32 x 30, 540 x 4, 60 x 4 incendiaries. Primary target: Berlin. There was 10/10 cloud. Bombed at 19.37 hours at 22,000 ft. Bombed in centre of Red and Green Flares. No Result noticed. Had encounter with enemy aircraft.

F/S. L.J.H. Whitbread R/Gunner until 01/03/1944.

27/01/1944 DS785 JI-D Bombing Berlin 17.49 20.30 01.48

Bomb load 1 x 8000 lb bomb. Primary target: Berlin. There was 10/10 cloud. Bombed at 20.30 hours at 21,000 ft. Red glow seen on clouds. P.Q.R. seen and useful. Attack should develop well. Markers concentrated. Photo attempted. Spoof markers between Hamburg and Bremen very effective and foxed jerry.

15/02/1944 DS785 JI-D Bombing Berlin 17.29 21.18 23.53

Bomb load 1 x 8000 lbs bomb. Primary target: Berlin. There was 10/10 cloud over the target. Bombed at 21.18 hrs. At 21,000 ft. Route very good. No fighters seen.

Sgt. J. Black was F/Engineer that day and F/S. E.A. Kingham 2nd Pilot.

19/02/1944 DS785 JI-D Bombing Leipzig 00.28 04.02 06.45

Bomb load 1 x 2000, 1 x 500 lb bomb, 40 x 30, 900 x 4 incendiaries. Primary target: Leipzig. There was 10/10 cloud. Bombed at 04.02 hours at 20,000 ft. 50 x 4 inc hung up. Appeared to be excellent attack. Large red glow over target seen shortly after bombing. Large blue flash seen slightly SE of A.P. just before bombing.

01/03/1944 LL733 JI-G Bombing Stuttgart 23.31 03.09 07.04

Bomb load 1 x 8000 lb bomb, 8 x 30, 90 x 4 incendiaries. Primary target: Stuttgart. There was 10/10 cloud. Bombed at 03.09 hours at 20,000 ft. Glows seen from wide area as aircraft was leaving.

15/03/1944 LL738 JI-D Bombing Stuttgart 19.22 23.09 02.23

Bomb load 1 x 1000 lb bomb, 1050 x 4, 90 x 4, 64 x 30 incendiaries. Primary target: Stuttgart. There was 3-5/10 cloud. Bombed at 23.29 hours from 20,000 feet. Many undershoots to the South of the target. Fair concentration of fires seen. Route good, marking was late and scattered, seemed a good effort.

22/03/1944 LL738 JI-D Bombing Frankfurt 18.32 21.59 00.48

Bomb load 1 x 1000 lb bomb, 64 x 30, 1161 x 4, 129 x 4 incendiaries. Primary target: Frankfurt. There was 5/10 cloud. Bombed at 21.59 hours from 20,000 feet. 1 x 1000 lb bomb hung up. Monica u/s. Many sticks of incendiaries criss-crossed over target. Made 4 orbits on NS leg to waste time. Target congested, just avoided collision on 3 occasions.

24/03/1944 LL738 JI-D Bombing Berlin 18.28 22.39 01.52

Bomb load 1 x 1000 lb bomb, 88 x 30, 810 x 4, 90 x 4 incendiaries. Primary target: Berlin. There was 8/10 cloud over the target. Bombed at 22.39 hours from 20,000 feet. 90 x 4 incendiaries hung up. Flash jammed in chute. Attacked by fighter, Mid Upper Gunner injured. Change of zero message received.

30/03/1944 LL738 JI-D Bombing Nuremburg 22.25 x x
Bomb load 1 x 1000 lb bomb, 96 x 30, 810 x 4, 90 x 4 incendiaries. Aircraft missing.

F/S. L.J.H. Whitbread was MU/Gunner that day.
Shot down by a night fighter JU88 while outbound 31/03/1944 possibly at 00.20 hours by Lt. Hans Raum of 9./NJG3, whilst holding course at 21,000 feet. The Lancaster crashed out of control into the southern outskirts of Sinzig at Westum.

Of those killed, three are buried in Rheinberg War Cemetery, but both Air Gunners and Sgt. West have no known grave and are commemorated on the Runnymede Memorial.

P/O. G.S. Hughes KIA, Sgt. H. West 1523926 KIA, P/O. L.S. Smith KIA, F/S. A.D. Hall 427199 POW, W/O. O.J. Goddard KIA, F/S. L.J.H. Whitbread KIA, Sgt. G.H. Thornton KIA.

F/S. A.D. Hall was interned in Camp L3, POW No.4187. After the war F/S Hall wrote: "Our aircraft was attacked and set on fire. I was the first to leave the aircraft. I regret being unable to give any information on the fate of the other six crew members."

F/L. Thomas W. Hurley

J14025   F/L. Thomas W. "Wes" Hurley, RCAF.   Pilot.
J40364   F/O. E. "Ernie" Woolls, RCAF.   A/Bomber.
R169461   F/S. F.J. Shepheard, RCAF.   Navigator.   3 ops.
Sgt.J.E. Banham.   Navigator.   4 ops.
171810 (1378131) F/O. Walter Eric Overbury.   Navigator.   1 op.
149340 (1562280) F/O. Talbot William Ledingham, DFC.   Navigator. 1 op.
Sgt.R.C. Webb.   Navigator.   1 op.
1397906   F/S. Sidney Smith.   Navigator.   1 op.
R163277   W/O. Robert "Bob" Fry, RCAF.   Navigator. 13 ops.
R255554   F/S. Joe W. Baker, RCAF.   WOP/AG.
R231245   W/O. Baxter M.W. Fillmore, RCAF. MU/Gunner. 22 ops.
R163118   Sgt. E. Doug Rogers, RCAF.   R/Gunner.
Sgt.G. "Gerry" Mazzina.   F/Engineer.
J10781   F/L. E.S. "Ted" Henderson, RCAF. 2nd Pilot.   19/02/1945
150868 (1805085) F/O. Robert Owen Blackall. 2nd Pilot.   09/04/1945

Passengers: 03/05/1945, 08/05/1945.

28/01/1945 PA186 A2-G Bombing Cologne-Gremberg   10.26 14.10
16.11   Bomb load 1 x 4000 HC, 10 x 500 ANM64, 2 x 500 GP, 3 x
250 GP. Primary target: Koln - Gremberg, Marshalling yards. Weather
10/10ths cloud en route clearing on approach to target where visibility
was good and nil cloud. Bombed at 14.10 hours from 19,500 feet on
Red flares (GH unserviceable).
   From his normal crew, only F/L. T.W. Hurley did the mission as 2nd
Pilot with F/L. J.F. Ness' crew.
29/01/1945 PD389 A2-J   Bombing Krefeld 10.24 13.58 15.55
   Bomb load 1 x 4000 HC, 10 x 500 ANM64, 2 x 500 GP, 4 x 250 GP.
Primary target: Krefeld Marshalling Yards. Weather 10/10ths low thin
cloud over target although clear patches en-route. Bombed at 13.58
hours from 20,000 feet on G.H. Leader.
   F/S. F.J. Shepheard Navigator until 02/02/1945.
01/02/1945 PD389 A2-J   Bombing Munchen-Gladbach 13.14 16.33
18.29
   Bomb load 1 x 4000 HC, 14 x No 14 Clusters. Primary target:
Munchen-Gladbach, Marshalling yards. Bombed at 16.33 hours from
18,400 feet on leading aircraft.

02/02/1945 PE209 JI-A Bombing Wiesbaden 20.50 00.01 02.52

Bomb load 1 x 4000 HC, 10 x 500 ANM64, 2 x 500 GP, 4 x 250 GP. Primary target: Wiesbaden. Weather 10/10ths cloud, winds very erratic. Bombed at 00.01 hours from 18,700 feet on Gee fix.

08/02/1945 NN776 A2-D Bombing Hohenbudberg 03.38 06.23

08.20 Bomb load 1 x 4000 HC, 2 x 500 MC, 4 x 250 GP, 4 x 500 GP, 6 x 500 ANM64. Primary target: Hohenbudberg, Marshalling yards. Weather 8/10ths cloud over target. Bombed at 06.23 hours from 18,500 feet on Red T.Is. Very large Red glow in target area.

Sgt. J.E. Banham Navigator that day.

13/02/1945 NG203 A2-C Bombing Dresden 21.49 01.40 06.55

Bomb load 1 x 500 MC, 15 x No. 14 Clusters. Primary target: Dresden. Weather 5/10ths cloud over target. Bombed at 01.40 hours from 19,500 feet on centre of Red T.I.s.

F/O. W.E. Overbury Navigator that day.

14/02/1945 NG203 A2-C Bombing Chemnitz 20.19 00.32 04.25

Bomb load 1 x 500 MC, 15 x No. 14 Clusters. Primary target: Chemnitz. Weather 8-10/10ths cloud, tops 15-16,000 feet with occasional breaks. Bombed at 00.32 hours from 19,500 feet on bomb bursts under clouds.

Sgt. J.E. Banham Navigator until 19/02/1945.

16/02/1945 PB423 A2-L Bombing Wesel 12.37 x 18.15

Bomb load 1 x 4000 HC, 4 x 500 GP, 2 x 500 MC L/Delay, 4 x 250 GP, 6 x 500 ANM64. Primary target: Wesel. Weather clear. Abortive sortie. Did not bomb, complete hang up over Wesel. Bombs that fell were concentrated centre of target. Jettisoned 1 x 4000 HC 5227N 0320E at 16.19 hours from 8,000 feet. Jettisoned 2 x 500 MC L/Delay 11 and 15 miles North at 16.22 hours from 8,000 feet.

19/02/1945 NF966 A2-H Bombing Wesel 12.59 16.37 19.30

Bomb load 1 x 4000 HC, 6 x 500 MC, 6 x 500 ANM64, 4 x 250 GP. Primary target: Wesel. Weather over target 5-7/10ths cloud. Bombed at 16.39 hours from 20,600 feet on centre of Red puffs.

F/L. E.S. Henderson 2nd Pilot that day.

23/02/1945 NG118 A2-H Bombing Gelsenkirchen 11.21 15.00 17.09

Bomb load 1 x 4000 HC, 9 x 500 ANM64, 2 x 500 MC, 4 x 250 GP. Primary target Gelsenkirchen. Weather 10/10ths cloud. Bombed at 15.00 hours from 20,200 feet on leading aircraft. On return landed at Stradishall.

F/O. T.W. Ledingham Navigator that day.

27/02/1945 NG118   A2-H   Bombing Gelsenkirchen 10.57 14.28 16.42

Bomb load 1 x 4000 HC, 2 x 500 MC (L/D 37B), 9 x 500 ANM64, 4 x 250 GP. Primary target: Gelsenkirchen (Alma Pluts) Benzin plant. Weather 10/10ths cloud, 6/10,000 feet tops. Bombed at 14.28 hours from 19,700 feet on G.H. Leader.

Sgt. R.C. Webb Navigator that day.

01/03/1945 NG203   A2-C   Bombing Kamen   12.16 15.06 17.50

Bomb load 1 x 4000 HC, 9 x 500 ANM64, 2 x 500 MC L/D, 4 x 250 GP. Primary target: Kamen, Coking plant. Weather 10/10ths cloud. Bombed at 15.06 hours from 21,000 feet on upwind edge of smoke puffs.

F/S. S. Smith Navigator that day.

27/03/1945 NG118   A2-H   Bombing Hamm Sachsen 10.26 14.03 15.55

Bomb load 12 x 1000 HC. Primary target: Hamm Sachsen, Benzol plant. Weather 10/10ths cloud. Bombed at 14.03 hours at 18,000 feet on G.H. Leader on Green smoke Puffs only.

W/O. R. Fry Navigator from that day.

04/04/1945 NG118   A2-H   Bombing Merseburg 18.51 22.59 03.11

Weather 5-10/10ths cloud, and 10/10ths over Merseburg. Bomb load 1 x 4000 HC, 6 x 500 ANM64. Bombed primary target Merseburg (Leuna) at 22.59 hours from 20,000 feet on Red/Green skymarker. M.B. heard to instruct "Bomb Skymarkers". Large area of yellow glow beneath cloud. 10/10th cloud. Large explosion 23.03 hours beneath the glow. Should be a good raid. Dummies numerous.

09/04/1945 PD389 A2-J   Bombing Kiel   19.40 22.42 01.30

Primary target: Kiel, Submarine Buildings Yards. Weather clear with slight haze. Bombed secondary target Hamburg. Bomb load 1 x 4000 HC and 12 x 500 ANM64. Bombed centre of Red/Green T.I.s at 22.42 hrs from 18,000 feet. Large fire seen on approach. 4 large fires seen on leaving target. One very large explosion seen. No fire after 21.48 hrs. D/R until 22.15 hrs when yellow illuminations were seen ahead. There were considerable Decoys. M/B heard to instruct bomb nearest green flares. These were seen to fall well to starboard. 22.30 turned starboard 190 degs ran in on 170 and bombed centre of Green T.I.s. G East chain U/S. Several 4000 lb seen to fall in the sea from 300 degs.

F/O. R.O. Blackall 2nd Pilot that day.

18/04/1945 NG118   A2-H   Bombing Heligoland 09.48 13.10 15.25

Bomb load 6 x 1000 MC, 10 x 500 ANM64. Primary target:

Heligoland, Naval base. Weather no cloud, slight haze. Bombed visual on yellow T.I.s at 13.10 hours from 19,000 ft. Overshoot yellow T.I. by two seen on M/B's instructions. Bomb bursts crashed across centre of smoke, 1 x 500 ANM64 hang up we did an orbit and released manually over target. Target area mass of smoke. Red dust with several fires.

29/04/1945 PD389 A2-J Manna The Hague   12.36 13.58 15.22

Dropping area: The Hague. Weather broken cloud above and clear below. Dropped 4 packs on white cross at 13.58 hours, 1 container brought back. Had to orbit twice as containers hang up. Successful sortie and Dutch people obviously delighted to receive our contributions.

01/05/1945 PD389 A2-J Manna The Hague   13.10 14.24 15.36

Dropping area The Hague. Weather clear over target. Dropped 4 Panniers on T.I.s and White Cross at 14.24 hrs. Dropping more concentrated than previous and ground seemed better. There was a person standing by each group of T.I.s. Cheering crowds as before. People on the Grandstand.

03/05/1945 PD389 A2-J Manna The Hague   11.14 12.28 13.35

Dropping area The Hague. Dropped 5 panniers clear on Red T.I.s and White Cross at 12.28 hrs. Delivery accurate. Still getting an enthusiastic reception. Many flags on view.

No Mid Upper Gunner that day.

Passenger: LAC. Green.

08/05/1945 RE120 A2-C Manna Rotterdam 12.48 14.12 15.25

Dropping area Rotterdam. Dropped 3 Packs on Red T.I.s and visually at 14.12 hours. Clear. 2 Packs hung up - brought back. Two aircraft seen to drop complete load in lake to south of release point.

No Mid Upper Gunner that day.

Passenger: LAC. Fyson.

11/05/1945 RA602   A2-H Exodus   Juvincourt - Tangmere 11.04 x 16.48

Duration 3.30. Outward 1.33 hours. Collected 24 ex P.O.Ws. Homeward 1.57 hours. No comment.

12/05/1945 RA602   A2-H Exodus   Brussels - Tangmere 12.00 x 18.47

Duration 3.19. Outward 1.18 hours. Homeward 2.01 hours. 10 Refugees to Brussels, 24 ex POWs to Tangmere. All O.K.

15/05/1945 PD389 A2-J   Exodus   Juvincourt - Wing 16.02 x 21.15

Duration 3 hrs 28 mins. Outward 1 hr 38 mins. Collected 24 POWs.

Homeward 1 hr 50 mins. Organisation good.

18/05/1945 RA602   A2-H   Exodus Brussels - Oakley 12.12 x 17.07
Duration 3 hrs 4 mins. Out 1 hr 07 mins. In 1 hr 57 mins. 10 Belgian refugees taken to Brussels. 24 ex POWs returned to U.K. Organisation good.

19/05/1945 RA602   A2-H   Exodus Brussels - Oakley 12.53 x 19.25
Duration 2 hrs 53 mins. Out 1 hr 12 mins. In 1 hr 41 mins. 12 Belgian refugees taken to Brussels. 24 ex POWs all military evacuated.

P/O. Harry Glyn Huyton

196041 (1581940) P/O. Harry Glyn Huyton.   Pilot.
164760 (1800540) F/O. Derrick Charles "Derek" Halford.   A/Bomber.
Sgt. Hubert B. Woodcraft.   Navigator.
Sgt. V.E. "Vic" Chapman.   WOP/AG.
Sgt. William F. "Bill" Wilkes. MU/Gunner. 8 ops.
  W/O. George Edgar Sales.   R/Gunner.   3 ops.
Sgt. G.N. Zanetti.   R/Gunner.   1 op.
  W/O. Doug Parker.   R/Gunner.   5 ops.
  F/S. E. Scotchbrook.   F/Engineer. 6 ops.
Sgt. Frank H. Close.   F/Engineer. 3 ops.

Passengers: 07/05/1945, 30/06/1945, 08/07/1945, 23/07/1945, 28/07/1945.

14/03/1945 ME364   JI-P Bombing Heinrichshutte   13.05   16.40
  18.35
Bomb load 1 x 4000 HC, 12 x 500 ANM64. Primary target: Heinrichshutte, Hattingen Steel works & Benzol plant. Weather 10/10ths cloud, tops 7/12,000 feet. Bombed at 16.40 hours from 18,000 feet on G.H. Considerable flak after crossing battle front. Hattingen Steel works & Benzol plant. Patchy clouds.
From his normal crew, only F/S. H.G. Huyton did the mission as 2nd Pilot with F/L. M.G.T. Allen's crew.

17/03/1945 ME355   JI-L Bombing August Viktoria 11.39   15.07
  17.10
Bomb load 1 x 4000 HC, 13 x 500 ANM64, 2 x 500 MC. Primary target: Auguste Viktoria, Marl-Hüls coal mine. Weather 10/10ths

L to R: D.C. Halford, V.E. Chapman, W.F. Wilkes, H.B. Woodcraft, D. Parker, F.H. Close, G.E. Sales, H.G. Huyton.

cloud, tops and contrails up to 23,000 feet. Bombed at 15.07 hours from 19,000 feet on G.H. aircraft.

F/S. E. Scotchbrook F/Engineer until 30/06/1945.

Sgt. G.N. Zanetti R/Gunner that day.

09/04/1945 ME387   JI-N Bombing Kiel   19.40   22.39   01.27

Bombed primary target: Kiel. Bomb load 1 x 4000 HC and 12 x 500 ANM64. at 22.39 hours from 20,000 feet on centre of Green T.I.s as per M.B.s instructions. Harbour identified visually. Two large explosions at 22.37 hours. Marking and bombing concentrated both A/Ps receiving attention. Fires seen one hour after leaving.

From his normal crew, only P/O. H.G. Huyton did the mission as 2nd Pilot with F/L. A.W. Tasker's crew.

18/04/1945 ME387   JI-N Bombing Heligoland 09.46 13.10   15.15

Bomb load 6 x 1000 MC, 10 x 500 ANM64. Primary target: Heligoland, Naval base. Weather no cloud, slight haze. Bombed on smoke and M/Bs instructions at 13.10 hours from 18,100 ft. Bombs burst on north end of island. Only pier and northern tip of island visible. Remainder of target covered with smoke and fires. Target area in sea 13.14 from 18,100 ft. 1 x 1000 MC due to hang up.

W/O. D. Parker R/Gunner until 30/06/1945.

20/04/1945 ME387   JI-N Bombing Regensburg 09.27 13.58   17.00

352

Bomb load 16 x 500 ANM64. Primary target: Regensburg. Weather clear over target and whole route. Bombed visually at 13.58 hours from 18,700 ft on end of oil dock. Many bomb bursts and explosions. Aircraft was following N/514 who apparently could not release. Raid appeared good and weather perfect.

03/05/1945 ME529   A2-F   Manna The Hague   11.12 12.28 13.50

Dropping area The Hague. Dropped 5 Panniers visually on White Cross and T.I.s at 12.28 hrs. 9/10 2,000 Base Hazy.

07/05/1945 ME359   JI-T Manna The Hague   12.17 13.48 14.53

Dropping area The Hague. Dropped 4 Packs visually on White Cross at 13.48 hours. 3/10 base 1000 hazy. One pack brought back.

AC. Turner was a passenger that day and there was no Mid Upper Gunner.

30/06/1945 RA599   JI-L Baedeker Tour over Continent 12.18 x 17.07

Passengers: Cpl. Best, Cpl. Cament, LAC. Edwards.

08/07/1945 ME336   JI-S Baedeker Tour over Continent 15.03 x 19.44

From that day Sgt. F.H. Close was F/Engineer and W/O. G.E. Sales R/Gunner.

Passengers: AC. Nemby, AC. Deal, AC. Holmes, AC. Peck, AC. Stevens.

23/07/1945 ME336   JI-S Baedeker Tour over Continent 10.04 x 14.41

Passengers: Cpl. Winston, Cpl. Chadwick (3 Grp), ACW. Bosworth (3 Grp), ACW. Hutt, ACW. Gilley.

28/07/1945 ME363   JI-R Baedeker Tour over Continent 09.33 x 13.40

Passengers: Cpl. Gotterson, Cpl. Simpson, AC. Lewis, 759. Spuffield (WAAF), 769. Forbes (WAAF).

P/O. Norman Jennings, DFC

179704 (1268456) P/O. Norman Jennings. DFC. Pilot.

Sgt. F.J. Nixey.   A/Bomber.

R177891   Sgt. S. Havelock. RCAF.   Navigator.

Sgt. P.J.A. Daly.   WOP/AG.

Sgt. H.J. Ball.   MU/Gunner.

Sgt. C.F. Haslam.   R/Gunner.

(*) Sgt. L. Foster.   F/Engineer. 27 ops.

1890339 (*) Sgt.   Thomas Henry "Tom" Harvell. F/Engineer. 3 ops.

(*) Due to incoherency in the ORBs, we cannot ascertain how many operations Sgt. T.H. Harvell did with this crew. Consequently Sgt. L. Foster's number of sorties is uncertain too.

14/06/1944 DS813 JI-H Bombing Le Havre   23.45 01.14 02.29
Bomb load 11 x 1000 MC, 4 x 500 GP. Primary target: Le Havre. Weather was clear. Bombed at 01.14 hours from 16,000 feet. Target easily identified and attack good. Master Bomber good and no interference.
(*) Possibly Sgt. L. Foster F/Engineer until 05/07/1944.
15/06/1944 DS813 JI-H Bombing Valenciennes 23.01 00.30 02.12
Bomb load 16 x 500 GP, 2 x 500 MC. Primary target: Valenciennes. Weather clear below cloud. Bombed at 00.38 hours from 8,000 feet on red and green T.I.s per Master Bomber's instructions after orbiting. Opposition Nil. Should be a successful raid.
17/06/1944 PB143 JI-B Bombing Montdidier 01.05 x 04.38
Bomb load 16 x 500 GP, 2 x 500 ANM64 GP. Primary target: Montdidier. There was 10/10ths cloud over target. Master Bomber heard to order return to Base. 2 x 500 GP jettisoned safe 5005N 0058E at 03.23 hours from 10,000 feet.
24/06/1944 ME841 JI-H Bombing Rimeux 23.26 00.35 02.19
Bomb load 18 x 500 GP. Primary target: Rimeux, Flying bomb installations. Weather clear. Bombed at 00.35 hours from 11,900 feet on two red T.I.s. Good trip, bombs seen bursting amongst red T.I.s. No troubles.
27/06/1944 LM180 JI-G Bombing Biennais   23.35 01.11 02.34
Bomb load 16 x 500 GP. 2 x 500 ANM64 GP. Primary target: Biennais, Flying bomb installations. There was 10/10ths cloud. Bombed at 01.11 hours from 13,000 ft. Red glow.
30/06/1944 ME858 JI-J Bombing Villers Bocage 18.05 19.59 21.25
Bomb load 11 x 1000 MC, 4 x 500 GP. Primary target: Villers Bocage. Weather clear. Bombed at 19.59 hours from 11,500 feet. Very successful attack.
02/07/1944 ME858 JI-J Bombing Beauvoir   12.41 14.37 16.00
Bomb load 11 x 1000 MC, 4 x 500 GP. Primary target: Beauvoir, Flying bomb supply site. Bombed at 14.37 hours from 11,500 feet on yellow T.I.s.
05/07/1944 ME858 JI-J Bombing Watten 22.45 00.10 01.22
Bomb load 11 x 1000 ANM65, 4 x 500 GP. Primary target: Watten, Constructional works. Bombed at 00.10 hours from 9,000 feet red

T.I.s.

10/07/1944 ME858   JI-J Bombing Nucourt   04.08   06.04½   07.52
Bomb load 11 x 1000 ANM65, 4 x 500 GP. Primary target: Nucourt, Constructional works. Bombed at 06.04 hours from 14,000 feet, Gee Fix.
(*) Possibly Sgt. T.H. Harvell F/Engineer that day.

12/07/1944 ME858   JI-J Bombing Vaires   17.47 x 21.41
Bomb load 18 x 500 GP. Primary target: Vaires, Marshalling yards. Abandoned mission as instructed by Master Bomber. Jettisoned at 20.43 hours from 14,000 feet, position 4956N 0038E 4 x 500 GP.
(*) Possibly Sgt. T.H. Harvell F/Engineer that day.

24/07/1944 ME841   JI-H Bombing Stuttgart   21.43   01.47   15.14
Bomb load 7 x 1000 MC, 4 x 500 GP. Primary target: Stuttgart. Weather 10/10ths cloud. Bombed at 01.47 hours from 20,000 feet on centre of concentration of green yellow and red T.I.s. Cloud made attack difficult to assess. Had combat with enemy aircraft.
(*) Possibly Sgt. L. Foster F/Engineer that day.

25/07/1944 HK572   JI-T Bombing Stuttgart   21.39   01.49   05.34
Bomb load 5 x 1000 MC, 1 x 500 GP. Primary target: Stuttgart. Weather clear amid 10/10ths cloud. Bombed at 01.49 hours from 18,000 feet centre of red T.I.s. Marking seen to be over built up area.
(*) Possibly Sgt. T.H. Harvell F/Engineer that day.

28/07/1944 ME841   JI-H Bombing Stuttgart   21.38½   01.50   05.25
Bomb load 7 x 1000 MC, 2 x 500 GP. Primary target: Stuttgart. Weather 9/10ths cloud. Bombed at 01.50 hours from 19,000 feet centre of green and red T.I.s. Trouble free route.
(*) Possibly Sgt. L. Foster F/Engineer from that day.

01/08/1944 ME841   JI-H Bombing Foret de Nieppe 19.17 20.47
21.40
Bomb load 11 x 1000 MC, 4 x 500 GP. Primary target: De Nieppe, constructional works. Bombed at 20.47 hours from 11,000 feet, on Gee Fix.

03/08/1944 ME841   JI-H Bombing Bois de Cassan 11.43 14.07
15.38
Bomb load 11 x 1000 MC, 4 x 500 GP. Primary target: Bois de Cassan, Flying bomb supply depot. Bombed at 14.07 hours from 14,500 feet centre of smoke.

04/08/1944 ME841   JI-H Bombing Bec D'Ambes   13.18 18.01
21.10
Bomb load 8 x 1000 MC, 2 x 500 GP. Primary target: Bec d'Ambes

depot. Weather 3/10ths cloud. Bombed at 18.01 hours from 7,500 feet, visual of tanks. Satisfactory effort. No trouble at all.

05/08/1944 ME841 JI-H Bombing Bassen 14.22 19.03 22.22

Bomb load 8 x 1000 MC, 2 x 500 GP. Primary target: Bassen Oil Depot. Weather clear. Bombed at 19.03 hours from 3,500 feet large yellow flame in target area. Target one mass of flames and smoke.

08/08/1944 LM285 JI-K Bombing Foret de Lucheux 21.39 23.48 01.17

Bomb load 18 x 500 GP. Primary target: Foret de Lucheux, Petrol dump. Weather clear. Bombed at 23.48 hours from 12,000 feet, green T.I.s. Fires seen beginning to obtain a good hold, much black smoke.

"Foret de Lucheux" is a forest between Lille and Amiens. During WWII, important fuel tanks were there.

09/08/1944 ME841 JI-H Bombing Fort d'Englos 21.47 23.16 00.15

Bomb load 14 x 1000 MC. Primary target: Fort d'Englos (Lille), Petrol dump. Weather clear. Bombed at 23.16 hours from 12,500 feet, undershot red T.I.s by two seconds. Good concentration of bombs bursting around red T.I.s.

The fort of Ennetières-en-Weppes, or "fort d'Englos" is one of a set of six forts surrounding Lille.

12/08/1944 PB143 JI-B Bombing Brunswick 21.42 x 23.30

Bomb load 1 x 2000 HC. 12 x 500 'J' type clusters. Target: Brunswick. Abortive sortie. Jettisoned at 22.46 hours at 5220N 0250E (Safe). Insufficient fuel pressure starboard outer engine.

14/08/1944 LM285 JI-K Bombing Hamel (Falaise) 13.44 15.51 17.18

Bomb load 11 x 1000 MC. 4 x 500 GP. Primary target: Hamel, Bombing of troop concentrations. Weather clear. Bombed at 15.51 hours from 8,500 feet, green T.I.s as instructed by Master Bomber. Instructions to cease bombing given at 15.55 hours, when target was obscured by smoke and dust.

31/08/1944 LM275 JI-E Bombing Pont-Remy 15.48 18.11 19.26

Bomb load 11 x 1000 MC, 4 x 500 GP Mk IV LD. Primary target: Pont Remy, Dump. Weather cloudy. Bombed at 18.11 hours from 15,500 feet on visual target.

10/09/1944 LM277 JI-F Bombing Le Havre 15.54 17.39 19.13

Bomb load 11 x 1000 MC, 4 x 500 GP. Primary target: Le Havre. Weather clear. Bombed at 17.39 hours from 11,000 feet. Undershot T.I.s red by 200 yards.

11/09/1944 PB426 JI-J Bombing Kamen 16.07 18.42 20.26

Bomb load 1 x 4000 HC, 16 x 500 GP. Weather clear. Primary target: Kamen. Bombed at 18.42 hours from 16,500 feet on yellow T.I.

14/09/1944 LM277 JI-F Bombing Wassenaar 12.52 14.30 15.38

Bomb load 11 x 1000 MC, 4 x 500 GP. Primary target: Wassenaar. Weather was good, nil cloud. Bombed at 14.30 hours from 11,600 feet, red T.I.s.

17/09/1944 PB426 JI-J Bombing Boulogne 10.47 x 13.37

Bomb load 11 x 1000 MC, 4 x 500 GP. Primary target: Boulogne, Aiming point 2. Weather clear below cloud. At 12.15 hours order given by Master Bomber to abandon mission. Jettisoned 3 x 1000 MC, brought remainder back.

20/09/1944 PB426 JI-J Bombing Calais 14.47 16.02 17.10

Bomb load 11 x 1000 MC, 4 x 500 GP. Primary target: Calais. Weather clear over target. Bombed at 16.02 hours from 2,500 feet.

25/09/1944 PB426 JI-J Bombing Pas de Calais 08.22 x 10.53

Bomb load 11 x 1000 MC, 4 x 500 GP. Primary target: Calais. Abandoned mission on Master Bomber's instructions. Jettisoned 3 x 1000, 1 x 500 at 5026N 0101E.

26/09/1944 NF968 JI-L Bombing Calais 11.27 12.46 13.47

Bomb load 11 x 1000 MC, 4 x 500 GP. Primary target: Calais 7D. Weather clear below cloud which was 3,500 feet. Bombed at 12.46 hours from 3,000 feet on red T.I. + 1 second.

27/09/1944 LM288 JI-C(*) Bombing Calais 07.39 08.49 10.26

Bomb load 11 x 1000 MC, 4 x 500 GP. Primary target: Calais 15. Weather, cloud 5,500 feet 10/10ths. Bombed at 08.49 hours from 5,500 feet, overshot red T.I.

(*) In ORBs F/O I.J. Bittner crew is noted using the same A/C at the same time, with comment as follows:

"Primary target: Calais. Bombed at 08.43 hours from 5,500 feet, overshot red T.I. by 1 second."

P/O. Charles James Johnson, DFM

177517 (1334210) P/O. Charles James Johnson, DFM. Pilot.
1575003 (177519) F/S. Eugene Lush.   A/Bomber.
657320   F/S. P. Henser.   Navigator.
1461473   Sgt. T.J. Green.   WOP/AG.   19 ops
1578078   F/S. D. Thom.   WOP/AG.   9 ops
199780 (1870250) F/S. James Poad, DFM.   MU/Gunner.
1600884   F/S. Roy Arthur Dymott, DFM. R/Gunner.
177639 (1288976) P/O. John Frederic Whitmore. F/Engineer.

07/03/1944 LL727 A2-C   Bombing Le Mans   19.43 x 23.33
   Bomb load 10 x 1000, 4 x 500 lb bomb. No attack. Could not identify the target. There was 10/10 cloud with tops 4/5000 feet. 4 x 500 lb bombs jettisoned. 6 x 1000 lb bombs brought back to Base. Aircraft came down to 9,000 feet over the target. Other aircraft seen at 6,000 feet still above cloud. Saw no red T.I. hence brought bombs back.
   From his normal crew, only F/S. C.J. Johnson did this mission as 2nd Pilot with L. Greenburgh's crew.

15/03/1944 LL670 A2-K   Bombing Stuttgart   19.31 x 22.47
   Bomb load 1 x 8000 lb bomb, 8 x 30 incendiaries. Returned early. Furthest point reached 15 miles W of Chartres. 1 x 8000 jettisoned to reduce weight, 8 x 30 incendiaries brought back. Navigator lost protractor. Navigator sick.
   From his normal crew, only F/S. C.J. Johnson did this mission as 2nd Pilot with E.R. Protheroe's crew.

22/03/1944 LL698 A2-J   Bombing Frankfurt   18.44   21.59   01.03
   Bomb load 1 x 1000 lb bomb, 64 x 30, 1161 x 4, 129 x 4 incendiaries. Primary target: Frankfurt. There was wispy cloud. Bombed at 21.59 hours from 19,500 feet. A good concentration of fires seen. Monica u/s. Good attack and good route. Many incendiaries jettisoned on return route giving away track of aircraft.
   Sgt. T.J. Green WOP/AG until 08/05/1944.

24/03/1944 LL698 A2-J   Bombing Berlin   18.41   22.33   01.41
   Bomb load 1 x 1000 lb bomb, 88 x 30, 810 x 4, 90 x 4 incendiaries. Primary target: Berlin. There was 4/10 cloud with tops 7,000. Bombed at 22.33 hours from 20,000 feet. Incendiaries and fires burning, built up area could be seen clearly in their glow. Very searchlights in target area, flak unexpectedly light. Glow of fires seen for 100 miles.

26/03/1944 LL698 A2-J   Bombing Essen   20.10   22.07   00.34

Bomb load 1 x 2000 lb bomb, 56 x 30, 1080 x 4, 120 x 4 incendiaries. Primary target: Essen. There was 10/10 cloud. Bombed at 22.07 hours from 20,500 feet. Nothing seen owing to 10/10 cloud, target obscured.

30/03/1944 DS633 A2-B   Bombing Nuremburg   22.12   01.29   05.14

Bomb load 1 x 1000 lb bomb, 96 x 30, 810 x 4, 90 x 4 incendiaries. Primary target: Nuremberg. There was 8/10 cloud. Bombed at 01.29 hours from 20,000 feet. Several good fires seen. Attack very good. Landed Tangmere, short of petrol - considered that aircraft had not sufficient petrol.

10/04/1944 DS795 A2-J   Bombing Laon   01.44   03.48   05.51

Bomb load 9 x 1000, 4 x 500 lb bombs. Primary target: Laon. Weather was clear. Bombed at 03.48 hours from 11,000 feet. There was a good concentration of T.I.s. Bomb bursts seen on target. Very successful attack.

18/04/1944 DS633 A2-B   Bombing Rouen   22.39   00.45   02.10

Bomb load 8 x 1000 MC, 2 x 1000 GP, 5 x 500 lb bomb. Primary target: Rouen. There was some ground haze, but no cloud. Bombed at 00.45 hours from 11,500 feet. A.P. visible (identified by loop in river and bridge over river. T.I.s appeared to be burning in concentration around this point. Route excellent. Photo attempted.

20/04/1944 DS633 A2-B   Bombing Cologne   00.16   02.07   03.58

Bomb load 1 x 1000 lb bomb, 945 x 4, 105 x 4, 88 x 30 lb incendiaries. Primary target: Koln. There was 10/10 cloud. Bombed at 02.07 hours from 20,000 feet. Bombed in centre of cluster red flares. Engines overheating. Route quiet.

22/04/1944 DS633 A2-B   Bombing Dusseldorf 23.09   01.25   03.09

Bomb load 1 x 1000 lb bomb, 96 x 30, 1140 x 4 incendiaries. Primary target: Dusseldorf. Bombed at 01.25 hours from 19,000 feet. Huge fires were concentrated. Good successful attack. Many aircraft jettisoned incendiaries after leaving target en route home up to 50 miles from Dusseldorf. Route OK.

24/04/1944 DS633 A2-B   Bombing Karlsruhe 22.37   01.03   03.48

Bomb load 1 x 1000 lb bomb, 1026 x 4, 114 x 4, 108 x 30 lb incendiaries. Primary target: Karlsruhe. There was 10/10 cloud with base 19,000. Bombed at 01.03 hours from 20,000 feet. No definite indicators in target - widely scattered incendiaries, some small fires, T.I.s died out by time area was reached. Monica u/s. Attack appeared to be scattered over a period of 50 or 60 miles. Had combat with enemy aircraft.

26/04/1944 DS633 A2-B Bombing Essen 22.59 01.30 03.15

Bomb load 1 x 2000 lb bomb, 84 x 30, 945 x 4, 105 x 4 lb incendiaries. Primary target: Essen. There was slight haze. Bombed at 01.30 hours from 21,000 feet. Bomb bursts seen among the T.I.s. Searchlights working in course, several aircraft held. Good fires burning as we left the target, visible from English Coast.

27/04/1944 LL677 A2-E Bombing Friedrichshafen 22.03 00.11 05.39

Bomb load 810 x 4, 80 x 30 lb incendiaries. Primary target: Friedrichshafen. Weather was clear over the target, patchy over route. Bombed at 02.11 hours from 20,000 feet. Bombs and incendiaries falling well round markers. Successful prang. Many large fires seen lighting up the water-front, smoke rising up to 20,000 feet. Route very quiet and satisfactory.

08/05/1944 LL677 A2-E Bombing Cap Gris Nez 22.57 23.52 00.45

Bomb load 14 x 1000 lb bombs. Primary target: Cape Gris Nez. Weather was clear. Bombed at 23.52 hours from 8,300 feet. Visual of cliff edges, bombed just inside on area estimated to contain gun sites. Bombs seen to burst in sea, but majority appeared concentrated on the target area. Bombed very early in the attack therefore impossible to estimate success of raid.

09/05/1944 LL677 A2-E Bombing Cap Gris Nez 03.10 04.09 05.25

Bomb load 1 x 1000 GP, 13 x 1000 MC. Primary target: Cape Gris Nez. Slight haze observed but visual of target and red T.I.s was obtained. Bombed at 04.09 hours from 7,000 feet. On instructions of Master Bomber bombs were aimed to left of red T.I.s. Bombs appeared to be falling over buildings to left of the guns positions themselves and seemed to be fairly concentrated. Believe target was successfully attacked.

F/S. D. Thom WOP/AG that day.

10/05/1944 LL677 A2-E Bombing Courtrai 22.20 23.28 01.05

Bomb load 7 x 1000 GP, 7 x 1000 MC. Primary target: Courtrai. Haze over target, but T.I.s seen. Bombed on Master Bomber's instruction at 23.28 hours from 8,000 feet. No visual of target possible, but bombing appeared very concentrated. Route satisfactory.

Sgt. T.J. Green WOP/AG that day.

27/05/1944 LL677 A2-E Bombing Aachen 00.35 02.31 04.10

Bomb load 7 x 1000 MC, 4 x 1000 ANM, 4 x 500 MC. Primary target: Aachen. Clear over target. Bombed at 02.31 hours from 14,000 feet. Visual of river obtained. Attack appeared concentrated.

Sgt. T.J. Green WOP/AG that day.

28/05/1944 LL677 A2-E Bombing Angers 18.55 23.55 01.45

Bomb load 5 x 1000 MC, 1 x 1000 USA, 4 x 500 MC. Primary target: Angers. Clear over target. Bombed as instructed by Master Bomber at 23.55 hours from 10,000 feet. A good visual of target and markers. Attack well concentrated. Route satisfactory.

F/S. D. Thom WOP/AG that day.

30/05/1944 LL677 A2-E Bombing Boulogne 23.05 00.06 01.05

Bomb load 6 x 1000 MC, 4 x 500 MC. Primary target: Boulogne Gun Batteries. Clear over target. Bombed red T.I.s at 00.06 hours from 8,000 feet. Two sticks to the North of the T.I.s. Flak was almost nil. No searchlights were seen. No trouble experienced.

Sgt. T.J. Green WOP/AG that day.

05/06/1944 LL677 A2-E Bombing Ouistreham 03.57 05.10 06.50

Bomb load 9 x 1000 MC and 2 x 500 MC. Primary target: Ouistreham. There was 5/10 cloud at target. Bombed at 05.10 hours from 11,000 feet. Red T.I. seen in the sea N.E. of target. Cloud prevented visual of the target. Results might not be too good due to lack of concentration in marking. Quiet trip and opposition negligible.

F/S. D. Thom WOP/AG until 12/06/1944.

06/06/1944 LL677 A2-E Bombing Lisieux 00.32 01.39 03.40

Bomb load 16 x 500 MC Nose Inst. and 2 x 500 MC LD. Primary target: Lisieux. Weather was clear below but cloud above. Bombed at 01.39 hours from 2,400 feet. Bombing seemed accurate but smoke obscured target area. Route quiet. Gunners assisted an ME110 into the sea, finishing a job apparently started by a Mosquito, although A/A fire was seen previously. Both F/Gunner and M/U Gunner fired bursts and strikes were seen. Aircraft crashed and exploded in the sea. Half claim made.

08/06/1944 DS795 A2-J Bombing Fougeres 21.55 00.24 02.30

Bomb load 16 x 500 GP and 2 x 500 MC LD. Primary target: Fougeres. Bombed as instructed by Master Bomber at 00.24 hours from 7,700 feet. Huge fire seen in area and a large explosion at 00.23 hours. A smaller fire about 2 miles S.W. Smoke billowing up to 5,000 feet.

10/06/1944 LL677 A2-E Bombing Dreux 23.10 01.03 03.28

Bomb load 16 x 500 GP, 2 x 500 LD. Primary target: Dreux. Bombed as instructed by Master Bomber at 01.03 hours from 8,000 feet. Too much smoke over target to see results. Much fighter activity.

An ME410 claimed as destroyed.

12/06/1944 LL620 JI-T Bombing Gelsenkirchen 23.39 01.07 03.00

Bomb load 1 x 4000 HC, 14 x 500 GP, 2 x 500 MC. Primary target: Gelsenkirchen. Clear over target. Bombed red and green T.I.s at 01.07 hours from 19,500 feet. Large fires seen in target area with black smoke up to 17,000 feet. Defences were much lighter than expected. Large explosion seen at 01.06 hours.

14/06/1944 LL677 A2-E Bombing Le Havre 23.38 01.16 02.40

Bomb load 11 x 1000 MC, 4 x 500 GP. Primary target: Le Havre. Weather clear. Bombed at 01.16 hours from 15,000 feet on green T.I. Large fires seen burning on arrival. Good raid - markers concentrated. Defences seldom in action. Successful combat in Fecamp area.

Sgt. T.J. Green WOP/AG that day.

15/06/1944 LL677 A2-E Bombing Valenciennes 22.57 00.40 02.17

Bomb load 16 x 500 GP, 2 x 500 MC. Primary target: Valenciennes. Weather clear below 10/10ths cloud above. Bombed at 00.40 hours from 8,000 feet on green T.I. with 2 seconds overshoot as instructed by Master Bomber. Trouble free route.

Sgt. T.J. Green WOP/AG that day.

21/06/1944 LL677 A2-E   Bombing Domleger 17.59 x 20.53

Bomb load 18 x 500 MC. Primary target: Domleger near Abbeville, V-1 flying bomb launch site. There was 8/10ths cloud. No T.I.s seen owing to low cloud. Sortie abandoned under Master Bomber's instructions. Jettisoned 4 x 500 MC at 19.41 hours from 11,000 feet, 5022N 0126E.

F/S. D. Thom WOP/AG that day.

24/06/1944 LL677 A2-E Bombing Rimeux 23.19 00.35 02.09

Bomb load 18 x 500 GP. Primary target: Rimeux, Flying bomb installations. Weather clear. Bombed at 00.35 hours from 12,500 feet cluster of three red and green T.I.s. Good concentration of markers. Numerous searchlights, slight flak. Trouble free trip.

F/S. D. Thom WOP/AG that day.

27/06/1944 LL728 A2-L Bombing Biennais 23.26 01.12 02.39

Bomb load 16 x 500 GP, 2 x 500 ANM64 GP. Primary target: Biennais, Flying bomb installations. There was 10/10ths cloud. Bombed at 01.12 hours from 13,000 feet red glow. Fires seen on leaving the target.

Sgt. T.J. Green WOP/AG from that day.

30/06/1944 LL677 A2-E Bombing Villers Bocage 18.11 19.58 21.07

Bomb load 11 x 1000 MC, 2 x 500 GP. Primary target: Villers

Bocage. Weather clear. Bombed at 19.58 hours from 12,000 feet T.I.s on cross-roads as instructed. Whole target covered with smoke. Very good concentrated attack.

F/L. E.G. Jones

F/L. E.G. Jones.   Pilot.
165487 (1607046) F/O. Robert Edward Augustus Lewis. A/Bomber.
Sgt. M. Beaumont.   Navigator.
Sgt. B. Davies.   WOP/AG.
Sgt. H.F. Underhill.   MU/Gunner.
Sgt. D.M. Gibbons.   R/Gunner.
Sgt. E.F.R. Tilley.   F/Engineer.

29/07/1945 RF230 JI-B Baedeker Tour over Continent 09.45 x 14.16
    Passengers: Cpl. Hickman, Cpl. Thomas (WAAF), LAC. Bradford, LAC. Willis, ACW. Pepler.

F/O. R. Jones

F/O. R. Jones.   Pilot.
154599 (1673169) F/O. Malcom Gray Dennison. A/Bomber.
    F/O. R.A. Hudson.   Navigator.
Sgt. E.G. or F.G. Pountain. WOP/AG.
Sgt. W. Gregory.   MU/Gunner.
Sgt. R.W. Frogley.   R/Gunner.
Sgt. R. Atkin.   F/Engineer.
188927 (1612704) P/O. Victor Reginald Thompson. 2nd Pilot.
04/04/1945

Passengers: 13/06/1945, 13/07/1945, 24/07/1945.

22/02/1945 ME355   JI-L Bombing Osterfeld   12.10   16.02   18.07
    Bomb load 1 x 4000 HC, 9 x 500 ANM64, 2 x 500 MC, 4 x 250 GP. Primary target: Osterfeld, Coking ovens. Weather at target clear, but hazy. Bombed at 16.02 hours from 20,500 feet. Bombed concentration of bomb bursts.

This crew is believed to be that of F/O. R. Jones (WMHM).

23/02/1945 ME355 JI-L BombingGelsenkirchen 11.17 15.02
18.25
Bomb load 1 x 4000 HC, 9 x 500 ANM64, 2 x 500 MC, 4 x 250 GP.
Primary target Gelsenkirchen. Weather 10/10ths cloud. Bombed at
15.02 hours from 20,500 feet on leading aircraft. On return landed at
Acklington.

26/02/1945 ME355 JI-L BombingDortmund 10.23 14.03 16.21
Bomb load 1 x 4000 HC, 2 x 500 MC L/Delay 37B, 9 x 500
ANM64, 4 x 250 GP. Primary target: Dortmund, Hoesch Benzin plant.
Weather 10/10ths cloud, tops 8/10,000 feet. Bombed at 14.03 hours
from 20,000 feet on G.H. Leader.

28/02/1945 ME355 JI-L BombingNordster 08.47 12.04 14.08
Bomb load 1 x 4000 HC, 9 x 500 ANM64, 2 x 500 MC L/D, 4 x
250 GP. Primary target: Nordstern (Gelsenkirchen). Weather 10/10ths
cloud. Bombed at 12.04 hours from 20,500 feet on leading aircraft.

02/03/1945 ME355 JI-L BombingKoln 12.49 x 18.24
Bomb load 1 x 4000 HC, 12 x 500 ANM64. Primary target: Koln.
Weather 10/10ths cloud over Koln, South and South-East of Koln
clear. Abortive sortie. All bombs brought back.

05/03/1945 ME355 JI-L BombingGelsenkirchen 10.24 14.07
15.52
Bomb load 1 x 4000 HC, 11 x 500 ANM64, 1 Skymarker Red.

364

Primary target: Gelsenkirchen, Benzol plant. Weather 10/10ths cloud over target with cirrus cloud at bombing height. Bombed at 14.07 hours from 21,000 feet on G.H.

06/03/1945 ME355   JI-L Bombing Salzbergen 08.17 12.15 14.08

Bomb load 1 x 4000 HC, 11 x 500 ANM64, 2 x 500 MC, 1 Skymarker Blue Puff. Primary target: Salzbergen, Wintershall oil plant. Weather 10/10ths cloud over target, tops 10,000 feet. Bombed at 12.15 hours from 21,000 feet on G.H.

07/03/1945 ME336   JI-S Bombing Dessau   17.08   22.03   01.55

Bomb load 1 x 4000 HC, 6 x Mk.17 Clusters. Primary target: Dessau. Weather 5 to 10/10ths thin cloud. Bombed at 22.03 hours from 20,000 feet on Red/Green stars.

11/03/1945 ME351   JI-U Bombing Essen   11.35 15.26 17.22

Bomb load 1 x 4000 HC, 13 x 500 ANM64, 2 x 500 MC. Primary target: Essen, Marshalling yards. Weather 10/10ths cloud, tops 7/8000 feet. Bombed at 15.26 hours from 19,000 feet on G.H.

14/03/1945 ME354   JI-M   Bombing   Heinrichshutte 13.06 16.40 18.33

Bomb load 1 x 4000 HC, 12 x 500 ANM64. Primary target: Heinrichshutte, Hattingen Steel works & Benzol plant. Weather 10/10ths cloud, tops 7/12,000 feet. Bombed at 16.40 hours from 18,000 feet on G.H.

21/03/1945 ME355   JI-L Bombing Munster   09.32 13.08 15.36

Bomb load 1 x 4000 HC, 13 x 500 ANM64, 2 x 500 MC, 1 Skymarker Blue Puff. Primary target Munster Viaduct and Marshalling Yards. Weather cloud nil to 2/10ths. 6 x 500 ANM64, 2x 500 MC, 1 Skymarker Blue Puff on target at 13.08 hours from 18,000 feet on G.H. 1 x 4000 HC, 7 x 500 ANM64 Jettisoned on village 5-6 miles South-east of target due to distributor failure.

04/04/1945 ME336   JI-S Bombing Merseburg (Leuna) 18.44 22.49 02.39

Weather 5-10/10ths cloud, and 10/10ths over Merseburg. Bombed primary Target: Merseburg. Bomb load 1 x 4000 HC, 6 x 500 ANM64. Bombed on Red T.I. with Green stars slightly to port at 22.49 hours from 20,000 feet. Large orange explosion seen. One large green explosion very bright area 2 miles square appeared to be in flames. Dropping of flares was late. On first run no markers to bomb on, orbited and made second run when markers had been dropped. A.P.I. U/S.

P/O. Victor Reginald Thompson 2nd Pilot that day.

13/04/1945 ME354   JI-M   Bombing Kiel   20.29 23.30 01.57

Bomb load 18 x 500 ANM64. Primary target: Kiel, Docks & ship yards. Weather 10/10ths cloud low and thin. Bombed on centre of Green T.I.s on instructions of M/B at 23.30 hours from 20,000 feet. Very bright red explosion seen at 23.31. Other explosions seen and mushrooms of smoke rising above cloud. Gee U/S. Believed good attack. Marking good.

20/04/1945 ME355   JI-L Bombing Regensburg 09.37 13.57 17.11

Bomb load 15 x 500 ANM64. Primary target: Regensburg. Weather clear over target and whole route. Bombed on G.H. at 13.57 hours from 19,000 ft. on blue smoke only. Bombs released by H2S switch, due to sticking distributor arm. Marker blue puff release on G.H. bombing overshot. Fair amount of overshooting and undershooting seen result disappointing due to technical failure. Railway bridge received direct hit.

29/04/1945 ME336   JI-S Manna The Hague   12.57 13.52 15.02

Dropping area: The Hague. Weather broken cloud above and clear below. Dropped 5 packs on red T.I.s. and white cross at 13.52 hours. Bags standing up in form of a pyramid, slightly to starboard of white cross. T.I. fell to port. Civilians in thousands dancing and waving from coast to dropping zone. Uniformed troops surrounding the dropping area apparently keeping back the crowds.

02/05/1945 ME358   JI-O Manna The Hague   10.58 x 13.20

Dropping area The Hague. Weather over dropping zone clear below cloud for the first arrivals changing later to heavy showers which marred visibility. 4 Panniers dropped on White Cross and Red T.I.'s. 1 Pannier hung up brought back. Dropping area very small.

14/05/1945 ME359   JI-T Exodus   Juvincourt - Oakley 10.16 x 16.37

Duration 4.04 hours. Outward 1.41 hours. Collected 24 P.O.Ws. Homeward 2.23 hours. Control at Oakley very slow.

17/05/1945 ME359   JI-T Exodus Brussels - Westcott 10.07 x 17.07

Duration 3 hrs 30 mins. Out 1 hr 36 mins. In 1 hr 54 mins. Arrived Brussels at 11.44 with 10 Belgian refugees. Evacuated 24 ex POW Organisation good.

18/05/1945 ME359   JI-T Exodus   Brussels - Oakley 11.59 x 16.46

Duration 3 hrs 02 mins. Out 1 hr. In 2 hrs 02 mins. 10 Belgian refugees taken to Brussels. 24 ex POWs returned to U.K. Organisation good.

23/05/1945 RA599   JI-L Exodus   Brussels - Oakley 12.02 x 17.06

Duration 2.55 hours. Out 1.46 hours. In 1.09 hours. 11 Belgian refugees returned to Brussels. 24 POWs evacuated. All OK.

24/05/1945 RA599 JI-L Exodus Brussels 12.06 x 15.27
Duration 2.18 hours. Out 1.06 hours. In 1.12 hours. 10 Belgian refugees. No POWs available.

25/05/1945 RA599 JI-L Exodus Brussels 12.02 x 15.48
Duration 2.18 hours. Out 1.10 hours. In 1.08 hours. 10 Belgian refugees returned to Brussels. No POWs home. Dakotas taxied on runway as A/C was about to land.

26/05/1945 RA599 JI-L Exodus Brussels - Ford 12.04 x 17.42
Duration 3.02 hours. Out 1.06 hours. In 1.56 hours. 10 Belgian refugees to Brussels. 24 ex POWs all military brought back.

13/06/1945 RA599 JI-L BaedekerTour over Continent 10.28 x 14.58
Passengers: LAC. M. Jermy, LAC. P. Dixon, AC1. J. Twinning, LAC. J. Brynan, Cpl. R. Bloomfield.

29/06/1945 ME422 JI-Q Post Mortem Special mission 10.05 x 15.48

03/07/1945 ME363 JI-R Post Mortem Special mission 14.28 x 19.40

13/07/1945 RA599 JI-L BaedekerTour over Continent 15.36 x 19.30
Passengers: Cpl. Bell, Cpl. Peape, Cpl. Bell (WAAF), Cpl. Oliver (WAAF), Cpl. Gregory (WAAF).

24/07/1945 RA599 JI-L BaedekerTour over Continent 10.08 x 14.27
Passengers: F/L. Bristol, Cpl. Diller, Cpl. Scott, LACW. Paddon, ACW. Hoskin.

F/L. Robert Jones

127236 (1388626) F/L. Robert "Robbie" "Bob" Jones. Pilot.
124321 (1315167) F/L. Kenneth Hedley "Ken" Loder. A/Bomber.
652896 Sgt. George Frederick "Robby" Robinson. Navigator.
1334090   F/S. Frank Stanley Jones.   WOP/AG.
1895981   Sgt. Robert "Bob" Lane.   MU/Gunner.
1875233   Sgt. Alfred Richard "Alf" Braine. R/Gunner.
1890339 (*) Sgt. Thomas Henry "Tom" Harvell. F/Engineer.
  ??(*) Sgt. L. Foster. ??   F/Engineer.

(*) Probably due to error in the ORBs, on 02/07/1944 Sgt. L. Foster was quoted as being in this crew while Sgt. H.T. Harvell was noted as being in P/O. N. Jennings' crew.

Clockwise from top left: Robert Jones, Frank R. Jones, Robert Lane, Thomas H. Harvell.

14/06/1944 DS842 JI-F Bombing Le Havre   23.52 01.15 02.28
   Bomb load 11 x 1000 GP, 4 x 500 GP. Primary target: Le Havre. Weather clear. Bombed at 01.15 hours from 15,000 feet on yellow and green markers as instructed. Bombs falling along the Quay. Perfect attack. No troubles.
   From his normal crew, only F/O. Robert Jones did this mission as 2nd Pilot with P/O. R. Langley's crew.

15/06/1944 LL734 JI-G Bombing Valenciennes 23.10 00.36 02.33
   Bomb load 16 x 500 GP, 2 x 500 MC. Primary target: Valenciennes. Weather clear below slight haze. Bombed at 00.36 hours from 7,000 feet on red and green T.I.s on Master Bomber's instructions. Sticks seen to burst south of T.I.s. Should be a good attack. Had combat with

E/A.

23/06/1944 LM206   JI-C Bombing L'Hey   23.05 00.15   01.24

Bomb load 11 x 1000 MC, 4 x 500 GP. Primary target: L'Hey, Flying bomb installations. Weather 10/10ths cloud. Bombed at 00.15 hours from 9,000 feet. Good bombing concentrated around red T.I.s. Gee target co-ordinates consisted with red T.I.s. Master Bomber not heard. Some air to air tracer seen.

27/06/1944 ME841   JI-H Bombing Biennais   23.36 01.10   02.47

Bomb load 16 x 500 GP. 2 x 500 ANM64 GP. Primary target: Biennais, Flying bomb installations. There was 10/10ths cloud. Bombed at 01.10 hours from 13,000 feet. Explosions seen at 01.15 hours and 01.17 hours.

30/06/1944 ME841   JI-H Bombing Villers Bocage   18.06 20.00 21.51

Bomb load 11 x 1000 MC, 4 x 500 GP. Primary target: Villers Bocage. Weather clear. Bombed at 20.00 hours from 3,600 feet. Splendid attack, bombing very concentrated.

02/07/1944 ME842   JI-K Bombing Beauvoir   12.45 14.36   15.51

Bomb load 11 x 1000 MC, 4 x 500 GP. Primary target: Beauvoir, Flying bomb supply site. Bombed at 14.36 hours from 10,300 feet on yellow T.I.s.

05/07/1944 ME842   JI-K Bombing Watten   22.44   00.08 01.03

Bomb load 11 x 1000 ANM 65, 4 x 500 GP. Primary target: Watten, Constructional works. Bombed at 00.08 hours from 8,000 feet red T.I.s.

23/07/1944 LM627   JI-D Bombing Kiel   22.20 01.24 03.51

Bomb load 10 x 1000 MC, 5 x 500 GP Special Nickels. Primary target: Kiel, Warehouses and docks. Weather 10/10ths cloud. Bombed at 01.24 hours from 20,000 feet centre of red and green T.I.s. Two long explosions at 01.20 hours and 01.22 hours. Defences accurate, no fighters.

24/07/1944 LM627   JI-D Bombing Stuttgart   21.41 01.42 05.13

Bomb load 7 x 1000 MC, 4 x 500 GP. Primary target: Stuttgart. Weather 10/10ths cloud with occasional small breaks. Bombed at 01.42 hours at 21,000 feet on red T.I. Quiet trip. Yellowish explosion at 01.41 hours.

28/07/1944 LM206   JI-C Bombing Stuttgart   21.41 x 01.17

Bomb load 7 x 1000 MC, 2 x 500 GP. Target Stuttgart. Aircraft missing.

Shot down by a JU88 flown by Oblt. Heinz Roekker of 2./NJG2

able to hide in clouds at 01.17 hours on 29th July 1944, just to the S of Coussey (Vosges) 7 km NW of Neufchateau, en route to target.

Those killed were buried in the Neufchateau Communal Cemetery, Vosges. Sgt. Thomas Henry Harvell was able to evade capture with the help of the French Resistance. Sgt. G.F. Robinson, was captured and held POW in Camp L7, POW No.625.

F/S. Alfred Kay

1437600   F/S. Alfred Kay.   Pilot.
1337038   F/S. John Joseph McKeown.   A/Bomber.
1395122   Sgt. John Handley David Fenwick.   Navigator.
1493956   Sgt. John Payne "Jackie" McCormick.   WOP/AG.
J87476 (R184021) P/O. Bertil Wilfred Bergquist, RCAF. MU/Gunner.
1128211   Sgt. Robert Harrison.   R/Gunner.
1603363   Sgt. Edward George Marchant.   F/Engineer.

Robert Harrison (left), Alfred Kay (top right), John P. McCormick (bottom right). (courtesy Susan Gray Mills)

21/02/1944 DS820 JI-A Bombing Stuttgart   00.29 04.06 07.00

Bomb load 1 x 4000 lbs bomb, 40 x 30, 690 x 4, 90 x 4 x incendiaries. Primary target: Stuttgart. There was 7/10 cloud. Bombed at 04.06 hours at 20,000 ft. Bright white fires seen in centre of T.I.s. Large orange explosion. Big blue flash just before bombs dropped. Little opposition encountered.

From his normal crew, only F/S. Alfred Kay did this mission as 2nd Pilot with P/O. R. Langley's crew.

24/02/1944 DS785 JI-D Bombing Schweinfurt 20.57 x 01.14

Bomb load 1 x 4000 lb bomb, 24 x 30, 420 x 4, 90 x 4 incendiaries. Aircraft missing. No news.

Crashed 25th February 1944 at 01:14 hours at Heidingsfeld, near Würzburg. Cause of crash unknown, but possibly a victim of Lt. Hans Raum, 9./NJG3, who claimed a 4-engined aircraft West of Wurzburg; however it is equally possible that the aircraft was a victim of flak.

All the crew were KIA. Originally buried in the cemetery at Heidingsfield, the crew were re-interred in Durnbach War Cemetery. This is believed to have been Sgt Kay's second sortie.

F/O. Holman Gordon Stanley Kerr

185226 (1482503) F/O. Holman Gordon Stanley Kerr. Pilot.
154941 (1579494) F/O. Frank Clarke.   A/Bomber.
1397906   F/S. Sidney Smith.   Navigator.
A434001   F/S. Allan Olsen, RAAF. WOP/AG.
2220626   Sgt. Christopher George Hogg. MU/Gunner.
605706 Sgt. Herbert Percival Thomas. R/Gunner.
1589746   Sgt. William Marsden. F/Engineer.

13/02/1945 PB419 A2-B Bombing Dresden 22.00 01.31 07.53

Bomb load 1 x 4000 MC, 15 x No. 14 Clusters. Primary target: Dresden. Weather 5/10ths cloud over target. Bombed at 01.31 hours from 20,000 feet on Red T.I.s.

From his normal crew, only F/O. H.G.S. Kerr did this mission as 2nd Pilot with S/L. E.B. Cozens' crew.

16/02/1945 PB419 A2-B Bombing Wesel   12.35 16.01 17.52

Allan Olsen (front row right) with what is believed to be the crew of F/O. Homan Kerr.

(courtesy Sally Olsen)

Bomb load 1 x 4000 HC, 4 x 500 GP, 2 x 500 MC L/Delay, 4 x 250 GP, 6 x 500 ANM64. Primary target: Wesel. Weather clear. Bombed at 16.01 hours from 20,000 feet on G.H. Leader.

From his normal crew, only F/O. H.G.S. Kerr did this mission as 2nd Pilot with S/L. E.B. Cozens' crew.

18/02/1945 PB419 A2-B Bombing Wesel   11.32 15.26 17.05

Bomb load 1 x 4000 HC, 4 x 500 GP, 2 x 500 MC L/Delay, 4 x 250 GP, 6 x 500 ANM64. Primary target: Wesel. Weather 10/10ths cloud. Bombed at 15.26 hours from 20,000 feet on G.H. Leader.

19/02/1945 PB419 A2-B Bombing Wesel   13.05 16.37 19.15

Bomb load 1 x 4000 HC, 6 x 500 MC, 6 x 500 ANM64, 4 x 250 GP. Primary target: Wesel. Weather over target 5-7/10ths cloud. Bombed at 16.37 hours from 20,000 feet on leading aircraft. Landed at Moreton in Marsh.

20/02/1945 PB419 A2-B Bombing Dortmund 21.45 01.06 03.28

Bomb load 1 x 4000HC, 6 x 500 Type 14 Clusters, 6 x 750 Type 15 Clusters. Primary target: Dortmund. Weather 8-10/10ths thin cloud at about 5,000 feet. Bombed at 01.06 hours from 21,000 feet on centre of Red glows through clouds, with a Green T.I. on each side.

22/02/1945 PB419 A2-B Bombing Osterfeld 12.20 16.01 17.54

Bomb load 1 x 4000 HC, 9 x 500 ANM64, 2 x 500 MC, 4 x 250 GP.

Primary target: Osterfeld, Coking ovens. Weather at target clear, but hazy. Bombed at 16.01 hours from 20,000 feet on G.H. Leader.

26/02/1945 NG203   A2-C   Bombing Dortmund 10.25   14.03   16.16
Bomb load 1 x 4000 HC, 2 x 500 MC L/Delay 37B, 9 x 500 ANM64, 4 x 250 GP. Primary target: Dortmund, Hoesch Benzin plant. Weather 10/10ths cloud, tops 8/10,000 feet. Bombed at 14.03 hours from 20,000 feet on G.H. Leader.

28/02/1945 NN775   A2-F   Bombing Nordstern 08.58   12.04   14.19
Bomb load 1 x 4000 HC, 9 x 500 ANM64, 2 x 500 MC L/D, 4 x 250 GP. Primary target: Nordstern (Gelsenkirchen). Weather 10/10ths cloud. Bombed at 12.04 hours from 21,000 feet on leading aircraft.

05/03/1945 NN775   A2-F   Bombing Gelsenkirchen 10.35 x   x
Bomb load 1 x 4000 HC, 12 x 500 ANM64. Primary target: Gelsenkirchen, Benzol plant. Weather 10/10ths cloud over target with cirrus cloud at bombing height. Aircraft missing.

No survivors from the crew when the aircraft crashed at Bunsbeek, a province of Brabant, Belgium. Circumstances of loss not stated but most likely due to flak damage as no fighter activity was noted on this daylight raid. The crew are buried at Heverlee War Cemetery, 30 km from Brussels.

Sgt. H.P. Thomas had enlisted in Canada, though he lived at Beckford Kraal, Clarendon on Jamaica.

P/O. Ernest Arthur Kingham

174119 (1216258)   P/O. Ernest Arthur Kingham.   Pilot.
1433953   F/S. Frank Richard Spencer.   A/Bomber. 23 ops.
1330751   F/S. William Henry Wyer.   A/Bomber. 1 op.
J20915   P/O. John Peake, DFC RCAF.   A/Bomber. 2 ops.
1575248   F/S. Raymond Harold Hutt.   Navigator.
1414792   F/S. Benjamin "Ben" Bloom.   WOP/AG.
1895351   Sgt. Frederick Neale Ansell.   MU/Gunner.
J92608 (R188172) P/O. Daniel George "Dan" Davis, RCAF. R/Gunner.
1531244   Sgt. Joseph Black.   F/Engineer.

15/02/1944 DS785 JI-D Bombing Berlin   17.29 21.18   23.53
Bomb load 1 x 8000 lbs bomb. Primary target: Berlin. There was 10/10 cloud over the target. Bombed at 21.18 hrs. At 21,000 ft. Route very good. No fighters seen.

L to R: R.H. Hutt, F.N. Ansell, B. Bloom, E.A. Kingham, D.G. Davies, J. Black, F.R. Spencer.
(courtesy Charlie Bloom)

From his normal crew, only P/O. E.A. Kingham did this mission as 2nd Pilot with P/O. G.S. Hughes' crew.

21/02/1944 DS785 JI-D Bombing Stuttgart   00.27 04.10 07.30

Bomb load 1 x 4000 lb bomb, 690 x 4, 90 x 4 incendiaries. Primary target: Stuttgart. There was 5/10 scattered cloud. Bombed at 04.10 hours at 21,000 ft. T.I.s well concentrated. 180 x 4 inc hung up. All clouds reflected with red glow. Buildings seen through cloud gaps to be blazing. Had encounter with enemy aircraft.

01/03/1944 LL690 JI-J Bombing Stuttgart   23.36 03.10 07.11

Bomb load 1 x 2000, 1 x 500 lb bomb, 40 x 30, 900 x 4 incendiaries. Primary target: Stuttgart. There was 10/10 cloud. Bombed at 03.10 hours at 20,000 ft. Glow of fires appeared concentrated in small area. Route very good. Photo attempted.

F/S. W.H. Wyer A/Bomber that day.

07/03/1944 LL690 JI-J Bombing Le Mans   19.42 x 23.51

Bomb load 10 x 1000, 4 x 500 lb bomb. No attack. Could not identify target. Red glow of T.I. seen through cloud. 4 x 500 lb bombs jettisoned. 10 x 1000 lb bombs brought back to Base.

P/O. John Peake A/Bomber that day.

15/03/1944 LL690 JI-J Bombing Stuttgart 19.19 23.23 02.52
Bomb load 1 x 1000 lb bomb, 72 x 30, 1050 x 4, 90 x 4 incendiaries. Primary target: Stuttgart. There was thin low cloud. Bombed at 23.23 hours from 21,000 feet. Some glows and reflections seen. Attack only moderate. Fires seen but rather scattered. Route OK.

18/03/1944 LL690 JI-J Bombing Frankfurt 19.46 22.03 00.54
Bomb load 1 x 4000 lb bomb, 32 x 30, 1140 x 4 incendiaries. Primary target: Frankfurt, Weather was hazy. Bombed at 22.03 hours from 21,000 feet. Many fires visible, spread over a large area.

24/03/1944 LL728 JI-B Bombing Berlin 18.31 22.30 02.00
Bomb load 1 x 1000 lb bomb, 88 x 30, 810 x 4, 90 x 4 incendiaries. Primary target: Berlin. There was 6/10 cloud over the target. Bombed at 22.30 hours from 20,000 feet. Scattered marking. No fires seen in area. Raid did not appear to be very good, commentated helpful. Change of zero hours heard on 22.00 Broadcast.
P/O. John Peake A/Bomber that day.

11/04/1944 LL690 JI-J Bombing Aachen 21.00 22.46 00.33
Bomb load 10 x 1000, 2 x 500 lb bombs, 160 x 4, 20 x 4 incendiaries. Primary target: Aachen. There was 6/10 cloud, broken at intervals. Bombed at 22.46 hours from 20,000 feet. Reddish fires seen in target area. Fires appeared to be spreading as Lancaster left. Photo attempted.

18/04/1944 LL690 JI-J Bombing Rouen 22.22 00.48 02.50
Bomb load 8 x 1000 MC, 2 x 1000 GP, 5 x 500 lb bomb. Primary target: Rouen. There was slight haze. Bombed at 00.48 hours from 12,500 feet. Two group of markers seen. M of C instructed to bomb the red T.I.s - second group were NW of A.P. M of C very helpful. Should be a good raid.

20/04/1944 LL690 JI-J Bombing Cologne 00.25 02.13 04.01
Bomb load 1 x 1000, 1026 x 4, 108 x 30 lb incendiaries. Primary target: Koln. There was 10/10 cloud. Bombed at 02.13 hours from 20,000 feet. Cloud prevented sight of target. Defences lighter than expected. Good red glow seen below cloud as far away as the E.C. (home). Route good. Landed at Woodbridge.

22/04/1944 LL690 JI-J Bombing Dusseldorf 23.13 01.27 03.19
Bomb load 1 x 8000 lb bomb, 48 x 30, 486 x 4, 54 x 4 incendiaries. Primary target: Dusseldorf. Weather was hazy with cloud above. Bombed at 01.27 hours from 20,000 feet. T.I.s. and attack concentrated. Target well alight on leaving. Many searchlights about.

24/04/1944 LL690 JI-J Bombing Karlsruhe 22.23 00.55 04.19

Bomb load 1 x 1000 lb bomb, 1026 x 4, 114 x 4, 108 x 30 lb incendiaries. Primary target: Karlsruhe. There was patchy cloud. Bombed at 00.55 hours from 19,000 feet. T.I.s well concentrated, and incendiaries also concentrated around T.I.s. Some large fires seen after leaving target area. Some buildings aflame.

26/04/1944 LL690 JI-J Bombing Essen 22.54 01.30 03.05

Bomb load 1 x 8000 lb bomb, 60 x 30, 405 x 4, 45 x 4 lb incendiaries. Primary target: Essen. There was slight cloud at 22,000 feet, clear below. Bombed at 01.30 hours from 22,000 feet. There was a good concentration of T.I.s with some incendiaries. A very good trip. Searchlights numerous and flak moderate. Few flak holes in fuselage also undercarriage doors.

30/04/1944 LL690 JI-J Catamount x x x

Only quoted in ORB summary. Op not detailed.

E.A. Kingham noted in logbook "Special exercise (CATAMOUNT)"

01/05/1944 LL690 JI-J Bombing Chambly 22.58 00.27 02.18

Bomb load 10 x 1000, 5 x 500 lb bombs. Primary target: Chambly. There was 1/10 cloud visibility OK. Bombed at 00.27 hours from 7,500 feet. T.I.s nicely concentrated and bombing close to T.I.s. River seen S of T.I.s where expected. H. flares helpful, and about where expected in relation to T.I. A good show. An explosion as we ran in and fires as we came away.

08/05/1944 LL690 JI-J Bombing Cap Gris Nez 22.58 23.57 00.58

Bomb load 14 x 1000 lb bombs. Primary target: Cape Gris Nez. Weather was clear. Bombed at 23.57 hours from 7,000 feet. Bombs appeared to burst in concentration on tip of Cape. A very concentrated effort.

10/05/1944 LL690 JI-J Bombing Courtrai 22.15 23.26 00.30

Bomb load 7 x 1000 GP, 7 x 1000 MC. Primary target: Courtrai. Clear conditions. Saw white flares followed by red and green T.I.s. Bombed as instructed by Master Bomber at 23.26 hours from 11,000 feet. Whitish yellow fire seen in target area. Bombs appeared to burst in good concentration around markers. Good attack. Fire seen during bombing run appeared to increase on leaving target.

24/05/1944 LL690 JI-J Bombing Boulogne 00.20 01.15 02.05

Bomb load 9 x 1000 MC, 1 x 1000 GP, 1 x 1000 ANM, 4 x 500 GP. Primary target: Boulogne, Gun Battery. Clear over target. Bombed at 01.15 hours from 9,000 feet and bombs seen to burst close to markers.

27/05/1944 LL690 JI-J Bombing Aachen   00.35 02.28 04.05

Bomb load 7 x 1000 MC, 4 x 1000 ANM, 4 x 500 MC. Primary target: Aachen. Clear over target but 10/10 cloud over sea. Bombed at 02.28 hours from 12,500 feet. A good concentration of markers and a fair amount of flak. Single-engine enemy aircraft seen at 02.25 hours in light of a Lancaster falling on fire.

30/05/1944 LL697 JI-E Bombing Boulogne   23.06 00.06 01.34

Bomb load 6 x 1000 MC, 4 x 500 MC. Primary target: Boulogne Gun Batteries. Clear over target. Bombed red T.I.s at 00.06 hours from 8,000 feet. Bomb bursts generally seemed concentrated except for a stick to the North. Pall of smoke seen. Slight light flak.

31/05/1944 LL690 JI-J Bombing Trappes 23.52 01.57 04.18

Bomb load 8 x 1000 MC, 8 x 500 MC. Primary target: Trappes. Clear at target. Perfect visual of marshalling yards obtained. Bombed as directed by Master Bomber at 01.57 hours from 8,000 feet. Bomb bursts seen on the yards and much smoke. Attack thought good. Route satisfactory but long.

06/06/1944 LL690 JI-J Bombing Lisieux   00.15 01.40 03.19

Bomb load 16 x 500 MC tail fused and 2 x 500 MC LD. Primary target: Lisieux. Weather was clear below but cloud above. Bombed red T.I.s at 01.40 hours from 5,600 feet. Marking was concentrated and bombing accurate. Smoke prevented a visual. Cloud more troublesome than the opposition. Attack thought good. Route quiet.

07/06/1944 LL690 JI-J Bombing Massy Palaiseau 00.23 02.15 04.18

Bomb load 18 x 500 MC. Primary target: Massy Palaiseau, Marshalling Yards. Cloud above 6,000 feet, hazy below. Bombed on Master Bomber's instructions at 02.15 hours from 6,400 feet. T.I.s were concentrated and bombs burst amongst them. Attack seemed concentrated. Some light flak south of the target.

10/06/1944 LL690 JI-J Bombing Dreux 23.09 00.56 03.05

Bomb load 16 x 500 GP, 2 x 500 LD. Primary target: Dreux. Bombed to starboard of green T.I.s on instructions of Master Bomber at 00.56 hours from 8,000 feet. Three sticks seen to burst across tracks. Perfect visual obtained by flares. Light flak was slight. Weather clear.

11/06/1944 LL690 JI-J Bombing Nantes 23.55 02.45 05.00

Bomb load 16 x 500 GP, 2 x 500 LD. Primary target: Nantes. Bombed centre of red and green T.I.s as instructed by Master Bomber at 02.45 hours from 2,500 feet. There was 10/10ths cloud but clear below base at 2,500 feet.

14/06/1944 LL690 JI-J Bombing Le Havre 23.51 01.14 02.31

Bomb load 11 x 1000 MC, 4 x 500 GP. Primary target: Le Havre.
Weather clear. Bombed at 01.14 hours from 15,500 feet on red and
green T.I.s. Number of large fires seen on arrival, more on leaving.
Slight opposition.

15/06/1944 LL690 JI-J Bombing Valenciennes 23.14 x 00.52

Bomb load 16 x 500 GP, 2 x 500 MC. Primary target: Valenciennes.
Aircraft missing.

Shot down on 16th June 1944, probably at 00.52 hours by a Bf 110
flown by Oblt. Peter Ehrhardt of 9/NJG5. The aircraft came down
between Iwuy (Nord) and Rieux-en-Cambresis, 9 km from Cambrai.
Five are buried in Rieux Communal Cemetery, while F/S. Hutt is
buried at Iwuy Communal Cemetery. Sgt. Bloom is commemorated on
the Runnymede Memorial.

F/L. Leonard John Kingwell

133610 (1338555) F/L. Leonard John Kingwell. Pilot.
J20915 F/O. John Peake. DFC. RCAF. A/Bomber. 10 ops.
1585341   Sgt. William Alexander Bates. A/Bomber. 1 op.
1396522   Sgt. George Edward Knight. Navigator.
1220052   F/S. Harold Marcus Whichelow. WOP/AG.
1581481   Sgt. Harry Taylor. MU/Gunner.
A409037   W/O. Harold Stanley Fidge, RAAF. R/Gunner.
1812145   Sgt. Dennis William Newbury. F/Engineer.
R133286 W/O. James David Dodding, RCAF. 2nd Pilot. 19/02/1944

20/12/1943 LL625 JI-C Bombing Frankfurt 17.41 19.50 22.49

Bomb load 1 x 4000, 48 x 30 incendiaries, 950 x 4 incendiaries, 100
x 4 incendiaries. Primary target: Frankfurt. 7/10 cloud, thin layer over
target. Few red and green T.I.s seen. Bombed at 19.50 at 19,000 feet.
Attack scattered at first, but on leaving target fires had a good hold.

F/O. J. Peake A/Bomber until 15/02/1944.

24/12/1943 LL625 JI-C Bombing Berlin 00.23 04.13 07.58

Bomb load 1 x 4000, 32 x 30 incendiaries, 450 x 4 incendiaries, 90
x 4 incendiaries. Primary target: Berlin. Broken cloud, 5/10. Bombed
at 04.13 hrs. At 19,000 ft. Huge orange coloured fire blasting. Had
three encounters with enemy aircraft.

29/12/1943 DS785 JI-D Bombing Berlin   17.05 20.19 23.49

Bomb load 1 x 2000, 40 x 30, 900 x 4, 90 x 4 incendiaries. Primary target: Berlin. There was 10/10 cloud with 10,000 tops. Bombed at 20.19 hours at 19,000 ft. Red flares with green stars seen. White glare underneath cloud. Sky markers well concentrated. Glare on cloud showed good fires burning underneath.

01/01/1944 DS785 JI-D Bombing Berlin   00.30 x 02.16

Bomb load 1 x 2000, 40 x 30, 900 x 4 lbs incendiaries. Returned early. Farthest point reached 5238N 03E. All bombs jettisoned. M/U Turret R.S.J. burst. Intercom and heating out of action.

14/01/1944 LL681 JI-J Bombing Brunswick 16.44 19.20 21.54

Bomb load 1 x 4000, 48 x 30 incendiaries. Primary target: Brunswick. 10/10 cloud with tops 5-8,000 ft. Bombed at 19.20 hours at 20,000 ft. Target well lit up. White glow illuminating clouds. Monica u/s. Very concentrated attack. Photo attempted.

20/01/1944 LL681 JI-J Bombing Berlin   16.09 19.38 23.25

Bomb load 1 x 4000, 32 x 30, 540 x 4, 60 x 4 incendiaries. Primary target: Berlin. There was 10/10 cloud. Bombed at 19.38 hours at 20,000 ft on 5 red and green sky markers. Markers well concentrated and should be a good attack. Some reflection of fires seen.

21/01/1944 LL681 JI-J Bombing Magdeburg 19.51 23.03 03.00

Bomb load 1 x 4000, 720 x 4, 90 x 4, 32 x 30 incendiaries. Primary target: Magdeburg. There was 4-7/10 broken cloud. Bombed at 23.03 hours at 20,000 ft. Good fires seen through breaks in cloud. Bullet holes in starboard fin rudder. Bomb doors holed by either fighter or flak. Crossed coast at Wilhelmshafen due to loss of Navigational Equipment during fighter attack. Fighters were over the target very quickly.

27/01/1944 LL624 JI-B Bombing Berlin   17.52 x 19.41

Bomb load 1 x 8000. Returned early. Farthest point reached 5317N 0250E. Poor engine performance. Bomb jettisoned.

30/01/1944 DS842 JI-F Bombing Berlin   17.10 20.27 23.36

Bomb load 1 x 4000 lb bomb, 600 x 4, 90 x 4, 32 x 30 incendiaries. Primary target: Berlin. There was 10/10 cloud with tops 8.000 ft. Bombed at 20.27 hours at 20,000 ft. Many flares well concentrated. Cloud prevented visual. Monica u/s. Incendiaries did not show through the cloud, but the red glow of fires could be seen 100 miles from target. Sky markers were good. Hundreds of fighter flares in target area and on the track.

15/02/1944 LL681 JI-J Bombing Berlin   17.27 21.23 00.08

Bomb load 1 x 4000 lbs bomb, 32 x 30, 540 x 4, 90 x 4 incendiaries. Primary target: Berlin. There was 10/10 cloud. Bombed at 21.23 hrs. At 20,000 ft. Sky markers well concentrated with the exception of one cluster one-mile W 21.16 hrs. Cloud prevented visual. No flak shooting at sky markers on this sortie. Markers well concentrated.

19/02/1944 LL681 JI-J Bombing Leipzig 00.17 x x

Bomb load 1 x 2000, 1 x 500 lbs. Bomb. 40 x 30, 900 x 4 incendiaries. Aircraft missing. No news. Lost 20th February 1944 without trace probably a victim of unidentified night fighter.

W/O. J.D. Dodding was 2nd Pilot that day and Sgt. W.A. Bates A/Bomber.

All 8 crew KIA and commemorated on the Runnymede Memorial.

FL. acting S/L. John Forbes Knight, DFC

J5133 S/L. John Forbes Knight, DFC RCAF. Pilot.
160956 (1333696) F/O. John Barwick Cushing, DFC. A/Bomber.
132915 F/L. Jeffrey Howard Canton, DFC. Navigator.
R193875 W/O. C.L. Calhoun, RCAF. WOP/AG.
Sgt. T.R. Pinder. MU/Gunner.
Sgt. W.D. Jones. R/Gunner.
Sgt. J. Dolby. F/Engineer.
NZ429076
P/O. Frederick L. "Freddie" Hookway, RNZAF. 2nd Pilot.
23/03/1945

Passengers: 07/05/1945

28/01/1945 PD389 A2-J Bombing Cologne-Gremberg 10.36 14.11 16.15

Bomb load 1 x 4000 HC, 10 x 500 ANM64, 2 x 500 GP, 3 x 250 GP. Primary target: Koln - Gremberg, Marshalling yards. Weather 10/10ths cloud en route clearing on approach to target where visibility was good and nil cloud. Bombed at 14.11 hours from 19,800 feet on G.H. Leader.

29/01/1945 LM728   JI-F
BombingKrefeld   10.24 13.59
15.35Bomb load 1 x 4000 HC,
10 x 500 ANM64, 2 x 500 GP, 4 x
250 GP. Primary target: Krefeld
Marshalling Yards. Weather
10/10ths low thin cloud over target
although clear patches en-route.
Bombed at 13.59 hours from
20,000 feet on G.H. Leader.
01/02/1945 PD334A2-D
BombingMunchen-Gladbach13.17
16.35 18.28
Bomb load 1 x 4000 HC, 14 x
No. 14 Clusters. Primary target:
Munchen-Gladbach, Marshalling

John Forbes Knight

yards. Bombed at 16.35 hours from 19,200 feet on leading aircraft.
13/02/1945 NG142   JI-J BombingDresden   21.48 01.28 06.48
Bomb load 1 x 4000 HC, 7 x No. 14 Clusters. Primary target:
Dresden. Weather 5/10ths cloud over target. Bombed at 01.28 hours
from 20,000 feet on centre of fires.
14/02/1945 NG142   JI-J BombingChemnitz 20.22 23.32 02.59
Bomb load 1 x 4000 HC, 6 x No. 14 Clusters. Primary target:
Chemnitz. Weather 8-10/10ths cloud, tops 15-16,000 feet with
occasional breaks. Aircraft returned early with hydraulics in rear turret
unserviceable. 1 x 4000 HC bomb hung up, jettisoned in area 5012N
0015W at 02.22 hours from 7,000 feet. Bombed last resort:
Lachsonheim airfield at 23.32 hours from 17,000 feet. Runway and
occult.
16/02/1945 NN782   JI-F Bombing Wesel 12.30 16.01 17.45
Bomb load 1 x 4000 HC, 4 x 500 GP, 2 x 500 MC L/Delay, 4 x 250
GP, 6 x 500 ANM64. Primary target: Wesel. Weather clear. Bombed at
16.01 hours from 20,000 feet on leading aircraft.
22/02/1945 PB142 JI-G BombingOsterfeld   12.14 16.00 17.37
Bomb load 1 x 4000 HC, 9 x 500 ANM64, 2 x 500 MC, 4 x 250 GP.
Primary target: Osterfeld, Coking ovens. Weather at target clear, but
hazy. Bombed at 16.00 hours from 20,000 feet on G.H. Leader.
25/02/1945 NF968 JI-B BombingKamen 09.33 12.47 15.05
Bomb load 1 x 4000 HC, 9 x 500 ANM64, 2 x 500 MC, 4 x 250 GP.
Primary target: Kamen. Weather 6-8/10ths cloud. Bombed at 12.47

hours from 19,700 feet on G.H. equipment.

27/02/1945 NF968 JI-B Bombing Gelsenkirchen   11.02   14.27   16.30
Bomb load 1 x 4000 HC, 2 x 500 MC (L/D 37B), 9 x 500 ANM64, 3 x 250 GP, 1 x 250 Blue Puff. Primary target: Gelsenkirchen (Alma Pluts) Benzin plant. Weather 10/10ths cloud, 6/10,000 feet tops. Bombed at 14.27 hours from 19,600 feet on G.H.

01/03/1945 NF968 JI-B Bombing Kamen   11.47   15.05   17.43
Bomb load 1 x 4000 HC, 10 x 500 ANM64, 2 x 500 MC L/D, 1 Blue smoke puff. Primary target: Kamen, Coking plant. Weather 10/10ths cloud. Bombed at 15.05 hours from 18,600 feet on leading G.H. aircraft.

02/03/1945 NF968 JI-B Bombing Koln   12.39   16.03   18.20
Bomb load 1 x 4000 HC, 11 x 500 ANM64. Primary target: Koln. Weather 10/10ths cloud over Koln, South and South-East of Koln clear. Bombed at 16.03 hours from 19,800 feet. Visual of Southern end of town on edge of River.

06/03/1945 PB142 JI-G Bombing Salzbergen   08.20   12.15   14.14
Bomb load 1 x 4000 HC, 12 x 500 ANM64, 2 x 500MC. Primary target: Salzbergen, Wintershall oil plant. Weather 10/10ths cloud over target, tops 10,000 feet. Bombed at 12.15 hours from 20,400 feet on G.H.

07/03/1945 NF968 JI-B Bombing Dessau   17.09   22.04   02.31
Bomb load 1 x 4000 HC, 6 x Mk. 17 Clusters. Primary target: Dessau. Weather 5 to 10/10ths thin cloud. Bombed at 22.04 hours from 20,100 feet on Skymarkers and Master Bomber.

17/03/1945 LM724   JI-H Bombing August Viktoria 11.32   15.06
17.07
Bomb load 1 x 4000 HC, 13 x 500 ANM64, 2 x 500 MC. Primary target: Auguste Viktoria, Marl-Hüls coal mine. Weather 10/10ths cloud, tops and contrails up to 23,000 feet. Bombed at 15.06 hours from 20,300 feet on G.H.

20/03/1945 LM285   JI-A Bombing Hamm   09.58   13.15   15.46
Bomb load 7 x 1000 ANM59, 8 x 500 ANM64, 1 Skymarker Green Puff. Primary target: Hamm, Marshalling yards. Weather 5/10ths cloud. Bombed at 13.15 hours from 17,800 feet on G.H. Partial failure of G.H. resulting in bombs falling on North-East part of town.

23/03/1945 ME351   JI-U Bombing Wesel   14.27 17.38   19.11
Bomb load 13 x 1000 ANM65. Primary target: Wesel, in support of ground troops. Weather perfect. Bombed at 17.38 hours from 19,900 feet on G.H.

P/O. F.L. Hookway 2nd Pilot that day.

29/03/1945 NF968 JI-B Bombing Salzgitter   12.20 16.43 19.11
Bomb load 1 x 4000 HC, 8 x 500 ANM64. Primary target: Salzgitter, Hallendorf works. Weather 10/10ths cloud. Bombed at 16.43 hours from 22,000 feet on G.H.

09/04/1945 NF968 JI-B Bombing Kiel   19.27 22.38 01.46
Bomb load 1 x 4000 HC and 12 x 500 ANM64. Primary target: Kiel, Submarine Buildings Yards. Weather clear with slight haze. Bombed at 22.38 hours from 20,000 feet on centre red/green T.I.s. Explosion seen in target 1 and 2. Great number of 4000 lbs seen to fall in the sea area from 0300E. Six were seen to fall at one time. Rear turret U/S oil had drained out. Good attack. Release of 4000 lb increased in frequency as dusk fell. Gee faded from 0500E. H2S u/s over target.

30/04/1945 RF230 JI-B Manna Rotterdam 16.53 18.10 19.23
Dropping area: Rotterdam. Weather intermittent showers and low cloud. Load 5 packs. Dropped 5 packs at 18.10 hours on white cross. Good reception from populace. Many of packs fell short some in water.

07/05/1945 RF230 JI-B Manna The Hague   12.24 13.50 14.54
Dropping area The Hague. Dropped 5 packs on White Cross at 13.50 hours. Clear. 5142N 0228E 13.08 1,500 ft. Several patches of yellow oil - 2 yellow cylinders and one white cylinder - pieces of floating wreckage.
No Mid Upper Gunner that day.
Passenger Sgt. George.

10/05/1945 ME530 JI-C Exodus   Juvincourt - Ford 11.07 x 14.21
Duration 3.49. Outward 1.30 hours. Collected 24 POWs. Homeward 1.59 hours. Tyre burst on landing at Ford, but nobody hurt. Returned to Base 11/05/1945 at 14.21 hours.

12/05/1945 RA600 JI-B Exodus   Brussels - Tangmere 11.45 x 17.14
Duration 2.15. Outward 1.05 hours. Homeward 1.10 hours. 10 Refugees to Brussels, 24 ex POWs. to Ford. Everything satisfactory.

15/05/1945 RA600 JI-B Exodus   Juvincourt - Wing 15.52 x 21.17
Duration 4 hrs 03 mins. Outward 2 hrs 14 mins. Collected 24 POWs. Homeward 1 hr 49 mins. All O.K.

18/05/1945 RA600 JI-B Exodus   Brussels - Oakley 12.11 x 22.56
Duration 2 hrs 28 mins. Out 1 hr 06 mins. In 1 hr 22 mins. 10 Belgians taken to Brussels. 24 ex POWs returned. All O.K.

19/05/1945 RF231 JI-A Exodus   Brussels - Oakley 12.00 x 17.21

Duration 2 hrs 54 mins. Out 1 hr 09 mins. In 1 hr 45 mins. 10 Belgian refugees to Brussels. 24 ex POWs (all military) evacuated.

F/O. John Rollo Laing

147526 (1056076) F/O. John Rollo Laing.   Pilot.
1044234   F/S. Jack Knights.   A/Bomber.
1533843   Sgt. Albert Vickers.   Navigator.
169554 (1076809) P/O. James Morton Hydes, DFC.   WOP/AG. 3 ops.
1023462 F/S. Gerald Eagleson "Gerry" Scott. WOP/AG. 12 ops.
R174878 F/S.   Ronald Bayne "Ron" McAllister, RCAF. MU/Gunner.
1451820   Sgt. Charles Arthur Salt.   R/Gunner.
1579492   Sgt. Philip Charles Knill Bennett. F/Engineer.
1337754 Sgt. Charles James "Charlie" Medland, DFM. 2nd Pilot. 07/03/44

29/12/1943 LL625 JI-C Bombing Berlin   17.08 20.31 23.43
    Bomb load 1 x 2000, 40 x 30 incendiaries, 900 x 4 incendiaries, 90 x 4 incendiaries. Primary target: Berlin. There was 10/10 cloud with one or two breaks. Bombed at 20.31 hours at 20,000 ft. Bomb sight used. Green star reflection, red in colour in cloud showing fires underneath. Late on target so cut across to join main force. Glare on leaving showed that good fires were burning under the cloud.
    P/O. J.M. Hydes WOP/AG until 02/01/1944.
01/01/1944 LL625 JI-C Bombing Berlin   00.43 03.19 07.28
    Bomb load 1 x 2000, 40 x 30, 900 x 4 lb incendiaries. Primary target: Berlin. There was 10/10 cloud with tops 18,000 feet. 5 Red sky markers seen which soon disappeared into cloud. Bombed at 03.19 hours at 20,000 feet. Too much cloud, but flash of own bombs seen. Not a good attack, too scattered.
02/01/1944 LL625 JI-C Bombing Berlin   00.17 02.48 06.31
    Bomb load 1 x 2000, 40 x 30, 900 x 4 incendiaries. Primary target: Berlin. There was 10/10 cloud. Bombed at 02.48 hours at 20,000 ft. Solid cloud to above 23,000 ft. Icing to 12 Dgs F. Route good. Little flak. T.I.s dead on target. Good concentration.
14/01/1944 LL625 JI-C Bombing Brunswick 16.52 19.16 22.11
    Bomb load 1 x 4000, 48 x 30 incendiaries. Primary target:

R.B. "Ron" McAllister (left) and G.E. "Gerry" Scott.
(courtesy Janelle McAllister)

Brunswick. There was 10/10 cloud. Bombed at 19.16 hours at 10,000 ft. Orange coloured glow through cloud seen. 12 x 30 inc hung up.

F/S. G.E. Scott WOP/AG from that day.

20/01/1944 LL625 JI-C Bombing Berlin   16.12 19.34   23.42

Bomb load 1 x 4000, 32 x 30, 540 x 4, 60 x 4 incendiaries. Primary target: Berlin. 8/10 cloud. Bombed at 19.34 hours at 20,000 ft. On red sky markers. Saw red glow through clouds.

27/01/1944 LL625 JI-C Bombing Berlin   17.52 20.36   01.26

Bomb load 1 x 4000, 32 x 30, 450 x 4, 90 x 4 incendiaries. Primary target: Berlin. There was 10/10 cloud. Bombed at 20.36 hours at 20,000 ft. 10/10 cloud prevented visual. Markers well concentrated although flak was being belted up round them. Red glow reflected through the clouds showing fires underneath. Large area well concentrated.

28/01/1944 LL625 JI-C Bombing Berlin   00.16 03.22   08.10

Bomb load 1 x 4000 lb bomb, 24 30, 180 x 4, 90 x 4 incendiaries. Primary target: Berlin. There was 10/10 cloud with one or two breaks. Bombed at 03.22 hours at 20,000 ft. Heavy concentration of sky markers and large red glow reflected through cloud. The best prang I have been on - P.F.F. were 'Bang On'. Fires red glow could be seen for 150 miles after leaving target. Had encounter with enemy aircraft.

30/01/1944 LL625 JI-C Bombing Berlin   17.11 20.25   23.54

Bomb load 1 x 4000 lb bomb, 600 x 4, 90 x 4, 32 x 30 incendiaries. Primary target: Berlin. There was 10/10 cloud. Bombed at 20.25 hours at 20,000 ft. No result seen in target, but fires seen on leaving. Not as good as last nights' raid. P.F.F. concentrated at first, appeared scattered later. Had encounter with enemy aircraft.

15/02/1944 LL625 JI-C Bombing Berlin   17.36 21.30 00.37

Bomb load 1 x 8000 lbs bomb. Primary target: Berlin. There was 10/10 cloud. Bombed at 21.30 hrs at 20,000 ft. Barrage of H.F. more intense than usual. Guns started firing before S/Ls exposed. S/Ls few in number below cloud. No fighters seen.

19/02/1944 LL625 JI-C Bombing Leipzig   00.14 04.12 07.00

Bomb load 1 x 2000, 1 x 500 lb bomb, 40 x 30, 900 x 4 incendiaries. Primary target: Leipzig. There was 10/10 cloud with tops 5/6,000 ft. Bombed at 04.12 hours at 20,000 ft. Good exhibition of sky marking. Red glow visible on leaving target. Route markers all seen and used - helpful. A good effort. Quiet route. P.F.F. exceptionally good.

25/02/1944 DS842 JI-F Bombing Augsburg   21.56 01.27 05.14

Bomb load 1 x 8000 lb bomb, 8 x 30, 90 x 4 incendiaries. Primary target: Augsburg. Weather, thin patchy cloud. Bombed at 01.27 hours at 19,000 ft. Northern part of target solid mass of fire. Monica u/s. Route very good. Pretty good effort. Total S/Ls (searchlights) about 60, mostly S and N of target. Solid concentration of fires seen from 200 miles.

01/03/1944 LL625 JI-C Bombing Stuttgart   23.38 03.04 07.15

Bomb load 1 x 8000 lb bomb. Primary target: Stuttgart. There was 10/10 cloud. Bombed at 03.04 hours at 20,000 ft. Bright white fires seen through a single break in the clouds. Monica u/s near target. Quiet route. Marking over target good, red glow seen on leaving the target.

07/03/1944 LL625 JI-C Bombing Le Mans   19.40 x 23.57

Bomb load 1 x 1000, 4 x 500 lb bomb. No attack. Target not accurately identified. 3 x 500 lbs bomb jettisoned. 10 x 1000, 1 x 500 lb bombs brought back. Made two orbits round target 21.39 to 21.55 hours up to 9,000 feet. Glow of red T.I.s seen through cloud from 7,500 feet. Tops of cloud 6,000 feet. Red glow covered wide area, bomb flashes seen, appeared scattered.

Sgt. C.J. Medland 2nd Pilot that day.

22/03/1944 LL625 JI-C Bombing Frankfurt   18.31 21.52 00.25

Bomb load 1 x 8000 lb bomb, 56 x 30 incendiaries. Primary target: Frankfurt. There was 3-5/10 cloud. Bombed at 21.52 hours from 20,000 feet. Spoof flares seen at Hannover but believed on S side of town about 9 seen. P.F.F. well on time. Concentration good, but sky markers only observed about 5 miles N.W. of the town.

24/03/1944 LL625 JI-C Bombing Berlin   18.29 x x

Bomb load 1 x 8000 lb bomb. Aircraft missing.

Homebound, crashed near Worlitz, a small town S of the Elbe and 12 km ENE of Dessau. Possibly shot down by Lt. Walter Briegleb of 10/NJG3, who claimed a 'Halifax' NNE of Bitterfeld, some 25 miles to the South. No other claims match the time and location of LL625's loss.

All crew KIA except F/S. R.B. McAllister who was interned in Camps 9C and L7, POW No.53122. Those killed were buried at Worlitz. They have been subsequently re-interred in the Berlin 1939-45 War Cemetery.

P/O. Robert Langley, DFC

172533 (1040312) P/O. Robert "Bob" Langley, DFC. Pilot.
928520 Sgt. Derek T. Bradsell. A/Bomber.
R148538 F/S. T.E. Francis, RCAF. A/Bomber. 2 ops.
151014 (968290) F/O. Donald Frank Henshaw. A/Bomber. 1 op.
1455046 F/S. Frank R. Jones. Navigator.
173122 (1319583) Sgt. Albert Bell, DFC. Navigator. 2 ops.
1450246 F/S. Charlie F. Wakeling. WOP/AG.
1821995 Sgt. Ron R. Smith. MU&R/Gunner.
Sgt. W. Wilson. MU&R/Gunner. 3 ops.
177708 (1813263) P/O. Herbert George "Bert" Oliver. R/Gunner. 34 ops.
56623 (573999) Sgt. Ronald Charles Parker. F/Engineer.
 (*) Sgt. G. Meghill or Meghee. MU/G or 2nd Pilot. 02/01/1944
1437600 F/S. Alfred Kay. 2nd Pilot. 21/02/1944
119080 (1386534)
 F/L. John Godfrey "Timmy" Timms, DFC. 2nd Pilot. 11/05/1944
182344 (740534)
 W/O. Cyril Ernest Williams, AFC DFC. 2nd Pilot. 22/05/1944
127236 (1388626) F/O. Robert "Robbie" Jones. 2nd Pilot. 14/06/1944

Passenger: 15/05/1944.

(*): According ORBs Sgt. G. Meghill was 2nd Pilot whereas R. Langley noted in his logbook "Sgt. MEGHEE M/U".

P/O. Bob Langley and his crew are believed to be the first 514 Squadron crew to complete a full tour of thirty operations with the squadron.

03/11/1943 DS787 JI-F Gardening Frisian Islands 18.25 x 20.31
   Aircraft carried 2 x B218, 4 x 200. Primary area Frisian Islands. Broken layer cloud 6/10 above and below, Gee fixed garden area. Monica. Satisfactory trip.
   Note: Sgt R Langley in DS787, JI-F commented in his log book 'Wizard night. Never saw a thing.' Although the time the mines were dropped is not recorded, the sorties took approximately two hours and the mining operation therefore occurred before the first 514 Squadron

L to R (back): Sgt. R.R. Smith, Sgt. C.F. Wakeling, Sgt. R.C. Parker, Sgt. H.G. Oliver. L to R (front): Sgt. F.R. Jones, Sgt. R. Langley, Sgt. D.T. Bradsell. (courtesy Marilyn Langley)

bombs were dropped on Düsseldorf. The crews taking part in this first operation were those of S/L. A.L. Roberts, F/O. G.H. Hinde, Sgt. R. Langley and F/S WL McGown - from "Striking Through Clouds", by Simon Hepworth and Andrew Porrelli, 2014.

11/11/1943 DS787JI-F Gardening La Tranche   17.34 x 00.51

Aircraft carried 4 x B204. Primary area La Tranche. No cloud. Visibility good. Slight damage to Bomb Bay door Starboard side of undercarriage and Starboard Main Plane.

R. Langley noted in his logbook: "Mining operations. Ille de Rey, La Rochelle. Heavy flak damage to aircraft over Nantes."

26/11/1943 DS787JI-F BombingBerlin   17.51 21.21   00.47

Bomb load 1 x 4000 HC, 24 x 30 incendiaries, 405 x 4, 45 x 4. Primary target: Berlin. Weather good, visibility good. Bombed target at 21.21 hours at 20,000 feet. Photo flash failed to release. An interesting trip.

02/12/1943 DS787JI-F BombingBerlin   17.05 x 19.21

Bomb load 1 x 2000 HC, 1 x 1000 MC, 40 x 30 incendiaries, 810 x 4 incendiaries, 90 x 4 incendiaries. Primary target: Berlin. Returned

389

P/O. Bob Langley DFC

(courtesy Marilyn Langley)

early due to engine trouble. Furthest point reached 5228 N 0210 deg. All bombs jettisoned. Icing troubles experienced both out and home at 19,000 feet.

20/12/1943 DS787 JI-F Bombing Frankfurt 17.52 x 19.38
Bomb load 1 x 8000, 16 x 30 incendiaries, 330 x 4 incendiaries, 30 x 4 incendiaries. Returned early. Landed at Woodbridge.

24/12/1943 DS787 JI-F Bombing Berlin 00.22 04.02 07.15
Bomb load 1 x 4000, 32 x 30 incendiaries, 450 x 4 incendiaries, 90 x 4 incendiaries. Primary target: Berlin. 9/10 cloud, tops 7,000/8,000. Visibility good. Bombed at 04.02 at 20,000 ft. Three green sky markers close together, probably the first to go down. Bomb sight used. Route markers red and yellow well placed. Slight icing, nothing to matter. No fires on arrival but a few as we left. Photo attempted.

R. Langley noted in his logbook: "Another quiet but really cold."

29/12/1943 DS787 JI-F Bombing Berlin 17.03 20.30 23.43
Bomb load 1 x 2000, 40 x 30, 900 x 4, 90 x 4 incendiaries. There was 9/10 cloud (medium). Skymarkers red and green stars seen. Bombed at 20.30 hours at 20,000 ft. Red glow below clouds seen. Monica u/s. Flak over target more than usual. Route good and trouble free. Photo attempted.

R. Langley noted in his logbook: "Quiet trip."

01/01/1944 DS787 JI-F Bombing Berlin 00.37 03.12 07.23
Bomb load 1 x 4000, 24 x 30, 450 x 4, 90 x 4 lb incendiaries. Primary target: Berlin. There was 10/10 cloud over the target. Bombed at 03.12 hrs at 20,000 feet. Markers flares glowing in cloud. P.F.F. appeared to be scattered, this may have been due to cloud obscuring flares.

02/01/1944 DS787 JI-F Bombing Berlin 00.09 02.46 06.42
Bomb load 1 x 4000, 24 x 30, 450 x 4, 90 x 4 incendiaries. Primary

target: Berlin. 7-8/10 cloud, tops at 12,000 ft. Bombed at 02.46 hours at 20,000 ft. Should be a good show. Numerous P.F.F. flares and red T.I. all concentrated. Photo flash did not go off.

According ORBs Sgt. G. Meghill was 2nd Pilot whereas R. Langley noted in his logbook "Sgt. MEGHEE M/U".

14/01/1944 DS786 JI-E Bombing Brunswick 17.05 19.21 22.19

Bomb load 1 x 4000, 48 x 30 incendiaries. Primary target: Brunswick. There was 7/10 cloud over the target. Red and green T.I.s seen also one sky marker. Bombed at 19.21 hours at 20,000 ft. Glow of green T.I.s seen through cloud. Glow of extensive fires seen. Attack concentrated. Photo attempted.

20/01/1944 DS842 JI-F Bombing Berlin 16.10 x 18.54

Bomb load 1 x 4000, 32 x 30, 540 x 4, 60 x 4 incendiaries. Returned early. Compasses u/s. Farthest point reached 53°53'N 03°00'E. Jettisoned total bomb load.

Sgt. A. Bell not listed that day in ORBs, but noted as "Nav." in R. Langley's logbook.

21/01/1944 LL624 JI-B Bombing Magdeburg x x x

Returned early - Intercom U/S.

Sortie not listed in ORBs that day but noted in R. Langley's logbook with Sgt. A. Bell as Navigator.

15/02/1944 DS842 JI-F Bombing Berlin 17.32 21.30 00.27

Bomb load 1 x 8000 lb bomb. Primary target: Berlin. There was 10/10 cloud. Bombed at 21.30 hrs. At 20,000 ft. Bombed on cascade of green T.I.s going down. Markers seemed fewer and too scattered to be a really good effort. Cloud prevented visual.

19/02/1944 DS820 JI-A Bombing Leipzig 00.12 x 02.00

Bomb load 1 x 2000, 1 x 500 lb bomb, 900 x 4, 40 x 30 incendiaries. Returned early and landed at Mepal. D.R. (Dead Reckoning) Compass u/s. P4 Compass not accurate. Port generator discharging. Landed at Mepal.

21/02/1944 DS820 JI-A Bombing Stuttgart 00.29 04.06 07.00

Bomb load 1 x 4000 lb bomb, 40 x 30, 690 x 4, 90 x 4 x incendiaries. Primary target: Stuttgart. There was 7/10 cloud. Bombed at 04.06 hours at 20,000 ft. Bright white fires seen in centre of T.I.s. Large orange explosion. Big blue flash just before bombs dropped. Little opposition encountered.

F/S. Alfred Kay 2nd Pilot that day.

24/02/1944 DS842 JI-F Bombing Schweinfurt 18.43 23.11 02.01

Bomb load 1 x 8000 lb bomb. Primary target: Schweinfurt. Weather was perfect. Bombed at 23.11 hours at 20,000 ft. Saw large orange explosion to South. Seemed a very good attack. Barrage of H.F. moderate. Large factory seen to be hit and set on fire by showers of incendiaries.

Sgt. W. Wilson R/Gunner that day.

01/03/1944 DS813 JI-H Bombing Stuttgart   23.29   03.03   06.57

Bomb load 1 x 8000 lb bomb. Primary target: Stuttgart. There was 10/10 cloud. Bombed at 03.03 hours at 20,000 ft. Clouds obscured the target. Rather a scattered effort with some good fires.

According ORBs Sgt. W. Wilson was MU/Gunner and Sgt. R. Smith R/Gunner. However, in R. Langley's logbook W. Wilson is not noted in the crew that day and it is reported "Bert's oxygen mask U/S. Does trip with pipe in his mouth. Face gets frostbitten". Bert is H.G. Oliver the rear gunner.

According ORBs F/S. T.E. Francis was A/Bomber that day but this Bomb Aimer replacement is not specified in R. Langley's logbook.

26/03/1944 LL733 JI-G Bombing Essen   19.56   22.01   00.19

Bomb load 1 x 8000, 96 x 30 incendiaries. Primary target: Essen. There was 10/10 cloud. Bombed at 22.01 hours from 20,000 feet. Glow of red T.I.s seen also flashes of bomb bursts. No fires seen through cloud. Moderate H.F.

According ORBs F/S. T.E. Francis A/Bomber that day but this Bomb Aimer replacement is not specified in R. Langley's logbook.

According ORBs Sgt. W. Wilson MU/Gunner and Sgt. R. Smith R/Gunner but in R. Langley's logbook W. Wilson not noted in the crew that day.

11/04/1944 DS842 JI-F Bombing Aachen   20.56   22.45   00.22

Bomb load 10 x 1000, 2 x 500 lb bombs, 160 x 4, 20 x 4 incendiaries. Primary target: Aachen. There was broken cloud. Bombed at 22.45 hours from 20,000 feet. A successful attack. A concentration of fires seen.

18/04/1944 DS842 JI-F Bombing Rouen   22.23 00.48   03.03

Bomb load 8 x 1000 MC, 2 x 1000 GP, 5 x 500 lb bomb. Primary target: Rouen. There was some haze. Bombed at 00.48 hours from 12,300 feet. Aircraft bombed on T.I.s South and East as directed by M of C. Too much conversation with M of C. Attack believed successful.

20/04/1944 DS842 JI-F Bombing Cologne   00.01   02.06   03.51

Bomb load 1 x 8000 lb bomb, 24 x 30, 216 x 4, 24 x 4 lb incendiaries. Primary target: Cologne. There was 10/10 cloud over target. Bombed at 02.06 hours from 19,500 feet. Green sky markers, but no stars seen - disappeared in cloud. Little seen except the one cluster of green sky markers. Attack considered very poor. P.F.F. late causing us to bomb 4 minutes late. A more pronounced marking was seen after we left the target.

22/04/1944 DS842 JI-F Bombing Dusseldorf 23.12 01.15 03.02
Bomb load 9 x 1000, 5 x 500 lb bombs. Primary target: Dusseldorf. There was ground haze, very thin cloud at 20,000 feet. Bombed at 01.15 hours from 18,500 feet. Visual of river and railway lines. Markers concentrated. Bombs appeared to fall in area lit up by T.I.s. Very successful raid.

09/05/1944 DS842 JI-F Bombing Cap Gris Nez 03.05 04.13 05.20
Bomb load 1 x 1000 GP, 13 x 1000 MC. Primary target: Cape Gris Nez. Clear conditions and visuals of coast and green T.I.s were obtained. On instructions of Master Bomber, bombs were aimed to left of red T.I.s at 04.13 hours from 6,400 feet. For a small target, markers appeared scattered at beginning of raid but concentrated towards the end. Bombs were seen to burst in centre of T.I. concentration. Attack improved later and bombs appeared to burst in area marked.

11/05/1944 DS842 JI-F Bombing Louvain 22.50 00.18 01.50
Bomb load 5 x 1000 GP, 5 x 1000 MC. Primary target: Louvain. Thin cloud over target area. Bombed yellow and white markers at 00.18 hours from 8,000 feet. Much smoke observed but P.F.F. markers scattered. Aircraft arrived late at target.

F/L. J.G. Timms 2nd Pilot that day. (No mention in ORBs but noted in R. Langley's logbook).

15/05/1944 DS842 JI-F Catamount Rushford Range 22.50 00.18 01.50
Only described in ORB summary. Sortie not detailed. Not counted as Op.

R. Langley noted in his logbooks "Special Nav. exercise". Passenger LAC. Fyson.

21/05/1944 DS842 JI-F Bombing Duisburg 22.45 01.13 02.45
Bomb load 1 x 8000 lb bomb, 96 x 30 incendiaries. Primary target: Duisberg. There was 10/10 cloud up to 20,000 feet. Bombed red T.I.s at 01.13 hours from 20,500 feet. Bombing appeared concentrated around the marker seen. Orange glow where T.I.s had gone down.

22/05/1944 DS842 JI-F Bombing Dortmund 22.45 x 00.20
Bomb load 1 x 2000 lb bomb, 96 x 30, 810 x 4, 90 x 4 incendiaries. Primary target: Dortmund. Returned early and landed at Woodbridge. Excessive icing encountered and aircraft could not maintain altitude as

a result.

W/O. C.E. Williams 2nd Pilot that day.

30/05/1944 DS842 JI-F Bombing Boulogne   23.00   00.07   01.00

Bomb load 6 x 1000 MC, 4 x 500 MC. Primary target: Boulogne Gun Batteries. Haze over target. Bombed red T.I.s at 00.07 hours from 6,000 feet. Only one large concentration of red T.I.s and bombs were bursting over them. Attack very concentrated.

12/06/1944 DS842 JI-F Bombing Gelsenkirchen   23.02   01.04   03.09

Bomb load 1 x 4000 HC, 12 x 500 GP, 4 x 500 MC. Primary target: Gelsenkirchen. Clear over target. Bombed red and green T.I.s at 01.04 hours from 20,000 feet. Marking and bombing appeared very concentrated and large explosion seen to North of T.I.s at 01.03 hours.

14/06/1944 DS842 JI-F Bombing Le Havre   23.52   01.15   02.28

Bomb load 11 x 1000 MC, 4 x 500 GP. Primary target: Le Havre, Weather clear. Bombed at 01.15 hours from 15,000 feet on yellow and green markers as instructed. Bombs falling along the Quay. Perfect attack. No troubles.

F/O. Robert "Robbie" Jones 2nd Pilot that day. (No mention in ORBs but noted in R. Langley's logbook).

15/06/1944 DS842 JI-F Bombing Valenciennes 23.15   00.37   01.50

Bomb load 16 x 500 GP, 2 x 500 MC. Primary target: Valenciennes. Weather clear. Bombed at 00.37 hours from 7,000 feet on red and green T.I.s overshooting by 2 seconds on Master Bomber's instructions. One stick went slightly N of T.I. and a second slightly South. Quiet route.

17/06/1944 DS842 JI-F Bombing Montdidier 01.07 02.56 04.34

Bomb load 16 x 500 GP, 2 x 500 ANM64 GP. Primary target: Montdidier. Weather was 10/10ths cloud. Over target 02.54 hours. 02.56 hours Master Bomber ordered return to Base. Tried to overtake flying bomb without success. Jettisoned 9 x 500 GP at 5044N 0112E.

21/06/1944 DS842 JI-F Bombing Domleger   17.57 x 20.43

Bomb load 18 x 500 MC. Primary target: Domleger near Abbeville, V-1 flying bomb launch site. There was 10/10ths cloud. Reached target area 19.29 hours at 12,500 feet, Master Bomber ordered abandon mission if T.I.s were not visible. No T.I.s seen, jettisoned safe 6 x 500 MC at 19.41 hours from 11,000 feet 5013N 0123E.

23/06/1944 DS842 JI-F Bombing L'Hey   23.07 00.16   01.07

Bomb load 11 x 1000 MC, 4 x 500 GP. Primary target: L'Hey, Flying bomb installations. There was 10/10ths cloud, tops 6,000 feet. Bombed at 00.16 hours from 9,000 feet. Bombed a further edge of red markers as instructed by Master Bomber. Master Bomber made aircraft bomb all edges and the centre of markers. Red markers seen about 5 miles S.E. of target. Photo taken.

24/06/1944 DS842 JI-F Bombing Rimeux   23.37   00.33   01.47

Bomb load 18 x 500 GP. Primary target: Rimeux, Flying bomb installations. Weather clear, a few patches of cloud. Bombed at 00.33 hours from 11,500 feet. Bomb bursts seen amongst T.I.s, which were well concentrated. Numerous searchlights, flak negligible. Three small fires seen.

27/06/1944 DS842 JI-F Bombing Biennais   23.39   01.10   03.16

Bomb load 16 x 500 GP, 2 x 500 ANM64 GP. Primary target: Biennais, Flying bomb installations. There was 10/10ths cloud. Bombed at 01.10 hours from 12,000 feet. Fires seen burning on leaving.

W/O. John Ludlow Lassam

1332109   W/O. John Ludlow Lassam. Pilot.
1052269   Sgt. Allan Roland Hope.   A/Bomber.
658221 Sgt. Walter Charles Taylor. Navigator.
1566046   F/S. William Young Anthony.   WOP/AG.
J90375 (R212331)
    P/O. Bernard Horace 'Chap' Cooper, RCAF. MU/Gunner.
J94826 (R202910) P/O. Donald Peter Manchul, RCAF.   R/Gunner.
564683   F/S. Ernest James Hack.   F/Engineer.
37994 W/C.   Michael 'Mike' Wyatt, DFC. Captain.   23/06/1944

23/06/1944 LL733 JI-S Bombing L'Hey   23.10 00.18   01.45

Bomb load 11 x 1000 MC, 4 x 500 GP. Primary target: L'Hey. There was 10/10ths cloud, tops 4/5,000 feet. Bombed at 00.18 hours from 9,000 feet. Bombed centre of red T.I. glow on Master Bomber's instructions. Uneventful trip.

All the crew did this mission with W/C. M. Wyatt as Captain and W/O. J.L. Lassam 2nd Pilot.

24/06/1944 LL666 JI-Q Bombing Rimeux   23.30   00.35   02.01

Bomb load 18 x 500 GP. Primary target: Rimeux, Flying bomb installations. Weather clear, slight haze. Bombed at 00.35 hours from 10,000 feet red T.I.s. Good bombing around T.I.s. Numerous searchlights.

30/06/1944 LL666 JI-Q Bombing Villers Bocage 18.16 20.00 21.27
Bomb load 11 x 1000 MC, 3 x 500 GP. Primary target: Villers Bocage. Weather clear below cloud. Bombed at 20.00 hours from 4,000 feet, red T.I.s. Clouds of smoke seen, attack concentrated.

02/07/1944 LL666 JI-Q Bombing Beauvoir 12.47 14.37 16.14
Bomb load 11 x 1000 MC, 4 x 500 GP. Primary target: Beauvoir, Flying bomb supply site. Bombed at 14.37 hours from 10,500 feet on yellow and red T.I.s.

07/07/1944 HK570 JI-P Bombing Vaires 22.36 01.33 03.13

Bernard Horace 'Chap' Cooper

Bomb load 11 x 1000 MC, 2 x 500 GP. Primary target: Vaires, Marshalling yards. Weather clear. Bombed at 01.33 hours from 13,500 feet centre of yellow and green T.I.s reds becoming obscured. Bomb bursts well placed.

10/07/1944 HK570 JI-P Bombing Nucourt 04.24 06.02 07.22
Bomb load 11 x 1000 ANM65, 4 x 500 GP. Primary target: Nucourt, Constructional works. Bombed at 06.02 hours from 16,000 feet on Gee.

12/07/1944 HK570 JI-P Bombing Vaires 17.46 x 22.13
Bomb load 18 x 500 GP. Primary target: Vaires, Marshalling yards. No attack made in accordance with Master Bomber's instructions. Jettisoned at 21.52 hours from 3,000 feet, position 5220N 0220E 4 x 500 GP.

15/07/1944 HK570 JI-P Bombing Chalons Sur Marne 21.34 01.29 03.49
Bomb load 18 x 500 GP. Primary target: Chalons sur Marne, Railway centre. 10/10ths cloud above. Bombed at 01.29 hours from 8,000 feet, red T.I.s. Markers well placed, ground detail very clear.

18/07/1944 HK570 JI-P Bombing Emieville 04.12 06.06 07.22
Bomb load 11 x 1000 MC, 4 x 500 GP. Primary target: Emieville,

Troop concentration. Slight haze. Bombed at 06.06 hours from 6,500 feet yellow T.I.s. Heavy flak over target. Good concentration of bombing.

20/07/1944 HK570   JI-P Bombing Homberg   23.13 x 01.59

Bomb load 1 x 4000 HC, 2 x 500 MC, 14 x 500 GP. Primary target: Homberg, Oil plant. Aircraft missing.

Shot down, possibly by either Hptm. Heinz-Martin Hadeball, 3./NGr.10, or Hptm. Ernst-Wilhelm Modrow, 1/NJG1. Crashed 01.59 hours on 21st June 1944 in the sea off the Dutch coast (presumably on return leg as the squadron aircraft bombed between 01.19hrs and 01.25hrs).

According to the Haamstede Mayor's report, Sgt. Taylor was washed up on the 21st June 1944 at Renesse (Zeeland) on the northern side of Schouwen Duiveland, 14 km NW from Zierikzee. "The mortal remains of Sergeant Walter Charles Taylor were initially buried in the cemetery in Haamstede. After the liberation the remains were reburied in the military cemetery in Bergen op Zoom. Have the other six crew members received a sailor's grave?". They are commemorated on the Runnymede War Memorial.

P/O.   John Lawrie

NZ428001 P/O. John Lawrie, RNZAF.   Pilot.
191661 (1801354) Sgt. Martin John Carter.   A/Bomber.
A424209   F/S. Denison Reginald "Reg" Orth, RAAF.   Navigator.
1582432 Sgt. Ellis George Durland.   WOP/AG.
A437391   F/S. Lindsay Rutland "Sam" Burford, RAAF. MU/Gunner.
A434592 (O18009)
        F/S. Robert Charles "Bob" Chester-Master, RAAF. R/Gunner.
1822876 Sgt. Thomas Davidsen "Tommy" Young. F/Engineer.
37994 W/C. Michael "Mike" Wyatt, DFC. Captain. 18/07/1944

18/07/1944 DS826 JI-U Bombing   Emieville 04.26 06.07 07.52

Bomb load 11 x 1000 MC, 4 x 500 GP. Primary target: Emieville, Troop concentration Operation Goodwood. Weather clear. Bombed at 06.07 hours from 8,000 feet yellow T.I.s. Much smoke, bomb bursts seen, a good attack. Slight shrapnel damage to the bomb doors.

All the crew did this mission with W/C. M. Wyatt as Captain and F/S. (later P/O, possibly posthumously) J. Lawrie 2nd Pilot.

18/07/1944 DS826 JI-U Bombing Aulnoye   22.37   00.54   02.32

Bomb load 18 x 500 GP. Primary target: Aulnoye, Railway junction. Weather clear. Bombed at 00.54 hours from 9,000 feet green T.I.s. Uneventful trip.   DS826 JI-U called 'THE SWOOSE'.

20/07/1944 DS826   JI-U Bombing   Homberg   23.26   01.21   02.51

Bomb load 1 x 4000 HC, 2 x 500 MC, 14 x 500 GP. Primary target: Homberg, Oil plant. Weather clear. Bombed at 01.21 hours from 20,000 feet centre of red T.I. Clouds of smoke rising to 10,000 feet. Fired on by an ME109, which missed. Returned fire. No claim made.

23/07/1944 LL731 JI-U Bombing   Kiel   22.42 x 00.27

Bomb load 6 x 1000 MC, 10 x 500 GP. Returned early, intercom u/s. Jettisoned at 5323N 0211E.

24/07/1944 LL731 JI-U Bombing   Stuttgart   21.46   01.49   04.23

Bomb load 5 x 1000 ANM 65, 3 x 500 GP. Primary target Stuttgart. Weather 9/10ths cloud. Bombed at 01.49 hours from 19,000 feet on eastern group of green and yellow sky markers. Attack moderate.

28/07/1944 LL731 JI-U Bombing   Stuttgart   21.43   01.51   05.36

Bomb load 13 x 500 GP. Primary target: Stuttgart. Weather 9/10ths cloud. Bombed at 01.51 hours from 17,000 feet green T.I.s. Glow of fires seen through the clouds. Trouble free route; fighter activity on last leg. Caught briefly by a searchlight.

01/08/1944 LL731 JI-U Bombing Foret de Nieppe 19.20 20.45 21.44

Bomb load 11 x 1000 MC, 4 x 500 GP. Primary target: De Nieppe, constructional works. Bombed at 20.45 hours from 12,000 feet leading aircraft.

03/08/1944 LL731 JI-U Bombing Bois de Cassan 11.48 14.04 15.46
Bomb load 11 x 1000 MC, 4 x 500 GP. Primary target: Bois de Cassan, Flying bomb supply depot. Bombed at 14.04 hours from 15,000 feet, centre of smoke.

04/08/1944 LM265 JI-E Bombing Bec d'Ambes 13.19 18.02 21.26
Bomb load 8 x 1000 MC, 2 x 500 GP. Primary target: Bec d'Ambes depot. Weather clear. Bombed at 18.02 hours from 8,000 feet, centre of large cloud of black smoke seen to be in centre of target area. 'Bang on', couldn't have been better.

08/08/1944 LL731 JI-U Bombing Foret de Lucheux 21.43 23.49 01.16
Bomb load 18 x 500 GP. Primary target: Foret de Lucheux, Petrol dump. Weather clear. Bombed at 23.49 hours from 12,000 feet, red T.I.s. About 4 fires seen burning among the red T.I.s, smoke up to 6,000 feet. Hydraulics damaged by enemy fire. Crash landed at base.

'Foret de Lucheux' is a forest between Lille and Amiens. During WWII, important fuel tanks were there.

11/08/1944 LL624 JI-R Bombing Lens 14.10 16.33 17.41
Bomb load 11 x 1000 MC. 4 X 500 GP. Primary target: Lens, Marshalling yards. Weather 4/10ths cloud over target. Bombed at 16.33 hours from 14,000 feet, cluster of yellow T.I.s. Cloud tops up to 10,000 feet. Cloud and smoke prevented observation. No opposition, appeared good attack.

12/08/1944 LM180 JI-G Bombing Russelsheim 21.44 x 01.30
Target: Russelsheim. Bomb load 1 x 4000 HC, 6 x 500 No. 14 clusters, 6 x (150 x 4) 10% X1 B. Also 1410 gallons of petrol which allowed approximately 6½ hours flying time. The anticipated duration of this flight was approximately 4 hours 45 minutes. Aircraft missing.

Shot down at 01.30hrs on 13th July 1944 by a night-fighter, probably flown by Uffz. Hermann Moeckel of 2./NJG4, crashing near Bavegem. This was Moeckel's only victim in his career as a night fighter pilot. He was himself shot down by an Allied night fighter on the night of 29th / 30th December 1944, surviving as a POW.

P/O. John Lawrie sacrificed his life by remaining at the controls in order to allow his crew escape. P/O. Lawrie is buried in Schoonselhof Cemetery, Antwerpen, having been brought here from a temporary grave at Fort Borsbeek. All the remaining crew evaded capture except for George Durland who was captured with an injured leg. However, he escaped from a prisoner convoy when strafed by a P-47, and got home to England before the others, all of whom were sheltered by the Belgians. F/S. D.R. Orth and F/S. R.C. Chester-Master arrived safe in UK on 10th September 1944, the same day as F/O. A.H. Morrison of P/O. C.F. Prowles' crew, shot down on 16th June 1944.

On arriving, Robert Chester-Master supplied the following information when interrogated by authority: 'On the return journey when South of Brussels the aircraft was attacked by enemy fighter aircraft at a height of 8,000 feet. Starboard inner on fire which spread to port outer. Crew ordered to prepare abandon as aircraft losing height rapidly. Port engines gave trouble and Captain ordered crew to bale out. Flight Sergeant Chester-Master abandoned the aircraft at a height of approximately 700 feet. Chester-Master safe also the Bomb Aimer safe Brussels, Navigator safe, no news fate Burford although believed baled out safely'. Eventually F/S. L.R. Burford returned safe to the UK on 22nd September 1944.

F/L.   Thomas Arthur Lever

120516 (1028757) F/L. Thomas Arthur Lever.   Pilot.
NZ415810 F/S. George Wirepa, RNZAF.   A/Bomber.
NZ416636 W/O. V.H. Hurrey, RNZAF. Navigator.
1543160   Sgt. A. Davis.   WOP/AG.
1405988   Sgt. J. or L.J.J. Glanville.   MU/Gunner.
A424440   (*) F/S. Max Noel McLaughlin, RAAF. R/Gunner.
1067301   Sgt. C.J. Howard.   F/Engineer.
J86219 (**)   F/O. Irvine Joseph Bittner, RCAF, DFC. 2nd Pilot.
18/08/1944.

(*) This service number is not traceable via. NAA records. Service numbers – O24303 and N247213 are attached to NAA files on this serviceman.
(**) By error, ORBs quote Pickler as 2nd Pilot on 18/08/1944. Cross check of logbooks allows to say that it was Bittner. See below 18/08/1944 operation.

3rd left: MN McLaughlin, 4th left: TA Lever, 6th left: G Wirepa (photo: Peter Anderson)

07/05/1944 LL652 JI-C Bombing Nantes   00.39   03.06   05.41
   Bomb load 1 x 4000, 14 x 500 lb bombs. Primary target: Nantes. Weather was clear. Bombed at 03.06 hours from 9,200 feet. Much smoke obscured target. One large explosion seen over target at 03.05 hours. A good attack.

09/05/1944 LL652 JI-C Bombing Cap Gris Nez   02.56   04.07   05.12
   Bomb load 1 x 1000 GP, 13 x 1000 MC. Primary target: Cape Gris Nez. Clear conditions obtained and coast line and Green T.I.s observed. Bombed at 04.07 hours from 6,000 feet and bombs appeared to fall along coast line. Bomb bursts were seen to straddle gun site. Target well illuminated and attack seemed a good one.

10/05/1944 LL666 JI-D Bombing Courtrai   22.05   23.26   01.00
   Bomb load 7 x 1000 GP, 7 x 1000 MC. Primary target: Courtrai. Conditions hazy. Bombed on instructions of Master Bomber at 23.26 hours from 9,800 feet. Bomb bursts concentrated between two clusters of White T.I.s. Attack seemed good. Photo attempted. Sighted enemy aircraft but no combat.

19/05/1944 LL734 JI-G Bombing Le Mans   22.15   00.37   03.25
   Bomb load 4 x 1000 USA, 5 x 1000 MC, 1 x 1000 GP, 4 x 500 GP. Primary target: Le Mans. Clear conditions below cloud. Bombed markers at 00.37 hours from 8,000 feet. Large fires seen and some scattered bombing.

401

21/05/1944 LL734 JI-G Bombing Duisburg   22.40 01.27 03.30

Bomb load 1 x 2000 lb bomb, 120 x 30, 600 x 4 incendiaries. Primary target: Duisberg. There was 10/10 cloud over target, tops 20,000 feet. Bombed Red T.I.s and flares at 01.27 hours from 21,000 feet. Made two orbits and waited 12 minutes in target area for markers which were seen but quickly disappeared in cloud. Attack seemed poor. Orbited the target twice.

24/05/1944 LL697 JI-E Bombing Boulogne   00.12 01.15 02.31

Bomb load 9 x 1000 MC, 1 x 1000 GP, 1 x 1000 ANM, 4 x 500 GP. Primary target: Boulogne, Gun Battery. Haze over target. Bombed markers at 01.15 hours from 8,000 feet. Bombs seen to burst around T.I.s. Request more trips like this one.

28/05/1944 LL734 JI-G Bombing Angers   18.51   23.54 01.39

Bomb load 5 x 1000 MC, 1 x 1000 USA, 4 x 500 MC. Primary target: Angers. Hazy condition at target. Bombed at 23.54 hours from 9,000 feet. Target well lit up. Made good run up. Master Bomber not clearly heard.

30/05/1944 LL734 JI-G Bombing Boulogne   22.50   00.05   01.33

Bomb load 6 x 1000 MC, 4 x 500 MC. Primary target: Boulogne Gun Batteries. Hazy over target. Bombed Red T.I.s at 00.05 hours from 8,000 feet. Many bomb bursts seen, mostly on T.I.s but some to the North.

05/06/1944 LL734 JI-G Bombing Ouistreham 03.37 05.09 06.47

Bomb load 9 x 1000 MC and 2 x 500 MC. There was 10/10ths cloud with tops at 10,000 feet. Bombed markers from 10,500 feet. Vision was obscured by cloud. Some amount of icing on return. Two large explosions to the West, where Green T.I.s had been dropped, were seen.

07/06/1944 LL734 JI-G Bombing Massy Palaiseau 00.23 x 03.59

Bomb load 18 x 500 MC. Returned early because D/R Compass was u/s after having reached Abbeville area. Approx. 30 miles off track at French Coast and was late. 14 x 500 MC were brought back and others jettisoned safe.

21/06/1944 ME842   JI-K Bombing Domleger 17.55 x 20.54

Bomb load 18 x 500 MC. Primary target: Domleger near Abbeville, V-1 flying bomb launch site. There was 10/10ths cloud. Reached target at 19.30 hours at 13,000 feet. Master Bomber instructed bomb Red T.I.s if visible, otherwise return to base. No T.I.s visible, returned to base. Slight predicted heavy flak encountered. Jettisoned safe 8 x 500 MC at 19.41 hours from 10,000 feet. 50.26N, 01.21E.

23/06/1944 ME842   JI-K Bombing L'Hey   23.02 00.16   01.13
Bomb load 11 x 1000 MC, 4 x 500 GP. Primary target: L'Hey, Flying bomb installations. Weather 10/10ths cloud. Bombed at 00.16 hours from 9,000 feet. A concentrated attack. Master Bomber only heard faintly.

24/06/1944 ME842   JI-K Bombing Rimeux   23.38   00.36   02.03
Bomb load 18 x 500 GP. Primary target: Rimeux, Flying bomb installations. Weather clear. Bombed at 00.36 hours from 12,500 feet centre of Red T.I.s. Attack appeared satisfactory, numerous searchlights seen.

30/06/1944 ME842   JI-K Bombing Villers Bocage   18.04   19.55   21.03
Bomb load 10 x 1000 MC, 3 x 500 GP. Weather 5/10ths cloud. Bombed at 19.55 hours from 12,000 feet. Fighter cover well in evidence. Very good attack.

10/07/1944 PB143 JI-B Bombing Nucourt   04.12   06.04   07.24
Bomb load 11 x 1000 ANM65, 4 x 500 GP. Primary target: Nucourt, Constructional works. Bombed at 06.04 hours from 15,000 feet on Gee Fix.

12/07/1944 PB185 JI-F Bombing Vaires   17.53 x 22.07
Bomb load 18 x 500 GP. Primary target: Vaires, Marshalling yards. Abandoned mission as instructed by Master Bomber. Jettisoned at 20.49 hours from 12,000 feet, position 49.55N, 00.30E, 4 x 500 GP.

15/07/1944 LM181   JI-E Bombing Chalons Sur Marne   21.48   01.30   03.58
Bomb load 18 x 500 GP. Primary target: Chalons sur Marne, Railway centre. Weather clear below 8,000 feet, patchy cloud 8-12,000 feet. Bombed from 8,000 feet centre of Red and Green T.I.s. Marking accurate, should have been a good raid.

18/07/1944 LM181   JI-E Bombing Emieville   04.10   06.07   07.28
Bomb load 11 x 1000 MC, 4 x 500 GP. Primary target: Emieville, Troop concentration. Slight haze. Bombed at 06.07 hours from 7,000 feet Yellow T.I.s. Appeared a good raid, target one mass of smoke.

28/07/1944 HK572   JI-T Bombing Stuttgart   21.34   01.52   05.34
Bomb load 17 x 500 GP. Primary target: Stuttgart. Bombed at 01.52 hours from 20,000 feet. Green T.I.s. Bunches of green T.I.s very widely scattered. Uneventful trip, yellowish explosion seen at 01.51 hours. Weather 10/10ths cloud.

01/08/1944 HK572   JI-T Bombing Foret de Nieppe 19.07 20.46   21.43

Bomb load 11 x 1000 MC, 4 x 500 GP. Primary target: De Nieppe, constructional works. Bombed at 20.46 hours from 10,500 feet on Lancaster ahead.

03/08/1944 HK572   JI-T Bombing Bois de Cassan   11.47   14.07   15.31

Bomb load 11 x 1000 MC, 4 x 500 GP. Primary target: Bois de Cassan, Flying bomb supply depot. Bombed at 14.07 hours from 15,200 feet on centre of smoke.

05/08/1944 HK572   JI-T Bombing Bassen   14.23   19.01   22.11

Bomb load 8 x 1000 MC, 2 x 500 GP. Primary target: Bassen Oil Depot. Weather clear below 4,800 feet. Bombed at 19.01 hours from 4,500 feet visually. Four small explosions followed by a large one with orange flames at 19.04 hours. Very good concentrated attack.

07/08/1944 HK572   JI-T Bombing Mare de Magne 21.51   23.44   01.12

Bomb load 11 x 1000 MC, 4 x 500 GP. Primary target: Mare de Magne (just past Caen). Weather clear, slight haze. Bombed at 23.44 hours from 8,000 feet on centre of Red T.I.s. Bomb bursts observed across Red T.I.s.

Mare-de-Magne: place between Caen and Fontenay le Marmion.

08/08/1944 HK572   JI-T Bombing Foret de Lucheux 21.44   23.52   01.08

Bomb load 18 x 500 GP. Primary target: Foret de Lucheux, Petrol dump. Clear sky. Bombed at 23.52 hours from 11,500 feet, centre of red T.I.s. Really good prang.

"Foret de Lucheux" is a forest between Lille and Amiens. During WWII, important fuel tanks were there.

11/08/1944 LM288   JI-C Bombing Lens   14.07   16.32   17.27

Bomb load 11 x 1000 MC. 4 X 500 GP. Primary target: Lens, Marshalling yards. Weather 5/10ths cloud. Bombed at 16.32 hours from 14,500 feet on Yellow T.I.s. Bomb bursts seen in Marshalling Yards. Very good attack.

12/08/1944 HK572   JI-T Bombing Russelsheim 21.48   00.17   02.32

Bomb load 1 x 4000 HC, 6 x 500 No.14 clusters and 6 x (150 x 4) 10% X1B. Primary target: Russelsheim. Aircraft landed at Woodbridge with brake troubles. Bombed at 00.17 hours from 18,000 feet.

15/08/1944 HK572   JI-T Bombing St Trond   09.52   12.09   13.21

Bomb load 11 x 1000 MC, 4 x 500 GP. Primary target St. Trond Airfield. Weather clear. Bombed at 12.09 hours from 17,000 feet on intersection of runways. All bombs within airfield, many craters on runways.

16/08/1944 HK572   JI-T Bombing Stettin   20.57 01.12   05.07

Bomb load 1 x 2000 HC, 12 x 500 lb clusters, 30lb. 'J' type. Primary target: Stettin. Weather 6-8/10ths cloud, tops 21,000 feet, base 14,000 feet. Bombed at 01.12 hours from 16,000 feet on centre of Red T.I.s. Fires just getting a hold as left target.

18/08/1944 HK572   JI-T Bombing Bremen   21.26   00.17   02.49

Bomb load 1 x 8000 HC, 48 x 30 incendiaries, 540 x 4 incendiaries, 60 x 4 Primary target: Bremen. Weather clear. Bombed at 00.17 hours, from 18,000 feet on Red T.I.s. Decoys in action. Good attack. Marking good.

F/O. I.J. Bittner 2nd Pilot that day.

Although quoted by ORBs in this crew, R.A. Pickler can't be in two crews at the same time. It is confirmed by Cossens logbook that he is already in Cossens' crew on that day at that time. 2nd pilot in this crew was F/O. Irvine Joseph Bittner according his logbook, target and time of flight.

25/08/1944 LL731 JI-U Bombing Vincly   18.31½ 20.30   21.57

Bomb load 11 x 1000 MC, 2 x 500 GP MK IV, 2 x 500 GP MK IV, LD. Primary target: Vincly. Weather, cloud patches. Bombed at 20.30 hours from 15,300 feet, visual of G.H. Leader. Flak over target area.

F/O. Ronald Frederick Limbert, DFC

143269 (1801437) F/O. Ronald Frederick "Ron" Limbert, DFC. Pilot.
152743 (1393295) F/O. Alan Robert Lionel Lundie.   A/Bomber.
106323   F/O. Herbert Leslie "Bertie" Hallam, DFC.   Navigator.
1835068   F/S. Derek Bolton.   WOP/AG.
1350917   Sgt. Albert Ivor Prescott.   MU/Gunner.
911222 Sgt. Charlie Stepney.   R/Gunner.
2205999   Sgt. Roger Scott.   F/Engineer.

07/08/1944 PB142 JI-A Bombing Mare de Magne 21.47   23.39   01.00

Bomb load 11 x 1000 MC, 4 x 500 GP. Primary target: Mare de Magne (just past Caen). Weather clear, slight haze. Bombed at 23.39 hours from 9,000 feet centre of red T.I.s. Bursts seen across and around T.I.s.

From his normal crew, only F/O. R.F. Limbert did this mission as 2nd Pilot with F/O. C.J. Thomson's crew.

The Ron Limbert Crew: photo taken at Chedburgh July 1944, few days before whole crew was posted to 514 Squadron RAF Waterbeach.

L to R: H.L. Hallam, R. Scott, A.I. Prescott, R.F. Limbert, A.R.L. Lundie, C. Stepney, D. Bolton. (courtesy Garry Scott - Tom Sharrad via Antony Jacubs)

08/08/1944 PB142 JI-A Bombing Foret de Lucheux 21.43   23.49
01.27

Bomb load 18 x 500 GP. Primary target: Foret de Lucheux, Petrol dump. Weather clear. Bombed at 23.49 hours from 12,000 feet, red T.I.s. Fires and much black smoke, good concentrated attack.

"Foret de Lucheux" is a forest between Lille and Amiens. During WWII, important fuel tanks were there.

09/08/1944 PB142 JI-A Bombing Fort d'Englos 21.43 23.13 00.19

Bomb load 14 x 1000 MC. Primary target: Fort d'Englos (Lille), Petrol dump. Weather clear over target. Bombed at 23.13 hours from 12,000 feet, red T.I.s. T.I.s did not appear concentrated. Vivid explosion seen, and some fires after bombing.

The fort of Ennetières-en-Weppes, or "fort d'Englos" is one of a set of six forts surrounding Lille.

29/08/1944 LM288   JI-C Bombing Stettin   21.18 02.06 06.46

Bomb load 1 x 500 GP, 1 x 1000 MC, 84 x 30, 756 x 4, 84 x 4 LB incendiaries. Primary target: Stettin. Weather 3/10ths cloud. Bombed at 02.06 hours from 17,000 feet, centre of red T.I.s. Fires and explosions seen around T.I.s. Concentrated attack, fires burning red on leaving target area.

05/09/1944 PB426 JI-J Bombing Le Havre   17.20 19.23 20.35

Bomb load 11 x 1000 MC, 4 x 500 GP. Primary target: Le Havre.

Bombed at 19.23 hours from 13,000 feet red T.I.

06/09/1944 PD265 JI-G Bombing Le Havre   16.37 18.43 20.11
    Bomb load 11 x 1000 MC, 4 x 500 GP. Primary target: Le Havre.
Bombed at 18.43 hours from 7,000 feet, red T.I.s.

17/09/1944 LM288   JI-C Bombing Boulogne   10.51 x 13.26
    Bomb load 11 x 1000 MC, 4 x 500 GP. Primary target: Boulogne,
Aiming point 2. Weather clear below cloud. At 12.15 hours order
given by Master Bomber to abandon mission. Jettisoned 2 x 1000 MC,
brought remainder back.

20/09/1944 LM288   JI-C Bombing Calais   14.42 16.01   17.23
    Bomb load 11 x 1000 MC, 4 x 500 GP. Primary target: Calais.
Weather clear over target. Bombed at 16.01 hours from 2,800 feet, red
T.I.s.

23/09/1944 LM288   JI-C Bombing Neuss   19.23 21.23   23.10
    Bomb load 11 x 1000 ANM59, 4 x 500 GP. Primary target: Neuss.
Weather 10/10ths cloud over target, tops 8/10,000 feet. Bombed at
21.23 hours from 20,000 feet slightly to port of red glow of red T.I.s.

25/09/1944 LM288   JI-C Bombing Pas de Calais 08.35 x 10.59
    Bomb load 11 x 1000 MC, 4 x 500 GP. Primary target: Calais.
Abandoned mission on Master Bomber's instructions. Jettisoned 6 x
1000, 1 x 500 safe at 5025N 0105E.

26/09/1944 LM288   JI-C Bombing Calais   11.38 12.46   14.06
    Bomb load 11 x 1000 MC, 4 x 500 GP. Primary target: Calais 7D.
Weather clear below cloud which was 3,500 feet. Bombed at 12.46
hours from 3,500 feet on red T.I. + 1 second.

28/09/1944 LM288   JI-C Bombing Calais   07.57 09.20   10.32
    Bomb load 11 x 1000 MC, 4 x 500 GP. Primary target: Calais 19.
Bombed at 09.20 hours from 9,500 feet red T.I.

05/10/1944 LM288   JI-C Bombing Saarbrucken 17.22   20.35 22.34
    Bomb load 11 x 1000 MC, 1 x 500 GP, 3 x 500 GP. Long Delay.
Primary target: Saarbrucken, Marshalling yards. Weather clear over
target. Bombed at 20.35 hours at 15,000 feet on green T.I.s.

06/10/1944 LM288   JI-C Bombing Dortmund 16.43 20.41 22.45
    Bomb load 1 x 4000 HC. 12 x No. 14 Clusters. Primary target:
Dortmund, Town and Railways. Weather over the target was clear with
slight ground haze. Bombed at 20.41 hours from 21,000 feet. Fires
South of river.

14/10/1944 LM288   JI-C Bombing Duisburg   07.19 09.05 11.16
    Bomb load 11 x 1000 MC. 4 x 500 GP Long Delay. Primary target:
Duisburg. Weather patchy cloud with gaps for bombing. Bombed at

09.05 hours from 18,500 feet. Built up area East bank of river North of Docks.

14/10/1944 LM288   JI-C Bombing Duisburg   23.09 01.29 03.27
Bomb load 1 x 4000 HC. 14 x No. 14 Clusters. Primary target: Duisburg. Weather was clear with small amount of cloud over the target. Bombed at 01.29 hours from 20,000 feet. Centre of red T.I.s.

18/10/1944 LM288   JI-C Bombing Bonn   08.21 11.00 13.12
Bomb load 1 x 4000 HC. 5 x 12 x 30 - 2 x 12 x 30 modified. 9 x No.14 Clusters. Primary target: Bonn. Weather varying cloud 2-7/10ths with break for bombing. Bombed at 11.00 hours from 17,000 feet. Visual of centre of town.

28/10/1944 NN717   JI-E Bombing Flushing   09.06 10.16 11.09
Bomb load 11 x 1000 MC. 4 x 500 GP. Primary target: Flushing. Weather over the target quite clear and conditions perfect, although believed to be only local, and some low cloud approaching. Bombed at 10.16 hours from 8,500 feet. Visual.

30/10/1944 LM288   JI-C Bombing Wesseling   09.01 12.01 13.23
Bomb load 1 x 4000 HC, 15 x 500 GP. Primary target: Wesseling. Weather was 10/10ths cloud - tops about 7,000 feet. Bombed at 12.01 hours from 15,500 feet on G.H.

31/10/1944 NG118   A2-E   Bombing Bottrop   12.06 15.01 16.23
Bomb load 1 x 4000 HC. 15 x 500 GP. 1 Flare. Primary target: Bottrop, Synth. Oil plants. Weather 10/10ths cloud over target. Bombed at 15.01 hours from 18,000 feet. Red flares.

02/11/1944 LM288   JI-C Bombing Homberg   11.15 14.10 15.40
Bomb load 1 x 4000 HC, 6 x 1000 ANM59, 6 x 500 MC. Primary target: Homberg. Weather variable cloud but clear for bombing. Target obscured by pall of smoke rising to 10,000 feet. Bombed at 14.10 hours from 19,000 feet on instruments.

04/11/1944 LM288   JI-C Bombing Solingen   11.24 14.07 15.42
Bomb load 1 x 4000 HC, 6 x 1000 ANM59, 4x 500 GP, 2 x 500 MC (L/Delay), 3 Flares. Primary target: Solingen. Weather 8-10/10ths cloud. Bombed at 14.07 hours from 21,000 feet on upwind edge of centre cluster of red flares.

05/11/1944 LM288   JI-C Bombing Solingen   10.45 13.03 15.18
Bomb load 1 x 4000 HC, 6 x 1000 ANM59, 4 x 500 GP, 2 x 500 GP (L/Delay), 3 Flares. Primary target: Solingen. Weather 10/10ths cloud over target. Bombed at 13.03 hours from 18,000 feet on Green and Red flares.

06/11/1944 LM288   JI-C Bombing Koblenz   17.05 19.32 22.05

Bomb load 1 x 4000 HC, 12 x 500 Clusters, 2 x 250 T.I.s. Primary target: Koblenz. Weather clear over target. Bombed at 19.32 hours from 18,000 feet on G.H.

08/11/1944 LM288   JI-C Bombing Homberg   08.11   10.30   12.02
Bomb load 1 x 4000 HC, 14 x No. 14 Clusters. Primary target: Homberg. Weather clear. Bombed at 10.30 hours from 18,000 feet on instruments.

11/11/1944 LM288   JI-C Bombing Castrop Rauxel 08.23   11.06   12.37
Bomb load 1 x 4000 HC, 15 x 500 GP, 1 Flare. Primary target: Castrop Rauxel, Oil refineries. Weather 10/10ths cloud. Bombed at 11.06 hours from 20,000 feet on G.H.

15/11/1944 LM288   JI-C Bombing Dortmund   12.49   15.40   18.05
Bomb load 1 x 4000 HC, 15 x 500 GP, 1 Red with Green star Flare. Primary target: Hoesch-Benzin Dortmund, Oil refineries. Weather 10/10ths cloud over the target. Bombed at 15.40 hours from 17,000 feet on G.H. Port outer engine smashed by falling bomb also port inner engine damaged. Another bomb came through the fuselage - beside main spar, remaining there until landing at Woodbridge. Yet another bomb struck the starboard outer engine. Crew behaved admirably.

21/11/1944 LM684   JI-C Bombing Homberg   12.45 x   x
Bomb load 1 x 4000 HC, 15 x 500 GP, 1 Red & Green Flare. Primary target: Homberg. Weather about 5/10ths cloud but clear for bombing. Aircraft missing. Crashed 1 km NW of Moers. Seen to explode as the aircraft approached the target. It is most likely that it was hit by Flak, for which Homberg was notorious. There were no survivors from the crew. Witnessed by F/L. Harry Yates in 'Luck and a Lancaster'.

All were buried locally. They have been subsequently re-interred in the Reichswald Forest War Cemetery.

Simon Hepworth, whilst researching the death of his great-uncle, F/S Gosnold, F/E of PD265, who was KIA on this operation, discovered an eye-witness from an adjacent aircraft who states that this aircraft was destroyed by its newly dropped 'cookie' being struck by another bomb and exploding underneath the aircraft.

F/L. Harold Thomas Lunson

130171 (1335758) F/L. Harold Thomas Lunson. Pilot.
160747 (1652919) F/O. George Stanley James Couchman. A/Bomber.
9 ops
163912 (1616284) F/O. William Charles Roberts.   Navigator.
200553 (1852169) P/O. Thomas Donald Blight. WOP/AG.
 Sgt. V.W. or B.W. Place.   MU/Gunner.
 Sgt. J. Jones.   R/Gunner.
  F/S. A. Marshall.   F/Engineer.
  F/S. W.H. Davey.   F/Engineer. 1 op.

Passengers: 04/06/1945, 18/06/1945, 26/06/1945, 07/07/1945,
13/07/1945, 31/07/1945

26/02/1945 NF968 JI-B Bombing Dortmund 10.14 14.03 16.02
   Bomb load 1 x 4000 HC, 2 x 500 MC L/Delay 37B, 9 x 500
ANM64, 3 x 250 GP, 1 Sky marker Red Puff. Primary target:
Dortmund, Hoesch Benzin plant. Weather 10/10ths cloud, tops
8/10,000 feet. Bombed at 14.03 hours from 20,000 feet on G.H.
equipment.
   From his normal crew, only F/L. H.T. Lunson did this mission as
2nd Pilot with F/L. R. Worthing's crew.
27/02/1945 LM285   JI-A Bombing Gelsenkirchen 11.00 14.30
   16.54
   Bomb load 1 x 4000 HC, 2 x 500 MC (L/D 37B), 9 x 500 ANM64,
4 x 250 GP. Primary target: Gelsenkirchen (Alma Pluts). Weather
10/10ths cloud, 6/10,000 feet tops. Bombed at 14.30 hours from
20,600 feet on leading aircraft.
01/03/1945 NG298   JI-E Bombing Kamen 11.41 15.07 17.44
   Bomb load 1 x 4000 HC, 9 x 500 ANM64, 2 x 500 MC L/D, 4 x
250 GP. Primary target: Kamen, Coking plant. Weather 10/10ths
cloud. Bombed at 15.07 hours from 19,900 feet on Blue smoke puffs.
05/03/1945 NG298   JI-E Bombing Gelsenkirchen 10.23 14.07
   16.24
   Bomb load 1 x 4000 HC, 12 x 500 ANM64. Primary target:
Gelsenkirchen, Benzol plant. Weather 10/10ths cloud over target with
cirrus cloud at bombing height. Bombed at 14.07 hours from 21,000
feet on G.H. Leader.

07/03/1945 LM724   JI-H Bombing Wesel   02.47 05.30   07.43

Bomb load 1 x 4000 HC, 13 x 500 ANM64, 2 x 500 GP. Primary target: Wesel, Troop & Transport concentration. Weather 10/10ths cloud, thin in places. Bombed at 05.30 hours from 18,000 feet on G.H.

From his normal crew, only F/L. H.T. Lunson did this mission as 2nd Pilot with S/L. K.G. Condict's crew.

17/03/1945 NG298   JI-E Bombing August Viktoria 11.30   15.06 17.04

Bomb load 1 x 4000 HC, 13 x 500 ANM64, 2 x 500 MC. Primary target: Auguste Viktoria, Marl-Hüls coal mine. Weather 10/10ths cloud, tops and contrails up to 23,000 feet. Bombed at 15.06 hours from 20,000 feet on G.H. Leader.

20/03/1945 NG298   JI-E Bombing Hamm   09.55 x 13.00

Bomb load 7 x 1000 MC, 9 x 500 ANM64. Primary target: Hamm, Marshalling yards. Weather 5/10ths cloud.   Abortive sortie. Turned back at 5038N 0228E owing to overspeeding of starboard outer engine, which would not feather but eventually caught fire. Fear of fire spreading prompted landing at Manston. 5 x 1000 MC, 1 x 500ANM64 jettisoned in Channel. 2 x 1000 MC, 8 x 500 ANM64 brought back to Base.

04/06/1945 RE137 JI-D Baedeker Tour over Germany   16.48 x 21.10

Passengers: F/O. H. Hughes, Sgt. R. Reynolds, AC. A. Charlton.

18/06/1945 NG298   JI-E Baedeker Tour over Continent 09.52 x 14.29

Passengers: Cpl. Murfitty, LAC. Watson, LAC. Rhodes, AC. Ribble.

26/06/1945 RE120 A2-C   Baedeker Tour over Continent 10.00   x 14.10

Passengers: Sq. Off. Denholm, S/O. Gray, 063 LAC. Saunders, 647 LAC. Gale, 410 LAC. Osgerley.

07/07/1945 RE116 JI-F Baedeker Tour over Continent 11.31 x 15.21

Passengers: Sgt. Wragge, Cpl. Amos, LAC. Roberts, Cpl. Porter (WAAF), LACW. Watts.

13/07/1945 ME535   JI-G Baedeker Tour over Continent 15.05 x 19.06

No Bomb Aimer that day.

Passengers: Cpl. Case, Hatton, Hart, Medcalfe, Smythe, Clare.

31/07/1945 RA601   JI-J Baedeker Tour over Continent 09.57 x 12.04

Returned early. Weather bad.

F/S. W.H. Davey was F/Engineer that day and no Bomb Aimer.

Passengers: LAC. Waters, LAC. Smith, LAC. Gordon, LACW. Truscott, LACW. Carroll.

411

F/L.   William Llewellyn Macdougald

150434 (1512417) F/L. William Llewellyn "Mac" Macdougald. Pilot.
J42261   F/O. H.B. Elvins, RCAF. A/Bomber. 6 ops.
  F/S. William "Bill" Elliott. A/Bomber. 6 ops.
J42227   F/O. J.A. Sutton, RCAF. Navigator. 6 ops.
164038 (1621350) F/O. Bertram "Bert" Evans.   Navigator. 6 ops.
A429706   W/O. Julius Angus, RAAF. WOP/AG. 6 ops.
177179   F/O. Terence "Locky" Lockwood. WOP/AG. 6 ops.
  Sgt. John "Red" Boswell.   MU/Gunner.
3030920   Sgt. Roy Conway Higgott. R/Gunner.
  F/S. John Edward "Johnny" Walker. F/Engineer.

Passengers: 08/06/1945, 28/06/1945, 15/07/1945, 18/07/1945,
22/07/1945.

29/03/1945 PD389 A2-J   Bombing Salzgitter   12.16 16.42 19.10
    Bomb load 1 x 4000 HC, 8 x 500 ANM64. Primary target:
Salzgitter, Hallendorf works. Weather 10/10ths cloud. Bombed at
16.42 hours from 21,000 feet on formation of four aircraft just
discernible in cloud. Lost leader on last leg in, due to cloud, picked up
formation of 4 A/C and bombed on them.
    Until 12/05/1945 F/O. H.B. Elvins A/Bomber, F/O. J.A. Sutton
Navigator, W/O. J. Angus WOP/AG.
13/04/1945 ME425 A2-L   Bombing Kiel   20.25 23.31 02.00
    Bomb load 18 x 500 ANM64. Primary target: Kiel, Docks & ship
yards. Weather 10/10ths cloud low and thin. Bombed on Green T.I.s
per M/B's instructions at 23.31 hours from 19,800 feet. Between two
lots of cascading green T.I.s. H2S good. If marking was accurate
attack should be good.
18/04/1945 PB419 JI-L Bombing Heligoland 09.58 13.08   15.30
    Bomb load 6 x 1000 MC, 10 x 500 ANM64. Primary target:
Heligoland, Naval base. Weather no cloud, slight haze. Bombed
visually up-wind edge of smoke at 13.08 hours from 16,500 ft. Many
bomb bursts seen amongst smoke. Should be an excellent raid. Much
smoke - Oil fire started on leaving. Pillar of black smoke rising.
22/04/1945 NN781   A2-B   Bombing Bremen 15.12 18.41 20.57
    Bomb load 1 x 4000 HC, 2 x 500 MC, 14 x 500 ANM 64. Primary
target: Bremen, in support of Troop concentration. Weather on
approaching target 4-5/10ths cloud. Bombed on leading A/C S/514 at

Background Lancaster Mk. 1 RF272 A2-F at Waterbeach in late June or July 1945

L to R (back): J.E. Walker, T. Lockwood, B. Evans, W.L. Macdougald. L to R (front R.C. Higgot, J. Boswell, W. Elliot. (courtesy Keith Higgott)

18.41 hours from 19,500 ft. Smoke seen on east bank of river. Slight damage to starboard inner. Formation good and raid concentrated

30/04/1945 NN781 A2-B Manna Rotterdam 16.59 18.18 19.35

Dropping area: Rotterdam. Weather intermittent showers and low cloud. Load 5 packs. Dropped 4 packs at 18.18 hours in field piled high with packs and surrounded with people. One pack hung up brought back. Very bad visibility. No identification seen. Population gave exuberant welcome.

12/05/1945 RE123 A2-K Exodus Juvincourt - Wing 09.09 x 14.50

Duration 4.00. Outward 2.01 hours. Collected 24 POWs. Homeward 1.59 hours. Very good control system at Juvincourt.

08/06/1945 RA602 A2-H Baedeker Tour over Continent 10.05 x 14.55

From that day F/S. W. Elliott was A/Bomber, F/O. B. Evans Navigator, F/O. T. Lockwood WOP/AG.

Passengers: LAC. R. Dix, LAC. Z. Bonsall, Cpl. G. Murphy.

413

25/06/1945 NN781   A2-B   Post Mortem Special mission   10.02   x 16.05

28/06/1945 RF272 A2-F   BaedekerTour over Continent 13.07 x 17.37

Passengers: F/L. Boston, Sgt. Wilson, Cpl. McGrath, LAC. Mortimer, LAC. Olley.

15/07/1945 RF272 A2-F   BaedekerTour over Continent 10.07 x 14.34

Passengers: LAC. Wood, ACW. Lewis, LAC. Bowells, LACW. Wright.

18/07/1945 RE159 A2-E   BaedekerTour over Continent 09.56 x 14.34

Passengers: Cpl. Ward, LAC. Hendy, LAC. Scutt, Cpl. White (WAAF), ACW. Hornett.

22/07/1945 RE158 A2-J Baedeker   Tour over Continent 10.15 x 14.34

Passengers: F/L. Eagles, Cpl. Penny, LAC. Milwane, LACW. Moore, ACW. Johnstone.

F/O. H. MacLean

J38094   F/O. H. MacLean, RCAF.   Pilot.
J41566   F/O. Lorne Henry Victor Gundlack, RCAF.   A/Bomber.
165037 (1490801) F/O. William John Graham.   Navigator.
Sgt. J.C. Tilley.   WOP/AG.
R279111 R192364 F/S. J.M. Moses, RCAF. MU/Gunner. 21 ops.
R181014   F/S. Earl Vernon "Vern" Flatekval. RCAF. R/Gunner.
Sgt. H.E. Freeman.   F/Engineer.
J26041   F/O. R.C. Foord, RCAF.   2nd Pilot. 04 & 20/04/1945

Passengers: 07/05/1945

16/01/1945 NN773   JI-K Bombing Wanne-Eickel   23.21   02.19 04.25

Bomb load 1 x 4000 HC, 10 x 500 ANM58, 4 x 250 GP - Primary target: Wanne-Eickel, Benzol plant. Weather 10/10ths thin low cloud. Bombed at 02.19 hours from 19,500 feet on Red flare with Green stars.

Earl Vernon 'Vern' Flatekval (left) and Lorne Henry Victor Gundlack (right).

From his normal crew, only F/O. H. MacLean did this mission as 2nd Pilot with F/O. M.D. Muggeridge's crew.

03/02/1945 PB423 A2-L Bombing Dortmund 16.45 19.50 21.45

Bomb load 1 x 4000 HC, 2 x 500 MC, 2 x 500 MC I/Delay, 6 x 500 ANM64, 2 x 500 GP, 3 x 250 GP. Primary target Dortmund-Huckarde, Coking plant. Weather clear with slight haze. Bombed at 19.50 hours from 19,500 feet on Red T.Is. Much smoke and fires.

08/02/1945 PB902 JI-A Bombing Hohenbudberg 03.42 x 07.37

Bomb load 1 x 4000 HC, 2 x 500 MC, 4 x 250 GP, 4 x 500 GP, 6 x 500 ANM64. Primary target: Hohenbudberg, Marshalling yards. Weather 8/10ths cloud over target. Farthest point reached 5035N 0055E. Jettisoned load at 5216N 0257E at 06.40 hours from 10,000 feet. Starboard outer engine feathered. Aircraft set course on three engines, but could not climb above 12,000 feet.

13/02/1945 NN782 JI-F Bombing Dresden 21.46 01.35 06.35

Bomb load 1 x 4000 HC, 6 x No. 14 Clusters. Primary target: Dresden. Weather 5/10ths cloud over target. Bombed at 01.35 hours from 20,000 feet on centre of Red T.I.s.

14/02/1945 NN782 JI-F Bombing Chemnitz 20.37 00.35 04.33

Bomb load 1 x 4000 HC, 8 x No. 14 Clusters. Primary target: Chemnitz. Weather 8-10/10ths cloud, tops 15-16,000 feet with occasional breaks. Bombed at 00.35 hours from 19,500 feet on upwind edge of flares.

25/02/1945 NN782　JI-F Bombing Kamen　09.31　12.46½　15.13

Bomb load 1 x 4000 HC, 9 x 500 ANM64, 2 x 500 MC, 2 x 250 GP. Primary target: Kamen. Weather 6-8/10ths cloud. Bombed at 12.46 hours from 20,000 feet on G.H. Leader.

27/02/1945 LM724　JI-H Bombing Gelsenkirchen　10.54　14.29　16.44

Bomb load 1 x 4000 HC, 2 x 500 MC (L/D 37B), 9 x 500 ANM64, 4 x 250 GP. Primary target: Gelsenkirchen (Alma Pluts). Weather 10/10ths cloud, 6/10,000 feet tops. Bombed at 14.29 hours from 19,000 feet. G.H. run satisfactory but all bombs hung up, and had to be released by jettisoning 30 seconds afterward.

01/03/1945 PB142 JI-G Bombing Kamen　11.51　15.06　17.53

Bomb load 1 x 4000 HC, 11 x 500 ANM64, 2 x 500 MC L/Delay37. Primary target: Kamen, Coking plant. Weather 10/10ths cloud. Bombed at 15.06 hours from 17,500 feet on G.H. Bombs hung up for 25 seconds and then jettisoned live.

05/03/1945 NN782　JI-F Bombing Gelsenkirchen　10.28　14.07　16.03

Bomb load 1 x 4000 HC, 12 x 500 ANM64. Primary target: Gelsenkirchen, Benzol plant. Weather 10/10ths cloud over target with cirrus cloud at bombing height. Bombed at 14.07 hours from 20,500 feet on G.H. Leader.

07/03/1945 LM285　JI-A Bombing Wesel　02.35　05.31　07.29

Bomb load 1 x 4000 HC, 13 x 500 ANM64, 2 x 500 GP. Primary target: Wesel, Troop & Transport concentration. Weather 10/10ths cloud, thin in places. Bombed at 05.31 hours from 17,800 feet on G.H. Bomb bursts appeared concentrated judging by flashes seen in cloud.

09/03/1945 LM285　JI-A Bombing Datteln　10.57　14.02　16.00

Bomb load 1 x 4000 HC, 13 x 500 ANM64, 2 x 500 HC L/Delay36. Primary target: Datteln, Synthetic oil plant. Weather 10/10ths cloud, tops 8-10,000 feet. Bombed at 14.02 hours from 20,400 feet on G.H.

04/04/1945 ME530　JI-C Bombing Merseburg (Leuna)　18.40　22.46　02.39

Bombed primary target. Bomb load 1 x 4000 HC, 6 x 500 ANM64. 5/10th to 10/10th thin cloud. Glow of fires and bursting bombed. Bombed at 22.46 hours from 20,000 feet. Bombed glow of fires, Red and Green Decoy Markers seen to port of track near target. W/T U/S and H2S U/S. Fires seen at Magdeberg on leg into target. No markers seen in our A/P so orbited on glow of fires.

F/O. R.C. Foord 2nd Pilot that day.

09/04/1945 ME530   JI-C Bombing Kiel   19.36   22.38   01.38

Bomb load 1 x 4000 HC and 12 x 500 ANM64. Primary target: Kiel, Submarine Buildings Yards. Weather clear with slight haze. Bombed at 22.38 hours from 19,500 feet on Green T.I.s on M.B.'s instructions. Fires and much smoke in target area. Very good attack. M.B. good and appeared satisfied with results.

13/04/1945 ME530   JI-C Bombing Kiel   20.18   23.59   02.00

Bomb load 1 x 4000 HC and 12 x 500 ANM64. Primary target: Kiel, Docks & ship yards. Weather 10/10ths cloud low and thin. Bombed at 23.59 hours from 19,500 feet on centre of Green T.I.'s per M.B.'s instructions. Red glow of fires seen round the marked A/P. Bombing seemed to be concentrated. Glow seen long after leaving area.

20/04/1945 ME380   JI-E Bombing Regensburg 09.30 13.57 17.07

Bomb load 15 x 500 ANM64. Primary target: Regensburg. Weather clear over target and whole route on G.H. at 13.57 from 18,500 feet. Good runs, bombs appeared to be falling N and S of oil plant. No black smoke. Success of attack doubtful, otherwise good trip. Perfect conditions for G.H. run.

F/O. R.C. Foord 2nd Pilot that day.

24/04/1945 ME530   JI-C Bombing Bad Oldesloe 07.16   10.45   13.03

Bomb load 6 x 1000 ANM65, 10 x 500 ANM 64. Primary target: Bad-Oldesloe, Rail and road junction and Marshalling Yards. Weather 3/10ths to nil cloud. Bombed on G.H. at 10.45 hours from 17,000 ft. Very satisfactory G.H. run. Bomb bursts seen in M/Y at 10.45 and huge red flash in target area rising to over 200ft burning red afterwards. Squadron formation good - splitting momentarily over Dutch coast due to flak. Good raid.

07/05/1945 RE116 JI-F Manna The Hague   12.26   13.53   14.57

Dropping area The Hague. Dropped 3 Packs on Red T.I.s and White Cross at 13.53 hours. Clear. Cloud above. All bags in the field - ground obscured. Some flour bags appeared to have burst.

AC. J. Sawyer was a passenger that day and there was no Mid Upper Gunner.

10/05/1945 RE116 JI-F Exodus Juvincourt - Ford   11.08 x 18.30

Duration 3.56. Outward 1.54 hours. Collected 24 ex POWs. Homeward 2.02 hours. Organisation O.K.

12/05/1945 RE116 JI-F Exodus   Juvincourt - Wing 08.56 x 17.42

Duration 3.34. Outward 1.35 hours. Collected 24 POWs. Homeward 1.59 hours. Organisation good.

14/05/1945 ME380   JI-E Exodus   Juvincourt - Oakley 10.13 x
Oakley

Duration 3.24 hours. Outward 1.46 hours. Collected 24 POWs.
Homeward 1.38 hours. Trouble with undercarriage caused 1½ hours
delay at Juvincourt. Left aircraft at Oakley with jammed throttle,
returned in 514/O. Organisation good.

17/05/1945 ME380   JI-E Exodus Brussels - Westcott 10.51 x 14.44

Duration 2 hrs 21 mins. Out 1 hr 12 mins. In 1 hr 10 mins. 10
Belgian refugees taken to Brussels. No POWs. brought back.
Everything satisfactory.

19/05/1945 ME380   JI-E Exodus   Brussels - Oakley 11.54 x 18.51

Duration 2 hrs 59 mins. Out 1 hr 19 mins. In 1 hr 40 mins. 10
Belgian refugees taken to Brussels. 24 ex POWs. returned to U.K.

23/05/1945 ME380   JI-E Exodus   Brussels - Oakley 12.06 x 18.14

Duration 2.58 hours. Out 1.10 hours. In 1.48 hours. 10 Belgian
refugees returned to Brussels. 24 ex POWs. evacuated. Organisation
good.

F/L.   Roy Henry "Marco" Marks

47225 (549527) F/L. Roy Henry "Marco" Marks.   Pilot.
55289 (591809) P/O. Timothy Terence Murphy.   A/Bomber.
164442 (1583325) F/O. Robert Arthur Edward Tidmarsh.   Navigator.
    F/S. C.V. Markell.   WOP/AG.
 Sgt. Gwynhefin Roberts "Gwyn" Morgan. MU/Gunner.
 Sgt. Robert Vipond.   R/Gunner.
 Sgt. T. Collins.   F/Engineer.
J20086   F/L. K.L. Ellwood, RCAF. 2nd Pilot. 14/03/1945
196313 (1601963) P/O. Ronald Frederick Etherington. 2nd Pilot.
04/04/1945

Passengers: 07/05/1945, 05/07/1945, 09/07/1945.

11/12/1944 NG118   A2-E   Bombing Osterfeld 08.41 11.06   12.51

Bomb load 1 x 4000 HC, 12 x 500 GP, 1 x 500 GP Long Delay, 2 x
500 MC, 1 Flare. Primary target: Osterfeld. Weather 10/10ths cloud,
tops 16,000 feet. Bombed at 11.06 hours from 20,000 feet on G.H.

From his normal crew, only F/L. R. Marks did this mission as 2nd
Pilot with F/L. R.A. Pickler's crew.

Back from left: 2nd G.R. Morgan, 3rd R.H. Marks. (courtesy Stuart Morgan)

02/01/1945 LM724   JI-H Bombing Nuremburg 15.26 19.33 22.44

Bomb load: 1 x 1000 ANM65, 1 x 500 ANM58, 10 x 80 x 4 IB, 120 x 4 lb. Primary target: Nuremburg. Weather clear. Bombed at 19.33 hours from 17,000 feet. - Overshot Red T.I.s as instructed by Master Bomber.

From his normal crew, only F/L. R. Marks did this mission as 2nd Pilot with F/L. K.G. Condict's crew.

07/01/1945 LM724   JI-H Bombing Munich 19.00 22.43   03.02

Bomb load 1 x 1000 ANM65, 1 x 500 ANM58, 1080 x 4lb I.B., 120 x 4lb I.B. Primary target: Munich. Weather 10/10ths cloud over target 6-8,000 feet with a thin layer altitude 16,000 feet. Bombed at 22.43 hours from 20,200 feet on Red and Green flares.

19/02/1945 ME365   JI-T Bombing Wesel 12.55 16.36 18.39

Bomb load 1 x 4000 HC, 6 x 500 MC, 6 x 500 ANM64, 4 x 250 GP. Primary target: Wesel. Weather over target 5-7/10ths cloud. Bombed at 16.36 hours from 19,000 feet on G.H. Leader.

20/02/1945 ME336   JI-S Bombing Dortmund 21.43 01.08 03.39

Bomb load 1 x 4000 HC, 5 x 500 Type 14 Clusters, 6 x 750 Type 15 Clusters. Primary target: Dortmund. Weather 8-10/10ths thin cloud at about 5,000 feet. Bombed at 01.08 hours from 21,000 feet on Red ground markers.

23/02/1945 ME364 JI-P Bombing Gelsenkirchen 11.15 15.03 18.08

Bomb load 1 x 4000 HC, 9 x 500 ANM64, 2 x 500 MC, 4 x 250 GP. Primary target Gelsenkirchen. Weather 10/10ths cloud. Bombed at 15.03 hours from 20,500 feet on Green smoke puffs. On return landed at Acklington.

26/02/1945 ME364 JI-P Bombing Dortmund 11.25 14.04 16.15

Bomb load 1 x 4000 HC, 2 x 500 MC L/Delay 37B, 9 x 500 ANM64, 4 x 250 GP. Primary target: Dortmund, Hoesch Benzin plant. Weather 10/10ths cloud, tops 8/10,000 feet. Bombed at 14.04 hours from 20,000 feet on G.H. equipment.

28/02/1945 ME365 JI-T Bombing Nordstern 08.40 12.04 14.00

Bomb load 1 x 4000 HC, 9 x 500 ANM64, 2 x 500 MC L/D, 4 x 250 GP. Primary target: Nordstern (Gelsenkirchen). Weather 10/10ths cloud. Bombed at 12.04 hours from 21,000 feet on leading aircraft.

02/03/1945 ME365 JI-T Bombing Koln 12.36 16.04 18.16

Bomb load 1 x 4000 HC, 12 x 500 ANM64. Primary target: Koln. Weather 10/10ths cloud over Koln, South and South-East of Koln clear. Bombed at 16.04 hours from 21,000 feet. Visually. Own bomb bursts seen among built up area.

11/03/1945 ME422 JI-Q Bombing Essen 11.29 15.25 17.15

Bomb load 1 x 4000 HC, 13 x 500 ANM64, 2 x 500 MC. Primary target: Essen, Marshalling yards. Weather 10/10ths cloud, tops 7/8000 feet. Bombed at 15.25 hours from 19,300 feet on G.H. 1 x 500 MC brought back to base due to hang up.

14/03/1945 ME422 JI-Q Bombing Heinrichshutte 13.00 16.39 18.30

Bomb load 1 x 4000 HC, 12 x 500 ANM64. Primary target: Heinrichshutte, Hattingen Steel works & Benzol plant. Weather 10/10ths cloud, tops 7/12,000 feet. Bombed at 16.39 hours from 18,500 feet on Red markers.

F/L. K.L. Ellwood 2nd Pilot that day.

27/03/1945 ME351 JI-U Bombing Hamm Sachsen 10.29 14.04 15.55

Bomb load 1 x 4000 HC, 13 x 500 ANM64, 2 x 500 MC. Primary target: Hamm Sachsen, Benzol plant. Weather 10/10ths cloud. Bombed at 14.04 hours at 17,500 feet on Green Puffs.

04/04/1945 ME354 JI-M Bombing Merseburg (Leuna) 18.55

22.54   02.55

Weather 5-10/10ths cloud, and 10/10ths over Merseburg. Bombed primary target. Bomb load 1 x 4000 HC, 6 x 500 ANM64. 9/10th cloud. Bombed on Sky-markers at 22.54 hours from 19,500 feet. 1 x 4000 jettisoned 45 secs after all other bombs released. Markings late and very widely dispersed. Master Bomber said "Bomb Skymarkers" then "Bomb visually" - not helpful.

P/O. R.F. Etherington 2nd Pilot that day.

13/04/1945 ME422   JI-Q Bombing Kiel   20.29   23.39   02.20

Bomb load 1 x 4000 HC and 12 x 500 ANM64. Primary target: Kiel, Docks & ship yards. Weather 10/10ths cloud low and thin. Bombed on centre of Green T.I.s at 23.39 hours from 19,000 feet. Well concentrated marking and flashes under cloud. Flashes from below cloud almost blinking. Attack seemed good. We orbited twice before bombing.

07/05/1945 ME422   JI-Q Manna The Hague   12.24   13.43   14.40

Dropping area The Hague. Dropped 5 Packs visually on White Cross and T.I.s at 13.43 hours. Clear - 3/10 Base 5000 hazy.

F/L. L.G. Blomfield was a passenger that day and there was no Mid Upper Gunner.

09/05/1945 ME422   JI-Q Exodus   Juvincourt - Dunsfold   07.29 x 12.59

Outward 1.40 hours. Collected 24 POW Homeward 1.51 hours. Operation well executed - impossible to get 24 people in front of the step.

11/05/1945 ME422   JI-Q Exodus   Juvincourt - Tangmere 11.16 x 16.39

Duration 3.25. Outward 1.28 hours. Collected 24 ex POWs. Homeward 1.28 hours. Landing procedure at Tangmere extremely poor.

12/05/1945 PD389 A2-J   Exodus Brussels - Tangmere   12.39 x 18.05

Duration 3.34. Outward 1.31 hours. Homeward 2.03 hours. 10 Refugees to Brussels, 24 ex POWs to Ford. Everything O.K.

16/05/1945 ME422   JI-Q Exodus   Brussels - Westcott 13.23 x 19.08

Duration 2 hrs 52 mins. Out 1 hr 6 mins. In 1 hr 46 mins. Arrived overseas A/F 14.23. Arrived reception A/F 18.29. 10 Belgian refugees taken to Brussels / Melsbroeck. 24 ex POW all military to Westcott.

18/05/1945 ME422   JI-Q Exodus   Brussels - Oakley 12.09 x 17.06

Duration 3 hrs 06 mins. Out 1 hr 02 mins. In 2 hrs 04 mins. 10 Belgian refugees taken to Brussels. 24 ex POWs returned to U.K.

Organisation O.K.

19/05/1945 ME422   JI-Q Exodus   Brussels - Oakley 12.09 x 17.31
    Evacuated 24 ex POWs. All military. 10 Belgian refugees taken to Brussels. Duration 2 hrs 52 mins. Out 1 hr 6 mins. In 1 hr 46 mins.

24/05/1945 ME422   JI-Q Exodus   Brussels 12.02 x 15.07
    Duration 2.12 hours. Out 1.03 hours. In 1.09 hours. 10 Belgian refugees returned to Brussels. No POWs available.

25/05/1945 ME422   JI-Q Exodus   Brussels 12.00 x 15.00
    Duration 2.10 hours. Out 1.02 hours. In 1.08 hours. 10 Belgian refugees returned to Brussels. No POWs. No trouble.

26/05/1945 ME422   JI-Q Exodus   Brussels - Ford 13.00 x 18.02
    Duration 3.05 hours. Out 1.03 hours. In 2.02 hours. 10 Belgian refugees to Brussels. 24 ex POWs all military brought back.

05/07/1945 RE139 JI-M   Baedeker Tour over Continent 14.19 x 18.33
    Passengers: F/L. Corless, Cpl. Pollicox, Cpl. Favell, A/S/O. Watts, LACW. Medhurst.

09/07/1945 ME422   JI-Q Baedeker Tour over Continent 09.51 x 14.05
    Passengers: F/O. Smith (M.T.O), Cpl. Trotman, Cpl. Hoyle, ACW. Morgan, ACW. Byrne.

F/O. Thomas Charles Marks, DFC

183874 (1295478) F/O. Thomas Charles "Tom" Marks, DFC. Pilot.
    F/S. John H. Jeffries.   A/Bomber.
    F/S. W.E. or W.L. "Bill" Harradine.   Navigator.
A419813   W/O.   Robert Edward "Bob" Jenkins, RAAF. WOP/AG.
    F/S. J.T. "Tom" Evans.   MU/Gunner.
    F/S. William "Bill" Hough.   R/Gunner.
Sgt. W.H. "Paddy" Mills.   F/Engineer.

23/09/1944 DS842 A2-J   Bombing Neuss   19.28 21.27 23.43
    Bomb load 8 x 1000 ANM59, 3 x 1000 ANM44, 4 x 500 GP. Primary target: Neuss. Weather 10/10ths cloud over target, tops 8/10,000 feet. Bombed at 21.27 hours from 19,500 feet on centre of glow.

03/10/1944 PD333 A2-K   Bombing Westkapelle   11.58 13.20 14.26
    Bomb load 1 x 4000 MC, 6 x 1000 MC, 1 x 500 GP L/Delay. Primary target: Westkapelle. Weather patchy-scattered cloud with base 5,000 feet. Bombed at 13.20 hours from 5,500 feet to starboard and undershot by width of red T.I.

514 Squadron RAF - Autumn 1944 (R.E. Jenkins collection)

L to R (back): J.H. Jeffrie, W. Harradine, T.C. Marks, R.E. Jenkins. L to R (front): F/Sgt. J.T. Evans, W. Hough.

Note: Sgt. W.H. Mills (F/Engineer) missed the photo.

05/10/1944 NG118   A2-E   Bombing Saarbrucken   17.40   20.34   22.37

Bomb load 11 x 1000 MC, 1 x 500 GP, 3 x 500 GP Long Delay. Primary target: Saarbrucken, Marshalling yards. Visibility O.K. Target confirmed by span on river on town. Dropped all bombs at 20.34 hours from 15,000 feet. Bombs fell about green T.I.

06/10/1944 PD334 A2-D   Bombing Dortmund   16.53   20.36   22.31

Bomb load 1 x 4000 HC, 12 x No. 14 Clusters. Primary target: Dortmund, Town and Railways. Weather over the target was clear with slight ground haze. Bombed at 20.36 hours from 22,000 feet on centre of red T.I.s.

14/10/1944 NG142   A2-H   Bombing Duisburg   06.58 09.04   11.26

Bomb load 11 x 1000 MC, 4 x 500 GP Long Delay. Primary target: Duisburg. Weather patchy cloud with gaps for bombing. Bombed at 09.04 hours from 18,000 feet. Red T.I. North of Docks.

14/10/1944 NG142   A2-H   Bombing Duisburg   22.58 01.34   03.55

Bomb load 1 x 4000 HC, 14 x No. 14 Clusters. Primary target: Duisburg. Weather was clear with small amount of cloud over the target. Bombed at 01.34 hours from 22,500 feet. Red T.I.

19/10/1944 NG142 A2-H Bombing Stuttgart 17.22 20.37 23.30

Bomb load 1 x 4000 HC, 3 x 500 Clusters, 7 x 150 x 4, 1 x 90 x 4 IB. Primary target: Stuttgart, A/P 'D' 1st attack. Weather 10/10ths cloud which broke to 6/10ths at the end of the period. Bombed at 20.37 hours from 18,000 feet. Glow of incendiaries as marker were visible when over target.

21/10/1944 PD333 A2-K Bombing Flushing 10.48 12.29 13.42

Bomb load 12 x 1000 MC, 2 x 500 GP. Primary target: Flushing 'B'. Weather clear. Bombed at 12.29 hours from 8,000 feet. Visual of A/P.

23/10/1944 PD334 A2-D Bombing Essen 16.40 19.29 21.35

Bomb load 1 x 4000 HC, 6 x 1000 MC, 6 x 500 MC. Primary target: Essen. Weather 10/10ths cloud over target - tops 12/14,000 feet with most appalling weather on route. Bombed at 19.29 hours from 19,000 feet. Green flares.

25/10/1944 PD334 A2-D Bombing Essen 13.16 15.47 17.23

Bomb load 1 x 4000 HC, 10 x No.14 Clusters, 4 x 15 x 4. Primary target: Essen. Weather over target 10/10ths low cloud, with one clear patch which appeared to fill up later in the attack. Bombed at 15.47 hours from 21,000 feet. Group of Red flares.

28/10/1944 PD334 A2-D Bombing Cologne 13.04 15.46 17.56

Bomb load 1 x 4000 HC, 12 x 150 x 4. Primary target: Cologne. Weather clear over target. Bombed at 15.46 hours from 19,000 feet. Red T.I.s.

30/10/1944 PD334 A2-D Bombing Wesseling 09.08 12.04 13.43

Bomb load 1 x 4000 HC, 16 x 500 GP. Primary target: Wesseling. Weather was 10/10ths cloud - tops about 7,000 feet. Bombed at 12.04 hours from 17,000 feet on leading G.H. aircraft.

31/10/1944 PD334 A2-D Bombing Bottrop 12.02 14.59 16.35

Bomb load 1 x 4000 HC, 16 x 500 GP. Primary target: Bottrop, Synth. Oil plants. Weather 10/10ths cloud over target. Bombed at 14.59 hours from 17,000 feet on leading aircraft.

02/11/1944 PD334 A2-D Bombing Homberg 11.20 14.09 15.47

Bomb load 1 x 4000 HC, 6 x 1000 ANM59, 6 x 500 MC. Primary target: Homberg. Weather variable cloud but clear for bombing. Target obscured by pall of smoke rising to 10,000 feet. Bombed at 14.09 hours from 20,500 feet.

15/11/1944 NG141 A2-J Bombing Dortmund 12.30 15.41 17.38

Bomb load 1 x 4000 HC, 16 x 500 GP. Primary target: Hoesch-Benzin Dortmund, Oil refineries. Weather 10/10ths cloud over the target. Bombed at 15.41 hours from 17,000 feet on Flares.

16/11/1944 NG141 A2-J BombingHeinsburg 13.07 15.32 17.35
   Bomb load 1 x 4000 HC, 6 x 1000 MC, 6 x 500 GP. Primary target: Heinsburg. Weather - nil cloud with slight haze over target. Bombed at 15.32 hours from 9,000 feet. Centre of upwind edge of smoke.

20/11/1944 NG141 A2-J BombingHomberg 12.39 15.17 17.17
   Bomb load 1 x 4000 HC, 16 x 500 MC. Primary target: Homberg. Weather 10/10ths cloud over target. Bombed at 15.17 hours from 20,500 feet. Bombed on main stream of aircraft.

21/11/1944 NG141 A2-J BombingHomberg 12.41 15.08 17.01
   Bomb load 1 x 4000 HC, 16 x 500 GP. Primary target: Homberg. Weather about 5/10ths cloud but clear for bombing. Bombed at 15.08 hours from 20,000 feet on Red T.I. in target area.

23/11/1944 NG298 A2-F BombingNordster 12.38 15.24 17.37
   Bomb load 1 x 4000 HC, 16 x 500 GP. Primary target: Nordstern, Gelsenkirchen Oil refineries. Weather 10/10ths cloud. Bombed at 15.24 hours from 18,000 feet. Centre of Red flares.

27/11/1944 NG298 A2-F BombingCologne 12.21 15.07 17.03
   Bomb load 1 x 4000 HC, 16 x 500 GP. Primary target: Cologne, Marshalling Yards. Weather patchy cloud. Bombed at 15.07 hours from 19,500 feet on G.H. Leader.

F/S. Paul Eugene Mason

NZ415771 F/S. Paul Eugene Mason, RNZAF. Pilot.
R153186   F/S. Arthur Edward Dimock, RCAF. A/Bomber.
NZ426364 F/S. James Stanley Gallagher, RNZAF. Navigator.
NZ417215 F/S. Lancelot Kell, RNZAF. WOP/AG.
R190931   Sgt. Ernest James Oakley, RCAF. MU/Gunner.
1308671 Sgt. John William Hennis. R/Gunner.
1583806 Sgt. Ronald Frederick Laishley. F/Engineer.

24/12/1943 DS816JI-O BombingBerlin 00.33 04.14 07.40
   Bomb load 1 x 8000. Primary target: Berlin. 7/10 cloud, haze. Bombed at 04.14 hrs at 18,000 feet. No markers seen. Good fires, very wide spread. Moderately good attack. Route O.K. Photo attempted.
   From his normal crew, only F/S. P.E. Mason did this mission as 2nd Pilot with S/L. A.L. Roberts' crew.

L to R (top): A.E. Dimock, R.F. Laishley, J.W. Hennis. L to R (bottom): E.J. Oakley, P.E. Mason, J.S. Gallagher and first graves plaque.

14/01/1944 LL679 A2-J Bombing Brunswick 17.22 x x

Bomb load 1 x 4000, 48 x 30. Aircraft missing.

All are buried in the Hannover War Cemetery. Probably victim of a night-fighter. It is stated on www.lostaircraft.com to have crashed at Lauenberg, SE of Dassel, however this appears to be a long way south of the bomber stream. It is possible that LL679 fell victim to Maj. Helmut Lent of Stab./NJG3 who is credited with an unidentified Lancaster at much the same time and place as LL685.

F/O. Merlin Leigh Matkin

J37099   F/O. Merlin Leigh Matkin, RCAF. Pilot.
J40946   FO. Joe A. Speare, RCAF.   A/Bomber.
J40778   F/O. Ray Bertram Hilchey, RCAF. Navigator.
1892880   Sgt. John Goodworth Brittain. WOP/AG.
J95536 (R279032) Sgt. Orval Clare "Shorty" Evers, RCAF.
MU/Gunner.
J95531 (R271567)
          Sgt. Robert MacPherson "Bob" Toms, RCAF. R/Gunner.
939832 Sgt. Alfred "Alf" McMurrugh.   F/Engineer.

13/01/1945 PA186 A2-G Bombing Saarbrucken 11.52 15.24 17.32
    Bomb load 1 x 4000 HC, 10 x 500 ANM58 or 64, 4 x 250 GP.
Primary target: Saarbrucken. Weather 3-5/10ths cloud, tops 4/5,000
feet. Bombed at 15.24 hours from 19,500 feet on G.H. All aircraft on
this operation were diverted on return to Exeter as weather at base was
unfit to land.

    From his normal crew, only F/O.
M.L. Matkin did this mission as 2nd
Pilot with F/L. F.P. Hendy's crew.
15/01/1945 LM627   A2-H
    Bombing Lagendreer   11.44
    15.00 16.40
    Bomb load 1 x 4000 HC, 10 x
500 ANM64, 4 x 250 GP. Primary
target: Lagendreer. Weather
10/10ths cloud. Bombed at 15.00
hours from 19,400 feet on G.H.
Leader.
16/01/1945 PB906 A2-B Bombing
    Wanne-Eickel 23.12 x x
    Bomb load 1 x 4000 HC, 10 x
500 ANM58, 4 x 250 GP. Primary
target: Wanne-Eickel, Benzol plant.
Weather 10/10ths thin low cloud.
Aircraft missing en route.
    Lost without trace on 17th

Merlin Leigh Matkin

January 1945. All of the crew are commemorated on the Runnymede Memorial.

From his normal crew, only F/O. M.L. Matkin did this mission as 2nd Pilot with F/O. G.D. Orr's crew.

From 01/02/1945, the remaining members of F/O. M.L. Matkin crew continued to fly together with F/O. L.J.W. Sutton as new skipper.

F/L.   Charles McBride

139981 (1370460) F/L. Charles McBride.   Pilot.
  Nil   A/Bomber.
131603 (1508455) F/L. Alan Hope Deadman. DFC. Navigator.
  F/S. V.H. Stevens.   WOP/AG.
111124? (1381275)? F/L. Jack? Noble? Airey? (*)   MU/Gunner.
  Nil   R/Gunner.
  F/S. R. Sherwood.   F/Engineer.

Passengers 17/06/1945
(*): surname not entirely legible in ORBs.

17/06/1945 ME336   JI-S BaedekerTour over Continent 10.04 x 15.36
  Passengers: Cpl. Thacker, LAC. Mitchell, Cpl. Burnk, LAC. Wood.
  No Air Bomber and no Rear Gunner that day.

F/L.   Bruce Kenneth McDonald, DFC

J27538   F/L. Bruce Kenneth McDonald, DFC, RCAF. Pilot.
J22614   F/O. W.R. "Walt" Hambley, RCAF. A/Bomber.
J29859   F/O. John Friesen, DFC, RCAF.   Navigator.
1587262 Sgt. B.A. "Bob" Hare.   WOP/AG.
1527504 Sgt. Horace Ernest "Ben" Bentley.   MU & R/Gunner.
R256011 Sgt. Donald R. "Don" Gardiner, RCAF.   MU & R/Gunner.
1867310 Sgt. A.B. "Tim" Mason.   F/Engineer.
171813 (1553846)
  F/O. John Herbert Gerard Harland. 2nd Pilot. 01/08/1944
186330 (1682052) P/O. Thomas Gilchrist.   2nd Pilot. 05/10/1944
185434 (1387393) P/O. John Henry Tolley. 2nd Pilot. 23/10/1944
J28107
F/O. Christopher Iltyd Hubert Nicholl. RCAF. 2nd Pilot. 28/10/1944

L to R: W.R. Hambley, B.A. Hare, J. Friesen, B.K. McDonald, D. Gardiner, H.E. Bentley, A.B. Mason. (courtesy Don Gardiner & David Bentley)

24/06/1944 LL728 A2-L Bombing Rimeux 23.36 00.37 02.22
Bomb load 18 x 500 GP. Primary target: Rimeux, Flying bomb installations. Weather clear. Bombed at 00.37 hours from 12,000 feet centre of red T.I.s, which appeared to be well plastered with bombs. Numerous searchlights.

02/07/1944 LL716 A2-G Bombing Beauvoir 12.55 14.36 16.20
Bomb load 11 x 1000 MC, 4 x 500 GP. Primary target: Beauvoir, Flying bomb supply site. Bombed at 14.36 hours from 8,800 feet, Gee Fix coinciding with visual.

05/07/1944 LL728 A2-L Bombing Watten 22.54 00.10 01.26
Bomb load 11 x 1000 ANM65, 4 x 500 GP. Primary target: Watten, Constructional works. Bombed at 00.10 hours from 8,800 feet red T.I.s.

07/07/1944 LL728 A2-L Bombing Vaires 22.47 01.37 03.24
Bomb load 7 x 1000 MC, 4 x 500 GP. Primary target: Vaires, Marshalling yards. Weather clear. Bombed at 01.37 hours from 12,000 feet, green T.I.s. Bombing concentrated, red glow in target area. Had combat with enemy aircraft.

10/07/1944 LL728 A2-L Bombing Nucourt 04.28 06.05 08.00
Bomb load 11 x 1000 ANM65, 4 x 500 GP. Primary target: Nucourt, Constructional works. Bombed at 06.05 hours from 16,000 feet on Gee.

12/07/1944 LL728 A2-L   Bombing Vaires   17.58 20.00 22.03

Bomb load 18 x 500 GP. Primary target: Vaires, Marshalling yards. Reached target 20.00 hours heard Master Bomber order abandon mission.

15/07/1944 LL728 A2-L   Bombing Chalons sur Marne 21.45 01.38 04.14

Bomb load 18 x 500 GP. Primary target: Chalons sur Marne, Railway centre. Weather clear below. Bombed at 01.38 hours from 9,000 feet yellow T.I.s as instructed. 1 x 500 GP hung up. Little evidence of bombing, Master Bomber good.

18/07/1944 LL728 A2-L   Bombing Emieville 04.23   06.08 07.45

Bomb load 11 x 1000 MC, 4 x 500 GP. Primary target: Emieville, Troop concentration. Weather clear. Bombed at 06.08 hours from 7,500 feet yellow T.I.s. Pall of smoke covered a large area. Starboard fin and rudder shot off tail-plane by heavy flak over target. Landed at Woodbridge.

Sgt. H.E. Bentley was MU/Gunner and Sgt. D.R. Gardiner R/Gunner that day.

20/07/1944 LL697 A2-B   Bombing Homberg 23.20 01.21 02.46

Bomb load 1 x 4000 HC, 2 x 500 MC, 14 x 500 GP. Primary target: Homberg, Oil plant. Weather clear. Bombed at 01.21 hours from 17,500 feet red T.I. and green T.I. Clouds of black smoke and explosion. Had combat with enemy aircraft.

23/07/1944 DS620 A2-D   Bombing Kiel   22.36 x 01.26

Bomb load 6 x 1000 MC, 10 x 500 GP. Returned early, Rear turret u/s. Jettisoned 4 x 1000 MC, 4 x 500 GP at 00.28 hours from 4,000 feet, position 5330N 0250E.

24/07/1944 DS620 A2-D   Bombing Stuttgart 21.53 x 00.40

Bomb load 5 x 1000 ANM 65, 3 x 500 GP. Returned early. D.R. Compass and 04 compass unreliable and starboard outer engine feathered. Jettisoned 4945N 0015W.

25/07/1944 DS813 JI-N Bombing Stuttgart   21.36 01.51 05.39

Bomb load 5 x 1000 MC, 3 x 500 GP. Primary target: Stuttgart. Weather clear, hazy below. Bombed at 01.51 hours from 19,000 feet red T.I. Good fires started.

27/07/1944 LL692 A2-C   Bombing Les Catelliers 16.42 x 20.11

Bomb load 18 x 500 GP. Primary target: Les Catelliers, Flying bomb site. Aircraft jettisoned bomb load owing to engine failure.

According H.E. Bentley's logbook "Hit by Flak".

30/07/1944 LL728 A2-L Bombing Caen   06.17   07.50   09.25

Bomb load 18 x 500 GP. Primary target: Caen 'B'. Weather 10/10 cloud. Bombed at 07.50 hours from 2,000 feet, red T.I.s. Port inner engine u/s at 08.35 hours. Starboard inner u/s at 08.52 hours. Necessary to land at Bassingbourne. Village believed well hit.

According to J. Friesen's logbook target "Amaye-sur-Seulles", next to Villers Bocage, 20 km west from Caen.

01/08/1944 LL677 A2-E Bombing Foret de Nieppe 19.22 x 21.46

Bomb load 11 x 1000 MC, 4 x 500 GP. Target: De Nieppe, constructional works. Jettisoned at 20.55 hours from 10,000 feet. 4 x 1000 MC, 4 x 500 GP at Posn. 5110N 0225E. Abandoned on Master Bomber's orders.

F/O. J.H.G. Harland 2nd Pilot that day.

03/08/1944 LM286   A2-F Bombing Bois de Cassan 11.37   14.07   15.53

Bomb load 11 x 1000 MC, 4 x 500 GP. Primary target: Bois de Cassan, Flying bomb supply depot. Bombed at 14.07 hours from 16,000 feet, centre of smoke.

25/08/1944 LM286   A2-F Bombing Russelsheim 20.25 01.04   04.25

Bomb load 1 x 4000 HC, 11 x 500 lb Clusters. Primary target: Russelheim. Weather clear. Bombed at 01.04 hours red T.I.s. Attacked early stage before raid developed. Bombed target from 18,000 feet.

26/08/1944 LL726 A2-H Bombing Kiel 20.16 23.09 01.48

Bomb load 1 x 8000 HC, 180 x 4 IB, 16 x 30 IB. Primary target: Kiel. Weather clear with slight haze. Bombed at 23.09 hours from 19,000 feet red and green T.I.s. Large explosion in target at 23.11 hours. A good attack.

05/09/1944 DS787 A2-G Bombing Le Havre 17.30 19.23 20.54

Bomb load 11 x 1000 MC, 4 x 500 GP. Primary target: Le Havre. Bombed at 19.23 hours from 13,500 feet red T.I.

08/09/1944 LL734 A2-B Bombing Le Havre 06.14 x 09.30

Bomb load 11 x 1000 MC, 4 x 500 GP. Primary target: Le Havre. Weather 10/10ths cloud down to 3,000 feet. Abandoned mission on Master Bomber's instructions.

11/09/1944 LL734 A2-B Bombing Kamen   16.09   18.43   20.27

Bomb load 1 x 4000 HC, 16 x 500 GP. Weather clear. Primary target: Kamen. Bombed at 18.43 hours from 16,500 feet on yellow T.I. per Master Bomber's instructions.

14/09/1944 LL734 A2-B Bombing Wassenaar 12.50 14.30 15.37
Bomb load 11 x 1000 MC, 4 x 500 GP. Primary target: Wassenaar. Weather was good, nil cloud. Bombed at 14.30 hours from 12,000 feet, red T.I.s. According to J. Friesen's logbook target "The Hague". Wassenaar is 10km from The Hague.

20/09/1944 LM286 A2-F Bombing Calais 14.36 16.01 17.16
Bomb load 11 x 1000 MC, 4 x 500 GP. Primary target: Calais. Weather clear over target. Bombed at 16.01 hours from 2,800 feet, red T.I.s.

05/10/1944 LM286 A2-F Bombing Saarbrucken 17.09 x 22.39
Bomb load 11 x 1000 MC, 1 x 500 GP, 3 x 500 GP. Long Delay. Primary target: Saarbrucken, Marshalling yards. Weather clear over target. Abandoned mission at position 5918N 0705E on instructions from Master Bomber heard to say they were unable to locate target and called "Abandon Mission - our troop in vicinity". Jettisoned 4 x 500 GP. At 20.38 from 9,000 feet - live, Remainder brought back.
According to H.E. Bentley's logbook "Flak damage".
P/O. T. Gilchrist 2nd Pilot that day.

06/10/1944 PD325 A2-L Bombing Dortmund 16.59 20.27 22.15
Bomb load 1 x 4000 HC, 12 x No. 14 Clusters. Primary target: Dortmund, Town and Railways. Weather over the target was clear with slight ground haze. Bombed at 20.27 hours from 22,000 feet on centre of mixed red and green T.I.s.

07/10/1944 PD325 A2-L Bombing Emmerich 12.20 14.28 16.00
Bomb load 1 x 4000 HC, 10 x No. 14 clusters, 4 x (150 x 4). Primary target: Emmerich. Weather clear with cloud at 13,000 feet. Bombed at 14.28 hours from 12,000 feet near edge of smoke pall.

14/10/1944 LM286 A2-F Bombing Duisburg 06.49 09.04 11.20
Bomb load 11 x 1000 MC, 4 x 500 GP Long Delay. Primary target: Duisburg. Weather patchy cloud with gaps for bombing. Bombed at 09.04 hours from 18,000 feet. Fires and smoke North of Docks.

14/10/1944 LM286 A2-F Bombing Duisburg 22.22 01.30 03.22
Bomb load 11 x 1000 MC, 4 x 500 GP Long Delay. Primary target: Duisburg. Weather was clear with small amount of cloud over the target. Bombed at 01.30 hours from 21,500 feet. Red T.I.s.
According to H.E. Bentley's logbook "2 Fighter attacks".

19/10/1944 LM286 A2-F Bombing Stuttgart 17.16 20.23 23.11
Bomb load 1 x 4000 HC, 6 x 1000 MC, 1 x 500 GP. Primary target: Stuttgart, A/P 'D' 1st attack. Weather 10/10ths cloud which broke to 6/10ths at the end of the period. Bombed at 20.23 hours from 19,000

feet on Gee.

21/10/1944 LM286   A2-F   Bombing Flushing 10.44 12.29 13.41
Bomb load 12 x 1000 MC, 2 x 500 GP. Primary target: Flushing 'B'. Weather clear. Bombed at 12.29 hours from 7,500 feet. Visual.

23/10/1944 LM286   A2-F   Bombing Essen 16.33 19.40 21.56
Bomb load 1 x 4000 HC, 6 x 1000 MC, 6 x 500 GP. Primary target: Essen. Weather 10/10ths cloud over target - tops 12/14,000 feet with most appalling weather on route. Bombed at 19.40 hours from 20,500 feet. Green flares. According to H.E. Bentley's logbook "Hit by Flak".
P/O. J.H. Tolley 2nd Pilot that day.

25/10/1944 NG118   A2-E   Bombing Essen 13.08 x 14.45
Bomb load 1 x 4000 HC, 6 x 1000 MC, 6 x 500 GP. Primary target: Essen. Abortive sortie. Aircraft returned early with starboard outer engine unserviceable. Jettisoned 40 miles East of Southwold.

28/10/1944 LM286   A2-F   Bombing Cologne 13.01 15.46 17.42
Bomb load 1 x 4000 HC, 12 x 150 x 4. Primary target: Cologne. Weather clear over target. Bombed at 15.46 hours from 18,000 feet. Yellow T.I.s.
F/O. C.I.H. Nicholl 2nd Pilot that day.

30/10/1944 LM286   A2-F   Bombing Wesseling 09.10 11.58 13.26
Bomb load 1 x 4000 HC, 16 x 500 GP. Primary target: Wesseling. Weather was 10/10ths cloud - tops about 7,000 feet. Bombed at 11.58 hours from 17,500 feet on G.H. aircraft ahead.

According H.E. Bentley's logbook "Bombs from Halifax through wing (PT)".

31/10/1944 LM286   A2-F   Bombing Bottrop 11.58 15.00 16.00
Bomb load 1 x 4000 HC, 16 x 500 GP. Primary target: Bottrop, Synth. Oil plants. Weather 10/10ths cloud over target. Bombed at 15.00 hours from 18,000 feet on Gee.

04/11/1944 ME841   JI-J   Bombing Solingen 11.35 14.10 15.55
Bomb load 1 x 4000 HC, 6 x 1000 ANM59, 6 x 500 GP. Primary target: Solingen. Weather 8-10/10ths cloud. Bombed at 14.10 hours from 20,500 feet on red flares.

05/11/1944 LM286   A2-F   Bombing Solingen 10.12 13.03 14.41
Bomb load 1 x 4000 HC, 6 x 1000 ANM59, 4 x 500 GP, 2 x 500 GP (L/Delay). Primary target: Solingen. Weather 10/10ths cloud over target. Bombed at 13.03 hours from 18,000 feet on Red flares with green stars.

433

F/L. William John McFetridge

110842 (655364) F/L. William John McFetridge. Pilot.
J29711 F/O. G.A. Rochefort, RCAF. A/Bomber.
153449 (1624529) F/O. James McInnes. Navigator.
1081021 Sgt. C. Sunley. WOP/AG.
1570475 Sgt. W. Corney. MU/Gunner.
187851 (1621603) Sgt. Ronald Wilfred "Ron" Britnell. R/Gunner.
1331645 Sgt. B.R. Apps. F/Engineer.

22/05/1944 DS795 A2-J Bombing Dortmund 22.55 x 01.20
Bomb load 1 x 2000 lb bomb, 96 x 30, 810 x 4, 90 x 4 incendiaries.
Primary target: Dortmund. Returned early. Severe icing and unable to
climb above 9,000 feet. Farthest point reached 5221N 0148E. All
bombs jettisoned safe at 00.49 hours.

24/05/1944 LL678 A2-L Bombing Boulogne 00.15 01.16 02.35
Bomb load 9 x 1000 MC, 1 x 1000 GP, 1 x 1000 ANM, 4 x 500 GP.
Primary target: Boulogne, Gun Battery. Clear over target. Bombed
green T.I.s at 01.16 hours from 8,000 feet. Bomb bursts seen mostly to
North of the T.I.s. Slight heavy and light flak over target but generally
an uneventful trip. Unidentified aircraft showing green light seen
homeward from target.

27/05/1944 LL678 A2-L Bombing Boulogne 00.15 01.16 02.20
Bomb load 7 x 1000 MC, 4 x 1000 ANM, 4 x 500 GP. Primary
target: Boulogne Gun Batteries. Clear at target. Bombed at 01.16 hours
from 8,500 feet. Bursts seemed accurate on the T.I.s. Two explosions
seen at 01.15 hours. Fighter flares observed on route to target.

28/05/1944 LL678 A2-L Bombing Angers 19.00 23.54 01.55
Bomb load 5 x 1000 MC, 1 x 1000 USA, 4 x 500 MC. Primary
target: Angers. Clear over target. Visual obtained of river and railway.
Bombed at 23.54 hours from 9,200 feet. Attack appeared good. Route
O.K. At 00.36 hours an unidentified aircraft was seen.

30/05/1944 LL678 A2-L Bombing Boulogne 23.05 00.06 01.15
Bomb load 6 x 1000 MC, 4 x 500 MC. Primary target: Boulogne
Gun Batteries. Haze over target. Bombed red T.I.s at 00.06 hours from
8,000 feet. Bombs seen to fall between two clusters of T.I.s. Defences
appeared strengthened since last attack. Part of one stick of bombs
seen to fall on coast line. Much smoke seen coming from target area.
At 00.06 hours sighted an enemy aircraft 1000 yards astern but evaded
successfully. At 00.11 hours an unidentified twin-engine aircraft

followed for 6 minutes before turning away.

31/05/1944 LL678 A2-L Bombing Trappes 00.06 02.01 03.50
Bomb load 8 x 1000 MC, 8 x 500 MC. Primary target: Trappes. Clear at target. Bombed as instructed by Master Bomber at 02.01 hours from 9,000 feet. Yards lit up by flares and one large fire and bursts in the yards were seen. Good attack, very concentrated. Master Bomber good.

05/06/1944 DS795 A2-J Bombing Ouistreham 03.41½ 05.10 06.58
Bomb load 9 x 1000 MC and 2 x 500 MC. Primary target: Ouistreham. There was 5/10 broken cloud over target and 10/10 over route. Bombed markers at 05.10 hours from 10,000 feet. Slight visual of target obtained. Two sets of red and one of green T.I.s were seen and they appeared rather scattered. Some bursts seen near the markers but not much could be seen owing to cloud.

07/06/1944 DS795 A2-J Bombing Massy Palaiseau 00.32 02.15 03.58
Bomb load 18 x 500 MC. Primary target: Massy Palaiseau, Marshalling Yards. Hazy below and 10/10 cloud above. Bombed on Master Bomber's instructions at 02.15 hours from 6,000 feet. Did not get a visual but bombing observed to be between red and green T.I.s. Moderate light flak. Quiet trip. Had Monica identification of a JU88 which crossed from port to starboard on homeward journey.

10/06/1944 LL716 A2-G Bombing Dreux 23.07 00.59 03.14
Bomb load 16 x 500 GP, 2 x 500 LD. Primary target: Dreux. Bombed as instructed by Master Bomber at 00.59 hours from 7,000 feet. Visual obtained of yards. No trouble experienced.

12/06/1944 LL697 JI-E Bombing Gelsenkirchen 23.04 01.07 03.05
Bomb load 1 x 4000 HC, 12 x 500 GP, 4 x 500 MC. Primary target: Gelsenkirchen. Clear over target. Bombed red and green T.I.s at 01.07 hours from 18,000 feet. Colossal fires and palls of smoke seen. Moderate amount of fighter flares and general activity experienced. Had combat with enemy aircraft.

14/06/1944 LL716 A2-G Bombing Le Havre 23.48 01.16 02.44
Bomb load 11 x 1000 MC, 4 x 500 GP. Primary target: Le Havre. Weather clear - save smoke. Bombed at 01.16 hours from 15,500 feet between red and green markers. Good marking and bombing. Big fires seen among warehouses. Master Bomber very clear. Photo taken.

15/06/1944 DS786 A2-F Bombing Valenciennes 23.12 00.36 02.01
Bomb load 16 x 500 GP, 2 x 500 MC. Primary target: Valenciennes. Weather clear below cloud. Bombed at 00.36 hours from 7,000 feet centre of red and green T.I.s. Master Bomber was clear and concise.

P/O. William Lachlan McGown, DFC & Bar

174120 (1118708)
  P/O. William Lachlan "Bill" McGown, DFC & Bar. Pilot.
173388 (1337757) P/O. Lyndon Warwick Clive Lewis.   A/Bomber.
203358 (1389896) F/S. Maurice James Bulled. A/Bomber. 1 op.
A413305   P/O. Archibald Norman Durham, RAAF. Navigator.
1323954   Sgt. Stanley William Ricketts.   Navigator. 1 op.
A410529   P/O. Kenneth Edward Bryan, RAAF. WOP/AG.
1873573   F/S. John George Shepherd Boanson. MU/Gunner.
1585622   Sgt. George A. "Hawkeye" Henry. MU/Gunner. 2 ops.
1590234   Sgt. John Oswald "Jack" Tanney. R/Gunner. 11 ops.
J92270 (R161202) Sgt. William Fraser Sutherland, RCAF. R/Gunner.
2 ops.
R119782   F/S. H.J. Dahle, RCAF.   R/Gunner. 1 op.
1565396   F/S. Robert Calder "Bert" Guy.   R/Gunner. 13 ops.
1581581   Sgt. John "Jack" Clarke.   F/Engineer.

03/11/1943 DS814 JI-M   Gardening Frisian Islands 18.10 x 20.21
  Aircraft carried 6 x B200. Primary Area FRISIAN ISLANDS. 7/10
Layer cloud. Good visibility. Gee Fix Garden. Monica. Satisfactory
Sortie.
  Sgt. J.O. Tanney was R/Gunner until 30/03/44 except 27 &
28/01/44.
26/11/1943 DS821 JI-S Bombing Berlin   17.55 21.30 01.13
  Bomb Load 1 x 4000 H.C., 24 x 30 incendiaries, 405 x 4
incendiaries, 45 x 4. Primary target BERLIN. No cloud, visibility
good, slight haze. Target attacked at 21.30 hrs at 20,000 feet. As we
approached closer fires had got a good hold, visible for 100 miles on
return. 1st Route marker was good but 2nd appeared north of route.
Photo flash hung up but was manually released after bombs had gone.
City well alight.
  Sgt. S.W. Ricketts was Navigator that day. ORBs omitted to quote
their names, but J.G.S Boanson's logbook and J.O. Tanney's
testimony prove that J.G.S. Boanson and J. Clarke took part in this
operation.
02/12/1943 DS821 JI-S Bombing Berlin   17.10 x 19.15
  Bomb load 1 x 4000 HC, 40 x 30 incendiaries, 810 x 4 incendiaries,
90 x 4 incendiaries. Primary target Berlin. Task abandoned. Starboard
inner engine u/s, high oil temperature, low pressure. 1 x 4000 HC safe.

630 x 4 jettisoned.

Foulsham Autumn 1943

L to R (back): J. Clark, J.O. Tanney, K.E. Bryan, L.W.C. Lewis. L to R (front): A.N. Durham, W.L. McGown, J.G.S. Boanson. (courtesy J.O. Tanney)

03/12/1943 DS818 JI-Q Bombing Leipzig 00.39 04.06 07.02

Bomb load 1 x 4000 HC, 24 x 30 incendiaries 450 x 4 incendiaries, 150 x 4 incendiaries. Primary target LEIPZIG. Satisfactory route with route markers effective. 10/10 cloud over target. Bombed total load 04.06 hours, 20,000 feet. Reflection of fires on cloud.

27/01/1944 LL683 JI-P Bombing Berlin 17.57 20.32 01.35

Bomb load 1 x 4000, 32 x 30, 450 x 4, 90 x 4 incendiaries. Primary target: Berlin. There was 10/10 cloud. Bombed at 20.32 hours at 18,000 ft. Cloud prevented visual. Sky markers were in three groups. Jerry putting flak up at markers. Many 'cookie' explosions in larger area.

Sgt. G.A. Henry was MU/Gunner that day and Sgt. W.F. Sutherland R/Gunner.

28/01/1944 LL683 JI-P Bombing Berlin 00.13 03.24 08.21

Bomb load 1 x 2000 lb bomb, 16 x 30, 750 x 4 incendiaries. Primary target: Berlin. There was 10/10 cloud. Bombed at 03.24 hours at 20,000 ft. Good concentration of fires reflected through cloud also

437

Robert Calder 'Bert' Guy - January 1944

(courtesy Jean & Sinclair Ronald)

seen through break. Attack seemed rather scattered. Sky markers seemed to be two or three miles apart. One big fire and many small fires seen. Good route, no trouble.

Sgt. G.A. Henry was MU/Gunner that day and Sgt. W.F. Sutherland R/Gunner.

15/02/1944 LL683 JI-P Bombing Berlin 17.36 21.34 00.43

Bomb load 1 x 4000 lb bomb, 32 x 30, 540 x 4, 90 x 4 incendiaries. Primary target: Berlin. There was 10/10 cloud. Bombed at 21.34 hrs at 20,000 ft. Glow seen through cloud. Route good. P.F.F. very scattered. Attack not concentrated.

19/02/1944 LL683 JI-P Bombing Leipzig 23.59 04.17 06.48

Bomb load 1 x 4000 lbs bomb, 32 x 30, 510 x 4, 90 x 4 incendiaries. Primary target: Leipzig. There was 10/10 cloud with top 8/10,000 ft. Bombed at 04.17 hours at 19,000 ft. Leipzig flak damaged port elevator 04.15 hours. Looked good prang. Markers were 'Bang on'. Cloud prevented visual.

21/02/1944 LL683 JI-P Bombing Stuttgart 00.17 04.12 07.07

Bomb load 1 x 4000 lb bomb, 40 x 30, 690 x 4, 90 x 4 incendiaries. Primary target: Stuttgart. There was 7/10 cloud. Dropped bombs on Dornberg airfield. Reached Stuttgart 03.50 hours turned too late to make second run. Bombed at 04.12 hours at 20,000 ft. Photo taken.

24/02/1944 LL683 JI-P Bombing Schweinfurt 20.47 01.12 04.26

Bomb load 1 x 4000 lb bomb, 24 x 30, 420 x 4, 90 x 4 incendiaries. Primary target: Schweinfurt. There was broken cloud with good visibility. Bombed at 01.12 hours at 20,000 ft. One mass of fires seen burning orange. A really successful raid. Mass of fires in target area.

18/03/1944 LL683 JI-P Bombing Frankfurt 19.34 22.04 01.00

Bomb load 1 x 4000 lb bomb, 1350 x 4, 90 x 4, 32 x 30 incendiaries. Primary target: Frankfurt. There was some low cloud with much haze. Bombed at 22.04 hours from 19,000 feet. A large explosion was seen at 22.02 hours. Not many other results. Route OK.

F/S. M.J. Bulled was A/Bomber that day.

22/03/1944 LL683 JI-P Bombing Frankfurt   18.46 22.02 01.12

Bomb load 1 x 1000 lb bomb, 64 x 30, 1161 x 4, 129 x 4 incendiaries. Primary target: Frankfurt. There was thin cloud, well broken. Bombed at 22.02 hours from 20,000 ft. Many fires widespread over target area. Good prang. Fires seen 80 miles from target. A few undershoots.

30/03/1944 LL683 JI-P Bombing Nuremburg 22.30 01.26 07.25

Bomb load 1 x 1000 lb bomb, 96 x 30, 810 x 4, 90 x 4 incendiaries. Primary target: Nuremberg. There was 9/10 cloud with tops 22,000 feet, with gaps. Bombed at 01.26 hours from 20,000 feet. Many incendiaries scattered. Attack very widespread. P.F.F. not considered good.

On return the crew diverted from Waterbeach to Stradishall but this airfield was also fog-bound and despite several attempts could not land there. Again the crew diverted and almost ran out of fuel, the fog cleared and the pilot promptly force landed his aircraft down in a field near RAF Sawbridgeworth, Hertfordshire.

Three of the crew had baled out, two were not seriously hurt, but the rear gunner Sgt. John Tanney broke his back on landing and did not fly again.

Contrary to ORBs, Boanson's logbook confirmed that he didn't fly in this mission which was also confirmed by J.O. Tanney on 9th March 2009. Consequently, the Mid Upper Gunner for this day is unknown.

18/04/1944 DS682 JI-N Bombing Rouen   22.46 00.49 02.54

Bomb load 8 x 1000 MC, 2 x 1000 GP, 5 x 500 bombs. Primary target: Rouen. There was 3/10 cloud. Bombed at 00.49 hours from 13,500 feet. Fires from previous attack seen. M of C was helpful and directed bombing 400 yards south of cluster at red and green T.I.s.

F/S. H.J. Dahle was R/Gunner that day.

20/04/1944 DS786 A2-F   Bombing Cologne 00.21 02.14 04.40

Bomb load 1 x 8000 lb bomb, 24 x 30, 216 x 4, 24 x 4 lb incendiaries. Primary target: Koln. There was 10/10 cloud. Bombed at 02.14 hours from 19,000 feet. Cloud only seen except glow of fires below cloud.

F/S. Robert Calder Guy was R/Gunner from that day.

22/04/1944 LL624 JI-P Bombing Dusseldorf 22.42 01.21 02.51

Bomb load 1 x 1000 lb bomb, 26 x 30, 1140 x 4 incendiaries. Primary target: Dusseldorf. There was slight haze. Bombed at 01.21

hours from 16,000 feet. Good fires were seen lighting up river. Starboard outer prop cowling u/s, both wings holed. Just before bombing aircraft damaged by falling bombs. Managed to get our run up and bombed as briefed. Fires had a good hold and were concentrated round the markers.

24/04/1944 DS822 JI-T Bombing Karlsruhe 22.27 00.55 05.00

Bomb load 1 x 1000 lb bomb, 1026 x 4, 114 x 30, 108 x 30 lb incendiaries. Primary target: Karlsruhe. There was 10/10 cloud over 17,000 feet, clear below. Bombed at 00.55 hours from 15,000 feet. 1 x 1,000 hung up. T.I.s concentrated. Fires seen in target area. Very successful attack. Route good. Flaps would not come down - caused Lancaster to land away from base, at Woodbridge.

27/04/1944 LL620 JI-N Bombing Friedrichshafen 22.09 02.07 05.25

Bomb load 1 x 4000, 2 x 1000, 1 x 500 lb bombs. Primary target: Friedrichshafen. Weather was hazy. Bombed at 02.07 hours from 20,000 feet. Visual of lake by light of flares. Markers were on the aiming point. Some incendiaries were seen to fall short. Large red explosion at 02.09 hours.

30/04/1944 DS816 JI-O Catamount x   23.10 x   x

Only quoted in ORB summary. Sortie not detailed. J.G.S. Boanson and R.C. Guy noted in their logbooks "Special exercise (CATAMOUNT)".

01/05/1944 LL620 JI-N Bombing Chambly   22.45 00.29 02.26

Bomb load 10 x 1000, 5 x 500 lb bombs. Primary target: Chambly. Weather was clear. Bombed at 00.29 hours from 7,500 feet. Good fires and smoke seen in target area. Very good effort. Route OK.

09/05/1944 LL739 JI-M Bombing Cap Gris Nez   03.10 04.06
05.10

Bomb load 1 x 1000 GP, 13 x 1000 MC. Primary target: Cape Gris Nez, Gun emplacement. Slight haze persisted but visuals obtained of target and markers. Bombed visually at 04.06 hours from 7,000 feet. Three green T.I.s seen 450 yards inland and these were ignored on instructions of Master Bomber. Bomb burst were observed. Believed successful attack.

15/05/1944 DS816 JI-O Catamount Rushford Range 23.00 x   x

Only quoted in ORB summary. Op not detailed. J.G.S. Boanson and R.C. Guy noted in their logbooks "Special exercise (CATAMOUNT)".

21/05/1944 LL620 JI-N Bombing Duisburg   22.55 01.22 03.20

Bomb load 1 x 8000 lb bomb, 96 x 30 incendiaries. Primary target: Duisberg. There was 10/10 cloud at target, tops 19,000 feet. Bombed markers at 01.22 hours from 19,000 feet. Markers quickly disappeared into the cloud and consequently attack was very scattered.

22/05/1944 LL620 JI-N Bombing Dortmund 22.55 00.50 02.45

Bomb load 1 x 8000 lb bomb, 48 x 30, 540 x 4, 60 x 4 incendiaries. Primary target: Dortmund. Weather was clear over target. Bombed markers at 00.50 hours from 19,000 feet. Appeared to be a good attack. Visual of built up area obtained with T.I.s well scattered and bombs falling amidst T.I.s. Had three sightings of unidentified enemy aircraft near target at 00.45 hours, 00.48 hours and 00.52 hours.

02/06/1944 LL635 JI-M Bombing Wissant 01.25 x 03.35

Bomb load 1 x 1000 GP, 10 x 1000 MC, 4 x 500 MC. Primary target: Wissant Gun Positions. Target not identified. Red T.I.s were dropped on approach but were extinguished before aircraft arrived. 3 x 1000 and 4 x 500 MCs jettisoned safe at 5221N 0214E. Remainder of bomb load brought back. Unable to bomb owing to cloud.

05/06/1944 LL620 JI-N Bombing Ouistreham 03.45 05.09 06.45

Bomb load 9 x 1000 MC and 2 x 500 MC. Primary target: Ouistreham. There was 2/10 broken cloud below but 10/10 above. Bombed at 05.09 hours from 9,000 feet. Good visual of target obtained. T.I. reds appeared to be 100 yards east of the aiming point but greens were well placed.

07/06/1944 DS822 JI-T Bombing Massy Palaiseau 00.37 x 02.40

The aircraft was loaded with 18 x 500 MC bombs, 9000 rounds of ammunition and 1450 gallons of fuel (enough for six and a half hours flying) and was detailed to attack Massy Palaiseau Marshalling Yards. The mission length was expected to be about 3 hours 15 minutes later but nothing further was heard from the aircraft and its crew and Lancaster DS822 were reported as missing.

They were one of a force of 337 aircraft sent to attack railway targets at Acheres, Juvisy, Versailles, and Massy-Palaiseau. The force comprised of 195 Halifax aircraft, 122 Lancasters and 20 Mosquitoes. 67 Lancasters (Main Force) and 3 Lancasters and 5 Mosquitoes (Pathfinder element) were allocated to the target at Massy-Palaiseau. All the targets were accurately bombed but, because the targets were further from the fighting in Normandy than those attacked in previous raids in support of the invasion forces, the German night fighters had more opportunity to attack the bombers. From the aircraft sent out to attack the targets, losses totalled 11 Halifaxes and 17 Lancasters including Lancaster DS822.

According to captured German documents DS822 had been shot

down by a night fighter and crashed at 02.40 hours on 8th June 1944 at La Celle-les-Bordes.

P/O. W.L. McGown evaded; Sgt. J. Clarke first evaded then became a POW; P/O. L.W.C. Lewis first evaded then became a POW; P/O. A.N. Durham evaded; P/O. K.E. Bryan KIA; F/S. J.G.S. Boanson KIA; F/S. R.C. Guy KIA.

F/O. Lamont Weir McLean

NZ422420 F/O. Lamont Weir McLean, RNZAF. Pilot.
NZ428982 F/S. William Simpson McIlRaith, RNZAF. A/Bomber.
NZ425298 F/S. Arthur Thompson Stone, RNZAF. Navigator.
NZ427967 F/S. Thomas Kerr Durie, RNZAF. WOP/AG.
910935 Sgt. Ronald Ernest Digby. MU/Gunner.
1826247 Sgt. Malcom Duncan. R/Gunner.
1852441 Sgt. George William "Bummy" Bumstead. F/Engineer.

20/07/1944 LM181 JI-E Bombing Homberg 23.08 x 01.22
Bomb load 1 x 4000 HC, 2 x 500 MC, 16 x 500 GP. Primary target: Homberg, Oil plant. Aircraft missing.
Probably shot down by Fw. Klaus Moller, 12./NJG3, or Ofw. Heinrich Schmidt, 2./NJG6. LM181 crashed 01.22 hours on 21st July 1944 in the target area possibly at Neukirchen where the crew were

F/O. Lamount Weir McLean's crew.

2nd from left L.W. McLean, far right M. Duncan, other positions unknown. (courtesy Tom Duncan)

initially buried. All crew KIA and now buried in the Reichswald Forest War Cemetery.

F/O. William Eugene McLean

J35287   F/O. William Eugene McLean, RCAF. Pilot.
  Sgt. S.W. Moore.   A/Bomber.
1583975 F/S. Norman William Nightingale. Navigator.
2204969 Sgt. Arthur Trevor Blackshaw. WOP/AG.
  Sgt. G.H. Berridge.   MU/Gunner.
1596012 Sgt. William Harvey.   R/Gunner.
1851647 Sgt. Frederick George Maunder. F/Engineer.

A.T. Blackshaw *(right)*
&
W.E. McLean *(left)*

13/01/1945 PB906 A2-D Bombing Saarbrucken 11.56 15.23 17.37
Bomb load 1 x 4000 HC, 10 x 500 ANM58 or 64, 4 x 250 GP.
Primary target: Saarbrucken. Weather 3-5/10ths cloud, tops 4/5,000

feet. Bombed at 15.23 hours from 19,500 feet on leading G.H. aircraft.

All aircraft on this operation were diverted on return to Exeter as the weather at base was unfit to land.

From his normal crew, only F/O. W.E. McLean did this mission as 2nd Pilot with F/O. G.D. Orr's crew.

22/01/1945 PD389 A2-J Bombing Hamborn 17.03 20.06 21.45

Bomb load 1 x 4000 HC, 7 x 500 ANM58 or 64, 2 x 500 GP (L/Delay), 3 x 250 GP. Primary target: Hamborn, Thyssen works. Weather over target clear and almost as bright as day. Bombed at 20.06 hours from 20,000 feet on centre of Green T.I.s.

According C.I.H. Nicholl's logbook target "Duisburg". Hamborn is a suburb of Duisburg.

From his normal crew, only F/O. W.E. McLean did this mission as 2nd Pilot with F/O. C.I.H. Nicholl's crew.

28/01/1945 PB423 A2-L Bombing Cologne-Gremberg 10.41 14.11 16.04

Bomb load 1 x 4000 HC, 10 x 500 ANM64, 2 x 500 GP, 3 x 250 GP. Primary target: Koln-Gremberg, Marshalling yards. Weather 10/10ths cloud en route clearing on approach to target where visibility was good and nil cloud. Bombed at 14.11 hours from 18,600 feet - visually.

From his normal crew, only F/O. W.E. McLean did this mission as 2nd Pilot with F/L. H.C. Mottershead's crew.

29/01/1945 NG142 JI-J Bombing Krefeld 10.22 14.00 15.38

Bomb load 1 x 4000 HC, 10 x 500 ANM64, 2 x 500 GP, 4 x 250 GP. Primary target: Krefeld Marshalling Yards. Weather 10/10ths low thin cloud over target although clear patches en-route. Bombed at 14.00 hours from 20,000 feet on G.H. Leader.

01/02/1945 LM627 A2-H Bombing Munchen-Gladbach 13.15 16.35 18.30

Bomb load 1 x 4000 HC, 14 x No. 14 Clusters. Primary target: Munchen-Gladbach, Marshalling yards. Bombed at 16.35 hours from 18,500 feet on leading aircraft.

02/02/1945 NN772 A2-C Bombing Wiesbaden 20.50 x x

Bomb load 1 x 4000 HC, 10 x 500 ANM64, 2 x 500 GP, 4 x 250 GP. Primary target: Wiesbaden. Weather 10/10ths cloud, winds very erratic. The aircraft was hit by flak, just after releasing its bomb load and came down at Springen, 6km W of Bad Schwalbach.

Those killed were initially buried at Springen. They have been subsequently re-interred in the Durnbach War Cemetery. The village of Springen is located about 19 km NW from the centre of Wiesbaden.

A detailed account of the last minutes of this aircraft was recorded by Squadron Commander, W/C P.L.B. Morgan as follows:

"On the night of the 2nd/3rd February 1945, the above named officer was detailed as pilot and captain of a four engined heavy bomber to attack Wiesbaden.

The target was a heavily defended one, and just after the bombs had been released there was a loud explosion in the aircraft. Flying Officer McLean was then heard to ask the Flight Engineer if the starboard inner engine had been hit. He got no reply but almost immediately he himself confirmed that it was the starboard inner engine and that it was now out of action. At this moment the Mid-Upper Gunner saw that the starboard inner engine was on fire. The Air Bomber, who was down in the bomb aimer's position when the explosion occurred, then came up to see if he could give any assistance. At this moment, a large piece of white-hot metal came into the aircraft and lodged between the pilot's feet just aft of the rudder bar. The Air Bomber attempted to remove this with the aid of a flying jacket, but was unable to do so. Seeing this, Flying Officer McLean ordered the crew to carry out the emergency procedure for abandoning the aircraft.

Flying Officer McLean continued to control the aircraft in spite of the white hot metal, which by now was quickly setting fire to everything in its vicinity, including Flying Officer McLean's boots and clothing. Just prior to leaving his turret, the Mid-Upper Gunner saw that the whole of the front part of the aircraft was on fire but the aircraft was still being kept steady which enabled him to reach the emergency exit and abandon the aircraft.

The Air Bomber, on his way to the emergency exit, noticed the Flight Engineer lying on the floor, apparently wounded or killed, so he called for a parachute pack, which he fastened to the Flight Engineer's harness. The pilot then told them to get out quickly. The Air Bomber then noticed that Flying Officer McLean was enveloped from head to foot in flames and that the whole cockpit was on fire. He then received a blow to the stomach and fell out of the aircraft.

The Air Bomber and the Mid-Upper Gunner were the only two survivors of the crew but they undoubtedly owe their lives to the outstanding bravery of the captain, Flying Officer McLean, who remained at the controls in order to steady the aircraft sufficiently to let his crew abandon it, completely disregarding his own safety and enduring what must have been extreme agony. Had he chosen, Flying Officer McLean was in a position to save himself but, crippled as the aircraft was, it is unlikely that any other members of the crew would have survived.

By his action, Flying Officer McLean set the highest example for outstanding bravery and courage, sacrificing his own life in attempting to save the lives of his crew and comrades.

It is very strongly recommended that this outstanding example of heroism be recognized by the posthumous award of the Victoria Cross to Flying Officer W.E. McLean."

F/O. McLean RCAF received a Mentioned in Despatches. Sgt. A.T. Blackshaw was captured upon landing by parachute and executed on 3rd February 1945. The perpetrator, SS Corporal Heinrich Franke, was later convicted and hanged (Heinrich Franke, b. 19 May 1899, d. 29 Oct 1948).

Sgt. S.W. Moore POW. Sgt. G.H. Berridge was confined to Hospital NK until Liberation. No POW No.

F/S.   Charles James Medland, DFM

1337754 F/S. Charles James "Charlie" Medland, DFM. Pilot.
1430699 F/S. Leonard J. "Len" Venus.   A/Bomber.
151314/141314 (1210258)
   F/O. Dennis Frank "Johnny" Walker. Navigator.
1321645 Sgt. Leslie "Les" Shimmons.   WOP/AG.
J89473 (R203266)
   P/O. Charles Edward "Chuck" Rose, RCAF. MU/Gunner.
1836434 Sgt. Benjamin Robert "Ben" Williams. R/Gunner.
1818874 Sgt. Anthony Ralph "Tony" Sealtiel.   F/Engineer.

07/03/1944 LL625 JI-C Bombing Le Mans   19.40 x 23.57
   Bomb load 1 x 1000, 4 x 500 lb bomb. No attack. Target not accurately identified. 3 x 500 lb bomb jettisoned. 10 x 1000, 1 x 500 lb bombs brought back. Made two orbits round target 21.39 to 21.55 hours up to 9,000 feet. Glow of red T.I.s seen through cloud from 7,500 feet, tops of cloud 6,000 feet. Red glow covered wide area, bomb flashes seen, appeared scattered.

   From his normal crew, only F/S. C.J. Medland did this mission as 2nd Pilot with F/O. J.R. Laing's crew.

24/03/1944 LL733 JI-G Bombing Berlin   18.26 22.46 01.54
   Bomb load 1 x 8000 lb bomb. Primary target: Berlin. There was

7/10 cloud, tops 6,000 feet. Bombed at 22.46 hours from 20,000 feet. Not a great deal seen in area and fires seemed wide spread. Monica u/s. Zero change not heard.

From his normal crew, only F/S. Sgt. C.J. Medland did this mission as 2nd Pilot with F/L. R.C. Chopping's crew.

17/03/1944 LL669 JI-K Air test Woodbridge x x x

Weather: Foggy, clearing towards noon. Non-Operational Flying: In the afternoon Air Tests and Cross Countries were carried out, and a number of Flapless Landing Practices at Woodbridge, on which 1 Aircraft crashed but without casualties.

Note: In fact, it appears that two aircraft crashed. DS820, JI-R, flown by F/S. Shearing, crash-landed at Martlesham Heath and LL669, JI-K, flown by F/S. C.J. Medland, crash-landed at Leiston.

26/03/1944 DS669 JI-C Bombing Essen 20.07 22.11 01.01

Bomb load 1 x 2000 lb bomb, 56 x 30, 1080 x 4, 120 x 4 incendiaries. Primary target: Essen. There was 10/10 cloud. Bombed at 22.11 hours from 20,000 feet. Red glow of fires seen. Flak very slight. Large fires appeared to be under the cloud as we left target.

30/03/1944 LL733 JI-G Bombing Nuremburg 22.28 01.17 06.30

Bomb load 1 x 1000 lb bomb, 96 x 30, 810 x 4, 90 x 4 incendiaries. Primary target: Nuremburg. There was 8/10 cloud. Bombed at 01.17 hours from 21,000 feet. Visual of built up area seen by photo flash, only a few fires seen. Low cloud and snow caused diversion. Landed at Woodbridge. After leaving the glow of many fires could be seen.

10/04/1944 LL695 JI-A Bombing Laon 01.28 03.50 05.39

Bomb load 9 x 1000, 4 x 500 lb bomb. Primary target: Laon. There was 3/10 cloud with full moon. Bombed at 03.50 hours from 10,500 feet. Well concentrated attack and T.I.s right on target. LL695 JI-A for "Able".

26/04/1944 LL695 JI-A Bombing Essen 23.05 x 02.15

Bomb load 1 x 2000 lb bomb, 84 x 30, 945 x 4, 105 x 4 lb incendiaries. Returned early. Farthest point reached 5355N 0535E. Total load jettisoned. Failure of Inter-comm.

27/04/1944 LL695 JI-A Bombing Friedrichshafen 22.05 02.08 05.43

Bomb load 1 x 4000 lb bomb, 32 x 30, 32 x 4, 36 x 4 incendiaries. Primary target: Friedrichshafen. Weather was clear with much smoke. Bombed at 02.08 hours from 19,800 feet. Many fires seen coinciding with T.I.s and incendiaries fires. A successful attack. Route O.K.

01/05/1944 LL695 JI-A Bombing Chambly 22.52 00.23 02.00

Bomb load 10 x 1000, 5 x 500 lb bombs. Primary target: Chambly.

Weather was clear. Bombed at 00.23 hours from 7,000 feet. Bombs seen bursting among sheds. The attack was good.

After leaving target an attack by a JU88 blew the starboard inner engine clean out. Rear and Mid Upper Gunners fired bursts claiming strikes. Lancaster corkscrewed and evaded successfully. Enemy aircraft claimed as damaged. Excessive vibration necessitated the port outer engine to be feathered and immediately afterwards at 00.34 hours an enemy aircraft attacked from port bow at 1500 yards, tracer passing below. Both gunners fired, no claim. Lancaster corkscrewed and evaded.

At 00.43 hours enemy aircraft approached on port beam at 700 yards, tracer passing above, again the Rear and Mid Upper Gunners fired (manually, as turrets were both u/s). Lancaster corkscrewed and evaded.

The last attack at 00.48 hours was from astern, tracer passing near. Lancaster continued to corkscrew and both gunners fired (manually), evaded successfully. The speed during the last three attacks was 143 I.A.S. After the first attack Lancaster went into a steep dive the preliminary warning to bale out was given, but we managed to pull out just below 6,000 feet and made for home. Landed at Woodbridge successfully.

08/05/1944 LL697 JI-E Bombing Cap Gris Nez   22.53   23.52   00.38

Bomb load 14 x 1000 lb bombs. Primary target: Cape Gris Nez. Weather was clear, good visibility. Bombed at 23.52 hours from 9,000 feet. There were numerous bomb bursts over the target. 3 bombs from another Lancaster seen to fall in sea, own bursts obscured by smoke. Bombing seemed accurate. Markers not seen until 23.57 hours. Large explosion seen 23.54 hours.

09/05/1944 LL666 JI-D Bombing Cap Gris Nez   03.00   04.08   04.50

Bomb load 1 x 1000 GP, 13 x 1000 MC. Primary target: Cape Gris Nez. Slight haze over target, but target and T.I.s were seen. Red and yellow T.I.s were bombed as instructed by Master Bomber at 04.08 hours from 8,000 feet. The coast was seen clearly but other detail obscured by glow of flares and by dust. Attack believed successful.

21/05/1944 LL695 JI-A Bombing Duisburg   22.42 x 01.38

Bomb load 1 x 2000 bomb, 120 x 30 incendiaries, 600 x 4 incendiaries. Aircraft missing.

Shot down by a night-fighter (Hptm Martin Drewes, III./NJG1) and crashed 01.38 22nd May 1944 at Geldrop (Noord-Brabant), 6 km ESE from the centre of Eindhoven, where those who were killed were buried on the 26th May 1944 in Woensel General Cemetery. The body of Sgt. Rose has since been taken to the Canadian War Cemetery at Groesbeek.

F/S. C.J. Medland DFM Injured POW, Sgt. A.E. Sealtiel KIA, F/O. D. Walker Evaded, F/S. L.J. Venus POW, Sgt. L. Shimmons Evaded, Sgt. C.E. Rose RCAF KIA, Sgt. B.R. Williams KIA.

F/S. C.J. Medland was confined to hospital due to injuries. No POW No. F/S. L.J. Venus initially evaded until captured on 13th July 1944 and interned in Camp L7, POW No.417.

P/O. acting F/O. Hubert Leon Merrett, DFC

182447 (1435615) F/O.Hubert Leon Merrett, DFC. Pilot.
 F/S. W.E. Williams. A/Bomber.
190511 (1549561) P/O.John Alfred Peduzie, DFM. Navigator.
 F/S. S. Blackett. WOP/AG.
 Sgt.F.D. Harding. MU/Gunner.
R172904 F/S. R.A. McNabb, RCAF. R/Gunner. 33 ops.
196933 (1333763) W/O. Harold George Everest Friend. R/Gunner. 1 op.
 Sgt.Sidney A. Brown. F/Engineer.
J16010 F/L. Ernest Brazier Cozens, DFC, RCAF. 2nd Pilot.
30/11/1944

03/08/1944 LL666 JI-Q Bombing Bois de Cassan 11.51 14.07 15.40
 Bomb load 11 x 1000 MC, 4 x 500 GP. Primary target: Bois de Cassan, Flying bomb supply depot. Bombed at 14.07 hours from 15,500 feet centre of smoke.
04/08/1944 HK577 JI-P Bombing Bec d'Ambes 13.27 18.01 21.24
 Bomb load 7 x 1000 MC, 4 x 500 GP. Primary target: Bec d'Ambes depot. Weather clear. Bombed at 18.01 hours from 8,500 feet oil storage tanks. A very successful attack. Target well ablaze.
07/08/1944 LL731 JI-U Bombing Mare de Magne 21.49 23.47 01.01
 Bomb load 9 x 1000 MC, 4 x 500 GP. Primary target: Mare de Magne (just past Caen). Weather clear. Bombed at 23.47 hours from 7,500 feet red T.I.s. Much smoke around T.I.s.
 Mare-de-Magne: A place between Caen and Fontenay le Marmion.
14/08/1944 LL635 JI-M Bombing Hamel (Falaise) 13.54 15.15 17.21
 Bomb load 11 x 1000 MC, 4 x 500 GP. Primary target: Hamel.

Sidney A. Brown. (courtesy Tracy Clarke)

Weather clear. Bombed at 15.15 hours from 8,500 feet centre of red T.I.s. Pall of smoke developed over target area. Bombing concentrated. Bombing of troop concentrations. According to logbooks: G.A. Wark, pilot, target: "Falaise", T.C. Clayton: (Wark crew) target 'Hamel'. Testimony of Corbett Stewart: (Heald crew) target 'Falaise'. There are several places named "Le Hamel" near Falaise. **18/08/1944** PB423 JI-S Bombing Bremen 21.37 00.15 02.54 Bomb load 1 x 4000 HC, 96 x 30 lb inc, 1080 x 4lb inc, 120 x 4lb x inc. Primary target: Bremen. Weather clear. Bombed at 00.15 hours from 18,500 feet, green T.I.s. Explosion in target at 00.14 hours.

25/08/1944 LM685   JI-Q Bombing Russelsheim 20.31   01.08   04.30
    Bomb load 1 x 4000 HC, 11 x 500 lb Clusters. Primary target: Russelheim. Weather clear. Bombed at 01.08 hours from 18,000 feet. Very concentrated attack. Plenty of fires seen.
26/08/1944 LM685   JI-Q Bombing Kiel   20.12   23.20   02.02
    Bomb load 1 x 4000 HC, 96 x 30 IB, 900 x 4 IB. Primary target: Kiel. Weather clear, slight haze. Bombed at 23.20 hours from 19,500 feet, red T.I.s. Large area of fire. Explosion area 23.18 hours. Very concentrated attack.
03/09/1944 LM685   JI-Q Bombing Eindhoven 15.16   17.34   18.56
    Bomb load 11 x 1000 MC, 4 x 500 GP. Primary target: Eindhoven airfield. Bombed at 17.34 hours from 16,500 feet, red T.I.s.
23/09/1944 LM685   JI-Q Bombing Neuss 19.24 21.26   23.16
    Bomb load 11 x 1000 ANM44, 4 x 500 GP. Primary target: Neuss. Weather 10/10ths cloud over target, tops 8/10,000 feet. Bombed at 21.26 hours from 20,000 feet on centre of dull red glow.
26/09/1944 LM685   JI-Q Bombing Calais 11.29 12.45   13.55
    Bomb load 11 x 1000 MC, 4 x 500 GP. Primary target: Calais 7D.

Weather clear below cloud which was 3,500 feet. Bombed at 12.45 hours from 3,000 feet on red T.I. + 1 second.

27/09/1944 LM685 JI-Q Bombing Calais 07.30 08.42 09.55
Bomb load 11 x 1000 MC, 4 x 500 GP. Primary target: Calais 15. Weather, cloud 5,500 feet 10/10ths. Bombed at 08.42 hours from 5,400 feet 100 yards to port of red T.I.

28/09/1944 LM685 JI-Q Bombing Calais 08.01 09.20 10.37
Bomb load 11 x 1000 MC, 4 x 500 GP. Primary target: Calais 19. Bombed at 09.20 hours from 9,200 feet red T.I.

03/10/1944 LM685 JI-Q Bombing Westkapelle 12.03 13.20 14.18
Bomb load 1 x 4000 MC, 6 x 1000 MC, 1 x 500 GP. L/Delay. Primary target: Westkapelle (Walcheren). Weather patchy-scattered cloud with base 5,000 feet. Bombed at 13.20 hours from 4,700 feet on red T.I.

06/10/1944 LM685 JI-Q Bombing Dortmund 16.50 20.29 22.26
Bomb load 1 x 4000 HC, 12 x No. 14 Clusters. Primary target: Dortmund, Town and Railways. Weather over the target was clear with slight ground haze. Bombed at 20.29 hours from 20,750 feet on centre of green T.I.s.

07/10/1944 NF968 JI-L Bombing Emmerich 12.15 14.28 15.53
Bomb load 1 x 4000 HC, 10 x No.14 clusters, 4 x (150 x 4). Primary target Emmerich. Weather clear with cloud at 13,000 feet. Bombed at 14.28 hours from 13,000 feet on South-west part of town as instructed by Master Bomber.

14/10/1944 LM685 JI-Q Bombing Duisburg 07.20 09.02 10.51
Bomb load 11 x 1000 MC, 4 x 500 GP Long Delay. Primary target: Duisburg. Weather patchy cloud with gaps for bombing. Bombed at 09.02 hours from 20,000 feet. Docks and River.

15/10/1944 LM685 JI-Q Bombing Wilhelmshaven 17.17 19.49 21.42
Bomb load 11 x 1000 MC, 4 x 500 GP. Primary target: Wilhelmshaven. Weather haze and thin cloud at first with thick cloud later. Bombed at 19.49 hours from 21,000 feet. Green T.I.s.

18/10/1944 PB426 JI-J Bombing Bonn 08.23 11.00 13.01
Bomb load 1 x 4000 HC, 5 x 12 x 30 - 2 x 12 x 30 modified, 9 x No.14 Clusters. Primary target: Bonn. Weather varying cloud 2-7/10ths with break for bombing. Bombed at 11.00 hours from 19,000 feet. Built up area slightly East of A/P.

21/10/1944 LM685 JI-Q Bombing Flushing 11.01 12.27 13.24
Bomb load 12 x 1000 MC, 2 x 500 GP. Primary target: Flushing 'B'.

451

Weather clear. Bombed at 12.27 hours from 9,000 feet. Visual.

22/10/1944 LM717   JI-T Bombing Neuss   13.14 16.04   17.32

Bomb load 1 x 4000 HC, 6 x 1000 MC, 6 x 500 GP. Primary target: Neuss. Weather 10/10ths cloud over target. Bombed at 16.04 hours from 18,000 feet. Bombed behind formation of 4 aircraft ahead. 1 x 1000 MC jettisoned at 5205N 0205E at 17.05 hours from 1,700 feet.

23/10/1944 LM685   JI-Q Bombing Essen   16.25 19.33   21.24

Bomb load 1 x 4000 HC, 2 x 1000 MC, 10 x 500 GP, 3 x 500 MC. Primary target: Essen. Weather 10/10ths cloud over target - tops 12/14,000 feet with most appalling weather on route. Bombed at 19.33 hours from 22,000 feet. Green flares.

26/10/1944 LM685   JI-Q Bombing Leverkusen   12.59 15.27   17.08

Bomb load 1 x 4000 HC, 6 x 1000 MC, 4 x 500 GP, 2 x 500 GP Long Delay. Primary target: Leverkusen. Weather over target and on route was 10/10ths cloud. Bombed at 15.27 hours from 18,000 feet on G.H.

04/11/1944 PB423 A2-G   Bombing Solingen   11.26 14.11   16.12

Bomb load 1 x 4000 HC, 6 x 1000 ANM59, 4 x 500 GP, 2 x 500 MC (L/Delay), 3 Flares. Primary target: Solingen. Weather 8-10/10ths cloud. Bombed at 14.11 hours from 20,000 feet on G.H.

05/11/1944 LM685   JI-Q Bombing Solingen   10.24   13.05   15.09

Bomb load 1 x 4000 HC, 6 x 1000 ANM59, 4 x 500 GP, 2 x 500 GP (L/Delay), 3 Flares. Primary target: Solingen. Weather 10/10ths cloud over target. Bombed at 13.05 hours from 14,800 feet. Red flares with Green stars.

08/11/1944 LM685   JI-Q Bombing Homberg   08.06 10.27 12.52

Bomb load 1 x 4000 HC, 6 x 1000 GP, 6 x 500 GP. Primary target: Homberg. Weather clear. Bombed at 10.27 hours from 18,000 feet on instruments. Aircraft hit by flak, 3 engines damaged. Aircraft returned on 2 engines.

11/11/1944 LM717   JI-T Bombing Castrop Rauxel 08.13   11.07 13.08

Bomb load 1 x 4000 HC, 15 x 500 GP, 1 Flare. Primary target: Castrop Rauxel, Oil refineries. Weather 10/10ths cloud. Bombed at 11.07 hours from 23,000 feet on G.H.

15/11/1944 LM734   JI-U Bombing Dortmund   12.48   15.40   17.32

Bomb load 1 x 4000 HC, 16 x 500 GP. Primary target: Hoesch-Benzin Dortmund, Oil refineries. Weather 10/10ths cloud over the target. Bombed at 15.40 hours from 18,000 feet on flares.

20/11/1944 PD389 JI-Q Bombing Homberg   12.48   15.18   17.23

Bomb load 1 x 4000 HC, 15 x 500 GP, 1 Red-Green Flare. Primary target: Homberg. Weather 10/10ths cloud over target. Bombed at 15.18 hours from 20,000 feet on G.H.

21/11/1944 PD389 JI-Q Bombing Homberg   12.40   15.08   16.30
Bomb load 1 x 4000 HC, 15 x 500 GP, 1 Red-Green Flare. Primary target: Homberg. Weather about 5/10ths cloud but clear for bombing. Bombed at 15.08 hours from 20,000 feet on G.H.

29/11/1944 PD389 JI-Q Bombing Neuss   03.00 05.33   07.06
Bomb load 1 x 4000 HC, 6 x 1000 MC, 6 x 500 GP, 3 Flares Red with Green stars. Primary target: Neuss. Weather 10/10ths cloud over target but the glow of fires was seen through cloud. Bombed at 05.33 hours from 20,000 feet. Centre of sky markers. Attack believed scattered.

W/O. H.G.E. Friend R/Gunner that day.

30/11/1944 PD389 JI-Q Bombing Osterfeld   10.55   13.09   14.36
Bomb load 1 x 4000 HC, 15 x 500 GP, 1 Red/Green flare. Primary target: Osterfeld, Coking plant. Weather 10/10ths cloud. Bombed at 13.09 hours from 20,000 feet on G.H.

F/L. E.B. Cozens 2nd Pilot that day.

02/12/1944 PB419 JI-N Bombing Dortmund   13.05   14.58   17.08
Bomb load 13 x 1000 HC, 1 Red/Green flare. Primary target: Dortmund, Benzol plant. Weather 10/10ths cloud. Bombed at 14.58 hours from 20,000 feet on G.H.

04/12/1944 PD389 JI-Q Bombing Oberhausen   12.00 14.06   15.55
Bomb load 1 x 4000 HC, 15 x 500 GP, 1 Flare. Primary target: Oberhausen, Built up area. Weather 10/10ths cloud. Bombed at 14.06 hours from 20,200 feet on G.H.

05/12/1944 PD389 JI-Q Bombing Hamm   09.08   11.30   14.08
Bomb load 1 x 4000 HC, 11 x 500 ANM58, 2 x 500 MC, 2 x 500 GP Long Delay, 1 Flare. Primary target: Hamm. Weather 10/10ths cloud over target, but otherwise varying from 6-10/10ths. Bombed at 11.30 hours from 21,500 feet on Red flares.

F/O. Thomas James Middleton

50885 (564052) F/O. Thomas James Middleton. Pilot.
152917 (1672305) F/O. Arnold George Burgess. A/Bomber.
J29575 F/O. Frederick Kenneth Beers, RCAF. Navigator.
970374 F/S. Thomas Derek Jones. WOP/AG.
3030323 Sgt. Alfred Bertram Ernest Booth. MU/Gunner.
1875016 Sgt. Cyril Brown. R/Gunner.
2203120 Sgt. Richard Winson Stafford. F/Engineer.

18/07/1944 LL666 JI-Q Bombing Emieville 04.28 06.08 07.31
Bomb load 11 x 1000 MC, 4 x 500 GP. Primary target: Emieville,
Troop concentration. Weather clear. Bombed at 06.08 hours from
8,000 feet centre of smoke. A good attack.
18/07/1944 LL666 JI-Q Bombing Aulnoye 22.40 00.58 02.30
Bomb load 18 x 500 GP. Primary target: Aulnoye, Railway junction.
Weather clear, slight haze. Bombed at 00.58 hours from 9,000 feet
green T.I.s, concentrated attack.
20/07/1944 LL666 JI-Q Bombing Homberg 23.24 01.20 02.53
Bomb load 1 x 4000 HC, 2 x 500 MC, 14 x 500 GP. Primary target:
Homberg, Oil plant. Weather clear. Bombed at 01.20 hours from
19,000 feet red and green T.I.s. Black smoke in dense cloud over T.I.s.
Lots of fighters.
23/07/1944 LL666 JI-Q Bombing Kiel 22.25 01.28 03.45
Bomb load 10 x 1000 MC, 5 x 500 GP Special Nickels. Primary
target: Kiel, Warehouses and docks. Weather 10/10ths cloud. Bombed
at 01.22 hours from 21,000 feet red T.I. Numerous fires in moderately
large area.
24/07/1944 PB185 A2-F Bombing Stuttgart 21.45 x 02.30
Bomb load 7 x 1000 MC, 4 x 500 GP. Aircraft missing.
Probably shot down 25th July 1944 at 02.33 hours by Hptm. Paul
Zorner of Stab III./NJG5 in the vicinity of Trier, returning from the
target. All crew lost. Despite Sgt. Stafford being identified at the time
he and the rest of the crew are commemorated on the Runnymede
Memorial, for aircrew with no known resting place.
At 37, Sgt. Brown was well above the average age for Bomber
Command aircrew.

F/O. Douglas Millar

53841 (566455) F/O.Douglas Millar.   Pilot.
1542381   Sgt. Harry Matthews Glansford. A/Bomber.
J35242   F/O. David Oscar Brown, RCAF.   Navigator.
1127147   Sgt. George Henry Holt. WOP/AG.
2221318   Sgt. William Edward Blore. MU/Gunner.
3030276   Sgt. Harold Edwin Long. R/Gunner.
1896733   Sgt. Norman Derham.   F/Engineer.

*Top row: D. Millar (left) & D.O. Brown (right). Above:
H.M. Glansford (left) & H.E. Long (right)*

10/07/1944 LM206   JI-C Bombing Nucourt 04.09 06.04 07.59
    Bomb load 11 x 1000 ANM65, 4 x 500 GP. Primary target: Nucourt,
Constructional works. Bombed at 06.04 hours from 15,000 feet on
E.T.A.

12/07/1944 LM206　JI-C Bombing Vaires　17.51 x 22.05

Bomb load 18 x 500 GP. Primary target: Vaires, Marshalling yards. No markers seen therefore sortie abandoned. Bombs brought back to Base.

15/07/1944 ME858　JI-J Bombing Chalons Sur Marne　21.33　01.33 04.01

Bomb load 18 x 500 GP. Primary target: Chalons sur Marne, Railway centre. Weather broken cloud. Bombed at 01.33 hours from 9,000 feet yellow T.I.s. Appeared good attack.

18/07/1944 ME858　JI-J Bombing Emieville　04.08　06.07　07.59

Bomb load 11 x 1000 MC, 4 x 500 GP. Primary target: Emieville, Troop concentration. Weather clear. Bombed at 06.07 hours from 8,000 feet yellow T.I.s.

20/07/1944 ME858　JI-J Bombing Homberg　23.07 x 01.16

Bomb load 1 x 4000 HC, 2 x 500 MC, 16 x 500 GP. Primary target: Homberg, Oil plant. Aircraft missing. All crew KIA.

Shot down at 01.14 by Uffz. Gustav Sarzio, 6./NJG1. Crashed approaching the target 01.16 hours 21st July 1944 approx. 1 km SW of Hunsel (Limburg), a small village close to the Belgian border and 10 km SE of the Dutch town of Weert where all are buried in the Roman Catholic Churchyard.

F/S.　Cecil George Miller

A412451 (O22004)　F/S. Cecil George Miller, DFC, RAAF.　Pilot.
1324718　Sgt. A.W. Clarke.　A/Bomber. 4 ops.
1585341　Sgt. William Alexander Bates.　A/Bomber. 3 ops.
177471 (1559304) Sgt. Raymond Wilcock.　Navigator.
183613 (1330208) Sgt. David Bertram John Hicks.　WOP/AG.
919869　Sgt.　E.G.H. or M.H. or G.H.M. Goodman. MU/Gunner. 5 ops.
F/S. J. Crawford.　MU/Gunner. 1 op.
179393 (1750524) Sgt. Ronald Charles Donaldson Baker. MU & R/Gunner
1399608　F/S. Sydney Loseby　R/Gunner. 1 op.
2202190　Sgt. A.C. or A.E. Edwards.　F/Engineer.

14/01/1944 LL684 A2-B Bombing Brunswick 17.00　19.29　22.22

Bomb load 1 x 4000, 48 x 30 incendiaries. Primary target:

Brunswick. There was 10/10 cloud. Bombed at 19.29 hours at 21,000 ft. Large fires concentrated seen from a distance of 100 miles. Should be a good raid.

Sgt. A.W. Clarke A/Bomber that day.

Sgt. Goodman MU/Gunner until 30/01/44.

20/01/1944 LL684 A2-B   Bombing Berlin   16.22 x 18.21

Bomb load 1 x 4000, 32 x 30, 540 x 4, 60 x 4 incendiaries. Primary target: Berlin. Returned early. Port inner engine u/s. Farthest point reached 53°35N 02°50E. Total load jettisoned.

Cecil George Miller. (AWM UK2169)

Sgt. W.A. Bates A/Bomber until 27/01/44.

21/01/1944 LL684 A2-B   Bombing Magdeburg   20.05   23.03   03.37

Bomb load 1 x 4000, 720 x 4, 90 x 4, 32 x 30 incendiaries. Primary target: Magdeburg. 10/10 cloud over route. Bombed at 23.03 hours at 21,000 ft. Green T.I.s seen with a large number of fires and incendiaries. Target well covered with fires. Monica seemed unreliable. Route good.

27/01/1944 LL684 A2-B   Bombing Berlin 17.48 20.45   01.49

Bomb load 1 x 4000, 7 Cans incendiaries. Primary target: Berlin. There was 10/10 cloud tops 10,000 ft. Bombed at 20.45 at 21,000 ft. Enemy fighters in target area. 1 Cannister incendiaries hung up. Owing to fuel shortage landed at Manston.

30/01/1944 LL684 A2-B   Bombing Berlin   17.15 x 20.48

Bomb load 1 x 2000 lb bomb, 1 x 500 lb bomb, 900 x 4, 48 x 30 incendiaries. Returned early. Farthest point reached 5415N 0601E. Rear and M/U turrets inter-comm u/s. M/U guns u/s 18.55 hours 19000 ft 5403N 0455E on Track. Heavy flak bursting 2,000 yards on starboard quarter slightly above. 12 gun flashes seen, Bomb Aimer aimed bombs at flashes. Bomb observed to explode. Photo attempted. Heading 260 M out line 2 ships near proximity seen.

Sgt. A.W. Clarke A/Bomber from that day.

25/02/1944 LL684 A2-B   Bombing Augsburg 21.59   01.19   05.19

457

Bomb load 1 x 4000 lb bomb, 32 x 30, 510 x4, 90 x 4 incendiaries. Primary target: Augsburg. Weather very clear. Bombed at 01.19 hours at 20,000 ft. Many large fires and columns of smoke seen. Very good attack. Route good.

Sgt. R.C.D. Baker was MU/Gunner that day and F/S. S. Loseby R/Gunner.

01/03/1944 LL684 A2-B Bombing Stuttgart 23.44 03.10 07.39

Bomb load 1 x 2000, 1 x 500 lb bomb, 40 x 30, 900 x 4 incendiaries. Primary target: Stuttgart. There was 10/10 cloud, bright above. Bombed at 03.10 hours at 20,000 ft. Very big fires seen after leaving - not much seen while actually over target. Route good. Attack appeared scattered to the South.

F/S. J. Crawford MU/Gunner that day.

Flight Sergeant Sydney Loseby was later awarded the DFM (Gazetted 12/12/44), while serving with No. 582 Squadron, having completed no less than 49 operational sorties, many of them as part of No. 8 Path Finder Group.

F/S. H.W. Moffatt

NZ4214515 F/S. H.W. Moffatt, RNZAF. Pilot.
NZ42832 F/O. N. Simmons, RNZAF. A/Bomber.
 F/S. L.F. Matsell. Navigator.
NZ4213875 F/S. J. Marriott, RNZAF. WOP/AG.
NZ437262 F/S. C.R. Boss, RNZAF. MU/Gunner.
NZ437294 F/O. W.H. Hawken, RNZAF. R/Gunner.
Sgt. F.W. Harrison. F/Engineer.

01/07/1945 ME336 JI-S Post Mortem Special mission 12.01 x 18.06
Landed on 3 engines.
05/07/1945 ME351 JI-U Post Mortem Special mission 13.20 x 18.21

F/O. Edward Monahan

J41845   F/O. Edward "Eddie" Monahan, RCAF. Pilot.
J41554   F/O. B.W. "Bill" Mosher, RCAF.   A/Bomber.
J39013   F/O. Leonard Stanley Robert "Smitty" Smith, RCAF.
   Navigator.
177174 (1870300) F/O. John Frederick "Johnny" Channell. WOP/AG.
R158869 Sgt. George Edward Gard, RCAF. MU/Gunner.
R269940 Sgt. M. "Mike" Furey, RCAF.   R/Gunner.
   Sgt. Desmond R. Chubbock.   F/Engineer.

Passengers: 07/05/1945

14/03/1945 NF966 A2-G Bombing Heinrichshutte 13.58 x 16.08
   Bomb load 1 x 4000 HC, 12 x 500 ANM64. Primary target:
Heinrichshutte, Hattingen Steel works & Benzol plant. Weather
10/10ths cloud, tops 7/12,000 feet. Farthest point reached 5023N
0008W. Port inner engine unserviceable. Jettisoned 1 x 4000 HC, 12 x
500 ANM64 at 5023N 0008W at 15.07 hours from 5,200 feet.
   From his normal crew, only F/O. E. Monahan did this mission as
2nd Pilot with F/L. R.E. Farvolden's crew.
09/04/1945 PB482 A2-K Bombing Kiel 19.36 22.42 01.31
   Bombed primary target: Kiel. Bomb load 1 x 4000 HC and 12 x 500
ANM64. Bombed centre of Green T.I.s. at 22.42 hours from 20,000
feet. M/B heard. Visual of Canal and harbour. Many fires started. Huge
explosion orange coloured 22.35. Concentration of bombing seemed to
be on the North of marking. Good attack. Fires seen from Sylt
outward.
   From his normal crew, only F/O. E. Monahan did this mission as
2nd Pilot with F/L. B.A. Audis' crew.
18/03/1945 NN717   A2-E Bombing Bruchstrasse 11.42   15.04
   17.11
   Bomb load 1 x 4000 HC, 13 x 500 ANM64, 2 x 500 MC. Primary
target: Bruchstrasse, Coal mine & coking plant. Weather 10/10ths
cloud, tops 6-12,000 feet. Bombed at 15.04 hours from 19,000 feet on
leading aircraft.
   According to G.E. Gard's logbook: "No damage. Flack: light-
moderate".
20/03/1945 LM724   JI-H Bombing Hamm   09.59 13.15 15.52
   Bomb load 7 x 1000 ANM59, 9 x 500 ANM64. Primary target:

Above:L to R (back): Sgt. G. Gard, F/O. S.R. Smith, Sgt. M. Furey. L to R (front): F/O. B.W. Mosher, F/O. E. Monahan, F/O. J.F. Channell. Left:: Sgt. D Chubbock - Cambridge 27/03/1945. (Photos courtesy William Gard)

Hamm, Marshalling yards. Weather 5/10ths cloud. Bombed at 13.15 hours from 18,000 feet on leading G.H. aircraft.

According to G.E. Gard's logbook "No damage. Attack concentrated. Flack - light".

22/04/1945 PB423 A2-C Bombing Bremen 15.04 x 20.49

Bomb load 1 x 4000 HC, 2 x 500 MC, 14 x 500 ANM64. Primary target: Bremen, in support of Troop concentration. Weather on approaching target 4-5/10ths cloud. 1 x 4000 HC jettisoned at 19.55 hrs at 5230N 0328E from 8,000 feet. 2 x 500 MC and 14 x 500 ANM64 brought back to Base. G.H. Leader 514/K2 did not bomb. Too late to pick up another leader so load brought back.

According to G.E. Gard's logbook: "Overshot target brought bombs back dropped 4000 lb in sea. Cloud 7/10. Flack moderate very accurate".

30/04/1945 RE123 A2-K Manna Rotterdam 16.58 18.24 19.43

Dropping area: Rotterdam. Weather intermittent showers and low cloud. Load 5 packs. Dropped 5 packs on white cross at 18.24 hours. Bomb doors holed by ?? units. Deliveries were accurate in spite of poor visibility. Roof tops covered with enthusiastic Dutch reception committee. House on fire.

02/05/1945 RE123 A2-K Manna The Hague 11.07 x 13.34

Dropping area The Hague. Weather over dropping zone clear below cloud for the first arrivals changing later to heavy showers which marred visibility. 5 Panniers brought back. Believed distributor failure.

07/05/1945 RE123 A2-K Manna The Hague 12.14 13.39 14.43

Dropping area The Hague. Dropped 5 packs on smoke from T.I.s visual on White Cross at 13.39 hours. Clear. 10/10 cloud 1000 ft. Good trip all packs dropped on the airfield. Timing of aircraft better than before. Every house had a flag. Germans being taken off Schouen in Barges.

According ORBs, no MU/Gunner that day, confirmed by note in G.E. Gard's logbook "was excused this flight".

Passenger: AC. J. Hayward.

11/05/1945 RE123 A2-K Exodus Juvincourt - Wing 17.20 x 21.43

Duration 3.08. Outward 1.27 hours. No POWs brought back. Homeward 1.41 hours. Aircraft could not take off with POWs on board before 20.00 hours so were ordered to return empty.

13/05/1945 RE117 A2-D Exodus Juvincourt - Tangmere 13.21 x 16.21 Duration 3.05 hours. Message received R.T.B. (Return to Base).

W/C. Philip Lawder Basil Morgan

39555   W/C.   Philip Lawder Basil Morgan. Pilot.
   Sgt. E.J. Slaughter.   A/Bomber. 1 op.
J37188 F/O.   Joseph Edward "Ted" Morrey, RCAF.   A/Bomber. 1 op.
160956 (1333696) F/O. John Barwick Cushing, DFC. A/Bomber. 1 op.
164120 or 172092 F/O. Joseph Burke.   Navigator. 1 op.
   Sgt. L. "Bill" Bailey.   Navigator. 1 op.
161741 (657060) F/O. Alfred Ernest Nye, DFC.   Navigator. 1 op.
   F/O. E.T. Williams.   Navigator. 1 op.
195188 (1673373) P/O. Alan Fairfax.   Navigator. 1 op.
   Sgt Reginald W. "Reg" Spencer. WOP/AG. 1 op.
   Sgt. Roy V. Rudling.   WOP/AG. 1 op.
176988 (1892590) F/O. Norman Sydney Warren. WOP/AG. 1 op.
103538 (902785) F/L. Vivian George Ivor Outen. WOP/AG. 1 op.
177174 (1870300) F/O. John Frederick "Johnny" Channell. WOP/AG.
1 op.
   Sgt. R. Shields.   MU/Gunner. 1 op.
R220987 F/S.   Sydney J. "Syd" South, RCAF.   MU/Gunner. 1 op.
141271 (1386976) F/L. Herbert Henry Wright, DFM. MU/Gunner. 1
op.
   Sgt. G.C. O'Brien.   R/Gunner. 1 op.
R279116 F/S.   L.J. "Joe" Kirwan, RCAF. R/Gunner. 1 op.
   Sgt. D. Vipond.   R/Gunner. 1 op.
179331 (944736) F/O. George Rothwell.   R/Gunner. 1 op.
   F/S. E.A. Cox.   F/Engineer. 1 op.
191847 (962612) P/O. Ralph Swift.   F/Engineer. 3 ops.
   F/L. T. Wake.   F/Engineer. 1 op.

Passengers: 22/06/1945, 05/07/1945, 22/07/1945.

14/02/1945 PB423 A2-L Bombing Chemnitz 20.30   00.37 05.02
   Bomb load 1 x 500 MC, 15 x No. 14 Clusters. Primary target:
Chemnitz. Weather 8-10/10ths cloud, tops 15-16,000 feet with
occasional breaks. Bombed at 00.37 hours from 20,000 feet on centre
of fires.
   Crew that day:
39555 W/C. Philip Lawder Basil Morgan. Pilot.
 Sgt. E.J. Slaughter.   A/Bomber
164120 or 172092 F/O. Joseph Burke.   Navigator.

F/S. E.A. Cox.   F/Engineer.
Sgt. Reginald W. "Reg" Spencer.   WOP/AG.
Sgt. R. Shields.   MU/Gunner.
Sgt. G.C. O'Brien.   R/Gunner.

06/03/1945 ME422   JI-Q Bombing Salzbergen 08.20 12.14 14.07
Bomb load 1 x 4000 HC, 12 x 500 ANM64, 2x 500MC. Primary target: Salzbergen, Wintershall oil plant. Weather 10/10ths cloud over target, tops 10,000 feet. Bombed at 12.14 hours from 21,000 feet on G.H.
Crew that day:
39555   W/C. Philip Lawder Basil Morgan. Pilot.
J37188   F/O. Joseph Edward "Ted" Morrey, RCAF. A/Bomber.
Sgt. L. "Bill" Bailey.   Navigator.
Sgt. Roy V. Rudling.   WOP/AG.
R220987 F/S.   Sydney J. "Syd" South, RCAF. MU/Gunner.
R279116 F/S.   L.J. "Joe" Kirwan, RCAF.   R/Gunner.
191847 (962612) P/O. Ralph Swift.   F/Engineer.

22/06/1945 ME422   JI-Q Baedeker Tour over Continent 15.12   x 19.42
Crew that day:
39555   W/C. Philip Lawder Basil Morgan. Pilot.
Nil   A/Bomber
161741 (657060) F/O. Alfred Ernest Nye. DFC.   Navigator.
176988 (1892590) F/O. Norman Sydney Warren.   WOP/AG.
Nil   MU/Gunner.
Nil   R/Gunner.
191847 (962612) P/O. Ralph Swift.   F/Engineer.
Passengers: F/O. Meason, S/L. O'Conner, F/L. Sallington, F/L. White, F/S. Hammond, F/L. Watson.

05/07/1945 ME530   JI-C Baedeker Tour over Continent 14.21 x 18.30
Crew that day:
39555   W/C. Philip Lawder Basil Morgan. Pilot.
Nil   A/Bomber
F/O. E.T. Williams.   Navigator.
103538 (902785) F/L. Vivian George Ivor Outen. WOP/AG.
Nil   MU/Gunner.
Sgt. D. Vipond.   R/Gunner.

F/L. T. Wake.   F/Engineer.
Passengers: Sgt. Harmer, F/S. Bramburg, Sgt. Last (WAAF), Cpl. Goodman, LAC. Godden.

22/07 to 26/07//1945
   ME422   JI-Q Dodge Italy   08.05 15.45 15.55
   22/07/1945 Waterbeach 08.05 - Italy 15.45 (in Summary report noted 08.15 & 16.41), 26/07/1945 Italy 09.45 - Waterbeach 15.55
   Crew:
39555 W/C. Philip Lawder Basil Morgan. Pilot.
160956 (1333696) F/O. John Barwick Cushing, DFC. A/Bomber.
195188 (1673373) P/O. Alan Fairfax.   Navigator.
177174 (1870300) F/O. John Frederick "Johnny" Channell. WOP/AG.
141271 (1386976) F/L. Herbert Henry Wright, DFM. MU/Gunner.
179331 (944736) F/O. George Rothwell.   R/Gunner.
191847 (962612) P/O. Ralph Swift.   F/Engineer.
   Passengers: G/Capt. Dabinett, W/C. Milward, W/C. Elliot, S/L. Brown.

F/O. Maurice Linden Morgan-Owen

151873 (1323722) F/O. Maurice Linden Morgan-Owen   Pilot.
A22102 F/O. George Alexander Jacobson, RAAF. A/Bomber.
1576157 F/S. Alan William Green.   Navigator.
1387535 Sgt. Frank Barrett.   WOP/AG.
1516394 Sgt. Ernest "Sunny" Gledhill.   WOP/AG.
614774   Sgt. Alfred Douglas Tetley.   MU/Gunner.
1151568 Sgt. Herbert Stanley "Bub" Hayward. R/Gunner.
535804 Sgt. Henry "Leo" Sadler.   F/Engineer.

10/04/1944 LL732 A2-H Bombing Laon 01.42 03.51 06.02
   Bomb load 8 x 1000, 6 x 500 lb bombs. Primary target: Laon. Weather was good but smoky. Bombed at 03.51 hours from 11,000 feet. Saw two cluster of green T.I.s about 300/400 yards apart N & S. We bombed Northern reds seen in target area, 4 or 5 were earlier but none as we bombed. Large fire seen about ½ mile S.E. of the Northern T.I. Good attack. Photo attempted but may be failure owing to our turning to avoid other aircraft.
   Sgt. F. Barrett WOP/AG that day.

Top row: Maurice Morgan-Owen (left), E. Gledhill (right).
Bottom row: H.S. Hayward (left), G.A. Jacobson (right)

18/04/1944 DS822 JI-T Bombing Rouen   22.41 00.52   03.10

Bomb load 10 x 1000 MC, 5 x 500 MC lb bombs. Primary target:
Rouen. Weather was clear, good visibility. Bombed at 00.52 hours
from 13,500 feet. Target identified visually. T.I.s markers were
scattered. Bombing was well concentrated. 1 x 1000 bomb hung up
and brought back. A successful mission. Good weather on route.

Sgt. E. Gledhill WOP/AG that day.

20/04/1944 DS822 JI-T Bombing Cologne   23.51   02.16   03.31

Bomb load 1 x 1000 lb bomb, 1026 x 4, 114 x 4, 108 x 30 lb
incendiaries. Primary target: Koln. There was 10/10 cloud. Bombed at
02.16 hours from 20,000 feet. R.P. flares disappeared and bombed
glow of red flares. Glows of fires seen and 1 large explosion at 02.15
hours. Attack late in opening. Some fires seen. Route satisfactory.

Sgt. F. Barrett WOP/AG that day.

22/04/1944 DS682 JI-N Bombing Dusseldorf 22.58 x   x

Bomb load 1 x 8000 lb bomb, 48 x 30, 486 x 4, 54 x 4 incendiaries.
Aircraft missing.

Crashed in the sea. Circumstances not stated. A SOS message was received at 02.56hrs giving his position over the sea at approximately 70 miles West of the Dutch Coast, position 5236N 0351E. From that time nothing further has been heard from this aircraft. No night fighter claim is recorded so it is likely that the aircraft sustained damage earlier in the raid and failed to make it home.

Sgt. E. Gledhill WOP/AG that day.

Five are commemorated on the Runnymede Memorial; Sgt Sadler, who was washed ashore on 21st June 1944, and Sgt Tetley are buried in Sage War Cemetery.

F/L. Frederick William Morrish

141716 (1312150) F/L. Frederick William 'Fred' Morrish. Pilot.
   F/S. Arthur Kenneth "Ken" Staveley. A/Bomber.
   W/O. R.I. or W.I. Sutcliffe. Navigator. 2 ops.
163912 (1616284) F/O. William Charles Roberts. Navigator. 1 op.
   F/S. L. "Bill" Bailey. Navigator. 6 op.
J40778 F/O. Ray Bertram Hilchey, RCAF. Navigator. 1 op.
161741 (657060) F/O. Alfred Ernest Nye, DFC. Navigator. 1 op.
Sgt.J.E. Banham. Navigator. 11 ops.
Sgt.H.W. "Harry" Grosvenor. WOP/AG.
Sgt.John T. "Jonny" Dowson. MU/Gunner. 21 ops.
   F/S. Jack "Ginger" Hall. R/Gunner.
   F/S. Reginald J. "Reg" Mann. F/Engineer. 20 ops.
   F/S. P. or T. Wilson. F/Engineer. 2 ops.

Passengers: 03/05/1945, 01/06/1945, 23/06/1945, 13/07/1945, 31/07/1945.

23/02/1945 ME336 JI-S Bombing Gelsenkirchen 11.13 15.03 16.54
   Bomb load 1 x 4000 HC, 9 x 500 ANM64, 2 x 500 MC, 4 x 250 GP.
Primary target Gelsenkirchen. Weather 10/10ths cloud. Bombed at 15.03 hours from 20,000 feet on G.H.

From his normal crew, only F/L. F.W. Morrish did this mission as 2nd Pilot with F/L. R. Worthing's crew.
26/02/1945 NN782 JI-F Bombing Dortmund 10.24 14.02 16.07
   Bomb load 1 x 4000 HC, 2 x 500 MC L/Delay 37B, 9 x 500

ANM64, 4 x 250 GP. Primary target: Dortmund, Hoesch Benzin plant. Weather 10/10ths cloud, tops 8/10,000 feet. Bombed at 14.02 hours from 20,000 feet on G.H. Leader.

W/O. R.I. or W.I. Sutcliffe was Navigator that day.

28/02/1945 ME336   JI-S Bombing Nordstern   08.45   12.05   14.10

Bomb load 1 x 4000 HC, 9 x 500 ANM64, 2 x 500 MC L/D, 4 x 250 GP. Primary target: Nordstern (Gelsenkirchen). Weather 10/10ths cloud. Bombed at 12.05 hours from 21,000 feet on Green markers.

F/O. W.C. Roberts was Navigator that day.

05/03/1945 NG142   JI-J Bombing Gelsenkirchen   10.25   14.07 16.09

Bomb load 1 x 4000 HC, 12 x 500 ANM64. Primary target: Gelsenkirchen, Benzol plant. Weather 10/10ths cloud over target with cirrus cloud at bombing height. Bombed at 14.07 hours from 21,000 feet on leading G.H. aircraft.

F/S. L. Bailey was Navigator that day.

06/03/1945 ME387   JI-N Bombing Wesel   18.20 21.08   23.31

Bomb load 1 x 4000 HC, 13 x 500 ANM64, 2x 500 MC. Primary

467

target: Wesel. Weather 10/10ths cloud, tops 16,000 feet preventing visual. Bombed at 21.08 hours from 18,100 feet on G.H.

From his normal crew, only F/L. F.W. Morrish did this mission as 2nd Pilot with F/L. J.S. Parnell's crew.

09/03/1945 PB482 A2-K Bombing Datteln 10.32 14.00 15.59

Bomb load 1 x 4000 HC, 13 x 500 ANM64, 2 x 500 MC L/Delay37. Primary target: Datteln, Synthetic oil plant. Weather 10/10ths cloud, tops 8-10,000 feet. Bombed at 14.00 hours from 21,000 feet on G.H. Leader. Checked up with bomb sight on 3 Blue smoke Puffs.

W/O. R.I. or W.I. Sutcliffe was Navigator that day.

11/03/1945 NN782 JI-F Bombing Essen 11.32 15.25 17.18

Bomb load 1 x 4000 HC, 13 x 500 ANM64, 2 x 500 MC. Primary target: Essen, Marshalling yards. Weather 10/10ths cloud, tops 7/8000 feet. Bombed at 15.25 hours from 19,000 feet on G.H. Leader.

F/O. R.B. Hilchey was Navigator that day.

27/03/1945 LM627 JI-D Bombing Hamm Sachsen 10.38 14.04 16.08

Bomb load 1 x 4000 HC, 13 x 500 ANM64, 2 x 500 MC. Primary target: Hamm Sachsen, Benzol plant. Weather 10/10ths cloud. Bombed at 14.04 hours from 18,000 feet.

F/O. A.E. Nye was Navigator that day.

04/04/1945 PB142 JI-K Bombing Merseburg (Leuna) 18.48 x 00.06

Weather 5-10/10ths cloud, and 10/10ths over Merseburg. Bomb load 1 x 4000 HC, 6 x 500 ANM64. Abortive. Returned early, furthest point reached 50N 0420E at 20.56. 1 x 4000 jettisoned safe at 50.23N 0002E at 22.57 hours from 6,000 feet. 6 x 500 ANM64 jettisoned safe at 42.59N 04.35E at 21.03 from 1000 feet. Port inner caught fire and was feathered, automatic boost control on starboard inner caught fire and was feathered immediately afterwards - To maintain height had to jettison immediately so dropped 6 x 500 ANM64 and jettisoned some of the petrol load and window. Starboard inner then gave signs of life then returned to sea to jettison 4000 HC.

Sgt. J.E. Banham Navigator until 17/05/45.

13/04/1945 NG142 JI-J Bombing Kiel 20.25 23.31 02.04

Bomb load 18 x 500 ANM64. Primary target: Kiel, Docks & ship yards. Weather 10/10ths cloud low and thin. Bombed centre of Green glow per M/B's instructions, at 23.31 hours from 20,000 feet. Reds seen well to port, had to turn on new heading per M/B's instructions. 1 x 500 ANM64 hang up. Bomb bursts seen accurately across T.I.s glow. Fires gaining hold as we left.

22/04/1945 LM627   JI-D Bombing Bremen   15.12   18.42   21.24

Bomb load 1 x 4000 HC, 2 x 500 MC, 14 x 500 ANM 64. Primary target: Bremen, in support of Troop concentration. Weather on approaching target 4-5/10ths cloud. Bombed on G.H. Leader 514/S at 18.42 hours from 18,500 ft. Many small fires seen amid huge pall of black smoke. Starboard fin holed by flak. Excellent raid - Bombing accurate - Own leaders' GH u/s picked another leader.

29/04/1945 RF231 JI-A Manna The Hague   13.02   13.57   15.18

Dropping area: The Hague. Weather broken cloud above and clear below. Dropped 5 packs on white cross at 13.57 hours. All bags dropped in small area to starboard of cross. Visibility was good. No vehicles to be seen in the Hague. Pinpoints for run in were easily picked opt. Cheering populace packed squares and streets and on roof tops.

01/05/1945 RE116 JI-F Manna The Hague   13.12 x 15.45

Dropping area The Hague. Weather clear over target. Dropped 5 Panniers on T.I.s, White cross and Visual. T.I.s better placed to-day, Bags well concentrated; no water near. Flags waving by crowds as before. Everything straight forward. Showers over the sea.

03/05/1945 RE123 A2-K   Manna The Hague 11.13 x 13.34

Dropping area The Hague. Dropped 4 panniers clear on T.I..s and White Cross (almost covered by Bags). Dropping concentrated. Usual waving crowds.

No Mid Upper Gunner that day.

Passengers: LAC. Irvine.

09/05/1945 RE116 JI-F Exodus   Juvincourt - Dunsfold 07.28 x 12.32

Outward 1.34 hours. Collected 24 POWs. Homeward 2.00 hrs. Good organisation.

11/05/1945 RE137 JI-D Exodus   Juvincourt - Tangmere 11.20 x 18.17

Duration 3.46. Outward 1.34 hours. Collected 24 ex POWs. Homeward 2.12 hours. Brought crew of 514/L from Tangmere.

12/05/1945 RE137 JI-D Exodus   Brussels - Tangmere 12.36 x 18.24

Duration 2.46. Outward 1.07 hours. Homeward 1.39 hours. 10 Refugees to Brussels. Told to take off from Brussels as weather was bad over U.K.

14/05/1945 RE137 JI-D Exodus   Juvincourt - Oakley 10.15 x 15.44

Duration 3.47 hours. Outward 1.33 hours. Collected 24 POWs. Homeward 2.14 hours.

17/05/1945 RE137 JI-D Exodus Brussels - Westcott 10.21 x 15.52

Duration 3 hrs 15 mins. Out 1 hr 23 mins. In 1 hr 52 mins. 10

Belgian refugees taken to Brussels. 24 Ex POWs returned to Westcott. Organisation O.K.

01/06/1945 RE137 JI-D Baedeker Tour over Germany 10.11 x 14.30
F/S. L. Bailey Navigator from that day.
Passengers: F/S. J.B. Blades, AC. P. Briggs, AC. W. Kilmaster.

23/06/1945 RE140 JI-H Baedeker Tour over Continent 09.56 x 14.21
Passengers: Cpl. Bennett, Cpl. Murphy, Cpl. Edwards, Cpl. Coking, A/C. Park.

25/06/1945 RE140 JI-H Post Mortem Special mission 09.45 x 16.08

13/07/1945 RE137 JI-D Baedeker Tour over Continent 09.32 x 13.50
F/S. P. or T. Wilson F/Engineer from that day.
Passengers: Cpl. Cartwright, LAC. Widdowson, LAC. Minifie, LACW. Prior, ACW. Bryan.

31/07/1945 RF230 JI-B Baedeker Tour over Continent 09.53 x 12.09
Returned early. Weather bad.
Passengers: Sgt. Lock, LAC. Wetherby, LAC. Hayes, LACW. Cayford, LACW. Bryan.

S/L.   Herbert Cooper Mottershead

46928 (655159) S/L. Herbert Cooper Mottershead. Pilot.
F/S. D. Flinders.   A/Bomber.
F/S. R.C. Webb.   Navigator.
F/S. G.E. Highmore.   WOP/AG.
F/S. G.A. Banks.   MU/Gunner. 31 ops.
Sgt. W.J. Cook.   R/Gunner.
F/S. J.F. Bremridge.   F/Engineer.
J35287   F/O. William Eugene McLean. RCAF.   2nd Pilot.
28/01/1945
134136 (1436422)
F/L. Frank Raymond Wilton England.   2nd Pilot. 25/02/1945
150868 (1805085)
F/O. Robert Owen "Robin" Blackall. 2nd Pilot. 23/03/1945

Passengers: 03/05/1945, 08/05/1945, 18/06/1945, 05/07/1945, 30/07/1945.

01/01/1945 LM728   A2-B   Bombing Vohwinkle 16.26 19.44 21.29
Bomb load 1 x 4000 HC, 12 x 500 ANM58, 2 x 500 GP. Primary

target: Vohwinkel. Weather clear. Bombed at 19.44 hours from 19,500 feet. Red and Green T.I.s.

From his normal crew, only F/L. H.C. Mottershead did this mission as 2nd Pilot with F/O. G.D. Orr's crew.

02/01/1945 PB142 JI-G Bombing Nuremburg 15.30 19.34 22.59

Bomb load: 1 x 1000 ANM65, 1 x 500 ANM58, 10 x 80 x 4 IB, 120 x 4. Primary target: Nuremburg. Weather clear. Bombed at 19.34 hours from 17,000 feet. Overshot Red T.I.s.

11/01/1945 PB423 A2-L Bombing Krefeld 11.41 15.13 16.47

Bomb load 1 x 4000 HC, 10 x 500 ANM64, 4 x 250 GP. Primary target: Krefeld. Weather 10/10ths cloud above and below. Visibility poor. Bombed at 15.13 hours from 18,800 feet on G.H. Leader.

13/01/1945 PB423 A2-L Bombing Saarbrucken 11.50 15.25 17.19

Bomb load 1 x 4000 HC, 10 x 500 ANM58 or 64, 4 x 250 GP. Primary target: Saarbrucken. Weather 3-5/10ths cloud, tops 4/5,000 feet. Bombed at 15.25 hours from 19,100 feet on G.H. Leader. All aircraft on this operation were diverted on return to Exeter as weather at base was unfit to land.

15/01/1945 PB423 A2-L Bombing Lagendreer 11.45 15.02 16.46

Bomb load 1 x 4000 HC, 10 x 500 ANM64, 4 x 250 GP. Primary target: Lagendreer. Weather 10/10ths cloud. Bombed at 15.02 hours from 18,200 feet on G.H. Leader.

16/01/1945 PB423 A2-L Bombing Wanne-Eickel 23.09 02.34 04.36

Bomb load 1 x 4000 HC, 10 x 500 ANM58, 4 x 250 GP. Primary target: Wanne-Eickel, Benzol plant. Weather 10/10ths thin low cloud. Bombed at 02.34 hours from 17,600 feet on centre of Red flares.

22/01/1945 PB423 A2-L Bombing Hamborn 16.58 20.07 22.05

Bomb load 1 x 4000 HC, 7 x 500 ANM58 or 64, 2 x 500 GP (L/Delay), 3 x 250 GP. Primary target: Hamborn (Duisburg), Thyssen works. Weather over target clear and almost as bright as day. Bombed at 20.07 hours from 20,000 feet on smoke and flames.

28/01/1945 PB423 A2-L Bombing Cologne 10.41 14.11 16.04

Bomb load 1 x 4000 HC, 10 x 500 ANM64, 2 x 500 GP, 3 x 250 GP. Primary target: Koln - Gremberg, Marshalling yards. Weather 10/10ths cloud en route clearing on approach to target where visibility was good and nil cloud. Bombed at 14.11 hours from 18,600 feet - visually.

F/O. W.E. McLean 2nd Pilot that day.

29/01/1945 PB423 A2-L Bombing Krefeld 10.16 13.57 15.46

Bomb load 1 x 4000 HC, 10 x 500 ANM64, 2 x 500 GP, 4 x 250 GP. Primary target: Krefeld Marshalling Yards. Weather 10/10ths low thin cloud over target although clear patches en-route. Bombed at 13.57 hours from 20,400 feet on G.H. Leader.

01/02/1945 PB423 A2-L Bombing Munchen-Gladbach 13.10 16.33 18.16

Bomb load 1 x 4000 HC, 14 x No. 14 Clusters. Primary target: Munchen-Gladbach, Marshalling yards. Bombed at 16.33 hours from 17,600 feet on leading aircraft.

02/02/1945 PB423 A2-L Bombing Wiesbaden 20.32 23.46 02.45

Bomb load 1 x 4000 HC, 6 x 500 ANM64, 6 x 500 GP, 4 x 250 GP. Primary target: Wiesbaden. Weather 10/10ths cloud, winds very erratic. Bombed at 23.46 hours from 20,000 feet on Gee fix.

25/02/1945 PB423 A2-L Bombing Kamen 09.35 12.46 15.02

Bomb load 1 x 4000 HC, 9 x 500 ANM64, 2 x 500 MC, 4 x 250 GP. Primary target: Kamen. Weather 6-8/10ths cloud. Bombed at 12.46 hours from 19,700 feet on G.H. Leader.

F/L. F.R.W. England 2nd Pilot that day.

28/02/1945 NG118 A2-H Bombing Nordstern 08.48 12.05 14.10

Bomb load 1 x 4000 HC, 9 x 500 ANM64, 2 x 500 MC L/D, 4 x 250 GP. Primary target: Nordstern (Gelsenkirchen). Weather 10/10ths cloud. Bombed at 12.05 hours from 19,700 feet on G.H.

01/03/1945 NG118 A2-H Bombing Kamen 11.55 15.08 17.32

Bomb load 1 x 4000 HC, 11 x 500 ANM64, 2 x 500 MC L/Delay37. Primary target: Kamen, Coking plant. Weather 10/10ths cloud. Bombed at 15.08 hours from 18,600 feet on Blue smoke puffs.

07/03/1945 NF966 A2-G Bombing Wesel 02.31 05.36 07.45

Bomb load 1 x 4000 HC, 13 x 500 ANM64, 2 x 500 GP. Primary target: Wesel, Troop & Transport concentration. Weather 10/10ths cloud, thin in places. Bombed at 05.36 hours from 17,900 feet on G.H.

17/03/1945 ME363 JI-R Bombing August Viktoria 11.39 15.14 17.15

Bomb load 1 x 4000 HC, 13 x 500 ANM64, 2 x 500 MC. Primary target: Auguste Viktoria, Marl-Hüls coal mine. Weather 10/10ths cloud, tops and contrails up to 23,000 feet. Bombed at 15.14 hours from 21,000 feet on navigational aids - Gee. No Leader available. 1 x 500 ANM64 hung up and brought back to base.

20/03/1945 ME425 A2-L Bombing Hamm 09.44 13.15 15.31

Bomb load 7 x 1000 ANM65, 8 x 500 ANM64, 1 Skymarker Green Puff. Primary target: Hamm, Marshalling yards. Weather 5/10ths cloud. Bombed at 13.15 hours from 17,200 feet on G.H.

23/03/1945 ME425 A2-L Bombing Wesel 14.30 17.40 19.15

Bomb load 1 x 1000 ANM65, 12 x 1000 MC. Primary target: Wesel, in support of ground troops. Weather perfect. Bombed at 17.40 hours from 19,600 feet on G.H. 1 x 1000 ANM65 hung up and brought back to Base.

F/O. R.O. Blackall 2nd Pilot that day.

29/03/1945 ME425   A2-L   Bombing Salzgitter   12.22 x 19.28

Bomb load 1 x 4000 HC, 8 x 500 ANM64. Primary target: Salzgitter, Hallendorf works. Weather 10/10ths cloud. Abortive sortie. H2S Mark II and G.H. unserviceable. Bombs returned to Base. Followed Vic of 3 into cloud, did not see another aircraft so waited hoping to find alternative target - cloud too thick so brought bombs back.

20/04/1945 ME425   A2-L   Bombing Regensburg   09.29   13.56 17.04

Bomb load 15 x 500 ANM64. Primary target: Regensburg. Weather clear over target and whole route. Bombed on G.H. (H2S Checked) at 13.56 hours from 19,000 feet. Target well hit with much smoke. Tending to undershoot. Large fire seen 10-15 miles east of Regensberg on the Danube. 1 x 500 ANM64 brought back - hang up. G.H. set working well. Satisfactory effort.

30/04/1945 ME425   A2-L   Manna Rotterdam   17.02   18.26   19.45

Dropping area: Rotterdam. Weather intermittent showers and low cloud. Load 5 packs. Dropped 5 packs on white cross between 18.26 and 18.30 hours. Splendid reception from locals. One house on fire may have been caused by red T.I. Much undershooting some packs fell in water. Rowing boats seen going to the rescue.

03/05/1945 ME425   A2-L   Manna The Hague   11.16   12.29   13.31

Dropping area The Hague. Dropped 4 panniers visually on smoke from T.I. at 12.29 hrs. Visibility good. Cloud Base 1,500/2,000 ft. A good collection of food packs obscured the White Cross.

No Mid Upper Gunner that day.

Passenger: AC. Wells.

08/05/1945 ME425   A2-L   Manna Rotterdam   12.43   14.15   15.21

Dropping area Rotterdam. Dropped 5 Packs on Red T.I. and visually at 14.15 hours. Clear. Area bad for dropping owing to drainage canals.

Passengers: AC. M. Reeves.

10/05/1945 ME425   A2-L   Exodus Juvincourt - Ford 11.25 x 18.01

Duration 3.44. Outward 1.50 hours. Collected 24 ex POWs. Homeward 1.54 hours. Organisation excellent throughout.

12/05/1945 ME425   A2-L   Exodus Brussels - Tangmere 12.16 x 18.36

Duration 3.26. Outward 2.16 hours. Homeward 1.10 hours. 10 Refugees to Brussels, told to return empty from Brussels as weather unsuitable over U.K.

16/05/1945 RE123 A2-K Exodus Brussels - Westcott 13.09 x 17.54
Duration 2 hrs 58 mins. Out 1 hr 7 mins. In 1 hr 51 mins. Arrived overseas A/F 14.17. Arrived reception A/F 17.03. 10 Belgian refugees all to Brussels / Melsbroeck. 24 ex POW all military taken to Westcott.

18/05/1945 ME425 A2-L Exodus Brussels - Oakley 12.48 x 17.32
Duration 3 hrs 03 mins. Out 1 hr 07 mins. In 1 hr 56 mins. 9 Belgian refugees taken to Brussels. 24 ex POWs returned to U.K. No difficulties.

18/06/1945 NN773 JI-K Baedeker Tour over Continent 09.55 x 15.10
Passengers: AC. Humphreys, LAC. Road, LAC. Kipper, Cpl. Evans.

25/06/1945 RE116 JI-F Post Mortem Special mission 09.50 x 15.54

03/07/1945 RA601 JI-J Post Mortem Special mission 14.08 x 19.55

05/07/1945 RA601 JI-J Baedeker Tour over Continent 15.15 x 18.23
Passengers: Pennyman, Lowe, Hudson, Stephenson. (Bomber Command personnel ranks and initials not given.)

24 to 26/07/1945
RA601 JI-J Dodge Italy 06.33 17.49 18.07
24/07/1945 Waterbeach 06.33 - Italy 17.49. -- 26/07/1945 Italy 10.00 - Waterbeach 18.07.

30/07/1945 RA601 JI-J Baedeker Tour over Continent 15.09 x 19.13
Passengers: Sgt. Gardiner, Sgt. Collins, Cpl. Gardner, LAC. Booth.

F/L. Murray David Muggeridge

NZ413103 F/L. Murray David Muggeridge, DFM, RNZAF. Pilot.
157197 F/O. Alan Washbrook, DFC. A/Bomber.
P/O. E. Williams. Navigator.
141012 (1112430) F/L. William Stuart Gregory. WOP/AG.
179331 (944736) F/O. George Rothwell. MU/Gunner. 14 ops.
R133292 W/O. J.S. Hatton, RCAF. MU/Gunner. 1 op.
R263534 F/S. W.G. Wheeler, RCAF. MU/Gunner. 4 ops.
F/S. E.D. Dixon. MU/Gunner. 1 op.
177925 (1809613) F/O. Anthony Ellwood, DFM. R/Gunner.
196200 (957153) P/O. Frederic Eric Hill, DFM. F/Engineer.
J38094 F/O. H. MacLean, RCAF. 2nd Pilot. 16/01/1945

122112 (1315400) F/L. Montague Grosvenor Tynsdale Allen. 2nd Pilot. 19&20/02/1945
150651 (1795353) F/O. William George Henry Thomas Gibson. 2nd Pilot. 06/03/1945
130318 (656066) F/L. Robert Geoffrey Keen Rice. 2nd Pilot. 09/03/1945

02/01/1945 LM627 A2-H
  Bombing Nuremburg
  15.29 19.32 23.03
  Bomb load: 1 x 1000 ANM65, 1 x 500 ANM58, 1080 x 4 IB. Primary target: Nuremburg. Weather clear. Bombed at 19.32 hours from 17,000 feet on centre of Red and Green T.I.s.
  F/O. G. Rothwell MU/Gunner that day.
05/01/1945 PB482 A2-K
  Bombing Ludwigshafen
  11.28 15.11 17.30
  Bomb load 1 x 4000 HC, 10 x 500 ANM58 or 64, 2 x 500 GP. Primary target:

Alan Washbrook, post WW2 whilst serving as a Flight Lieutenant with No. 49 Squadron, Operation Grapple, H-bomb - May 1957.

Ludwigshafen, Marshalling yards. Weather clear over target. Bombed at 15.11 hours from 19,000 feet on built up area. Bombs could not be released and finally released manually. Bomb doors hit by flak.
  W/O. J.S. Hatton RCAF MU/Gunner that day.
07/01/1945 PD389 A2-J   Bombing Munich 19.02 22.13 03.32
  Bomb load 1 x 1000 ANM65, 1 x 500 ANM58, 1080 x 4 lb IB, 120 x 4 IB. Primary target: Munich. Weather 10/10ths cloud over target 6-8,000 feet with a thin layer altitude 16,000 feet. Bombed at 22.13 hours from 20,500 feet to port on Red and Green flares.
  F/O. G. Rothwell MU/Gunner until 27/02/45.
13/01/1945 PB419 JI-J Bombing Saarbrucken 11.58 15.24 18.06
  Bomb load 1 x 4000 HC, 10 x 500 ANM58 or 64, 4 x 250 GP. Primary target: Saarbrucken. Weather 3-5/10ths cloud, tops 4/5,000 feet. Bombed at 15.24 hours from 19,000 feet on leading G.H. aircraft. All aircraft on this operation were diverted on return to Exeter as

weather at base was unfit to land.

16/01/1945 NN773 JI-K Bombing Wanne-Eickel 23.21 02.19 04.25

Bomb load 1 x 4000 HC, 10 x 500 ANM58, 4 x 250 GP. Primary target: Wanne-Eickel, Benzol plant. Weather 10/10ths thin low cloud. Bombed at 02.19 hours from 19,500 feet on Red flare with Green stars.

F/O. H. MacLean 2nd Pilot that day.

19/02/1945 ME354 JI-M Bombing Wesel 12.53 16.36 18.20

Bomb load 1 x 4000 HC, 6 x 500 MC, 6 x 500 ANM64, 3 x 250 GP, 1 Skymarker Red puff. Primary target: Wesel, communications. Weather over target 5-7/10ths cloud. Bombed at 16.36 hours from 18,700 feet on G.H.

F/L. M.G.T. Allen 2nd Pilot that day.

20/02/1945 ME355 JI-L Bombing Dortmund 21.44 01.06 03.38

Bomb load 1 x 4000 HC, 6 x 500 Type 14 Clusters, 6 x 750 Type 15 Clusters. Primary target: Dortmund. Weather 8-10/10ths thin cloud at about 5,000 feet. Bombed at 01.06 hours from 20,300 feet on glow of Red T.I. through thin cloud. 10/10 Cloud 5000' - 3/4 Moon - Strong fighter reaction.

F/L. M.G.T. Allen 2nd Pilot that day.

23/02/1945 ME354 JI-M Bombing Gelsenkirchen 11.10 14.59 16.58

Bomb load 1 x 4000 HC, 9 x 500 ANM64, 2 x 500 MC, 3 x 250 GP, 1 Green Puff. Primary target Gelsenkirchen. Weather 10/10ths cloud. Bombed at 14.59 hours from 19,500 feet on G.H.

27/02/1945 ME354 JI-M Bombing Gelsenkirchen 10.46 14.27 16.35

Bomb load 1 x 4000 HC, 2 x 500 MC (L/D 37B), 9 x 500 ANM64, 3 x 250 GP, 1 x 250 Blue Puff. Primary target: Gelsenkirchen (Alma Pluts). Weather 10/10ths cloud, 6/10,000 feet tops. Bombed at 14.27 hours from 19,500 feet on G.H.

05/03/1945 ME354 JI-M Bombing Gelsenkirchen 10.19 14.07 16.20

Bomb load 1 x 4000 HC, 11 x 500 ANM64, 1 Skymarker Red. Primary target: Gelsenkirchen, Benzol plant. Weather 10/10ths cloud over target with cirrus cloud at bombing height. Bombed at 14.07 hours from 21,000 feet on G.H.

F/S. W.G. Wheeler RCAF MU/Gunner until 12/03/45.

06/03/1945 ME354 JI-M Bombing Wesel 18.11 21.10 23.20

Bomb load 1 x 4000 HC, 13 x 500 ANM64, 2 x 500MC. Primary target: Wesel. Weather 10/10ths cloud, tops 16,000 feet preventing visual. Bombed at 21.10 hours from 18,000 feet on G.H. Bombing concentrated.

F/O. W.G.H.T. Gibson 2nd Pilot that day.

09/03/1945 ME354   JI-M   Bombing Datteln   10.30   14.01   15.58

Bomb load 1 x 4000 HC, 13 x 500 ANM64, 2 x 500 MC L/Delay37. Primary target: Datteln, Synthetic oil plant. Weather 10/10ths cloud, tops 8-10,000 feet. Bombed at 14.01 hours from 20,000 feet on G.H.

All aircraft seemed to be dropping bombs in the same place.

F/L. R.G.K. Rice 2nd Pilot that day.

12/03/1945 PB142 JI-G Bombing Dortmund   13.00   16.57   18.05

Bomb load 1 x 4000 HC, 13 x 500 ANM64, 1 Skymarker Red Puff. Primary target: Dortmund. Weather 10/10ths cloud over target, tops 6/10,000 feet. Bombed at 16.57 hours from 19,000 feet on G.H.

18/03/1945 ME354   JI-M   Bombing Bruchstrasse   11.41   15.04   17.11

Bomb load 1 x 4000 HC, 13 x 500 ANM64, 2 x 500 MC, 1 Skymarker Blue Puff. Primary target: Bruchstrasse, Coal mine & coking plant. Weather 10/10ths cloud, tops 6-12,000 feet. Bombed at 15.04 hours from 18,500 feet on G.H.

F/S. E.D. Dixon MU/Gunner that day.

27/03/1945 ME354   JI-M   Bombing Hamm Sachsen 10.25   14.03   16.43

Bomb load 1 x 4000 HC, 13 x 500 ANM64, 2 x 500 MC. Primary target: Hamm Sachsen, Benzol plant. Weather 10/10ths cloud. Bombed at 14.03 hrs at 18,000 feet on G.H.

F/O. G. Rothwell MU/Gunner from that day.

29/03/1945 ME354   JI-M   Bombing Salzgitter   12.12   16.43   19.32

Bomb load 1 x 4000 HC, 8 x 500 ANM64. Primary target: Salzgitter, Hallendorf works. Weather 10/10ths cloud. Bombed at 16.43 hours from 22,000 feet on G.H. Leader. Weather prevented effective formation, cloud tops being above on last leg - doubtful of success.

09/04/1945 ME354   JI-M   Bombing Kiel   19.35   22.37   01.45

Bomb load 1 x 4000 HC and 12 x 500 ANM64. Primary target: Kiel, Submarine Buildings Yards. Weather clear with slight haze. Bombed at 22.37 hours from 19,000 feet on centre of Red T.I.s. (green intermingled) heard M.B.'s instructions. Good visual of canal and harbour. Marking appeared accurate. Excellent raid, bombing-marking accurate.

18/04/1945 ME354   JI-M   Bombing Heligoland 09.50 13.08 15.30
Bomb load 6 x 1000 MC, 10 x 500 ANM64. Primary target: Heligoland, Naval base. Weather no cloud, slight haze. Bombed visually on red markers and M/B at 13.08 hours from 18,500 ft. Used emergency sight angle. Only northern tip of island visible. Remainder smoke and fires oil smoke. Large explosion 13.27. 1 x 1000 MC brought back. Bomb sight u/s. Very good show.

22/04/1945 ME355   JI-M   Bombing Bremen 15.09 18.41 21.16
Bomb load 1 x 4000 HC, 2 x 500 MC, 14 x 500 ANM 64. Primary target: Bremen, in support of Troop concentration. Weather on approaching target 4-5/10ths cloud. Bombed on G.H. at 18.41 hours from 19,200 ft. Good concentration of bombs on eastern bank river. Much smoke seen. Port tyre burst - damage to fuselage and bomb doors, appeared concentrated raid. Formation on average good.

02/05/1945 ME422   JI-Q Manna The Hague   11.00 12.16 13.18
Dropping area The Hague. Weather over dropping zone clear below cloud for the first arrivals changing later to heavy showers which marred visibility. Dropped 5 panniers on Red T.I. and White Cross at 12.16 hours. All Panniers appeared to go in dropping area.

F/L.   Alexander Edward Munro

A418705   F/L. Alexander Edward Munro, RAAF. Pilot.
F/S. F.E. Coe.   A/Bomber.
195188 (1673373) P/O. Alan Fairfax.   Navigator.
A409317   W/O. Sydney Alfred Pope, RAAF.   WOP/AG.
F/S. O.H. Taylor.   MU/Gunner.
F/S. G.W. Scott.   R/Gunner.
3010919   Sgt. Lesley James "Jimmy" Fieldhouse. F/Engineer.

29/11/1944 ME841   JI-J Bombing Neuss 02.52 05.36 07.26
Bomb load 1 x 4000 HC, 6 x 1000 MC, 6 x 500 GP. Primary target: Neuss. Weather 10/10ths cloud over target but the glow of fires was seen through cloud. Bombed at 05.36 hours from 20,000 feet. Centre of Red and Green Markers. Red glow seen through cloud.

From his normal crew, only P/O. A.E. Munro did this mission as 2nd Pilot with F/O. D.W. Parks' crew.

L to R (back): 2ⁿᵈ A. Fairfax, 3ʳᵈ L.J. Fieldhouse, 4ᵗʰ A.E. Munro.

L to R (front): 3ʳᵈ Sydney Alfre Pope.

30/11/1944 NG350   JI-C Bombing Osterfeld   10.55   13.06   14.49
   Bomb load 1 x 4000 HC, 16 x 500 GP. Primary target: Osterfeld, Coking plant. Weather 10/10ths cloud. Bombed at 13.06 hours from 19,500 feet on G.H. Leader. Aircraft slightly damaged by flak.

04/12/1944 NG350   JI-C Bombing Oberhausen   11.47 14.06   16.10
   Bomb load 1 x 4000 HC, 6 x 1000 MC, 6 x 500 GP. Primary target: Oberhausen, Built up area. Weather 10/10ths cloud. Bombed at 14.06 hours from 20,000 feet on G.H. Leaders' release.

05/12/1944 LM733   JI-F Bombing Hamm   08.35   11.30   13.44
   Bomb load 1 x 4000 H.C, 1950 x 4 lb incendiaries. Primary target: Hamm. Weather 10/10ths cloud over target, but otherwise varying from 6-10/10ths. Bombed at 11.30 hours from 20,000 feet on G.H. Leader.

06/12/1944 PB419 JI-N Bombing Merseburg 16.54 20.48 00.14
   Bomb load 1 x 4000 HC, 8 x 500 GP and 1 x 500 GP Long Delay. Primary target: Merseburg. Weather 10/10ths cloud with odd breaks.

479

Bombed at 20.48 hours from 20,000 feet on centre of T.I.s.

08/12/1944 NG350   JI-C Bombing Duisburg   08.40   11.05   13.10
   Bomb load 14 x 1000 ANM59. Primary target: Duisberg. Weather
10/10ths cloud. Bombed at 11.05 hours from 20,000 feet on G.H.
Leader. Landed at Woodbridge with flaps unserviceable.

11/12/1944 PB756 JI-B Bombing Osterfeld   08.38   11.08   12.55
   Bomb load 12 x 1000 ANM65, 2 x 1000 ANM59. Primary target:
Osterfeld. Weather 10/10ths cloud, tops 16,000 feet. Bombed at 11.08
hours from 20,500 feet on G.H. Leader.

31/12/1944 LM717   JI-C Bombing Vohwinkle   11.33   14.43   16.29
   Bomb load 1 x 4000 HC, 3 x 1000 MC, 2 x 500 GP, 2 x 500
ANM64, 5 x 250 GP. Primary target: Vohwinkel. Weather 10/10ths
cloud on approaching target although the target itself was clear.
Bombed at 14.43 hours from 20,000 feet on G.H. Leader.

02/01/1945 PB426 JI-D Bombing Nuremburg   15.30   19.34   22.48
   Bomb load: 1 x 4000 HC, 7 x 500 Clusters - Primary target:
Nuremburg. Weather clear. Bombed at 19.34 hours from 18,000 feet.
Centre of smoke, fires and Red T.I.s.

05/01/1945 LM717   JI-C Bombing Ludwigshafen   11.22   15.07
   17.25
   Bomb load 1 x 4000 HC, 10 x 500 ANM58 or 64, 2 x 500 GP.
Primary target: Ludwigshafen, Marshalling yards. Weather clear over
target. Bombed at 15.07 hours from 19,000 feet on leading aircraft.
Aircraft hit by flak, hydraulics lead damaged.

06/01/1945 PB902 JI-A Bombing Neuss   15.51   18.48   20.24
   Bomb load 1 x 4000 HC, 2 x 500 ANM58, 12 x 500 ANM64.
Primary target: Neuss. Weather 8-10/10ths cloud over target. Bombed
at 18.48 hours from 20,000 feet on Green and Red flares.

13/01/1945 PB142 JI-G Bombing Saarbrucken   11.50   15.23   17.42
   Bomb load 1 x 4000 HC, 10 x 500 ANM58 or 64, 4 x 250 GP.
Primary target: Saarbrucken. Weather 3-5/10ths cloud, tops 4/5,000
feet. Bombed at 15.23 hours from 20,000 feet on leading aircraft.
Visual check. All aircraft on this operation were diverted on return to
Exeter as weather at base was unfit to land.

16/01/1945 PB142 JI-G Bombing Wanne-Eickel   23.22   02.22   04.15
   Bomb load 1 x 4000 HC, 10 x 500 ANM58, 4 x 250 GP. Primary
target: Wanne-Eickel, Benzol plant. Weather 10/10ths thin low cloud.
Bombed at 02.22 from 19,000 feet on Red and Green flares.

19/02/1945 ME336   JI-S Bombing Wesel   12.54   16.36   18.22
   Bomb load 1 x 4000 HC, 6 x 500 MC, 6 x 500 ANM64, 3 x 250 GP,

1 Skymarker Red puff. Primary target: Wesel. Weather over target 5-7/10ths cloud. Bombed at 16.36 hours from 19,500 feet on G.H.

22/02/1945 ME336 JI-S Bombing Osterfeld 11.59 16.01 17.30
  Bomb load 1 x 4000 HC, 9 x 500 ANM64, 2 x 500 MC, 3 x 250 GP.
Primary target: Osterfeld, Coking ovens. Weather at target clear, but hazy. Bombed at 16.01 hours from 20,000 feet on G.H. Leader.

23/02/1945 ME351 JI-U Bombing Gelsenkirchen 11.13 15.01 17.34
  Bomb load 1 x 4000 HC, 9 x 500 ANM64, 2 x 500 MC, 3 x 250 GP,
1 Green Puff. Primary target Gelsenkirchen. Weather 10/10ths cloud. Bombed at 15.01 hours from 19,500 feet on GH. On return landed at Acklington.

26/02/1945 ME336 JI-S Bombing Dortmund 10.41 14.02 16.05
  Bomb load 1 x 4000 HC, 2 x 500 MC L/Delay 37B, 9 x 500
ANM64, 3 x 250 GP, 1 Red Puff. Primary target: Dortmund, Hoesch Benzin plant. Weather 10/10ths cloud, tops 8/10,000 feet. Bombed at 14.02 hours from 20,000 feet on G.H.

28/02/1945 ME351 JI-U Bombing Nordstern 08.39 12.04 13.58
  Bomb load 1 x 4000 HC, 9 x 500 ANM64, 2 x 500 MC L/D, 3 x 250 GP, 1 Green Puff. Primary target: Nordstern (Gelsenkirchen). Weather 10/10ths cloud. Bombed at 12.04 hours from 20,000 feet on G.H.

02/03/1945 ME422 JI-Q Bombing Koln 12.37 x 18.17
  Bomb load 1 x 4000 HC, 11 x 500 ANM64. Primary target: Koln. Weather 10/10ths cloud over Koln, South and South-East of Koln clear. Abortive sortie. Total bomb load brought back.

06/03/1945 ME336 JI-S Bombing Salzbergen 08.10 12.15 14.09
  Bomb load 1 x 4000 HC, 11 x 500 ANM64, 2x 500 MC, 1
Skymarker Blue Puff. Primary target: Salzbergen, Wintershall oil plant. Weather 10/10ths cloud over target, tops 10,000 feet. Bombed at 12.15 hours from 21,000 feet on G.H.

07/03/1945 ME336 JI-S Bombing Wesel 02.37 05.33 07.36
  Bomb load 1 x 4000 HC, 13 x 500 ANM64, 2 x 500 GP. Primary target: Wesel, Troop & Transport concentration. Weather 10/10ths cloud, thin in places. Bombed at 05.33 hours from 18,000 feet on G.H.

09/03/1945 ME351 JI-U Bombing Datteln 10.36 13.56 15.51
  Bomb load 1 x 4000 HC, 13 x 500 ANM64, 2 x 500 MC L/Delay37,
1 Skymarker Blue Puff. Primary target: Datteln, Synthetic oil plant. Weather 10/10ths cloud, tops 8-10,000 feet. Bombed at 13.56 hours from 21,000 feet on leading G.H. aircraft. (Own G.H. unserviceable). 1 Skymarker Blue Puff brought back.

There is an error in the ORBs that day, as Munro's crew being noted twice at the same time in 2 different planes whereas Gibson's crew was missed in records.

12/03/1945 ME336   JI-S Bombing Dortmund   12.59 16.57 18.54
Bomb load 1 x 4000 HC, 13 x 500 ANM64, 1 Skymarker Red Puff. Primary target: Dortmund. Weather 10/10ths cloud over target, tops 6/10,000 feet. Bombed at 16.57 hours from 19,100 feet on G.H.

29/03/1945 ME355   JI-L Bombing Salzgitter   12.16 16.42 19.04
Bomb load 1 x 4000 HC, 8 x 500 ANM64. Primary target: Salzgitter, Hallendorf works. Weather 10/10ths cloud. Bombed at 16.42 hours from 21,000 feet on G.H. & H.2.S. Damage on fuselage.

09/04/1945 ME336   JI-S Bombing Kiel   19.44 x 22.50
Bomb load 1 x 4000 HC and 12 x 500 ANM64. Primary target: Kiel, Submarine Buildings Yards. Weather clear with slight haze. Farthest point reached 5430N 0400E. 7 x 500 ANM64 jettisoned at 5229N 0311E at 22.08 hours from 8,000 feet to reduce weight. 1 x 4000 HC and 5 x 500 ANM64 brought back to Base. Intercom 12 pin plug loose in socket sufficient to put w/t u/s, leaving inter-com unserviceable. Fault found out too late to allow carrying on with attack.

13/04/1945 ME336   JI-S Bombing Kiel   20.12 23.35 02.11
Bomb load 18 x 500 ANM64. Primary target: Kiel, Docks & ship yards. Weather 10/10ths cloud low and thin. Bombed on centre of Green T.I.s per M.B.'s instructions at 23.35 hours from 20,000 feet. Bomb sight U/S. Bombed on M.B.s estimate. Huge explosion 23.36 hrs. Bombing accurately placed on markers. Glow seen many miles from target.

20/04/1945 ME336   JI-S Bombing Regensburg 09.25 13.55 16.54
Bomb load 15 x 500 ANM64. Primary target: Regensburg. Weather clear over target and whole route. Bombed on G.H. and H.2.S and visual of river and docks at 13.55 hours from 19,000 ft. G.H. and H.2.S and target on bomb sight. All instruments perfect. Bombs seen to straddle docks. Much smoke. Very large explosion seen at 48.50N 11.30E. Cause unknown no aircraft in vicinity. The beginnings of a very good attack. Railway Bridge definitely hit.

24/04/1945 ME336   JI-S Bombing Bad Oldesloe 07.21 10.43 13.04
Bomb load 6 x 1000 ANM65, 10 x 500 ANM 64. Primary target: Bad-Oldesloe, Rail and road junction and Marshalling Yards. Weather 3/10ths to nil cloud. Bombed on G.H. at 10.43 hours from 17,800 ft. Excellent G.H. run. Southern part of town covered with smoke pall.

Huge red flash or explosion at 10.45 in south-eastern part of target. Squadron formation very good. The attack should be accurate.

30/04/1945 ME336   JI-S MannaRotterdam 16.50 18.18 19.33

Dropping area: Rotterdam. Weather intermittent showers and low cloud. Load 5 packs. Dropped 4 packs on white cross at 18.18 hours orbit due to hang up. One pack hung up. Supplies dropping accurately. House on fire NW of A/P. Route lined with cheering crowds evidently enthusiastic in spite of inclement weather.

13/05/1945 ME336   JI-S Exodus Juvincourt - Tangmere 13.07 x 16.13

Duration 3.08 hours. Message "Return to Base" at 14.46 hrs.

14/05/1945 ME336   JI-S Exodus   Juvincourt - Oakley 10.18 x 15.38

Duration 3.27 hours. Outward 1.35 hours. Collected 24 POWs. Homeward 1.52 hours. Organisation O.K.

17/05/1945 ME336   JI-S Exodus   Brussels - Westcott 10.00 x 14.43

Duration 3 hrs 2 mins. Out 1 hr 10 mins. In 1 hr 52 mins. 10 Belgian refugees to Brussels. 24 Ex POWs brought back. Everything O.K.

19/05/1945 NN776   A2-G Exodus Brussels - Oakley 11.53 x 17.23

Duration 3 hrs 1 min. Out 1 hr 15 mins. In 1 hr 46 mins. 10 Belgian refugees to Brussels. 24 ex POWs all military evacuated.

23/05/1945 ME364   JI-P Exodus   Brussels - Oakley 11.52 x 17.08

Duration 2.55 hours. Out 1.08 hours. In 1.47 hours. 7 Belgian refugees returned to Brussels. 24 ex POWs evacuated. Organisation O.K.

F/L. John Freeland Ness, DFC

J18394   F/L. John Freeland Ness, DFC, RCAF. Pilot.
J93901or81 (R185460) P/O. B. Vineberg, RCAF.   A/Bomber.
164193 (1802887)   F/O. Martin Arthur Catty.   Navigator.
 Sgt. S.B. Highfield. WOP/AG. 36 ops.
NZ412324
     F/O. Oliver Lawrence Goldsmith, DFC, RNZAF. WOP/AG. 2
   ops.
159964 (1605076) F/O. Kenneth Dundonald Bailey.   WOP/AG. 1 op.

NZ425546
   F/O. Albert George "Chatty" Chatfield, DFC, RNZAF. MU/Gunner.
1 op.
   F/S. George Edgard Sales.   MU/Gunner. 1 op.
   Sgt. W. Hough.   MU/Gunner.   19 ops.
   Sgt. J.T. Evans.   MU & R/Gunner.   8 ops.
   F/S. William John "Bill" Meredith. MU & R/Gunner. 10 ops.
   Sgt. R. Bridge.   MU & R/Gunner.
   Sgt. P. Rahill.   F/Engineer.
116005 (1379910) F/L. Royston Worthing. 2nd Pilot. 01/01/1945
40160 later C94073
   S/L. Hugh Clayton George Wilcox, RCAF. 2nd Pilot. 05/01/1945
J14025 F/L.   Thomas W. "Wes" Hurley, RCAF. 2nd Pilot. 28/01/1945
J40283 F/O. Harold A. Pickersgill.   2nd Pilot. 02/02/1945

31/10/1944 ME841   JI-C Bombing Bottrop   11.54 15.01 16.47
   Bomb load 1 x 4000 HC, 16 x 500 GP. Primary target: Bottrop,
Synth. Oil plants. Weather 10/10ths cloud over target. On leading
aircraft.
   F/O. A.G. Chatfield was MU/Gunner that day and Sgt. R. Bridge
R/Gunner.
02/11/1944 NN717   JI-E Bombing Homberg   11.30 14.09 15.37
   Bomb load 1 x 4000 HC, 6 x 1000 ANM59, 6 x 500 MC. Primary
target: Homberg. Weather variable cloud but clear for bombing. Target
obscured by pall of smoke rising to 10,000 feet. Bombed at 14.09
hours from 20,000 feet. Green flares.
   F/S. W.J. Meredith was MU/Gunner that day and Sgt. R. Bridge
R/Gunner.
05/11/1944 NG203   JI-A Bombing Solingen   10.21 13.06 15.02

Bomb load 1 x 4000 HC, 14 x 500 Clusters. Primary target: Solingen. Weather 10/10ths cloud over target. Bombed at 13.06 hours from 17,500 feet on Red flares with Green stars concentrated.

Sgt. R. Bridge MU/Gunner and F/S. W.J. Meredith R/Gunner until 06/12/44.

06/11/1944 NG203   JI-A Bombing Koblenz   16.48 19.35 22.18

Bomb load 1 x 4000 HC, 2100 x 4 lb IB. Primary target: Koblenz. Weather clear over target. Bombed at 19.35 hours from 18,000 feet on centre of fires.

11/11/1944 NG203   JI-A Bombing Castrop Rauxel 08.27   11.08   12.50

Bomb load 1 x 4000 HC, 16 x 500 GP. Primary target: Castrop Rauxel, Oil refineries. Weather 10/10ths cloud. Bombed at 11.08 hours from 21,500 feet on Red flares.

15/11/1944 NG203   JI-A Bombing Dortmund 12.34 15.40 17.20

Bomb load 1 x 4000 HC, 16 x 500 GP. Primary target: Hoesch-Benzin Dortmund, Oil refineries. Weather 10/10ths cloud over the target. Bombed at 15.40 hours from 17,000 feet on leading aircraft.

16/11/1944 NG203   JI-A Bombing Heinsburg 13.08   15.31   17.07

Bomb load 1 x 4000 HC, 6 x 1000 MC, 6 x 500 GP. Primary target: Heinsburg. Weather - nil cloud with slight haze over target. Bombed at 15.31 hours from 9,000 feet. Starboard of smoke as instructed by the Master Bomber.

20/11/1944 NG203   JI-A Bombing Homberg   12.49 15.15 17.04

Bomb load 1 x 4000 HC, 16 x 500 GP. Primary target: Homberg. Weather 10/10ths cloud over target. Bombed at 15.15 hours from 21,000 feet on leading G.H. aircraft.

F/O. O.L. Goldsmith WOP/AG that day.

21/11/1944 NG203   JI-A Bombing Homberg   12.32 15.06 16.31

Bomb load 1 x 4000 HC, 16 x 500 GP. Primary target: Homberg. Weather about 5/10ths cloud but clear for bombing. Bombed at 15.06 hours from 20,000 feet on G.H. Leader.

F/O. O.L. Goldsmith WOP/AG that day.

04/12/1944 NN717   JI-E Bombing Oberhausen 11.50 14.08 16.15

Bomb load 1 x 4000 HC, 6 x 1000 MC, 6 x 500 GP. Primary target: Oberhausen, Built up area. Weather 10/10ths cloud. Bombed at 14.08 hours from 20,000 feet on upwind edge of Red flares.

06/12/1944 NF966 JI-R Bombing Merseburg 17.01 20.50 00.20

Bomb load 1 x 4000 HC, 8 x 500 GP and 1 x 500 GP Long Delay. Primary target: Merseburg (Leuna Oil) . Weather 10/10ths cloud with odd breaks. Bombed at 20.50 hours from 20,000 feet on Red/Green flare.

08/12/1944 NN717 JI-E Bombing Duisburg 08.36 11.05 12.53

Bomb load 14 x 1000 ANM59. Primary target: Duisberg. Weather 10/10ths cloud. Bombed at 11.05 hours from 20,000 feet on GH Leader.

F/S. E.G. Sales was MU/Gunner that day and Sgt. R. Bridge R/Gunner.

12/12/1944 ME841 JI-J Bombing Witten 11.13 14.07 15.54

Bomb load 1 x 4000 HC, 5 x 500 GP, 6 x 500 ANM58, 4 x 500 ANM64, 1 Flare. Primary target: Witten. Weather 10/10ths cloud, tops 14/16,000 feet. Bombed at 14.07 hours from 20,000 feet on G.H.

Sgt. W. Hough was MU/Gunner that day and Sgt. R. Bridge R/Gunner.

16/12/1944 NG203 JI-A Bombing Siegen 11.23 15.00 16.52

Bomb load 1 x 4000 HC, 5 x 1000 MC, 7 x 500 GP, 1 Flare. Primary target: Siegen. Weather very bad on route with icing and cloud. Bombed at 15.00 hours from 18,000 feet on G.H. Leader. Moderate icing.

Sgt. R. Bridge was MU/Gunner that day and Sgt. J.T. Evans R/Gunner.

21/12/1944 ME354 JI-F Bombing Trier 12.22 15.02 16.55

Bomb load 1 x 4000 HC. 10 x 500 GP. 6 x 250 GP. Primary target: Trier, Marshalling yards. Weather 10/10 cloud, tops 6/9000 feet. Bombed at 15.02 hours from 17,500 feet on G.H.

Sgt. W. Hough MU/Gunner that day and Sgt. R. Bridge R/Gunner.

23/12/1944 LM727 JI-F Bombing Trier 11.48 14.33 16.30

Bomb load 1 x 4000 HC, 10 x 500 GP, 2 x 250 GP, 4 x 250 T.I. red. Primary target: Trier. Weather clear over target. Bombed at 14.33 hours on G.H.

Sgt. R. Bridge was MU/Gunner that day and Sgt. J.T. Evans R/Gunner.

28/12/1944 LM717 JI-C Bombing Cologne Gremberg 12.25 15.06 16.56

Bomb load 1 x 4000 HC, 10 x 500 GP, 5 x 250 GP, 1 Flare. Primary target: Koln Gremberg, Marshalling yards. Weather 10/10ths cloud or fog. Bombed at 1506 hours from 19,500 feet on G.H.

Sgt. J.T. Evans was MU /Gunner that day and Sgt. R. Bridge R/Gunner.

31/12/1944 LM724 JI-H Bombing Vohwinkle 11.32 14.42 16.25

Bomb load 1 x 4000 HC, 3 x 1000 M65, 2 x 500 M64, 2 x 500 GP, 2 x 500 GP L/Delay, 1 x 250 GP, 4 x 250 T.Is. Primary target: Vohwinkel. Weather 10/10ths cloud on approaching target although the target itself was clear. Bombed at 14.42 hours from 19,000 feet on G.H.

Sgt. J.T. Evans was MU /Gunner that day and Sgt. R. Bridge R/Gunner.

01/01/1945 LM724　JI-H Bombing Vohwinkle　16.24　19.45　21.40

Bomb load 1 x 4000 HC, 10 x 500 ANM64, 2 x 500 GP, 1 x 250 Green T.I. Primary target: Vohwinkel. Weather clear. Bombed at 19.45 hours from 21,000 feet on G.H.

Until 06/01/45 Sgt. R. Bridge MU/Gunner and Sgt. J.T. Evans R/Gunner.

F/L. R. Worthing 2nd Pilot that day.

03/01/1945 LM275　JI-F Bombing Dortmund Buckarde　12.55　15.32　17.35

Bomb load 1 x 4000 HC, 12 x 500 ANM58 or 64, 3 x 500 GP, 1 Flare. Primary target: Dortmund Buckarde. Weather 10/10ths cloud over target.

05/01/1945 PB419 JI-J Bombing Ludwigshafen　11.18　15.09　17.20

Bomb load 1 x 4000 HC, 10 x 500 ANM58 or 64, 1 x 500 GP, 1 Flare, Primary target: Ludwigshafen, Marshalling yards. Weather clear over target. Bombed at 15.09 hours from 19,500 feet. North part of Marshalling Yard.

S/L. H.C.G. Wilcox 2nd Pilot that day.

06/01/1945 LM724　JI-H Bombing Neuss　15.49　18.48　20.25

Bomb load 1 x 4000 HC, 10 x 500 ANM64, 4 x 250 Red T.I.s. Primary target: Neuss. Weather 8-10/10ths cloud over target. Bombed at 18.48 hours from 20,000 feet on G.H.

22/01/1945 PB426 JI-D Bombing Hamborn　17.06　20.03　21.39

Bomb load 1 x 4000 HC, 7 x 500 ANM58 or 64, 2 x 500 GP (L/Delay), 3 x 250 GP. Primary target: Hamborn (Duisburg), Thyssen works. Weather over target clear and almost as bright as day. Bombed at 20.03 hours from 19,000 feet. Bomb sight not used as aircraft had to take evasive action from flak.

From that day Sgt. W. Hough was MU/Gunner and Sgt. R. Bridge R/Gunner.

28/01/1945 PA186 A2-G Bombing Cologne　10.26　14.10　16.11

Bomb load 1 x 4000 HC, 10 x 500 ANM64, 2x500 GP, 3 x 250 GP. Primary target: Koln - Gremberg, Marshalling yards. Weather 10/10ths cloud en route clearing on approach to target where visibility was good and nil cloud. Bombed at 14.10 hours from 19,500 feet on Red flares (G.H. unserviceable).

F/L. T. W. Hurley 2nd Pilot that day.

29/01/1945 NF968 JI-B Bombing Krefeld   10.21   13.59½   15.32

Bomb load 1 x 4000 HC, 10 x 500 ANM64, 2 x 500 GP, 4 x 250 GP. Primary target: Krefeld Marshalling Yards. Weather 10/10ths low thin cloud over target although clear patches en-route. Bombed at 13.59 hours from 19,700 feet on G.H.

01/02/1945 NF968 JI-B Bombing Munchen-Gladbach   13.22   16.33   18.20

Bomb load 1 x 4000 HC, 10 x 500 ANM64, 2 x 500 GP, 3 x 250 GP, 1 Blue smoke T.I. Primary target: Munchen-Gladbach, Marshalling yards.

02/02/1945 LM728   JI-F Bombing Wiesbaden   20.35   23.52   02.35

Bomb load 1 x 4000 HC, 12 x 500 GP, 4 x 250 GP. Primary target: Wiesbaden. Weather 10/10ths cloud, winds very erratic. Bombed at 23.52 hours from 21,000 feet on East position of bomb bursts. Gee unserviceable.

F/O. H.A. Pickersgill 2nd Pilot that day.

03/02/1945 LM728   JI-F Bombing Dortmund   16.17   19.38   21.30

Bomb load 1 x 4000 HC, 2 x 500 MC, 2 x 500 MC L/Delay, 6 x 500 ANM64, 2 x 500 GP, 1 x 250 GP, 2 Red T.I.s. Primary target Dortmund-Huckarde, Coking plant. Weather clear with slight haze. Bombed at 19.38 hours from 20,500 feet on G.H. Explosions in target area. Slight damage to fuselage due to heavy flak.

08/02/1945 PB426 JI-D Bombing Hohenbudberg   03.35   06.22   07.55

Bomb load 1 x 4000 HC, 2 x 500 MC, 2 x 250 GP, 4 x 500 GP, 6 x 500 ANM64, 2 x 250 Red T.I.s. Primary target: Hohenbudberg, Marshalling yards. Weather 8/10ths cloud over target. Bombed at 06.22 hours from 18,500 feet on Red T.I.s. T.I.s brought back, G.H. unserviceable. Few markers visible.

14/02/1945 PB426 JI-D Bombing Chemnitz   20.24   00.31   04.30

Bomb load 1 x 4000 HC, 8 x No. 14 Clusters. Primary target: Chemnitz. Weather 8-10/10ths cloud, tops 15-16,000 feet with occasional breaks. Bombed at 00.31 hours from 19,500 feet on Red and Green sky markers.

16/02/1945 PB426 JI-D Bombing Wesel   12.28 16.01   17.34

Bomb load 1 x 4000 HC, 4 x 500 GP, 2 x 500 MC L/Delay, 3 x 250 GP, 6 x 500 ANM64, 1 Red Puff. Primary target: Wesel. Weather clear.

Bombed at 16.01 hours from 19,500 feet on G.H.

18/02/1945 NF968 JI-B Bombing Wesel   11.24 15.24   17.00

Bomb load 1 x 4000 HC, 4 x 500 GP, 2 x 500 MC L/Delay, 3 x 250 GP, 6 x 500 ANM64. Primary target: Wesel. Weather 10/10ths cloud. Bombed at 15.24 hours from 19,500 feet on G.H.

F/O. K.D. Bailey WOP/AG that day.

28/02/1945 LM724   JI-H Bombing Nordstern   08.44 12.04   14.05

Bomb load 1 x 4000 HC, 9 x 500 ANM64, 2 x 500 MC L/D, 3 x 250 GP, 1 Green Puff. Primary target: Nordstern (Gelsenkirchen). Weather 10/10ths cloud. Bombed at 12.04 hours from 21,000 feet on G.H.

Nordstern is an industrial place at Gelsenkirchen.

10/03/1945 PB142 JI-G Bombing Gelsenkirchen   12.01 15.36   17.30

Bomb load 1 x 4000 HC, 13 x 500 ANM64, 2 x 500 MC, 1 Skymarker Blue Puff. Primary target: Gelsenkirchen. Weather 10/10ths cloud at target, tops 8,000 feet. Bombed at 15.36 hours from 19,000 feet on G.H.   Bomb aimer's panel damaged by flak.

17/03/1945 NF968 JI-B Bombing August Viktoria 11.38 15.06   17.00

Bomb load 1 x 4000 HC, 13 x 500 ANM64, 2 x 500 MC. Primary target: Auguste Viktoria, Marl-Hüls coal mine. Weather 10/10ths cloud, tops and contrails up to 23,000 feet. Bombed at 15.06 hours from 20,500 feet on G.H. According J.F. Ness' logbook target was Reklinghausen - August Viktoria is a coal mine at Marl-Hüls 5 miles N.W. of Reklinghausen.

20/03/1945 NF968 JI-B Bombing Hamm   10.02   13.13   15.47

Bomb load 7 x 1000 ANM59, 8 x 500 ANM64, 1 Skymarker Green Puff. Primary target: Hamm, Marshalling yards. Weather 5/10ths cloud. Bombed at 13.13 hours from 18,000 feet on G.H.

23/03/1945 NF968 JI-B Bombing Wesel   14.20 17.38   19.05

Bomb load 13 x 1000 MC. Primary target: Wesel, in support of ground troops. Weather perfect. Bombed at 17.38 hours from 20,000 feet on G.H.

27/03/1945 NF968 JI-B Bombing Hamm Sachsen 10.30   14.04   15.58

Bomb load 1 x 4000 HC, 13 x 500 ANM64, 2 x 500 MC. Primary target: Hamm Sachsen, Benzol plant. Weather 10/10ths cloud. Bombed at 14.04 hours from 18,400 feet on Green smoke puffs.

04/04/1945 NF968 JI-B Bombing Merseburg (Leuna)   18.39 22.50 02.29

Bomb load 1 x 4000 HC, 6 x 500 ANM64. Bombed on R/Green Sky markers at 22.50 hours from 20,000 feet. 10/10th cloud over target with patchy cloud around. Attack seemed good, Green and Red T.I.s seen dropped in Magdeburg area which attracted some bombing, attack on Merseburg opened late.

F/O. acting F/L.Cyril William Nichol

134092 (1325070) F/L. Cyril William Nichol.   Pilot.
J23133   F/O. Keith Douglas Deans, RCAF. A/Bomber.
1324521 (*)   Sgt. Percy "Steve" Stevens-Hoare. Navigator.
1179569   F/S. Arthur John Elliott. WOP/AG. 15 ops.
1485703 F/S.John Edward "Johnny" Richardson.   WOP/AG. 1 op.
1407182   Sgt. Arthur Reginald Bird. MU/Gunner. 1 op.
179008 (1377495) F/S. Albert Vincent Jackson.   MU/Gunner. 15 ops.
1262356   Sgt. George Charles Fearman.   R/Gunner.
1615097.   Sgt. Fred C. Townshend.   F/Engineer.
NZ416582
F/S.Bernard William Windsor, DFM, RNZAF. 2nd Pilot. 15/03/1944

(*): Contrary to ORBs information (Hoare), according Stalag Luft 1 list and London Gazette, true surname is Percy STEVENS-HOARE.

16/12/1943 DS815 JI-N Bombing Berlin   16.50 20.04 00.07
   Bomb load 1 x 2000, 5 x 30 incendiaries, 7 x 4 incendiaries.
Primary target: Berlin. 10/10 cloud. Bombed target at 20.04 at 21,500.
Small hole in bomb bay and B/Aimer's compartment. Good trip. After zero hours not many fires seen. Many fighter flares seen. Fairly good glow seen. Had combat with enemy aircraft. Landed at Downham Market.
   F/S. A.J. Elliott WOP/AG until 15/03/44.
   Sgt. A.R. Bird was MU/Gunner that day, subsequently KIA on 20/12/43, DS817 JI-P of F/S G.J. Davis' crew.
24/12/1943 DS815 JI-N Bombing Berlin   00.19 x 02.34
   Bomb load 1 x 4000, 32 x 30, 450 x 4, 90 x 4 incendiaries. Sortie abandoned. Excessive spark trail port outer-engine. Bombs jettisoned.
   F/S. A.V. Jackson MU/Gunner from that day.
29/12/1943 DS815 JI-N Bombing Berlin   17.04 20.16 00.14
   Bomb load 1 x 2000, 40 x 30, 900 x 4, 90 x 4 incendiaries. Primary target: Berlin. There was 10/10 cloud. Bombed at 20.16 hours at 21,500 ft. Several red flares with green stars were seen. Fires seen and

large explosion at 20.27 hours. Photo attempted. Route O.K.

14/01/1944 DS815 JI-N Bombing Brunswick 16.55 19.16 21.56

Bomb load 1 x 4000, 48 x 30 incendiaries. Primary target: Brunswick. There was 10/10 cloud with one or two breaks. Bombed at 19.16 hours at 20,000 ft. Glow of many concentrated fires seen through the cloud. Monica u/s. Opening attack rather scattered but appeared to be more concentrated before leaving target. Red T.I.s cascaded 3 minutes ahead of zero hour.

20/01/1944 DS815 JI-N Bombing Berlin 16.15 19.38 23.32

Bomb load 1 x 4000, 32 x 30, 540 x 4, 60 x 4 incendiaries. Primary target: Berlin. There was 10/10 cloud. Bombed at 19.38 hours at 21,000 ft. One good concentration of red and green markers. One large explosion to S of target at 19.42. Concentrated glow of fires seen on leaving.

21/01/1944 DS815 JI-N Bombing Magdeburg 19.50 23.06 02.50

Bomb load 1 x 4000, 720 x 4, 90 x 4, 32 x 30 incendiaries. Primary target: Magdeburg. There was 5/10 cloud. Bombed at 23.06 hours at 20,000 ft. String of fires seen merging into one. Poor route especially route in and out over coast. No help from Pathfinders. Attack good and concentrated. Photo flash failure.

27/01/1944 DS815 JI-N Bombing Berlin 17.43 20.42 02.03

Bomb load 1 x 8000 lb bomb. Primary target: Berlin. There was 10/10 cloud. Bombed at 20.42 hours at 20,000 ft P.F.F. not too good with route markers. Red glow seen in sky 100 miles away on homeward route from target.

28/01/1944 DS815 JI-N Bombing Berlin 00.23 03.28 07.40

Bomb load 1 x 4000 lb bomb, 24 x 30, 180 x 4, 90 x 4 incendiaries. Primary target: Berlin. There was 9/10 cloud, clear in patches. Bombed at 03.28 hours at 20,000 ft. Cluster of green T.I.s seen through breaks in clouds. Just after leaving target saw long narrow line of concentrated fires over target. Route satisfactory.

15/02/1944 DS815 JI-N Bombing Berlin 17.42 21.30 00.32

Bomb load 1 x 8000 lb bomb. Primary target: Berlin. There was 10/10 cloud with tops 10/12,000 ft. Bombed at 21.30 hrs at 21,000 ft. Markers scattered over 10/15 mile area. Cloud prevented visual, but cookies seemed to be bursting close together. Large explosions at 21.36 hrs, white flash penetrated cloud. Sky markers not too good.

19/02/1944 DS815 JI-N Bombing Leipzig 23.58 04.03 06.36

Bomb load 1 x 4000 lb bomb, 510 x 4, 90 x 4, 32 x 30 incendiaries. Primary target: Leipzig. There was 10/10 cloud. Bombed at 04.03

hours at 21,000 ft. Monica semi-u/s. P.F.F. markers well concentrated. Met winds valueless at start of operation therefore necessitating orbiting on route to make up time.

21/02/1944 DS815 JI-N Bombing Stuttgart   00.15 04.03 06.46

Bomb load 1 x 8000 lb bomb, 16 x 30, 90 x 4 incendiaries. Primary target: Stuttgart. There was 6/10 cloud. Bombed at 04.03 hours at 21,000 ft. Green T.I.s seen through cloud. Reddish glow and much smoke seen at a distance of 200 miles from target. Incendiaries seen burning in forest north of target, believed jettisoned too early - all other flares on target. Photo attempted.

24/02/1944 DS815 JI-N Bombing Schweinfurt 20.59 01.13 04.27

Bomb load 1 x 8000 lb bomb, 8 x 30 incendiaries; Primary target: Schweinfurt. Weather good, no cloud but much smoke, visual of railway on run up. Bombed at 01.13 hours at 22,000 ft. Many fires seen with 10/10 smoke obscuring vision. Route satisfactory. A good attack.

07/03/1944 DS815 JI-N Bombing Le Mans   19.38 21.42 23.48

Bomb load 10 x 1000, 4 x 500 lb bombs. Primary target: Le Mans. There was 10/10 cloud. Bombed at 21.42 hours from 13,000 feet. Red T.I.s seen to fall followed by another 'bang on top' about 4 minutes apart. Slight light flak over target. Tracer coming up through glow of T.I.s. One burst of H.F. in run up, later appeared to be about 6 guns.

15/03/1944 DS815 JI-N Bombing Stuttgart DFM 19.50 23.20 02.45

Bomb load 1 x 8000 lb bomb, 8 x 30 incendiaries. Primary target: Stuttgart. There was thin cloud over the target. Bombed at 23.20 hours from 20,000 feet. 1 Red T.I. seen in sight. Sky markers very scattered. Red T.I.s seen dropping over existing fires as aircraft left. Route O.K. Attack slow opening but improving later.

F/S. B.W. Windsor 2nd Pilot that day.

18/03/1944 LL703 JI-L Bombing Frankfurt   19.28 22.05 00.40

Bomb load 1 x 4000 lb bomb, 1350 x 4, 90 x 4, 32 x 30 incendiaries. Primary target: Frankfurt. Weather, wispy cloud much haze. Bombed at 22.05 hours from 20,000 feet. Some fires seen coinciding with position of red T.I.s. Cookies seen bursting in area. Built up area seen. Aircraft arrived early and orbited waiting for the markers. Route O.K.

F/S. J.E. Richardson WOP/AG that day.

22/03/1944 DS815 JI-N Bombing Frankfurt   18.33 x 00.15

Bomb load 1 x 1000 lb bomb, 64 x 30, 1161 x 4, 12 x 4 incendiaries. Aircraft missing.

Intercepted on the return leg on 23/03/44 at 00.15 hours by a night-fighter flown by Hptm. Ludwig Meister of 1./NJG4, which opened fire, killing F/S. Elliott and injuring F/O. Deans and Sgt. Townshend. On fire and with port engines faltering, F/L. Nichol skilfully landed the aircraft 400 metres west of La Californie (Pas de Calais) 4 km SW of the village of Ruminghem.

F/S. A.J. Elliott WOP/AG that day was the sole member of the crew KIA. He is buried in Longuenesse (St-Omer) Souvenir Cemetery.

F/S. A.V. Jackson Evaded, Sgt. G.C. Fearman Evaded. F/O. K.D. Deans was injured and interned in Camps 9C/L3, POW No.1851. Sgt. P. Stevens-Hoare in Camp L1, POW No.3821. F/L. C.W. Nichol in Camp L3, POW No.4903. Sgt. F.C. Townsend injured and interned in Camps 9C/L7, POW No.52298.

F/O. Christopher Iltyd Hubert Nicholl, DFC

J28107   F/O. Christopher Iltyd Hubert Nicholl, DFC, RCAF. Pilot.
154338 (1586703) F/O. Bernard Lethaby.   A/Bomber.
J38221   F/O. H.W. Robinson, RCAF.   Navigator.
Sgt. A.H.S. Francis.   WOP/AG.
Sgt. T. Smyth.   MU/Gunner.
Sgt. E.B. Dobbin.   R/Gunner.
Sgt. F.H. Davis.   F/Engineer.
J40219   F/O. H.C. Snow, RCAF.   2nd Pilot. 13/01/1945
J35287   F/O. William Eugene McLean, RCAF.   2nd Pilot. 22/01/1945
191610 (1394302) W/O.   Harry Stanley Butcher. 2nd Pilot. 16/02/1945
174335 (1430412) F/O. George Robertson.   2nd Pilot. 20/02/1945
J7741   F/L.   R.E. Farvolden, RCAF.   2nd Pilot. 07/03/1945

28/10/1944 LM286   A2-F   Bombing Cologne 13.01 15.46 17.42
   Bomb load 1 x 4000 HC, 12 x 150 x 4. Primary target: Cologne. Weather clear over target. Bombed at 15.46 hours from 18,000 feet. Yellow T.I.s.

   From his normal crew, only F/O. C.I.H. Nicholl did this mission as 2nd Pilot with F/L. B.K. McDonald's crew.

Christopher Iltyd Hubert Nicholl

31/10/1944 PD324A2-B BombingBottrop 11.59 15.01 16.40 Bomb load 1 x 4000 HC. 16 x 500 GP. Primary target: Bottrop, Synth. Oil plants. Weather 10/10ths cloud over target. Bombed at 15.01 hours from 17,500 feet on G.H. aircraft ahead.

02/11/1944 PD333A2-K BombingHomberg 11.24 14.06 15.43 Bomb load 1 x 4000 HC, 6 x 1000 ANM59, 6 x 500 MC. Primary target: Homberg. Weather variable cloud but clear for bombing. Target obscured by pall of smoke rising to 10,000 feet. Bombed at 14.06 hours from 18,000 feet. Visually. Aircraft hit by flak. Pilot's windscreen and Air Bomber's panel damaged, also tail plane.

05/11/1944 PD334A2-D BombingSolingen 10.19 13.01 14.38 Bomb load 1 x 4000 HC, 6 x 1000 ANM59, 4 x 500 GP, 2 x 500 GP (L/Delay), 3 Flares. Primary target: Solingen. Weather 10/10ths cloud over target. Bombed at 13.01 hours from 19,000 feet on flares.

06/11/1944 PD324A2-B BombingKoblenz 16.45 19.36 22.03 Bomb load 1 x 4000 HC, 12 x 500 Clusters, 300 x 4 lb IB. Primary target: Koblenz. Weather clear over target. Bombed at 19.36 hours from 17,500 feet overshooting to the North of the town.

15/11/1944 LM286 A2-F BombingDortmund 12.28 15.41 17.23 Bomb load 1 x 4000 HC, 16 x 500 GP. Primary target: Hoesch-Benzin Dortmund, Oil refineries. Weather 10/10ths cloud over the target. Bombed at 15.41 hours from 17,000 feet on leaving aircraft.

16/11/1944 PD333A2-K BombingHeinsburg 13.12 15.35 17.29 Bomb load 1 x 4000 HC, 6 x 1000 MC, 6 x 500 GP. Primary target: Heinsburg. Weather - nil cloud with slight haze over target. Bombed at 15.35 hours from 9,000 feet; Centre of town.

20/11/1944 PD333A2-K BombingHomberg 12.42 x 17.24 Bomb load 1 x 4000 HC, 16 x 500 GP. Primary target: Homberg. Weather 10/10ths cloud over target. Brought bombs back. Target not identified accurately.

21/11/1944 PD333 A2-K Bombing Homberg 12.30 15.08 16.44
    Bomb load 1 x 4000 HC, 16 x 500 GP. Primary target: Homberg. Weather about 5/10ths cloud but clear for bombing. Bombed at 15.08 hours from 20,000 feet on chimney stacks.
27/11/1944 NG142 A2-H Bombing Cologne 12.38 15.05 17.05
    Bomb load 1 x 4000 HC, 16 x 500 GP. Primary target: Cologne, Marshalling Yards. Weather patchy cloud. Bombed at 15.05 hours from 18,400 feet on G.H. Leader.
29/11/1944 NG118 A2-E Bombing Neuss 02.53 05.36 07.20
    Bomb load 1 x 4000 HC, 6 x 1000 MC, 6 x 500 GP, 3 Flares Red with Green stars. Primary target: Neuss. Weather 10/10ths cloud over target but the glow of fires was seen through cloud. Bombed at 05.36 hours from 20,000 feet. Centre of flares.
04/12/1944 NG141 A2-J Bombing Oberhausen 11.59 14.09 16.08
    Bomb load 1 x 4000 HC, 6 x 1000 MC, 6 x 500 GP. Primary target: Oberhausen, Built up area. Weather 10/10ths cloud. Bombed at 14.09 hours from 20,500 feet with G.H. Leader.
05/12/1944 NG141 A2-J Bombing Hamm 08.49 11.29 13.42
    Bomb load 1 x 4000 HC, 12 x 500 ANM58, 2 x 500 GP, 2 x 500 GP Long Delay. Primary target: Hamm. Weather 10/10ths cloud over target, but otherwise varying from 6-10/10ths. Bombed at 11.29 hours from 20,000 feet on G.H. Leader.
06/12/1944 NG141 A2-J Bombing Merseburg 17.09 20.53 00.21
    Bomb load 1 x 4000 HC, 8 x 500 GP and 1 x 500 GP Long Delay. Primary target: Merseburg. Weather 10/10ths cloud with odd breaks. Bombed at 20.53 hours from 23,500 feet on Red/Green flares.
23/12/1944 LM685 JI-K Bombing Trier 12.08 14.33 16.13
    Bomb load 1 x 4000 HC, 10 x 500 GP, 6 x 250 GP. Primary target: Trier. Weather clear over target. Bombed at 14.33 hours from 18,000 feet on centre of smoke on A.P.
27/12/1944 NG141 A2-J Bombing Rheydt 12.24 14.59 16.39
    Bomb load 7 x 1000 MC, 6 x 500 GP, 3 x 250 GP. Primary target: Rheydt, Marshalling yards. Weather clear. Bombed at 14.59 hours from 20,000 feet. Centre of Yellow T.I.
28/12/1944 NG141 A2-J Bombing Cologne Gremberg 12.18 15.06 17.02
    Bomb load 1 x 4000 HC, 10 x 500 GP, 6 x 250 GP. Primary target: Koln Gremberg, Marshalling yards. Weather 10/10ths cloud or fog. Bombed at 15.06 hours from 20,000 feet on G.H. Leader.
31/12/1944 PB426 JI-D Bombing Vohwinkle 11.34 14.44 16.33

Bomb load 1 x 4000 HC, 3 x 1000 M65, 2 x 500 GP, 2 x 500 ANM64, 2 x 500 GP L/Delay, 5 x 250 GP. Primary target: Vohwinkel. Weather 10/10ths cloud on approaching target although the target itself was clear. Bombed at 14.44 hours from 19,000 feet on G.H. Leader.

02/01/1945 PD389 A2-J   Bombing Nuremburg 15.33 19.29 22.41

Bomb load: 1 x 4000 HC, 7 x 500 Clusters - Primary target: Nuremburg. Weather clear. Bombed at 19.29 hours from 18,000 feet on centre of Red and Green T.I.s. Rear Gunner fired 2 bursts at twin-engine fighter - No claim.

05/01/1945 PB902 JI-A Bombing Ludwigshafen   11.52 15.08 17.41

Bomb load 1 x 4000 HC, 10 x 500 ANM58 or 64, 2 x 500 GP. Primary target: Ludwigshafen, Marshalling yards. Weather clear over target. Bombed at 15.08 hours from 19,700 feet on leading G.H. aircraft. Aircraft hit by flak.

06/01/1945 PD389 A2-J   Bombing Neuss 15.48 18.49 20.26

Bomb load 1 x 4000 HC, 10 x 500 ANM64, 4 x 250 Red T.Is. Primary target: Neuss. Weather 8-10/10ths cloud over target. Bombed at 18.49 hours from 19,500 feet on Red T.I.

11/01/1945 PD389 A2-J   Bombing Krefeld   11.55 15.12 16.32

Bomb load 1 x 4000 HC, 10 x 500 ANM64, 4 x 250 GP. Primary target: Krefeld. Weather 10/10ths cloud above and below. Visibility poor. Bombed at 15.12 hours from 19,000 feet on G.H. Leader.

13/01/1945 PD389 A2-J   Bombing Saarbrucken 11.58   15.24   18.12

Bomb load 1 x 4000 HC, 10 x 500 ANM58 or 64, 4 x 250 GP. Primary target: Saarbrucken. Weather 3-5/10ths cloud, tops 4/5,000 feet. Bombed at 15.24 hours from 19,000 feet on leading aircraft. All aircraft on this operation were diverted on return to Exeter as weather at base was unfit to land.

F/O. H.C. Snow 2nd Pilot that day.

15/01/1945 PD389 A2-J   Bombing Lagendreer 11.48 15.01 16.56

Bomb load 1 x 4000 HC, 10 x 500 ANM64, 4 x 250 GP. Primary target: Lagendreer. Weather 10/10ths cloud. Bombed at 15.01 hours from 20,000 feet on G.H. Leader.

16/01/1945 LM627   A2-H Bombing Wanne-Eickel 23.27 02.19 04.28

Bomb load 1 x 4000 HC, 10 x 500 ANM58, 4 x 250 GP. Primary target: Wanne-Eickel, Benzol plant. Weather 10/10ths thin low cloud. Bombed at 02.19 hours from 19,500 feet on Red T.I.s.

22/01/1945 PD389 A2-J   Bombing Hamborn   17.03 20.06 21.45

Bomb load 1 x 4000 HC, 7 x 500 ANM58 or 64, 2 x 500 GP

(L/Delay), 3 x 250 GP. Primary target: Hamborn, Thyssen works. Primary target: Hamborn (Duisburg). Weather over target clear and almost as bright as day. Bombed at 20.06 hours from 20,000 feet on centre of Green T.I.s.

According to C.I.H. Nicholl's logbook the target was "Duisburg". Hamborn is a suburb of Duisburg.

F/O. W.E. McLean 2nd Pilot that day.

02/02/1945 PD389 A2-J Bombing Wiesbaden 20.44 23.42 02.26
Bomb load 1 x 4000 HC, 10 x 500 ANM64, 2 x 500 GP, 4 x 250 GP. Primary target: Wiesbaden. Weather 10/10ths cloud, winds very erratic. Bombed at 23.42 hours from 20,000 feet on Gee.

03/02/1945 PD389 A2-J Bombing Dortmund 16.24 19.36 21.30
Bomb load 1 x 4000 HC, 2 x 500 MC, 2 x 500 MC L/Delay, 6 x 500 ANM64, 2 x 500 GP, 3 x 250 GP. Primary target Dortmund-Huckarde, Coking plant. Weather clear with slight haze. Bombed at 19.36 hours from 18,500 feet on Red T.I.

08/02/1945 PD389 A2-J Bombing Hohenbudberg 03.38 06.25 08.11
Bomb load 1 x 4000 HC, 2 x 500 MC, 4 x 250 GP, 4 x 500 GP, 6 x 500 ANM64. Primary target: Hohenbudberg, Marshalling yards. Weather 8/10ths cloud over target. Bombed at 06.23 hours from 18,000 feet on Red T.I.s.

13/02/1945 NN717 A2-E Bombing Dresden 21.52 01.31 06.44
Bomb load 1 x 500 MC, 15 x No. 14 Clusters. Primary target: Dresden. Weather 5/10ths cloud over target. Bombed at 01.31 hours from 20,000 feet. Overshot Green T.I.s.

14/02/1945 NN717 A2-E Bombing Chemnitz 20.28 00.31 04.34
Bomb load 1 x 500 MC, 15 x No. 14 Clusters. Primary target: Chemnitz. Weather 8-10/10ths cloud, tops 15-16,000 feet with occasional breaks. Bombed at 00.31 hours from 18,000 feet. Downwind of flares.

16/02/1945 NN717 A2-E Bombing Wesel 12.32 16.01 17.48
Bomb load 1 x 4000 HC, 4 x 500 GP, 2 x 500 MC L/Delay, 4 x 250 GP, 6 x 500 ANM64. Primary target: Wesel. Weather clear. Bombed at 16.01 hours from 20,500 feet on leading aircraft.

W/O. H.S. Butcher 2nd Pilot that day.

20/02/1945 PD389 A2-J Bombing Dortmund 21.53 01.07 03.18
Bomb load 1 x 2000 HC, 12 x 750 Type 15 Clusters. Primary target: Dortmund. Weather 8-10/10ths thin cloud at about 5,000 feet. Bombed at 01.07 hours from 21,000 feet on centre of Red/Green T.I.s.

F/O. G. Robertson 2nd Pilot that day.

23/02/1945 PD389 A2-J Bombing Gelsenkirchen 11.18 15.01
18.02

Bomb load 1 x 4000 HC, 9 x 500 ANM64, 2 x 500 MC, 4 x 250 GP. Primary target Gelsenkirchen. Weather 10/10ths cloud. Bombed at 15.01 hours from 20,000 feet on leading aircraft. On return landed at Acklington.

28/02/1945 PD389 A2-J Bombing Nordstern 08.49 12.04 14.13

Bomb load 1 x 4000 HC, 9 x 500 ANM64, 2 x 500 MC L/D, 4 x 250 GP. Primary target: Nordstern (Gelsenkirchen). Weather 10/10ths cloud. Bombed at 12.04 hours from 20,400 feet on leading aircraft.

According to C.I.H. Nicholl's logbook the target was "Gelsenkirchen". Nordstern is an industrial place at Gelsenkirchen.

02/03/1945 PD389 A2-J Bombing Koln 13.08 x 18.30

Bomb load 1 x 4000 HC, 12 x 500 ANM64. Primary target: Koln. Weather 10/10ths cloud over Koln, South and South-East of Koln clear. Abortive sortie. Total bomb load brought back to Base.

06/03/1945 PD389 A2-J Bombing Salzbergen 08.14 12.14 14.02

Bomb load 1 x 4000 HC, 12 x 500 ANM64, 2 x 500MC. Primary target: Salzbergen, Wintershall oil plant. Weather 10/10ths cloud over target, tops 10,000 feet. Bombed at 12.14 hours from 21,500 feet on G.H. Leader. 1 x 500 ANM64 hung up and jettisoned at 12.21 hours from 21,000 feet at 5201N 0708E.

07/03/1945 PD389 A2-J Bombing Dessau 17.01 22.18 02.09

Bomb load 1 x 500 ANM64, 15 x No. 15 Clusters. Primary target: Dessau. Weather 5 to 10/10ths thin cloud. Bombed at 22.18 hours from 20,300 feet on Skymarkers and Master Bomber.

F/L. R.E. Farvolden 2nd Pilot that day.

10/03/1945 PD389 A2-J Bombing Gelsenkirchen 11.59 15.36
17.25

Bomb load 1 x 4000 HC, 13 x 500 ANM64, 2 x 500 MC. Primary target: Gelsenkirchen. Weather 10/10ths cloud at target, tops 8,000 feet. Bombed at 15.36 hours from 19,000 feet on G.H. Leader.

11/03/1945 ME529 A2-F Bombing Essen 11.36 15.25 17.31

Bomb load 1 x 4000 HC, 13 x 500 ANM64, 2 x 500 MC. Primary target: Essen, Marshalling yards. Weather 10/10ths cloud, tops 7/8,000 feet. Bombed at 15.25 hours from 19,300 feet on G.H. Leader. Should be an excellent attack.

F/O. Maurice Raymond Oliver, DFC

NZ42705   F/O.Maurice Raymond Oliver, DFC, RNZAF. Pilot.
NZ4213727 F/S. R.K. Sligo, RNZAF.   A/Bomber.
NZ425739 F/S. Alexander John Crawford, RNZAF. Navigator.
Sgt. C.F. Bolton.   WOP/AG.
Sgt. W.J. Larter.   MU/Gunner.
NZ425161 P/O. J.T. Mephan.   R/Gunner.
Sgt. F.K. Burville.   F/Engineer. 35 ops
Sgt. Thomas Charles "Tom" Clayton.   F/Engineer. 1 op

25/07/1944 LL697 A2-B Bombing Stuttgart 21.47 01.35 05.26
   Bomb load 5 x 1000 MC, 3 x 500 GP. Abortive sortie. Jettisoned at
01.35 hours from 17,000 feet, position 4821N 0714E. Unable to
maintain height. Fighter attacks by an ME110, JU88 and a S/E aircraft,
no claims, no damage.
28/07/1944 DS786 A2-H Bombing Stuttgart 21.56 x 23.51
   Bomb load 13 x 500 GP. Target: Stuttgart. Abortive sortie.
Jettisoned at 5220N 0235E at 23.07 hours from 5,000 feet. Starboard
outer engine fluctuating, temperature and pressure oil leak on port
inner.
30/07/1944 DS620 A2-D Bombing Caen 06.16 07.51 09.45
   Bomb load 18 x 500 GP. Primary target: Caen 'B'. Weather cloud
base 2,000 feet. Bombed at 07.51 hours from 2,000 feet red T.I.s. A
good attack. Landed at Woodbridge.
01/08/1944 LL716 A2-G Bombing Foret de Nieppe 19.23 20.45
   21.50
   Bomb load 11 x 1000 MC, 4 x 500 GP. Primary target: De Nieppe,
constructional works. Bombed at 20.45 hours from 12,000 feet on
leading aircraft.
03/08/1944 DS620 A2-D Bombing Bois de Cassan 11.54   14.06
   15.33
   Bomb load 11 x 1000 MC, 4 x 500 GP. Primary target: Bois de
Cassan, Flying bomb supply depot. Bombed at 14.06 hours from
15,500 feet, centre of smoke.
07/08/1944 DS826 A2-C Bombing Mare de Magne 21.59 23.46
   01.05
   Bomb load 9 x 1000 MC, 4 x 500 GP. Primary target: Mare de
Magne (just past Caen). Slight haze. Bombed at 23.46 hours from

7,300 feet red T.I.s. Bombing appeared concentrated around T.I.s.

Mare-de-Magne: place between Caen and Fontenay le Marmion.

08/08/1944 DS826 A2-C Bombing Foret de Lucheux 21.52 23.50 01.12

Bomb load 18 x 500 GP. Primary target: Foret de Lucheux, Petrol dump. Weather clear. Bombed at 23.50 hours from 12,000 feet, nearest edge of large fires as instructed by Master Bomber. Large fires left burning the centre of the wood, and much black smoke.

"Foret de Lucheux" is a forest between Lille and Amiens. During WWII, important fuel tanks were stored there.

11/08/1944 DS826 A2-C Bombing Lens 14.17 16.34 17.33

Bomb load 11 x 1000 MC, 4 X 500 GP. Primary target: Lens, Marshalling yards. Small amount of cloud. Bombed at 16.34 hours from 14,000 feet, yellow T.I. Good concentrated attack.

14/08/1944 LM286 A2-F Bombing Hamel (Falaise) 13.51 15.51 17.16

Bomb load 11 x 1000 MC, 4 x 500 GP. Primary target: Hamel. Weather clear. Bombed at 15.51 hours from 8,500 feet, other bombs seen bursting across T.I.s. Bombing of troop concentrations.

16/08/1944 DS826 A2-C Bombing Stettin 21.15 01.11 05.23

Bomb load 1 x 2000 HC, 9 x 500 lb 'J' type clusters. Primary target: Stettin. Weather 10/10ths cloud on run-up, clear over target. Bombed at 01.11 hours from 20,000 feet red T.I.s. Bombs appeared scattered over fairly wide area, some fires started.

18/08/1944 DS826 A2-C Bombing Bremen 21.49 00.16 02.46

Bomb load 1 x 2000 HC, 96 x 30 lb inc, 810 x 4lb inc, 90 x 4lb x inc. Primary target: Bremen. Weather clear. Bombed at 00.16 hours from 20,000 feet, red T.I.s. Large fires and black smoke. Appeared to be concentrated raid.

25/08/1944 DS826 A2-C Bombing Vincly 18.38 20.37 22.06

Bomb load 11 x 1000 MC, 2 x 500 GP MK IV, 2 x 500 GP MK IV, LD. Primary target: Vincly. Weather: cloud patches. Bombed at 20.37 hours from 15,000 feet, visual of G.H. Leader.

26/08/1944 DS826 A2-C Bombing Kiel 20.23 23.13 01.41

Bomb load 1 x 4000 HC, 72 x 30 IB, 600 x 4 IB, 90 x 4 IB. Primary target: Kiel. Weather clear. Bombed at 23.13 hours from 18,500 feet centre of red T.I.s. Few T.I.s scattered. One large fire S of T.I.s.

10/09/1944 DS826 A2-C Bombing Le Havre 15.47 17.38 19.07

Bomb load 11 x 1000 MC, 4 x 500 GP. Primary target: Le Havre. Weather clear. Bombed at 17.38 hours from 10,000 feet. Undershot red

T.I.s by 200 yards.

12/09/1944 NF966 JI-R Bombing Frankfurt   18.45   23.05   01.16
Bomb load 1 x 4000 HC, 14 x 500 Clusters 4lb. Target: Frankfurt - Main. Weather clear over the target. Bombed at 23.05 hours from 18,700 feet at centre of red T.I.s.

17/09/1944 DS826 A2-C   Bombing Boulogne   10.57 x 13.46
Bomb load 11 x 1000 MC, 4 x 500 GP. Primary target: Boulogne Aiming Point 2. Weather clear below cloud. At 12.15 hours order given by Master Bomber to abandon mission. Jettisoned 2 x 1000 MC, brought remainder back.

20/09/1944 DS826 A2-C   Bombing Calais   14.58   16.02   17.25
Bomb load 11 x 1000 MC, 4 x 500 GP. Primary target: Calais. Weather clear over target. Bombed at 16.02 hours from 4,000 feet, red T.I.s.

23/09/1944 DS826 A2-C   Bombing Neuss   19.31 x 21.21
Bomb load 4 x 1000 ANM 59, 7 x 1000 ANM 44, 3 x 500 GP. Primary target: Neuss. Abortive sortie. Returned early with starboard inner engine u/s.
Sgt. T.C. Clayton F/Engineer that day, as confirmed by his logbook.

28/09/1944 NG118   A2-E   Bombing Calais   08.03 x 10.39
Bomb load 11 x 1000 MC, 4 x 500 GP. Primary target: Calais 19. Abortive sortie. At 09.28 hours Master Bomber gave abandon mission. Jettisoned 4 x 1000 MC.

05/10/1944 LM734   A2-C   Bombing Saarbrucken   17.32 x 22.28
Bomb load 11 x 1000 MC, 1 x 500 GP. Primary target: Saarbrucken, Marshalling yards. Weather clear over target. Abandoned mission on instructions from Master Bomber heard to say they were unable to locate target and called "Abandon Mission - our troop in vicinity". Full bomb load brought back to Base.

06/10/1944 LM734   A2-C   Bombing Dortmund 16.55   20.32   22.18
Bomb load 1 x 4000 HC, 12 x No. 14 Clusters. Primary target: Dortmund, Town and Railways. Weather over the target was clear with slight ground haze. Bombed at 20.32 hours from 21,000 feet on centre of red and green T.I.s.

07/10/1944 LM734   A2-C   Bombing Emmerich 12.24   14.29   15.51
Bomb load 1 x 4000 HC. 10 x No. 14 clusters, 4 x (150 x 4). Primary target Emmerich. Weather clear with cloud at 13,000 feet. Bombed at 14.29 hours from 13,000 feet on South side of smoke as instructed.

14/10/1944 LM734   A2-C   Bombing Duisburg 22.36 01.29   03.18

Bomb load 11 x 1000 MC, 4 x 500 GP Long Delay. Primary target: Duisburg. Weather was clear with small amount of cloud over the target. Bombed at 01.29 hours from 19,000 feet. Centre of red T.I.s.

15/10/1944 NG121 JI-H Bombing Wilhelmshaven 17.36 19.49 21.50

Bomb load 11 x 1000 MC, 4 x 500 GP. Primary target: Wilhelmshaven. Weather haze and thin cloud at first with thick cloud later. Bombed at 19.49 hours from 17,000 feet. Centre of red T.I.s.

19/10/1944 LM734 A2-C Bombing Stuttgart 17.19 20.34 23.22

Bomb load 1 x 4000 HC, 3 x 500 Clusters, 7 x 150 x 4, 1 x 90 x 4 IB. Primary target: Stuttgart, A/P 'D' 1st attack. Weather 10/10ths cloud which broke to 6/10ths at the end of the period. Bombed at 20.34 hours from 16,000 feet. Red flares and yellow stars.

28/10/1944 LM734 A2-C Bombing Flushing 09.02 x 11.14

Bomb load 11 x 1000 MC, 4 x 500 GP. Primary target: Flushing. Weather over the target quite clear and conditions perfect, although believed to be only local, and some low cloud approaching. Abortive sortie - did not bomb owing to intercom being unserviceable. Accuracy would have been too uncertain. Aircraft hit by flak over the target. Jettisoned 40 miles off Southwold.

30/10/1944 NG118 A2-E Bombing Wesseling 09.17 12.01 13.30

Bomb load 1 x 4000 HC, 16 x 500 GP. Primary target: Wesseling. Weather was 10/10ths cloud - tops about 7,000 feet. Bombed at 12.01 hours from 19,000 feet on leading G.H. aircraft.

31/10/1944 PD333 A2-K Bombing Bottrop 12.04 15.01 16.28

Bomb load 1 x 4000 HC, 16 x 500 GP. Primary target: Bottrop, Synth. Oil plants. Weather 10/10ths cloud over target. Bombed at 15.01 hours from 18,000 feet on Gee.

05/11/1944 NG236 A2-C Bombing Solingen 10.19 13.01 14.38

Bomb load 1 x 4000 HC, 14 x 500 Clusters. Primary target: Solingen. Weather 10/10ths cloud over target. Bombed at 13.01 hours from 18,000 feet on Red flares with Green stars.

06/11/1944 NG236 A2-C Bombing Koblenz 17.02 x 19.43

Bomb load 1 x 4000 HC, 12 x 500 Clusters, 300 x 4 lb IB. Primary target: Koblenz. Abortive. Returned early with rear turret unserviceable.

08/11/1944 NG236 A2-C Bombing Homberg 08.05 10.23 12.01

Bomb load 1 x 4000 HC, 14 x No. 14 Clusters. Primary target: Homberg. Weather clear. Bombed at 10.23 hours from 17,000 feet on leading aircraft. Aircraft hit by flak. Mid upper turret damaged.

15/11/1944 NG236   A2-C   BombingDortmund 12.31   15.41   17.15
   Bomb load 1 x 4000 HC, 16 x 500 GP. Primary target: Hoesch-Benzin Dortmund, Oil refineries. Weather 10/10ths cloud over the target. Bombed at 15.41 hours from 16,500 feet. Upwind edge of Red flares.

16/11/1944 NG236   A2-C   BombingHeinsburg 13.17   15.31   16.51
   Bomb load 1 x 4000 HC, 6 x 1000 MC, 6 x 500 GP. Primary target: Heinsburg. Weather - nil cloud with slight haze over target. Bombed at 15.31 hours from 9,500 feet. Centre of town.

20/11/1944 NG236   A2-C   BombingHomberg 12.44 15.15   17.05
   Bomb load 1 x 4000 HC, 4 x 500 GP, 12 x 500 MC. Primary target: Homberg. Weather 10/10ths cloud over target. Bombed at 15.15 hours from 20,500 feet on G.H. Leader.

21/11/1944 NG236   A2-C   BombingHomberg 12.56 15.07   16.26
   Bomb load 1 x 4000 HC, 16 x 500 GP. Primary target: Homberg. Weather about 5/10ths cloud but clear for bombing. Bombed at 15.07 hours from 20,000 feet on Factory.

23/11/1944 NG236   A2-C   BombingNordstern 12.42   15.22   16.52
   Bomb load 1 x 4000 HC, 16 x 500 GP. Primary target: Nordstern, Gelsenkirchen Oil refineries. Weather 10/10ths cloud. Bombed at 15.22 hours from 20,000 feet. Red flares.

F/O. George Davidson Orr

150425 (1339926) F/O. George Davidson Orr. Pilot.
591822   F/S. Thomas Frederick Wilcox. A/Bomber.
1670036 F/S. James Bryson.   Navigator.
642488   F/S. Anthony McGlone.   WOP/AG.
1291345 F/S. Henry Edward Bishop.   MU/Gunner. 25 ops.
141271 (1386976) F/O Herbert Henry Wright, DFM MU/Gunner. 1 op.
937528   F/S. George Spencer.   R/Gunner.
2205575 Sgt. Roy Werrill.   F/Engineer.
J88748   P/O. Joseph Norman Gallicano, RCAF. 2nd Pilot. 9/11/1944
46928 (655159) F/L. Herbert Cooper Mottershead. 2nd Pilot. 1/1/1945
J35287   F/O. William Eugene McLean, RCAF. 2nd Pilot. 13/01/1945
J37099   F/O. Merlin Leigh Matkin, RCAF. 2nd Pilot. 16/01/1945

20/09/1944 LM685   JI-Q Bombing Calais   14.52 16.03 17.49
    Bomb load 11 x 1000 MC, 4 x 500 GP. Primary target: Calais.
Weather clear over target. Bombed at 16.03 hours from 2,300 feet, red
T.I.s.
23/09/1944 NG118   A2-E Bombing Neuss   19.30 21.29 23.26
    Bomb load 8 x 1000 ANM59, 3 x 1000 ANM44, 4 x 500 GP.
Primary target: Neuss. Weather 10/10ths cloud over target, tops

8/10,000 feet. Bombed at 21.29 hours from 20,300 feet on glows of fires seen below cloud.

26/09/1944 NG118   A2-E   Bombing Calais   11.24   12.46   14.10
   Bomb load 11 x 1000 MC, 4 x 500 GP. Primary target: Calais 7D. Weather clear below cloud which was 3,500 feet. Bombed at 12.46 hours from 3,200 feet on red T.I. + 1 second.

28/09/1944 LM286   A2-F   Bombing Calais   08.05   09.21   10.36
   Bomb load 11 x 1000 MC, 4 x 500 GP. Primary target: Calais 19. Bombed at 09.21 hours from 9,000 feet red T.I.

05/10/1944 PD334 A2-D   Bombing Saarbrucken   17.15 x 22.52
   Bomb load 11 x 1000 MC, 1 x 500 GP, 3 x 500 GP. Long Delay. Primary target: Saarbrucken, Marshalling yards. Weather clear over target. Abandoned mission on instructions from Master Bomber heard to say they were unable to locate target and called "Abandon Mission - our troop in vicinity". Jettisoned 3 x 500 safe at 5220N 0241E at 21.14 hours from 10,000 feet. Remainder brought back.

06/10/1944 LM735   A2-G   Bombing Dortmund 16.34   20.39   22.50
   Bomb load 1 x 4000 HC, 12 x No. 14 Clusters. Primary target: Dortmund, Town and Railways. Weather over the target was clear with slight ground haze. Bombed at 20.39 hours from 20,500 feet on centre of green T.I.s.

15/10/1944 LM719   A2-E   Bombing Wilhelmshaven 17.09   19.55   21.57
   Bomb load 11 x 1000 MC, 4 x 500 GP. Primary target: Wilhelmshaven. Weather haze and thin cloud at first with thick cloud later. Bombed at 19.55 hours from 17,000 feet. Flames.

19/10/1944 NG141   A2-J   Bombing Stuttgart   17.17   20.37   23.36
   Bomb load 1 x 4000 HC, 3 x 500 Clusters, 7 x 150 x 4, 1 x 90 x 4 IB. Primary target: Stuttgart, A/P 'D' 1st attack. Weather 10/10ths cloud which broke to 6/10ths at the end of the period. Bombed at 20.37 hours from 17,000 feet. Fires - H2S was unserviceable. Flash accidently jettisoned at 5155N 0021W in a field at 18.06 hours from 2,000 feet.
   F/O. H.H. Wright MU/Gunner that day.

21/10/1944 LM734   A2-C   Bombing Flushing 10.50 12.27 13.30
   Bomb load 12 x 1000 MC, 2 x 500 GP. Primary target: Flushing 'B'. Weather clear. Bombed at 12.27 hours from 8,000 feet. Visual.

23/10/1944 LM734   A2-C   Bombing Essen 16.27 19.34 21.26
   Bomb load 1 x 4000 HC, 6 x 1000 MC, 6 x 500 GP. Primary target: Essen. Weather 10/10ths cloud over target - tops 12/14,000 feet with

most appalling weather on route. Bombed at 19.34 hours from 19,500 feet. Red flares.

04/11/1944 NG141 A2-J Bombing Solingen 11.39 14.09 16.07
Bomb load 1 x 4000 HC, 14 x 500 Clusters. Primary target: Solingen. Weather 8-10/10ths cloud. Bombed at 14.09 hours from 21,000 feet on red flares.

05/11/1944 PD324 A2-B Bombing Solingen 10.11 13.05 14.51
Bomb load 1 x 4000 HC, 14 x 500 Clusters. Primary target: Solingen. Weather 10/10ths cloud over target. Bombed at 13.05 hours from 18,500 feet on leading aircraft.

08/11/1944 PD324 A2-B Bombing Homberg 07.59 10.32 12.21
Bomb load 1 x 4000 HC, 14 x No. 14 Clusters. Primary target: Homberg. Weather clear. Bombed at 10.32 hours from 18,500 feet on leading aircraft.

15/11/1944 PD324 A2-B Bombing Dortmund 12.31 15.41 17.32
Bomb load 1 x 4000 HC, 16 x 500 GP. Primary target: Hoesch-Benzin Dortmund, Oil refineries. Weather 10/10ths cloud over the target. Bombed at 15.41 hours from 18,000 feet on leading aircraft.

20/11/1944 PD324 A2-B Bombing Homberg 12.36 15.18 17.09
Bomb load 1 x 4000 HC, 3 x 500 GP, 13 x 500 MC. Primary target: Homberg. Weather 10/10ths cloud over target. Bombed at 15.18 hours from 20,000 feet on G.H. Leader.

23/11/1944 PD324 A2-B Bombing Nordstern 12.34 15.20 17.16
Bomb load 1 x 4000 HC, 16 x 500 GP. Primary target: Nordstern, Gelsenkirchen Oil refineries. Weather 10/10ths cloud. Bombed at 15.20 hours from 20,000 feet with leading aircraft.

27/11/1944 PD324 A2-B Bombing Cologne 12.23 15.05 16.44
Bomb load 1 x 4000 HC, 16 x 500 GP. Primary target: Cologne, Marshalling Yards. Weather patchy cloud. Bombed at 15.05 hours from 20,000 feet on G.H. Leader.

29/11/1944 PD324 A2-B Bombing Neuss 02.48 05.36 07.02
Bomb load 1 x 4000 HC, 14 x 150 x 4 incendiaries. Primary target: Neuss. Weather 10/10ths cloud over target but the glow of fires was seen through cloud. Bombed at 05.36 hours from 20,000 feet, Centre of flares.
P/O. J.N. Gallicano 2nd Pilot that day.

28/12/1944 PD324 A2-B Bombing Cologne 12.20 15.05 16.49
Bomb load 7 x 1000 MC, 7 x 500 GP, 3 x 250 GP. Primary target: Koln Gremberg, Marshalling yards. Weather 10/10ths cloud or fog. Bombed at 15.05 hours from 20,000 feet on leading G.H. aircraft.

01/01/1945 LM728   A2-B   Bombing Vohwinkle 16.26 19.44 21.29

Bomb load 1 x 4000 HC, 12 x 500 ANM58, 2 x 500 GP. Primary target: Vohwinkel. Weather clear. Bombed at 19.44 hours from 19,500 feet. Red and Green T.I.s.

F/L. H.C. Mottershead 2nd Pilot that day.

02/01/1945 LM728   A2-B   Bombing Nuremburg   15.32 19.36 22.37

Bomb load: 1 x 1000 ANM65, 1 x 500 ANM58, 8 (150 x 4) 10 x IB, 120 x 4. Primary target: Nuremburg. Weather clear. Bombed at 19.36 hours from 17,500 feet. Red and Green T.I.s.

05/01/1945 LM728   A2-B   Bombing Ludwigshafen 11.25 15.07 17.15

Bomb load 1 x 4000 HC, 10 x 500 ANM58 or 64, 2 x 500 GP. Primary target: Ludwigshafen, Marshalling yards. Weather clear over target. Bombed at 15.07 hours from 20,000 feet on G.H. Leader. Aircraft hit by flak - Pilot's half panel and starboard wing damaged.

07/01/1945 LM627   A2-H   Bombing Munich x x x

Bomb load 1 x 4000 HC, 7 x 500 clusters. Primary target: Munich. Weather 10/10ths cloud over target 6-8,000 feet with a thin layer altitude 16,000 feet. Failed to take off owing to oil leak in starboard inner engine.

13/01/1945 PB906 A2-D Bombing Saarbrucken 11.56 15.23 17.37

Bomb load 1 x 4000 HC, 10 x 500 ANM58 or 64, 4 x 250 GP. Primary target: Saarbrucken. Weather 3-5/10ths cloud, tops 4/5,000 feet. Bombed at 15.23 hours from 19,500 feet on leading G.H. aircraft. All aircrafts on this operation were diverted on return to Exeter as weather at base was unfit to land.

F/O. W.E. McLean 2nd Pilot that day.

15/01/1945 PB906 A2-B Bombing Lagendreer   11.46 15.02 16.35

Bomb load 1 x 4000 HC, 10 x 500 ANM64, 4 x 250 GP. Primary target: Lagendreer. Weather 10/10ths cloud. Bombed at 15.02 hours from 19,000 feet on G.H. Leader.

16/01/1945 PB906 A2-B Bombing Wanne-Eickel 23.12 x x

Bomb load 1 x 4000 HC, 10 x 500 ANM58, 4 x 250 GP. Primary target: Wanne-Eickel, Benzol plant. Weather 10/10ths thin low cloud. Aircraft missing en route.

F/O. M.L. Matkin 2nd Pilot that day.

Lost without trace 17th January 1945. All the crew are commemorated on the Runnymede Memorial.

F/O. Donald Wilson Parks, DFC

1st Crew

169025   F/O. Donald Wilson "Don" Parks, DFC. Pilot.
154582 (1389582) F/O. Charles William "Chas" Pfaff. A/Bomber.
A422481   F/O. Donald Leslie "Don" Forwood, RAAF. Navigator.
A429191   F/S. Kevin Albert "Bunny" Warren, RAAF. WOP/AG.
Sgt. Henry George "Tich" Taylor. MU/Gunner.
Sgt. I.R. "Ron" Clarke. R/Gunner.
Sgt. Eric J. "Clem" Clempson. F/Engineer.

L to R: I.R. Clarke, K.A. Warren, C.W. Pfaff, D.W. Parks, H.G. Taylor, D.L. Forwood, E.J. Clempson. (courtesy Kevin Taylor)

10/09/1944 PD265 JI-G Bombing Le Havre   15.50 17.39 19.12
    Bomb load 11 x 1000 MC, 4 x 500 GP. Primary target: Le Havre. Weather clear. Bombed at 17.39 hours from 10,000 feet. Undershot T.I.s red by 200 yards.
14/09/1944 LM724   JI-B Bombing Wassenaar 12.54 14.30 15.43
    Bomb load 11 x 1000 MC, 4 x 500 GP. Primary target: Wassenaar. Weather was good, nil cloud. Bombed at 14.30 hours from 12,000 feet, red T.I.s.
17/09/1944 PD265 JI-G Bombing Boulogne   10.54 x 13.11
    Bomb load 11 x 1000 MC, 4 x 500 GP. Primary target: Boulogne,

Aiming point 2. Weather clear below cloud. At 12.15 hours order given by Master Bomber to abandon mission. Jettisoned 2 x 1000 MC, brought remainder back.

23/09/1944 PB426 JI-J Bombing Neuss   19.25 21.26 23.29
Bomb load 11 x 1000 ANM59, 4 x 500 GP. Primary target: Neuss. Weather 10/10ths cloud over target, tops 8/10,000 feet. Bombed at 21.26 from 19,000 feet on centre of glow.

28/09/1944 NN717   JI-E Bombing Calais   07.59 x 10.51
Bomb load 11 x 1000 MC, 4 x 500 GP. Primary target: Calais 19. Abortive sortie. At 09.28 hours Master Bomber gave abandon mission. Jettisoned 6 x 1000.

03/10/1944 PB426 JI-J Bombing Westkapelle 12.29   13.53 14.53
Bomb load 1 x 4000 MC, 6 x 1000 MC, 1 x 500 GP L/Delay. Primary target: Westkapelle (Walcheren). Weather patchy-scattered cloud with base 5,000 feet. Bombed at 13.53 hours from 6,000 feet slight undershot red T.I.

According to H.G. Taylor's logbook: "Walcheren Isle Sea Wall we did it".

05/10/1944 PB426 JI-J Bombing Saarbrucken   17.39 x 23.01
Bomb load 11 x 1000 MC, 1 x 500 GP, 3 x 500 GP. Long Delay. Primary target: Saarbrucken, Marshalling yards. Weather clear over target. Abandoned mission on instructions from Master Bomber heard to say they were unable to locate target and called "Abandon Mission - our troop in vicinity". Jettisoned 3 x 500 GP Long Delay at 22.27 hours from 8,500 feet 30 miles East of Southwold. Remainder brought back.

06/10/1944 PB426 JI-J Bombing Dortmund 16.44 20.26 22.12
Bomb load 1 x 4000 HC, 12 x No. 14 Clusters. Primary target: Dortmund, Town and Railways. Weather over the target was clear with slight ground haze. Bombed at 20.26 hours from 21,500 feet on centre of red and green T.I.s.

14/10/1944 PB426 JI-J Bombing Duisburg   07.07 09.04 11.17
Bomb load 11 x 1000 MC, 4 x 500 GP Long Delay. Primary target: Duisburg. Weather patchy cloud with gaps for bombing. Bombed at 09.04 hours from 20,000 feet. Built up area North of Docks and South of T.I.s.

According to H.G. Taylor's logbook: "Town & Docks".

14/10/1944 PB426 JI-J Bombing Duisburg   23.07 01.34 03.51
Bomb load 1 x 4000 HC, 14 x No. 14 Clusters. Primary target: Duisburg. Weather was clear with small amount of cloud over the

target. Bombed at 01.34 hours from 20,000 feet. Centre of green T.I.s. According to H.G. Taylor's logbook: "Town & Docks".

19/10/1944 PB426 JI-J Bombing Stuttgart   22.02 01.12 04.11
Bomb load 1 x 4000 HC, 6 x 1000 MC, 1 x 500 GP. Primary target: Stuttgart, A/P 'E' 2nd attack. Weather 10/10ths low cloud over target and all crew arrived late owing to winds not as forecast. Bombed at 01.12 hours from 18,500 feet. Wanganui sky markers.

Port inner damaged by flak. Hydraulics to Mid-upper turret severed - direct hit by flak at 4833N 05.35E at 01.56 hours.

Combat with FW190 at 00.47 hours 4908N 0650E 19,000 feet. Rear Gunner fired 3 long bursts M/U Gunner long burst - no claim. M/U Gunner wounded. According to H.G. Taylor's logbook written by Forwood due to Taylor injury: "Marshalling Yards - Wounded in left leg - Combat with FW190. Hits noticed".

2nd Crew

169025   F/O. Donald Wilson "Don" Parks, DFC. Pilot.
154582 (1389582) F/O. Charles William "Chas" Pfaff.   A/Bomber.
Sgt. J. Murray.   A/Bomber. 1 op.
A422481   F/O. Donald Leslie "Don" Forwood, RAAF. Navigator.
A429191   F/S. Kevin Albert "Bunny" Warren, RAAF. WOP/AG.
56195 (544317) P/O. Cyril Marjoram.   MU/Gunner.
J90779 (R190691) P/O. Douglas R. Bacon, RCAF. R/Gunner.
Sgt. Eric J. "Clem" Clempson. F/Engineer.
A418705 P/O. Alexander Edward Munro, RAAF. 2nd Pilot 29/11/1944

28/10/1944 NG203   JI-A Bombing Flushing   09.01 10.15 11.15
Bomb load 11 x 1000 MC, 4 x 500 GP. Primary target: Flushing. Weather over the target quite clear and conditions perfect, although believed to be only local, and some low cloud approaching. Bombed at 10.15 hours from 9,500 feet. Visual.

30/10/1944 NG203   JI-A Bombing Wesseling 09.23 11.57 13.23
Bomb load 1 x 4000 HC, 16 x 500 GP. Primary target: Wesseling. Weather was 10/10ths cloud - tops about 7,000 feet. Bombed at 11.57 hours from 18,000 feet on leading G.H. aircraft's release.

31/10/1944 NN717   JI-E Bombing Bottrop   11.46 15.01 16.32
Bomb load 1 x 4000 HC, 15 x 500 GP, 1 Flare. Primary target: Bottrop, Synth. Oil plants. Weather 10/10ths cloud over target. Bombed at 15.01 hours from 18,500 feet on G.H. aircraft ahead.

02/11/1944 ME841   JI-J   Bombing Homberg   11.20   14.10   15.47

Bomb load 1 x 4000 HC, 6 x 1000 ANM59, 6 x 500 MC. Primary target: Homberg. Weather variable cloud but clear for bombing. Target obscured by pall of smoke rising to 10,000 feet. Bombed at 14.10 hours from 18,000 feet. Green flares.

04/11/1944 LM733   JI-F   Bombing Solingen   11.37   14.10   16.05

Bomb load 1 x 4000 HC, 14 x 500 Clusters. Primary target: Solingen. Weather 8-10/10ths cloud. Bombed at 14.10 hours from 20,000 feet on upwind edge of red flares.

06/11/1944 LM285   JI-K   Bombing Koblenz   17.03   19.31   22.01

Bomb load 1 x 4000 HC, 12 x 500 Clusters, 300 x 4 lb IB. Primary target: Koblenz. Weather clear over target. Bombed at 19.31 hours from 18,500 feet on Red and Green T.I.s.

15/11/1944 NG121   JI-H Bombing Dortmund   12.50   15.39   17.18

Bomb load 1 x 4000 HC, 16 x 500 GP. Primary target: Hoesch-Benzin Dortmund, Oil refineries. Weather 10/10ths cloud over the target. Bombed at 15.59 hours from 17,000 feet on Red flares.

16/11/1944 NG121   JI-H Bombing Heinsburg 13.13   15.32   17.24

Bomb load 1 x 4000 HC, 6 x 1000 MC, 6 x 500 GP. Primary target: Heinsburg. Weather - nil cloud with slight haze over target. Bombed at 15.32 hours from 9,000 feet. Centre of town.

21/11/1944 LM733   JI-F   Bombing Homberg   12.47   15.07   16.41

Bomb load 1 x 4000 HC, 16 x 500 GP. Primary target: Homberg. Weather about 5/10ths cloud but clear for bombing. Bombed at 15.07 hours from 20,000 feet on G.H. Leader.

23/11/1944 ME841   JI-J   Bombing Nordstern   12.41   15.21   17.22

Bomb load 1 x 4000 HC, 15 x 500 GP, 1 Red flare with Green stars. Primary target: Nordstern, Gelsenkirchen Oil refineries. Weather 10/10ths cloud. Bombed at 15.21 hours from 20,000 feet on Red T.I.

Sgt. J. Murray A/Bomber that day.

29/11/1944 ME841   JI-J   Bombing Neuss   02.52 05.36   07.26

Bomb load 1 x 4000 HC, 6 x 1000 MC, 6 x 500 GP. Primary target: Neuss. Weather 10/10ths cloud over target but the glow of fires was seen through cloud. Bombed at 05.36 hours from 20,000 feet. Centre of Red and Green Markers. Red glow seen through cloud.

P/O. A.E. Munro 2nd Pilot that day.

11/12/1944 LM627   A2-H   Bombing Osterfeld 08.49 11.05   12.48

Bomb load 1 x 4000 HC, 13 x 500 GP, 2 x 500 MC. Primary target: Osterfeld. Weather 10/10ths cloud, tops 16,000 feet. Bombed at 11.05 hours from 20,000 feet on G.H.

12/12/1944 LM724   JI-H Bombing Witten   11.21 14.06   15.55

Bomb load 1 x 4000 HC, 5 x 500 GP, 6 x 500 ANM58, 4 x 500 ANM64, 1 Flare. Primary target: Witten. Weather 10/10ths cloud, tops 14/16,000 feet. Bombed at 14.06 hours from 20,800 feet on G.H.

16/12/1944 ME841   JI-J Bombing Siegen   11.26 x 15.00

Bomb load 1 x 4000 HC, 5 x 1000 MC, 7 x 500 GP, 1 Flare. Primary target: Siegen. Weather very bad on route with icing and cloud. Aircraft returned early, landed at Woodbridge. Port outer engine and hydraulics U/S. Jettisoned safe 5220N 0239E.

21/12/1944 NG203   JI-A Bombing Trier   12.17   15.03   16.54

Bomb load 1 x 4000 HC, 6 x 250 GP. Primary target: Trier, Marshalling yards. Weather 10/10 cloud, tops 6/9000 feet. Bombed at 15.03 hours from 18,000 feet on G.H.

23/12/1944 NG203   JI-A Bombing Trier   11.53   14.29   16.07

Bomb load 1 x 4000 HC, 10 x 500 GP, 2 x 250 GP, 4 x 250 T.I. Red. Primary target: Trier. Weather clear over target. Bombed at 14.29 hours from 18,000 feet visually.

28/12/1944 PB419 JI-J Bombing Cologne Gremberg   12.24   15.06   17.00

Bomb load 7 x 1000 MC, 5 x 500 GP, 4 x 250 Red T.I.s. Primary target: Koln Gremberg, Marshalling yards. Weather 10/10ths cloud or fog. Bombed at 15.06 hours from 20,000 feet on G.H.

31/12/1944 PB419 JI-J Bombing Vohwinkle 11.42   14.44   16.30

Bomb load 1 x 4000 HC, 3 x 1000 M65, 2 x 500 ANM58, 2 x 500 M64, 2 x 500 GP, 2 x 500 GP L/Delay, 1 x 250 GP, 1 Flare. Primary target: Vohwinkel. Weather 10/10ths cloud on approaching target although the target itself was clear. Bombed at 14.44 hours from 20,000 feet on G.H.

01/01/1945 LM275   JI-F Bombing Vohwinkle 16.19   19.43   21.25

Bomb load 1 x 4000 HC, 12 x 500 ANM58, 2 x 500 GP. Primary target: Vohwinkel. Weather clear. Bombed at 19.43 hours from 20,500 feet on G.H.

F/L.   James Stuart Parnell

138092 (1113875) F/L. James Stuart "Jimmy" Parnell. Pilot.
154311 (1398362) F/O. Ronald "Ron" Goulding. . A/Bomber. 36 ops.
Sgt. J. Murray.   A/Bomber.   2 ops.
154526 (1586844) F/O. Leslie Charles "Les" Seaward. Navigator.
A429763   W/O.   Donald Ernest Matson, RAAF.   WOP/AG. 32 ops.
Sgt. B.A. Robus.   WOP/AG.   5 ops.
F/S. G.A. Brown.   WOP/AG.   1 op.
Sgt. H.L. "Harry" Griffiths. MU/Gunner. 37 ops.
Sgt. Leslie E. "Les" Gurr.   R/Gunner.
Sgt. Brian R. Prudden.   F/Engineer.
J28322   F/O. Campbell George Fiset, RCAF. 2nd Pilot. 30/11/1944
J40283   F/O. Harold A. Pickersgill, RCAF. 2nd Pilot. 19/02/1945
141716 (1312150) F/L. Frederick William Morrish. 2nd Pilot.
06/03/1945

Passengers: 04/05/1945, 12/06/1945.

28/10/1944 PB482 JI-P Bombing Cologne   13.11   15.47   17.37
    Bomb load 1 x 4000 HC, 8 x 150 x 4. Primary target: Cologne.
Weather clear over target. Bombed at 15.47 hours from 20,000 feet.
Smoke trails as instructed.
    From his normal crew, only F/O. J.S. Parnell did this mission as 2nd
Pilot with F/O. A.D.J. Uffindell's crew.
30/10/1944 LM728   JI-U Bombing Wesseling 09.12   12.04   13.50
    Bomb load 1 x 4000 HC, 15 x 500 GP. Primary target: Wesseling.
Weather was 10/10ths cloud - tops about 7,000 feet. Bombed at 12.04
hours from 16,500 feet on release by G.H. Leader.
31/10/1944 LM727   JI-S Bombing Bottrop   12.11   15.01   16.51
    Bomb load 1 x 4000 HC, 16 x 500 GP. Primary target: Bottrop,
Synth. Oil plants. Weather 10/10ths cloud over target. Bombed at
15.01 hours from 18,000 feet on G.H. Leader.
04/11/1944 LM727   JI-S Bombing Solingen   11.41   14.10   16.13
    Bomb load 1 x 4000 HC, 14 x 500 Clusters. Primary target:
Solingen. Weather 8-10/10ths cloud. Bombed at 14.10 hours from
19,500 feet on upwind edge of red flares.
06/11/1944 LM727   JI-S Bombing Koblenz   16.54   19.40   22.14
    Bomb load 1 x 4000 HC, 12 x 500 Clusters, 300 x 4 lb IB. Primary
target: Koblenz. Weather clear over target. Bombed at 19.40 hours

from 17,500 feet on centre of 3 T.I. Green.

08/11/1944 LM727   JI-S Bombing Homberg   07.55 10.30 12.31
Bomb load 1 x 4000 HC, 14 x No. 14 Clusters. Primary target: Homberg. Weather clear. Bombed at 10.30 hours from 17,500 feet on leading aircraft.

15/11/1944 LM717   JI-T Bombing Dortmund   12.35 15.40 17.40
Bomb load 1 x 4000 HC, 16 x 500 GP. Primary target: Hoesch-Benzin Dortmund, Oil refineries. Weather 10/10ths cloud over the target. Bombed at 15.40 hours from 16,500 feet on leading aircraft.

16/11/1944 LM727   JI-S Bombing Heinsburg 13.10 15.33 17.39
Bomb load 1 x 4000 HC, 6 x 1000 MC, 6 x 500 GP. Primary target: Heinsburg. Weather - nil cloud with slight haze over target. Bombed at 15.33 hours from 9,000 feet. Starboard of smoke.

20/11/1944 LM727   JI-S Bombing Homberg   12.56 15.14 17.20
Bomb load 1 x 4000 HC, 13 x 500 GP, 3 x 500 MC. Primary target: Homberg. Weather 10/10ths cloud over target. Bombed at 15.14 hours from 20,000 feet on G.H. Leader.

23/11/1944 LM734   JI-U Bombing Nordstern   12.49 15.20 17.07
Bomb load 1 x 4000 HC, 16 x 500 GP. Primary target: Nordstern, Gelsenkirchen Oil refineries. Weather 10/10ths cloud. Bombed at 15.20 hours from 20,000 feet. Red T.I.s with G.H. Leader.

27/11/1944 LM727   JI-S Bombing Cologne   12.33 15.05 17.00
Bomb load 1 x 4000 HC, 16 x 500 GP. Primary target: Cologne, Marshalling Yards. Weather patchy cloud. Bombed at 15.05 hours from 20,000 feet on G.H. Leader.

30/11/1944 PB767 JI-G Bombing Osterfeld   11.00 13.11 14.41
Bomb load 1 x 4000 HC, 16 x 500 GP. Primary target: Osterfeld, Coking plant. Weather 10/10ths cloud. Bombed at 13.11 hours from 19,500 feet on G.H. Leader.

F/O. C.G. Fiset 2nd Pilot that day.

08/12/1944 LM727   JI-S Bombing Duisburg   08.46 11.05 12.52
Bomb load 14 x 1000 ANM59. Primary target: Duisberg. Weather 10/10ths cloud. Bombed at 11.05 hours from 20,000 feet on G.H. Leader.

Sgt. J. Murray was A/Bomber that day and F/S. G.A. Brown WOP/AG.

11/12/1944 PD389 JI-Q Bombing Osterfeld   08.49 11.06 13.03
Bomb load 1 x 4000 HC, 12 x 500 GP, 2 x 500 MC, 1 Flare. Primary target: Osterfeld. Weather 10/10ths cloud, tops 16,000 feet. Bombed at 11.06 hours from 19,000 feet on E.T.A.

Sgt. J. Murray A/Bomber that day.

12/12/1944 PD389 JI-Q Bombing Witten   11.24 14.06   15.50

Bomb load 1 x 4000 HC, 5 x 500 GP, 6 x 500 ANM58, 4 x 500 ANM64, 1 Flare. Primary target: Witten. Weather 10/10ths cloud, tops 14/16,000 feet. Bombed at 14.06 hours from 20,300 feet on G.H.

16/12/1944 PD389 JI-Q Bombing Siegen   11.30   15.00   17.05

Bomb load 1 x 4000 HC, 5 x 1000 MC, 7 x 500 GP, 1 Flare. Primary target: Siegen. Weather very bad on route with icing and cloud. Bombed at 15.00 hours from 17,500 feet on G.H. Leader.

01/02/1945 LM728   JI-F Bombing Munchen-Gladbach   13.21   16.34   18.15

Bomb load 1 x 4000 HC, 10 x 500 ANM64, 2 x 500 GP, 4 x 250 GP. Primary target: Munchen-Gladbach, Marshalling yards. Bombed at 16.34 hours from 19,000 feet on G.H.

19/02/1945 ME351   JI-U Bombing Wesel   13.09 16.35   18.59

Bomb load 1 x 4000 HC, 6 x 500 MC, 6 x 500 ANM64, 3 x 250 GP, 1 Skymarker Red puff. Primary target: Wesel. Weather over target 5-7/10ths cloud. Bombed at 16.35 hours from 19,200 feet on G.H.

F/O. H.A. Pickersgill 2nd Pilot that day.

25/02/1945 ME336   JI-S Bombing Kamen   09.28   12.46   15.04

Bomb load 1 x 4000 HC, 9 x 500 ANM64, 2 x 500 MC, 3 x 250 GP, 1 x 250 Blue Puff. Primary target: Kamen. Weather 6-8/10ths cloud. Bombed at 12.46 hours from 19,900 feet on G.H. equipment.

27/02/1945 ME351   JI-U Bombing Gelsenkirchen   10.52   14.27   16.26

Bomb load 1 x 4000 HC, 2 x 500 MC (L/D 37B), 9 x 500 ANM64, 3 x 250 GP, 1 x 250 Blue Puff. Primary target: Gelsenkirchen (Alma Pluts). Weather 10/10ths cloud, 6/10,000 feet tops. Bombed at 14.27 hours from 20,000 feet on G.H.

01/03/1945 ME355   JI-L Bombing Kamen   11.47   15.05   17.48

Bomb load 1 x 4000 HC, 10 x 500 ANM64, 2 x 500 MC L/Delay37, 1 SM Blue puff. Primary target: Kamen, Coking plant. Weather 10/10ths cloud. Bombed at 15.05 hours from 18,500 feet on G.H.

06/03/1945 ME387   JI-N Bombing Wesel   18.20 21.08   23.31

Bomb load 1 x 4000 HC, 13 x 500 ANM64, 2 x 500MC. Primary target: Wesel. Weather 10/10ths cloud, tops 16,000 feet preventing visual. Bombed at 21.08 hours from 18,100 feet on G.H.

F/L. F.W. Morrish 2nd Pilot that day.

29/03/1945 ME351   JI-U Bombing Salzgitter   12.26   16.42   19.23

Bomb load 1 x 4000 HC, 8 x 500 ANM64. Primary target:

Salzgitter, Hallendorf works. Weather 10/10ths cloud. Bombed at 16.42 hours from 21,000 feet on G.H. & H.2.S. Difficult for followers, green puffs dispersed.

09/04/1945 ME351   JI-U Bombing Kiel   19.32   22.37   01.57

Bomb load 1 x 4000 HC and 12 x 500 ANM64. Primary target: Kiel, Submarine Buildings Yards. Weather clear with slight haze. Bombed at 22.37 hours from 20,000 feet on Red and Green T.I.s. M/B too scrambled to be heard. Fairly well concentrated. Very successful raid.

18/04/1945 ME351   JI-U Bombing Heligoland 09.45 13.07 15.11

Bomb load 6 x 1000 MC, 10 x 500 ANM64. Primary target: Heligoland, Naval base. Weather no cloud, slight haze. Bombed visually at wind edge of smoke at 13.07 hours from 18,200 ft. Smoke pall with much black smoke to south. Attack on both islands very successful.

30/04/1945 ME363   JI-R Manna Rotterdam 16.51 18.19 19.36

Dropping area: Rotterdam. Weather intermittent showers and low cloud. Load 5 packs. Dropped 5 packs at 18.19 hours in field piled high with packs and surrounded with people. One pack hung up. Orbited to starboard dropping remaining pack on white cross where few packs had been dropped as area appeared marshy.

04/05/1945 ME422   JI-Q Manna The Hague   11.56 13.22 14.29

Dropping area The Hague. Dropped 5 Panniers on White Cross and Red T.I. at 13.22 hours. Clear cloud - Base 1,000 ft. All Panniers fell in area marked.

No Mid Upper Gunner that day.

Passenger: Cpl. Wilson.

09/05/1945 ME351   JI-U Exodus   Juvincourt - Dunsfold 07.33 x 14.40

Arrived Dunsfold 12.48 hours, collected 24 P.O.Ws. Organisation good. Suggest that arrival of aircraft at Dunsfold should be staggered, to avoid jamming up the R.T.

11/05/1945 ME351   JI-U Exodus   Juvincourt - Tangmere 11.09 x 18.15

Duration 3.41. Outward 1.32 hours. Collected 24 ex POWs. Homeward 2.09 hours. Wheel changed at Juvincourt.

12/05/1945 ME530   JI-C Exodus   Brussels - Tangmere 11.49 x 18.19

Duration 3.28. Outward 1.23 hours. Homeward 2.05 hours. 10 Refugees to Brussels, 24 POW to Ford. All O.K.

17/05/1945 RE117 A2-D Exodus   Brussels - Westcott 12.00 x 18.34

Duration 2 hrs 24 mins. Out 1 hr 12 mins. In 1 hr 12 mins. 10 Belgian refugees taken to Brussels. No POWs available. Delay due to overheating engines at Brussels, plus a terrific dust storm.

19/05/1945 ME535 JI-G Exodus Brussels - Oakley 11.49 x 17.37
Duration 3 hrs 09 mins. Out 1 hr 17 mins. In 1 hr 27 mins. 10 Belgian refugees taken to Brussels. 24 ex POWs returned to U.K.

23/05/1945 ME351 JI-U Exodus Brussels - Oakley 12.10 x 18.13
Duration 2.59 hours. Out 1.12 hours. In 1.47 hours. 9 Belgian refugees returned to Brussels. 24 ex POWs evacuated. All OK.

24/05/1945 ME351 JI-U Exodus Brussels 12.04 x 15.19
Duration 2.23 hours. Out 1.07 hours. In 1.16 hours. 10 Belgian refugees returned to Brussels. No ex POWs to be brought back.

25/05/1945 ME351 JI-U Exodus Brussels 12.04 x 15.10
Duration 2.21 hours. Out 1.07 hours. In 1.14 hours. 10 Belgian refugees to Brussels. No POWs. All OK.
Sgt. B.A. Robus WOP/AG from that day.

26/05/1945 ME351 JI-U Exodus Brussels - Ford 11.57 x 17.25
Duration 3.11 hours. Out 1.08 hours. In 2.03 hours. 10 Belgian refugees to Brussels. 24 ex POWs all military brought back.

12/06/1945 ME351 JI-U Baedeker Tour over Continent 12.23 x 17.07
29/06/1945 ME364 JI-P Post Mortem Special mission 10.03 x 15.53
Passengers: F/O. O. Howard, Cpl. B. Maxwell.

03/07/1945 ME351 JI-U Post Mortem Special mission 14.39 x 19.49

F/O. Thomas Harry Pashley

153592 (1582441) F/O. Thomas Harry Pashley.   Pilot.
165300 (1622311) F/O. Maurice Cecil Stamford.   A/Bomber.
Sgt. E.O. James.   Navigator.
NZ4213316 F/S. T. Willcox, RNZAF.   WOP/AG.
Sgt. K.G. Bateman.   MU/Gunner. 15 ops.
Sgt. G.T. Bain.   R/Gunner.
F/S. W. King Whiteford.   F/Engineer.

Passengers: 04/05/1945, 02/06/1945, 14/06/1945, 26/07/1945, 28/07/1945.

27/02/1945 PD389 A2-J Bombing Gelsenkirchen 11.00 14.28 16.25
Bomb load 1 x 4000 HC, 2 x 500 MC (L/D 37B), 9 x 500 ANM64, 4 x 250 GP. Primary target: Gelsenkirchen (Alma Pluts) Benzin plant.

Weather 10/10ths cloud, 6/10,000 feet tops. Bombed at 14.28 hours from 19,500 feet on G.H.

From his normal crew, only F/O. T.H. Pashley did this mission as 2nd Pilot with P/O. A.W. Tasker's crew.

28/02/1945 ME364   JI-P Bombing Nordstern   08.49   12.05   14.07

Bomb load 1 x 4000 HC, 9 x 500 ANM64, 2 x 500 MC L/D, 4 x 250 GP. Primary target: Nordstern (Gelsenkirchen). Weather 10/10ths cloud. Bombed at 12.05 hours from 20,000 feet on leading aircraft.

10/03/1945 NG118   A2-H Bombing Gelsenkirchen 12.30 15.37 17.36

Bomb load 1 x 4000 HC, 13 x 500 ANM64, 2 x 500 GP. Primary target: Gelsenkirchen. Weather 10/10ths cloud at target, tops 8,000 feet. Bombed at 15.37 hours from 19,000 feet on G.H. Leader. Cluster of 5 Blue Puffs seen as we bombed.

12/03/1945 NG142   JI-J Bombing Dortmund 13.03   16.57   18.54

Bomb load 1 x 4000 HC, 13 x 500 ANM64. Primary target: Dortmund. Weather 10/10ths cloud over target, tops 6/10,000 feet. Bombed at 16.57 hours from 19,000 feet on G.H. Leader. Should be a good attack.

18/03/1945 ME336   JI-S Bombing Bruchstrasse   12.16   15.05   17.25

Bomb load 1 x 4000 HC, 13 x 500 ANM64, 2 x 500 MC. Primary target: Bruchstrasse, Coal mine & coking plant. Weather 10/10ths cloud, tops 6-12,000 feet. Bombed at 15.05 hours from 19,000 feet on leading G.H. aircraft. Blue Puff seen as bombs released.

20/03/1945 ME336   JI-S Bombing Hamm   09.43   13.15   15.33

Bomb load 7 x 1000 ANM65, 9 x 500 ANM64. Primary target: Hamm, Marshalling yards. Weather 5/10ths cloud. Bombed at 13.15 hours from 18,000 feet on leading aircraft. Slight damage to Mid-upper turret by heavy flak over the target.

04/04/1945 ME387   JI-N Bombing Merseburg (Leuna)   18.52 x 02.57

Weather 5-10/10ths cloud, and 10/10ths over Merseburg. Bombed primary target. Bomb load 1 x 4000 HC, 6 x 500 ANM64. 7/10th cloud (Stratus). Bombed on starboard of middle stick red green stars. Bright bluish green explosion seen. Some smoke. Several bombs seen to drop outside the target area. P.F.F. was late and scattered in four different areas.

From his normal crew, only F/O. T.H. Pashley did this mission as 2nd Pilot with S/L. H.C.G. Wilcox's crew.

13/04/1945 PB419 JI-L Bombing Kiel   20.17   23.31   02.34

Bomb load 1 x 4000 HC and 12 x 500 ANM64. Primary target:

Kiel, Docks & ship yards. Weather 10/10ths cloud low and thin. Bombed at 23.31 hours from 18,000 feet on Red T.I.s. M/B indistinct. Cookie bursts seen among T.I.s. Starboard inner and port inner had to be nursed due to high oil pressure. Could not get height. Bombing appeared concentrated. Should be an effective raid.

20/04/1945 ME358   JI-O Bombing Regensburg 09.39 13.56   17.17

Bomb load 16 x 500 ANM64. Primary target: Regensburg. Weather clear over target and whole route. Bombed visually at 13.56 hours from 18,000 ft. G.H. set caught fire believed oil depots. Smoke and explosions. Good raid and little trouble. Concentrated bombing.

24/04/1945 ME358   JI-O Bombing Bad Oldesloe 07.03   10.46   13.12

Bomb load 6 x 1000 ANM65, 10 x 500 ANM 64. Primary target: Bad-Oldesloe, Rail and road junction and Marshalling Yards. Weather 3/10ths to nil cloud. Bombed on furthest upwind sky-blue puff at 10.46 hours from 17,000 ft G.H. u/s no pulses received. Large fire seen in target area. Explosions seen. Hydraulic fluid appears to have flowed over R/F unit. Cause not known. Effective. Good concentration.

01/05/1945 ME364   JI-P Manna The Hague   13.29   14.43   15.53

Dropping area The Hague. Weather clear over target. Dropped 5 Panniers on Red T.I. and White Cross at 14.43 hrs. Good concentration of bags.

04/05/1945 ME363   JI-R Manna The Hague   12.05   13.23   14.35

Dropping area The Hague. Dropped 5 panniers on Red T.I.s and White Cross at 13.23 hours. Clear. Delivery OK. "We thank you" written on ground before D.Z. (Drop Zone).

No Mid Upper Gunner that day.

Passengers: AC2. Marran.

08/05/1945 ME359   JI-T Manna Rotterdam 12.42   14.09   15.10

Dropping area Rotterdam. Dropped 5 Packs on T.I.s and food packs at 14.09 hours. Clear. Good concentration of packs. T.I.s were late.

02/06/1945 RE139 JI-M   Baedeker Tour over Germany   09.48 x 15.35

Passengers: S/L. W. McIntyre, F/O. G. Masters, Sgt. P. Pounds.

14/06/1945 RE139 JI-M   Baedeker Tour over Continent 12.26 x 17.03

Passengers: LAC. Bowman, LAC. Willis, LAC. Burrows, Sgt. Jones.

25/06/1945 RA599   JI-L Post Mortem Special mission x x x

P.O. Engine Magneto failed to switch off.

26/07/1945 RE139 JI-M   Baedeker Tour over Continent 10.10 x 14.18

Passengers: F/L. Williams, Cpl. Sayers, LAC. Pennington, LACW.

Watts, LACW. Sparks.

28/07/1945 RE139 JI-M   Baedeker Tour over Continent 10.00 x 14.06
    Passengers: Cpl. Horseman, LAC. Brackpoll, LAC. Roberts, 647.
Jones, 132. Goodier.

F/L. acting S/L. Colin Payne DFC

149559 (1451625) S/L. Colin Payne. DFC. Pilot.
132709 (1206772) F/O. Kenneth Wilfred Armstrong, DFC. Navigator.
171685 (1324883) P/O. Stanley Charles Young. A/Bomber.
174249 (978911) P/O. John Brewer Robinson. WOP/AG.
A421309 P/O. David N. or W. Bennett, RAAF. MU/Gunner. 15 ops.
981579 Sgt. Alexander Nicholson. MU/Gunner. 1 op.
171595 (1396800) P/O. Peter Anthony Sydney Twinn. R/Gunner.
186764 (1336682) Sgt. Alexander Charles Gilbert. F/Engineer. 15 ops.
51707 (570208) F/O. Howard Hall. F/Engineer. 1 op.
F/O. A. Soaper. 2nd Pilot. 01/01/1944

03/11/1943 DS786 JI-E Bombing Dusseldorf 18.08 19.51 21.33
    Aircraft carried 1 x 4000, 720 x 4 lb incendiaries, 32 x 30 lb
incendiaries (including 60 x 4 lb). Attacked target at 19.51 hours,
height 20,600 feet 040 degs. 150 MPH. Good visibility. Ground
markers seen to the South. Large fires seen in main target area and
some fires seen on out Tag. Photos attempted but no flash. Very
satisfactory raid.

The crew whilst at No. 9 Squadron, August 1943.

18/11/1943 DS786 JI-E Bombing Berlin   17.44 21.01   01.10

Bomb load 1 x 4000, 16 x 30, 270 x 4. Primary target Berlin. Visibility poor with 10/10 cloud in target area. No Green T.I.s seen and only one Red T.I. seen so bombs were dropped on latter at 21.01 hours, 20,000 feet. Bomb Markers were seen on the way to the target, but not on return journey. P.F.F Green T.I.s were dropped late.

22/11/1943 DS786 JI-E Bombing Berlin   17.37 20.22   23.09

Bomb load 1 x 4000, 360 x 4 incendiaries, 90 x 4 incendiaries, 24 x 30 incendiaries. Primary target: Berlin. 10/10 cloud Tops 10/12,000 feet. P.F.F. Flares. Very large glow beneath cloud. An exceptionally big explosion at 20.22 hours. Think it must have been a good PRANG as so many Lancs could be seen in target area.

23/11/1943 DS786 JI-E Bombing Berlin   17.35 x 00.01

Bomb load 1 x 4000 HC, 32 x 30 incendiaries, 540 x 4 incendiaries, 90 x 4. Primary target: Berlin. 10/10 cloud Tops 8,000/10,000 feet. Visibility good above. Skymarkers red flares, green stars and green T.I.s. Bombed on estimated centre of green T.I.s which were fairly well concentrated. Glow of fire seen through cloud. 30 x 4 incendiaries hung up over target and brought back. Route markers were useful. Diverted to Cranfield on return.

26/11/1943 DS735 JI-A Bombing Berlin   17.52 21.17   00.20

Bomb load 1 x 4000 HC, 24 x 30 incendiaries, 405 x 4 incendiaries, 45 x 4. Primary target: Berlin. No cloud, visibility good. Attacked target at 21.17 hrs at 21,500 ft. A very large explosion was seen to light up a large factory. Good fires seen when leaving, visible for 100 miles.

Sgt. Alexander Nicholson MU/Gunner that day.

02/12/1943 DS706 JI-G Bombing Berlin   17.07 20.17   23.22

Bomb load 1 x 8000, 160 x 4 incendiaries, 20 x 4 incendiaries. Primary target: Berlin. 6-8/10 cloud with tops at 4,000 ft. Bombed on Red and Green T.I.s 20.17 hrs at 21,500 ft. Few fires taking hold as aircraft left target. Camera u/s.

F/O. H. Hall F/Engineer that day.

16/12/1943 DS786 JI-E Bombing Berlin   16.45 x 18.55

Bomb load 1 x 4000, 450 x 4, 90 x 4 incendiaries. Port undercarriage could not be raised due to burst Hydraulic pipe. Tried to hand pump but this proved ineffective so we returned to Base after reducing load by jettisoning.

20/12/1943 DS706 JI-G Bombing Frankfurt   17.33   19.43   22.26

Bomb load 1 x 8000, 16 x 30 incendiaries, 330 x 4 incendiaries, 30 x 4 incendiaries. Primary target: Frankfurt. 9/10 cloud. Lack of markers. Bombed target at 19.43 at 19,000 ft. Column of smoke seen up to 6,000 ft. Good red glow showing through cloud could be seen 100 miles away.

24/12/1943 DS786JI-E Bombing Berlin   00.25 04.09   07.27

Bomb load 1 x 8000. Primary target: Berlin. Broken cloud. Bombed at 04.09 at 20,000 ft. Target well slight. Two large explosions 04.14 hrs. Fires taking good hold before we left the target.

29/12/1943 DS786JI-E Bombing Berlin   17.00 20.06   23.26

Bomb load 1 x 4000, 24 x 30 incendiaries, 540 x 4 incendiaries, 90 x 4 incendiaries. Primary target: Berlin. There was 10/10 cloud with tops 8/10,000. Bombed at 20.06 hours at 21,000 ft. All bombs dropped except 90 x 4 incendiaries which hung up and brought back. 10/10 cloud prevented observation. Rear Gunner reported red glow beneath cloud seen from 40 miles.

01/01/1944 DS786JI-E Bombing Berlin   00.25 03.10   06.59

Bomb load 1 x 4000, 24 x 30, 450 x 4, 90 x 4 lb incendiaries. Primary target: Berlin. There was 10/10 cloud over the target. Red and green stars and marker flares seen. Bombed at 03.10 hrs at 20,000 feet. Weather very poor.

F/O. A. Soaper 2nd Pilot that day.

02/01/1944 DS786JI-E Bombing Berlin   00.06 02.48   06.37

Bomb load 1 x 4000, 24 x 30, 450 x 4, 90 x 4 incendiaries. Primary target: Berlin. There was 10/10 cloud, tops 10,000 ft. Very thick. Bombed at 02.48 hours at 21,000 ft. Sky markers well concentrated, too much cloud to see fires or explosion.

15/02/1944 DS786A2-F Bombing Berlin   17.34 21.34   00.57

Bomb load 1 x 8000 lb bomb. Primary target: Berlin. There was 10/10 cloud. Bombed at 21.34 hrs. At 20,000 ft. Route satisfactory. P.F.F. markers scattered. Difficult to ascertain result of the raid.

21/02/1944 DS786A2-F Bombing Stuttgart 00.25 04.02   06.30

Bomb load 1 x 8000 lb bomb, 16 x 30, 90 x 4 incendiaries. Primary target: Stuttgart. There was 2-4/10 broken cloud. Bombed at 04.07 hours at 20,000 ft. T.I.s concentrated but seemed to be burning in open fields. Curious blue and green flash seen 04.06 hours.

10/04/1944 DS786A2-F Bombing Laon   01.25   03.48   05.25

Bomb load 9 x 1000, 4 x 500 lb bomb. Primary target: Laon. Weather was clear. Bombed at 03.48 hours from 9,500 feet. Saw 12 bombs burst. T.I.s concentrated. Railway lines quite visible. Attack considered quite successful. Bombing very concentrated. One fairly large fire seen.

18/04/1944 LL678 A2-L Bombing Rouen 22.26 00.46 02.07
Bomb load 8 x 1000 MC, 2 x 1000 GP, 5 x 500 lb bombs. Primary target: Rouen. Weather was hazy. Bombed at 00.46 hours from 13,500 feet. Bomb bursts seen and fires at Southern A.P. Too early to ascertain result of raid. Route O.K.
Tour expired after this trip.

F/O. Kaiho Thomas Penkuri

J20187 F/O. Kaiho Thomas "Tommy" Penkuri, RCAF. Pilot.
1547059 F/S. Donald Joseph Kilner. A/Bomber.
J85314 (R64521) P/O. Lawrence Alvin "Larry" Wry, RCAF. Navigator.
1316364 Sgt. Thomas Yeandle Owen. WOP/AG.
1891075 Sgt. Kenneth Edwin "Ken" Peake. MU/Gunner. 8 ops.
A415845 F/S. Richard Hiden White, RAAF. MU/Gunner. 1 op.
Sgt. W. Wilson. MU/Gunner. 1 op.
J92270 P/O. William Fraser Sutherland, RCAF. R/Gunner. 4 ops.
1126069 Sgt. J. Crawford. R/Gunner. 6 ops.
1025606 Sgt. Gilbert "Gil" Cosgrove. F/Engineer. 9 ops.
1330027 Sgt. M.C.L. Bristow (or Bristowe). F/Engineer. 1 op.
NZ422270 F/S. Kenneth Drummond, RNZAF. 2nd Pilot. 15/03/1944

14/01/1944 DS813 JI-H Bombing Brunswick 16.45 19.19 22.11
Bomb load 1 x 4000, 48 x 30 incendiaries. Primary target: Brunswick. There was 9/10 cloud. Bombed at 19.19 hours at 20,000 ft. Monica not used. Route good. Fires scattered at first but merged later. Photo attempted.
F/S. R.H. White was MU/Gunner that day and Sgt. J. Crawford R/Gunner.

20/01/1944 DS813 JI-H Bombing Berlin 16.21 x 19.23
Bomb load 1 x 4000, 32 x 30, 540 x 4, 60 x4 incendiaries. Primary target: Berlin. Returned early. Rear turret intercom and oxygen u/s. Farthest point reached 5403N 0432E. Total load jettisoned.
P/O. W.F. Sutherland R/Gunner that day.

21/01/1944 DS813 JI-H Bombing Magdeburg 19.59 23.12 03.04
Bomb load 1 x 4000, 720 x 4, 90 x 4, 32 x 30 incendiaries. Primary target: Magdeburg. There was broken cloud 7/10. Bombed at 23.12 hours at 20,000 ft. Considerable amount of undershooting but T.I.s well placed. Very deep red fire with great quantity of smoke. Good

L to R (top): K.T. Penkuri, G. Cosgrove, K. Drummond. L to R (bottom): W.F. Sutherland (believed to be), L.A. Wry, K.E. Peake. (courtesy Villars-le-Pautel Mayor)

fires burning when leaving target.

Sgt. J. Crawford R/Gunner until 30/01/44.

27/01/1944 DS786 JI-E Bombing Berlin   18.01 20.38 02.15

Bomb load 1 x 4000, 32 x 30, 450 x 4, 90 x 4 incendiaries. Primary target: Berlin. There was 10/10 cloud. Bombed at 20.38 hours at 20,000 ft. Flashes seen through clouds which were lit up by S/Ls. Little to be seen on arrival, concentration of fires seen some time after leaving.

30/01/1944 DS785 JI-D Bombing Berlin   17.12 20.27 23.57

Bomb load 1 x 8000 lb bomb. Primary target: Berlin. There was 10/10 cloud. Bombed at 20.27 hours at 20,000 ft. Glow of fires through cloud. Target ringed with fighter flares 'More than ever'. Nice widespread fires after left the target. Very good attack. Route good. Had encounter with enemy aircraft.

21/02/1944 LL653 JI-E Bombing Stuttgart   00.22 04.01 06.50

Bomb load 1 x 8000 lb bomb, 16 x 30, 90 x 4 incendiaries. Primary target: Stuttgart. There was no cloud. Bombed at 04.01 hours at 20,000 ft. Some small fires obtaining hold. Large fires seen on leaving North side of town. Believed good attack. Two greenish explosions seen at 04.00 hours. Route satisfactory. Arrived slightly early.

Sgt. W. Wilson was MU/Gunner that day and P/O. W.F. Sutherland R/Gunner.

24/02/1944 LL653 JI-E Bombing Schweinfurt 18.42 23.20 02.16

Bomb load 1 x 8000 lb bomb. Primary target: Schweinfurt. Weather was perfect. Bombed at 23.20 hours at 18,000 ft. Saw one mass of incendiaries and fires on South of river. Well concentrated attack and moderate H.F. Many fighter flares about.

Sgt. J. Crawford R/Gunner that day.

25/02/1944 LL653 JI-E Bombing Augsburg 21.52 01.18 04.47

Bomb load 1 x 2000 lb bomb, 48 x 30, 900 x4 incendiaries. Primary target: Augsburg. There was good visibility, no cloud. Bombed at 01.18 hours at 21,000 ft. Target a solid mass, burning red. Very good attack. Marking OK. Fires very well concentrated.

P/O. W.F. Sutherland R/Gunner that day.

01/03/1944 LL653 JI-E Bombing Stuttgart 23.27 03.30 07.26

Bomb load 1 x 4000 lb bomb, 24 x 30, 600 x 4, 90 x 4 incendiaries. Primary target: Stuttgart. There was 10/10 cloud. Bombed at 03.07 hours and 03.30 hours. Pipe line in forward turret fractured by flak. Attack appeared concentrated. Fires seen after leaving target. Route good.

Sgt. M.C.L. Bristow (or Bristowe) was F/Engineer that day and Sgt. J. Crawford R/Gunner.

15/03/1944 LL653 JI-E Bombing Stuttgart 19.17 x x

Bomb load 1 x 8000 lb. Bomb, 8 x 30 incendiaries. Aircraft missing.

Probably shot down by a night fighter flown by Hptm. Eckart-Wilhelm von Bonin, Stab II./NJG1, exploding and crashing between Blondefontaine and Villars-le-Pautel two villages in Haute-Saone, 32 km and 34 km NNW respectively from Vesoul, France.

P/O. W.F. Sutherland was R/Gunner and F/S. K. Drummond 2nd Pilot.

All of the crew were KIA and are buried in Villars-le-Pautel Communal Cemetery.

P/O. Leslie Mitchell Petry, DFC

NZ422315 P/O. Leslie Mitchell "Les" Petry, DFC, RNZAF. Pilot.
NZ422205 F/O. F.J. "Freddy" Parker, RNZAF. A/Bomber.
1444526 F/S. Eric J. Reid.   Navigator. 25 ops.
151336 (992963 F/O.Hamish Cran MacLennan, DFC Navigator 2 ops.
1539935 F/S. Ronald Fox.   Navigator. 2 ops.
J10722 F/L. James Douglas "Doug" Trick, RCAF. Navigator. 1 op.
F/S.Harry T. "Adge" Boal.   WOP/AG.
A428053   F/S. Ronald Allan "Ronnie" Pitt, RAAF. MU/Gunner.
221176 Sgt. W.B. Watt.   R/Gunner. 13 ops.
992807 F/S. A. "Sandy" MacLean.   R/Gunner. 17 ops.
179379 (955440) P/O.Herbert Edward "Bert" Chandler. F/Engineer.

15/02/1944 LL620 A2-G Bombing Berlin   17.39 21.24 00.40
   Bomb load 1 x 2000, 1 x 1000 lb bomb, 24 x 30, 900 x 4
incendiaries. There was 10/10ths cloud. Bombed from 21,000 feet.
Sky markers scattered over a wide area. No fighter flares on run up but
area encircled after leaving. Spoof fighter flares seen to east and west.
   F/S. A. MacLean R/Gunner until 07/06/44.

L to R: Sandy MacLean, Bert Chandler, Eric Reid, Les Petry, Adge Boal, Freddy Parker, Ronnie Pitt. (WMHM)

24/02/1944 LL691 A2-D Bombing Schweinfurt 20.55 01.16 04.31

Bomb load 1 x 4000 lb bomb, 24 x 30, 420 x 4, 90 x 4 incendiaries. Primary target: Schweinfurt. There was no cloud, visibility good. Bombed at 01.16 hours at 20,000 feet. There were many fires covering the target area. T.I.s were late in going down, F/F were being pulled out as we left. T.I.s very concentrated and the whole target was a mass of fire although a big undershoot to the South West. A good effort. Thick black smoke rising to 20,000 feet.

25/02/1944 LL691 A2-D Bombing Augsburg 21.53 01.16 04.39

Bomb load 1 x 4000 lb bomb, 32 x 30, 510 x 4, 90 x 4 incendiaries. Primary target: Augsburg. Weather clear, visibility good. Bombed at 01.16 hours at 21,000 feet. Good concentration of fires burning red, black smoke billowing over area. Several small red explosions in target area at 01:08 hours. Route both ways trouble free.

07/03/1944 LL691 A2-D Bombing Le Mans 19.48 x 00.17

Bomb load 10 x 1000 and 4 x 500 lb bombs. There was 10/10ths cloud. No markers seen so we circled 10 minutes during 3 runs over target still no markers seen, so as briefed we brought bombs back. 4 x 500 lb bombs jettisoned safe. Remainder brought back.

22/03/1944 LL691 A2-D Bombing Frankfurt 18.40 22.04 00.59

Bomb load 1 x 8000 lb bomb, 56 x 30 incendiaries. Primary target: Frankfurt. There was clear weather over the target. Bombed at 22.04 hours from 21,000 feet. Attack successful, fires well alight, PPF on time but scattered. Glow of fires seen 250 miles on way home, streets easily visible.

24/03/1944 LL691 A2-D Bombing Berlin 18.43 22.35 01.40

Bomb load 1 x 1000 lb bomb 88 x 30, 810 x 4, 90 x 4 incendiaries. Primary target: Berlin. There was 5/10ths cloud. Bombed at 22.35 hours from 21,000 feet. Scattered T.I.s burning streets. Fires scattered. P.F.F. monitor heard.

26/03/1944 LL691 A2-D Bombing Essen 20.13 22.08 00.41

Bomb load 1 x 8000 lb bomb, 96 x 30 incendiaries. Primary target: Essen. There was 10/10 cloud. Bombed at 22.08 hours from 21,000 feet. Nothing seen. Spoof flares seen to go down but nothing visible at target.

30/03/1944 LL691 A2-D Bombing Nuremburg 22.17 01.15 05.10

Bomb load 1 x 8000 lb bomb, 90 x 4 incendiaries. Primary target: Nuremburg. Bombed Erlangen. There was 5/10 cloud. Bombed at 01.15 hours from 20,000 feet. There was ground haze, but fires had been started, burning red as we left. Arrived 01.09 hours, no markers seen, but fires had already been started. We did and orbit still no markers seen, so we bombed on fires below.

11/04/1944 LL620 A2-G Bombing Aachen 21.07 22.47 00.13

Bomb load 10 x 1000, 2 x 500 lb bombs, plus 160 x 4 and 20 x 4 incendiaries. Weather was clear. Bombed at 22.47 hours from 20,000 feet. Incendiaries falling short, bombs dropping in railway yards and many concentrated fires seen. Successful attack. Good bombing. Route OK.

18/04/1944 LL691 A2-D Bombing Rouen 22.44 00.47 02.27

Bomb load 8 x 1000 MC, 2 x 1000 GP and 5 x 500 lb bombs. There was slight haze. Visibility good. Bombed at 00.47 hours from 13,500 feet. Markers seen to be right in the T.I. concentration. Should be a good effort. Explosions seen when leaving.

20/04/1944 LL691 A2-D Bombing Cologne 00.19 02.08 03.54

Bomb load 1 x 1000 lb bomb, 1026 x 4, 114 x 4, 108 x 30 lb incendiaries. Primary target: Koln. There was 10/10ths cloud. Bombed at 02.08 from 21,000 feet. Cloud prevented visual. Attack late by 10 minutes. Markers fairly numerous but rather scattered. Glow of fires visible from English Coast. Route quiet.

22/04/1944 LL691 A2-D Bombing Dusseldorf 23.19 01.26 03.06

Bomb load 1 x 2000 lb. bomb, 84 x 30, 1050 x 4 incendiaries. There was slight haze, much vapour trails. Bombed at 01.26 hours from 20,500 feet. T.I.s were concentrated. Incendiaries falling short. Bombs seen to fall in target area. P.F.F. rather late approx 3 minutes.

24/04/1944 LL691 A2-D Bombing Karlsruhe 22.25 00.47 03.55

Bomb load 1 x 8000 lb bomb, 24 x 30, 216 x 4, 24 x 4 incendiaries. Primary target: Karlsruhe. There was 10/10ths cloud over target and over most of route. Bombed at 00.47 hours from 18,000 feet. Bombed area of scattered incendiaries. Nothing seen except scattered incendiaries. Some tendency for controls to ice up and difficult to maintain speed. Attack appeared to be very scattered and did not appear successful.

11/05/1944 LL677 A2-E Bombing Louvain 22.58 00.18 01.41

Bomb load 5 x 500 MC, 5 x 1000 GP, 5 x 1000 MC. Primary target: Louvain. Clear over target and green markers seen. Bombed at 00.18 hours from 8,000 feet. Smoke and scattered fires visible. Main force arrived late and attack seemed very scattered.

F/O. H.C. MacLennan Navigator that day.

30/05/1944 DS786 A2-F Bombing Boulogne 23.15 00.06 00.55

Bomb load 6 x 1000 MC, 4 x 500 MC. Primary target: Boulogne

Gun Batteries. Clear at target. Bombed red T.I.s at 00.06 hours from 8,000 feet. Should be a good attack. Flak was negligible.

F/O. H.C. MacLennan Navigator that day.

06/06/1944 LL716 A2-G Bombing Lisieux 00.33 01.40 03.06

Bomb load 16 x 500 MC Nose Inst. and 2 x 500 MC LD. Primary target: Lisieux. F/S. R. Fox. - Navigator. Weather was clear below but cloud above. Bombed at 01.40 hours from 3,600 feet. Own stick seen to burst across T.I.s and visual of the village showed the marking to be accurate. T.I.s seen to be split on several occasions by bomb bursts. Route good.

F/S. R. Fox Navigator that day.

07/06/1944 LL677 A2-E Bombing Massy Palaiseau 00.40 02.19 03.51

Bomb load 18 x 500 MC. Primary target: Massy Palaiseau, Marshalling Yards. There was cloud at 7/8,000 feet, clear below. Bombed at 02.19 hours from 6,000 feet as instructed by Master Bomber. Raid thought satisfactory. Much fighter activity in target area and on route home. Flak damage to rear turret was sustained at Paris, Gunner Sgt. "Sandy" McLean injured. At 02:40 hours enemy aircraft sighted and one burst fired, dived and successfully evaded. It is believed that F/S. MacLean lost his leg as a result of wounds.

According to J.D. Trick's logbook target "Paris" but in R.A. Pitt's logbook target "Massy-Palaiseau". Massy Palaiseau is 20km South from Paris.

F/L. J.D. Trick was Navigator that day.

11/06/1944 DS787 A2-D Bombing Nantes 23.58 02.45 05.02

Bomb load 16 x 500 GP, 2 x 500 LD. Primary target: Nantes. Bombed on centre of T.I.s at 02.45 hours from 8,000 feet as instructions of Master Bomber to bomb below not heard. T.I.s seen through 10/10ths cloud. Vapour trails of fighters seen over target.

Sgt. W.B. Watt R/Gunner from that day.

F/S. E.J. Reid Navigator until 14/06/44.

12/06/1944 DS787 A2-D Bombing Gelsenkirchen 23.15 01.08 02.56

Bomb load 1 x 4000 HC, 14 x 500 GP, 2 x 500 MC. Primary target: Gelsenkirchen. Clear over target. Bombed red and green T.I.s at 01.08 hours from 19,000 feet. Searchlights were numerous but rather aimless. Large orange explosion seen at 01.05 hours.

14/06/1944 DS787 A2-D Bombing Le Havre 23.54 01.16 02.32

Bomb load 11 x 1000 MC, 4 x 500 GP. Primary target: Le Havre. Weather clear. Bombed at 01.16 hours from 15,000 feet on red T.I.s.

Many fires seen burning on arrival. Stick seen to burst across jetty. Very successful raid. Marking best seen.

23/06/1944 DS787 A2-D Bombing L'Hey   23.16 00.16 01.22

Bomb load 11 x 1000 MC, 4 x 500 GP. Primary target: L'Hey, Flying bomb installations. There was 10/10ths cloud. Bombed at 00.16 hours from 9,000 feet. Bomber stream concentrated, no difficulties.

Error in ORBs. F/S. MacLean lost his leg as a result of wounds on 7/8 June, thus he could not be in the crew for this mission.

F/S. R. Fox Navigator that day.

27/06/1944 DS787 A2-D Bombing Biennais 23.34 01.10 02.24

Bomb load 16 x 500 GP, 2 x 500 ANM 64 GP. Primary target: Biennais, Flying bomb installations. There was 10/10ths cloud. Bombed at 01.10 hours from 13,500 feet red glow. Combat with a single engined enemy aircraft, no claim.

F/S. E.J. Reid Navigator from that day.

02/07/1944 DS787 A2-D Bombing Beauvoir 12.59 14.37 16.12

Bomb load 11 x 1000 MC, 4 x 500 GP. Primary target: Beauvoir, Flying bomb supply site. Bombed at 14.37 hours from 12,000 feet on yellow T.I.s.

05/07/1944 DS787 A2-D Bombing Watten   23.02 00.11 00.58

Bomb load 11 x 1000 ANM 65, 4 x 500 GP. Primary target: Watten, Constructional works. Bombed at 00.11 hours from 10,000 feet on red T.I.s.

10/07/1944 DS787 A2-D Bombing Nucourt 04.31 06.05 07.48

Bomb load 11 x 1000 ANM 65, 4 x 500 GP. Primary target: Nucourt, Constructional works. Bombed at 06.05 hours from 16,000 feet on Gee.

12/07/1944 DS787 A2-D Bombing Vaires   18.04 20.40 21.46

Bomb load 18 x 500 GP. Primary target: Vaires, Marshalling yards. Abortive attack on Vaires. Bosville Railway Sidings attacked. Weather at Bosville clear, 10/10ths cloud over Paris. Bombed at 20.40 hours from 15,000 feet. Bombs slightly overshot target and fell in field, sidings seen clearly.

15/07/1944 LL670 A2-K Bombing Chalons sur Marne 21.49 01.35 04.20

Bomb load 18 x 500 GP. Primary target: Chalons sur Marne, Railway centre. Weather hazy below cloud, 10/10ths above. Bombed at 01.35 hours from 9,000 feet on green T.I.s. Well lit up. Attack seemed good.

17/07/1944 DS787 A2-D Bombing Paris

514 Squadron Operational Record Books do not make any mention of this raid, reported as a DNCO (Did Not Complete) mission in some 514 Sqn crew's logbooks and in that of R.A. Pitt as follows: "OPS BOMBING PARIS D.N.C.O. (RECALLED)". Bomber Command War Diaries Stated for that day - "Flying Bomb Sights - 132 Aircraft. 72 Halifaxes, 28 Stirlings, 20 Lancasters, 11 Mosquitos, and 1 Mustang attacked 3 V-weapons sites without loss. Few details of results were recorded."

18/07/1944 DS787 A2-D Bombing Emieville 04.33 06.08 07.37

Bomb load 11 x 1000 MC, 4 x 500 GP. Primary target: Emieville, Troop concentration. Bombed at 06.08 hours from 6,500 feet on yellow T.I.s. Whole target area covered in the heavy concentrated bombing.

18/07/1944 LL677 A2-E Bombing Aulnoye 22.39 00.58 02.00

Bomb load 18 x 500 GP. Primary target: Aulnoye, Railway junction. Weather clear. Bombed at 00.58 hours from 9,000 feet on green T.I.s. Bombing appeared rather scattered.

P/O. D.T. Pettit

NZ40429   P/O. D.T. Pettit, RNZAF.   Pilot.
NZ43165   F/O. G.F. McGimpsey, RNZAF.   A/Bomber.
NZ436031 F/O. R. Barclay, RNZAF.   Navigator.
F/S. A. Williams.   WOP/AG.
Sgt. G.P. Morgan.   MU/Gunner.
Sgt. W. Agnew.   R/Gunner.
Sgt. N. Greenhow.   F/Engineer.

Passengers: 15/07/1945, 23/07/1945, 25/07/1945.

29/06/1945 ME363   JI-R Post Mortem Special mission 09.57 x 16.06
15/07/1945 ME358   JI-O Baedeker Tour over Continent 10.10 x 14.55
23/07/1945 RE139 JI-M   Baedeker Tour over Continent 10.02 x 14.25
25/07/1945 ME363   JI-R Baedeker Tour over Continent 09.37 x 19.27
16/08/1945 ME355   A2-G Dodge Italy (Bari) ca.07.06 to 10.53 x x
    Recalled VHF U/S.

14 a/c airborne for Italy. One a/c went u/s. All aircrew landed safely at Bari, Italy.

The mission is described in the ORB summary only. The following details and crew composition for 16 and 16 to 20 August come from M.G.T. Allen's logbook.

From his normal crew, only P/O. D.T. Pettit did this mission as 2nd Pilot with F/L. M.G.T. Allen's crew.

16 to 20/08/1945

LM544   JI-A Dodge Italy   A.M.   ca.20.20 P.M.

16 August Waterbeach ca. 07.06 to 10.53 - Bari ca. 20.20.

Returned 20th August 1945, Bari xx.xx, landing at Waterbeach
ca.15.19 to 17.14.

Repatriation of 20 Army personnel.

From his normal crew, only P/O. D.T. Pettit did this mission as 2nd Pilot with F/L. M.G.T. Allen's crew.

P/O. Richard Oastler Pick, DFC

178795 (1382432) P/O. Richard Oastler Pick, DFC   Pilot.
A420854   F/S. George Edward Barrow, RAAF. A/Bomber.
A413783   F/O. William Graham Mayes, DFC, RAAF. Navigator.
A424262   F/S. Charles Albert Carrigan, RAAF. WOP/AG.
1149149   Sgt. A.W. Hanson.   MU/Gunner.
1604483   Sgt. W. Aston.   R/Gunner.
574751 Sgt. J. Edmundson.   F/Engineer.

10/04/1944 LL690 JI-J Bombing Laon   01.19   03.42   05.42
Bomb load 8 x 1000, 6 x 500 lb bombs. Primary target: Laon. Weather was clear. Bombed at 03.42 hours from 11,000 feet. Aircraft had to evade another Lancaster in target area and believed photo spoilt. Attack believed satisfactory. Route OK.

18/04/1944 LL695 JI-A Bombing Rouen   22.26 00.43   03.01
Bomb load 10 x 1000, 5 x 500 lb bomb. Primary target: Rouen. There was some thin cloud. Bombed at 00.43 hours from 12,500 feet. Some fires seen as directed by M of C. Too much conversation by M of C. Attack believed to fall too far West. Had combat with enemy aircraft.

20/04/1944 LL695 JI-A Bombing Cologne   23.56   02.08   04.25
Bomb load 1 x 1000 lb bomb, 1026 x 4, 114 x 4 incendiaries, 108 x 30 lb incendiaries. Primary target: Koln. There was 10/10 cloud on target. Bombed at 02.08 hours from 21,000 feet. Only red sky flares seen. Sky markers very scattered approx. Over a distance of 4 miles.

Two reds with yellow stars were observed.

22/04/1944 LL695 JI-A Bombing Dusseldorf 22.59 01.22 03.13
Bomb load 1 x 2000 lb bomb, 84 x 30, 1050 x 4 incendiaries.
Primary target: Dusseldorf. Weather was clear with slight haze.
Bombed at 01.22 hours from 19,000 feet. Many fires seen with red
T.I.s on top. Very successful attack. Route satisfactory.

26/04/1944 LL733 JI-G Bombing Essen 22.57 01.33 03.19
Bomb load 1 x 2000 lb bomb, 84 x 30, 945 x 4, 105 x 4 lb
incendiaries. Primary target: Essen. There was hazy with light layer of
cloud at 21,000 feet. Bombed at 01.33 hours from 20,000 feet. T.I.s
were rather scattered. Incendiaries well concentrated round T.I.s.
Attack appeared to be going well, T.I.s although scattered, were in an
area of approximately a mile - incendiaries had taken a good hold.
Route extremely satisfactory.

27/04/1944 LL690 JI-J Bombing Friedrichshafen 21.58 02.08 05.45
Bomb load 810 x 4, 80 x 30 lb incendiaries. Primary target:
Friedrichshafen. There was slight haze otherwise visibility was good.
Bombed at 02.08 hours from 20,000 feet. There was a good
concentration of T.I.s and bombs falling very close to markers.
Successful attack. Many large fires seen with column of smoke rising
up to 15,000 feet.

01/05/1944 DS842 JI-F Bombing Chambly 22.51 00.22 01.55
Bomb load 10 x 1000, 5 x 500 lb bombs. Primary target: Chambly.
Weather was clear. Bombed at 00.22 hours from 10,000 feet. Visual of
river and rail depot. Bombs seen exploding round T.I.s. Instructed to
bomb yellow T.I.s and commended results. No red T.I.s seen only
yellow.

19/05/1944 LL666 JI-D Bombing Le Mans 22.31 00.25 02.59
Bomb load 4 x 1000 USA, 5 x 1000 MC, 1 x 1000 GP, 4 x 500 GP.
Primary target: Le Mans. 10/10 cloud at 8,000/9,000 feet. Marshalling
Yards and markers visible and bombed at 00.25 hours from 7,500 feet.
Two large explosions seen 3 miles S.E. at 00.24 hours. Markers
seemed well placed.

21/05/1944 LL666 JI-D Bombing Duisburg 22.40 01.13 03.10
Bomb load 1 x 2000 lb bomb, 120 x 30 incendiaries, 600 x 4
incendiaries. Primary target: Duisberg. There was 10/10 cloud.
Bombed red T.I. at 01.13 hours from 22,000 feet. Large explosion seen
at 01.11 hours in target area. Many fighter flares seen on the
homeward route.

22/05/1944 LL666 JI-D Bombing Dortmund 22.45 00.49 03.00

Bomb load 1 x 2000 lb, bomb, 96 x 30, 810 x 4, 90 x 4 incendiaries. Primary target: Dortmund. Clear over target. Bombed red and green T.I.s at 00.49 hours from 19,000 feet. Aircraft holed on port side of fuselage by falling incendiary. Owing to searchlight glare could not see much of the target area but what was seen seemed to indicate a good raid. Many bomb bursts seen and many fires started. Over base ice formed at 6,000 feet and for some considerable time difficulty was experienced in gaining height over 9,700 feet.

27/05/1944 DS813 JI-H Bombing Aachen 00.30 02.28 04.00

Bomb load 7 x 1000 MC, 4 x 1000 ANM, 4 x 500 MC. Primary target: Aachen. Hazy over target. Bombed at 02.28 hours from 14,000 feet. Few bomb bursts seen around T.I.s. Dinghy inflated and left aircraft on take-off. Single engine enemy aircraft seen at 02.24 hours following an aircraft in flames.

28/05/1944 DS813 JI-H Bombing Angers 18.40 23.55 02.10

Bomb load 5 x 1000 MC, 1 x 1000 USA, 4 x 500 MC. Primary target: Angers. Slight haze over target. Bombed at 23.55 hours from 10,000 feet. Trouble free route and attack seemed good. Burst hydraulic pipe rendered rear turret u/s. Rear turret U/S due to a burst hydraulic pipe.

31/05/1944 DS813 JI-H Bombing Trappes 00.13 02.00 04.25

Bomb load 8 x 1000 MC, 8 x 500 MC. Primary target: Trappes. Clear at target. Moon bright. Bombed at 02.00 hours from 9,500 feet as directed by Master Bomber. Bomb bursts appeared to be on the target but no big fires visible. Weather unexpectedly good.

05/06/1944 LL697 JI-E Bombing Ouistreham 03.53 05.08 07.00

Bomb load 9 x 1000 MC and 2 x 500 MC. Primary target: Ouistreham. Slightly dispersed cloud at target. Bombed markers at 05.08 hours from 9,500 feet. Bomb bursts seen to be concentrated and attack thought successful. Route trouble free.

06/06/1944 LL697 JI-E Bombing Lisieux 00.10 01.35 03.07

Bomb load 16 x 500 MC tail fused and 2 x 500 MC LD. Primary target: Lisieux. Weather was clear over target. Overshot red T.I.s and bombed visually on the centre of a built-up area. A good visual of target obtained. Only 1 red T.I. was seen and some bombs were bursting around it. Insufficient time before first wave bombed, for Master Bomber to indicate to the Bomber Stream the accuracy of the markers. Total time margin was 2 minutes. Master Bomber heard clearly. Bombed at 01.35 hours from 5,500 feet.

08/06/1944 LL697 JI-E Bombing Fougeres 22.03 00.19 02.22

Bomb load 16 x 500 GP and 2 x 500 MC LD. Primary target: Fougeres. Bombed as instructed by Master Bomber at 00.19 hours from 8,500 feet. Bombs appeared to be fell towards the north-east of the town. Good effort. Concentration of aircraft on route and over target was good in spite of clouds.

10/06/1944 LL666 JI-D Bombing Dreux   23.05 00.56   03.25

Bomb load 16 x 500 GP, 2 x 500 LD. Primary target: Dreux. Master Bomber not heard. T.I.s seen to be off to port so bombed on visual at 00.56 hours from 8,000 feet. Two sticks seen to burst across yards. ME109 encountered near Cherbourg and claimed as damaged. Weather clear with a few patches of cloud.

11/06/1944 LL666 JI-D Bombing Nantes   23.51   02.49   05.19

Bomb load 16 x 500 GP, 2 x 500 LD. Primary target: Nantes. Bombed as instructed by Master Bomber at 02.49 hours from 2,500 feet in centre of Red and Green T.I.s. Lancaster coned by 3 searchlights before run up and held until evaded by climbing into cloud. 10/10ths cloud above but clear at 2,500 feet.

14/06/1944 LL666 JI-D Bombing Le Havre   23.53   01.14   02.23

Bomb load 11 x 1000 MC, 4 x 500 GP. Primary target: Le Havre. Weather was clear. Bombed at 01.14 hours from 15,000 feet on yellow and green markers o top of each other. Bombs and flares close together and glow of fires just to the North. Good attack. Photo attempted.

15/06/1944 LL666 JI-D Bombing Valenciennes 23.06   00.39   02.08

Bomb load 16 x 500 GP, 2 x 500 MC. Primary target: Valenciennes. Weather clear below cloud - base 10,000 feet. Bombed at 00.39 hours from 9,000 feet on green T.I.s as instructed by Master Bomber. Good concentrated bombing. Much interference on R/T. Route very good.

30/06/1944 LM627   JI-D Bombing Villers Bocage 18.08 20.01   21.25

Bomb load 10 x 1000 MC, 3 x 500 GP. Primary target: Villers Bocage. Weather clear. Bombed at 20.01 hours from 12,000 feet red T.I.s. Target covered with smoke. Good effort. Target well pranged. Trouble free route.

02/07/1944 LM627   JI-D Bombing Beauvoir   12.44   14.35   16.11

Bomb load 11 x 1000 MC, 4 x 500 GP. Primary target: Beauvoir, Flying bomb supply site. Bombed at 14.35 hours from 8,500 feet on yellow T.I.s.

05/07/1944 LL666 JI-Q Bombing Watten   22.59   00.11   01.05

Bomb load 11 x 1000 ANM65, 4 x 500 GP. Primary target: Watten, Constructional works. Bombed at 00.11 hours from 9,000 feet red T.I.s.

07/07/1944 LL666 JI-Q Bombing Vaires   22.53 01.32 03.04

Bomb load 7 x 1000 MC, 4 x 500 GP. Primary target: Vaires, Marshalling yards. Weather clear. Bombed at 01.32 hours from 12,000 feet centre of red and green T.I.s as instructed by Master Bomber. One large explosion at 01.36 hours. Good satisfactory raid.

10/07/1944 HK572   JI-T Bombing Nucourt 04.40 06.05 07.36

Bomb load 11 x 1000 ANM65, 4 x 500 GP. Primary target: Nucourt, Constructional works. Bombed at 06.05 hours from 15,500 feet on Gee.

12/07/1944 LL666 JI-Q Bombing Vaires   18.02 20.00 21.47

Bomb load 18 x 500 GP. Primary target: Vaires, Marshalling yards. Reached target 20.00 hours at 15,000 feet. Master Bomber said "Bomb yellow T.I.s, and later "abandon mission". Rather disgusted to meet large Halifax and Lancaster formations going out as we returned.

15/07/1944 LL666 JI-Q Bombing Chalons Sur Marne   21.51 01.31 03.53

Bomb load 18 x 500 GP. Primary target: Chalons sur Marne, Railway centre. Weather clear below 8,000 feet. Bombed at 01.31 hours from 8,000 feet concentration of red and green T.I.s. Markers very accurate, good attack.

18/07/1944 LL733 JI-S Bombing Emieville   04.27 06.07 07.36

Bomb load 11 x 1000 MC, 4 x 500 GP. Primary target: Emieville, Troop concentration. Weather clear. Bombed at 06.07 hours from 7,000 feet pall of smoke. One mass of smoke, good attack.

20/07/1944 LL733 JI-S Bombing Homberg   23.33 01.21 02.40

Bomb load 1 x 4000 HC, 2 x 500 MC, 14 x 500 GP. Primary target: Homberg, Oil plant. Weather clear. Bombed at 01.21 hours from 19,500 feet red and green T.I.s. Black smoke rising to 12,000 feet with a red glow at base.

24/07/1944 LL733 JI-S Bombing Stuttgart   21.47 01.48 05.03

Bomb load 5 x 1000 ANM65, 3 x 500 GP. Primary target Stuttgart. Weather 10/10ths cloud. Bombed at 01.48 hours from 20,200 feet on green sky markers with yellow stars. Quite a successful attack.

F/O. Harold A. Pickersgill

J40283 F/O. Harold A. Pickersgill, RCAF. Pilot.
J37188 (R157354) F/O. Joseph Edward "Ted" Morrey, RCAF.
  A/Bomber.
Sgt. L. "Bill" Bailey.   Navigator.
Sgt. Roy V. Rudling.   WOP/AG.
R220987   F/S. Sydney J. "Syd" South, RCAF. MU/Gunner.
R279116   F/S. L.J. "Joe" Kirwan, RCAF.   R/Gunner.
Sgt. Dennis S. Tomlin.   F/Engineer.

02/02/1945 LM728   JI-F Bombing Wiesbaden 20.35 23.52 02.35
   Bomb load 1 x 4000 HC, 12 x 500 GP, 4 x 250 GP. Primary target:
Wiesbaden. Weather 10/10ths cloud, winds very erratic. Bombed at
23.52 hours from 21,000 feet on position east of bomb bursts. Gee
unserviceable.
   From his normal crew, only F/O. H.A. Pickersgill did this mission
as 2nd Pilot with F/L. J.F. Ness' crew.
03/02/1945 PB426 JI-D Bombing Dortmund-Huckarde 16.16 19.39
   21.32
   Bomb load 1 x 4000 HC, 12 x 500 GP, 3 x 250 GP. Primary target
Dortmund-Huckarde, Coking plant. Weather clear with slight haze.
Bombed at 19.39 hours from 20,000 feet on Red T.I. Much smoke, few
fires.
   According to J.E. Morrey's logbook "(Harckle Oil Plant) 12,500
lbs."
19/02/1945 ME351   JI-U Bombing Wesel 13.09 16.35 18.59
   Bomb load 1 x 4000 HC, 6 x 500 MC, 6 x 500 ANM64, 3 x 250 GP,
1 Skymarker Red puff. Primary target: Wesel. Weather over target 5-
7/10ths cloud. Bombed at 16.35 hours from 19,200 feet on G.H.
   From his normal crew, only F/O. H.A. Pickersgill did this mission
as 2nd Pilot with F/L. J.S. Parnell's crew.
18/03/1945 ME355   JI-L Bombing Bruchstrasse 11.35 15.05 17.05
   Bomb load 1 x 4000 HC, 13 x 500 ANM64, 2 x 500 MC. Primary
target: Bruchstrasse, Coal mine & coking plant. Weather 10/10ths
cloud, tops 6-12,000 feet. Bombed at 15.05 hours from 19,000 feet on
G.H.
   According to J.E. Morrey's logbook target "Bochum".
20/03/1945 ME355   JI-L Bombing Hamm 09.54 13.15 15.52
   Bomb load 7 x 1000 ANM65, 9 x 500 ANM64. Primary target:

L to R (back): Dennis Tomlin, Roy Rudling, Harold Pickersgill, Joe Kirwan, Syd South.
L to R (front): Ted Morrey, Bill Bailey. (courtesy Sandra Morrey)

Hamm, Marshalling yards. Weather 5/10ths cloud. Bombed at 13.15 hours from 17,000 feet on G.H. Perspex holed by heavy flak. According to J.E. Morrey's logbook "Hamm (2 Flak holes)".

27/03/1945 ME355   JI-L Bombing Hamm Sachsen 10.34   14.04   16.03

Bomb load 1 x 4000 HC, 13 x 500 ANM64, 2 x 500 MC. Primary target: Hamm Sachsen, Benzol plant. Weather 10/10ths cloud. Bombed at 14.04 hours at 17,000 feet on H2S and Green Puffs.

04/04/1945 ME523   A2-G Bombing Merseburg 18.56   22.59   03.05

Weather 5-10/10ths cloud, and 10/10ths over Merseburg (Leuna). Bombed primary target Merseburg. Bomb load 1 x 4000 HC, 6 x 500 ANM64 on single Red T.I. plus M.B.'s comments to bomb red T.I.s. 5/10th cloud. Red glow seen beneath cloud. Bomb doors holed by flak. Arrived at 22.41 and had to orbit for 18 minutes. Eventually finding correct target with M.B.'s instructions. Numerous confusing dummies.

According to J.E. Morrey's logbook "Intense flak".

13/04/1945 ME387   JI-N Bombing Kiel   20.24   23.29   02.03

Bomb load 1 x 4000 HC and 12 x 500 ANM64. Primary target: Kiel, Docks & ship yards. Weather 10/10ths cloud low and thin. Bombed on centre of Green T.I.s per M.B.'s instructions at 23.29 hours from 20,000 feet. Red T.I. seen to port of track. Red glow seen through cloud round green T.I.s. Should be a good raid. Large explosion seen

538

23.30 hrs.

20/04/1945 ME422   JI-Q Bombing Regensburg   09.41 13.56   17.23

Bomb load 15 x 500 ANM64. Primary target: Regensburg. Weather clear over target and whole route. Bombed on G.H. at 13.56 hours from 18,200 ft. G.H. fairly good run, but tracers were jittery. Our bombs straddled target. Bombing generally undershot. Fairly good attack, bombing concentrated but tended to undershoot. Good trip otherwise.

29/04/1945 ME359   JI-T Manna The Hague   12.30   13.48   15.12

Dropping area: The Hague. Weather broken cloud above and clear below. Dropped 4 packs at 13.48 hours, 1 container brought back. Many people waving along the complete route overland, even the roof tops were crowded with gleeful "bods". Weather poor - operation successful.

According to J.E. Morrey's logbook: "Food supplies to Dutch people. 6280 lbs dropped on Ypenburg drome near The Hague".

01/05/1945 ME422   JI-Q Manna The Hague   13.28 x 16.00

Dropping area The Hague. Weather clear over target. Dropped 4 Panniers on smoke from T.I.s and visual of racecourse. Showers over the sea and some icing. Better than before. Fields packed with bags. A few sacks fell outside the woods and persons grabbed them and made off. Usual greetings from the crowds.

According to J.E. Morrey's logbook: "Food supplies to Dutch people. 6730 lbs dropped on R.C. near The Hague".

07/05/1945 RA599   JI-L Manna The Hague   12.22   13.44   14.51

Dropping area The Hague. Dropped 4 Packs on Red T.I.s to the port of White Cross at 13.44 hours. Clear. Supplies dropped accurately. "Gate" still numerous and enthusiastic.

According to J.E. Morrey's logbook: "Dropped on Ypenburg near The Hague".

11/05/1945 ME535   JI-G Exodus Juvincourt - Tangmere 11.21 x 17.47

Duration 3.23. Outward 1.31 hours. Collected 24 ex POWs. Homeward 1.52 hours. No complaint from POWs - no snags.

13/05/1945 ME358   JI-O Exodus Juvincourt - Tangmere 13.08 x 16.15

Duration 3.07 hours. Circled Juvincourt about 10 mins. Message R.T. Base received 14.47 hours.

F/L. Ronald Arthur Pickler, DFC

128922 (1432982) F/L. Ronald Arthur Pickler, DFC. Pilot.
W/O. B.A. Clifford.   A/Bomber. 22 ops.
Sgt.J. Murray.   A/Bomber.   7 ops.
188943 (1685202) P/O. Laurence Woodroofe, DFM.   Navigator.
Sgt.N. Coultous.   WOP/AG.
R224436   F/S. G. Coulson, RCAF.   MU/Gunner.
R213423   F/S. E.D. Craig, RCAF.   R/Gunner.
189122 (1895450) P/O. Alfred Cyril Gair.   F/Engineer.
47225 (549527)F/L. Roy Henry "Marco" Marks 2nd Pilot 11/12/1944

Ronald Arthur Picker

18/08/1944 LL635 JI-M
Bombing Bremen 21.41
00.15 02.40
Bomb load 1 x 2000 HC, 96 x 30 lb incendiaries, 810 x 4 lb incendiaries, 90 x 4 lb incendiaries. Primary target: Bremen. Weather clear over target. Bombed at 00.15 hours from 17,500 feet red T.I.s. T.I.s well concentrated. Long rows of fires burning. Excellent concentrated attack.
    From his normal crew, only F/O. R.A. Pickler did this mission as 2nd Pilot with F/O. E.T. Cossens' crew.
31/08/1944 LL731 JI-U
Bombing Pont-Remy 16.12 18.13 19.52
Bomb load 11 x 1000 MC, 2 x 500 GP Mk IV LD.
Primary target: Pont Remy, Dump. Weather cloudy. Bombed at 18.13 hours from 14,500 feet on Leading aircraft.
    W/O. B.A. Clifford A/Bomber until 30/11/44.
05/09/1944 LL734 A2-B Bombing Le Havre 17.33 19.23 20.42
Bomb load 11 x 1000 MC, 4 x 500 GP. Primary target: Le Havre.

Bombed at 19.23 hours from 13,500 feet red T.I.

17/09/1944 NF966 JI-R Bombing Boulogne 10.55 x 13.44

Bomb load 11 x 1000 MC, 4 x 500 GP. Primary target: Boulogne Aiming Point 2. Weather clear below cloud. At 12.15 hours order given by Master Bomber to abandon mission. Jettisoned 2 x 1000 MC, brought remainder back.

20/09/1944 LM719 JI-M Bombing Calais 14.45 16.02 17.50

Bomb load 11 x 1000 MC, 4 x 500 GP. Primary target: Calais. Weather clear over target. Bombed at 16.02 hours from 3,500 feet, red T.I.s.

25/09/1944 LM719 JI-M Bombing Pas de Calais 08.15 x 11.05

Bomb load 11 x 1000 MC, 4 x 500 GP. Primary target: Calais. Abandoned mission on Master Bomber's instructions. Jettisoned 3 x 1000, 1 x 500.

27/09/1944 LM719 JI-M Bombing Calais 07.31 08.42 10.19

Bomb load 11 x 1000 MC, 4 x 500 GP. Primary target: Calais 15. Weather, cloud 5,500 feet 10/10ths. Bombed at 08.42 hours from 5,500 feet on green T.I. and visual of A/P.

06/10/1944 LM719 JI-M Bombing Dortmund 16.49 20.28 22.25

Bomb load 1 x 4000 HC, 12 x No. 14 Clusters. Primary target: Dortmund, Town and Railways. Weather over the target was clear with slight ground haze. Bombed at 20.28 hours from 20,400 feet on green T.I.s.

14/10/1944 LM275 JI-M Bombing Duisburg 07.15 09.04 11.15

Bomb load 11 x 1000 MC, 4 x 500 GP Long Delay. Primary target: Duisburg. Weather patchy cloud with gaps for bombing. Bombed at 09.04 hours from 19,000 feet. Area North of Docks.

14/10/1944 LM275 JI-M Bombing Duisburg 22.51 01.31 03.34

Bomb load 11 x 1000 MC, 4 x 500 GP Long Delay. Primary target: Duisburg. Weather was clear with small amount of cloud over the target. Bombed at 01.31 hours from 22,000 feet. Centre of green T.I.s.

18/10/1944 LM275 JI-M Bombing Bonn 08.24 11.02 13.16

Bomb load 1 x 4000 HC, 5 x 12 x 30 - 2 x 12 x 30 modified, 9 x No. 14 Clusters. Primary target: Bonn. Weather varying cloud 2-7/10ths with break for bombing. Bombed at 11.02 hours from 17,400 feet visually. Bombing good on built up area.

21/10/1944 LM275 JI-M Bombing Flushing 10.57 12.27 13.32

Bomb load 12 x 1000 MC, 2 x 500 GP. Primary target: Flushing 'B'. Weather clear. Bombed at 12.27 hours from 7,600 feet. A/P in bomb sight.

22/10/1944 LM685 JI-Q Bombing Neuss 13.33 15.56 17.26

Bomb load 1 x 4000 HC, 6 x 1000 MC, 6 x 500 GP. Primary target: Neuss. Weather 10/10ths cloud over target. Bombed at 15.56 hours from 18,300 feet on G.H. leader.

23/10/1944 PB419 JI-N Bombing Essen 17.18 19.34 21.21

Bomb load 1 x 4000 HC, 2 x 1000 MC, 10 x 500 GP, 3 x 500 MC. Primary target: Essen. Weather 10/10ths cloud over target - tops 12/14,000 feet with most appalling weather on route. Bombed at 19.34 hours from 21,300 feet. Green flares.

25/10/1944 LM685 JI-Q Bombing Essen 13.11 15.41 17.14

Bomb load 1 x 4000 HC, 6 x 1000 MC, 6 x 500 GP. Primary target: Essen. Weather over target 10/10ths low cloud, with one clear patch which appeared to fill up later in the attack. Bombed at 15.41 hours from 21,000 feet. Green flares.

02/11/1944 LM685 JI-Q Bombing Homberg 11.38 14.06 15.30

Bomb load 1 x 4000 HC, 6 x 1000 ANM59, 6 x 500 MC. Primary target: Homberg. Weather variable cloud but clear for bombing. Target obscured by pall of smoke rising to 10,000 feet. Bombed at 14.04 hours from 20,000 feet visually.

04/11/1944 PB419 JI-N Bombing Solingen 11.19 14.06 15.54

Bomb load 1 x 4000 HC, 6 x 1000 ANM59, 4 x 500 GP, 2 x 500 MC (L/Delay), 3 Flares. Primary target: Solingen. Weather 8-10/10ths cloud. Bombed at 14.06 hours from 19,500 feet on G.H.

05/11/1944 PB482 JI-P Bombing Solingen 10.15 13.06 14.48

Bomb load 1 x 4000 HC, 6 x 1000 ANM59, 4 x 500 GP, 2 x 500 GP (L/Delay), 3 Flares. Primary target: Solingen. Weather 10/10ths cloud over target. Bombed at 13.06 hours from 17,000 feet on instruments.

08/11/1944 PB423 A2-G Bombing Homberg 07.53 10.32 12.16

Bomb load 1 x 4000 HC, 6 x 1000 GP, 6 x 500 GP. Primary target: Homberg. Weather clear. Bombed at 10.32 hours from 17,500 feet on instruments. Aircraft hit by flak. Bomb doors and rear turret damaged.

15/11/1944 PB423 A2-G Bombing Dortmund 12.42 15.40 17.26

Bomb load 1 x 4000 HC, 15 x 500 GP, 1 Red with Green star Flare. Primary target: Hoesch-Benzin Dortmund, Oil refineries. Weather 10/10ths cloud over the target. Bombed at 15.40 hours from 16,600 feet on G.H.

27/11/1944 PB423 A2-G Bombing Cologne 12.27 15.04 16.33

Bomb load 1 x 4000 HC, 15 x 500 GP, 1 Flare. Primary target: Cologne, Marshalling Yards. Weather patchy cloud. Bombed at 15.04 hours from 19,800 feet on Red T.I. Flare brought back as G.H.

unserviceable. At 15.01 hours aircraft hit by flak making it very difficult to control. Bombing run completed and aircraft kept under control and flown back by combined efforts of pilot, engineer, air bomber, navigator and rear gunner on stick plus a length of rope. Mid upper gunner wounded in the head by flak. Captain comments that the crew behaved splendidly. Landed at Woodbridge.

30/11/1944 NG118   A2-E   Bombing Osterfeld 10.39 13.18 14.52

Bomb load 1 x 4000 HC, 15 x 500 GP, 1 Red/Green flare. Primary target: Osterfeld, Coking plant. Weather 10/10ths cloud. Bombed at 13.18 hours from 19,900 feet on G.H. Flares fairly concentrated. Satisfactory trip.

04/12/1944 NG118   A2-E   Bombing Oberhausen 11.38 14.09 15.59

Bomb load 1 x 4000 HC, 15 x 500 GP, 1 Flare. Primary target: Oberhausen, Built up area. Weather 10/10ths cloud. Bombed at 14.09 hours from 20,000 feet on G.H.

Sgt. J. Murray A/Bomber until 06/12/44.

05/12/1944 ME841   JI-J   Bombing Hamm   09.05   11.30   13.52

Bomb load 1 x 4000 HC, 2 x 500 MC, 12 x 500 GP, 2 x 500 GP Long Delay. Primary target: Hamm. Weather 10/10ths cloud over target, but otherwise varying from 6-10/10ths. Bombed at 11.30 hours from 20,000 feet on G.H.

06/12/1944 PA186 A2-G Bombing Merseburg 17.05 20.46 00.25

Bomb load 1 x 4000 HC, 8 x 500 GP and 1 x 500 GP Long Delay. Primary target: Merseburg. Weather 10/10ths cloud with odd breaks. Bombed at 20.46 hours from 22,500 feet on centre of wanganui flares.

11/12/1944 NG118   A2-E   Bombing Osterfeld 08.41 11.06 12.51

Bomb load 1 x 4000 HC, 12 x 500 GP, 1 x 500 GP Long Delay, 2 x 500 MC, 1 Flare. Primary target: Osterfeld. Weather 10/10ths cloud, tops 16,000 feet. Bombed at 11.06 hours from 20,000 feet on G.H.

F/L. R.H. Marks was 2nd Pilot that day and W/O. B.A. Clifford A/Bomber.

12/12/1944 LM627   A2-H   Bombing Witten   11.16   14.05   16.07

Bomb load 1 x 4000 HC, 5 x 500 GP, 6 x 500 ANM58, 4 x 500 ANM64. Primary target: Witten. Weather 10/10ths cloud, tops 14/16,000 feet. Bombed at 14.05 hours from 20,000 feet on G.H.

Sgt. J. Murray A/Bomber from that day.

16/12/1944 PA186 A2-G Bombing Siegen   11.20   15.00   17.03

Bomb load 1 x 4000 HC, 5 x 1000 MC, 7 x 500 GP, 1 Flare. Primary target: Siegen. Weather very bad on route with icing and cloud. Bombed at 15.00 hours from 18,000 feet on G.H. Leader.

Aircraft hit by Flak, bomb doors damaged.

21/12/1944 PA186 A2-G Bombing Trier   12.10   14.58   16.59

Bomb load 1 x 4000 HC, 10 x 500 GP, 2 x 250 GP, 4 x 250 T.I. Red. Primary target: Trier, Marshalling yards. Weather 10/10 cloud, tops 6/9000 feet. Bombed at 14.58 hours from 18,000 feet on G.H.

Richard Dimbleby from the BBC flew in "G2" with F/L. R.A. Pickler, DFC.

23/12/1944 PA186 A2-G Bombing Trier   11.51   14.29   16.33

Bomb load 1 x 4000 HC, 10 x 500 GP, 4 x 250 T.I. Red. Primary target: Trier. Weather clear over target. Bombed at 14.29 hours from 18,000 feet on centre of town.

F/O. Alan Frederick Henry Plant

173553 (1322337) F/O. Alan Frederick Henry Plant. Pilot.

F/S. A.J. Snape.   A/Bomber.

F/S. J.L. Welsh.   Navigator.

F/S. L.G. Reeves.   WOP/AG.

Sgt. G.McK. Graham.   MU/Gunner.

Sgt. J. McLean.   R/Gunner.

Sgt. D.B. Finlay.   F/Engineer.

Passengers: 06/07/1945, 21/07/1945.

29/06/1945 ME355 A2-G Post Mortem Special mission 10.16 x 16.05

05/07/1945 RE159 A2-E Post Mortem Special mission 14.32 x 18.20

06/07/1945 RE117 A2-D Baedeker Tour over Continent 10.19 x 14.55

Passengers: F/S. Tomkins (WAAF), Sgt. Latter, Sgt. Green.

21/07/1945 RF272 A2-F Baedeker Tour over Continent 15.15x 19.50

Passengers: Cpl. Rilsron, LAC. Nunn, LAC. Parker, Sgt. Modge (WAAF), LACW. McNiven.

F/L. acting S/L. Harry Edward Tony Prager, DSO, DFC

1st crew.

138695 (1146886) S/L. Harry Edward Tony Prager, DSO, DFC. Pilot.
170457 (1585089) F/O.   Victor Francis Dobell Meade. A/Bomber.
135676 (1317703) F/O.   Harry James.   Navigator.
NZ414385   W/O. W.T.L. Mack, RNZAF.   WOP/AG.
A415845   P/O. Richard Hiden White, RAAF. MU/Gunner.
A410114   P/O. Geoffrey George Williams, RAAF. R/Gunner.
183649 (1608232) Sgt. Ronald James O'Donnell.   F/Engineer.

Note: R.J. O'Donnell and V.F.D. Meade subsequently died in a crash on 17/05/1945 whilst at No. 630 Squadron.

31/05/1944 DS842 JI-F Bombing Trappes 23.45 02.00 04.15
    Bomb load 8 x 1000 MC, 8 x 500 MC. Primary target: Trappes. Clear at target. Visual obtained of target. Bombed as directed by Master Bomber at 02.00 hours from 8,500 feet. 4 sticks of bombs seen bursting across railway tracks. Attack thought good. Route rather long.
02/06/1944 LL697 JI-E Bombing Wissant 01.25 02.14 03.00
    Bomb load 1 x 1000 GP, 10 x 1000 MC, 4 x 500 MC. Primary target: Wissant Gun Positions. There was 10/10ths cloud with base at 4,700 feet. Bombed red T.I.s at 02.14 hours from 4,700 feet. Markers and coast-line visible. Bombs seen bursting on markers.
05/06/1944 LL690 JI-J Bombing Ouistreham 03.40 05.10 06.25
    Bomb load 9 x 1000 MC and 2 x 500 MC. Primary target: Ouistreham. There was patchy cloud at target and slight haze. Bombed markers at 05.10 hours from 9,000 feet. Bombs appeared to fall west of target, although markers appeared to be to east of target. No flak or fighters seen over target.
06/06/1944 DS795 A2-J   Bombing Lisieux 00.28 01.41 03.45
    Bomb load 16 x 500 MC Nose Inst. and 2 x 500 MC LD. Primary target: Lisieux. Weather was clear below but cloud above. Overshot T.I.s and bombed visually. Bombs seen to fall in the town, at 01.41 hours from 3,500 feet. Red T.I. appeared to be off the town. Fires seen in target area, and attack good. Master Bomber not heard.
08/06/1944 DS813 JI-H Bombing Fougeres   21.50 00.19 02.08
    Bomb load 16 x 500 GP and 2 x 500 MC LD. Primary target:

James Douglas Trick. (courtesy Brent Sheldon)

Fougeres. Bombed as instructed by Master Bomber at 00.19 hours from 9,500 feet. Visual of town obtained but could not see where bombs fell. Attack believed successful. Tiring trip and weather most troublesome. Congestion of aircraft. Four Lancasters were seen over the sea with lights on.

15/07/1944 ME841 JI-H Bombing Chalons Sur Marne 21.38 01.33 03.59

Bomb load 18 x 500 GP. Primary target: Chalons sur Marne, Railway centre. Weather clear below 8,000 feet, green T.I.s. Bomb bursts seen across yards. Marking accurate.

18/07/1944 ME841 JI-H Bombing Emieville 04.07 06.05 07.07

Bomb load 11 x 1000 MC, 4 x 500 GP. Primary target: Emieville, Troop concentration. Weather clear. Bombed at 06.05 hours from 8,000 feet yellow T.I.s. Bombing accurate.

18/07/1944 ME841 JI-H Bombing Aulnoye 22.22 00.55 01.55

Bomb load 18 x 500 GP. Primary target: Aulnoye, Railway junction. Weather clear. Bombed at 00.55 hours from 11,500 feet, green T.I.s. A good attack.

23/07/1944 ME841 JI-H Bombing Kiel 22.16 01.19 03.20

Bomb load 10 x 1000 MC, 5 x 500 GP. Primary target: Kiel, Warehouses and docks. Weather 10/10ths cloud. Bombed at 01.19 hours from 20,000 feet starboard red as instructed by Master Bomber. Large explosion at 01.21 hours.

2nd crew.

138695 (1146886) S/L. Harry Edward Tony Prager, DSO, DFC. Pilot.
J16632 F/L. Maurice Coles Smith, DFC, RCAF. A/Bomber.
J10722 F/L. James Douglas "Doug" Trick, DFC, RCAF. Navigator.
J9067 F/L. John Wilfred Hoffman, DFC, RCAF. WOP/AG.

221176 Sgt. W.B. Watt.   MU/Gunner.
J18874 (R61306) F/O Aurele Mederic Sauve, DFC, RCAF R/Gunner.
53741 (616330) F/O. Alfred James Henry Ames, DFM. F/Engineer.

Passenger: 07/08/1944

07/08/1944 ME841   JI-H Bombing Mare de Magne 21.53 23.42 00.56
   Bomb load 11 x 1000 MC, 4 x 500 GP. Primary target: Mare de
Magne (just past Caen). Thin cloud over target. Bombed at 23.42
hours from 8,500 feet red T.I.s.
   Passenger: Maj Gen. F. Crawford CB MC.
Special comment by Major General Crawford: - On approach to target
I noticed gun flashes and gun fire on ground and Bofors tracer very
clear. Searchlights appeared after bombing, red T.I.s dropped in
identical position as Red Star Shells. Bombing very concentrated."
   According to J.D. Trick & M.C. Smith's logbooks target: "Caen".
Mare-de-Magne: place between Caen and Fontenay le Marmion.
08/08/1944 ME841   JI-H Bombing Foret de Lucheux 21.45   23.50
   00.59
   Bomb load 18 x 500 GP. Primary target: Foret de Lucheux, Petrol
dump. Weather clear. Bombed at 23.50 hours from 12,000 feet, red
T.I.s. Good fires and black smoke up to 10,000 feet.
   Foret de Lucheux is a forest between Lille and Amiens. During
WWII, important fuel tanks were there.
11/08/1944 ME841   JI-H Bombing Lens   14.05 16.33 17.24
   Bomb load 11 x 1000 MC, 4 X 500 GP. Primary target: Lens,
Marshalling yards. Weather 4/10ths cloud. Bombed at 16.33 hours
from 14,000 feet, red and yellow T.I.s as instructed by Master Bomber.
Very good concentrated raid.
12/08/1944 ME841   JI-H Bombing Brunswick 21.39 00.10 02.25
   Bomb load 1 x 2000 HC, 12 x 500 'J' type clusters. Primary target:
Brunswick. Weather 10/10ths cloud. Bombed at 00.10 hours from
20,000 feet. Smoke rising above clouds. Bombing appeared accurate.
Flak damage to aircraft over target. Attack should be satisfactory.
15/08/1944 LM285   JI-K Bombing St Trond   09.55 12.09 13.25
   Bomb load 11 x 1000 MC, 4 x 500 GP. Primary target St. Trond
Airfield. Bombed at 12.09 hours from 17,000 feet, red T.I.s and
runways. Weather clear. Concentrated attack, palls of smoke prevented
visual of attack.

05/09/1944 LM275 JI-E Bombing Le Havre 17.25 19.23 20.28
Bomb load 11 x 1000 MC, 4 x 500 GP. Primary target: Le Havre.
Bombed at 19.23 hours from 13,000 feet red T.I.
06/09/1944 ME841 JI-H Bombing Le Havre 16.31 18.40 19.45
Bomb load 11 x 1000 MC, 4 x 500 GP. Primary target: Le Havre.
Bombed at 18.40 hours from 7,000 feet red T.I.s.
08/09/1944 ME841 JI-H Bombing Le Havre 05.59 07.51 09.08
Bomb load 11 x 1000 MC, 4 x 500 GP. Primary target: Le Havre.
Weather 10/10ths cloud down to 3,000 feet. Jettisoned in target area at
07.51 hours from 5,000 feet. Saw green T.I.s well to the North.
Aircraft hit by flak which caused a fire in the bomb bay when hit by
flak which started a fire in the bomb bay. Navigator and M/U Gunner
extinguished fire.
11/09/1944 LM274 JI-B Bombing Kamen 16.03 18.42 20.21
Bomb load 1 x 4000 HC, 16 x 500 GP. Weather clear. Primary
target: Kamen. Bombed at 18.42 hours from 16,000 feet. T.I. yellow
and flames of fires.
20/09/1944 NG121 JI-H Bombing Calais 14.54 16.01 17.04
Bomb load 11 x 1000 MC, 4 x 500 GP. Primary target: Calais.
Weather clear over target. Bombed at 16.01 hours from 3,500 feet, red
T.I.s.
23/09/1944 NG121 JI-H Bombing Neuss 19.27 21.23 22.56
Bomb load 8 x 1000 ANM 59, 3 x 1000 ANM 44, 4 x 500 GP.
Primary target: Neuss. Weather 10/10ths cloud over target, tops
8/10,000 feet. Bombed at 21.23 hours from 21,000 feet on red glow of
T.I.s.
26/09/1944 NG121 JI-H Bombing Calais (Cap Gris Nez) 11.44 12.44
14.03
Bomb load 11 x 1000 MC, 4 x 500 GP. Primary target: Calais 7D.
Weather clear below cloud which was 3,500 feet. Bombed at 12.44
hours from 4,000 feet on red T.I. + 1 second.
"According J.D. Trick & M.C. Smith's logbook target: "Cap Gris
Nez".
27/09/1944 NG121 JI-H Bombing Calais 07.42 08.43 09.48
Bomb load 11 x 1000 MC, 4 x 500 GP. Primary target: Calais 15.
Weather, cloud 5,500 feet 10/10ths. Bombed at 08.43 hours from
5,500 feet on port ahead of red T.I.
28/09/1944 NG121 JI-H Bombing Calais 07.56 09.20 10.31
Bomb load 11 x 1000 MC, 4 x 500 GP. Primary target: Calais 19.
Bombed at 09.20 hours from 9,000 feet red T.I.

05/10/1944 NG121   JI-H Bombing Saarbrucken 17.11 x 22.16

Bomb load 11 x 1000 MC, 1 x 500 GP, 3 x 500 GP. Long Delay. Primary target: Saarbrucken, Marshalling yards. This aircraft was a supporter to P.F.F. Weather clear over target. Orbited the target for 16 minutes. Abandoned mission on instructions from Master Bomber heard to say they were unable to locate target and called "Abandon Mission - our troop in vicinity". Jettisoned 3 x 500 Long Delay 40 miles East of Southwold from 5,000 feet at 21.42 hours. Remainder brought back.

18/10/1944 PB142 JI-A Bombing Bonn   08.17 11.03 12.59

Bomb load 1 x 4000 HC. 5 x 12 x 30 - 2 x 12 x 30 modified, 9 x No. 14 Clusters. Primary target: Bonn. Weather varying cloud 2-7/10ths with break for bombing. Bombed at 11.03 hours from 17,000 feet. Smoke on A/P.

19/10/1944 NG121   JI-H Bombing Stuttgart   17.39 20.27 23.31

Bomb load 1 x 4000 HC, 6 x 1000 MC, 1 x 500 GP. Primary target: Stuttgart, A/P 'D' 1st attack. Weather 10/10ths cloud which broke to 6/10ths at the end of the period. Bombed at 20.27 hours from 18,000 feet on H2S. Checked by wanganui.

23/10/1944 NG121   JI-H Bombing Essen 16.55 19.33 21.09

Bomb load 1 x 4000 HC, 14 x 500 Clusters. Primary target: Essen. Weather 10/10ths cloud over target - tops 12/14,000 feet with most appalling weather on route. Bombed at 19.33 hours from 20,000 feet. Red markers.

25/10/1944 NG121   JI-H Bombing Essen   13.00 15.29 16.49

Bomb load 1 x 4000 HC, 6 x 1000 MC, 6 x 500 GP. Primary target: Essen. Weather over target 10/10ths low cloud, with one clear patch which appeared to fill up later in the attack. Bombed at 15.29 hours from 23,000 feet. Red T.I.s.

26/10/1944 LM627   JI-D Bombing Leverkusen 13.02 15.29 17.05

Bomb load 1 x 4000 HC, 6 x 1000 MC, 4 x 500 GP, 2 x 500 GP Long Delay. Primary target: Leverkusen. Weather over target and on route was 10/10ths cloud. Bombed at 15.29 hours from 16,500 feet on G.H.

P/O. John Prescott

195832 (657512) P/O. John Prescott.   Pilot.
Sgt. D.J. Morgan.   A/Bomber.
P/O.E.T. or G.T. Rushton. Navigator.
F/S. W. Townshend.   WOP/AG.
Sgt. A. Goodwin.   MU/Gunner.
Sgt. K.S. Cracknell.   R/Gunner.
Sgt. R.T. Vane. F/Engineer.

29/06/1945 RE140 JI-H Post Mortem Special mission 10.01 x 15.52
03/07/1945 ME380   JI-E Post Mortem Special mission 14.15 x 20.00

P/O. Elmer Richard Protheroe

54223 (552769) P/O.Elmer Richard "Dick" Protheroe. Pilot.
1332664   F/S. P.W.B. Sach.   A/Bomber.
1576433   F/S. F.A. Kesterton.   Navigator.
1559148   Sgt. David Kellock.   Navigator. 2 ops.
1246248   Sgt. R.G. Law.   WOP/AG.
1568243   Sgt. Andrew Wilson Birse. MU/Gunner.
1823872   Sgt. Robert Moffat Collins. R/Gunner.
1676325   Sgt. Sam Proctor.   F/Engineer.
1283636   F/S. Frederick "Fred" Gregory. 2nd Pilot. 19/02/1944
177517(1334210)F/S Charles James Johnson DFM 2nd Pilot 15/3/1944

29/12/1943 DS813 JI-H Bombing Berlin   17.13 20.07 23.58
    Bomb load 1 x 2000, 40 x 30 incendiaries, 900 x 4 incendiaries, 90
x 4 incendiaries. Primary target: Berlin. There was 10/10 cloud.
Bombed at 20.07 hours at 19,000 feet. Route was O.K.
    From his normal crew, only F/S. E. R. Protheroe did this mission as
2nd Pilot with P/O. E.A. Greenwood's crew.
14/01/1944 LL670 A2-K Bombing Brunswick 17.25 19.28 22.15
    Bomb load 1 x 4000, 48 x 30 incendiaries. Primary target:
Brunswick. There was 10/10 cloud. Bombed at 19.28 hours at 20,000
ft. Several large fires burning orange showing through cloud. Good
raid, fires burning well visible 60 miles away. Route markers seemed
to be too scattered.

20/01/1944 LL670 A2-K
Bombing Berlin   16.18
19.42 00.01
Bomb load 1 x 4000, 32 x
30, 540 x 4, 60 x 4
incendiaries. Primary target:
Berlin. 10/10 cloud. Bombed
at 19.42 hours at 20,000 ft.
On red and green T.I.s.
Orange glow seen on leaving
target.
21/01/1944 LL670 A2-K
Bombing Magdeburg
20.14 23.10 03.22
Bomb load 1 x 4000, 720
x 4, 90 x 4, 32 x 30
incendiaries. Primary target:
Magdeburg. Cloud very light
2-3/10. Bombed at 23.10
hours at 20,000 ft. 2 Red
T.I.s together. One very large

Elmer Richard Protheroe

fire orangey red and 6 smaller fires of same colour. T.I.s and flares
very well placed. Fires appeared to be gaining control all over target
area.

27/01/1944 LL670 A2-K Bombing Berlin   17.55 20.30 01.40
Bomb load 1 x 4000, 32 x 30, 450 x 4. Primary target: Berlin. There
was 10/10 cloud. Starboard bomb door holed by flak. Bombed at 20.30
hours at 20,000 ft. Red glow seen on leaving. Small flak hole on
starboard bomb door. Sky markers dropped dead on time and well
concentrated. On leaving red glow reflected evidence of fires beneath
cloud.

28/01/1944 LL670 A2-K Bombing Berlin   00.21 03.21 08.43
Bomb load 1 x 4000 lb bomb, 24 x 30, 180 x 4, 90 x 4 incendiaries.
Primary target: Berlin. There was 10/10 cloud thin. Bombed at 03.21
hours at 21,000 ft. Many concentrated fires and 1 large explosion at
03.20 hours. Route satisfactory and very good attack.

15/02/1944 LL670 A2-K Bombing Berlin   17.28 21.19 00.04
Bomb load 1 x 8000 lb bomb. Primary target: Berlin. There was
10/10 cloud. Bombed at 21.19 hrs. At 20,000 ft. Flares and T.I.s very
prominent. Route good. Photo attempted.

19/02/1944 LL670 A2-K Bombing Leipzig 00.15 04.06 06.54

Bomb load 1 x 4000 lb bomb. 32 x 30, 510 x 4, 90 x 4 x incendiaries. Primary target: Leipzig. There was 10/10 cloud. Bombed at 04.06 hours at 20,000 ft. Four large fires and smaller ones seen over a wide area. Northern route OK. Aircraft arrived too early and had to waste time in Willenberg area. Attack very widespread.

F/S. F. Gregory 2nd Pilot that day.

07/03/1944 LL684 A2-B Bombing Le Mans 19.46 22.05 00.23

Bomb load 10 x 1000, 4 x 500 lb bombs. Primary target: Le Mans. There was 10/10 cloud with occasional breaks. River and Marshalling Yard visual. Bombed at 22.05 hours from 5,500 feet. One large and six small fires seen clearly. Bombed on visual as no markers were seen.

15/03/1944 LL670 A2-K Bombing Stuttgart 19.31 x 22.47

Bomb load 1 x 8000 lb bomb, 8 x 30 incendiaries. Returned early. Furthest point reached 15 miles W. of Chartres. 1 x 8000 jettisoned to reduce weight, 8 x 30 incendiaries brought back. Navigator lost protractor. Navigator sick.

F/S. C.J. Johnson 2nd Pilot that day.

24/03/1944 LL670 A2-K Bombing Berlin 18.51 23.15 02.37

Bomb load 1 x 1000 lb. bomb, 88 x 30, 810 x 4, 90 x 4 incendiaries. Primary target: Berlin. There was 8/10 cloud over the target. Bombed at 23.15 hours from 20,000 feet. Fires were large and scattered. 1 large and 4 small fires seen through one gap, many others seen. Attack considered successful, but P and F winds not sufficiently strong.

Sgt. D. Kellock Navigator from that day.

30/03/1944 LL670 A2-K Bombing Nuremburg 22.07 01.26 06.01

Bomb load 1 x 1000 lb bomb, 96 x 30, 810 x 4, 90 x 4 incendiaries. Primary target: Nuremburg. There was 8/10 cloud with tops 15,000 feet. Bombed at 01.28 hours from 20,000 feet. P.F.F. were not too good, nothing to be seen in target area. Fires non-existent. Raid poor.

P/O. Charles Frank Prowles

L to R (top): Charles Frank Prowles, Arnold Hughes Morrison. Centre: Jack Porrelli. L to R (bottom): Arthur Albert Holmes, Ronald Bernard Spencer.

177531 (1600548) P/O. Charles Frank "Ted" Prowles. Pilot.

A425771 F/S. Ronald Bernard "Spence" Spencer, RAAF, Bomb Aimer.

A411168   F/O. Arnold Hughes Morrison, DFC, RAAF. Navigator.

1670154 Sgt. Raymond Surtees.   WOP/AG.

Sgt. R.D. Keen.   MU/Gunner. 1 op.

519212 Sgt. Arthur Albert "Bert" Holmes, MU&R/Gunner.

R87920 WO2. William Ernest "Ernie""Bill" Egri, RCAF, DFM.
   R/Gunner. 1 op.

1594519 Sgt. John "Jack" Porrelli.   R/Gunner. 13 or 14 ops.

1715000 Sgt. Henry Albert "Harry" Osborn.   F/Engineer.

22/04/1944 DS826 JI-L Bombing Dusseldorf 22.52 01.21 03.15

Bomb load 1 x 2000 lb bomb, 1050 x 4 lb incendiaries. Primary target: Dusseldorf. There was no cloud. Bombed at 01.21 hours from 19,000 feet. Many fires seen surrounding the T.I.s. Very good attack. Searchlights numerous, accurate flak, too accurate for comfort. Route good. Large explosion seen 01.38 hours.

Sgt. R.D. Keen was MU/Gunner that day and Sgt. A.A. Holmes R/Gunner.

26/04/1944 LL734 JI-S Bombing Essen 22.50 01.40 03.31

Bomb load 1 x 2000 lb bomb, 84 x 30, 945 x 4, 105 x 4 lb incendiaries. Primary target: Essen. Weather was clear. Bombed at 01.40 hours from 19,000 feet. A large concentration of fires seen covered with smoke. Glimpse of river on approach. Attack seemed spread, markers were to the East of main concentration. Moderate heavy flak, no fighters.

Contrary to ORBs, in his logbook J. Porrelli noted that he did this operation and no mention of this operation in W.E. Egri logbook.

Sgt. A.A. Holmes MU/Gunner from that day.

01/05/1944 DS816 JI-O Bombing Chambly 22.42 00.23 02.22

Bomb load 10 x 1000, 5 x 500 lb bombs. Primary target: Chambly. Weather was clear. Bombed at 00.23 hours from 9,000 feet. Saw bombs bursting round T.I.s inside railway yard. Chatter between M of C made it difficult to hear A/B instructions. Had combat with enemy aircraft.

07/05/1944 LL739 JI-M Bombing Nantes 00.27 03.05 05.55

Bomb load 1 x 4000, 14 x 500 lb bombs. Primary target: Nantes. Weather was clear. Bombed at 03.05 hours from 9,700 feet. Bombs seen bursting on T.I.s. There was a heavy pall of smoke covering whole area. Raid appeared rather scattered. Route good.

10/05/1944 DS816 JI-O Bombing Courtrai 22.20 23.27 00.50

Bomb load 7 x 1000 GP, 7 x 1000 MC. Primary target: Courtrai. There was no cloud but general mist. Bombed at 23.27 hours from 11,000 feet. Red glow seen in centre of target area. All bombs seen to fall in area indicated by Master Bomber.

11/05/1944 DS816 JI-O Bombing Louvain 22.57 00.18 01.32

Bomb load 5 x 1000 GP, 5 x 1000 MC, 5 x 500 MC. Primary target: Louvain. Clear over target. Bombed as ordered by Master Bomber at 00.18 hours from 8,800 feet. T.I.s appeared concentrated and bombs fell in area marked. Large deep red explosion at 00.14 hours.

19/05/1944 DS822 JI-T Bombing Le Mans   22.38 00.25 03.08

Bomb load 4 x 1000 USA, 5 x 1000 MC, 1 x 1000 GP, 4 x 500 GP. Primary target: Le Mans. 6-10/10 cloud over target. Bombed on Master Bomber's instructions at 00.25 hours from 8,000 feet. Large explosion seen near buildings. After bombing, second explosion seen giving a brilliant white flash. Attack appeared well concentrated. On return landed at Bourn in mistake.

Contrary to ORBs, in his logbook W.E. Egri noted that he did this operation as Rear Gunner, and no mention of this operation in Porrelli logbook.

21/05/1944 DS816 JI-O Bombing Duisburg   22.55 01.24 03.25

Bomb load 1 x 2000 lb bomb, 120 x 30, 600 x 4 incendiaries. Primary target: Duisberg. There was 10/10 cloud with tops at 18,000 feet. Bombed markers at 01.24 hours from 21,000 feet. Cloud prevented any visual. Fighter flares seen from target to coast on homeward route. Sighted 4 enemy aircraft at 00.26 hours which crossed above from port to starboard at 20,000 feet. At 01.20 hours aircraft was fired on by an unidentified enemy aircraft over target. Again at 02.04 hours unidentified enemy aircraft approached from astern firing a short burst but Lancaster evaded.

Contrary to ORBs, according to J. Porrelli's logbook he did not fly this operation. Consequently the Rear Gunner that day is unknown.

24/05/1944 DS816 JI-O Bombing Boulogne   00.25 01.13 02.25

Bomb load 9 x 1000 MC, 1 x 1000 GP, 1 x 1000 ANM, 4 x 500 GP. Primary target: Boulogne, Gun Battery. Very slight haze over the target. Bombed at 01.13 hours from 8,100 feet. 1 searchlight and a few bursts of flak seen. No T.I. markers seen at first on arrival, only bomb bursts.

27/05/1944 DS816 JI-O Bombing Aachen   00.36 02.29 04.05

Bomb load 7 x 1000 MC, 4 x 1000 ANM, 4 x 500 MC. Primary target: Aachen. Clear at target. Bombed markers at 02.29 hours from 14,000 feet. One stick seen to fall among red T.I.s but heavy smoke pall prevented visual. Flak moderate. Trouble free trip. Unidentified twin-engine aircraft approached at 02.15 hours but Lancaster evaded.

28/05/1944 DS816 JI-O Bombing Angers   19.00   23.59   01.50

Bomb load 5 x 1000 MC, 1 x 1000 USA, 4 x 500 MC. Primary target: Angers. Clear over target. Bombed at 23.59 hours from 9,000 feet. A good visual of target. Whole target area seemed covered with flames and smoke. Route satisfactory.

30/05/1944 DS816 JI-O Bombing Boulogne   23.10   00.05   01.15

Bomb load 6 x 1000 MC, 4 x 500 MC. Primary target: Boulogne Gun Batteries. Clear over target. Bombed at 00.05 hours from 7,100 feet. Bomb bursts concentrated on T.I.s.

10/06/1944 DS816 JI-O Bombing Dreux   23.17 01.00   03.20

Bomb load 16 x 500 GP, 2 x 500 LD. Primary target: Dreux. Bombed to starboard of green T.I.s as instructed by Master Bomber at 01.00 hours from 8,000 feet. Bombs seen to burst across yards. No trouble experienced. Weather clear with slight haze.

12/06/1944 DS816 JI-O Bombing Gelsenkirchen   23.10 01.08 03.01

Bomb load 1 x 4000 HC, 12 x 500 GP, 4 x 500 MC. Primary target: Gelsenkirchen. Clear over target. Bombed red and green T.I.s at 01.08 hours from 19,700 feet. Close concentration of bomb bursts seen in area of T.I.s with smoke and fires.

14/06/1944 DS816 JI-O Bombing Le Havre   23.49 01.16 02.43

Bomb load 11 x 1000 MC, 4 x 500 GP. Primary target: Le Havre. Weather clear. Much smoke. Bombed at 01.16 hours from 15,000 feet on green markers. Good concentration of bombs markers. Big area of fire in docks and town to the North. One aircraft seen shot down.

15/06/1944 DS816 JI-O Bombing Valenciennes 23.08 x   x

Bomb load 16 x 500 GP, 2 x 500 MC. Aircraft missing.

Shot down, probably at 00.51 hours by Bf 110 flown by Hptm. Hubert Rauh of Stab II/.NJG4. Crashed at Croisilles (Pas de Calais) where those who died are buried in the British Cemetery.

F/S. C.F. Prowles KIA, Sgt. H.A. Osborn KIA, F/O. A.H. Morrison Evaded, F/S. R.B. Spencer KIA, Sgt. R. Surtees KIA, Sgt. J. Porrelli KIA, Sgt. A.A. Holmes KIA.

S/L. Eric George Brodie Reid, DFC

70816   S/L.   Eric George Brodie "Barney" Reid, DFC. Pilot.
170457 (1585089) P/O. Victor Francis Dobell Meade. A/Bomber.
135676 (1317703) F/O. Harry James.   Navigator.
NZ414385   F/S. W.T.L. Mack, RNZAF.   WOP/A.G.
138423 (984424) F/O Jackson Nisbet Pollock, DFC MU/Gunner. 1 op.
A415845   F/S. Richard Hiden White, RAAF. MU/Gunner. 10 ops.
A410114   P/O. Geoffrey George Williams, RAAF. R/Gunner.
183649 (1608232) Sgt. Ronald James O'Donnell.   F/Engineer.
70126 F/L. Ralph Campbell Chopping, DFC.   2nd Pilot. 15/02/1944

R.J. O'Donnell and V.F.D. Meade subsequently died on 17/05/1945
whilst serving with No. 630 Squadron.

11/11/1943 DS783 JI-B Gardening La Tranche   17.33 x 00.54
    Aircraft carried 2 x H802, 2 x G714. Primary area La Tranche. No
cloud.
    F/O. J.N. Pollock MU/Gunner that day.
16/12/1943 DS706 JI-G Bombing Berlin   16.44 20.04   00.19
    Bomb load 1 x 4000, 90 x 4 incendiaries. Primary target: Berlin.
10/10 cloud over target. Green T.I.s seen; Bombed at 20.04 at 22,000
ft. Very good fires seen. Landed at Downham Market.
    F/S. R.H. White MU/Gunner from that day.
24/12/1943 LL624 JI-B Bombing Berlin   00.28 x 07.35
    Bomb load 1 x 8000. Primary target: Berlin. 10/10 cloud, Tops
8,000 ft, visibility OK. Green T.I.s with 4 Sky markers 2 miles ahead.
Red glow of big fire seen through cloud also several incendiaries
which had not yet taken hold. Photo attempted.
29/12/1943 LL624 JI-B Bombing Berlin   17.10 20.08   23.36
    Bomb load 1 x 4000, 24 x 30 incendiaries, 90 x 4 incendiaries, 540
x 4 incendiaries. Primary target: Berlin. There was 10/10 cloud with
tops 10,000ft. Bombed at 20.08 hours at 22,000. Cloud prevented
visual observation. All markers were seen excepting marker North of
Stendal not seen. Flak all the way round to Bremen. Smoke above
cloud tops and glow seen on leaving target.
28/01/1944 LL624 JI-B Bombing Berlin   00.09 03.19   07.59
    Bomb load 1 x 2000 lb. bomb, 16 x 30, 750 x 4 incendiaries.
Primary target: Berlin. There was 10/10 cloud with tops 5000 ft.

Bombed at 03.19 hours at 21.000 ft. Very good attack. Good concentration of fires.

15/02/1944 LL728 JI-B Bombing Berlin   17.24 21.25   00.11

Bomb load 1 x 4000 lb bomb, 32 x 30, 540 x 4, 90 x 4 x incendiaries. Primary target: Berlin. There was 10/10 cloud with tops at 1,000 ft. Bombed at 21.25 hrs at 21,000 ft. P.F.F. scattered. Few results noticed. Believed decoy dark green markers SW of Berlin.

F/L. R.C. Chopping 2nd Pilot that day.

21/02/1944 LL728 JI-B Bombing Stuttgart   00.29   04.10   06.31

Bomb load 1 x 8000 lb bomb, 16 x 30, 300 x 4 incendiaries. Primary target: Stuttgart. There was 6/10 cloud. Bombed at 04.10 hours at 20,000 ft. No visual details. Incendiaries over a wide area. Ground snow covered. Route OK.

24/02/1944 LL728 JI-B Bombing Schweinfurt 18.48   23.12   01.57

Bomb load 1 x 8000 lb bomb. Primary target: Schweinfurt. Weather was perfect. Bombed at 23.12 hours at 21,000 ft. Successful attack. Good red fires to North on leaving. Little opposition over target and on route.

25/02/1944 LL728 JI-B Bombing Augsburg   21.55   01.17   04.38

Bomb load 1 x 8000 lb bomb, 8 x 30, 9 x 4 incendiaries. Primary target: Augsburg. There was some low cloud over the target. Bombed at 01.17 hours at 19,000 ft. A good mass of fires seen. A number of fires seen at junction of river and railway which were outlined by snow. Very little opposition. Route good.

01/03/1944 LL728 JI-B Bombing Stuttgart   23.39   03.05   07.00

Bomb load 1 x 8000 lb bomb. Primary target: Stuttgart. There was 10/10 cloud. Bombed at 03.05 hours at 21,000 ft. Some fires were seen as aircraft left. Route good.

01/05/1944 LL728 JI-B Bombing Chambly   22.41   00.28   02.08

Bomb load 10 x 1000, 5 x 500 lb bombs. Primary target: Chambly. Weather was clear. Bombed at 00.28 hours from 5,000 feet. A good number of fires were seen in target area. Aircraft returned at 2,000 feet to French Coast - Good attack. Route OK - no opposition over target. One fire seen south of target, either jettison or crashed aircraft.

F/L. Robert Geoffrey Keen Rice

130318 (656066) F/L. Robert Geoffrey Keen Rice. Pilot.
F/S. W.J. Jenkinson. A/Bomber. 18 ops.
159990 (1650697) F/O. David Philip Bartlett. A/Bomber. 2 ops.
164196 (1624262) F/O. George Edward Kiley. Navigator.
176987 (1892606) F/O. Douglas Reginald Warren. WOP/AG. 9 ops.
189643 (1504777) F/O. Colin Pratt.   WOP/AG. 11 ops.
Sgt. H.G. Allam.   MU/Gunner. 19 ops.
Sgt. R.H. Chambers. R/Gunner.
 F/S.D.S. Tungate.   F/Engineer.

Passengers: 07/05/1945, 19/06/1945, 13/07/1945, 17/07/1945,
19/07/1945.

07/03/1945 NF966 A2-G Bombing Dessau   17.07 22.08 02.28
   Bomb load 1 x 4000 HC, 6 x Mk. 17 Clusters. Primary target:
Dessau. Weather 5 to 10/10ths thin cloud. Bombed at 22.08 hours
from 19,500 feet on Red T.Is.
   From his normal crew, only F/L. R.G.K. Rice did this mission as
2nd Pilot with F/L. F.P. Hendy's crew.
09/03/1945 ME354   JI-M Bombing Datteln   10.30 14.01 15.58
   Bomb load 1 x 4000 HC, 13 x 500 ANM64, 2 x 500 MC L/Delay37.
Primary target: Datteln, Synthetic oil plant. Weather 10/10ths cloud,
tops 8-10,000 feet. Bombed at 14.01 hours from 20,000 feet on G.H.
   All aircraft seemed to be dropping bombs in the same place.
   From his normal crew, only F/L. R.G.K. Rice did this mission as
2nd Pilot with F/L. M.D. Muggeridge's crew.
10/03/1945 NN717   A2-E Bombing Gelsenkirchen 12.11 15.38
   17.37
   Bomb load 1 x 4000 HC, 13 x 500 ANM64, 1 x 500 MC, 1 x 500
GP. Primary target: Gelsenkirchen. Weather 10/10ths cloud at target,
tops 8,000 feet. Bombed at 15.38 hours from 19,000 feet on leading
G.H. aircraft.
   F/S. W.J. Jenkinson A/Bomber until 26/05/45.
   F/O. D.R. Warren WOP/AG until 09/04/45.
20/03/1945 ME529   A2-F Bombing Hamm   09.45 13.15 16.22
   Bomb load 7 x 1000 ANM59, 9 x 500 ANM64. Primary target:
Hamm, Marshalling yards. Weather 5/10ths cloud. Bombed at 13.15

hours from 18,000 feet on leading G.H. aircraft. Heavy flak holes between port inner and port outer engines and in Mid-upper turret perspex.

21/03/1945 NN781 A2-B Bombing Munster 09.28 13.08 15.29

Bomb load 1 x 4000 HC, 13 x 500 ANM64, 2 x 500 MC. Primary target Munster Viaduct and Marshalling Yards. Weather cloud nil to 2/10ths. Bombed at 13.08 hours from 18,500 feet on leading G.H. aircraft. Heavy flak damage to aircraft. Pilot slightly grazed on forehead by piece of flak after perspex broken.

29/03/1945 PB426 A2-E Bombing Salzgitter 12.14 16.42 19.15

Bomb load 1 x 4000 HC, 8 x 500 ANM64. Primary target: Salzgitter, Hallendorf works. Weather 10/10ths cloud. Bombed at 16.42 hours from 21,500 feet on leading G.H. aircraft.

04/04/1945 PB419 A2-C Bombing Merseburg (Leuna) 18.38 x 02.44

Weather 5-10/10ths cloud, and 10/10ths over Merseburg. Abortive. Farthest point reached 5142N 1040E at 22.24 hours. 18,500 feet. Bomb load 1 x 4000 HC, 6 x 500 ANM64 jettisoned at 5015N 0000 at 01.49 hrs from 15,000 feet. Starboard outer feathered at 5142N 1040E Oil pressure very low from set course.

09/04/1945 PB423 A2-C Bombing Kiel 19.48 22.43 02.09

Bomb load 1 x 4000 HC and 12 x 500 ANM64. Primary target: Kiel, Submarine Buildings Yards. Weather clear with slight haze. Bombed at 22.43 hours from 20,000 feet on centre starboard of Red/Green T.I.s. M/B's instructions. Explosions seen in area of T.I.s. Explosions seen over Hamburg area. Good attack well concentrated on T.I.s area of flame smoke and explosion area of sq. 8 miles.

01/05/1945 RE123 A2-K Manna The Hague 13.10 14.26 15.31

Dropping area The Hague. Weather clear over target. Dropped four Panniers on Red T.I. and White Cross at 14.26 hours. Large notice on roof of house at Flardingen: "Thanks R.A.F".

F/O. Colin Pratt WOP/AG that day.

07/05/1945 ME425 A2-L Manna The Hague 12.12 13.41 14.49

Dropping area The Hague. Dropped 3¼ Packs on White Cross and Red T.I.s at 13.41 hours. Clear. 3/4 packs hung up, brought back.

Passenger: AC. L. Collins. No Mid Upper Gunner that day.

F/O. D.R. Warren WOP/AG until 17/05/45.

11/05/1945 RE159 A2-E Exodus Juvincourt - Tangmere 11.02 x 17.43

Duration 3.46. Outward 1.34 hours. Collected 24 ex POWs.

Homeward 2.12 hours. POWs arranged too near perimeter track danger from taxiing aircraft.

17/05/1945 RE159 A2-E   Exodus   Brussels - Westcott 10.04 x 16.04
 Duration 3 hrs 22 mins. Out 1 hr 30 mins. In 1 hr 52 mins. 10 Belgian refugees taken to Brussels. 24 Ex POWs delivered to Westcott. 5 Balloons at Cardington flying at 3,000ft on return trip. Everything satisfactory at Brussels.

18/05/1945 RE159 A2-E   Exodus   Brussels - Oakley 12.05 x 20.05
 Duration 3 hrs 34 mins. Out 1 hr 8 mins. In 1 hr 54 mins. 11 Belgian refugees taken to Brussels. 24 ex POWs Returned to U.K. Organisation excellent throughout.
 F/O. Colin Pratt WOP/AG from that day.

23/05/1945 RE159 A2-E   Exodus Brussels - Oakley 12.13 x 18.20
 Duration 3 hrs 16 mins. Out 1 hr 14 mins. In 2 hrs 02 mins. 10 Belgian refugees returned to Brussels. 24 ex POWs evacuated. All OK.

24/05/1945 RE159 A2-E   Exodus   Brussels   11.58 x 16.34
 Duration 2.15 hours. Out 1.04 hours. In 1.11 hours. 10 Belgian refugees to Brussels.

25/05/1945 RE159 A2-E   Exodus   Brussels   12.06 x 16.06
 Duration 2.26 hours. Out 1.10 hours. In 1.16 hours. 10 Belgian refugees to Brussels. No POWs back. No troubles.

26/05/1945 ME355   A2-G   Exodus   Brussels - Ford 11.52 x 18.12
 Duration 3.17 hours. Out 1.09 hours. In 2.00 hours. 10 Belgian refugees to Brussels. 24 ex POWs all military brought back.

19/06/1945 RE159 A2-E   Baedeker Tour over Continent 09.40 x 14.08
 F/O. D.P. Bartlett A/Bomber that day.
 Passengers: A/Cdre. H.H. Down, Sgt. Meeds, Sgt. Mylechreest, Cpl. Swan, Cpl. Brow.

25/06/1945 RE159 A2-E   Post Mortem Special mission 09.58 x 15.57
 F/O. D.P. Bartlett A/Bomber that day.

13/07/1945 ME355   A2-G   Baedeker Tour over Continent 15.20 x 19.45
 F/S. W.J. Jenkinson A/Bomber from that day.
 Passengers: Sgt. Predergat, Sgt. Sackett, LAC. Gear, Sgt. Machell (WAAF), LACW. Brown (WAAF).

17/07/1945 RE159 A2-E   Baedeker Tour over Continent 09.32 x 13.47

Passengers: LAC. Chanter, Cpl. Lorton, LAC. Brown, ACW.
Clarke, ACW. Robinson
19/07/1945 RE159 A2-E Baedeker Tour over Continent 15.16 x
19.29
    Passengers: Sgt. Pringle, Sgt. Smyth, Cpl. Machew, LAC. Hallow,
LACW. Sanders.

P/O. Edgar Richardson

179944 (1431070) P/O. Edgar Richardson.   Pilot.
1391956   Sgt. George Henry Trigwell.   A/Bomber.
550259   F/S. William James McIntosh.   Navigator.
1379027   F/S. Cecil Burnley Robertshaw. WOP/AG.
1486527   Sgt. Bernard Reginald Vince. MU/Gunner.
1868834   Sgt. Philip Raymond Smith.   R/Gunner.
2212994   Sgt. G.M. Holt.   F/Engineer.
A434016   P/O. Henry Frederick Roome, RAAF. 2nd Pilot.
12/08/1944

L to R: Edgar Richardson, Hendy Frederick Roome, George Henry Trigwell.

18/07/1944 LL624 JI-R Bombing Aulnoye   22.35 00.59 02.23
    Bomb load 18 x 500 GP. Primary target: Aulnoye, Railway junction.
Weather clear. Bombed at 00.59 hours from 9,000 feet green T.I.s. A
good attack.
20/07/1944 DS813 JI-N Bombing Homberg   23.23 01.22 03.00
    Bomb load 1 x 4000 HC, 2 x 500 MC, 14 x 500 GP. Primary target:
Homberg, Oil plant. Weather clear, slight haze. Bombed at 01.22 hours

from 18,500 feet red and green T.I.s. Clouds of smoke from fires in target area. Fighters much in evidence. We had five fighter attacks within 30 miles of target out and home.

23/07/1944 HK572   JI-T Bombing Kiel   22.26 01.25 03.12

Bomb load 10 x 1000 MC, 5 x 500 GP Special Nickels. Primary target: Kiel, Warehouses and docks. Weather 10/10ths cloud occasional breaks. Bombed at 01.25 hours from 20,000 feet centre of green and red T.I.s. Glow of bomb bursts seen below clouds. No fighters.

24/07/1944 HK572   JI-T Bombing Stuttgart   21.46 01.55 05.29

Bomb load 7 x 1000 MC, 4 x 500 GP. Primary target Stuttgart. Weather 10/10ths cloud. Bombed at 01.55 hours from 18,500 feet on green sky markers. Bombs appeared to fall in area marked. A quiet trip.

27/07/1944 HK572   JI-T Bombing Les Catelliers   16.59 18.50 20.09

Bomb load 18 x 500 GP. Primary target: Les Catelliers, Flying bomb site. Bombed at 18.50 hours from 16,000 feet on Mosquito.

30/07/1944 HK572   JI-T Bombing Caen   06.02 07.50 10.02

Bomb load 18 x 500 GP. Primary target: Caen 'B'. Weather 10/10ths cloud. Bombed at 07.50 hours from 18,500 feet southern edge of smoke pall on instructions from Master Bomber. Bomb bursts concentrated around smoke and T.I.s.

04/08/1944 HK572   JI-T Bombing Bec D'Ambes   13.22 17.58 21.07

Bomb load 7 x 1000 MC, 4 x 500 GP. Primary target: Bec d'Ambes depot. Weather clear. Bombed at 17.58 hours from 8,000 feet, visual of tip of bomb sight. Aircraft orbited target after bombing. Rear Gunner and Mid Upper Gunner fired burst at 2 tankers in the river at 2,000 feet.

07/08/1944 HK577   JI-P Bombing Mare de Magne 21.43 23.43 01.02

Bomb load 11 x 1000 MC, 4 x 500 GP. Primary target: Mare de Magne (just past Caen). Weather clear, slight ground haze. Bombed at 23.43 hours from 8,000 feet port edge of red T.I.s as instructed by Master Bomber. Bomb bursts seen round and across T.I.s and star shells dropping amidst T.I.s.

Mare-de-Magne: place between Caen and Fontenay le Marmion.

08/08/1944 HK577   JI-P Bombing Foret de Lucheux 21.38 23.50 01.04

Bomb load 18 x 500 GP. Primary target: Foret de Lucheux, Petrol dump. Weather clear. Bombed at 23.50 hours from 12,000 feet, fires in centre of wood. Small bunches of flames seen in the target area, large explosion at 23.51 hours.

"Foret de Lucheux" is a forest between Lille and Amiens. During WWII, important fuel tanks were there.

12/08/1944 LM265 JI-E Bombing Russelsheim 21.45 x 00.30

Bomb load 1 x 4000 HC, 6 x 500 No. 14 clusters, 6 x (150x4). Aircraft missing.

Cause not stated. The aircraft crashed at 00.30 hours on the 13th August 1944 in the village of Engegstadt, about 10 miles south west of Mainz, Germany. Possibly shot down by Lt. Otto Teschner, 11./NJG1, who claimed a 4-engine aircraft at 00.30 hours in the Bad Kreuznach area, which is the appropriate vicinity.

P/O. H.F. Roome 2nd Pilot that day.

All crew KIA except Sgt. G.M. Holt who was interned in Camp L7, POW No.592. Those killed are now buried in the Reichswald Forest War Cemetery.

F/O. Hugh Christopher Richford, DFC

183740 (1320653) F/O Hugh Christopher "Richie" Richford, DFC, Pilot.
J91186 (R157166) W/O. E. "Ernie" Emmett, RCAF. A/Bomber.
F/S. A. Dix.   Navigator. 24 ops.
Sgt. William E. or L."Bill" Harradine.   Navigator. 1 op.
161741 (657060) F/O. Alfred Ernest Nye, DFC. Navigator. 1 op.
149340 (1562280) F/O.   Talbot William "Bill" Ledingham, DFC. Navigator. 4 ops.
Sgt. Geoffrey "Geoff" Norris. WOP/AG. 29 ops.
F/S. G.A. Brown.   WOP/AG. 1 op.
Sgt. Denis R. "Rats" Ratcliffe.   MU/Gunner.
Sgt. W. "Wally" Morrison. R/Gunner.
Sgt. Harry B. Dison.   F/Engineer.
J36160 F/O. Glen A. Hanson, RCAF. 2nd Pilot. 11/12/1944

Last trip to Trier on 21st December 1944. The two FFI women were Mlle H. Edouard and Mlle H. Carion of the French Resistance who had assisted shot-down airmen. L to R: "Rats" Ratcliffe, Harry Dison, "Geoff" Norris, "Bill" Ledingham, "Ernie" Emmett, "Wally" Morrison, "Richie" Richford. (courtesy Chris Richford)

09/08/1944 DS620 A2-D Bombing Fort d'Englos 21.53   22.53   23.54

Bomb load 13 x 1000 MC. Target: Fort d'Englos (Lille), Petrol dump. Returned early, Gee and W/T receiver U/S. Jettisoned at 22.53 hours from 10,000 feet, 8 x 1000 MC, position 5132N, 0223E.

F/S. A. Dix Navigator until 06/10/44.

Sgt. G. Norris WOP/AG for all operations except 16/12/44.

The fort of Ennetières-en-Weppes, or "fort d'Englos" is one of a set of six forts surrounding Lille.

11/08/1944 LL728 A2-L Bombing Lens 14.19   16.34   17.34

Bomb load 11 x 1000 MC, 4 X 500 GP. Primary target: Lens, Marshalling yards. Weather 4/10ths cloud. Bombed at 16.34 hours from 14,000 feet yellow T.I.s. Concentrated bomb bursts and smoke.

12/08/1944 DS842 A2-J Bombing Russelsheim 21.52   00.16   02.50

Bomb load 1 x 2000 HC, 12 x 500 No. 14 Clusters. Primary target: Russelsheim. Weather clear. Bombed at 00.18 hours from 17,000 feet, centre of red T.I.s. Three fighter attacks seen at Brunswick. Should be

565

good attack.

15/08/1944 DS842 A2-J   Bombing St Trond   10.10 12.09 13.28

Bomb load 11 x 1000 MC, 4 x 500 GP. Primary target St. Trond Airfield. Weather clear, bombed at 12.09 hours from 17,000 feet, undershot intersection of runways as per Master Bomber.

25/08/1944 PB426 JI-J Bombing   Russelsheim 20.33 01.00 04.29

Bomb load 1 x 4000 HC, 11 x 500 LB Clusters. Primary target: Russelheim. Weather clear. Bombed at 01.00 hours from 17,000 feet centre of red T.I.s. T.I.s well scattered by bomb bursts. Should be a good attack.

29/08/1944 LM286   A2-F   Bombing Stettin   21.15 02.11 06.43

Bomb load 1 x 4000 HC, 52 x 30, 486 x 4, 54 x 4 lb incendiaries. Primary target: Stettin. Weather thin layer 8/10ths cloud. Bombed at 0211 hours from 17000 feet, centre of red and green T.I.s. Fires seen among T.I.s, gaining hold, smoke billowing. Should be good raid.

31/08/1944 LM286   A2-F   Bombing Pont-Remy 16.07 18.18 19.47

Bomb load 11 x 1000 MC, 4 x 500 GP Mk IV LD. Primary target: Pont Remy, Dump. Weather cloudy. Bombed at 18.18 hours from 15,000 feet on G.H. Leading aircraft.

06/09/1944 LL677 A2-E   Bombing Le Havre 16.42 18.41 20.12

Bomb load 11 x 1000 MC, 4 x 500 GP. Primary target: Le Havre. Bombed at 18.41 hours from 7,000 feet, red T.I.s.

10/09/1944 DS842 A2-J   Bombing Le Havre   15.49 17.38 19.08

Bomb load 11 x 1000 MC, 4 x 500 GP. Primary target: Le Havre. Weather clear. Bombed at 17.38 hours from 9,700 feet. Undershot T.I.s red by 200 yards.

11/09/1944 LL666 A2-K   Bombing Kamen   16.14 18.43 20.34

Bomb load 1 x 4000 HC, 16 x 500 GP. Weather clear. Primary target: Kamen. Bombed at 18.43 hours from 16,900 feet on centre of fires as per Master Bomber's instructions.

14/09/1944 LL666 A2-K   Bombing Wassenaar 12.49 14.30 15.35

Bomb load 11 x 1000 MC, 4 x 500 GP. Primary target: Wassenaar. Weather was good, nil cloud. Bombed at 14.30 hours from 12,000 feet, red T.I.s. 1 x 1000 jettisoned safe in sea.

25/09/1944 NG118   A2-E   Bombing Pas de Calais 08.26 x 11.15

Bomb load 11 x 1000 MC, 4 x 500 GP. Primary target: Calais. Abandoned mission on Master Bomber's instructions. Jettisoned 4 x 1000 MC.

26/09/1944 PD325 A2-L   Bombing Calais   11.31 12.46 13.52

Bomb load 11 x 1000 MC, 4 x 500 GP. Primary target: Calais 7D.

Weather clear below cloud which was 3,500 feet. Bombed at 12.46 hours from 3,000 feet on red T.I. + 2 seconds.

06/10/1944 NG118   A2-E   Bombing Dortmund 16.45   20.39   22.14
   Bomb load 1 x 4000 HC, 12 x No. 14 Clusters. Primary target: Dortmund, Town and Railways. Weather over the target was clear with slight ground haze. Bombed at 20.39 hours from 22,000 feet on centre of green T.I.s.

07/10/1944 NG118   A2-E   Bombing Emmerich 12.18   14.28   16.13
   Bomb load 1 x 4000 HC, 10 x No. 14 clusters, 4 x (150 x 4). Primary target Emmerich. Weather clear with cloud at 13,000 feet. Bombed at 14.28 hours from 13,800 feet on South side of smoke.
   Sgt. W. Harradine Navigator that day.

14/10/1944 NG118   A2-E   Bombing Duisburg 07.01 09.04   11.04
   Bomb load 11 x 1000 MC, 4 x 500 GP Long Delay. Primary target: Duisburg. Weather patchy cloud with gaps for bombing. Bombed at 09.04 hours from 18,500 feet. Visual of river and docks.
   F/S. A. Dix Navigator until 21/10/44.

14/10/1944 NG118   A2-E   Bombing Duisburg 22.31 01.28   03.15
   Bomb load 11 x 1000 MC, 4 x 500 GP Long Delay. Primary target: Duisburg. Weather was clear with small amount of cloud over the target. Bombed at 01.28 hours from 21,500 feet. Centre of red T.I.s.

19/10/1944 LM719   A2-E   Bombing Stuttgart 17.20   20.36   23.30
   Bomb load 1 x 4000 HC, 3 x 500 Clusters, 7 x 150 x 4, 1 x 90 x 4 I.B. Primary target: Stuttgart, A/P 'D' 1st attack. Weather 10/10ths cloud which broke to 6/10ths at the end of the period. Bombed at 20.36 hours from 18,000 feet. Centre of red T.I. with yellow.

21/10/1944 NG118   A2-E   Bombing Flushing 10.21   12.27   13.49
   Bomb load 12 x 1000 MC, 2 x 500 GP. Primary target: Flushing 'B'. Weather clear. Bombed at 12.27 hours from 8,300 feet. Visual of A/P.

23/10/1944 NG118   A2-E   Bombing Essen 16.37   19.45   22.03
   Bomb load 1 x 4000 HC 2 x 1000 MC, 11 x 500 GP, 2 x 500 MC. Primary target: Essen. Weather 10/10ths cloud over target - tops 12/14,000 feet with most appalling weather on route. Bombed at 19.45 hours from 22,300 feet. Red flares.
   F/O. A.E. Nye Navigator that day.

05/11/1944 NG141   A2-J   Bombing Solingen   10.12   13.05   15.05
   Bomb load 1 x 4000 HC, 6 x 1000 ANM59, 4 x 500 GP, 2 x 500 GP (L/Delay). Primary target: Solingen. Weather 10/10ths cloud over target. Bombed at 13.05 hours from 17,500 feet on leading aircraft.
   F/S. A. Dix Navigator until 02/12/44.

11/11/1944 PD334A2-D Bombing Castrop Rauxel 08.13 11.06 12.49
Bomb load 1 x 4000 HC, 16 x 500 GP. Primary target: Castrop
Rauxel, Oil refineries. Weather 10/10ths cloud. Bombed at 11.06 hours
from 21,000 feet on G.H. Leader.
15/11/1944 PD334A2-D Bombing Dortmund 12.41 15.42 17.27
Bomb load 1 x 4000 HC, 16 x 500 GP. Primary target: Hoesch-
Benzin Dortmund, Oil refineries. Weather 10/10ths cloud over the
target. Bombed at 15.42 hours from 17,300 feet on Red flares.
16/11/1944 PD334A2-D Bombing Heinsburg 13.11 15.34 17.03
Bomb load 1 x 4000 HC, 6 x 1000 MC, 6 x 500 GP. Primary target:
Heinsburg. Weather - nil cloud with slight haze over target. Bombed at
15.34 hours from 8,500 feet. Upwind edge of smoke on Master
Bomber's instructions.
27/11/1944 NG236 A2-C Bombing Cologne 12.26 15.05 16.59
Bomb load 1 x 4000 HC, 16 x 500 GP. Primary target: Cologne,
Marshalling Yards. Weather patchy cloud. Bombed at 15.05 hours
from 19,000 feet on G.H. Leader's release.
02/12/1944 NG141 A2-J Bombing Dortmund 12.56 14.56 17.07
Bomb load 14 x 1000 HC. Primary target: Dortmund, Benzol plant.
Weather 10/10ths cloud. Bombed at 14.56 hours from 19,800 feet with
G.H. Leader. Aircraft hit by flak - Wing damaged badly.
08/12/1944 NG236 A2-C Bombing Duisburg 08.30 11.05 13.10
Bomb load 14 x 1000 ANM59. Primary target: Duisberg. Weather
10/10ths cloud. Bombed at 11.05 hours from 19,000 feet on G.H.
Leader.
F/O. T.W. Ledingham Navigator from that day.
11/12/1944 NG141 A2-J Bombing Osterfeld 08.45 11.05 12.50
Bomb load 9 x 1000 ANM65, 5 x 1000 ANM59. Primary target:
Osterfeld. Weather 10/10ths cloud, tops 16,000 feet. Bombed at 11.05
hours from 20,000 feet on G.H. Leader.
F/O. G.A. Hanson 2nd Pilot that day.
16/12/1944 NG118 A2-E Bombing Siegen 11.30 15.03 17.10
Bomb load 1 x 4000 HC, 14 x No. 14 Clusters. Primary target:
Siegen. Weather very bad on route with icing and cloud. Bombed at
15.03 hours from 17,500 feet. Red and Green flares.
F/S. G.A. Brown WOP/AG that day.
21/12/1944 PD334A2-D Bombing Trier 12.25 15.00 16.50
Bomb load 1 x 4000 HC, 10 x 500 GP, 6 x 250 GP. Primary target:
Trier, Marshalling yards. Weather 10/10 cloud, tops 6/9000 feet.
Bombed at 15.00 hours from 18,000 feet on leader.

S/L. Alan Lestocq Roberts, DFC & Bar

115023 (1169273) S/L. Alan Lestocq Roberts, DFC & Bar. Pilot.
939667 F/S. Roger Foggin. A/Bomber.
173122 (1319583) P/O. Albert Bell, DFC. Navigator.
1336538 Sgt. Peter William Upton. WOP/AG. 8 ops.
169554 (1076809) P/O. James Morton Hydes, DFC. WOP/AG. 14 ops.
A424001 Sgt. Clement Herbert Henn, RAAF. MU/Gunner. 1 op.
1873573 F/S. John George Shepherd Boanson. MU/Gunner. 1 op.
1238470 Sgt. Geoffrey Clewlow, DFM. MU/Gunner. 17 ops.
940758 Sgt. T.G. Kilfoyle. MU&R/Gunner. 3 ops.
R119782 Sgt. H.J. Dahle, RCAF. MU&R/Gunner.
951033 Sgt. R.A. Bannister. F/Engineer.
NZ415771 F/S. Paul Eugene Mason, RNZAF. 2nd Pilot. 24/12/1943
J87679 (R168202) F/S. Richard Albert John Bennett, RCAF. 2nd Pilot.
29/12/1943 F/L. A.L. Parry. 2nd Pilot. 01/01/1944
120090 (742232) F/O. Robert Julian Curtis, DFM. 2nd Pilot.
14/01/1944
176275 (1389988) F/S. Norman James Tutt. 2nd Pilot. 15/02/1944
174413 (1238964) F/S. Derek Anthony Duncliffe. 2nd Pilot.
19/02/1944
1084862 F/S. John Clare Gilbertson-Pritchard. 2nd Pilot. 24/02/1944
NZ424433 Sgt. Argyle Bruce "Sly" Cunningham, RNZAF 2nd Pilot
07/03/1944

SS/L Alan Roberts (right) with crew members on the wing of DS816, JI-O.

03/11/1943 DS816 JI-O Gardening Frisian Islands 18.09 x 20.28

Aircraft carried 6 x B200. Primary area Frisian Islands. 9/10 cloud. Tops about 500 feet and some high clouds. Monica.

Sgt. P.W. Upton WOP/AG until 14/01/44.

Sgt. T.G. Kilfoyle was MU/Gunner that day and Sgt. H.J. Dahle R/Gunner.

26/11/1943 DS816 JI-O Bombing Berlin 17.59 x 19.28

Bomb load 1 x 4000 HC, 24 x 30 incendiaries, 405 x 4 incendiaries, 45 x 4. No attack. Returned owing to engine trouble. Jettisoned entire bomb load.

Sgt. H.J. Dahle was MU/Gunner that day and Sgt. T.G. Kilfoyle R/Gunner.

16/12/1943 DS816 JI-O Bombing Berlin 16.51 20.08 00.28

Bomb load 1 x 4000, 540 x 4 incendiaries, 40 x 30 incendiaries. Primary target: Berlin. 10/10 cloud. Bombed at 20.08 at 22,000 ft. Very good job by P.F.F. Flak moderate to heavy barrage. Plenty of fighters coming out of target. Landed at Downham Market.

Sgt. T.G. Kilfoyle MU/Gunner that day.

Sgt. H.J. Dahle R/Gunner from that day.

20/12/1943 DS816 JI-O Bombing Frankfurt 17.35 x 19.03

Bomb load 1 x 8000, 16 x 30 incendiaries, 330 x 4 incendiaries, 30 x 4 incendiaries. Primary target: Frankfurt. Sortie abandoned. Returned early. Port inner u/s. Engine appeared normal after bomb jettisoned.

Sgt. C.H. Henn MU/Gunner that day.

24/12/1943 DS816 JI-O Bombing Berlin 00.33 04.14 07.40

Bomb load 1 x 8000, Primary target: Berlin. 7/10 cloud, haze. Bombed at 04.14 hrs at 18,000 feet. No markers seen. Good fires, very wide spread. Moderately good attack. Route K. Photo attempted.

F/S. J.G.S. Boanson was MU/Gunner that day and F/S. P.E. Mason 2nd Pilot.

29/12/1943 DS816 JI-O Bombing Berlin 17.07 20.16 00.14

Bomb load 1 x 4000, 24 x 30 incendiaries, 540 x 4 incendiaries, 90 x 4 incendiaries. Primary target: Berlin. There was 10/10 cloud with tops 8/10,000. Bombed at 20.16 hours at 18,000 ft. 8 x 30 incendiaries hung up and brought back. Cloud prevented observation other than bomb flashes. Flak rather heavier than usual.

Sgt. Geoffrey Clewlow MU/Gunner from that day.

F/S. R.A.J. Bennett 2nd Pilot that day.

01/01/1944 DS816 JI-O Bombing Berlin 00.34 03.12 07.43

Bomb load 1 x 4000, 24 x 30, 450 x 4, 90 x 4 lb incendiaries. Primary target: Berlin. There was 10/10 cloud over the target. Bombed at 03.12 hrs at 21,000 feet. 1 Green T.I. cascading and disappearing into cloud. Column of smoke seen rising above cloud. Attack rather scattered, not deemed satisfactory. Route OK. Poor weather grounded enemy fighters. Photo attempted.

F/L. A.L. Parry 2nd Pilot that day.

14/01/1944 DS823 JI-M   Bombing Brunswick 16.56 19.17 22.05

Bomb load 1 x 4000, 48 x 30 incendiaries. Primary target: Brunswick. There was 8/10 cloud. Bombed at 19.17 hours at 21,000 feet. Some fires seen rather scattered. Monica u/s. P.F.F. opened attack too early and T.I. very scattered, appeared to be scattered raid. Photo attempted.

F/O. R.J. Curtis 2nd Pilot that day.

27/01/1944 DS816 JI-O Bombing Berlin 17.58 20.37 01.55

Bomb load 1 x 8000 lb bomb. Primary target: Berlin. There was 10/10 cloud. Bombed at 20.37 hours at 20,000 ft. Smoke seen from large fire above cloud on leaving target. Sky markers well concentrated.

P/O. J.M. Hydes WOP/AG from that day.

28/01/1944 LL703 JI-L Bombing Berlin 23.58 x 03.04

Bomb load 1 x 2000 lb. bomb, 16 x 30, 750 x 4 incendiaries. Returned early. Farthest point reached 5403N 0438E. Instrument panel u/s. Load jettisoned.

30/01/1944 LL703 JI-L Bombing Berlin 17.25 20.22 23.47

Bomb load 1 x 2000 lb bomb, 900 x 4, 90 x 4, 24 x 30 incendiaries. Primary target: Berlin. There was 10/10 cloud. Bombed at 20.22 hours at 21,000 ft. Cluster of 4 Red flares, green stars. Green T.I.s dropping just as we bombed. Cloud prevented visual. Attack very scattered - best I've seen as far as the sky marking was concentrated. There appeared to be a good red glow underneath the cloud when we were leaving the target.

15/02/1944 DS816 JI-O Bombing Berlin 17.31 21.31 01.00

Bomb load 1 x 8000 lb bomb. Primary target: Berlin. There was 10/10 cloud. Bombed at 21.31 hrs at 21,000 ft. Red glow seen below cloud. Fighter flares were scattered. No fighter opposition, but heavier flak. Skymarkers appeared to be scattered. Route in conjunction with weather gave trouble-free trip.

F/S. N.J. Tutt 2nd Pilot that day.

571

19/02/1944 DS816 JI-O Bombing Leipzig   23.54   03.59   06.38

Bomb load 1 x 4000 lb bomb, 32 x 30, 510 x 4, 90 x 4 incendiaries. Primary target Leipzig. There was 10/10 cloud. Bombed at 03.59 hours at 21,000 ft. Aircraft arrived 12½ minutes early on target - orbited. Route OK. Photo attempted.

F/S. D.A. Duncliffe 2nd Pilot that day.

24/02/1944 DS816 JI-O Bombing Schweinfurt   20.42   01.07   04.48

Bomb load 1 x 8000 lb bomb. Primary target: Schweinfurt. Weather clear, much smoke. Bombed at 01.07 hours at 11,000 ft. Bomb jettisoned on Schweinfurt at 01.07 hours - a 4 lb incendiary dropped from above fell in aircraft by Navigator's table and thrown to safety by WOP. Inter-com I.F.F. Pilots nerves affected by falling incendiary. Slight damage to Navigator's table. Wonderful attack. Route good. Aircraft flew at 11,000 ft whole sortie on account of oxygen failure. Fuselage holed by incendiaries from above. Wireless Operator threw them out.

F/S. J.C. Gilbertson-Pritchard 2nd Pilot that day.

01/03/1944 DS815 JI-N Bombing Stuttgart   23.52 x 06.58

Bomb load 1 x 8000 lb bomb. Primary target: Stuttgart. There was 10/10 cloud with occasional clear patches. Glow from fires as far as miles short of A.P. (Aiming Point). It appeared that first 14 mins of attack was very scattered. Glow of fires seen on return route at approx 100 miles.

07/03/1944 DS816 JI-O Bombing Le Mans   19.31 x 23.38

Bomb load 10 x 1000, 4 x 500 lb bomb. No attack made, bombs brought back. Target not identified visually. 2 x 1000, 2 x 500 lb. Bombs jettisoned safe to reduce weight for landing.

Sgt. A.B. Cunningham 2nd Pilot that day.

15/03/1944 DS816 JI-O Bombing Stuttgart   19.18   23.20   02.50

Bomb load 1 x 8000 lb bomb, 8 x 30 incendiaries. Primary target: Stuttgart. There was broken cloud. Bombed at 23.20 hours from 20,000 feet. Attack began very scattered, improved as attack progressed.

30/03/1944 DS816 JI-O Bombing Nuremburg 22.23 01.23   06.24

Bomb load 1 x 1000 lb bomb, 80 x 30, 900 x 4 incendiaries. Primary target: Nuremberg. Weather was cloudy with 8/10-10/10 cloud. Bombed at 01.23 hours from 20,000 feet. Red flares and yellow stars, concentrated. Many good fires. Badly chosen route. Attack good.

20/04/1944 DS818 JI-Q Bombing Cologne   00.14   02.08   04.04

Bomb load 1 x 1000 lb bomb, 1026 x 4, 108 x 30 lb incendiaries.

Primary target: Koln. There was 10/10 cloud. Bombed at 02.08 hours from 20,000 feet. 2 x 12 x 30 hang up. Little effort to defend target. Route very quiet.

27/04/1944 DS818 JI-Q Bombing Friedrichshafen 22.54 02.06 03.21
Bomb load 1 x 4000, 2 x 1000, 1 x 500 lb bombs. Primary target: Friedrichshafen. Weather was clear. Bombed at 02.06 hours from 17,000 feet. There was a good area of fires among markers. Town could be seen clearly in the glow. A very concentrated effort. Should be a good attack. Defences flak moderate, searchlights ineffective. Two large explosions seen at 02.09 hours.

08/05/1944 DS816 JI-O Bombing Cap Gris Nez   22.50 23.54 00.47
Bomb load 14 x 1000 lb bombs. Primary target: Cape Gris Nez. Weather was clear, good visibility. Bombed at 23.54 hours from 8,300 feet. Numerous bomb bursts and smoke seen. A very good effort. P.F.F. Markers not dropped until 23.57 hours, seen to drop amidst the smoke.

09/05/1944 DS816 JI-O Bombing Cap Gris Nez   03.10 04.10 05.25
Bomb load 1 x 1000 GP, 13 x 1000 MC. Primary target: Cape Gris Nez. Clear conditions. Green T.I.s seen followed by red and yellow. Visual of coastline obtained. Made two attacks on target dropping 7 bombs each time – 1st on red and yellow T.I.s at 04.10 hours from 6,000 feet and 2nd on red and yellow T.I.s at 04.14 hours from 5,500 feet. Bomb bursts appeared concentrated in target area. Area well covered by bomb bursts. Large white explosion seen at 04.12 hours on top of Cape.

F/O. George Robertson, AFC

174335 (1430412) F/O. George Robertson, AFC. Pilot.
163634 (1800578) F/O. William John Briggs.   A/Bomber.
197201 (1523227) P/O. John Lawson Besford. Navigator.
Sgt. J.C. Hill.   WOP/AG.
F/S. R.S. Marshall.   MU/Gunner. 24 ops.
Sgt. M.C. or M.S. Hodge.   R/Gunner. 20 ops.
F/S. E.R. Griffiths. R/Gunner. 5 ops.
 Sgt. H. Jepson.   F/Engineer.
150919 (1586715) F/O. Ronald Tembey "Ron" Gill. 2nd Pilot.
11/03/1945

Passengers: 08/07/1945, 17/07/1945, 22/07/1945.

In front of Lancaster Mk3 RE123 A2-K L to R: J.C. Hill, H. Jepson, W.J. Briggs, G. Robertson, J.L. Besford, R.S. Marshall, M.C. Hodge, unknown (possibly E.R. Griffiths). (courtesy WMHM)

16/02/1945 NN776   A2-D   Bombing Wesel   12.30 16.00 18.10

Bomb load 1 x 4000 HC, 4 x 500 GP, 2 x 500 MC L/Delay, 4 x 250 GP, 6 x 500 ANM64. Primary target: Wesel. Weather clear. Bombed at 16.00 hours from 21,000 feet on leading aircraft. Aircraft hit by flak - port inner engine damaged and had to be feathered.

From his normal crew, only F/O. G. Robertson did this mission as 2nd Pilot with F/O. J.N. Gallicano's crew.

18/02/1945 PB902 JI-A Bombing Wesel 11.27 15.25 17.04

Bomb load 1 x 4000 HC, 4 x 500 GP, 2 x 500 MC L/Delay, 4 x 250 GP, 6 x 500 ANM64. Primary target: Wesel. Weather 10/10ths cloud. Bombed at 15.25 hours from 20,000 feet on leading aircraft.

Sgt. M.C. Hodge R/Gunner until 26/05/45.

19/02/1945 NN781   A2-D   Bombing Wesel   12.57 16.35 19.10

Bomb load 1 x 4000 HC, 6 x 500 MC, 6 x 500 ANM64, 4 x 250 GP. Primary target: Wesel. Weather over target 5-7/10ths cloud. Bombed at 16.35 hours from 19,500 feet on leading aircraft. Landed at Moreton in Marsh.

574

20/02/1945 PD389 A2-J   Bombing Dortmund 21.53 01.07 03.18

Bomb load 1 x 2000 HC, 12 x 750 Type 15 Clusters. Primary target: Dortmund. Weather 8-10/10ths thin cloud at about 5,000 feet. Bombed at 01.07 hours from 21,000 feet on centre of Red/Green TIs.

From his normal crew, only F/O. G. Robertson did this mission as 2nd Pilot with F/O. C.I.H. Nicholl's crew.

22/02/1945 NN781   A2-D Bombing Osterfeld 12.11 16.02 17.56

Bomb load 1 x 4000 HC, 9 x 500 ANM64, 2 x 500 MC, 4 x 250 GP. Primary target: Osterfeld, Coking ovens. Weather at target clear, but hazy. Bombed at 16.02 hours from 20,000 feet visually.

26/02/1945 NN781   A2-D Bombing Dortmund 10.17 14.06 16.22

Bomb load 1 x 4000 HC, 2 x 500 MC L/Delay 37B, 9 x 500 ANM64, 4 x 250 GP. Primary target: Dortmund, Hoesch Benzin plant. Weather 10/10ths cloud, tops 8/10,000 feet. Bombed at 14.06 hours from 20,000 feet on G.H. Leader.

27/02/1945 PB423 A2-L   Bombing Gelsenkirchen 10.58 14.27 16.32

Bomb load 1 x 4000 HC, 2 x 500 MC (L/D 37B), 9 x 500 ANM64, 4 x 250 GP. Primary target: Gelsenkirchen (Alma Pluts) Benzin plant. Weather 10/10ths cloud, 6/10,000 feet tops. Bombed at 14.27 hours from 19,500 feet on G.H. Leader.

01/03/1945 PB423 A2-L   Bombing Kamen   11.44 15.06 17.30

Bomb load 1 x 4000 HC, 11 x 500 ANM64, 2 x 500 MC L/Delay37. Primary target: Kamen, Coking plant. Weather 10/10ths cloud. Bombed at 15.06 hours from 19,000 feet on G.H. Leader.

05/03/1945 NN781   A2-D Bombing Gelsenkirchen 10.17 14.08 16.18

Bomb load 1 x 4000 HC, 12 x 500 ANM64. Primary target: Gelsenkirchen, Benzol plant. Weather 10/10ths cloud over target with cirrus cloud at bombing height. Bombed at 14.08 hours from 21,000 feet on leading aircraft.

07/03/1945 NN717   A2-E Bombing Dessau   17.00 22.07 02.21

Bomb load 1 x 4000 HC, 6 x Mk. 17 Clusters. Primary target: Dessau. Weather 5 to 10/10ths thin cloud. Bombed at 22.07 hours from 20,000 feet on Red/Green stars. One ME109 seen.

09/03/1945 ME529   A2-F Bombing Datteln 10.55 14.00 16.03

Bomb load 1 x 4000 HC, 13 x 500 ANM64, 13 x 500 MC L/Delay37B. Primary target: Datteln, Synthetic oil plant. Weather 10/10ths cloud, tops 8-10,000 feet. Bombed at 14.00 hours from 20,500 feet on G.H. Leader.

11/03/1945 NG203   A2-C Bombing Essen 11.31 15.25 17.17

Bomb load 1 x 4000 HC, 13 x 500 ANM64, 2 x 500 MC. Primary target: Essen, Marshalling yards. Weather 10/10ths cloud, tops 7/8,000 feet. Bombed at 15.25 hours from 18,500 feet. Followed G.H. Leader. 3 Blue Puffs seen on aiming point and flares seen to port from the other attack.

F/O. R.T. Gill 2nd Pilot that day.

14/03/1945 NN717   A2-E   Bombing Heinrichshutte 13.13 16.40 18.48

Bomb load 1 x 4000 HC, 12 x 500 ANM64. Primary target: Heinrichshutte, Hattingen Steel works & Benzol plant. Weather 10/10ths cloud, tops 7/12,000 feet. Bombed at 16.40 hours from 17,500 feet on leading G.H. aircraft. 1 x 500 ANM64 hung up, brought back to Base.

18/03/1945 ME529   A2-F   Bombing Bruchstrasse 11.34 15.05 17.08

Bomb load 1 x 4000 HC, 13 x 500 ANM64, 2 x 500 MC. Primary target: Bruchstrasse, Coal mine & coking plant. Weather 10/10ths cloud, tops 6-12,000 feet. Bombed at 15.05 hours from 19,000 feet on leading aircraft.

21/03/1945 ME529   A2-F   Bombing Munster 09.24 13.08 15.07

Bomb load 1 x 4000 HC, 13 x 500 ANM64, 2 x 500 MC. Primary target Munster Viaduct and Marshalling Yards. Weather cloud nil to 2/10ths. Bombed at 13.08 hours from 18,500 feet on leading G.H. aircraft. Heavy flak holes in starboard nacelles.

18/04/1945 ME523   A2-G   Bombing Heligoland 09.54 13.07 15.27

Bomb load 6 x 1000 MC, 10 x 500 ANM64. Primary target: Heligoland, Naval base. Weather no cloud, slight haze. Bombed visually on centre of smoke at 13.07 hours from 18,000 ft. Islands covered in smoke. Very successful raid and no trouble. Instructed to bomb on Red T.I. which were lost. Smoke then on Pickwick.

29/04/1945 RE123 A2-K Manna The Hague 12.35 13.56 15.14

Dropping area: The Hague. Weather broken cloud above and clear below. Dropped 5 packs of rations at 13.56 hrs. Slight damage to bomb doors due to sliding back in wind and hitting bomb doors as they closed. Packs seen to fall approx. 10 yards to starboard of white cross.

02/05/1945 ME425   A2-L   Manna The Hague 11.11 x 13.35

Dropping area The Hague. Weather over dropping zone clear below cloud for the first arrivals changing later to heavy showers which marred visibility. 5 Panniers brought back. 10/10 cloud.

05/05/1945 RE123 A2-K Manna The Hague 06.07 07.35 08.31

Dropping area: The Hague. Dropped 5 Panniers on White Cross and T.I.'s visually at 07.35 hours. 10/10 cloud, Base 1,500, Hazy. Landplane seen at 07.09, 1,000ft. 5147N 0343E, circling then turned north.

No Mid Upper Gunner that day.

10/05/1945 RE123 A2-K Exodus Juvincourt - Ford 11.23 x 17.35

Duration 3.08. Outward 1.55 hours. Collected 24 ex POWs. Homeward 1.13 hours. Organisation good - needless waste of time parading to the control tower at Ford.

25/05/1945 RA602 A2-H Exodus Brussels 12.01 x 16.25

Duration 2.34 hours. Out 1.18 hours. In 1.16 hours. 10 Belgian refugees to Brussels. No POWs home. Dakotas taxied on runway as a/c about to land, caused own a/c to make another circuit.

26/05/1945 RA602 A2-H Exodus Brussels - Ford 12.13 x 18.17

Duration 3.20 hours. Out 1.11 hours. In 2.08 hours. 10 Belgian refugees to Brussels. 24 ex POWs all military brought back.

25/06/1945 RE123 A2-K Post Mortem Special mission 09.48 x 16.11

19,000 could not reach 20,000 ft.

F/S. E.R. Griffiths R/Gunner from that day.

01/07/1945 RE123 A2-K Post Mortem Special mission 12.08 x 18.05

08/07/1945 RE120 A2-C Baedeker Tour over Continent 15.00 x 19.12

Passengers: Cpl. Parker, LAC. Paths, AC. James, AC. Fix, Sgt. Cox.

17/07/1945 RA602 A2-H Baedeker Tour over Continent 14.57 x 19.11

Passengers: F/O. Pickett, Sgt. Nuttall, Sgt. Preston, Sgt. Taylor, Cpl. Jacques.

22/07/1945 RE159 A2-E Baedeker Tour over Continent 09.55 x 14.18

Passengers: S/L. Brain, LAC. Holmes, LAC. Healey, LACW. Dalto, ACW. Hockley.

F/O. Leonard James Saltmarsh, DFC

1600189 (174576) F/O. Leonard James "Len" Saltmarsh, DFC. Pilot.
183731 (1389641) P/O. John David Smith. A/Bomber.
183193 (1324610) P/O. Wilfred George Jeffery. Navigator.
201216 (1470138) Sgt. James Albert Smith. WOP/AG.
3040869 Sgt. Henry Carter. MU/Gunner.
1821925 Sgt. Finlay Graham Coghill. R/Gunner.
F/S. A.R. Thompson. F/Engineer. 19 ops.
Sgt. J. Donaldson. F/Engineer. 4 ops.
160960 (813254) F/L. John Aubrey Wake, DFC. F/Engineer. 1 op.

23/06/1944 Bombing L'Hey ca.23.05 x x
Primary target: L'Hey, Flying bomb installations. There was 10/10ths cloud.
From his normal crew, only F/O. L.J. Saltmarsh did this mission as 2nd Pilot
with an unknown crew.
24/06/1944 LL734 JI-O Bombing Rimeux 23.21 00.37 02.14
Bomb load 18 x 500 GP. Primary target: Rimeux, Flying bomb installations.
Weather clear. Bombed at 00.37 hours from 11,000 feet centre of red T.I.s. No
trouble.
F/S. A.R. Thompson F/Engineer until 26/08/44 except for 25/08/44.
30/06/1944 LL734 JI-O Bombing Villers Bocage 18.21 20.04 21.42
Bomb load 8 x 1000 MC, 2 x 500 GP. Primary target: Villers Bocage.
Weather clear. Target obscured by smoke. Bombed at 20.04 hours from 12,000
feet. A good prang.
02/07/1944 LL734 JI-O Bombing Beauvoir 12.51 14.36 16.27
Bomb load 11 x 1000 MC, 4 x 500 GP. Primary target: Beauvoir, Flying
bomb supply site. Bombed at 14.36 hours from 11,500 feet on yellow T.I.s.
07/07/1944 LL624 JI-R Bombing Vaires 22.56 01.33 03.23
Bomb load 7 x 1000 MC, 4 x 500 GP. Primary target: Vaires, Marshalling
yards. Weather clear. Bombed at 01.33 hours from 11,500 feet red T.I.s.
Several explosions seen and much smoke. Good precise effort.
10/07/1944 LL624 JI-R Bombing Nucourt 04.19 06.05 07.46
Bomb load 11 x 1000 ANM65, 4 x 500 GP. Primary target: Nucourt,
Constructional works. Bombed at 06.05 hours from 15,500 feet on Gee.
12/07/1944 LL624 JI-R Bombing Vaires 18.05 x 21.52
Bomb load 18 x 500 GP. Primary target: Vaires, Marshalling yards. Weather
over target 10/10ths cloud, no markers seen, mission abandoned.
15/07/1944 LL624 JI-R Bombing Chalons Sur Marne 21.52 01.34
04.22
Bomb load 18 x 500 GP. Primary target: Chalons sur Marne, Railway centre.
Weather clear below 9,000 feet. Bombed at 01.34 hours from 8,000 feet,
yellow T.I.s as instructed by Master Bomber. A good effort. Trouble free route.

Fighter seem active in target area.

18/07/1944 LL624 JI-R Bombing Emieville   04.39   06.08   07.44

Bomb load 11 x 1000 MC, 4 x 500 GP. Primary target: Emieville, Troop concentration. Slight haze. Bombed at 06.08 hours from 8,000 feet yellow T.I.s. Mass of smoke and flames left behind.

20/07/1944 LL624 JI-R Bombing Homberg   23.32   01.23   02.56

Bomb load 1 x 4000 HC, 2 x 500 MC, 14 x 500 GP. Primary target: Homberg, Oil plant. Weather clear. Bombed at 01.23 hours from 18,500 feet red T.I. Many explosions and black smoke.

23/07/1944 LL624 JI-R Bombing Kiel   22.41   01.24   03.53

Bomb load 10 x 1000 MC, 5 x 500 GP. Primary target: Kiel, Warehouses and docks. Weather 9/10ths thin low cloud. Bombed at 01.24 hours from 18,000 feet centre of red and green T.I.s. Good effort. Tracer up to 20,000 feet.

24/07/1944 LL624 JI-R Bombing Stuttgart 21.48   01.45   05.11

Bomb load 5 x 1000 ANM65, 3 x 500 GP. Primary target Stuttgart. Weather 10/10ths cloud. Bombed at 01.45 hours from 17,500 feet on red T.I. slight to the east as Master Bomber instructed. Glow seen under the clouds.

27/07/1944 LL624 JI-R Bombing Les Catelliers 16.58   18.52   20.07

Bomb load 18 x 500 GP. Primary target: Les Catelliers, Flying bomb site. Bombed at 18.52 hours from 16,500 feet on Mosquito.

30/07/1944 LL731 JI-U Bombing Caen   06.11   07.50   09.16

Bomb load 18 x 500 GP. Primary target: Caen 'B'. Weather low base. Bombed at 07.50 hours from 1,800 feet, glow of red T.I.s. as instructed. Numerous bomb bursts in target area. Master Bomber very poor reception.

03/08/1944 LL624 JI-R Bombing Bois de Cassan   11.53   14.07   15.20

Bomb load 11 x 1000 MC, 4 x 500 GP. Primary target: Bois de Cassan, Flying bomb supply depot. Bombed at 14.07 hours from 15,000 feet, up wind smoke.

12/08/1944 LL624 JI-R Bombing Russelsheim 22.00 00.19   02.36

Bomb load 1 x 2000 HC, 12 x 500 No. 14 Clusters. Primary target: Russelsheim. Bombed at 00.19 hours from 17,000 feet. Red and green T.I.s. T.I.s very scattered also fires. Master Bomber not heard after initial conversation with his deputy.

15/08/1944 LL624 JI-R Bombing St Trond   10.03   12.09   13.34

Bomb load 11 x 1000 MC, 4 x 500 GP. Primary target St. Trond Airfield. Weather clear, slight haze. Bombed at 12.09 hours from 17,000 feet between red T.I.s and intersection of runways. Starboard outer feathered 15 miles before target, attacked target and returned on three engines which were giving trouble. Very concentrated attack.

16/08/1944 LL731 JI-U Bombing Stettin   21.08   01.00   05.05

Bomb load 1 x 2000 HC, 9 x 500 lb 'J' type clusters. Primary target: Stettin. Weather cloud tops at 15,000 feet. Bombed at 01.00 hours from 16,000 feet, centre of red and green T.I.s. Fires well alight, markers concentrated. Landed at Foulsham.

18/08/1944 LL624 JI-R Bombing Bremen 21.52 00.14 02.36

Bomb load 1 x 2000 HC, 96 x 30 lb inc, 810 x 4lb inc, 90 x 4lb x inc. Primary target: Bremen. Weather clear. Bombed at 00.14 hours from 16,000 feet, red T.I.s. A very good show.

25/08/1944 LL624 JI-R Bombing Vincly ca. 18.35 x x

Primary target: Vincly. Weather: cloud clearing near target.

F/L. J.A. Wake F/Engineer that day. Only Pilots and F/Engineer's names are reported with certainty. The others are believed to be from Saltmarsh's crew.

Details supplied by F/L. J.A. Wake, DFC, AE for Waterbeach Museum: "Fully loaded with bomb and fuel was taking off for an attack on Vincly, France. During take off, a tyre on the starboard side burst and the starboard wing dropped causing the propellers to ground on the runway. The outboard engine on the starboard wing was ripped from its mounting, and the aircraft skidded over the airfield out of control. The crew abandoned the aircraft while it was still moving. Fortunately, the aircraft did not catch fire and none of the munitions exploded."

LL624 did not fly again.

Lancaster Mk2 LL624 JI-R jacked up for the removal of the bomb load after failing to take off from Waterbeach (Waterbeach Military Heritage Musuem)

26/08/1944 LL731 JI-U Bombing Kiel 20.18 23.12 01.40

Bomb load 1 x 4000 HC, 72 x 30 IB, 600 x 4 IB, 90 x 4 IB. Primary target:

Kiel. Weather clear. Bombed at 23.12 hours from 18,000 feet, centre of red and green T.I.s. Number of undershoots. Many bombs bursting among T.I.s.

05/09/1944 NF966 JI-R Bombing Le Havre 17.28 19.24 20.58

Bomb load 11 x 1000 MC, 4 x 500 GP. Primary target: Le Havre. Bombed at 19.24 hours from 13,000 feet red T.I.

Sgt. J. Donaldson F/Engineer from that day.

05/10/1944 NF966 JI-R Bombing Saarbrucken 17.26 20.37 22.35

Bomb load 11 x 1000 MC, 1 x 500 GP, 3 x 500 GP. Long Delay. Primary target: Saarbrucken, Marshalling yards. Weather clear over target. Bombed at 20.37 hours from 11,000 feet on red and green T.I.s. Master Bomber not heard clearly, saw much heavy smoke over target obscuring T.I.s.

06/10/1944 NF966 JI-R Bombing Dortmund 16.52 20.47 22.37

Bomb load 1 x 4000 HC, 12 x No. 14 Clusters. Primary target: Dortmund, Town and Railways. Weather over the target was clear with slight ground haze. Bombed at 20.47 hours from 20,000 feet on centre of fires. T.I.s not visual due to fires.

07/10/1944 NF966 JI-R Bombing Emmerich 12.13 14.27 15.49

Bomb load 1 x 4000 HC, 10 x No. 14 clusters, 4 x (150 x 4). Primary target Emmerich. Weather clear with cloud at 13,000 feet. Bombed at 14.27 hours from 11,000 feet on South edge of pall of smoke as instructed by Master Bomber.

W/C. Arthur James Samson, DFC

W/C. A.J. Samson.

20/12/1943 DS821 JI-S Bombing Frankfurt   17.28   19.50   22.29
Bomb load 1 x 4000, 48 x 30 incendiaries, 950 x 4 incendiaries, 100 x 4 incendiaries. Primary target: Frankfurt. 8/10 cloud (thin). Bombed target at 19.50 at 20,000 ft. Scattered fires in target area. Undershooting up to 30 miles. Explosion seen at 19.45 hrs. Very moderate raid.

Crew:
78850 (741089) W/C. Arthur James Samson, DFC.   Pilot.
44828 (534190) W/C.   William David Gordon Watkins, DSO, DFC, DFM. A/Bomber.
1579592 Sgt. P.C. Davies.   Navigator.
169554 (1076809) Sgt. James Morton Hydes, DFC.   WOP/AG.
1126069 Sgt. J. Crawford.   MU/Gunner.
1399608 Sgt. Sydney Loseby.   R/Gunner.
173829 (1393193) P/O. Donald Albert "Don" Winterford.   F/Engineer.

W/C. W.D.G. "Lofty" Watkins. (courtesy Lorne Watkins)

15/03/1944 LL731 JI-U Bombing Stuttgart 19.11 23.22 03.16
Bomb load 1 x 8000 lb. bomb, 90 x 4 incendiaries. Primary target: Stuttgart. There was 8/10 thin patchy cloud. Bombed at 23.22 hours from 20,000 feet. Some red fires seen from 100 miles away. Red T.I.s slightly overshooting sky markers in vicinity.

Crew:
78850 (741089) W/C. Arthur James Samson, DFC.   Pilot.
J20915 F/O. John Peake, DFC, RCAF. A/Bomber.
1579592 Sgt. P.C. Davies.   Navigator.
115327 (1059813) F/L. Ronald Thompson, DFC. WOP/AG.
1238470 Sgt. Geoffrey Clewlow, DFM. MU/Gunner.
138423 (984424) F/L. Jackson Nisbet Pollock, DFC. R/Gunner.
173829 (1393193) P/O. Donald Albert "Don" Winterford.   F/Engineer.

10/04/1944 LL624 JI-P Bombing Laon   01.12   03.39   05.21
Bomb load 9 x 1000, 4 x 500 lb bombs. Primary target: Laon. Weather was

clear. Bombed at 03.39 hours from 10,000 feet. Perfect markings and visual means of locomotive depot seen. 2 fires burning and later covered with smoke. Very good attack, well marked.

Crew:
78850 (741089) W/C. Arthur James Samson, DFC.   Pilot.
J20915   F/O. John Peake, DFC, RCAF. A/Bomber.
J10722   F/L. James Douglas "Doug" Trick, DFC, RCAF. Navigator.
1485703 F/S. John Edward "Johnny" Richardson. WOP/AG.
143598 (1397354)   F/O. Harold Cherberd Bryant, DFC.   MU/Gunner.
138423 (984424) F/L. Jackson Nisbet Pollock, DFC. R/Gunner.
173829 (1393193)   P/O. Donald Albert "Don" Winterford.   F/Engineer.

J.D. Trick is J10722 in ORBs and rcafassociation.ca, and J10772 in London Gazette DFM award.

W/Cdr. Samson, who was 514 Squadron's first CO, survived the war itself, only to be killed on 8th September 1945 when flying a No.117 Squadron Dakota carrying sick POWs recently released from Japanese captivity. The aircraft exploded just off the coast of Burma with the loss of all 4 crew and 24 passengers. He is commemorated Column 445 at The SINGAPORE MEMORIAL which stands in Kranji War Cemetery, 22 kilometres north of Singapore city.

F/S.   Kenneth Frederick Samuels

1291787 F/S.   Kenneth Frederick "Ken" Samuels. Pilot.
1454683 Sgt.   Peter Drake Martindale.   A/Bomber.
1600694 Sgt.   Lawrence Sidney John Adkin.   Navigator.
1311211 Sgt.   W. Muskett.   WOP/A.G. 2 ops.
1382810 Sgt.   John Dowding.   WOP/A.G. 1 op.
981579   Sgt.   Alexander Nicholson.   MU/Gunner.
R165360 Sgt.   Leo Wilton, RCAF.   R/Gunner. 1 op.
1128920 Sgt.   K.F. Murphy.   R/Gunner. 1 op.
1338959 Sgt.   Reginald Arthur Duncan Mirams.   R/Gunner. 1 op.
1815316 Sgt.   Peter William Webb.   F/Engineer. 2 ops.
1523926 Sgt.   Harry West.   F/Engineer. 1 op.

11/11/1943 DS784 JI-C Gardening La Tranche 17.37 x 01.05
Aircraft carried 2 x G710, 2 x G714. Primary area La Tranche. No cloud.
Sgt. P.W. Webb was F/Engineer that day, Sgt. W. Muskett WOP/AG and Sgt. L. Wilton R/Gunner.

18/11/1943 DS706 JI-G Bombing Mannheim 17.23 x 23.46

Bomb load 1 x 4000, 16 x 30, 720 x 4. Primary target Mannheim. Visibility good, no cloud. T.I.s were well concentrated with 20 large fires burning and many incendiaries. Bombed centre of green T.I.s.

Sgt. H. West was F/Engineer that day and Sgt. K.F. Murphy R/Gunner.

14/01/1944 DS706 JI-G Bombing Brunswick 16.57 x 18.50

Bomb load 1 x 4000, 48 x 30 incendiaries. Returned early. Pilot sick. Farthest point reached 5255N 0257E. Load jettisoned.

Sgt. P.W. Webb was F/Engineer that day, Sgt. J. Dowding WOP/A.G and Sgt. R.A.D. Mirams R/Gunner.

P/O. Charles Bertram Sandland

172944 (1602762)   P/O. Charles Bertram "Bert" Sandland. Pilot.
200762 (658786) Sgt. Herbert Victor "Bert" Thornley. A/Bomber.
R171545   F/S. Ross Angus Flemming, RCAF.   Navigator.
158614 (1602650)   F/O. Michael Alan "Mickey" Shingleton. WOP/AG.
R193539   Sgt. Ernest "Ernie" Gordon, RCAF. MU/Gunner.
R190999 Sgt. James D. "Doug" McLaughlin, RCAF. R/Gunner.
1584289 Sgt. Stanley H. "Stan" Sedgwick   F/Engineer.

07/05/1944 DS818 JI-Q Bombing Nantes   00.28 03.04   05.51

Bomb load 1 x 4000, 13 x 500 lb bombs. Primary target: Nantes. Weather was clear. Bombed at 03.04 hours from 9,200 feet. Fires seen in target area from Coast on leaving. Uneventful trip. Raid appeared successful.

L to R (back): H.V. Thornley, C.B. Sandland, R.A. Flemming, E. Gordon.

L to R (front): S.H. Sedgwick, M.A. Shingleton, J.D. McLaughlin.

585

08/05/1944 DS826 JI-L Bombing Cap Gris Nez 22.55 23.51 00.45

Bomb load 14 x 1000 lb bombs. Primary target: Cape Gris Nez. Weather was clear. Bombed at 23.51 hours from 8,000 feet. Judged distance from coastline on area of Gun Emplacements. T.I.s seen later to fall in this area. Very concentrated attack. Bomb bursts appeared on tip of Cape.

10/05/1944 DS822 JI-T Bombing Courtrai 22.12 23.26 00.38

Bomb load 7 x 1000 GP, 7 x 1000 MC. Primary target: Courtrai. Hazy conditions. Bombed Yellow and White T.I.s at 23.26 hours from 10,800 feet. Bombs concentrated around T.I.s. Reddish glow seen after leaving target area. Attack appeared successful.

11/05/1944 DS826 JI-L Bombing Louvain 22.53 00.17 01.38

Bomb load 5 x 1000 GP, 5 x 1000MC, 5 x 500 MC. Primary target: Louvain. Hazy conditions over target. Bombed markers at 00.17 hours from 7,500 feet. Some Red fires seen but attack seemed very moderate. Master Bomber scarcely heard because of R/T (radio transmitter) jamming.

19/05/1944 LL620 JI-N Bombing Le Mans 22.28 00.26 03.16

Bomb load 4 x 1000 USA, 5 x 1000 MC, 1 x 1000 GP, 4 x 500 GP. Primary target: Le Mans. 8/10ths cloud at target. Bombed Yellow T.I. markers at 00.26 hours from 9,200 feet. Numerous bomb bursts seen but attack thought to be moderate.

21/05/1944 LL635 JI-M Bombing Duisburg 22.50 01.15 03.25

Bomb load 1 x 2000 lb bomb, 120 x 30, 600 x 4 incendiaries. Primary target: Duisberg. There was 10/10 cloud over the target. Bombed at 01.15 hours from 22,000 feet. Cloud prevented visual but Red glow seen under cloud.

24/05/1944 LL635 JI-M Bombing Boulogne 00.08 01.15 02.28

Bomb load 9 x 1000 MC, 1 x 1000 GP, 1 x 1000 ANM, 4 x 500 GP. Primary target: Boulogne, Gun Battery. Clear over target except for slight haze. Bombed at 01.15 hours from 7,000 feet and bombs burst amongst T.I.s. No troubles encountered.

27/05/1944 LL635 JI-M Bombing Boulogne 00.15 01.15 01.55

Bomb load 7 x 1000 MC, 4 x 1000 ANM, 4 x 500 GP. Primary target: Boulogne Gun Batteries. Clear at target. Bombed at 01.15 hours from 8,000 feet. Bomb bursts and explosions seen at 01.17 hours. Rear turret was u/s.

28/05/1944 LL635 JI-M Bombing Angers 19.09 23.56 02.17

Bomb load 5 x 1000 MC, 1 x 1000 USA, 4 x 500 MC. Primary target: Angers. Slight haze over target. Bombed at 23.56 hours from 8,500 feet. Orbited to port over target and bombed as instructed by Master Bomber.

31/05/1944 LL635 JI-M Bombing Trappes 23.57 01.57 03.57

Bomb load 8 x 1000 MC, 8 x 500 MC. Primary target: Trappes. Clear at target. Bombed as instructed by Master Bomber at 01.57 hours from 9,600 feet. Target well lit up but no ground detail visible. Markers seemed scattered. Two fires seen at NE end of the marshalling yards.

05/06/1944 LL635 JI-M Bombing Ouistreham 03.48 05.10 06.33

Bomb load 9 x 1000 MC and 2 x 500 MC. Primary target: Ouistreham.

There was 5/10ths cloud at target. Bombed markers at 05.10 hours from 9,600 feet. Target area obscured by cloud when bombs went but visual of coast line obtained after.

07/06/1944 LL635 JI-M Bombing Massy Palaiseau 00.28 02.12   04.20

Bomb load 18 x 500 MC. Primary target: Massy Palaiseau, Marshalling Yards. Hazy below and cloud above. Bombed on Master Bomber's instructions at 02.12 hours from 5,400 feet. T.I.s. seemed well placed. Many exchanges of tracer seen on approach to and on leaving target. Unable to assess results of bombing.

11/06/1944 LL635 JI-M Bombing Nantes 23.46 02.51   05.28

Bomb load 16 x 500 GP, 2 x 500 LD. Primary target: Nantes. Bombed as instructed by Master Bomber at 02.51 hours from 2,500 feet. There was poor visibility and haze and nothing seen except large red flash.

12/06/1944 LL635 JI-M Bombing Gelsenkirchen 23.03 01.02   03.08

Bomb load 1 x 4000 HC, 12 x 500 GP and 4 x 500 MC. Clear over target. Bombed Red and Green T.I.s at 01.02 hours from 20,000 feet. S/Ls (searchlights) stayed in cones almost stationary. Flak was moderate.

14/06/1944 LL635 JI-M Bombing Le Havre   23.42   01.12   02.16

Bomb load 11 x 1000 MC, 4 x 500 GP. Primary target: Le Havre. Weather clear. Bombed at 01.12 hours from 15,000 feet. T.I.s seen close together. Fires covering wide area on arrival. Little flak.

15/06/1944 LL635 JI-M Bombing Valenciennes   23.02   00.35   02.41

Bomb load 16 x 500 GP, 2 x 500 MC. Primary target: Valenciennes. Weather clear. Bombed at 00.35 hours from 9,000 feet. Bombs seen bursting around T.I.s.

23/06/1944 LL635 JI-M Bombing L'Hey 23.15   00.16   01.18

Bomb load 11 x 1000 MC, 4 x 500 GP. Primary target: L'Hey, Flying bomb installations. There was 10/10ths cloud. Bombed at 00.16 hours from 9,000 feet. Bombed centre of red glow of T.I.s which seemed to burn whitish yellow colour on leaving the target. Trouble free route.

24/06/1944 LL635 JI-M Bombing Rimeux   23.29   00.34   02.07

Bomb load 18 x 500 GP. Primary target: Rimeux, Flying bomb installations. Weather clear. Bombed at 00.34 hours from 12,000 feet, centre of red T.I.s. Good concentration of markers. Defences negligible.

30/06/1944 LL635 JI-M Bombing Villers Bocage 18.17   20.00   21.34

Bomb load 10 x 1000 MC, 3 x 500 GP. Primary target: Villers Bocage. Bombed at 20.00 hours from 4,000 feet. Weather 4/10ths cloud at 6,000 feet. Clouds of smoke obscuring target. The aircraft received damage by flak to nose, also on port and starboard side of Mid Upper Turret. Much heavy flak. Good photo taken. Lancaster aircraft just astern received direct hit by flak which broke tail off. Seen to hit the ground, no survivors. Thought to be T/514 (LL620 JI-T).

02/07/1944 LL635 JI-M Bombing Beauvoir   12.49   14.37   16.25

Bomb load 11 x 1000 MC, 4 x 500 GP. Primary target: Beauvoir, Flying bomb supply site. Bombed at 14.37 hours from 11,500 feet on yellow T.I.s.

05/07/1944 LL734 JI-O Bombing Watten   22.55 00.12   01.20

Bomb load 11 x 1000 ANM65, 4 x 500 GP. Primary target: Watten, Constructional works. Bombed at 00.12 hours from 8,600 feet red T.I.s.

07/07/1944 LL635 JI-M Bombing Vaires   22.51   01.29   03.02

Bomb load 7 x 1000 MC, 4 x 500 GP. Primary target: Vaires, Marshalling yards. Bombed at 01.29 hours from 13,500 feet red T.I.s. T.I.s well placed and bombing concentrated.

10/07/1944 LL731 JI-L Bombing Nucourt x x x

Bomb load 11 x 1000 ANM65, 4 x 500 GP. To attack Nucourt, Constructional works. Failed to take off.

12/07/1944 LL635 JI-M Bombing Vaires   18.00 x 21.56

Bomb load 18 x 500 GP. Abandoned mission as instructed by Master Bomber. Jettisoned at 20.43 hours from 10,000 feet, position 4955N 0030E 14 x 500 GP.

15/07/1944 LL635 JI-M Bombing Chalons sur Marne   21.44 x 04.24

Bomb load 18 x 500 GP. Primary target: Chalons sur Marne, Railway centre. No attack made. 10/10ths cloud at 12,000 feet. Heard Master Bomber say base of cloud 10,000 feet.

17/07/1944 LL635 JI-M Bombing Paris   12.25 x   x

Whole crew composition is believed as 514 Squadron Operational Record Books (ORBs) do not make any mention of this raid, reported as a DNCO (Did Not Complete) mission in some 514 Sqn crew's logbooks and in that of J.D. McLaughlin as follows: "OPS RECALLED".

Bomber Command War Diaries Stated for that day:

"Flying Bomb Sights - 132 Aircraft. 72 Halifaxes, 28 Stirlings, 20 Lancasters, 11 Mosquitos, and 1 Mustang attacked 3 V-weapons sites without loss. Few details of results were recorded."

18/07/1944 LL635 JI-M Bombing Emieville   04.27   06.09   07.49

Bomb load 11 x 1000 MC, 4 x 500 GP. Primary target: Emieville, Troop concentration. Bombed at 06.09 hours from 8,000 feet South edge of smoke area. Area covered by pall of smoke. Many bomb bursts seen in target area.

18/07/1944 LL635 JI-M Bombing Aulnoye 22.42   00.58   02.16

Bomb load 18 x 500 GP. Primary target: Aulnoye, Railway junction. Weather hazy. Bombed at 00.58 hours from 9,700 feet green T.I. Bombing concentrated.

20/07/1944 LL635 JI-M Bombing Homberg   23.27   01.20   03.02

Bomb load 1 x 4000 HC, 2 x 500 MC, 14 x 500 GP. Primary target: Homberg, Oil plant. Weather clear, slight haze. Bombed at 01.20 hours from 19,000 feet. Bomb bursts well concentrated.

23/07/1944 LL635 JI-M Bombing Kiel   22.45   01.23   03.58

Bomb load 10 x 1000 MC, 5 x 500 GP. Primary target: Kiel, Warehouses and docks. Thin layer of cloud. Bombed at 01.23 hours from 19,000 feet green T.I. Attack believed rather scattered.

24/07/1944 LL635 JI-M Bombing Stuttgart 21.33 x 03.04
Bomb load 5 x 1000 ANM 65, 3 x 500 GP. Returned early with port outer engine U/S. Jettisoned 4350N, 0320E.
27/07/1944 LL734 JI-O Bombing Les Catelliers 16.57 18.50 20.03
Bomb load 18 x 500 GP. Primary target: Les Catelliers, Flying bomb site. Bombed at 18.50 hours from 16,400 feet on Mosquito.
30/07/1944 LL734 JI-O Bombing Caen 06.18 07.51 09.03
Bomb load 18 x 500 GP. Primary target: Caen 'B'. Weather 8-9/10ths cloud. Bombed at 07.51 hours from 2,000 feet red T.I.s. Bombing accurate, target covered with smoke, Master Bomber very helpful.

F/S.   Edward Henry John Shearing

1388915 F/S. Edward Henry John Shearing. Pilot.
1230758 Sgt. Robert James Rigden.   A/Bomber. 6 ops.
J20915 P/O. John Peake, DFC, RCAF. A/Bomber. 1 op.
1168418 F/S. Victor Henry Tayton. Navigator.
1544531 Sgt. Reginald Marshall, DFC. WOP/AG.
J92607 (R204001) P/O.   Joseph Lloyd Clinton Masson, RCAF. MU/Gunner.
R185925   Sgt. Murray H. Smart, RCAF. R/Gunner. 6 op.
A410114 P/O. Geoffrey George Williams, RAAF. R/Gunner. 1 op.
1811667 Sgt. Arthur Thomas Blunden. F/Engineer.

L to R (back): R. Marshall, J.L.C. Masson, V.H. Tayton.

L to R (front): M.H. Smart, E.H.J. Shearing, R.J. Rigden. (courtesy Peter Rigden)

15/03/1944 DS820 JI-A Bombing Stuttgart 19.30 23.36 03.28

Bomb load 1 x 1000 lb bomb, 1050 x 4, 90 x 4 x incendiaries. Primary target: Stuttgart. There was a thin cloud; Bombed at 23.36 hours from 20,000 feet. Monica u/s over 2,000 feet. Fires were scattered. Several large ones, tending to undershoot. Route satisfactory.

From his normal crew, only F/S. E.H.J. Shearing did this mission as 2nd Pilot with F/O. P.J.K. Hood's crew.

17/03/1944 DS820 JI-R Bombing Woodbridge   x x x

Weather: Foggy, clearing towards noon. Non-Operational Flying: In the afternoon Air Tests and Cross Countries were carried out, and a number of Flapless Landing Practices at Woodbridge, on which 1 Aircraft crashed but without casualties.

Note: In fact, it appears that two aircraft crashed. DS820 JI-R, flown by F/S. Shearing, crash-landed at Martlesham Heath. LL669, JI-K, flown by F/S. C.J. Medland, crash-landed at Leiston.

26/03/1944 LL728 JI-B Bombing Essen 20.06 22.08 00.56

Bomb load 1 x 2000 lb bomb, 56 x 30, 1080 x 4, 120 x 4 incendiaries. Primary target: Essen. There was 10/10 cloud over the target. Bombed at 22.08 hours from 20,000 feet. Glow of T.I.s only, one fire seen N of target. Spoof markers seen. Gee fuse blow, u/s on homeward run, came home on beacons and Q.M.s. P.F.F. went on time and on arrival attack seemed to be in full swing.

10/04/1944 LL728 JI-B Bombing Laon   01.24 03.50 05.56

Bomb load 9 x 1000, 4 x 500 lb bomb. Primary target: Laon. There was ground haze, no cloud. Bombed at 03.50 hours from 10,000 feet. T.I.s well concentrated. Bombs appeared to fall in area marked. Quiet trip. Route excellent.

P/O. G.G. Williams R/Gunner that day.

07/05/1944 LL690 JI-J Bombing Nantes 00.32 03.03 05.59

Bomb load 1 x 4000, 14 x 500 lb bombs. Primary target: Nantes. Weather was clear. Bombed at 03.03 hours from 9.000 feet. Target well illuminated by flares, also much smoke. Attack appeared successful. One large explosion seen at 03.05 hours leaving huge column of black smoke.

09/05/1944 LL690 JI-J Bombing Cap Gris Nez 03.10   04.11   05.10

Bomb load 1 x 1000 GP, 13 x 1000 MC. Primary target: Cape Gris Nez. Slight haze prevailed but target and markers seen. On instructions of Master Bomber bombs were aimed slightly left of red T.I. at 04.11 hours from 6,000 feet. Much smoke and a large explosion were observed at 04.12 hours. Appeared to be a good attack.

10/05/1944 LL728 JI-B Bombing Courtrai 22.10 23.27 01.05

Bomb load 7 x 1000 GP, 6 x 1000 MC. Primary target: Courtrai. Hazy conditions over target, but green and yellow markers seen. Bombed centre of green and yellow T.I.s at 23.27 hours from 11,000 feet. Unable to hear Master

Bomber. Target well illuminated. Sighted enemy aircraft (ME109) below.

19/05/1944 LL641 JI-K Bombing Le Mans 22.30 00.30 03.10

Crashed at Chippenham. Bomb load 4 x 1000 USA, 5 x 1000 MC, 1 x 1000 GP, 4 x 500 GP. Primary target: Le Mans, railway yards. Bombed markers at 00.30 hours from 7,500 feet. 1 x 1000 MC hung up and was jettisoned safe in the English Channel near French Coast. Homebound, aircraft spun and crashed at 03:10 on 20th May 1944 at Chippenham, Cambridgeshire, some 4 miles NNE from the airfield at Newmarket. The cause is unknown.

P/O. John Peake who was A/Bomber that day, baled out successfully and the Rear Gunner was thrown clear, but sustained injuries. All remaining members of the crew were killed. Those killed are buried in various UK cemeteries. Two, Sgt. Blunden and F/S. Taylor, at 37 and 35 respectively, were well above the average age of Bomber Command aircrew.

F/O. F.E. Sider

J29301   F/O. F.E. Sider, RCAF. Pilot.
J40945   F/O. H.D. Fulcher, RCAF. A/Bomber.
J40779   F/O. E.S. MacTier, RCAF. Navigator.
Sgt. B.A. Robus.   WOP/AG.
R264534 F/S. W.G. Wheeler, RCAF. MU/Gunner.   8 ops.
Sgt. J.S. McLintock. MU/Gunner. 11 ops.
Sgt. J.D. Gundlack.   MU/Gunner. 2 ops.
R217362 F/S. J.A. Moran, RCAF.   R/Gunner.
Sgt. J. Taylor-Lowen. F/Engineer.
196042 (1564681) P/O. Joseph McLaws McLellan Cameron. 2nd Pilot.
04/04/1945

Passengers: 07/05/1945.

16/12/1944 NF966 JI-R Bombing Siegen 11.22 14.59 16.55

Bomb load 1 x 4000 HC, 5 x 1000 MC, 7 x 500 GP. 1 Flare. Primary target: Siegen. Weather very bad on route with icing and cloud. Bombed at 14.59 hours from 17,750 feet on G.H. Leader.

From his normal crew, only F/O. F.E. Sider did this mission as 2nd Pilot with F/L. L.L. Currie's crew.

08/02/1945 NG142 JI-J Bombing Hohenbudberg 03.29 06.23 08.08

Bomb load 1 x 4000 HC, 2 x 500 MC, 4 x 250 GP, 4 x 500 GP, 6 x 500 ANM64. Primary target: Hohenbudberg, Marshalling yards. Weather 8/10ths cloud over target. Bombed at 06.23 hours from 19,500 feet on Red T.I.s. Bombing fairly concentrated.

From his normal crew, only F/O. F.E. Sider did this mission as 2nd Pilot with F/O. G.C. Fiset's crew.

19/02/1945 PB426 JI-D Bombing Wesel 13.06 16.36 19.22

Bomb load 1 x 4000 HC, 6 x 500 MC, 6 x 500 ANM64, 4 x 250 GP. Primary target: Wesel. Weather over target 5-7/10ths cloud. Bombed at 16.36 hours from 20,000 feet on leading aircraft. Landed at Moreton in Marsh.

F/S. W.G. Wheeler MU/Gunner until 17/03/45 except 05/03/45.

22/02/1945 ME351 JI-U Bombing Osterfeld 12.11 16.00 17.51

Bomb load 1 x 4000 HC, 9 x 500 ANM64, 2 x 500 MC, 4 x 250 GP. Primary target: Osterfeld, Coking ovens. Weather at target clear, but hazy. Bombed at 16.00 hours from 19,500 feet on G.H. Leader.

23/02/1945 NN782 JI-F Bombing Gelsenkirchen 11.20 15.01 16.57

Bomb load 1 x 4000 HC, 9 x 500 ANM64, 2 x 500 MC, 4 x 250 GP. Primary target Gelsenkirchen. Weather 10/10ths cloud. Bombed at 15.01 hours from 19,500 feet on leading aircraft.

26/02/1945 LM275 JI-C Bombing Dortmund 10.29 14.04 16.14

Bomb load 1 x 4000 HC, 2 x 500 MC L/Delay 37B, 9 x 500 ANM64, 4 x 250 GP. Primary target: Dortmund, Hoesch Benzin plant. Weather 10/10ths cloud, tops 8/10,000 feet. Bombed at 14.04 hours from 20,100 feet on G.H.

01/03/1945 LM724 JI-H Bombing Kamen 11.39 15.06 17.36

Bomb load 1 x 4000 HC, 11 x 500 ANM64, 2 x 500 MC L/Delay37. Primary target: Kamen, Coking plant. Weather 10/10ths cloud. Bombed at 15.06 hours from 18,900 feet on G.H.

02/03/1945 ME364 JI-P Bombing Koln 12.37 16.02 18.20

Bomb load 1 x 4000 HC, 12 x 500 ANM64. Primary target: Koln. Weather 10/10ths cloud over Koln, South and South-East of Koln clear. Bombed at 16.02 hours from 20,500 feet on leading aircraft.

05/03/1945 ME336 JI-S Bombing Gelsenkirchen 10.32 14.11 16.05

Bomb load 1 x 4000 HC, 12 x 500 ANM64. Primary target: Gelsenkirchen, Benzol plant. Weather 10/10ths cloud over target with cirrus cloud at bombing height. Bombed at 14.11 hours from 20,500 feet on G.H. Attacked last resort target: Wattenscheid Area.

Sgt. J.S. McLintock MU/Gunner that day.

07/03/1945 LM728 JI-R Bombing Wesel 02.29 05.32 07.41

Bomb load 1 x 4000 HC, 13 x 500 ANM64, 2 x 500 GP. Primary target: Wesel, Troop & Transport concentration. Weather 10/10ths cloud, thin in places. Bombed at 05.32 hours from 18,100 feet on G.H.

17/03/1945 ME351 JI-U Bombing August Viktoria 11.41 15.07 17.06

Bomb load 1 x 4000 HC, 13 x 500 ANM64, 2 x 500 MC. Primary target: Auguste Viktoria, Marl-Hüls coal mine. Weather 10/10ths cloud, tops and contrails up to 23,000 feet. Bombed at 15.07 hours from 21,400 feet on G.H.

20/03/1945 ME351 JI-U Bombing Hamm 09.55 13.15 15.43

Bomb load 7 x 1000 MC, 9 x 500 ANM64. Primary target: Hamm, Marshalling yards. Weather 5/10ths cloud. Bombed at 13.15 hours from 17,500 feet on G.H. and visual. Aircraft hit by heavy flak.

Sgt. J.S. McLintock MU/Gunner until 15/05/45 except 07/05/45.

21/03/1945 ME351JI-U Bombing Munster 09.35 13.08 15.17

Bomb load 1 x 4000 HC, 13 x 500 ANM64, 2 x 500 MC. Primary target Munster Viaduct and Marshalling Yards. Weather cloud nil to 2/10ths. Bombed at 13.08 hours from 17,500 feet on G.H. Slight heavy flak damage.

23/03/1945 ME358JI-O Bombing Wesel 14.24 17.39 19.09

Bomb load 2 x 1000 ANM65, 11 x 1000 MC. Primary target: Wesel, in support of ground troops. Weather perfect. Bombed at 17.39 hours from 19,500 feet on G.H. 1 x 1000 MC hang up and brought back to Base.

29/03/1945 ME530JI-C Bombing Salzgitter 12.23 16.45 19.14

Bomb load 1 x 4000 HC, 8 x 500 ANM64. Primary target: Salzgitter, Hallendorf works. Weather 10/10ths cloud. Bombed at 16.45 hours from 22,000 feet on leading aircraft.

04/04/1945 ME363JI-R Bombing Merseburg (Leuna) 18.46 22.48 03.08

Weather 5-10/10ths cloud, and 10/10ths over Merseburg. Bombed Primary Target: Merseburg. Bomb load 1 x 4000 HC, 6 x 500 ANM64. Bombed on Red T.I. on ground at 22.48 hrs from 19,900 feet. 1 x 500 ANM64 jettisoned live at 01.53 hrs from 7,000 feet, 5018N 0000E. Timing rather poor - Red and Green T.I. seen dropped to port in Magdeberg area. Master bomber not heard.

P/O. J McLaws McLellan Cameron 2nd Pilot that day.

13/04/1945 ME364JI-P Bombing Kiel 20.16 23.39 02.08

Bomb load 18 x 500 ANM64. Primary target: Kiel, Docks & ship yards. Weather 10/10ths cloud low and thin. Bombed on centre of Green T.I.s per M.B.s instructions at 23.39 hours from 20,000 feet. Red glow seen round markers. Bomb bursts seen across T.I.s.

30/04/1945 ME364JI-P Manna Rotterdam 16.52 18.16 19.31

Dropping area: Rotterdam. Weather intermittent showers and low cloud. Load 5 packs. Dropped 2 visually in field full of packs at 18.16 hours. A/C were congested at dropping. Packs well together. Populace waving and cheering. House seen burning.

02/05/1945 RE120 A2-C Manna The Hague 11.08 12.27 13.31

Dropping area The Hague. Weather over dropping zone clear below cloud for the first arrivals changing later to heavy showers which marred visibility. Dropped 4 panniers on Red T.I.s visual of racecourse at 12.27 hours.

07/05/1945 ME351JI-U Manna The Hague 12.19 13.46 14.46

Dropping area The Hague. Dropped 4 Packs on Red T.I.s ahead of White Cross at 13.46 hours. Clear. 1 pack returned to Base due to hang-up. Delivery O.K. Usual cheerful reception - message "Many thanks" on roof of Hague building.

No Mid Upper Gunner that day.

Passenger: Sgt. Shelmar.

10/05/1945 ME351 JI-U Exodus Juvincourt - Ford 11.18 x 17.46

Duration 3.54. Outward 1.50 hours. Collected 24 ex POWs. Homeward 2.04 hours. Delay at Ford. Otherwise organisation OK.

12/05/1945 ME351 JI-U Exodus Juvincourt - Wing 09.02 x 14.38

Duration 4.08. Outward 2.14 hours. Collected 24 POWs. Homeward 1.54 hours. No trouble experienced.

15/05/1945 ME363 JI-R Exodus Juvincourt - Wing 15.55 x 21.39

Duration 3 hrs 55 mins. Outward 1 hr 54 mins. Collected 10 POWs. Homeward 2 hrs 1 mins. All OK.

18/05/1945 ME336 JI-S Exodus Brussels - Oakley   12.07 x 17.12

Duration 3 hrs 25 mins. Out 1 hr 19 mins. In 2 hrs 6 mins. 9 Belgians taken to Brussels. 24 ex POWs. returned to UK. All OK.

Sgt. J.D. Gundlack MU/Gunner from that day.

19/05/1945 RA599 JI-L Exodus Brussels - Oakley   12.06 x 19.30

Duration 3 hrs 09 mins. Out 1 hr 24 mins. In 1 hr 45 mins. 10 Belgians taken to Brussels. 24 ex POWs. evacuated.

S/L.   Ernest Frank Sly DFC

46091 (566485) S/L.   Ernest Frank Sly, DFC, AFM.   Pilot.
J18090 (R92293) F/O. Edwin Horton Thomas, DFM, RCAF. A/Bomber.
J16339 F/O. John Livingstone Martin, RCAF. Navigator.
NZ405487   F/O. William Leonard Harvey, DFM. RNZAF.   WOP/AG.
J17725 (R121611)   F/O. James Allan Sneddon, DFM, RCAF. MU/Gun.
155354 (901620) F/O. Frank George Rosher, DFM.   R/Gunner.
52159 (569294) F/O.   Philip Pullyn Boulter.   F/Engineer.

29/12/1943 LL685 A2-G Bombing Berlin 17.09 20.21 23.53

Bomb load 1 x 4000, 24 x 30, 540 x 4, 90 x 4 incendiaries. Primary target: Berlin. There was 10/10 cloud. Red flares and green stars seen. Bombed at 20.21 hours at 20,000 ft. Circle of fires seen on cloud, beneath tending to undershoot. Outward journey good. Photo attempted.

01/01/1944 LL685 A2-G Bombing Berlin 00.35 03.13 07.41

Bomb load 1 x 4000, 24 x 30, 450 x 4, 90 x 4 lb incendiaries. Primary target: Berlin. There was 10/10 cloud with tops at 20,000 feet. Sky markers with red and green stars seen. Bombed at 03.13 hr at 20,000 feet. Very few sky markers scattered over 5 miles. Photo attempted.

02/01/1944 LL685 A2-G Bombing Berlin 00.07 02.48 06.58

Bomb load 1 x 4000, 24 x 30, 450 x 4, 90 x 4 incendiaries. Primary target: Berlin. There was 10/10 cloud at 19,500 ft. Bombed at 02.48 hours at 19,500 ft. Starboard outer engine failed over the target. Starboard inner failed over the Dutch Wart. Both engines icing trouble, started again at lower altitudes. More flak than last night. Big glow of fires seen below clouds.

14/01/1944 LL685 A2-G Bombing Brunswick 17.06 x 19.05

Bomb load 1 x 4000, 48 x 30. Aircraft missing.

Intercepted by a night-fighter flown by Hptm. Walter Barte of Stab III./NJG3 at 19.05 800 metres W of Bennebostel, 5 km S of Celle, where all were buried on 15th January 1944. They have been subsequently re-interred in the Hanover War Cemetery.

P/O. Harvey had won an immediate DFM while serving with 149 Sqn, the citation Gazetted on 16th March 1943 paid tribute to his devotion to duty despite having been wounded in the head. The awards gained by P/O. Thomas, F/O. Sneddon and P/O. Rosher, were Gazetted on 14th May 1943, 9th July 1943, and 11th June 1943 respectively.

James Allan Sneddon (left) and William Leonard Harvey (right).

F/O. Gordon Wood Smith

176513 (1434073)   F/O. Gordon Wood Smith, DFC. Pilot.
R186008   Sgt. D.L. Paterson, RCAF. A/Bomber.
187032 (1685406) P/O. John Spencer Thomas, DFC. Navigator.
Sgt. G. Bailey.   WOP/AG.
Sgt. P. Woolloff.   MU/Gunner. 5 ops.
A434518 (O16108 Q151003) F/S. Lewis McGregor Douglas Shaw, RAAF.
MU/Gunner. 29 ops.
Sgt. A.B. Ashton.   R/Gunner.
Sgt. C. Watson.   F/Engineer. 32 ops.
Sgt. A.T. Millar.   F/Engineer. 2 ops.
A425772 F/O. Frederick Stephens, DFC, RAAF.   2nd Pilot. 05/10/1944

F/O. Gordon Wood Smith, DFC.

09/08/1944 LL666 JI-Q Bombing Fort d'Englos 21.44 23.16 00.23
Bomb load 13 x 1000 MC. Primary target: Fort d'Englos (Lille), Petrol dump. Weather clear. Bombed at 23.16 hours from 13,000 feet, centre of concentration of red and green T.I.s. Defences slight.

The fort of Ennetières-en-Weppes, or "fort d'Englos" is one of a set of six forts surrounding Lille.

11/08/1944 LL666 JI-Q Bombing Lens   14.17   16.34   17.37
Bomb load 11 x 1000 MC, 4 x 500 GP. Primary target: Lens, Marshalling yards. Broken cloud, 5/10ths over target. Bombed at 16.34 hours from 14,000 feet, yellow T.I. and visual. Good concentration of bombing. Whole area covered in smoke.

12/08/1944 LL666 JI-Q Bombing Russelsheim 21.43 00.20 02.44
Bomb load 1 x 2000 HC, 12 x 500 No. 14 clusters. Primary target: Russelsheim. Weather clear. Bombed at 00.20 hours from 17,000 feet, centre of fires as instructed by Master Bomber. Target well alight. Master Bomber clearly heard. Many fighters on route. Good prang.

15/08/1944 LL666 JI-Q Bombing St Trond 10.01 12.10 13.32
Bomb load 11 x 1000 MC, 4 x 500 GP. Primary target St. Trond Airfield. Weather clear. Bombed at 12.10 hours from 17,000 feet, red T.I.s. Concentrated bombing, palls of smoke.

16/08/1944 LL666 JI-Q Bombing Stettin 20.58 01.12 05.04

596

Bomb load 1 x 2000 HC, 9 x 500 lb 'J' type clusters. Primary target: Stettin. Weather base of cloud 14,000 feet. Bombed at 01.12 hours from 12,000 feet. Came down to 12,000 feet and on breaking cloud saw scattered red T.I.s. Starboard outer engine u/s over target. Port outer engine feathered at 5440N 0500E. Landed at Woodbridge on two engines.

25/08/1944 HK572 JI-T Bombing Russelsheim 20.25 01.00 04.34

Bomb load 1 x 4000 HC, 12 x 500 LB Clusters. Primary target: Russelheim. Weather clear. Bombed at 01.00 hours, mixed red and green T.I.s. Visual of river bank slightly to N of red and green T.I.s indicated good marking. Perspex blown from mid-upper turret by flak over target.

26/08/1944 PB426 JI-J Bombing Kiel 20.28 23.13 01.54

Bomb load 1 x 4000 HC, 96 x 30 IB, 900 x 4 IB. Primary target: Kiel. Weather clear. Bombed at 23.13 hours from 19,000 feet, green and red T.I.s. T.I.s rather scattered. Undershot due to starboard inner engine u/s in Kiel area. Dull red explosion at 23.16 hours.

05/09/1944 NF968 JI-L Bombing Le Havre 17.21 19.23 20.39

Bomb load 11 x 1000 MC, 4 x 500 GP. Primary target: Le Havre. Bombed at 19.23 hours from 13,000 feet red T.I.

20/09/1944 LM684 JI-O Bombing Calais 14.38 16.02 17.19

Bomb load 11 x 1000 MC, 4 x 500 GP. Primary target: Calais. Weather clear over target. Bombed at 16.02 hours from 3,500 feet, red T.I.s.

23/09/1944 LM719 JI-M Bombing Neuss 19.14 21.25 23.08

Bomb load 8 x 1000 ANM59, 3 x 1000 ANM44, 4 x 500 GP. Primary target: Neuss. Weather 10/10ths cloud over target, tops 8/10,000 feet. Bombed at 21.25 hours from 20,000 feet on green glow beneath cloud.

25/09/1944 LM684 JI-O Bombing Pas de Calais 08.18 x 10.54

Bomb load 11 x 1000 MC, 4 x 500 GP. Primary target: Calais. Abandoned mission on Master Bomber's instructions. Jettisoned 3 x 1000, 4 x 500 at 5029N 0100E.

26/09/1944 LM684 JI-O Bombing Calais 11.25 12.47 13.56

Bomb load 11 x 1000 MC, 4 x 500 GP. Primary target: Calais 7D. Weather clear below cloud which was 3,500 feet. Bombed at 12.47 hours from 3,000 feet on red T.I.

03/10/1944 LM684 JI-O Bombing Westkapelle 12.29 14.00 15.22

Bomb load 1 x 4000 MC, 6 x 1000 MC, 1 x 500 GP. L/Delay. Primary target: Westkapelle (Walcheren). Weather patchy-scattered cloud with base 5,000 feet. Bombed at 14.00 hours from 5,000 feet on visual, short of red T.I.s per Master Bomber's instructions.

05/10/1944 LM684 JI-O Bombing Saarbrucken 17.03 x 22.44

Bomb load 11 x 1000 MC, 1 x 500 GP, 3 x 500 GP. Long Delay. Primary target: Saarbrucken, Marshalling yards. Weather clear over target. Abandoned mission on instructions from Master Bomber heard to say they were unable to locate target and called "Abandon Mission - our troop in vicinity". Jettisoned 4 x 500 GP at 5130N 0150E at 22.03 hours from 2,000 feet. Remainder brought back.

14/10/1944 LM684 JI-O Bombing Duisburg   06.54   09.04   10.47

Bomb load 11 x 1000 MC, 4 x 500 GP Long Delay. Primary target: Duisburg. Weather patchy cloud with gaps for bombing. Bombed at 09.04 hours from 18,000 feet. Smoke North of Docks. Undershot red T.I.

14/10/1944 LM684 JI-O Bombing Duisburg   22.40   01.31   03.30

Bomb load 11 x 1000 MC, 4 x 500 GP Long Delay. Primary target: Duisburg. Weather was clear with small amount of cloud over the target. Bombed at 01.31 hours from 21,500 feet. Red T.I.

18/10/1944 LM684 JI-O Bombing Bonn 08.25 x 12.55

Bomb load 1 x 4000 HC. 5 x 12 x 30 - 2 x 12 x 30 modified, 9 x No. 14 Clusters. Primary target: Bonn. Weather varying cloud 2-7/10ths with break for bombing. Bomb doors and starboard wing damaged by flak on the bombing run, which dislodged the cookie short of the target. Landed at Lille Vendeville at 12.55 hours, partly owing to flak damage and severe icing experienced on leaving target and shortage of petrol.

Returned at Base on 19/10/1944 12.50 hours.

21/10/1944 LM684 JI-O Bombing Flushing 10.58   12.29   13.28

Bomb load 12 x 1000 MC, 2 x 500 GP. Primary target: Flushing 'B'. Weather clear. Bombed at 12.29 hours from 8,000 feet. Area containing A/P.

22/10/1944 LM684 JI-O Bombing Neuss 13.08   15.55   17.21

Bomb load 1 x 4000 HC, 14 x No. 14 Clusters. Primary target: Neuss. Weather 10/10ths cloud over target. Bombed at 15.55 hours from 18,000 feet on G.H.

23/10/1944 LM684 JI-O Bombing Essen 16.31   19.27   22.01

Bomb load 1 x 4000 HC, 2 x 1000 MC, 10 x 500 GP, 3 x 500 MC. Primary target: Essen. Weather 10/10ths cloud over target - tops 12/14,000 feet with most appalling weather on route. Bombed at 19.27 hours on H2S.

26/10/1944 PB419 JI-N Bombing Leverkusen 13.13   15.30   17.15

Bomb load 1 x 4000 HC, 6 x 1000 MC, 4 x 500 GP, 2 x 500 GP Long Delay. Primary target: Leverkusen. Weather over target and on route was 10/10ths cloud. Bombed at 15.30 hours from 17,500 feet on G.H.

28/10/1944 LM727 JI-S Bombing Flushing 09.05   10.16   11.11

Bomb load 11 x 1000 MC, 6 x 1000 MC, 4 x 500 GP. Primary target: Flushing. Weather over the target quite clear and conditions perfect, although believed to be only local, and some low cloud approaching. Bombed at 10.16 hours from 8,000 feet. Visual of jetty.

29/10/1944 LM684 JI-O Bombing Flushing 10.06   11.36   12.23

Bomb load 11 x 1000 ANM59, 4 x 500 GP. MC. Primary target: Flushing, Gun installations. Weather clear over target. Bombed at 11.36 hours from 6,000 feet. Starboard of Red T.I.s as instructed.

31/10/1944 LM684 JI-O Bombing Bottrop 12.09 15.00   16.42

Bomb load 1 x 4000 HC, 16 x 500 GP. Primary target: Bottrop, Synth. Oil plants. Weather 10/10ths cloud over target. Bombed at 15.00 hours from

18,500 feet on G.H. Leader.

02/11/1944 LM684 JI-O Bombing Homberg   11.26   14.11   15.46
Bomb load 1 x 4000 HC, 6 x 1000 ANM59, 6 x 500 MC. Primary target: Homberg. Weather variable cloud but clear for bombing. Target obscured by pall of smoke rising to 10,000 feet. Bombed at 14.11 hours from 18,000 feet.

04/11/1944 LM684 JI-O Bombing Solingen 11.20   14.10   16.00
Bomb load 1 x 4000 HC, 6 x 1000 ANM59, 4 x 500 GP, 2 x 500 MC (L/Delay), 3 Flares. Primary target: Solingen. Weather 8-10/10ths cloud. Bombed at 14.10 hours from 20,000 feet on G.H.

06/11/1944 LM684 JI-O Bombing Koblenz 16.57   19.34   21.49
Bomb load 1 x 4000 HC, 12 x 500 Clusters, 2 x 250 T.I.s. Primary target: Koblenz. Weather clear over target. Bombed at 19.34 hours from 19,000 feet on mass of fires and smoke a mile square.

08/11/1944 LM684 JI-O Bombing Homberg   08.02   10.29   12.12
Bomb load 1 x 4000 HC, 6 x 1000 GP, 6 x 500 GP. Primary target: Homberg. Weather clear. Bombed at 10.29 hours from 18,000 feet on instruments. Aircraft damaged by flak. Port inner and front turret hit.

15/11/1944 PB142 JI-O Bombing Dortmund   12.36   15.41   17.21
Bomb load 1 x 4000 HC, 2 x 500 MC, 13 x 500 GP, 1 Red with Green star Flare. Primary target: Hoesch-Benzin Dortmund, Oil refineries. Weather 10/10ths cloud over the target. Bombed at 15.41 hours from 16,500 feet on G.H. Leader. G.H. unserviceable. Best concentration of flares yet seen.

16/11/1944 PB142 JI-O Bombing Heinsburg 13.24 15.38   17.02
Bomb load 1 x 4000 HC, 6 x 1000 MC, 4 x 500 GP, 4 x 250 lb T.I.s. Primary target: Heinsburg. Weather - nil cloud with slight haze over target. Bombed at 15.38 hours from 12,000 feet. Upwind edge of smoke on town.

20/11/1944 PB142 JI-O Bombing Homberg   12.53   15.17   17.03
Bomb load 1 x 4000 HC, 15 x 500 GP, 1 Red-Green Flare. Primary target: Homberg. Weather 10/10ths cloud over target. Bombed at 15.17 hours from 21,000 feet on G.H.

23/11/1944 PB142 JI-O Bombing Nordstern   12.31   15.20   17.11
Bomb load 1 x 4000 HC, 12 x 500 GP, 4 x 250 Red T.I.s. Primary target: Nordstern, Gelsenkirchen Oil refineries. Weather 10/10ths cloud. Bombed at 15.20 hours from 20,000 feet on G.H.

04/12/1944 PB142 JI-O Bombing Oberhausen 11.51 14.06 15.54
Bomb load 1 x 4000 HC, 15 x 500 GP, 1 Flare. Primary target: Oberhausen, Built up area. Weather 10/10ths cloud. Bombed at 14.06 hours from 20,000 feet on G.H.

05/12/1944 PB142 JI-O Bombing Hamm 08.59 11.29   14.08
Bomb load 1 x 4000 HC, 2 x 500 MC, 11 x 500 GP, 2 x 500 GP Long Delay, 1 Flare. Primary target: Hamm. Weather 10/10ths cloud over target, but otherwise varying from 6-10/10ths. Bombed at 11.29 hours from 20,000 feet on G.H.

F/O. H.C. Snow

J40219 F/O.   H.C. Snow, RCAF.   Pilot.
R195837 F/S. R.A. Moran, RCAF.   A/Bomber.
J40887 F/O.   B.E. Freano, RCAF.   Navigator.
Sgt. D.C. Bradbury.   WOP/AG.
R119986 F/S. G.C. Angus, RCAF.   MU/Gunner.
R255188 F/S. D.G. Thompson, RCAF.   R/Gunner.
Sgt. L.J. Thatcher.   F/Engineer.
NZ429076 F/OFrederick Louis "Freddie" Hookway, RNZAF 2nd Pilot.
4/4/1945

Passengers: 02/05/1945, 05/05/1945.

13/01/1945 PD389 A2-J Bombing Saarbrucken 11.58 15.24   18.12
Bomb load 1 x 4000 HC, 10 x 500 ANM58 or 64, 4 x 250 GP. Primary target: Saarbrucken. Weather 3-5/10ths cloud, tops 4/5,000 feet. Bombed at 15.24 hours from 19,000 feet on leading aircraft.
All aircraft on this operation were diverted on return to Exeter as weather at base was unfit to land.
From his normal crew, only F/O. H.C. Snow did this mission as 2nd Pilot with F/O. C.I.H. Nicholl's crew.
15/01/1945 PB142 JI-G Bombing Lagendreer 11.43   15.00   16.40
Bomb load 1 x 4000 HC, 10 x 500 ANM64, 4 x 250 GP. Primary target: Lagendreer. Weather 10/10ths cloud. Bombed at 15.00 hours from 18,500 feet on G.H. Leader.
13/02/1945 LM627 A2-H   Bombing Dresden 21.5001.38   06.36
Bomb load 1 x 4000 HC, 6 x No. 14 Clusters. Primary target: Dresden. Weather 5/10ths cloud over target. Bombed at 01.38 hours from 19,500 feet on centre of Red T.I.s.
14/02/1945 PB142 JI-G Bombing Chemnitz   20.35   00.32   04.18
Bomb load 1 x 4000 HC, 6 x No. 14 Clusters. Primary target: Chemnitz. Weather 8-10/10ths cloud, tops 15-16,000 feet with occasional breaks. Bombed at 00.32 hours from 19,000 feet on Red flares.
16/02/1945 LM627 A2-H   Bombing Wesel 12.34   16.00   17.47
Bomb load 1 x 4000 HC, 4 x 500 GP, 2 x 500 MC L/Delay, 4 x 250 GP, 6 x 500 ANM64. Primary target: Wesel. Weather clear. Bombed at 16.00 hours from 20,000 feet on leading aircraft. Aircraft hit by flak. 12 heavy flak holes.
18/02/1945 PB426 JI-D Bombing Wesel 11.33   15.29   16.50
Bomb load 1 x 4000 HC, 4 x 500 GP, 2 x 500 MC L/Delay, 4 x 250 GP, 6 x 500 ANM64. Primary target: Wesel. Weather 10/10ths cloud. Bombed at 15.29 hours from 20,000 feet on G.H. Leader.
22/02/1945 ME354 JI-M Bombing Osterfeld   12.18   16.01   17.55
Bomb load 1 x 4000 HC, 9 x 500 ANM64, 2 x 500 MC, 4 x 250 GP. Primary

target: Osterfeld, Coking ovens. Weather at target clear, but hazy. Bombed at 16.01 hours from 19,500 feet on G.H. equipment.

26/02/1945 LM724JI-H Bombing Dortmund   10.15   14.05   16.25

Bomb load 1 x 4000 HC, 2 x 500 MC L/Delay 37B, 9 x 500 ANM64, 4 x 250 GP. Primary target: Dortmund, Hoesch Benzin plant. Weather 10/10ths cloud, tops 8/10,000 feet. Bombed at 14.05 hours from 20,000 feet. Followed another aircraft.

28/02/1945 LM275JI-C Bombing Nordstern   08.53   12.05   14.23

Bomb load 1 x 4000 HC, 9 x 500 ANM64, 2 x 500 MC L/D, 4 x 250 GP. Primary target: Nordstern (Gelsenkirchen). Weather 10/10ths cloud. Bombed at 12.05 hours from 20,500 feet on G.H.

02/03/1945 NF966 A2-G   Bombing Koln   12.50 x 18.40

Bomb load 1 x 4000 HC, 12 x 500 ANM64. Primary target: Koln. Weather 10/10ths cloud over Koln, South and South-East of Koln clear. Abortive sortie. Jettisoned 2 x 500 ANM64 at 17.54 hours from 7,000 feet at 5214N 0306E. Brought back 1 x 4000 HC and 10 x 500 ANM64.

06/03/1945 NF968 JI-B Bombing Salzbergen 08.1812.15   14.15

Bomb load 1 x 4000 HC, 12 x 500 ANM64, 2 x 500MC. Primary target: Salzbergen, Wintershall oil plant. Weather 10/10ths cloud over target, tops 10,000 feet. Bombed at 12.15 hours from 20,500 feet on G.H. Bombing believed concentrated.

07/03/1945 PB482 A2-K   Bombing Wesel 02.48   05.31   07.40

Bomb load 1 x 4000 HC, 13 x 500 ANM64, 2 x 500 GP. Primary target: Wesel, Troop & Transport concentration. Weather 10/10ths cloud, thin in places. Bombed at 05.31 hours from 18,000 feet on G.H.

09/03/1945 PB142 JI-G Bombing Datteln   10.36 14.00   15.59

Bomb load 1 x 4000 HC, 13 x 500 ANM64, 2 x 500 MC L/Delay37, 1 Skymarker Blue Puff. Primary target: Datteln, Synthetic oil plant. Weather 10/10ths cloud, tops 8-10,000 feet. Bombed at 14.00 hours from 20,500 feet on G.H.

11/03/1945 LM724JI-H Bombing Essen   11.30   15.25   17.16

Bomb load 1 x 4000 HC, 13 x 500 ANM64, 2 x 500 MC, 1 Skymarker Blue Puff. Primary target: Essen, Marshalling yards. Weather 10/10ths cloud, tops 7/8000 feet. Bombed at 15.25 hours from 19,500 feet on G.H.

04/04/1945 ME380JI-E Bombing Merseburg (Leuna) 18.40   22.55 02.53

Weather 5-10/10ths cloud, and 10/10ths over Merseburg. Bombed primary target. Bomb load 1 x 4000 HC, 6 x 500 ANM64. 10/10th cloud. Bombed on Sky Markers at 22.55 hours from 20,000 feet in centre of red flares with green stars. Very concentrated bombing, H.2.S. D.R. Compass U/S. Marking not good, had to bomb on incorrect heading in order to get bombs away before flares died out.

F/O. F.L. Hookway 2nd Pilot that day.

09/04/1945 ME380JI-E Bombing Kiel   19.34   22.35   01.34

Bomb load 1 x 4000 HC and 12 x 500 ANM64. Primary target: Kiel, Submarine Buildings Yards. Weather clear with slight haze. Bombed at 22.35 hours from 20,000 feet on Green ground markers and M/B's instructions. Well concentrated fires starting up. Excellent raid.

18/04/1945 ME380JI-E Bombing Heligoland 09.5513.10 15.28

Bomb load 6 x 1000 MC, 10 x 500 ANM64. Primary target: Heligoland, Naval base. Weather no cloud, slight haze. Bombed on smoke and M/B at 13.10 hours from 18,500 ft. Saw bombs fall across northeast harbour. Only north tip of island visible. Remainder obscured by smoke. Very good attack.

29/04/1945 RE116 JI-F Manna The Hague 12.24 13.50 15.02

Dropping zone: The Hague. Weather broken cloud above and clear below. Dropped 3 packs on white cross and red T.I. at 13.50 hours. 2 packs hang up due to failure in release gear. Orbited but could not release on second run.

02/05/1945 ME380JI-E Manna The Hague 11.13 12.34 13.41

Dropping area The Hague. Weather over dropping zone clear below cloud for the first arrivals changing later to heavy showers which marred visibility. Dropped 5 panniers at 12.34 hours on Red T.I.s - White Cross. Slight rain. Delivery OK - Crowds as numerous as ever and just as enthusiastic - One or two loads overshooting into the woods.

Passengers: A.C. Carter.

05/05/1945 ME380JI-E Manna The Hague 06.0107.19 08.20

Dropping area: The Hague. Dropped 5 Panniers visually on White Cross and T.I.s at 07.19 hours. 10/10 cloud - 1000 ft base, Hazy. T.I.s scattered.

Passengers: Cpl. Murphy.

10/05/1945 RE140 JI-H Exodus Juvincourt - Ford 11.10 x 17.19

Duration 3.48. Outward 1.50 hours. Collected 24 ex POWs. Homeward 1.58 hours. Unnecessary delay caused by signing on at control tower at Ford. Otherwise OK.

11/05/1945 RE140 JI-H Exodus Juvincourt - Wing 17.07 x 22.21

Duration 3.42. Outward 2.15 hours. Collected 24 ex POWs. Homeward 1.27 hours. Flying control at Wing very slow in landing a/c.

13/05/1945 RF231 JI-A Exodus Juvincourt - Tangmere 13.18 x 16.16

Duration 2.58 hours. "All aircraft on circuit to return to Base" message received 14.47 hours.

16/05/1945 ME530JI-C Exodus Brussels - Westcott 13.03 x 17.45

Duration 2 hrs 57 mins. Arrived overseas A/F 14.15. Out 1 hr 11 mins. In 1 hr 46 mins. Arrived reception A/F 17.09. 10 Belgian refugees taken to Brussels / Melsbroeck. 24 ex POWs all military evacuated to Westcott.

18/05/1945 ME380JI-E Exodus Brussels - Oakley 11.48 x 16.42

Duration 2 hrs 57 mins. Out 1 hr 08 mins. In 1 hrs 49 mins. 10 Belgians taken to Brussels. 24 ex POWs returned to UK. No troubles.

19/05/1945 ME530JI-C Exodus Brussels - Oakley 11.50 x 17.17

Duration 3 hrs 05 mins. Out 1 hr 10 mins. In 1 hr 55 mins. 10 Belgian refugees to Brussels. 24 ex POWs (all military) evacuated.

F/L. Arthur Charles Southward

47481 (523741) F/L.   Arthur Charles Southward. Pilot.
F/S. J.A. Woods.   A/Bomber.
164586 (1581895)   F/O. Stanley Talbot.   Navigator.
F/S. C.N. Jones.   WOP/AG.
Sgt. R.W.J. Williams.   MU/Gunner. 19 ops.
Sgt. G.W. Miller.   R/Gunner.
Sgt. C.W. Rogers.   F/Engineer.

Passengers: 04/06/1945, 12/07/1947.

05/03/1945 NN773 JI-K Bombing Gelsenkirchen 10.24   14.07   15.52
Bomb load 1 x 4000 HC, 12 x 500 ANM64. Primary target: Gelsenkirchen, Benzol plant. Weather 10/10ths cloud over target with cirrus cloud at bombing height. Bombed at 14.07 hours from 20,800 feet on G.H. Leader.
From his normal crew, only F/L. A.C. Southward did this mission as 2nd Pilot with P/O. L.J.W. Sutton's crew.
04/04/1945 LM724 JI-H Bombing Merseburg (Leuna) 18.43   22.53   02.50
Weather 5-10/10ths cloud, and 10/10ths over Merseburg. Bombed Magdeburg area. Bomb load 1 x 4000 HC, 6 x 500 ANM64. Bombed on Red and Green T.I.s and River Elbe. Cloud 5/10th. Bombed at 22.53 hours from 20,000 feet. Attack on Mersenberg opened late. Red/Green T.I. dropped NE of Target. A/C circled three times for further means of identifying sky markers later seen at Merseburg.
From his normal crew, only F/L. A.C. Southward did this mission as 2nd Pilot with F/L. J.D.K. Crooks' crew.
06/03/1945 NN773 JI-K Bombing Salzbergen 08.24 12.14   14.24
Bomb load 1 x 4000 HC, 12 x 500 ANM64, 2 x 500MC. Primary target: Salzbergen, Wintershall oil plant. Weather 10/10ths cloud over target, tops 10,000 feet. Bombed at 12.14 hours from 21,000 feet on G.H. Leader. Gee set caught fire over French coast but fire was extinguished.
17/03/1945 NG142 JI-J Bombing August Viktoria (Hüls) 11.35   x 16.54
Bomb load 1 x 4000 HC, 13 x 500 ANM64, 2 x 500 MC. Primary target: Auguste Viktoria, Marl-Hüls coal mine. Weather 10/10ths cloud, tops and contrails up to 23,000 feet. Abortive sortie. Starboard inner engine gave trouble and finally gave out just as formation, which had been lost in clouds, was found. Jettisoned 1 x 4000 HC, 4 x 500 ANM64 at 5110N 0517E at 14.39 hours from 18,000 feet. 9 x 500 ANM64 and 2 x 500 MC brought back to Base.
20/03/1945 NN773 JI-K Bombing Hamm 09.58 13.15   15.54
Bomb load 7 x 1000 ANM59, 9 x 500 ANM64. Primary target: Hamm, Marshalling yards. Weather 5/10ths cloud. Bombed at 13.15 hours from

18,000 feet on G.H. Leader.

21/03/1945 LM627 JI-D Bombing Munster 09.40 13.11 15.26

Bomb load 1 x 4000 HC, 13 x 500 ANM64, 2 x 500 MC. Primary target Munster Viaduct and Marshalling Yards. Weather cloud nil to 2/10ths. Bombed at 13.11 hours from 18,500 feet on leading aircraft.

29/03/1945 NN773 JI-K Bombing Salzgitter 12.22 16.43 19.20

Bomb load 1 x 4000 HC, 8 x 500 ANM64. Primary target: Salzgitter, Hallendorf works. Weather 10/10ths cloud. Bombed at 16.43 hours from 22,000 feet on E.T.A. and Green Smoke Puffs. Lost Leader in cloud, tried unsuccessfully to find another Leader. Bombed on ETA 45 secs after Bombs Gone.

09/04/1945 NG142 JI-J Bombing Kiel 19.37 22.36 01.32

Bomb load 1 x 4000 HC and 12 x 500 ANM64. Primary target: Kiel, Submarine Buildings Yards. Weather clear with slight haze. Bombed at 22.36 hours from 20,000 feet on centre of Red T.I.s (M/B not heard). Very large fire burning red, surrounded by numerous smaller fires. Bombing concentrated. Good attack, marking well grouped. Two distinct areas of markers.

22/04/1945 NN782 JI-K Bombing Bremen 15.07 18.41 20.43

Bomb load 1 x 4000 HC, 2 x 500 MC, 14 x 500 ANM 64. Primary target: Bremen, in support of Troop concentration. Weather on approaching target 4-5/10ths cloud. Bombed on G.H. Leader 514/M at 18.41 hours from 19,000 ft. Accurate bombing seen north of river bend. Much black/brown smoke up to 6,000 ft. Successful raid. Formation good. Own G.H. Leader u/s. Picked up G.H. Leader 514/M.

29/04/1945 ME535 JI-G Manna The Hague 12.23 13.47 14.57

Dropping area: The Hague. Weather broken cloud above and clear below. Dropped 5 packs on red T.I. at 13.47 hours. Packs seen to drop in northeast corner of airfield.

02/05/1945 RF231 JI-A Manna The Hague 11.15 12.31 13.37

Dropping area The Hague. Weather over dropping zone clear below cloud for the first arrivals changing later to heavy showers which marred visibility. 5 Panniers dropped visually on T.I. and White Cross at 12.31 hrs.

No Mid Upper Gunner that day.

Passenger: A.C. Evans.

07/05/1945 RE137 JI-D Manna The Hague 12.27 13.52 15.00

Dropping area The Hague. Dropped 5 Packs on Red T.I.s each side of White Cross at 13.52 hours. Clear. Supplies delivered OK. Oil patch and pieces of wreckage seen 5143N 0224E 13.05 hours.

09/05/1945 ME535 JI-G Exodus Juvincourt - Dunsfold 07.26 x 13.00

Outward 1.40 hours. Collected 24 POWs. Homeward 1.50 hrs. Impossible to get 24 people forward of step, otherwise everything went well.

11/05/1945 RE116 JI-F Exodus Juvincourt - Tangmere 11.21 x 16.38

Duration 3.28. Outward 1.34 hours. Collected 24 ex POWs. Homeward 1.53 hours. Excellent reception at Tangmere.

12/05/1945 RE140 JI-H ExodusBrussels - Tangmere 12.27 x 18.30

Duration 3.58. Outward 2.01 hours. Homeward 1.57 hours. 3 Refugees to Brussels, 24 ex POWs to Ford. Flying control at Brussels very slow.

14/05/1945 ME530JI-C ExodusJuvincourt - Oakley 10.17 x 16.26

Duration 4.08 hours. Outward 1.38 hours. Collected 24 POWs. Homeward 2.30 hours. All OK.

17/05/1945 RA600 JI-B ExodusBrussels - Westcott 10.30 x 16.01

Duration 3 hrs 12 mins. Out 1 hr 17 mins. In 1 hr 55 mins. 11 Belgian refugees taken to Brussels. 24 Ex POWs returned to Westcott. R.T. very weak at Brussels.

19/05/1945 RE140 JI-H ExodusBrussels - Oakley 11.59 x 18.55

Duration 3 hrs 06 mins. Out 1 hr 27 mins. In 1 hr 39 mins. 10 Belgian refugees taken to Brussels. 24 ex POWs evacuated.

23/05/1945 RA600 JI-B ExodusBrussels - Oakley 12.11 x 18.00

Duration 2.56 hours. Out 1.13 hours. In 1.43 hours. 10 Belgian refugees returned to Brussels. 24 ex POWs evacuated. Organisation excellent.

04/06/1945 ME535JI-G Baedeker Tour over Germany 16.50 x 21.12

Passengers: AC. T. Evans, AC. D. Davis, AC. G. Griffiths.

12/07/1945 RF230 JI-B Baedeker Tour over Continent 10.21 x 14.35

Passengers: Cpl. Browsword, LAC. Bromley, LAC. Poultney, LACW. Butters, ACW. Johnston.

24 to 26/07/1945

ME530JI-C Dodge Italy 06.2617.52 17.48

24/07/1945 Waterbeach 06.26 - Italy 17.52 - 26/07/1945 Italy 10.03 - Waterbeach 17.48.

F/S. Frederick Charles Victor Steed

179073 (1333416) F/S. Frederick Charles Victor Steed. Pilot.
203358 (1389896) F/S. Maurice James Bulled. A/Bomber.
185898 (1433260) Sgt. Allen Watts. Navigator.
651820 W/O. Arthur McRobbie Robertson. WOP/AG.
1651741 Sgt. W.H. Sweet. MU/Gunner.
R78082 F/S. C.A. Forsythe. RCAF. R/Gunner.
1566622 Sgt. James Cumming. F/Engineer.

11/11/1943 DS786 JI-E Gardening La Tranche x x x

Aircraft carried 3 x G710, 1 x H802. Primary area La Tranche. No cloud. Visibility good. Hole in Rear Gunner's Turret. T.R. 1196 aerial shot away. Route satisfactory.

18/11/1943 DS818 JI-Q Bombing Mannheim 17.28 x 20.43

Bomb load 1 x 4000, 16 x 30, 720 x 4. Primary target Mannheim. Aircraft developed engine trouble at 12,000 feet and was forced to return to base 19.16 hours. 4000 lb bomb was jettisoned. 720 x 4 and 16 x 30 brought back to base.

02/12/1943 DS815 JI-N Bombing Berlin 17.07 20.23 00.06

Bomb load 1 x 4000, 40 x 30 incendiaries, 650 x 4 incendiaries, 70 x 4 incendiaries. Primary target: Berlin. 4/10 cloud. Bombed on Green T.I.s at 20.23 at 20,300 ft. 4 lb inc, bomb, presumably from another aircraft, fell through perspex behind Nav. table, and was thrown overboard. Port aileron holed by a 30lb inc. Log blown through hole in aircraft. Encounter with enemy aircraft reported.

29/12/1943 DS818 JI-Q Bombing Berlin 17.11 x 19.23

Bomb load 1 x 2000, 40 x 30 incendiaries, 900 x 4 incendiaries, 90 x 4 incendiaries. Returned early. All four engines overheating, oil temp. rising, oil pressure decreasing. Bombs jettisoned. 990 x 4 incendiaries brought back to Base.

01/01/1944 DS818 JI-Q Bombing Berlin 00.33 03.15 07.43

Bomb load 1 x 4000, 24 x 30, 450 x 4, 90 x 4 lbs. Incendiaries. Primary target: Berlin. There was 10/10 cloud. Several R.G. sky markers seen as we approached, soon disappeared. Bombed at 03.15 hours at 20,500 feet. Nothing seen, too much cloud. Photo flash shaken out of tri-cell by avoiding action. Glow of fires seen from 25/30 miles away after leaving target. Took avoiding action over the target.

02/01/1944 LL683 JI-P Bombing Berlin 00.01 x 02.11

Bomb load 1 x 4000, 24 x 30, 450 x 4, 90 x 4 lbs. Incendiaries. Returned early, farthest point reached 5235N 0300E. Rear turret completely u/s. Pilot could not get oxygen. Bombs jettisoned.

14/01/1944 DS818 JI-Q Bombing Brunswick 16.54 x 19.16

Bomb load 1 x 4000, 48 x 30 incendiaries. Returned early. Airscrew control u/s. Farthest point reached 5306N 0359E. 1 x 4000 bomb jettisoned.

20/01/1944 DS818 JI-Q Bombing Berlin 16.20 x 19.55

Bomb load 1 x 4000, 32 x 30, 540 x 4, 60 x 4 incendiaries. Returned early. Lack of oxygen on pilot's connection. Farthest point reached 54°10'N 05°E. Jettisoned 1 x 4000.

21/01/1944 DS818 JI-Q Bombing Magdeburg 19.58 23.05 03.07

Bomb load 1 x 4000, 720 x 4, 90 x 4, 32 x 30 incendiaries. Primary target: Magdeburg. There was 4/10 cloud broken. Bombed at 23.05 hours at 20,000 ft. Concentrated fires burning.

28/01/1944 DS818 JI-Q Bombing Berlin 00.04 03.24 07.53

Bomb load 1 x 2000 lb bomb, 16 x 30, 750 x 4 incendiaries. Primary target: Berlin. There was 10/10 cloud with tops 6,000 ft. Bombed at 03.24 hours at 20,500 ft. During run in sky lit up by flash of large explosions. Route markers easily identified. Route good. Fighter opposition conspicuous by its absence.

15/02/1944 DS818 JI-Q Bombing Berlin 17.41 x 19.53

Bomb load 1 x 2000, 1 x 1000 lb bomb, 24 x 30, 900 x 4 incendiaries. Returned early. Starboard outer cutting out, also excessive vibration. Farthest point reached 53.50N 0234E. Total load jettisoned safe to reduce weight.

25/02/1944 DS818 JI-Q Bombing Augsburg   21.38   01.15   04.58

Bomb load 1 x 4000 lb bomb, 32 x 30, 510 x 4, 90 x 4 incendiaries. Primary target: Augsburg. Weather very clear. Bombed at 01.15 hours at 18,000 ft. Mass of flames and smoke. Arrived 4 minutes early. Route good and no troubles. A marvellous attack.

01/03/1944 DS818 JI-Q Bombing Stuttgart   23.49   03.11   06.52

Bomb load 1 x 4000 lb bomb, 24 x 30, 600 x 4, 90 x 4 incendiaries. Primary target: Stuttgart. There was 10/10 cloud with occasional breaks. Bombed at 03.11 hours at 20,000 ft. Fires seen through one small break, otherwise cloud prevented visual. Route satisfactory. Target area well lit up.

15/03/1944 DS818 JI-Q Bombing Stuttgart   19.16   23.20   02.27

Bomb load 1 x 1000 lb bomb, 72 x 30, 1050 x 4, 90 x 4 incendiaries. Primary target: Stuttgart. There was thin patchy cloud over the target. Bombed at 23.20 hours from 20,000 feet. Small fires seen but rather widespread. Believed slight petrol leak due to flak over target. Route OK. Attack only moderate.

22/03/1944 DS818 JI-Q Bombing Frankfurt   18.39   21.54   00.04

Bomb load 1 x 1000 lb bomb, 64 x 30, 1161 x 4, 129 x 4 incendiaries. Primary target: Frankfurt. There was thin cloud, with breaks. Bombed at 21.54 hours from 20,000 feet. Incendiaries fires burning among red and green T.I.s. Attack seemed quite good. River showed up plainly in glare of incendiaries. Bomb tit did not work when pressed, so we overshot by approx 3 seconds.

24/03/1944 DS818 JI-Q Bombing Berlin 18.35   22.33   01.37

Bomb load 1 x 1000 lb. bomb, 88 x 30, 810 x 4, 90 x 4 incendiaries. Primary target: Berlin. There was 3/10 cloud with gaps. Bombed at 22.33 hours from 20,500 feet. Considered P.F.F. about 4 minutes late or revised zero hour - few T.I.s seen but these were concentrated fires, could be seen from Hannover on way home.

10/04/1944 DS818 JI-Q Bombing Laon   01.14   03.38   05.27

Bomb load 9 x 1000, 4 x 500 lb bomb. Primary target: Laon. There was ground haze and no cloud. Bombed at 03.38 hours from 10,000 feet. T.I.s very well concentrated. All explosions seen to occur in area marked. Very well concentrated attack. Photo attempted.

26/04/1944 DS818 JI-Q Bombing Essen   22.54   01.35   03.21

Bomb load 1 x 2000 lb bomb, 84 x 30, 945 x 4, 105 x 4 lb incendiaries. Primary target: Essen. Weather was clear below, broken above. Bombed at 01.35 hours from 20,000 feet. There was a number of fires. Centre of target covered with smoke. Markers right on time but main force started bombing just before zero. Attack well concentrated. Much H.F. but bursting below. Searchlights numerous but not effective. Nearly collided with another Lancaster. Fires still seen from enemy coast.

01/05/1944 DS818 JI-Q Bombing Chambly   22.40   00.22   01.40

Bomb load 10 x 1000, 5 x 500 lb bombs. Primary target: Chambly. Weather was clear. Bombed at 00.22 hours from 9,500 feet. Target illuminated by white flares. Yellow T.I. dropped by M of C and instruction given to bomb on same. Route OK. Aircraft had right wing down when bombing.

10/05/1944 LL734 JI-S Bombing Courtrai 22.10 23.27 00.55

Bomb load 7 x 1000 GP, 7 x 1000 MC. Primary target: Courtrai. Hazy conditions. Bombed as ordered by Master Bomber at 23.27 hours from 7,000 feet. Bombing appeared well concentrated. Route satisfactory. No opposition. Bombed at low height to get good photo with colour film.

F/O. Frederick Stephens DFC

A425772 F/O. Frederick Stephens, DFC, RAAF. Pilot.
Sgt. F. Daldry. A/Bomber.
Sgt. E. Knowles. Navigator. 24 ops.
Sgt. W.L. Harradine. Navigator. 4 ops.
A436049 F/S. Alan Walter Bennington, RAAF. WOP/AG.
F/S. Martin Harvey Hanley. MU/Gunner. 27 ops.
F/S. Davis. MU/Gunner. 1 op.
Sgt. P.E. Steele. R/Gunner.
Sgt. D.J. Taylor. F/Engineer.

26/09/1944 NF966 JI-R Bombing Calais 11.26 12.46 14.04

Bomb load 11 x 1000 MC, 4 x 500 GP. Primary target: Calais 7D. Weather clear below cloud which was 3,500 feet. Bombed at 12.46 hours from 3,500 feet on red T.I. + ½ second.

27/09/1944 NF966 JI-R Bombing Calais 07.30 08.47 10.17

Bomb load 11 x 1000 MC, 4 x 500 GP. Primary target: Calais 15. Weather, cloud 5,500 feet 10/10ths. Bombed at 08.47 hours from 5,000 feet on red T.I.

05/10/1944 LM684 JI-O Bombing Saarbrucken 22.44 x x

Bomb load 11 x 1000 MC, 1 x 500 GP, 3 x 500 GP Long Delay. Abandoned mission on instructions from Master Bomber heard to say they were unable to locate target and called "Abandon Mission - our troop in vicinity". Jettisoned 4 x 500 GP at 5130N 0150E at 22.03 hours from 2,000 feet. Remainder brought back. Abandoned on Master Bomber's orders.

From his normal crew, only F/O. F. Stephens did this mission as 2nd Pilot with P/O. G.W. Smith's crew.

06/10/1944 LM728 JI-U Bombing Dortmund 16.40 20.32 22.20

Bomb load 1 x 4000 HC, 12 x No. 14 Clusters. Primary target: Dortmund, Town and Railways. Weather over the target was clear with slight ground haze.

L to R (back): 2nd A.W. Bennington, 3rd F. Stephens, 4th M.H. Hanley. Other crewmen unknown. (courtesy Suzy McCullough (Bennington))

Bombed at 20.32 hours from 21,000 feet on Northern part of green T.I. concentration. Combat with single engine aircraft at 21.00 hours 5115N 0530E at 20,000 feet - no claim.

14/10/1944 NF966 JI-R Bombing Duisburg   07.03   09.03   10.49

Bomb load 11 x 1000 MC, 4 x 500 GP Long Delay. Primary target: Duisburg. Weather patchy cloud with gaps for bombing. Bombed at 09.04 hours from 18,000 feet. River Docks. Bombed at 09.03 hours from 19,000 feet. Built up area adjacent to East end of Bridge.

14/10/1944 NF966 JI-R Bombing Duisburg   22.49   01.32   03.21

Bomb load 1 x 4000 HC, 14 x No. 14 Clusters. Primary target: Duisburg. Weather was clear with small amount of cloud over the target. Bombed at 01.32 hours from 21,500 feet. Red T.I.s. Had two combats - one at 00.52 hours at 5022N 0340E aircraft crossed port - starboard opening fire - Rear Gunner replied - no claim. Second at 01.23 hours at 5118N 0620E - believed jet-propelled aircraft fired from below - Rear Gunner replied - no claim.

The ORBs report that M.H. Hanley was the M/U Gunner, but according to the combat report, the M/U Gunner was a F/S. Davis.

18/10/1944 NF966 JI-R Bombing Bonn 08.27   11.01   13.05

Bomb load 1 x 4000 HC, 5 x 12 x 30 - 2 x 12 x 30 modified, 9 x No. 14 Clusters. Primary target: Bonn. Weather varying cloud 2-7/10ths with break for bombing. Bombed at 11.01 hours from 20,000 feet. Built up area, believed just North of A/P.

19/10/1944 LM727 JI-S Bombing Stuttgart 21.53 01.10 03.56
Bomb load 1 x 4000 HC, 3 x 500 Clusters, 7 x 150 x 4, 1 x 90 x 4. Primary target: Stuttgart, A/P 'E' 2nd attack. Weather 10/10ths low cloud over target and all crew arrived late owing to winds not as forecast. Bombed at 01.10 hours from 22,500 feet. Position where markers had been.

21/10/1944 NF966 JI-R Bombing Flushing 11.02 12.27 13.20
Bomb load 12 x 1000 MC, 2 x 500 GP. Primary target: Flushing 'B'. Weather clear. Bombed at 12.27 hours from 8,000 feet. A/P.

22/10/1944 PB482 JI-P Bombing Neuss 13.11 15.56 17.19
Bomb load 1 x 4000 HC, 14 x No. 14 Clusters. Primary target: Neuss. Weather 10/10ths cloud over target. Bombed at 15.56 hours from 18,000 feet following aircraft 'O'.

25/10/1944 LM727 JI-S Bombing Essen 13.17 15.39 17.12
Bomb load 1 x 4000 HC, 6 x 1000 MC, 6 x 500 GP. Primary target: Essen. Weather over target 10/10ths low cloud, with one clear patch which appeared to fill up later in the attack. Bombed at 15.39 hours from 23,000 feet. Yellow flares.

26/10/1944 LM717 JI-T Bombing Leverkusen 12.49 15.29 17.13
Bomb load 1 x 4000 HC, 6 x 1000 MC, 4 x 500 GP, 2 x 500 GP Long Delay. Primary target: Leverkusen. Weather over target and on route was 10/10ths cloud. Bombed at 15.29 hours from 18,000 feet on G.H.

28/10/1944 LM685 JI-Q Bombing Cologne 13.09 15.46 17.38
Bomb load 1 x 4000 HC, 12 x 500 lb clusters, 2 x 150 x 4. Primary target: Cologne. Weather clear over target. Bombed at 15.46 hours from 20,000 feet. Visual.

30/10/1944 LM275 JI-M Bombing Wesseling 09.03 12.01 13.24
Bomb load 1 x 4000 HC, 15 x 500 GP. Primary target: Wesseling. Weather was 10/10ths cloud - tops about 7,000 feet. Bombed at 12.01 hours from 18,000 feet on G.H.

02/11/1944 LM717 JI-T Bombing Homberg 11.25 14.09 15.32
Bomb load 1 x 4000 HC, 6 x 1000 ANM59, 6 x 500 MC. Primary target: Homberg. Weather variable cloud but clear for bombing. Target obscured by pall of smoke rising to 10,000 feet. Bombed at 14.09 hours from 19,000 feet. Upwind edge of smoke.

04/11/1944 PB482 JI-P Bombing Solingen 11.21 14.07 15.51
Bomb load 1 x 4000 HC, 6 x 1000 ANM59, 4 x 500 GP, 2 x 500 MC (L/Delay), 3 Flares. Primary target: Solingen. Weather 8-10/10ths cloud. Bombed at 14.07 hours from 21,000 feet on upwind edge of red flares.

21/11/1944 PB142 JI-O Bombing Homberg 12.34 15.07 16.35
Bomb load 1 x 4000 HC, 15 x 500 GP, 1 Red-Green Flare. Primary target: Homberg. Weather about 5/10ths cloud but clear for bombing. Bombed at 15.07 hours from 21,000 feet on bomb bursts South of Red T.I.s.

23/11/1944 PB419 JI-N Bombing Nordstern 13.02 15.20 17.17

Bomb load 1 x 4000 HC, 15 x 500 GP, 1 Red flare with Green stars. Primary target: Nordstern, Gelsenkirchen Oil refineries. Weather 10/10ths cloud. Bombed at 15.20 hours from 20,500 feet on G.H.

27/11/1944 PB142 JI-O Bombing Cologne 12.25 15.06 16.45

Bomb load 1 x 4000 HC, 15 x 500 GP, 1 Flare. Primary target: Cologne, Marshalling Yards. Weather patchy cloud. Bombed at 15.06 hours from 21,000 feet on G.H.

29/11/1944 PB142 JI-O Bombing Neuss 02.50 05.29 06.55

Bomb load 1 x 4000 HC, 6 x 1000 MC, 4 x 500 GP, 4 x 250 T.I.s. Primary target: Neuss. Weather 10/10ths cloud over target but the glow of fires was seen through cloud. Bombed at 05.29 hours from 19,000 feet on G.H.

02/12/1944 PB142 JI-O Bombing Dortmund 12.57 14.58 17.00

Bomb load 13 x 1000 HC, 1 Red/Green flare. Primary target: Dortmund, Benzol plant. Weather 10/10ths cloud. Bombed at 14.58 hours from 20,000 feet with G.H. Leader.

04/12/1944 LM627 JI-R Bombing Oberhausen 11.40 14.07 15.55

Bomb load 1 x 4000 HC, 15 x 500 GP, 1 Flare. Primary target: Oberhausen, Built up area. Weather 10/10ths cloud. Bombed at 14.07 hours from 20,000 feet on G.H.

05/12/1944 LM724 JI-H Bombing Hamm 09.01 11.30 13.38

Bomb load 1 x 4000 HC, 6 x 500 ANM58, 7 x 500 GP, 2 x 500 GP Long Delay, 1 Flare. Primary target: Hamm. Weather 10/10ths cloud over target, but otherwise varying from 6-10/10ths. Bombed at 11.30 hours from 20,000 feet on G.H.

08/12/1944 NF966 JI-R Bombing Duisburg 08.30 11.05 12.47

Bomb load 13 x 1000 ANM59, 1 Red/Green flare. Primary target: Duisberg. Weather 10/10ths cloud. Bombed at 11.05 hours from 20,000 feet on G.H.

11/12/1944 PB482 JI-P Bombing Osterfeld 08.41 11.04 11.50

Bomb load 4 x 1000 ANM65, 9 x 1000 ANM59, 1 Flare. Primary target: Osterfeld. Weather 10/10ths cloud, tops 16,000 feet. Bombed at 11.04 hours from 20,000 feet on G.H.

16/12/1944 PB142 JI-O Bombing Siegen 11.35 15.01 16.48

Bomb load 1 x 4000 HC, 14 x No. 14 clusters. Primary target: Siegen. Weather very bad on route with icing and cloud. Bombed at 15.01 hours from 18,000 feet on leading G.H. aircraft.

Sgt. W.L. Harradine Navigator from that day.

27/12/1944 PD325 A2-L Bombing Rheydt 12.55 15.00 16.30

Bomb load 7 x 1000 MC, 6 x 500 GP, 3 x 250 GP. Primary target: Rheydt, Marshalling yards. Weather clear. Bombed at 15.00 hours from 20,000 feet. Centre of Red T.I.s.

28/12/1944 PD325 A2-L Bombing Cologne 12.15 15.06 16.45

Bomb load 1 x 4000 HC, 10 x 500 GP, 6 x 250 GP. Primary target: Koln Gremberg, Marshalling yards. Weather 10/10ths cloud or fog. Bombed at

15.06 hours from 20,000 feet on bunch of Red/Green flares.

31/12/1944 LM685 JI-K Bombing Vohwinkle 11.25 14.43 16.20

Bomb load 1 x 4000 HC, 3 x 1000 M65, 2 x 500 M58, 2 x 500 ANM64, 2 x 500 GP, 2 x 500 GP L/Delay. Primary target: Vohwinkel. Weather 10/10ths cloud on approaching target although the target itself was clear. Bombed at 14.43 hours from 20,000 feet on leading G.H. aircraft.

F. Stephens was later killed in a flying accident on 27th September 1946 at Craigton Hill, Milngavie, Scotland. The aircraft, a Scottish Airways de Havilland Dragon Rapide G-AFFF, crashed with the loss of all on board. He is buried in Soham, Cambridgeshire.

S/L. Derek William Arthur Stewart DFC

132602 (1330605) S/L. Derek William Arthur Stewart, DFC. Pilot.
F/S. R.J. "Bob" Armit. A/Bomber.
137605 (1552887) F/O. Kenneth Stewart Murdoch. Navigator.
F/S. J.F.B. Redfern. WOP/AG.
1347006 F/S. Patrick Francis "Jock" Moakler. MU/Gunner.
148013 (1867527) F/O. DermotGerald Rearden. R/Gunner.
Sgt. R.J. Baker. F/Engineer.

Note: Contrary to the ORBs, in his logbook P.F. Moakler always noted his position as M/U Gunner.

24/05/1944 LL677 A2-E Bombing Boulogne 00.15 01.15 02.05

Bomb load 9 x 1000 MC, 1 x 1000 GP, 1 x 1000 ANM, 4 x 500 GP. Primary target: Boulogne, Gun Battery. Clear over the target. Bombed green T.I.s at 01.15 hours from 8,500 feet. Received impression that attack was to North of the aiming point. Good uneventful trip. Flak moderate.

27/05/1944 LL726 A2-H Bombing Boulogne 00.15 01.15 01.55

Bomb load 7 x 1000 MC, 4 x 1000 ANM, 4 x 500 GP. Primary target: Boulogne Gun Batteries. Clear at target. Bombed at 01.15 hours from 7,000 feet. Attack thought good. Many fighter flares seen.

31/05/1944 LL716 A2-G Bombing Trappes 00.10 01.58 04.22

Bomb load 8 x 1000 MC, 8 x 500 MC. Primary target: Trappes. Clear at target. Bombed at 01.58 hours from 8,500 feet. Whole area illuminated by flares. Good concentrated bombing. Route good but long. At 02.04 hours whilst on the way home, a twin-engined aircraft was seen shooting down a four engined aircraft.

05/06/1944 LL716 A2-G Bombing Ouistreham 03.51 05.10 06.37

Bomb load 9 x 1000 MC and 2 x 500 MC. Primary target: Ouistreham. There was 5/10 broken cloud. Bombed at 05.10 hours from 10,500 feet. No visual possible. Three red T.I.s were seen in line but could not bomb these because of other aircraft, therefore bombed slightly to east of them.

07/06/1944 LL716 A2-G

Bombing Massy Palaiseau 00.27 02.14 04.20

Bomb load 18 x 500 MC. Primary target: Massy Palaiseau, Marshalling Yards. Ground haze, 10/10 cloud above. Bombed on Master Bomber's instructions at 02.14 hours from 5,500 feet. Haze prevented visual. Route quiet until Paris area was reached. Flak slight. Was approached from below by a JU88 but evaded successfully.

F/S. Patrick Francis "Jock" Moakler. (courtesy Stewart Moakler)

11/06/1944 LL716 A2-G Bombing Nantes 23.41 02.46 05.08

Bomb load 16 x 500 GP, 2 x 500 LD. Primary target: Nantes. Bombed at 02.46 hours from 8,000 feet in 10/10ths cloud as instructions of Master Bomber not heard. L/F moderate, occasional bursts of H/F.

12/06/1944 LL716 A2-G Bombing Gelsenkirchen 23.00 01.07 03.02

Bomb load 1 x 4000 HC, 12 x 500 GP, 4 x 500 MC. Primary target: Gelsenkirchen. Clear over target. Bombed red and green T.I.s at 01.07 hours from 16,000 feet. Very good fires and palls of smoke seen. Lancaster coned over target on bombing.

15/06/1944 LL716 A2-G Bombing Valenciennes 23.07 00.41 02.57

Bomb load 16 x 500 GP, 2 x 500 MC. Primary target: Valenciennes. Cloud in layer 10/10ths at 10,000 feet, clear below. Bombed at 00.41 hours from 9,000 feet, bunch of red and green markers close together allowing a two second overshoot as instructed by Master Bomber. No results seen except markers dying out.

17/06/1944 LL716 A2-G Bombing Montdidier 01.11 02.56 04.31

Bomb load 16 x 500 GP, 2 x 500 ANM64 GP. Primary target: Montdidier. Bombed at 02.56 hours from 10,000 feet glow of red T.I.s. 02.56 Master Bomber said retain height, immediately after we had bombed he instructed return to base. Flying bombs seen over London area.

21/06/1944 LL716 A2-G Bombing Domleger 17.55 19.29 20.41

Bomb load 18 x 500 MC. Primary target: Domleger near Abbeville, V-1

613

flying bomb launch site. There was 10/10ths cloud. Reached target area 19.29 hours at 13,000 feet. No attack made as no T.I.s seen under Master Bomber's instructions. Jettisoned safe 8 x 500 MC at 19.39 hours from 10,000 feet at 5020N 0125E.

23/06/1944 LL716 A2-G Bombing L'Hey 22.57 00.15 01.33

Bomb load 11 x 1000 MC, 4 x 500 GP. Primary target: L'Hey, Flying bomb installations. There was 10/10ths cloud. Bombed at 00.15 hours from 9,000 feet edge of glow of T.I.s as instructed by Master Bomber. Bang on. No trouble.

27/06/1944 LL716 A2-G Bombing Biennais 23.24 01.10 02.23

Bomb load 16 x 500 GP, 2 x 500 ANM 64 GP. Primary target: Biennais, Flying bomb installations. There was 10/10ths cloud. Bombed at 01.10 hours from 12,000 feet, red glow.

10/07/1944 LL716 A2-G Bombing Nucourt 04.26 06.03 07.42

Bomb load 11 x 1000 ANM 65, 4 x 500 GP. Primary target: Nucourt, Constructional works. Bombed at 06.03 hours from 16,000 feet on Gee.

12/07/1944 HK572 JI-T Bombing Vaires 18.15 19.58 21.38

Bomb load 18 x 500 GP. Primary target: Vaires, Marshalling yards. Target reached at 19.58 hours, Master Bomber said bomb yellow T.I.s, followed almost immediately by Abandon mission.

15/07/1944 LL716 A2-G Bombing Chalons s/Marne 21.41 01.31 04.11

Bomb load 18 x 500 GP. Primary target: Chalons sur Marne, Railway centre. Weather clear below 8,000 feet. Bombed at 01.31 hours from 8,500 feet, white T.I.s as instructed by Master Bomber. Good route. Should be an excellent attack.

17/07/1944 LL716 A2-G Bombing Paris x x x

This is believed to be the crew composition as 514 Squadron Operational Record Books (ORBs) do not make any mention of this raid, reported as a DNCO (Did Not Complete) mission in some 514 Sqn crew's logbooks and in that of P.F. Moakler as follows: "OPS BOMBING PARIS D.N.C.O. (RECALLED)"

Bomber Command War Diaries stated for that day: "Flying Bomb Sights - 132 Aircraft, 72 Halifaxes, 28 Stirlings, 20 Lancasters, 11 Mosquitos, and 1 Mustang attacked 3 V-weapons sites without loss. Few details of results were recorded."

18/07/1944 LL716 A2-G Bombing Emieville 04.20 06.07 07.47

Bomb load 11 x 1000 MC, 4 x 500 GP. Primary target: Emieville, Troop concentration. Weather clear. Bombed at 06.07 hours from 9,000 feet yellow T.I.s. One pall of smoke left. Very good concentration.

18/07/1944 LL716 A2-G Bombing Aulnoye 22.31 00.56 02.07

Bomb load 18 x 500 GP. Primary target: Aulnoye, Railway junction. Weather clear. Bombed at 00.56 hours from 9,000 feet, green T.I.s. Two large explosions at 00.56 hours.

F/O. Leslie John William Sutton, DFC

1st Crew

186268 (1289916)   F/O. Leslie John William "Les" Sutton, DFC. Pilot.
A416222   F/O. Sydney Graham McRostie, RAAF. A/Bomber.
A425592 P/O. Charles Louis "Lou" Brimblecombe, RAAF. Navigator.
159964 (1605076) F/O. Kenneth Dundonald Bailey.   WOP/AG. 13 ops.
Sgt. W.H.E. Gray. WOP/AG. 6 ops.
J19707 F/O.   Frank Harold Rowan, DFC, RCAF. WOP/AG. 3 ops.
F/S. W. Carr.   MU/Gunner.
F/S. J.A. Wood.   R/Gunner.
Sgt. J.B. Robertson.   F/Engineer.

07/06/1944 LL727 A2-C   Bombing Massy Palaiseau 00.27 x 02.55
Bomb load 18 x 500 MC. Primary target: Massy Palaiseau, Marshalling
Yards. Set on fire by a night fighter over the target area, the crew escaped from
their attacker, received further flak damage before finally being shot down by
the JU88 of Hptm. Herbert Lorenz of 1/NJG2. Crashed 08/06/1944 02.55
hours at St-Eusoye (Oise), 20 km NE of Beauvais.
From his normal crew, only W/O. L.J.W. Sutton did this mission as 2nd
Pilot with F/O. L. Greenburgh's crew.
F/O. L. Greenburgh Evaded, W/O. L.J.W. Sutton Evaded, F/S. R. Fox
Evaded, F/S. E.G. Rippingale Evaded.
There is an unconfirmed report that Sgt. F.J. Carey evaded until captured on
6th July 1944 and was interned in Camp L7. PoW No. 384, with Sgt. F.
Collingwood, PoW No. 80059.
F/S. R.J. Woosnam initially evaded until captured on 3rd July 1944 and
interned in Camp L7, PoW No. 424.
The sole casualty, F/S G.H. Stromberg who died of his injuries in Amiens
Hospital on 9th June 1944, is buried at Amiens St-Pierre Cemetery.
25/10/1944 LM684JI-O Bombing Essen 13.12   15.43   17.11
Bomb load 1 x 4000 HC, 6 x 1000 MC, 6 x 500 GP. Primary target: Essen.
Weather over target 10/10ths low cloud, with one clear patch which appeared
to fill up later in the attack. Bombed at 15.43 hours from 20,000 feet. Red
flares.
From his normal crew, only P/O. L.J.W. Sutton did this mission as 2nd Pilot
with F/O. A.D.J. Uffindell's crew.
30/10/1944 NF968 JI-L Bombing Wesseling   09.00 12.04 13.46
Bomb load 1 x 4000 HC, 15 x 500 GP. Primary target: Wesseling. Weather
was 10/10ths cloud - tops about 7,000 feet. Bombed at 12.04 hours from
16,000 feet on G.H.
F/O. K.D. Bailey WOP/AG until 28/12/44.

02/11/1944 PB419 JI-N Bombing Homberg   11.12   14.07   15.53

Bomb load 1 x 4000 HC, 6 x 1000 ANM59, 6 x 500 MC. Primary target: Homberg. Weather variable cloud but clear for bombing. Target obscured by pall of smoke rising to 10,000 feet. Bombed at 14.07 hours from 19,000 feet. Visually and Green flares.

04/11/1944 PD265 JI-G Bombing Solingen 11.23   14.08   16.02

Bomb load 1 x 4000 HC, 6 x 1000 ANM59, 4 x 500 GP, 2 x 500 MC (L/Delay), 3 Flares. Primary target: Solingen. Weather 8-10/10ths cloud. Bombed at 14.08 hours from 19,500 feet on G.H.

06/11/1944 PB482 JI-P Bombing Koblenz 16.54   19.31   22.08

Bomb load 1 x 4000 HC, 12 x 500 Clusters, 2 x 250 T.I.s. Primary target: Koblenz. Weather clear over target. Bombed at 19.31 hours from 17,500 feet on centre of Red and Green T.I.s.

20/11/1944 LM734 JI-U Bombing Homberg   12.41   15.16   17.16

Bomb load 1 x 4000 HC, 7 x 500 MC, 9 x 500 GP. Primary target: Homberg. Weather 10/10ths cloud over target. Bombed at 15.16 hours from 20,000 feet on G.H. Leader. Landed at Woodbridge.

27/11/1944 PB767 JI-G Bombing Cologne 12.20   15.05   16.56

Bomb load 1 x 4000 HC, 15 x 500 GP, 1 Flare. Primary target: Cologne, Marshalling Yards. Weather patchy cloud. Bombed at 15.05 hours from 19,500 feet. Visually.

30/11/1944 PB142 JI-O Bombing Osterfeld   10.47   13.12   14.49

Bomb load 1 x 4000 HC, 15 x 500 GP, 1 Red/Green flare. Primary target: Osterfeld, Coking plant. Weather 10/10ths cloud. Bombed at 13.12 hours from 19,600 feet on G.H.

02/12/1944 LM728 JI-T Bombing Dortmund   13.02   14.56   17.02

Bomb load 13 x 1000 HC, 1 Red/Green flare. Primary target: Dortmund, Benzol plant. Weather 10/10ths cloud. Bombed at 14.56 hours from 19,200 feet on G.H.

12/12/1944 PB482 JI-P Bombing Witten 11.19 14.05   15.53

Bomb load 1 x 4000 HC, 5 x 500 GP, 6 x 500 ANM58, 4 x 500 ANM64, 1 Flare. Primary target: Witten. Weather 10/10ths cloud, tops 14/16,000 feet. Bombed at 14.05 from 20,000 feet on G.H.

15/12/1944 PB482 JI-P Bombing Siegen ca.11.30 x ca.14.00

Between 11.19 to 11.36 hours 19 aircraft took off to attack Siegen. At 12.30 hours, all aircraft recalled as fighters were unable to take off. All aircraft and landed from 13.39 to 14.18.

Operation only reported in ORBs "Summary of events", no trace in ORBs "Detail of Work carried out - Details of sorties of flight". Reported in C.L. Brimblecombe's logbook.

16/12/1944 PB482 JI-P Bombing Siegen 11.24 x 14.05

Bomb load 1 x 4000 HC, 5 x 1000 MC, 7 x 500 GP, 1 Flare. Primary target: Siegen. Weather very bad on route with icing and cloud. Aircraft returned early, icing, and after circling for about an hour had insufficient fuel to for trip.

Jettisoned safe at 5213N 0322E 13.03 hours 9,000 feet.

23/12/1944 LM724 JI-H Bombing Trier 11.43 14.30 16.06

Bomb load 1 x 4000 HC, 10 x 500 GP, 2 x 250 GP, 4 x 250 T.I. Red. Primary target: Trier. Weather clear over target. Bombed at 14.30 hours from 18,000 feet on Red T.I.

28/12/1944 LM627 A2-H Bombing Cologne 12.16 15.06 16.58

Bomb load 7 x 1000 MC, 5 x 500 GP, 4 x 250 Red T.I.s. Primary target: Koln Gremberg, Marshalling yards. Weather 10/10ths cloud or fog. Bombed at 15.06 hours from 20,000 feet on G.H.

06/01/1945 PB426 JI-D Bombing Neuss 15.50 18.47 20.18

Bomb load 1 x 4000 HC, 2 x 500 ANM58, 12 x 500 ANM64, 1 flare. Primary target: Neuss. Weather 8-10/10ths cloud over target. Bombed at 18.47 hours from 20,000 feet on G.H.

Sgt. W.H.E. Gray WOP/AG until 16/01/45.

07/01/1945 PB426 JI-D Bombing Munich 18.58 x 23.19

Bomb load 1 x 4000 HC, 7 x 500 clusters. Primary target: Munich. Weather 10/10ths cloud over target 6-8,000 feet with a thin layer altitude 16,000 feet. Abortive sortie. Returned early with inter-communication unserviceable, 1 x 4000 HC jettisoned at 5020N 0050E.

11/01/1945 PB142 JI-G Bombing Krefeld x x x

Bomb load 1 x 4000 HC, 10 x 500 ANM64, 4 x 250 GP, 1 Flare. Primary target: Krefeld. Weather 10/10ths cloud above and below. Visibility poor.

Failed to take off - Radiator change necessary.

13/01/1945 PB426 JI-D Bombing Saarbrucken 11.48 15.23 17.37

Bomb load 1 x 4000 HC, 10 x 500 ANM58 or 64, 4 x 250 GP. Primary target: Saarbrucken. Weather 3-5/10ths cloud, tops 4/5,000 feet. Bombed at 15.23 hours from 20,000 feet on G.H. All aircraft on this operation were diverted on return to Exeter as weather at base was unfit to land.

15/01/1945 PB419 JI-J Bombing Lagendreer 11.37 15.00 16.37

Bomb load 1 x 4000 HC, 10 x 500 ANM64, 4 x 250 GP, 1 Flare. Primary target: Lagendreer. Weather 10/10ths cloud. Bombed at 15.00 hours from 19,000 feet on G.H.

16/01/1945 NG203 JI-C Bombing Wanne-Eickel 23.19 02.24 04.10

Bomb load 1 x 4000 HC, 10 x 500 ANM58, 4 x 250 GP. Primary target: Wanne-Eickel, Benzol plant. Weather 10/10ths thin low cloud. Bombed at 02.24 hours from 20,000 feet on G.H.

22/01/1945 NN773 JI-K Bombing Hamborn (Duisburg) 17.00 20.05 21.45

Bomb load 1 x 4000 HC, 7 x 500 ANM58 or 64, 2 x 500 GP (L/Delay), 3 x 250 GP. Primary target: Hamborn, Thyssen works. Weather over target clear and almost as bright as day. Bombed at 20.05 hours from 20,500 feet on Red T.I.s.

F/O. F.H. Rowan WOP/AG until 29/01/45.

28/01/1945 LM275 JI-C Bombing Cologne-Gremberg 10.22 14.12

15.55

Bomb load 1 x 4000 HC, 10 x 500 ANM64, 2 x 500 GP, 3 x 250 GP. Primary target: Koln- Gremberg, Marshalling yards. Weather 10/10ths cloud en route clearing on approach to target where visibility was good and nil cloud. Bombed at 14.12 hours from 20,000 feet on G.H.

29/01/1945 LM275 JI-C Bombing Krefeld 10.15 13.57 15.29

Bomb load 1 x 4000 HC, 10 x 500 ANM64, 2 x 500 GP, 3 x 250 GP. Primary target: Koln - Gremberg, Marshalling yards. Weather 10/10ths cloud en route clearing on approach to target where visibility was good and nil cloud. Bombed at 13.57 hours from 20,000 feet on G.H.

2nd Crew

186268 (1289916) F/O. Leslie John William "Les" Sutton, DFC. Pilot.
J40946 F/O. Joe A. Speare, RCAF. A/Bomber.
J40778 F/O. Ray Bertram Hilchey, RCAF. Navigator.
1892880 F/S. John Goodworth Brittain. WOP/AG.
J95536 (R279032) P/O. Orval Clare "Shorty" Evers, RCAF. MU/Gunner.
J95531 (R271567) P/O. Robert MacPherson "Bob" Toms, RCAF. R/Gunner.
939832 F/S. Alfred "Alf" McMurrugh. F/Engineer.
191303 (1386380)
P/O. William Allwright Frederick Winkworth. 2nd Pilot. 13/02/1945
47481 (523741)
F/L. Arthur Charles Southward. 2nd Pilot. 05/03/1945
A417741 O35137
F/O. Peter Geoffrey Dean, RAAF. 2nd Pilot. 07/03/1945
F/O. A. Hugues. 2nd Pilot. 21/03/1945
163588 (1802442)
F/O. Norman James "Jim" Eley. 2nd Pilot. 04/04/1945

01/02/1945 NN773 JI-K Bombing Munchen-Gladbach 13.13 16.33 18.13

Bomb load 1 x 4000 HC, 14 x No. 14 Clusters. Primary target: Munchen-Gladbach, Marshalling yards. Bombed at 16.33 hours from 19,000 feet on G.H. aircraft.

02/02/1945 NN773 JI-K Bombing Wiesbaden 20.41 23.41 02.35

Bomb load 1 x 4000 HC, 12 x 500 GP, 4 x 250 GP. Primary target: Wiesbaden. Weather 10/10ths cloud, winds very erratic. Bombed at 23.41 hours from 20,000 feet on Gee fix.

08/02/1945 NN773 JI-K Bombing Hohenbudberg 03.32 06.24 08.06

Bomb load 1 x 4000 HC, 2 x 500 MC, 4 x 250 GP, 4 x 500 GP, 6 x 500

L to R: O.C. Evers, A. McMurrugh, R.B. Hilchey, J.G. Brittain, R.M. Toms, J.A. Speare, L.J.W. Sutton

ANM64. Primary target: Hohenbudberg, Marshalling yards. Weather 8/10ths cloud over target. Bombed at 06.24 hours from 19,000 feet slightly to port of Red T.I. Many bomb bursts around Red T.I.s which appeared concentrated.

13/02/1945 NN773 JI-K Bombing Dresden 21.42 01.33 06.15

Bomb load 1 x 4000 HC, 7 x No. 14 Clusters. Primary target: Dresden. Weather 5/10ths cloud over target. Bombed at 01.33 hours from 20,000 feet on Red and Green T.I.s.

P/O. W.AF. Winkworth 2nd Pilot that day.

14/02/1945 NN773 JI-K Bombing Chemnitz 20.16 00.34 04.30

Bomb load 1 x 4000 HC, 8 x No. 14 Clusters. Primary target: Chemnitz. Weather 8-10/10ths cloud, tops 15-16,000 feet with occasional breaks. Bombed at 00.34 hours from 20,300 feet on Red/Green star flare.

25/02/1945 LM285 JI-A Bombing Kamen 09.37 12.47 15.14

Bomb load 1 x 4000 HC, 9 x 500 ANM64, 2 x 500 MC, 4 x 250 GP. Primary target: Kamen. Weather 6-8/10ths cloud. Bombed at 12.47 hours from 19,100 feet on G.H. Leader.

27/02/1945 NN773 JI-K Bombing Gelsenkirchen 10.58 14.27 16.28

Bomb load 1 x 4000 HC, 2 x 500 MC (L/D 37B), 9 x 500 ANM64, 4 x 250 GP. Primary target: Gelsenkirchen (Alma Pluts) Benzin plant. Weather 10/10ths cloud, 6/10,000 feet tops. Bombed at 14.27 hours from 19,300 feet on leading aircraft.

01/03/1945 NN773 JI-K Bombing Kamen 11.46 15.05 17.40

Bomb load 1 x 4000 HC, 11 x 500 ANM64, 2 x 500 MC L/Delay 37. Primary target: Kamen, Coking plant. Weather 10/10ths cloud. Bombed at 15.05 hours from 18,800 feet on leading aircraft.

619

05/03/1945 NN773 JI-K Bombing Gelsenkirchen 10.24   14.07   15.52

Bomb load 1 x 4000 HC, 12 x 500 ANM64. Primary target: Gelsenkirchen, Benzol plant. Weather 10/10ths cloud over target with cirrus cloud at bombing height. Bombed at 14.07 hours from 20,800 feet on G.H. Leader.

F/L. A.C. Southward 2nd Pilot that day.

07/03/1945 NN773 JI-K Bombing Dessau 16.55 22.06   02.17

Bomb load 1 x 500 ANM64, 15 x No. 15 Clusters. Primary target: Dessau. Weather 5 to 10/10ths thin cloud. Bombed at 22.06 hours from 20,000 feet on Red/Green flares.

F/O. P.G. Dean 2nd Pilot that day.

09/03/1945 NN773 JI-K Bombing Datteln 10.33 14.00   15.52

Bomb load 1 x 4000 HC, 13 x 500 ANM64, 2 x 500 MC L/Delay 37. Primary target: Datteln, Synthetic oil plant. Weather 10/10ths cloud, tops 8-10,000 feet. Bombed at 14.00 hours from 21,000 feet on G.H. Leader.

12/03/1945 NN773 JI-K Bombing Dortmund   12.54   16.56   18.47

Bomb load 1 x 4000 HC, 13 x 500 ANM64. Primary target: Dortmund. Weather 10/10ths cloud over target, tops 6/10,000 feet. Bombed at 16.56 hours from 18,900 feet on G.H. Leader.

14/03/1945 NG142 JI-J Bombing Heinrichshutte 13.13 x 18.20

Bomb load 1 x 4000 HC, 12 x 500 ANM64. Primary target: Heinrichshutte, Hattingen Steel works & Benzol plant. Weather 10/10ths cloud, tops 7/12,000 feet. Returned early. Farthest point reached 5050N 0615E. Jettisoned 1 x 4000 HC, 11 x 500 ANM64 at 5215N 0310E at 15.33 hours from 17,500 feet. 1 x 500 ANM64 brought back to base.

18/03/1945 LM627 JI-D Bombing Bruchstrasse 11.54 15.04   17.15

Bomb load 1 x 4000 HC, 13 x 500 ANM64, 2 x 500 MC. Primary target: Bruchstrasse, Coal mine & coking plant. Weather 10/10ths cloud, tops 6 - 12,000 feet. Bombed at 15.04 hours from 19,000 feet on G.H. Leader.

21/03/1945 NN773 JI-K Bombing Munster 09.31   13.07   15.11

Bomb load 1 x 4000 HC, 13 x 500 ANM64, 2 x 500 MC. Primary target Munster Viaduct and Marshalling Yards. Weather cloud nil to 2/10ths. Bombed at 13.07 hours from 18,000 feet on G.H. aircraft and visually. Aircraft hit by flak. Bomb bursts on junction and along tracks.

F/O. A. Hugues 2nd Pilot that day.

04/04/1945 ME535 JI-G Bombing Merseburg (Leuna) 18.37   22.45
02.40

Weather 5-10/10ths cloud, and 10/10ths over Merseburg. Bombed primary target. Bomb load 1 x 4000 HC and 6 x 500 ANM64. 9/10 cloud. Bombed on single red T.I. at 22.45 hours from 20,000 feet. Glow seen through cloud appeared to be fires. Excessive vibration caused star inner on return. Numerous dummies over a large area including Magdeberg. Bombing rather scattered.

F/O. N.J. Eley 2nd Pilot that day.

13/04/1945 NN782 JI-K Bombing Kiel   20.23   23.27   01.48

Bomb load 1 x 4000 HC and 12 x 500 ANM64. Primary target: Kiel, Docks & ship yards. Weather 10/10ths cloud low and thin. Bombed on Red T.I.s at 23.27 hours from 19,500 ft. Brought back 1 x 500 ANM64 due to hang up. Good concentration of marking, were near first to bomb, too early to assess.

F/O. Alfred Edward Sweeney

54909 (573980) F/O. Alfred Edward "Todd" Sweeney.   Pilot.
W/O.   Joseph Eley.   A/Bomber.
137538 (866622) F/L. Charles Sydney Huddart.   Navigator.
172736 (1290831)   F/O. Roy Victor Weavers.   WOP/AG.
185658 (1810652)   F/O. William Albert Monk.   MU/Gunner.
185657 (1810654)   F/O. Alfred Henry Monk.   R/Gunner.
W/O.   Thomas Smith Redpath.   F/Engineer.

Passengers: 28/06/1945, 03/07/1945, 05/07/1945, 28/07/1945.

Date Aircraft Duty Target Up Drop Down

25/06/1945 ME351 JI-U Post Mortem   Special mission   09.53   x 15.52

28/06/1945 ME364 JI-P Baedeker Tour over Continent 12.54 x 17.08

Passengers: Sgt. Phillips, Sgt. Fox, Cpl. Rowlands, Sgt. Holloway, LAC. Duffield.

03/07/1945 ME359 JI-T Baedeker Tour over Continent 09.59 x 14.25

Passengers: Sgt. Lindley, Cpl. Bayes, LAC. Holland, Sgt. Stone (WAAF), LACW. Dodman.

05/07/1945 ME364 JI-P Baedeker Tour over Continent 15.22 x 19.30

Passengers: LACW. Evans, LACW. McAnney, LAC. Cooper, Cpl. Cannel, Sgt. Verlander.

W/O. Thomas Smith Redpath, F/Engineer. (courtesy Georgene Bentley (Redpath))

28/07/1945 ME351 JI-U Baedeker Tour over Continent 09.55 x 14.08

Passengers: Cpl. Rennix, Cpl. Jubb, Cpl. Hailey, LAC. Johnston, LAC. Michael.

F/S. Horace Albert Symmons

1319783 F/S. Horace Albert Symmons. Pilot.
1392790 Sgt. Eric George Rippingale. A/Bomber.
1559148 Sgt. David Kellock. Navigator.
1485703 Sgt. John Edward "Johnny" Richardson. WOP/AG.
1851507 Sgt. William Charles "Bill" Udell. MU/Gunner.
1565396 Sgt. Robert Calder "Bert" Guy. R/Gunner.
1624295 Sgt. Eric Charles Coles. F/Engineer.
978968 F/S. Norman Hall. 2nd Pilot. 27/01/1944

L to R (back): E.C. Coles, R.C. "Bert" Guy, J.E. "Johnny" Richardson. L to R (front): D. Kellock, H.A. Symmons, W.C. "Bill" Udell, E.G. Rippingdale. (courtesy Mark Rippingdale, Jean & Sinclair Ronald)

20/12/1943 LL653 A2-F Bullseye   x x x

Reported in ORB summary. Sortie not detailed. Also reported in E.G. Rippingale's logbook with flying time 2.50 hours.

"Bullseye" was a mock bombing raid that was close to being a combat simulation, complete with searchlights and flares. A Bullseye exercise was a simulated night bombing operation against a 'target' town or city designed to give crews the experience of an operational sortie but without crossing into enemy territory. Crews would be given a flight plan to follow and a target to simulate bombing.

29/12/1943 LL674 A2-D Bombing Berlin 17.34 20.20 00.09

Bomb load 1 x 2000, 40 x 30 incendiaries, 900 x 4 incendiaries, 90 x 4 incendiaries. Primary target: Berlin. There was 10/10 cloud. Bombed at 20.20 hours at 19,000 ft. Glow of fires seen below clouds. Route markers seen on way put. Photo taken.

27/01/1944 LL674 A2-D Bombing Berlin 17.10 x 20.20

Aborted the operation and overran the runway and crashed into a ditch on return. Touched down at 20.20 hours. No injuries reported. Apart from the names of the 'two pilots', taken from the accident record card, no crew details were recorded in ORBs as it omits all reference to the incident. Such omissions, although not unique, are relatively uncommon.

F/S. H.A. Symmons was Captain and F/S. N. Hall 2nd pilot.

Both the Rear Gunner R.C. Guy and the Bomb Aimer E.G. Rippingale noted simply in their logbooks "OPS E/R PRANGED BERLIN".

Rest of crew his believed to be the usual one of H.A. Symmons.

The RAF Waterbeach ORB notes that F/S. Symmons was sick, and the aircraft was flown home by F/S Norman Hall who, fortuitously, was flying as 'second dickie'. On landing LL674 overran the runway, coming to rest in a ditch with the wing obstructing the Ely road, fortunately without injury to the crew or passing motorists. Aircraft SOC 26/02/1944.

F/L. Russel Frank Talbot

63477 (1375830) F/L. Russel Frank Talbot. Pilot.
Sgt. F.W. Rae.   A/Bomber.
F/S. A.B. Carthew.   Navigator. 2 ops.
F/S. L.F. Matsell. Navigator. 2 ops.
F/S. R. Jacobs.   WOP/AG.
Sgt. R.B. Rowcliffe. MU/Gunner.
Sgt. F. Stephenson.   R/Gunner.
Sgt. P.S. Hartigan. F/Engineer.

Passengers: 30/06/1945, 09/07/1945, 19/07/1945.

25/06/1945 RE117 A2-D Post Mortem Special mission 09.54 x 16.01
F/S. A.B. Carthew was Navigator that day and on the next operation.
30/06/1945 RA602 A2-H Baedeker Tour over Continent 12.35 x 16.54
Passengers: LAC. Whittle, LAC. Brown, AC. Dyke
09/07/1945 ME529 A2-B Baedeker Tour over Continent 09.45 x 14.16
F/S. L.F. Matsell was Navigator from that day.
Passengers: Cpl. Law, LAC. Ritz, AC. Riley, Sgt. Grimes, Sgt. Hanns.
19/07/1945 RE158 A2-J Baedeker Tour over Continent 09.16 x 14.00
Passengers: Sgt. Bye, Cpl. Wheeler, LAC. Brind, LACW. Judd, LACW. Leggett.

F/O. Alfred William Tasker

186502 (1128949)   F/O. Alfred William Tasker.   Pilot.
F/S. D. Sutton.   A/Bomber.
F/S. C.F. Jeffery.   Navigator.
Sgt. H.G. Gale.   WOP/AG.
R215675   F/S. T.R. Satterthwaite, RCAF.   MU/Gunner. 32 ops.
Sgt. F.C. Vincent.   MU/Gunner. 7 ops.
R214447   F/S. J. Chaytor, RCAF.   R/Gunner. 30 ops.
F/S. E.D. Dixon.   R/Gunner. 1 op.
Sgt. J.A. Walker.   R/Gunner. 7 ops.
Sgt. V. Graham.   F/Engineer.
153592 (1582441)   F/O. Thomas Harry Pashley. 2nd Pilot. 27/02/1945.
196041 (1581940)   P/O. Harry Glyn Huyton. 2nd Pilot. 09/04/1945.

Passengers: 07/05/1945, 08/06/1945, 17/06/1945, 14/07/1945, 23/07/1945.

11/12/1944 PA186 A2-G Bombing Osterfeld 08.46 11.05 12.52
    Bomb load 1 x 4000 HC, 13 x 500 GP, 2 x 500 MC. Primary target: Osterfeld. Weather 10/10ths cloud, tops 16,000 feet. Bombed at 11.05 hours from 20,000 feet on G.H. Leader.
    From his normal crew, only F/O. A.W. Tasker did this mission as 2nd Pilot with P/O. W. McD. Coyle's crew.
12/12/1944 PA186 A2-G Bombing Witten 11.15 14.03 16.15
    Bomb load 1 x 4000 HC, 14 x 500 Clusters. Primary target: Witten. Weather 10/10ths cloud, tops 14/16,000 feet. Bombed at 14.03 hours from 20,000 feet on G.H. Leader.
    F/S. T.R. Satterthwaite MU/Gunner until 24/05/45 except for 17/05/45.
    F/S. J. Chaytor R/Gunner until 24/05/45, except for 05/01, 07/05 & 17/05/45.
16/12/1944 NG141 A2-J Bombing Siegen 11.27 15.00 17.10
    Bomb load 1 x 4000 HC, 5 x 1000 MC, 7 x 500 GP. Primary target: Siegen. Weather very bad on route with icing and cloud. Bombed at 15.00 hours from 17,000 feet. Red flares.
23/12/1944 PD324 A2-B Bombing Trier 11.55 14.32 16.20
    Bomb load 1 x 4000 HC, 10 x 500 GP, 6 x 250 GP. Primary target: Trier. Weather clear over target. Bombed at 14.32 hours from 18,000 feet on centre of the town.
27/12/1944 LM727 A2-F Bombing Rheydt 12.47 14.59 16.55
    Bomb load 7 x 1000 MC, 6 x 500 GP, 3 x 250 GP. Primary target: Rheydt, Marshalling yards. Weather clear. Bombed at 14.59 hours from 20,000 feet. Red T.I.s.
28/12/1944 NG142 A2-C Bombing Cologne 12.26 15.06 17.05

Bomb load 1 x 4000 HC, 10 x 500 GP, 6 x 250 GP. Primary target: Koln Gremberg, Marshalling yards. Weather 10/10ths cloud or fog. Bombed at 15.06 hours from 21,000 feet on leading G.H. aircraft.

02/01/1945 NG142 A2-C Bombing Nuremburg 15.37 19.37 23.03

Bomb load: 1 x 4000 HC, 7 x 500 Clusters - Primary target: Nuremburg. Weather clear. Bombed at 19.37 hours from 18,500 feet. Red T.Is.

05/01/1945 NG142 A2-C Bombing Ludwigshafen 11.40 15.12 17.50

Bomb load 1 x 4000 HC, 10 x 500 ANM58 or 64, 2 x 500 GP. Primary target: Ludwigshafen, Marshalling yards. Weather clear over target. Bombed 15.12 hours from 19,000 feet on leading aircraft. Aircraft hit by flak - nose and tail damaged.

F/S. E.D. Dixon R/Gunner that day.

07/01/1945 PD334 A2-D Bombing Munich 19.21 22.40 02.52

Bomb load 1 x 4000 HC, 7 x 500 clusters - Primary target: Munich. Weather 10/10ths cloud over target 6-8,000 feet with a thin layer altitude 16,000 feet. Bombed at 22.40 hours from 19,500 feet on Red and Green flares.

11/01/1945 PB906 A2-B Bombing Krefeld   12.00 15.12 16.37

Bomb load 1 x 4000 HC, 2 X 500 ANM58, 8 x 500 ANM64, 4 x 250 GP. Primary target: Krefeld. Weather 10/10ths cloud above and below. Visibility poor. Bombed at 15.12 hours from 19,800 feet on G.H. Leader.

13/01/1945 LM627 A2-H Bombing Saarbrucken   12.00 x 14.50

Bomb load 1 x 4000 HC, 10 x 500 ANM58 or 64, 4 x 250 GP. Primary target: Saarbrucken. Weather 3-5/10ths cloud, tops 4/5,000 feet. Abortive sortie. Aircraft returned early with W/T unserviceable. Jettisoned bombs at 5010N 0005E.

16/01/1945 NN772 A2-C Bombing Wanne-Eickel 23.18 02.23 04.35

Bomb load 1 x 4000 HC, 10 x 500 ANM58, 4 x 250 GP. Primary target: Wanne-Eickel, Benzol plant. Weather 10/10ths thin low cloud. Bombed at 02.23 hours from 20,000 feet on Red and Green markers.

28/01/1945 NN772 A2-C Bombing Cologne 10.35 14.13 16.02

Bomb load 1 x 4000 HC, 10 x 500 ANM64, 2 x 500 GP, 3 x 250 GP. Primary target: Koln - Gremberg, Marshalling yards. Weather 10/10ths cloud en route clearing on approach to target where visibility was good and nil cloud. Bombed at 14.13 hours from 20,000 feet on G.H. Leader.

19/02/1945 ME359 JI-N Bombing Wesel 12.56 16.34 19.35

Bomb load 1 x 4000 HC, 6 x 500 MC, 6 x 500 ANM64, 4 x 250 GP. Primary target: Wesel. Weather over target 5-7/10ths cloud. Bombed at 16.34 hours from 18,000 feet on G.H. Landed at Moreton in Marsh.

22/02/1945 ME359 JI-N Bombing Osterfeld   11.57 15.57 18.07

Bomb load 1 x 4000 HC, 9 x 500 ANM64, 2 x 500 MC, 4 x 250 GP. Primary target: Osterfeld, Coking ovens. Weather at target clear, but hazy. Attacked secondary target at 5135N 0636E. Bombed at 15.57 hours from 16,600 feet. Landed at Woodbridge.

25/02/1945 NG203 A2-C Bombing Kamen   09.32 12.47 14.55

Bomb load 1 x 4000 HC, 9 x 500 ANM64, 2 x 500 MC, 4 x 250 GP. Primary target: Kamen. Weather 6-8/10ths cloud. Bombed at 12.47 hours from 19,500 feet on G.H. Leader.

27/02/1945 PD389 A2-J Bombing Gelsenkirchen 11.00   14.28   16.25

Bomb load 1 x 4000 HC, 2 x 500 MC (L/D 37B), 9 x 500 ANM64, 4 x 250 GP. Primary target: Gelsenkirchen (Alma Pluts) Benzin plant. Weather 10/10ths cloud, 6/10,000 feet tops. Bombed at 14.28 hours from 19,500 feet on G.H.

F/O. T.H. Pashley 2nd Pilot that day.

10/03/1945 ME336 JI-S Bombing Gelsenkirchen 12.15   15.36   17.23

Bomb load 1 x 4000 HC, 13 x 500 ANM64, 2 x 500 MC. Primary target: Gelsenkirchen. Weather 10/10ths cloud at target, tops 8,000 feet. Bombed at 15.36 hours from 18,500 feet on G.H. Blue Puffs well together.

11/03/1945 ME364 JI-P Bombing Essen 11.25   15.25   17.15

Bomb load 1 x 4000 HC, 13 x 500 ANM64, 2 x 500 MC, 1 Skymarker Blue Puff. Primary target: Essen, Marshalling yards. Weather 10/10ths cloud, tops 7/8000 feet. Bombed at 15.25 hours from 19,000 feet on G.H.

14/03/1945 NG203 A2-C   Bombing Heinrichshutte 13.20   16.40   18.53

Bomb load 1 x 4000 HC, 11 x 500 ANM64, 1 Skymarker Red Puff. Primary target: Heinrichshutte, Hattingen Steel works & Benzol plant. Weather 10/10ths cloud, tops 7/12,000 feet. Bombed at 16.40 hours from 18,500 feet on G.H.

21/03/1945 ME387 JI-N Bombing Munster 09.27   13.08   15.10

Bomb load 1 x 4000 HC, 13 x 500 ANM64, 2 x 500 MC, 1 Skymarker Blue Puff. Primary target Munster Viaduct and Marshalling Yards. Weather cloud nil to 2/10ths. Bombed at 13.08 hours from 18,500 feet on G.H. 6   Blue smoke puffs seen well together.

27/03/1945 ME387 JI-N Bombing Hamm Sachsen 10.28 14.03   15.56

Bomb load 1 x 4000 HC, 13 x 500 ANM64, 2 x 500 MC. Primary target: Hamm Sachsen, Benzol plant. Weather 10/10ths cloud. Bombed at 14.03 hours at 18,200 feet on G.H. Leader.

09/04/1945 ME387 JI-N Bombing Kiel   19.40   22.39   01.27

Bombed primary target: Kiel, Submarine Buildings Yards. Weather clear with slight haze. Bomb load 1 x 4000 HC and 12 x 500 ANM64. Bombed at 22.39 hours from 20,000 feet on centre of Green T.I.s as per M.B.s instructions. Harbour identified visually. Two large explosions at 22.37 hours and 22.37½ hours. Marking and bombing concentrated both A/Ps receiving attention. Fires seen one hour after leaving.

P/O. H.G. Huyton 2nd Pilot that day.

22/04/1945 ME336 JI-S Bombing Bremen   15.22   18.42   21.04

Bomb load 1 x 4000 HC, 2 x 500 MC, 14 x 500 ANM64. Primary target: Bremen, in support of Troop concentration. Weather on approaching target 4 - 5/10ths cloud. Bombed on G.H. at 18.42 hours from 18,500 ft. Satisfactory G.H. run. Pall of smoke over area. Tail plane B/A compartment holed by flak.

Good raid.

29/04/1945 ME358 JI-O Manna The Hague 12.32 13.49 15.10

Dropping area: The Hague. Weather broken cloud above and clear below. Dropped 5 packs on red T.I.s and white cross through broken cloud, at 13.49 hours. Cheering and waving crowds lining all streets. Excellent trip 3/4 weather poor.

02/05/1945 ME336 JI-S Manna The Hague 10.58 12.19 13.24

Dropping area The Hague. Weather over dropping zone clear below cloud for the first arrivals changing later to heavy showers which marred visibility. Dropped 5 panniers on Red T.I.s and White Cross at 12.19 hours. Slight rain. Excellent delivery - Usual cheering crowds as reception committee.

07/05/1945 ME336 JI-S Manna The Hague 12.20 13.46 14.50

Dropping area The Hague. Dropped 4 Packs visual on White Cross at 13.46 hours. Clear, cloud above. Same as usual. Bags well together on airfield. Dropping zone could be seen 3 miles away, but spurts of dust rising from the ground.

No Rear Gunner that day.

Passenger: LAC. Brown.

09/05/1945 ME363 JI-R Exodus Juvincourt - Dunsfold 07.03 x 14.26

Outward 2.04 hours. Collected 24 POWs. Homeward 2.29 hrs. Engine trouble delayed departure from Juvincourt.

11/05/1945 ME358 JI-O Exodus Juvincourt - Tangmere 11.15 x 18.01

Duration 3.42. Outward 1.40 hours. Collected 24 ex POWs. Homeward 2.02 hours. No comment.

14/05/1945 RE140 JI-H Exodus Juvincourt - Oakley 10.14 x 15.27

Duration 3.50 hours. Outward 1.40 hours. Collected 24 POWs. Homeward 2.10 hours. Organisation OK.

17/05/1945 JI-J Exodus Brussels - Westcott 10.58 x 15.15

Duration 2 hrs 20 mins. Out 1 hr 5 mins. In 1 hr 15 mins. 10 Belgian refugees taken over to Brussels. No POWs available. Everything satisfactory.

Sgt. F.C. Vincent was MU/Gunner that day and Sgt. J.A. Walker R/Gunner.

19/05/1945 RE123 A2-K Exodus Brussels - Oakley 11.52 x 17.38

Duration 3 hrs 13 mins. Out 1 hr 18 mins. In 1 hr 55 mins. 10 Belgian refugees to Brussels. 24 POWs all military evacuated.

23/05/1945 ME363 JI-R Exodus Brussels - Oakley 12.01 x 17.41

Duration 3.25 hours. Out 1.15 hours. In 2.10 hours. 9 Belgian refugees returned to Brussels. 24 ex POWs evacuated. All O.K.

24/05/1945 ME363 JI-R Exodus Brussels 11.58 x 17.10

Duration 2.22 hours. Out 1.10 hours. In 1.12 hours. 10 Belgian refugees to Brussels.

25/05/1945 NN782 JI-K Exodus Brussels 12.41 x 15.55

Duration 3.14 hours. Out 1.03 hours. In 1.11 hours. 10 Belgian refugees taken to Brussels. No POWs. No troubles.

From that day Sgt. F.C. Vincent was MU/Gunner and Sgt. J.A. Walker

627

R/Gunner.
26/05/1945 ME366 JI-S Exodus Brussels - Ford 11.55 x 18.36
Duration 3.17 hours. Out 1.02 hours. In 2.15 hours. 6 Belgian refugees to Brussels. 24 ex POWs all military brought back.
08/06/1945 RA599 JI-L Baedeker Tour over Continent 14.57 x 19.19
Passengers: G/Capt. G. Rutter, F/O. S. Simmon, Sgt. R. Gilman, F/Lt. J. Buswell, Cpl. J. Stafford.
17/06/1945 ME387 JI-N Baedeker Tour over Continent 10.00 x 13.59
Passengers: F/O. Chatfield, Cpl. Bishop, Cpl. Wauncott, LAC. Phillips.
14/07/1945 ME387 JI-N Baedeker Tour over Continent 09.45 x 14.05
Passengers: W/O. Montgomery, LAC. Sanabury, AC. Hughes, ACW. Seed, ACW. Pe???le.
23/07/1945 RA599 JI-L Baedeker Tour over Continent 15.03 x 19.17
Bomber Command personnel ranks and initials not given.
Passengers: Borman, Pierce, Painter, Hunt, Goldsmith.

F/L. Lloyd Charles Alexander Taylor

A425812 F/L. Lloyd Charles Alexander Taylor, RAAF. Pilot.
A426708 F/S. Cecil Keith Thomas, RAAF. A/Bomber.
1483346 Sgt. James Frederick Vincent. Navigator.
A422083 F/S. Stanley William Newman, RAAF. WOP/AG.
158285 F/O. Frederick Brearley "Brea" Hill. MU/Gunner.
2210653 Sgt. Richard Gill. R/Gunner.
568729 Sgt. Alan Roderick. F/Engineer.
182344 (740534) W/O. Cyril Ernest Williams, DFC, AFC. 2nd Pilot.
24/05/1944.

09/04/1944 LL697 JI-E Bombing Villeneuve St Georges 21.56 00.01
01.57
Bomb load 8 x 1000 lb bomb, 6 x 500 lb bomb. Primary target: Villeneuve Marshalling Yards. There was no cloud, visibility good. Bombed at 00.01 hours from 13,500 feet. Some bomb bursts seen. No visible identification. 1 large fire seen and many bomb bursts. Markers clearly seen. Route satisfactory.
10/04/1944 DS842 JI-F Bombing Laon 01.17 03.38 05.19
Bomb load 9 x 1000, 4 x 500 lb bomb. Primary target: Laon. Weather was clear. Bombed at 03.38 hours from 11,000 feet. Bomb bursts seen in vicinity of T.I.s. Gee u/s. Good attack. Route satisfactory.
18/04/1944 LL697 JI-E Bombing Rouen 22.20 00.48 03.06

L to R (back): S.W. Newman, F.B. Hill, C.K. Thomas. L to R (front): R. Gill, L.C.A. Taylor, J.F. Vincent. (courtesy Belgian Aviation History Association)

Bomb load 8 x 1000 MC, 2 x 1000 GP, 5 x 500 lb bomb. Primary target: Rouen. Weather was clear. Bombed at 00.48 hours from 12,500 feet. Group of markers seen N of river. M of C instructed to bomb on Southern markers. T.I.s rather scattered for the size of the target. M of C talked too much. Route good.

20/04/1944 LL697 JI-E Bombing Cologne 00.06 02.15 04.35

Bomb load 1 x 8000 lb bomb, 24 x 30, 216 x 4, 24 x 4 lb incendiaries. Primary target: Koln. There was 10/10 cloud. Bombed at 02.15 hours from 20,000 feet. Saw only 3 red flares which were scattered and soon disappeared through cloud.

22/04/1944 LL697 JI-E Bombing Dusseldorf 23.07 01.30 03.16

Bomb load 1 x 2000 lb bomb, 84 x 30, 1050 x 4 incendiaries. Primary target: Dusseldorf. There was slight haze. Bombed at 01.30 hours from 19,000 feet. River visual. Markers seemed bang on, fires starting. Attack seemed very scattered, a lot of jettisons seen on the way into the target. Broken oil pipe Mid Upper Turret going out making turret u/s.

24/04/1944 LL697 JI-E Bombing Karlsruhe 22.24 00.48 03.57

Bomb load 1 x 1000 lb bomb, 1026 x 4, 114 x 4, 108 x 30 lb incendiaries. Primary target: Karlsruhe. Weather was cloudy. Bombed at 00.48 hours from 15,000 feet. Fires were well concentrated. No trouble on route. Good attack.

26/04/1944 DS813 JI-H Bombing Essen 22.56 01.32 03.24

Bomb load 1 x 2000 lb bomb, 84 x 30, 945 x 4, 105 x 4 lb incendiaries. Primary target: Essen. There was very light scattered cloud. Bombed at 01.32 hours from 18,000 feet. T.I.s concentrated. Incendiaries fell in area marked. A well concentrated raid. Route good.

01/05/1944 LL652 JI-C Bombing Chambly   22.50   00.23   01.59

Bomb load 10 x 1000, 5 x 500 lb bombs. Primary target: Chambly. There was no cloud. Bombed at 00.23 hours from 8,000 feet. Green markers seen to be off the target. Fires could be seen in target area. Emergency intercom. used, commentator not heard, so bombed on visual. Many bombs seen to burst in the yards. Explosion seen at 00.22 hours.

10/05/1944 LL652 JI-C Bombing Courtrai 22.10   23.27   00.25

Bomb load 7 x 1000 GP, 7 x 1000 MC. Primary target: Courtrai. Slight haze over target, but red T.I.s and white flares seen. Bombed at 23.27 hours from 10,500 feet on yellow T.I.s as instructed by Master Bomber. Flares slightly scattered, but target seen visually. Attack thought to be successful. Some fires observed. Route good and defences negligible.

19/05/1944 LL652 JI-C Bombing Le Mans 22.32   00.25   02.43

Bomb load 4 x 1000 USA, 5 x 1000 MC, 1 x 1000 GP, 4 x 500 GP. Primary target: Le Mans. Cloud base 8,000 feet at target but clear below. Bombed markers at 00.25 hours from 7,500 feet, and bomb burst seen. Was at target too early to form an opinion as to the effectiveness of the bombing.

22/05/1944 LL652 JI-C Bombing Dortmund   22.42   00.49   02.48

Bomb load 1 x 2000 lb, bomb, 96 x 30, 810 x 4, 90 x 4 incendiaries. Primary target: Dortmund. Clear conditions over target. Bombed red and green markers at 00.49 hours from 17,000 feet. Bombing seemed accurate if markers correctly placed, but some severe undershoots noticed. Large explosion seen to North of aiming point. Fighter flares seen on whole route out to the target.

24/05/1944 LL652 JI-C Bombing Boulogne   00.10   01.13   02.00

Bomb load 9 x 1000 MC, 1 x 1000 GP, 1 x 1000 ANM, 4 x 500 GP. Primary target: Boulogne, Gun Battery. Clear over target. Bombed at 01.13 hours from 7,500 feet. Uneventful trip. Attack considered good but some overshoots were noticed.

W/O. Cyril Ernest Williams 2nd Pilot that day.

27/05/1944 LL652 JI-C Bombing Aachen 00.31 x x

Bomb load 7 x 1000 MC, 4 x 1000 ANM, 4 x 500 MC. Aircraft missing.

All crew KIA. Shot down 28th May 1944 by a night-fighter and crashed at Ophasselt (Oost-Vlaanderen), some 5 km N of Geraardsbergen, where they are all buried in the Communal Cemetery.

P/O.   Noel William Faulkner Thackray

A409973 P/O. Noel William Faulkner "Bill" Thackray. R.A.A.F. Pilot.
A415482 F/S. John Russel "Jack" Moulsdale, RAAF.   A/Bomber.
642170 Sgt. Edward Leo Humes.   Navigator.   6 ops.
1579592 Sgt. P.C. Davies.   Navigator. 11 ops.
1575442 Sgt. Patrick "Jock" Hughes.   WOP/AG.
A424001 F/S. Clement Herbert Henn, RAAF.   M/U. Gunner. 16 ops.
542541 Sgt. Douglas Kenny.   M/U. Gunner. 1 op.
A424363 F/S. Reginald Ernest "Reg" Bromley, RAAF. R/Gunner.
1832773 Sgt. Clive Walter Banfield.   F/Engineer.
A410039 P/O. Walter Evan Chitty, RAAF.   2nd Pilot. 22/03/1944.

11/11/1943 DS817 JI-P Gardening   La Tranche   17.50 x 23.13
Aircraft carried 2 x G710, 2 x D404. Primary area La Tranche. Did not drop owing to Navigational error.
Sgt. E.L. Humes Navigator until 24/12/1943.
Sgt. D. Kenny M/U Gunner that day.

L to R (top): Noel William Faulkner Thackray, John Russel Moulsdale.

L to R (bottom): Reginald Ernest Bromley, Clement Herbert Henn.

25/11/1943 DS824 JI-U Gardening SW France 17.40 x 00.40

Bomb load 4 Veg. Primary area S.W. France. 10/10 cloud, Tops 17,000 feet along whole route. Came down to 24,000 feet. 4 Veg planted as ordered. Diverted to Exeter.

F/S. C.H. Henn M/U. Gunner from that day.

02/12/1943 DS736 JI-L Bombing Berlin 17.09 20.20 23.41

Bomb load 1 x 4000, 40 x 30 incendiaries, 650 x 4 incendiaries, 70 x 4 incendiaries. Primary target: Berlin. 6/10 cloud. Bombed at 20.20 hours, 20,000 feet. Almost collided with another Lancaster which passed within 3 yards over target area. Flak caused several holes in wings and bomb bay.

16/12/1943 LL627 JI-U Bombing Berlin 16.53 20.07 00.12

Bomb load 1 x 2000, 5 x 30 incendiaries, 7 x 4 incendiaries. Primary target: Berlin. 10/10 cloud over target. Bombed at 20.07 at 20,300 ft. Good red glow seen through cloud. A good trip. Had combat with enemy aircraft. Landed at Downham Market.

24/12/1943 LL627 JI-U Bombing Berlin 00.24 04.17 08.15

Bomb load 1 x 8000. Primary target: Berlin. 4/10 cloud below. Ground and markers seen. Bombed at 04.17 hrs at 20,000 ft. Big area concentrated fires burning well. Photo flash brought back, found on floor of a/c when WOP went back just before target. Came N of track on route home before entering coast to 10/10 cloud and a desire to avoid other a/c area bases. Very satisfactory sortie. Leipzig burning nicely.

20/01/1944 LL627 JI-U Bombing Berlin 16.22 19.39 23.56

Bomb load 1 x 4000, 32 x 30, 540 x 4, 60 x 4 incendiaries. Primary target: Berlin. There was 10/10 cloud. Bombed at 19.39 hours at 20,000 ft on main concentration of flares.

Sgt. P.C. Davies Navigator until 30/03/1944.

27/01/1944 LL703 JI-L Bombing Berlin 17.59 x 20.08

Bomb load 1 x 4000, 32 x 30, 450 x 4, 90 x 4 incendiaries. Returned early. Farthest point reached 5317N 0312E. Poor engine performance. Load jettisoned.

28/01/1944 DS816 JI-O Bombing Berlin 00.06 03.27 08.40

Bomb load 1 x 4000 lb bomb, 24 x 30, 180 x 4, 90 x 4 incendiaries. Primary target: Berlin. There was 10/10 cloud, tops 7,000 with gaps. Bombed at 03.27 hours at 20,000 ft. During run in large part of sky lit up by flash of big explosion. Route markers P.Q.R. seen, very useful. Attack appears to have been well concentrated. Large glow of fires seen through cloud.

30/01/1944 DS823 JI-M Bombing Berlin 17.24 x 19.31

Bomb load 1 x 2000 lb bomb, 1 x 500 lb bomb, 90 x 4, 48 x 30 incendiaries. Returned early. Farthest point reached 5330N 0320E. Burst Oil pipe Rear Turret. Load jettisoned.

15/02/1944 LL731 JI-U Bombing Berlin 17.40 21.30 00.13

Bomb load 1 x 2000, 10 x 1000 lb bomb, 24 x 30, 900 x 4 incendiaries. Primary target: Berlin. There was 10/10 cloud. Bombed at 21.30 hrs. At 20,000 ft. Intensity of flak indicated that attack was good. No fighters seen.

19/02/1944 LL731 JI-U Bombing Leipzig 23.56 04.02 06.34

Bomb load 1 x 4000 lb bomb, 32 x 30, 510 x 4, 90 x 4 incendiaries. Primary target: Leipzig. There was 10/10 cloud with tops 5/8000 ft. Bombed at 04.02 hours at 20,000 ft. Cloud prevented visual but reddish glow showed through as we left. Best concentration of sky markers I have ever seen. The sea turning point out the sky was black with kites orbiting with Nav lights on - seen for 8/10 minutes. If markers were on the raid should be first class.

07/03/1944 LL731 JI-U Bombing Le Mans 19.32 21.59 00.07

Bomb load 10 x 1000, 4 x 500 lb bombs. Primary target: Le Mans. There was 10/10 cloud with tops 6,000 feet. Gee fix and fires reflected through cloud. Bombed at 21.59 hours from 13,000 feet. Large explosions seen from own bombs. Orange glow seen and occasional bombs bursting.

18/03/1944 LL731 JI-U Bombing Frankfurt 19.32 22.04 00.54

Bomb load 1 x 8000 lb bomb, 32 x 30 incendiaries. Primary target: Frankfurt. Weather was clear. Ground markers and shape of river seen. Bombed at 22.04 hours from 20,000 feet. Concentrated fires round T.I.s especially to the North. A concentrated attack.

22/03/1944 LL731 JI-U Bombing Frankfurt 18.42 22.04 00.51

Bomb load 1 x 8000 lb bomb, there was 6/10 thin cloud. Primary target: Frankfurt. Bombed at 22.04 hours from 20,000 feet. Good fires coinciding with position of markers with a slight undershoot. A good attack, fires seen from over 100 miles. Route OK.

P/O. W.E. Chitty 2nd Pilot that day.

24/03/1944 LL731 JI-U Bombing Berlin 18.36 22.31 02.08

Bomb load 1 x 1000 lb bomb, 88 x 30, 810 x 4, 90 x 4 incendiaries. Primary target: Berlin. There was 5/10 cloud. Bombed at 22.31 hours from 20,000 feet. Few cookies seen to explode, fires starting. Route markers would have been helpful, P and F winds were not.

30/03/1944 LL731 JI-U Bombing Nuremburg 22.24 01.25 06.29

Bomb load 1 x 1000 lb bomb, 96 x 30, 810 x 4, 90 x 4 incendiaries. Primary target: Nuremberg. There was 10/10 cloud. Bombed at 01.25 hours from 20,000 feet. Many fires seen. Route markers and spoof attack, Cologne seen. Attack considered successful although T.I.s rather scattered. Glow of fires seen for 150 miles after leaving target.

11/04/1944 LL639 JI-R Bombing Aachen 21.01 x x

Bomb load 10 x 1000, 2 x 500 lb bomb, 160 x 4, 20 x 4 incendiaries. Aircraft missing.

Sgt. E.L. Humes Navigator that day.

Crashed near St Truiden. On the way back to England the plane was hit by flak which set the right outer engine on fire. As the blazing engine fell away which made the aircraft uncontrollable, the pilot ordered the crew to abandon the aircraft. Only one of the seven crewmembers survived, Sgt E.L. Humes (PoW in camp L3). The bomber crashed in a field near Molenbeersel

(Belgium), 9 km NW of Merseyck.

Funeral services for the six airmen killed were conducted at St-Truiden in Belgium 15th April 1944. They have since been subsequently re-interred in the Heverlee War Cemetery.

P/O. Stanley Philip Iltid Thomas

156310 (1320091) P/O. Stanley Philip Iltid Thomas.   Pilot.
1334913 Sgt. Ronald William Fontaine.   A/Bomber.
1612568 Sgt. James Lawrence Brent. Navigator.
1048366 Sgt. Frank Thomas.   WOP/A.G.
1818663 Sgt. Henry Alan Lucas.   MU/Gunner.
A415979 F/S. Bernard Smith "Bernie" Haines, RAAF. R/Gunner.
1332705 Sgt. Harry Herbert Stagg.   F/Engineer.

11/11/1943 DS738 JI-J Gardening   La Tranche 17.36 x 00.48

Aircraft carried 2 x G710, 2 x D404. Primary area La Tranche. No cloud. Visibility good.

18/11/1943 DS784 JI-C Bombing Mannheim 17.24 x x

Bomb load 1 x 4000, 16 x 30, 720 x 4. Primary target Mannheim. Aircraft failed to return.

Cause of loss not established. Crashed at Assesse (Namur) 16 km SE of

L to R (back): B.S. Haines, F. Thomas, H.H. Stagg, H.A. Lucas. L to R (back): R.W. Fontaine, S.P.I. Thomas, J.L. Brent. (courtesy Bernard Haines via Rene Romainville)

Namur, Belgium. There are two German night fighter pilots who made claims in the area: Hptm. Evers from Stab/I/NJG6 who claimed a kill at 22.10hrs and Lt. Peters from Stab I/NJG4 at 22.11hrs.

Those killed are buried in Assesse Communal Cemetery. P/O. S.P.I. Thomas KIA, Sgt. H.H. Stagg KIA, Sgt. J.L. Brent KIA, Sgt. R.W. Fontaine KIA, Sgt. F. Thomas KIA. Sgt. H.A. Lucas Evaded, F/S. B.S. Haines, RAAF PoW.

Sgt. H.A. Lucas successfully evaded and reached Brussels, where he remained until the city was liberated in September 1944. F/S. B.S. Haines at first escaped, then was captured on 20th November 1943 and was interned in Camp 4B, PoW No.267163. Eventually escaped after three unsuccessful attempts, re-captured by the Soviets, he was finally liberated by the Americans.

F/O. Victor Reginald Thompson

188927 (1612704)   F/O. Victor Reginald Thompson. Pilot.
Sgt. E.J. Weir.   A/Bomber.
Sgt. H.I. Padfield.   Navigator.
Sgt. R.L. Smith.   WOP/AG.
Sgt. G.J. Slevin.   MU/Gunner. 12 ops.
Sgt. A. Cooper.   R/Gunner.
F/S. R. MacKenzie.   F/Engineer.

Passengers: 04/05/1945, 09/06/1945, 17/06/1945, 23/07/1945, 25/07/1945, 26/07/1945

17/03/1945 ME422 JI-Q Bombing August Viktoria 12.04 15.03   17.20
Bomb load 1 x 4000 HC, 13 x 500 ANM64, 2 x 500 MC. Primary target: Auguste Viktoria, Marl-Hüls coal mine. Weather 10/10ths cloud, tops and contrails up to 23,000 feet. Bombed at 15.03 hours from 21,500 feet on G.H.
According Sieloff's logbook: "F/O. Thompson 2nd Dicky" and target "Huls",
From his normal crew, only P/O. V.R. Thompson did this mission as 2nd Pilot with F/O. C.A. Dunn's crew.
18/03/1945 NN781 A2-B   Bombing Bruchstrasse   11.42   15.04   17.23
Bomb load 1 x 4000 HC, 13 x 500 ANM64, 2 x 500 MC. Primary target: Bruchstrasse, Coal mine & coking plant. Weather 10/10ths cloud, tops 6 - 12,000 feet. Bombed at 15.04 hours from 19,000 feet on leading aircraft.
04/04/1945 ME336 JI-S Bombing Merseburg (Leuna) 18.44   22.49
02.39
Weather 5 - 10/10ths cloud, and 10/10ths over Merseburg. Bombed primary Target: Merseburg. Bomb load 1 x 4000 HC, 6 x 500 ANM64. Bombed on

Red T.I. with Green stars slightly to port at 22.49 hours from 20,000 feet.

Large orange explosion seen. One large green explosion very bright area 2 miles square appeared to be in flames. Dropping of flares was late. On first run no markers to bomb on, orbited and made second run when markers had been dropped. A.P.I. U/S.

From his normal crew, only P/O. V.R. Thompson did this mission as 2nd Pilot with F/O. R. Jones' crew.

18/04/1945 ME363 JI-R Bombing Heligoland 09.59 13.08 15.32

Bomb load 6 x 1000 MC, 10 x 500 ANM64. Primary target: Heligoland, Naval base. Weather no cloud, slight haze. Bombed on yellow T.I.s. and M/Bs instructions at 13.08 hours from 18,500 ft. Our bombs bursts in the middle of the inferno. Only northern tip of island visible.

20/04/1945 ME363 JI-R Bombing Regensburg 09.25 13.56 17.00

Bomb load 16 x 500 ANM64. Primary target: Regensburg. Weather clear over target and whole route. Bombed visually at 13.56 hours from 19,000 feet. Split up formation at release point so bombed visually on blue marker. Oil tank hit on North side of haven. Flash and much smoke. Railway bridge hit then a further tank exploded 13.58 hours. Bombing observed to be accurate on the refinery. Excellent attack.

24/04/1945 ME359 JI-T Bombing Bad Oldesloe 07.00 10.45 13.00

Bomb load 6 x 1000 ANM65, 10 x 500 ANM64. Primary target: Bad-Oldesloe, Rail and road junction and Marshalling Yards. Weather 3/10ths to nil cloud. Bombed on G.H. aircraft 514/O at 10.45 hours from 18,000 ft. Our fourth or fifth bomb caused a large orange explosion. No bomb bursts and craters were seen outside target area. Bang on.

01/05/1945 ME363 JI-R Manna The Hague 13.25 14.48 16.00

Dropping area The Hague. Weather clear over target. Dropped 5 Panniers at 14.48 hours on T.I.s and visual of racecourse. Showers of sleet over sea. Target well covered with bags, crowds of people waving flags.

04/05/1945 ME336 JI-S Manna The Hague 11.58 13.24 14.34

Dropping area The Hague. Dropped 5 panniers on Red T.I.s visual on White Cross at 13.24 hours. Clear. 10/10 cloud at 1,000. Our bags dropped on the White Cross and another a/c's load just missed. Dropping was concentrated. Many people seen round the T.I.s on the southerly dropping zone. A green very light was fired from the ground just after we dropped our load.

No Mid Upper Gunner that day.

Passenger: Cpl. Beat.

09/06/1945 ME359 JI-T Baedeker Tour over Continent 10.11 x 15.58

Passengers: F/O. J. Bailey, LAC. K. Budger, LAC. L.O. Scutt, LAC. K. Thompkins.

17/06/1945 ME363 JI-R Baedeker Tour over Continent 14.47 x 18.43

Passengers: Cpl. Fielder, LAC. Charman, LAC. Hudson, LAC. Waterman, LAC. Youeno.

01/07/1945 ME359 JI-T Post Mortem Special mission 12.04 x 17.48

05/07/1945 ME359 JI-T Post Mortem Special mission 13.10 x 18.03
23/07/1945 ME351 JI-U Baedeker Tour over Continent 15.21 x 20.02
Passengers: S/O. Condey, F/O. Kidson, Sgt. Martin, LAC. Morton, W/O. Hysten.
25/07/1945 RA599 JI-L Baedeker Tour over Continent 09.54 x 13.22
Passengers: LAC. Kershaw, LAC. Morris, LACW. Southerton, LACW. Holford.
26/07/1945 ME351 JI-U Baedeker Tour over Continent 10.39 x 14.36
Passengers: S/L. Bow, Cpl. James, LACW. Rees, LAC. Salisbury, LAC. Gautier.

F/O. Cedric Jeffrey Thomson

A417904   F/O. Cedric Jeffrey Thomson, RAAF. Pilot.
A418888   F/S. Harold Thodey, RAAF. A/Bomber.
182472 (1396812) P/O. Ronald George James "Ron" Cooper. Navigator.
A426599   P/O. Roy Edward Holdcroft, RAAF. WOP/AG.
1897052 Sgt. Derek A. Gee.   MU/Gunner.
1891250 Sgt. Gerald R. Lawrence. R/Gunner.
1430544 Sgt. G. Wadeley.   F/Engineer. 31 ops.
51707 (570208) F/O. Howard Hall. F/Engineer. 1 op.
143269 (1801437)
F/O. Ronald Frederick "Ron" Limbert, DFC. 2nd Pilot. 07/08/1944.

07/05/1944 LL733 JI-G Bombing
Nantes 00.30 03.04 05.53
Bomb load 1 x 4000, 13 x 500 lb bombs. Primary target: Nantes. Weather was clear. Bombed at 03.04 hours from 10,000 feet. Bombs appeared concentrated. Large white fire seen with smoke rising rapidly to 10,000 feet. Good raid. Route good. Monica u/s.
08/05/1944 LL733 JI-G Bombing Cap Gris Nez 22.52 23.51 00.52
Bomb load 14 x 1000 lb bombs. Primary target: Cape Gris Nez. Weather was clear with good visibility. Bombed at 23.51 hours from 8,000 feet. Numerous bomb bursts seen. A good attack, markers not seen until after bombing.

Cedric Jeffrey Thomson (AWM UK1741)

10/05/1944 LL733 JI-G Bombing Courtrai 22.07 23.24 00.47

Bomb load 7 x 1000 GP, 7 x 1000 MC. Primary target: Courtrai. Clear conditions. White flares illuminated town and red T.I.s were in approximate position of railway marshalling yards. Bombed red T.I. at 23.24 hours from 10,000 feet. Bombs appeared to burst in concentration around red T.I. which Master Bomber ordered to be bombed. A successful attack. Warned by Master Bomber to beware enemy fighters.

11/05/1944 LL733 JI-G Bombing Louvain 23.01 00.22 01.34

Bomb load 5 x 1000 GP, 5 x 1000 MC. Primary target: Louvain. Clear conditions at target but ground haze. Bombed at 00.22 hours from 8,500 feet. Very few markers seen and bomb bursts scattered. On homeward journey engaged in combat at 00.23 hours near Charleroi.

F/O. H. Hall. F/Engineer that day.

19/05/1944 LL690 JI-J Bombing Le Mans 22.14 00.26 03.03

Bomb load 4 x 1000 USA, 5 x 1000 MC, 1 x 1000 GP, 4 x 500 GP. Primary target: Le Mans. Cloudy over target. Green T.I.s bombed at 00.28 hours from 8,000 feet. Visual obtained of Marshalling Yards and markers seemed accurately placed. Seems to be a good attack. Aiming point photo achieved, spent 35mins corkscrewing to avoid fighter attacks.

21/05/1944 LL690 JI-J Bombing Duisburg 22.44 01.14 02.59

Bomb load 1x2000 lb. bomb, 120 x 30, 600 x 4 incendiaries. Primary target: Duisberg. There was 10/10 cloud at target. Bombed red T.I.s at 01.14 hours from 21,000 feet. Cloud precluded any observation being made but many bomb flashes seen. At 01.54 hours sighted an unidentified enemy aircraft (17,000 feet) which later became lost in cloud. Made two bombing runs.

22/05/1944 LL690 JI-J Bombing Dortmund x x x

Bomb load 1 x 2000 lb bomb, 96 x 30, 810 x 4, 90 x 4 incendiaries. Could not climb above 10,000 feet because of icing and therefore returned early. All bombs jettisoned safe at Rushford Range at 00.06 hours. Farthest point reached 5210N 0120E.

27/05/1944 DS822 JI-T Bombing Boulogne 00.10 01.15 02.21

Bomb load 7 x 1000 MC, 4 x 1000 ANM, 4 x 500 GP. Primary target: Boulogne Gun Batteries. Clear at target. Bombed at 01.15 hours from 8,000 feet. Concentrated attack around T.I.s and believed good. Route OK.

28/05/1944 DS822 JI-T Bombing Angers 19.05 23.58 02.10

Bomb load 5 x 1000 MC, 1 x 1000 USA, 4 x 500 MC. Primary target: Angers. Clear over target. Bombed as instructed by Master Bomber at 23.58 hours from 7,500 feet. Visual obtained of target, and good concentration of bombs around T.I.s.

30/05/1944 DS813 JI-H Bombing Boulogne 22.58 00.04 01.11

Bomb load 6 x 1000 MC, 4 x 500 MC. Primary target: Boulogne Gun Batteries. Clear over target. Bombed red T.I.s at 00.04 hours from 7,000 feet and sticks seen to burst across T.I.s. Markers well concentrated and attack thought to be successful. No trouble experienced. Flak slight.

05/06/1944 LL692 JI-A Bombing Ouistreham 03.50 05.07 06.43

Bomb load 9 x 1000 MC and 2 x 500 MC. Primary target: Ouistreham. Broken cloud at target. Obtained visual of coast and target and bombed at 05.07 hours from 9,000 feet. Unable to assess results as little to be seen for ice on the panel.

07/06/1944 LL692 JI-A Bombing Massy Palaiseau 00.20 x x

Bomb load 18 x 500 MC. Primary target: Massy Palaiseau, Marshalling Yards. Weather was clear below cloud, base at 7,500 feet. Bombed green T.I. at 02.13 hours from 6,000 feet. Bomb bursts were seen and raid was thought satisfactory. Monica was u/s. Master Bomber was clear and precise.

17/06/1944 LL697 JI-E Bombing Montdidier 01.06 x 04.36

Bomb load 16 x 500 GP, 2 x 500 ANM 64 GP. Primary target: Montdidier. Weather 10/10ths cloud. Master Bomber heard faintly giving return to Base. No attack, jettisoned 6 x 500 GP 5000N 0055E at 03.25 hours from 8,000 feet.

21/06/1944 PB142 JI-A Bombing Domleger 17.45 x 20.47

Bomb load 18 x 500 MC. Primary target: Domleger near Abbeville, V-1 flying bomb launch site. Returned to Base as instructed by Master Bomber as T.I.s were not visible. Jettisoned safe 8 x 500 MC at 19.43 hours from 12,000 feet 5013N 0123E.

23/06/1944 PB142 JI-A Bombing L'Hey 23.08 00.15 01.07

Bomb load 11 x 1000 MC, 4 x 500 GP. Primary target: L'Hey, Flying bomb installations. There was 10/10ths cloud. Bombed at 00.15 hours from 9,000 feet centre of red glow. Route trouble free, flak negligible.

24/06/1944 PB142 JI-A Bombing Rimeux 23.34 00.33 01.43

Bomb load 18 x 500 GP. Primary target: Rimeux, Flying bomb installations. Weather clear. Bombed at 00.33 hours from 9,500 feet centre of red T.I.s. Two sticks were seen burst N.W. of T.I.s. Marking seemed concentrated. Numerous searchlights, otherwise trouble free trip.

30/06/1944 PB142 JI-A Bombing Villers Bocage 18.01 20.00 21.23

Bomb load 11 x 1000 MC, 4 x 500 GP. Primary target: Villers Bocage. Weather clear. Bombed at 20.00 hours from 4,000 feet, red T.I. as instructed by the Master Bomber. Good prang. Trouble free trip. Many aircraft did not come down to 4,000 feet to bomb.

02/07/1944 PB142 JI-A Bombing Beauvoir 12.37 14.36 16.04

Bomb load 11 x 1000 MC, 4 x 500 GP. Primary target: Beauvoir, Flying bomb supply site. 5-10/10ths broken drifting cloud. Bombed at 14.36 hours from 8,000 feet on yellow T.I.s.

05/07/1944 PB142 JI-A Bombing Watten 22.48 00.07 01.10

Bomb load 11 x 1000 ANM 65, 4 x 500 GP. Primary target: Watten, Constructional works. Bombed at 00.07 hours from 8,000 feet red T.I.s.

10/07/1944 PB142 JI-A Bombing Nucourt 04.05 06.03 07.23

Bomb load 11 x 1000 ANM 65, 4 x 500 GP. Primary target: Nucourt, Constructional works. Bombed at 06.03 hours from 15,000 feet Gee Fix.

12/07/1944 PB142 JI-A Bombing Vaires 17.50 20.00 21.58

Bomb load 18 x 500 GP. Primary target: Vaires, Marshalling yards. Weather 8/10ths cloud, one thin patch. Bombed at 20.00 hours from 15,000 feet yellow T.I.s. Stream of aircraft port of track on run up to target. T.I.s clearly seen.

18/07/1944 PB142 JI-A Bombing Aulnoye 22.23 00.53 02.22

Bomb load 18 x 500 GP. Primary target: Aulnoye, Railway junction. Weather clear, slight haze. Bombed at 00.53 hours from 7,800 feet, red T.I. One stick seen to burst across eastern railway line. Should be a good attack.

20/07/1944 PB142 JI-A Bombing Homberg 23.12 01.19 02.43

Bomb load 1 x 4000 HC, 2 x 500 MC, 14 x 500 GP. Primary target: Homberg, Oil plant. Weather hazy. Bombed at 01.19 hours from 20,000 feet, red T.I.s. Bomb bursts well centred on red T.I.s. Very successful attack. Fuselage and elevators damaged by flak.

25/07/1944 PB142 JI-A Bombing Stuttgart 21.37 01.55 05.45

Bomb load 7 x 1000 MC, 4 x 500 GP. Primary target: Stuttgart. Weather 3/10ths cloud. Bombed at 01.55 hours from 20,000 feet centre of red T.I.s. Explosive bursts of flame seen in target area, bomb bursts seen across T.I.s. Made two bombing runs. Evaded searchlights and fighters while returning.

04/08/1944 PB142 JI-A Bombing Bec D'Ambes 13.16 17.59 21.11

Bomb load 8 x 1000 MC, 2 x 500 GP. Primary target: Bec d'Ambes depot. Weather clear. Bombed at 17.59 hours from 8,000 feet, oil storage tanks. Flames seen to appear near target area, together with dense black smoke up to 5/6000 feet. Some bombs fell on large ship in the river. Very successful attack. Bombs seen straggling target. Yellow flames bursting from oil tanks. Satisfactory effort. Uneventful trip.

07/08/1944 PB142 JI-A Bombing Mare de Magne 21.47 23.39 01.00

Bomb load 11 x 1000 MC, 4 x 500 GP. Primary target: Mare de Magne (just past Caen). Weather clear, slight haze. Bombed at 23.39 hours from 9,000 feet centre of red T.I.s. Bursts seen across and around T.I.s.

F/O. R.F. Limbert 2nd Pilot that day.

Mare-de-Magne: place between Caen and Fontenay le Marmion.

18/08/1944 JB228 JI-L Bombing Bremen 21.51 00.14 02.41

Bomb load 1 x 4000 HC, 96 x 30 lb incend, 1080 x 4lb incend, 120 x 4lb incend. Primary target: Bremen. Bombed at 00.14 hours from 20,000 feet, incendiary fires and red T.I.s. Numerous concentrated fires merging into one mass. Coned by searchlights.

25/08/1944 PB142 JI-A Bombing Russelsheim 20.27 00.57 04.13

Bomb load 1 x 4000 HC, 11 x 500 LB Clusters. Primary target: Russelheim. Weather clear, slight haze. Bombed at 00.57 hours from 18,000 feet, undershot red and green T.I.s. Red and green T.I.s clearly seen on both S and N banks of river. Bomb bursts seen across target.

31/08/1944 PB142 JI-A Bombing Pont-Remy 16.06 18.07 19.31

Bomb load 11 x 1000 MC, 4 x 500 GP Mk IV LD. Primary target: Pont Remy, Dump. Weather cloudy. Bombed at 18.07 hours from 16,000 feet on Leader's release of bombs. Slight flak.

03/09/1944 LM277 JI-F Bombing Eindhoven 15.00 x 17.55

Bomb load 11 x 1000 MC, 4 x 500 GP. Target: Eindhoven airfield. Returned early. Hydraulics u/s.

05/09/1944 LM277 JI-F Bombing Le Havre   17.23   19.24   20.52

Bomb load 11 x 1000 MC, 4 x 500 GP. Primary target: Le Havre. Bombed at 19.24 hours from 13,000 feet red T.I.

06/09/1944 PB142 JI-A Bombing Le Havre   16.40   18.39   19.52

Bomb load 11 x 1000 MC, 4 x 500 GP. Primary target: Le Havre. Bombed at 18.39 hours from 7,000 feet. Overshot on green T.I.s.

P/O. Robert Jack Thornton

NZ412612 P/O. Robert Jack Thornton, RNZAF. Pilot.
1323518 Sgt. George Alfred Hubbard.   A/Bomber.
153630 (1393286) F/O. Paul Bernard Bailey. Navigator.
1163754 W/O. John William Hall.   WOP/AG.
R195309 F/S. Charles L. "Charlie" Robinson, RCAF.   MU/Gunner.
545186 F/S. D.R. Burns.   R/Gunner.
1796603 Sgt. G.F. Good.   F/Engineer.

18/08/1944 LM286 A2-F   Bombing Bremen 21.38 00.23   03.06

Bomb load 1 x 4000 HC, 96 x 30 lb incend, 1080 x 4lb incend, 120 x 4lb incend. Primary target: Bremen. Weather clear. Bombed at 00.23 hours from 19,000 feet. Centre of red and green T.I.s. Fires well spread and gaining good hold. Large column of black smoke up to 15,000 feet. Should be good attack.

25/08/1944 LM285 JI-K Bombing Russelsheim 20.30 01.00   04.24

Bomb load 1 x 4000 HC, 11 x 500 LB Clusters. Primary target: Russelheim. Weather clear. Bombed at 01.00 hours from 18,000 feet, centre of red and green T.I.s. Bomb bursts seen amid T.I.s. Incendiaries seen to have been dropped before zero hour. Should be a good attack.

31/08/1944 DS842 A2-J Bombing Pont-Remy 16.13   18.11   19.40

Bomb load 11 x 1000 MC, 2 x 500 GP Mk IV LD. Primary target: Pont Remy, Dump. Weather cloudy. Bombed at 18.11 hours from 15,000 feet on Gee H Leading aircraft.

06/09/1944 LL734 A2-B   Bombing Le Havre 16.41   18.41   20.00

Bomb load 11 x 1000 MC, 4 x 500 GP. Primary target: Le Havre. Bombed at 18.41 hours from 7,000 feet, red T.I.s.

10/09/1944 LL726 A2-H   Bombing Le Havre 15.48   17.42   19.06

Bomb load 11 x 1000 MC, 4 x 500 GP. Primary target: Le Havre. Weather clear. Bombed at 17.42 hours from 10,000 feet. Undershot T.I.s red by 600 yards.

11/09/1944 DS787 A2-G   Bombing Kamen   16.11 x 18.42

Bomb load 1 x 4000 HC, 16 x 500 GP. Weather clear. Target: Kamen.

Aircraft missing.

Crashed at 18.42 hours onto a road at Lerche, 5 km from the centre of Kamen. This was the only aircraft lost on the Kamen raid and it is believed to have been hit by a bomb from another aircraft.

Four of the crew were KIA. They are buried in Reichswald Forest War Cemetery, Germany.

C.L. Robinson POW camp L6 POW No. 225530, D.R. Burns POW camp L7 POW No. 893, G.F. Good POW.

FL. acting S/L. John Godfrey Timms, DFC

119080 (1386534)   S/L. John Godfrey "Timmy" Timms, DFC. Pilot.
174890 (1431402)   F/O. Wilfred Arthur Hadley. A/Bomber.
146376 (1581749)   F/O. Kenneth Walter Hall, DFC. Navigator. 29 ops.
F/O. J. Baker.   Navigator. 2 ops.
139955 (1068058)   F/O. Edward Ellin.   WOP/AG. 26 ops.
NZ412324 F/O. Oliver Lawrence Goldsmith, DFC. WOP/AG. 3 ops.
103538 (902785) F/L. Vivian George Ivor Outen, DFC. WOP/AG. 1 op.
Sgt. C.A. Brown.   WOP/AG. 1 op.
1117683 W/O.   John Moran, DFC.   MU/Gunner.
182656 (1127881)   P/O. Edward John Rosling, DFC. R/Gunner.
1094472 Sgt. L. Hammond.   F/Engineer.
Sgt. J.A. Attwood.   2nd Pilot. 05/06/1944.

John Godfrey Timms

11/05/1944DS842 JI-F Bombing Louvain
22.50   00.18   01.50
Bomb load 5 x 1000 GP, 5 x 1000 MC. Primary target: Louvain. Thin cloud over target area. Bombed yellow and white markers at 00.18 hours from 8,000 feet. Much smoke observed but P.F.F. markers scattered. Aircraft arrived late at target.

From his normal crew, only F/L. J.G. Timms did this mission as 2nd Pilot with P/O. R. Langley's crew.

21/05/1944LL652 JI-C Bombing Duisburg
22.55   01.23   03.20
Bomb load 1 x 2000 bomb, 120 x 30 incendiaries, 600 x 4 incendiaries. Primary target: Duisburg. There was 10/10 cloud. Bombed red T.I. at 01.23 hours from 21,000 feet. Opposition thought slight and searchlights ineffective. Arrived at Duisberg at 01.11 hours and orbited twice.

F/O. K.W. Hall Navigator until 02/11/1944.

F/O. E. Ellin WOP/AG until 03/10/1944.

24/05/1944 DS842 JI-F Bombing Boulogne   00.11   01.16   02.39

Bomb load 9 x 1000 MC, 1 x 1000 GP, 1 x 1000 ANM, 4 x 500 GP. Primary target: Boulogne, Gun Battery. Clear over the target. Bombed at 01.16 hours from 8,500 feet. Bombs burst among T.I.s. No troubles. Attack thought good.

27/05/1944 DS842 JI-F Bombing Boulogne   00.11   01.17   02.05

Bomb load 7 x 1000 MC, 4 x 1000 ANM, 4 x 500 GP. Primary target: Boulogne Gun Batteries. Slight haze over target. Bombed centre of markers at 01.17 hours from 8,500 feet. Two explosions seen in target area at 01.18 hours. Attack was concentrated. Route satisfactory.

28/05/1944 DS842 JI-F Bombing Angers 18.53 23.57   02.06

Bomb load 5 x 1000 MC, 1 x 1000 USA, 4 x 500 MC. Primary target: Angers. Clear with slight haze. Bombed at 23.57 hours from 8,000 feet. Bombed as instructed by Master Bomber, bursts falling across T.I.s. Good effort. Trouble free route.

05/06/1944 DS842 JI-F Bombing Ouistreham 03.50   05.09   06.45

Bomb load 9 x 1000 MC and 2 x 500 MC. Primary target: Ouistreham. There was 5/10 cloud at target. Bombed markers at 05.09 hours from 10,000 feet. One stick was seen to overshoot but attack generally thought good. Route quiet.

Sgt. J.A. Attwood 2nd Pilot that day.

06/06/1944 DS842 JI-F Bombing Lisieux 00.19 01.35   03.09

Bomb load 16 x 500 MC tail fused and 2 x 500 MC LD. Primary target: Lisieux. Break in cloud on target. Bombed red markers at 01.35 hours from 6,000 feet and bombs seen to burst on markers. Master Bomber was unintelligible at first. Timing was difficult and success of the raid impossible to ascertain.

08/06/1944 DS842 JI-F Bombing Fougeres   21.54   00.19   02.16

Bomb load 16 x 500 GP and 2 x 500 MC LD. Primary target: Fougeres. Bombed as instructed by Master Bomber at 00.19 hours from 7,300 feet. T.I.s were scattered and a built-up area was seen to south-east of the T.I. dropped. Opposition slight. Weather as forecast.

11/06/1944 DS842 JI-F Bombing Nantes 23.48 02.50 05.17

Bomb load 16 x 500 GP, 2 x 500 LD. Primary target: Nantes. Bombed as instructed by Master Bomber at 02.50 hours from 2,400 feet. Orbited target before identifying. Obtained visual of river. Conditions hazy below cloud.

24/06/1944 ME858 JI-J Bombing Rimeux   23.23   00.33   01.56

Bomb load 18 x 500 GP. Primary target: Rimeux, Flying bomb installations. Weather clear. Bombed at 00.33 hours from 12,000 feet centre of red T.I.s. Two sticks seen to burst over red T.I.s. Trouble free route, good concentration of markers.

27/06/1944 ME858 JI-J Bombing Biennais 23.40   01.12   02.29

Bomb load 16 x 500 GP, 2 x 500 ANM 64 GP. Primary target: Biennais,

Flying bomb installations. There was 10/10ths cloud. Bombed at 01.12 hours from 13,100 feet red glow.

30/06/1944 PB185 JI-F Bombing Villers Bocage 18.02   20.00   21.14

Bomb load 11 x 1000 MC, 4 x 500 GP. Primary target: Villers Bocage. Weather clear. Bombed at 20.00 hours from 4,000 feet, red T.I. - bang on the village - very good attack.

02/07/1944 PB185 JI-F Bombing Beauvoir   12.38   14.37   16.06

Bomb load 11 x 1000 MC, 4 x 500 GP. Primary target: Beauvoir, Flying bomb supply site. Bombed at 14.37 hours from 12,000 feet on yellow T.I.s.

05/07/1944 PB185 JI-F Bombing Watten 22.41 00.09   00.55

Bomb load 11 x 1000 ANM 65, 4 x 500 GP. Primary target: Watten, Constructional works. Bombed at 00.09 hours from 9,000 feet red T.I.s.

07/07/1944 PB185 JI-F Bombing Vaires 22.37   01.31   03.01

Bomb load 11 x 1000 ANM65. Primary target: Vaires, Marshalling yards. Weather clear. Bombed at 01.31 hours from 12,000 feet centre of T.I.s. Large red glare from explosions at 01.34 hours, appeared good attack.

15/07/1944 PB185 JI-F Bombing Chalons Sur Marne 21.32   01.32   03.58

Bomb load 18 x 500 GP. Primary target: Chalons sur Marne, Railway centre. Weather 7/10 cloud above. Bombed at 01.32 hours from 10,000 feet yellow T.I.s. Markers concentrated. A good prang.

18/07/1944 PB185 JI-F Bombing Emieville   04.09   06.06   07.50

Bomb load 11 x 1000 MC, 4 x 500 GP. Primary target: Emieville, Troop concentration. Weather clear. Bombed at 06.06 hours from 7,000 feet yellow T.I.s. A mass of smoke left behind.

20/07/1944 DS786 A2-F   Bombing Homberg 23.31   01.21   02.49

Bomb load 1 x 4000 HC, 2 x 500 MC, 14 x 500 GP. Primary target: Homberg, Oil plant. Weather clear. Bombed at 01.21 hours from 15,000 feet red T.I.s. Many large fires and columns of smoke. Had combat with enemy aircraft.

25/07/1944 LL716 A2-G   Bombing Stuttgart 21.46   02.00   05.53

Bomb load 5 x 1000 MC, 3 x 500 GP. Primary target: Stuttgart. Weather no cloud, ground haze. Bombed at 02.00 hours from 16,500 feet green T.I.s. Scattered attack.

01/08/1944 LM286 A2-F   Bombing Foret de Nieppe   19.12 x 21.38

Bomb load 11 x 1000 MC, 4 x 500 GP. Target: De Nieppe, constructional works. Abandoned on Master Bomber's orders. Jettisoned, position 5106N 0230E at 20.54 hours from 9.000 feet 4 x 1000 MC.

11/08/1944 LM286 A2-F   Bombing Lens 14.09 16.34   17.29

Bomb load 11 x 1000 MC. 4 X 500 GP. Primary target: Lens, Marshalling yards. Weather 6/10ths cloud. Bombed at 16.34 hours from 14,000 feet, yellow T.I.s. Bomb bursts observed above Marshalling yards.

26/08/1944 LM286 A2-F   Bombing Kiel 20.15 23.14   01.31

Bomb load 1 x 4000 HC, 96 x 30 IB, 900 x 4 IB. Primary target: Kiel.

Weather clear. Bombed at 23.14 hours from 17,500 feet centre of red T.I.s. 8 x 30 IB hung up. Many fires gaining hold.

06/09/1944 PB419 JI-N Bombing Le Havre   16.30   18.48   20.02

Bomb load 11 x 1000 MC, 4 x 500 GP. Primary target: Le Havre. Bombed at 18.48 hours from 7,000 feet, red T.I.s.

14/09/1944 DS786 A2-L   Bombing Wassenaar   12.47   14.30   15.31

Bomb load 11 x 1000 MC, 4 x 500 GP. Primary target: Wassenaar. Weather was good, nil cloud. Bombed at 14.30 hours from 12,100 feet, red T.I.s.

03/10/1944 LM286 A2-F   Bombing Westkapelle   11.57   13.20   14.15

Bomb load 1 x 4000 MC, 6 x 1000 MC, 1 x 500 GP. L/Delay. Primary target: Westkapelle (Walcheren). Weather patchy-scattered cloud with base 5,000 feet. Bombed at 13.20 hours from 6,000 feet at start of red T.I.

06/10/1944 LM286 A2-F   Bombing Dortmund 16.42 20.25   22.04

Bomb load 1 x 4000 HC, 12 x No. 14 Clusters. Primary target: Dortmund, Town and Railways. Weather over the target was clear with slight ground haze. Bombed at 20.25 hours from 20,000 feet on red T.I.s.

F/O. O.L. Goldsmith WOP/AG that day.

07/10/1944 LM286 A2-F   Bombing Emmerich   12.17   14.27   16.12

Bomb load 1 x 4000 HC. 10 x No.14 clusters. 4 x (150 x 4). Primary target Emmerich. Weather clear with cloud at 13,000 feet. Bombed at 14.27 hours from 14,000 feet on visual.

F/O. E. Ellin WOP/AG that day.

15/10/1944 LM286 A2-F   Bombing Wilhelmshaven   17.08   19.50 21.46

Bomb load 11 x 1000 MC, 4 x 500 GP. Primary target: Wilhelmshaven. Weather haze and thin cloud at first with thick cloud later. Bombed at 19.50 hours from 14,500 feet. Centre of red T.I.s.

F/L. V.G.I. Outen WOP/AG that day.

25/10/1944 LM286 A2-F   Bombing Essen   12.53   15.30   16.54

Bomb load 1 x 4000 HC, 6 x 1000 MC, 6 x 500 GP. Primary target: Essen. Weather over target 10/10ths low cloud, with one clear patch which appeared to fill up later in the attack. Bombed at 15.30 hours from 22,000 feet port of Red T.I.s.

Sgt. C.A. Brown WOP/AG that day.

02/11/1944 PD324 A2-B   Bombing Homberg 11.19 14.10   15.36

Bomb load 1 x 4000 HC, 6 x 1000 ANM 59, 6 x 500 MC. Primary target: Homberg. Weather variable cloud but clear for bombing. Target obscured by pall of smoke rising to 10,000 feet. Bombed at 14.10 hours from 20,500 feet. Centre of smoke.

F/O. O.L. Goldsmith WOP/AG that day.

30/11/1944 PD325 A2-L   Bombing Osterfeld 10.39 13.10   14.55

Bomb load 1 x 4000 HC, 16 x 500 GP. Primary target: Osterfeld, Coking plant. Weather 10/10ths cloud. Bombed at 13.10 hours from 20,000 feet on G.H. Leader.

F/O. J. Baker Navigator from that day.

F/O. O.L. Goldsmith WOP/AG that day.

02/12/1944 PD325 A2-L   Bombing Dortmund 12.52 14.56   16.57

Bomb load 14 x 1000 HC. Primary target: Dortmund, Benzol plant. Weather 10/10ths cloud. Bombed at 14.56 from 20,000 feet on leading aircraft. Aircraft hit by flak. Mid upper turret and starboard inner and outer engines damaged. Mid upper gunner wounded by flak.

F/O. E. Ellin WOP/AG that day.

F/O. John Henry Tolley, DFC

1st crew

185434 (1387393)   F/O. John Henry Tolley. DFC. Pilot.

Sgt. A. Griffiths.   A/Bomber. 7 ops.

Sgt. A.D. Horne.   A/Bomber. 1 op.

F/S. K. Greenwood   Navigator.

1673010 Sgt. W.K. Campin.   WOP/AG. 7 ops.

A419813 W/O. Robert Edward "Bob" Jenkins, RAAF.   WOP/AG. 1 op.

Sgt. W.J. McDermott.   MU/Gunner.

W/O. C.J. or C.K. Fudge.   R/Gunner. 1 op.

1380157 Sgt. W.H. Ellis.   R/Gunner. 7 ops.

Sgt. L. Haworth.   F/Engineer.

23/10/1944 LM286 A2-F   Bombing Essen 16.33   19.40   21.56

Bomb load 1 x 4000 HC, 6 x 1000 MC, 6 x 500 GP. Primary target: Essen. Weather 10/10ths cloud over target - tops 12/14,000 feet with most appalling weather on route. Bombed at 19.40 hours from 20,500 feet. Green flares.

According to H.E. Bentley's logbook: "Hit by Flak".

From his normal crew, only P/O. J.H. Tolley did this mission as 2nd Pilot with F/L. B.K. McDonald's crew.

25/10/1944 LM734 A2-C   Bombing Essen 13.04   15.36   17.16

Bomb load 1 x 4000 HC, 10 x No. 14 Clusters, 4 x 150 x 4. Primary target: Essen. Weather over target 10/10ths low cloud, with one clear patch which appeared to fill up later in the attack. Bombed at 15.36 hours from 23,000 feet. Red flares.

28/10/1944 PB423 A2-G   Bombing Cologne 13.33 15.47   17.44

Bomb load 1 x 4000 HC, 8 x 150 x 4. Primary target: Cologne. Weather clear over target. Bombed at 15.47 hours from 19,000 feet, visually.

30/10/1944 PB423 A2-G   Bombing Wesseling 09.18 11.59   13.33

Bomb load 1 x 4000 HC, 16 x 500 GP. Primary target: Wesseling. Weather was 10/10ths cloud - tops about 7,000 feet. Bombed at 11.59 hours from 18,000 feet on G.H. aircraft ahead.

02/11/1944 NG118 A2-E   Bombing Homberg 11.24   14.08   15.29

Bomb load 1 x 4000 HC, 6 x 1000 ANM59, 6 x 500 MC. Primary target: Homberg. Weather variable cloud but clear for bombing. Target obscured by pall of smoke rising to 10,000 feet. Bombed at 14.08 hours from 21,000 feet. Visual.

11/11/1944 PD333 A2-K   Bombing Castrop Rauxel   08.22   11.07
12.53

Bomb load 1 x 4000 HC, 16 x 500 GP. Primary target: Castrop Rauxel, Oil refineries. Weather 10/10ths cloud. Alternative target: Wuppertal. Bombed at 11.11 hours from 20,000 feet on G.H. Leader.

15/11/1944 NG142 A2-H   Bombing Dortmund 12.45 15.41   17.30

Bomb load 1 x 4000 HC, 16 x 500 GP. Primary target: Hoesch-Benzin Dortmund, Oil refineries. Weather 10/10ths cloud over the target. Bombed at 15.41 hours from 16,800 feet on flares.

21/11/1944 NG121 JI-H Bombing Homberg   12.44   15.06   15.47

Bomb load 1 x 4000 HC, 16 x 500 GP. Primary target: Homberg. Weather about 5/10ths cloud but clear for bombing. Bombed at 15.06 hours from 20,000 feet on leading aircraft. Hit by flak on approaching target. Aircraft crash landed in Belgium near Antwerp.

Witnessed by F/L. Harry Yates in 'Luck and a Lancaster'

Presumed engaged by enemy action as Sgt. Ellis baled out. The rest of the crew managed to get the aircraft back over Allied held territory and crash-landed 15.47 apx. 8 km S of Antwerpen. No injuries to the crew were reported but the Lancaster was subsequently SOC. Sgt W.H. Ellis was interned in Camp L1, no PoW No.

05/01/1945 LM685 JI-K Bombing Ludwigshafen 11.35   15.08   17.25

Bomb load 1 x 4000 HC, 10 x 500 ANM58 or 64, 2 x 500 GP. Primary target: Ludwigshafen, Marshalling yards. Weather clear over target. Bombed at 15.08 hours from 20,000 feet on leading G.H. aircraft. Aircraft hit by flak - Air Bomber's panel damaged.

Sgt. A.D. Horne was A/Bomber that day, W/O. R.E. Jenkins WOP/AG and W/O. C.J. Fudge R/Gunner.

2nd crew

185434 (1387393)   F/O. John Henry Tolley, DFC. Pilot.
F/S. A.D. Horne.   A/Bomber. 14 ops.
Sgt. J.A. Murray.   A/Bomber. 1 op.
J94421 (R169804)   P/O. D.L. Cressman, RCAF. A/Bomber. 6 ops.
159990 (1650697)   F/O. David Philip Bartlett. A/Bomber. 3 ops.
149340 (1562280)   F/O. Talbot William "Bill" Ledingham, DFC. Navigator. 14 ops.

R175321 W/O. Gordon Harrison "Butch" Bate, RCAF Navigator. 7 ops.
195188 (1673373) P/O. Alan Fairfax. Navigator. 3 ops.
A419813 W/O. Robert Edward "Bob" Jenkins, RAAF. WOP/AG. 15 ops.
F/S. B.A. Brown. WOP/AG. 9 ops.
Sgt. W.J. McDermott. MU & R/Gunner.
W/O. C.J. or C.K. Fudge. MU & R /Gunner. 21 ops.
Sgt. G.N. Zannetti. R/Gunner. 3 ops.
Sgt. A.T. Millar. F/Engineer.
J37983 F/O. William Mark "Skip" Wiseman. RCAF. 2nd Pilot. 25/02/1945
54040 (580110) F/O. Joseph Holmes Wilson. 2nd Pilot. 09/04/1945

16/01/1945 NN775 A2-F Bombing Wanne-Eickel 23.15 02.23 04.20
Bomb load 1 x 4000 HC, 10 x 500 ANM58, 4 x 250 GP. Primary target:
Wanne-Eickel, Benzol plant. Weather 10/10ths thin low cloud. Bombed at
02.23 hours from 18,000 feet on upwind edge of wanganui flares.
Sgt. A.D. Horne A/Bomber, F/O. T.W. Ledingham Navigator until
17/03/1945.
W/O. R.E. Jenkins WOP/AG until 09/04/1945.
W/O. C.J. or C.K. Fudge R/Gunner until 10/05/1945.
22/01/1945 NN775 A2-F Bombing Hamborn 17.05 20.04 21.40
Bomb load 1 x 4000 HC, 7 x 500 ANM 58 or 64, 2 x 500 GP (L/Delay), 3
x 250 GP. Primary target: Hamborn (Duisburg), Thyssen works. Weather over
target clear and almost as bright as day. Bombed at 20.04 from 20,000 feet on
centre of Red and Green T.I.s and the river.
28/01/1945 NN775 A2-F Bombing Cologne 10.29 14.13 15.50
Bomb load 1 x 4000 HC, 10 x 500 ANM64, 2 x 500 GP, 3 x 250 GP. Primary
target: Koln - Gremberg, Marshalling yards. Weather 10/10ths cloud en route
clearing on approach to target where visibility was good and nil cloud.
Bombed at 14.13 hours from 20,000 feet on G.H. Leader.
29/01/1945 NN775 A2-F Bombing Krefeld 10.18 14.00 15.30
Bomb load 1 x 4000 HC, 10 x 500 ANM 64, 2 x 500 GP, 4 x 250 GP. Primary
target: Krefeld Marshalling Yards. Weather 10/10ths low thin cloud over target
although clear patches en-route. Bombed at 14.00 hours from 20,000 feet on
Red and Green flares.
01/02/1945 NN775 A2-F Bombing Munchen-Gladbach 13.10 16.35 18.08
Bomb load 1 x 4000 HC, 14 x No. 14 Clusters. Primary target: Munchen-
Gladbach, Marshalling yards. Bombed at 16.35 hours from 18,000 feet on
leading aircraft.
02/02/1945 NN775 A2-F Bombing Wiesbaden 20.30 23.48 02.15
Bomb load 1 x 4000 HC, 12 x 500 GP, 4 x 250 GP. Primary target:
Wiesbaden. Weather 10/10ths cloud, winds very erratic. Bombed at 23.48
hours from 18,000 feet on Gee fix.
25/02/1945 NG118 A2-H Bombing Kamen 09.30 12.46 14.50
Bomb load 1 x 4000 HC, 9 x 500 ANM64, 2 x 500 MC, 3 x 250 GP and

L to R: R.E. Jenkins, A.T.Millar, C.J. Fudge, J.H. Tolley, T.W. Ledingham, A.D. Horne, W.J. McDermott.

Smoke Puff. Primary target: Kamen. Weather 6-8/10ths cloud. Bombed at 12.46 hours from 19,000 feet on G.H. Leader.

F/O. W.M. Wiseman 2nd Pilot that day.

27/02/1945 NN775 A2-F   Bombing Gelsenkirchen 10.50   14.28   16.42

Bomb load 1 x 4000 HC, 2 x 500 MC (L/D 37B), 9 x 500 ANM64, 4 x 250 GP. Primary target: Gelsenkirchen (Alma Pluts) Benzin plant. Weather 10/10ths cloud, 6/10,000 feet tops. Bombed at 14.28 hours from 20,000 feet on G.H. Leader.

01/03/1945 NN775 A2-F   Bombing Kamen   11.37   15.05   17.16

Bomb load 1 x 4000 HC, 9 x 500 ANM 64, 2 x 500 MC L/D37, 4 x 250 GP. Primary target: Kamen, Coking plant. Weather 10/10ths cloud. Bombed at 15.05 hours from 18,000 feet on G.H. aircraft.

02/03/1945 NN775 A2-F   Bombing Koln   12.47 16.02   18.10

Bomb load 1 x 4000 HC, 12 x 500 ANM 64. Primary target: Koln. Weather 10/10ths cloud over Koln, South and South-East of Koln clear. Bombed at 16.02 hours from 20,500 feet on leading G.H. aircraft.

06/03/1945 NN782 JI-F Bombing Salzbergen 08.18 12.15   14.15

Bomb load 1 x 4000 HC, 12 x 500 ANM64, 2 x 500 MC. Primary target: Salzbergen, Wintershall oil plant. Weather 10/10ths cloud over target, tops 10,000 feet. Bombed at 12.15 hours from 20,500 feet on leading G.H. aircraft.

07/03/1945 ME529 A2-F   Bombing Dessau   17.00   22.15   02.00

Bomb load 1 x 4000 HC, 6 x Mk.17 Clusters. Primary target: Dessau.

649

Weather 5 to 10/10ths thin cloud. Bombed at 22.15 hours from 20,500 feet on Red/Green Skymarkers.

14/03/1945 ME529 A2-F   Bombing Heinrichshutte 13.10   16.40   18.37

Bomb load 1 x 4000 HC, 12 x 500 ANM64. Primary target: Heinrichshutte, Hattingen Steel works & Benzol plant. Weather 10/10ths cloud, tops 7/12,000 feet. Bombed at 16.40 hours from 19,500 feet on leading G.H. aircraft.

17/03/1945 ME529 A2-F   Bombing August Viktoria   11.27   15.06   16.58

Bomb load 1 x 4000 HC, 13 x 500 ANM64, 2 x 500 MC. Primary target: Auguste Viktoria, Marl-Hüls coal mine. Weather 10/10ths cloud, tops and contrails up to 23,000 feet. Bombed at 15.06 hours from 20,500 feet on leading G.H. aircraft.

W/O. C.J. or C.K. Fudge was MU/Gunner that day and Sgt. W.J. McDermott was R/Gunner.

09/04/1945 ME529 A2-F   Bombing Kiel   19.41 22.44   01.39

Bombed primary target: Kiel, Submarine Buildings Yards. Weather clear with slight haze. Bomb load 1 x 4000 HC and 12 x 500 ANM64. Bombed at 22.44 hours at 20,000 feet undershooting on Green T.I.s. on M/B's instructions. Visual of whole area with distinct sets of markers - all in dock area. Believed good attack. Marking was good, M/B excellent but some interference. Lanc arrived early 22.28 saw lighted area to South and tracked towards then attack started 22.31 so orbited and bombed (lighted area believed decoy).

Sgt. J.A. Murray was A/Bomber that day and F/O. J.H. Wilson 2nd Pilot.

W/O. G.H. Bate Navigator until 10/05/1945.

R.E. Jenkins noted in his logbook "Orbited target, Good Prang, Plenty of light flak, 'Admiral Scheer' sunk during raid."

13/04/1945 ME359 JI-T Bombing Kiel   20.13   23.38   01.48

Bomb load 1 x 4000 HC and 12 x 500 ANM64. Primary target: Kiel, Docks & ship yards. Weather 10/10ths cloud low and thin. Bombed on Green T.I.s at 23.38 hours from 20,000 feet. Glow of bomb bursts seen through cloud. Fire in Fishpond extinguished. Arrived early but later Green T.I.s dropped in centre of reds. Had a good run up.

P/O. D.L. Cressman A/Bomber until 10/05/1945.

From that day F/S. B.A. Brown WOP/AG.

20/04/1945 PD389 A2-J Bombing Regensburg 09.27   14.00 x

Bomb load 16 x 500 ANM 64. Primary target: Regensburg. Weather clear over target and whole route. Reached Regensburg 14.00 hrs on G.H., but bombs hung up in spite of every effort to release. After orbiting brought then back. Bombing was seen N + S of oil plant but not on it. Weather was clear, heavy flak was slight. Took photo manually, 5 secs after target 3 miles NNW. Very disappointed. Perfect trip otherwise.

24/04/1945 RE123 A2-K   Bombing Bad Oldesloe 07.08 10.54   12.58

Bomb load 6 x 1000 ANM 65, 10 x 500 ANM 64. Primary target: Bad-

Oldesloe, Rail and road junction and Marshalling Yards. Weather 3/10ths to nil cloud. Bombed on G.H. at 10.54 hours from 17,300 ft. Good G.H. run. Heavy smoke over centre of target area and explosions along rail tracks. Good concentration in centre of M/Y, some bombs fell along residential area. Smoke and fires on junction. Bang on. Formation good but our followers not with us, over target.

30/04/1945 ME529 A2-F Manna Rotterdam 16.55 18.22 19.35

Dropping area: Rotterdam. Weather intermittent showers and low cloud. Load 5 packs. Dropped two packs on red T.I.s at 18.22 hours. Three packs brought back due to hang up. Target area congested a/c proceeding on all headings which with the poor visibility made the run up difficult. Dutch people lined up cheering - flags flying.

02/05/1945 ME529 A2-F Manna The Hague 11.03 12.24 13.26

Dropping area The Hague. Weather over dropping zone clear below cloud for the first arrivals changing later to heavy showers which marred visibility. Dropped 4 panniers dropped on White Cross and Red T.I.s at 12.24 hours. 1 pannier hung up brought back. Clear patch over target area. Bomb doors slightly damaged by panniers. Area very small for dropping.

10/05/1945 ME529 A2-F Exodus Juvincourt - Ford 11.21 x 18.07

Duration 3.55. Outward 1.56 hours. Collected 24 ex POWs. Homeward 1.59 hours. Good organisation.

24/05/1945 ME529 A2-F Exodus Brussels 12.52 x 16.34

Duration 2.25 hours. Out 1.13 hours. In 1.12 hours. 10 Belgian refugees to Brussels.

From that day F/O. D.P. Bartlett was A/Bomber, P/O. A. Fairfax Navigator and Sgt. G.N. Zannetti R/Gunner.

25/05/1945 NN781 A2-B Exodus Brussels 12.11 x 16.41

Duration 2.16 hours. Out 1.07 hours. In 1.09 hours. 10 Belgian refugees to Brussels. No POWs back. No troubles.

26/05/1945 NN781 A2-B Exodus Brussels - Ford 12.14 x 18.56

Duration 3.12 hours. Out 1.12 hours. In 2.00 hours. 10 Belgian refugees to Brussels. 24 ex POWs all military brought back.

F/O. John Backhouse Topham, DFC

178865 (1476474)   F/O. John Backhouse "Toppy" Topham, DFC. Pilot.
J29670 (R163578)   F/O. J Ralph McClenaghan, RCAF. A/Bomber. 24 ops.
1230758 F/S. Robert James Rigden.   A/Bomber. 7 ops.
151338 (1543004)   F/O. Stuart Baxter.   Navigator.
1845143 F/S. Harold "Harry" Gilmore. WOP/AG.
1546284 Sgt. James "Jim" Scully. MU/Gunner.
1308261 Sgt. P Anstey. R/Gunner. 4 ops.
A415845   F/S. Richard Hiden White, RAAF. R/Gunner. 6 ops.
1565396 F/S. Robert Calder "Bert" Guy. R/Gunner. 1 op.
141271 (1386976)   F/O. Herbert Henry Wright, DFM. R/Gunner. 1 op.
R87920   (*)
W/O2. William Ernest "Ernie" Egri, DFM, RCAF. R/Gunner. 19 ops.
A437587 (**)
F/S. Francis William "Frank" Dennehy, RAAF. Mid Under Gunner. 1 op.
1675129 Sgt. John Davies "Jack" Reid. F/Engineer.

(*) - W.E. Egri in several sources quoted by error as W.E. Eyre. (References: Logbook and Granddaughter's testimony)
(**) - Also known as "Dauntless Dennehy" during WWII.

Francis William "Frank" Dennehy. (courtesy John Harrington)

18/03/1944 LL727 A2-C
Bombing Frankfurt   19.44 x 00.49
Bomb load 1 x 8000 lb bomb, 450 x 4, 90 x 4, 32 x 30 incendiaries. No attack. Markers not seen while in target area. Monica u/s from take off. A poor show. After we had been over target for 5 minutes we were coned by S/Ls. Fighter flares around us so we let the load go, but no T.I.s visible at the time.

From his normal crew, only F/S. J.B. Topham did this mission as 2nd Pilot with F/O. L. Greenburgh's crew.

22/03/1944 LL620 A2-G
Bombing Frankfurt 18.30 x 01.05
Bomb load 1 x 1000 lb bomb, 64 x 30, 1161 x 4, 129 x 4 incendiaries.

Primary target: Frankfurt. No attack. Distributor trouble over target which released photo flash and took photo but did not release bombs. Two fighter attacks between Osnabruck and target, one over the target and one attack after leaving target. Fighter flare dropped by our aircraft tail on bombing run.

F/O. J.R. McClenaghan A/Bomber until 28/05/44.

Sgt. P. Anstey R/Gunner until 30/03/44.

26/03/1944 DS813 JI-H Bombing Essen 20.15 x 21.45

Bomb load 1 x 2000 lb bomb, 56 x 30, 1080 x 4, 120 x 4 incendiaries. Returned early. Farthest point reached 5255N 0240E. Mid Upper Gunner ill. Load jettisoned.

30/03/1944 LL677 A2-E Bombing Nuremburg 22.15 01.21 05.52

Bomb load 1 x 1000 lb bomb, 96 x 30, 810 x 4, 90 x 4 incendiaries. Primary target: Nuremburg. There was 6/10 cloud with gaps. Bombed at 01.21 hours from 21,000 feet. Many fires seen also T.I.s red and green and sky markers. P.F.F. considered successful, good concentration of markers.

10/04/1944 LL677 A2-E Bombing Laon 01.34 03.52 05.58

Bomb load 9 x 1000, 4 x 500 lb bomb. Primary target: Laon. There was slight haze, visibility good. Bombed at 03.52 hours from 10,500 feet. There was a good concentration of at least 3 green T.I.s with stick of bombs just before we dropped ours. Several of the bombs seen as we ran up. A good attack. One red T.I. fell just as we left. Two bullet holes in fuselage near oil gauge, cause not known. Starboard outer oil pressure gauge damaged.

F/S. R.H. White R/Gunner that day.

11/04/1944 DS795 A2-J Bombing Aachen 21.06 22.44 00.19

Bomb load 10 x 1000, 2 x 500 lb bombs, 160 x 4, 20 x 4 incendiaries. Primary target: Aachen. There was 8/10 cloud, but over target clear. Bombed at 22.44 hours from 17,500 feet. T.I.s well concentrated. Many fires seen. Attack appeared very successful. Fires seen burning in target area.

Sgt. P. Anstey R/Gunner that day.

18/04/1944 LL670 A2-K Bombing Rouen 22.34 00.47 02.47

Bomb load 8 x 1000 MC, 2 x 1000 GP, 5 x 500 lb bombs. Primary target: Rouen. Weather was clear. Bombed at 00.47 from 12,000 feet. Markers were scattered. 1 x 500 lb bomb brought back to Base - hung up. Letter seen in target area.

F/S. Robert Calder Guy was R/Gunner that day.

Contrary to ORBs, Robert Calder Guy noted this mission as Rear Gunner in his logbook. According his own James Scully confirms that he was the other Air Gunner.

20/04/1944 LL670 A2-K Bombing Cologne 00.11 02.08 04.09

Bomb load 1 x 1000 lb bomb, 1026 x 4, 108 x 30 lb incendiaries. Primary target: Koln. There was 10/10 cloud. Bombed at 02.08 hours from 19,000 feet. Cloud only seen with red flares. 150 x 4 lb incendiaries hung up and brought back. Route quiet. Defences slight.

F/S. R.H. White R/Gunner until 27/04/44.

22/04/1944 DS786 A2-F Bombing Dusseldorf 23.11 x 01.04

Bomb load 1 x 2000 lb bomb, 84 x 30, 1050 x 4 incendiaries. Returned early. Bombs jettisoned safe at 5130N 0251E. Farthest point reached 00.13 hours 14,000 feet. Port inner engine overheated. Ran into static cloud for 20 minutes after crossing coast. A number of bomb-loads seen to be jettisoned over the sea.

24/04/1944 LL670 A2-K Bombing Karlsruhe 22.29 x 00.17

Bomb load 1 x 1000 lb bomb, 1026 x 4, 114 x 4, 108 x 30 incendiaries. Returned early. Farthest point reached 5212N 0300E. Total load jettisoned to reduce weight. Navigator sick.

26/04/1944 LL670 A2-K Bombing Essen 23.04 01.31 03.13

Bomb load 1 x 8000 lb bomb, 60 x 30, 405 x 4, 45 x 4 lb incendiaries. Primary target: Essen. Weather was clear. Bombed at 01.31 hours from 18,000 feet. A good concentration, incendiaries fell close to markers. Route satisfactory.

27/04/1944 LL670 A2-K Bombing Friedrichshafen 23.04 02.07 03.13

Bomb load 810 x 4, 80 x 30 lb incendiaries. Primary target: Friedrichshafen. Weather was clear. Bombed at 02.07 hours from 18,000 feet. There was a good concentration of reds and mixed T.I.s. Incendiaries falling near markers. A very successful attack.

01/05/1944 LL670 A2-K Bombing Chambly 22.56 00.28 02.13

Bomb load 10 x 1000, 5 x 500 lb bombs. Primary target: Chambly. Weather was clear. Bombed at 00.28 hours from 10,000 feet. Target illuminated by flares. Fuselage and wings damaged by flak over Dieppe. A good trip and successful sortie. Route OK.

F/O. H.H. Wright DFM was R/Gunner that day.

19/05/1944 DS842 JI-F Bombing Le Mans 22.21 00.28 03.10

Bomb load 4 x 1000 USA, 5 x 1000 MC, 1 x 1000 GP, 4 x 500 GP. Primary target: Le Mans. Cloud extended from 8,500 feet upwards. Bombed as instructed by Master Bomber at 02.28 hours from 7,500 feet. Arrived rather early and made orbit. Attack thought to be good. At 00.59 hours FW 190 seen about 250 yards away but become lost in clouds. When 30 miles from Le Mans on outward journey JU 88 approached and Rear Gunner fired short burst at it. Enemy aircraft approached again and both Gunners fired bursts claiming several hits.

From his normal crew, only F/S. J.B. Topham did this mission as Captain with F/O. E.A. Campbell's crew.

22/05/1944 DS786 A2-F Bombing Dortmund 22.55 00.51 02.50

Bomb load 1 x 2000 lb, bomb, 96 x 30, 810 x 4, 90 x 4 incendiaries. Primary target: Dortmund. Clear over target. Bombed at 00.51 hours from 17,000 feet. Rain and icing at take-off. Numerous fires seen around aiming point. No difficulties encountered except searchlight belt at Cologne-Dusseldorf. Sighted enemy aircraft at 00.51 hours dropping flares shortly after leaving target and at 00.53 hours saw combat between two unidentified aircraft.

W/O2. W.E. Egri R/Gunner from that day.

28/05/1944 LL670 A2-K Bombing Angers 18.55 23.59 02.00

Bomb load 5 x 1000 MC, 1 x 1000 USA, 4 x 500 MC. Primary target: Angers. Clear at target. Bombed markers at 23.59 hours from 7500 feet. Several explosions seen in target area. Smoke up to 10,000 feet prevented visual. Quiet route. At 23.29 hours unidentified twin engine aircraft was seen 800 yards astern, Lancaster evaded.

10/06/1944 LL670 A2-K Bombing Dreux 23.08 01.00 03.35

Bomb load 16 x 500 GP, 2 x 500 LD. Primary target: Dreux. Bombed as instructed by Master Bomber at 01.00 hours from 8,000 feet. Large explosion seen at 01.00 hours. Defences slight. No trouble experienced.

F/S. R.J. Rigden was A/Bomber until 24/06/44.

11/06/1944 LL670 A2-K Bombing Nantes 23.49 02.45 05.04

Bomb load 16 x 500 GP. 2 x 500 LD. Primary target: Nantes. Bombed at 02.45 hours from 6,000 feet, on glow of green T.I.s in 10/10ths cloud. Trip uneventful.

14/06/1944 LL670 A2-K Bombing Le Havre 23.41 01.14 02.20

Bomb load 11 x 1000 MC, 4 x 500 GP. Primary target: Le Havre. Weather almost clear. Bombed at 01.14 hours from 13,500 feet on green and yellow T.I.s. Fires seen from previous attack illuminated whole dock area. A very good attack.

15/06/1944 LL670 A2-K Bombing Valenciennes 22.58 00.36 02.23

Bomb load 16 x 500 GP, 2 x 500 MC. Primary target: Valenciennes. Weather clear. Bombed at 00.36 hours from 9,000 feet centre of red and green T.I.s. Tremendous orange explosion at 00.46 hours followed by a large white one.

17/06/1944 LL670 A2-K Bombing Montdidier 01.04 x 04.45

Bomb load 16 x 500 GP, 2 x 500 ANM 64 GP. Primary target: Montdidier. There was 10/10ths cloud. Aircraft orbited target, no T.I.s seen. Heard Master Bomber instruct return to Base. Jettisoned safe 03.25 hours from 9,000 feet, 5007N 0100E, 2 x 500 GP.

21/06/1944 LL670 A2-K Bombing Domleger 18.01 x 20.36

Bomb load 18 x 500 MC. Primary target: Domleger near Abbeville, V-1 flying bomb launch site. There was 10/10ths cloud. Master Bomber ordered bomb red T.I.s if visible, otherwise return to Base. No T.I.s seen. Jettisoned safe 12 x 500 MC at 19.40 hours from 12,000 feet at 5020N 0128E.

24/06/1944 LL670 A2-K Bombing Rimeux 23.25 00.34 01.52

Bomb load 18 x 500 GP. Primary target: Rimeux, Flying bomb installations. Weather clear. Bombed at 00.34 hours from 11,000 feet concentration of red T.I.s. Attack appeared well concentrated. Many yellow flares seen.

27/06/1944 LL670 A2-K Bombing Biennais 23.32 01.13 02.21

Bomb load 16 x 500 GP, 2 x 500 ANM64 GP. Primary target: Biennais, Flying bomb installations. There was 10/10ths cloud. Bombed at 01.13 hours from 13,500 feet red glow. Several explosions seen.

F/O. J.R. McClenaghan A/Bomber from that day.

02/07/1944 LL670 A2-K Bombing Beauvoir 12.56 x 15.00

Bomb load 11 x 1000 MC, 4 x 500 GP. To attack Beauvoir, Flying bomb supply site. Abortive sortie. Jettisoned at 14.12 hours from 7,500 feet 5040N 0107E. Starboard inner engine U/S.

There is an error in the ORBs as P.F. Carter's crew is reported twice at the same time in two different aircraft. See at ME841 JI-H. This has been corrected ref James Scully and W.E. Egri logbooks.

17/07/1944 LL670 A2-K Bombing Paris x x x

The is believed to be the composition of the crew as the 514 Squadron Operational Record Books (ORBs) do not make any mention of this raid, it is reported as a DNCO (Did Not Complete) mission in some 514 Sqn crew's logbooks and in those of W.E. Egri and J. Scully as follows: "OPS PARIS (RECALLED by GROUP)".

Bomber Command War Diaries Stated for that day –

"Flying Bomb Sights – 132 Aircraft. 72 Halifaxes, 28 Stirlings, 20 Lancasters, 11 Mosquitos, and 1 Mustang attacked 3 V-weapons sites without loss. Few details of results were recorded."

18/07/1944 LL670 A2-K Bombing Aulnoye 22.33 00.54 02.05

Bomb load 18 x 500 GP. Primary target: Aulnoye, Railway junction. Weather clear. Bombed at 00.54 hours from 8,500 feet green T.I.s. Bomb bursts well on T.I.s, visual of river.

20/07/1944 LL670 A2-K Bombing Homberg 23.21 x 01.03

Bomb load 1 x 4000 HC, 2 x 500 MC, 14 x 500 GP. Primary target: Homberg, Oil plant. Returned early, starboard inner engine u/s. Jettisoned at 00.30 hours from 9,000 feet, 36 miles East of Southwold.

23/07/1944 LL670 A2-K Bombing Kiel 22.40 01.26 04.06

Bomb load 6 x 1000 MC, 2 x 500 GP. Primary target: Kiel, Warehouses and docks. Weather 10/10ths low cloud. Bombed at 01.26 hours from 18,500 feet cluster of green T.I.s. Moderate raid, rather dispersed.

24/07/1944 LL670 A2-K Bombing Stuttgart 21.56 01.54 05.27

Bomb load 5 x 1000 ANM65, 3 x 500 GP. Primary target Stuttgart. Weather 10/10ths cloud. Bombed at 01.54 hours from 19,000 feet on green flares and yellow stars. Results doubtful.

27/07/1944 LL697 A2-B Bombing Les Catelliers 17.01 18.52 20.04

Bomb load 18 x 500 GP. Primary target: Les Catelliers, Flying bomb site. Bombed at 18.52 hours from 16,500 feet on Mosquito.

28/07/1944 LL716 A2-G Bombing Stuttgart 21.45 01.54 05.26

Bomb load 13 x 500 GP. Primary target: Stuttgart. Weather 10/10ths cloud. Bombed at 01.54 hours from 18,000 feet, green sky markers. Several fires burning in target area. A quiet trip. Sky markers seemed scattered.

03/08/1944 LL716 A2-G Bombing Bois de Cassan 11.58 x 14.10

Bomb load 11 x 1000 MC, 4 x 500 GP. Target: Bois de Cassan, Flying bomb supply depot. Aircraft missing.

Shot down at 14.10, crashing some 10 km S of Beaumont (Oise), France. Baxter states that their Lancaster was hit from above by bombs dropped by a Halifax.

F/S. Dennehy was flying as mid-under gunner, a role unique to the Mk. II Lancs.

F/O. J.B. Topham Evaded, Sgt. J.D. Reid PoW, F/O. S.Baxter PoW, F/S. J.R. McClenaghan PoW, F/S. H. Gilmore PoW, F/S. F.W. Dennehy Evaded, Sgt. J. Scully PoW, WO2 W.E. Egri PoW.

W.E. Egri (given W.E. Eyre by some sources) was interned in Camp L7, PoW No. 574 with Sgt J.Scully, PoW No. 627. F/O. S. Baxter initially evaded but was captured in Paris on 9th August 1944. He was incarcerated in the notorious Parisian Prison at Fresnes and eventually transported to Buchenwald. Luftwaffe officers obtained his release and he was interned in Camp L3. No PoW No. Also held captive in Buchenwald, Sgt J.D. Reid also evaded until captured in Paris with his comrades on 9th August 1944 and joined them in Buchenwald before internment in Camp L3, PoW No.8113.

WO2 W.E. Egri (Eyre), as a Flight Sergeant had a narrow escape from death following a crash whilst flying with No. 15 Sqn.

LL716 A2-G wreckage

F/O. Trevor Gordon Neville Trask DFC

A419921 F/O. Trevor Gordon Neville Trask, DFC, RAAF. Pilot.
A410425 F/O. Charles Albert "Chuck" Beresford, RAAF. A/Bomber.
Sgt. E.J. McKay.   Navigator. 18 ops.
152708 (1318086) F/O. Peter Gordon Lankester. Navigator. 6 ops.
F/S. D.L. Lewis.   Navigator. 6 ops.Sgt. D.W. King.   WOP/AG.
Sgt. P. Foster.   MU/Gunner.
Sgt. J.F. Lewis.   R/Gunner. 14 ops.
F/S. J. Tranter.   R/Gunner. 5 ops.
Sgt. W.A. Dabbs.   R/Gunner. 11 ops.
195353 (1896500) Sgt.Walter Peyton Edward Matterson. F/Engineer. 3 ops.
Sgt. R.E.G. Collins.   F/Engineer. 8 ops.
Sgt. A.T. Millar.   F/Engineer. 7 ops.
1714996 F/S. Leonard Arthur "Len" Ive. F/Engineer. 12 ops.

15/08/1944 DS787 A2-G Bombing St Trond 10.07   12.10   13.26
   Bomb load 11 x 1000 MC, 4 x 500 GP. Primary target St. Trond Airfield.
Bombed at 12.10 hours from 17,200 feet, intersection of runways and red T.I.s.
Successful attack.
   Sgt. Walter Peyton Edward Matterson F/Engineer until 26/08/44.
   Sgt. E.J. McKay Navigator until 22/10/44.
   Sgt. J.F. Lewis R/Gunner until 14/10/44.
25/08/1944 DS842 A2-J Bombing Russelsheim   20.36   01.09   04.50
   Bomb load 1 x 4000 HC, 6 x 500 lb Clusters. Primary target: Russelheim.
Weather clear. Bombed at 01.09 hours from 18,000 feet. Dropped on E.T.A.
No T.I.s visible.
26/08/1944 DS842 A2-J Bombing Kiel 20.19 23.07 01.38
   Bomb load 1 x 8000 HC, 180 x 4 IB, 16 x 30 IB. Primary target: Kiel.
Weather clear. Bombed at 23.07 hours from 17,500 feet centre of concentration
of red T.I.s. Many fires and much smoke seen.
05/09/1944 DS786 A2-L   Bombing Le Havre 17.35 19.25   20.30
   Bomb load 11 x 1000 MC, 4 x 500 GP. Primary target: Le Havre. Bombed
at 19.25 hours from 13,000 feet red T.I.
   Sgt. R.E.G. Collins F/Engineer until 03/10/44.
10/09/1944 DS787 A2-G Bombing Le Havre 15.45   17.38   19.03
   Bomb load 11 x 1000 MC, 4 x 500 GP. Primary target: Le Havre. Weather
clear. Bombed at 17.38 hours from 10,000 feet. Undershot T.I.s red by 100
yards.
12/09/1944 DS842 A2-J Bombing Frankfurt 18.43 23.01   01.20
   Bomb load 1 x 1000 MC, 16 x 500 Clusters 4lb. Primary target: Frankfurt -
Main. Weather clear over the target. Bombed at 23.01 hours from 17,600 feet
on red and green T.I.s.

14/09/1944 LM285 JI-K Bombing Wassenaar 13.07 14.29 15.36

Bomb load 11 x 1000 MC, 4 x 500 GP. Primary target: Wassenaar. Weather was good, nil cloud. Bombed at 14.29 hours from 12,000 feet. Overshooting slightly port red T.I.s.

17/09/1944 NG118 A2-E Bombing Boulogne 10.26 11.43 12.52

Bomb load 11 x 1000 MC, 4 x 500 GP. Primary target: Boulogne Aiming Point 3. Weather clear below cloud. Bombed at 11.43 hours from 2,500 feet, red T.I.s.

25/09/1944 PD324 A2-B Bombing Pas de Calais 08.25 x 11.07

Bomb load 11 x 1000 MC, 4 x 500 GP. Primary target: Calais. Abandoned mission on Master Bomber's instructions. Jettisoned 3 x 1000 MC, 1 x 500 GP.

27/09/1944 PD324 A2-B Bombing Calais 07.27 08.41 10.13

Bomb load 11 x 1000 MC, 4 x 500 GP. Primary target: Calais 15. Weather, cloud 5,500 feet 10/10ths. Bombed at 08.41 hours from 5,000 feet overshot green T.I. by 100 yards.

03/10/1944 LM734 A2-C Bombing Westkapelle 12.02 13.20 14.11

Bomb load 1 x 4000 MC, 6 x 1000 MC, 1 x 500 GP L/Delay. Primary target: Westkapelle (Walcheren). Weather patchy-scattered cloud with base 5,000 feet. Bombed at 13.20 hours from 5,000 feet undershot width of red T.I.

05/10/1944 PB423 JI-Z Bombing Saarbrucken x x x

Bomb load 11 x 1000 MC, 1 x 500 GP, 3 x 500 GP. Long Delay. Primary target: Saarbrucken, Marshalling yards. Failed to take off - Rear turret U/S.

Sgt. A.T. Millar was F/Engineer until 22/10/44.

14/10/1944 NG141 A2-J Bombing Duisburg 06.52 09.05 11.22

Bomb load 11 x 1000 MC, 4 x 500 GP Long Delay. Primary target: Duisburg. Weather patchy cloud with gaps for bombing. Bombed at 09.05 hours from 19,000 feet. Built up area North of Docks area.

14/10/1944 NG141 A2-J Bombing Duisburg 22.54 01.28 03.24

Bomb load 1 x 4000 HC, 14 x No. 14 Clusters. Primary target: Duisburg. Weather was clear with small amount of cloud over the target. Bombed at 01.28 hours from 20,000 feet. Centre of red and green T.I.s.

18/10/1944 PB423 A2-G Bombing Bonn 08.29 11.00 12.58

Bomb load 1 x 4000 HC, 5 x 12 x 30 - 2 x 12 x 30 modified, 9 x No. 14 Clusters. Primary target: Bonn. Weather varying cloud 2-7/10ths with breaks for bombing. Bombed at 11.00 hours from 18,500 feet on G.H. G.H. checked visually and found OK.

F/S. J. Tranter was R/Gunner until 06/11/44.

19/10/1944 PD334 A2-D Bombing Stuttgart 17.23 20.32 23.37

Bomb load 1 x 4000 HC, 3 x 500 Clusters, 7 x 150 x 4, 1 x 90 x 4 I.B. Primary target: Stuttgart, A/P 'D' 1st attack. Weather 10/10ths cloud which broke to 6/10ths at the end of the period. Bombed at 20.32 hours from 18,000 feet. Wanganui flares.

21/10/1944 PD334 A2-D Bombing Flushing 10.55 12.28 13.46

Bomb load 12 x 1000 MC, 2 x 500 GP. Primary target: Flushing 'B'. Weather clear. Bombed at 12.28 hours from 8,000 feet.

22/10/1944 LM627 JI-D Bombing Neuss 13.15   16.03   17.43

Bomb load 1 x 4000 HC, 6 x 1000 MC, 6 x 500 GP. Primary target: Neuss. Weather 10/10ths cloud over target. Bombed at 16.03 hours from 17,800 feet following bombs of leading aircraft. G.H. equipment failed on approach to target - D.R. compass - H2S - A.S.I. - all unserviceable.

06/11/1944 NG118 A2-E   Bombing Koblenz 16.52 19.36   22.06

Bomb load 1 x 4000 HC, 12 x 500 Clusters, 2 x 250 T.I.s. Primary target: Koblenz. Weather clear over target. Bombed at 19.36 hours from 17,500 feet on estimated position of A/P.

F/O. P.G. Lankester was Navigator until 23/11/44.

F/S. L.A. Ive was F/Engineer from that day.

11/11/1944 NG118 A2-E   Bombing Castrop Rauxel   08.03   11.07 12.43

Bomb load 1 x 4000 HC, 15 x 500 GP, 1 Flare. Primary target: Castrop Rauxel, Oil refineries. Weather 10/10ths cloud. Bombed at 11.07 hours from 19,500 feet on G.H.

Sgt. W.A. Dabbs R/Gunner from that day.

16/11/1944 NG118 A2-E   Bombing Heinsburg   13.20   15.37   17.35

Bomb load 1 x 4000 HC, 11 x 500 GP, 4 x 250 lb T.I.s. Primary target: Heinsburg. Weather - nil cloud with slight haze over target. Bombed at 15.37 hours from 11,000 feet. Slightly to edge of smoke on Master Bomber's instructions.

Error in ORBs (double entry). At the same time R.W. Vickers' crew is recorded in both NF968 JI-L and NG118 A2-E. Thanks to D.V. Donnelly's logbook it appears R.W. Vickers crew was in A/C NF968 JI-L. Due to the number of aircraft detailed for this operation and some others reasons, the crew of NG118 A2-E is believed that of T.G.N. Trask.

20/11/1944 NG118 A2-E   Bombing Homberg 12.37 x 17.20

Bomb load 1 x 4000 HC, 3 x 500 GP, 12 x 500 MC. Primary target: Homberg. Weather 10/10ths cloud over target. Jettisoned at 10 seconds before G.H. indicated time owing to aircraft being out of control over target area. Aircraft dived steeply to starboard, pulled out at 17,000 feet.

21/11/1944 NG118 A2-E   Bombing Homberg 12.34   15.08   16.40

Bomb load 1 x 4000 HC, 15 x 500 GP, 1 Red-Green Flare. Primary target: Homberg. Weather about 5/10ths cloud but clear for bombing. Bombed at 15.08 hours from 19,500 feet on G.H.

23/11/1944 NG118 A2-E   Bombing Nordstern 12.51 15.19   17.51

Bomb load 1 x 4000 HC, 15 x 500 GP, 1 Red flare with Green stars. Primary target: Nordstern, Gelsenkirchen Oil refineries. Weather 10/10ths cloud. Bombed at 15.19 hours from 19,500 feet on G.H.

30/11/1944 PD333 A2-K   Bombing Osterfeld 10.40   13.09   15.08

Bomb load 1 x 4000 HC, 16 x 500 GP. Primary target: Osterfeld, Coking plant. Weather 10/10ths cloud. Bombed at 13.09 hours from 19,500 feet. Centre of sky markers. Very concentrated bombing.

F/S. D.L. Lewis was Navigator from that day.

08/12/1944 PD334 A2-D Bombing Duisburg 08.37 11.07 13.03

Bomb load 14 x 1000 ANM59. Primary target: Duisberg. Weather 10/10ths cloud. Bombed at 11.07 hours from 20,200 feet on centre of flares.

11/12/1944 PD334 A2-D Bombing Osterfeld 08.55 11.07 13.05

Bomb load 1 x 4000 HC, 12 x 500 GP, 3 x 500 MC. Primary target: Osterfeld. Weather 10/10ths cloud, tops 16,000 feet. Bombed at 11.07 hours from 20,000 feet on green flares.

16/12/1944 PD325 A2-L Bombing Siegen 11.35 15.01 17.10

Bomb load 1 x 4000 HC, 14 x No. 14 clusters. Primary target: Siegen. Weather very bad on route with icing and cloud. Bombed at 15.01 hours from 18,000 feet on leading aircraft.

21/12/1944 PD325 A2-L Bombing Trier 12.24 15.04 17.10

Bomb load 1 x 4000 HC, 10 x 500 GP, 6 x 250 GP. Primary target: Trier, Marshalling yards. Weather 10/10 cloud, tops 6/9,000 feet. Bombed at 15.04 hours from 18,000 feet on G.H.

23/12/1944 PD334 A2-D Bombing Trier 11.49 14.32 16.18

Bomb load 1 x 4000 HC, 10 x 500 GP, 6 x 250 GP. Primary target: Trier. Weather clear over target. Bombed at 14.32 hours from 18,000 feet on Red T.I. in centre of town.

F/S. Norman Turner

1795136 F/S. Norman Turner.   Pilot.

J92606 (R153503) P/O. Richard Frederick "Dick" Eason, RCAF.
     A/Bomber.

1542922 Sgt. Augustine Whitehead.   Navigator.

1547914 Sgt. William Winkley.   WOP/AG.

1894853 Sgt. Percival Frank Whale.   MU/Gunner.

1890418 Sgt. Victor George Childs.   R/Gunner.

973493 Sgt. William Hopkirk Lamond.   F/Engineer.

1623526 AC1. George Robinson. Super Numerary Crew.

Notes: In many documents and also CWGC, R.F. Eason is quoted by error as R.F. Easen. *(Source: his nephew Richard Alan "Dick" Eason).*

30/04/1944 LL691 A2-D Bullseye English Channel x x 00.15

Whilst on a training flight, LL691crashed on 01/05/1944 at 00.15 hours in the English Channel off Dover. All crew were killed and are commemorated on the Runnymede Memorial. The crew were only recently posted to 514 Squadron on 29th April 1944.

Only recorded in ORB summary. Crew death dated 1st May 1944 in CWGC

P/O. Richard Frederick "Dick" Eason, RCAF.
(courtesy Richard Alan Eason)

database where Eason's name is mispelled Easen.

AC1 Robinson was an armourer, a ground crewman, being carried as a passenger. This was a routine event on non-operational flights and was officially condoned, the passenger being officially recorded and issued with a parachute. Family sources suggest that the aircraft was shot down; however there is no record of a night fighter claim.

"Bullseye" was a mock bombing raid that was a combat simulation, complete with searchlights and flares. A Bullseye exercise was a simulated night bombing operation against a 'target' town or city designed to give crews the experience of an operational sortie but without crossing into enemy territory. Crews would be given a flight plan to follow and a target to simulate bombing.

F/S. Norman James Tutt

176275 (1389988) F/S. Norman James Tutt. Pilot.
1321473 Sgt. Richard Harry Ames. A/Bomber.
1458651 Sgt. Harold Harris. Navigator.
1385979 Sgt. Robert F. Boots. WOP/AG.
1807151 Sgt. C.A. or J.P. Pemble. MU/Gunner.
1851135 Sgt. R.A. Tyrrell. R/Gunner. 2 ops.
1560436 F/S. William James Clubb. R/Gunner. 1 op.
622838 F/S. Sidney Parr. F/Engineer.

15/02/1944 DS816 JI-O Bombing Berlin 17.31 21.31 01.00
Bomb load 1 x 8000 lb bomb. Primary target: Berlin. There was 10/10 cloud. Bombed at 21.31 hrs at 21,000 ft. Red glow seen below cloud. Fighter flares were scattered. No fighter opposition, but heavier flak. Skymarkers appeared to be scattered. Route in conjunction with weather gave trouble-free trip.

From his normal crew, only F/S. N.J. Tutt did this mission as 2nd Pilot with S/L. A.L. Roberts' crew.
19/02/1944 LL684 A2-B Bombing Leipzig 00.07 04.10 07.06
Bomb load 1 x 4000 lb bomb, 32 x 30, 510 x 4, 90 x 4 incendiaries. Primary

662

target: Leipzig. There was 10/10 cloud. Bombed at 04.10 hours at 20,000 ft (incendiaries only). Mid Upper turret u/s. No lights on bomb panel. Attack appeared concentrated. Glow of fires seen below cloud. Good route.

24/02/1944 LL684 A2-B Bombing Schweinfurt 20.52 01.08 04.57

Bomb load 1 x 4000 lb bomb, 24 x 30, 90 x 4, 420 x 4 incendiaries. Primary target: Schweinfurt. Weather was clear with much smoke. Bombed at 01.08 hours at 20,000 ft. Mass of fires and smoke seen. Route good. Good attack.

25/02/1944 LL670 A2-K Bombing Augsburg 21.57 01.18 05.26

Bomb load 1 x 4000 lb bomb, 32 x 30, 90 x 4 incendiaries. Primary target: Augsburg. Weather clear but pall of smoke seen hanging over town. Bombed at 01.18 hours at 20,000 ft. Monica partially u/s. Fires burning on arrival. Smoke clouds to 10,000 ft.

F/S. W.J. Clubb R/Gunner that day.

Note: Later on the night of 15th-16th June 1944 on an operation to Lens whilst at No. 582 Squadron, five of the crew were involved in the crash of Lancaster MK. III ND502 60-N. The aircraft crashed in the North West suburbs of Arras. It is likely the aircraft was shot down by a night fighter. N.J. Tutt, S. Parr, H. Harris and R.H. Ames were KIA, while R.F. Boots survived and evaded successfully. Harris was hit and mortally wounded while attempting to open escape hatch to enable the crew to bail out.

F/O. Alfred Desmond Joseph Uffindell, DFC

NZ425302 F/O. Alfred Desmond Joseph "Des" Uffindell, DFC, RNZAF. Pilot.

NZ429058 F/S. N.C. Sotham, RNZAF. A/Bomber.

NZ429020 F/S. L.M. "Red" Emanuel, RNZAF. Navigator.

F/S. G. Coulthard. WOP/AG.

R212856 F/S. J.F. Wilson, RCAF. MU/Gunner.

183647 (1335707) P/O.Archibald Edward "Max" Clark, DFC R/Gunner 21 ops.

NZ425546 F/O.Albert George "Chatty" Chatfield, DFC, RNZAF. R/Gunner. 9 ops.

Sgt. W.A. Saunders. F/Engineer.

186268 (1289916) P/O. Leslie John William "Les" Sutton, DFC. 2nd Pilot. 25/10/1944

138092 (1113875) F/O. James Stuart Parnell. 2nd Pilot. 28/10/1944

04/08/1944 LL624 JI-R Bombing Bec d'Ambes 13.28 18.04 21.17

Bomb load 5 x 1000 MC, 4 x 500 GP. Primary target: Bec d'Ambes Depot. Weather - visibility very good. Bombed at 18.04 hours from 8,000 feet. Yellow T.I.s in the midst of much black smoke and yellow flames. 3 tanks exploded

A.D.J. "Des" Uffindell crew and ground crew (courtesy David Clark).

as our bombs were going down. Very good attack, smoke from attack up to 12,000 feet.

From his normal crew, only F/O. A.D.J. Uffindell did this mission as 2nd Pilot with F/O. E.T. Cossens' crew.

05/08/1944 HK577 JI-P Bombing Bassen 14.25 19.01 22.15

Bomb load 8 x 1000 MC, 4 x 500 GP. Primary target: Bassen Oil Depot. Weather clear below 5,000 feet. Bombed at 19.01 hours from 4,500 feet at base of fires. One large fire in NW corner of target, two small fires south.

A.E. Clark Rear Gunner until 31/10/44.

14/08/1944 LL624 JI-R Bombing Hamel (Falaise) 13.53 15.52 17.20

Bomb load 11 x 1000 MC, 4 x 500 GP. Primary target: Hamel, bombing of troop concentrations. Weather clear but much smoke. Bombed at 15.52 hours, 8,500 feet to starboard of green T.I.s as directed by Master Bomber. Very good concentrated attack.

18/08/1944 HK577 JI-P Bombing Bremen 21.47 00.16 02.45

Bomb load 1 x 8000 HC, 48 x 30 inc, 540 x 4 inc, 60 x 4 inc. Primary target: Bremen. Weather clear. Bombed at 00.16 hours, 18,500 feet, red T.I.s. Bombing very concentrated believed successful.

25/08/1944 HK577 JI-P Bombing Russelsheim 20.29 01.13 04.33

Bomb load 1 x 4000 HC, 12 x 500 LB Clusters. Primary target: Russelsheim. Weather clear. Bombed at 01.13 hours from 18,500 feet, centre of fires (T.I.s burnt out). Many scattered fires. Explosions among T.I.s. Large area of fires rather too scattered but should show good results.

26/08/1944 HK577 JI-P Bombing Kiel   20.04   23.09   01.27

Bomb load 1 x 4000 HC, 96 x 30 IB, 900 x 4 IB. Primary target: Kiel. Weather clear. Bombed at 23.09 hours from 19,000 feet single red T.I. On run-up attacked by 2 M.E.109s. Rear Gunner successful in sending 1 E/A down in flames which was seen to hit dock by M.U. Gunner. Successful raid.

23/09/1944 PB482 JI-P Bombing Neuss 19.19   21.36   00.15

Bomb load 11 x 1000 ANM 59, 4 x 500 GP. Primary target: Neuss. Weather 10/10ths cloud over target, tops 8/10,000 feet. Bombed at 21.36 hours from 20,000 feet on centre of glow.

28/09/1944 NF968 JI-L Bombing Calais 08.00   09.21   10.33

Bomb load 11 x 1000 MC, 4 x 500 GP. Primary target: Calais 19. Bombed at 09.21 hours from 9,500 feet red T.I.

03/10/1944 PB482 JI-P Bombing Westkapelle 12.33   13.51   14.50

Bomb load 1 x 4000 MC, 6 x 1000 MC, 1 x 500 GP L/Delay. Primary target: Westkapelle (Walcheren). Weather patchy-scattered cloud with base 5,000 feet. Bombed at 13.51 hours, 5,000 feet on Red T.I.

05/10/1944 PB482 JI-P Bombing Saarbrucken 17.25 22.45

Bomb load 11 x 1000 MC, 1 x 500 GP, 3 x 500 GP. Long Delay. Abandoned mission on instructions from Master Bomber heard to say they were unable to locate target and called "Abandon Mission - our troop in vicinity". Jettisoned 1 x 1000 MC, 2 x 500 Long Delay at position 5220N 0233E at 22.15 hours from 4,000 feet. Remainder brought back.

06/10/1944 PB482 JI-P Bombing Dortmund   16.46   20.26   21.58

Bomb load 1 x 4000 HC, 12 x No. 14 Clusters. Primary target: Dortmund, Town and Railways. Weather over the target was clear with slight ground haze. Bombed at 20.26 hours from 20,000 feet on Green T.I.s. Combat at 20.25 hours at 20,000 feet with M.E.410. Rear Gunner fired 3 bursts, M.U. Gunner 1 burst. Strikes observed. Enemy aircraft claimed damaged.

14/10/1944 PB482 JI-P Bombing Duisburg   07.11   09.03   10.52

Bomb load 11 x 1000 MC, 4 x 500 GP. Long Delay. Primary target: Duisburg. Weather patchy cloud with gaps for bombing. Bombed at 09.03 hours from 18,000 feet. North of Docks.

14/10/1944 PB482 JI-P Bombing Duisburg   22.58   01.31   03.19

Bomb load 1 x 4000 HC, 14 x No. 14 Clusters. Primary target: Duisburg. Weather was clear with small amount of cloud over the target. Bombed at 01.31 hours from 20,000 feet. Red and Green T.I.s.

15/10/1944 PB482 JI-P Bombing Wilhelmshaven 17.21 19.48   21.40

Bomb load 11 x 1000 MC, 4 x 500 GP. Primary target: Wilhelmshaven. Weather haze and thin cloud at first with thick cloud later. Bombed at 19.48 hours from 16,000 feet. Red T.I. and incendiaries.

18/10/1944 PB482 JI-P Bombing Bonn 08.26 11.02 12.56

Bomb load 1 x 4000 HC, 5 x 12 x 30 - 2 x 12 x 30 modified, 9 x No. 14 Clusters. Primary target: Bonn. Weather varying cloud 2-7/10ths with break for bombing. Bombed at 11.02 hours from 17,000 feet. Visual of centre of town.

19/10/1944 PB482 JI-P Bombing Stuttgart 22.06 01.10 03.48

Bomb load 1 x 4000 HC, 3 x 500 Clusters, 7 x 150 x 4, 1 x 90 x 4 IB. Primary target: Stuttgart, A/P 'E' 2nd attack. Weather 10/10ths low cloud over target and all crew arrived late owing to winds not as forecast. Bombed at 01.10 hours from 18,000 feet. Red flares with Yellow stars. Combat with twin-engine aircraft over target 01.10 hours. Rear Gunner could not fire.

21/10/1944 PB482 JI-P Bombing Flushing 11.01 12.27 13.20

Bomb load 12 x 1000 MC, 2 x 500 GP. Primary target: Flushing 'B'. Weather clear. Bombed at 12.27 hours from 6,000 feet. Visual.

23/10/1944 PB482 JI-P Bombing Essen 16.34 19.32 21.08

Bomb load 1 x 4000 HC, 2 x 1000 MC, 11 x 500 GP, 2 x 500 MC. Primary target: Essen. Weather 10/10ths cloud over target - tops 12/14,000 feet with most appalling weather on route. Bombed at 19.32 hours from 20,000 feet. Red flares.

25/10/1944 LM684 JI-O Bombing Essen 13.12 15.43 17.11

Bomb load 1 x 4000 HC, 6 x 1000 MC, 6 x 500 GP. Primary target: Essen. Weather over target 10/10ths low cloud, with one clear patch which appeared to fill up later in the attack. Bombed at 15.43 hours from 20,000 feet. Red flares.

P/O. L.J.W. Sutton 2nd Pilot that day.

28/10/1944 PB482 JI-P Bombing Cologne 13.11 15.47 17.37

Bomb load 1 x 4000 HC, 8 x 150 x 4. Primary target: Cologne. Weather clear over target. Bombed at 15.47 hours from 20,000 feet. Smoke trails as instructed.

F/O. J.S. Parnell 2nd Pilot that day.

30/10/1944 PB482 JI-P Bombing Wesseling 09.18 12.00 13.18

Bomb load 1 x 4000 HC, 15 x 500 MC. Primary target: Wesseling. Weather was 10/10ths cloud - tops about 7,000 feet. Bombed at 12.00 hours from 17,000 feet on G.H.

31/10/1944 PB482 JI-P Bombing Bottrop 12.07 15.00 16.27

Bomb load 1 x 4000 HC, 15 x 500 GP, 1 Flare. Primary target: Bottrop, Synth. Oil plants. Weather 10/10ths cloud over target. Bombed at 15.00 hours from 16,500 feet on G.H.

11/11/1944 PB482 JI-P Bombing Castrop Rauxel 08.25 11.06 12.45

Bomb load 1 x 4000 HC, 15 x 500 GP, 1 Flare. Primary target: Castrop Rauxel, Oil refineries. Weather 10/10ths cloud. Bombed at 11.06 hours from 18,500 feet on G.H.

F/O. A.G. Chatfield R/Gunner from that day.

15/11/1944 PB482 JI-P Bombing Dortmund 12.51 15.42 17.12 Bomb load 1 x 4000 HC, 2 x 500 MC, 13 x 500 GP, 1 Red with Green star Flare. Primary target: Hoesch-Benzin Dortmund, Oil refineries. Weather 10/10ths cloud over the target. Bombed at 15.42 hours from 16,500 feet on G.H. Raid should be successful.

20/11/1944 PB482 JI-P Bombing Homberg 12.54 15.14 16.54 Bomb load 1 x 4000 HC, 15 x 500 GP, 1 Red-Green Flare. Primary target: Homberg. Weather 10/10ths cloud over target. Bombed at 15.14 hours from 20,000 feet on G.H.

21/11/1944 PB482 JI-P Bombing Homberg 12.45 15.13 16.37 Bomb load 1 x 4000 HC, 15 x 500 GP, 1 Red & Green Flare. Primary target: Homberg. Weather about 5/10ths cloud but clear for bombing. Bombed at 15.13 hours from 18,500 feet on fires and smoke.

P/O. Archibald Edward "Max" Clark DFC (courtesy David Clark).

27/11/1944 PB482 JI-P Bombing Cologne 12.35 15.03 16.46 Bomb load 1 x 4000 HC, 15 x 500 GP, 1 Flare. Primary target: Cologne, Marshalling Yards. Weather patchy cloud. Bombed at 15.03 hours from 19,000 feet on G.H.

29/11/1944 PB482 JI-P Bombing Neuss 03.04 05.35 07.03 Bomb load 1 x 4000 HC, 6 x 1000 MC, 6 x 500 GP, 3 Flares Red with Green stars. Primary target: Neuss. Weather 10/10ths cloud over target but the glow of fires was seen through cloud. Bombed at 05.35 hours from 19,000 feet on G.H. Bright glow seen through cloud.

02/12/1944 PB482 JI-P Bombing Dortmund 13.07 14.57 16.50 Bomb load 13 x 1000 HC, 1 Red/Green flare. Primary target: Dortmund, Benzol plant. Weather 10/10ths cloud. Bombed at 14.57 hours from 19,500 feet on G.H.

04/12/1944 PB482 JI-P Bombing Oberhausen 12.01 14.08 15.49 Bomb load 1 x 4000 HC, 15 x 500 GP, 1 Flare. Primary target: Oberhausen, Built up area. Weather 10/10ths cloud. Bombed at 14.08 hours from 20,000 feet on G.H.

05/12/1944 PB482 JI-P Bombing Hamm 09.11 11.30 13.35 Bomb load 1 x 4000 HC, 13 x 500 GP, 2 x 500 GP Long Delay, 1 Flare.

667

Primary target: Hamm. Weather 10/10ths cloud over target, but otherwise varying from 6-10/10ths. Bombed at 11.30 hours from 20,000 feet on G.H.

F/S. John Bernard Underwood

1454510 F/S. John Bernard Underwood. Pilot.
J24235 F/O. W.D. McPhee, RCAF. A/Bomber.
136818 (1410296) F/O. Ivor John Frederick Rich. Navigator.
1238225 Sgt. Richard Jock Day. WOP/AG.
J89472 (R104854 R184854 ?) P/O. R.C. Sime, RCAF. MU/Gunner.
1656081 Sgt. Howell John. R/Gunner.
1607088 Sgt. Albert William Johnson. F/Engineer.

07/03/1944 DS786 A2-F   Bombing Le Mans 19.45   22.06   23.54
Bomb load 10 x 1000, 4 x 500 lb. bombs. Primary target: Le Mans. There was 10/10 cloud over the target with one or two breaks. Bombed at 22.06 hours from 10,000 feet. Buildings clearly outlined. No markers seen, target circled for 6 minutes when break in the cloud allowed visual of fires and buildings. Choose bombing on fires rather than bringing bombs back.
15/03/1944 DS786 A2-F   Bombing Stuttgart 19.29 23.21   03.26
Bomb load 10 x 1000 lb bombs, 1050 x 4, 90 x 4 incendiaries. Primary target: Stuttgart. There was 5/10 thin cloud. Bombed at 23.21 hours from 16,000 feet. There was a good concentration of T.I.s, red and green with fires around. Port outer engine airscrew blades and exhaust manifold wiped off in collision with F.W.190. Cannon shell through rear turret. We were attacked by an F.W.190. Combat with F.W.190 few seconds before dropping bombs. E/A collided with Lancaster and was claimed as destroyed. On examination later it was found that the Lancaster had sustained severe damage on the port side and round the Rear turret due to cannon shells. Parts of the Enemy aircraft airscrew and perspex cockpit were found embedded in the engine nacelle on the port side.
18/03/1944 LL684 A2-B   Bombing Frankfurt 19.43 x 21.53
Bomb load 1 x 4000 lb bomb, 1350 x 4, 90 x 4, 32 x 30 incendiaries. Returned early. Furthest point reached 5117N 0220E. Total bomb load jettisoned. Aircraft difficult to control and unable to gain height. Cluster of about a dozen red lights seen approx 10 miles W. of Dunkirk and about 5 to 10 miles inland from coast observed.
22/03/1944 LL684 A2-B   Bombing Frankfurt 18.26 x   x
Bomb load 1 x 1000 lb bomb, 64 x 30, 1161 x 4, 129 x 4 incendiaries. Aircraft missing. Crashed near Nieuw Dordrecht (Drenthe), 8 km SE of Emmen, Holland.

The five killed were buried on 27th March 1944 in Emmen (Nieuw Dordrecht) General Cemetery. F/O W.D. McPhee was interned in Camp L1, PoW No.3831 with Sgt R.C. Sime, PoW No.3841.

John Bernard Underwood's crew. H. John 2nd from left.

Left: Sgt. Howell John. Right: Ivor John Frederick Rich (courtesy Jayne Thomas).

F/O. Robert Walter Vickers, DFC

A424481   F/O. Robert Walter "Bob" Vickers, DFC. RAAF. Pilot.
F/S. Abie Hearn.   A/Bomber.
F/S.   W.E. Williams.*   A/Bomber.
55235 (658150) F/O.   Ivan Marshall "Ivanhoe" Lumsden. Navigator.
Sgt. Basil Dale.   WOP/AG. 29 ops.
189643 (1504777)   F/S. Colin Pratt.   WOP/AG.   1 op.
F/S.   S. Blackett.*   WOP/AG.
Sgt. Geoffrey F. Gill.   MU/Gunner. 27 ops.
W/O.   I.M. Davies.   MU/Gunner.   1 op.
196933 (1333763) W/O.   Harold George Everest Friend. MU/Gunner. 2 ops.
187670 (800653) P/O.   Dennis Vincent "Don" Donnelly. R/Gunner.
Sgt. Harold Burrows.   F/Engineer.

* The operation to Oberhausen on 04/12/1944 is the only operation quoted in ORBs for both of these airmen with this crew. However, they are also listed at the same time in their usual crew in PD389 JI-Q captained by H.L. Merrett. Consequently it is thought that they did not fly the mission with R.W. Vickers.

Robert Vickers wrote:

Souls of Airmen

I have seen her face.
Through flak and flame and death,
Flesh torn and burned;
Ten thousand crosses far and wide await.
The firestorm cold.
The grief and tears but yesterday.

Not for us the cheering throng
The years of love and sound of children's feet
We journey back where brothers lie,
The tarmac, silent now and grey, and
Wildflowers grow where once we flew.

The flights and squadrons, wing on wing
and group on group ascend.
Up, on and up, till earth's horizons fade.
While former foes and suffering victims
Merge and join the stream. One purpose now.
Without the trials of innocence or guilt.

No Orpheus here.
No fleeting glimpse and then forever lost.
The golden beams like searchlights
point the way to journey's end.
The shining face and waiting arms of Hope.

08/08/1944 LL624 JI-R Bombing Foret de Lucheux 21.46 23.50 01.25

Bomb load 18 x 500 GP. Primary target: Foret de Lucheux, Petrol dump. Weather clear. Bombed at 23.50 hours port of green T.I.s as instructed by Master Bomber. Columns of black smoke up to 6,000 feet over target.

"Foret de Lucheux" is a forest between Lille and Amiens. During WWII, important fuel tanks were there.

09/08/1944 LL731 JI-U Bombing Fort d'Englos 21.45 23.18 00.17

Bomb load 13 x 1000 MC. Primary target: Fort d'Englos (Lille), Petrol dump. Weather clear. Bombed at 23.18 hours from 13,000 feet, yellow T.I. per Master Bomber's instructions. Only smoke from bomb bursts seen, nothing to show that target had been hit.

According D.V. Donnelly's logbook "Port outer engine feathered over the target".

The fort of Ennetières-en-Weppes, or "fort d'Englos" is one of a set of six forts surrounding Lille.

12/08/1944 DS620 A2-D Bombing Russelsheim 21.55 00.19 02.54

Bomb load 1 x 2000 HC, 14 x (150 x 4). Primary target: Russelsheim. Opel Motors works. Weather clear. Bombed at 00.19 hours from 17,000 feet, centre of red T.I.s. 1 x 150 x 4 brought back due to hung up. Attacked by M.E. 410 in target area, evaded. Enemy fighter damaged. Good attack.

29/08/1944 PB423 JI-S Bombing Stettin 21.22 02.08 06.16

Bomb load 1 x 4000 HC, 52 x 30, 486 x 4, 54 x 4 lb incendiaries. Primary target: Stettin. Weather cloud 5/10ths. Bombed at 02.08 hours, centre of red T.I.s. Fires taking hold. Large explosions at 02.08 hours.

D.V. Donnelly noted in his logbook "Docks. 1 x 4000."

03/09/1944 ME841 JI-H Bombing Eindhoven 15.30 17.31 18.48

Bomb load 11 x 1000 MC, 4 x 500 GP. Primary target: Gilze-Rijen. Bombed at 17.31 hours from 14,000 feet, visually.

D.V. Donnelly noted in his logbook "Gilze-Rijen-G. Airfield–Holland…"

17/09/1944 NF968 JI-L Bombing Boulogne 10.41 12.15 13.31

Bomb load 11 x 1000 MC, 4 x 500 GP. Primary target: Boulogne, Aiming point 2. Weather clear below cloud. Bombed at 12.15 hours from 3,500 feet, 200 yards port of red T.I.s.

D.V. Donnelly noted in his logbook "Garrison…"

20/09/1944 NF968 JI-L Bombing Calais 14.43 16.05 17.35

Bomb load 11 x 1000 MC, 4 x 500 GP. Primary target: Calais. Weather clear

November 1944 – in front of NF968 JI-L "London Avenger" (courtesy Trevor Sims)

over target. Bombed at 16.05 hours from 2,500 feet, red T.I.s.

D.V. Donnelly noted in his logbook "Garrison..."

03/10/1944 NF968 JI-L Bombing Westkapelle 12.33 13.52 14.52

Bomb load 1 x 4000 MC, 6 x 1000 MC, 1 x 500 GP L/Delay. Primary target: Westkapelle (Walcheren). Weather patchy-scattered cloud with base 5,000 feet. Bombed at 13.52 hours from 5,000 feet to port of red T.I.s.

D.V. Donnelly noted in his logbook "Sea Wall Walcheren Island..."

05/10/1944 NF968 JI-L Bombing Saarbrucken 17.22 x 22.48

Bomb load 11 x 1000 MC, 4 x 500 GP. Primary target: Saarbrucken, Marshalling yards. Weather clear over target. Abandoned mission on instructions from Master Bomber heard to say they were unable to locate target and called "Abandon Mission - our troop in vicinity". Jettisoned 3 x 1000 MC at position 5220N 0237E at 22.15 hours from 7,000 feet. Remainder brought back.

06/10/1944 NF968 JI-L Bombing Dortmund 17.01 20.52 22.45

Bomb load 1 x 4000 HC, 12 x No. 14 Clusters. Primary target: Dortmund, Town and Railways. Weather over the target was clear with slight ground haze. Bombed at 20.52 hours from 20,000 feet. Unable to use bomb sight on account of evasion from fighter.

D.V. Donnelly noted in his logbook "Dortmund City..."

14/10/1944 NF968 JI-L Bombing Duisburg 06.59 09.07 11.09

Bomb load 11 x 1000 MC, 4 x 500 GP Long Delay. Primary target: Duisburg. Weather patchy cloud with gaps for bombing. Bombed at 09.07 hours from 18,000 feet. Fires at Railway junction North of Docks.

14/10/1944 NF968 JI-L Bombing Duisburg 22.52 01.29 03.13

Bomb load 11 x 1000 MC, 4 x 500 GP Long Delay. Primary target: Duisburg. Weather was clear with small amount of cloud over the target. Bombed at 01.29 hours from 20,000 feet; Red T.I. and visual of Docks.

18/10/1944 ME841 JI-Y Bombing Bonn 08.17 11.01 13.08

Bomb load 1 x 4000 HC, 5 x 12 x 30 - 2 x 12 x 30 modified. 9 x No.14

Clusters. Primary target: Bonn. Weather varying cloud 2-7/10ths with break for bombing. Bombed at 11.01 hours from 19,000 feet on G.H. Bursts seen among built up area each side of the river. Bomb Aimer's perspex bombing panel shattered. Bomb aimer's perspex and bombing panel shattered by enemy fire.

D.V. Donnelly noted in his logbook "Rail. Centre...."

19/10/1944 NF968 JI-L Bombing Stuttgart 22.03 01.10 04.04

Bomb load 1 x 4000 HC. 6 x 1000 MC. 1 x 500 GP. Primary target: Stuttgart, A/P 'E' 2nd attack. Weather 10/10ths low cloud over target and all crew arrived late owing to winds not as forecast. Bombed at 01.10 hours from 20,000 feet. Glow of fires and Red and Yellow markers.

D.V. Donnelly noted in his logbook "Industrial area..."

21/10/1944 NF968 JI-L Bombing Flushing 10.53 12.25 13.34

Bomb load 12 x 1000 MC, 2 x 500 GP. Primary target: Flushing 'B'. Weather clear. Bombed at 12.25 hours from 8,000 feet. Visual.

D.V. Donnelly noted in his logbook "Heavy Gun installations..."

W/O. H.G.E. Friend MU/Gunner that day.

23/10/1944 NF968 JI-L Bombing Essen 16.53 x 20.42

Bomb load 1 x 4000 HC, 14 x 500 Clusters. Primary target: Essen. Weather 10/10ths cloud over target - tops 12/14,000 feet with most appalling weather on route. Aircraft returned early with A.S.I. and port inner engine unserviceable. Jettisoned at 19.51 hours 40 miles East of Southwold.

25/10/1944 NF968 JI-L Bombing Essen 13.02 15.35 16.52

Bomb load 1 x 4000 HC, 6 x 1000 MC, 6 x 500 GP. Primary target: Essen. Weather over target 10/10ths low cloud, with one clear patch which appeared to fill up later in the attack. Bombed at 15.35 hours from 20,200 feet. White smoke as instructed.

D.V. Donnelly noted in his logbook "Industrial area..."

26/10/1944 NF968 JI-L Bombing Leverkusen 13.15 15.29 17.14

Bomb load 1 x 4000 HC, 6 x 1000 MC, 4 x 500 GP, 2 x 500 GP Long Delay. Primary target: Leverkusen. Weather over target and on route was 10/10ths cloud. Bombed at 15.29 hours from 17,500 feet on G.H.

D.V. Donnelly noted in his logbook "Chemical plants..."

29/10/1944 NF968 JI-L Bombing Flushing 10.04 11.34 12.27

Bomb load 11 x 1000 ANM59, 4 x 500 GP. Primary target: Flushing, Gun installations. Weather clear over target. Bombed at 11.34 hours from 6,000 feet. Starboard of Red T.I.

D.V. Donnelly noted in his logbook "Westkapelle. Heavy Gun installations..."

31/10/1944 PB423 A2-G Bombing Bottrop 12.01 14.59 16.29

Bomb load 1 x 4000 HC, 15 x 500 GP, 1 Flare. Primary target: Bottrop, Synth. Oil plants. Weather 10/10ths cloud over target. Bombed at 14.59 hours from 17,500 feet on G.H. Aircraft hit by flak on run up - Starboard fin and rudder damaged.

02/11/1944 PB482 JI-P Bombing Homberg   11.17   14.09   15.28

Bomb load 1 x 4000 HC, 6 x 1000 ANM59, 6 x 500 MC. Primary target: Homberg. Weather variable cloud but clear for bombing. Target obscured by pall of smoke rising to 10,000 feet. Bombed at 14.09 hours from 20,000 feet on instruments. Bomb doors hit by flak.

11/11/1944 NF968 JI-L Bombing Castrop Rauxel 08.19   11.08   12.50

Bomb load 1 x 4000 HC, 15 x 500 GP, 1 Flare. Primary target: Castrop Rauxel, Oil refineries. Weather 10/10ths cloud. Bombed at 11.08 hours from 21,000 feet on centre of Red flares.

Contrary to ORBs, according his logbook, D.V. Donnelly was Rear Gunner that day. As ORBs state that H.G.E. Friend was present, he could have taken the place of MU/Gunner.

15/11/1944 NF968 JI-L Bombing Dortmund   12.42   15.41   17.12

Bomb load 1 x 4000 HC, 2 x 500 MC, 13 x 500 GP, 1 Red with Green star Flare. Primary target: Hoesch-Benzin Dortmund, Oil refineries. Weather 10/10ths cloud over the target. Bombed at 15.41 hours from 16,500 feet on Red flares. G.H. unserviceable. Bombing concentrated.

16/11/1944 NF968 JI-L Bombing Heinsburg 13.24 15.38   17.22

Bomb load 1 x 4000 HC, 6 x 1000 MC, 4 x 500 GP, 4 x 250 lb T.I.s. Primary target: Heinsburg. Weather - nil cloud with slight haze over target. Bombed at 15.38 hours from 9,500 feet. Centre of town.

F/S. Colin Pratt WOP/AG that day.

D.V. Donnelly noted in his logbook "Troop concentration, Ammo stores…"

There is a double entry in the ORBs. At the same time this crew is recorded in both NF968 JI-L and NG118 A2-E. Thanks to D.V. Donnelly's logbook it appears R.W. Vickers crew was actually in A/C NF968 JI-L. Due to the number of aircraft detailed for this operation and other reasons, the crew of NG118 A2-E is believed to be that of T.G.N. Trask.

21/11/1944 NF968 JI-L Bombing Homberg   12.40   15.07   16.38

Bomb load 1 x 4000 HC, 15 x 500 GP, 1 Red & Green Flare. Primary target: Homberg. Weather about 5/10ths cloud but clear for bombing. Bombed at 15.07 hours from 19,500 feet slightly west of target.

D.V. Donnelly noted in his logbook "Oil refineries…"

23/11/1944 NF968 JI-L Bombing Nordstern   12.45   15.20   17.07

Bomb load 1 x 4000 HC, 12 x 500 GP, 4 x 250 Red T.I.s. Primary target: Nordstern, Gelsenkirchen Oil refineries. Weather 10/10ths cloud. Gelsenkirchen bombed at 15.20 hours from 20,000 feet on G.H.

27/11/1944 NF968 JI-L Bombing Cologne 12.30   15.05   16.45

Bomb load 1 x 4000 HC, 15 x 500 GP, 1 Flare. Primary target: Cologne, Marshalling Yards. Weather patchy cloud. Bombed at 15.05 hours from 20,000 feet. Visually.

30/11/1944 NF968 JI-L Bombing Osterfeld   10.51   13.09   14.56

Bomb load 1 x 4000 HC, 15 x 500 GP, 1 Red/Green flare. Primary target: Osterfeld, Coking plant. Weather 10/10ths cloud. Bombed at 13.09 hours from

19,800 feet on G.H.

W/O. H.G.E. Friend MU/Gunner that day.

02/12/1944 NF968 JI-L Bombing Dortmund 13.00 14.58 16.54

Bomb load 13 x 1000 HC, 1 Red/Green flare. Primary target: Dortmund, Benzol plant. Weather 10/10ths cloud. Bombed at 14.58 hours from 19,700 feet on G.H.

04/12/1944 PB426 JI-D Bombing Oberhausen 11.57 14.08 15.57

Bomb load 1 x 4000 HC, 15 x 500 GP, 1 Flare. Primary target: Oberhausen, Built up area. Weather 10/10ths cloud. Bombed at 14.08 hours from 20,000 feet on G.H.

W/O. I.M. Davies was MU/Gunner that day.

For F/S. W.E. Williams and F/S. S. Blackett, 04/12/1944 is the only operation with this crew quoted in ORBs. However they are stated at the same time with their usual crew in PD389 JI-Q captained by H.L. Merrett. Consequently it is believed they did not fly with R.W. Vickers that day.

P/O. Victor Hugh Jeffery Vizer

161383 (1265713) P/O. Victor Hugh Jeffery Vizer. Pilot.
1399054 Sgt. Charles James McLoughlin. A/Bomber.
652649Sgt. Edward Sidney Lowe. Navigator.
1313419 Sgt. Edward James Pitman. WOP/AG.
1624738 Sgt. John Douglas Barker. MU/Gunner.
1626043 Sgt. Leslie Theodore Gardiner. R/Gunner.
1686490 Sgt. Kenneth Foyle. F/Engineer.
125519 (1321297) F/O. Peter James Kendrick Hood. 2nd Pilot. 02/01/44
A425136 F/S. Herbert Samuel "Bertie" "Dellie" Delacour, RAAF. 2nd Pilot. 14/01/44

29/12/1943 LL653 A2-F Bombing Berlin 17.14 20.17 23.46

Bomb load 1 x 4000, 24 x 30 incendiaries, 54 x 4 incendiaries, 90 x 4 incendiaries. Primary target: Berlin. There was 10/10 cloud well below. Bombed at 20.17 hours at 19,000 ft. In centre of about 12 concentrated red and green sky markers. Glow of fires seen below. All route markers on way to target seen in correct positions and effective. Route markers not seen on return journey. Monica not used. Would have been a good raid if PFF were right. One or two fighter flares either side of target were seen.

02/01/1944 LL653 A2-F Bombing Berlin 00.21 03.02 06.53

Bomb load 1 x 4000, 24 x 30, 450 x 4, 90 x 4 incendiaries Primary target: Berlin. There was 10/10 cloud, very thick. Bombed at 03.02 hours at 9,000 ft. Sky markers (red) very scattered but green T.I.s nicely concentrated. Orange glow through cloud but could identify it as fires etc. M.U. Turret u/s. Hit by flak.

F/O. P.J.K. Hood was 2nd Pilot that day.

14/01/1944 LL680 A2-H Bombing Brunswick 16.58 19.21 22.25

Bomb load 1 x 4000, 48 x 30 incendiaries. Primary target: Brunswick. There was 8/10 cloud. Bombed at 19.21 hours at 20,000 ft. Large glow of fires seen while over target and still visible 60 miles away on homeward journey. Very good and effective effort. Photo attempted.

F/S. H.S. Delacour was 2nd Pilot that day.

20/01/1944 LL680 A2-H Bombing Berlin 16.24 19.40 23.40

Bomb load 1 x 4000, 32 x 30, 540 x 4, 60 x 4 incendiaries. Primary target: Berlin. There was 10/10 cloud. Bombed at 19.40 hours at 20,000 ft. On red and green sky markers. Should be a good show.

Sgt. Leslie Theodore Gardiner, R/Gunner

21/01/1944 LL680 A2-H Bombing Magdeburg ca.20.00 x x

Bomb load 1 x 4000, 720 x 4, 90 x 4, 32 x 30 incendiaries. Aircraft missing.

While outbound at 21,000 feet, intercepted and shot down by a night fighter. As aircraft disintegrated, P/O. V.H.J. Vizer was thrown clear through the Perspex canopy and survived though badly injured. He was confined in Hospital due to injuries until repatriation. He was repatriated on 2nd February 1945 aboard the SS Letitia.

The rest of crew were KIA and buried in Hanover War Cemetery.

P/O acting F/O. George Arthur Wark, DFC

J88101 F/O. George Arthur "Art" Wark, DFC, RCAF. Pilot.
J36229 F/O. E.J. La Chance, RCAF.   A/Bomber.
J35544 F/O. J.W.R. Wilson, RCAF.   Navigator.
 Sgt. G.J. Whitcombe.   WOP/AG.
 Sgt. J. McCluskey.   MU/Gunner.
 Sgt. H. McKellar.   R/Gunner.
 Sgt. Thomas Charles "Tom" Clayton.   F/Engineer.

09/08/1944 N/K Bombing Fort d'Englos (Lille)ca.21.45 x ca.01.15

Not recorded in ORBs, but according to F/O G.A. Wark's own list of operations reported at rcafassociation.ca, he flew this sortie (Lille) of 02.30 flying time. As the rule was to fly in operation one or two times as 2nd Pilot just before to be the Skipper, it is believed he did this sortie as 2nd Pilot with an unknown crew.

Fort of Ennetières-en-Weppes, or "Fort d'Englos" is one of a set of six forts surrounding Lille.

12/08/1944 LL635 JI-M Bombing Russelsheim 21.57 00.15 02.41

Bomb load 1 x 8,000 HC, 6 x 500 No. 14 clusters. Primary target: Russelsheim. Weather clear. Bombed at 00.15 hours from 17,500 feet. red T.I.s. Large number of flares seen over target. Markers appeared to be well concentrated. Master Bomber not clearly heard.

From his normal crew, only F/S. G.A. Wark did this mission as 2nd Pilot with F/O. E.T. Cossens' crew.

14/08/1944 DS620 A2-D Bombing Hamel (Falaise) 13.53 15.50 17.24

Bomb load 11 x 1000 MC. 4 x 500 GP. Primary target: Hamel. Weather clear, slight haze. Bombed at 15.50 hours from 8,500 feet. Bomb bursts concentrated amongst T.I.s.

According to logbooks: G.A. Wark pilot target "Falaise", T.C. Clayton's "target Hamel".

25/08/1944 LL726 A2-H Bombing Russelsheim 20.40 01.04 04.40

Bomb load 1 x 4000 HC, 6 x 500 LB Clusters. Primary target: Russelheim. Weather clear. Bombed at 01.04 from 17,500 feet centre of cluster of red T.I.s. Bomb bursts well concentrated round T.I.s.

31/08/1944 DS786 A2-L Bombing Pont-Remy 16.15 18.11 19.45

Bomb load 11 x 1000 MC, 2 x 500 GP Mk IV LD. Primary target: Pont Remy, Dump. Weather cloudy. Bombed at 18.11 hours from 15,000 feet on visual of target.

03/09/1944 DS786 A2-L Bombing Eindhoven 15.20 17.30 18.59

Bomb load 11 x 1000 MC, 4 x 500 GP. Primary target: Eindhoven airfield. Bombed at 17.30 hours from 16,000 feet red T.I.s.

06/09/1944 DS786 A2-L Bombing Le Havre 16.43 18.40 19.55

Bomb load 11 x 1000 MC, 4 x 500 GP. Primary target: Le Havre. Bombed at 18.40 hours from 7-5,000 feet starboard green T.I.s. 1 x 1000 MC brought back.

08/09/1944 DS786 A2-L Bombing Le Havre 06.03 x 09.32

Bomb load 11 x 1000 MC, 4 x 500 GP. Primary target: Le Havre. Weather 10/10ths cloud down to 3,000 feet. Abandoned mission on Master Bomber's instructions.

11/09/1944 DS786 A2-L Bombing Kamen 16.15 18.43 20.31

Bomb load 1 x 4000 HC, 16 x 500 GP. Weather clear. Primary target: Kamen. Bombed at 18.43 hours from 17,000 feet on red T.I.s per Master Bomber's instructions.

14/09/1944 PD265 JI-G Bombing Wassenaar 12.55 14.30 15.45

Bomb load 11 x 1000 MC, 4 x 500 GP. Primary target: Wassenaar. Weather was good, nil cloud. Bombed at 14.30 hours from 11,500 feet, red T.I.s.

20/09/1944 NG118 A2-E   Bombing Calais   14.44   16.03   17.36

Bomb load 11 x 1000 MC, 4 x 500 GP. Primary target: Calais. Weather clear over target. Bombed at 16.03 hours from 2,500 feet, red T.I.s.

25/09/1944 PD325 A2-L   Bombing Pas de Calais 08.29 x 11.09

Bomb load 11 x 1000 MC, 4 x 500 GP. Primary target: Calais. Abandoned mission on Master Bomber's instructions. Jettisoned 4 x 1000 MC.

27/09/1944 PD325 A2-L   Bombing Calais   07.36   08.43   10.23

Bomb load 11 x 1000 MC, 4 x 500 GP. Primary target: Calais 15. Weather, cloud 5,500 feet 10/10ths. Bombed at 08.43 hours from 4,500 feet, 150 yards to port of green T.I.

03/10/1944 PD325 A2-L   Bombing Westkapelle 12.00   13.29   14.29

Bomb load 1 x 4000 MC, 6 x 1000 MC, 1 x 500 GP L/Delay. Primary target: Westkapelle (Walcheren). Weather patchy-scattered cloud with base 5,000 feet. Bombed at 13.29 hours from 5,000 feet between 2 red T.I.s.

According to G.A. Wark's logbook the target was "Walcheren". Westkapelle is a place of Walcheren Island.

05/10/1944 PD325 A2-L   Bombing Saarbrucken   17.36 x 22.55

Bomb load 11 x 1000 MC, 1 x 500 GP, 3 x 500 GP. Long Delay. Primary target: Saarbrucken, Marshalling yards. Weather clear over target. Abandoned mission on instructions from Master Bomber heard to say they were unable to locate target and called "Abandon Mission - our troop in vicinity". Jettisoned 3 x 500 at position 5223N 0228E time 22.19 from 8,000 feet. Remainder brought back.

14/10/1944 PD325 A2-L   Bombing Duisburg 06.50   09.05   11.15

Bomb load 11 x 1000 MC, 4 x 500 GP Long Delay. Primary target: Duisburg. Weather patchy cloud with gaps for bombing. Bombed at 09.05 hours from 19,000 feet. Built up area East bank of River.

14/10/1944 PD325 A2-L   Bombing Duisburg 22.27   01.26   03.38

Bomb load 11 x 1000 MC, 4 x 500 GP Long Delay. Primary target: Duisburg. Weather was clear with small amount of cloud over the target. Bombed at 01.26 hours from 20,000 feet. Red T.I.s.

19/10/1944 PD325 A2-L   Bombing Stuttgart 17.26   20.37   23.45

Bomb load 1 x 4000 HC, 3 x 500 Clusters, 7 x 150 x 4, 1 x 90 x 4 IB. Primary target: Stuttgart, A/P 'D' 1st attack. Weather 10/10ths cloud which broke to 6/10ths at the end of the period. Bombed at 20.37 hours from 17,000 feet. Red T.I.

21/10/1944 PD325 A2-L   Bombing Flushing 10.52   12.27   13.42

Bomb load 12 x 1000 MC, 2 x 500 GP. Primary target: Flushing 'B'. Weather clear. Bombed at 12.27 hours from 8,500 feet. What appeared to be square building adjoining A/P.

23/10/1944 PD325 A2-L   Bombing Essen 16.36   19.43   22.11

Bomb load 1 x 4000 HC, 6 x 1000 MC, 6 x 500 GP. Primary target: Essen.

Weather 10/10ths cloud over target - tops 12/14,000 feet with most appalling weather on route. Bombed at 19.43 hours from 20,000 feet. Red flares.

25/10/1944 PD325 A2-L Bombing Essen 13.19 15.47 17.21

Bomb load 1 x 4000 HC, 6 x 1000 MC, 6 x 500 GP. Primary target: Essen. Weather over target 10/10ths low cloud, with one clear patch which appeared to fill up later in the attack. Bombed at 15.47 hours from 21,500 feet. Red flares.

28/10/1944 PD325 A2-L Bombing Flushing 08.52 10.16 11.20

Bomb load 11 x 1000 MC, 4 x 500 GP. Primary target: Flushing. Weather over the target quite clear and conditions perfect, although believed to be only local, and some low cloud approaching. Bombed at 10.16 hours from 8,000 feet. Visual.

30/10/1944 PD325 A2-L Bombing Wesseling 09.20 12.01 13.35

Bomb load 1 x 4000 HC, 16 x 500 GP. Primary target: Wesseling. Weather was 10/10ths cloud - tops about 7,000 feet. Bombed at 12.01 hours from 18,500 feet on G.H. aircraft ahead.

31/10/1944 PD325 A2-L Bombing Bottrop 12.05 15.01 16.46

Bomb load 1 x 4000 HC, 16 x 500 GP. Primary target: Bottrop, Synth. Oil plants. Weather 10/10ths cloud over target. Bombed at 15.01 hours from 18,500 feet on leading G.H. aircraft.

06/11/1944 PD325 A2-L Bombing Koblenz 16.5819.35 21.55

Bomb load 1 x 4000 HC, 2100 x 4 lb IB. Primary target: Koblenz. Weather clear over target. Bombed at 19.35 hours from 17,000 feet on Red and green T.I.s.

15/11/1944 PD325 A2-L Bombing Dortmund 12.33 15.41 17.20

Bomb load 1 x 4000 HC, 16 x 500 GP. Primary target: Hoesch-Benzin Dortmund, Oil refineries. Weather 10/10ths cloud over the target. Bombed at 15.41 hours from 16,000 feet on leading aircraft.

16/11/1944 PD325 A2-L Bombing Heinsburg 13.02 15.36 17.36

Bomb load 1 x 4000 HC, 6 x 1000 MC, 6 x 500 GP. Primary target: Heinsburg. Weather - nil cloud with slight haze over target. Bombed at 15.36 hours from 9,000 feet. Smoke.

20/11/1944 PD325 A2-L Bombing Homberg 12.40 15.14 17.10

Bomb load 1 x 4000 HC, 16 x 500 GP. Primary target: Homberg. Weather 10/10ths cloud over target. Bombed at 15.14 hours from 20,000 feet on leading G.H. aircraft.

21/11/1944 PD325 A2-L Bombing Homberg 12.38 15.08 16.46

Bomb load 1 x 4000 HC, 16 x 500 GP. Primary target: Homberg. Weather about 5/10ths cloud but clear for bombing. Bombed at 15.08 hours from 19,500 feet on Factory.

04/12/1944 PD324 A2-B Bombing Oberhausen 11.46 14.09 16.12

Bomb load 1 x 4000 HC, 2100 x 4 lb incendiaries. Primary target: Oberhausen, Built up area. Weather 10/10ths cloud. Bombed at 14.09 hours from 20,000 feet on leading G.H. aircraft.

P/O. Michael John Warner

1396311 (173432)   P/O. Michael John Warner, Croix de Guerre.   Pilot.

183730 (1479323)   P/O. Cyril Holmes.   A/Bomber.

1567997   Sgt. J.P. Tait.   Navigator.

188440 (1377392)   W/O.   James Gordon George Foyle.   WOP/AG.

3005223   Sgt. Bertram F. Hammond.   MU/Gunner.

1577910   Sgt. Donald N. Sheppard.   R/Gunner.

1387916   Sgt. R.A. Norton.   F/Engineer. 26 ops.

1692208   Sgt. T. Buchanan.   F/Engineer. 5 ops.

37994   W/C.   Michael Wyatt, DFC. Captain. 30/05/45

B.F. Hammond (left), D.N. Sheppard (bottom right), M.J. Warner (top right) (source WMHC)

30/05/1944 LL620 JI-N Bombing Boulogne   23.10   00.05   01.34

Bomb load 6 x 1000 MC, 4 x 500 MC. Primary target: Boulogne Gun Batteries. Clear over target. Bombed red T.I.s at 00.05 hours from 8,000 feet. Sticks seen to burst to North of T.I.s. Trouble free trip.

That day this crew was captained by W/C. M. Wyatt, P/O. M.J. Warner acting as 2nd Pilot.

31/05/1944 LL620 JI-N Bombing Trappes   00.04   02.07   04.40

Bomb load 8 x 1000 MC, 8 x 500 MC. Primary target: Trappes. Clear at target. Bombed at 02.07 hours from 8,500 feet. Uncertain of target at first and so made an orbit. Seemed a long interval between red T.I.s and backers-up. Could not understand the Master Bomber.

02/06/1944 DS816 JI-O Bombing Wissant   01.21 x 03.35

Bomb load 1 x 1000 GP, 10 x 1000 MC, 4 x 500 MC. Primary target: Wissant Gun Positions. Target not identified because of cloud and therefore did not bomb. 4 x 1000 MC and 4 x 500 MC jettisoned safe 30 miles East of Southwold. Remainder of bomb load was brought back.

06/06/1944 DS816 JI-O Bombing Lisieux 00.11 01.37   03.02

Bomb load 16 x 500 MC tail fused and 2 x 500 MC LD. Primary target: Lisieux. Broken cloud. Red T.I.s appeared to be in centre of town. Visual of streets obtained. Bombed red T.I. at 01.37 hours from 5,500 feet. Bombs burst across a built-up area. Monica was u/s.

07/06/1944 DS816 JI-O Bombing Massy Palaiseau 00.30 02.16   04.16

Bomb load 18 x 500 MC. Primary target: Massy Palaiseau, Marshalling Yards. Clear below cloud. Bombed red and green T.I.s at 02.16 hours from 6,500 feet. Master Bomber not heard. Bomb bursts amongst T.I.s and smoke. Raid appeared satisfactory and huge columns of smoke seen in target area.

11/06/1944 DS816 JI-O Bombing Nantes 23.43 02.46   05.21

Bomb load 16 x 500 GP, 2 x 500 LD. Primary target: Nantes. Bombed as instructed by Master Bomber at 02.46 hours from 2,500 feet. Bombs burst alongside and among T.I.s. Master Bomber's instructions heard clearly. 10/10ths cloud but clear below at 2,500 feet.

12/06/1944 DS826 JI-U Bombing Gelsenkirchen 23.08 x 00.33

Bomb load 1 x 4000 HC, 12 x 500 GP, 4 x 500 MC. On taking off A.S.I.s were found to be u/s. The bomb load was jettisoned (safe) at 53.15N 00.48E at 23.47 hours and Lancaster landed at Woodbridge at 00.33 hours.

14/06/1944 DS826 JI-U Bombing Le Havre   23.44   01.14   02.25

Bomb load 11 x 1000 MC, 4 x 500 GP. Primary target: Le Havre. Weather clear. Bombed at 01.14 hours from 15,500 feet on Master Bomber's instructions. Two fires seen on arrival. Seemed a very good attack.

Sgt. T. Buchanan was F/Engineer that day.

21/06/1944 LL734 JI-G Bombing Domleger 18.06 x 20.44

Bomb load 18 x 500 MC. Primary target: Domleger near Abbeville, V-1 flying bomb launch site. T.I.s not seen obeyed Master Bomber's instructions to return to Base. Jettisoned safe 8 x 500 MC at 19.41 hours from 12,000 feet, 5017N 0130E.

23/06/1944 DS816 JI-O Bombing L'Hey 23.13 00.17 01.30

Bomb load 11 x 1000 MC, 4 x 500 GP. Primary target: L'Hey, Flying bomb installations. There was 10/10ths cloud, tops 5,000 feet. Bombed at 00.17 hours from 8,500 feet. Bombed centre of glow as directed by Master Bomber. Target identified by T.I.s falling through cloud and Gee Fix. Blue flash seen in red glow at time of bombing. Photo attempted.

27/06/1944 LL734 JI-O Bombing Biennais 23.38 01.11 02.38

Bomb load 16 x 500 GP. 2 x 500 ANM 64 GP. Primary target: Biennais, Flying bomb installations. There was 10/10ths cloud. Bombed at 01.11 hours from 13,000 feet red glow.

10/07/1944 LL734 JI-O Bombing Nucourt 04.25 06.07 08.02

Bomb load 11 x 1000 ANM 65, 4 x 500 GP. Primary target: Nucourt, Constructional works. Bombed at 06.07 hours from 15,000 feet on Gee.

12/07/1944 LL734 JI-O Bombing Vaires 18.01 x 22.06

Bomb load 18 x 500 GP. Primary target: Vaires, Marshalling yards. Instructed to bomb yellow T.I.s or abandon mission. No T.I.s seen. Jettisoned at 20.44 hours from 13,000 feet, position 4952N 0029E 4 x 500 GP.

15/07/1944 LL734 JI-O Bombing Chalons Sur Marne 21.50 01.31 04.05

Bomb load 18 x 500 GP. Primary target: Chalons sur Marne, Railway centre. Clear below cloud base at 8,500 feet. Bombed at 01.31 hours from 8,000 feet yellow T.I.s. A good attack.

18/07/1944 LL734 JI-O Bombing Emieville 04.34 06.09 07.50

Bomb load 11 x 1000 MC, 4 x 500 GP. Primary target: Emieville, Troop concentration. Weather clear. Bombed at 06.09 hours from 7,700 feet yellow T.I.s. Much smoke all around T.I.s, also fires. A very successful attack.

18/07/1944 LL734 JI-O Bombing Aulnoye 22.44 00.56 02.08

Bomb load 18 x 500 GP. Primary target: Aulnoye, Railway junction. Weather clear. Bombed at 00.56 hours from 9,000 feet green T.I.s. Markers well placed.

20/07/1944 LL734 JI-O Bombing Homberg 23.29 01.20 02.38

Bomb load 1 x 4000 HC, 2 x 500 MC, 14 x 500 GP. Primary target: Homberg, Oil plant. Weather clear, slight haze. Bombed at 01.20 hours from 19,500 feet red T.I.

23/07/1944 LL734 JI-O Bombing Kiel 22.34 01.20 03.49

Bomb load 10 x 1000 MC, 5 x 500 GP. Primary target: Kiel, Warehouses and docks. Weather 10/10ths cloud. Bombed at 01.20 hours from 21,000 feet red T.I. No searchlights, some flak.

25/07/1944 LL734 JI-O Bombing Stuttgart 21.45 01.53 05.56

Bomb load 5 x 1000 MC, 3 x 500 GP. Primary target: Stuttgart. Weather clear, slight haze. Bombed at 01.53 hours from 19,000 feet centre of red T.I.s. Explosions in target area at 01.53 hours and 02.30 hours. Several scattered fires amongst T.I.s.

28/07/1944 LL734 JI-O Bombing Stuttgart 21.50 01.51 05.28

Bomb load 13 x 500 GP. Primary target: Stuttgart. Weather 9/10ths cloud. Bombed at 01.51 hours from 18,000 feet green T.I.s as instructed by Master Bomber. Fairly large fire burning W of T.I.s. Explosion seen east of T.I.s at 01.46 hours. Trouble free route.

01/08/1944 LL624 JI-R Bombing Foret de Nieppe 19.11 x 21.45

Bomb load 11 x 1000 MC, 4 x 500 GP. Target: De Nieppe, constructional works. Jettisoned at 20.54 hours from 9,000 feet 4 x 1000 MC, position 5106N 0230E. Abandoned on Master Bomber's orders.

03/08/1944 LL734 JI-O Bombing Bois de Cassan   11.55   14.06   15.42

Bomb load 11 x 1000 MC, 4 x 500 GP. Primary target: Bois de Cassan, Flying bomb supply depot. Bombed at 14.06 hours from 16,500 feet centre of smoke.

07/08/1944 LL734 JI-O Bombing Mare de Magne 21.54 23.43   00.58

Bomb load 9 x 1000 MC, 4 x 500 GP. Primary target: Mare de Magne (just past Caen). Weather clear over target. Bombed at 23.43 hours from 8,500 feet centre of red T.I.s on Master Bomber's instructions. Much black smoke seen rising over target. Mare-de-Magne: place between Caen and Fontenay le Marmion.

09/08/1944 LL635 JI-M Bombing Fort d'Englos (Lille)21.41 23.13
00.10

Bomb load 13 x 1000 MC. Primary target: Fort d'Englos, Petrol dump. Weather clear. Bombed at 23.13 hours from 10,500 feet, undershot red T.I.s by two seconds on instructions of Master Bomber. Much white flame in target area, followed by palls of black smoke.

Sgt. T. Buchanan was F/Engineer that day.

Fort of Ennetières-en-Weppes, or "Fort d'Englos" is one of a set of six forts surrounding Lille.

18/08/1944 LL734 JI-O Bombing Bremen   21.46   00.12   02.31

Bomb load 1 x 2000 HC, 96 x 30 lb incendiaries, 810 x 4lb incendiaries 90 x 4lb x incendiaries. Primary target: Bremen. Weather clear with slight haze. Bombed at 00.12 hours from 20,000 feet. Red and green T.I.s.

Sgt. T. Buchanan was F/Engineer that day.

25/08/1944 LM684 JI-O Bombing Russelsheim 20.34 01.06   04.22

Bomb load 1 x 4000 HC, 11 x 500 lb Clusters. Primary target: Russelheim. Weather no cloud, slight haze. Bombed at 01.06 hours from 18,000 feet, centre of red T.I.s. T.I.s. partially obscured by smoke which covered whole target area. Difficult to assess results owing to smoke concentration.

26/08/1944 LM684 JI-O Bombing Kiel   20.10   23.12   01.29

Bomb load 1 x 4000 HC, 96 x 30 IB, 900 x 4 IB. Primary target: Kiel. Weather clear. Bombed at 23.12 hours from 18,000 feet, centre of red T.I.s. 2 red explosions seen at 23.10 hours and 23.12 hours. Very good attack. Rear Gunner reported 2 large reddish explosions at 23.14 hours and 23.15 hours, fires were spreading over whole target.

29/08/1944 LM684 JI-O Bombing Stettin 21.26 02.08 06.27

Bomb load 1 x 500 GP, 1 x 1000 MC, 84 x 30, 756 x 4, 84 x 4 LB incendiaries. Primary target: Stettin. Weather clear. Bombed at 02.08 hours from 15,000 feet centre of red T.I.s. Scattered fires seen to merge into one large fire.

03/09/1944 LM684 JI-O Bombing Eindhoven 15.15 x 18.30

Bomb load 11 x 1000 MC, 4 x 500 GP. Primary target: Eindhoven airfield. Primary target not bombed. Returned early. Navigation error.

Sgt. T. Buchanan was F/Engineer that day.

05/09/1944 LM684 JI-O Bombing Le Havre 17.22 19.23 20.29

Bomb load 11 x 1000 MC, 4 x 500 GP. Primary target: Le Havre. Bombed at 19.23 hours from 13,000 feet red T.I.

Sgt. T. Buchanan was F/Engineer that day.

06/09/1944 LM684 JI-O Bombing Le Havre 16.39 18.40 19.44

Bomb load 11 x 1000 MC, 4 x 500 GP. Primary target: Le Havre. Bombed at 18.40 hours from 7-5,000 feet, red T.I.s.

P/O. William Martin Watkins, DFC

176915 P/O. William Martin "Bill" Watkins, DFC. Pilot.
55903 (536929) P/O. Walter Thomas. A/Bomber. 30 ops.
1392790 Sgt. Eric George Rippingale. A/Bomber. 1 op.
R71332 W/O. A.J. Jamieson, RCAF. Navigator.
189715 (1321974) F/S. William Luke Dymond. WOP/AG.
1592295 Sgt. Peter Dawson, DFM. MU/Gunner.
1623889 Sgt. Bernard Ferries, DFM. R/Gunner.
182463 (1607133) Sgt. Leslie William Warren. F/Engineer.

10/04/1944 LL691 A2-D Bombing Laon 01.40 03.51 06.01

Bomb load 8 x 1000, 6 x 500 lb bombs. Primary target: Laon. Weather was clear with very slight haze. Bombed at 03.51 hours from 10,000 feet. One large explosion seen orange in colour leaving a fire which continued to burn. Attack considered very successful. After bombing and before photo flash exploded Rear Gunner ordered corkscrew owing to close proximity of another Lancaster, then resumed course.

18/04/1944 DS795 A2-J Bombing Rouen 22.43 00.48 03.13

Bomb load 10 x 1000, 5 x 500 lb bomb. Primary target: Rouen. Weather was clear. Bombed at 00.48 hours from 13,500 feet. Marshalling Yards seen by bomb flashes. Believed successful attack.

According his logbook, E.G. Rippingale was the Bomb Aimer for this operation. He noted "OPS ROUEN RLY YDS 700 yds west of A.P. 1000lb 500lb".

20/04/1944 DS795 A2-J Bombing
Cologne 00.12 02.01 04.27
Bomb load 1 x 1000, 1026 x 4, 114 x 4, 108 x 30 lb incendiaries. Primary target: Koln. There was 10/10 cloud. Bombed at 02.01 hours from 21,000 feet. Cloud prevented visual. Markers well concentrated. Route quiet. Vibration seen on leaving Koln. Returned Koln, Antwerp, Knocke, Orfordness, Base. Navigator had black out.

22/04/1944 DS795 A2-J Bombing
Dusseldorf 22.56 01.30 03.19
Bomb load 1 x 2000 lb bomb, 84 x 30, 1050 x 4 incendiaries. Primary target: Dusseldorf. There was 5/10 cloud at 20,000 feet. Bombed at 01.30 hours from 20,000 feet. Very large fires seen spreading backwards. T.I.s appeared rather scattered. Very successful attack. Route good.

P/O. William Martin "Bill" Watkins, DFC (copyright Glamorgan Cricket Archives)

24/04/1944 DS795 A2-J Bombing Karlsruhe   22.18 00.48 04.28
Bomb load 1 x 1000 lb bomb, 1026 x 4, 114 x 4, 108 x 30 lb incendiaries. Primary target: Karlsruhe. Weather was clear. Bombed at 00.48 hours from 19,000 feet. Red T.I.s concentrated, but some scattered incendiaries.

26/04/1944 DS786 A2-F Bombing Essen 22.53 01.29 03.02
Bomb load 1 x 2000 lb bomb, 84 x 30, 945 x 4, 105 x 4 lb incendiaries. Primary target: Essen. There was a thin film of cloud at 21,000 feet, clear below. Bombed at 01.29 hours from 20,000 feet. T.I.s appeared concentrated and bombs fell in area marked. Orange coloured fires seen. A very successful attack. Route good.

27/04/1944 DS786 A2-F Bombing Friedrichshafen 22.53 02.12 03.02
Bomb load 1 x 4000 lb bomb, 32 x 30, 36 x 4, 36 x 4 lb incendiaries. Primary target Friedrichshafen. Weather was clear. Bombed at 02.12 hours from 20,000 feet. T.I.s were well concentrated. One large fire seen with column of black smoke rising up to 12,000 feet. Route satisfactory.

01/05/1944 DS786 A2-F Bombing Chambly 22.49 00.23 02.28
Bomb load 10 x 1000, 5 x 500 lb bombs. Primary target: Chambly. Weather was clear. Bombed at 00.23 hours from 9,000 feet. Green T.I.s seen to be off target. A good attack. Fighters gave us plenty to think about, had six attacks between the target and the coast, homeward.

07/05/1944 LL726 A2-H   Bombing Nantes   00.24   03.05   05.38

Bomb load 1 x 4000, 14 x 500 lb bombs. Primary target: Nantes. Weather was clear. Bombed at 03.05 hours from 9,000 feet. Red T.I.s appeared scattered, one set of white then yellow T.I.s followed. Had visual of river. Good attack but conditions too bright.

09/05/1944 LL726 A2-H   Bombing Cap Gris Nez 03.00   04.09   05.10

Bomb load 1 x 1000 GP, 13 x 1000 MC. Primary target: Cape Gris Nez. Visibility good and bombs were released on red and yellow T.I.s at 04.09 hours from 6,000 feet. First batch of T.I.s were dropped off the mark and instructions were given to bomb the second batch. Palls of smoke observed and attack believed to be successful.

19/05/1944 LL726 A2-H   Bombing Le Mans   22.20   00.33   03.30

Bomb load 4 x 1000 USA, 5 x 1000 MC, 1 x 1000 GP, 4 x 500 GP. Primary target: Le Mans. 10/10 cloud at 9,000 feet over target. Bombed red T.I. markers at 00.33 hours from 6,000 feet. Attack appeared very successful if markers correctly placed.

21/05/1944 LL726 A2-H   Bombing Duisburg 22.50   01.13   03.05

Bomb load 1 x 2000 lb bomb, 120 x 30, 600 x 4 incendiaries. Primary target: Duisberg. There was 10/10 cloud at target. Bombed red flares at 01.13 hours from 20,000 feet. Considered a poor attack and bombing appeared scattered. Port inner engine feathered on homeward journey.

24/05/1944 LL726 A2-H   Bombing Boulogne 00.10   01.19   02.25

Bomb load 9 x 1000 MC, 1 x 1000 GP, 1 x 1000 ANM, 4 x 500 GP. Primary target: Boulogne, Gun Battery. Clear over target. Bombed green T.I.s at 01.19 hours from 7,000 feet. Bombs seen to burst around markers. Uneventful trip and a good one. Sighted a single-engined enemy aircraft outward from Boulogne.

05/06/1944 LL726 A2-H   Bombing Ouistreham 03.55   05.11   07.03

Bomb load 9 x 1000 MC and 2 x 500 MC. Primary target: Ouistreham. There was 2/10 broken cloud. Bombed at 05.11 hours from 9,300 feet. Visual of the estuary obtained. T.I.s appeared very scattered and in three groups. Some icing experienced over the target.

07/06/1944 DS786 A2-F   Bombing Massy Palaiseau 00.40 x 04.13

Bomb load 18 x 500 MC. No attack. Bombs were jettisoned live at 4845N 0210E owing to attack by a JU.88. Mission was upset by fighter activity. Nine aircraft were seen shot down. At 02.12 hours was attacked by JU.88 from starboard quarter down. Rear and M.U. Gunners both fired and Lancaster evaded. Was again attacked when homeward bound by ME.410 from astern; Rear Gunner fired and enemy aircraft dived away as Lancaster corkscrewed.

10/06/1944 LL726 A2-H   Bombing Dreux 23.10   00.58   03.43

Bomb load 16 x 500 GP, 2 x 500 LD. Primary target: Dreux. Bombed on green T.I.s as Master Bomber not heard, at 00.58 hours from 8,000 feet. Large explosion seen 01.10 hours. Bombs very concentrated. Fighters active in target area.

12/06/1944 LL670 A2-K   Bombing Gelsenkirchen 23.01   01.08   03.12

Bomb load 1 x 4000 HC, 12 x 500 GP, 4 x 500 MC. Primary target: Gelsenkirchen. Clear over target. Bombed red and green T.I.s at 01.08 hours from 16,000 feet. Large explosion seen at 01.05 hours and large fires with much smoke. Route quiet but track marked by succession of 4 red Balls. Flak barrage and intense searchlights over target. Twin engined aircraft claimed destroyed.

15/06/1944 DS787 A2-D   Bombing Valenciennes 23.00   00.37   02.00

Bomb load 16 x 500 GP, 2 x 500 MC. Primary target: Valenciennes. Weather clear below cloud. Bombed at 00.37 hours from 9,000 feet red and green T.I.s. Good cloud cover on route. Target had to be remarked as first set of T.I.s. fell to starboard.

17/06/1944 DS787 A2-D   Bombing Montdidier   01.00 x 04.56

Bomb load 16 x 500 GP, 2 x 500 ANM 64 GP. Primary target: Montdidier. Heard Master Bomber instruct Pathfinders not to illuminate target and later order main force to return to Base. Jettisoned safe 03.13 hours from 10,000 feet 4 x 500 5012N 0117E.

21/06/1944 LL726 A2-H   Bombing Domleger   18.00 x 21.00

Bomb load 18 x 500 MC. Primary target: Domleger near Abbeville, V-1 flying bomb launch site. There was 10/10ths cloud. Sortie abandoned in accordance with Master Bomber's instructions. Odd bursts of heavy flak slightly below.

23/06/1944 LL726 A2-H   Bombing L'Hey 23.02   00.19   01.35

Bomb load 11 x 1000 MC, 4 x 500 GP. Primary target: L'Hey, Flying bomb installations. There was 10/10ths cloud, tops 4/5000 feet. Bombed at 00.19 hours from 8,000 feet N.W. side of red glow as instructed by Master Bomber; Large explosion at 00.23 hours in centre of glow. Trouble free route, cloud prevented estimate of attack.

27/06/1944 LL726 A2-H   Bombing Biennais 23.26   01.13   02.51

Bomb load 16 x 500 GP. 2 x 500 ANM 64 GP. Primary target: Biennais, Flying bomb installations. There was 10/10ths cloud. Bombed at 01.15 hours from 13,000 feet on Gee Fix.

30/06/1944 LL726 A2-H   Bombing Villers Bocage 18.22   20.00   21.09

Bomb load 10 x 1000 MC, 4 x 500 GP. Primary target: Villers Bocage. Weather clear, patch over target. Bombed at 20.00 hours from 3,800 feet red T.I. One mass of concentrated smoke was left behind. Light flak over target damaged perspex in bomb aimer's compartment, bomb aimer slightly injured. Master Bomber instructed aircraft to come below cloud, this was not necessary as cloud cleared. Very good attack.

02/07/1944 LL726 A2-H   Bombing Beauvoir 12.53   14.37   16.21

Bomb load 11 x 1000 MC, 4 x 500 GP. Primary target: Beauvoir, Flying bomb supply site. Bombed at 14.37 hours from 11,000 feet on yellow T.I.s and visual.

05/07/1944 LM181 JI-E   Bombing Watten 23.18 00.12   01.06

Bomb load 11 x 1000 ANM 65, 4 x 500 GP. Primary target: Watten, Constructional works. Bombed at 00.12 hours from 8,000 feet red T.I.s.

15/07/1944 LL726 A2-H Bombing Chalons Sur Marne 21.43 x 01.59

Bomb load 18 x 500 GP. Primary target: Chalons sur Marne, Railway centre. Returned early Pilot sick. Furthest reached 4935N 0253W. Jettisoned 30 East of Southwold.

18/07/1944 LL726 A2-H Bombing Emieville 04.16 06.06 07.54

Bomb load 11 x 1000 MC, 4 x 500 GP. Primary target: Emieville, Troop concentration. Weather clear. Bombed at 06.06 hours from 8,000 feet yellow T.I.s. Much smoke, a good attack.

18/07/1944 LL726 A2-H Bombing Aulnoye 22.30 00.56 02.21

Bomb load 18 x 500 GP. Primary target: Aulnoye, Railway junction. Weather hazy. No cloud. Bombed at 00.56 hours from 9,000 feet, green T.I.s. Concentrated attack. More backing up flares needed.

20/07/1944 LL726 A2-H Bombing Homberg 23.14 01.21 02.58

Bomb load 1 x 4000 HC, 2 x 500 MC, 14 x 500 GP. Primary target: Homberg, Oil plant. Weather clear. Jettisoned at 01.21 hours from 16,000 feet in target area due to fighter attack, numerous fighters and flares.

23/07/1944 LL716 A2-G Bombing Kiel 22.31 01.22 03.55

Bomb load 6 x 1000 MC, 10 x 500 GP. Primary target: Kiel, Warehouses and docks. Weather 10/10ths cloud. Bombed at 01.22 hours from 18,000 feet red and green T.I.s. 3 large red glows seen through cloud.

24/07/1944 LL716 A2-G Bombing Stuttgart 21.37 01.47 04.57

Bomb load 5 x 1000 ANM 65, 3 x 500 GP. Primary target Stuttgart. Weather 10/10ths cloud. Bombed at 01.47 hours from 17,500 feet on green flares and yellow stars; Flak defences intense. Had combat with enemy aircraft.

F/L.   Frederick John Wheeler, DFC, AFC

145669 (1237645) F/L. Frederick John Wheeler, DFC, AFC. Pilot.

F/O. J.W. Hughes. A/Bomber.

F/O. W.T. Jones. Navigator.

185888 (1034350) F/O. John Robert O'Hanlon. WOP/AG.

183711 (1319414) F/O. John Francis Coules, DFM. MU/Gunner.

172813 (1335750) F/O. Harry Douglas White. R/Gunner.

185061 (1522652) F/O. Oswald Ethan Mee. F/Engineer.

Passengers: 28/06/1945, 08/07/1945, 30/07/1945.

25/06/1945 ME363 JI-R Post Mortem Special mission 09.47 x 16.09

28/06/1945 RF231 JI-A Baedeker Tour over Continent 12.43 x 17.20

Passengers: Cpl. Edwards, S/O. Lynton, Sgt. Everett, LAC. Summers, LAC. Holey.

01/07/1945 RF230 JI-B Post Mortem   Special mission   12.00 x 18.03
08/07/1945 RE116 JI-F Baedeker Tour over Continent 15.01 x 19.22
Passengers: S/L. Lovell, Dr. Dickwell, Dr. St. Joseph, Mr. Game.
30/07/1945 RE117? A2-D Baedeker Tour over Continent 13.52 x
18.19
Conflict in ORBs: Etherington's crew recorded at the same time with the
same aircraft serial.
Passengers: LAC. Fleck, LAC. Benyon, AC. Crossinggun, LACW.
Harbour, ACW. While.

P/O. Kenneth George Whitting

A413058 P/O. Kenneth George Whitting, RAAF. Pilot.
1319553 F/S. Roger William Basey.   A/Bomber.
1315509 F/S. Desmond Edwards.   Navigator.
998689 Sgt. William Anthony Casey. WOP/AG.
A413635 F/S. John Edward Moloney, RAAF.   MU/Gunner.
R172037 Sgt. Per Arne Theodore Nelson, RCAF. R/Gunner.
1445497 Sgt. Leslie Frederick Bostock. F/Engineer.

24/12/1943 LL671 A2-B   Bombing
Berlin 00.37 x   x
Bomb load 1 x 4000, 32 x 30
incendiaries, 450 x 4 incendiaries, 90
x 4 incendiaries. Aircraft missing.
Aircraft carrying 6400 rounds of
ammunition, 1900 gallons of petrol
sufficient for 8 hours flying time, with
the trip estimated to take 7 hours.
According to the only survivor F/S.
Moloney it is believed that P/O.
Whitting, the pilot, was killed during
an attack on the aircraft. The aircraft
crashed at Ostheim, approx 10 miles
N.E. of Frankfurt and 10 miles S.E. of
Friedberg.
J.E. Moloney was taken prisoner and

P/O. Kenneth George Whitting, RAAF

interned at Camp 4B as POW No 269792. Those killed are buried in the
Durnbach War Cemetery, Germany.

P/O acting F/O. John Anthony Whitwood, DFC

178864   F/O. John Anthony Whitwood, DFC. Pilot.

J25348   F/O. Donald J. "Don" McEwen, RCAF. A/Bomber.

152708 (1318086) F/O. Peter Gordon Lankester. Navigator.

Sgt. D. "Jock" Cargill.   WOP/AG.

86817 F/O. Henry Charles Alfred Chapman. MU/Gunner. 4 ops.

R209030 Sgt. J.V. Gillespie, RCAF.   MU/Gunner. 23 ops.

1584931 F/S. Geoffrey Albert "Geoff" Payne. MU/Gunner. 2 ops.

1867675 Sgt. Thomas Aubrey "Tommy" Birch, DFM. R/Gunner.

183650 (1162011) P/O. Kenneth "Ken" Thomas. F/Engineer.

Passenger 14/10/1944:William Troughton, Daily Express War Correspondent

06/06/1944 LL734 JI-G Bombing Lisieux 00.19 01.37 03.23

Bomb load 16 x 500 MC tail fused and 2 x 500 MC LD. Primary target: Lisieux. Weather was clear for bombing. Bombed between red T.I.s from 8,000 feet. Built up area was seen and bombs seemed well on. Many bomb bursts seen & much smoke from the T.I.s. One fire was seen on leaving the target.

F/O. H.C.A. Chapman was MU/Gunner that day.

14th October 1944 – Lancaster Mk1 PD265 JI-G just landed from Duisburg.L to R (back): S. Putman, E. Basford, W. Bell, (three of the ground crew). L to R (front): D.J. McEwen, W.M. Troughton (war correspondent), T.A. Birch, K. Thomas, D. Cargill, P.G. Lankester, J.V. Gillespie, J.A. Whitwood.

08/06/1944 LL690 JI-J Bombing Fougeres   21.52   00.21   02.34

Bomb load 16 x 500 GP and 2 x 500 MC LD. Primary target: Fougeres. Bombed as instructed by Master Bomber at 00.21 hours from 8,000 feet. Visual of street obtained and billows of smoke seen. Bomb bursts on the T.I.s. No opposition met with. At 00.17 hours outward bound and again at 00.26 hours homeward bound, had Monica indications of unidentified aircraft. Evaded.

10/06/1944 LL734 JI-G Bombing Dreux 23.05   00.58   03.49

Bomb load 16 x 500 GP, 2 x 500 LD. Bombed on green T.I.s on instructions of Master Bomber at 00.58 hours from 6,500 feet. Hit by flak. Target reception very poor. Unidentified S/E aircraft claimed as destroyed. Weather Clear. Shot down an unidentified single engined aircraft.

F/O. H.C.A. Chapman was MU/Gunner that day.

11/06/1944 LL734 JI-G Bombing Nantes 23.56 02.51   04.23

Bomb load 16 x 500 GP, 2 x 500 LD. Primary target: Nantes. Bombed yellow T.I.s on Master Bomber's instructions at 02.51 hours from 2,000 feet. There were few searchlights and some light flack. Lancaster coned by searchlights below cloud, and gunners fired at searchlights.

14/06/1944 LL734 JI-G Bombing Le Havre   23.50   01.15   02.41

Bomb load 11 x 1000 MC, 4 x 500 GP. Primary target: Le Havre. Weather was clear. Bombed at 01.15 hours from 15,000 feet, centre of red and green T.I.s. Some fires seen on arrival, much smoke. Attack concentrated. Docks clearly seen on run in.

15/06/1944 LL641 JI-K Bombing Valenciennes   23.04 x 02.46

Bomb load 16 x 500 GP, 2 x 500 MC. No attack. Just crossed French Coast. All navigational aids at fault. 2 x 500 MC jettisoned, 16 x 500 brought back.

F/O. H.C.A. Chapman was MU/Gunner that day.

21/06/1944 ME841 JI-H Bombing Domleger   17.56 x 21.07

Bomb load 18 x 500 MC. Primary target: Domleger near Abbeville, V1 flying bomb launch site. No T.I.s visible, returned to base as per Master Bombers instructions. Jettisoned safe 6 x 500 MC from 12,000 feet, 5025N 0120E.

23/06/1944 LL734 JI-G Bombing L'Hey 23.07   00.16   01.07

Bomb load 11 x 1000 MC, 4 x 500 GP. Primary target: L'Hey, Flying bomb installations. Weather 10/10ths cloud. Bombed at 00.16 hours from 8,000 feet. A Yank reading a news bulletin was heard on channel "B", also much interference of channel "D". Large explosion seen astern at 00.30 hours.

F/O. H.C.A. Chapman was MU/Gunner that day.

24/06/1944 LM180 JI-G Bombing Rimeux 23.27   00.35   02.18

Bomb load 18 x 500 GP. Primary target: Rimeux, Flying bomb installations. Weather clear. Bombed at 00.35 hours from 10,000 feet centre of red T.I.s. Many bomb bursts seen amongst red T.I.s. Numerous searchlights. Clouds of smoke seen.

07/07/1944 LM180 JI-G Bombing Vaires 22.59   01.37   03.33

Bomb load 7 x 1000 MC, 4 x 500 GP. Primary target: Vaires, Marshalling yards. Bombed at 01.37 hours from 12,000 feet green T.I.s as directed by Master Bomber. One 1000 lb bomb hung up over target and eventually dropped at 01.46 hours position 48.42N 02.13E. Should be good attack. Many fighter flares seen.

F/S. G.A. Payne was MU/Gunner that day.

By F/Sgt. Geoffrey Payne – September 2014.

"Reporting to the Gunnery Office July the 7th, to my delight was informed that I would be flying that night with F/S. Whitwood's crew as MU gunner, as their own gunner was off sick with a bad stomach. Target for the night was Vaires railway marshalling yard Paris and was part of the plan to disrupt the German supply route to the Normandy battlefields. Take off time 22.30 just as darkness was falling. Flying as a MU gunner was a new experience for me with great views all around. A fairly direct route to the target, plenty of searchlight activity but the flak was nowhere near as heavy as my experience of German targets. A well concentrated attack without the loss of aircraft possibly due to another attack on a flying bomb storage depot at St-Leu-d'Esserent, north of Paris where enemy fighters claimed thirty aircraft. Landed back at base after a 4hr 45min flight."

10/07/1944 LM180JI-G Bombing Nucourt 04.02 06.08 07.41

Bomb load 11 x 1000 ANM 65, 4 x 500 GP. Primary target: Nucourt, Constructional works. Bombed from 15,000 feet on Gee fix.

F/S. G.A. Payne was again MU/Gunner that day.

By F/Sgt. Geoffrey Payne – September 2014.

"On the 10th of July I was with F/S. Whitwood's crew again on my first daylight raid for an attack on a flying bomb dump at Nucourt. Take-off time 04.04hrs. Uneventful trip with light flak at the target area which was covered in cloud. Landed back at base at 07.45hrs. F/S. Whitwood's crew completed their tour of ops and all survived the war. Five days later I was to join a crew (the Cossens' Crew) whose R/gunner (Sgt. Peter Brown – badly injured on 7th June 1944 during operations on Massy Palaiseau) had lost a foot from a predicted flak shell which had penetrated his turret and continued on to its predicted height before exploding."

15/07/1944 LM180JI-G Bombing Chalons Sur Marne 21.34 01.35 04.02

Bomb load 18 x 500 GP. Primary target: Chalons sur Marne, Railway centre. Weather clear. Bombed at 01.35 hours from 8,000 feet on green T.I.s. A good attack, Master Bomber good and concise.

20/07/1944 LM180JI-G Bombing Homberg 23.09 01.23 02.41

Bomb load 1 x 4000 HC, 2 x 500 MC, 16 x 500 GP. Primary target: Homberg, Oil plant. Slight haze. Bombed at 01.23 hours from 19,000 feet on red and green T.I.s. Good raid and columns of black smoke.

23/07/1944 LM180JI-G Bombing Kiel 22.21 01.21 03.31

Bomb load 10 x 1000 MC, 5 x 500 GP. Primary target: Kiel, Warehouses and docks. Weather 10/10ths cloud. Bombed at 01.21 hours from 19,500 feet centre of 3 red T.I.s. T.I.s well concentrated.

25/07/1944 LL624 JI-R Bombing Stuttgart 21.41 01.55 05.50

Bomb load 5 x 1000 MC, 3 x 500 GP. Primary target: Stuttgart. Weather clear over target. Bombed at 01.55 hours from 19,000 feet green T.I.s. Attack rather scattered. Slight icing in cloud.

28/07/1944 LM180 JI-G Bombing Stuttgart 21.36 01.54 05.38

Bomb load 7 x 1000 MC, 2 x 500 GP. Primary target: Stuttgart. Weather 10/10ths thin cloud. Bombed at 01.54 hours from 19,500 feet green T.I.s. Appeared to be a decoy red T.I. N.W. Of target. Not very satisfactory.

03/08/1944 LM180 JI-G Bombing Bois de Cassan 11.39 14.07 15.34

Bomb load 11 x 1000 MC, 4 x 500 GP. Primary target: Bois de Cassan, Flying bomb supply depot. Bombed at 14.07 hours from 15,000 feet centre of smoke.

04/08/1944 LM180 JI-G Bombing Bec D'Ambes 13.17 18.01 21.04

Bomb load 8 x 1000 MC, 2 x 500 GP. Primary target: Bec d'Ambes depot. Weather – clear patch over target. Bombed at 14.07 hours from 8,500 feet, visual A/P. Reddish flames and black smoke up to 7,000 feet. Good effort. Uneventful trip.

05/08/1944 LM288 JI-C Bombing Bassen 14.24 18.59 22.03

Bomb load 8 x 1000 MC, 2 x 500 GP. Primary target: Bassen Oil Depot. Weather thunder cloud down to 5,000 feet, clear below. Bombed at 18.59 hours from 5,500 feet visually and at base of smoke. Large column of smoke up to 5,000 feet, huge explosion at 19.02 hours, orange red in column.

08/08/1944 LM180 JI-G Bombing Foret de Lucheux 21.41 23.50 01.11

Bomb load 18 x 500 GP. Primary target: Foret de Lucheux, Petrol dump. Weather clear. Bombed at 23.50 hours from 11,700 feet, red T.I. Large red fires and much black smoke observed.

"Foret de Lucheux" is a forest between Lille and Amiens. During WWII, important fuel tanks were there.

09/08/1944 PB143 JI-B Bombing Fort d'Englos (Lille)21.49 23.13 00.17

Bomb load 14 x 1000 MC. Primary target: Fort d'Englos, Petrol dump. Bombed at 23.13 hours from 12,000 feet. Red T.I.s. Very good concentration of bomb bursts just short of red T.I.s. Orange coloured fires seen as aircraft left target.

Fort of Ennetières-en-Weppes, or "Fort d'Englos" is one of a set of six forts surrounding Lille.

31/08/1944 PD265 JI-G Bombing Pont-Remy 16.01 18.17 19.45

Bomb load 11 x 1000 MC, 4 x 500 GP Mk IV LD. Primary target: Pont Remy, Dump. Weather cloudy. Bombed at 18.17 hours from 15,000 feet on Gee H.

05/09/1944 PD265 JI-G Bombing Le Havre 17.26 19.23 20.44

Bomb load 11 x 1000 MC, 4 x 500 GP. Primary target: Le Havre. Bombed at 19.23 hours from 13,000 feet red T.I.

08/09/1944 PD265 JI-G Bombing Le Havre 06.04 08.04 09.23

Bomb load 11 x 1000 MC, 4 x 500 GP. Primary target: Le Havre. Weather 10/10ths cloud down to 3,000 feet. Bombed at 08.04 hours from 2/3,000 feet, red T.I.s.

11/09/1944 PD265 JI-G Bombing Kamen 16.08 18.43 20.25

Bomb load 1 x 4000 HC, 16 x 500 GP. Weather clear. Primary target: Kamen. Bombed at 18.43 hours from 16,600 feet between red and yellow T.I.s.

06/10/1944 PD265 JI-G Bombing Dortmund 16.38 20.28 22.14

Bomb load 1 x 4000 HC, 12 x No. 14 Clusters. Primary target: Dortmund, Town and Railways. Weather over the target was clear with slight ground haze. Bombed at 20.28 hours from 20,000 feet on centre of red and green T.I.s.

07/10/1944 PD265 JI-G Bombing Emmerich 12.02 14.28 16.03

Bomb load 1 x 4000 HC, 10 x No. 14 clusters. 4 x (150 x 4). Primary target Emmerich. Weather clear with cloud at 13,000 feet. Bombed at 14.28 hours from 13,000 feet on North of smoke as ordered by the Master Bomber. 1 cluster of incendiaries fell 50 miles East of Southwold at 13.37 hours when checking bombing doors.

14/10/1944 PD265 JI-G Bombing Duisburg 07.10 09.07 11.02

Bomb load 11 x 1000 MC, 4 x 500 GP Long delay. Primary target: Duisburg. Weather patchy cloud with gaps for bombing. Bombed at 09.07 hours from 18,200 feet, built up area north of docks.

Daily Express War correspondent William M. Troughton aboard.

15/10/1944 PD265 JI-G Bombing Wilhelmshaven 17.20 19.55 21.58

Bomb load 11 x 1000 MC, 4 x 500 GP. Primary target: Wilhelmshaven. Weather haze and thin cloud at first with thick cloud later. Bombed from 12,500 feet, centre of red and green T.I.s.

S/L. Hugh Clayton George Wilcox

Service number RAF 40160, transferred to RCAF (C94073) on 8 June 1945, released 9 March 1946. Subsequently rejoined the RAF.

40160 S/L. Hugh Clayton George Wilcox. Pilot.
J22066 F/O. T.S. Falconer, RCAF. A/Bomber.
J39944 F/O. B. Cohen, RCAF. Navigator.
F/S. V.H. Stevens. WOP/AG.
R256481 F/S. John Joseph Ciancio, RCAF. MU/Gunner.
R280958 F/S. H.B.G. Conrad, RCAF. R/Gunner.
****651 Sgt. Donald Albert Poole. F/Engineer.
131794 (1109283) F/L. William Gilson Bainbridge. 2nd Pilot.
01&07/03/45
153592 (1582441) F/O. Thomas Harry Pashley. 2nd Pilot. 04/04/1945

Passengers: 03/06/1945

05/01/1945 PB419 JI-J Bombing Ludwigshafen 11.18 15.09 17.20
Bomb load 1 x 4000 HC, 10 x 500 ANM58 or 64, 1 x 500 GP, 1 Flare, Primary target: Ludwigshafen, Marshalling yards. Weather clear over target. Bombed at 15.09 hours from 19,500 feet. North part of Marshalling Yard.
From his usual crew, only S/L. H.C.G. Wilcox did this mission as 2nd Pilot with F/O. J.F. Ness' crew.
16/01/1945 PA186 A2-G Bombing Wanne-Eickel 23.10 02.27 04.19
Bomb load 1 x 4000 HC, 10 x 500 ANM58, 4 x 250 GP, 1 Flare. Primary target: Wanne-Eickel, Benzol plant. Weather 10/10ths thin low cloud. Bombed at 02.27 hours from 18,000 feet on G.H.
From his usual crew, only S/L. H.C.G. Wilcox did this mission as 2nd Pilot with F/L. F.P. Hendy's crew.
28/01/1945 NN781 A2-B Bombing Cologne 10.40 14.13 16.15
Bomb load 1 x 4000 HC, 10 x 500 ANM64, 2 x 500 GP, 3 x 250 GP. Primary target: Koln-Gremberg, Marshalling yards. Weather 10/10ths cloud en route clearing on approach to target where visibility was good and nil cloud. Bombed at 14.13 hours from 21,000 feet on G.H. Leader.
29/01/1945 PB426 JI-D Bombing Krefeld 11.00 13.58 15.42
Bomb load 1 x 4000 HC, 10 x 500 ANM64, 2 x 500 GP, 4 x 250 GP. Primary target: Krefeld Marshalling Yards. Weather 10/10ths low thin cloud over target although clear patches en-route. Bombed at 13.58 hours from 20,000 feet on G.H. Leader.
25/02/1945 ME354 JI-M Bombing Kamen 09.31 12.46 15.15
Bomb load 1 x 4000 HC, 9 x 500 ANM64, 2 x 500 MC, 4 x 250 GP. Primary target: Kamen. Weather 6-8/10ths cloud. Bombed at 12.46 hours from 19,000 feet on G.H. Leader.

Lancaster III ME387 JI-N 514 Squadron RAF "B Flight" – 1945 – L to R: H.B.G. Conrad, V.H. Stevens, B. Cohen, HCG Wilcox, T.S. Falconer, D.A. Poole, J.J. Ciancio (courtesy Tony Poole)

27/02/1945 ME387JI-N Bombing Gelsenkirchen 10.51   14.27   17.05

Bomb load 1 x 4000 HC, 9 x 500 ANM64, 2 x 250 GP. Primary target: Gelsenkirchen (Alma Pluts) Benzin plant. Weather 10/10ths cloud, 6/10,000 feet tops. Bombed last resort target Solingen. Dropped 1 x 4000 HC at 14.27 hours from 20,000 feet. Jettisoned 9 x 500 ANM64, 2 x 250 GP at 15.54 hours from 3,000 feet at position 5215N 0315E. Gee fix taken.

01/03/1945 ME387JI-N Bombing Kamen   11.48   15.05   17.54

Bomb load 1 x 4000 HC, 11 x 500 ANM64, 2 x 500 MC L/Delay. Primary target: Kamen, Coking plant. Weather 10/10ths cloud. Bombed at 15.05 hours from 18,500 feet on leading G.H. aircraft and Blue puffs. 1 x 500 ANM64 hung up and brought back.

F/L. W.G. Bainbridge was 2nd Pilot that day.

07/03/1945 ME387JI-N Bombing Dessau   17.11   21.58   01.52

Bomb load 1 x 4000 HC, 6 x Mk 17 Clusters. Primary target: Dessau. Weather 5 to 10/10ths thin cloud. Bombed at 21.58 hours from 20,000 feet on Red flares with Green stars.

F/L. W.G. Bainbridge was 2nd Pilot that day.

18/03/1945 ME363JI-R Bombing Bruchstrasse   11.45   15.05   17.18

Bomb load 1 x 4000 HC, 13 x 500 ANM64, 2 x 500 MC, 1 Skymarker Blue Puff. Primary target: Bruchstrasse, Coal mine & coking plant. Weather 10/10ths cloud, tops 6-12,000 feet. Bombed at 15.05 hours from 18,500 feet

696

on G.H.

23/03/1945 ME387JI-N Bombing Wesel 14.25 17.39 19.05

Bomb load 13 x 1000 MC. Primary target: Wesel, in support of ground troops. Weather perfect. Bombed at 17.39 hours from 20,000 feet on G.H.

04/04/1945 ME387JI-N Bombing Merseburg (Leuna) 18.52 x 02.57

Bombed primary target Merseburg. Bomb load 1 x 4000 HC, 6 x 500 ANM64. 7/10th cloud (Stratus). Bombed on starboard of middle stick red green stars. Bright bluish green explosion seen. Some smoke. Several bombs seen to drop outside the target area. P.F.F. working was late and scattered in four different areas.

F/O. H.T. Pashley was 2nd Pilot that day.

22/04/1945 ME387JI-N Bombing Bremen 15.17 18.42 21.05

Bomb load 1 x 4000 HC, 2 x 500 MC, 14 x 500 ANM 64. Primary target: Bremen, in support of Troop concentration. Weather on approaching target 4-5/10ths cloud. Bombed on G.H. Leader at 18.42 hours from 18,500 ft. Bomb seen to fall in target area. Flak. Appeared effective concentration affected by flak. Fighter cover not close.

03/05/1945 ME364JI-P Manna The Hague 11.09 12.25 13.31

Dropping area The Hague. Dropped 5 Panniers on smoke from T.I.s and White Cross at 12.25 hrs. Visibility good. Cloud base 15/2,000 ft. Satisfactory and good collection of Bags.

10/05/1945 RA599 JI-L Exodus Juvincourt - Ford 11.28 x 17.09

Duration 3.30. Outward 1.35 hours. Collected 24 ex POWs. Homeward 1.55 hours. Better facilities for collecting of documents from aircraft who are landing at Ford and taking off immediately.

12/05/1945 ME359JI-T Exodus Brussels -Tangmere 12.13 x 18.07

Duration 3.33. Outward 1.23 hours. Homeward 2.10 hours. 10 Refugees to Brussels, 24 POWs to Ford. All OK.

17/05/1945 RE139 JI-M Exodus Brussels - Westcott 10.25 x 14.51

Duration 2 hrs 44 mins. Out 1 hr 25 mins. In 1 hr 20 mins. 10 Belgian refugees taken to Brussels. No POWs back. Organisation OK at Brussels.

03/06/1945 ME387JI-N Baedeker Tour over Germany 09.41 x 14.07

Passengers: G/C. H.E. Hills, AC. H. Hannakin, AC. J. Davis, AC. T. Atkinson.

F/O. Harold Gordon Wilkinson

176508 (1434961)   F/O. Harold Gordon Wilkinson. Pilot.
  F/S. E.W. Holmes.   A/Bomber.
 Sgt. G. Lightowler.   Navigator.
175748 (1387471)   F/O. Edwin Stanley Spinks. WOP/AG.
  F/O. A.W. Jones.   MU/Gunner.
  W/O.   E.T. Inions.   R/Gunner. 5 ops.
 Sgt. R.T. Roles.   F/Engineer

Passengers: 07/07/1945, 08/07/1945, 19/07/1945, 22/07/1945.

29/06/1945 RE120 A2-C   Post Mortem Special mission 09.59   x 16.04
No Rear Gunner that day.
01/07/1945 RE117 A2-D   Post Mortem Special mission 12.03   x 18.08
07/07/1945 RE120 A2-C   Baedeker Tour over Continent 10.56   x 15.56
   Passengers: LAC. Handley, F/O. Spierenburg, Cpl. Pritchard (WAAF).
08/07/1945 RF272 A2-F   Baedeker Tour over Continent 10.47   x 15.37
   Passengers: Cpl. Mackintosh (WAAF), LACW. Blyne, LAC. Appleby, F/S. Hinton, AC. Curphy.
19/07/1945 RA602 A2-H   Baedeker Tour over Continent 09.59   x 14.06
   Passengers: F/L. Fowler (3 Group), Cpl. Stacey, LAC. Hendry, ACW. Blundell, ACW. Lingard.
22/07/1945 RA602 A2-H   Baedeker Tour over Continent 09.59   x 14.28
   Passengers: Sgt. Delanoy, LAC. Beck, LAC. Brown, ACW. Morrie, ACW. Reiley.

P/O. Cyril Ernest Williams, DFC, AFC

182344 (740534) P/O. Cyril Ernest Williams. DFC. AFC. Pilot.
570047   F/S. L. Price-Stephens. A/Bomber.
51634 (581284)F/O.Percy Albert Edward Grinter, DFC. Navigator. 20 ops.
J16828   F/O. Allan Harry Fallis, DFC, RCAF. Navigator. 8 ops.
1078195 Sgt. W. Littler.   WOP/AG.
547837   Sgt. J. Kelly.   MU/Gunner.
178476 (1151582) P/O.   Edward Ernest "Ted" de Joux, DFM, CGM. R/Gunner. 20 ops.
W/O. C. Hughes.   R/Gunner. 8 ops.
Sgt. B.R. Apps.   F/Engineer. 4 ops.
913879   Sgt. R.O. Mowe.   F/Engineer. 24 ops.

22/05/1944 DS842 JI-F Bombing Dortmund 22.45 x 00.20

Bomb load 1 x 2000 lb bomb, 96 x 30, 810 x 4, 90 x 4 incendiaries. Primary target: Dortmund. Returned early and landed at Woodbridge. Excessive icing encountered and aircraft could not maintain altitude as a result.

From his usual crew, only W/O. C.E. Williams did this mission as 2nd Pilot with P/O. R. Langley's crew.

24/05/1944 LL652 JI-C Bombing Boulogne 00.10 01.13 02.00

Bomb load 9 x 1000 MC, 1 x 1000 GP, 10 x 1000 ANM, 4 x 500 GP. Primary target: Boulogne, Gun Battery. Clear over target. Bombed at 01.13 hours from 7,500 feet. Uneventful trip. Attack considered good but some overshoots were noticed.

P/O. Edward Ernest "Ted" de Joux, DFM, CGM (courtesy Simon de Joux)

From his usual crew, only W/O. C.E. Williams did this mission as 2nd Pilot with F/O. L.C.A. Taylor's crew.

27/05/1944 LL728 JI-B Bombing Boulogne 00.09 01.16 02.02

Bomb load 7 x 1000 MC, 4 x 1000 ANM, 4 x 500 GP. Primary target: Boulogne Gun Batteries. Clear at target. Bombed centre of the markers at 01.16 hours from 10,000 feet. Flak slight and bursting beneath. Fighter flares seen on the run-in to the target.

LL728 JI-B was known as "Black Bess".

F/O.P.A.E. Grinter was Navigator until 25/07/1944 and P/O. E.A. de Joux was R/Gunner.

Sgt. B.R. Apps was F/Engineer until 31/05/1944.

28/05/1944 LL728 JI-B Bombing Angers 19.00 23.55 01.41

Bomb load 5 x 1000 MC, 1 x 1000 USA, 4 x 500 MC. Primary target: Angers. Clear at target. Bombed at 23.55 hours from 8,000 feet. Good trip and route OK. Master Bomber clearly heard. Red flares seen on reaching enemy coast.

30/05/1944 LL728 JI-B Bombing Boulogne 23.00 00.05 01.50

Bomb load 6 x 1000 MC, 4 x 500 MC. Primary target: Boulogne Gun

699

Batteries. Clear over target. Bombed red T.I.s at 00.05 hours from 8,000 feet. Light and heavy flak commenced as soon as T.I.s fell. Flak slightly more than on previous occasion.

31/05/1944 LL728 JI-B Bombing Trappes   23.51   02.02   04.35

Bomb load 8 x 1000 MC, 8 x 500 MC. Primary target: Trappes. Clear at target. Visual obtained of lake and T.I.s. Bombed at 02.02 hours from 8,000 feet. Unable to assess effect of the attack. 1 x 1,000 MC hung up.

05/06/1944 LL728 JI-B Bombing Ouistreham 03.43   05.10   06.42

Bomb load 9 x 1000 MC and 2 x 500 MC. Primary target: Ouistreham. Patchy cloud and slight haze at target. Bombed markers at 05.10 hours from 9,000 feet. Results of attack not seen, cloud prevented visual after bombing. Route quiet.

Sgt. R.O. Mowe became F/Engineer from that day.

07/06/1944 LL697 JI-E Bombing Massy Palaiseau 00.18 02.13   04.25

Bomb load 18 x 500 MC. Primary target: Massy Palaiseau, Marshalling Yards. Slight haze below and cloud above. Bombed as directed by Master Bomber at 02.13 hours from 6,500 feet. Railway lines seen by light of the flash with T.I.s on either side. Previous bombs seen to fall between T.I.s. Attack thought successful. Route fairly quiet.

10/06/1944 LL692 JI-A Bombing Dreux   23.04   00.55   03.18

Bomb load 16 x 500 GP, 2 x 500 LD. Primary target: Dreux. Bombed on visual T.I.s seen to be off to the N.E. as Master Bomber not heard at 00.55 hours from 5,000 feet. Bombs seen to burst across the yards. Weather clear. Had combat with enemy aircraft.

11/06/1944 LL692 JI-A Bombing Nantes   23.47 02.47   05.13

Bomb load 16 x 500 GP. 2 x 500 LD. Primary target: Nantes. Bombed as instructed by Master Bomber at 02.47 hours from 2,300 feet. No visual obtained. Conditions hazy below cloud base of 2,700 feet. Port outer engine u/s on return.

14/06/1944 LL692 JI-A Bombing Le Havre   23.36   01.14   02.36

Bomb load 11 x 1000 MC, 4 x 500 GP. Primary target: Le Havre. Weather was clear. Bombed at 01.14 hours from 16,000 feet on red and green T.I.s. Very good attack. Explosions and fires seen 70 miles from target.

23/06/1944 LL666 JI-D Bombing L'Hey   22.59   00.16   01.26

Bomb load 11 x 1000 MC, 4 x 500 GP. Primary target: L'Hey, Flying bomb installations. There was 10/10ths cloud. Bombed at 00.16 hours from 9,000 feet red T.I. Quiet trip. Bomb bursts concentrated amongst markers position of which coincided with Gee target co-ordinates.

27/06/1944 LM206 JI-C Bombing Biennais 23.37   01.11   02.46

Bomb load 16 x 500 GP, 2 x 500 ANM 64 GP. Primary target: Biennais, Flying bomb installations. There was 10/10ths cloud. Bombed at 01.11 hours from 13,000 feet. Red glow seen.

30/06/1944 LM206 JI-C Bombing Villers Bocage 18.09   20.02   21.05

Bomb load 11 x 1000 MC, 4 x 500 GP. Primary target: Villers Bocage.

Weather clear. Bombed at 20.02 hours from 12,000 feet on visual of town, checked by Gee. Markers not seen. Town covered with smoke.

02/07/1944 LM206 JI-C Bombing Beauvoir   12.46   14.36   16.07

Bomb load 11 x 1000 MC, 4 x 500 GP. Primary target: Beauvoir, Flying bomb supply site. Bombed at 14.36 hours from 3,000 feet visual.

05/07/1944 LM206 JI-C Bombing Watten   22.42   00.07   00.53

Bomb load 11 x 1000 ANM 65, 4 x 500 GP. Primary target: Watten, Constructional works. Bombed at 00.07 hours from 8,000 feet red T.I.s.

07/07/1944 PB142 JI-A Bombing Vaires   22.42   01.33   02.59

Bomb load 11 x 1000 ANM65. Primary target: Vaires, Marshalling yards. Weather clear. Bombed at 01.33 hours from 12,000 feet red and yellow T.I.s as instructed. Red fires and huge explosion at 01.37 hours. Good concentration of markers.

18/07/1944 LM206 JI-C Bombing Emieville   04.11   06.04   07.10

Bomb load 11 x 1000 MC, 4 x 500 GP. Primary target: Emieville, Troop concentration. Weather clear. Bombed at 06.04 hours from 7,000 feet further edge of yellow T.I.s, as instructed by Master Bomber. All bombs well concentrated, Master Bomber very clear.

18/07/1944 LM206 JI-C Bombing Aulnoye   22.25   00.53   01.58

Bomb load 18 x 500 GP. Primary target: Aulnoye, Railway junction. Weather hazy but no cloud. Bombed at 00.53 hours from 9,000 feet green T.I.s. Markers accurately placed. Large sheds seen clearly to the north of target. Large yellow explosion at 00.56 hours.

20/07/1944 LM206 JI-C Bombing Homberg   23.06   01.20   02.34

Bomb load 1 x 4000 HC, 2 x 500 MC, 14 x 500 GP. Primary target: Homberg, Oil plant. Weather slight haze. Bombed at 01.20 hours from 20,000 feet red T.I.s. Satisfactory raid. Considerable number of fighters.

24/07/1944 PB142 JI-A Bombing Stuttgart   21.40   01.46   05.08

Bomb load 7 x 1000 MC, 4 x 500 GP. Primary target: Stuttgart. Weather 10/10ths cloud. Bombed at 01.46 hours from 21,000 feet glow of red T.I.s. Results difficult to assess owing to cloud.

25/07/1944 LM206 JI-C Bombing Stuttgart   21.34   01.53   05.24

Bomb load 7 x 1000 MC, 4 x 500 GP. Primary target: Stuttgart. Weather clear, slight ground haze. Bombed at 01.53 hours from 20,000 feet centre of T.I.s. Markers spread over a large area, bomb bursts concentrated in centre of area marked.

08/08/1944 LM288 JI-C Bombing Foret de Lucheux 21.42   23.48   00.58

Bomb load 18 x 500 GP. Primary target: Foret de Lucheux, Petrol dump. Weather clear. Bombed at 23.48 hours from 11,000 feet, centre of wood. Several small explosions followed by two large ones at 23.50 hours.

F/O. A.H. Fallis became Navigator from this day and W/O. C. Hughes R/Gunner.

"Foret de Lucheux" is a forest between Lille and Amiens. During WWII, important fuel tanks were there.

12/08/1944 LM288 JI-C Bombing Brunswick 21.39 00.03 02.34

Bomb load 1 x 2000 HC, 12 x 500 'J' type clusters. Primary target: Brunswick. Weather 10/10ths cloud. Bombed at 00.03 hours from 20,000 feet between two fires. Glow of fires spread over large area. Port inner engine seized and had to be feathered just after leaving target. Result of attack doubtful.

31/08/1944 LM288 JI-C Bombing Pont-Remy 16.04 18.07 19.36

Bomb load 11 x 1000 MC, 4 x 500 GP Mk IV LD. Primary target: Pont Remy, Dump. Weather cloudy. Bombed at 18.07 hours from 15,000 feet on visual target.

03/09/1944 LM288 JI-C Bombing Eindhoven 15.10 17.38 18.57

Bomb load 11 x 1000 MC, 4 x 500 GP. Primary target: Eindhoven airfield. Bombed at 17.38 hours from 16,000 feet, visual.

08/09/1944 LM288 JI-C Bombing Le Havre 05.50 x 09.26

Bomb load 11 x 1000 MC, 4 x 500 GP. Primary target: Le Havre. Weather 10/10ths cloud down to 3,000 feet. Abandoned mission on Master Bomber's instructions.

10/09/1944 LM288 JI-C Bombing Le Havre 15.53 17.38 19.14

Bomb load 11 x 1000 MC, 4 x 500 GP. Primary target: Le Havre. Weather clear. Bombed at 17.38 hours from 11,000 feet. Undershot T.I.s red by 200 yards.

11/09/1944 LM288 JI-C Bombing Kamen 16.05 18.42 20.23

Bomb load 1 x 4000 HC, 16 x 500 GP. Weather clear. Primary target: Kamen. Bombed at 18.42 hours from 17,000 feet on very large orange red fire.

12/09/1944 LM288 JI-C Bombing Frankfurt 18.32 23.00 01.02

Bomb load 1 x 4000 HC, 14 x 500 Clusters 4lb. Target: Frankfurt - Main. Weather clear over the target. Bombed at 23.00 hours from 19,000 feet on red T.I.s.

F/O. Eric Ellis Williams, DFC

A423963 F/O. Eric Ellis Williams, DFC, RAAF. Pilot.
A420266 F/O. Kenneth Pritchard, DFC, RAAF. A/Bomber. 20 ops.
F/L. F. Wilson. A/Bomber. 14 ops.
A429215 F/S. Albert William Morgan Cassidy, DFM, RAAF. Navigator.
Sgt. W.H.E. Gray. WOP/AG. 28 ops
F/S. B.A. Brown. WOP/AG. 3 ops.
636773 W/O. George Beadle Stratford, DFC. WOP/AG. 3 ops.
Sgt. W.T. Peck. MU/Gunner. 32 ops.
F/S. George Edgard Sales. MU/Gunner. 2 ops.
2227465 Sgt. George Albert Banks. R/Gunner.
Sgt. W.T. Spurge. F/Engineer.
J29160 F/O. Leslie Flack, RCAF. 2nd Pilot. 29/11/1944

Note: E.E. Williams died in an air crash 18 February 1948 at Amberley, Australia with his 5 crew members and 10 passengers.

25/07/1944 LL666 JI-Q
Bombing Stuttgart 21.43
02.14 06.05
Bomb load 5 x 1000 MC, 3 x 500 GP. Primary target: Stuttgart. Weather clear. Bombed at 02.14 hours from 18,000 feet fires. Several small fires surrounding one large fire.

F/O. K. Pritchard was A/Bomber until 18/10/1944.

Sgt. W.H.E. Gray was WOP/AG until 02/11/1944.

Sgt. W.T. Peck was MU/Gunner until 14/10/1944.

28/07/1944 LL624 JI-R
Bombing Stuttgart 21.47
01.51 05.43
Bomb load 13 x 500 GP. Primary target: Stuttgart. Weather 9/10ths cloud. Bombed at 01.51 hours from 18,000 feet green markers and yellow stars. Little evidence of bombing.

Sgt. George Albert Banks, R/Gunner (courtesy Kevin Banks)

01/08/1944 LL666 JI-Q Bombing Foret de Nieppe 19.19 20.45 21.50
Bomb load 11 x 1000 MC, 4 x 500 GP. Primary target: De Nieppe, constructional works. Bombed at 20.45 hours from 12,000 feet on Lancaster ahead.

04/08/1944 LL734 JI-O Bombing Bec D'Ambes 13.29 18.01 21.16
Bomb load 5 x 1000 MC, 4 x 500 GP. Primary target: Bec d'Ambes depot. Weather clear. Bombed at 18.01 hours from 8,000 feet, visually. Good effort, no trouble.

05/08/1944 LL734 JI-O Bombing Bassen 14.18 19.03 22.12
Bomb load 8 x 1000 MC, 4 x 500 GP. Primary target: Bassen Oil Depot. Weather cloud from 15,000 feet down to 5,000 feet, clear below. Bombed at 19.03 hours from 5,000 feet at base of fires. Two large red fires with columns of black smoke to 4,000 feet.

07/08/1944 LL666 JI-Q Bombing Mare de Magne 21.51 23.45 01.12
Bomb load 9 x 1000 MC, 4 x 500 GP. Primary target: Mare de Magne (just past Caen). Weather clear over target. Bombed at 23.45 hours from 8,000 feet red T.I.s on Master Bomber's instructions. Concentration of bombs were seen

to fall on eastern side of red T.I.s.

Mare-de-Magne: place between Caen and Fontenay le Marmion.

09/08/1944 HK577 JI-P Bombing Fort d'Englos (Lille) 21.48   23.20 00.23

Bomb load 13 x 1000 MC. Primary target: Fort d'Englos, Petrol dump. Weather clear. Bombed at 23.20 hours from 13,600 feet yellow T.I.s. Bomb bursts seen short of yellow T.I.s. Defences negligible.

Fort of Ennetières-en-Weppes, or "Fort d'Englos" is one of a set of six forts surrounding Lille.

31/08/1944 PB423 JI-S Bombing Pont-Remy 15.58   18.11   19.27

Bomb load 11 x 1000 MC, 4 x 500 GP Mk IV LD. Primary target: Pont Remy, Dump. Weather cloudy. Bombed at 18.11 hours from 15,000 feet on Gee H leading aircraft.

05/09/1944 LM288 JI-C Bombing Le Havre   17.16   19.22   20.35

Bomb load 11 x 1000 MC, 4 x 500 GP. Primary target: Le Havre. Bombed at 19.22 hours from 13,000 feet red T.I.

20/09/1944 LM727 JI-S Bombing Calais 14.41   16.04   17.30

Bomb load 11 x 1000 MC, 4 x 500 GP. Primary target: Calais. Weather clear over target. Bombed at 16.04 hours from 2,500 feet, red T.I.s.

23/09/1944 LM727 JI-S Bombing Neuss 19.15   21.33   23.36

Bomb load 8 x 1000 ANM 59, 3 x 1000 ANM 44, 4 x 500 GP. Primary target: Neuss. Weather 10/10ths cloud over target, tops 8/10,000 feet. Bombed at 21.33 hours from 19,000 feet on red glow beneath cloud.

25/09/1944 LM727 JI-S Bombing Pas de Calais   08.20 x 11.10

Bomb load 11 x 1000 MC, 4 x 500 GP. Primary target: Calais. Abandoned mission on Master Bomber's instructions. Jettisoned 8 x 1000 MC.

26/09/1944 LM727 JI-S Bombing Calais 11.36   12.44   14.05

Bomb load 11 x 1000 MC, 4 x 500 GP. Primary target: Calais 7D. Weather clear below cloud which was 3,500 feet. Bombed at 12.44 hours from 3,000 feet on red T.I. + 1 second.

28/09/1944 LM684 JI-O Bombing Calais   08.40 x 10.51

Bomb load 11 x 1000 MC, 4 x 500 GP. Primary target: Calais 19. Abortive sortie. At 09.28 hours Master Bomber gave abandon mission. Jettisoned 4 x 1000.

03/10/1944 LM727 JI-S Bombing Westkapelle 12.08   13.21   14.25

Bomb load 1 x 4000 MC, 6 x 1000 MC, 1 x 500 GP. L/Delay. Primary target: Westkapelle (Walcheren). Weather patchy-scattered cloud with base 5,000 feet. Bombed at 13.21 hours from 5,000 feet on junction of middle of fields near T.I. red.

06/10/1944 LM727 JI-S Bombing Dortmund   16.49   20.34   22.23

Bomb load 1 x 4000 HC, 12 x No. 14 Clusters. Primary target: Dortmund, Town and Railways. Weather over the target was clear with slight ground haze. Bombed at 20.34 hours from 20,000 feet on red T.I.

07/10/1944 LM727 JI-S Bombing Emmerich 12.16 14.26   16.14

Bomb load 1 x 4000 HC, 10 x No.14 clusters. 4 x (150 x 4). Primary target Emmerich. Weather clear with cloud at 13,000 feet. Bombed at 14.26 hours from 13,000 feet on South-West corner as instructed by Master Bomber.

14/10/1944 LM727 JI-S Bombing Duisburg   07.18   09.06   11.29

Bomb load 11 x 1000 MC, 4 x 500 GP Long Delay. Primary target: Duisburg. Weather patchy cloud with gaps for bombing. Bombed at 09.06 hours from 18,000 feet by H25. No visual confirmation.

14/10/1944 LM727 JI-S Bombing Duisburg   22.59   01.32   03.53

Bomb load 1 x 4000 HC, 14 x No. 14 Clusters. Primary target: Duisburg. Weather was clear with small amount of cloud over the target. Bombed at 01.32 hours from 20,000 feet. Red T.I.

F/S. E.G. Sales was MU/Gunner until 18/10/1944.

18/10/1944 LM724 JI-B Bombing Bonn   08.20 x 12.50

Bomb load 1 x 4000 HC, 5 x 12 x 30 - 2 x 12 x 30 modified. 9 x No. 14 Clusters. Primary target: Bonn. Weather varying cloud 2-7/10ths with break for bombing. Aircraft jettisoned on approach to target when aircraft was hit by direct heavy flak, aircraft peeled off immediately. Numerous flak holes in fuselage and starboard wing.

Landed at Woodbridge with severe flak damage. Starboard inner engine C.S.U U/S. Rudder trims U/S. DR compass U/S. Bomb Aimer F/O. Pritchard fractured leg.

30/10/1944 PB419 JI-N Bombing Wesseling   09.15   11.58   13.40

Bomb load 1 x 4000 HC, 15 x 500 GP. Primary target: Wesseling. Weather was 10/10ths cloud - tops about 7,000 feet. Bombed at 11.58 hours from 18,000 feet on G.H. aircraft in formation ahead.

Sgt. W.T. Peck was MU/Gunner from that day.

Contrary to the entry in the ORBs, F/O. K. Pritchard could not have been in the crew due to the fractured leg he suffered on 18/10/44. Consequently, it is believed that F/L. F. Wilson was A/Bomber that day.

31/10/1944 LM685 JI-Q Bombing Bottrop 11.57 15.00   16.48

Bomb load 1 x 4000 HC. 16 x 500 GP. Primary target: Bottrop, Synth. Oil plants. Weather 10/10ths cloud over target. Bombed at 15.00 hours from 19,000 feet on G.H.

Contrary to the entry in the ORBs, F/O. K. Pritchard could not have been in the crew due to the fractured leg he suffered on 18/10/44. Consequently, it is believed that F/L. F. Wilson was A/Bomber that day.

02/11/1944 LM727 JI-S Bombing Homberg   11.30   14.10   15.38

Bomb load 1 x 4000 HC, 6 x 1000 ANM59, 6 x 500 MC. Primary target: Homberg. Weather variable cloud but clear for bombing. Target obscured by pall of smoke rising to 10,000 feet. Bombed at 14.10 hours from 20,000 feet. Green flares (not very clear).

F/L. F. Wilson was A/Bomber from that day.

05/11/1944 LM727 JI-S Bombing Solingen 10.15   13.01   14.43

Bomb load 1 x 4000 HC, 14 x 500 Clusters. Primary target: Solingen.

Weather 10/10ths cloud over target. Bombed at 13.01 hours from 18,500 feet on Red flares.

F/S. B.A. Brown was WOP/AG that day.

06/11/1944 LM717JI-T Bombing Koblenz 16.48 19.36 21.53

Bomb load 1 x 4000 HC, 12 x 500 Clusters, 2 x 250 T.I.s. Primary target: Koblenz. Weather clear over target. Bombed at 19.36 hours from 17,500 feet on fires in the town.

F/S. B.A. Brown was WOP/AG that day.

11/11/1944 LM727JI-S Bombing Castrop Rauxel 08.12 11.10 12.46

Bomb load 1 x 4000 HC, 16 x 500 GP. Primary target: Castrop Rauxel, Oil refineries. Weather 10/10ths cloud. Alternative target: Wuppertal. Bombed at 11.10 hours from 19,000 feet on G.H. Leader 514/'R'.

W/O. G.B. Stratford was WOP/AG until 16/11/1944.

15/11/1944 LM727JI-S Bombing Dortmund 12.53 15.40 17.23

Bomb load 1 x 4000 HC, 16 x 500 GP. Primary target: Hoesch-Benzin Dortmund, Oil refineries. Weather 10/10ths cloud over the target. Bombed at 15.40 hours from 16,500 feet on leading aircraft.

16/11/1944 LM717JI-T Bombing Heinsburg 13.28 15.41 17.28

Bomb load 1 x 4000 HC, 6 x 1000 MC, 4 x 500 GP, 4 x 250 lb T.I.s. Primary target: Heinsburg. Weather - nil cloud with slight haze over target. Bombed at 15.41 hours from 9,000 feet. Undershot Pickwick per Master Bomber.

20/11/1944 PB423 A2-G Bombing Homberg 12.44 x 14.33

Bomb load 1 x 4000 HC, 15 x 500 GP, 1 Red-Green Flare. Primary target: Homberg. Abortive sortie. Jettisoned at 13.56 hours from 7,000 feet 4 miles East of Southwold. Elevator control jammed, rear turret unserviceable.

F/S. B.A. Brown was WOP/AG that day.

23/11/1944 PD389 JI-Q Bombing Nordstern 12.47 15.14 17.18

Bomb load 1 x 4000 HC, 15 x 500 GP, 1 Red flare with Green stars. Primary target: Nordstern, Gelsenkirchen Oil refineries. Weather 10/10ths cloud. Bombed at 15.19 hours from 20,000 feet. Red flares.

Sgt. W.H.E. Gray was WOP/AG from that day.

27/11/1944 LM627JI-R Bombing Cologne 12.25 15.06 17.05

Bomb load 1 x 4000 HC, 15 x 500 GP, 1 Flare. Primary target: Cologne, Marshalling Yards. Weather patchy cloud. Bombed at 15.06 hours from 20,000 feet on Gee fix and flares in bomb sight.

29/11/1944 LM727JI-S Bombing Neuss 02.55 05.33 07.05

Bomb load 1 x 4000 HC, 14 x 150 x 4 incendiaries. Primary target: Neuss. Weather 10/10ths cloud over target but the glow of fires was seen through cloud. Bombed at 05.33 hours from 20,000 feet on H2S.

F/O. Leslie Flack was 2nd Pilot that day.

02/12/1944 NG203 JI-A Bombing Dortmund 13.05 14.56 16.50

Bomb load 13 x 1000 HC, 1 Red/Green flare. Primary target: Dortmund, Benzol plant. Weather 10/10ths cloud. Bombed at 14.56 hours from 20,000 feet on G.H.

04/12/1944 PB419 JI-N Bombing Oberhausen 11.50 14.06 15.53

Bomb load 1 x 4000 HC, 15 x 500 GP, 1 Flare. Primary target: Oberhausen, Built up area. Weather 10/10ths cloud. Bombed at 14.06 hours from 20,000 feet on G.H.

P/O. John Kenneth Williams

161058 (1020779) P/O. John Kenneth Williams. Pilot.
151014 (968290) F/O. Donald Frank Henshaw. A/Bomber.
1334196 F/S. Leslie Noel Millis. Navigator.
A417157 F/S. Wilbur Henry Chapman, RAAF. WOP/AG.
914246 Sgt. Arthur Pratt. MU & R/Gunner.
932746 F/S. Ernest Allan Lane. MU & R/Gunner.
1570038 Sgt. James Richard Keenen. F/Engineer.

Foulsham October 1943. L to R (back): Ernest Allan Lane, Arthur Pratt, James Richard Keenen, Leslie Noel Millis. L to R (front): Donald Frank Henshaw, John Kenneth Williams, Wilbur Henry Chapman (courtesy Peter Thomas)

11/11/1943 DS823 JI-K Gardening La Tranche 17.33 x 01.01

Aircraft carried 4 x G710. Primary area La Tranche. No enemy aircraft seen and very little flak encountered. Visibility good.

F/S. E.A. Lane was MU/Gunner that day and Sgt. A. Pratt R/Gunner.

18/11/1943 DS823 JI-K Bombing Mannheim 17.26 x 23.33

Bomb load 1 x 4000, 16 x 30, 720 x 4. Primary target Mannheim. Patchy cloud at 20,000 feet. Red T.I.s in a circle. Build up area and several good fires going. Turning point yellow markers not seen Red Hlbb fires seen 10 miles astern at 21.06. Monica not used. Returned over French coast at Calais.

Sgt. A. Pratt was MU/Gunner from this day and F/S. E.A. Lane R/Gunner.

02/12/1943 DS824 JI-K Bombing Berlin   17.08 x 19.59

Bomb load 1 x 4000, 40 x 30, 650 x 4 incendiaries, 70 x 4 incendiaries. Primary target: Berlin. Task abandoned. Starboard inner engine u/s. All bombs jettisoned in North Sea. Made good 3 engine landing.

16/12/1943 LL625 JI-C Bombing Berlin   17.07   20.02   23.41

Bomb load 1 x 2000, 6 x 150 incendiaries, 2 x 90 incendiaries, 4 x 30 incendiaries. Primary target: Berlin. 10/10 cloud. Bombed target at 20.02 at 21,000 ft. Raid seemed rather scattered. Red and Green T.I.s and Markers seen. Landed at Downham Market.

01/01/1944 DS824 JI-K Bombing Berlin   00.33   03.12   07.45

Bomb load 1 x 4000, 24 x 30, 450 x 4, 90 x 4 lbs. Incendiaries. Primary target: Berlin. There was 10/10 cloud over the target. Bombed at 03.12 hours at 21,000 feet. Gee u/s on homeward route. Fixed arial came away. Course unknown. P.F.F. widely scattered and backing up poor.

02/01/1944 DS824 JI-K Bombing Berlin   00.18   02.48   06.35

Bomb load 1 x 4000, 24 x 30, 450 x 4, 90 x 4 incendiaries. Primary target: Berlin. There was 10/10 cloud. Bombed at 02.48 hours at 21,000 ft. Route satisfactory. P.F.F. appeared concentrated. Had encounter with an enemy aircraft.

14/01/1944 DS824 JI-K Bombing Brunswick 16.47 19.16   21.51

Bomb load 1 x 4000, 48 x 30 incendiaries. Primary target: Brunswick. There was 7-9/10 cloud, with one or two breaks. Bombed at 19.16 hours at 20,000 ft. Incendiaries seen burning below cloud. Raid concentrated providing markers were placed correctly - Raid "Bang On". Cloud preventing visual of raid.

21/01/1944 DS824 JI-K Bombing Magdeburg 19.56 x   x

Bomb load 1 x 4000, 720 x 4, 90 x 4, 32 x 30 incendiaries. Aircraft missing. Shot down by Oblt. Martin Drewes, 11/NJG1. Crashed in the Ijsselmeer.

All crew members were KIA. Four, including P/O. Williams who was on his second tour, are buried in cemeteries along the Friesland coast, while F/O. D.F. Henshaw; Sgt. A. Pratt and Sgt. J.R. Keenen are commemorated on the Runnymede Memorial. F/S. Lanes's wife, Dorothy Mary Lane, lived in Winnipeg, Manitoba.

F/O. Joseph Holmes Wilson

54040 (580110) F/O. Joseph Holmes Wilson. Pilot.
Sgt. W.J. Bailey.   A/Bomber.   4 ops.
  F/S. F.E. Coe.   A/Bomber.   4 ops.
  F/S. A.H. Brown.   Navigator.
  F/S. F. Tranter.   WOP/AG.
Sgt. L. Lithgow.   MU/Gunner.   7 ops.
Sgt. G.W. Lomas.   R/Gunner.
  F/S. J.F.S. Forster.   F/Engineer.

Passengers: 07/05/1945, 05/06/1945, 13/07/1945, 20/07/1945.

09/04/1945 ME529 A2-F   Bombing Kiel   19.41 22.44   01.39
  Bombed primary target: Kiel. Bomb load 1 x 4000 HC and 12 x 500 ANM64. Bombed at 22.44 hours at 20,000 feet undershooting on Green T.I.s. on M/B's instructions. Visual of whole area with distinct sets of markers - all in dock area. Believed good attack. Marking was good, M/B excellent but some interference. Lanc arrived early 22.28 saw lighted area to South and tracked towards then attack started 22.31 so orbited and bombed (lighted area believed decoy).
  From his usual crew, only F/O J.H. Wilson did this mission as 2nd Pilot with F/O J.H. Tolley's crew.

13/04/1945 PD389 A2-J Bombing Kiel   20.18   23.36   02.17
  Bomb load 1 x 4000 HC and 12 x 500 ANM64. Primary target: Kiel, Docks & ship yards. Weather 10/10ths cloud low and thin. One Red T.I. to port. We bombed on centre of Green T.I.s per M/B's instructions, at 23.36 hours from 20,000 feet.
  Huge red explosion at 23.35 hrs. Glow indicated good fires beneath cloud. Port outer feathered over Kiel. Good raid.

30/04/1945 PD389 A2-J Manna Rotterdam   16.53 18.22   19.39
  Dropping area: Rotterdam. Weather intermittent showers and low cloud. Load 5 packs. Dropped 3 packs at 18.22 hours on white cross with red light in centre. 2 packs hung up brought back. Very good welcome from population.

02/05/1945 PD389 A2-J Manna The Hague   11.05   12.25   13.29
  Dropping area The Hague. Weather over dropping zone clear below cloud for the first arrivals changing later to heavy showers which marred visibility. Dropped 5 panniers visually on White Cross and T.I.s at 12.25 hours. 10/10 cloud.

07/05/1945 RE117 A2-D   Manna The Hague 12.09 x 14.33
  Dropping area The Hague. Dropped 4 Packs visually on White Cross and T.I.s. 5/10 Base 1000 Good visibility. 1 pack brought back.
  No Mid Upper Gunner that day.

Passenger: Sgt. J. James.

05/06/1945 RE158 A2-J Baedeker Tour over Germany 07.53 x 11.54
Passengers: F/L. H. Flannagan, LAC. T. Trotman, AC. R. Rudder.

03/07/1945 ME529 A2-B Post Mortem Special mission 14.10 x 19.57

13/07/1945 RA602 A2-H Baedeker Tour over Continent 09.42 x 14.30
Passengers: Sgt. Bagg, Cpl. White, LAC. Minorette, LACW. Mitchinson, LACW. Marywell.

20/07/1945 RE120 A2-C Baedeker Tour over Continent 09.27 x 13.40
Passengers: F/S. Linton, Cpl. Hurley, LAC. Coggle, LACW. Bruce, LACW. Thackeray.

P/O acting F/O. Stanley Ewart Wilson, DFC

179940 (1432463) F/O. Stanley Ewart "Stan" Wilson, DFC. Pilot.
F/S. J.E. Atkin. A/Bomber.
183734 (1815445) P/O. Donald Harry Curzon. Navigator.
F/S. A.M. Williams. WOP/AG.
Sgt. J.P. Golden. MU & R/Gunner.
Sgt. Ronald Cooper. MU & R/Gunner.
F/S. F. Webb. F/Engineer.

F/O. Stanley Ewart "Stan" Wilson, DFC

18/07/1944 DS842 A2-J Bombing Emieville   04.31 06.08 07.43

Bomb load 11 x 1000 MC, 4 x 500 GP. Primary target: Emieville, Troop concentration. Weather clear. Bombed at 06.08 hours from 6,500 feet yellow T.I.s. Bombing appeared concentrated. One flak hole near the port outer engine near No.2 petrol tank.

20/07/1944 LL716 A2-G   Bombing Homberg 23.25 x 01.33

Bomb load 1 x 4000 HC, 2 x 500 MC, 14 x 500 GP. Primary target: Homberg, Oil plant. Returned early - unable to climb above 15,000 feet. Jettisoned at 00.39 hours from 12,000 feet at position 5221N 0232E.

23/07/1944 PB142 JI-A Bombing Kiel   22.24   01.20   03.47

Bomb load 10 x 1000 MC, 5 x 500 GP. Primary target: Kiel, Warehouses and docks. Weather 10/10ths cloud. Bombed at 01.20 hours from 20,000 feet centre of red and green T.I.s. Large explosion giving an orange glow at 0121 hours. Special Nickels carried.

25/07/1944 DS826 JI-J   Bombing Stuttgart 21.38 x 00.01

Bomb load 5 x 1000 MC, 3 x 500 GP. Abortive sortie. Jettisoned 23.25 hours from 5,000 feet 5220N 0239E. Rear turret and mid upper u/s.

27/07/1944 DS826 JI-J   Bombing Les Catelliers 16.55   18.51   20.17

Bomb load 18 x 500 GP. Primary target: Les Catelliers, Flying bomb site. Bombed at 18.51 hours from 16,000 feet on Mosquito.

30/07/1944 DS826 JI-J   Bombing Caen   06.15 x 10.00

Bomb load 18 x 500 GP. Primary target: Caen 'B'. Weather low cloud. Bombed at 07.50 hours from 3,500 feet, red T.I.s south end as instructed. A good effort. Landed at Debach.

01/08/1944 DS826 JI-J   Bombing Foret de Nieppe 19.13 20.46   21.57

Bomb load 11 x 1000 MC, 4 x 500 GP. Primary target: De Nieppe, constructional works. Bombed at 20.46 hours from 11,500 feet on leading aircraft.

03/08/1944 LM285 JI-K Bombing Bois de Cassan   11.45   14.05   15.43

Bomb load 11 x 1000 MC, 4 x 500 GP. Primary target: Bois de Cassan, Flying bomb supply depot. Bombed at 14.05 hours from 15,500.

04/08/1944 LM285 JI-K Bombing Bec d'Ambes   13.24   18.00   21.08

Bomb load 8 x 1000 MC, 2 x 500 GP. Primary target: Bec d'Ambes depot. Weather clear. Bombed at 18.00 hours from 8,000 feet, oil storage tanks. Tank set on fire with 1st stick of bombs. Bombing well concentrated. Attack considered very concentrated.

05/08/1944 LM285 JI-K Bombing Bassen 14.27 18.59   22.08

Bomb load 8 x 1000 MC, 2 x 500 GP. Primary target: Bassen Oil Depot. Clear over target. Bombed at 18.59 hours from 7,000 feet visually oil storage tanks. Two storage tanks seen afire with dense black smoke. Bombs concentrated on target.

08/08/1944 LM265 JI-E Bombing Foret de Lucheux 21.53   23.49   01.03

Bomb load 18 x 500 GP. Primary target: Foret de Lucheux, Petrol dump.

Weather clear, slight haze. Bombed at 23.49 hours from 12,000 feet, yellow T.I.s. Several fires in target area. Fighter attack on run up, should be good attack.

"Foret de Lucheux" is a forest between Lille and Amiens. During WWII, important fuel tanks were there.

09/08/1944 LM285 JI-K Bombing Fort d'Englos (Lille) 21.49 23.16 00.17

Bomb load 14 x 1000 MC. Primary target: Fort d'Englos, Petrol dump. Weather clear. Bombed at 23.16 hours from 13,000 feet. Red T.I.s. Master Bomber not heard. Doubtful whether target was hit.

Fort of Ennetières-en-Weppes, or "Fort d'Englos" is one of a set of six forts surrounding Lille.

08/09/1944 LM285 JI-K Bombing Le Havre   06.02   08.04   09.21

Bomb load 11 x 1000 MC, 4 x 500 GP. Primary target: Le Havre. Weather 10/10ths cloud down to 3,000 feet. Bombed at 08.04 hours from 5,500 feet, red T.I.s.

12/09/1944 LM285 JI-K Bombing Frankfurt   18.30   23.00   01.07

Bomb load 1 x 4000 HC, 14 x 500 clusters 4lb. Target: Frankfurt - Main. Weather clear over the target. Bombed at 23.00 hours from 17,500 feet on centre of red and green T.I.s.

20/09/1944 LL666 A2-K   Bombing Calais   14.56   16.01   17.20

Bomb load 11 x 1000 MC, 4 x 500 GP. Primary target: Calais. Weather clear over target. Bombed at 16.01 hours from 3,500 feet, red T.I.s.

25/09/1944 NG121 JI-H Bombing Pas de Calais   08.23 x 10.55

Bomb load 11 x 1000 MC, 4 x 500 GP. Primary target: Calais. Abandoned mission on Master Bomber's instructions. Jettisoned 4 x 1000 at 5026N 0101E.

27/09/1944 LM724 JI-B Bombing Calais   07.41   08.43   09.57

Bomb load 11 x 1000 MC, 4 x 500 GP. Primary target: Calais 15. Weather, cloud 5,500 feet 10/10ths. Bombed at 08.43 hours from 5,500 feet on port of green T.I.

06/10/1944 LM285 JI-K Bombing Dortmund   17.05   20.26   22.08

Bomb load 1 x 4000 HC, 12 x No. 14 Clusters. Primary target: Dortmund, Town and Railways. Weather over the target was clear with slight ground haze. Bombed at 20.26 hours from 22,500 feet on centre of red and green T.I.s.

07/10/1944 LM285 JI-K Bombing Emmerich 12.04 14.27   15.56

Bomb load 1 x 4000 HC, 10 x No.14 clusters. 4 x (150 x 4). Primary target Emmerich. Weather clear with cloud at 13,000 feet. Bombed at 14.27 hours from 13,500 feet on Southern edge of smoke as instructed by Master Bomber.

21/10/1944 LM285 JI-K Bombing Flushing 10.47   12.28   13.36

Bomb load 12 x 1000 MC, 2 x 500 GP. Primary target: Flushing 'A'. Weather clear. Bombed at 12.28 hours from 8,000 feet. A/P. 'A'.

22/10/1944 LM285 JI-K Bombing Neuss 13.09   15.55   17.17

Bomb load 1 x 4000 HC, 6 x 1000 MC, 6 x 500 GP. Primary target: Neuss. Weather 10/10ths cloud over target. Bombed at 15.55 hours from 18,000 feet on GH.

23/10/1944 LM285 JI-K Bombing Essen 16.25 19.31 21.13

Bomb load 1 x 4000 HC, 2 x 1000 MC, 10 x 500 GP. Primary target: Essen. Weather 10/10ths cloud over target - tops 12/14,000 feet with most appalling weather on route. Bombed at 19.31 hours from 19,000 feet. Green flares.

26/10/1944 LM285 JI-K Bombing Leverkusen 13.28 15.29 17.11

Bomb load 1 x 4000 HC, 6 x 1000 MC. 4 x 500 GP. 2 x 500 GP Long Delay. Primary target: Leverkusen. Weather over target and on route was 10/10ths cloud. Bombed at 15.29 hours from 18,000 feet on G.H. aircraft ahead.

28/10/1944 LM288 JI-C Bombing Cologne 13.26 15.46 17.39

Bomb load 1 x 4000 HC, 8 x 150 x 4. Primary target: Cologne. Weather clear over target. Bombed at 15.46 hours from 22,000 feet; Red T.I. as instructed.

30/10/1944 PD265 JI-G Bombing Wesseling 09.05 11.58 13.24

Bomb load 1 x 4000 HC, 15 x 500 GP. Primary target: Wesseling. Weather was 10/10ths cloud - tops about 7,000 feet. Bombed at 11.58 hours from 18,000 feet on G.H.

31/10/1944 PD265 JI-G Bombing Bottrop 11.53 15.01 16.22

Bomb load 1 x 4000 HC, 15 x 500 GP. 1 Flare. Primary target: Bottrop, Synth. Oil plants. Weather 10/10ths cloud over target. Bombed at 15.01 hours from 18,000 feet on G.H.

02/11/1944 LM627 JI-D Bombing Homberg 11.16 14.09 15.33

Bomb load 1 x 4000 HC, 6 x 1000 ANM59, 6 x 500 MC. Primary target: Homberg. Weather variable cloud but clear for bombing. Target obscured by pall of smoke rising to 10,000 feet. Bombed at 14.09 hours from 19,000 feet. Centre of Green flares.

04/11/1944 LM285 JI-K Bombing Solingen 11.25 14.09 15.48

Bomb load 1 x 4000 HC, 6 x 1000 ANM59, 4 x 500 GP, 2 x 500 MC (L/Delay), 3 Flares. Primary target: Solingen. Weather 8-10/10ths cloud. Bombed at 14.09 hours from 20,000 feet on G.H.

05/11/1944 LM285 JI-K Bombing Solingen 10.29 13.04 14.45

Bomb load 1 x 4000 HC, 6 x 1000 ANM59, 4 x 500 GP, 2 x 500 GP (L/Delay), 3 Flares. Primary target: Solingen. Weather 10/10ths cloud over target. Bombed at 13.04 hours from 17,500 feet on instruments.

08/11/1944 LM285 JI-K Bombing Homberg 08.08 10.32 12.06

Bomb load 1 x 4000 HC, 6 x 1000 GP, 6 x 500 GP. Primary target: Homberg. Weather clear. Bombed at 10.32 hours from 18,000 feet on instruments.

11/11/1944 LM285 JI-K Bombing Castrop Rauxel 08.18 11.06 12.44

Bomb load 1 x 4000 HC, 16 x 500 GP. Primary target: Castrop Rauxel, Oil refineries. Weather 10/10ths cloud. Bombed at 11.06 hours from 19,500 feet on G.H. Leader.

15/11/1944 LM285 JI-K Bombing Dortmund 12.49 15.41 17.16

Bomb load 1 x 4000 HC, 2 x 500 MC, 13 x 500 GP, 1 Red with Green star Flare. Primary target: Hoesch-Benzin Dortmund, Oil refineries. Weather

10/10ths cloud over the target. Bombed at 15.41 hours from 18,000 feet on G.H. Formation. GH and Gee unserviceable. Raid believed satisfactory.

16/11/1944 LM285 JI-K Bombing Heinsburg 13.25 15.41 17.15

Bomb load 1 x 4000 HC, 6 x 1000 MC, 4 x 500 GP, 4 x 250 lb T.I.s. Primary target: Heinsburg. Weather - nil cloud with slight haze over target. Bombed at 15.41 hours from 10,000 feet. Centre of town on G.H.

20/11/1944 NG121 JI-H Bombing Homberg 12.53 15.17 16.58

Bomb load 1 x 4000 HC, 2 x 500 GP, 14 x 500 MC. Primary target: Homberg. Weather 10/10ths cloud over target. Bombed at 15.17 hours from 20,000 feet on G.H. Leader.

21/11/1944 LM285 JI-K Bombing Homberg 13.02 15.09 16.33

Bomb load 1 x 4000 HC, 15 x 500 GP, 1 Red & Green Flare. Primary target: Homberg. Weather about 5/10ths cloud but clear for bombing. Bombed at 15.09 hours from 20,000 feet on G.H.

23/11/1944 LM285 JI-K Bombing Nordstern 12.50 15.20 16.58

Bomb load 1 x 4000 HC, 15 x 500 GP, 1 Red flare with Green stars. Primary target: Nordstern, Gelsenkirchen Oil refineries. Weather 10/10ths cloud. Bombed at 15.20 hours from 20,000 feet on G.H.

P/O. Bernard William Windsor, DFM

1st crew

NZ416582 P/O. Bernard William Windsor, DFM, RNZAF. Pilot.
1577855 Sgt. K.A. Attwood. A/Bomber.
1506247 Sgt. G.K. Hardwick. Navigator.
1575129 F/S. Robert Donald Langford. WOP/AG.
1893040 Sgt. Lewis Harold David Warren. MU/Gunner.
543703 Sgt. Leonard Douglas "Len" Blackford. R/Gunner.
527589 Sgt. Frank Leonard Dolamore, DFM. F/Engineer.

15/03/1944 DS815 JI-N Bombing Stuttgart 19.50 23.20 02.45

Bomb load 1 x 8000 lb bomb, 8 x 30 incendiaries. Primary target: Stuttgart. There was thin cloud over the target. Bombed at 23.20 hours from 20,000 feet. 1 red T.I. seen in sight. Sky markers very scattered. Red T.I.s seen dropping over existing fires as aircraft left. Route OK. Attack slow opening but improving later.

From his usual crew, only F/S. B.W. Windsor did this mission as 2nd Pilot with F/O. C.W. Nichol's crew.

18/03/1944 DS818 JI-Q Bombing Frankfurt 19.33 22.01 00.37

Bomb load 1 x 4000 lb bomb, 1350 x 4, 90 x 4, 32 x 30 incendiaries. Primary target: Frankfurt. Weather very hazy, visibility bad. Bombed at 22.01 hours from 21,000 feet. 3 Red T.I.s seen after bombing owing to bad visibility.

Monica behaved erratically. Attack not considered concentrated. Many small fires seen. P.F.F. not successful.

22/03/1944 LL703 JI-L Bombing Frankfurt   18.39 x 01.20

Bomb load 1 x 1000 lb. bomb, 64 x 30, 1161 x 4, 129 x 4 incendiaries. No attack. Attacked by fighter, 2 long bursts from level astern. Rear Gunner fired and said "Dive", went into almost vertical dive, during which aircraft became uncontrollable (due to damage caused to elevators by E/A fire), when 2 bursts from fighter killed Rear Gunner Sgt. L.D. Blackford and M/U Gunner Sgt. L.H.D. Warren, setting fire to aircraft in bomb bay. Bombs jettisoned. The Pilot with the assistance of the Engineer resumed control of the aircraft, but meanwhile Bomb Aimer and Navigator had bailed out after Captain's orders.

Sgt. K.A. Attwood was captured and became POW 3798 at Camp L1 and Sgt. G.K. Hardwick POW 3463 at Camp L6.

2nd crew

NZ416582 P/O.   Bernard William Windsor, DFM, RNZAF.   Pilot.

R155985 W/O2. William Earle Brown, RCAF. A/Bomber.

1549227 Sgt. Gordon Kenneth Woodward. Navigator.

1575129 F/S. Robert Donald Langford. WOP/AG.

811039 Sgt. Ernest Walter "Ernie" Haigh. MU/Gunner.

1600760 Sgt. Jack Birch.   R/Gunner.   4 op.

1238470 F/S. Geoffrey Clewlow, DFM. R/Gunner. 1 op.

1852412 Sgt. Keith Russell Baker. R/Gunner. 2 op.

527589 Sgt. Frank Leonard Dolamore, DFM. F/Engineer.

09/04/1944 DS822 JI-T Bombing Villeneuve St George 21.37   00.01   02.01

Bomb load 8 x 1000 lb bomb, 6 x 500 lb bomb. Primary target: Villeneuve-Saint-Georges, Marshalling Yards. Visibility clear. Bombed at 00.01 hours from 13,000 feet. Good concentration of T.I.s and sticks of bombs seen exploding on yards. 1 x 1000 lb bomb hung up, presence unknown until return. Bomb release faulty. Very successful attack. One very large explosion seen at 00.02 hours.

Sgt. Jack Birch was R/Gunner that day.

10/04/1944 LL639 JI-R Bombing Laon   01.18   03.38   05.34

Bomb load 9 x 1000, 4 x 500 lb bomb. Primary target: Laon. There was 8/10 cloud, full moon, visibility very good. Bombed at 03.38 hours from 10,500 feet. Two lots of red T.I.s seen both in same place, 3 greens more scattered. Several sticks of bombs fell round reds, and 3 more scattered among the greens. A good attack. Monica not used. An easy trip and a good show. Big explosion on the target 3 minutes after we bombed.

Sgt. Jack Birch was R/Gunner that day.

18/04/1944 LL731 JI-U Bombing Rouen 22.35 00.48 02.43

Bomb load 8 x 1000 MC, 5 x 500 MC, 2 x 1000 GP. Primary target: Rouen.

Top: B.W. Windsor. L to R (bottom): G.K. Woodward, K. Birch, E.W. Haigh.

There was 2/10 cloud and haze. Bombed at 00.48 hours from 14,000 feet. Fires seen burning in built up area. M of C not heard. Attack appeared scattered for small target. Rear Gunner saw stick of bombs across buildings including a church.

F/S. Geoffrey Clewlow was R/Gunner that day.

20/04/1944 LL731 JI-U Bombing Cologne 23.54 02.08 04.04

Bomb load 1 x 1000 lb bomb, 1026 x 4, 114 x 4, 108 x 30 lb incendiaries. Primary target: Koln. There was 10/10 cloud tops 3000/4000 feet, visibility Air to Ground Nil. Bombed at 02.08 hours from 21,000 feet. Glow of T.I. only seen through cloud. No fires or explosions. Sky markers rather scattered first red marker seen at Z + 4. No greens seen.

Sgt. Jack Birch was R/Gunner that day.

22/04/1944 LL731 JI-U Bombing Dusseldorf 22.53 01.30 03.22

Bomb load 1 x 2000 lb bomb, 84 x 30, 1050 x 4 incendiaries. Primary target: Dusseldorf. Weather hazy with 3/10-5/10 cloud at 20,000 feet. Bombed at 01.30 hours from 20,000 feet. Good concentration of T.I.s. Some fires burning and bombs seen to fall around T.I.s. Bombing appeared to be well concentrated and successful. Route quite good.

Sgt. K.R. Baker was R/Gunner that day.

19/05/1944 DS781 JI-R Bombing Le Mans 22.20 00.27 02.55

Bomb load 4 x 1000 USA, 5 x 1000 MC, 1 x 1000 GP, 4 x 500 GP. Primary target: Le Mans. Cloud tops 10,000 feet, base 8,500 feet. Bombed green T.I.s on Master Bomber's instructions at 00.27 hours from 8,000 feet. Attack appeared to be good and well directed by the Master Bomber. Large explosion, orange with black smoke, seen at 00.26 hours. No trouble experienced en route. Unidentified aircraft, believed to be an enemy, seen at 6,000 over the target at 00.25 hours.

Sgt. K.R. Baker was R/Gunner that day.

21/05/1944 DS781 JI-R Bombing Duisburg 22.45 x x

Bomb load 1 x 2000 lb bomb, 120 x 30, 600 x 4 incendiaries. Aircraft missing.

Sgt. Jack Birch was R/Gunner that day.

Crashed 22/05/1944 in the North Sea all crew KIA. There are several claims by night-fighter crews for Lancasters shot down as they left the Dutch coast and it is most likely that DS781 fell victim to one of these.

Sgt. Haigh is buried in Kiel War Cemetery; the rest are commemorated on the Runnymede Memorial.

P/O. Windsor and Sgt. Dolamore were both awarded DFMs for actions in the most hazardous circumstances during the operation to Frankfurt in March. The awards were Gazetted on 25th April 1944.

P/O acting F/O. William Allwright Frederick Winkworth

191303 (1386380) F/O. William Allwright Frederick Winkworth. Pilot.
Sgt. E.J. Slaughter. A/Bomber.
164120 or 172092 F/O. Joseph Burke. Navigator.
Sgt. Reginald W. "Reg" Spencer. WOP/AG.
Sgt. R. Shields. MU/Gunner. 15 ops.
Sgt. G.C or G.J. O'Brien. R/Gunner.
F/S. E.A. Cox. F/Engineer.
NZ414255 F/O. Leslie A. "Les" Adams, RNZAF. 2nd Pilot. 17/03/1945

Passengers: 03/05/1945, 08/05/1945, 01/06/1945.

13/02/1945 NN773 JI-K Bombing Dresden 21.42 01.33 06.15

Bomb load 1 x 4000 HC, 7 x No. 14 Clusters. Primary target: Dresden. Weather 5/10ths cloud over target. Bombed at 01.33 hours from 20,000 feet on Red and Green T.I.s.

From his usual crew, only P/O W.A.F. Winkworth did this mission as 2nd Pilot with P/O L.J.W. Sutton's crew.

16/02/1945 NG298 JI-E Bombing Wesel 12.26 16.00 17.33

Bomb load 1 x 4000 HC, 4 x 500 GP, 2 x 500 MC L/Delay, 4 x 250 GP, 6 x 500 ANM64. Primary target: Wesel. Weather clear. Bombed at 16.00 hours from 20,000 feet on centre of built up area.

From his usual crew, only P/O W.A.F. Winkworth did this mission as 2nd Pilot with F/L F.P. Hendy crew.

27/02/1945 NG298 JI-E Bombing Gelsenkirchen 10.50 14.28 16.45

Bomb load 1 x 4000 HC, 2 x 500 MC (L/D 37B), 9 x 500 ANM64, 2 x 250 GP. Primary target: Gelsenkirchen (Alma Pluts) Benzin plant. Weather 10/10ths cloud, 6/10,000 feet tops. Bombed at 14.28 hours from 20,000 feet on leading aircraft.

01/03/1945 NG142 JI-J Bombing Kamen 11.50 15.05 17.47

Bomb load 1 x 4000 HC, 11 x 500 ANM64, 2 x 500 MC L/Delay. Primary target: Kamen, Coking plant. Weather 10/10ths cloud. Bombed at 15.05 hours from 18,200 feet on G.H. Leader. 4 Blue markers checked in both sight as we bombed.

02/03/1945 NG142 JI-J Bombing Koln 12.44 x 18.12

Bomb load 1 x 4000 HC, 12 x 500 ANM64. Primary target: Koln. Weather 10/10ths cloud over Koln, South and South-East of Koln clear. Abortive sortie. All bombs brought back.

06/03/1945 NG142 JI-J Bombing Salzbergen 08.44 12.15 14.28

Bomb load 1 x 4000 HC, 12 x 500 ANM64, 2x 500 MC. Primary target: Salzbergen, Wintershall oil plant. Weather 10/10ths cloud over target, tops 10,000 feet. Bombed at 12.15 hours from 21,500 feet on G.H. Leader. 4 Blue markers slightly to starboard as we bombed.

07/03/1945 NN782 JI-F Bombing Dessau 17.29 22.04 01.56

Bomb load 1 x 500 ANM64, 15 x No. 15 Clusters. Primary target: Dessau. Weather 5 to 10/10ths thin cloud. Bombed at 22.04 hours from 20,000 feet. Visual. Saw horseshoe bend in river and town.

10/03/1945 NG142 JI-J Bombing Gelsenkirchen 12.03 15.37 17.26

Bomb load 1 x 4000 HC, 13 x 500 ANM64, 1 x 500 MC, 1 x 500 GP. Primary target: Gelsenkirchen. Weather 10/10ths cloud at target, tops 8,000 feet. Bombed at 15.37 hours from 18,800 feet. Followed G.H. Leader. Aircraft hit by heavy flak. Perspex damaged.

17/03/1945 NN782 JI-F Bombing August Viktoria 11.37 15.06 17.22

Bomb load 1 x 4000 HC, 13 x 500 ANM64, 2 x 500 MC. Primary target: Auguste Viktoria, Marl-Hüls coal mine. Weather 10/10ths cloud, tops and contrails up to 23,000 feet. Bombed at 15.06 hours from 20,400 feet on G.H. Leader.

F/O. L.A. Adams was 2nd Pilot that day.

20/03/1945 NN782 JI-F Bombing Hamm 09.59 13.14 15.49

Bomb load 7 x 1000 ANM59, 9 x 500 ANM64. Primary target: Hamm, Marshalling yards. Weather 5/10ths cloud. Bombed at 13.14 hours from 18,300 feet on G.H. aircraft. Checked with bomb sight. Hit by heavy flak.

13/04/1945 ME535 JI-G Bombing Kiel   20.19   23.39   02.13

Bomb load 1 x 4000 HC and 12 x 500 ANM64. Primary target: Kiel, Docks & ship yards. Weather 10/10ths cloud low and thin. Bombed on centre of Green at 23.39 hours from 21,000 feet. Green T.I.'s seen through cloud. Very disappointing from visual view.

20/04/1945 LM724 JI-H Bombing Regensburg 09.43   13.55   17.27

Bomb load 15 x 500 ANM64. Primary target: Regensburg. Weather clear over target and whole route. Bombed G.H. and visual. G.H. tracking pulse. Released visually as release pulse was unsatisfactory. At 13.55 hours from 19,000 ft. Bomb bursts seen across target. Some undershooting seen. Formation poor although the attack should be successful.

01/05/1945 ME380 JI-E Manna The Hague   13.16   14.35   15.42

Dropping area The Hague. Weather clear over target. 5 Panniers dropped at 14.35 hrs. Clear. Supplies were dropping 'Bang on' spot to-day. Excellent delivery.

03/05/1945 ME380 JI-E Manna The Hague   11.02   12.21   13.21

Dropping area The Hague. Dropped 5 Panniers on White Cross and Red T.I.'s at 12.21 hrs. 4/5 - 10ths Cloud - Base 2,000 ft. All Panniers fell in area.

No Mid Upper Gunner that day.

Passenger: LAC. Watts.

08/05/1945 RE116 JI-F Manna Rotterdam   12.41   14.06   15.12

Dropping area Rotterdam. Dropped 5 Packs on White Cross at 14.06 hours. Clear. Area dry. Bags well clustered.

Passengers: LAC. K. Niyhes.

11/05/1945 ME380 JI-E Exodus Juvincourt - Tangmere 11.18 x 17.45

Duration 3.30. Outward 1.34 hours. Collected 24 ex POWs. Homeward 1.56 hours. Tangmere gave very good reception.

13/05/1945 ME380 JI-E Exodus Juvincourt - Tangmere 13.17 x 16.19

Duration 3.01 hours. Mess received "Return to Base" 14.47 hrs.

01/06/1945 ME380 JI-E Baedeker Tour over Germany 10.14 x 14.12

Passengers: F/O. B. Zealey, AC. M. Forster, AC. W. Cowley.

P/O. Alan Barker Lloyd Winstanley DFC

170661 (1236018)   P/O. Alan Barker Lloyd Winstanley, DFC. Pilot.
1586607   Sgt. R.B.G. or R.P.C. Scrase. A/Bomber.   8 ops.
1392790   Sgt. Eric George Rippingale. A/Bomber.   1 op.
Sgt. D.L. Bazent.   A/Bomber.   1 op.
1575003   Sgt. E. Lush.   A/Bomber.   1 op.
NZ415810   F/S. George Wirepa, RNZAF. A/Bomber.   1 op.
J20915   F/O. John Peake, DFC, RCAF.   A/Bomber.   3 op.
1319844   F/S. H. Tysoe.   Navigator. 12 ops.
135676 (1317703)   F/O. Harry James.   Navigator.   3 ops.
1125643   Sgt. Norman Dixon, DFM. WOP/AG.
1544912   Sgt. William Wilson. MU/Gunner. 1 op.
1301325   Sgt. J.S. Johnson.   MU/Gunner. 11 ops.
1520937 or 1520957   Sgt. E. Buckley.   MU/Gunner. 3 ops.
1579675   Sgt. Harold Roy Hill. R/Gunner.   1 op.
J92270 (R181202)   Sgt. William Fraser Sutherland, RCAF.   R/Gunner. 2 ops.
R161431   F/S. S.J. Everitt, RCAF. R/Gunner. 12 ops.
1582209   Sgt. G.H. Homer.   F/Engineer.
F/S. W. Bishop.   2nd Pilot. 29/12/1943.

29/12/1943 LL677 A2-E   Bombing Berlin   17.09   20.20   23.31
F/S. W. Bishop, 2nd Pilot for this mission. Bomb load 1 x 2000, 40 x 30 incendiaries, 900 x 4incendiaries, 90 x 4 incendiaries. Primary target: Berlin. There was 10/10 cloud. Bombed at 20.20 hours at 19,000 ft. Good concentration of red and green markers seen. Glow of fires seen below clouds. Route markers on way out seen and all effective in right place. No route markers seen on route home.
F/S. W. Bishop was 2nd Pilot that day and Sgt. H.R. Hill R/Gunner.
F/S. H. Tysoe was Navigator until 24/03/1944.
Sgt. R. Scrase was A/Bomber until 15/02/1944.
Sgt. E. Buckley was MU/Gunner until 20/01/1944.
14/01/1944 LL677 A2-E   Bombing Brunswick   17.02 x 19.07
Bomb load 1 x 4000, 48 x 30 incendiaries. Returned early. Heating Mid Upper turret. Furthest point reached 5258N 020E. 1 x 4000 bomb jettisoned.
Sgt. W.F. Sutherland was R/Gunner that day.
20/01/1944 LL677 A2-E   Bombing Berlin   16.23 x 22.23
Bomb load 1 x 4000, 32 x 30, 540 x 4, 60 x 4 incendiaries. Primary target: Berlin. Returned early. Attacked by fighter. Half starboard propeller shot off. Tyre punctured. Starboard inner tank holed and all petrol lost. Mid Upper and

front turrets u/s. Total load jettisoned 10 miles of Hamburg.

Sgt. W.F. Sutherland R/Gunner that day.

28/01/1944 DS786 A2-F   Bombing Berlin 00.17 x 07.54

Bomb load 1 x 2000 lb bomb, 16 x 30, 750 x 4 incendiaries. Primary target: Berlin. There was 10/10 cloud. Large dumb-bell shaped fire running S to N surrounded by searchlights. Attack appeared very concentrated - should have good photo.

Sgt. W. Wilson was MU/Gunner that day.

F/S. S.J. Everitt was R/Gunner from that day.

15/02/1944 LL684 A2-B   Bombing Berlin 17.38   21.24   00.01

Bomb load 1 x 2000, 1 x 1000 lb bomb, 24 x 30, 900 x 4 incendiaries. Primary target: Berlin. There was 10/10 cloud with tops at 10,000 ft. Bombed at 21.24 hrs. at 21,000 ft. Too early to ascertain results. Many flares shot up on homeward journey. Had encounter with enemy aircraft before dropping bombs.

Sgt. J.S. Johnson was MU/Gunner from that day.

19/02/1944 DS786 A2-F   Bombing Leipzig   00.07   04.07   06.41

Bomb load 1 x 2000 lb bomb, 1 x 500 lb bomb, 40 x 30, 900 x 4 incendiaries. Primary target: Leipzig. There was 10/10 cloud with 6,000 ft. Tops. Bombed at 04.07 hours at 21,000 ft. Raid very successful. Some visual evidence of fires as we bombed. Markers very good for concentration.

78 out of 823 bombers were lost on this operation.

According E.G. Rippingale's logbook he was the Bomb Aimer that day.

24/02/1944 LL677 A2-E   Bombing Schweinfurt 20.48   01.09   04.19

Bomb load 1 x 4000 lb bomb, 420 x 4, 90 x 4, 24 x 30 incendiaries. Primary target: Schweinfurt. Weather clear. Bombed at 01.09 hours at 22,000 ft. Green flares scattered, reds well concentrated. Bend in river seen. Marvellous attack. 3 masses of blood red fires joined together by orange fires on bank of river.

Sgt. D.L. Bazent was A/Bomber that day.

25/02/1944 LL677 A2-E   Bombing Augsburg 22.00   01.16   04.45

Bomb load 1 x 4000 lb bomb, 32 x 30, 510 x 4, 90 x 4 incendiaries. Primary target: Augsburg. Weather was clear. Bombed at 01.16 hours at 21,000 ft. Mass of flames and smoke rising to 20,000 ft as we were leaving. Good route. Concentrated fires spreading more than 2 miles.

Sgt. R. Scrase was A/Bomber that day.

01/03/1944 LL677 A2-E   Bombing Stuttgart 23.33 x 02.45

Bomb load 1 x 4000 lb bomb, 24 x 30, 600 x 4, 90 x 4 incendiaries. Primary target: Stuttgart. Returned early. Furthest point reached 5010N 0025E. Port outer engine u/s. Bomb load jettisoned.

Sgt. R. Scrase was A/Bomber that day.

15/03/1944 LL677 A2-E   Bombing Stuttgart 19.26   23.26   03.15

Bomb load 1 x 1000 lb bomb, 72 x 30, 90 x 4 incendiaries. Primary target: Stuttgart. There was 7/10 cloud. Bombed at 23.26 hours from 21,000 feet. Attack very scattered. Incendiary fires 10 miles S of main attack with green

T.I. in vicinity. Route OK.

Sgt. E. Lush was A/Bomber that day.

18/03/1944 LL677 A2-E   Bombing Frankfurt 19.38 22.03 00.57

Bomb load 1 x 4000 lb bomb, 1350 x 4, 40 x 30 incendiaries. Primary target: Frankfurt. Weather very hazy, visibility bad. Bombed at 22.03 hours from 21,000 feet. T.I.s well concentrated with a ring of green T.I.s. Bomb doors damaged by cookie. Route good. Coned. Flak moderately heavy up to 22,000 feet. P.F.F. fairly good and on time. Attack considered successful.

F/S. George Wirepa was A/Bomber that day.

24/03/1944 LL677 A2-E   Bombing Berlin 18.44 22.40 02.22

Bomb load 1 x 1000 lb bomb, 88 x 30, 810 x 4, 90 x 4 incendiaries. Primary target: Berlin. There was 7/10 cloud. Bombed at 22.40 hours from 19,000 feet. Monica u/s. Main fires seemed well alight as we left target. Change of zero given too late.

Sgt. R. Scrase was A/Bomber that day.

20/04/1944 LL678 A2-L   Bombing Cologne 00.1302.08 03.56

Bomb load 1 x 1000 lb bomb, 1026 x 4, 108 x 30 lb. incendiaries. Primary target: Koln. There was 10/10 cloud. Bombed at 02.08 hours from 21,000 feet. Too early to form opinion. D.R. Compass u/s. P.F.F. 5 minutes late. Yellow stars scarcely distinguishable. Glow of fires seen from Dutch Coast. Route satisfactory.

From that day F/O. H. James was Navigator and F/O. J. Peake A/Bomber.

22/04/1944 LL678 A2-L   Bombing Dusseldorf 22.55 01.19 03.00

Bomb load 9 x 1000, 5 x 500 lb bomb. Primary target: Dusseldorf. Weather was hazy. Bombed at 01.19 hours from 22,000 feet. Good fires seen burning round the markers. T.I.s well concentrated. Flak slight in loose barrage. If the markers were on the bombing was excellent.

24/04/1944 LL678 A2-L   Bombing Karlsruhe 22.29 00.30 03.40

Bomb load 1 x 1000 lb bomb, 1026 x 4, 114 x 4, 108 x 30 lb incendiaries. Primary target: Karlsruhe not bombed. Off track owing to Navigator's oxygen failure. Bombed Darmstadt 00.30 hours from 22,000 feet. Concentration of flak and searchlights penetrating cloud.

F/O. William Mark Wiseman

J37983 F/O. William Mark "Skip" Wiseman, RCAF. Pilot.
J40517 F/O. Gilbert Vernon "Dewey" Dewitt, RCAF. A/Bomber.
J40830 F/O. D.C. "Mac" MacGorman, RCAF. Navigator.
Sgt. C.E. or E.S. Steele.   WOP/AG.
2222979 Sgt. Wilfred "Joe" King.   MU/Gunner. 16 ops.
J268399 F/S. Samuel "Sammy" Folino, RCAF. R/Gunner.
Sgt. George W. Sumner.   F/Engineer.

L to R (bottom): G.W. Sumner, W.M. Wiseman, G.V. Dewitt. L to R (top): D.C. MacGorman, W. King, S. Folino, "Red" Steele (courtesy Gary King, nephew of "Joe" King)

25/02/1945 NG118 A2-H Bombing Kamen   09.30   12.46   14.50
Bomb load 1 x 4000 HC, 9 x 500 ANM 64, 2 x 500 MC, 3 x 250 GP and Smoke Puff. Primary target: Kamen. Weather 6-8/10ths cloud. Bombed at 12.46 hours from 19,000 feet on G.H. Leader.
From his usual crew, only F/O W.M. Wiseman did this mission as 2nd Pilot with P/O J.H. Tolley's crew.
26/02/1945 NG118 A2-H Bombing Dortmund 10.23 15.03 16.19
Bomb load 1 x 4000 HC, 2 x 500 MC L/Delay 37B, 9 x 500 ANM64, 4 x 250 GP. Primary target: Dortmund, Hoesch Benzin plant. Weather 10/10ths cloud, tops 8/10,000 feet. Bombed at 15.03 hours from 21,000 feet on G.H. Leader.
28/02/1945 NF966 A2-G Bombing Nordstern 08.55 12.05 14.18

Bomb load 1 x 4000 HC, 9 x 500 ANM64, 2 x 500 MC L/D, 4 x 250 GP. Primary target: Nordstern (Gelsenkirchen). Weather 10/10ths cloud. Bombed at 12.05 hours from 20,000 feet on leading aircraft.

10/03/1945 NG203 A2-C Bombing Gelsenkirchen 12.10 15.38 17.30

Bomb load 1 x 4000 HC, 13 x 500 ANM 64, 2 x 500 GP. Primary target: Gelsenkirchen. Weather 10/10ths cloud at target, tops 8,000 feet. Bombed at 15.38 hours from 19,200 feet on G.H. Leader.

12/03/1945 NG203 A2-C Bombing Dortmund 13.01 17.06 19.01

Bomb load 1 x 4000 HC, 13 x 500 ANM 64. Primary target: Dortmund. Weather 10/10ths cloud over target, tops 6/10,000 feet. Bombed at 17.06 hours from 19,000 feet on G.H.

21/03/1945 ME363 JI-R Bombing Munster 09.35 13.09 15.18

Bomb load 1 x 4000 HC, 13 x 500 ANM 64, 2 x 500 MC. Primary target Munster Viaduct and Marshalling Yards. Weather cloud nil to 2/10ths. Bombed at 13.09 hours from 18,000 feet on G.H. Slight damage on tail-plane and astrodome.

23/03/1945 ME363 JI-R Bombing Wesel 14.24 17.39 19.12

Bomb load 13 x 1000 ANM 65. Primary target: Wesel, in support of ground troops. Weather perfect. Bombed at 17.39 hours from 20,000 feet on G.H. 2 x 1000 ANM65 hung up and jettisoned at 5217N 0302E at 18.27 hours from 10,000 feet.

27/03/1945 ME425 A2-L Bombing Hamm Sachsen 10.32 14.03 16.00

Bomb load 1 x 4000 HC, 13 x 500 ANM 64, 2 x 500 MC. Primary target: Hamm Sachsen, Benzol plant. Weather 10/10ths cloud. Bombed at 14.03 hours at 17,500 feet on G.H. Leader.

04/04/1945 NN781 A2-B Bombing Merseburg (Leuna) 18.43 22.38 03.12

Weather 5-10/10ths cloud, and 10/10ths over Merseburg. Target not attacked. Bomb load 1 x 4000 HC, 6 x 500 ANM 64 brought back. Arrived at 22.38, Orbit as no markers were down - saw skymarkers go down at 22.45 by the time we got on correct heading they had disappeared. Accurately engaged by intense flak we had to take evasive action after which there were no markers visible. Decided to bring bombs back owing to proximity of bomb line. Second bombing run at approx 23.05.

From his usual crew, only F/O W.M. Wiseman did this mission as 2nd Pilot with S/L E.B. Cozens' crew.

09/04/1945 ME523 A2-G Bombing Kiel 19.50 22.35 01.55

Bomb load 1 x 4000 HC and 12 x 500 ANM 64. Primary target: Kiel, Submarine Buildings Yards. Weather clear with slight haze. Bombed at 22.35 hours from 20,000 feet on Green T.I.s cascading into Red T.I.s. Large orange explosion at 22.33 on our A/P. Concentrated attack. Very good attack. M/B not audible.

22/04/1945 ME523 A2-G Bombing Bremen 15.08 18.43 20.54

Bomb load 1 x 4000 HC, 2 x 500 MC, 14 x 500 ANM 64. Primary target: Bremen, in support of Troop concentration. Weather on approaching target 4-5/10ths cloud. Bombed on G.H. at 18.43 hours from 18,000 ft. Excellent G.H. run. Many cookie bursts seen amid smoke north of river. Good formation through target, results accurate.

30/04/1945 RE117 A2-D Manna Rotterdam 17.01 18.21 19.41

Dropping area: Rotterdam. Weather intermittent showers and low cloud. Load 5 packs. Dropped 4 packs visually on white cross at 18.21 hours. Our load dropped to port of the cross. Some loads fell in water others caused a splash when dropped in land. A lower dropping height would be an advantage.

People were picking up the bags almost as they were dropped. Populace waving with sheets and clothing.

02/05/1945 RE117 A2-D Manna The Hague 11.09 12.22 13.30

Dropping area The Hague. Weather over dropping zone clear below cloud for the first arrivals changing later to heavy showers which marred visibility. Dropped 4 panniers on Red T.I. and White Cross at 12.22 hours. Showers - Poor visibility. Low cloud on outward journey - Good collection of panniers.

05/05/1945 ME529 A2-F Manna The Hague 06.08 07.24 08.26

Dropped 5 panniers on Red T.I. and White Cross at 07.24 hours. Low cloud - Poor visibility. Many Union Jacks and Dutch Flags flown - racecourse covered with panniers.

No Mid Upper Gunner that day.

11/05/1945 ME529 A2-F Exodus Juvincourt - Tangmere 11.12 x 17.03

Duration 3.33. Outward 1.27 hours. Collected 24 ex POWs. Homeward 2.06 hours. No comment. Operation Exodus. This dealt with the repatriation of some of the British prisoners of war from Europe.

13/05/1945 ME529 A2-F Exodus Juvincourt - Tangmere 13.22 x 16.24

Duration 3.01 hours. "Return to Base" received at 14.50 hrs.

17/05/1945 PD389 A2-J Exodus Brussels - Westcott 10.01 x 15.40

Duration 3 hrs 17 mins. Out 1 hr 33 mins. In 1 hr 44 mins. 10 Belgian refugees taken to Brussels. 24 Ex POWs returned (including 18 British Indians). No troubles.

18/05/1945 PD389 A2-J Exodus Brussels - Oakley 13.00 x 17.34

Duration 3 hrs 27 mins. Out 1 hr 25 mins. In 2 hrs 2 mins. 9 Belgian refugees returned to Brussels. 24 ex POWs. Returned to U.K. Organisation good.

23/05/1945 RA602 A2-H Exodus Brussels - Oakley 12.16 x 18.25

Duration 3 hrs 49 mins. Out 1 hr 27 mins. In 2 hrs 22 mins. 10 Belgian refugees returned. 3 POWs. evacuated. All OK.

P/O. Norman Robertson Wishart, DFC

177530 (1550859) P/O. Norman Robertson Wishart, DFC. Pilot.
1494877 F/S. A. or J. or W.J. Thornber. A/Bomber.
R155800 W/O. A. Gray, RCAF. Navigator.
1345701 Sgt. Norman James Turner. WOP/AG.
1452207 Sgt. T.J. Saint. MU & R/Gunner.
1398893 Sgt. F. Fairbrass. MU & R/Gunner.
2209045 Sgt. L. Cartwright. F/Engineer.

18/03/1944 LL728 JI-B Bombing Frankfurt   19.37   22.06   00.42
Bomb load 1 x 4000 lb bomb, 1350 x 4, 90 x 4, 32 x 30 incendiaries. Primary target: Frankfurt. Weather was hazy. Bombed at 22.06 hours from 20,000 feet. Glows seen through clouds tending to undershoot. Attack promised well. Route OK. Arrived before time and had to orbit.

22/03/1944 LL697 JI-E Bombing Frankfurt   18.36   21.53   00.55
Bomb load 1 x 1000 lb bomb, 64 x 30, 1161 x 4, 129 x 4 incendiaries. Primary target: Frankfurt. There was 3/10 cloud over the target. Bombed at 21.53 hours from 20,400 feet. Good concentration, T.I.s and many small fires also concentrated. Spoof attack flares at Hannover seen. A very good prang, well concentrated.

24/03/1944 LL697 JI-E Bombing Berlin 19.27   22.35   01.32
Bomb load 1 x 1000 lb bomb, 88 x 30, 810 x4, 90 x 4 incendiaries. Primary target: Berlin. There was 8/10 cloud. Bombs dropped 22.35 hours from 14,000 feet. Total load jettisoned about 7 miles N. of aiming point due to loss of height, down to 14,000 feet. Lancaster went into a spiral dive. Although load jettisoned due to engine trouble we still hit Berlin, many fires seen beneath us when we jettisoned. Change of zero hour heard on 22.00 broadcast.

26/03/1944 LL697 JI-E Bombing Essen 20.00   22.05   00.29
Bomb load 1 x 2000 lb bomb, 56 x 30, 1080 x 4, 120 x 4 incendiaries. Primary target: Essen. There was 10/10 cloud with occasional breaks. Bombed at 22.05 hours from 21,000 feet. Glow of green T.I.s seen through the cloud. No trouble on route, cloud prevented visual but fire glows showed over a large area. Would have been a help had Wanganuii S/Ls not in evidence.

30/03/1944 LL697 JI-E Bombing Nuremburg 22.31   01.17   05.41
Bomb load 1 x 1000 lb bomb, 96 x 30, 810 x 4, 90 x 4 incendiaries. Primary target: Nuremberg. There was 7/10 cloud with tops 12,000 feet. Bombed at 01.17 hours from 21,000 feet. Good concentrated fires - coinciding with position of both red and green markers and sky markers. Spoof fighter flares seen. Believed good attack. P.F.F. markers concentrated.

11/04/1944 LL728 JI-B Bombing Aachen 21.04 22.40   00.35
Bomb load 10 x 1000, 2 x 500 lb bomb, 160 x 4, 20 x 4 incendiaries. Primary target: Aachen. There was broken cloud. Bombed at 22.40 hours from 20,000

feet. Red T.I.s concentrated and many good fires seen. Good successful attack. Route OK.

26/04/1944 LL697 JI-E Bombing Essen 22.49 01.34 03.25

Bomb load 1 x 2000 lb bomb, 84 x 30, 945 x 4, 105 x 4 lb incendiaries. Primary target: Essen. Weather was clear but cloud above. Bombed at 01.34 hours from 20,800 feet. Many round fires seen about the A/P. Fires tending to undershoot. Very good effort. Good route.

27/04/1944 LL697 JI-E Bombing Friedrichshafen 21.50 02.14 05.54

Bomb load 10 x 4000 lb bomb, 32 x 30, 32 x 4 incendiaries. Primary target: Friedrichshafen. Weather was clear. Bombed at 02.14 hours from 20,000 feet. A large concentration of fires seen among the T.I.s. An extremely good attack. Large bright red explosion in target area at 02.17 hours. Route good.

01/05/1944 LL697 JI-E Bombing Chambly 22.45 00.22 02.01

Bomb load 10 x 1000, 5 x 500 lb bombs. Primary target: Chambly. Weather was clear. Visual of river and railways. Bombed at 00.22 hours from 9,500 feet. Bombs seen exploding round yellow T.I.s on E side of railway yard, green T.I.s just off the yard to N.E. One fire seen after leaving. M of C very helpful.

07/05/1944 LL697 JI-E Bombing Nantes 00.23 03.02 05.42

Bomb load 1 x 4000, 14 x 500 lb bombs. Primary target: Nantes. Weather was clear. Bombed at 03.02 hours from 10,000 feet. Everything seen clearly. Very large explosion seen just after bombing - Orange coloured flame and heavy black smoke rose to about 9,000 feet. Extinguished rapidly afterwards. Attack very good. Bombs seen to drop on target.

Sgt. F. Fairbrass was MU/Gunner that day and Sgt. T.J. Saint R/Gunner.

09/05/1944 LL697 JI-E Bombing Cap Gris Nez 03.00 04.12 05.20

Bomb load 1 x 1000 GP, 13 x 1000 MC. Primary target: Cape Gris Nez. There was no cloud but slight haze, visibility OK. No T.I.s or flares seen on arrival but orbited for 7 minutes and then saw first yellow T.I. followed by red. Coast line and Cape Gris Nez visible but not in detail. Bombed red T.I. on instructions from Master Bomber at 04.12 hours from 5,800 feet. Attack seemed nicely spread around red T.I. Some delay experienced on getting Pathfinders to drop flares, but when this was done, everything was OK. Seemed a good prang.

Sgt. F. Fairbrass was MU/Gunner that day and Sgt. T.J. Saint R/Gunner.

19/05/1944 LL697 JI-E Bombing Le Mans 22.15 00.26 03.35

Bomb load 4 x 1000 USA, 5 x 1000 MC, 1 x 1000 GP, 4 x 500 GP. Primary target: Le Mans. Cloud over target with base at 8,000 feet. Bombed markers at 00.26 hours from 8,000 feet. Numerous bomb bursts and one large fire seen. Satisfactory attack.

21/05/1944 LL697 JI-E Bombing Duisburg 22.40 01.14 03.20

Bomb load 1 x 2000 lb bomb, 120 x 30 incendiaries, 600 x 4 incendiaries. Primary target: Duisburg. 10/10 wispy cloud in layers over target. Bombed at 01.14 hours from 21,000 feet. Nothing seen but glow of T.I.s and bomb flashes. Unable to assess effectiveness of raid because of cloud.

22/05/1944 LL697 JI-E Bombing Dortmund   22.45 x 00.30

Bomb load 1 x 2000 lb bomb, 96 x 30, 810 x 4, 90 x 4 incendiaries. Primary target: Dortmund. Returned early because of severe icing. Farthest point reached 5232N 0206E and all bombs jettisoned safe at that position at 23.37 hours. Turrets, guns and engine all frozen. Aerial flopping around prop and aircraft would not climb above 6500 feet.

27/05/1944 LL697 JI-E Bombing Aachen   00.30 02.28   04.10

Bomb load 7 x 1000 MC, 4 x 1000 ANM, 4 x 500 MC. Primary target: Aachen. Clear over target but 10/10 cloud over sea. Bombed T.I.s at 02.28 hours from 14,000 feet. Visual seen of built up area by light photo flash. Some heavy flak over target. Route good. Unidentified aircraft seen dropping flares on outward journey at 02.12 hours.

28/05/1944 LL697 JI-E Bombing Angers   18.45 23.55   01.45

Bomb load 5 x 1000 MC, 1 x 1000 USA, 4 x 500 MC. Primary target: Angers. Clear at target. Bombed at 23.55 hours from 10,000 feet. Good visual obtained. Markers concentrated. Route satisfactory.

31/05/1944 LL697 JI-E Bombing Trappes   23.45   01.59   04.30

Bomb load 8 x 1000 MC, 8 x 500 MC. Primary target: Trappes. Clear with slight haze at target. Bombed at 01.59 hours from 7,000 feet. Visual obtained of shower bursts across railway yards. Attack thought good. Fire seen at east end of yards. Opposition slight. Monica u/s at French coast home.

10/06/1944 DS842 JI-F Bombing Dreux 23.12   00.56   03.31

Bomb load 16 x 500 GP, 2 x 500 LD. Primary target: Dreux. Bombed as instructed by Master Bomber at 00.56 hours from 6,000 feet. Many bomb bursts near T.I.s seen and smoke at end of yards. Weather clear, generally quiet trip.

11/06/1944 DS813 JI-H Bombing Nantes 23.54 02.48   04.59

Bomb load 16 x 500 GP. 2 x 500 LD. Primary target: Nantes. Bombed as instructed by Master Bomber at 02.48 hours from 2,500 feet. Conditions clear below 2,500 feet. Base of cloud lit up by bomb bursts. Flak moderate.

14/06/1944 LL697 JI-E Bombing Le Havre   23.43   01.12   02.18

Bomb load 11 x 1000 MC, 4 x 500 GP. Primary target: Le Havre. Weather was clear. Bombed at 01.12 hours from 14,500 feet on Master Bomber's instructions on yellow T.I.s. Large fire burning North of A/P on arrival and several smaller fires in Dock area. 2 ships seen to be on fire. Fighters not in evidence early part of attack.

15/06/1944 LL697 JI-E Bombing Valenciennes   22.59   00.38   02.39

Bomb load 16 x 500 GP, 2 x 500 MC. Primary target: Valenciennes. Weather clear below cloud. Bombed at 00.38 hours from 8,000 feet on red and green T.I.s. close together. Many bomb bursts across T.I.s. Master Bomber instructed crew to hold bombing till he marked target again. Aircraft orbited and banked on southerly course.

21/06/1944 LL697 JI-E Bombing Domleger   17.58 x 20.45

Bomb load 18 x 500 MC. Primary target: Domleger near Abbeville, V-1 flying bomb launch site. Unable to see T.I.s obeyed Master Bomber's instructions to return to Base. Jettisoned safe 8 x 500 MC at 19.40 hours from 10,000 feet 5030N 0120E.

23/06/1944 ME841 JI-H Bombing L'Hey 23.06 00.16 01.12

Bomb load 11 x 1000 MC, 4 x 500 GP. Primary target: L'Hey, Flying bomb installations. There was 10/10ths cloud, tops 5/6,000 feet. Bombed at 00.16 hours from 9,000 feet. Glow of red T.I.s. Flak slight, glow of T.I.s clearly seen; should have been a good concentration of bombing. Trouble free route.

30/06/1944 LM181 JI-E Bombing Villers Bocage 18.03 20.00 21.01

Bomb load 11 x 1000 MC, 4 x 500 GP. Primary target: Villers Bocage. Weather clear, wispy cloud above. Bombed at 20.00 hours from 4,000 feet. Clouds of black smoke and dust seen. Good raid, target well pranged. Opposition moderate.

02/07/1944 LM181 JI-E Bombing Beauvoir 12.39 14.36 15.43

Bomb load 11 x 1000 MC, 4 x 500 GP. Primary target: Beauvoir, Flying bomb supply site. Bombed at 14.36 hours from 13,500 feet on yellow T.I.s.

07/07/1944 LM181 JI-E Bombing Vaires 22.34 01.30 03.06

Bomb load 11 x 1000 ANM 65. Primary target: Vaires, Marshalling yards. Weather clear. Bombed at 01.30 hours from 12,500 feet, centre of all T.I.s as per Master Bomber's instructions. Bombs seen falling in marshalling yards. Marking good and bombing concentrated. Large red flash in target area at 01.33 hours. Flak bursts holed aircraft over target.

10/07/1944 PB185 JI-F Bombing Nucourt 04.01 06.04 07.23

Bomb load 11 x 1000 ANM 65, 4 x 500 GP. Primary target: Nucourt, Constructional works. Bombed at 06.04 hours from 15,500 feet, Gee.

12/07/1944 LM180 JI-G Bombing Vaires 17.48 x 21.37

Bomb load 18 x 500 GP. Primary target: Vaires, Marshalling yards. Master Bomber instructed "return to Base". Jettisoned 4 x 500 GP. At 20.42 hours from 12,000 feet, position 4953N 0034E.

23/07/1944 LM206 JI-C Bombing Kiel 22.17 01.19 03.39

Bomb load 10 x 1000 MC, 5 x 500 GP. Special Nickels. Primary target: Kiel, Warehouses and docks. There was 10/10ths thin cloud. Bombed at 01.19 hours from 19,500 feet centre of red T.I.s. Cloud prevented visual. Defences fairly accurate, searchlights ineffective.

25/07/1944 PB143 JI-B Bombing Stuttgart 21.30 01.52 05.21

Bomb load 7 x 1000 MC, 4 x 500 GP. Primary target: Stuttgart. Clear space among 10/10ths cloud, tops 2,500 feet over target. Bombed at 01.52 hours from 21,000 feet centre of red T.I. Bomb bursts seen amongst T.I.s, markers rather scattered.

F/O. Stanley Paul Witchell

178789 (1601470)   F/O. Stanley Paul Witchell.   Pilot.
160956 (1333696)   F/O. John Barwick Cushing, DFC.   A/Bomber.
195188 (1673373)   P/O. Alan Fairfax.   Navigator.
177174 (1870300)   F/O. John Frederick "Johnny" Channell. WOP/AG.
179331 (944736) F/O. George Rothwell.   MU/Gunner.
Sgt. D.W.F. Sawyer.   R/Gunner.
191847 (962612) P/O. Ralph Swift.   F/Engineer

01/07/1945 RF231 JI-A Post Mortem   Special mission 12.05 x 17.39

F/O. Douglas Austin Woods

A420731   F/O. Douglas Austin "Doug" Woods, RAAF. Pilot.
1384669 F/S. Ernest Thomas Shanks.   A/Bomber.
138083 (1528349)   F/O. Francis Longson.   Navigator.
1143288 Sgt. Kenneth Royston Heron. WOP/AG.
1586017 Sgt. GR Hutton.   MU/Gunner. 1 op.
1851507 Sgt. William Charles "Bill" Udell. MU/Gunner. 26 ops.
178475 (1357729)   P/O. Hilary Louis Doherty.   R/Gunner.
1330027 Sgt. M.C.L. Bristow or Bristowe.   F/Engineer. 1 op.
1624295 Sgt. Eric Charles Coles.   F/Engineer. 26 ops.

19/02/1944 LL732 JI-R Bombing Leipzig   00.03 x 01.50
Bomb load 1 x 4000 lb bomb, 510 x 4, 90 x 4, 32 x 30 incendiaries. Returned early. Farthest point reached 5313N 0140E. Load jettisoned. Starboard outer engine completely u/s and had to be feathered and port outer and starboard inner failing. Intercom u/s also.
Sgt. G.R. Hutton was MU/Gunner that day and Sgt. M.C.L. Bristow F/Engineer.
24/02/1944 LL731 JI-U Bombing Schweinfurt 18.46 23.25   02.13
Bomb load 1 x 4000 lb bomb, 24 x 30, 510 x 4, 90 x 4 incendiaries. Primary target: Schweinfurt. Weather clear - no clouds. Bombed at 23.25 hours at 18,000 ft. Concentration of fires late on target, no T.I.s visible. There was smoke to approx. 4,000 ft. 3 very large fires appeared to be spreading. Route very good.
25/02/1944 LL732 JI-R Bombing Augsburg   21.37 x 05.00
Bomb load 1 x 4000 lb bomb, 32 x 30, 510 x 4, 90 x 4 incendiaries. Primary target: Augsburg. Weather was clear, no cloud. Lancaster orbited on last leg of track before reaching target in order to lose time. Fires raging in city. Glow seen 100 miles before arrival, seen also at same distance on return.

F/O. Douglas Austin "Doug" Woods, RAAF (courtesy Alan Henry)

01/03/1944 LL731 JI-U Bombing Stuttgart 23.50   03.16   07.13

Bomb load 1 x 8000 lb. bomb. Primary target: Stuttgart. There was 10/10 cloud. Bombed at 03.16 hours at 20,000 ft. Large glow of fires seen below cloud. Appearance of a few explosions on run up. Raid appeared somewhat scattered. Photo attempted.

15/03/1944 LL739 JI-M Bombing Stuttgart 19.12   23.18   02.43

Bomb load 1 x 1000 lb bomb, 1050 x 4, 90 x 4, 72 x 30 incendiaries. Primary target: Stuttgart. There was 8-9/10 cloud over the target. Bombed at 23.18 hours from 20,000 feet. There was scattered fires under the cloud. Attack slow in opening, fires seemed to become more numerous on leaving target. Route good. Marking poor.

18/03/1944 LL739 JI-M Bombing Frankfurt   19.31 x 00.34

Bomb load 1 x 4000 lb bomb, 1350 x 4, 90 x 4, 32 x 30 incendiaries. Weather was clear. No attack. Total load jettisoned to reduce weight. Holes in wing inspection panel. Rear turret out of action. Starboard outer hit. No T.I.s seen so decided to bring bombs back. Uncomfortable time with fighter and forced to jettison later.

24/03/1944 LL739 JI-M Bombing Berlin 18.33   22.32   01.49

Bomb load 1 x 1000 lb bomb, 88 x 30, 810 x 4, 90 x 4 incendiaries. Primary target: Berlin. There was 8-10/10 cloud with gaps. Bombed at 22.32 hours from 20,000 feet. Attack did not appear to have developed, only sky markers seen. Mid Upper turret u/s and petrol tanks holed, starboard No. 1 and port No.1 and 2. On return flow about 100 miles S of track, winds believe to be cause. Considered attack successful. P.F.F. a little late.

26/03/1944 LL731 JI-U Bombing Essen 19.59   22.11   01.02

731

Bomb load 1 x 2000 lb bomb, 56 x 30, 1080 x 4, 120 x 4 incendiaries. Primary target: Essen. There was 10/10 cloud over the target. Bombed at 22.11 hours from 22,000 feet. Glow seen beneath cloud - some fires but appeared scattered. Attack seemed scattered. P.F.F. believed late in opening attack. Spoof markers seen about 2 miles N. of target.

30/03/1944 LL739 JI-M Bombing Nuremburg 22.20 x 02.47

Bomb load 1 x 1000 lb bomb, 96 x 30, 810 x 4, 90 x 4 incendiaries. Returned early and landed at Woodbridge. Attacked by ME410 five times. Starboard wing and starboard tail damaged. Rear Guns frozen, Mid Upper guns would only fire 4 rounds at a time. Saw 15 to 20 aircraft shot down by fighter on outward route S. of Ruhr.

The damage sustained by LL739 JI-M on the night of 30-31 March 1944

10/04/1944 DS822 JI-T Bombing Laon 01.13 03.40 05.13

Bomb load 9 x 1000, 4 x 500 lb bomb. Primary target: Laon. Weather was clear. Bombed at 03.40 hours from 11,000 feet. Dull reddish glow seen from area under T.I. markers. Route excellent. Attack appeared to be very concentrated. Photo attempted.

11/04/1944 DS822 JI-T Bombing Aachen 20.57 x 00.10

Bomb load 10 x 1000, 2 x 4000 lb bombs, 160 x 4, 20 x 4 incendiaries. Primary target: Aachen. There was ground haze but no cloud. T.I.s appeared stretched out in line - not concentrated. Monica u/s on homeward leg from target. Raid appeared very scattered due to lack of concentration of T.I.s. Photo attempted.

26/04/1944 LL731 JI-U Bombing Essen 22.48 01.32 03.11

Bomb load 1 x 2000 lb bomb, 84 x 30, 945 x 4, 105 x 4 lb incendiaries.

Primary target: Essen. Weather was clear with slight haze. Bombed at 01.32 hours from 16,000 feet. Saw one fire burning when we bombed. Fires seen as far as English Coast. Seemed a good effort. Route good.

27/04/1944 LL731 JI-U Bombing Friedrichshafen 22.08 02.13 05.48

Bomb load 1 x 4000 lb bomb, 32 x 30, 324 x 4, 36 x 4 incendiaries. Primary target: Friedrichshafen. Weather was clear with some haze. Bombed at 02.13 hours from 12,000 feet. Many fires seen. A good concentrated attack - aircraft late and bombed at 12,000 feet to arrive in time. Holes in starboard main plane and No. 3 petrol tank - Hole in port main plane - Fighter attack.

01/05/1944 LL739 JI-M Bombing Chambly 23.00 00.27 01.51

Bomb load 10 x 1000, 5 x 500 lb bombs. Primary target: Chambly. Weather was clear. Bombed at 00.27 hours from 7,000 feet. Monica u/s. A good attack. Two large fires seen on leaving. Well directed by M of C who instructed us to bomb on yellow T.I.s and said attack well placed.

09/05/1944 DS822 JI-T Bombing Cap Gris Nez 03.15 04.07 04.45

Bomb load 1 x 1000 GP, 13 x 1000 MC. Primary target: Cape Gris Nez. Slight haze over target, but red and green T.I.s seen. Bombed on instructions from Master Bomber at 04.07 hours from 3,000 feet. Coast was seen clearly but owing to T.I.s could not distinguish detail of other landmarks. Bombs believed to fall on target. Own bombs seemed to produce something more than an actual burst.

11/05/1944 DS822 JI-T Bombing Louvain 23.00 x 00.12

Bomb load 5 x 1000 GP, 5 x 1000 MC, 5 x 500 MC. Primary target: Louvain. Slight defect in port inner engine, A.S.I. and Altimeter also u/s. Jettisoned bombs at 23.37 hours at 5147N 0212E and returned to Base. Would have carried on but for A.S.I. Later discovered that trouble was caused by a bee in the pitot head.

21/05/1944 DS822 JI-T Bombing Duisburg 22.46 x 00.58

Bomb load 1 x 2000 lb bomb, 120 x 30, 600 x 4 incendiaries. Primary target: Duisberg. Aircraft returned early as pilot was sick. Farthest point reached 5252N 0323E. 10 x 2000 bomb and 48 x 30 incendiaries jettisoned in sea at 00.08 hours from 17,000 feet. Remainder of bombs brought back to Base.

24/05/1944 DS822 JI-T Bombing Boulogne 00.05 01.17 01.55

Bomb load 9 x 1000 MC, 1 x 1000 GP, 1 x 1000 ANM, 4 x 500 GP. Primary target: Boulogne, Gun Battery. Clear over the target. Bombed green T.I.s at 01.17 hours from 9,000 feet. Good attack. Slight flak seen but trip uneventful.

02/06/1944 LL731 JI-L Bombing Wissant 01.29 02.12 03.03

Bomb load 1 x 1000 GP, 10 x 1000 MC, 4 x 500 MC. Primary target: Wissant Gun Positions. There was 10/10 cloud at target with tops at 6,000 feet. Bombed on the glow from red T.I.s in conjunction with a Gee fix at 02.12 hours from 8,000 feet. Bomb bursts were seen. Route was OK.

05/06/1944 DS822 JI-T Bombing Ouistreham 03.25 05.11 06.35

Bomb load 9 x 1000 MC and 2 x 500 MC. Primary target: Ouistreham. There was 10/10 cloud on route and 3/10 broken over target. Bombed markers at 05.11 hours from 10,000 feet. Bombs concentrated around T.I.s but T.I.s appeared to be inaccurately placed. Could not see much but some smoke was visible and glow of T.I.s seen through cloud.

06/06/1944 DS822 JI-T Bombing Lisieux 00.12 01.37 02.55

Bomb load 16 x 500 MC tail fused and 2 x 500 MC LD. Primary target: Lisieux. Weather was clear over target at 6000 feet. Bombed markers at 01.37 hours from 6,000 feet. Bombs seen bursting round the only red T.I. Effort well concentrated. A good visual obtained of the target.

08/06/1944 LL620 JI-T Bombing Fougeres   21.57 00.23 02.36

Bomb load 16 x 500 GP and 2 x 500 MC LD. Primary target: Fougeres. Bombed fires and markers at 00.23 hours from 4,000 feet. White T.I.s seen with growing fires near, which spread around the railway track area. Bombs falling on tracks appeared to lift trucks into the air. Good concentrated attack with fires visible 80 miles away. Photograph was taken during a steep turn to port to avoid another aircraft.

10/06/1944 LL620 JI-T Bombing Dreux 23.18 01.00 03.12

Bomb load 16 x 500 GP, 2 x 500 LD. Primary target: Dreux. Bombed on green and yellow T.I.s on instructions of Master Bomber at 01.00 hours from 8,000 feet. Did not see much of attack. Weather broken cloud and haze.

23/06/1944 DS826 JI-U Bombing L'Hey 23.14 00.15 01.32

Bomb load 11 x 1000 MC, 4 x 500 GP. Primary target: L'Hey, Flying bomb installations. There was 10/10ths cloud, tops 4,000 feet. Bombed at 00.15 hours from 8,000 feet. Concentrated bombing amongst T.I.s. Some heavy and light flak.

24/06/1944 LL620 JI-T Bombing Rimeux 23.29 00.33 02.07

Bomb load 18 x 500 GP. Primary target: Rimeux, Flying bomb installations. Slight haze. Bombed at 00.33 hours from 10,000 feet. Bombed on concentration of red T.I.s. Several combats seen.

27/06/1944 LL620 JI-T Bombing Biennais 23.27 01.11 02.55

Bomb load 16 x 500 GP, 2 x 500 ANM 64 GP. Primary target: Biennais, Flying bomb installations. There was 10/10ths cloud. Bombed at 01.11 hours from 12,000 feet, red glow.

30/06/1944 LL620 JI-T Bombing Villers Bocage 18.19 x   x

Bomb load 11 x 1000 MC, 3 x 500 GP. Primary target: Villers Bocage to bomb a key road junction in tactical support of Allied ground forces. Seen by LL635 JI-M to be hit by flak over target, which broke tail off, and then to hit ground at Coulvain (Calvados), 5 km SW of Villers-Bocage. There were no survivors.

All are buried in Coulvain Churchyard. The Rear Gunner, Sgt. Doherty, came from Castlepollard in County West Meath of the Irish Republic. So successful was this attack that tanks of the German 2nd and 9th Panzer Divisions had to abandon their planned counter attack on the nearby allied held beaches.

F/L.   Royston Worthing

116005 (1379910)   F/L. Royston Worthing. Pilot.
163638 (1676072)   F/O. Stanley Sanderson Gill. A/Bomber.
164189 (1805737)   F/O. Alfred William Tarry. Navigator.
NZ4212883 F/O.T.F. Haworth, RNZAF.   WOP/AG.
176562 (1228022)   F/O. William Boughton "Bill" Parker. MU & R/Gunner.
Sgt. P.J. Norton.   MU & R/Gunner.
Sgt. H.J. Salter. F/Engineer. 19 ops.
939832Sgt. Alfred "Alf" McMurrugh.   F/Engineer. 1 op.
191247 (1581759)
P/O. Stephen "Steve" Abel, DFC.   2nd Pilot. 13&16/02/45
150651 (1795353)
F/O.William George Henry Thomas Gibson. 2nd Pilot. 18/02/1945
141716 (1312150)   F/L. Frederick William Morrish. 2nd Pilot. 23/02/1945
130171 (1335758)   F/L. Harold Thomas Lunson. 2nd Pilot. 26/02/1945
153171 (1562823)   F/O. William "Bill" Allan. 2nd Pilot. 14/03/1945

21/12/1944 LM724 JI-H Bombing Trier   12.15 x 17.12
Bomb load 1 x 4000 HC, 10 x 500 GP, 2 x 250 GP, 4 x 250 GP. Primary target: Trier. Primary target: Trier, Marshalling yards. Weather 10/10 cloud, tops 6/9,000 feet. Abortive - bombs could not be released on target.
From his usual crew, only F/L R. Worthing did this mission as 2nd Pilot with F/L K.G. Condict's crew.
23/12/1944 NN717 JI-E Bombing Trier   11.44   14.32   16.24
Bomb load 1 x 4000 HC, 10 x 500 GP, 6 x 250 GP. Primary target: Trier. Weather clear over target. Bombed at 14.32 hours from 18,000 feet on centre of Red T.I.
F/O. W.B. Parker was MU/Gunner that day and Sgt. P.J. Norton R/Gunner.
31/12/1944 LM275 JI-F Bombing Vohwinkle 11.30 14.44 16.35
Bomb load 1 x 4000 HC, 3 x 1000 M65, 2 x 500 M64, 2 x 500 GP, 2 x 500 long delay, 5 x 250 GP. Primary target: Vohwinkel. Weather 10/10ths cloud on approaching target although the target itself was clear. Bombed at 14.44 hours from 19,000 feet on G.H. Leader.
From that day Sgt. P.J. Norton was MU/Gunner and F/O. W.B. Parker R/Gunner.
01/01/1945 LM724 JI-H Bombing Vohwinkle 16.24 19.45   21.40
Bomb load 1 x 4000 HC, 10 x 500 ANM 64, 2 x 500 GP, 1 x 250 Green T.I. Primary target: Vohwinkel. Weather clear. Bombed at 19.45 hours from 21,000 feet on G.H.
From his usual crew, only F/L R. Worthing did this mission as 2nd Pilot with F/O J.F. Ness' crew.

02/01/1945 LM275 JI-F Bombing Nuremburg 15.28 19.29 22.58

Bomb load: 1 x 1000 ANM 65, 1 x 500 ANM 58, 10 x 80 x 4 IB, 120 x 4, - Primary target: Nuremburg. Weather clear. Bombed at 19.29 hours from 18,000 feet. Point between Groups of T.Is.

05/01/1945 PB142 JI-G Bombing Ludwigshafen 11.15 15.10 17.21

Bomb load 1 x 4000 HC, 10 x 500 ANM58 or 64, 2 x 500 GP. Primary target: Ludwigshafen, Marshalling yards. Weather clear over target. Bombed at 15.10 hours from 20,000 feet. Works just east of Marshalling Yards before the River.

07/01/1945 LM685 JI-K Bombing Munich 18.52 22.30 02.27

Bomb load 1 x 1000 ANM65, 1 x 500 ANM58, 1080 x 4 lb IB, 120 x 4 X.I.B. Primary target: Munich. Weather 10/10ths cloud over target 6-8,000 feet with a thin layer altitude 16,000 feet. Bombed at 22.30 hours from 20,000 feet on Red and Green flares.

11/01/1945 LM685 JI-K Bombing Krefeld 11.40 15.12 16.44

Bomb load 1 x 4000 HC, 2 X 500 ANM 58, 8 x 500 ANM64, 4 x 250 GP. Primary target: Krefeld. Weather 10/10ths cloud above and below. Visibility poor. Bombed at 15.10 hours from 20,000 feet on G.H. Leader.

15/01/1945 NF968 JI-B Bombing Lagendreer 11.37 15.02 16.46

Bomb load 1 x 4000 HC, 10 x 500 ANM 64, 4 x 250 GP. Primary target: Lagendreer. Weather 10/10ths cloud. Bombed at 15.02 hours from 19,000 feet on G.H. Leader.

16/01/1945 NF968 JI-B Bombing Wanne-Eickel 23.11 02.28 04.27

Bomb load 1 x 4000 HC, 10 x 500 ANM 58, 4 x 250 GP. Primary target: Wanne-Eickel, Benzol plant. Weather 10/10ths thin low cloud. Bombed at 02.28 hours from 20,000 feet on centre of Wanganui flare.

28/01/1945 PB902 JI-A Bombing Cologne-Gremberg 10.19 14.11 15.58

Bomb load 1 x 4000 HC, 10 x 500 ANM 64, 2 x 500 GP, 3 x 250 GP. Primary target: Koln - Gremberg, Marshalling yards. Weather 10/10ths cloud en route clearing on approach to target where visibility was good and nil cloud. Bombed at 14.11 hours from 20,000 feet on G.H. Leader.

Sgt. A. McMurrugh was F/Engineer that day.

01/02/1945 NG142 JI-J Bombing Munchen-Gladbach 13.16 16.33 18.19

Bomb load 1 x 4000 HC, 14 x No 14 Clusters. Primary target: Munchen-Gladbach, Marshalling yards. Bombed at 16.33 hours from 19,000 feet on leading aircraft.

13/02/1945 NG298 JI-E Bombing Dresden 21.42 01.30 06.07

Bomb load 1 x 4000 HC, 7 x No. 14 Clusters. Primary target: Dresden. Weather 5/10ths cloud over target. Bombed at 01.30 hours from 20,000 feet. Overshot Green T.Is.

P/O. S. Abel was 2nd Pilot that day.

14/02/1945 NF968 JI-B Bombing Chemnitz   20.23 00.31 04.20

Bomb load 1 x 4000 HC, 8 x No. 14 Clusters. Primary target: Chemnitz. Weather 8-10/10ths cloud, tops 15-16,000 feet with occasional breaks. Bombed at 00.31 hours from 20,000 feet on upwind edge of flares.

Courtesy Will Theakston – Grandson of F/O. S.S. Gill

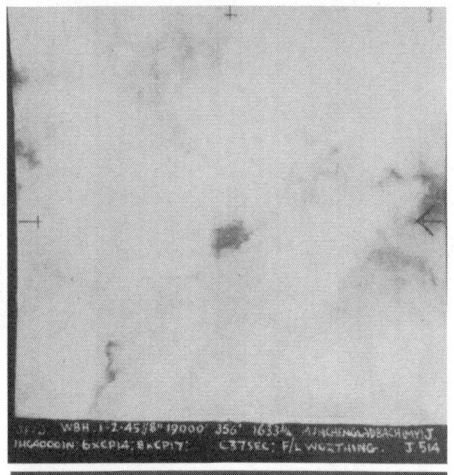

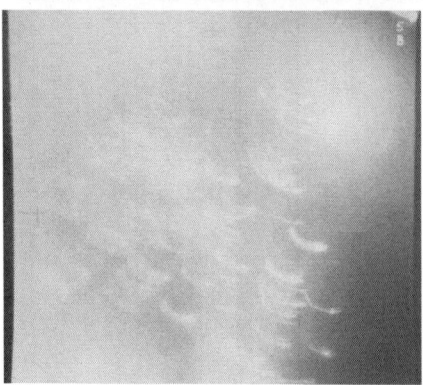

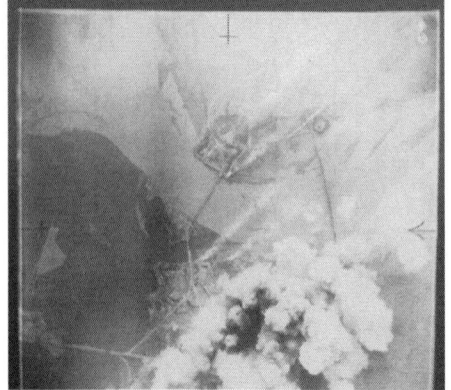

A selection of aiming point photos taken by the Worthington crew (courtesy of Will Theakston).

16/02/1945 PB902 JI-A Bombing Wesel 12.26 16.00 17.48

Bomb load 1 x 4000 HC, 4 x 500 GP, 2 x 500 MC L/Delay, 4 x 250 GP, 6 x 500 ANM 64. Primary target: Wesel. Weather clear. Bombed at 16.00 hours from 20,000 feet on leading aircraft.

P/O. S. Abel was 2nd Pilot that day.

18/02/1945 NN773 JI-K Bombing Wesel 11.21 15.24 16.51

Bomb load 1 x 4000 HC, 4 x 500 GP, 2 x 500 MC L/Delay, 4 x 250 GP, 6 x 500 ANM 64. Primary target: Wesel. Weather 10/10ths cloud. Bombed at 15.24 hours from 19,400 feet on G.H. Leader.

F/O. W.G.H.T. Gibson was 2nd Pilot that day.

23/02/1945 ME336 JI-S Bombing Gelsenkirchen 11.13 15.03 16.54

Bomb load 1 x 4000 HC, 9 x 500 ANM64, 2 x 500 MC, 4 x 250 GP. Primary target Gelsenkirchen. Weather 10/10ths cloud. Bombed at 15.03 hours from 20,000 feet on G.H.

F/L. F.W. Morrish was 2nd Pilot that day.

26/02/1945 NF968 JI-B Bombing Dortmund 10.14 14.03 16.02

Bomb load 1 x 4000 HC, 2 x 500 MC L/Delay 37B, 9 x 500 ANM 64, 3 x 250 GP, 1 Sky marker Red Puff. Primary target: Dortmund, Hoesch Benzin plant. Weather 10/10ths cloud, tops 8/10,000 feet. Bombed at 14.03 hours from 20,000 feet on G.H. equipment.

F/L. H.T. Lunson was 2nd Pilot that day.

28/02/1945 PB426 JI-D Bombing Nordstern 08.41 12.05 14.02

Bomb load 1 x 4000 HC, 9 x 500 ANM 64, 2 x 500 MC L/D, 4 x 250 GP. Primary target: Nordstern (Gelsenkirchen). Weather 10/10ths cloud. Bombed at 12.05 hours from 20,000 feet on G.H.

10/03/1945 LM724 JI-H Bombing Gelsenkirchen 12.01 15.37 17.19

Bomb load 1 x 4000 HC, 13 x 500 ANM 64, 2 x 500 MC, 1 Skymarker Blue Puff. Primary target: Gelsenkirchen. Weather 10/10ths cloud at target, tops 8,000 feet. Bombed at 15.37 hours from 19,200 feet on G.H.

12/03/1945 LM724 JI-H Bombing Dortmund 12.52 16.58 18.43

Bomb load 1 x 4000 HC, 13 x 500 ANM 64, 1 Skymarker Red Puff. Primary target: Dortmund. Weather 10/10ths cloud over target, tops 6/10,000 feet. Bombed at 16.58 hours from 19,000 feet on G.H.

14/03/1945 NF968 JI-B Bombing Heinrichshutte 13.02 16.40 18.33

Bomb load 1 x 4000 HC, 11 x 500 ANM 64, 1 Skymarker Red Puff. Primary target: Heinrichshutte, Hattingen Steel works & Benzol plant. Weather 10/10ths cloud, tops 7/12,000 feet. Bombed at 16.40 hours from 17,500 feet on G.H. Aircraft hit by heavy flak.

F/O. W. Allan was 2nd Pilot that day.

F/O. Stanley Grover Wright, DFC

J26104   F/O. Stanley Grover "Stan" Wright, DFC, RCAF.   Pilot.
R190706 F/S. L.E. "Pete" Jewell, RCAF. A/Bomber. 23 ops.
   Sgt. John H. Jeffries.   A/Bomber. 9 ops.
J37746   F/O. K.D. "Ken" Ridley, RCAF.   Navigator. 29 ops.
J35544   F/O. J.W.R. Wilson, RCAF.   Navigator. 3 ops.
R181437 Sgt. N. "Nick" Andreashuk, RCAF.   WOP/AG.
NZ425546
F/O. Albert George "Chatty" Chatfield, DFC, RNZAF.   MU/Gunner. 6 ops.
J41051   P/O. A.J. "Jake" Stansbury, RCAF.   MU&R/Gunner. 29 ops.
J41274   P/O. W.W. "Curly" Maynes, RCAF.   MU&R/Gunner. 29 ops.
   Sgt. Oscar Joseph "Joe" Dibley.   F/Engineer.
37994 W/C.   Michael "Mike" Wyatt, DFC. Captain.

23/09/1944 PD265 JI-G Bombing Neuss 19.17 x 22.03
   Bomb load 7 x 1000 ANM 59, 4 x 1000 ANM 44, 4 x 500 GP. Primary
target: Neuss. Returned early through navigation error. Jettisoned 5 x 1000.
   F/S. L.E. Jewell was A/Bomber until 06/12/1944.
25/09/1944 LM627 JI-D Bombing Pas de Calais   08.19 x 11.04
   Bomb load 11 x 1000 MC, 4 x 500 GP. Primary target: Calais. Abandoned
on Master Bomber's orders. Jettisoned 6 x 1000, 3 x 500 at 5025N 0105E.
   W/C. M. Wyatt was Captain of this crew that day and F/O. S.G. Wright 2nd
Pilot.

*PB765 JI-B, 20-21 November 1944 Homberg. L to R (standing): Jock, Shag, Taffy (all
ground crew), "Curly" Maynes, "Ken" Ridley, "Stan" Wright and "Jake" Stansbury. L to
R (kneeling): Yorkie (ground crew), "Pete" Jewell, "Nick" Andreashuk and "Joe" Dibley
(both photos courtesy Garth Ridley).*

26/09/1944 PD334 A2-D Bombing Calais 11.49 12.45 14.15

Bomb load 11 x 1000 MC, 4 x 500 GP. Primary target: Calais 7D. Weather clear below cloud which was 3,500 feet. Bombed at 12.45 hours from 3000 feet on red T.I. + 1 second.

03/10/1944 LM288 JI-C Bombing Westkapelle 12.35 13.51 15.06

Bomb load 1 x 4000 MC, 6 x 1000 MC, 1 x 500 GP L/Delay. Primary target: Westkapelle (Walcheren). Weather patchy-scattered cloud with base 5,000 feet. Bombed at 13.51 hours from 5,000 feet short of red T.I.

06/10/1944 NN717 JI-E Bombing Dortmund 16.37 20.22 22.05

Bomb load 1 x 4000 HC, 12 x No. 14 Clusters. Primary target: Dortmund, Town and Railways. Weather over the target was clear with slight ground haze. Bombed at 20.22 hours from 22,500 feet on red T.I.s.

07/10/1944 PB426 JI-J Bombing Emmerich 12.06 14.28 15.47

Bomb load 1 x 4000 HC, 10 x No. 14 clusters, 4 x (150 x 4). Primary target Emmerich. Weather clear with cloud at 13,000 feet. Bombed at 14.28 hours from 13,000 feet on South side of pall of smoke as instructed.

14/10/1944 LM285 JI-K Bombing Duisburg 06.55 09.05 10.58

Bomb load 11 x 1000 MC, 4 x 500 GP Long Delay. Primary target: Duisburg. Weather patchy cloud with gaps for bombing. Bombed at 09.05 hours from 18,500 feet. Built up area North-west of Docks.

14/10/1944 LM285 JI-K Bombing Duisburg 23.01 01.32 03.31

Bomb load 1 x 4000 HC, 14 x No. 14 Clusters. Primary target: Duisburg. Weather was clear with small amount of cloud over the target. Bombed at 01.32 hours from 21,500 feet. Centre of red T.I.s.

19/10/1944 LM285 JI-K Bombing Stuttgart 22.00 01.10 04.03

Bomb load 1 x 4000 HC, 6 x 1000 MC, 1 x 500 GP. Primary target: Stuttgart, A/P 'E' 2nd attack. Weather 10/10ths low cloud over target and all crew arrived late owing to winds not as forecast. Bombed at 01.10 hours from 18,500 feet. Wanganui flares.

23/10/1944 LM719 JI-B Bombing Essen 16.19 19.32 21.25

Bomb load 1 x 4000 HC, 6 x 1000 MC, 6 x 500 GP. Primary target: Essen. Weather 10/10ths cloud over target - tops 12/14,000 feet with most appalling weather on route. Bombed at 19.32 hours from 18,000 feet. Port of Red flares. Attacked by fighter at 5145N 0640E at 19.40 hours at 14,000 feet. MU Gunner fires 1 burst. Rear turret guns frozen and rear turret unserviceable by flak.

25/10/1944 LM285 JI-K Bombing Essen 12.55 15.33 16.57

Bomb load 1 x 4000 HC, 6 x 1000 MC, 6 x 500 GP. Primary target: Essen. Weather over target 10/10ths low cloud, with one clear patch which appeared to fill up later in the attack. Bombed at 15.33 hours from 22,500 feet. White smoke as instructed by Master Bomber.

28/10/1944 LM719 JI-B Bombing Cologne 13.14 x 15.13

Bomb load 1 x 4000 HC, 12 x 500 Clusters, 2 x 150 x 4. Primary target: Cologne. Weather clear over target. Abortive sortie. W/T receiver unserviceable. Aircraft jettisoned at 14.36 hours 5228N 0230E, 12,000 feet.

30/10/1944 NG121 JI-H Bombing Wesseling   09.08   11.59   13.46

Bomb load 1 x 4000 HC, 16 x 500 GP. Primary target: Wesseling. Weather was 10/10ths cloud - tops about 7,000 feet. Bombed at 11.59 hours from 19,000 feet on release of G.H. Leader's bombs.

02/11/1944 NG203 JI-A Bombing Homberg   11.29   14.10   15.50

Bomb load 1 x 4000 HC, 6 x 1000 ANM 59, 6 x 500 MC. Primary target: Homberg. Weather variable cloud but clear for bombing. Target obscured by pall of smoke rising to 10,000 feet. Bombed at 14.10 hours from 21,000 feet. North end of smoke.

15/11/1944 PB756 JI-B Bombing Dortmund   12.40   15.40   17.35

Bomb load 1 x 4000 HC, 16 x 500 GP. Primary target: Hoesch-Benzin Dortmund, Oil refineries. Weather 10/10ths cloud over the target. Bombed at 15.40 hours from 17,000 feet on leading aircraft.

16/11/1944 PB756 JI-B Bombing Heinsburg 13.14 15.32   17.22

Bomb load 1 x 4000 HC, 6 x 1000 MC, 6 x 500 GP. Primary target: Heinsburg. Weather - nil cloud with slight haze over target. Bombed at 15.32 hours from 9,800 feet. South-west corner of town.

20/11/1944 PB756 JI-B Bombing Homberg   12.45   15.15   17.12

Bomb load 1 x 4000 HC, 12 x 500 GP, 4 x 500 MC. Primary target: Homberg. Weather 10/10ths cloud over target. Bombed at 15.15 hours from 20,000 feet on G.H.

21/11/1944 PB756 JI-B Bombing Homberg   12.31   15.06   16.42

Bomb load 1 x 4000 HC, 16 x 500 GP. Primary target: Homberg. Weather about 5/10ths cloud but clear for bombing. Bombed at 15.06 hours from 20,000 feet visually.

23/11/1944 PB756 JI-B Bombing Nordstern   12.50   15.21   17.24

Bomb load 1 x 4000 HC, 16 x 500 GP. Primary target: Nordstern, Gelsenkirchen Oil refineries. Weather 10/10ths cloud. Bombed at 15.21 hours from 20,000 feet on G.H. Leader.

27/11/1944 NG350 JI-C Bombing Cologne   12.35   15.05   17.07

Bomb load 1 x 4000 HC, 16 x 500 GP. Primary target: Cologne, Marshalling Yards. Weather patchy cloud. Bombed at 15.05 hours from 20,000 feet on G.H. Leader.

02/12/1944 PB756 JI-B Bombing Dortmund   13.03   14.57   17.15

Bomb load 14 x 1000 HC. Primary target: Dortmund, Benzol plant. Weather 10/10ths cloud. Bombed at 14.57 hours from 19,000 feet on G.H. Leader.

F/O. J.W.R. Wilson was Navigator until 06/12/1944.

05/12/1944 LM285 JI-K Bombing Hamm   09.03   11.31   13.56

Bomb load 1 x 4000 HC, 9 x 500 ANM 59, 4 x 500 GP, 2 x 500 GP Long Delay, 1 Flare. Primary target: Hamm. Weather 10/10ths cloud over target, but otherwise varying from 6-10/10ths. Bombed at 11.31 hours from 19,000 feet on G.H.

06/12/1944 PB756 JI-B Bombing Merseburg 17.00 20.52   00.28

Bomb load 1 x 4000 HC, 8 x 500 GP and 1 x 500 GP Long Delay. Primary

742

target: Merseburg. Weather 10/10ths cloud with odd breaks. Bombed at 20.52 from 23,000 feet on red glow.

16/12/1944 ME355 JI-L Bombing Siegen 11.29 x 15.13

Bomb load 1 x 4000 HC, 5 x 1000 MC, 7 x 500 GP. Primary target: Siegen. Weather very bad on route with icing and cloud. Aircraft returned early with CSU and starboard outer engine U/S. Jettisoned safe 5220N 0235E at 5,000 feet 14.28 hours.

Sgt. J.H. Jeffries was A/Bomber from that day.

21/12/1944 ME355 JI-L Bombing Trier 12.21 15.03 17.05

Bomb load 1 x 4000 HC, 10 x 500 GP, 6 x 250 GP. Primary target: Trier, Marshalling yards. Weather 10/10 cloud, tops 6/9000 feet. Bombed at 15.03 hours from 18,000 feet on G.H.

23/12/1944 PB419 JI-J Bombing Trier 11.45 14.31 16.05

Bomb load 1 x 4000 HC, 10 x 500 GP, 6 x 250 GP. Primary target: Trier. Weather clear over target. Bombed at 14.31 hours from 18,000 feet on Red T.I.

28/12/1944 PB426 JI-D Bombing Cologne Gremberg 12.22 15.07 17.04

Bomb load 7 x 1000 MC, 6 x 500 GP, 2 x 250 GP, 1 Flare. Primary target: Koln Gremberg, Marshalling yards. Weather 10/10ths cloud or fog. Bombed at 15.07 hours from 19,700 feet on G.H.

F/O. A.G. Chatfield was MU/Gunner until 01/01/1945 and P/O. W.W. Maynes R/Gunner.

31/12/1944 NF968 JI-B Bombing Vohwinkle 11.28 14.42 16.24

Bomb load 1 x 4000 HC, 3 x 1000 M65, 2 x 500 GP, 2 x 500 ANM 64, 2 x 500 GP L/Delay, 4 x 250 GP, 1 Flare. Primary target: Vohwinkel. Weather 10/10ths cloud on approaching target although the target itself was clear. Bombed at 14.42 hours from 19,500 feet on leading G.H. aircraft.

01/01/1945 NF968 JI-B Bombing Vohwinkle 16.15 19.45 21.22

Bomb load 1 x 4000 HC, 12 x 500 GP, 4 Red T.I.s. Primary target: Vohwinkel. Weather clear. Bombed at 19.45 hours from 20,500 feet on G.H.

03/01/1945 NF968 JI-B Bombing Dortmund Buckarde 12.51 15.33 17.41

Bomb load 1 x 4000 HC, 12 x 500 ANM 58 or 64, 3 x 500 GP, 1 Flare. Primary target: Dortmund Buckarde. Weather 10/10ths cloud over target. Bombed at 15.33 hours from 19,100 feet on G.H.

F/O. A.G. Chatfield was MU/Gunner from that day and P/O. A.J. Stansbury R/Gunner.

05/01/1945 NF968 JI-B Bombing Ludwigshafen 11.20 15.08 17.16

Bomb load 1 x 4000 HC, 10 x 500 ANM 58 or 64, 2 x 500 GP, 1 Flare. Primary target: Ludwigshafen, Marshalling yards. Weather clear over target. Bombed at 15.08 hours from 20,000 feet on G.H. Landed at Woodbridge.

F/O Stanley Grover Wright, DFC citation.

Early January 1945 L to R (standing): "Chatty" Chatfield, "Josh" Dibley, John Jefferies, a member of the ground crew, "Stan" Wright, "Nick" Andreashuk and "Jake" Stansbury. L to R (kneeling): "Ken" Ridley and three of the ground crew.

"This officer has completed a large number of attacks against heavily defended targets in Germany. He is a skilful pilot who has always displayed great courage and determination in the face of the enemy and who has never let either adverse weather or enemy opposition deter him from completing his allotted task. On one occasion in January 1945, Flying Officer Wright was detailed for a daylight attack against Ludwigshafen. Whilst en route to the target several of his flying instruments became unserviceable and while over the target his aircraft was severely damaged by heavy anti-aircraft fire. Despite this, Flying Officer Wright pressed home a telling attack and afterwards flew his damaged bomber safely back to base."

11/01/1945 PB426 JI-D Bombing Krefeld 11.47 15.15 16.34

Bomb load 1 x 4000 HC, 10 x 500 ANM 64, 4 x 250 GP. Primary target: Krefeld. Weather 10/10ths cloud above and below. Visibility poor. Bombed at 15.15 hours from 20,000 feet on G.H.

W/C. Michael Wyatt, DFC

514 Squadron's second CO, Wing Commander "Mike" Wyatt did all his missions as Captain with the following 2nd Pilots. The crew for each mission was the usual of the 2nd Pilot. The operations are detailed in this book with those of the crew concerned.

37994 W/C. Michael "Mike" Wyatt, DFC. Pilot.

30/05/1944
173432 (1396311) P/O. Michael John Warner.   2nd Pilot.
183730 (1479323) F/S. Cyril Holmes, DFC.   A/Bomber.
1567997 Sgt. J.P. Tait.   Navigator.
188440 (1377392) W/O. James Gordon George Foyle. WOP/AG.
3005223 Sgt. B.F. Hammond.   MU/Gunner.
1577910 Sgt. Donald N. Sheppard. R/Gunner.
1387916 Sgt. R.A. Norton.   F/Engineer.

05/06/1944

105193 (1378130)   F/L. Philip Barber Clay, DFC.   2nd Pilot.

J29880   F/O.   R.E. Bayliss, RCAF.   A/Bomber.

1566160   Sgt. Ronald James Wilson, DFM.   Navigator.

153266 (1487602)   F/O. John Rogers, DFC.   WOP/AG.

187639 (1896360)   Sgt. Thomas Henry Cousins.   MU/Gunner.

3040512   Sgt. D. Cox.   R/Gunner.

55894 (643636) Sgt.Roy Douglas Simpson.   F/Engineer.

10/06/1944

66013   F/L. Marcus Dods, DFC.   2nd Pilot.

182294 (1610232)   Sgt. Roy Perkins.   A/Bomber.

A424502   Sgt. Douglas Leslie Wright, DFC, RAAF.   Navigator.

A424380   F/S. Brian McLennan Crapp, RAAF.   WOP/AG.

1180797   Sgt. R.K. Redfern.   MU/Gunner.

909712Sgt. J. Edwards.   R/Gunner.

12893311   Sgt. F. Widowson.   F/Engineer.

23/06/1944

1332109   W/O.   John Ludlow Lassam.   2nd Pilot.

1052269   F/S. Allan Roland Hope.   A/Bomber.

658221Sgt.   Walter Charles Taylor.   Navigator.

1566046   Sgt. William Young Anthony.   WOP/AG.

J90375 (R212331)   Sgt. Bernard Horace "Chap" Cooper, RCAF. MU/Gun.

J94826 (R202910)   Sgt. Donald Peter Manchul. RCAF.   R/Gunner.

564683Sgt.   Ernest James Hack.   F/Engineer.

05/07/1944

179705 (1511708)   F/S. Geoffrey Charles France.   2nd Pilot.

J29701   F/O.   Kenneth Hubert "Ken" Barker, RCAF.A/Bomber.

161585 (1605263)   F/O. Frederick James "Fred" Eisberg.   Navigator.

1705084   Sgt. Ronald William "Ron" Harding. WOP/AG.

 Sgt. William John "Bill" Meredith.   MU/Gunner.

1894366   Sgt. Leslie Peter Coles.   R/Gunner.

1891510   Sgt. Peter Andrew "Pete" Gosnold.   F/Engineer.

18/07/1944

NZ428001   F/S.   John Lawrie, RNZAF.   2nd Pilot.

191661 (1801354)   Sgt. Martin John Carter.   A/Bomber.

A424209   Sgt. Denison Reginald "Reg" Orth, RAAF.Navigator.

1582432   Sgt. Ellis George Durland.   WOP/AG.

A437391   Sgt. Lindsay Rutland "Sam" Burford, RAAF. MU/Gunner.

A434592 (O18009)Sgt.   Robert Charles "Bob" Chester-Master, RAAF.

R/Gunner.
1822876 Sgt. Thomas Davidsen "Tommy" Young.   F/Engineer.

25/09/1944

J26104 F/O. Stanley Grover "Stan" Wright, DFC, RCAF. 2nd Pilot.
R190706   F/S. L.E. "Pete" Jewell.   A/Bomber.
J37746 F/O. K.D. "Ken" Ridley, RCAF.   Navigator.
R181437   Sgt. N. "Nick" Andreashuk, RCAF. WOP/AG.
J41274 P/O. W.W. "Curly" Maynes, RCAF. MU/Gunner.
J41051 P/O. A.J. "Jake" Stansbury, RCAF. R/Gunner.
Sgt. Oscar Joseph "Joe" Dibley.   F/Engineer.

Glossary

△: Target

△ or **TOT:** Time on Target

AA or A/A gun: Anti-Aircraft gun batteries

A/C: Aircraft

A/F: Airfield

A/P: Aiming Point

A.S.I: Air Speed Indicator,

Baedeker: Used to fly ground crews over Germany to see the results of their sustained efforts, under a scheme known as Operation Baedeker.

Bullseye: "Bullseye" was a mock bombing raid that was to close to being combat simulation, complete with searchlights and flares. A Bullseye exercise was a simulated night bombing operation against a 'target' town or city designed to give crews the experience of an operational sortie but without crossing into enemy territory. Crews would be given a flight plan to follow and a target to simulate bombing. In the early days before cameras were fitted Personnel on the ground would report on how close aircraft came to the 'target'. These exercises could also include co-operation with fighter units, balloon units and of course anti aircraft guns.

Catamount: Special Night Navigation Exercise in which was incorporated Infra-red Photography and Night Bombing.

Dodge: Operation Dodge was the return to the UK of Prisoners of War held by the Japanese. Initially flown into Italy by the Americans, Bomber Command then took over this, one of the last and most rewarding operations carried out by the Command.

D.R.C. / D.R. compass: Dead Reckoning Compass, compass with dead reckoning navigation tools. In navigation, dead reckoning or dead-reckoning (also ded for deduced reckoning or DR) is the process of calculating one's current position by using a previously determined position, or fix, and advancing that position based upon known or estimated speeds over elapsed time and course.

E/A: Enemy Aircraft

E.C: Enemy Coast

E.C.O: Enemy Coast Out

E.T.A: Estimated Time of Arrival (sometimes called ETOA)

Exodus: Operation Exodus. This was the repatriation of some of the British prisoners of war from Europe. Operation Exodus continued throughout May 1945. Former POWs were brought home, landing at Westcott, Oakley, Ford or Tangmere.

Gardening: Mine-laying operations, sowing mines in rivers, ports and oceans from low heights.

Gee: Sometimes written GEE, was the code name given to a radio navigation system used by the Royal Air Force during World War II. It measured the time delay between two radio signals to produce a "fix", with accuracy on the order of a few hundred yards at ranges up to about 350 miles (560 km). It was the first hyperbolic navigation system to be used operationally, entering service with RAF Bomber Command in 1942.

GeeH: Gee-H, sometimes written G-H or GEE-H, was a radio navigation system developed by Britain during World War II to aid RAF Bomber Command. The name refers to the system's use of the earlier Gee equipment, as well as its use of the "H principle" or "twin-range principle" of location determination. Its official name was AMES Type 100.

Gee-H was used to supplant the Oboe bombing system, both of which worked along similar lines. By measuring the distance to a radio station, the bomber was able to navigate along an arc in the sky, dropping their bombs when they reached a set distance from another station. The main difference between Oboe and Gee-H was the location of the equipment; Oboe used very large displays in ground stations to take very accurate measurements but could only direct one aircraft at a time. Gee-H used much smaller gear on board the aircraft and was somewhat less accurate but could direct as many as 80 aircraft at a time.

Gee-H entered service in October 1943 and first used successfully in November against the Mannesmann steel works at Düsseldorf on the night of 1/2 November when about half of the sets failed leaving only 15 aircraft to bomb the factory on Gee-H. Gee-H remained in use throughout the war, although it was subject to considerable jamming from the Germans.

G.H. equipment: British scientists kept working to give the RAF a technological advantage and produced the even more advanced 'GH' in 1944. GH equipment onboard RAF bombers sent radio pulses to two ground stations in Britain, which re-transmitted them back to the aircraft. By measuring the time interval between the outgoing and returning pulses on an oscilloscope display the navigator could direct the pilot towards the target and determine the precise point for accurate bomb-release. This system only could be used by a limited number of aircraft at any one time and had the same range as OBOE (around 300 miles) but it improved the RAF's bombing accuracy even further. This was stated to be within 150 feet at 300 miles range from the transmitter.

H2S: Originally designated "BN (Blind Navigation)". H2S was the first airborne, ground scanning radar system. It was developed in Britain during World War II for the Royal Air Force and was used in various RAF bomber aircraft from 1943. It was designed to identify targets on the ground for night and all-weather bombing, allowing attack outside the range of the various radio navigation aids like Gee or Oboe which were limited to about 500 km. The early variants of the transmitter/receiver equipment were officially known as TR3159 (H2S Mk I/ASV VIB) or TR3191 (H2S Mk II).

H.F: High Frequency (radio).

I.B: Incendiary Bomb

I.F.F: Identification Friend or Foe. A way to identify friendly aircraft fro enemy aircraft by assigning a unique identifier code to aircraft transponders

LD or L/D or L/Delay: Long Delay bomb.

Manna: Operation Manna was humanitarian food drops, carried out to relieve a famine in German-occupied Holland, and undertaken by Allied bomber crews, during the final days of World War II in Europe. Manna was carried out by British RAF units, as well as squadrons from the Australian, Canadian, New Zealand and Polish air forces, between 29 April and 8 May 1945.

M/B: Master Bomber

M/Y: Marshalling yards

ORB: Operations Record Book

P.F.F: Path Finder Force

Post Mortem: Operation Post Mortem involved crews, after VE Day, flying at operational height towards the continent in a simulated Main Force attack whilst specialist radar crew tracked the bomber stream using captured German 'Flensburg' radar equipment. The purpose was to check the equipment's efficiency and to allow Bomber Command to try out defence tactics.

S.C: South Coast

T.I.s: Target Indicators

Vic: The Vic formation is a formation devised for military aircraft and first used during World War I. It comprises three or sometimes more aircraft flying in close formation with the leader at the apex and the rest of the flight en echelon to left and right, the whole resembling the letter "V". The name is derived from the term for the letter V in the phonetic alphabet of the time.

Wanganui: This was also known as "sky marking". Wanganui was used when the target was obscured by cloud, industrial haze, or a smoke screen. Oboe radio signal or H2S was used to release the markers over the unseen target. The target indicators used were on parachutes to give an aiming point that could be seen by the main force.

W/T receiver: Wireless Telegraphy (radio) receiver.

Printed in Great Britain
by Amazon